INTRODUCTION TO PARALEGALISM

Perspectives, Problems, and Skills

FIFTH EDITION

The West Paralegal Series

Your options keep growing with West Publishing.
Each year our list continues to offer you more options for every course, new or existing, and on-the-job reference materials. We now have over 140 titles from which to choose.

We are pleased to offer books in the following subject areas:

Administrative Law
Alternative Dispute Resolution
Bankruptcy
Business Organizations/Corporations
Civil Litigation and Procedure
CLA Exam Preparation
Client Accounting
Computer in the Law Office
Constitutional Law
Contract Law
Criminal Law and Procedure
Document Preparation
Environmental Law
Ethics

Family Law
Federal Taxation
Intellectual Property
Introduction to Law
Introduction to Paralegalism
Law Office Management
Law Office Procedures
Legal Research, Writing, and Analysis
Legal Terminology
Paralegal Employment
Real Estate Law
Reference Materials
Torts and Personal Injury Law
Will, Trusts, and Estate Administration

You will find unparalleled, practical teaching support.
Each text is enhanced by instructor and student supplements to ensure the best learning experience possible to prepare for this field. We also offer custom publishing and other benefits such as West's Student Achievement Award. In addition, our sales representatives are ready to provide you with needed and dependable service.

We want to hear from you.
The most important factor in improving the quality of our paralegal texts and teaching packages is active feedback from educators in the field. If you have a question, concern, or observation about any of our materials or you have written a proposal or manuscript, we want to hear from you. Please do not hesitate to contact your local representative or write us at the following address:

West Paralegal Series, 3 Columbia Circle, P.O. Box 15015, Albany, NY 12212-5015.

For additional information point your browser to
http://www.westpub.com/Educate and **http://www.delmar.com**

West Publishing — *Your Paralegal Publisher*
an imprint of Delmar Publishers

an International Thomson Publishing company I(T)P®

INTRODUCTION TO PARALEGALISM

► *Perspectives, Problems, and Skills*

FIFTH EDITION

William P. Statsky

West Publishing Company
a division of International Thomson Publishing I(T)P®

Minneapolis/St. Paul • Albany • Bonn • Boston
Cincinnati • Detroit • London • Madrid • Melbourne
Mexico City • New York • Pacific Grove • Paris
San Francisco • Singapore • Tokyo • Toronto • Washington

NOTICE TO THE READER

Publisher does not warrant or guarantee any of the products described herein or perform any independent analysis in connection with any of the product information contained herein. Publisher does not assume, and expressly disclaims, any obligation to obtain and include information other than that provided to it by the manufacturer.

The reader is expressly warned to consider and adopt all safety precautions that might be indicated by the activities herein and to avoid all potential hazards. By following the instructions contained herein, the reader willingly assumes all risks in connection with such instructions.

The Publisher makes no representation or warranties of any kind, including but not limited to, the warranties of fitness for particular purpose or merchantability, nor are any such representations implied with respect to the material set forth herein, and the publisher takes no responsibility with respect to such material. The publisher shall not be liable for any special, consequential, or exemplary damages resulting, in whole or part, from the readers' use of, or reliance upon, this material.

West Legal Studies Staff:

Design: Lois Stanfield, LightSource Images
Cover design: Lois Stanfield, LightSource Images
Cover image: Gary Conner/PhotoEdit
Art: Parkwood Composition Service, Inc.
Composition: Parkwood Composition Service, Inc.

Netscape Communications, the Netscape Communications logo, Netscape, and Netscape Navigator are trademarks of the Netscape Communications Corporation. Netscape screen captures are ©1996 by Netscape Communications Corporation.

Printed in the United States of America
5 6 7 8 XXX 04 03 02 01 00

For more information, contact Delmar, 3 Columbia Circle, PO Box 15015, Albany, NY 12212-0515; or find us on the World Wide Web at http://www.westlegalstudies.com

For permission to use material from this text or product contact us by Tel (800) 730-2214; Fax (800) 730-2215; www.thomsonrights.com

Library of Congress Cataloging-in-Publication Data

Statsky, William
    Introduction to paralegalism : perspectives, problems, and skills
/ William P. Statsky — 5th ed.
      p. cm.
    Includes bibliographical references and index.
    ISBN 0-314-20147-5 (hard cover : alk. paper)
     1. Legal assistants—United States. 2. Legal assistants—
Vocational guidance—United States. I. Title.
KF320.L4S73   1997
340'.02373—dc21   97-4932
                                     CIP

For Patricia Farrell Statsky:
A person whose ability and love have
sustained more than she knows

BY THE SAME AUTHOR

Case Analysis and Fundamentals of Legal Writing, 4th edition, St. Paul: West Publishing Company, 1995 (with J. Wernet)

Essentials of Paralegalism, 2nd ed. St. Paul: West Publishing Company, 1993

Essentials of Torts. St. Paul: West Publishing Company, 1994

Family Law: The Essentials St. Paul: West Publishing Company, 1997

Family Law, 4th ed. St. Paul: West Publishing Company, 1996

Inmate Involvement in Prison Legal Services: Roles and Training Options for the Inmate as Paralegal, American Bar Association, Commission on Correctional Facilities and Services, 1974

Legal Desk Reference. St. Paul: West Publishing Company, 1990 (with B. Hussey, M. Diamond & R. Nakamura)

The Legal Paraprofessional as Advocate and Assistant: Training Concepts and Materials. New York: Center on Social Welfare Policy and Law, 1971 (with P. Lang)

Legal Research and Writing: Some Starting Points, 4th ed. St. Paul: West Publishing Company, 1993

Legal Thesaurus/Dictionary: A Resource for the Writer and Computer Researcher. St. Paul: West Publishing Company, 1985

Legislative Analysis and Drafting, 2d ed. St Paul: West Publishing Company, 1984

Paralegal Employment: Facts and Strategies for the 1990s, 2d ed. St. Paul: West Publishing Company, 1993

Paralegal Ethics and Regulation, 2d ed. St. Paul: West Publishing Company, 1993

Torts: Personal Injury Litigation, 3d ed. St. Paul: West Publishing Company, 1995

Rights of the Imprisoned: Cases, Materials, and Directions. Indianapolis: Bobbs-Merrill Company, 1974 (with R. Singer)

What Have Paralegals Done? A Dictionary of Functions. Washington D.C.: National Paralegal Institute, 1973

The pain and the excitement of paralegalism, and indeed of the law itself, are that the problem we are given will often be smaller than the problem we find.

Contents in Brief

CONTENTS

PREFACE

Four editions ago—in 1974—many were asking the question, "What's a paralegal?" That day has long past, although there is still a great deal of information that people need to have in order to appreciate the outstanding contribution paralegals have made in the delivery of legal services. This book seeks to provide that information and, at the same time, to introduce you to the fundamental skills needed to thrive in this still-developing career— a career whose members may one day outnumber attorneys in the traditional and untraditional law office. A great deal has happened since 1974. Yet the dominant themes of the field continue to be challenge, promise, and the opportunity to rethink the question of what is the most effective way to meet the legal needs of the public.

CHANGES IN THE FIFTH EDITION

In addition to the updating material in the book on employment, salaries, roles, ethics, and regulation, a number of particular changes in the fifth edition should be mentioned:

- Chapter 1 includes the World Wide Web home pages of the National Federation of Paralegal Associations and the National Association of Legal Assistants.
- Additions to chapter 2 include a chart on the most commonly used job-search methods, resources on the Internet and the World Wide Web for finding employment, choice of language in résumés, a new record keeping job search form, etc.
- Two of the large charts in chapter 2 (one on private employment and the other on state government employment) have been moved to the end of chapter 2 as chapter appendixes. The private employment chart now includes large corporations that have legal departments.
- Chapter 3 contains more techniques of preventing miscommunication on the job and a discussion of CLE (Continuing Legal Education) requirements of paralegal associations.
- The networking discussion of chapter 3 now includes online networking, particularly through listservs where paralegals can ask job-related questions of potentially thousands of other paralegals.
- The recommendations and implications of the long-awaited report of the Commission on Nonlawyer Practice of the American Bar Association are included in chapter 4.
- Chapter 4 also provides a summary of the latest regulatory developments in Arizona, California, Florida, Illinois, Minnesota, and Oregon.
- Chapter 4 previews the licensing proposal of the National Federation of Paralegal Associations and the Federation's advanced certification examination (PACE). A major new chart compares the certification exams of NALA and NFPA.
- The four major state-specific certification examinations are also covered in chapter 4: the California Advanced Specialty Program, the Certified Florida Legal Assistant Exam, the Texas Legal Assistant Specialty Certification Exam, and the Louisiana Certified Paralegal Exam.
- Chapter 4 also contains new material on overtime compensation for paralegals, and a clarification of the multiple meanings of the word, "certified."

- The ethics material in chapter 5 has been expanded in areas such as billing practices and conflict of interest.
- Charts have been included in chapter 5 that compare the variety of attorney and paralegal ethical codes that are now available.
- A topic of the paralegal as whistle blower has been added to chapter 5, including a recent dramatic court opinion on this issue.
- The discussion of federalism, checks and balances, and our adversarial system in chapter 6 have been expanded.
- Chapter 7 introduces the IRAC technique of legal analysis used in many law schools.
- Chapter 8 on interviewing has been substantially revised. A new kind of case—one involving personal injury—is now used as the basis of the dialogue between a paralegal interviewer and the client being interviewed.
- Chapter 8 includes a sample retainer, extensive checklists of interviewing techniques on topics that range from preparing for an interview to ending one. There is also a checklist on ways to improve your interviewing skills.
- Several chapters, particularly chapter 8, include a discussion of being a paralegal in an environment where lawyer bashing has become commonplace.
- Online investigation resources have been added to chapter 9 on investigation.
- Chapter 9 makes investigation techniques more concrete through a discussion of common automobile accidents and of locating the assets of debtors.
- The material added to chapter 10 on litigation include the paralegal's role in summary/advisory juries, techniques of serving process and filing documents, time-line summaries of discovery documents, etc.
- The introduction to chapter 11 on legal research has been revised for greater clarity.
- The terminology of legal research chart has been broken into two charts: a chart covering the essentials of legal research terminology and a chart providing a comprehensive list of legal research terminology.
- The role of the Internet in legal research has been added to chapter 11. An example is using World Wide Web to find primary authority.
- The citation material in chapter 11 includes the revisions made in the 16th edition of the Bluebook.
- Chapter 11 covers the controversy over genetic citation, also called electronic citation or public domain citation.
- Chapter 12 includes more guidance on writing fundamentals such as the use of the active/passive voice.
- There are new materials in chapter 13 on computers on Windows 95, natural language database searching, fonts/points in printing, scanners, text arrangement with word processors, etc.
- Chapter 13 also includes a broad discussion of many of the important features of the Internet including listservs, bulletin board systems, e-mail, newsgroups, Internet relay chat, hypertext, the search engines of the World Wide Web, and attorney profiles available on the Internet.
- Chapter 14 now covers the limited liability company and the limited liability partnership as options for the organization attorneys in the practice of law.
- Chapter 14 includes more exhibits on billable hours and timekeeping documents.
- Value billing has been added to the discussion of the funding of legal services in chapter 14.
- Chapter 15 provides a chart presentation of the components of procedural due process and the relationship of these components to formal administrative advocacy where paralegals are allowed to represent clients.
- There is a new appendix on Internet legal resources (K).

- Appendix L contains information about online searching for federal government paralegal jobs.
- Appendix F includes a state-by-state overview of the practice of law, ethical guidelines, and court cases involving paralegals and other nonattorneys.
- Other new appendix material includes lists of depository libraries (H), appellate courts (I), and state resources (J) for every state.

TEACHING AIDS AND SUPPLEMENTS

- **Instructor's Manual:** Written by the text author, the instructor's manual includes Class Ideas, such as lecture ideas and suggestions for using selected Assignments. The instructor's manual also includes detailed competency lists for each chapter.
- **Test Bank,** prepared by Dorothy Moore, contains over 1000 test questions. Each chapter contains a variety of questions in true/false, multiple-choice and essay format.
- **WESTEST Computerized Test Bank:** The printed test bank is also available on the latest version of WESTEST, a computerized test system. WESTEST allows instructors to select and edit questions from the test bank, add their own questions, and print exams in a variety of formats. WESTEST is available for IBM PC and compatible microcomputers or the Macintosh family of microcomputers.
- **Transparency Masters,** containing approximately 50 Exhibits from the text, provide helpful illustration for instructor lectures.
- **Transparency Acetates** provide an additional 25 Exhibits, in color, from the text.
- **Study Guide and Workbook:** Written by the text author, the Study Guide and Workbook includes review questions, short writing exercises, and additional enrichment materials, such as legislative documents.
- **Survival Manual for Paralegal Students,** written by Bradene Moore and Kathleen Reed of the University of Toledo, provides tips for making the most of paralegal courses.
- **Strategies and Tips for Paralegal Educators,** written by Anita Tebbe and Johnson County Community College, provides teaching strategies specifically designed for paralegal educators. It concentrates on how to teach and is organized in three parts: the WHO of paralegal education—students and teachers; the WHAT of paralegal education—goals and objectives, and the HOW of paralegal education—methods of instruction, methods of evaluation, and other aspects of teaching. A copy of this pamphlet is available to each adopter of a West text.
- **West's Law Finder,** a brief 77-page pamphlet that describes various legal research sources and how they can be used. Classroom quantities are available.
- **Sample Pages, Third Edition.** This 231-page pamphlet introduces all of West's legal research materials. The accompanying *Instructor's Manual* gives ideas for effectively using the material in the classroom. Classroom quantities are available.
- **Citation-At-A-Glance, Revised Edition.** This handy reference card provides a quick, portable reference to the basic rules of citation for the most commonly cited legal sources, including judicial opinions, statutes and secondary sources, such as legal encyclopedias and legal periodicals. *Citation-At-A-Glance, Revised Edition* uses the rules set forth in *A Uniform System of Citation,* Sixteenth Edition (1996). A free copy of this card is included with every student text.
- **How to Shepardize: Your Guide to Complete Legal Research Through Shepard's Citations** is a brief (64-page) pamphlet that helps students understand the research technique of Shepardizing citations. The pamphlet is available in classroom quantities (one copy for each student who purchases a new text.)

- **WESTLAW,** West's online computerized legal research system, offers students "hands-on" experience with a system commonly used in law offices. Qualified adopters can receive 10 free hours of WESTLAW.
- **WESTMATE Tutorial** (for DOS and Windows) is an interactive tutorial for WEST-MATE software that introduces students to WESTLAW capabilities. It is available free to qualified adopters.
- **West's Paralegal Video Library** includes:
  - The Drama of the Law II: Paralegal Issues video
  - *I Never Said I Was a Lawyer* paralegal ethics video
  - The Making of a Case video
  - Mock Trial Videos—Business Litigation
  - Mock Trial Videos—Trial Techniques: A Products Liability Case
  - Arguments to the United States Supreme Court video
  - West's Introduction to Legal Research

These videos are available to qualified adopters.

ACKNOWLEDGMENTS

It is difficult to name all the individuals who have provided guidance in the preparation of the five editions of this book. Looking back over the years, there are a number of people who have played important roles in my initiation and growth as a student of paralegal education. I owe a debt to Jean and Edgar Cahn, founders of the Legal Technician Program at Antioch School of Law where I worked; Bill Fry, Director of the National Paralegal Institute and a valued colleague since our days together at Columbia Law School, where he was my dean in one of the first paralegal training programs in the country, the Program for Legal Service Assistants; Dan Oran, who helped me plan the first edition; Michael Manna, Ed Schwartz; Bill Mulkeen; and finally, Juanita Hill, Willie Nolden, and Linda Saunders, some of my early students who taught me so much.

I wish to thank the following people at West Publishing Company: Elizabeth Hannan, Patricia Bryant, John Lindley, Peter Krall, and Karen Laird.

Finally, a word of thanks to the reviewers who made valuable suggestions for improving the text:

Laura Barnard
Lakeland Community College, OH

Michele G. Bradford
Gadsden State Community College, AL

Toni Volza Esposito
Briarwood College, CT

Karl Freedman
Professional Career Development
Institute, GA

Nancy L. Hart
Midland College, TX

Diana D. Juettner
Mercy College, NY

H. Margaret Nickerson
William Woods University, MO

Virginia Noonan
Northern Essex Community College, MA

Gina-Marie Reitano
St. John's University, NY

James N. Sheperd
New Hampshire Technical College

Cynthia Weishapple
Chippewa Valley Technical College, WI

Mary A. Whiting
Brooklyn College, NY

Andrea E. Williams
Central Florida Community College

■ *The "expanded use of well-trained assistants, sometimes called 'paralegals,' has been an important development. Today there are . . . double the number of . . . schools for training paralegals [than the number of schools for training attorneys]. . . . The advent of the paralegal enables law offices to perform high quality legal services at a lower cost. Possibly we have only scratched the surface of this development."*

Warren E. Burger, Chief Justice
of the United States Supreme Court, February 3, 1980

■ *"Paralegals are an absolutely essential component of quality legal services in the future."*

James Fellers, President
American Bar Association, April 4, 1975

■ *"[T]he number of job openings for paralegals is expected to increase significantly through the year 2005 . . . [accompanied by] keen competition for jobs. . . ."*

U.S. Department of Labor
Occupational Outlook Handbook, 1996–1997

How to Study Law in the Classroom and on the Job

► *Outline*

Section A
CLASSROOM LEARNING

Education does not come naturally to most of us. It is a struggle. This is all the more true for someone entering a totally new realm of training such as legal education. Much of the material will seem foreign and difficult. There is a danger of becoming overwhelmed by the vast quantity of laws and legal material that confronts you. How do you study law? How do you learn law? What is the proper perspective that a student of law should have about the educational process? These are our concerns in this introduction to the process of studying law. In short, our theme is training to be trained—the art of effective learning.

The first step is to begin with a proper frame of mind. Too many students have false expectations of what legal education can accomplish. This substantially interferes with effective studying.

1. Your legal education has two phases. Phase I begins now and ends when you complete this training program. Phase II begins when this training program ends and is not completed until the last day of your employment as a paralegal.

You have entered a career that will require you to be a perpetual student. The learning never ends. This is true not only because the boundary lines of law are vast, but also because the law is changing every day. No one knows all of the law. Phase I of your legal education is designed to provide you with the foundation that will enable you to become a good student in Phase II.

2. Your legal education has two dimensions: the content of the law (the rules) and the practical techniques of using that content in a law office or other legal environment (the skills).

Rules

There are two basic kinds of rules or laws:

Substantive Law: Those nonprocedural rules that govern rights and duties; for example, the requirements for the sale of land;

Procedural Law: Those rules that govern the mechanics of resolving a dispute in court or in an administrative agency; for example, the number of days within which a party must respond to a claim stated in a complaint.

The law library contains millions of substantive and procedural laws written by courts (in volumes called *reporters*), by legislatures (in volumes called *statutory codes*), and by administrative agencies (in volumes called *administrative codes*). A substantial portion of your time in school will involve a study of the substantive and procedural law of your state, and often of the federal government as well.

Skills

By far the most important dimension of your legal education will be the skills of using rules. Without the skills, the content of the law is close to worthless. Examples of legal skills include:

- How to interview a client (see chapter 8).
- How to investigate the facts of a case (see chapter 9).

- How to draft a complaint, the document that initiates a lawsuit (see chapter 10).
- How to digest or summarize documents in a case file (see chapter 10).
- How to do legal research in a law library (see chapter 11).

The overriding skill that, to one degree or another, is the basis for all others is the skill of legal analysis (see chapter 7). Some make the mistake of concluding that legal analysis is the exclusive domain of the attorney. Without an understanding of at least the fundamentals of legal analysis, however, paralegals cannot understand the legal system and cannot intelligently carry out many of the more demanding tasks they are assigned.

3. You must force yourself to suspend what you already know about the law in order to be able to absorb (a) that which is new and (b) that which conflicts with your prior knowledge and experience.

Place yourself in the position of training students to drive a car. Your students undoubtedly already know something about driving. They have watched others drive and maybe have even had a lesson or two from friends. It would be ideal, however, if you could begin your instruction from point zero. There is a very real danger that the students have picked up bad habits from others. This will interfere with their capacity to *listen* to what you are saying. The danger is that they will block out anything you say that does not conform to previously learned habits and knowledge. If the habits or knowledge are defective, your job as a trainer is immensely more difficult.

The same is true in studying law. Everyone knows something about the law from government or civics courses as a teenager and from the various treatments of the law in the media. Some of you may have been involved in the law as a party or as a witness in court. Others may have worked, or currently work, in law offices. Will this prior knowledge and experience be a help or a hindrance to you in your future legal education? For some it will be a help. For most of us, however, there is a danger of interference.

This is particularly so with respect to the portrayal of the law on TV and in the movies. Those who grew up with TV's *Perry Mason* probably came to the conclusion that most legal problems are solved by dramatically tricking a hostile witness on the stand into finally telling the truth. Not so. The practice of law is not an endless series of confessions and concessions that are pried loose from opponents. Nor was the more recent TV program *L.A. Law* much more realistic. Every attorney does not spend all day engaged in the kind of case that makes front page news. Recently, a paralegal left her job as a paralegal with a solo practitioner to take another paralegal position with a firm that she thought was going to be like *L.A. Law*. Three months later, she begged her old boss to take her back. She had discovered that there was a great gap between reality and *L.A. Law*.

Another potentially misleading portrayal of the law came in the O. J. Simpson criminal and civil trials that captivated the nation from 1995 to 1997. Very few parties to litigation have teams of attorneys, investigators, and experts ready to do battle with each other. The overwhelming number of legal disputes are never litigated in court. Most are either settled or are simply dropped by one or both parties. Of the small number that are litigated, the vast majority involve parties with one attorney each who may use an expert witness or two. In short, it is rare for the legal system to become the spectacle—some would say the circus—that the occasional high-profile case leads us to believe is common in the practice of law.

While excitement and drama can be part of the legal system, they are not everyday occurrences. What is dominant is painstaking and meticulous hard work. This reality is almost never portrayed in the media.

Therefore, it is strongly recommended that you place yourself in the position of a stranger to the material you will be covering in your courses, regardless of your background and exposure to the field. Cautiously treat everything as a new experience. Temporarily suspend what you already know. Resist the urge to pat yourself on the back by saying, "I already knew that" or "I already know how to do that." For many students, such statements lead to relaxation. They do not work as hard once they have convinced themselves that there is nothing new to learn. No problem exists, of course, if these students are right. The danger, however, is that they are wrong or that they are only partially right. Students are not always the best judge of what they know and of what they can do. Do not become too comfortable. Adopt the following healthy attitude: "I've heard about that before or I've already done that, but maybe I can learn something new about it." Every new teacher, every new supervisor, every new setting is an opportunity to add a dimension to your prior knowledge and experience. Be open to these opportunities. No two people practice law exactly the same way. Your own growth as a student and as a paralegal will depend in large part on your capacity to listen for, explore, and absorb this diversity.

4. Be sure that you know the goals and context of every assignment.

Throughout your education, you will be given a variety of assignments: class exercises, text readings, drafting tasks, field projects, research assignments, etc. You should ask yourself the following questions about each one:

- What are the goals of this assignment? What am I supposed to learn from it?
- How does this assignment fit into what I have already learned? What is the context of the assignment?

Successfully undertaking the assignment depends in part on your understanding of its goals and how these goals relate to the overall context of the course. How do you identify goals and context?

- Carefully listen to and take notes on what your teachers tell the class about the assignment.
- Ask teachers questions about their expectations for assignments. Demonstrate a polite but probing interest.
- If the teacher has given a particular assignment before to other classes, ask former students. If they have had any papers returned to them by the teacher, try to read some of them to determine what comments/criticisms the teacher has made on them. These observations will be additional clues to what the teacher is after.
- Take note of what the authors of your texts have expressly or implicitly told you about the importance or purpose of certain tasks.
- Ask your classmates about their understanding of purpose and context.

In short, be preoccupied by these concerns. *Do not undertake assignments in isolation or in a vacuum.*

As we will see in greater detail later, this advice applies on the job as well as in school. A strong indication of one's commitment—an essential ingredient for progress and advancement—is a sincere interest in the broader picture. Avoid gaining a reputation as someone who simply wants to "get the job done and get out as quickly as possible." While speed is sometimes critical, speed is never a substitute for efficiency and professionalism. The latter are directly dependent on the extent of your involvement, interest, and enthusiasm in carrying out a task. Boredom and incompetence often feed on each other.

This is not to say that you must be wildly enthusiastic about everything you do. Sustaining such enthusiasm is unrealistic. At a minimum, you want to avoid undertaking tasks routinely—even routine tasks! One way to accomplish this goal is to have a constant eye on the broader picture. Why are you being asked to do something in a certain way? Has it always been done this way? Are there more efficient ways? After the pressure of the immediate need has passed, can you think about and eventually propose a more effective *system* of handling the task?

Of course, there is a danger of going to the opposite extreme. You cannot be so preoccupied with purpose, context, and systems that you fail to complete the immediate job before you. Timing is important. Often the office will have no tolerance for suggestions for improvement until immediate deadlines have passed. This simply means that you must always be operating at two levels. First, the *now* level: Mobilize all of your resources to complete the task as efficiently as possible under the present work environment. Second, the *systems* level: Keep your mind open, and challenge your creativity to identify steps and procedures that might be taken in the future to achieve greater efficiency in accomplishing the task.

5. Design a study plan.

Make current *lists* of everything that you must do. Update them regularly. Divide every list into long-term projects (what is due next week or at the end of the semester) and short-term projects (what is due tomorrow). Have a plan for each day. Establish the following norm for yourself: every day you will focus in some way on *all* of your assignments. Every day you will review your long-term and short-term list. Priority, of course, will be given to the short-term tasks. Yet some time, however small, will also be devoted to the long-term tasks. At a minimum, this time can be used simply to remind yourself that these tasks are hanging over you and that you must make concrete commitments to devote substantial blocks of time to them in the immediate future. Make and renew these commitments every day. If possible, go beyond this. On a day that you will be mainly working on the short-term projects, try to set aside 5 percent of your time to the long-term projects, for instance, by doing some background reading or by preparing a very rough first draft of an outline. It is critical that you establish *momentum* toward the accomplishment of *all* your tasks. This is done by never letting anything sit on the back burner. Set yourself the goal of making at least *some* progress on everything every day. Without this goal, the momentum may be very difficult to sustain.

Once you have decided what tasks you will cover on a given study day, the next question is: In what *order* will you cover them? There are a number of ways in which you can classify the things that you must do—for example: (a) easy tasks that will require a relatively short time to complete, (b) complex tasks requiring more time, (c) tasks with time demands that will be unknown until you start them. At the beginning of your study time, spend a few seconds preparing an outline of the order in which you will cover the tasks that day and the approximate amount of time that you will set aside for each task. You may want to start with some of the easier tasks so that you can feel a sense of accomplishment relatively soon. Alternatively, you may want to devote early study time to the third kind of task listed above ("c") so that you can obtain a clearer idea of the scope and difficulty of such assignments. The important point is that you establish a *schedule*. It does not have to be written in stone. Quite the contrary—it is healthy that you have enough flexibility to revise your day's schedule so that you can respond to unfolding realities as you study. Adaptation is not a sign of disorganization, but the total absence of an initial plan is.

6. Add 50 percent to the time you initially think you will need to study a subject.

You are kidding yourself if you have not set aside a *substantial* amount of time to study law outside the classroom. The conscientious study of law takes time—lots of it. It is true that some students must work and take care of family responsibilities. You cannot devote time that you do not have. Yet the reality is that limited study time leads to limited education.

Generally, people will find time for what they want to do. You may *wish* to do many things for which there will never be enough time. You will find the time, however, to do what you really *want* to do. Once you have decided that you want something badly enough, you will find the time to do it.

Most people waste tremendous amounts of time by worrying about all the things that they have to do and in taking rest periods from this worrying through socializing or other casual pursuits. How much of each work hour do you spend in *productive* time? For most of us the answer is about twenty minutes. The rest of the hour is spent worrying, relaxing, repeating ourselves, socializing, etc. One answer to the problem of limited time availability is to increase the amount of *productive* time that you derive out of each work hour. You may not be able to add any new hours to the clock, but you can add to your net productive time. How about moving up to thirty minutes an hour? Forty? You will be amazed at the time that you can "find" simply by making a conscious effort to remove some of the waste. When asked how a masterpiece was created, a great sculptor once responded: "You start with a block of stone and you cut away everything that is not art." In your study habits, start with a small block of time and work to cut away everything that is not productive.

There are no absolute rules on how much time you will need. It depends on the complexity of the subject matter you must master. It is probably accurate to say that most of us need to study more than we do—as a rule of thumb, about 50 percent more. You should be constantly on the alert for ways to increase the time you have available or, more accurately, to increase the productive time that you can make available.

Resolving time-management problems as a student will be good practice for you when you are confronted with similar (and more severe) time-management problems as a working paralegal. Many law offices operate at a hectic pace. One of the hallmarks of a professional is a pronounced reverence for deadlines and the clock in general. Time is money. An ability to find and handle time effectively can also be one of the preconditions for achieving justice in a particular case.

Soon you will be gaining a reputation among other students, teachers, supervisors, and employers. You should make a concerted effort to make sure you acquire a reputation for hard work, punctuality, and conscientiousness about the time you devote to your work. In large measure, success follows from such a reputation. It is as important, if not more important, than raw ability or intelligence.

7. Create your own study area free from distractions.

It is essential that you find study areas that are quiet and free from distractions. Otherwise, concentration is obviously impossible. It may be that the worst places to study are at home or at the library, unless you can find a corner that is cut off from noise and people who want to talk. Do not make yourself too available. If you study in the corridor, at the first table at the entrance to the library, or at the kitchen table, you are inviting distraction. You need to be able to close yourself off for two to three hours at a time. It is important for you to interact with other people—but not while you are studying material that requires considerable concentration. You will be tempted to digress and to socialize. You are in the best position to know where these temptations are. You are also the most qualified person to know how to avoid the temptations.

8. Conduct a self-assessment of your prior study habits and establish a program to reform the weaknesses.

If you were to describe the way you study, would you be proud of the description? Here is a partial list of some of the main weaknesses of attitude or practice that students have in studying:

- They have done well in the past with only minimal study effort. Why change now?
- No one else in the class appears to be studying very much. Why be different?
- They learn best by listening in class. Hence, instead of studying on their own, why not wait until someone explains it in person?
- They simply do not like to study; there are more important things to do in life.
- They can't concentrate.
- They study with the radio on or with other distractions.
- They get bored easily. "I can't stay motivated for long."
- They do not understand what they are supposed to study.
- They skim read.
- They do not stop to look up strange words or phrases.
- They study only at exam time—they cram for exams.
- They do not study at a consistent pace. They spend an hour here and there and have no organized, regular study times.
- They do not like to memorize.
- They do not take notes on what they are reading.

What other interferences with effective studying can you think of? Or more important, which of the above items apply to you? How do you plead? In law, it is frequently said that you cannot solve a problem until you obtain the facts. What are the facts in the case of your study habits? Make your personal list of attitude problems, study patterns, or environmental interferences. Place these items in some order. Next, establish a plan for yourself. Which item on the list are you going to try to correct tonight? What will the plan be for this week? For next week? For the coming month? What specific steps will you take to try to change some bad habits? Do not, however, be too hard on yourself. Be determined but realistic. The more serious problems are obviously going to take more time to correct. Improvement will come if you are serious about improvement and regularly think about it. If one corrective method does not work, try another. If the fifth does not work, try a sixth. Discuss techniques of improvement with other students and with teachers. Prove to yourself that change is possible.

9. Conduct a self-assessment on grammar, spelling, and composition, and design a program to reform weaknesses.

The legal profession lives by the written word. Talking is important for some activities, but writing is crucial in almost every area of law. You cannot function in this environment without a grasp of the basics of spelling, grammar, and composition. A major complaint made by employers today is that paralegals are consistently violating these basics. The problem is very serious.

Step One

You must take responsibility for your training in grammar, spelling, and composition. Do not wait for someone to teach you these basics. Do not wait until someone points out your weaknesses. You must make a personal commitment to train yourself. If English courses are available to you, great. It is essential, however, that you understand that a weekly class will probably not be enough.

Step Two

Raise your consciousness about the writing around you. Your training in writing should not be compartmentalized. You must be constantly thinking about and worrying about writing. The concern should be a preoccupation. When you are reading a newspaper, for example, you should be conscious of the use of semicolons and paragraph structure in what you are reading. At least occasionally you should ask yourself why a certain punctuation mark was used by a writer. You are surrounded by writing. You read this writing for content. You must begin a conscious effort to focus on the structure of this writing as well.

Step Three

Purchase several grammar books. Do not rely on only one grammar book. There are hundreds of texts on the market, and they each explain things differently, so you should consult more than one grammar book on difficult points. It must be admitted that some grammar books are poorly written! They are not always easy to use. They may give examples of grammar rules without clearly defining the rules. Or they may define the rules without giving clear examples of their application. A grammar book may be excellent for some areas of writing but weak for others. Hence, have more than one grammar book in your personal library.

You may have saved grammar books you used earlier in your education. In addition, go to second-hand bookstores. They often have a section on textbooks. Some of the best grammar books are old elementary texts that provide excellent overviews of the basics. Another way to cut down on the expense of purchase is to consider paperback texts. The characteristics to look for in making a purchase are:

- A comprehensive index.
- Clearly defined rules covering the basics.
- Numerous examples of the application of the rules.
- Exercises on the rules *with answers* so that you can check your own progress.

Step Four

Use the grammar books almost as frequently as you would a dictionary. Have the books at your side every time you write. Force yourself to use these books regularly. The more often you use them now, the less you will need them later as you continue to improve. You will never be able to discard them entirely, however. You will need to consult them when doing any serious writing in the law. How often will you have to consult them? It depends on the extent of the weaknesses that you have and the frequency with which you begin consulting them now.

Step Five

Improve your spelling. Use a dictionary often. Begin making a list of words that you are spelling incorrectly. Work on these words. Ask other students, relatives, or friends to test you on them by reading the words to you one by one. Spell the words out loud or on paper. You can drill yourself into spelling perfection, or close to it, by this method. When you have the slightest doubt about the spelling of a word, check the dictionary. Add difficult words to your list. Again, the more often you take this approach now, the less often you will need to use the dictionary later.

As we will see in chapter 13 on computers, many word processing programs have "spell checkers" that not only identify words you may have misspelled but also provide suggested corrections. Does this new technology mean that your spelling problems have been solved forever? Hardly. Spell checkers can catch many spelling blunders, but they can be very misleading. First of all, they don't catch misspelled proper names such as the surnames of individuals (unless you add these names to the base of words being checked). An even more serious problem is that spell checkers don't alert you to improper word choices. Every word in the following sentence, for example, is incorrect, but a spell checker would tell you that the sentence has no spelling problems:

"Its to later too by diner."

Here is what should have been written:

"It's too late to buy dinner."

Since the first sentence has no misspellings, you are led—misled—to believe that you have written a flawless sentence.

Step Six

Enroll in English and writing courses. Check offerings at local schools like adult education programs in the public schools or at colleges.

Step Seven

Find out which law courses in your curriculum require the most writing from students. If possible, take these courses—no matter how painful you find writing to be. In fact, the more painful it is, the more you need to place yourself in an environment where writing is demanded of you on a regular basis.

Step Eight

Simplify your writing. Cut down the length of your sentences. Minimize the use of semicolons that extend the length of sentences. Many people have the mistaken idea that legal writing must be "heavy," august, and flowery. This usually leads to verbosity. The best legal writing, no matter how technical, is evenly paced, clear, and concise.

Step Nine

Prepare a self-assessment of your weaknesses. Make a list of what you must correct. Then set a schedule for improvement. Set aside a small amount of time each day, say, ten minutes, during which you work on your writing weaknesses. Be consistent about this time. Do not wait for the weekend or for next semester when you will have more time. The reality is that you will probably never have substantially more time than you have now. The problem is not so much the absence of time as it is an unwillingness to dig into the task. Progress will be slow and you will be on your own. Hence, there is a danger that you will be constantly finding excuses to put it off.

10. Consider forming a student study group, but be cautious.

Students sometimes find it useful to form study groups. A healthy exchange with your colleagues can be very productive. One difficulty is finding students with whom you are compatible. Trial and error may be the only way to identify such students. A more serious concern is trying to define the purpose of the study group. It should not be used as a substitute for your own individual study. It would be inappropriate to divide a course into parts, with members of the group having responsibility for preparing notes on and teaching the assigned parts to the remainder of the group.

The group can be very valuable for mutual editing on writing assignments. Suppose, for example, that you are drafting complaints in a course. Photocopy a complaint that one member of the group drafts. The group then collectively comments upon and edits the complaint according to the standards discussed in class and in the course materials. Similarly, you could try to obtain copies of old exams in the course and collectively examine answers prepared by group members. Ask your teacher for fact situations that could be the basis of legal analysis memos (see chapter 7) or other drafting assignments. Make up fact situations of your own. The student whose work is being scrutinized must be able to take constructive criticism. The criticism should be intense if it is to be worthwhile.

Students should be asked to rewrite the draft after incorporating suggestions made. The rewrite should later be subjected to another round of mutual editing. Occasionally, you might want to consider asking your teacher to meet with your group in order to obtain further help in legal writing.

Do not hesitate to subject your writing to the scrutiny of other students. You can learn a great deal from each other.

11. Use your legal research skills to help you understand components of a course that are giving you difficulty.

The law library is more than the place to go to find law that governs the facts of a client's case. A great deal of the material in the law library consists of explanations/ summaries/overviews of the same law that you will be covering in your courses. You need to learn how to gain access to this material as soon as possible. In chapter 11, a series of techniques is presented on doing background research through texts such as legal dictionaries, legal encyclopedias, treatises, annotations, etc. (See Exhibit 11.14 in chapter 11.) You should become acquainted with these kinds of law books. They will prove invaluable as outside reading to help resolve conceptual and practical difficulties you are having in class.

12. Organize your learning through definitions or definitional questions.

One of the most sophisticated questions an attorney or paralegal can ask is: What does that word or phrase mean? What's the definition? To a very large extent, the practice of law is a probing for definitions of key words or phrases in the context of facts that have arisen. Can a five year old be liable for negligence? (What is *negligence?*) Can the government tax a church-run bingo game? (What is the *free exercise of religion?*) Can attorneys in a law firm strike and obtain the protection of the National Labor Relations Act? (What is a *covered* employee under the labor statute?) Can a person rape his or her spouse? (What is the definition of *rape?*) Can a citizen slander the president of the United States? (What is a *defamatory statement* and what are the definitions of the defenses to a slander action?) Etc.

For every course that you take, you will come across numerous technical words and phrases in class and in your readings. Begin compiling a list of these words and phrases for each class. Try to limit yourself to what you think are the major ones. When in doubt about whether to include something on your list, resolve the doubt by including it.

Then pursue definitions. Find definitions in your text and in the law library, for instance, in *Words and Phrases,* legal encyclopedias, treatises, annotations, legal periodical literature, statutory codes, etc. (See chapter 11.) Ask your teacher for guidance in finding definitions.

For some words, you may have difficulty obtaining definitions. Do not give up your pursuit. Keep searching. Keep probing. Keep questioning. For some words, there may be more than one definition. Others may require definitions of the definitions.

Of course, you cannot master a course simply by knowing the definitions of all the key words and phrases involved. Yet these words and phrases are the *vocabulary* of the course and are the foundation and point of reference for learning the other aspects of the course. Begin with vocabulary.

Consider a system of three-by-five or two-by-three cards to help you learn the definitions. On one side of the card, place a single word or phrase. On the other side, write the definition with a brief page reference or citation to the source of the definition. Using the cards, test yourself periodically. If you are in a study group, ask other members to test you. Ask a relative to test you. Establish a plan of ongoing review.

13. Studying ambiguity—coping with unanswered questions.

Legal studies can be frustrating because there is so much uncertainty in the law. Legions of unanswered questions exist. Definitive answers to legal questions are not always easy to find, no matter how good your legal research techniques are. Every new fact situation presents the potential for a new law. Every law seems to have an exception. Furthermore, advocates frequently argue for exceptions to the exceptions. As indicated, when terms are defined, the definitions often need definitions. A law office is not always an easy environment in which to work because of this reality.

The study of law is in large measure an examination of ambiguity that is identified, dissected, and manipulated.

The most effective way to handle frustration with this state of affairs is to be realistic about what the law is and isn't. Do not expect definitive answers to all legal questions. Search for as much clarity as you can, but do not be surprised if the conclusion of your search is further questions. A time-honored answer to many legal questions is: "It depends!" Become familiar with the following equation since you will see it used often:

If "X" is present, then the conclusion is "A," but if "Y" is so, then the conclusion is "B," but if "Z" is . . .

The practice of law may sometimes appear to be an endless puzzle. Studying law, therefore, must engage you in similar thinking processes. Again, look for precision and clarity, but do not expect the puzzle to disappear.

14. Translate important rules into checklists—develop your own practice manual.

It is important that you learn how to write checklists that could be part of a manual. Every rule that you are told about or that you read about can be translated into a checklist. Checklist formulation should eventually become second nature to you. The sooner you start thinking in terms of dos, don'ts, models, etc., the better. You won't have time to translate every rule you study into a checklist. Nevertheless, try doing the translation for at least several of the major rules you encounter in each course.

Suppose that you have before you the following statute of your state:

§1742. No marriage shall be solemnized without a license issued by the county clerk of any county of this state not more than thirty days prior to the date of the solemnization of the marriage.

One way to handle this statute is to create a checklist of questions that you would ask a client in order to determine whether the statute applies. (Breaking a statute down into its *elements* will assist you in identifying such questions, as you will see in chapter 7.) Some of the questions would be:

1. Did you have a marriage license?
2. Where did you get the license? Did you obtain it from a county clerk in this state?
3. On what date did you obtain the license?
4. On what date did you go through the marriage ceremony (solemnization)? Were there more than thirty days between the date you obtained the license and the date of the ceremony?

These are the questions that must be asked as part of a large number of questions concerning the validity of a marriage. If you were creating a manual, the above questions in your checklist for section 1742 could go under the manual topic of "Marriage Formation" or "Marriage License." Whenever you have a class on this topic or analyze any law on this topic, translate the lecture into checklists such as the brief one presented above.

To be sure, checklists written by others are already in existence. They are found, for example, in manuals and practice books. Why create your own? First of all, your check-lists are *not* intended as a substitute for those in manuals or practice books. You will undoubtedly make extensive use of the latter. You are encouraged to do so. Your check-lists will supplement the others. More significantly, two of the best ways for you to learn how to use manuals are (a) to write checklists of your own and (b) to see the connection between the law (for example, a statute) and the guidelines and techniques within a checklist.

15. Develop the skill of note taking.

Note taking is essential in the law. You will regularly be told to "write it down" or "put it in a memo." Effective note taking is often a precondition to being able to do *any* kind of writing in the law.

First, take notes on what you are reading for class preparation and for research assign-ments. Do not rely exclusively on your memory. After reading hundreds of pages (or more), you will not be able to remember what you have read at the end of the semester, or even at the end of the day. Copy what you think are the essential portions of the mate-rials you are reading. Be sure to include definitions of important words and phrases as indicated in guideline 12 above.

To be sure, note taking will add time to your studying. Yet you will discover that it was time well spent, particularly when you begin reviewing for an exam or writing your mem-orandum.

Second, take notes in class. You must develop the art of taking notes while simultane-ously listening to what is being said. On the job, you may have to do this frequently. For example, when:

- Interviewing a client
- Interviewing a witness during field investigation
- Receiving instructions from a supervisor
- Talking with someone on the phone
- Taking notes during a deposition
- Taking notes while a witness is giving testimony at trial

A good place to begin learning how to write and listen at the same time is during your classes.

Most students take poor class notes. This is due to a number of reasons:

- They may write slowly.
- They may not like to take notes; it's hard work.
- They may not know if what is being said is important enough to be noted until after it is said—when it is too late because the teacher has gone on to something else.
- They do not think it necessary to take notes on a discussion that the teacher is having with another student.
- They take notes only when they see other students taking notes.
- Some teachers ramble.

A student who uses these excuses for not taking comprehensive notes in class will even-tually be using similar excuses on the job when precise note taking is required for a case. This is unfortunate. You must overcome whatever resistances you have acquired to the admittedly difficult task of note taking. Otherwise you will pay the price in your school-work and on the job.

Of course, you do not want to write down everything, even if this were physically possible. You ought to make the assumption, however, that if it is important enough for someone to tell you something, it is important enough for you to make note of it.

If you do not know how to take shorthand, develop your own system of abbreviations. (See the list of common abbreviations in Exhibit A.) Sometimes you will have to begin taking notes at the moment the person starts talking rather than wait until the end of what he or she is saying. Try different approaches to increasing the completeness of your notes.

If you are participating in class by talking with the teacher, it will obviously be difficult for you to take notes at the same time. After class, take a few moments to jot down some notes on what occurred during the discussion. Then ask someone else who was in class to review these notes for accuracy and completeness.

16. Studying rules—the role of memory.

Memory plays a significant role in the law. Applicants for the bar, for example, are not allowed to take notes into the exam room. An advocate in court or at an administrative hearing may be able to refer to notes, but the notes are of little value if the advocate does not have a solid grasp of the case. Most of the courses you will be taking have a memory

---

Exhibit A — Common Abbreviations Used in Note Taking by Students in Litigation Classes

π	plaintiff	lee	lessee	jdr	joinder
Δ	defendant	CN	contributory	b/p	burden of proof
θ	third party		negligence	s/l	statute of limitations
c.l.	common law	CpN	comparative	s/f	statute of frauds
c/a	cause of action		negligence	K	contract
JV/π	jury verdict for	rsb	reasonable	T	tort
	plaintiff	A/R	assumption of risk	IT	intentional tort
R&R	reversed &	cz	cause	N	negligence
	remanded	px cz	proximate cause	SL	strict liability
Dem	demurrer	ab dg	abnormally	A&B	assault & battery
$	suppose		dangerous	4cb	foreseeable
Q	question	inj	injunction	dfm	defamation
O	owner	bfp	bona fide	Dct	deceit
stat	statute		purchaser	lbl	libel
L	liable, liability	br/wrt	breach of	sld	slander
nj	injury		warranty	impl	implied
dmg	damages	dft	defect	impt	imputed
dfs	defense	dsn	design	jfc	justification
Tp	trespass	WD	wrongful death	std	standard
pvg	privilege	Svv	survival	vln	violation
Tfz	tortfeasor	m-	mal-, mis-	pun	punitive
lz	license	m-pr	malpractice	stfn	satisfaction
lzc	licensee	m-rep	misrepresentation	rls	release
tpr	trespasser	n-	non-	rem	remedy
ktb	contribution	[	not, un-	p.f.	prima facie
lr	lessor	[4cf	unforeseeable		

Source: Prosser, Wade & Schwartz, *Cases and Materials on Torts*, 1263 (Foundation Press, 1976).

component. This is true even for open-book exams, since you will not have time to go through all the material while responding to the questions.

Students often make two mistakes with respect to the role of memory:

- They think that memorizing is beneath their dignity.
- They think that because they understand something, they know it sufficiently to be able to give it back in an examination.

Of course, you should not be memorizing what you do not understand. Rote memorization is close to worthless. This is not the case for important material that you comprehend. Yet simply understanding something does not necessarily mean that you have a sufficient grasp of it for later use.

Many systems for memorizing material can be effective:

- Reading it over and over
- Copying it
- Writing questions to yourself about it and trying to answer the questions
- Having other students ask you questions about it
- Making summaries or outlines of it
- Etc.

If you do not have a photographic mind, you must resort to such techniques. Try different systems. Ask other students for tips on how they make effective use of their memory.

You will have to find out from your teacher what material you will be expected to know for the course. You can also check with other students who have had this teacher in the past. It may not always be easy to find out how much a teacher expects you to know from memory. Teachers have been known to surprise students on examinations! Some teachers do not like to admit that they are asking their students to memorize a lot of material for their courses, yet they still give examinations that require a lot of memory preparation.

17. Studying skills—the necessity of feedback.

Memory obviously plays a less significant role in learning the skills of interviewing, investigation, legal analysis, drafting, coordinating, digesting, and advocacy. These skills have their own vocabulary that you must know, but it is your judgmental rather than your memory faculties that must be developed in order to become competent and excel in these skills.

They are developed primarily by *doing*—practice drills or exercises are essential. The learning comes from the feedback that you obtain while engaged in the skill exercises. What are the ways that a student obtains feedback?

- Evaluations on assignments and exams
- Role-playing exercises that are critiqued in class
- Comparisons between your work (particularly writing projects) with models provided by the teacher or that you find on your own in the library
- Critiques that you receive from students in study groups

You must constantly be looking for feedback. Do not wait to be called on. Do not wait to see what feedback is planned for you at the end of the course. Take the initiative immediately. Seek conferences with your teachers. Find out who is available to read your writing or to observe your performance in any of the other skills. Set up your own role-playing sessions with your fellow students. Seek critiques of your rewrites even if rewriting was not required. Look for opportunities to critique other students on the various skills. Ask other students for permission to read their graded examinations so that you can compare their papers with your own. Create your own hypotheticals for analysis in study groups. (A *hypothetical* is simply a set of facts invented for the purpose of discussion and analysis.) Do additional reading on the skills. Become actively involved in your own skills development.

18. The value of speed-reading courses in the study of law.

In the study of law, a great deal of reading is required. Should you, therefore, take a speed-reading course? No, unless the course helps you *slow down* the speed of your reading! This advice may be quite distasteful to advocates (and salespersons) of speed-reading courses. The reality, however, is that statutes, regulations, and court opinions cannot be speed-read. They must be carefully picked apart and read word for word, almost as if you were translating from one language into another. If you are troubled by how long it takes you to read, do not despair. Do not worry about having to read material over and over again. Keep reading. Keep rereading. The pace of your reading will pick up as you gain experience. Never strive, however, to be able to fly through the material. Strive for comprehensiveness. Strive for understanding. For most of us, this will come through the slow process of note taking and rereading. It is sometimes argued that comprehension is increased through speed. Be careful of this argument. Reading law calls for careful thinking about what you read—and taking notes on these thoughts. There may be no harm in rapidly reading legal material for *the first time*. At your second, third, and fourth reading, however, speed is of little significance.

Section B
ON-THE-JOB LEARNING: THE ART OF BEING SUPERVISED

A great deal of learning will occur when you are on the job. Some of it may come through formal in-house office training and by the study of office procedure manuals. Most of the learning, however, will come in day-to-day interaction with your supervisors as you are given assignments. The learning comes through *being* supervised. Being supervised is not always easy. It will take some effort on your part to maximize the learning potential of the experience. The following guidelines are designed to assist you in increasing this potential.

Don't play "king's clothes" with the instructions that you receive.

Recall the story of the king's (or emperor's) clothes. The king was naked, but everybody kept saying what a beautiful wardrobe he had on. As new people arrived, they saw that he had no clothes, but they heard everyone talking as if he were fully dressed. The new people did not want to appear stupid, so they too began admiring the king's wardrobe. When paralegals are receiving instructions on an assignment, they play king's clothes when they pretend that they understand all the instructions but in fact do not. They do not want to appear to be uninformed or unintelligent. They do not want to give the impression that they are unsure of themselves. For obvious reasons, this is a serious mistake.

Whenever you are given an assignment in a new area—that is, an assignment on something that you have not done before—there should be a great deal that you do not understand. This is particularly true during your first few months on the job, when just about everything is new! Do not pretend to be something you are not. Constantly ask questions about new things. Do not be reluctant to ask for explanations. Learn how to ask for help. *It will not be a sign of weakness.* Quite the contrary. People who take steps to make sure that they fully understand all their instructions will soon gain a reputation for responsibility and conscientiousness.

Repeat the instructions to your supervisor before you leave the room.

Once your supervisor has told you what he or she wants you to do, do not leave the room in silence or with the general observation, "I'll get on that right away." Repeat the instructions back to the supervisor *as you understand them.* Make sure that you and your supervisor are on the same wavelength by explaining back what you think you were told to do. This will be an excellent opportunity for the supervisor to determine what you did or did not understand, and to provide you with clarifications where needed.

Supervisors will not always be sure of what they want you to do. By trying to obtain clarity on the instructions, you are providing them with the opportunity to think through what they want done. In the middle of the session with you, the supervisor may change his or her mind on what is to be done.

Write your instructions down.

Never go to your supervisor without pen and paper. Preferably, keep an instructions notebook, diary, or journal (p. 168) in which you record the following information:

- Notes on what you are asked to do
- The date you got the assignment
- The date by which the supervisor expects you to complete all or part of the assignment
- The date you actually complete the assignment
- Comments made by supervisors or others on what you submit

The notes will serve as your memory bank. Whenever any questions arise about what you were supposed to do, you have something concrete to refer to.

Exhibit B contains an assignment checklist on which you can record this kind of data for every major assignment you receive.

Insist on a due date and on a statement of priorities.

You need to know when an assignment is due. Ask for a due date *even if the supervisor tells you to "get to it when you can."* This phrase may mean "relatively soon" or "before the end of the month" to your supervisor, but not to you. If the supervisor says he or she does not know when it should be done, ask for an approximate due date. Tell the supervisor you want to place the assignment on your calendar so that it will not slip through the cracks because of all the other assignments.

Also ask what priority the assignment has. Where does it fit in with your other assignments? If you have more than enough to fill the day, you need to know what takes priority. If you do not ask for a priority listing, the supervisor may assume you are under no time pressures.

If the instructions appear to be complicated, ask your supervisor to separate and prioritize the tasks.

As you receive instructions, you may sometimes feel overwhelmed by all that is being asked of you. Many supervisors do not give instructions in clear, logical patterns. They may talk in a rambling, stream-of-consciousness fashion. When confronted with this situation, simply say:

OK, but can you break that down for me a little more so that I know what you want me to do first? I think I will be able to do the entire assignment, but it would help if I approach it one step at a time. Where do you want me to start?

Exhibit B   Checklist for Major Assignments

Name of supervisor for the assignment:

What you have been asked to do:

Specific areas or tasks you have been told *not* to cover, if any:

Format supervisor expects, e.g., rough draft, final copy ready for supervisor's signature:

Date you are given the assignment:

Expected due date:

Is the task billable to a client? If so, to what account?

Location of samples or models in the office to check as possible guides (where would the supervisor look if the supervisor was performing the assignment?):

Possible resource people in the office you may want to contact for help:

Practice manuals or treatises in the library that might provide background or general guidance:

Dates you contacted supervisor or others for help before due date:

Date you completed the assignment:

Positive, negative, or neutral comments from supervisor or others on the quality of your work on the assignment:

Things you would do differently the next time you get an assignment of this kind:

As often as possible, write your instructions and what you do in the form of checklists.

A methodical mind is one that views a project in "do-able" steps and that tackles one step at a time. You need to have a methodical mind in order to function in a busy law office. One of the best ways to develop such a mind is to think in terms of checklists. A checklist is simply a chronological sequencing of tasks that must be done in order to complete a project. Convert the instructions from your supervisor into checklists in the same way you would translate rules into checklists as discussed earlier. In the process of actually carrying out instructions, you go through many steps—all of which could become part of a detailed checklist. The steps you went through to complete the task become a checklist of things to do in order to complete such a task in the future. To be sure, it can be time-consuming to draft checklists. Keep in mind, however, that:

- The checklists can be invaluable for other employees who are given similar assignments in the future.
- The checklists will be a benefit to you in organizing your own time and in assuring completeness.

You will not be able to draft checklists for everything that you do. Perhaps you will not be able to write more than one checklist a week. Perhaps you will have to use some of your own time to write checklists. Whatever time you can devote will be profitably spent so long as you are serious about writing and using the checklists. They may have to be rewritten or modified later. This should not deter you from the task, since most things that are worth doing require testing and reassessment.

Once you have a number of checklists, you have the makings of a how-to-do-it manual that you have written yourself.

Find out what manuals and checklists already exist in your office.

It does not make sense to reinvent the wheel. If manuals and checklists on the topic of your assignment already exist in your office, you should find and use them. (Also check in computer databases where the office may store frequently used forms and instructions.) The problem is that how-to-do-it information is usually buried in the heads of the attorneys, paralegals, and secretaries of the office. No one has taken the time to write it all down (see chapter 3). If this is *not* the case, you should find out where it is written down and try to adapt what you find to the assignment on which you are working.

Ask for a model.

One of the best ways to make sure you know what a supervisor wants is to ask whether he or she knows of any models that you could use as a guide for what you are being asked to do. Such models may be found in closed case files, manuals, formbooks, practice texts, etc. Care must be applied in using such material. Every new legal problem is potentially unique. What will work in one case may not work in another. A model is a guide, a starting point—and nothing more.

Do some independent legal research on your own on the instructions you are given.

Often you will be told what to do without being given more than a cursory explanation of why it needs to be done that way. But all the instructions you are given have some basis in the law. A complaint, for example, is served on an opposing party in a designated way because the law has imposed rules on how such service is to be made. You may be asked to serve a complaint in a certain way without being told what section of the state code (or of your court rules) *requires* it to be served in that way. It would be highly impractical to read all the law that is the foundation for an assigned task. It is not necessary to do so and you would not have time to do so.

What can you do, however, is to select certain instructions on certain assignments and do some background legal research to gain a greater appreciation for why the instructions were necessary. You will probably have to do such legal research on your own time unless the assignment you are given includes doing some legal research (see chapter 11). Research can be time-consuming, but you will find it enormously educational. It can place a totally new perspective on the assignment and, indeed, on your entire job.

Get on the office mailing lists for new publications.

A law office frequently buys publications for its law library that are relevant to its practice. The publications often include legal treatises and legal periodicals (to be discussed later in chapter 11). Before these publications are shelved in the library, they are often routed to the attorneys in the office so that they can become acquainted with current legal writing that will be available in the library. Each attorney usually keeps the publication for a few hours or a few days for review before passing it on to the next person on the mailing list.

Ask to get on these mailing lists. The publications are often excellent self-education opportunities, particularly the articles in the legal periodicals.

Ask secretaries and other paralegals for help.

Secretaries and paralegals who have worked in the office for a long period of time can be very helpful to you if you approach them properly. Everybody wants to feel important. Everybody wants to be respected. When someone asks for something in a way that gives the impression he or she is *entitled* to what is being sought, difficulties usually result. Think of how you would like to be approached if you were in the position of the secretary or paralegal. What would turn you off? What would make you want to go out of your way to cooperate with and assist a new employee who needs your help? Your answers (and sensitivity) to questions such as these will go a long way toward enabling you to draw on the experience of others in the office.

Obtain feedback on an assignment before the date it is due.

Unless the assignment you are given is a very simple one, do not wait until the date that it is due to communicate with your supervisor. If you are having trouble with the assignment, you will want to check with your supervisor as soon as possible and as often as necessary. It would be a mistake, however, to contact the supervisor only when trouble arises. Of course, you want to avoid wasting anyone's time, including your own. You should limit your contacts with a busy supervisor to essential matters. You could take the following approach with your supervisor:

> Everything seems to be going fine on the project you gave me. I expect to have it in to you on time. I'm wondering, however, if you could give me a few moments of your time. I want to bring you up to date on where I am so that you can let me know if I am on the right track.

Perhaps this contact could take place on the phone or during a brief office visit. Suppose that you have gone astray on the assignment without knowing it? It is obviously better to discover this before the date the assignment is due. The more communication you have with your supervisor, the more likely it is that you will catch such errors before a great deal of time is wasted.

Ask to participate in office and community training programs.

Sometimes a law office conducts training sessions for its attorneys. You should ask that you be included. Bar associations and paralegal associations often conduct all-day seminars on legal topics relevant to your work. Seek permission to attend some of them if they are held during work hours. If they are conducted after hours, invest some of your own time to attend. If your employer won't pay the enrollment fee, ask if part of the fee could be paid. Even if you must pay the entire cost, it will be a worthwhile long-term investment.

Ask to be evaluated regularly.

For a number of reasons, evaluations may not be given or may not be helpful when they are given:

- Evaluations can be time-consuming.
- Evaluators are reluctant to say anything negative, especially in writing.
- Most of us do not like to be evaluated: it's too threatening to our ego.

Go out of your way to let your supervisor know that you want to be evaluated and that you can handle criticism. If you are defensive when you are criticized, you will find that the evaluations of your performance will go on behind your back! Such a work environment is obviously very unhealthy. Consider this approach that a paralegal might take with a supervisor:

I want to know what you think of my work. I want to know where you think I need improvement. That's the only way I'm going to learn. I also want to know when I'm doing things correctly, but I'm mainly interested in your suggestions on what I can do to increase my skills.

If you take this approach *and mean it,* the chances are good that you will receive some very constructive criticism and gain a reputation for professionalism.

Proceed one step at a time.

Perhaps the most important advice you can receive in studying law is to concentrate on what is immediately before you. Proceed one step at a time. What are your responsibilities in the next fifteen minutes? Block everything else out. Make *the now* as productive as you can. Your biggest enemy is worry about the future: worry about the exams ahead of you, worry about your family, worry about the state of the world, worry about finding employment, etc. Leave tomorrow alone! Worrying about it will only interfere with your ability to make the most of what you must do now. Your development in the law will come slowly, in stages. Map out these stages in very small time blocks—beginning with the time that is immediately ahead of you. If you must worry, limit your concern to how to make the next fifteen minutes a more valuable learning experience.

S u m m a r y

Legal education is a lifelong endeavor; a competent paralegal never stops learning about the law and the skills of applying it. A number of important guidelines will help you become a good student in the classroom and on the job. Do not let the media blur your understanding of what the practice of law is actually like. To avoid studying in a vacuum, be sure that you know the goals of an assignment, and how it fits into the other assignments. Organize your day around a study plan. Since the time demands on you will probably be greater than you anticipated, it is important that you design a system of studying. Step one is to assess your own study habits, such as how you handle distractions or how you commit things to memory. Then promise yourself that you will do something about your weaknesses.

Increase your proficiency in the basics of writing. How many of the rules about the comma can you identify? Do you know when to use *that* rather than *which* in your sentences? How many of your paragraphs have topic sentences? Are there zero spelling errors on every page of your writing? You have entered a field where the written word is paramount. You must take personal responsibility—now—for the improvement of your grammar, spelling, and composition skills.

Use the law library to help you understand difficult areas of the law. But don't expect absolute clarity all the time. Seek out evaluations of your work. Become a skillful note taker. Get into the habit of looking for definitions and of translating rules into checklists.

These suggestions also apply once you are on the job. Don't pretend you understand what you don't. Repeat instructions back to your supervisor before you begin an assignment. Ask for due dates and priorities if you are given several things to do. Write down your instructions in your own notebook or journal. Find out if an assignment has been done by others in the past. If so, seek their help. Try to find a model and adapt it as needed. Be prepared to do some independent research. Get on internal office mailing lists for new publications. Participate in training programs at the law office and in the legal community. Ask to be evaluated regularly. Seek feedback before an assignment is due.

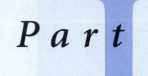

Part I

THE PARALEGAL IN THE LEGAL SYSTEM

► Contents

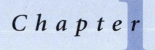

INTRODUCTION TO A NEW CAREER IN LAW

► *Chapter Outline*

Section A
QUESTIONS, FRUSTRATION, AND CHALLENGE

Welcome to the field! You probably fall into one or more of the following categories:

- You have never worked in a law office and have many questions about the career of a paralegal.
- You are or once were employed in a law office and now want to upgrade your skills.
- You have not made up your mind about whether to become an attorney and see the paralegal career as a way to learn more about the legal profession.

As Chief Justice Warren Burger points out in the quotation at the beginning of this book (page xix), the paralegal career is still developing. By definition, therefore, a number of important questions remain. The task of the first part of this book is to address these questions:

- What is a paralegal?
- Where do paralegals work?
- What are the functions of a paralegal?
- How do I obtain a job?
- What is the difference between an attorney and a paralegal?
- What is the difference between a paralegal and the clerical staff of a law office?
- What problems do paralegals encounter on the job and how can these problems be resolved?
- How is the paralegal field regulated? Who does the regulating and for what purposes?
- What are the ethical guidelines that govern paralegal conduct?
- What is the future of the paralegal field?

> "Paralegals: a novelty in the sixties, an asset in the seventies, a necessity" today.
>
> —Hon. Richard A. Powers III, Magistrate, United States District Court for the Eastern District of Pennsylvania.

Unfortunately *and* fortunately, these questions do not yet have definitive answers. As we shall see, considerable controversy surrounds many of them. It would be foolhardy for anyone to enter the field without having a comprehensive understanding of what the controversies are. According to Deanna Shimko-Herman, a paralegal in Milwaukee, "It is incumbent upon paralegals to be fully informed of the issues, and to operate from that informed base."[1] At times, however, the controversy seems to breed more confusion than constructive dialogue. This confusion can be frustrating to someone new to the field. From another point of view, however, this state of affairs presents you with the ultimate challenge of shaping your own answers to these questions. Someone once said that the most effective way to cope with change is to help create it. If Chief Justice Burger is correct that "we have only scratched the surface" of paralegal development, the creative opportunities that exist for you are boundless. You will not simply be performing a job—you will be *helping to create a new profession*. This challenge would not exist if all the answers to the fundamental questions were already written in stone.

> "Our profession is still growing and evolving. Be part of this evolution!"
>
> —Bobbi J. McFadden, President, Cincinnati Paralegal Association.

Section B
DO YOU KNOW WHAT TIME IT IS?

Perhaps you're wondering what working in the law will be like. As we will see, there is great diversity in the field. In five years, if you meet the person sitting next to you now

---

[1]Shimko-Herman, *Should Paralegals Be Regulated with Limited Licensing?* 17 On Point 10 (National Capital Area Paralegal Ass'n, February 1991).

in class and compare notes on what your workdays are like as paralegals, you will probably be startled by the differences. Of course, there will also be similarities.

One way to gauge what working in a law office might be like is to answer a particular question. Stop what you are doing for a moment and answer this question:

Do you know what time it is?

Depending on when you are reading this book, you probably will look at your watch or the clock on the wall and answer, 9:45 A.M., 1:30 P.M., 3:32 P.M., 11:28 P.M., etc. There are hundreds of possible answers. But if you answered in this manner, you've made your first mistake in the study and practice of law. Look at the question again. Read it slowly. You were *not* asked, *what time is it?* You were asked, *Do you know* what time it is? There are *only* two possible answers to this question: *yes* or *no*.

Welcome to the law! One of the singular characteristics of the field you are about to enter is its *precision* and *attention to detail*. Vast amounts of time can be wasted answering the wrong question.[2] In fact, attorneys will tell you that one of the most important skills in the law is the ability to identify the question—the issue—that needs to be resolved.

Developing this sensitivity begins with the skill of *listening*—listening very carefully. It also involves thinking before responding, noting distinctions, noting what is said and what is not said, being aware of differences in emphasis, being aware that slight differences in the facts can lead to dramatically different conclusions.

In short, you have a great deal ahead of you in the study of law; it's going to be a fascinating adventure.

Section C
MAJOR PLAYERS: THE BIG FIVE

During this course, we will meet many organizations. Five in particular have had a dramatic influence on the development of paralegalism. These five (not necessarily listed in order of influence) are as follows:

- National Federation of Paralegal Associations (**NFPA**)
- National Association of Legal Assistants (**NALA**)
- American Bar Association (**ABA**)
- Your state's bar association
- Your local paralegal association

While these organizations will be covered in some detail throughout the remaining chapters of the book, a brief word about each will be helpful at this point.

NATIONAL FEDERATION OF PARALEGAL ASSOCIATIONS (NFPA)

The NFPA is an association of over sixty state and local paralegal associations throughout the country—representing more than 17,000 paralegals. (See Appendix B). Individual paralegals cannot be members of the NFPA. From its national headquarters in Kansas City, Missouri, the NFPA promotes paralegalism through continuing legal education (CLE) programs and political action. As we will see in chapter 4, the NFPA recently launched its voluntary certification exam for *advanced* paralegals called PACE—Paralegal Advanced Certification Exam. The NFPA opposes certification for *entry-level* paralegals, i.e., those with no paralegal experience.

---

[2]See Jane Cracroft, *Developing Effective Witnesses,* The Legal Investigator, 7 (August 1991).

Voting at the annual convention of the National Federation of Paralegal Associations. 21 National Paralegal Reporter 28 (Fall 1996). Used by permission of the National Federation of Paralegal Association.

NATIONAL ASSOCIATION OF LEGAL ASSISTANTS (NALA)

NALA is primarily an association of individual paralegals, although eighty-nine state and local paralegal associations are affiliated with the organization. (See Appendix B.) More than 17,000 paralegals in the country are represented by NALA; 7,737 of them have passed NALA's *entry-level* certification exam called the CLA (Certified Legal Assistant) exam. This voluntary exam has been in existence since 1976. From its national head-quarters in Tulsa, Oklahoma, NALA is equally active in the continuing legal education and political arenas.

Over the years NALA and the NFPA have carried on a lively debate on major issues such as whether there should be entry-level certification. This debate has contributed greatly to the vitality of the field. Both associations can be reached by their "snail" mail street address (see Appendix B) and on the Internet (see Exhibit 1.1).

AMERICAN BAR ASSOCIATION (ABA)

The ABA is a voluntary association of attorneys; no attorney must be a member. Yet it is a powerful entity because of its resources, prestige, and the large number of attorneys who have joined. The ABA has a Standing Committee on Legal Assistants that has had a significant impact on the growth of the field. Recently, paralegals have been allowed to become Associate Members of the ABA, a development not everyone initially welcomed as we will see in chapter 4.

STATE BAR ASSOCIATION OF YOUR STATE

Every state has at least one bar association that plays a major role in regulating attorneys under the supervision of the state's highest court. (See Appendix C.) Most of the state bar associations have taken formal positions (in guidelines or ethical opinions) on

Exhibit 1.1 Reaching the Major National Paralegal Associations (NFPA and NALA) on the Internet

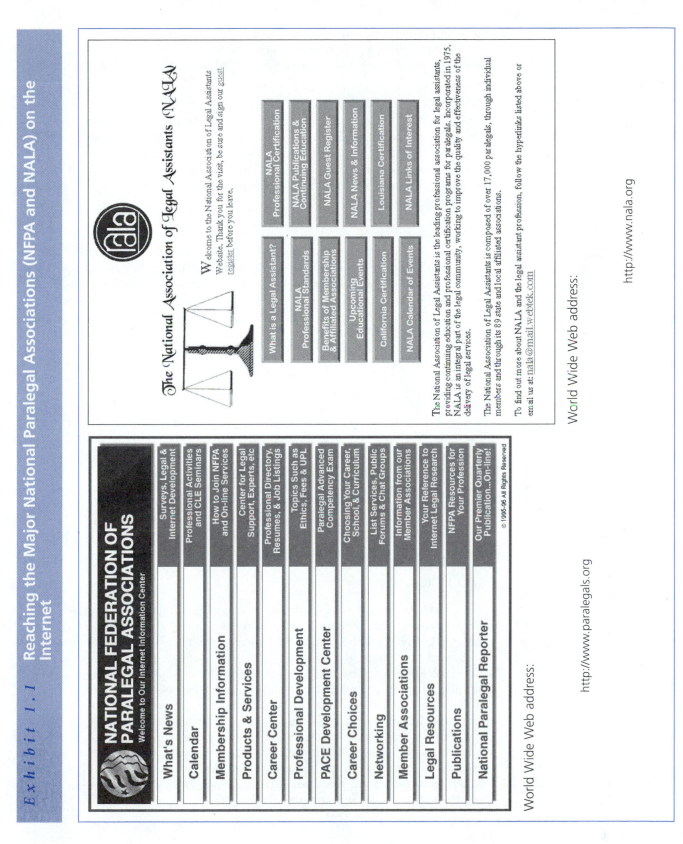

E x h i b i t 1.1 **Reaching the Major National Paralegal Associations (NFPA and NALA) on the Internet**

NATIONAL FEDERATION OF PARALEGAL ASSOCIATIONS
Welcome to Our Internet Information Center

What's News — Surveys, Legal & Internet Development

Calendar — Professional Activities and CLE Seminars

Membership Information — How to Join NFPA and On-line Services

Products & Services — Center for Legal Support, Experts, etc

Career Center — Professional Directory, Resumes, & Job Listings

Professional Development — Topics Such as Ethics, Fees & UPL

PACE Development Center — Paralegal Advanced Competency Exam

Career Choices — Choosing Your Career, School, & Curriculum

Networking — List Services, Public Forums & Chat Groups

Member Associations — Information from our Member Associations

Legal Resources — Your Reference to Internet Legal Research

Publications — NFPA Resources for Your Profession

National Paralegal Reporter — Our Premier Quarterly Publication...On-line!

© 1995-96 All Rights Reserved

World Wide Web address:

http://www.paralegals.org

The National Association of Legal Assistants (NALA)

Welcome to the National Association of Legal Assistants Website. Thank you for the visit, be sure and sign our guest register before you leave.

What is a Legal Assistant? — NALA Professional Certification

NALA Professional Standards — NALA Publications & Continuing Education

Benefits of Membership & Affiliated Associations — NALA Guest Register

Upcoming Educational Events — NALA News & Information

California Certification — Louisiana Certification

NALA Calendar of Events — NALA Links of Interest

The National Association of Legal Assistants is the leading professional association for legal assistants, providing continuing education and professional certification programs for paralegals. Incorporated in 1975, NALA is an integral part of the legal community, working to improve the quality and effectiveness of the delivery of legal services.

The National Association of Legal Assistants is composed of over 17,000 paralegals, through individual members and through its 89 state and local affiliated associations.

To find out more about NALA and the legal assistant profession, follow the hyperlinks listed above or email us at: nala@mail.webtek.com

World Wide Web address:

http://www.nala.org

the use of paralegals by attorneys. (See Appendix F.) A few have followed the lead of the ABA and have allowed paralegals to become associate members. Whenever a paralegal issue arises, you will inevitably hear people ask, "What has the bar said about the issue?"

YOUR LOCAL PARALEGAL ASSOCIATION

There are three main kinds of local paralegal associations: statewide, county or region-wide, and citywide. In Appendix B, you will find a list of every local association in the country with an indication of whether it is affiliated with NFPA, affiliated with NALA, or not affiliated with any national association. A great many paralegals in the country have found major career support and inspiration through active participation in their local paralegal association.

While these five organizations will dominate our discussion of paralegalism, we will also be referring to other important groups, such as **LAMA,** the Legal Assistant Management Association (an association of people who supervise other paralegals in large law offices); **AAfPE,** the American Association for Paralegal Education (an association of paralegal schools); and **ALA,** the Association of Legal Administrators (an association of people who manage law offices).

Assignment 1.1

It is not too early in your education to make contact with paralegal associations. In the back of this book, after the index, you will find several forms: "Paralegal Associations: Local" and "Paralegal Associations: National." By filling out and mailing the forms now, you can begin this contact.

Section D
JOB TITLES

For convenience, this book uses the job title **paralegal.** An equally common and synonymous term is **legal assistant.** Not everyone uses one of these titles. In fact, there is considerable diversity in the job titles that are used. Job titles have also led to controversy (for example, a recent lawsuit was brought to prevent certain people from calling themselves paralegals or legal assistants) and confusion (for example, some licensed attorneys work under the title of legal assistant, particularly in the government).

To begin sorting through the maze, we examine three categories of people: employees of attorneys (the dominant category), self-employed individuals who work for attorneys (a growing but much smaller category), and self-employed individuals who provide their services directly to the public without attorney supervision (the smallest but most controversial category). In none of these categories is there universal agreement on what job title should be used. Some titles (paralegal, legal technician) are used in more than one category, but not always on a consistent basis.

1. EMPLOYEES OF ATTORNEYS

The vast majority (over 95 percent) are employees of attorneys. They may be called:

paralegal	lawyer's aide
legal assistant	legal service assistant
certified legal assistant	paralegal specialist
lawyer's assistant	legal analyst
attorney assistant	legal technician
project assistant	legal paraprofessional
lay assistant	

The most commonly used titles are *paralegal* and *legal assistant.* As indicated, these titles are synonymous.[3] They are as interchangeable as the words *lawyer* and *attorney.*

Most of these individuals are full-time employees. A fairly large number, however, are temporary employees who work part-time or who work full-time for a limited period when a law firm needs temporary help, usually from paralegals with experience in a particular area of the law.

If a law firm has a relatively large number of paralegals, it might call its entry-level people:

junior legal assistant	depo summarizer[4]
junior paralegal	legal assistant clerk
project assistant	paralegal clerk
document clerk	

Large, very sophisticated law firms may also have individuals who help recruit, train, and supervise all the paralegals in the office. (See the later discussion of career ladders.) This supervisor might be called:

paralegal supervisor	director of legal assistants
legal assistant supervisor	director of practice support
supervising legal assistant	paralegal coordinator
paralegal manager	senior legal assistant
manager of paralegal services	legal assistant coordinator
legal assistant manager	case manager
director of paralegal services	paralegal administrator
director of legal assistant services	legal assistant administrator

All of the titles listed thus far are generic in the sense that they do not tell you what area of law the person works in. Other employee job titles are more specific:

litigation assistant	conflict-of-interest coordinator
corporate paralegal	family law paralegal

---

[3]Someone once proposed that the word *paralegal* be used primarily as an adjective and the phrase *legal assistant* primarily as a noun. Under this proposal, a legal assistant would perform paralegal tasks. The proposal has never been considered seriously.

[4]A depo summarizer is someone who summarizes (or digests) depositions. As we will see in later chapters, a **deposition** is a pretrial question-and-answer session with a party or witness, usually conducted outside court. Its purpose is to obtain information that will help a side prepare for trial. Paralegals often digest transcripts of these depositions.

"In the continuing debate over how we should designate members of our profession, the lines are poorly drawn. The preference of name varies with the speaker. . . ."
—Lu Ann Trevino, Houston Legal Assistants Association.

probate specialist	welfare paralegal
personal injury paralegal	international trade paralegal
real estate paralegal	worker's compensation paralegal
bankruptcy paralegal	claims negotiator
water law paralegal	

Occasionally, when the office wants its paralegal to perform more than one job, hybrid titles are used. For example, an office might call an employee a *paralegal/investigator,* a *paralegal/librarian,* or a *paralegal/legal secretary.*

Perhaps the strangest—and thankfully the rarest—hybrid title you may see is *attorney/paralegal.* Recently, a law firm placed an ad in a Los Angeles legal newspaper looking for an individual who would work under this title. What's going on? One of the realities of the job market is that many parts of the country are flooded with unemployed attorneys, particularly those just graduating from law school. A recent article in the American Bar Association Journal was entitled *Post-School Job May Be as Paralegal.*[5] Some law firms are willing to hire a desperate attorney at a paralegal's salary because the firm can charge clients a higher billing rate for an attorney's time than for a paralegal's time. Most law firms, however, think it is unwise to hire an attorney for a paralegal's position because the two fields are separate employment categories and the firms know that the attorneys are not interested in careers as paralegals. Yet there will continue to be attorneys available for paralegal positions and law firms willing to hire them, particularly when the firms need temporary legal help.

2. SELF-EMPLOYED INDIVIDUALS WORKING FOR ATTORNEYS

All of the above titles we have examined thus far cover people who are employees of attorneys in one law office. They are known as **traditional paralegals** because they work under the supervision of attorneys. Another kind of traditional paralegal—although much smaller in number—is the **independent contractor** who has formed his or her own business that provides services *to attorneys* from more than one office. (Independent contractors are self-employed persons who control the *methods* of performing tasks; the *objectives* or end products of the tasks are controlled by those who buy their services.) They move from office to office for relatively short-term projects and periods, or they work in their own office on projects mailed to them (or transmitted by "fax" machine or by computer) from different attorneys around town. Such self-employed individuals have different titles such as:

freelance paralegal	contract paralegal
freelance legal assistant	legal technician
independent paralegal	temporary paralegal

3. SELF-EMPLOYED INDIVIDUALS SERVING THE PUBLIC

Finally, there is a controversial category of people who do not work for (and who are not supervised by) attorneys. They sell their services directly to the public. Among the titles used by such practitioners are:

paralegal	independent paralegal
legal technician	freelance paralegal
forms practitioner	legal scrivener
forms preparer	limited practice officer
legal typist	certified closing officer

---

[5] 81 ABAJ 14 (March 1995).

Bar associations have often tried to prosecute these individuals for **unauthorized practice of law.** Yet there is a movement, in the form of limited licensing, toward legitimizing some of their activities. We will examine this in chapter 4.

Established paralegals are not always happy with the diversity of titles. For example, a number of paralegal associations object to anyone in the third category (self-employed individuals serving the public) using the word *paralegal* in his or her title. To avoid confusion in the mind of the public, such associations want to limit that word to those who work under the supervision of an attorney. They prefer the title **legal technician,** for example, to the title *independent paralegal.* One paralegal association refers to everyone in the third category as "nonparalegals"! For similar reasons, the National Association of Legal Assistants recently asked a court to prevent inmates from using the title of paralegal or legal assistant. They had completed a course in legal research to allow them to work on their own legal problems and those of other inmates.[6] Since they would not always be working under the supervision of attorneys, NALA wanted them to use a title other than paralegal or legal assistant. Such efforts to restrict the use of titles have generally been unsuccessful.

There may come a time when a legislature or court will establish definitive titles for certain categories of individuals in this area. At the present time, however, official titles do not exist. There is no requirement, for example, that individuals be licensed by the state in order to work in any of the three categories listed above. Hence there are no rules on who can use titles such as paralegal or legal assistant. If a form of licensing is instituted, this may change. Again we will discuss this possibility in chapter 4.

Section E
JOB DEFINITIONS

What comes to mind when people think of a paralegal? Perhaps the most common definition is: a nonattorney who helps an attorney. While essentially correct, this definition has some problems—as we will see. In this book, the following definition is used:

> A paralegal is a person with legal skills who works under the supervision of an attorney or who is otherwise authorized to use those skills; this person performs tasks that do not require all the skills of an attorney and that most secretaries are not trained to perform.

The American Bar Association, the National Association of Legal Assistants, and the National Federation of Paralegal Associations have all formulated definitions. American Bar Association:

> Persons who, although not members of the legal profession, are qualified through education, training, or work experience, are employed or retained by a lawyer, law office, governmental agency, or other entity in a capacity or function which involves the performance, under the ultimate direction and supervision of an attorney, of specifically delegated substantive legal work, which work, for the most part, requires a sufficient knowledge of legal concepts that, absent that legal assistant, the attorney would perform the task.

---

[6]*Alan Gluth et al vs. Arizona Department of Corrections* (CB-84-1626 PHX CAM) (United States Court of Appeals for the Ninth Circuit). See 17 Facts & Findings 6 (NALA, Fall 1990).

National Association of Legal Assistants:

> Legal Assistants [also known as paralegals] are a distinguishable group of persons who assist attorneys in the delivery of legal services. Through formal education, training, and experience, legal assistants have knowledge and expertise regarding the legal system and substantive and procedural law which qualify them to do work of a legal nature under the supervision of an attorney.

National Federation of Paralegal Associations:

> A paralegal/legal assistant is a person qualified through education, training, or work experience to perform substantive legal work that requires knowledge of legal concepts and is customarily, but not exclusively, performed by a lawyer. This person may be retained or employed by a lawyer, law office, governmental agency, or other entity, or may be authorized by administrative, statutory or court authority to perform this work.

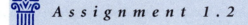

Assignment 1.2

Assume that Jones is authorized by law to represent clients in social security hearings for a fee. Jones is a nonattorney who works alone. Is Jones a legal assistant or paralegal under the ABA definition? Under the NALA definition? Under the NFPA definition? For each answer, explain why or why not.

In chapter 3, we will discuss the issue of career ladders within the paralegal field. Unless a law office employs a relatively large number of paralegals, career ladders usually do not exist. Yet career ladders are becoming increasingly common when an office has three or more paralegals. Then more than one definition of a paralegal is needed to reflect the different steps on the ladder—from the entry-level paralegal to the paralegal manager. In Exhibit 1.2, you will find an example of the definitions proposed by the Legal Assistant Management Association (LAMA), an organization of over 400 legal assistant managers. Of course, not all large offices use these titles or definitions, but their use is increasing.

A number of points need to be made about the definition of a paralegal—or the absence of a definition about which everyone can agree:

1. *To date, there is no official terminology imposed by law.*

    A person becomes a paralegal in three ways: by experience, by training, and by fiat.[7] See Exhibit 1.3. Twenty years ago, the first route was the most common way to become a paralegal. Today, the second route is the most common. While the third route still exists, it is becoming increasingly rare. Those who enter the field this way are sometimes resented by paralegals who entered the field by experience or training.

    Why do these three methods of becoming a paralegal exist? Primarily because there are no licensing or other laws on who can be a paralegal, at least at the present time. Consequently, there is nothing to prevent a law office from calling its messenger a paralegal! Bar associations, paralegal associations, and educators have attempted to formulate definitions, as we have seen, but nothing that has emerged

---

[7]Malone, *Let Your Staff Shine as "Paralegals,"* The Compleat Lawyer 4 (Winter 1990).

E x h i b i t   1 . 2   **Sample Job Descriptions of Paralegals in a Large Law Office Where a Career Ladder Exists**

Legal Assistant Clerk

A person who, under the supervision of a legal assistant, performs clerical tasks such as document numbering, alphabetizing of documents, labeling folders, filing, and any other project that does not require substantive knowledge of the transaction or litigation.

Legal Assistant [also called a Paralegal]

A person who assists attorneys in the practice of law. Responsibilities may include factual research, document analysis, cite checking and shepardizing, drafting certificates and corporate transactional documentation, drafting pleadings, coordinating document productions, administering trusts and estates, assisting with pension plan administration, assisting with real estate transactions, and handling substantive functions in practice areas that do not require a law degree.

Senior Legal Assistant

Someone who has been a legal assistant or case manager and has the ability to supervise or train other legal assistants. He or she may have met the firm's criteria for senior status and/or is a specialist in a specific practice area.

Supervising Legal Assistant

Someone who typically spends about 50% of his or her time supervising legal assistants and about 50% as a legal assistant.

Case Manager

An experienced legal assistant who has the proficiency to coordinate or direct legal assistant activities on a major case or transaction.

Legal Assistant Manager [also called Paralegal Administrator, Paralegal Coordinator, Director of Legal Assistant Services, and Supervisor]

A person responsible for recruiting, interviewing, and hiring legal assistants. May also be responsible for training legal assistants, monitoring their work assignments, and handling personnel and administrative matters that relate to legal assistants. May have budget responsibility for the legal assistant program, and play a role in salary and billing rate administration. The legal assistant manager works few or no billable hours.

Source: Ernst & Young, *Legal Assistant Managers and Legal Assistants,* 388 (3rd ed. 1989), Legal Assistants Management Association.

E x h i b i t   1 . 3   **Three Ways to Become a Paralegal**

By experience: A secretary, office clerk, or other member of the clerical staff starts to perform paralegal responsibilities. Eventually, he or she is given the title of paralegal.

By training: A graduate of a paralegal training program who has never worked in a law office is hired as a paralegal.

By fiat: An office hires an individual with the title of paralegal even though he or she has never had any law office experience or paralegal training.

is universally acceptable. To some, this state of affairs is healthy since the absence of official terminology encourages diversity. To others, it is frustrating:

> Unfortunately, some law firms seem to be using the phrases "legal assistant" and "paralegal" with alarming regularity without regard to the tasks being performed. And firms are hiring these people at a lower pay scale, thus lowering the salary of the average paralegal.[8]

2. *Definitions are often phrased in the negative.*

Some definitions do a better job of telling us what a paralegal is *not* than what one *is*. A paralegal is *not* an attorney, *not* a secretary, *not* a **law clerk** (in America, a law clerk is someone who is working in a law office while studying to be an attorney), etc. This can be frustrating, as evidenced by the following statement of Karen Dodge, an Oregon paralegal: "I am, along with thousands of other legal assistants, more than a non-lawyer!"[9]

3. *Many definitions have four main components.*

- The paralegal is not an attorney.
- The paralegal has legal knowledge and skills.
- The paralegal works under the supervision of an attorney.
- The paralegal does not practice law.

4. *There are problems with each of these four components.*

First, as we saw earlier, some attorneys *are* working as paralegals. In the same sense, there are attorneys working in America who are licensed in a foreign country. States consider such attorneys to be paralegals unless they become attorneys under our law. Occasionally, a suspended or disbarred attorney will try to continue work in the law as a paralegal. Under certain circumstances, as we will see in chapter 5, such work is ethical and legal.

Second, we learn very little when we are told that a paralegal has legal knowledge and skills. So do attorneys, law clerks, legal secretaries, investigators, many real estate brokers, bankers, etc.

Third, not all paralegals work under the supervision of an attorney. As we will see later, many paralegals working for the government are not supervised by attorneys. There are also special laws that permit nonattorneys to engage in legal work independent of attorneys. To be sure, most paralegals work in private law offices under the supervision of an attorney. Yet some are otherwise situated.

Fourth, it is inaccurate to say that paralegals cannot practice law. The more correct statement of the principle is that paralegals cannot engage in the *unauthorized* practice of law. The existence of rules on the *un*authorized practice of law governing paralegals presupposes the existence of an *authorized* practice of law by paralegals. It is true that the spectrum of authorized practice for paralegals is quite narrow—but it does exist. In our society, the practice of law is not the exclusive domain of the attorney. This will be explored in detail in chapters 4 and 5.

5. *The definitions that we have require further definitions.*

In law, the presence of a definition usually prompts a search for a definition of the definition! Paralegal definitions sometimes contain words and phrases such as *supervision, substantive legal work, practice of law, assistance,* etc. We must be con-

---

[8]*Ka L'eo O* (Hawaii Ass'n of Legal Assistants, February 1983).
[9]Karen Dodge, Paragram (Oregon Legal Assistants Ass'n, September 1984).

cerned about what these words and phrases mean—they must be defined. These definitions will then probably require clarifications that are, in effect, further definitions. This phenomenon is not peculiar to paralegalism. The process of legal analysis itself calls for an extended series of definitions and subdefinitions, as we will demonstrate in Part II of this book.

Other disciplines face the same difficulty. In the medical profession, for example, a close counterpart to the paralegal is the *physician assistant*. The following is a definition of this career:

> Physician assistant means an individual who is qualified by academic and clinical training to provide patient care services under the supervision and responsibility of a doctor of medicine or osteopathy.[10]

Among the major phrases in this definition that require further defining are "qualified," "patient care services," and "supervision."

6. *A title and definition should serve three main functions.*

In the quest for an acceptable title and definition, there is a danger of losing sight of the reasons that should govern the search. A title and definition should:

- Convey enough information about the field to a prospective student.
- Convey enough information about the field to a prospective employer.
- Convey enough information about the field to the public, as prospective clients.

7. *Unanimity may be unnecessary, undesirable, and impossible to achieve.*

The above three purposes can arguably be served without ever achieving total agreement on terminology. We bang our heads against a stone wall when we insist on terminology that:

- Precisely and definitively distinguishes this career from that of other law office personnel.
- Includes everyone who should be included.
- Excludes everyone who should be excluded.

This is simply too much to ask because of the great diversity in the field. We do not yet know all the boundary lines. The wiser course at this stage of development is *not* to insist on trying to achieve unanimity.

8. *Terminology and credentialization.*

It does not seem to disturb anyone that we do not have a definitive definition of an attorney. An attorney is someone with a license to practice law. Attorneys are defined primarily by the *credential* that they hold. Any attempt to provide a descriptive definition poses substantial difficulties. There has been endless litigation, for example, on trying to define the *practice of law* (see Appendix F). The same is true of terms such as *legal advice* and *professional judgment*. We will explore some of this controversy in chapters 4 and 5. The point, however, is that a precise definition of an attorney (in terms of what an attorney does) is no more easy to identify than a precise definition of a paralegal. We should not ask of paralegalism that it achieve a level of definitional precision that the legal profession has never been able to achieve.

When people in a career are having difficulty defining the career, they sometimes try to use **credentialization** as a way out of the difficulty. The paralegal career may

---

[10]44 Federal Register 36,177 (No. 121, 6/21/79).

also move in this direction. A paralegal may someday be defined primarily as some-one with a license or a certificate to be a paralegal. If this happens, the debate on role will not end. Shifting the question from "What is a paralegal?" to "What credentials should a paralegal have?" will not stop the controversy.

9. *Functional definition.*

While many organizations and individuals are engaged in a theoretical debate over the definition of a paralegal, the marketplace may be forcing a practical definition on us. As we will see in a moment, there are several kinds of cases in which the winning party can force the losing party to pay the attorney fees *and the paralegal fees* of the winning party. (When this occurs, the paralegal fees, of course, go to the supervising attorney of the paralegal; they do not go directly to the paralegal.) But everything a paralegal does on a case does *not* qualify for an award of paralegal fees. Consequently, if attorneys want to increase the chance of obtaining an award of paralegal fees, they must make sure that the tasks of the paralegal fit within the criteria for such an award. The main criterion is that the paralegal is performing tasks that are not purely secretarial or clerical. This reality may lead to a practical or functional definition of a paralegal: a person who performs nonclerical tasks that qualify for an award of paralegal fees.

▥ *A s s i g n m e n t   1 . 3*

In this assignment, we explore what the world thinks a paralegal or legal assistant is. Much will depend on what the public has heard about this field. It is not as well known as other new occupations such as *paramedic.* In many parts of the country, the word *paramedic* is printed in large bold print on ambulances racing throughout the city. This visibility has increased the public's understanding of what a paramedic is. Media attention is also important. Many paralegals were disappointed, for example, when the prime-time attorney soap opera *L.A. Law* failed to include a paralegal in the law firm that was the center of this very popular television program. Some wrote to the program producer to protest this glaring omission, but to no avail. This does not mean, however, that any kind of media attention would be welcomed. Shelly Widoff, a paralegal consultant in Boston, has her fingers crossed: "I just hope we all don't cringe when the media get hold of us on a TV sitcom."[11] Recently, many paralegals not only cringed but also vigorously protested when *Quincy,* a medical television program, portrayed a paralegal as an arch villain. Thankfully this occurred in only one episode!

Douglas Parker, a litigation paralegal, believes that the public has "as many different perceptions of our occupational status as there are craters on the moon."[12] To gauge whether this is true in your community, contact the following individuals in your area. Ask each of them the question: "What is a paralegal or legal assistant?" (Your teacher may want you to contact all of these people on your own or as part of a team effort in which a small number of students in the class divide up the number of individuals to be contacted.)

(a) A neighbor or friend who does not work in a law office and who has probably never been in a law office.

(b) A neighbor or friend who does not work in a law office but who has hired an attorney at least once in his or her life.

(c) A legal secretary.

---

[11]S. Widoff, *On the Docket,* 4 Legal Assistant Today 10 (January/February 1987).
[12]Parker, *Legal Assistants: A Case of Uncertain Identity,* 7 Legal Professional 10 (September/October 1989).

(d) An attorney who has never hired a paralegal.

(e) An attorney who has hired a paralegal.

(f) A working paralegal who is not now in school.

(g) A high school student.

(h) A student in a law school studying to be an attorney.

(i) A police officer.

(j) A person who runs a small business.

(k) A clerk in a local court.

(l) A local judge.

Take careful notes on their answers to the question. Compare the answers.

- What common ideas or themes did you find in the definitions?
- What two definitions were the most different? List the differences.
- Do you think that your survey raises any problems about the perception of paralegals in your area? If so, what are these problems, and how can they be solved?

Section F
PARALEGAL SALARIES

How much do paralegals make? Although some data are available to answer this question, there is no definitive answer because of the great variety of employment settings. Here are some relevant statistics:

- According to a 1993 survey of just over 3,500 paralegals by the National Federation of Paralegal Associations, the national average salary of paralegals was $31,706, with an average annual bonus of $1,620. The paralegals who responded to this survey had about ten years of experience. This survey also covered the starting salary of *entry-level* paralegals. Here is the breakdown of entry-level salaries:
  - 8.8 percent earned between $14,000 and $16,000.
  - 16.6 percent earned between $16,001 and $18,000.
  - 14.8 percent earned between $18,001 and $20,000.
  - 14.7 percent earned between $20,001 and $22,000.
  - 18.3 percent earned between $22,001 and $25,000.[13]
- According to a 1995 survey of just under 900 paralegals by *Legal Assistant Today,* a national paralegal magazine, the average salary of paralegals was $31,503 (not including bonus). Its 1996 survey showed a national average salary of $32,415. Most of these paralegals had up to nine years of experience. In the 1995 survey, those with less than one year of experience earned an average of $23,017.[14]

Experienced paralegals do very well. If they have good résumés and have developed specialties that are in demand, they usually improve their financial picture significantly.

---

[13]NFPA, *Findings of Paralegal Compensation and Benefits Survey* 17 (1993). See also a 1995 study of just over 2,600 paralegals by the National Association of Legal Assistants. It concluded that the mean national salary of paralegals was $30,038, with an annual bonus of $2,200. Most of the paralegals who responded to this survey had between one and fifteen years of experience. NALA, *The Legal Assistant Profession: 1995 National Utilization and Compensation Survey* 3, 37 (1995).

[14]J. Barge, *Hot Job of the 90s? 1995 Salary Survey Results,* 13 Legal Assistant Today 25 (January/February 1996). Also: 14 Legal Assistant Today 23 (January/February 1997).

A number of other generalizations can be made about salaries across the country:

- Paralegals who work in the law departments of corporations (banks, insurance companies, other businesses) tend to make more than those who work in private law firms. In a 1996 survey of corporate law departments, the average salary for a paralegal was $36,158.[15]
- Paralegals who work in large private law firms tend to make more than those who work in smaller private law firms.
- Paralegals who work in large metropolitan areas (over a million in population) tend to make more than those who work in rural areas.
- Paralegals who work for the government in civil service positions tend to make less than those who work for large private law firms or corporations. (Government paralegals earned a national average of $28,289 in 1996.)
- Paralegals who work in legal aid or legal service offices that are funded by government grants and charitable contributions tend to make less than all other paralegals.
- Paralegals working for attorneys who understand the value of paralegals tend to make more than those working for attorneys who have a poor or weak understanding of what paralegals can do.
- Paralegals who work in an office where there is a career ladder for paralegals, plus periodic evaluations and salary reviews, tend to make more than those who work in offices without these options.
- Paralegals who are career-oriented tend to make more than those less interested in a long-term commitment to paralegal work.
- Salary projections to the year 2000 are found in Exhibit 1.4.

E x h i b i t 1 . 4	**Salary Projections in the "Hot Careers"**
JOB	**PROJECTED SALARY IN 2000**
Accountant	$41,600
Computer programmer	$48,960
Dental hygienist	$39,800
Dentist	$120,480
Electrical engineer	$64,000
Employment interviewer	$25,600–$48,000
Legal assistant	**$39,840**
Management consultant	$58,100–$70,400
Nurse	$42,900
Nurse-anesthetist	$54,400–$78,400
Photographer	$31,700–$64,800
Physical therapist	$45,600–$96,000
Publicist	$46,400
Real estate agent	$32,880
Real estate broker	$63,700
Retail salesperson	$20,000–$26,800
Travel agent	$29,120

Source: Gates, *Hot Careers for the '90s,* Working Mother 68 (May 1989).

---

[15]14 Legal Assistant Today 23, 27 (January/February 1997).

There are a few paralegals in the country—*very few*—who command salaries of over $100,000. Lee Henderson, for example, is such a paralegal; she works for a large Dallas law firm. "Lee Henderson, a paralegal with 25 years' experience in the mortgage banking business, supervises a staff of 38. Her department manages closings for residential mortgage loans. She has also helped develop computer programs to assist other departments."[16] Again, such salaries, while possible, are rare.

In addition to the payment of bonuses, other fringe benefits must also be considered, e.g., vacation time, health insurance, parking facilities. A comprehensive list of such benefits will be presented in chapter 2. (See Exhibit 2.14.)

One final point to keep in mind about salaries. Once a person has gained training *and experience* as a paralegal, this background may be used to go into other law-related positions. For example, a corporate paralegal in a law firm might leave the firm to take a higher-paying position as a securities analyst for a corporation, or an estates paralegal at a law firm might leave for a more lucrative position as a trust administrator at a bank. A more extensive list of these law-related jobs will be given at the end of chapter 2. (See Exhibit 2.18.)

Section G
HISTORICAL PERSPECTIVE

In the late 1960s, most attorneys would draw a blank if you mentioned the words *paralegal* or *legal assistant*. According to Webster's *Ninth New Collegiate Dictionary*, the earliest recorded use of the word *paralegal* in English occurred in 1971. Today, the situation has changed radically. There are few offices that do not employ paralegals or are not seriously thinking about hiring them. A recent survey reports that there is one paralegal for every four attorneys in law firms and one paralegal for every two attorneys in the law departments of corporations.[17] It has been estimated that the number of paralegals may eventually exceed the number of attorneys in the practice of law. The United States Bureau of Labor Statistics has projected that paralegals will constitute one of the fastest growing fields in the country, with a growth of 86 percent between the years 1992 and 2005 (see Exhibit 1.5).

What has caused this dramatic change? The following factors have been instrumental in bringing paralegalism to its present state of prominence:

1. The pressure of economics.
2. The call for efficiency and delegation.
3. The promotion by bar associations.
4. The organization of paralegals.

1. THE PRESSURE OF ECONOMICS

Perhaps the greatest incentive to the development of paralegals has been arithmetic. Law firms simply add up what they earn without paralegals, add up what they could earn with paralegals, compare the two figures, and conclude that the employment of paralegals is profitable. There "can be little doubt that the principal motivation prompting law firms to hire legal assistants is the economic benefit enjoyed by the firm."[18] The key to increased profits is **leveraging**. Leverage, often expressed as a ratio, is the ability to make

"The past two decades have witnessed a remarkable transformation of the legal market, converting once loyal and steadfast clients into sophisticated consumers of legal products in a competitive legal marketplace. A critical component of this transformed legal market is the incorporation of paralegals providing a wide range of legal services into the law firm tapestry, a component brought about by the cost-effectiveness of employing an intermediate level of professional to handle matters beyond the ken of the average legal secretary but not demanding the full education, experience, or skill of a licensed attorney."

—Judge Becker, United States Court of Appeals for the Third Circuit

In Re Busy Beaver Building Centers, 19 F.3d 833, 851–2 (3rd Cir. 1994).

---

[16]Marcotte, *$100,000 a Year for Paralegals?* 73 American Bar Association Journal 19 (October 1987).

[17]Ernst & Young, *Legal Assistant Managers and Legal Assistants*, xi (3rd ed. 1989).

[18]*The Expanding Role of Legal Assistants in New York State*, 7 (N.Y. State Bar Association, Subcommittee on Legal Assistants).

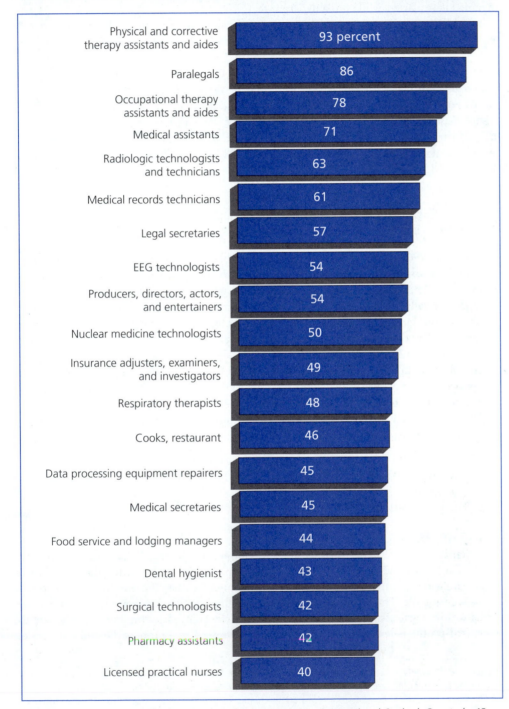

Exhibit 1.5   Fastest Growing Occupations Requiring Some Postsecondary Training or Extensive Employer Training, Projected 1992–2005

Occupation	Percent
Physical and corrective therapy assistants and aides	93 percent
Paralegals	86
Occupational therapy assistants and aides	78
Medical assistants	71
Radiologic technologists and technicians	63
Medical records technicians	61
Legal secretaries	57
EEG technologists	54
Producers, directors, actors, and entertainers	54
Nuclear medicine technologists	50
Insurance adjusters, examiners, and investigators	49
Respiratory therapists	48
Cooks, restaurant	46
Data processing equipment repairers	45
Medical secretaries	45
Food service and lodging managers	44
Dental hygienist	43
Surgical technologists	42
Pharmacy assistants	42
Licensed practical nurses	40

Source: U.S. Department of Labor, Bureau of Labor Statistics, *Occupational Outlook Quarterly,* 43 (Fall 1993).

a profit from the income-gathering work of others. The higher the ratio of paralegals to partners in the firm, the more profit to the partners (assuming everyone is generating income from billable time).[19]

In the best of all worlds, some of this increased profit will result in lower fees to the client. For example, Chief Justice Warren Burger felt that some attorneys charge "excessive fees for closing real-estate transactions for the purchase of a home. A greater part of that work can be handled by trained paralegals, and, in fact, many responsible law firms are doing just that to reduce costs for their clients."[20]

Exhibit 1.6 provides an example of the economic impact of using a paralegal. In the example, a client comes to a lawyer to form a corporation.[21] We will compare (a) the economics of an attorney and secretary working on the case, assuming a fee of $2,500, and (b) the economics of an attorney, secretary, *and* paralegal working on the same case, assuming a fee of $2,000. As you can see, with a paralegal added to the team, the firm's profit is increased about 18 percent in spite of the lower fee, and the attorney has more billable time to spend elsewhere. Some studies have claimed an even higher profit increase because of the effective use of paralegals.

The example assumes that the attorney's fee is $250 per hour and that the attorney billed the client $60 per hour for the paralegal's time. According to a 1995 survey, the average billing rate that firms charged clients for paralegal work was between $60 and $65 an hour, and the average billable hours requirement for each paralegal was 1,420 per year.[22] Not everything a paralegal does is billable to a client. For example, if a paralegal spends time helping to organize the law library, a client will not be charged for this time— it is nonbillable. In many firms, paralegals are expected to turn in a minimum number of billable hours per week. This is known as a **billable hours quota.**

When a law firm bills clients for paralegal time, the paralegal becomes a *profit center* in the firm. In such cases, paralegals are not simply part of the cost of doing business reflected in the firm's **overhead;**[23] they generate revenue (and, therefore, profit) for the firm. To calculate the amount of profit, the **rule of three** is often used as a general guideline. To be profitable, a paralegal must bill three times his or her salary. Of the total revenue brought in through paralegal billing, one-third is allocated to salary, one-third to overhead, and one-third to profit. Phrased another way, when the gross revenue generated through paralegal billing equals three times the paralegal's salary, the firm has achieved its minimum profit expectations.

For example:

Paralegal's salary:	$30,000
Paralegal rate:	$35 per hour
Billings the firm hopes this paralegal will generate:	$90,000
Rule-of-three allocation:	
—paralegal salary:	$30,000
—overhead for this paralegal:	$30,000
—profit to the law firm:	$30,000[24]

---

[19]The same, of course, is true of associates in the firm. The higher the ratio of associates to partners, the greater the profit to the partners.

[20]U.S. News & World Rep., February 22, 1982 at 32.

[21]Adapted from Jespersen, *Paralegals: Help or Hindrance?* The Houston Lawyer 111, 114–16 (March/April 1977).

[22]Barge, supra note 14 at p. 31.

[23]Overhead includes the cost of office space, furniture, equipment, and insurance, plus the cost of secretarial or other clerical staff whose time is usually not billed separately to clients.

[24]Adapted from State Bar of Texas, *Attorneys' Guide to Practicing with Legal Assistants,* VI(3) (1986).

Exhibit 1.6 The Profitability of Using Paralegals

TASK: TO FORM A CORPORATION

a. Attorney and Secretary

Function	Time Attorney	Secretary
1. Interviewing	1.0	0.0
2. Advising	1.0	0.0
3. Gathering information	1.0	0.0
4. Preparing papers	2.0	4.0
5. Executing and filing papers	1.0	1.0
	6.0	5.0

Assume that the attorney's hourly rate is $250 per hour and that the overhead cost of maintaining a secretary is $25 per hour.

Attorney (6 X $250)	$1,500
Secretary (5 X $25)	125
Total cost	$1,625
Fee	$2,500
Less cost	1,625
Gross profit	$ 875

b. Attorney, Secretary, *and* Paralegal

Function	Time Attorney	Paralegal	Secretary
1. Interviewing	0.5	0.5	0.0
2. Advising	1.0	0.0	0.0
3. Gathering information	0.0	1.0	0.0
4. Preparing papers	0.5	1.5	4.0
5. Executing and filing papers	0.5	0.5	1.0
	2.5	3.5	5.0

Assume a paralegal hourly rate of $60 per hour.

Attorney (2.5 X $250)	$625
Paralegal (3.5 X $60)	210
Secretary (5 X $25)	125
Total cost	$960
Fee	$2,000
Less cost	960
Gross profit	$1,040

COMPARISON

Fee: a. Attorney and Secretary	$2,500
b. Attorney, Secretary, and Paralegal	$2,000
Saving to client	$500
Increased profitability to attorney ($1,040 vs. $875)	$165

By using a paralegal on the case, the attorney's profit increases about 18% over the profit realized without the paralegal. Furthermore, the attorney has 3.5 hours that are suddenly available to work on other cases, bringing in additional revenue of $875 (3.5 X the attorney's hourly rate of $250).

LAUNCHING YOUR PARALEGAL CAREER

STEPS TO TAKE NOW

SUCCESS AS A PARALEGAL

Your success as a paralegal will depend on the following factors:

❍ The knowledge and skills you acquire in this paralegal program;
❍ The work habits and native intelligence you brought with you to the program
❍ Your zeal in pursuing self-education;
❍ Your determination and creativity in designing a strategy for finding employment.

In the following discussion, we will concentrate on the last two factors by making the following recommendations:

1. Start networking.
2. Start learning more about computers.
3. Start *re*-studying the basics of writing.
4. Start volunteering.

A word of caution before we begin exploring these recommendations. They will not apply to every paralegal student in every area of the country. Follow the guidance of your program director as to whether any of these recommendations do not apply to you. Most paralegal students in the country, however, need to give serious consideration to adopting all of the recommendations. Some of them may be covered elsewhere in the program and in your student materials. The focus here is on what you need to consider doing now *on your own*.

The last concept is very important—*on your own*. You have entered a career that places a premium on being a self-starter and a self-learner. The most successful paralegals are self-motivated. They take the initiative to find out what needs to be done, and then they do it. They know the value of *self-education*. To be sure, they are also ready to learn whatever is offered by formal training programs. In the curriculum of this paralegal program, you will encounter a great deal of valuable knowledge and skill that will be indispensable to the goal of achieving satisfying work as a paralegal. But more is needed from you. You need to seize every opportunity within and beyond the curriculum to train yourself. In short, you need to go on the offensive to get yourself ready for one of the most challenging and demanding fields in existence—the law.

START NETWORKING

Networking simply means making potentially useful contacts and allowing yourself to become a potentially useful contact for others. Here are the basic components of networking:

❍ You identify a large number of people that you meet socially and professionally,
❍ You make notes on what they do and how you can reach them,
❍ You organize these notes so that you can renew the contacts in the future as the need arises.

There are two main reasons why you need to be part of such a network.

First, you want to start establishing job leads:

❍ You want to find someone who's looking to hire a paralegal, or
❍ you want to find someone who knows someone who's looking to hire a paralegal, or
❍ you want to find someone who knows someone who knows someone who . . . .

How do you find these people? By aggressively building a network.

Second, when you are employed as a paralegal, you will always be on the lookout for resources that can help you do your job better and perhaps one day help you explore other job opportunities in the paralegal field and in related fields where legal knowledge and skills are needed. How do you obtain this kind of help? Networking is one of the best ways.

Here are three categories of individuals with whom to begin your networking: paralegals, classmates, attorneys.

Paralegals

As soon as possible, you need to locate employed paralegals. Begin by contacting your local paralegal association. You want to find out:

○ if you can join as a student member;
○ when and where its next meetings are held and whether you can attend; and
○ how to subscribe to its newsletter.

meeting? Proofread the newsletter? Take every opportunity to interact with the leaders and with the rank and file of the association. You will meet some wonderful people.

Classmates

Get to know your classmates. You will want to stay in contact with them throughout your paralegal career. Start now. Later we will suggest some concrete things that classmates can do for each other. For now, reach out and make contact. One day you will be extremely grateful when a former classmate gives you a job lead he or she does not want to pursue. And vice versa. One day on the job you will be extremely grateful when you are able to call a former classmate about a resource you need for a case. And vice versa.

Attorneys

Start making a list of attorneys who were once hired by any of the following: you, a member of your family, your business, your church, your friends, your accountant, your doctor, your dentist, etc. Also include attorneys who are related to or are friends of any of these individuals. Start collecting a file on each attorney. Try to include information such as name, address, and phone number; how you know the attorney or the nature of your relationship to the person who knows the attorney; the kind of practice he or she is in; whether he or she has ever hired paralegals or used paralegals as volunteers; etc. If you ever call or meet the attorney, add the date and circumstances of the contact to your file. Don't worry that collecting this information may take some time. It will be worth the effort.

Be persistent and be patient. Sometimes you will not know which networking contacts will be useful (or in what manner they will be useful) until months or even years after the contacts are made.

START LEARNING MORE ABOUT COMPUTERS

We all know that we live in the age of the computer. This is dramatically so in the practice of law. Hence it is imperative that you learn as much as you can about the basic categories of computer programs such as word

In Appendix B of this book, there is a list of the paralegal associations in the country. Since addresses change often, ask your teacher if the address for the association nearest you is correct.

It is never too soon to become involved with and to support your local paralegal association. Try to go to its functions. And go often—even if the meetings and training seminars cover things that you won't understand this early in your career. Your goals are to meet people, introduce yourself, ask people about their jobs, make notes on the specialty areas of the law different people work in, obtain tips on breaking into the field, etc. In short, your goal is to network.

Volunteer to help the association. Ask what you can do. Stuff envelopes? Answer the phones? Clean up after a processing, database management, spreadsheets, and communications. (See the definitions in chapter 13 of the text.) Regardless of the amount of attention given to computers in this paralegal program, you need to take the initiative by learning more on your own. Here are some of the things you can do.

Surfing the Internet

Find out if your local public library or your central public library offers free access to the Internet. If so, use it. Sign up for time on the World Wide Web. If there are introductory or basic classes or tutorials available, take them. Do this *even if you have access to the Internet elsewhere*. Different people explain things differently. You will invariably learn something new when different people or programs are teaching you the same thing.

Try to find something related to law on the Internet, e.g., a law or case on abortion. Don't worry that you have not yet had a course on legal research. Simply spend as much time as possible searching for legally related topics. Don't wait to be taught how to do this in school. Jump in on your own.

Exchanging Tutorials

Most people know how to do something on a computer, e.g., write a letter, copy a file in DOS, copy a file in Windows, create a macro, merge a file, write a simple spreadsheet, search a database. Ask a classmate what he or she knows how to do. If this skill is something you don't know how to do, ask the student to teach it to you. In exchange, offer to teach something about computers the other student does not know how to do. These tutorials do not have to be related to the law. They can cover any basic skill relating to word processing, database management, spreadsheets, and communications programs. Find a mutually acceptable place to meet where a computer is available. Try to keep the tutorial to one or two hours. Hence, the skill being taught should be relatively narrow. Suppose, for example, that you know how to write letters on WordPerfect, but have never used Microsoft Word. Find a fellow student who knows Microsoft Word and ask him or her to give you a brief tutorial on the basics of the Word program. If the first few attempts at mutual tutorials are not successful, keep trying. You will eventually find other students who are able to give you valuable hands-on experience.

Taking Courses

In many localities, free or low-cost adult education programs are available. They may be offered at local high schools or at community colleges. Frequently, long- and short-term computer courses are taught. For example, there may be a Saturday morning session on Introduction to Windows. Find out what is available. Try to fit some of these courses into your schedule. If a course runs longer than the time you have available, maybe you could attend the first few sessions. Sometimes the schools have workshops where you use workbooks that allow you to practice on the computer at your own pace and level.

When you apply for your first job, you want to be able to list on your résumé the computer programs you have studied. Of course, you must be truthful on the résumé. You can't say, "Proficient in WordPerfect 7" if you only attended an afternoon introduction to this program. The

truthful statement would be, "Some experience with WordPerfect 7." But *at least* you will be able to make such statements on your résumé that will be infinitely better than having a résumé that is silent on computers.

Again, don't worry that these courses in the community do not involve the law directly. At a minimum, you need extensive familiarity with the basic concepts of computer terminology and programs.

START RE-STUDYING THE BASICS OF WRITING

If you taught English for ten years before deciding to become a paralegal, you may not need the recommendations in this section. The rest of us need to take heed.

The legal profession proceeds on paper. It is true that a great deal happens on the phone, in the hallway, in the conference room, and in court. Yet before, during, and

after many of these events, something is inevitably presented in writing. No matter how much law you know, your reputation may "take a dive" the moment a conscientious supervisor, colleague, client, or public official notices misspellings or grammatical errors in your writing. For example:

❍ You submit a memo containing the following misspelled words: "accomodate," "forseeable," "compatable," "attornies." [1]
❍ You write a letter containing the following sentence in which the subject and verb do not agree: "The costs of the trial is listed in the report." [2]

There may be no problem with the *legal* component of your writing. *The problem concerns the fundamentals of*

---

[1] Correct spellings: accommodate, foresseable, compatible, attorneys.
[2] Correct grammar: The costs of the trial are listed in the report.

spelling and grammar in *all* the writing that we submit.

What can be done? Here are some minimal things you can do. Find out which teachers have the strictest standards for evaluating the writing of their students. Enroll in any courses these teachers offer. As indicated earlier, free or low-cost adult education programs are available in many localities. Find out what writing courses are offered. If any fit within your schedule, enroll. Finally, purchase several grammar books and study them on your own. Used books are often adequate if they have exercises and answers to at least some of the exercises so that you can check your progress. The last suggestion may be the most difficult to follow. It will take a great deal of discipline from you to set aside a specific period of time—preferably each day—in which you will read these texts and drill yourself on the exercises in them. Do you have this discipline?

START VOLUNTEERING

In some parts of the country, obtaining a job without paralegal experience is difficult. The competition for entry-level jobs in these areas is keen. Most paralegal students, however, have never worked in a law office.

Volunteering is an option. It may allow you to say on your résumé that you have worked in a law office, even if for only a short period of time. Of course, when you graduate from your paralegal program and start looking

for full-time work, you may not be able to compete with a veteran who has ten years of paralegal experience in the area of law a prospective employer wants. Yet you can increase your chances of finding employment by being able to present a résumé that shows at least *some* legal experience.

But as a new student with limited legal skills, what can you offer as a volunteer? It is true that you don't have much legal expertise at the present time. But many law offices need unskilled help collating records, delivering documents, mailing solicitation letters, answering the phones, etc. Be willing to do *whatever* is needed for an hour or two a week. Once you are in the office (with your proverbial foot in the door) and have gained a reputation as a conscientious and dependable worker, there is a good chance, but no guarantee, that you will be given the opportunity to provide more substantive help on ongoing legal cases in the office.

At a minimum, you should be able to talk informally with attorneys about one or more of their cases. There are many questions you could ask about a particular case. What is the case about? Who is bringing it? How did the office get the case? What stage is the case in? What is the next step? Even if you have not yet had a class on litigation, an inquisitive mind can learn a great deal.

Of course, you must be tactful. You can't let your questioning get in the way of the work flow of the office. Busy attorneys rarely have time to sit down and chat about their cases. You'll have to do the best you can, often catching a moment while the attorney is between tasks.

If you do find a volunteer position, be very careful about confidentiality. *Everything* you learn in the office about specific cases must not be revealed to anyone. This includes your spouse, your relatives, your friends, etc.

Some attorneys and law offices do not take volunteers. How do you find out which ones might want volunteers? Ask your program director for leads. Also ask your local paralegal association. It often can provide lists of organizations that need free (sometimes called *pro bono*) services.

Here are some categories of attorneys who might want some volunteer help:

Attorneys in organizations:
- Legal Aid Society or Legal Service Office (offers free legal services to the poor)

- ○ Volunteer Lawyer's Association (offers low- or no-fee legal services to the poor)
- ○ Local chapter of the American Civil Liberties Union (ACLU)
- ○ Environmental law public interest group
- ○ Domestic violence legal service group
- ○ Women's political group
- ○ Children's advocacy group
- ○ Union

Attorneys in public offices:
- ○ City Attorney's office
- ○ U.S. Attorney's office
- ○ Attorneys working in city agencies in your area
- ○ Attorneys working in state agencies in your area
- ○ Attorneys working in federal agencies in your area

Attorneys in private practice:

Earlier we listed attorneys that you should start collecting information about for purposes of networking. Many of these attorneys are in private practice. You might consider asking one of them if he or she could use a volunteer for a short period of time, e.g., an hour a week, a couple of hours a month.

CONCLUSION

These recommendations demand a good deal of initiative and determination from you—the kind of initiative and determination that are often characteristic of the most successful paralegals who are out there in the work world making a name for themselves and preparing the way for you.

Assignment 1.4

(a) In the example just given, how many billable hours per year would this paralegal have to produce in order to generate $30,000 per year in profits for the firm? Is this number realistic? If not, what must be done?

(b) Assume that a paralegal seeks a salary of $25,000 a year and that the law firm would like to be able to pay this salary. Using the "rule of three," if this person is able to generate 1,400 billable hours per year, at what hourly rate must this paralegal's time be billed in order for the attorney and the paralegal to be happy?

Paralegals can be even more profitable to the firm in cases where clients pay a fixed fee or a contingency fee. A **fixed fee** (e.g., $20,000) is paid regardless of the number of hours it takes the firm to complete the case—and regardless of the outcome of the case. A **contingency fee** is usually a percentage (e.g., 33 percent) that is paid only if the client wins, regardless of the number of hours it takes the firm to complete the case. In most cases where a client pays a fixed fee or a contingency fee, there is no hourly billing. Greater use of paralegals on such cases can lead to greater profits. The "more the attorney uses legal assistant services as opposed to attorney services," the less cost is incurred, "thereby maintaining more of the fee as a profit."[25]

Not every law firm agrees, however, that hiring paralegals inevitably leads to greater profits for the firm. A number of factors complicate the attempt to determine the economic effect of hiring paralegals. For example:

- Some firms have a relatively high turnover of paralegals. This means increased in-house training costs for newly hired paralegals and, therefore, higher overhead.
- As indicated earlier, many attorneys are looking for work, particularly recent law school graduates. Some are working part-time for law firms,[26] or are accepting comparatively low-paying **staff attorney**[27] positions at the firms. These attorneys have no hope of ever becoming partners in the firm—unlike the traditional **associates** at the firm. In fee-generating cases, some firms may be more likely to delegate work to a part-time attorney or to a staff attorney than to paralegals, since the firm can bill an attorney's time at a higher rate. This tendency is even greater if the salary of this attorney is not significantly different from the salary of the paralegals in the firm. When low-salaried attorneys are available, some firms are not as convinced that it's economical to hire paralegals.
- An experienced legal secretary can sometimes earn more than a new paralegal. Where this is so, a firm might be tempted to assign some secretarial tasks to the paralegal. When this occurs, the profitability of paralegals may diminish, since a firm cannot bill paralegal rates for secretarial tasks.

Yet such factors have not diminished the movement toward hiring increased numbers of paralegals. Furthermore, the cost-effectiveness of a paralegal should not be judged solely by the amount of revenue directly generated by his or her efforts. Paralegals often perform valuable but *nonbillable* tasks, such as recruiting new employees, managing other paralegals, helping to maintain the law library, updating and organizing pleadings files,

---

[25]L. Hangley, "The Role of the Legal Assistant" in *The Team Approach to Practice Development,* 5 (Professional Education Systems, 1989).
[26]Part-time attorneys are sometimes called **contract attorneys** or **project attorneys.**
[27]Also referred to as **second-tier attorneys.**

and doing most of the work on cases that the attorney would normally do for free (e.g., probating the estate of the attorney's brother-in-law). This, of course, enables attorneys to direct more of their efforts to fee-generating matters. Furthermore, if a paralegal is not as profitable as an employer had hoped, the problem may be the lack of an effective strategy to incorporate paralegals into the office and to manage them effectively. "In fact, if the hiring, allocation and utilization of paralegals is not actively planned and managed by the law firm, productivity and profitability will not be improved."[28] We will examine this theme in greater depth later.

🏛 *A s s i g n m e n t   1 . 5*

The following historical overview provides two theories to explain the development of paralegals. Why do you think the author feels that the "second has held the profession back"?

"Historically, the legal assistant's role evolved from efficient use of legal secretaries. There are two theories as to how this happened. One theory suggests that the attorney, seeing the benefit to his clients in providing increased services through the use of his legal secretary, provided his secretary with further education and training and she then performed substantive legal services. The other theory is that the attorney, looking for areas where he might bill his client for the secretary's service, determined that if he called his secretary a legal assistant, he could more easily charge for the secretarial services. Both of these approaches contributed to the evolution. While the first concept has elevated the paralegal profession, the second has held the profession back."[29]

Thus far the focus of our discussion has been law firm profit when the revenue generated by the law firm comes from the firm's own clients—through hourly fees, a fixed fee, or a contingent fee. Earlier we briefly mentioned another kind of case where the paralegal can play another significant role in the firm's profit picture. There are a number of special cases (for example, employment discrimination and antitrust violations), where *the losing side pays the attorney fees of the winning side.* Most courts agree that in addition to recovering attorney fees, the winning side can recover for its paralegal time spent in litigation. But in what amount? Two possibilities exist:

(a) *Prevailing Market Rate for Paralegals.* The **market rate** is the amount a law firm charges its clients for paralegal time, e.g., $60 an hour.

(b) *Actual Cost to the Law Firm.* The actual cost is the amount that the law firm pays to keep its paralegal, e.g., $20 an hour, to cover the paralegal's salary, fringe benefits, and other overhead items related to the paralegal.

There can be a dramatic difference between market rate and actual cost, since the former includes the profit that the firm makes through the paralegal. When a losing party must pay for the paralegal time of the winning party, how much is paid? Market rate or actual cost? Different states answer this question in different ways when the litigation involves a state matter.

---

[28]A. Olson, *Law Firms, Paralegals and Profitability,* 4 Journal of Paralegal Education and Practice 31, 32 (October 1987).
[29]L. Hangley, "The Role of the Legal Assistant" in *The Team Approach to Practice Development,* 3 (Professional Education Systems, 1989).

For certain kinds of *federal* cases, however, the United States Supreme Court settled the question in the very important 1989 opinion of *Missouri v. Jenkins* when it ruled that the prevailing market rate was to be the standard of recovery. The relevant portions of this opinion are reprinted below.

The case involved a Kansas City suit in which a claim was made under § 1988 of the Civil Rights Act. The lower court awarded the winning party $40 an hour for paralegal time, which was the prevailing rate in Kansas City at the time. On appeal, the losing party argued that it should pay no more than $15 an hour, which represented the actual cost to the law firm of employing the paralegal. The United States Supreme Court did not accept this position.

Case
Missouri v. Jenkins
United States Supreme Court
491 U.S. 274, 109 S. Ct. 2463,
105 L. Ed. 2d 229 (1989)

Justice BRENNAN delivered the opinion of the Court. . . . [T]o bill paralegal work at market rates . . . makes economic sense. By encouraging the use of lower-cost paralegals rather than attorneys wherever possible, permitting market-rate billing of paralegal hours "encourages cost-effective delivery of legal services and, by reducing the spiraling cost of civil rights litigation, furthers the policies underlying civil rights statutes." *Cameo Convalescent Center, Inc. v. Senn,*

738 F.2d 836, 846 (CA7 1984), cert. denied, 469 U.S. 1106, 105 S. Ct. 780, 83 L. Ed. 2d 775 (1985).*

Such separate billing appears to be the practice in most communities today.** In the present case, Missouri concedes that "the local market typically bills separately for paralegal services," Transcript of Oral Argument 14, and the District Court found that the requested hourly rates of $35 for law clerks, $40 for paralegals, and $50 for recent law graduates were the prevailing rates for such services in the Kansas City area. . . . Under these circumstances, the court's decision to award separate compensation at these rates was fully in accord with § 1988 [of the Civil Rights Act] . . . .

---

*It has frequently been recognized in the lower courts that paralegals are capable of carrying out many tasks, under the supervision of an attorney, that might otherwise be performed by a lawyer and billed at a higher rate. Such work might include, for example, factual investigation, including locating and interviewing witnesses; assistance with depositions, interrogatories, and document production; compilation of statistical and financial data; checking legal citations; and drafting correspondence. Much such work lies in a gray area of tasks that might appropriately be performed either by an attorney or a paralegal. To the extent that fee applicants under § 1988 are not permitted to bill for the work of paralegals at market rates, it would not be surprising to see a greater amount of such work performed by attorneys themselves, thus increasing the overall cost of litigation.

Of course, purely clerical or secretarial tasks should not be billed at a paralegal rate, regardless of who performs them. What the

court in *Johnson v. Georgia Highway Express, Inc.,* 488 F.2d 714, 717 (CA5 1974), said in regard to the work of attorneys is applicable by analogy to paralegals: "It is appropriate to distinguish between legal work, in the strict sense, and investigation, clerical work, compilation of facts and statistics and other work which can often be accomplished by non-lawyers but which a lawyer may do because he has no other help available. Such non-legal work may command a lesser rate. Its dollar value is not enhanced just because a lawyer does it."

**Amicus* National Association of Legal Assistants reports that 77 percent of 1,800 legal assistants responding to a survey of the association's membership stated that their law firms charged clients for paralegal work on an hourly billing basis. Brief for National Association of Legal Assistants as *Amicus Curiae* 11.

Many consider this opinion to be a great victory for the paralegal movement. "Waves from the ripple effect" of the opinion "will wash the doorsteps of virtually every law office which employs or which is contemplating utilizing legal assistants in its delivery of legal services."[30] The highest Court in the land not only acknowledged the value of paralegals, but also provided a clear demonstration of how profitable paralegals can be in these kinds

---

[30]*The Paralegal Factor,* 9 The California Lawyer 47 (June 1989).

of cases. Equally important is the admonition of the Court's footnote that "purely clerical or secretarial tasks [performed by a paralegal] should not be billed at a paralegal rate." If a law firm wants to recover paralegal fees at market rates from the opposing side, the firm must provide paralegal timesheets or other records showing that the firm gave the paralegal substantial, nonsecretarial tasks to perform in the case. As we shall see later, a major complaint of some paralegals is that they are not delegated enough challenging tasks. *Missouri v. Jenkins* should help combat this problem. Attorneys will be more inclined to use paralegals properly when they see that their economic livelihood is enhanced by doing so.[31] (See also Appendix F for summaries of cases on this topic.)

It must be noted, however, that some courts do *not* adopt the approach of the United States Supreme Court in *Missouri v. Jenkins*. This opinion involved the interpretation of the Civil Rights Act. If another court is interpreting a different statute, it might reach a different conclusion on how to handle paralegal time. A few courts refuse to allow any separate compensation for paralegal time. In such courts, paralegal fees are simply not recoverable. Yet the trend is definitely in the direction of the approach taken in *Missouri v. Jenkins*.

🏛 *A s s i g n m e n t   1 . 6*

(a) Earlier in this chapter, you were given sample job descriptions of paralegals in a large law office: legal assistant clerk, legal assistant, senior legal assistant, supervising legal assistant, case manager, and legal assistant manager. (See Exhibit 1.2.) Assume that the law firm of Smith & Smith is large enough to have employees in all of these categories and that employees in each category work on a major case for which an award of paralegal fees can be made. In the light of *Missouri v. Jenkins,* how would a court make a determination of paralegal fees in this case?

(b) What has been the impact of *Missouri v. Jenkins* in your state?

2. THE CALL FOR EFFICIENCY AND DELEGATION

Attorneys are overtrained for a substantial portion of the tasks that they perform in a law office. This is one of the major reasons that traditional law offices are charged with inefficiency. Paralegals have been seen as a major step toward reform. The results have been quite satisfactory, as evidenced by the following comments from attorneys who have hired paralegals:[32]

A competent legal assistant for several years has been effectively doing 25% to 35% of the actual work that I had been doing for many years prior to that time.

The results of our 3 attorney–3 paralegal system have been excellent. Our office's efficiency has been improved and our clients are receiving better service.

---

[31]These fee-award cases have another dimension that should also be considered. Suppose that an attorney seeks an award of *attorney* fees to cover time spent on tasks that the attorney should have delegated to a paralegal. In such a case, a court might refuse to award the attorney his or her normal hourly fee. One court phrased the problem this way: "Routine tasks, if performed by senior partners in large firms, should not be billed at their usual rates. A Michelangelo should not charge Sistine Chapel rates for painting a farmer's barn." *Ursic v. Bethlehem Mines,* 719 F.2d 670, 677 (3rd Cir. 1983).
[32]Oregon State Bar, Legal Assistants Committee, *Legal Assistant Survey* (1977).

It has been our experience that clients now ask for the legal assistant. Client calls to the attorneys have been reduced an estimated 75%.

It has taken a *very* long time for attorneys to realize that something was wrong with the way they practiced law. The following historical perspective presents an overview of how attorneys came to this realization.[33]

During the American colonial period, the general populace distrusted attorneys because many of them sided with King George III against the emerging independent nation. Some colonies tolerated the existence of attorneys, but established roadblocks to their practice. In 1641, for example, the Massachusetts Bay Colony prohibited freemen from hiring attorneys for a fee:

> "Every man that findeth himself unfit to plead his own cause in any court shall have libertie to employ any man against whom the court doth not except, to help him, Provided he gave him noe fee or reward for his pains."[34]

Furthermore, almost anyone could become an attorney without having to meet rigorous admission requirements.

Up until the nineteenth century, the attorney did not have assistants other than an occasional apprentice studying to be an attorney himself. The attorney basically worked alone. He carried "his office in his hat."[35] A very personal attachment and devotion to detail were considered to be part of the process of becoming an attorney and of operating a practice. In the early nineteenth century, George Wythe commented that:

> It is only by drudgery that the exactness, accuracy and closeness of thought so necessary for a good lawyer are engendered.[36]

The same theme came from Abraham Lincoln in his famous "Notes for a Law Lecture":

> If anyone . . . shall claim an exemption from the drudgery of the law, his case is a failure in advance.[37]

Attorneys would be somewhat reluctant to delegate such "drudgery" to someone working for them, according to this theory of legal education.

During this period, attorneys often placed a high premium on the personal relationship between attorney and client. As late as 1875, for example, Seward and his partners "would have none of the newfangled typewriters" because clients would "resent the lack of personal attention implied in typed letters."[38] The coming of the Industrial Revolution, however, brought the practice of law closer to industry and finance. Some law offices began to specialize. As attorneys assumed new responsibilities, the concern for organization and efficiency grew. To be sure, large numbers of attorneys continued to carry their law offices "in their hats" and to provide an essentially one-to-one service. Many law offices in the 1850s took a different direction, however.

---

[33]The research for part of the section on the historical background of paralegals was conducted by the author and subsequently used with his permission in the following article: Brickman, *Expansion of the Lawyering Process through a New Delivery System: The Emergence and State of Legal Paraprofessionalism*, 71 Columbia Law Review 1153, 1169ff (1971).

[34]"Body of Liberties," cited in R. Warner, *Independent Paralegal's Handbook*, 8 (Nolo Press, 1986).

[35]Lee, *Large Law Offices*, 57 American Law Review 788 (1923).

[36]Lewis, ed., "George Wythe," in Great American Lawyers: A History of the Legal Profession in America, vol. 1, 55 (1907).

[37]Nicolay & Hay, eds., "Notes for a Law Lecture," in Complete Works of Abraham Lincoln, 142 (1894). See also Frank, *Lincoln as a Lawyer*, 3 (1961).

[38]Swaine, *The Cravath Firm and Its Predecessors: 1819–1947*, vol 1, 365, 449.

Machines created new jobs. The typewriter introduced the typist. Librarians, investigators, bookkeepers, office managers, accountants, tax and fiduciary specialists, and research assistants soon found their way into the large law office. Although nonattorneys were primarily hired to undertake clerical or administrative responsibilities, they soon were delegated more challenging roles. As one study of a law firm noted with respect to several female employees who had been with the firm a number of years:

> In addition, these women were given considerable responsibility in connection with their positions as secretary or head bookkeeper. The head bookkeeper acted as assistant secretary to the partner-secretary of certain charitable corporations the firm represented. In this capacity, she recorded minutes of director's meetings, issued proxy statements, supervised the filing of tax returns for the organization and attended to other significant administrative matters.[39]

In this fashion, attorneys began delegating more and more nonclerical duties to their clerical staff. This was not always done in a planned manner. An employee might suddenly be performing dramatically new duties as emergencies arose on current cases and as new clients arrived in an already busy office. In such an environment, an attorney may not know what the employee is capable of doing until the employee does it. Despite its haphazard nature, the needs of the moment and **OJT** (on-the-job training) worked wonders for staff development.

By the 1960s, attorneys started to ask whether a new category of employee should be created. Instead of expanding the duties of a secretary, why not give the new duties to a new category of employee—the paralegal? A number of studies were conducted to determine how receptive attorneys would be to this idea on a broad scale. The results were very encouraging. The conclusion soon became inevitable that attorneys can delegate many tasks to paralegals without sacrificing quality of service. Today this theme has become a dominant principle of law office management. Most attorneys no longer ask, "Can I delegate?" Rather they ask, "Why *can't* this be delegated?" Or, "How can the delegation be effectively managed?" It is a given that substantial delegation is a necessity.

This is not to say, however, that all attorneys immediately endorse the paralegal concept with enthusiasm. Many are initially hesitant, as demonstrated by the following report on the hiring of legal assistants within the California Department of Health, Education, and Welfare (HEW):

> When the legal assistant program began in early 1977 in HEW, it was met with some skepticism, especially in offices in cities other than Sacramento. There was concern that the quality of the work might be diminished by legal assistants. However, team leaders and deputies are not only no longer skeptical, they are now enthusiastic supporters of the legal assistant program. The attorneys feel that the work product is at least as good, and more thorough, than that provided by attorneys, mainly because the legal assistants have developed an expertise in a narrow area of the law and the work is more stimulating to the legal assistants than it was to the attorneys. The legal assistants processed 152 cases in fiscal year 1977/78 and 175 cases in 1978/79. It was estimated that legal assistants are as efficient as attorneys in processing the preliminary phase of these cases. As a result, a legal assistant in this instance produces as many pleadings as a deputy attorney general would have produced in the same amount of time. For this reason the section has been able to provide a faster turnaround time for the client agencies.[40]

---

[39]Dodge, *Evolution of a City Law Office,* 1955 Wisconsin Law Review 180, 187.
[40]*Study of Paralegal Utilization in the California Attorney General's Office,* 23, Management Analysis Section. California Department of Justice (December 1980).

Proponents of greater use of paralegals in government argue that, in addition to efficiency, considerable savings can result from such use. For example, in order to save money and increase efficiency, a bill was introduced into the California Assembly:

"to require each state agency and department that employs attorneys to begin to utilize a combination of hiring practices and attrition which will result in a ratio of one paralegal . . . to every 5 attorneys employed by the state by January 1, 1990."[41]

Unfortunately, this bill was not enacted into law—largely because of opposition from government attorneys.

Another call for more cost-effective methods of practicing law by the government came from the Council for Citizens Against Government Waste (the "Grace Commission"), which recommended that the United States Department of Justice increase the ratio of paralegals to attorneys in order to achieve a savings of $13.4 million over three years. Soon thereafter, legislation was proposed in Congress to establish an Office of Paralegal Coordination and Activities in the Department of Justice to work toward the increased use of paralegals in the department.[42] Although Congress did not pass this proposal, the effort is typical of the momentum toward paralegal use throughout the practice of law.

3. THE PROMOTION BY BAR ASSOCIATIONS

The bar associations assumed a large role in the development of paralegals. This has given great visibility to the field. In 1968, the House of Delegates of the American Bar Association established a Special Committee on Lay Assistants for Lawyers (subsequently renamed the Standing Committee on Legal Assistants), and resolved:

(1) That the legal profession recognize that there are many tasks in serving client's needs which can be performed by a trained, non-lawyer assistant working under the direction and supervision of a lawyer;

(2) That the profession encourage the training and employment of such assistants. . . .[43]

Most of the state bar associations now have committees that cover the area of paralegal utilization. As we will see in chapter 5 and in Appendix F, some of these committees have established guidelines for the use of paralegals in a law office. The real impact on the growth of paralegalism, however, has come from those bar association committees that deal with legal economics and law office management. Such committees have sponsored numerous conferences for practicing attorneys. These conferences, plus articles in bar association journals, have extensively promoted paralegals.

4. THE ORGANIZATION OF PARALEGALS

Paralegals have been organizing. There are approximately 200 paralegal organizations throughout the country. (See list in Appendix B.) This has greatly helped raise everyone's consciousness about the potential of paralegalism. As indicated earlier, there are two major national associations, the National Federation of Paralegal Associations (NFPA) and the National Association of Legal Assistants (NALA). We will examine the work and the impact of these associations in the chapter on regulation. It is no longer true that attorneys are the sole organized voice speaking for paralegals and shaping the development of the field.

---

[41]Assembly Bill No. 2729 (January 21, 1986).
[42]H.R. 5107, 99th Cong., 2d Sess.
[43]Proceedings of the House of Delegates of the American Bar Association, 54 American Bar Association Journal 1017, 1021 (1968).

NOTE ON THE DELIVERY OF LEGAL SERVICES IN OTHER COUNTRIES

England

The English legal profession has two main branches, consisting of solicitors and barristers. The **solicitor** handles the day-to-day legal problems of the public but has only limited rights to represent clients in certain lower courts. The bulk of litigation in the higher courts is conducted by the **barrister.** When representation in such courts is needed, the solicitor arranges for the barrister to enter the case. Solicitors often employ one or more **Legal Executives,** who are the equivalent of the American paralegal. Legal Executives are delegated many responsibilities under the supervision of the solicitor. They undergo extensive training programs and take rigorous examinations at the Institute of Legal Executives. Once qualified, the Legal Executive obtains Fellowship in the Institute and is entitled to use the letters "F.Inst.L.Ex." after his or her name. There is also an Institute of Legal Executives in Australia.

Canada

"Legal assistants became a part of the legal community in Canada more than 60 years ago, practicing first in Montreal, then in Toronto, ... Although no exact figures are available, there are an estimated 3,000 legal assistants in Canada today. Among the first were former legal executives from England. . . . The ratio of legal assistant to lawyer ranges from 1:1 in small specialist firms to 10:1 or more in the large firms where legal assistants are often departmentalized. . . . The term 'legal assistant' is emerging as the most commonly used title in Canada and the term is recognized by the Law Society of British Colombia and the Canadian Bar Association. A unique situation exists in Ontario where the Law Society of Upper Canada requires legal assistants to be designated as **law clerks.** . . . ." The word "paralegal" commonly refers to a nonlawyer who offers certain services to the public for a fee and who does *not* work under the supervision of a Canadian lawyer. Hence legal assistants who work for lawyers generally do not call themselves paralegals.[44] In a sign of solidarity with America, the Manitoba Association of Legal Assistants recently became an affiliate member of the National Federation of Paralegal Associations.

Japan

Attorneys *(bengoshi)* are not the only providers of legal services in Japan. A separate category of workers called *judicial scriveners (shihoo shoshi)* has special authority to assist the public in preparing legal documents such as contracts and deeds. The granting of this authority is conditioned on the successful completion of an examination.

Cuba

In Cuba, legal assistants work with attorneys in law offices or collectives called *bufetes.* The assistants draft legal documents, interview clients, conduct legal research, file papers in court, negotiate for trial dates, etc.

Russia

Attorneys-at-law in Russia are organized in lawyers' colleges. Membership in the colleges is granted to three kinds of individuals: first, graduates from university law schools;

---

[44]Patricia Hicks, *The Legal Assistant in Canada,* 8 The LAMA Manager 5 (Legal Assistant Management Ass'n, October 1992).

second, individuals with legal training of six months or more, with experience in judicial work, or at least one year as a judge, governmental attorney, investigator, or legal counsel; and third, persons without legal training but with at least three years' experience. There are also nonlawyer notaries who prepare contracts and wills for the public.

Finland

In Finland, only members of the Finnish Bar Association can use the title of advocate. Advocates, however, do not enjoy an exclusive right of audience in the courts. Litigants can plead their own case or retain a representative who does not have to be an advocate.

Germany

The main providers of legal services in Germany are the lawyer *(Rechtsanwalt)* and the notary *(notar)*. The notary provides assistance in drafting contracts, wills, and other legal documents. To become a notary, an individual must be an attorney who has been in practice at least ten years. "A third type of individual providing legal services is the *Rechtsberater,* which means 'legal assistant.' " While *Rechtsberaters* often operate like American paralegals, they are "also permitted under German law to operate independently of attorney supervision. *Rechtsberaters* can open their own offices and provide legal services to the public in a limited range of areas. . . . This includes small claims matters, no-contest domestic matters, etc." A *Rechtsberater* must pass a licensing exam and maintain liability insurance.[45]

Section H
STAGES IN THE DEVELOPMENT OF PARALEGALISM

Paralegalism became a self-conscious movement in the 1960s. The following stages, or eras, of development summarize the progress of the field since then. See Exhibit 1.7. Each era is characterized by a single theme, although there is some overlap in that all five themes have been discussed throughout the history of paralegalism. Yet one theme dominates in each era.

1. THE ERA OF DISCOVERY

During the 1960s, we were finding out what paralegals are and what they can do. It was a time of discovery. Attorneys experimented with new roles for nonattorneys in the delivery of legal services. Surveys and studies were undertaken. The results were reported at national conferences and within the literature. Since the results were impressive, the news spread quickly. Attorneys were told that there was a new way to practice law. The

---

Exhibit 1.7   Paralegal Development

1. The era of **discovery**
2. The era of **education**
3. The era of **politics**
4. The era of **management**
5. The era of **credentialization**

---

[45]Robert Loomis, *Practicing Law in Germany,* 11 WSPA Findings and Conclusions 6 (Washington State Paralegal Ass'n, January 1995).

discovery of paralegals generated considerable enthusiasm, debate, and controversy. There is little doubt that paralegals are now a fixture in the vast majority of settings where law is practiced. The one possible exception is in some rural areas of the country where attorneys are taking a little longer to integrate paralegals into the practice of law. To this extent, the discovery of paralegals is still going on.

This is not to say that most attorneys hire paralegals or use them effectively. The expansion and development of paralegalism have by no means reached their peak. The point, however, is that the day has long passed when it was common within the legal profession to ask, "What's a paralegal?"

2. THE ERA OF EDUCATION

In the early 1970s, there was an explosion in the creation of paralegal training programs. The American Bar Association introduced a controversial plan to approve paralegal schools, as we will see in chapter 4. Law publishers began to produce texts for paralegals. At times, it appeared that few schools were *not* considering the creation of a paralegal program. Today the growth in programs has leveled off; new programs are not as common as they were in the early 1970s.

A more recent development in the field has been the creation of programs for *continuing* education for employed paralegals (**CLE: continuing legal education**). Almost every newsletter of paralegal associations throughout the country announces an upcoming seminar on substantive law topics (such as securities fraud or condominium conversions) or on paralegalism issues (such as overtime compensation or networking). These seminars may last several days or part of an afternoon in conjunction with the association's regularly scheduled monthly or annual meeting.

3. THE ERA OF POLITICS

Politics, of course, has always been part of paralegal history. For example, during the era of education, paralegals began to organize into local and national associations to protect their own interests as well as to pursue their professional development. The early 1980s, however, were a period of intense political debate both among paralegals and between paralegals and attorneys. While the debate continues today, it is no longer the dominant theme, as it was in those years. For example,

- The lines were sharply drawn between the National Federation of Paralegal Associations and the National Association of Legal Assistants on the issue of whether the certification of paralegals was premature. Today both associations have national certification exams, but they are significantly different in many ways (see Exhibit 4.8 in chapter 4).
- Paralegal associations undertook intensive lobbying drives to slow down regulatory efforts of some bar associations and to insure that paralegals would be close participants with attorneys in this regulation. Most paralegal associations developed strategies on how to combat problems common to paralegals.
- New local paralegal associations were formed with the active encouragement of the older associations. Considerable debate took place within some of these new associations over whether to affiliate with the National Federation of Paralegal Associations or with the National Association of Legal Assistants, or to remain unaffiliated.

4. THE ERA OF MANAGEMENT

Earlier in this chapter, factors such as economics and efficiency were listed as major reasons for the rapid expansion of paralegal use. While this enthusiasm has not died down, it became clear that the field needed a period of consolidation. Many law offices hired proportionately large numbers of paralegals within a short time. They were encouraged to expand by the promotional literature of the bar associations and by the increased income that the employment of the first paralegal generated. Some studies, however, have shown that a law office's increase in income tends to level off when larger numbers of paralegals are hired.[46]

Furthermore, not all offices are equipped to deal with the administrative problems that occur in an office with diverse personnel. Attorneys, for example, "who endorse the paralegal concept and hire recent graduates are often those whose workload is already too heavy. They have little time to provide individualized on-the-job training. The result is that paralegals feel frustrated with their lack of adequate preparation, and employers are disillusioned with their new employees."[47]

Attorneys are not trained as managers, yet management skills are fundamental to the effective use of paralegals. Hiring law office managers has helped, as has development of the relatively new career of legal administrator, but they have not eliminated the need for attorneys to educate themselves in the principles of management and systemization.

The mentality of the attorney is to work alone. Attorneys are trained to view each case as unique—every case can eventually be fought to the Supreme Court. This mentality and approach do not always encourage the attorney to delegate responsibility effectively. They certainly do not always prepare the attorney to run an office in a businesslike and efficient manner. The skills required to have a law declared unconstitutional are radically different from the skills required to manage people. Unfortunately, paralegals can be one of the victims of this defect in attorney training. It is not enough that paralegals are competent; they must also be *used* competently. Paralegals must be challenged and be secure in their relationship with attorneys and with other law office personnel. This is easier said than done, as we will see in chapter 3 on employment dynamics.

There are visible signs of change, however. Many law schools are giving more attention to the problems of law office administration. The bar associations are also intensifying their efforts in this direction. Slowly, attorneys have come to realize that incorporating paralegals into an office requires careful planning and an understanding of human nature. Management assistance is becoming available. There is now a vast body of experience on which to draw.

As we saw earlier, an important sign that change is on the way is the relatively recent creation of a new position in the larger law office—the legal assistant manager or paralegal administrator. Many firms with four or more paralegals have added a paralegal administrator to oversee the recruitment, training, assignment, and management of the office paralegals. The paralegal administrator often reports to an individual with broader management responsibility in the office, such as a legal administrator, office manager, managing partner, or chairperson of the management committee. Almost always, the paralegal administrator is someone with several years of experience as a paralegal who is intrigued by the invitation to move into management. Depending on the size of the office, some still perform paralegal duties on client cases in addition to their management duties. (See Exhibit 1.2.) The number of paralegal administrators is growing every day. As indicated earlier, they recently formed a national organization—the Legal Assistant Management Association (LAMA).

Attorneys now realize that they need this kind of specialized help to incorporate paralegals into the practice of law. In the old days, many attorneys had the mistaken notion

---

[46]Bower, *Can Paralegals Be Profitable?* Michigan Bar Journal 173 (March 1980).
[47]American Bar Association, *NFPA/NALA Focus: Two Perspectives,* 3 Legal Assistant Update 90 (1983).

that they could immediately make a lot of money simply by hiring paralegals. Thankfully, we are moving out of this era.

5. THE ERA OF CREDENTIALIZATION

The dust has not yet settled from all the controversies surrounding paralegalism. By the early 1990s none of the credentialing issues had been settled. Most people agreed that it was premature to launch extensive programs of licensing or certification. While some efforts in this direction were taken, as we will see in chapter 4, the consensus was that more time was needed to sort out all the factors involved in a program of credentialization.

It is anticipated, however, that this will change. A 1995 study reported that "nearly half the state legislatures are considering proposals" to regulate paralegals.[48] Momentum is building toward developing some form of official credentialization, such as limited licensing. According to Kay Field, former president of the National Association of Legal Assistants:

> Those of us who have worked hard to become qualified legal assistants resent the law firm who hires a high school girl to do the filing, [and] calls her a legal assistant, . . . We all agree that there needs to be some specific standards, but unfortunately we cannot all agree first of all who is to prepare them, secondly how stringent they will be, and lastly, who will enforce them. I say to you, however, that these matters must be addressed by us before they are done for us.[49]

President Field and her organization do not advocate licensing, but they do advocate action before it is too late. Intense debate rages among paralegals over the issue of credentialization, which we will examine in chapter 4. There is a very real danger that while paralegals continue to fight among themselves over the issue, attorneys and legislatures might suddenly step in to impose a scheme of regulation and control that will satisfy no one. Unless paralegals resolve the issue, it will be resolved for them. How could this happen? One possible scenario is as follows: The legislature imposes a license requirement after widespread publicity is given to an incident of negligence committed by an untrained and unqualified paralegal. To prevent such precipitate action by the legislature, it is critical that paralegals collectively decide what they want and how it should be achieved. The next four chapters are designed to provide you with the data you need to participate in this still-emerging aspect of paralegalism.

---

[48]New York State Bar Ass'n Ad Hoc Committee on Non-Lawyer Practice, *Final Report* 2 (May, 1995).
[49]K. Field, *Legal Assistants: Where Do We Go from Here?* 10 Facts and Findings 17, 18 (National Association of Legal Assistants, May/June 1984).

C h a p t e r   S u m m a r y

A *paralegal* is a person with legal skills who works under the supervision of an attorney or who is otherwise authorized to use those skills; this person performs tasks that do not require all the skills of an attorney and that most secretaries are not trained to perform. It is an exciting time to become a paralegal, even though many questions about the field remain to be resolved. There are three main categories of paralegals: those who are employed by attorneys (the largest), self-employed people working for attorneys, and self-employed people providing their services directly to the public. Within these categories, there is great diversity over the titles that are used. Nor is there universal agreement over the definition of a paralegal, or of the different kinds of paralegals. This diversity and lack of agreement are primarily caused by the fact that at present there are no licensing requirements to be a paralegal. People continue to enter the field by one of three routes: experience, training, or fiat. They do not enter through the vehicle of a unifying licensing system.

Paralegal salaries are influenced by a number of factors: experience, level of responsibility, kind of employer, geographic area, the employer's understanding of the paralegal's role, and the extent to which the paralegal is committed to the field as a career.

Bar associations and paralegal associations have promoted the value of paralegals extensively. The economic impact they have had on the practice of law is the major reason paralegals have flourished and grown so rapidly. In a properly leveraged firm, paralegals can be a "profit center" without any sacrifice in the quality of the service delivered by the firm. In every state, attorneys can charge their clients paralegal fees in addition to traditional attorney fees. Furthermore, under *Missouri v. Jenkins,* in some cases a firm can obtain an award of paralegal fees at market rates from losing parties in litigation. Also, a paralegal can help attorneys redirect some of their energies from nonbillable to billable tasks.

A firm operates more efficiently and profitably when it consistently and systematically delegates tasks to competent people with lower billing rates, so that other people with higher billing rates will be available to perform more complex tasks at higher rates. This is not to say, however, that paralegals are always profitable to a firm. Proper use and supervision of paralegals are key components of profitability.

Since the 1960s, paralegalism has gone through a number of stages. During the era of discovery, people were finding out what paralegals were capable of. This knowledge encouraged hundreds of institutions throughout the country to open paralegal schools during the era of education. The era of politics gave us a proliferation of paralegal associations at the national and local levels to address the emerging issues of this new field. In the era of management, greater attention was given to the ingredients of a successful paralegal-attorney relationship. Recognizing that attorneys have never been famous for their management skills, specialists emerged —for example, legal assistant managers—to help attorneys better integrate paralegals into an office. Today we are in the era of credentialization, during which we are likely to see limited licensing or other forms of official regulation.

KEY TERMS

NFPA, 5
NALA, 5
ABA, 5
LAMA, 8
AAfPE, 8
ALA, 8
paralegal, 8
legal assistant, 8
deposition, 9
traditional paralegals, 10
independent contractor, 10

unauthorized practice of law, 11
legal technician, 11
legal assistant clerk, 13
senior legal assistant, 13
supervising legal assistant, 13
case manager, 13
legal assistant manager, 13
law clerk (America), 14
credentialization, 15

leveraging, 19
billable hours quota, 21
overhead, 21
rule of three, 21
fixed fee, 23
contingency fee, 23
contract attorneys, 23
project attorneys, 23
second-tier attorneys, 23
staff attorney, 23
associates, 23

market rate, 24
Missouri v. Jenkins, 25
OJT, 28
solicitor, 30
barrister, 30
Legal Executives, 30
law clerk (Ontario), 30
CLE, 32

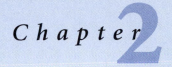

PARALEGAL EMPLOYMENT

➤ *Chapter Outline*

Section A
THE JOB MARKET

For many paralegals seeking their first job, these are difficult times. Even many attorneys are having a hard time obtaining their first job. Most employers are inundated with job applications. According to one expert, for every $10,000 in salary you hope to earn as a paralegal, you will need to set aside one month of search time. "So if you want $25,000 per year, your search should take about two and one-half months. But do not be disappointed if it takes longer."[1]

Competition for paralegal jobs is likely to come from several sources:

- Other recent graduates from paralegal training programs
- Secretaries and clerks now working in law offices who want to be promoted into paralegal positions
- Paralegals with a year or more of experience who are seeking a job change
- People with no legal training or experience who walk into an office "cold" seeking a job
- People with no legal training or experience but who have connections (a friend of an important client, a relative of a partner)
- Frustrated attorneys applying for paralegal jobs!

Fortunately, the last category is relatively small, but such attorneys exist.[2] Recently, for example, a paralegal job announcement drew more than 100 responses from paralegals, plus "four from attorneys."[3]

In this environment, the two keys to success are *information* about the employment scene and *techniques* to market yourself. With these objectives in mind, we turn now to the following themes:

- Places where paralegals work
- Paralegal specialties
- Effective job-finding strategies
- Alternative career options

Section B
WHERE PARALEGALS WORK

There are ten major locations where paralegals work. They are summarized in Exhibit 2.1, along with the approximate percentage of paralegals working in each location.

In general, the more attorneys in a law firm, the greater the likelihood that significant numbers of paralegals will be working there. Where do attorneys work? Appendix 2.A at the end of this chapter tries to identify some of the large employers of attorneys in the country (see page 123).

---

[1]Wagner, *Tips & Traps for the New Paralegal,* 8 Legal Assistant Today 78 (March/April 1991).

[2]Some unemployed attorneys are angry at bar associations for promoting the hiring of paralegals. "In the current market, a young attorney might well work for the same salary as a paralegal." After all, "bar associations represent lawyers, not paralegals. It must be pointed out that paralegals steal jobs from lawyers recently admitted to the bar." Anonymous, *Buddy, Can You Spare a Job,* 46 The Shingle 25 (Philadelphia Bar Ass'n, Fall 1983).

[3]Zavalney, *The Price of Success,* 6 Texas Lawyer 10 (January 21, 1991).

Exhibit 2.1 Where Do Paralegals Work and in What Percentages?

I. Traditional private law firms
 A. Small firm—1–10 lawyers (26%)
 B. Medium firm—11–50 lawyers (15%)
 C. Large firm—over 50 lawyers (30%)
II. Untraditional private law firms (3%)
III. Government
 A. Federal government (4%)
 B. State government (2%)
 C. Local government (1%)
IV. Legal service/legal aid offices (civil law) (3%)
V. Law departments of corporations, banks, insurance companies, and other businesses (8%)
VI. Special interest groups or associations (1%)
VII. Criminal law offices
 A. Prosecution (1%)
 B. Defense (1%)
VIII. Freelance or independent paralegals (1%)
IX. Service companies/consulting firms (1%)
X. Related fields (3%)
 A. Law librarian
 B. Paralegal teacher
 C. Paralegal supervisor/office administrator
 D. Miscellaneous

1. TRADITIONAL PRIVATE LAW FIRMS

Almost 75 percent of paralegals work for **private law firms.** Although the need for paralegals may be just as great in the other categories, the traditional private law firms have been doing most of the hiring. A "private" law firm is simply one that generates its income primarily from the fees of individual clients. On the number of paralegals within these firms, see the ratio data in Exhibit 2.2.

Exhibit 2.2 Ratio of Paralegals to Attorneys in Private Law Firms
(.24 means 24 paralegals per 100 attorneys)

	REGION							
BREAKOUT OF DATA	California	West	South Central	West Central	East Central	South	Northeast	ALL FIRMS
POPULATION								
Under 100,000	.21	.36	.37	.45	.31	.20	.21	.30
100,000–249,999	.36	.26	.25	.23	.17	.24	.29	.26
250,000–499,999	.22	.13	.44	.19	.19	.27	.24	.24
500,000–1 Million	—	.24	.27	.16	.21	.33	.24	.22
Over 1 Million	.26	.35	.19	.19	.16	.22	.25	.23
SIZE OF FIRM								
Under 9 Attorneys	.23	.25	.44	.41	.23	.75	.22	.36
9 to 20 Attorneys	.24	.26	.27	.26	.28	.21	.27	.26
21 to 40 Attorneys	.27	.21	.24	.22	.17	.25	.26	.23
41 to 74 Attorneys	.19	.35	.20	.19	.20	.27	.26	.24
75 or More Attorneys	—	—	—	.14	.15	.27	.24	.20
ALL FIRMS	.24	.28	.25	.22	.17	.27	.25	.24

Source: 1996 Survey of Law Firm Economics (Altman, Weil, Pensa Publications, Inc.)

Paralegals working for traditional private law firms, particularly the larger ones in metropolitan areas, have the following characteristics:

- They are among the highest paid paralegals.
- They tend to experience more law office management and personnel problems than other paralegals.
- They tend to specialize more and hence have less variety in their work assignments.
- They have been the most politically active paralegals in forming associations and in dealing with the bar associations.
- They are predominantly women.

2. UNTRADITIONAL PRIVATE LAW FIRMS

Since the mid-1970s a new kind of private law firm has come into existence. It also receives its income from fees, but it differs from the traditional law firm in a number of respects:

- It tends to charge lower fees.
- It tends to serve the middle class.
- It has branch offices that are storefront in character (as opposed to a single downtown office in a plush suite on the eleventh floor).
- It tends to hire more paralegals per attorney than the traditional private law firm.
- It is more likely to advertise and to use such devices as credit-card payment.

Such law firms have been controversial in the past. For example, the traditional bar initially went to court to try to prevent these firms from advertising. The bar lost this battle, although the debate over advertising continues today, as we will see in chapter 5.

The number of untraditional law firms is relatively small, but they are growing. The fear of losing business has caused many small traditional firms to begin imitating some of the characteristics of the more aggressive new breed.

3. GOVERNMENT

The civil service departments of federal, state, and local governments have established standards and classifications for many different kinds of government paralegals. These paralegals work in four main areas of government:

- In the office of the chief government attorney (e.g., attorney general, city attorney) for an entire jurisdiction
- In the office of the chief attorney (often called the general counsel) for individual government agencies
- In the office of the chief attorney (again often called the general counsel) for units within an individual government agency, e.g., civil rights division, enforcement bureau
- In the office of individual legislators, legislative committees, legislative counsel, or the legislative drafting office of the legislature

Federal Government

Thousands of paralegals work for the federal government in the capital (Washington, D.C.) and the main regional cities of the federal government (Atlanta, Boston, Chicago, Dallas, Denver, Kansas City, New York, Philadelphia, San Francisco, and Seattle). The most important job classification for this position is the **Paralegal Specialist** (GS-950).[4] This

---

[4]GS stands for **General Schedule,** which is the main pay-scale system used by the federal government. The number 950 is the occupational code for the Paralegal Specialist.

position is described in the following excerpt from the *Office of Personnel Management Handbook,* X-118. Note the extensive responsibility that these individuals have. The last line of this description is quite remarkable: paralegals perform "duties requiring discretion and independent judgment" that "may or may not be performed under the direction of a lawyer." There is no doubt that government paralegals have a range of responsibility that is broader than paralegals working anywhere else in the country.

Paralegal Specialist: Description of Work

Paralegal specialist positions involve such activities as (a) legal research, analyzing legal decisions, opinions, rulings, memoranda, and other legal material, selecting principles of law, and preparing digests of the points of law involved; (b) selecting, assembling, summarizing and compiling substantive information on statutes, treaties, contracts, other legal instruments, and specific legal subjects; (c) case preparation for civil litigation, criminal law proceedings or agency hearings, including the collection, analysis and evaluation of evidence, e.g., as to fraud and fraudulent and other irregular activities or violations of laws; (d) analyzing facts and legal questions presented by personnel administering specific Federal laws, answering the questions where they have been settled by interpretations of applicable legal provisions, regulations, precedents, and agency policy, and in some instances preparing informative and instructional material for general use; (e) adjudicating applications or cases on the basis of pertinent laws, regulations, policies and precedent decisions; or (f) performing other paralegal duties requiring discretion and independent judgment in the application of specialized knowledge of particular laws, regulations, precedents, or agency practices based thereon; these duties may or may not be performed under the direction of a lawyer.

The largest numbers of Paralegal Specialists are employed in the following units of the federal government:[5]

U.S. Department of Justice	U.S. Department of State
U.S. Department of Health and Human Services	U.S. Department of Energy
	U.S. Department of the Interior
U.S. Court System (nationwide)	U.S. Office of Personnel Management
U.S. Department of Treasury	Small Business Administration
U.S. Department of the Army	U.S. Department of Veterans Affairs
U.S. Department of Transportation	Environmental Protection Agency
U.S. Department of the Navy	U.S. Equal Employment Opportunity Commission
U.S. Department of Labor	

Paralegal Specialists are not the only individuals using special legal skills in the federal government. The following law-related occupations, filled mainly by nonattorneys, should be considered:

Legal Clerk	Clerk of Court
Legal Technician	Social Services Representative
Immigration Specialist	Equal Employment Opportunity Specialist
Civil Rights Analyst	
Claims Examiner	Equal Opportunity Assistant

---

[5] *The Paralegal's Guide to U.S. Government Jobs,* 100 (Federal Reports, 1993).

Hearings and Appeals Officer

Legal Instruments Examiner

Public Utilities Specialist

Tax Law Specialist

Internal Revenue Agent

Patent Advisor

Patent Examiner

Patent Technician

Contract Administrator

Contract Specialist

Contract Representative

Contracts Examiner

Labor Relations Specialist

Employee Relations Specialist

Wage and Hour Compliance Specialist

Mediation Specialist

Mediator

Investigator

Regulatory Analyst

Foreign Affairs Analyst/Officer

Import Specialist

Legislative Analyst

Legal Documents Examiner

Land Law Examiner

Copyright Examiner

Copyright Technician

Railroad Retirement Claims Examiner

Intelligence Analyst

Internal Revenue Officer

Environmental Protection Specialist

Security Specialist

Freedom of Information Act Specialist

Estate Tax Examiner

Fiduciary Accounts Examiner

Workers' Compensation Claims Examiner

Unemployment Compensation Claims Examiner

Unemployment Insurance Specialist

Corrections Assistant

Utilities Industry Analyst

When there is an opening for a Paralegal Specialist or for one of the positions listed above, the individual agency with this opening may do its own recruiting or may recruit through the **Office of Personnel Management**[6] (formerly called the Civil Service Commission), which oversees hiring procedures throughout the federal government. For a list of job information centers in your area where you can inquire about paralegal and other law-related positions in the federal government, see Appendix L at the end of the book.

State Government

When looking for work as a paralegal in the *state* government, find out if your state has established civil service classification standards for paralegal positions. See Appendix 2.B (at the end of this chapter) for some of this data. In addition, locate a directory of agencies, commissions, boards, or departments for your state, county, and city governments. You want to find a list of all (or most of the major) government offices. Many local public libraries will have a government directory. Alternatively, check the offices of state and local politicians, such as the governor, mayor, commissioner, alderman, representative, or senator. They will probably have such a directory. Finally, check your local

---

[6]1900 E. St. NW, Wash. D.C. 20415 (202-606-1800).

phone book for the sections on government offices. Contact as many of them as you can to find out whether they employ paralegals. If you have difficulty obtaining an answer to this question, find out where their attorneys are located. Sections or departments that employ attorneys will probably be able to tell you about paralegal employment opportunities. In your search, include a list of all the courts in the state. Judges and court clerks may have legal positions open for nonattorneys.

In addition to the statewide personnel departments listed in Appendix 2.B, many government offices have their own personnel department that will list employment openings. Also, whenever possible, talk with attorneys and paralegals who already work in these offices. They may know of opportunities that you can pursue.

Do not limit your search to paralegal or legal assistant positions. Legal jobs for nonattorneys may be listed under other headings, such as research assistant, legal analyst, administrative aide, administrative officer, executive assistant, examiner, clerk, and investigator. As we have seen, this is also true for employment in the federal government.

4. LEGAL SERVICE/LEGAL AID OFFICES (CIVIL LAW)

Community or neighborhood legal service offices and legal aid offices exist throughout the country. (See *Directory of Legal Aid & Defender Offices*, published by the National Legal Aid & Defender Association.) They obtain most of their funds from the government, often in the form of yearly grants to provide legal services to **indigents**—those without funds to hire an attorney. The clients do not pay fees. These offices make extensive use of paralegals with titles such as:

Administrative Benefits Representative	Information and Referral Specialist
Administrative Hearing Representative	Legal Assistant
Bankruptcy Law Specialist	Legal Research Specialist
Case Advocate	Legislative Advocate
Case Specialist	Paralegal
Community Law Specialist	Paralegal Coordinator
Disability Law Specialist	Paralegal Supervisor
Domestic Relations Specialist	Public Entitlement Specialist
Employment Law Specialist	Senior Citizen Specialist
Food Stamp Specialist	Social Security Specialist
Generalist Paralegal	Tribal Court Representative
Health Law Specialist	Veterans Law Specialist
Housing/Tenant Law Specialist	Wills Procedures Specialist
Immigration Paralegal	

As we will see in chapter 4, many administrative agencies permit nonattorneys to represent citizens at hearings before those agencies. Legal service and legal aid offices take advantage of this authorization. Their paralegals undertake extensive agency representation. (See Exhibit 2.3 for a sample job announcement that lists paralegal duties, including work at hearings, on behalf of clients.) The distinction between attorneys and paralegals in such offices is less pronounced than in many other settings. Unfortunately,

| *E x h i b i t 2 . 3* | **Sample Job Description for Paralegal in Legal Service Office** |

Gulf Coast Legal Foundation

Positions Open for Paralegals Experienced in Welfare

The Gulf Coast Legal Foundation, formerly the Houston Legal Foundation, has three positions open for paralegals with experience in welfare law. However, if experienced persons do not apply, we will seriously consider applicants with no more educational qualifications than a GED. We are discouraging law students and law graduates from applying. Our program has five neighborhood offices in Houston and Galveston and will expand to Fort Bend and Brazoria Counties. Our paralegals are assigned to specialty units. These positions are for the welfare unit where the goal is to increase the number of AFDC (Aid to Families with Dependent Children) families by 12,000 in the county and the number of SSI (Supplemental Social Security Income) recipients by 1,500 in the county, and to increase the level of benefits. The welfare unit represents the local welfare rights organization, which has ten years of history, parent councils of Title XX day care centers, and in cooperation with another unit, groups of handicapped people. The paralegal would maintain a direct service caseload of state welfare appeals and SSI hearings as well as some unemployment, health claims and other administrative matters. Each paralegal will be expected to handle six pending hearings and perform one research task each month after a training period of half a year. And do their own typing. The paralegal would also maintain a library of state manuals and social security materials. The paralegal would also be expected to participate in saturation leafleting, to attend some group meetings, and to perform minor educational services. The supervising attorney of the welfare unit would supervise the paralegal. The unit will have a total of five lawyers and six paralegals.

Because of inadequate public transportation, the paralegal would be responsible for transporting clients to welfare centers and maintaining a personal automobile.

Applicants should furnish their scores on the SAT or GRE exam, a writing sample, and detailed information concerning any prior legal services experience. We will give preference to experienced paralegals who intend to continue a career as a paralegal. Our program also has an affirmative action policy for the hiring of women and members of minority groups. Our program serves a substantial Mexican-American population and must give an additional preference to applicants who speak Spanish fluently.

The salary range can go up to the equivalent of a moderately experienced attorney.

however, these paralegals are among the lowest paid because of the limited resources of the offices where they work.

Legal service or legal aid offices are not the only way the government helps provide legal services to indigents. Many cities and counties have "volunteer lawyer" organizations that recruit private attorneys to provide **pro bono** (i.e., free) legal services. These organizations often employ paralegals.

In addition, there are several other settings in which paralegals have important roles:

- Paralegals may work in special institutions such as mental health hospitals or prisons.
- Paralegals who are senior citizens may provide legal services to senior citizens at nursing homes, neighborhood centers, and similar locations.

5. LAW DEPARTMENTS OF CORPORATIONS, BANKS, INSURANCE COMPANIES, AND OTHER BUSINESSES

Not every corporation or business in the country uses a law firm to handle all of its legal problems. Many have their own in-house law department under the direction of an attorney who is often called the **corporate counsel** or the general counsel.[7] The attorneys in this department have only one client—the corporation or business itself. Examples include manufacturers, retailers, transportation companies, publishers, general insurance

---

[7]Even when a corporation has its own law department, however, it may still occasionally hire an outside law firm in special situations such as legal disputes that involve complex litigation.

companies, real estate and title insurance companies, estate and trust departments of large banks, hospitals, universities, etc. In increasing numbers, paralegals are being hired in these settings. The average corporate law department employs five paralegals and seventeen staff attorneys. Paralegal salaries are relatively high because the employer (like the large traditional private law office) can often afford to pay good wages.

6. SPECIAL INTEREST GROUPS OR ASSOCIATIONS

Many **special interest groups** exist in our society: unions, business associations, environmental protection groups, taxpayer associations, consumer protection groups, trade associations, citizen action groups, etc. The larger groups have their own offices, libraries, and legal staff, including paralegals. The legal work often involves monitoring legislation, lobbying, preparing studies, etc. Direct legal services to individual members of the groups are usually not provided. The legal work relates to the needs (or a cause) of the organization as a whole. Occasionally, however, the legal staff will litigate test cases of individual members that have a broad impact on the organization's membership.

A different concept in the use of attorneys and paralegals by such groups is **group legal services.** Members of unions or groups of college students, for example, pay a monthly fee to the organization for which they are entitled to designated legal services, such as preparation of a will or divorce representation. The members pay *before* the legal problems arise. Group legal service systems are a form of **legal insurance** that operates in a manner similar to health insurance. Designated services are provided *if* the need for them arises. The group legal service office will usually employ paralegals.

7. CRIMINAL LAW OFFICES

Criminal cases are brought by government attorneys called prosecutors, district attorneys, or attorneys general. Defendants are represented by private attorneys if they can afford the fees. If they are indigent, they might be represented by **public defenders** who are attorneys working full-time in a special office funded by the government to represent the poor in criminal cases. Public defenders are usually government employees. Another option is the use of **assigned counsel** who are private attorneys who work on individual cases by court appointment. The use of paralegals in the practice of criminal law is increasing, particularly due to the encouragement of organizations such as the National District Attorneys Association and the National Legal Aid & Defender Association.

8. FREELANCE PARALEGALS

As we learned in chapter 1, most **freelance paralegals** are self-employed individuals who sell their services to attorneys. They are also called *independent paralegals* and *contract paralegals.* They perform their services in their own office or in the offices of the attorneys who hire them for special projects. Often they advertise in publications read by attorneys, such as legal newspapers and bar association journals. Such an ad might look something like this:

> Improve the quality and
> ****cost-effectiveness****
> of your practice with the help of:
> Lawyer's Assistant, Inc.

In addition, these paralegals will usually have a flyer or brochure that describes their services. Here is an excerpt from such a flyer:

Our staff consists of individuals with formal paralegal training and an average of five years of experience in such areas as estates and trusts, litigation, real estate, tax, and corporate law. Whether you require a real estate paralegal for one day or four litigation paralegals for one month, we can provide you with reliable qualified paralegals to meet your specific needs.

The attorneys in a law firm may be convinced of the value of paralegals but not have enough business to justify hiring a full-time paralegal employee. A freelance paralegal is an alternative.

For an overview on how to start a freelance business, see Appendix M.

As we saw in chapter 1, there are also self-employed paralegals who sell their services directly to the public. They, too, are sometimes called freelance paralegals, although the terms *legal technician* and *independent paralegal* are more common. Relatively few paralegals are engaged in this kind of business. This may change, however, as a number of states seriously consider a form of limited licensing to authorize what they do. We will examine this possibility in chapter 4.

9. SERVICE COMPANIES/CONSULTING FIRMS

Service companies and consulting firms also sell services to attorneys, but usually on a broader and more sophisticated scale than an individual freelance paralegal does. Examples of their services include:

- Selecting a computer system for a law office
- Designing and managing a computer-assisted document control system for a large case
- Digesting discovery documents
- Helping a law firm establish a branch office
- Designing a filing or financial system for the office
- Incorporating a new company in all fifty states
- Conducting a trademark search
- Undertaking a UCC (Uniform Commercial Code) search and filing in all fifty states

To accomplish such tasks, these service companies and consulting firms recruit highly specialized staffs of management experts, accountants, economists, former administrators, etc. More and more paralegals are joining these staffs; many of them are paralegals with prior law office experience, particularly computer experience.

10. RELATED FIELDS

Experienced paralegals have also been using their training and experience in a number of nonpractice legal fields. Many are becoming law librarians at firms. Paralegal schools often hire paralegals to teach courses and to work in administration, in such areas as admissions, internship coordination, placement, etc. Law offices with large numbers of paralegals have hired paralegal administrators or supervisors to help recruit, train, and manage the paralegals. Some paralegals have become legal administrators or office managers with administrative responsibilities throughout the firm. It is clear that we have not seen the end of the development of new roles for paralegals within the law firm or in related areas of the law. At the end of the chapter, a more extensive list of such roles will be provided. (See Exhibit 2.18 on page 121.)

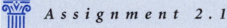 *A s s i g n m e n t   2 . 1*

(a) Find want ads for every category of employment mentioned in Exhibit 2.1. Try to find at least three ads for each category. Cut each ad out and tape it on a sheet of paper.

Beneath the ad, state where it was published, the date, and the page of the publication. You can use general circulation newspapers, legal newspapers, magazines, newsletters, the Internet, etc.

(b) Find at least one job description for every category of employment mentioned in Exhibit 2.1. These will be more difficult to obtain than the want ads. You can ask employed paralegals for a copy of their job description, or you can interview them about their job duties. Except for government employers, employers are often reluctant to send out job descriptions.

Section C
PARALEGAL SPECIALTIES: A DICTIONARY OF FUNCTIONS

We now examine forty-five areas of specialty work throughout the ten categories of paralegal employment just discussed. Paralegals often work in more than one of these specialties, and there is considerable overlap in the functions performed. The trend, however, is for paralegals to specialize. This follows the pattern of most attorneys.

For each specialty, you will find a listing of some of the major duties performed by paralegals. Most of the specialties also include comments from paralegals or their supervisors about the paralegal's work in the specialty. Finally, for the six specialties where most paralegals work (corporate law, estates, family law, litigation, real estate law, and tort law), you will also find excerpts from want ads to give you an idea of what employers are looking for when hiring for those specialties.

Paralegal Specialties

1. Administrative law
2. Admiralty law
3. Advertising law
4. Antitrust law
5. Banking law
6. Bankruptcy law
7. Civil rights law
8. Collections law
9. Communications law
10. Construction law
11. Contract law
12. Corporate law
13. Criminal law
14. Employee benefits law
15. Entertainment law
16. Environmental law
17. Estates, trusts, and probate law
18. Ethics and professional responsibility
19. Family law
20. Government contract law
21. Immigration law
22. Insurance law
23. Intellectual property law
24. International law
25. Judicial administration
26. Labor and employment law
27. Landlord and tenant law
28. Law librarianship
29. Law office administration
30. Legislation
31. Litigation (civil)
32. Military law
33. Municipal finance law
34. Oil and gas law
35. Parajudge
36. Pro bono work
37. Public sector
38. Real estate law
39. Social security law
40. Tax law
41. Tort law
42. Tribal law
43. Water law
44. Welfare law
45. Worker's compensation law
Note: Paralegal in the White House

> "The question so often asked of us is, 'what exactly do you do?'"
>
> —Douglas Parker, Paralegal, Pasadena, California

> "Each employer has a somewhat individual interpretation when it comes to selecting the responsibilities" of his or her legal assistant.
>
> —Mary K. Bronson, President, Nebraska Association of Legal Assistants

1. Administrative Law

I. Government Employment

Many paralegals work for specific administrative agencies. (See also Appendix 2.B for a list of paralegal functions in state agencies.) They might:

A. Handle questions and complaints from citizens.
B. Draft proposed regulations for the agency.
C. Perform legal research.
D. Provide litigation assistance in the agency and in court.
E. Represent the government at administrative hearings where authorized.
F. Manage the law office.
G. Train and supervise other nonattorney personnel.

II. Representation of Citizens

Some administrative agencies authorize nonattorneys to represent citizens at hearings and other agency proceedings. (See also *immigration law, pro bono work, public sector, social security law,* and *welfare law.*)

A. Interview client.
B. Conduct investigation.
C. Perform legal research.
D. Engage in informal advocacy at the agency.
E. Represent the client at agency hearing.
F. Draft documents for submission at hearing.
G. Monitor activities of the agency—for example, attend rule-making hearings to take notes on matters relevant to particular clients.
H. Prepare witnesses, reports, and exhibits designed to influence the drafting of regulations at the agency.

● *Comment on Paralegal Work in This Area:*

We "have a great deal of autonomy and an opportunity to develop expertise in particular areas." We have our "own caseloads, interview clients and then represent those clients at administrative hearings." Georgia Ass'n of Legal Assistants, *Sallye Jenkins Sapp, Atlanta Legal Aid; Sharon Mahaffey Hill, Georgia Legal Services,* 10 ParaGraph 5 (1987).

When I got my first case at a hearing before the State Department of Mental Health, I was "scared to death!" But the attorneys in the office were very supportive. "They advised me to make a good record, noting objections for the transcript, in case of future appeal. Making the right objections was scary." Milano, *New Responsibilities Being Given to Paralegals,* 8 Legal Assistant Today 27, 28 (November/December 1990).

2. Admiralty Law

This area of the law, also referred to as *maritime law,* covers accidents, injuries, and death connected with vessels on nav-igable waters. Special legislation exists in this area, such as the Jones Act. (See also *international law, litigation,* and *tort law.*)

I. Investigation
A. Obtain the facts of the event involved.
B. Arrange to board the vessel to photograph the scene of the accident.
C. Collect facts relevant to the seaworthiness of the vessel.
D. Take statements from witnesses.

II. Legal Research
A. Research liability under the applicable statutes.
B. Research special procedures to obtain compensation.

III. Subrogation
A. Handle small cargo subrogation files.
B. Prepare status reports for clients.

IV. Litigation
A. Draft complaints and other pleadings.
B. Respond to discovery requests.
C. Monitor all maritime files needed to keep track of discovery deadlines.
D. Coordinate projects by expert witnesses.
E. Provide general trial assistance.

● *Comment on Paralegal Work in This Area:*

Jimmie Muvern, CLA (Certified Legal Assistant), works for a sole practitioner in Baton Rouge, Louisiana, who specializes in maritime litigation: "If there is a doubt regarding the plaintiff's status as a Jones Act seaman, this issue is generally raised by a motion for summary judgment filed well in advance of trial, and it is good practice for the legal assistant who may be gathering facts regarding the client's accident to also gather facts from the client and from other sources which might assist the attorney in opposing summary judgment on the issue of the client's status as a Jones Act seaman." J. deGravelles & J. Muvern, *Who Is a Jones Act Seaman?* 12 Facts & Findings 34 (NALA, April 1986).

3. Advertising Law

(See also *administrative law* and *intellectual property law.*)

I. Compliance Work
A. *Advertising:* Review advertising of company products to identify claims made in the advertising about the product. Collect data needed to support the accuracy of the claims pursuant to regulations of the Federal Trade Commission, state laws, and company guidelines.
B. *Labels:* Review labels of company products to insure compliance with the regulations on deception of the Fed-

eral Trade Commission. Monitor compliance with the Food & Drug Administration and company policy on:

1. Product identity,
2. New weight statement,
3. Ingredient list,
4. Name and address of manufacturer/distributor,
5. Nutrition information.

C. *Product promotions:* Review promotions for company products (coupons, sweepstakes, bonus packs, etc.) to insure compliance with Federal Trade Commission guidelines, state laws, and company policy.

II. Inquiries and Complaints

A. Keep up-to-date on government regulations on advertising.
B. Help company attorney respond to inquiries and complaints from the public, a competitor, the Federal Trade Commission, the Food & Drug Administration, the state's attorney general, etc.

● *Comment on Paralegal Work in This Area:*

"On the surface, my job certainly does not fit the 'traditional' paralegal role. [Years ago, if] a fortune teller had ever read my coffee grounds, I might have learned that my paralegal career would include being part of the production of commercials and labels for household products I had grown up with." "My employer, the Procter & Gamble Company, is one of the largest consumer product companies in the United States." Its "Legal Division consists of forty attorneys and nine paralegals. Advertising law is challenging. It requires ingenuity, fast thinking and mastery of tight deadlines." Kothman, *Advertising Paralegal Finds Own Label,* National Paralegal Reporter 12 (NFPA, Spring 1990).

4. Antitrust Law

(See also *administrative law, corporate law, criminal law,* and *litigation.*)

I. Investigation/Analysis

A. Accumulate statistical and other technical data on a company or industry involved in litigation. Check Securities & Exchange Commission (SEC) filings, annual reports, advertising brochures, etc.
B. Prepare reports on economic data.
C. Obtain data from government bodies.
D. Find and interview potential witnesses.

II. Administrative Agency

A. Monitor the regulations and decisions of the Federal Trade Commission.
B. Prepare drafts of answers to requests for information from the Federal Trade Commission.

III. Litigation

A. Assist in drafting pleadings.
B. Request company witness files and other documents in preparation for deposition.
C. Schedule depositions.
D. Draft interrogatories.
E. Prepare special exhibits.
F. Organize, index, and digest voluminous records and lengthy documents.
G. Prepare trial notebook.
H. Attend trial and take notes on testimony of witnesses.
I. Cite check briefs of attorneys.
J. Provide general trial assistance.

● *Comment on Paralegal Work in This Area:*

When Mitchell became a permanent employee at the firm, "he was given three days' worth of files to read in order to familiarize himself with the [antitrust] case. At this point in the case, the firm had already gone through discovery of 27,000 documents. Mitchell analyzed and summarized documents with the other ten paralegals hired to work on the case. With a major case such as this one, paralegals did not have a regular nine to five work day. Mitchell frequently worked seventy hours a week (for which he was paid overtime). In January, Mitchell and his team were sent across the country to take depositions for the case. His air transportation, accommodations, and meals were all 'first class,' but this was not a vacation; he worked around the clock." R. Berkey, *New Career Opportunities in the Legal Profession,* 47 (Arco, 1983).

5. Banking Law

Paralegals employed by banks often work in the bank trust department. They also work in the bank's legal department, where they become involved with litigation, real estate, bankruptcy, consumer affairs, and securities law. In addition to banks, paralegals work for savings and loan institutions and other commercial lenders. Finally, some paralegals are employed in law firms that specialize in banking law. The following overview of duties is limited to the paralegal working for the legal department of a bank. (See also *administrative law, corporate law, estates law,* and *municipal finance law.*)

I. Claims

Assist legal staff in assessing bank liability for various claims, such as negligence and collection abuse.

II. Compliance Analysis

Determine whether the bank is complying with the regulations and statutes that regulate the banking industry.

III. Monitoring

Keep track of the rule-making and other activities of the various banking regulatory agencies and the bill-drafting activities of the legislative committees with jurisdiction over banks.

IV. Litigation

Assist attorneys litigating claims.

V. Miscellaneous

A. Draft and/or review loan applications and accompanying credit documents.
B. Perform document analysis on:
　1. Financial statements,
　2. Mortgages,
　3. Assignments,
　4. Security agreements.
C. Conduct UCC (Uniform Commercial Code) searches.
D. Assemble closing documents.
E. Arrange for and attend loan closings.
F. Prepare notarization of documents.
G. Monitor recordation.
H. Act as liaison among the supervising attorney at the bank, the loan officer, and the customer.
I. Perform routine legal research and analysis for the Compliance Department.

● *Comment on Paralegal Work in This Area:*

Ruth Sendecki is "the first legal assistant" at Merchants National Bank, one of the Midwest's largest bank holding companies. Most paralegals employed at banks today work in the trust department; Ruth, however, works with "general banking" at Merchants. Before this job, she worked at a bank, but not in a legal capacity. "You don't have to limit yourself to a law firm. You can combine being a legal assistant with other interests." Her "primary responsibility is in the commercial loan department. . . . She also serves the mortgage loan, correspondent banking and the international banking departments." According to her supervisor at the bank, "She is readily accessible for the benefit of the attorney, the loan officer and the customer to facilitate completion of the arrangements for both sides." Furthermore, she "is expanding her knowledge base, and other departments are drawing on her knowledge." Kane, *A Banker with the $oul of a Legal Assistant*, 5 Legal Assistant Today 65 (July/August 1988).

6. Bankruptcy Law

Paralegals in this area of law may be employed by a law firm that represents the debtor (e.g., an individual, a business); a creditor (e.g., a bank-mortgagee); or the trustee in bankruptcy. (A trustee in bankruptcy does not have to be a lawyer. Some paralegals with bankruptcy experience have in fact become trustees.) A few paralegals work directly for a bankruptcy judge as a clerk or deputy in Bankruptcy Court. The following overview assumes the paralegal works for a firm that represents the debtor. (See also *banking law, collections law, contract law,* and *litigation*.)

I. Interviewing/Data Collection

A. Help client fill out an extensive questionnaire on assets and liabilities. May visit client's place of business to determine the kinds of records kept there.
B. Help client assemble documents:
　1. Loan agreements,
　2. Deeds of trust,
　3. Security agreements,
　4. Creditor lists,
　5. Payables lists,
　6. Employment contracts,
　7. Financial statements,
　8. Leases, etc.

II. Investigation

A. Confirm amounts of indebtedness.
B. Identify secured and unsecured claims of creditors.
C. Check UCC (Uniform Commercial Code) filings at the secretary of state's office and at the county clerk's office.
D. Check real property records in the clerk's office in the county where the property is located.
E. Verify taxes owed; identify tax liens.
F. Identify exempt property.

III. Asset Control

A. Open bankruptcy file.
B. Prepare inventories of assets and liabilities.
C. Arrange for valuation of assets.

IV. Creditor Contact

A. Answer inquiries of creditors on the status of the case.
B. Request documentation from creditors on claims.

V. Drafting

A. Original bankruptcy petition.
B. Schedule of liabilities.
C. Statement of affairs.
D. Status reports.
E. Final account.

VI. Coordination

A. Serve as liaison with trustee in bankruptcy.
B. Coordinate meeting of creditors.
C. Prepare calendar of filing and other deadlines.

● *Comment on Paralegal Work in This Area:*

"As a legal assistant, you can play a major role in the representation of a Chapter 11 debtor. From prefiling activities through confirmation of the plan of reorganization, there are numerous duties which you can perform to assist in the successful reorganization of the debtor." Morzak, *Organizing Reorganization,* 5 Legal Assistant Today 33 (January/February 1988).

"Bankruptcy work is unusual in a number of ways—extremely short statutes of limitation, for example. . . . The field is one in which there's lots of opportunity for paralegals. The paralegal does everything except sign the papers. . . . Most attorneys do not like bankruptcy, but if you do all the legwork for them, you can make a lot of money for them." Johnson, *The Role of the Paralegal/Legal Assistant in Bankruptcy and Foreclosure,* AALA News 7 (Alaska Ass'n of Legal Assistants, March 1987).

7. Civil Rights Law

(See also *labor and employment law, pro bono work,* and *public sector.*)

I. Government Paralegal
A. Help identify and resolve discrimination complaints (based on sex, race, age, disability, etc.) made by government employees against the government.
B. Help government attorneys litigate discrimination complaints (based on sex, race, age, disability, etc.) brought by citizens against the government, against other citizens, or against companies.

II. Representation of Citizens

Assist law firms representing citizens in their discrimination complaints filed against the government, other citizens, or companies:
A. In court.
B. In special agencies created to hear discrimination cases, such as the Equal Employment Opportunity Commission or the Human Rights Commission.

● *Comment on Paralegal Work in This Area:*

"One aspect that Matthews likes is that each case is a different story, a different set of facts. 'There is a lot of interaction with people in the courts and with the public. We do a great deal of civil rights litigation, everything from excessive police force to wrongful termination. Sometimes there are as many as 60 witnesses. The lawyers depend on me to separate the witnesses out and advise them which ones would do best in the courtroom. A lot of time the lawyer does not know the witness and has not seen the witness until the person is in the courtroom testifying.' For one case,

Matthews reviewed more than 1,000 slides taken in a nightclub, looking for examples of unusual or rowdy behavior. The slides include everything from male strippers to people flashing. Autopsy and horrible injury photographs are also part of the job." *Broadening into the Paralegal Field,* 39 The Docket 7 (NALS, January/February 1991).

8. Collections Law[8]

(See also *banking law, bankruptcy law, contract law,* and *litigation.*)

I. Acceptance of Claims
A. Open file.
B. Prepare index of parties.
C. Prepare inventory of debts of debtor.

II. Investigation
A. Conduct asset check.
B. Verify address.
C. Verify filings at secretary of state's office and county clerk's office (e.g., UCC filings).
D. Contact credit bureau.
E. Verify information in probate court, registry of deeds, etc.

III. Litigation Assistant (Civil Court, Small Claims Court, etc.)
A. Draft pleadings.
B. Arrange for witnesses.
C. File documents in court.
D. Assist in settlement/negotiation of claim.
E. Assist in enforcement work, such as:
    1. Wage attachment (prejudgment attachment),
    2. Supplementary process,
    3. Execution,
    4. Seizure of personal property.

● *Comment on Paralegal Work in This Area:*

"O.K.—So, [collections work] is not the nicest job in the world, but somebody has to do it, right? If the attorney you work for does not want to do it, there are plenty more in town who will. For a paralegal working in this area, there is always something new to learn. . . . It is sometimes difficult to see the results of your labor right away in this kind of work, as very few files are paid in full and closed in a short period of time. It is disheartening to go through many steps and possibly spend a great deal of time just trying to get someone served or to locate someone, and then end up with nothing. I will admit that collections can be very frustrating, but boring they are not!" Wexel, *Collections: Persistence Pay$ Off,* The Paraview (Metrolina Paralegal Ass'n, April 1987).

---

[8]See Commercial Law League of America, Seminar, *A Paralegal Approach to the Practice of Commercial Law* (November 14, 1975).

"I currently have responsibility for some 400 collection cases. My days are spent on the phone talking to debtors, drafting the necessary pleadings, executing forms, and hopefully depositing the money collected. The exciting part of collection is executing on a judgment. We were successful in garnishing an insurance company's account for some $80,000 when they refused to pay a judgment that had been taken against them. We have also gone with the Sheriff to a beer distributorship two days before St. Patrick's Day to change the locks on the building housing gallons and gallons of green beer. The debtor suddenly found a large sum of money to pay us so that we would release the beer in time for St. Patrick's Day." R. Swoagerm, *Collections Paralegal,* The Citator 9 (Legal Assistants of Central Ohio, August 1990).

9. Communications Law

(See also *administrative law* and *entertainment law.*)

I. Government Paralegal

Assist attorneys at the Federal Communications Commission (FCC) in regulating the communications industry—for example, help with rule-making, license applications, and hearings.

II. Representation of Citizens or Companies
A. Draft application for licenses.
B. Prepare compliance reports.
C. Prepare exemption applications.
D. Prepare statistical analyses.
E. Monitor activities of the FCC.
F. Assist in litigation.
   1. Within the FCC,
   2. In court.

● *Comment on Paralegal Work in This Area:*

The current specialty of Carol Woods is the regulation of television and radio. "I am able to do work that is important and substantive, and am able to work independently. I have an awful lot of contact with clients, with paralegals at the client's office, and with government agencies. One of the liabilities of private practice for both attorneys and paralegals is that there is so much repetition and you can get bored. A lot of times as a paralegal you can't call the shots or know everything that goes into the planning of a project. However, when you can participate in all facets of a project, it's great!" A. Fins, *Opportunities in Paralegal Careers,* 84 (Nat'l Textbook Co., 1979).

10. Construction Law

(See also *contract law, litigation,* and *tort law.*)

I. Claims Assistance
A. Work with engineering consultants in the preparation of claims.

II. Data Collection
A. Daily manpower hours,
B. Amount of concrete poured,
C. Change orders.

III. Document Preparation
A. Prepare graphs.
B. Prepare special studies—for example, compare planned with actual progress on construction project.
C. Prepare documents for negotiation/settlement.
D. Help draft arbitration claim forms.

IV. Assist in litigation.

● *Comment on Paralegal Work in This Area:*

"Because of the complex factual issues that arise with construction disputes, legal assistants are critical in identifying, organizing, preparing, and analyzing the extensive relevant factual information. In many cases, whether a party wins or loses depends on how effectively facts are developed from documents, depositions, interviews, and site inspections. Thus, a successful construction litigation team will generally include a legal assistant skilled in organization and management of complex and voluminous facts. . . . Construction litigation also provides legal assistants with a very distinctive area for expertise and specialization." M. Gowen, *A Guide for Legal Assistants* 229 (Practicing Law Institute, 1986).

11. Contract Law

The law of contracts is involved in a number of different paralegal specialties. See *advertising law, antitrust law, banking law, bankruptcy law, collections law, construction law, corporate law, employee benefits law, entertainment law, family law, government contract law, insurance law, intellectual property law, international law, labor and employment law, landlord and tenant law, municipal finance law, oil and gas law, real estate law,* and *tax law.*

I. Contract Review
A. Review contracts to determine compliance with terms.
B. Investigate facts involving alleged breach of contract.
C. Do legal research on the law of contracts in a particular specialty.

II. Litigation Assistance

III. Preparation of Contract Forms
A. Separation agreements,
B. Employment contracts,
C. Contracts for sale, etc.

● *Comment on Paralegal Work in This Area:*

"The . . . paralegal also assists two attorneys in drafting, reviewing, researching, revising and finalizing a variety of contracts, including Entertainment, Participant and Operational Agreements. Much of the . . . paralegal's time is spent studying existing contracts looking for provisions that may answer any inquiries or disputes. With hundreds of agreements presently active, researching, reviewing, amending, terminating, revising and executing contracts is an everyday activity for [the] . . . Legal Department." Miquel, *Walt Disney World Company's Legal Assistants: Their Role in the Show,* 16 Facts and Findings 29, 30 (NALA, January 1990).

"Initially, my primary job was to review contracts, and act as Plan Administrator for the 401(k). I was also involved in the negotiation and development of a distributor agreement to market SPSS software to the Soviet Union. Most contract amendments were to software license agreements. The pace picked up when I was promoted to Manager of Human Services, while retaining all of my previous responsibilities." Illinois Paralegal Ass'n, *Spotlight on . . . Laurel Bauer,* 20 Outlook 21 (Winter 1991).

12. Corporate Law

Paralegals involved in corporate law mainly work in one of two settings: law firms that represent corporations, and legal departments of corporations. (See also *banking law, employee benefits law, insurance law, labor and employment law, real estate law,* and *tax law.*)

I. Incorporation and General Corporate Work
A. Preincorporation.
  1. Check availability of proposed corporate name and, if available, reserve it.
  2. Draft preincorporation subscriptions and consent forms for initial board of directors where required by statute.
  3. Record Articles of Incorporation.
  4. Order corporate supplies.
B. Incorporation.
  1. Draft and file Articles of Incorporation with appropriate state agency for:
    a. Subchapter S corporation,
    b. Close corporation,
    c. Nonprofit corporation.
  2. Draft minutes of initial meetings of incorporators and directors.
  3. Draft corporate bylaws.
  4. Obtain corporate seal, minute book, and stock certificate book.

  5. Prepare necessary documents to open a corporate bank account.
C. Directors meetings.
  1. Prepare and send out waivers and notices of meetings.
  2. Draft minutes of directors meetings.
  3. Draft resolutions to be considered by directors:
    a. Sale of stock,
    b. Increase in capitalization,
    c. Stock splits,
    d. Stock option,
    e. Pension plan,
    f. Dividend distribution,
    g. Election of officers.
D. Shareholders meetings (annual and special).
  1. Draft sections of annual report relating to business activity, officers, and directors of company.
  2. Draft notice of meeting, proxy materials, and ballots.
  3. Prepare agenda and script of meeting.
  4. Draft oath, report of judge of elections, and other compliance documents when required.
  5. Maintain corporate minute books and resolutions.
E. Draft and prepare general documents:
  1. Shareholder agreement,
  2. Employment contract,
  3. Employee benefit plan,
  4. Stock option plan,
  5. Trust agreement,
  6. Tax return,
  7. Closing papers on corporate acquisition.
  8. See also drafting tasks listed above for directors and shareholders meetings.

II. Public Sale of Securities
A. Compile information concerning officers and directors for use in Registration Statement.
B. Assist in research of blue sky requirements.
C. Closing:
  1. Prepare agenda,
  2. Obtain certificates from state agencies with respect to good standing of company and certified corporate documents,
  3. Prepare index and organize closing binders.

III. Research
A. Legislative monitoring: keep track of pending legislation that may affect office clients.
B. Extract designated information from corporate records and documents.
C. Assemble financial data from records on file at SEC and state securities regulatory agencies.
D. Undertake short- and long-term statistical and financial research on companies.

E. Perform legal research.

IV. General Assistance

A. Maintain tickler system (specifying, for example, dates of next corporate meeting, shareholder meeting, upcoming trial, appellate court appearance).

B. Monitor the daily law journal or legal newspaper in order to identify relevant cases on calendars of courts, current court decisions, articles, etc. and forward such data in the journal or newspaper to appropriate office attorneys.

C. Act as file managers for certain clients: index, digest, and monitor documents in the file, prepare case profiles, etc.

D. Maintain corporate forms file.

V. Miscellaneous

A. Prepare documents for qualification to do business in foreign jurisdictions.

B. Prepare filings with regulatory agencies.

C. Provide assistance in processing patent, copyright, and trademark applications.

D. Coordinate escrow transactions.

E. Work on certificates of occupancy.

F. Prepare documents needed to amend Bylaws or Articles of Incorporation.

G. Prepare interrogatories.

H. Digest deposition testimony.

I. Perform cite checks.

● *Comment on Paralegal Work in This Area:*

"When the majority of people describe a legal assistant or a paralegal, they often think of courtroom battles, million dollar lawsuits and mountains of depositions. For those of us in the corporate area, these sights are replaced with board room battles, million dollar mergers and mountains of prospectus. Some of us have NEVER seen the inside of a courtroom or have never touched a pleading. I guess it can be said that 'we don't do windows, we don't type, and we don't do litigation.' A corporate paralegal is never without a multitude of projects that offer excitement or anxiety. This isn't to say, however, that the corporate field is without its fair share of boredom. . . . The future is only limited by your imagination. Not every paralegal wants the drama of a landmark case. Some of us are quite content seeing a client's company written up in the *Wall Street Journal* for the first time!" D. Zupanovich, *The Forming of a Corporate Paralegal,* 2 California Paralegal 4 (July/September 1990).

"The company I work for is a major worldwide producer of chemicals. . . . I recently had to obtain some technical information about the computer system at a hotel in a foreign country in order to set up documents on a diskette that would be compatible with the computer system in that country before one of the attorneys went there for contract negotiations." "One of the most thrilling experiences I have had since working for the company was that of working on the closing of a leveraged buyout of a portion of our business in Delaware. To experience first-hand the intensity of the negotiating table, the numerous last-minute changes to documents, the multitudinous shuffle of papers, and the late, grueling hours was both exhausting and exhilarating." Grove, *Scenes from a Corporate Law Department,* The Paraview 2 (Metrolina Paralegal Ass'n, February 1990).

"Even 'dream jobs' have their moments of chaos. After only two months on the job [at Nestle Foods Corporation] Cheryl had to prepare for a Federal Trade Commission Second Request for Production of Documents relating to an acquisition. She suddenly was thrown into the job of obtaining and organizing over 6,000 documents from around the world, creating a document database and managing up to 10 temporary paralegals at a time. Of course, this preparation included weekends and evenings for a six-week period. Cheryl calls December the 'lost month.' "Scior, *Paralegal Profile: Corporate Paralegal,* Post Script 14 (Manhattan Paralegal Ass'n, April/May 1990).

● *Quotes from Want Ads:*

Law firm seeks paralegal for corporate work: "Ideal candidate is a self-starter with good communications skills and is willing to work overtime." "Ability to work independently is a must." Paralegal needed to assist corporate secretary: "Analytical, professional attitude essential. Knowledge of state and/or federal regulatory agencies required." "Ability to work under pressure." "All candidates must possess excellent writing and drafting skills." "Ideal candidate is a self-starter with good communication/research skills and is willing to work overtime." "Candidate having less than three years experience in general corporate legal assistance need not apply." Position requires "word processing experience and ability to manage multiple projects." Position requires "intelligent, highly motivated individual who can work with little supervision." "Great opportunity to learn all aspects of corporate business transactions." Position requires "career-minded paralegal with excellent organizational and communications skills, keen analytical ability and meticulous attention to detail." Position requires "an experienced paralegal with a strong blue-sky background, particularly in public and private real estate syndication." Applicant must have "excellent academic credentials, be analytical, objective, and dedicated to performing thorough quality work and to displaying a professional attitude to do whatever it takes to get the job done and meet deadlines."

13. Criminal Law[9]

(See also *litigation* and *military law.*)

I. Paralegal Working for Criminal/Civil Division Prosecutor
A. Log incoming cases.
B. Help office screen out cases that are inappropriate for arrest, cases that are eligible for diversion, etc.
C. Act as liaison with police department and other law enforcement agencies.
D. Prepare statistical caseload reports.
E. Interview citizens who are seeking the prosecution of alleged wrongdoers; prepare case files.
F. Help the Consumer Fraud Department resolve minor consumer complaints—for instance, contact the business involved to determine whether a settlement of the case is possible without prosecution.
G. Conduct field investigations as assigned.
H. Prepare documents for URESA cases (Uniform Reciprocal Enforcement of Support Act).
I. Monitor status of URESA cases.
J. Help office maintain its case calendar.
K. Act as liaison among the prosecutor, the victim, and witnesses while the case is being prepared for trial and during the trial.
L. Act as general litigation assistant during the trial and the appeal.

II. Paralegal Working for Defense Attorney
A. Interview defendants to determine eligibility for free legal defense (if the paralegal works for a public defender).
B. Conduct comprehensive interview of defendant on matters relevant to the criminal charge(s).
C. Help the defendant gather information relevant to the determination of bail.
D. Help the defendant gather information relevant to eligibility for diversion programs.
E. Conduct field investigations; interview witnesses.
F. Help obtain discovery, particularly through police reports and search warrants.
G. Act as general litigation assistant during the trial and the appeal.

● *Comment on Paralegal Work in This Area:*

"Ivy speaks with an obvious love for her current job in the State Attorney's office. In fact, she said she would not want to do anything else! She also said there is no such thing as a typical day in her office, which is one of the many aspects of her job she enjoys. She not only helps interview witnesses and prepare them for trial, but she often must locate a witness, requiring some detective work! Ivy assisted in a case involving an elderly woman who was victimized after the death of her husband. The woman was especially vulnerable because of her illiteracy. Through the help of the State Attorney's office, the woman was able to recover her money and get assistance with housing and learning to read. Ivy continues to keep in touch with the woman and feels the experience to be very rewarding." Frazier, *Spotlight on Ivy Hart-Daniel,* JLA News 2 (Jacksonville Legal Assistants, Inc., January 1989).

"Kitty Polito says she and other lawyers at McClure, McClure & Kammen use the firm's sole paralegal not only to do investigations but 'to pick cases apart piece by piece.' Polito credits legal assistant Juliann Klapp with 'cracking the case' of a client who was accused by a co-defendant of hitting the victim on the back of the head. At trial, the pathologist testified that the victim had been hit from left to right. Klapp passed a note to the attorneys pointing out that such a motion would have been a back-handed swing for their right-handed client. Thus it was more likely that the co-defendant, who is left-handed, was the one who hit the victim. The defendant won." Brandt, *Paralegals' Acceptance and Utilization Increasing in Indy's Legal Community,* 1 The Indiana Lawyer 1 (June 20, 1990).

14. Employee Benefits Law[10]

Employee benefits paralegals work in a number of different settings: in law firms, banks, large corporations, insurance companies, or accounting firms. The following overview of tasks covers a paralegal working for a law firm. (See also *contract law, corporate law, labor and employment law, social security law,* and *worker's compensation law.*)

I. Drafting of Employee Plans
A. Work closely with the attorney, the plan sponsor, the plan administrator, and the trustee in preparing and drafting qualified employee plans, such as:
1. Stock bonus plans,
2. Profit sharing plans,
3. Money purchase pensions,
4. Other pension plans,
5. Trust agreements,
6. Individual Retirement Account (IRA) plans,
7. Annuity plans,

---

[9]See J. Stein & B. Hoff, *Paralegals and Administrative Assistants for Prosecutors* (Nat'l District Attorneys Ass'n, 1974); and J. Stein, *Paralegals: A Resource for Defenders and Correctional Services* (1976).

[10]Rocky Mountain Legal Assistants Association, *The Use of the Legal Assistant* (1975).

8. HR-10 or Keogh plans,
9. Employee stock ownership plans,
10. Life and health insurance plans,
11. Worker's compensation plans,
12. Social security plans.

II. Document Preparation and Program Monitoring
A. Gather information.
B. Determine eligibility for participation and benefits.
C. Notify employees of participation.
D. Complete input forms for document assembly.
E. Assemble elections to participate.
F. Determine beneficiary designations.
G. Record elections to contribute.
H. Allocate annual contributions to the individual participant accounts.
I. Prepare annual account statements for participants.
J. Identify potential discrimination problems in the program.

III. Government Compliance Work Pertaining to:
A. Tax requirements for qualifications, amendment, and termination of plan.
B. Department of Labor reporting and disclosure requirements.
C. Insurance requirements.
D. Welfare and Pension Plans Disclosure Act requirements.
E. ERISA requirements (Employee Retirement Income Security Act).
F. Pension Benefit Guaranty Corporation requirements.

IV. Miscellaneous
A. Help draft summary plan descriptions for distribution to employees.
B. Help prepare and review annual reports of plans.
C. Continue education in current law of the field—for instance, study to become a Certified Employee Benefit Specialist (CEBS).

● *Comment on Paralegal Work in This Area:*

"Michael Montchyk was looking to use his undergraduate degree in statistics. . . . He now works for attorneys specializing in employee benefits, where understanding numbers and familiarity with the law are key skills." Lehren, *Paralegal Work Enhancing Careers of Many,* Philadelphia Business Journal 9B (August 6, 1990).

"This area is not for everybody. To succeed, you need considerable detail orientation, solid writing skills, self-motivation, the ability to keep up with a legal landscape that is never the same, and a knack for handling crisis situations which arise when least expected." Germani, *Opportunities in*

Employee Benefits, SJPA Reporter 7 (South Jersey Paralegal Ass'n, January 1989).

15. Entertainment Law

(See also *contract law, corporate law,* and *intellectual property law.*)

I. Types of Client Problem Areas
A. *Copyright and trademark law:* Applying for government protection for intellectual property, such as plays, films, video, music, and novels.
B. *Contract law:* Help negotiate and draft contracts, and insure their enforcement.
C. *Labor law:* Assist a client to comply with the contracts of unions or guilds.
D. *Corporate law:*
   1. Assist in formation of business organizations.
   2. Work on mergers.
   3. Maintain compliance with federal and state reporting laws and regulations.
E. *Tax law:* Planning and compliance.
   1. Report passive royalty income, talent advances, residuals, etc.
   2. Allocate expenditures to specific projects.
F. *Family law:* Assist with prenuptial agreements, divorces, child custody, etc.

II. Tasks
A. Register copyrights.
B. Help a client affiliate with his or her guild.
C. Monitor remake and sequel rights to films.
D. Prepare documents to grant a license to use client's music.
E. Check title registrations with the Motion Picture Association of America.
F. Read scripts to determine whether clearances are needed for certain kinds of material and references.
G. Apply for permits and licenses.
H. Calculate costs of property rights.

● *Comment on Paralegal Work in This Area:*

"I am a paralegal in the field of entertainment law, one of the fastest growing, and, to me, most exciting areas of the paralegal profession, and one whose duties are as varied as the practices of the lawyers for whom we work. . . . I started in a very large Century City firm whose entertainment practice covers everything from songwriters to financing of major motion pictures, and from major recording stars and producers to popular novelists. . . . My specialty (yes, a specialty within a specialty) is music. . . . My husband is also an entertainment paralegal who works for 20th Century Fox. . . . Never, ever a dull moment!" Birkner, *Entertainment Law: A Growing Industry for the Paralegal,* 2 California Paralegal Magazine 7 (April/June 1990).

16. Environmental Law[11]

(See also *legislation, litigation, oil and gas law, real estate law,* and *water law.*)

I. Research
A. Research questions pertaining to the environment, land use, water pollution, and the National Environmental Policy Act.
  1. Locate and study pertinent state and federal statutes, case law, regulations, and law review articles.
  2. Obtain secondary materials (maps, articles, books) useful for broadening the information base.
  3. Contact, when appropriate, government officials or other informants for data or answers.
  4. Obtain and develop personality profiles of members of Congress, members of relevant bureaucracies, and other political figures.
  5. Help prepare memoranda of findings, including citations and supporting documents.
B. Develop research notebooks for future reference. When new topics arise in environmental law, prepare notebooks to facilitate future research on similar topics.
C. Prepare bibliographies on environmental topics.

II. Drafting
A. Draft memoranda regarding new federal and state laws, regulations, or findings of research.
B. Draft memoranda discussing pertinent issues, problems, and solutions regarding public policy developments.
C. Draft narrative histories of legislation regarding political impulses, the impact of administrative and court rulings, and substantive and technical differences between drafts of legislation or results of amendments.
D. Draft and edit articles on coastal management programs and problems, conservation, water pollution, and the National Environmental Policy Act.
E. Edit environmental impact statements.
F. Assist in the preparation of briefs.
  1. Check citations for pertinence and accuracy.
  2. Develop table of contents, list of authorities, and certificate of service.

III. Hearing Participation
A. Locate and schedule witnesses.
B. Gather pertinent research materials (including necessary local documents, maps, and specific subject matter).

IV. Litigation: Provide General Trial Assistance

● **Comment on Paralegal Work in This Area:**

Mary Peterson's firm has made a specialty of environmental and land use law. In a recent major hazardous waste case, "we will try to prove that the paint companies, dry cleaning stores and even the federal government, which used the property to build aircraft during the war" are responsible. "Some of the toxic waste dumped there were cited by federal agencies even back to 1935." Her job is to investigate the types of hazardous wastes and, with the help of the Freedom of Information Act, gather all available evidence. Then she studies it, duplicates, indexes, and writes summaries, which she distributes to the partners and associates. It's a case that has taken eight months so far and may go on for several years "because you don't know what you will uncover tomorrow. The toxins and pollutants could be different. There is no standard, just a constantly changing picture." Edwards, *The General Practice Paralegal,* 8 Legal Assistant Today 49, 55 (March/April 1991).

17. Estates, Trusts, and Probate Law

(See also *banking law, collections law, employee benefits law, family law,* and *social security law.*)

I. Estate Planning
A. Collect data (birth dates, fair market value of assets, current assets and liabilities, etc.).
B. Using computer-generated forms, prepare preliminary drafts of wills or trusts.
C. Perform investment analysis in order to provide attorney who is fiduciary of estate with information relevant to investment options.

II. Office Management
A. Maintain tickler system.
B. Maintain attorney's calendar.
C. Open, index, monitor, and keep current all components of the office file on the client's trust and estate case.
D. Using computer programs, manage the accounting aspects of trusts and estates administered by the office.
E. Act as office law librarian (keeping loose-leaf texts up-to-date, etc.).
F. Train secretaries and other paralegals in the system used by the office to handle trusts, estates, and probate cases.
G. Selectively discard certain mail and underline significant parts of other mail.

---

[11]Colorado Bar Association Legal Assistant Committee. These tasks have been approved by the Committee, not by the Board of Governors of the Colorado Bar.

III. Estate of Decedent
A. Assets phase.
  1. Collect assets (such as bank accounts, custody accounts, insurance proceeds, social security death benefits, safety deposit box contents, and apartment contents).
  2. Assist in the valuation of assets.
  3. Maintain records (for example, wills and trusts, vault inventories, powers of attorney, property settlements, fee cards, bill-payment letters).
  4. Record and file wills and trusts.
  5. Notify beneficiaries.
  6. Prepare profiles of wills and trusts for attorney review.
B. Accounting phase.
  1. Prepare preliminary drafts of federal and state death tax returns.
  2. Apply the income-principal rules to the estate.
  3. Organize data relevant to the tax implications of estates.
  4. Prepare accountings: final and accounts current (for example, set up a petition for a first and final accounting).
C. Termination-distribution phase.
  1. Apply for the transfer of securities into the names of the people entitled.
  2. Draw checks for the signature of executors.
  3. Monitor legacies to charitable clients.
  4. File and prepare tax waivers.
  5. Assist with the closing documents.
  6. Calculate distributable net income.
  7. Follow up on collection and delivery.

IV. Litigation
  1. Perform legal research.
  2. Conduct factual research (investigation)—for instance, track down the names and addresses of all possible claimants and contact them.
  3. Prepare sample pleadings.
  4. Digest depositions (review, condense, point out inconsistencies, etc.).
  5. Prepare drafts of interrogatories.
  6. Prepare drafts of answers to interrogatories.
  7. Notarize documents.
  8. Act as court witness as to decedent's signature and other matters.
  9. Assist with litigation.

● *Comment on Paralegal Work in This Area:*

"What I like best about estate planning is that you work with people on a very individual basis. I don't think that in many other areas of law you get that one-on-one contact with the client. . . . You're working with people while they are thinking about the most important things in their lives— their families, their wealth and how to distribute it, and what they want to happen after they pass on. A lot of the clients contact me directly with their questions for the attorneys. Some of the widows especially are more comfortable calling me with their questions. They seem to think their questions might be 'stupid' and they're embarrassed to ask the attorneys directly. I can take their questions and see that the attorneys respond to them promptly." Bassett, *Top Gun Patricia Adams: Legal Assistant of the Year,* 6 Legal Assistant Today 70, 74 (July/August 1990).

"The position can be very stressful. But it is seldom boring. My typical day involves responding to many telephone inquiries from clients, dictating memos, or letters requesting additional information concerning life insurance policies, valuation of assets, or simply sending notice of an upcoming hearing "to all persons entitled," etc. I draft virtually all documents needed in the administration of an estate, beginning with the initial petition for probate. . . . The decedent may have had an interest in a closely-held business, or leave minor or handicapped children, or leave a spouse with no knowledge of the family assets; these all require additional attention. Every case is different. Probate paralegals to some extent must be 'snoopy,' because you do learn a great deal about people, both deceased and living. In most cases your client is facing a difficult time with trepidation and it is your role to provide confidence. The end results are very rewarding." Rose, *Still a Probate Paralegal,* 12 The Journal 5 (Sacramento Ass'n of Legal Assistants, August 1990).

● *Quotes from Want Ads:*

Law firm seeks someone with "good communication and organizational skills, [who] is self-motivated, relates well with attorneys, clients, and staff, is detail oriented, has a teamwork attitude, a pleasant personality, and is a nonsmoker." Bank has opening for "trust tax administrator, with emphasis on personal and trust planning." Paralegal must have "technical understanding of wills and estate plans and terminology. Must be self-starter." "This is a full-time position with extensive responsibility for both court-supervised and noncourt-supervised estates and trusts." Position requires a person who "enjoys writing and proofreading, and who has excellent grammatical skills." Job is "for individual who enjoys the complexity and detail of accounting and bookkeeping in a legal environment." "Applicants must be prepared to handle tax work."

18. Ethics and Professional Responsibility

Paralegals in this area work in two main settings: (1) in large law firms as a **conflicts specialist,** helping the firm determine whether conflicts of interest exist between prospective clients and current or former clients, and (2) in state disciplinary agencies that investigate complaints against attorneys for unethical behavior.

I. Law Firm (*Conflicts Specialist* or *Manager*)
A. Research
   1. Identify all persons or companies with a personal or business relationship with the prospective client.
   2. Determine whether the firm has ever represented the prospective client and/or any of its related parties.
   3. Determine whether the firm has ever represented an opponent of the prospective client and/or any of its related parties.
B. *Reports:* Notify attorney of data indicating possible conflict of interest.
C. *Database work:* Update information in client database on current and past clients for purposes of future conflicts checks.

II. Disciplinary Agency
A. Screen incoming data on new ethical complaints against attorneys.
B. Help investigate complaints.
C. Provide general litigation assistance to disciplinary attorneys during the proceedings at the agency and in court.

● *Comment on Paralegal Work in This Area:*

   Jane Palmer "does all the research on every prospective client, identifying all the related parties." Her computerized database tells her if the firm has ever represented a party on either side, or been adverse to them. "The most valuable thing has been my experience with the firm, developing somewhat of a corporate memory. The job takes extreme attention to detail. You may not always have all the information you need, so you have to be a detective. Quick response is important; so is making sure to keep things confidential." Sacramento Ass'n of Legal Assistants, *New Responsibilities Given to Paralegals,* The Journal 5 (February 1991).

19. Family Law[12]

(See also *contract law, employee benefits law, estates law, litigation, pro bono work,* and *public sector.*)

I. Telephone Screening of Clients

II. Commencement of Action
A. Interview client to obtain initial information for pleadings.

B. Prepare initial pleadings, including petition, summons and waiver of service, affidavit as to children, and response.
C. Draft correspondence to be sent to clients, courts, and other attorneys.
D. Arrange for service of process.

III. Temporary Orders
A. Prepare motions for temporary orders or temporary injunctions.
B. Draft notice and set hearings.
C. Assist in settlement negotiations.
D. Draft stipulations for temporary orders after negotiations.

IV. Financial Affidavits
A. Help clients gather and compile financial information.
B. Analyze income and expense information provided by client.
C. Work with accountants, financial advisors, brokers, and other financial experts retained by client.
D. Retain appraisers for real estate, business, and personal property.
E. Prepare financial affidavits.

V. Discovery
A. Prepare discovery requests.
B. Help clients organize documents and data to respond to discovery requests.
C. Help prepare responses to discovery requests.
D. Organize, index, and summarize discovered materials.

VI. Settlement Negotiations
A. Assist attorney in analysis of proposed settlements.
B. Research legal questions and assist in drafting briefs and memoranda.
C. Assist in drafting separation agreements.

VII. Hearings
A. Help prepare for hearings on final orders.
B. Research legal questions and assist in drafting briefs and memoranda.
C. Assist in the preparation of trial exhibits and trial notebooks.
D. Arrange for expert witnesses and assist in preparing witnesses and clients for trial.
E. Attend hearings.
F. Prepare decree.

VIII. Post-Decree
A. Prepare documents for transfers of assets.
B. Arrange to file and record all transfer documents.
C. Review bills for tax-deductible fees and help prepare opinion letter to client.
D. Draft pleadings for withdrawal from case.

---

[12]See footnote 11.

IX. Special Projects
A. Develop forms for gathering information from client.
B. Maintain files on separation-agreement provisions, current case law, resource materials for clients, and experts in various fields (e.g., custody, evaluation, and business appraisals).

● *Comment on Paralegal Work in This Area:*

Karen Dunn, a family law paralegal, "draws considerable satisfaction from a divorce case where the client was a woman in her sixties whose husband had left her, a situation which created predictable distress, notably during discussion of financial aspects. She was able to tell me things she couldn't tell the attorney. I found out she had a thyroid condition, so she was able to get more money in the end. I worked with her on the financial affidavit and drafted temporary orders to provide child support and spousal maintenance until the decree was entered." Edwards, *The General Practice Paralegal,* 8 Legal Assistant Today 49, 54 (March/April 1991).

"As the only paralegal in a one-attorney family law practice, my job responsibilities are numerous. I work for an attorney who believes her paralegal should handle nearly all the legal functions she does, with the exception of appearing in court on behalf of clients, taking depositions and giving legal advice. My skills are used to the maximum, as I gather and organize all case information, allowing the attorney to prepare for court and be more cost-effective. I am the liaison person between clients and the attorney. I am able to deal with the human, emotional aspects of our clients, and not just the technical aspects of the law. As each person is different, so is every case, which makes this job a continuing challenge." Lenihan, *Role of the Family Law Paralegal,* 10 Paragram 6 (Oregon Legal Assistants Ass'n, August 1987).

● *Quotes from Want Ads:*

Position is "excellent for a highly motivated person with excellent organizational skills and the ability to interface with clients." "Two swamped attorneys need reliable paralegal to work in fully computerized office. Must have excellent research and writing skills." Applicant must be "self-motivated, well-organized person who has initiative and can assume responsibility." Position requires "ability, experience, and attention to detail." "Looking for very professional applicants."

---

20. Government Contract Law[13]

(See also *administrative law, construction law, contract law, litigation,* and *water law.*)

I. Calendar
A. Maintain calendar for court and appeals board appearances.
B. Record dates briefs are due, etc.

II. Claims
A. Gather, review, summarize, and index client files.
B. Assist in drafting contract claims.
C. Conduct preliminary research on selected legal issues.

III. Appeals
A. Draft and answer interrogatories and requests for production of documents.
B. Summarize and index answers to discovery.
C. Assist in drafting appeal.
D. Prepare questions for witnesses and summarize their prior testimony.
E. Maintain documents during hearing.

IV. Post-Hearing Briefs
A. Summarize and index transcripts.
B. Assist with analysis of government's brief.
C. Conduct preliminary research on selected issues.
D. Assist in drafting the post-hearing brief.

21. Immigration Law

(See also *administrative law, family law, international law, labor and employment law,* and *public sector.*)

I. Problem Identification
A. Help individual who has difficulty in obtaining:
1. Visa,
2. Permanent residency based on occupation,
3. Nonimmigrant status,
4. Citizenship status.
B. Help individuals who are faced with deportation proceedings.

II. Providing Information on:
A. Visa process,
B. Permanent residency process,
C. Nonimmigrant status process,
D. Registration process,
E. Citizenship process,
F. Deportation process.

III. Investigation

Assist the individual in obtaining data and documentation on birth, travel, residency, etc.

---

[13]Berg, C., *Annual Survey* (San Francisco Ass'n of Legal Assistants, Dec. 19, 1973).

IV. Referral

Refer individuals to foreign consulates, nationality organizations, government officials, etc., for assistance concerning their immigration status.

V. Applications/Forms

Assist the individual in filling out visa applications, permanent residency applications, etc.

VI. Monitor Consular Processing Procedure

● ***Comment on Paralegal Work in This Area:***

"This is not a specialty for the faint-hearted or the misanthrope. The immigration paralegal may deal with much more than the timely filing of paperwork. One distinguishing feature of immigration work is our knowledge of intensely personal aspects of the client's life. We know his criminal record, the success and failure of his personal life, how much money he makes, and his dreams and aspirations. . . . Some clients have a very laissez-faire attitude towards perjury, and may invite the paralegal to participate without a blush. In America, [said one client] you lie *to* your attorney. In my country, you cook up the lie *with* your attorney." Myers & Raman, *Sweet-Talking Clients and Intransigent Bureaucrats*, 15 National Paralegal Reporter 4 (NFPA, Winter 1991).

22. Insurance Law

Paralegals in this area work for law firms that represent insurance companies who are defendants in litigation, often personal injury (PI) litigation. They also work for insurance companies themselves. The following overview covers the latter. (See also *corporate law, employee benefits law, litigation, social security law,* and *worker's compensation law.*)

I. Compliance
A. Analyze government regulations on the insurance industry.
B. Prepare applications for new insurance products to obtain approval from Department of Insurance.

II. Claims
A. Assist in processing disputed claims.
B. Provide trial assistance by coordinating activities of company attorneys with outside counsel to represent the company.

III. Monitoring and Research
A. Monitor regulations of agencies and statutes of the legislatures that affect the insurance industry, particularly the committees of the legislature with jurisdiction over the industry.

B. Provide factual and legal research on inquiries that come into the office from agents and brokers.

● ***Comment on Paralegal Work in This Area:***

"Compliance is an insurance industry term which refers to keeping the company and its products in compliance with state and federal law, and procuring licenses for the company in unlicensed states. Compliance is a good field for paralegals because there is opportunity to work autonomously and also to advance within most companies." I am a "Senior Compliance Analyst" at a life insurance company. "I have met many paralegals who are compliance analysts, compliance specialists, and compliance managers." Maston, *Insurance*, The Citator 8 (Legal Assistants of Central Ohio, August 1990).

23. Intellectual Property Law

Paralegals in this area work on copyrights, patents, and trademarks. (See also *contract law* and *entertainment law.*)

I. Copyrights
A. Application
  1. Help client apply for registration of a copyright for a novel, play, or other work with the Copyright Office.
  2. Help client apply for protection in foreign countries.
  3. Collect data, such as nature of the work, date completed, name of creator/author, name of the work, owner, etc., for application.
  4. Help identify the classification for the copyright.
  5. Examine accuracy of certificate-of-copyright registration.
B. Marketing
  1. Identify potential users/licensees of the copyright.
  2. Help prepare contracts.
C. Infringement
  1. Conduct investigations to determine whether an infringement exists—for example, compare the copyrighted work with the alleged infringing work.
  2. Provide general litigation assistance.

II. Patent
A. Application
  1. Help the inventor apply for a patent with the U.S. Patent and Trademark Office.
  2. Help the inventor describe the invention—for example, assemble designs, diagrams, and notebooks.
  3. Conduct a patent search. Check technical libraries to determine the current state of the art.
  4. Determine filing fees.
  5. Help the client apply for protection in foreign countries.
  6. Monitor the responses from government offices.

7. Examine certificate of patent for accuracy.

B. Marketing the invention
1. Help identify licensees. Solicit bids, conduct financial checks, study the market, etc.
2. Help prepare contracts.

C. Infringement
1. Conduct investigation on products that may have violated the patent.
2. Provide general litigation assistance.

III. Trademarks

A. Registration
1. Research trademark files or order search of trademark or trade name preliminary to an application before the U.S. Patent and Trademark Office.
2. Examine indexes and directories.
3. Conduct investigations to determine when the mark was first used, where, on what products, etc.
4. Prepare foreign trademark applications.
5. Respond to official actions taken by government offices.
6. Examine the certificate of trademark for accuracy.
7. Maintain files for renewals.

B. Infringement
1. Conduct investigations into who else used the mark, when, where, in what market, etc.
2. Provide general litigation assistance.

● *Comment on Paralegal Work in This Area:*

"With the right training, trademark paralegals can find richly rewarding experiences waiting for them, whether they remain in paralegal work or go on to build careers in some other facet of trademark law. Trademark work is very dynamic." Wilkinson, *The Case for a Career in Trademark Law,* 7 Legal Professional 29 (November/December 1989).

"Paula Rein was a trademark paralegal before such a job title was even invented. Her career has spanned over 19 years, leading her to some of the biggest corporations and law firms in New York City. Her extensive knowledge of trademark administration has made her one of the most resourceful trademark paralegals in her occupation. In her current 'diversified position,' at a law firm that specializes in intellectual property, she works on the cases of clients in the food and service industries and professional associations. Paula thrives in her current position." Scior, *Paralegal Profile,* Postscript 13 (Manhattan Paralegal Ass'n, December 1989).

24. International Law

Example: a paralegal working on a "dumping" case in international trade.

I. Investigation
A. Examine the normal behavior in the industry or market affected by the alleged dumping.
B. Do statistical research (cost and price data).
C. Prepare profiles of domestic competitors.

II. Preparation of Documents
A. Help prepare for presentation before the Commerce Department.
B. Help prepare for presentation before the Court of International Trade.

III. Accounting Research

IV. Coordination of Data from:
A. Members of Congress,
B. Foreign embassies,
C. State Department,
D. U.S. Special Trade Representative.

● *Comment on Paralegal Work in This Area:*

Steven Stark works "40–50 hours a week, specializing in international legal assisting, a hot area, while the Japanese are busy buying up American properties. [Steve became the liaison for the firm's Tokyo branch office. He originally expected to stay at the firm only three years, but found that] the longer you're here, the more they value you. New things still come up. You work with the constant tension of everyone being expected to perform at a very high level, at all times. This is a high-stakes game, with million and billion dollar deals. It's a peaked, emotional atmosphere, with long hours." Milano, *Career Profiles,* 8 Legal Assistant Today 35, 38 (September/October 1990).

25. Judicial Administration

Most courts have clerks to help with the administrative aspects of deciding cases. In addition, a few courts have paralegals that work for the court. They perform some of the functions of the administrative clerks, such as determining whether the parties have been properly notified of trial dates, checking filings and proposed orders from attorneys to determine whether anything appears inappropriate or premature, or obtaining additional information for a judge.

● *Comment on Paralegal Work in This Area:*

"The Shreveport City Court has employed me as its paralegal in the civil department for the past six years. The Baton Rouge City Court employs several paralegals." We handle many matters such as determining if the legal delays for pleading have expired "before initialing the pleading and passing it on to the clerk or judge for signature. The most important task is the handling of default judgments. I must certify that proper service has been made. Perhaps I could be called a 'nitpicker' about these cases, but the judge acts on my certificate that everything is in order. It is always challenging to stay informed on our constantly changing procedural laws; I must keep a set of the Civil Procedure [laws] at my desk." Waterman, *The Court's Paralegal*, 3 NWLPA News 5 (Northwest Louisiana Paralegal Ass'n, November 1990).

26. Labor and Employment Law

(See also *civil rights law, contract law, employee benefits law,* and *worker's compensation law.*)

I. Investigation

Look into:

A. Sexual harassment.
B. Wrongful discharge.
C. Violation of occupational safety and health laws.
D. Violation of labor laws involving collective bargaining, union organization, grievance and arbitration procedures.
E. Violation of Civil Rights Act protecting against discrimination on the basis of race, national origin, sex, or physical handicap.
F. Violation of Age Discrimination in Employment Act.
G. Violation of Americans with Disabilities Act.

II. Compliance

Assist companies in the design and implementation of policies on:

A. Drug and alcohol testing.
B. AIDS in the workplace.
C. Race, sex, disability, and age discrimination.

III. Litigation Assistance

A. Help handle labor disputes before the National Labor Relations Board, State Labor Relations Board, Civil Service Commission, Human Rights Board, and the courts.
B. Perform a variety of tasks:
   1. Maintain the files.
   2. Digest and index data in files.
   3. Arrange for depositions.
   4. Help draft petition and other pleadings.
   5. Maintain tickler system of due dates.
   6. Prepare exhibits.
   7. Prepare statistical data.
   8. Help prepare appeal.

● *Comment on Paralegal Work in This Area:*

"My experience in the labor and employment area has proven to be both diverse and unique. It is diverse because of the various labor-related issues accessible to me as a paralegal. It is unique because it is an area of specialty which involves very few paralegals in my part of the state. Batke, *Labor and Employment Paralegal*, The Citator 3 (Legal Assistants of Central Ohio, August 1990).

"In the labor law area, I was responsible for doing background research, preparing witnesses and drafting arbitration briefs. I also assisted with the drafting of revised language during contract negotiations with unions." Diebold, *A Paralegal of Another Kind*, 16 Facts and Findings 38 (NALA, March 1990).

27. Landlord and Tenant Law

Paralegals in real estate law firms occasionally become involved in commercial lease cases, such as a dispute over the interpretation of the lease of a supermarket at a large shopping mall. Such landlord-tenant cases, however, are not as common as the cases that arise between landlords and tenants who live in the apartments they rent. For example, a landlord of a small apartment seeks to evict a tenant for nonpayment of rent. Many of these cases are handled by publicly funded legal service or legal aid offices that do not charge fees. (See *public sector, oil and gas law,* and *real estate law.*)

● *Comment on Paralegal Work in This Area:*

"The Legal Action Center is the largest non-governmental social service agency in the state. As a paralegal, Virginia Farley handles all eviction calls to the landlord-tenant unit. Three afternoons a week are designated intake times. She screens all eviction cases, determines whether the applicant is eligible for free assistance according to the Center's guidelines, recommends a plan once a case is accepted and assists in carrying out the plan under an attorney's supervision. [After arriving in the city], Virginia made a commitment to work directly with the poor and started serving as a volunteer in five organizations until a job opened up for her at the Legal Action Center." Roche, *Paralegal Profile*, 4 Findings and Conclusions 5 (Washington Ass'n of Legal Assistants, November 1987).

28. Law Librarianship

There is a separate degree that a law librarian can obtain. This degree, however, is not a requirement to be a law librarian. A number of small or medium-sized law offices are hiring paralegals to perform library chores exclusively or in combination with paralegal duties on cases. (See also *law office administration* and *litigation*.)

I. Administration
A. Order books for law library.
B. File loose-leaf material and pocket parts in appropriate volumes.
C. Pay bills of library vendors.
D. Test and recommend computer equipment, software, and services for the law library.
E. Prepare budget for library.

II. Cite Checking
A. Check the citations in briefs, speeches, articles, opinion letters, and other legal documents to determine the accuracy of quoted material.
B. Check the citations to determine the accuracy of citation format according to the Uniform System of Citation (the Bluebook), local court rules, or other citation guidelines required by the office.

III. Research
A. Perform factual research.
B. Perform legal research.

IV. Training
A. Train office staff in traditional legal research techniques.
B. Train office staff in computer research, for example, WESTLAW, LEXIS.
C. Train office staff in cite checking.

● *Comment on Paralegal Work in This Area:*

"I suppose my entry into the law librarianship profession might be considered unorthodox because I had no formal educational courses in librarianship. My experience was that of working first as a legal secretary and later evolving into a legal assistant. My job in a small general practice firm included taking care of the office library such as filing supplements and pocket parts (because no one else would do it!!); doing the bookkeeping and paying the bills." I did some legal research "as an extension of legal drafting." "In all my working years (and they are many) I had the greatest satisfaction from my work as a law librarian because each day I learned new things." Lewek, *The Legal Assistant as Law Librarian*, 17 Facts & Findings 28 (NALA, March 1991).

29. Law Office Administration

At the beginning of chapter 14, you will find a detailed job description of the legal administrator and of the legal assistant manager. (See Exhibits 14.2 and 14.3.) Some experienced paralegals move into management positions at a law office. This might involve helping to administer the *entire*

office, or *one component* of it, such as the administration of all the legal assistants in the office, the administration of the legal assistants and other support personnel working on a large case, or the administration of the computer operation in the office. Some smaller law offices seek paralegals to perform office management duties along with paralegal duties. (See also *law librarianship* and *litigation*.)

● *Comment on Paralegal Work in This Area:*

In 1984, the partners at the firm decided to upgrade their legal assistant program and needed a nonlawyer to run it. They offered Linda Katz the new position. "The firm is segmented into practice areas, with legal assistants dispersed throughout the areas. They report to supervising attorneys for work assignments each day. I serve as administrative supervisor, assuring consistency in how legal assistants are treated and utilized, and what opportunities they have for benefits and advancement." Milano, *Career Profiles*, 8 Legal Assistant Today 35 (September/October 1990).

"A good paralegal litigation manager [in a large document case] has both strong paralegal skills and strong management skills. Such a manager must be able to analyze the case's organizational needs, develop methods to cope with them effectively, and often must act as paralegal, office manager and computer expert—all in a day's work." Kaufman, *The Litigation Manager*, 6 Legal Professional 55 (July/August 1989).

30. Legislation

I. Monitoring

Keep track of all events, persons, and organizations involved in the passing of legislation relevant to the clients of the firm.

II. Legislative History

Compile the legislative history of a statute.

III. Drafting of Proposed Legislation

IV. Lobbying
A. Prepare reports and studies on the subject of proposed legislation.
B. Arrange for and help prepare witnesses who will testify at legislative hearings.

● *Comment on Paralegal Work in This Area:*

Margo Horner "is a legislative analyst for the Nat'l Federation of Independent Business (NFIB). With paralegal training and a masters degree in history, her job is research, creating legislative strategy, working with [legislators] and their staffs to produce legislation favorable to [NFIB]. Margo likes the frenetic tempo of her life." Smith, *Margo*, 1 Legal Assistant Today 14 (Summer 1984).

31. Litigation (Civil)

Civil litigation involves court disputes in every area of the law other than a case where the government is charging (prosecuting) someone for the commission of a crime. Hence civil litigation can potentially involve every specialty other than criminal law.

I. File Monitoring
A. Index all files.
B. Write case profile based on information in the files.
C. Read attorney briefs to check accuracy of the information in the litigation file.
D. Organize, index, and digest documents obtained through answers to interrogatories, depositions, and other discovery devices.
E. Code documents into a computer database.

II. Investigation
A. Gather documents:
   1. Medical records,
   2. Police records,
   3. Birth and death records,
   4. Marriage records,
   5. Adoption and custody records,
   6. Incorporation records.
B. Research records. For example:
   1. Prepare a profit history report of a company.
   2. Identify corporate structure of a parent company and its subsidiaries.
   3. Trace UCC (Uniform Commercial Code) filings.
   4. Find out from court dockets if a particular merchant is being sued, has sued before, etc. Does any pattern exist?
   5. Identify the "real owner" of an apartment building.
   6. Check housing code agency to find out if a landlord has other building code violations against it on record.
C. Gather facts (other than from documents). In a wide range of cases (such as real estate, corporate, divorce, and custody), the investigator substantiates facts, follows leads for possible evidence in connection with litigation, etc.

III. Discovery
A. Draft interrogatories.
B. Draft answers to interrogatories.
C. Draft deposition questions.
D. Prepare witnesses for deposition.
E. Prepare witness books for deposition.
F. Arrange time and place of deposition.
G. Draft requests for admissions.
H. Draft answers to requests for admissions.
I. Draft requests for production of documents.
J. Draft answers to requests for production of documents.
K. Index and digest discovery data.
L. Work with computer programmer in designing a system to manage discovery documents.

IV. Filings/Serving
File and/or serve documents in court, at agencies, on parties, on attorneys, etc.

V. General Assistance
A. Arrange for clients and others to be interviewed.
B. Arrange for expert witnesses to appear in court or at depositions.
C. Reconstruct (from a large collection of disparate records and other evidence) what happened at a particular time and place.
D. Assist clients in completing information questionnaire, especially in class-action cases.
E. Help organize the *trial notebook* containing items the attorney will need during the trial, such as charts and tables to be used as exhibits at trial.
F. Sit at counsel's table at trial to take notes and suggest questions for attorney to ask witnesses.
G. Attend (and report on) hearings in related cases.
H. Supervise document encodation on a computer project related to a case in litigation.
I. Prepare and evaluate prospective jurors from jury book and during voir dire.
J. Help prepare appeal documents—for example, the notice of appeal.

VI. Legal Research
A. Shepardize cited authority; perform cite check.
B. Write preliminary memos and briefs.
C. Prepare bibliographies of source materials related to a case in litigation.

VII. Pleadings
Write preliminary draft of pleadings using standard forms and/or adapting other pleadings written by attorneys on similar cases.

VIII. Expert Analysis
Assist in obtaining expert opinions for attorneys on:
A. Taxation.
B. Accounting.
C. Statistics.
D. Economics (e.g., calculation of damages).

IX. Court Witness
A. Act as witness as to service of process.
B. Act as witness as to data uncovered or photographed (e.g., the condition of an apartment building).

- *Comment on Paralegal Work in This Area:*

"There are boxes and boxes with an infinite number of documents to be indexed. There are depositions to be summarized. There are cases whose cites need checking. There are trips to the courthouse downtown. There is red-lining of documents to determine changes between two documents. There is Bates-stamping of documents. And there are the exciting trips to visit clients." Lasky, *Impressions of a New Paralegal,* 17 Reporter 5 (Los Angeles Paralegal Ass'n, February 1988).

"I organized. I tabbed and tagged, listed and labelled, hoisted and hole-punched, folded and filed, boxed and Bates-stamped, indexed and itemized, sorted and summarized." Klinkseick, *Aim High,* 16 On Point 4 (Nat'l Capital Area Paralegal Ass'n, July/August 1990).

"Initially, it was overwhelming with the number of files and the names to learn and things to remember, but with help, I learned skills and techniques and polished them day after day as each new case brought with it new quirks and new challenges. I've attended depositions, PTO shaft inspections, and pig farm operations. I've calculated medical expenses, reviewed medical records, and been baffled at how salesmen keep time records! But the ultimate of all experiences, I have to admit, are the trials. You prepare and prepare and hope that you haven't missed any of the details. Then before you know it, the jury has been selected and you're off! The trials keep your adrenaline flowing. They frazzle your patience. They show you your limitations. They elevate you when you win. They shake your confidence when you lose." Riske, *In the Limelight,* 7 Red River Review 4 (Red River Valley Legal Assistants, North Dakota, August 1990).

"For almost six years now . . . , I've experienced the variety (and the drudgery) of preparing civil cases for trial. I've spent countless hours photocopying documents never read by any judge or jury, or worst of all, by anyone else. I've tracked down witnesses and encouraged them to talk only to find out that they know nothing about the case. In this business of endless paper where no two cases are alike, I've come to understand . . . that flexibility is essential and a sense of humor is invaluable in dealing with people, be they stressed-out attorneys or reluctant witnesses." Vore, *A Litigation Recipe,* 16 On Point 4 (Nat'l Capital Area Paralegal Ass'n, November 1990).

Rebecca McLaughlin tells of a particularly memorable event during her experience as a paralegal. "It was a few minutes after 12:00 noon on Friday, and presiding Judge Barbour always recesses court at precisely 12:30 on Fridays. The Government's star witness was on the stand and denied

he had ever seen a certain letter. One of the trial attorneys motioned me to counsel table and asked if we had any proof that the witness had, in fact, seen this letter." Since there were well over 900 defense exhibits, almost 300 Government exhibits, and well over 40 file cabinets filled with supporting documents, Rebecca felt little hope for success [in finding out quickly]. "She hurried across the street to the office, found the witness' original copy of the letter with his handwritten notes in the margin, and returned to the courtroom with a BIG SMILE. The witness was impeached with his own document minutes before recess." "Later, Rebecca received a well-deserved standing ovation from the attorneys, and all the trial team members. It was the highlight of her career." Johnson, *MALA Spotlight: Rebecca McLaughlin,* 8 The Assistant 17 (Mississippi Ass'n of Legal Assistants, July 1989).

- *Quotes from Want Ads:*

"Excellent writing skills and attention to detail are absolute requirements." "Plaintiff's medical malpractice firm seeks non-smoker with word processing abilities." Position requires "extensive writing, document summarizing, and medical records research." Must have an ability "to work independently in handling cases from inception through trial preparation; familiarity with drafting law motions pleadings is essential." High-energy candidate "needs to be assertive and should have an excellent academic background." "Wanted: a sharp, take-charge litigation paralegal." "Knowledge of computerized litigation support is a plus; good communications and organizational skills are a must." "Applicant must possess a thorough working knowledge of all phases of trial work." "Successful candidate will be professional, prompt, pleasant and personable. No egomaniacs or job hoppers, please." "Overtime flexibility required." "Defense litigation paralegal needed. Must be a self-starter with the ability to accept unstructured responsibility." "Applicant must have a thorough knowledge of state and federal court procedures." Position requires an ability "to organize and manage documents in large multi-party litigation." "Applicants must possess strong supervisory, analytic, writing, and investigative skills, and an ability to perform under pressure." "Position requires good analytical and writing skills, and the ability to organize and control several projects simultaneously." "Deposition summarizer needed; work in your own home on your own computer." "Part-time proofreader for deposition summaries needed."

32. Military Law

In the Navy, a nonattorney who assists attorneys in the practice of law is called a **legalman.** Depending upon the assignment, the legalman can work in a large variety of areas of

the law—for exa[...]
justice. The follo[...]
ited to any parti[...]

I. Military Proce[...]
A. Assist in proc[...]
  1. Special co[...]
  2. General c[...]
  3. Courts of[...]
  4. Line-of-d[...]
  5. Reclassific[...]
B. Prepare all s[...]
  special and ge[...]
C. Assure that charges are properly prepared and that specifications are complete and accurate.
D. Make initial determination on jurisdiction of court, status of accused, and subject matter of offenses.
E. Examine completed records of investigations and other records requiring legal review to insure that they are administratively correct.
F. Prepare special court-martial orders promulgating sentence.
G. Assure that records of court-martial are correct and complete before disposing of case.
H. Transmit bad-conduct discharge court-martial cases to appropriate officials.

II. Claims against the Government
A. Conduct examinations.
B. Process claims against the United States—for instance, federal tort claims.
C. Manage claim funds.
D. Undertake research on FLITE (Federal Legal Information Through Electronics).
E. Write briefs.

III. Administrative Duties
A. Maintain control records of all court-martial and claims cases within command.
B. Maintain law library.
C. Examine and distribute incoming correspondence, directives, publications, and other communications.
D. Supervise cataloging and filing of books, periodicals, newsletters, etc.
E. Maintain records of discipline within command.
F. Administer office budget.
G. Orient new personnel and monitor their training.

IV. Court Reporting
A. Use the steno-mask for recording legal proceedings.
B. Prepare charges to the jury.
C. Mark exhibits as they are entered into evidence.
D. Transcribe and assemble records of the proceeding.

[...]ment on Paralegal Work in This Area:

"[...]ve been working for the Office of the Staff Judge [...]e (SJA) at Fort Ord, California. The SJA is the [...]awyer. We serve a military community of just over [...]eople. Staff within the SJA consists of a combina-[...]nilitary and civilian attorneys, paralegals, legal clerks [...]rt reporters. I am responsible for claims filed against [...]ral government under the Federal Tort Claims Act. I [...]onsible for discovery and investigative efforts, deter-[...]legal issues, writing memorandums of law and rec-[...]ding settlement or denial. Job satisfaction for para-[...]ofessionals is high in the U.S. government. I know that, should I desire to re-enter the civilian work sector, my experience and knowledge of the government legal systems will uniquely qualify me to work for any firm which deals with the government." Richards, *Marching to a Different Drummer: Paralegal Work in the Military,* 2 California Paralegal Magazine 8 (October/December 1990).

33. Municipal Finance Law[14]

(See also *banking law* and *corporate law.*)

I. Document Preparation
A. Basic documents:
  1. Prepare first drafts of basic documents, including bonds, indentures of trust, financing agreements, and all other related documents.
  2. Attend drafting sessions and note changes required to initial drafts.
  3. Prepare second and subsequent drafts by incorporating revisions.
B. Closing documents:
  1. Prepare first drafts of all closing documents.
  2. Prepare second and subsequent drafts by incorporating revisions and red-line changes.
C. Draft official statement/private offering memorandum:
  1. Prepare first drafts.
  2. Attend drafting sessions.
  3. Perform due diligence to verify the information and data contained in the offering document.
  4. Prepare second and subsequent drafts by incorporating revisions and red-line changes.

II. Coordination
A. Establish timetable and list of participants.
B. Distribute documents to participants.
C. Coordinate printing of bonds and offering documents.
D. File all documents as required.
E. Coordinate publication of notices of meetings and elections, ordinances, public hearing notices, etc.

---

[14]See footnote 11.

III. Closing
A. Prepare checklist.
B. Arrange and assist in preclosing and closing.
C. File any documents necessary to be filed prior to closing.
D. Secure requisite documents to be prepared or furnished by other participants.
E. Perform all post-closing procedures, including:
    1. File all documents or security agreements.
    2. Supervise preparation of closing binders.

IV. Formation of Special Districts
A. Prepare documents necessary to organize the district.
B. File documents with municipality or county and district court.
C. Prepare documents for organizational meeting of district.

V. Elections (Formation of District or for Bond Election)

Draft election documents and obtain all necessary election materials.

VI. Develop and Maintain Research Files
A. IDB procedures for municipalities.
B. Home rule charters.
C. Demographic and economic statistics.
D. Memoranda noting statutory changes.
E. Interoffice research memoranda.
F. Checklists for each type of financing.

34. Oil and Gas Law

Some paralegals who work in the area of oil and gas law are referred to as **land technicians** or **landmen.** (See also *real estate law.*)

I. Collect and analyze data pertaining to land ownership and activities that may affect the procurement of rights to explore, drill for, and produce oil or gas.

II. Help acquire leases and other operating rights from property owners for exploration, drilling, and producing oil, gas, and related substances.

III. Monitor the execution of the leases and other operating agreements by insuring that contract obligations are fulfilled (e.g., payment of rent).

IV. Help negotiate agreements with individuals, companies, and government agencies pertaining to the exploration, drilling, and production of oil or gas.

V. Assist in acquiring oil and gas producing properties, royalties, and mineral interests.

VI. Process and monitor the termination of leases and other agreements.

VII. Examine land titles.

● *Comment on Paralegal Work in This Area:*

"As an oil and gas paralegal, my practice encompasses many different areas of law including real estate, litigation, bankruptcy, and securities, as well as contact with various county, state, and federal government agencies. I frequently spend time searching real estate records in counties . . . for information on leases to determine such things as who has been assigned an interest in the lease. I have worked in mechanic's lien foreclosures, partition actions, and bankruptcy cases. While researching such things as regulatory information and oil prices, I have obtained information from the Federal Energy Regulatory Commission offices in Washington. The variety of work requires a working knowledge of several areas of law, and is always challenging and interesting." Hunt, *Oil and Gas,* The Citator (Legal Assistants of Central Ohio, August 1990).

35. Parajudge

In many states, the judge presiding in certain lower courts does not have to be an attorney. Such courts include justice of the peace courts and local magistrates courts.

Administrative agencies often hold hearings conducted by hearing officers, referees, or administrative law judges (ALJ). Frequently, these individuals are not attorneys, particularly at state and local agencies.

36. Pro Bono Work

Pro bono work refers to services provided to another person at no charge. Law firms often give their attorneys time off so they can take pro bono cases—for example, to defend a poor person charged with a crime. Paralegals are also encouraged to do pro bono work. This is done on their own time or on law firm time with the permission of their supervisor. The following are examples of the variety of pro bono work performed by paralegals:

I. Abused Women
A. Draft request for protective order.
B. Draft divorce pleadings.

II. AIDS Patients
A. Interview patients and prepare a memorandum of the interview for the pro bono attorney on the case.
B. Assist patients with guardianship problems.
C. Draft powers of attorney.

III. Homeless
A. Handle Supplemental Social Security claims (SSI).
B. Make referrals to shelters and drug programs.

● *Comment on Paralegal Work in This Area:*

"Asked to share her favorite pro bono experience, Therese Ortega, a litigation paralegal, answered that to choose was too difficult; any time her efforts result in a benefit to the client, 'I get a warm glow.' One occasion she obviously cherishes was the fight on behalf of some low-income kidney dialysis patients whose eligibility for transportation to and from treatment was threatened. 'Perseverance and appeals paid off,' she says. Rides were re-established through the hearing process, then by information conferences. Finally, the cessation notices stopped." *Spotlight on Therese Ortega,* 13 The Journal 3 (Sacramento Ass'n of Legal Assistants, March 1991).

37. Public Sector

A paralegal in the *private sector* works in an office whose funds come from client fees or from the budget of the corporate treasury. Every other setting is generally considered the *public sector.* More specifically, the latter refers to those law offices that provide civil or criminal legal services to the poor for free. Often, the services consist of helping clients obtain government benefits such as public housing, welfare, medical care, etc. Such services are referred to as **public benefits,** and providing such assistance is called practice of public benefits law. Some of the paralegals who are employed by these offices are called Public Benefits Paralegals. The offices operate with government grants, charitable contributions, and the efforts of volunteers. They are called Legal Aid Society, Legal Aid Foundation, Legal Services Office, Office of the Public Defender, etc. For examples of the kinds of functions performed by paralegals in these offices, see *administrative law, bankruptcy law, civil rights law, criminal law, family law, landlord and tenant law, litigation, pro bono work, social security law, welfare law,* and *worker's compensation law.*

● *Comment on Paralegal Work in This Area:*

"If someone asked me what I disliked most about my job, I would have to answer: the size of my paycheck. That is the only drawback of working for a nonprofit law firm—[the Community Legal Aid Society which represents elderly and handicapped persons]. Everything else about my job is positive." For example, to "be an integral part of a case where a landlord is forced by the Courts to bring a house up to code and prevent a tenant from being wrongfully evicted is a great feeling." The positive aspects of the job "more than compensate for the size of the paycheck." Hartman, *Job Profile,* Delaware Paralegal Reporter 5 (Delaware Paralegal Ass'n, November 1988).

"Mr. Watnick stressed that the organization doesn't have the luxury of using paralegals as "xeroxers" or errand run-ners. Staff paralegals have their own caseloads and represent clients before Administrative Law Judges—with a dramatically high rate of success." Shays, *Paralegals in Human Service,* Postscript 16 (Manhattan Paralegal Ass'n, March/April 1990).

38. Real Estate Law

(See also *banking law, contract law,* and *landlord and tenant law.*)

I. General

Assist law firms, corporations, and development companies in transactions involving land, houses, condominiums, shopping malls, office buildings, redevelopment projects, civic centers, etc.

A. Research zoning regulations.

B. Prepare draft of the contract of sale.

C. Title work:
   1. If done outside, order title work from the title company; arrange title insurance.
   2. If done in-house:
      a. Examine title abstracts for completeness,
      b. Prepare a map based on a master title plat or the current government survey map,
      c. Help construct a chain of title noting defects, encumbrances, liens, easements, breaks in the chain, etc.,
      d. Obtain releases of liens, payoff statements for existing loans, etc.
      e. Help draft a preliminary title opinion.

D. Mortgages:
   1. Assist in obtaining financing,
   2. Review mortgage application,
   3. Assist in recording mortgage.

E. Closing:
   1. Arrange for a closing time with buyer, seller, brokers, and lender. Obtain letter confirming date of closing.
   2. Collect the data necessary for closing. Prepare checklist of expenses:
      a. Title company's fee,
      b. Lender's fee,
      c. Attorney's fee,
      d. Taxes and water bills to be prorated,
      e. Tax escrow, discharge of liens.
   3. Prepare and organize the documents for closing:
      a. Deed,
      b. Settlement statement,
      c. Note and deed of trust,
      d. Corporate resolutions,
      e. Performance bond,
      f. Waivers.

4. Check compliance with the disclosure requirements of the Real Estate Settlement Act.
5. Arrange for a rehearsal of the closing.
6. Attend and assist at the closing—for example, take minutes, notarize documents.

F. Foreclosure:
1. Order foreclosure certificate.
2. Prepare notice of election and demand for sale.
3. Compile a list of parties to be notified.
4. Monitor publication of the notice.
5. Assist with sale documents—for example, prepare bid letter.

G. Eminent Domain:
1. Photograph or videotape the property taken or to be taken by the state.
2. Prepare inventory of the property taken.
3. Help client prepare business records pertaining to the value of the property.
4. Arrange for appraisals of the property.
5. Order and review engineering reports regarding soil.
6. Review tax appeal records on values claimed by the property owner.
7. Mail out notice of condemnation.

H. Office management:
1. Maintain office tickler system.
2. Maintain individual attorney's calendar.
3. Be in charge of the entire client's file (opening it, keeping it up-to-date, knowing where parts of it are at all times, etc.).
4. Train other staff in the office system of handling real estate cases.

II. Tax-exempt Industrial Development Financing
A. Undertake a preliminary investigation to establish facts relevant to:
1. Project eligibility,
2. The local issuer,
3. Cost estimates of the financing.
B. Prepare a formal application to the issuer.
C. Prepare a timetable of approvals, meetings, and all other requirements necessary for closing.
D. Prepare a preliminary draft of portions of the proposal memorandum (relating to the legal structure of the financing) that is submitted to prospective bond purchasers.
E. Obtain confirmation from the Treasury Department that the company is in compliance with the financing covenants of current external debt instruments.
F. Obtain insurance certificates.
G. Write the first draft of the resolutions of the board of directors.

H. Write the preface and recital of documents for the legal opinion of the company.
I. Contact the bank to confirm the account numbers, amount of money to be transferred, and investment instructions.
J. Prepare a closing memorandum covering the following documents:
1. Secretary's certificate including resolutions of the board of directors, the certified charter and bylaws of the company, and the incumbency certificate,
2. UCC-1 financing statements,
3. Requisition forms,
4. Certificate of authorized company representative,
5. Deed,
6. Legal opinion of the company,
7. Transfer instruction letter,
8. Officer's certificate.
K. Confirm that the money has been transferred to the company's account on the day of closing.
L. Order an updated good-standing telegram.
M. Send a copy of the IRS election statement.
N. Assemble, monitor, and distribute documents to appropriate departments.

● *Comment on Paralegal Work in This Area:*

"Although it may look boring to the untrained eye, and sound boring to the untrained ear, for those of us whose livelihoods depend upon it, real estate law is *interesting* and *exciting*. There is always something new to learn or a little flaw to resolve. What can be better than having clients come to you and thank you for your assistance in what would have been a complete disaster without your knowledge and expertise to get them through? I call that total job satisfaction. I am now capable of doing everything in a real estate settlement from opening the file to walking into the settlement room and disbursing the funds. It is not uncommon for me to receive calls from attorneys in the area asking me how certain problems can be solved. That boosts my ego more than any divorce case ever could!" Jaeger, *Real Estate Law Is a Legal Profession Too!,* 14 On Point 9 (Nat'l Capital Area Paralegal Ass'n, June 1988).

At a paralegal conference, Virginia Henderson made a seminar presentation on her duties as a paralegal. Her "candor and energetic enthusiasm concerning her profession were encouraging and motivating. She was very explicit about her duties as a commercial real estate paralegal, explaining that attorney supervision is lessened once the paralegal assumes more responsibility and exhibits initiative as far as his/her duties are concerned. It was refreshing to listen to a veteran of the paralegal profession speak so optimistically about the profession's limitless potential. Here's to

having more paralegals as seminar speakers!" Troiano, *Real Estate,* Newsletter 12 (Western New York Paralegal Ass'n, November/December 1987).

"As a foreclosure legal assistant, one of my worst fears is to have a client call and say, 'Remember the Jones property you foreclosed for us last year? Well, we're trying to close on this and it seems there's a problem with the title. . . .' Oh no, what *didn't* I do! Mortgage foreclosure litigation is fraught with all kinds of pitfalls for the inexperienced and the unwary. An improper or faulty foreclosure could not only be disastrous for the client, it can also be a malpractice nightmare for the law firm." Hubbell, *Mortgage Foreclosure Litigation: Avoiding the Pitfalls,* 16 Facts and Findings 10 (NALA, November 1989).

● *Quotes from Want Ads:*

"Ideal candidate must possess exceptional organization, communication, writing and research skills and be willing to work overtime." "We need a team player with high energy." Position requires an ability to work independently on a wide variety of matters and to meet deadlines." "Experience in retail real estate or real estate financing a must." "Should be assertive and have excellent analytical skills." Position requires a "self-motivated person. We seek a TIGER who can accomplish much with a minimum of supervision." "Knowledge of state and federal securities law a plus." "Must be flexible and possess high integrity." Position requires a "self-starter able to deal effectively with executive management, outside counsel, escrow and title companies, brokers, leasing agents, and clients."

39. Social Security Law

(See also *administrative law, public sector,* and *welfare law.*)

I. Problem Identification

Identify whether:
A. Person is denied benefits.
B. Recipient is terminated from disability payments.
C. Recipient is charged with receiving overpayment.
D. Medicare waivers/appeals are involved.

II. Case Preparation
A. Investigate relevant facts.
B. Perform legal research.
C. Engage in informal advocacy with Social Security employees.

III. Representation
A. Represent clients at administrative hearings regarding SSI (Supplemental Security Income).
B. Represent clients at administrative hearings regarding SSD (Social Security Disability).

IV. Appeal
A. Help attorney prepare a court appeal of the Social Security Administration's decision.

● *Comment on Paralegal Work in This Area:*

"Paralegal representation of a claimant in a Social Security Disability hearing is the closest to a judicial setting that a paralegal may expect to become involved in. For the paralegal, this can be a very complex and challenging field. It can also be extremely rewarding, bringing with it the satisfaction of successfully representing a claimant in a quasi-judicial setting." Obermann, *The Paralegal and Federal Disability Practice in Maine,* MAP Newsletter (Maine Ass'n of Paralegals, January 1988).

40. Tax Law

(See also *corporate law, employee benefits law, estates law,* and *real estate law.*)

I. Compile all necessary data for the preparation of tax returns:
A. Corporate income tax,
B. Employer quarterly tax,
C. Franchise tax,
D. Partnership tax,
E. Sales tax,
F. Personal property tax,
G. Individual income tax,
H. Estate tax,
I. Gift tax.

II. Miscellaneaous Tasks
A. Communicate with client to obtain missing information.
B. Compile supporting documents for the returns.
C. Draft extensions-of-time requests for late filings.
D. Make corrections in the returns based upon new or clarified data.
E. Compute the tax liability or transfer client information to computer input sheets for submission to a computer service that will calculate the tax liability.
F. Organize and maintain client binder.
G. Compute cash flow analysis and other calculations needed for proposed real estate syndication.
H. Compile documentation on the valuation of assets.
I. Maintain the tax law library.
J. Read loose-leaf tax services and other periodic tax data to keep current on tax developments. Bring such developments to the attention of others in the office.
K. Supervise and train other nonattorney staff within the tax department of the office.

● *Comment on Paralegal Work in This Area:*

"A legal assistant with the firm for the past thirteen years, Pat [Coleman] spends a lot of time in her office. She is surrounded by her work, and one gets the idea that Pat knows exactly what is in every file and could put her hand on any information that is needed. Notes are taped next to the light switch; the firm's monthly calendar highlighting important meetings is readily available, and helps her track her many deadlines. Pat is an *Enrolled Agent* (which permits her to practice before the Treasury Department), has a lot of tax background, and is competent in that area as well as bookkeeping. One of her least favorite tax forms is the 990 required of not-for-profit organizations. The 990 tax form is second only to private foundation returns when it comes to being pesky and tricky." Howard, *Patricia Coleman of Chicago Creates Her Niche in Taxes, Trusts and ERISA,* 3 Legal Assistant Today 40 (Winter 1986).

41. Tort Law

A **tort** is a civil wrong that has injured someone. Paralegals who work on **PI** (personal injury) cases are mainly litigation assistants. The major torts are negligence, defamation, strict liability, and wrongful death. Paralegals in this area are also often involved in worker's compensation cases for injuries that occur on the job. (See *admiralty law, litigation,* and *worker's compensation.*)

● *Comment on Paralegal Work in This Area:*

"Personal injury/products liability cases can be fascinating, challenging, and educational. They also can be stressful, aggravating and very sad. I have been involved in a great many cases in my career, on both sides of the plaintiff/defendant fence. Some of the cases seemed frivolous and somewhat 'ambulance chasing' in nature. Others were significant cases in which the plaintiff had wrongfully suffered injury. There are many talents a good personal injury/products liability paralegal must have. He or she must be creative, tenacious, observant and able to communicate well with people." Lee, *Personal Injury/Products Liability Cases,* 11 Newsletter 7 (Dallas Ass'n of Legal Assistants, November 1987).

"Recently, Mary Mann, a paralegal who works on product liability litigation, was asked by her attorney to track down a specific medical article [on a subject relevant to a current case]. The attorney only had a vague description of the article, a possible title, and the name of the organization that might have published it. In her search Mary spoke by phone to people in New York, Atlanta, Washington, and finally to a doctor in Geneva, Switzerland, who spoke very little English. In her effort to make herself understood by the doctor, Mary continued to speak louder and louder in very simplistic and basic English phrases, as people tend to do when confronted by a language barrier. She is sure her efforts to maintain a professional demeanor were humorous to those passing by her office. However, she did succeed in getting the article and in the process gained a friend in Switzerland!" Fisher, *Spotlight: Mary Mann,* 7 The Assistant 14 (Mississippi Ass'n of Legal Assistants, April/June 1988).

"Asbestos litigation . . . opened up in the late 1970's with the lawsuits initiated against the Johns-Mansville Corporation. In 1982 Mansville filed a Chapter 11 bankruptcy to protect its assets from the thousands of claims being filed against it." Huge numbers of paralegals were employed in this litigation. For those paralegals working *for* Johns-Mansville on the defense team, "the question of morality arose. I get asked about the morality of my job constantly. For me, personal moral judgment does not enter into it. Our legal system is based on the availability of equal representation for both sides. I think I play a small part in making that system work." Welsh, *The Paralegal in Asbestos Litigation,* 10 Ka Leo O' H.A.L.A. 6 (Hawaii Ass'n of Legal Assistants, February/March 1987) (reprint from newsletter of the East Bay Ass'n of Legal Assistants).

● *Quotes from Want Ads:*

"Medical malpractice law firm seeks paralegal who is a self-starter, has good communication skills, is organized and detail-oriented." Position in PI [personal injury] firm requires "a take-charge person to handle case details from beginning to end." "Prefer person with experience in claims adjustment, medical records, or nursing." Position requires "dynamic, highly-motivated individual who will enjoy the challenge of working independently and handling a wide variety of responsibilities." "Excellent writing skills a must." "Should be able to perform under pressure." Manufacturer of consumer products "seeks paralegal with engineering background." Must be mature enough to handle "heavy client contact." Position requires "ability to read and summarize medical records."

42. Tribal Law

Tribal courts on Indian reservations have jurisdiction over many civil and criminal cases in which both parties are Native Americans. Parties are often represented by tribal court advocates who are nonattorney Native Americans. In addition, the judges are often nonattorneys. (See *litigation.*).

43. Water Law[15]

(See also *administrative law* and *real estate law.*)

---

[15]See footnote 11.

I. Water Rights

Investigate and analyze specific water rights and water rights associated with property:

A. Do research at Department of Water Resources regarding decrees, tabulations, well permits, reservoirs, diversion records, maps, and statements.

B. Communicate in writing and orally with Department of Water Resources personnel regarding status of water rights and wells.

C. Communicate in writing and orally (including interviews) with District Water Commissioners regarding status of water rights and wells, historic use, and use on land.

D. Communicate in writing and orally (including interviews) with property owners and managers, ranch managers, ditch company personnel, etc. regarding status of water rights and wells, historic use, and use on land.

E. Do research at other agencies and offices (such as the Bureau of Land Management, state archives, historical societies, public libraries).

F. Prepare historic use affidavits.

G. Prepare reports regarding investigation and analysis of the status of water rights and wells, historic use, and use on land.

H. Prepare maps, charts, diagrams, etc. regarding status of water rights and wells, historic use, and use on land.

II. Real Estate Transactions

A. Draft documents for the purchase and sale, encumbrance, or lease of water rights and wells.

B. Perform standup title searches in county clerk and recorder's offices.

C. Perform due diligence investigations.

D. Prepare for and assist at closings.

III. Well Permit Applications

A. Prepare well permit documents for filing—applications, land ownership affidavits, statements of beneficial use, amendments to record, extensions of time.

B. Coordinate and monitor the well permitting and drilling process.

C. In writing and orally, communicate with Department of Water Resources personnel, well drillers, and client.

IV. Water Court Proceedings—

Certain district courts have special jurisdiction over water right proceedings. Proceedings are governed by the Rules of Civil Procedure for District Courts and by local water court and district court rules.

A. Prepare water court documents for filing—applications, statements of opposition, draft rulings and orders, stipulations, withdrawals of opposition and affidavits.

B. Maintain diligence filing tickler system. Work with client to record and maintain evidence of diligence.

C. Review, route, and maintain a file of water court resumes.

D. Review, route, and maintain file of term day notices and orders. Prepare attorneys for term day and/or attend term day.

V. Monitor Publications

Read *Reporter,* water court resumes, and register for new water law cases and Department of Water Resources regulations.

44. Welfare Law

(See also *administrative law, pro bono work, public benefits,* and *social security law.*)

I. Problem Identification

A. Perform preliminary interview:

1. Identify nonlegal problems for referral to other agencies.

2. Open a case file or update it.

3. Using a basic fact sheet (or form), record the information collected during the interview.

4. Determine next appointment.

5. Instruct client on what to do next, such as obtain medical and birth records, etc.

6. Arrange for client to see office attorney.

B. Categorize welfare problems:

1. Help client learn what benefits exist in programs such as:

   a. Welfare

   b. Social Security

   c. Medicare

2. Help client fill out application forms.

3. Deal with client who objects to home visits by caseworkers or attempts by welfare department to force him or her to take a job or enter a training program.

4. Help client when welfare department wants to reduce the amount of client's welfare check or terminate public assistance altogether.

II. Problem Resolution

A. Consult with attorney immediately:

1. Summarize facts for the attorney.

2. Submit the case record to the attorney.

3. Obtain further instructions from attorney.

B. Refer nonlegal problems to other agencies:

1. Search for an appropriate agency.

2. Contact agency for the client.

C. Investigate:

1. Verify information (call caseworker, visit welfare office, etc.).
2. Search for additional information.
3. Record relevant facts.
4. Consult with attorney on difficulties encountered.

D. Analyze laws:
1. Check office welfare law manual.
2. Consult with office attorneys.
3. Contact legal service attorneys outside office.
4. Do research in law library.

E. Be an informal advocate (to determine if the problem can be resolved without a hearing or court action).
1. Make sure everyone (welfare department, client, etc.) understands the issue.
2. Provide missing information.
3. Pressure the welfare department (with calls, letters, visits, etc.).
4. Maintain records such as current and closed files.

F. Be a formal advocate:
1. Prior hearing (administrative review)
   a. Determine if such hearing can be asked for and when request must be made.
   b. Draft letter requesting such hearing.
   c. Prepare for hearing (see "Fair Hearing" below).
   d. Conduct hearing (see "Fair Hearing" below).
   e. Follow-up (see "Fair Hearing" below).
2. Fair Hearing
   a. Determine if the hearing can be asked for and when request must be made.
   b. Draft letter requesting the hearing.
   c. Prepare for the hearing:
      i. In advance of hearing, request that the welfare department send you the documents it will rely on at the hearing.
      ii. In advance of hearing, make sure that everyone (department representatives, client, etc.) is going to the hearing on the same issues.
      iii. Organize other relevant documents such as canceled check stubs.
      iv. Find witnesses.
      v. Prepare all witnesses (for example, explain what hearing will be about; conduct a brief role-playing experience to acquaint them with the format and what you will be seeking from the witnesses).
      vi. Map out a preliminary strategy to use in conducting the hearing.
      vii. Make a final attempt to resolve the issues without a hearing.
      viii. Make sure client and other witnesses will appear (e.g., give address of the hearing, take

them to the hearing on the date of the hearing).
   d. Conduct the hearing:
      i. Make sure the name, address, and title of everyone present are identified for the record.
      ii. Make opening statement summarizing client's case.
      iii. Ask for a postponement if the client has not appeared or if an emergency has arisen requiring more time to prepare.
      iv. Clearly state what relief the client is seeking from the hearing.
      v. If confusion exists on the issues, fight for a statement of the issues most favorable to the client.
      vi. Take notes on the opening statement of the welfare department representative.
      vii. Complain if welfare department failed to provide sufficient information in advance of the hearing.
      viii. Present the client's case:
         a. Submit documents.
         b. Conduct direct examination of the client's witnesses, including the client.
         c. Conduct re-direct examination of witnesses (if allowed).
         d. Cite the law.
      ix. Rebut case of welfare department:
         a. Raise objections to their documents and their interpretation of the law.
         b. Cross-examine their witnesses.
         c. Re-cross-examine their witnesses (if allowed).
      x. Make closing statement summarizing the case of the client and repeating the result the client is seeking.
   e. Follow-up:
      i. Pressure the hearing officer to reach a result without undue delay.
      ii. Request a copy of the transcript of the hearing.
      iii. When a result is reached, pressure the welfare department to abide by it.
      iv. Consult with attorney to determine whether the hearing result should be appealed in court.
3. Court
   a. Assist the attorney in gathering the documents for appeal; interview the witnesses, etc.
   b. Prepare preliminary draft of the legal argument to be made to trial court handling the appeal.
   c. Be a general assistant for the attorney at court proceedings.

    d. File papers in court.
    e. Serve the papers on opponents.
G. Miscellaneous
  1. Train other paralegals.
  2. Write pamphlets on welfare law for distribution in the community.
  3. Organize the community around welfare issues.

45. Worker's Compensation Law

(See also *administrative law, labor and employment law,* and *litigation.*)

I. Interviewing
A. Collect and record details of the claim (date of injury, nature and dates of prior illness, etc.).
B. Collect or arrange for the collection of documents, such as medical records and employment contract.
C. Schedule physical examination.

II. Drafting
A. Draft claim for compensation.
B. Draft request for hearing.
C. Draft medical authorization.
D. Draft demand for medical information in the possession of respondent or insurance carrier.
E. Draft proposed summary of issues involved.

III. Advocacy
A. Informal: Contact (call, visit, write a letter to) the employer and/or the insurance carrier to determine whether the matter can be resolved without a formal hearing or court action.
B. Formal: Represent claimant at the administrative hearing.

IV. Follow-up
A. Determine whether the payment is in compliance with the award.

B. If not, draft and file statutory demand for proper payment.
C. If such a statutory demand is filed, prepare a tickler system to monitor the claim.

● *Comment on Paralegal Work in This Area:*

"I have been working as a paralegal in this area for more than seven years. This is one of the areas of the law [in this state] in which a paralegal can perform almost all of the functions to properly process a Workers' Compensation claim. A Workers' Compensation practice must be a very high volume in order to be [profitable]. Thus paralegal assistance in handling a large case load is an absolute necessity. An extensive volume of paperwork is processed on a daily basis. Client contact is a major portion of a paralegal's responsibilities. With a large case load, it is physically impossible for an attorney to communicate with each and every client on a regular basis. It is not unusual for a paralegal in this field to work on several hundred files each week." Lindberg, *Virtually Limitless Responsibilities of a Workers' Compensation Paralegal,* Update 6 (Cleveland Ass'n of Paralegals, July 1989).

"The Company's two worker's compensation paralegals are responsible for reviewing each claimant's file, preparing a summary of medical reports, outlining the issues, and reviewing with the adjusters any questions or circumstances of the case before the claimant's deposition. In addition, they draft any necessary subpoenas, witness lists and settlement stipulations for their respective attorneys, and collect information and draft letters to the Special Disability Trust Fund outlining the Company's theory of reimbursement for second injury cases." Miquel, *Walt Disney World Company's Legal Assistants: Their Role in the Show,* 16 Facts and Findings 29, 30 (NALA, January 1990).

A Paralegal in the White House

Meg Shields Duke
New Roles in the Law Conference Report, 93 (1982)

[After working as a paralegal on the Reagan-Bush Campaign Committee], I'm a paralegal in the White House Counsel's office. I believe I'm the first paralegal in this office, in the White House. They've had law clerks in the past, but never have they hired a paralegal. There's one paralegal to nine attorneys at the moment. I think that's ridiculous and I hope we'll change that in the next several months to a year. But my responsibilities here are varied. Everybody is still trying to determine what their turf is. But for the first couple of months I've worked on a lot of transition matters, which might be

A Paralegal in the White House—continued

expected. I was the coordinator for our transition audit, congressional transition audit, from the Hill, which just ended a few weeks ago. I have engaged in drafting correspondence concerning the use of the president's name; the use of his image; our policy on gifts acceptance by public employees; drafting standards of conduct for public employees in the White House; job freeze litigation; those few controversial things. The last few weeks of my time have been devoted to the Lefever nomination. It's all been fascinating. Anyway, there are a number of areas that we also get involved in, the ethics of government act, for example. It's the first time it has been applied across the board to a new administration. It has been very, very time consuming for all our staff. I've been assisting in that, reviewing each individual file for high level government employees. As I said, I'm in the counsel's office now and intend to stay for a couple of years. But I would like to start my own paralegal firm. I have a close friend who started her own paralegal firm in Florida and we've talked often in the past of expanding it to Washington and a few other cities West where we'd like to spend some time. We're investigating the possibilities of reopening another firm here in Washington at some point, maybe in the next year and a half. But I think there is a place for more paralegals in the public sector, at least in the White House area, and I understand the Department of Justice of course has many, but I'd like to see it expanded and I'd also like to see more people branching out and trying this independent approach because I think it's fun. It's risky, but it's worth it.

Section D
FINDING A JOB: EMPLOYMENT STRATEGIES

There are many different strategies for finding employment. Exhibit 2.4 lists those most commonly used for every category of job, including those in the law. The strategies discussed in this section are primarily for individuals who have had very little or no employ-

"In my experience, most entry-level candidates are unprepared to effectively market themselves to law firms and corporations in this increasingly competitive marketplace. It is no longer enough simply to have a paralegal certificate. An individual must be able to sell him or herself effectively through the use of a well-written résumé and cover letter, and be prepared to develop strong interviewing skills."

—Tami M. Coyne, May 1990.

Exhibit 2.4   Most Commonly Used Job-Search Methods

PERCENTAGE OF TOTAL JOB-SEEKERS USING THE METHOD	METHOD	EFFECTIVENESS RATE*
66.0%	Applied directly to employer	47.7%
50.8	Asked friends about jobs where they work	22.1
41.8	Asked friends about jobs elsewhere	11.9
28.4	Asked relatives about jobs where they work	19.3
27.3	Asked relatives about jobs elsewhere	7.4
45.9	Answered local newspaper ads	23.9
21.0	Private employment agency	24.2
12.5	School placement office	21.4
15.3	Civil Service test	12.5
10.4	Asked teacher or professor	12.1

*A percentage obtained by dividing the number of job-seekers who actually found work using the method, by the total number of job-seekers who tried to use that method, whether successfully or not.

Source: U.S. Department of Labor, *Tips for Finding the Right Job,* 8 (1991).

ment experience with attorneys. Many of the strategies, however, are also relevant to peo-ple who have worked in law offices as secretaries or who are paralegals and wish to find other employment opportunities in the field.

GENERAL STRATEGIES FOR FINDING EMPLOYMENT

1. Begin now.
2. Start compiling a Job Hunting Notebook.
3. Organize an employment workshop.
4. Locate working paralegals.
5. Go on informational interviews.
6. Locate potential employers.
7. Surf the Internet.
8. Prepare a résumé, cover letter, and writing sample.
9. Prepare for the job interview.

Strategy 1: Begin Now

You should begin preparing for the job hunt on the first day of your first paralegal class. Do *not* wait until the program is almost over. Whether or not your school has place-ment assistance, you should assume that obtaining a job will be your responsibility. For most students, the job you get will be the job *you* find.

While in school, your primary focus should be on compiling an excellent academic record. *In addition,* you must start the job search now. It is not too early, for example, to begin compiling the lists called for in the Job Hunting Notebook that we will examine later. When school is over, be prepared to spend a substantial amount of additional time looking for employment. Since most students in the country will not have employment lined up before they graduate, time must be set aside for the search. How much time? There is, of course, no absolute answer to this question. It is clear, however, that a half-hearted, part-time effort will probably not be successful. Simply sitting back and sending out a stack of résumés is rarely effective! Since this is a "buyer's market" where there are many more applicants than available jobs, a conscientious search could involve four-to-six hours a day for several months. This may surprise—and disappoint—many graduates of paralegal programs. Yet this time frame is a reality throughout the legal profession. It applies to the majority of attorneys and legal administrators looking for work as well as to paralegals.

Being a paralegal requires determination, assertiveness, initiative, and creativity. *Find-ing* paralegal work will require these same skills. This is not a field for the faint of heart who are easily discouraged.

It may be that you are still very uncertain about the kinds of employment options that exist. How can you begin looking for a job if you don't yet know what kind of job you would like to have? First of all, many of the suggested steps in this chapter will be help-ful regardless of the kind of job you are pursuing. More important, however, the very process of going through these steps will help you clarify your employment objectives. As you begin seeking information and leads, the insights will come to you. At this point, keep an open mind, be conscientious, and begin now.

Strategy 2: Begin Compiling a Job Hunting Notebook

Later in this chapter, you will find an outline for a Job Hunting Notebook that you should start preparing now. (See Exhibit 2.16.) Following the outline, there are sample pages for the various sections in the Notebook.

> "Getting the job you want requires planning, determination, hard work, and follow-through. Don't give up!"
>
> —Lindi Massey, January 1991.

Strategy 3: Organize an Employment Workshop

Exhibit 2.1 at the beginning of this chapter gave you a list of the major categories (and subcategories) of paralegal employment. As a group project, your class should begin organizing an employment conference or workshop consisting of a panel of paralegals from as many of the categories and subcategories of paralegals as you can locate in your area. Try to find at least one paralegal to represent each category and subcategory. The guest paralegals could be asked to come to an evening or Saturday session to discuss the following topics:

- What I do (what a typical day consists of)
- How I obtained my job
- My recommendations for finding work
- Dos and don'ts in the employment interview
- What were the most valuable parts of my legal education, etc.

While you might want to ask a teacher or the director of the program at your school to help you organize the workshop, it is recommended that you make it a student-run workshop. It will be good practice for you in taking the kind of initiative that is essential in finding employment. You might want to consider asking the nearest paralegal association to co-sponsor the workshop with your class. (See question 5 in the letter found at the end of the index of this book.)

Have a meeting of your class and select a chairperson to help coordinate the event. Then divide up the tasks of contacting participants, arranging for a room, preparing an agenda for the workshop, etc. You may want to invite former graduates of your school to attend as panel speakers or as members of the audience. The ideal time for such a workshop is a month or two after you begin your coursework. This means that you need to begin organizing immediately.

Strategy 4: Locate Working Paralegals

Perhaps the most significant step in finding employment is to begin talking with paralegals who are already employed. They are the obvious experts on how to find a job! They are probably also very knowledgeable about employment opportunities in their office and in similar offices in the area. (See Job Hunting Notebook, p. 117.)

Attend paralegal association meetings. See Appendix B for a list of paralegal associations. Contact the one nearest you and ask about joining. There may be special dues for students.

Ask if the association has a **job bank** service. Here is what a paralegal who used this service had to say:

> I gained access to an opening to a wonderful job at a law firm exclusively listed in the Minnesota Association of Legal Assistants (MALA) Job Bank. . . . I would never have heard about the position if I hadn't been a member of MALA. *Merrill Advantage* (Spring 1990).

Not all associations have job bank services, however, and those that do have them may not make them available to students. (See question 4 in the letter found at the end of the index of this book.)

Try to obtain copies of current and past issues of the monthly or bimonthly newsletters of all the local paralegal associations in your area. Some of these newsletters give listings of job openings that mention specific employers. If so, try to contact the employers to determine if the position is still open. If it is no longer open, ask if you could send your résumé to be kept on file in the event a position becomes available in the future. Also, try to speak to the paralegal who filled the position in order to ask for leads to openings elsewhere. When you are told that the position is filled, simply ask, "Is there a chance that I could speak for a moment on the phone to the person who was hired? I'd like to get a general idea about working in this area of the law." If the person is hesitant to grant this request, say, "Would you be kind enough to give this paralegal my name and number and ask him (or her) to give me a call so that I could ask a few brief questions? I would really appreciate it."

Ask the local paralegal association if it has a *job-finding manual* for paralegals in your area. Find out about attending various association meetings. Try to participate in committees. The more active you are as a student member, the more contacts you will make. If there is no paralegal association near you, organize one—beginning with your own student body and past graduates of your school.

Paralegal newsletters often announce continuing education conferences and seminars for paralegals. Similar announcements are found in the newsletters of the two major national paralegal associations: the National Federation of Paralegal Associations *(National Paralegal Reporter),* and the National Association of Legal Assistants *(Facts and Findings).* Employed paralegals attend these events in large numbers. Hence they are excellent places to meet experienced paralegals.

Paralegals sometimes attend continuing education conferences conducted by the local bar association, particularly those bar associations where paralegals are allowed to become associate members. You should also find out if there is an association of legal secretaries and of legal administrators in your area. If so, they might conduct workshops or meetings that you can attend. At such meetings and elsewhere, try to talk with individual legal secretaries and legal administrators about employment opportunities for paralegals where they work.

Strategy 5: Go on Informational Interviews

An **informational interview** is an opportunity for you to sit down with someone, preferably where he or she works, to learn about a particular kind of employment. Unlike a job interview, where you are the one interviewed, *you* do the interviewing in an informational interview. You ask questions that will help you learn what working at that kind of office is like.

> If, for example, you are a real "people" person who finds antitrust theory fascinating, you should listen to antitrust paralegals discussing their day-to-day work. You may hear that most of them spend years in document warehouses with one lawyer, two other paralegals and a pizza delivery man as their most significant personal contacts. That information may influence your decision about antitrust as a career path.[16]

Informational interviews are time-consuming, though, so many employers do not allow their employees to give them during office hours.

Do *not* try to turn an informational interview into a job interview. While on an informational interview, it is inappropriate to ask a person for a job. Toward the end of the interview, you can delicately ask for leads to employment and you can ask how the person obtained his or her job, but these inquiries should be secondary to your primary purpose of obtaining information about the realities of work at that kind of office. Do not use an informational interview as a subterfuge for a job interview that you are having difficulty obtaining.

---

[16]Gainen, *Information Interviews: A Strategy,* Paradigm (Baltimore Ass'n of Legal Assistants, November/December 1989).

The best people to interview are employed paralegals whom you have met through the steps outlined in Strategy 4. While some attorneys and legal administrators may also be willing to grant you informational interviews, the best people to talk to are those who were once in your shoes. Simply say to a paralegal you have met, "Would it be possible for me to come down to the office where you work for a brief informational interview?" If he or she is not familiar with this kind of interview, explain its limited objective. Many will be too busy to grant you an interview, but you have nothing to lose by asking, even if you are turned down. As an added inducement, consider offering to take the paralegal to lunch. In addition to meeting this paralegal, you also want to try to have at least a brief tour of the office where he or she works. Observing how different kinds of employees interact with each other and with available technology in the office will be invaluable.

Here are some of the questions you should ask on an informational interview.

- What is a typical day for you in this office?
- What kinds of assignments do you receive?
- How much overtime is usually expected? Do you take work home with you?
- How do the attorneys interact with paralegals in this kind of practice? Who does what? How many different attorneys does a paralegal work with? How are assignment priorities set?
- How do the paralegals interact with secretaries and other support staff in the office?
- What is the hierarchy of the office?
- What kind of education best prepares a paralegal to work in this kind of office? What courses are most effective?
- What is the most challenging aspect of the job? The most frustrating?
- How are paralegals perceived in this office?
- Are you glad you became this kind of paralegal in this kind of office? Would you do it over again?
- What advice would you give to someone who wants to become a paralegal like yourself?

Several of these questions are also appropriate in a job interview, as we will see later.

One final word of caution. Any information you learn at the office about clients or legal matters must be kept confidential, even if the person you are interviewing is casual about revealing such information to you. This person may not be aware that he or she is acting unethically by disclosing confidential information. Carelessness in this regard is not uncommon.

Strategy 6: Locate Potential Employers

There are a number of ways to locate attorneys:

a. Placement office
b. Personal contacts
c. Ads
d. Through other paralegals
e. Employment agencies
f. Directories and other lists of attorneys
g. Courts and bar association meetings

(See Job Hunting Notebook, p. 117).

For every attorney that you contact, you want to know the following:

- Has the attorney hired paralegals in the past?
- If so, is the attorney interested in hiring more paralegals?

- If the attorney has never hired paralegals before, might he or she consider hiring one?
- Does the attorney know of other attorneys who might be interested in hiring paralegals?

The last point is particularly important. Attorneys from different firms often talk with each other about their practice, including their experiences with paralegals or their plans for hiring paralegals. Hence always ask about other firms. If you obtain a lead, begin your contact with the other firm by mentioning the name of the attorney who gave you the lead. You might say, "Mary Smith told me that you have hired paralegals in the past and might be interested in hiring another paralegal," or "John Rodriguez suggested that I contact you concerning possible employment at your firm as a paralegal."

a. Placement Office   Start with the placement office of your paralegal school. Talk with staff members and check the bulletin board regularly, e.g., daily. If your school is part of a university that has a law school, you might want to check the placement office of the law school as well. While paralegal jobs are usually not listed there, you may find descriptions of law firms with the number of attorneys and paralegals employed. (See also Appendix 2.A at the end of this chapter.) It might be useful for you to identify the major resources for obtaining *attorney* jobs, such as special directories, lists or ads in bar publications, legal newspapers, etc. In particular, try to find the following resource used by unemployed attorneys and law students: *National Directory of Legal Employers,* which is published by the National Association of Law Placement. (The Directory can also be used on WESTLAW, page 624, if you have access to this computer legal research system.) Such resources might provide leads on contacting offices about paralegal employment.

b. Personal Contacts   Make a list of attorneys who fall into the following categories:

- Personal friends
- Friends of friends
- Attorneys you have hired
- Attorneys your relatives have hired
- Attorneys your former employers have hired
- Attorneys your friends have hired
- Attorneys your church has hired
- Teachers
- Politicians
- Neighbors
- Etc.

You should consider contacting these attorneys about their own paralegal hiring plans as well as for references to other attorneys. Don't be reluctant to take advantage of any direct or indirect association that you might have with an attorney. Such contacts are the essence of **networking,** which simply means establishing contacts with people who may be helpful to you now or in the future. (See Job Hunting Notebook, page 118.)

c. Ads   You should regularly check the classified pages of your daily and Sunday newspaper as well as the legal newspaper for your area. (See Exhibit 2.5 for some of the common abbreviations used in ads.) If you are seeking employment in another city, the main branch of your public library and the main library of large universities in your area may have out-of-town newspapers. If you have friends in these other cities, they might be willing to send you clippings from the classified ads of their newspapers. There are several *national* legal newspapers that sometimes have paralegal employment ads. These include the *National Law Journal* and the *American Lawyer.* Law libraries often subscribe to such newspapers.

Exhibit 2.5 Classified Ad Abbreviations

ABBREVIATION	TRANSLATION	ABBREVIATION	TRANSLATION
2+	plus means "or more" (years of experience)	gd	good
		immed	immediate
acctg	accounting	inq	inquire
advc	advancement	k	thousands (usually annual salary in dollars)
agcy	agency		
appt	appointment		
asst	assistant	LLC	Limited Liability Company
atty	attorney		
begnr	beginner	loc	location or located
bkpg	bookkeeping	mfg	manufacturing
bnfts	benefits	mgmt	management
clk	clerk	ofc	office
co	company (mjr co means major company)	opty	opportunity
		ovtm	overtime
		pd vac	paid vacation
col grad	college graduate	p/t	part-time
col	college	pub	public
dept	department	refs	references
dict	dictation	secty	secretary
EOE	Equal Opportunity Employer	sr	senior (usually means experienced)
eves	evenings	w/	with (w/wo means with or without)
exp nec	experience necessary		
exp pfd	experience preferred	wkend	weekend
f/pd	fee paid	wpm	words per minute
f/t	full-time	yr	year

Source: *Finding a Job in the Want Ads* (New Mexico SOICC).

Look for ads under the headings "Paralegal" or "Legal Assistant." For example:

PARALEGAL
TRUST ACCOUNTANTS
For details see our ad in this section headed
ACCOUNTANT

PARALEGALS Fee Pd. Salary Open. Corporate & Real Estate positions. Superior writing ability is a necessity. Must be able to work under pressure. Superior opportunities. Contact . . .

PARALEGAL
(CORPORATE)
Large downtown Boston law firm seeks expd Corporate Paralegal. Opportunity for responsibility and growth. Must have strong academic background. Computer literacy a plus. Salary commensurate with exp. Send résumé in confidence to: X2935 TIMES

LEGAL ASSISTANT
Large West Palm Beach, Florida firm wishes to employ legal assistant with immigration/naturalization experience, in addition to civil litigation, research & pleading abilities. Knowledge of Germanic languages helpful. Full fringe benefits/profit sharing. Salary negotiable. Contact . . .

For detailed quotes from want ads for a variety of different kinds of paralegal jobs, see pages 54–72.

The ad may not give the name and address of the employer seeking the paralegal. Instead, it will direct interested parties to an intermediary, such as a newspaper, which forwards all responses to the employer. Such ads are called **blind ads.** Some ads are placed by private employment agencies that specialize in legal placements.

You will find that most want ads seek paralegals with experience in a particular area of practice. Hence, if you are a recent graduate of a paralegal school who is looking for a beginning or entry-level position, you may not meet the qualifications sought in the ads.[17] Should you apply for such positions nevertheless? Suppose, for example, that an ad seeks "a corporate paralegal with two years of experience." You might consider answering such an ad as follows:

> I am responding to your ad for a corporate paralegal. I do not have the experience indicated in the ad, but I did take an intensive course on corporate law at my paralegal school, and I'm wondering whether I could send you my résumé so that you can consider what I have to offer.

Or, phrased more positively:

> I am responding to your ad for a corporate paralegal. I feel that I qualify for the position even though I don't have the experience indicated in the ad. I took an intensive course in corporate law in my paralegal school. Could I send you my résumé so that you can consider what I have to offer?

If the answer is no, you can certainly ask for leads to anyone else who might be hiring individuals like yourself.

When reading want ads, do not limit yourself to the entries for "Paralegal" and "Legal Assistant." Also look for headings for positions that may be law related, such as "Research Assistant," "Legislative Aide," "Law Library Assistant." For example:

RESEARCH ASSISTANT

IMMEDIATE POSITION
Social Science Research Institute in downtown looking for coder/editor of survey instruments. Post Box L3040.

PROOFREADER
Leading newspaper for lawyers has an immediate opening for a proofreader of manuscripts and galleys. Attention to detail, some night work. Past exp pfd. Call Nance, 964-9700, Ext. 603.

LEGISLATIVE ASSISTANT/ SECRETARY—Good skills essential, dwntwn location, send résumé/sal. requirements to Post Box M 8341.

---

[17]At the end of this chapter, we will examine the Catch-22 problem of "no job/no experience" and "no experience/no job" when we discuss "your second job." (See page 119.)

> RECRUITMENT
> COORDINATOR
> Local office of national law firm seeks individual to coordinate the attorney recruiting and the paralegal program. B.A. required and 1–3 years' personnel, recruitment, or paralegal experience preferred. Salary commensurate with experience. E.O.E. Please send résumé and salary requirements to LT Box 9-24-2101.

> LEGISLATIVE ASSISTANT/ ADMINISTRATOR—If you are looking for that foot in the door, apply on CAPITOL HILL, here's the job for you. Newsmaking Congressman seeks dedicated indiv to handle challenging & rewarding duties. Track legislation, handle corresp & mailing. Get involved in the world of Capitol Hill. Good typg. Call Tues–Fri 8:30–4.

> LIBRARY/CLERICAL— permanent, full-time pos. at lge law firm library. Duties include looseleaf filing, processing new books & current periodicals, shelving books, and some typing. Exper. w/looseleaf filing pref. Good benefits and excel. leave policy. Respond to Post Box No. M8272.

> ADMINISTRATOR—LAW
> Medium-size established law firm seeks manager with administrative, financial & personnel experience and EDP familiarity to supervise all non-legal office activities. Salary will be commensurate with experience. Equal opportunity employer. Applicants should send résumés with salary requirements to LT Box 9-17-2085.

> When asked how fast you can type, the answer depends on how badly you need a job. If desperate, the answer is,
> "About 50 with some mistakes."
> Otherwise, the answer is,
> "Oh, I'm sorry. I thought you were looking for a paralegal, not a secretary."
> —Deborah Orlik, 1993

Of course, some of the above jobs may not be what you are looking for. They may not be directly related to your legal training and experience. Nevertheless, you should read such ads carefully. Some might be worth pursuing.

On most classified pages, you will find many ads for legal secretaries, docket clerks, and word processors. You might want to respond to such ads as follows:

> I saw your ad for a legal secretary. I am a trained paralegal and am wondering whether you have any openings for paralegals. If not, I would greatly appreciate your referring me to any attorneys you know who may be looking for competent paralegals.

What about *applying* for a clerical position in a law office? Many paralegals take the view that this would be a mistake. In a tight employment market, however, some paralegals believe that a secretarial or typing job would be a way to "get a foot in the door," and hope that they will eventually be able to graduate into a position in the office that is commensurate with their paralegal training. Such a course of action is obviously a very personal decision that you must make on your own. Clerical staff *do* commonly get promoted to paralegal positions in a firm, but people also can get stuck in clerical positions.

Should you ever respond to want ads *for attorneys*? Such ads regularly appear in legal newspapers and magazines. Of course, a paralegal cannot claim to be an attorney. But any office that is looking for attorneys obviously has a need for legal help. Hence, consider these possible reasons for responding to such ads, particularly when they give the name and address of the office seeking the attorney:

- Perhaps the office is *also* looking for paralegal help but is simply not advertising for it (or you have not seen the want ad for paralegals).

- Perhaps the office is having difficulty finding the attorney it is seeking and would consider hiring a paralegal for a temporary period of time to perform paralegal tasks *while* continuing the search for the attorney.
- Perhaps the office has never considered hiring a paralegal *instead of* an attorney, but would be interested in exploring the idea.

Many of these employers may be totally uninterested in a response by a paralegal to an ad for an attorney. Yet none of the possibilities just described is irrational. The effort might be productive. Even if you receive a flat rejection, you can always use the opportunity to ask the person you contact if he or she knows of any other offices that are hiring paralegals.

Finally, a word about want ads placed *by a paralegal* seeking employment. Should you ever place an ad in a publication read by attorneys, such as the journal of the bar association or the legal newspaper for your area? Such ads can be expensive and are seldom productive. Nevertheless, if you have a particular skill—for example, if you are a nurse trained as a paralegal and are seeking a position in a medical malpractice firm, an ad might strike a responsive chord.

d. Through Other Paralegals   In Strategy 4 above, we discussed methods to contact working paralegals. Once you talk with a paralegal, you can, of course, obtain information about contacting the employing attorney of that paralegal.

e. Employment Agencies   There have always been employment agencies for the placement of attorneys. Many of these agencies also handle placements for full-time and temporary paralegal positions. Recently, a number of agencies have been opened to deal primarily with paralegal placement. Here is an example of an ad from such an agency:

Help Wanted
Paralegal Agency   **Fee Paid** **Paralegal Placement Experts Recognized by** **Over 200 Law Firms and Corporations** **PENSIONS** Outstanding law firm seeks 1+ yrs pension paralegal exper. Major responsibilities, quality clients & liberal benefits. Salary commensurate w/exper. **LITIGATION** SEVERAL positions open at LAW FIRMS for litigation paralegals. Major benefits incl bonus. **MANAGING CLERK** Midtown law firm seeks 1+ yrs exper as a managing clerk. Work directly w/top management. Liberal benefits.
These are just a few of the many paralegal positions we have available. Call us for professional career guidance.

Look for such ads in the classified pages of general circulation and legal newspapers. Paralegal association newsletters and special paralegal magazines such as *Legal Assistant Today* may also have this kind of ad. Check your yellow pages under "Employment Agencies." If you are not sure which of the listed agencies cover legal placements, call several at random and ask which agencies in the city handle paralegal placement or legal placement in general. Caution is needed in using such agencies, however. Some of them know very little about paralegals, in spite of their ads claiming to place paralegals. You may find that the agency views a paralegal as a secretary with a little extra training.

All employment agencies charge a placement fee. You must check whether the fee is paid by the employer or by the employee hired through the agency. Read the agency's service contract carefully before signing. Question the agency about the jobs they have available—for instance, whether evening work is expected or what typing requirements there are, if any.

Finally, you should find out if there is a paralegal **staffing agency** in your area. This is a temporary employment agency that provides short-term employment at law offices. Most of the people placed are paralegals with experience in a particular area of practice. The paralegals are often paid by the agency, which in turn is paid by the offices. Law firms and corporate law departments may prefer temporary paralegals because of the low overhead costs involved, the availability of experienced people on short notice for indefinite periods, and the ability to end the relationship without having to go through the sometimes wrenching experience of terminating permanent employees.

f. Directories and Other Lists of Attorneys   Find out whether there is a directory or list of attorneys in your area. Ask a librarian at any law library in your area. Your yellow pages will also list attorneys generally or by specialty.

Also check with a librarian about national directories of attorneys. One of the major directories is the **Martindale-Hubbell Law Directory,** which gives descriptions of law firms by state and city or county (see Exhibit 2.6). For each firm, you are given brief biographies of the attorneys (listing bar memberships, colleges attended, etc.) as well as the firm's areas of practice. (In 1992, Martindale-Hubbell started to include information on paralegals and other legal support personnel in law firms. See the bottom of Exhibit 2.6. Paralegals are listed as part of a firm; they cannot be listed individually.) Also inquire about the availability of specialty lists of attorneys. Examples include criminal law attorneys, corporate counsel, bankruptcy attorneys, black attorneys, women attorneys, etc. Read whatever biographical data is provided on the attorneys. If you have something in common with a particular attorney (for example, you were both born in the same small town or you both went to the same school), you might want to mention this fact in a cover letter or phone conversation.

If you have access to either of the two major computer research systems—WESTLAW and LEXIS—you can locate attorneys on-line. LEXIS gives you the entire *Martindale-Hubbell Law Directory.* WESTLAW has created its own directory: *West's Legal Directory.* See Exhibit 2.7.

Finally, you may want to examine the *Directory of Legal Employers,* published by the National Association of Law Placement. As mentioned earlier, it lists the names and addresses of law firms and corporations that hire attorneys. But it will also indicate the number of paralegals employed by the offices listed in the directory. You can find this directory in two places: in the placement offices of most law schools and on WESTLAW.

In a moment we will discuss the role of the Internet in a job search. For now it is important to note that two of the major attorney directories discussed in this section (*West's Legal Directory* and *Martindale-Hubbell Law Directory*) are available on the Internet at the following sites:

```
http://www.wld.com

http://www.martindale.com
```

Exhibit 2.6   Excerpt from a Page in *Martindale-Hubbell Law Directory*

POYATT, ROYCROFT & MACDONALD
Established In 1968

731 SHADY LANE
DALLAS, TEXAS 75202
Telephone: 214-555-6720
Fax: 214-555-6730
Fort Worth, Texas Office: 34 Main Street, Suite 10, 77001
Telephone: 817-555-9224.   Fax: 817-555-9220

Poyatt, Roycroft & MacDonald was founded in 1968 by Kathleen Poyatt, Greg Roycroft and Julie MacDonald, former class-mates and graduates of the University of Texas Law School. Starting with a local general practice, the firm now serves the entire state and maintains two fully-staffed offices offering a wide range of legal services. The firm encourages continuing professional development, and all partners and associates participate in continuing legal education seminars, professional association activities and civic affairs.

MEMBERS OF FIRM

KATHLEEN POYATT, born Plano, Texas, May 13, 1940; admitted to bar, 1967, Texas and U.S. Court of Appeals, Fifth Circuit. *Education:* Tulane University (B.A., with honors, 1962); University of Texas (J.D., cum laude, 1967). Phi Beta Kappa; Phi Delta Phi; Order of the Coif. Associate Editor, Texas Law Review, 1966–1967. Certified Public Accountant, Texas, 1971. Member, Advisory Board, Dallas Family Planning Council, 1982–1984. Legal Counsel, Dallas Board of Realtors, 1986–1987. *Member:* Dallas and American Bar Associations; State Bar of Texas (Chair, Committee on Trust Administration, Estate Planning and Probate Section, 1989–); American Judicature Society. (Board Certified, Estate Planning and Probate Law, Texas Board of Legal Specialization). LANGUAGES: Spanish and French. SPECIAL AGENCIES: Texas Council on Charitable Trusts. REPORTED CASES: Mastalia v. Fairty, 145 S.E.2d 1405. TRANSACTIONS: Bankruptcy of Braniff Airlines, 1982; The Keepwell Foundation, 1990. AREAS OF CONCENTRATION: Trust Administration, Banking and Creditors' Rights, Trial, Litigation and Real Estate.

JULIE MACDONALD, born Nashville, Tennessee, August 29, 1940; admitted to bar, 1967, Texas and U.S. District Court, Northern District of Texas. *Education:* University of Tennessee at Memphis (B.A., with honors, 1962); University of Texas (J.D., with honors, 1967). Alpha Lambda Delta; Phi Kappa Phi; Phi Beta Kappa. Member, Tennessee State Board of Professional Responsibility, 1983–1984; Dallas Association of Young Lawyers; The Association of Trial Lawyers of America. *Member:* Dallas (*Member:* Real Estate and Commercial Real Estate Morning Section; Continuing Education Committee) and American (*Member:* Real Property Section; Continuing Education Committee). Bar Associations; State Bar of Texas; Dallas Association of Young Lawyers; The Association of Trial Lawyers of America, LANGUAGES: Spanish and Italian. SPECIAL AGENCIES: Texas Council on Taxation Trusts. REPORTED CASES: Cuneo v. Banks, 466 S.E.2d 6609; Kyle v. Smily, 432 S.E.2d 4599. TRANSACTIONS: The Hines foundation, 1989. AREAS OF CONCENTRATION: Trials and Appeals, Estate Planning, Real Estates, Banking and Taxation.

LEGAL SUPPORT PERSONNEL
PARALEGAL

LINDA DAVIS, born Maurice, Louisiana, August 16, 1962. *Education:* Interstate Paralegal Institute. Certified Legal Assistant, Texas, 1985. President, Dallas Paralegal Association, 1987. Secretary, Legal Assisstant Division Texas Bar Association, 1996. *Member:* National, State and Local Paralegal Association. Legal Research, Drafting Legal Pleadings, Client Correspondence, Deposition Summaries and File Investigations.

g. Courts and Bar Association Meetings   You can also meet attorneys at the courts of your area—for example, during a recess or at the end of the day. Bar association committee meetings are sometimes open to nonattorneys. The same may be true of **CLE** (Continuing Legal Education) seminars conducted for attorneys. When the other strategies for contacting attorneys do not seem productive, consider going to places where attorneys

Exhibit 2.7 **Sample Screen from *West's Legal Directory***

Name:	Jones, James E
City:	Boston
State:	Massachusetts
Position:	Partner
Firm:	Smith, Jones & White
Address:	1000 State Street, Exchange Plaza, Boston, MA 90001
Phone:	(617)722-7777
Electronic Mail:	Fax Area Code (617) Phone 722-7776
Born:	May 20, 1947, Dallas, TX. U.S.A.
Education:	Baylor University, Waco, Texas (J.D., 1973), Cum Laude
	University of Texas, Austin, Texas (B.A., 1969)
Admitted:	Massachusetts 1975
	Texas 1973
	Federal Court 1979
Fraternities:	Phi Alpha Delta
Directorships:	Massachusetts Commerce Association, 1980–Present
Affiliations:	American Bar Association
	State Bar of Massachusetts
Representative Clients:	Semi-Conductor, Inc.
	BCA National Bank
Representative Cases:	Thayer v. Smith, 560 S.W.2d 137 (1989)
Practice:	50% Patent, Trademark, Copyright
	25% Corporations Law
	25% Litigation
Foreign Languages:	Russian
Certified Specialty:	Patent, Trademark, Copyright--U.S. Patent & Trademark Office
Published Works:	*Corporations and Business Law,* 1981, CAB Publishing Company

congregate. Simply introduce yourself and ask if they know of paralegal employment opportunities at their firms or at other firms. If you meet an attorney who practices in a particular specialty, it would be helpful if you could describe your course work or general interest in that kind of law. If you are doing some research in that area of the law, you might begin by asking for some research leads before you ask about employment.

h. Miscellaneous   Look for ads in legal newspapers in which an attorney is seeking information about a particular product involved in a suit that is contemplated or underway. Or read feature stories in a legal newspaper on major litigation that is about to begin. If the area of the law interests you, contact the law firms involved (using the directories just described) to ask about employment opportunities for paralegals. Many firms hire additional paralegals, particularly for large cases.

Find the bar journal of your local or state bar associations in the law library. The articles in the journal are often written by attorneys from the state. If the subject of an article interests you, read it and call or write the author. Ask a question or two about the topic of the article and the area of the law involved. Then ask about employment opportunities for paralegals in that area.

Strategy 7: Surf the Internet

The **Internet** (which we will examine in greater detail later in chapters 11 and 13) is opening up a whole new universe of information, including mostly free information relevant to a job search. Although not many people now can tell you that they found their job on the Internet, this situation may change soon as the Internet's information and technology constantly expand. If you have access to the Internet, here are some of the things you can do, particularly by searching (sometimes called "surfing") the **World Wide Web** on the Internet:

- Locate want ads from newspapers all over the country.
- Obtain information about a law firm or corporation to which you are thinking about applying.
- Post your own résumé announcing your availability for work; others can locate it through standard search indexes on the web.

A number of general on-line job-search services are available where you can search for nonlegal as well as legal jobs. For example:

```
http://www.careerpath.com
```

```
http://www.careermosaic.com
```

```
http://www.jobcenter.com
```

```
http://www.jobweb.org
```

```
http://www.joblocator.com/jobs/
```

```
http://www.nationjob.com
```

```
http://www.employmentedge.com/employment.edge/
```

```
http://www.ajb.dni.us
```

```
http://www.espan.com
```

```
http://www.fedworld.gov
```

The last site mentioned covers jobs in the federal government. At any of these sites, type in **paralegal** or **"legal assistant"** to see what's available. Some of these sites require you to register before you can conduct a job search.

There are services directed specifically at attorneys. For example:

```
http://www.lawjobs.com
```

Try the same search terms (**paralegal** or **"legal assistant"**) to find out if any of the employers are looking for paralegals as well as attorneys.

Soon we will see on-line services specifically for paralegals. One of the first is the World Wide Paralegal Résumé Service of the National Federation of Paralegal Associations. On the World Wide Web, go to:

```
http://www.paralegals.org
```

Then press ⌐Career Center¬ to get access to job listings throughout the country as well as a list of recruiters. (See Exhibit 2.8.) Here is an example of a job listing from this service:

```
Probate Legal Assistants—Bay Area

Two positions available in San Francisco and East Bay. Firm offers
excellent compensation and work environment. Call . . . .
```

Exhibit 2.8	**Finding Employment On-Line: The World Wide Paralegal Résumé Service of the National Federation of Paralegal Associations**

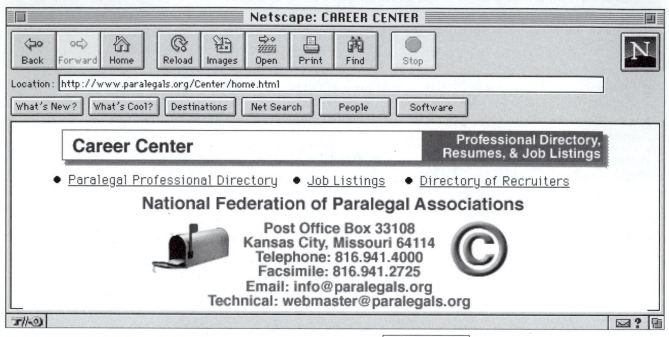

On the World Wide Web, go to **http://www.paralegals.org** and press **Career Center.**

Since the service is relatively new, there is not a great deal of information on it, but it is growing. Many of the job openings are for experienced paralegals. For a fee, you can place your résumé in the service's Program Directory.[18] If a prospective employer sees your résumé on the Web, he or she can contact you at an E-mail address that the National Federation provides.

Another way to use the Internet is to locate information about a particular law office or company where you are thinking of applying. For example:

```
http://www.wld.com
http://www.ljx.com
http://www.martindale.com
```

These resources can be an excellent way to do the kind of background research discussed later. (See page 95.) For examples of attorney profiles on the Internet, see Exhibit 14.22 at the end of Chapter 14.

🏛 *A s s i g n m e n t   2 . 2*

(a) Use some of the Internet sites mentioned above to find a job opening for a paralegal in a city where you hope to work. If you can't find an opening in that city, check openings for the entire state. Where did you find this information on the Internet?

---

[18]In 1997, the fee was $15 for six months and $24 for a year.

(b) Use some of the Internet sites mentioned above to locate a law firm in your state that employs more than ten attorneys. State the name, address, and phone number of this firm. How many attorneys does it have? What kind of law does it practice? Where did you find this information on the Internet?

Strategy 8: Prepare Your Résumé, Cover Letter, and Writing Sample

The cardinal principle of résumé writing is that the résumé must fit the job you are seeking. Hence you must have more than one résumé or you must rewrite your résumé for each kind of paralegal job you are seeking. A résumé is an *advocacy* document. You are trying to convince someone (a) to give you an interview and ultimately (b) to offer you a job. You are not simply communicating information about yourself. A résumé is *not* a summary of your life or a one-page autobiography. It is a very brief *commercial* in which you are trying to sell yourself as a person who can make a contribution to a particular prospective employer. Hence the résumé must stress what would appeal to this employer. You are advocating (or selling) yourself effectively when the form and content of the résumé have this appeal. Advocacy is required for several reasons. First, there are probably many more applicants than jobs available. Second, most prospective employers ignore résumés that are not geared to their particular needs.

Before examining sample résumés, we need to explore some general guidelines that apply to *any* résumé.

Guidelines on Drafting an Effective Résumé

1. Be concise and to the point. Generally, the résumé should fit on one page. A longer résumé is justified only if you have a unique education or experience that is directly related to law or to the particular law firm or company in which you are interested.

2. Be accurate. Studies show that about 30 percent of all résumés contain inaccuracies. Recently, a legal administrator felt the need to make the following comment (to other legal administrators) about job applicants: "I'm sure we have all had experiences where an applicant has lied on an application about experience, previous salary scales, length of time with previous employers, training, skills, and anything else they can think of that will make them appear more attractive."[19] While you want to present yourself in the best possible light, it is critical that you not jeopardize your integrity. All of the data in the résumé should be verifiable. Prospective employers who check the accuracy of résumés usually do so themselves, although some use outside organizations such as the National Credential Verification Service.

3. Include personal data—that is, name, address, zip code, and phone (with area code) where you can be reached. (If someone is not always available to take messages while you are away, invest in an answering machine.) Do not include a personal photograph or data on your health, height, religion, or political party. You do not have to include information that might give a prospective employer a basis to discriminate against you illegally, such as your marital status or the names and ages of your children. Later we will discuss how to handle such matters in a job interview.

4. Provide a concise statement of your career objective at the top of the résumé. (It should be pointed out, however, that some people recommend that this statement

---

[19]Jacobi, *Back to Basics in Hiring Techniques,* The Mandate, 1 (Ass'n of Legal Administrators, San Diego Chapter, October 1987).

be included in the cover letter rather than in the résumé.) The career objective should be a quick way for the reader to know whether your goal fits the needs of the prospective employer. Hence, *the career objective should be targeted to a particular employer* and therefore needs to be rewritten just about every time you send out a résumé to a different employer. An overly general career objective gives the unfortunate effect of a "mass-mailing résumé." Suppose, for example, you are applying for a position as a litigation paralegal at a forty-attorney law firm that is looking for someone to help with scheduling and document handling on several cases going on simultaneously.

Don't say: **Career Objective**—A position as a paralegal at an office where there is an opportunity for growth.

Do say: **Career Objective**—A position as a litigation paralegal at a medium-sized law firm where I will be able to use and build on the organizational skills I developed in my prior employment and the case management skills that I have learned to date.

The first statement is too flat and uninformative. Its generalities could fit just about *any* paralegal job. Even worse, its focus is on the needs of the applicant. The second statement is much more direct. While also referring to the needs of the applicant, the second statement goes to the heart of what the employer is looking for—someone to help create order out of the complexity of events and papers involved in litigation.

5. Next, state your prior education and training.[20] (See Job Hunting Notebook, pages 114 ff.) List each school or training institution and the dates attended. Use a reverse chronological order—that is, start the list with the most current and work backward. Do not include your high school unless you attended a prestigious high school, you have not attended college, or you are a very recent high school graduate. When you give your legal education:

a. List the major courses.
b. State specific skills and tasks covered in your courses that are relevant to the job you are applying for. Also state major topic areas covered in the courses that demonstrate a knowledge of (or at least exposure to) material that is relevant to the job. For example, if you are applying for a corporate paralegal job, relevant courses could be stated as follows:

Corporate Law: This course examined the formation of a corporation, director and shareholder meetings, corporate mergers, and the dissolution of corporations; we also studied sample shareholder minutes and prepared proxy statements. Grade received: B+.

Legal Bibliography: This course covered the basic law books relevant to researching corporate law, including the state code. We also covered the skills of using practice books, finding cases on corporate law through the digests, etc. Grade received: A−.

c. List any special programs in the school, such as unique class assignments, term papers, extensive research, moot court, internship, or semester projects. Give a

---

[20]If you already have experience as a paralegal and are seeking to change jobs, the next section of the résumé should be work experience, followed by education and training.

brief description if any of these programs are relevant to the job you are applying for.

    d. State any unusually high grades: give overall grade point average (GPA) only if it is distinctive.

List any degrees, certificates, or other recognition that you earned at each school or training institution. Include high aptitude or standard test scores. If the school or institution has any special distinction or recognition, mention this as well.

6. State your work experience. (See Job Hunting Notebook, pages 111 ff.) List the jobs you held, your job title, the dates of employment, and the major duties that you performed. (Do not state the reason you left each job, although you should be prepared to discuss this if you are granted an interview.) Again, work backward. Start with the most current (or your present) employment. The statement of duties is particularly important. If you have legal experience, emphasize specific duties and tasks that are directly relevant to the position you are seeking—for example, include that you drafted corporate minutes or prepared incorporation papers. Give prominence to such skills and tasks on the résumé. Nonlegal experience, however, can also be relevant. Every prior job says something about you as an individual. Phrase your duties in such jobs in a manner that will highlight important personality traits. (See p. 113.) In general, most employers are looking for people with the following characteristics:

- Emotional maturity
- Intelligence
- Willingness to learn
- Ability to get along with others
- Ability to work independently (someone with initiative and self-reliance who is not afraid of assuming responsibility)
- Problem-solving skills
- Ability to handle time pressures and frustration
- Ability to communicate—orally, on paper, on-line
- Loyalty
- Stability, reliability
- Energy

As you list duties in prior and current employment settings, do *not* use any of the language just listed. But try to state duties that tend to show that these characteristics apply to you. For example, if you had a job as a camp counselor, state that you supervised eighteen children, designed schedules according to predetermined objectives, prepared budgets, took over in the absence of the director of the camp, etc. A listing of such duties will say a lot about you as a person. You are someone who can be trusted, you know how to work with people, you are flexible, etc. These are the kind of conclusions that you want the reader of your résumé to reach. Finally, try to present the facts to show a growth in your accomplishments, development, and maturity.

7. Use *action verbs* throughout the résumé. Note that the examples just given used the verbs mentioned in the following lists:

Action Verbs to Use[21]

Creative skills	Financial skills	Management skills	Technical skills
conceptualized	administered	administered	assembled
created	analyzed	analyzed	built

---

[21]U.S. Department of Labor, *Tips for Finding the Right Job,* 17 (1991).

Creative skills	**Financial skills**	**Management skills**	**Technical skills**
(cont.)	(cont.)	(cont.)	(cont.)
designed	balanced	coordinated	calculated
established	budgeted	developed	designed
fashioned	forecast	directed	operated
illustrated	marketed	evaluated	overhauled
invented	planned	improved	remodeled
performed	projected	supervised	repaired

Helping skills	**Research skills**	**Clerical skills**	**Communication skills**
assessed	clarified	arranged	arranged
coached	evaluated	catalogued	addressed
counseled	identified	compiled	authored
diagnosed	inspected	generated	drafted
facilitated	organized	organized	formulated
represented	summarized	processed	persuaded
		systematized	

Non-Action Verbs to Avoid

was involved in	had a role in
was a part of	was related to

Non-action verbs are vague. They give the impression that you are not an assertive person.

8. State other experience and skills that do not fall within the categories of education and employment mentioned above. (See Job Hunting Notebook, p. 113.) Perhaps you have been a homemaker for twenty years, raised five children, worked your way through college, were the church treasurer, a Cub Scout volunteer, etc. In a separate category on the résumé called "Other Experience," list such activities and state your duties in the same manner mentioned above to demonstrate relevant personality traits. Hobbies can be included (without using the word "hobby") when they are distinctive and illustrate special talents or achievement.

9. State any special abilities (for example, that you can design a database or speak a foreign language), awards, credentials, scholarships, membership associations, leadership positions, community service, publications, etc., that have not been mentioned elsewhere on the résumé.

10. No one has a perfect résumé. There are facts about all of us that we would prefer to downplay or avoid, e.g., sudden change in jobs, school transfer because of personal or family difficulties, low aptitude test scores. There is no need to point out these facts, but in a job interview you must be prepared to discuss any obvious gaps or problems that might be evident from your résumé. Thus far we have been outlining the format of a **chronological résumé,** which presents your education, training, and experience in a chronological sequence starting with the present and working backward. (See Exhibit 2.10.) Later we will examine how a **functional résumé** might be more effective than a chronological résumé in handling difficulties such as sudden changes or gaps in employment. (See Exhibit 2.11.)

11. At the end of the résumé, say, "References available on request." On a separate sheet of paper, type the names, work addresses, and phone numbers of people who know your abilities and who could be contacted by a prospective employer. If the latter is seriously considering you for a position, you will probably be asked for the list. This will most likely occur during a job interview. Generally, you should seek the permission of people you intend to use as references. Call them up and ask if you can list them as references in your job search.

12. Do not include salary requirements or your salary history on the résumé. Leave this topic for the interview. If you are responding to an ad that asks for this history, include it in the cover letter.

13. The résumé should be neatly typed, grammatically correct, and readable. Be sure that there are no spelling errors or smudge spots from erasures or fingerprints. In this regard, if you can't make your résumé *perfect*, don't bother submitting it. Avoid abbreviations except for items such as street, state, degrees earned, etc. Do not make any handwritten corrections; retype the résumé after you make the corrections. Proofread carefully. Also ask someone else to proofread the résumé for you to see if you missed anything.

    You do not have to use complete sentences in the résumé. Sentence fragments are adequate as long as you rigorously follow the grammatical rule on **parallelism.**[22] For example, say, "research*ed* securities issues, draft*ed* complaints, serv*ed* papers on opposing parties." Do not say, "researched securities, drafting complaints, and I served papers on opposing parties." When you present a series or a list, be consistent in using words ending in "ed" or in "ing," etc. Do not suddenly change from an "ed" word to an "ing" word or use personal pronouns with only some of the items in the series or list. Finally, avoid jumping from past tense to present tense, or vice versa. Do not say, "prepared annual budgets and manages part-time personnel." Say, "prepare budgets and manage part-time personnel" or "prepared budgets and managed part-time personnel."

    Leave generous margins. Cluster similar information together and use consistent indentation patterns so that readers can easily scan the résumé and quickly find those categories of information in which they are most interested.

    The résumé should have a professional appearance. Consider having your résumé typeset on quality paper (with matching envelopes) by a commercial printing company or word processing service. Obtain multiple copies of your résumé. Avoid submitting a résumé that was obviously reproduced on a poor-quality photocopy machine at a corner drugstore. The résumé is often the first contact that a prospective employer will have with you. You want to convey the impression that you know how to write and organize data. Furthermore, it is a sign of respect to the reader when you show that you took the time and energy to make your résumé professionally presentable. Law offices are *conservative* environments. Attorneys like to project an image of propriety, stability, accuracy, and order. Be sure that your résumé also projects this image.

14. Again, the résumé concentrates on those facts about you that show you are particularly qualified *for the specific job you are seeking.* The single most important theme you want to convey in the résumé is that you are a person who can make a contribution to *this* organization. As much as possible, the reader of the résumé should have the impression that you prepared the résumé for the particular position that is open. In style and content, the résumé should emphasize what will be pleasing to the reader and demonstrate what you can contribute to a particular office. (See Exhibit 2.9.)

    The last guideline is very important. You cannot comply with it unless you have done some *background research* on the law office where you are applying and, if possible, on the person who will be receiving the résumé. How do you do this back-

---

[22]Using a consistent (i.e., parallel) grammatical structure when phrasing ideas in a list that are logically related. In a list of related ideas, be consistent in the use of words ending in *ed, ing,* and *tion;* the use of infinitives; the use of clauses; the use of phrases; the use of active voice, etc.

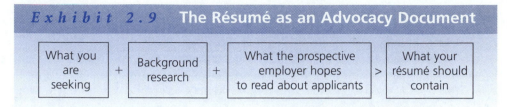

Exhibit 2.9   The Résumé as an Advocacy Document

What you are seeking + Background research + What the prospective employer hopes to read about applicants > What your résumé should contain

ground research? First and foremost, whenever practical, try to contact employees, particularly paralegals, who work there now or who once worked there. That's why Strategy 4, outlined above, on ways to locate working paralegals is so important.

In addition, consult one of the directories of attorneys, such as the *Martindale-Hubbell Law Directory* or *West's Legal Directory,* discussed earlier. Ask a librarian for a current directory of attorneys used in your state. Many large firms have brochures on their firms that are part of marketing strategies to find new clients. They may also have newsletters that they send to their current clients. Such brochures and newsletters may not be available to the general public unless someone within the firm gives you access to them.

If you are applying for a position in the law department of a large corporation, call the public relations office of the corporation and ask for promotional literature and a copy of its annual report. Many law libraries have directories of corporate counsel that you should check. In addition, most general libraries have directories, such as *Standard & Poor's Register of Corporations, Directors and Executives,* and *Moody's Bank and Finance Manual,* that provide information on such companies. Ask the librarian what other sources provide profiles of businesses.

Here is a partial checklist of information you want to obtain through background research on a prospective employer or job (see also page 106):

- Why has the office decided to hire a paralegal now? What needs or problems prompted this decision?
- What kind of law is practiced at the office? What are its specialties?
- How is the office structured and governed? By management committee?
- How old is the office? Has it expanded recently? If so, in what areas?
- What kinds of clients does the office have? A variety of small clients? Several large clients that provide most of the fees?
- If the office is the law department of a corporation, what are the company's main products or services?
- How many attorneys are in the office?
- How many paralegals? What kind of work do they do? Does the office understand the role of paralegals? What kinds of complaints have the paralegals had about the office? What are the advantages and disadvantages of working in the office?
- Has the office had personnel problems? High turnover?
- Does the office operate through systems? If not, how does it feel about developing such systems?

If you do your homework on a prospective employer, you will have begun collecting answers to such questions so that you can tailor your résumé to these answers. You will select those aspects of your prior employment or education, for example, that suggest or demonstrate you are able to handle the demands of the job.

Of course, for many jobs, you will *not* be able to obtain answers to these questions, no matter how much background research you do. You will simply have to do the best you can to predict what the "correct" answers are and structure your résumé, cover letter, and writing sample accordingly.

The main point, however, is that a lot of preparation is needed before you approach a prospective employer. Much time and energy must be expended. A conscientious and organized job search will be good preparation for the career ahead of you. *The same kind of motivation, creativity, and aggressiveness that is needed to find a good job is also needed to perform effectively as a paralegal and to advance in this field.* The cornerstone of achievement and success is a heavy dose of old-fashioned hard work.

Exhibit 2.10 is an example of a *chronological résumé,* the traditional format and the one most commonly used by applicants today. As indicated earlier, this résumé presents your

---

Exhibit 2.10   Sample Chronological Résumé

John J. Smith
43 Benning Road SE
Salem, Maryland 21455
(301) 456-0427

CAREER OBJECTIVE
Position as a paralegal at a small law firm in the area of probate, trusts, and estates in a firm where my accounting and legal skills will be used and where there are opportunities for growth.

EDUCATION
Jan. 1989–Jan. 1990 Maynard Paralegal Institute.
Courses:

Trusts and Estates:	The course presented an overview of probate procedure in Maryland. We covered how to conduct a client conference to collect the basic facts and how to prepare the 105 short form.
Tax I:	An introduction to the taxation of estates and general income tax; fundamentals of accounting; valuation of personal and real assets.

Introduction to Law   Civil Procedure
Family Law   Legal Research
Litigation

Internship:	Part of the curriculum at Maynard involved a six-week internship placement at a law firm; I was placed at Donaldson and Tannance, a general practice firm in Salem. Tasks undertaken at the internship: drafted answers to interrogatories in a divorce case on the ground of mental cruelty, maintained the office's tickler system, completed cite checking and shepardizing for an appellate brief.

Sept. 1987–June 1988 Jefferson Junior College Courses:

Business Law   Sociology
English I, II   Chemistry
Introduction to Psychology Creative Writing
French I

EMPLOYMENT
1985–1988   Teller, Salem National Bank
Responsibilities: Receiving deposit and withdrawal requests; training new tellers, supervising note department in the absence of the assistant manager.
1980–1984   Driver, ABC Biscuit Company

HONORS
1985 Junior Achievement Award for Outstanding Marketing

ASSOCIATIONS
Financial Secretary, Salem Paralegal Association; Regional Representative, National Federation of Paralegal Associations; Member, National Association of Legal Assistants

REFERENCES
Available on request.

education, training, and work history in reverse chronological sequence, beginning with the most recent events and working backward.

A *functional résumé,* on the other hand, clusters certain skills or talents together regardless of the period in which they were developed. See Exhibit 2.11. This style of résumé can be particularly useful when you want to downplay large gaps in education, when you are making a radical change of careers, or when your skills were not gained in paralegal education, training, or employment. The functional résumé should not, however, ignore the chronological sequence of the major training and work events of your life, since a prospective employer will want to know what this sequence is. Note that the functional résumé in Exhibit 2.11 has a skill cluster early in the résumé, followed by the historical overview in reverse chronological order. Using this format puts the emphasis of the résumé on the skills or abilities highlighted at the beginning.

Cover Letter   The **cover letter** should state how you learned about the office. It should also highlight and amplify those portions of the résumé that are relevant to the position you are seeking. Without repeating the résumé unduly, explain how you are qualified for the job. Like the résumé itself, the cover letter should give the impression that you are a professional. It is also important that you communicate a sense of enthusiasm about the position.

Note that the cover letter in Exhibit 2.12 is addressed to a specific person. Try to avoid sending a "To Whom It May Concern" letter unless you are responding to a blind ad. Whenever possible, find out the exact name of the person to whom the résumé should be sent. If you are not sure, call the office and ask.

One final, critically important point about the cover letter: it must be grammatically correct and contain no spelling errors. Do you see any problem with the following sentence from a cover letter?

"The description of responsibilities in the want ad fit my experience."

This sentence alone might cause a prospective employer to throw the letter, and its accompanying résumé, in the trash can. The subject and verb don't agree. The sentence should read:

"The description of responsibilities in the want ad fit*s* my experience."

There must be no lapses in your grammar and spelling. Your standard must be perfection. While this is also true of the résumé, it is particularly true of the cover letter. When the envelope is opened, the first thing that is read is the cover letter. The vast majority of us are *unaware of how poor our grammar is.* We have been lulled into a sense of security because readers of what we write—including teachers—seldom complain unless we make an egregious error. People read primarily for content; they do not focus on grammar and spelling. Hence you must provide this focus on your own. In the section on studying at the beginning of this book, there are suggestions for improving your writing skills. In the meantime, proofread, proofread, proofread; and then find others to proofread everything that you intend to submit in writing to a prospective employer. An additional technique used by careful writers is to read your cover letter (and résumé) *backward*—word by word, punctuation mark by punctuation mark. This will help you catch spelling and grammatical errors, particularly the blatant ones.

Exhibit 2.11   Sample Functional Résumé[23]

Jane Doe
18 East 7th Avenue
Denver, Colorado 80200
303-555-1198

JOB OBJECTIVE

A position in a legal office requiring skills in communications, research, and organization, leading toward training for and work as a paralegal.

BRIEF SUMMARY OF BACKGROUND

Bachelor of Arts and Bachelor of Science (Education) with major in English and minor in Library Science. Taught creative writing and communications to high school juniors and seniors; worked several years as research and index assistant in records and research department of large international organization; worked part-time on a volunteer basis in schools and libraries as librarian and reading tutor.

PROFESSIONAL SKILLS RELATED TO CAREER OBJECTIVE

Communications Skills

Taught communications to high school seniors; read extensively in international publications during nonworking years; conducted workshops on library skills and storytelling to children and young adults; participated in workshops with educators on reading skills; served as Circulation Representative for *The Christian Science Monitor,* which included promoting and selling subscriptions by telephone and in person. Gained considerable writing experience while working toward college degrees in English.

Clerical Skills

Facility with [a] vocabulary and spelling; [b] rules of diction and usage; [c] typing (80 wpm); [d] filing (helped revise and maintain many files including administrative, subjective, alpha-chrono combinations); [e] systems (maintained and circulated library collections and maintained catalog card files).

Research Skills

As librarian: helped students and teachers research and retrieve information and materials on various subjects; ordered, received, processed, and shelved library materials.

As research assistant: indexed correspondence; researched files for information using subject index; collated information on various subjects.

Analytical and Organizational Skills

Handled all phases of management of school library; planned for materials needed; ordered to meet those needs; supervised assistants; set up revised filing systems; helped engineer departmental move to new quarters.

EMPLOYMENT HISTORY

9/84–Present	Lincoln Elementary School
	100 Oak Street, Denver, Colorado 80203
	Title: Teacher's Aide (part-time)
6/76–6/84	International Church Center
	Executive Department, Records and Research Section
	465 E. 8th St., Boston, Massachusetts 02127
	Title: Research and Index Assistant (1 year full-time; 7 years part-time)
4/84–6/84	Latin Preparatory School
	16 Adams Court, Dorchester, Massachusetts 02139
	Title: School Librarian (substitute)
2/83–6/84	James P. O'Reilly Elementary School
	74 Statler Road, Boston, Massachusetts 02140
	Title: School Librarian (volunteer)
9/74–6/75	Roosevelt High School
	16 Main St., Minneapolis, Minnesota 55162
	Title: English Teacher

EDUCATION

1983–1984	University of Massachusetts, Boston Campus
	Special courses included: Library and Urban Children; Design Management
1979–1980	Harvard Extension, Problems in Urban Education
1969–1973	University of Minnesota, Minneapolis, B.S., *Major:* English *Minor:* Library Science

SCHOOL ACTIVITIES

National Honor Society; Dramatic Club; Creative Writing Club; YWCA; Member, Minnesota Dance Company, 1969–1973.

REFERENCES

Available on request.

---

[23]Rocky Mountain Legal Assistants Association, *Employment Handbook for Legal Assistants,* 26–8, (1979).

Assignment 2.3

Find a want ad from a law office seeking an entry-level paralegal. Try to locate an ad as detailed as possible in terms of what the employer is looking for.

(a) Prepare a résumé for this job. Make it a real résumé except for the following information, which you can make up:

- You can assume that you have already had course work in the areas involved in the job.
- You can assume that you once had a part-time summer position with a lawyer, but it was in an area of the law that is different from the area practiced in the law office seeking the paralegal.

Attach a copy of the ad to the résumé you hand in, and indicate where you obtained it.

(b) Prepare a cover letter to go with this résumé. You can make up identifying information the ad may not provide, e.g., the name and address of the person to whom you will be sending the résumé and letter. Assume that you called to obtain this information.

Writing Samples

You should be constantly thinking about writing samples based upon the course work you do and any legal employment or internship experiences you have had. If your writing sample comes from a prior job or internship, be sure that the confidentiality of actual parties is protected by "whiting out" or changing their names.[24] In addition, consider preparing other writing samples *on your own.* For example:

- A brief memorandum of law on the application of a statute to a set of facts that you make up (see chapter 12)
- A pleading such as a complaint (see chapter 10)
- A set of interrogatories (see chapter 10)
- Articles of incorporation and bylaws for a fictitious corporation
- An analysis of a recent court opinion (see chapters 7 and 11)
- An intake memorandum of law based on an interview that you role-play with another student (see chapter 8)
- An annotated bibliography on a particular topic (see chapter 11)
- A brief article that you write for a paralegal newsletter on an aspect of your legal education or work experience as a paralegal (see Appendix B)

Prepare a file of all your writing samples. (See Job Hunting Notebook, page 117.) If possible, try to have a teacher, practicing attorney, or paralegal review each sample. Rewrite it based on their comments. You must take the initiative in preparing writing samples and in soliciting feedback from knowledgeable contacts that you make. You need to have a large pool of diverse writing samples from which to choose once you begin the actual job hunt. Start preparing these samples now.

Strategy 9: The Job Interview

Once you have overcome the hurdles of finding a prospective employer who will read your cover letter and résumé, the next problem is to arrange for a job interview. In your

---

[24]"It is always inappropriate to hand a prospective employer anything that has current, active case information anywhere in it: case names and numbers, court and internal file numbers, names, addresses, telephone numbers of deponents, names of plaintiffs, defendants, and third parties in the body of the document." Fitzgerald, *Ethics and the Job Hunting Paralegal,* 18 Reporter (Los Angeles Paralegal Ass'n, November 1989).

Exhibit 2.12　　**Cover Letter**

43 Benning Road SE
Salem, Maryland 21455
301/456-0427
March 13, 1990

Linda Stenner, Esq.
Stenner, Skidmore & Smith
438 Bankers Trust Bldg.
Suite 1200
Salem, Maryland 21458

Dear Ms. Stenner:

   Michael Diamond, Esq. told me that your firm may have an opening for a trusts and estates paralegal. I am enclosing my resume for your consideration. I am very interested in working in the field of probate, trusts, and estates. The course work that I did at Maynard Institute and my prior work at the Salem National Bank provided me with an appreciation of the complexity of this area of the law. I find the field fascinating.

   I am fully aware of the kind of attention to detail that a paralegal in this field must have. If you decide to check any of my references, I am confident that you will be told of the high level of discipline and responsibility that I bring to the tasks I undertake.

   I have two writing samples that may be of interest to you: a draft of a will that I prepared in my course on trusts and estates, and a memorandum of law on the valuation of stocks. These writing samples are available on request.

   I would appreciate the opportunity to be interviewed for the paralegal position at your firm. I feel confident that my training and experience have prepared me for the kind of challenge that this position would provide.

                                         Sincerely,

                                         John J. Smith

---

cover letter, you may want to add the following sentence at the end: "Within the next two weeks, I will give you a call to determine whether an interview would be possible." This strategy does not leave the matter entirely up to the prospective employer as to whether there will be further contact with you. You must be careful, however, not to appear too forward. Some may resent this approach. On the other hand, you have little to lose by trying it several times to see what response you obtain.

   Whenever possible, try to have a paralegal, attorney, administrator, or secretary in the office arrange the interview for you with the person who will be doing the hiring and/or interviewing. Hopefully, your background research into the office will enable you to identify such an in-house person who will put in a word for you.

Job Interview Guidelines

(See Job Hunting Notebook, page 118.)

   "Attired in your best interviewing suit, you nervously navigate your way to the reception area of what you hope will be your future employer's office. You are a comfortable ten minutes early. Upon arrival you are directed to the office of the interviewer, whom you greet with a smile and pleasant handshake. She offers you a cup of coffee, which you wisely refuse, since you may spill it. She then looks you in the eye and poses her first question. 'Why are you interested in working for this company?' [Suddenly you go blank!] All thoughts leave your mind as you pray for the ability to speak." Cunningham, *A Planned Approach to Interviewing,* 5 The LAMA Manager 1 (Legal Assistants Management Association, Fall 1989).

1. Be sure you have the exact address, room number, and time of the interview. Give yourself sufficient time to find the office. If the area is new to you, be sure you have precise directions. It would be unfortunate to start your contact with the office by having to offer excuses for being late. Arrive at least ten minutes early. You will probably be nervous and will need to compose yourself before the interview. It is important that you are as relaxed as possible.

2. Try to find out in advance who will be interviewing you. (Don't be surprised, however, if the person who greets you is a substitute for the person originally scheduled to conduct the interview.) A number of different kinds of people might conduct the interview depending upon the size of the office: the law office manager, the managing attorney, the supervising attorney for the position, the paralegal supervisor, a staff paralegal, or a combination of the above if you are interviewed by different people on the same day or on different days. The style of the interview may be quite different depending on who conducts it. Someone with management responsibility might stress the interpersonal dimensions of the position, whereas a trial attorney might give you the feeling that you are being cross-examined. Try to determine whether you are being interviewed by the person who has the final authority to hire you. In many offices, you will be interviewed by someone whose sole task is to screen out unacceptable applicants. If you make it through this person, the next step will usually be an interview with the ultimate decision-maker. Whenever you know or suspect that you will be interviewed by an attorney, try to obtain his or her professional biography through *West's Legal Directory* (see Exhibit 2.7), *Martindale-Hubbell,* or other directories. (*Martindale-Hubbell* also has information on many key nonattorneys working in the office. See Exhibit 2.6.) You might be lucky enough to get to talk with someone who has been interviewed by this person before (such as a paralegal now working at the office, another job seeker, or someone at the local paralegal association) so that you can obtain a sense of what to expect.

3. Although relatively uncommon, you may have to face a **group interview** in which several interviewers question you at once. Alternatively, one or more interviewers could interview you along with, and at the same time as, other candidates for the job.

4. Make sure that you are prepared for the interview. Review the guidelines discussed above on writing your résumé. (Bring copies of your résumé.) In the résumé and in the interview, you are trying to sell yourself. Many of the principles of résumé writing apply to the interview. Know the kinds of questions you will probably be asked. Rehearse your responses. Write down a series of questions (tough ones) and ask a friend to role-play an interview with you. Have your friend ask you the questions and critique your responses. Also take the role of the interviewer and question your friend so that you can gauge both perspectives. Be prepared to handle a variety of questions. See Exhibit 2.13. Keep in mind, however, that no matter how much preparation you do, you may still be surprised by the course the interview takes. Be flexible enough to expect the unexpected. If you are relaxed, confident, *and prepared,* you will do fine.

5. You are not required to answer potentially illegal questions—for instance, "Are you married?" Some employers use the answers to such irrelevant questions to practice

Exhibit 2.13   The Six Categories of Job Interview Questions

● **Open-Ended Questions** (which are calculated to get you to talk, giving the listener an idea of how you organize your thoughts)

  (1) Tell me about yourself.

  (2) What kind of position are you seeking?

  (3) What interests you about this job?

● **Closed-Ended Questions** (which can be answered by one or two words)

  (4) When did you receive your paralegal certificate?

  (5) Did you take a course in corporate law?

● **Soft-Ball Questions** (which should be fairly easy to answer if you are prepared)

  (6) What are your interests outside of school and work?

  (7) What courses did you enjoy the most? Why? Which were least rewarding? Why?

  (8) Do your grades reflect your full potential? Why or why not?

  (9) Why did you leave your last job?

  (10) How have you grown or developed in your prior jobs? Explain.

  (11) How were you evaluated in your prior jobs?

  (12) What are your strengths as a worker?

  (13) Describe an ideal work environment. What would your "dream job" be?

  (14) What factors make a job frustrating? How would you handle these factors?

  (15) What do you hope to be doing in ten years? What are your long-term goals?

  (16) If you are hired, how long are you prepared to stay?

  (17) Are you interested in a job or a career? What's the difference?

  (18) Why did you become a paralegal?

  (19) What problems do you think a paralegal might face in a busy law office? How would you handle these problems?

  (20) Can you work under pressure? When have you done so in the past?

  (21) How flexible are you in adapting to changing circumstances? Give examples of your flexibility in the last year.

  (22) How do you feel about doing routine work?

  (23) Do you prefer a large or a small law office? Why?

  (24) What accomplishment in your life are you most proud of? Why?

  (25) What salary expectations do you have? What was your salary at your last position?

  (26) What other questions do you think I should ask in order to learn more about you?

  (27) What questions would you like to ask me about this office?

● **Tension Questions** (which are calculated to put you on the spot to see how you handle yourself)

  (28) No one is perfect. What are your weaknesses as a worker?

  (29) Have you ever been fired from a position? Explain the circumstances.

  (30) Why have you held so many jobs?

  (31) Name some things that would be unethical for an attorney to do. What would you do if you found out that the attorney supervising you was doing these things?

  (32) Are you a competitive person? If not, why not? If you are, give some examples over the last six months that demonstrate this characteristic.

  (33) Is there something in this job that you hope to accomplish that you were not able to accomplish in your last job?

  (34) Do you type? If not, are you willing to learn?

  (35) Do you smoke? If so, how would you handle a work environment that is totally smoke-free, including the wash rooms?

  (36) Where else have you interviewed for a job? Have you been turned down?

Exhibit 2.13   The Six Categories of Job Interview Questions—continued

(37) Why wouldn't you want to become an attorney now?

(38) Everyone makes mistakes. What is the biggest mistake that you made in any of your prior jobs and how did you handle it?*

(39) No job is perfect. What is the least appealing aspect of the job you are seeking here?

(40) There are over fifty applicants for this one position. Why do you think you are the most qualified?

(41) If you are offered this position, what are the major concerns that you would have about taking it?

(42) What would make you want to quit a job?

(43) Give some examples of when you have shown initiative over the last six months in school or at your last job.

● **Hypothetical Questions** (in which you are asked how you would handle a stated fact situation)

(44) If you were told, "This isn't any good, do it again, and get it right this time," what would you do?

(45) If you find out on Friday afternoon that you're expected to come in on Saturday, what would you do?**

(46) Assume that you are given the position here and that you work very closely on a day-to-day basis with an attorney. After a six-month period, what positive and negative comments do you think this attorney would make about you as a worker?

(47) Suppose that your first assignment was to read through and summarize 4,000 documents over an eight-month period. Could you do it? Would you want to do it?

(48) Assume that two airplanes crash into each other and that your firm represents one of the passengers who was killed. What kind of discovery would you recommend?

● **Potentially Illegal Questions** (because the questions are not relevant to the candidate's fitness and ability to do most jobs)

(49) Are you married? Do you plan to marry?

(50) Do you have any children? If so, how old are they? Who takes care of your children?

(51) If you do not have any children now, do you plan to have any in the future?

(52) How old are you?

(53) What is your religion?

(54) What is your political affiliation?

*Moralez, *Sample Interview Questions,* 11 Paragram (Oregon Legal Assistant Ass'n, May 1988).
**Wendel, *You the Recruiter,* 5 Legal Assistant Today 31 (September/October 1987).

illegal sex discrimination. You need to decide in advance how you will handle them if they are asked. You may want to ask why the question is relevant. Or you may simply decide to steer the interview back to the qualifications that you have and the commitment that you have made to a professional career. A good response might be, "If you're concerned that my marital status may affect my job performance, I can assure you that it will not." Follow this up with comments about dedication and job commitment. It may be the perfect time to offer references.[25] Whatever approach you take, be sure to remain courteous.

6. Avoid being critical of anyone. Do not, for example, "dump on" your prior employer or school. Criticizing or blaming other organizations, even if justified, is likely to give the interviewer the impression that you will probably end up blaming *this* organization if you get the job and difficulties arise.

7. What about being critical of yourself? You will be invited to criticize yourself when you are asked the seemingly inevitable question, "What are your weaknesses?" You

---

[25]Reitz, *Be Steps Ahead of Other Candidates: Understand the Interview Game,* 5 Legal Assistant Today 24, 84 (March/April 1988).

may want to pick a *positive* trait and express it as a negative. For example: "I tend to get frustrated when I'm not given enough to do. My goal is not just to collect a paycheck. I want to make a contribution." Or: "I think I sometimes have expectations that are too high. There is so much to learn, and I want it all now. I have to pace myself, and realize that the important goal is to complete the immediate task, even if I can't learn every conceivable aspect of that task at the present time." Or: "I get irritated by carelessness. When I see someone turn in sloppy work, or work that is not up to the highest standards, it bothers me."

If you use any of these approaches, be sure that you are able to back them up when you are asked to explain what you mean. You will probably be asked to give concrete examples of such "weaknesses."

8. If you have done the kind of background research on the office mentioned earlier, you will have a fairly good idea what the structure and mission of the office are. Interviewers are usually impressed by applicants who demonstrate this kind of knowledge during the interview. It will be clear to them which applicants have done their homework. A major goal of the interview is to relate your education and experience to the needs of the office. To the extent possible, you want to know what these needs are before the interview so that you can quickly and forcefully demonstrate that you are the person the office is looking for. Most offices decide to hire someone because they have a problem—for example, they need someone with a particular skill, they need someone to help them expand, or they need someone who can get along with a particularly demanding supervising attorney. If you are not sure, ask the interviewer directly why the office has decided to add a paralegal. The success of the interview is directly related to your ability to identify the problem of the office and to demonstrate how you can solve it for them.

9. If the paralegal job is in a certain specialty, such as probate or corporate law, you must be prepared to discuss that area of the law. You may be asked questions designed to assess your familiarity with the area. Prior to the interview, spend some time reviewing your class notes. Skim through a standard practice book for that area of the law in the state. Be sure that you can back up anything you said in your résumé about prior involvement with the area in your school or work experience. Such discussions are always an excellent opportunity for you to present writing samples in that field of the law. (Be sure to bring extra copies of such writing samples.)

10. Dress conservatively. "It is recommended that a man be clean shaven, wear a dark suit (gray or navy blue), a white shirt, and a muted-tone tie. Shoes should be polished. A woman should wear a skirt-suit or a blazer and skirt, plain blouse, neutral-colored stockings, and a simple hairdo. A minimal amount of jewelry and no perfume are the rule." "To complete these 'uniforms,' a briefcase is a necessity. It symbolizes that you are a professional. Women may want to keep their purses in their briefcases."[26] You want interviewers to remember what you said, not what you wore.

11. Be sure that you project yourself positively. Take the initiative in greeting the interviewer. A firm handshake is recommended. Maintain good posture and eye contact. Remember that everything you do will be evaluated. The interviewer will be making mental notes on your body language. Avoid appearing ill at ease or fidgety. Many feel that the practice of law is a battlefield. The interviewer will be forming an opinion of whether you "fit in."

---

[26]Berkey, *Successful Interviewing*, 5 Legal Assistant Today 66 (September/October 1987).

12. Try to avoid the topic of salary until the end of the interview when you have completed the discussion of the job itself. Preferably, let the interviewer raise the issue. Think through how you will handle the topic, but try to avoid discussing it until the appropriate time arises. If asked what salary you are seeking, give a salary range rather than a single rigid figure. Always relate salary to the specific skills and strengths that you would be able to bring to the office, rather than to the "going rate." You need to know what the going rate is—check recent salary surveys of local and national paralegal associations—so that the salary range you seek is realistic. But avoid using the going rate as the first and sole reason for your position on salary.

13. Be an active participant in the interview even though you let the interviewer conduct the interview. Help keep the discussion going.

14. Be enthusiastic, but not overly so. You want to let the office know that you really want the job, not because you are desperate but because you see it as a challenge offering professional development. You are qualified for the job and you feel that the office is the kind of place that recognizes valuable contributions from its workers.

15. Be yourself. Do not try to overwhelm the interviewer with your cleverness and charm.

16. Be prepared to leave the following documents with the interviewer: extra copies of your résumé, a list of references, and writing samples. Bring a transcript of your school grades (if they are impressive) and offer to leave a copy.

17. Ask the interviewer if you can have an opportunity to talk with one or more paralegals currently working at the office. It will be another sign of your seriousness.

18. Ask your own questions of the interviewer. In effect, you are interviewing the office as much as the other way around. Come with a written list and don't be afraid to let the interviewer see that you have a checklist of questions that you want to ask. It is a sign of an organized person. There is a great deal of information about the job that you could inquire about. From your background research about the job, you should already have some of this information, but you can now verify what you know. You want to ask pertinent and intelligent questions that will communicate to the interviewer that you are serious about the paralegal field, that you are prepared, and that you grasp what the interviewer has been telling you about the job and the office.

    Below are some topics you could cover in your own questions. See also Exhibits 2.14 and 2.15 for more ideas for questions.

    - What type of person is the office seeking to hire?
    - What prompted the office to seek this type of person?
    - What are some examples of paralegal responsibilities? Will the paralegal specialize in certain tasks or areas of the law? (Ask for a description of a typical workday of a paralegal at the firm.)
    - What skills will the paralegal need for the job? Digesting? Investigation? Research? Drafting? Interviewing?
    - How many attorneys are in the firm? Is the number growing, declining, remaining constant?
    - How is the firm managed or governed? Managing partner? Management committees? Legal administrator? Is there a policy manual for the firm?
    - How many paralegals are in the firm? Is the number growing, declining, remaining constant? Are all the paralegals at the firm full-time? Does the firm use part-time or freelance paralegals? Has the firm considered hiring a paralegal coordinator?
    - Is there a career ladder for paralegals in the firm?
    - How long has the firm used paralegals? What is the average length of time a paralegal stays with the firm? What are the feelings of firm members on the value of

(cont. on page 108)

Exhibit 2.14	**Checklist of Possible Paralegal Fringe Benefits**

Compensation:

____ Salary Increase Policy (amount or range? criteria for determining? frequency of review? who reviews?)

____ Overtime (frequency? method of compensation?)

____ Bonus (method for determining? frequency?)

____ Cost-of-Living Adjustment (frequency? method for determining?)

____ Other Incentive Programs, like Profit Sharing Plan

____ Pension/Retirement Plan (defined benefit? defined contribution? other?)

____ Tax Deferred Savings Plan

____ Other Investment Plan

Insurance:

____ Basic Medical (full coverage? partial?)

____ Major Medical (full coverage? partial?)

____ Dependent Medical Insurance (fully paid? partially paid?)

____ Supplemental Medical (fully paid? partially paid?)

____ Dental (full coverage? partial?)

____ Maternity Leave (full coverage? partial?)

____ Eye Care/Glasses (full coverage? partial?)

____ Life Insurance (fully paid? partially paid?)

____ Physical Disability (short term? long term? full coverage? partial?)

____ Sick Days (number? carryover of unused sick leave allowed?)

Professional Activities:

____ Time Off for Association Events

____ Association Dues Paid (full? partial?)

____ Association Dinner Events Paid

____ Tuition Reimbursement for Paralegal Classes

____ Tuition Reimbursement for Law School

Other:

____ Vacation (number of days? carry over of unused vacation allowed?)

____ Personal Leave Days (number allowed?)

____ Child Care Assistance

____ Paid Holidays (number?)

____ Parking (fully paid? partially paid?)

____ Leased Car

____ Mileage Allowance

____ Club Membership

____ Fitness Center

____ Refreshments on the Job

____ Sports Tickets

____ Entertainment Allowance

____ Free Legal Advice and Representation by the Firm on Personal Matters

Comparability:

____ Paralegal Fringe Benefits Similar/Dissimilar to Those of New Attorneys?

____ Paralegal Fringe Benefits Similar/Dissimilar to Those of Secretaries?

Exhibit 2.15 **Checklist of Factors that Help Determine the Quality of the Work Environment of a Paralegal**

____ Policy Manual on Paralegal Use in Office (available?)
____ Evaluation (method? frequency?)
____ Career Ladder for Paralegals in Office (criteria for advancement?)
____ Supervision of Paralegal (by attorney? by paralegal manager? by legal administrator?)
____ Supervision by Paralegal (secretary? assistant to paralegal?)
____ Work Assignments (who delegates? one attorney? several? paralegal manager?)
____ Availability of Secretarial Assistance
____ Paralegal Turnover in Office (low? high?)
____ Client Contact (frequent? rare?)
____ Attendance at Trials (frequent? rare?)
____ Sit at Counsel's Table (frequent? rare?)
____ Billable Hours: hourly rate?
____ Billable Hours: quota? (monthly quota? annual quota?)
____ Time Spent on Non-Billable Matters (frequent? rare? type?)
____ Office Space (private? shared?)
____ Use of Computers (frequent? rare?)
____ Availability of Word Processing Department to Paralegal (frequent? rare?)
____ Typing (own work? attorney's work?)
____ How Management Perceives Paralegals (professionals? administrative? support staff? combination?)
____ Flexible Work Schedule
____ Travel Required (frequent? rare? type?)
____ Attendance at Attorney Strategy Meetings (frequent? rare?)
____ Attendance at Management Meetings (frequent? rare?)
____ Office Training for Paralegals (kind? frequency?)
____ In-House Attorney Training Available to Paralegals (frequent? rare?)
____ CLE *(Continuing Legal Education)* for Attorneys Available to Paralegals (frequent? rare?)
____ Business Cards Provided
____ Name on Door
____ Name on Letterhead Stationery of Law Office
____ Has Own Letterhead Stationery
____ Office Correspondence (does paralegal ever sign under own name?)
____ Attendance at Attorney Retreats (frequent? rare?)
____ Attendance at Attorney Social Functions (frequent? rare?)

paralegals to the firm? Why is this so? How would firm members describe an ideal paralegal employee? Do all members of the firm feel the same about paralegals? What reservations, if any, do some members of the firm have about paralegals?

- What other personnel does the firm have (secretaries, computer staff, library staff, clerks, messengers, part-time law students, etc.)? How many of each are there? What relationship does the paralegal have with each?
- What kind of supervision does a paralegal receive? Close supervision? From one attorney? Several?
- Will the paralegal work for one attorney? Several? Will the paralegal have his or her own case load? Is there a paralegal pool available to many attorneys?

- What kind of client contact will the paralegal have? Phone? Meetings? Interviews? Document inspection at client's office?
- What kind of writing will the paralegal be doing? Letters that the paralegal will sign? Letters for attorney to sign? Memos?
- What opportunities does a paralegal have for further learning? Office training programs? (Do paralegals attend new-attorney training sessions?) Does the firm encourage outside training for paralegals, e.g., from paralegal associations, bar associations, area schools?
- Will the paralegals be attending staff meetings? Strategy sessions with attorneys?
- How are paralegals evaluated in the office? Written evaluations? Oral? How often?
- Are paralegals required to produce a set number of billable hours? Per day? Per week? Per month? Annually? What is the hourly rate at which a paralegal's time is billed to a client? Do different paralegals in the office bill at different rates? If so, what determines the difference?
- How often are paralegals required to record their time? Daily, hourly, in ten-minute segments, etc.?
- What secretarial assistance is available to the paralegal? None? A personal secretary? Secretary shared with an attorney? Use of a secretarial pool? Will the paralegal do any typing? Light typing? His or her own typing? Typing for others?
- Does the job require travel?
- What equipment will the paralegal be using? Computer, fax machine, copier, dictaphone? What software does the firm use for its major tasks? Word processing? Database management?
- Office space for the paralegal? Private office? Shared office? Partitioned office?
- Compensation and benefits—see Exhibit 2.14, Checklist of Possible Paralegal Fringe Benefits.

19. **Don't contaminate the law firm!** Later in chapter 5, when you study **conflict of interest,** you will learn that a new employee can contaminate an entire office. Here is an example of how this could happen: the paralegal once worked or volunteered for an office that represented a client who is now an opponent of a current client of the office where the paralegal is seeking employment. If the paralegal is hired, there is a possibility that the entire law firm would be disqualified from continuing to represent its client—all because of the paralegal's prior work on behalf of an opponent of this client.[27] To avoid contamination the law office must find out if prospective new employees (attorneys, paralegals, or secretaries) might bring a conflict of interest to the office because of their prior legal work. Hence you must be prepared to let prospective employers know the names of the clients for whom you worked in prior employment or volunteer settings. This disclosure, however, usually does not need to occur until it is clear that the office is very interested in you and asks for a list of such clients. Never volunteer to show the list to anyone. The names of clients are confidential. But limited disclosure will be needed to avoid a disqualification due to a conflict of interest.

20. After you have thoroughly explored the position during the interview, if you still want the job, ask for it. Be sure that you make a specific request. Some interviewers go out of their way to stress the difficult aspects of the job in order to gauge your

---

[27]As we will see in chapter 5, disqualification might be avoided if the new employer effectively screens the contaminated or tainted paralegal from work on the case and if this paralegal does not disclose anything he or she learned while working for the other law office.

reaction. Don't leave the interviewer with the impression that you may be having second thoughts if in fact you still want the job after you have had all your questions answered.

Follow-Up Letter

After the interview, always send a letter to the person who interviewed you. In a surprising number of cases, the follow-up letter is a significant factor in obtaining the job. In the letter:

- Thank the person for the interview.
- Tell the person that you enjoyed the interview and the opportunity to learn about the office.
- State that you are still very interested in the position.
- Briefly restate why you are qualified for the position.
- Clarify any matters that arose during the interview.
- Submit references or writing samples that may have been asked for during the interview.

Keep a copy of all such letters. In a notebook, maintain accurate records on the dates you sent out résumés, the kinds of résumés you sent, the dates of interviews, the names of people you met, your impressions, the dates when you made follow-up calls, etc. (See page 120.)

If you are turned down for a job, find out why. Call the office to try to obtain more information than is provided in standard rejection statements. Politely ask what could have improved your chances. Finally, use the occasion to ask for any leads to other prospective employers.

🏛 *Class Exercise 2.A*

Role-play an interview in class. The instructor will decide what kind of job the interview will be for and will select students to play the role of interviewer and interviewee. The interviewer should ask a variety of questions such as those presented above in the guidelines for handling a job interview. The rest of the class will evaluate the performance of the interviewee. What mistakes did he or she make? How should he or she have dealt with certain questions? Was he or she confident? Overconfident? Did he or she ask good questions of the interviewer? Were these questions properly timed? What impressions did the interviewee convey of himself or herself? Make a list of do's and don'ts for such interviews.

Section E
THE JOB HUNTING NOTEBOOK

Purchase a large three-ring, loose-leaf notebook for your Job Hunting Notebook. Include in it the outline of sections presented in Exhibit 2.16. Following the outline, create at least one page for each section.

There are a number of purposes for the Notebook:

- To help you identify your strengths based on past legal or nonlegal employment, training, and other life experience.

Exhibit 2.16   Outline of Job Hunting Notebook

Part I. Résumé and Writing Sample Preparation

1. Prior and Current Nonlegal Employment—Analysis Sheet
2. Prior and Current Legal Employment—Analysis Sheet
3. Prior and Current Volunteer Activity—Analysis Sheet
4. Other Life Experiences—Analysis Sheet
5. Nonlegal Education and Training—Analysis Sheet
6. Legal Education and Training—Analysis Sheet
7. Notes on Résumé Writing
8. Draft of General Résumé
9. Drafts of Specialized Résumés
10. Writing Samples

Part II. Contacts for Employment

11. Contacts—Attorneys You Already Know or with Whom You Have Any Indirect Association
12. Contacts—Employed Paralegals
13. Contacts and Tasks—General

Part III. Legwork in the Field

14. Job Interview Checklist
15. Job Interview—Analysis Sheet
16. Record Keeping

- To help you organize this data for your résumés.
- To provide you with checklists of contacts that you should start making immediately.
- To help you prepare for job interviews.
- To provide a place to store copies of résumés, cover letters, writing samples, follow-up letters, notes on job leads and strategies, personal impressions, etc.
- To keep a calendar on all aspects of the job search.

The Notebook is your own personal document. No one else will see it unless you choose to share its contents with others.

1. Prior and Current Nonlegal Employment—Analysis Sheet

2. Prior and Current Legal Employment—Analysis Sheet

3. Prior and Current Volunteer Activity—Analysis Sheet

We begin by analyzing three areas together: your experience in nonlegal jobs (e.g., cashier, truck driver); then in legal jobs (e.g., legal secretary, investigator); and finally in volunteer activity (e.g., church sale coordinator, political campaign assistant). Make a list of these jobs and volunteer activities. Start a separate sheet of paper for each entry on your list, and then do the following:

- State the name, address, and phone number of the place of employment or location of the volunteer work.

- State the exact dates you were there.
- State the names of your supervisors there. (Circle the name of supervisors who had a favorable impression of you. Place a double circle around the name of each supervisor who would probably write a favorable recommendation for you, if asked.)
- Make a list of every major task you performed there. Number each task, starting with number 1. (As you write this list, leave a three-inch *left-hand margin* on the paper. In front of the number for each task, place all of the following letters that apply to that task. When an explanation or description is called for, provide it on attached sheets of paper.)

B   The task required you to conform to a *budget*. (Briefly describe the budget, including its size and who prepared it.)

C   There was some *competition* in the office about who was most qualified to perform the task. (Briefly describe why you were the most qualified.)

E   You were *evaluated* on how well you performed the task. (Briefly describe the evaluation of you.)

EI   To perform the task, you occasionally or always had to *exercise initiative;* you did not just wait for detailed instructions. (Briefly describe the initiative you took.)

ET   You occasionally or frequently had to devote *extra time* to perform the task. (Briefly describe the circumstances.)

J/C   It was not a mechanical task; you had to exercise some *judgment* and/or *creativity* to perform it. (Briefly describe the kind of judgment or creativity you exhibited.)

M   *Math* skills were involved in performing the task. (Briefly describe what kind of math you had to do.)

OD   *Others depended* on your performing the task well. (Briefly describe who had to rely on your performance and why.)

OT   You always or regularly performed the task *on time.*

OW   To perform the task, you had to coordinate your work with *other workers;* you did not work alone. (Briefly describe the nature of your interaction with others.)

P   You had some role in *planning* how the task would be performed; you were not simply following someone else's plan. (Briefly describe your planning role.)

PI   You did not start out performing the task; you were formally or informally *promoted into* it. (Briefly describe what you did before being asked to perform this task and the circumstances of the promotion.)

PP   You are *personally proud* of the way you performed the task. (Briefly describe why.)

R   You made *recommendations* on how the task could be more efficiently performed or better integrated into the office. (Briefly describe the recommendations you made and what effect they had.)

RR   You *received recognition* because of how well you performed the task. (Briefly describe the recognition you received and from whom.)

SE   To perform the task, you had to operate *some equipment* such as computers or motor vehicles. (Briefly describe the equipment and the skills needed to operate it.)

SO   To perform the task, you had to *supervise others* or help supervise others. (Briefly describe whom you supervised and what the supervision entailed.)

T   You *trained* others to perform the task. (Briefly describe this training.)

TP   You had to work under *time pressures* when you performed the task; you didn't have forever to perform it. (Briefly describe these pressures.)

W   Performing the task involved some *writing*. (Briefly describe what kind of writing you did.)

Include other characteristics of the task that are not covered in this list.

4. Other Life Experiences—Analysis Sheet

Circle *each* of the following experiences that you have had. Do not include experiences that required schooling, since these experiences will be covered elsewhere in the Notebook. Do not include experiences that involved volunteer work unless you have not already included them elsewhere in the Notebook. Attach additional sheets as indicated and where more space is needed.

- Raised a family alone
- Helped raise a family
- Traveled extensively
- Read extensively in a particular field on your own
- Learned to operate computer programs on your own
- Learned a language on your own
- Learned a craft on your own, such as weaving or fixing cars
- Learned an art on your own, such as painting or sculpture
- Developed a distinctive hobby requiring considerable skill
- Other life experiences (list each)

Attach a separate sheet of paper for *each* of the life experiences or activities that you listed above. Write the activity at the top of the sheet. Answer the following questions for each activity:

a. How long did you engage in this activity?
b. Have you ever tried to teach this activity to someone else? If so, describe your efforts.
c. Do you think you could teach this activity to others? Explain your answer.
d. Which of the following characteristics do you think are necessary or helpful in being able to perform the activity competently? Do not focus at this point on whether you possess these characteristics. Simply compile a list of what would be helpful or necessary.

Intelligence	Compassion	Patience
Creativity	Responsibility	Dependability
Perseverance	Punctuality	Determination
Drive	Self-confidence	Stamina
Independence	Poise	Self-control
Talent	Efficiency	Grace
Understanding	Skill	Dexterity
Cleverness	Competitiveness	Sophistication
Spirit	Congeniality	Stick-to-itiveness
Conviction	Judgment	Will power
Fortitude	Strength	Zeal
Ambition	Know-how	Experience
Ability to work with others	Imagination	Others? (list)

  e. Ask *someone else* (whom you trust and who is familiar with you) to look at the list. Ask this person if he or she would add anything to the list. Then ask him or her to identify which of these characteristics apply to *you* for this activity.

  f. Now it's your turn. Which of these characteristics do *you* think apply to you for this activity?

  g. If there are any major differences in the answers to (e) and (f) above, how do you explain the discrepancy? Are you too hard on yourself? Do you tend to put yourself down and minimize your strengths?

5. Nonlegal Education and Training—Analysis Sheet

On a separate sheet of paper, list every school or training program *not* involving law that you have attended or are now attending (whether or not you completed it), starting with the most recent. Include four-year colleges, two-year colleges, vocational training schools, weekend seminars, work-related training programs, internships, church training programs, hobby training programs, self-improvement training, etc. Include everything since high school.

Devote a separate sheet of paper to each school or training program, writing its name at the top of the sheet and answering the following questions for it. If more than one course was taught, answer these questions for two or three of the most demanding courses.

  a. What were the exact or approximate dates of attendance?

  b. Did you complete it? What evidence do you have that you completed it? A grade? A certificate? A degree? A transcript?

  c. Were you required to attend? If so, by whom? If not, why did you attend?

  d. How did you finance your attendance?

  e. What requirements did you meet in order to attend? Was there competition to attend? If so, describe in detail.

  f. Describe the subjects taught. What was the curriculum?

  g. How were you evaluated?

  h. What evidence of these evaluations do you have? Could you obtain copies of them? Do you have a transcript of your record?

  i. Describe in detail any writing that you had to do, such as exams or reports. Do you have copies of any of these written items? If not, could you obtain copies?

  j. What skills other than writing did you cover, such as organization, research, computer use, speaking, reading, manual dexterity, machine operation, interpersonal relations?

  k. What evidence do you have or could you obtain that shows you covered these skills and how well you did in them?

  l. Did you receive any special award or distinction? If so, describe it and state what evidence you have or could obtain that you received it.

  m. Make a list of every favorable comment you can remember that was made about your work. What evidence of these comments do you have or could you obtain?

  n. Was the experience meaningful in your life? If so, explain why. How has it affected you today?

  o. What, if anything, did you do that called for extra effort or work on your part beyond what everyone else had to do?

  p. Have you ever tried to teach someone else what you learned? If so, describe your efforts. If not, could you? Describe what you could teach.

  q. List each teacher who knew you individually. Circle the name of each teacher who would probably write you a letter of recommendation if asked.

r. Would any other teacher or administrator be able to write you a letter of recommendation based on the records of the school or program? If so, who?

s. Does the school or program have a reputation for excellence? If so, describe its reputation.

6. Legal Education and Training—Analysis Sheet

On a separate sheet of paper, list every *legal* course or training program that you have ever taken—formal or informal. Include individual classes, seminars, internships, etc., at formal schools, on the job, or through associations. Devote a separate sheet of paper to each course or program, writing its name at the top of the sheet and answering the following questions for it.

a. What were the exact dates of attendance?

b. Did you complete it? What evidence do you have that you completed it? A grade? A certificate?

c. What requirements did you meet in order to attend? Was there competition to attend? If so, describe in detail.

d. What text(s) did you use? Photocopy the table of contents in the text(s) and circle those items that you covered.

e. Attach a copy of the syllabus and circle those items in the syllabus that you covered.

f. Make two lists: a list of the major themes or subject areas that you were required to *know* or understand (content) and a list of the things that you were asked to *do* (skills).

g. Make a detailed list of everything that you were asked to write for the course or program, such as exams, memos, research papers, other reports. For every written work product other than exams, give the specific topic of what you wrote. Describe this topic in at least one sentence.

h. Which of these written work products could you now *rewrite* as a writing sample? Whom could you ask to evaluate what you rewrite to insure that it meets high standards?

i. Describe in detail everything else you were asked to do other than mere reading assignments. Examples: role-play a hearing, visit a court, verbally analyze a problem, interview a client, evaluate a title abstract, search a title, operate a computer, find something in the library, find something on the Internet, investigate a fact.

j. How were you evaluated? What evidence do you have or could you obtain of these evaluations? Do you have a transcript of your record?

k. Did you receive any special award or distinction? If so, describe it and state what evidence you have or could obtain that you received it.

l. Make a list of every favorable comment you can remember that was made about your work. What evidence of these comments do you have or could you obtain?

m. What, if anything, did you do that called for extra work or effort on your part beyond what everyone else had to do?

n. Describe the most valuable aspect of what you learned.

o. Have you ever tried to teach anyone else what you learned? If so, describe your efforts. If not, could you? Describe what you could teach.

p. Describe every individual who evaluated you. Could you obtain a letter of recommendation from these individuals?

7. Notes on Résumé Writing

It is important that you have an open mind about résumés. There is no correct format. Different people have different views. In the best of all worlds, you will be able to do some background research on the law office where you are applying for work and will learn what kind of résumé (in form and content) that office prefers. When this type of research is not possible, you must do the best you can to predict what kind of a résumé will be effective.

On this page in the Notebook, you should collect ideas about résumés from a wide variety of people such as:

Teachers   Program administrators
Working paralegals   Unemployed paralegals
Paralegal supervisors   Legal administrators
Fellow students   Attorneys whom you know
Personnel officers   Authors of books and articles on
Placement officers   finding employment
Legal secretaries   Others?

You want to collect different points of view on questions such as:

- What is an ideal résumé?
- What are the major mistakes that a résumé writer can make?
- What is the best way to phrase a career objective?
- How long should the résumé be?
- In what order should the data in the résumé be presented?
- How detailed should the résumé be?
- What kind of personal data should be included and omitted?
- How do you phrase educational experiences to make them relevant to the job you are seeking?
- How do you phrase employment experiences to make them relevant to the job you are seeking?
- How do you show that nonlegal experiences (school or work) can be relevant to a legal job?
- How do you handle potentially embarrassing facts, e.g., frequent job changes, low course grades?
- What should the cover letter for the résumé say?

8. Draft of General Résumé

Prepare a general résumé and include it here. We are calling it general because it is not directed at any specific job. It should be comprehensive with no page limitation. Use the guidelines, questions, and checklists in this Notebook to help you identify your strengths. The résumés you write for actual job searches will be shorter, specialized, and tailored to the job you are seeking. Before you write specialized résumés, however, you should write a general one that will be your main point of reference in preparing these other résumés. The general résumé will probably never be submitted anywhere. Take at least one full day to compile the general résumé after carefully thinking about the data needed for it.

9. Drafts of Specialized Résumés

Every time you write a résumé that is tailored to a specific job, include a copy here. Also include several practice copies of specialized résumés. While taking a course in corporate law, for example, write a résumé in which you pursue an opening at a law office for a corporate paralegal. For each résumé that you write (practice or real), solicit the comments of teachers, administrators, other students, working paralegals, attorneys, etc. Include these comments in this section of the Notebook.

10. Writing Samples

The importance of collecting a fairly large pool of writing samples cannot be overemphasized. Even if you eventually use only a few of them, the value of preparing them is enormous. The following characteristics should apply to *each* writing sample:

- It is your own work.
- It is clearly and specifically identified. The heading at the top tells the reader what the writing is.
- It is typed (handwritten work should be typed).
- There are no spelling or grammatical errors in it.
- Its appearance is professional.
- Someone whom you respect has evaluated it before you put it in final form.
- You feel that it is a high-quality product.
- It does not violate anyone's right to privacy or confidentiality. (If the sample pertains to real people or events, you have disguised all names or other identifying features.)

There are two main kinds of writing samples: those that are assigned in school or at work and those you generate on your own.

Examples of Required Work That You Could Turn into a Writing Sample

- A memorandum of law
- A legal research report or memo
- An answer to a problem in a textbook
- An exam answer
- An intake memorandum of law
- A complaint
- An answer to a complaint
- A motion
- A set of interrogatories
- Answers to a set of interrogatories
- An index to discovery documents
- A digest of one or more discovery documents
- Other memos, studies, or reports
- Articles of incorporation and bylaws

Any of the above writing samples could be generated on your own if they are not required in your coursework. Ask your teachers or supervisors to help you identify written pieces that you could create. Also consider writing an article for one of the many newsletters of paralegal associations (see Appendix B). The article could cover an aspect of your education or work experience. You could write about why you want to become a paralegal. You might write a response or reaction to someone else's article in a paralegal newsletter or magazine. Even if what you write is not published in a newsletter, it might still become a writing sample if it meets the criteria listed above.

11. Contacts—Attorneys You Already Know or with Whom You Have Any Indirect Association

Make a list of attorneys as described in Strategy 6 in this chapter, page 80. Include their names, addresses, and phone numbers. Not only do you want to know whether any of these attorneys are interested in hiring paralegals, but equally important, you want to know if they can give you any leads to other employers who might be interested in hiring.

12. Contacts—Employed Paralegals

You want to talk with as many employed paralegals as you can to obtain leads to possible positions, as well as general guidelines for the job search. Make a list of the names, addresses, and phone numbers of all the paralegals that you contact. Include notes on what they told you. If they have nothing useful to say at the present time, ask them if you could check back with them in several months and if you could leave your name and number with them in the event that they come across anything in the future. See page 78 for ideas on how to locate employed paralegals for this kind of networking.

13. Contacts and Tasks—General

Below you will find a general checklist of contacts and tasks that you should consider in your job search. Take notes on the results of these contacts and tasks and include these notes here if they are not included elsewhere in the Notebook. Your notes should include what you did, when, whom you contacted, their address and phone number, what was said, what follow-up is still needed, etc.

- Attorneys with whom you already have a direct or indirect association
- Employed paralegals
- Other paralegals searching for work; they may be willing to share leads that were unproductive for them, especially if you do likewise
- Contacts provided by your placement office
- Want ads in general circulation newspapers
- Want ads in legal newspapers
- Want ads and job bank openings listed in paralegal newsletters
- General directories of attorneys, such as *Martindale-Hubbell* and *West's Legal Directory*
- Special directories of attorneys, such as the *Directory of Corporate Counsel*
- Information from placement offices of local law schools
- Employment agencies specializing in paralegal placement
- Staffing agencies specializing in support staff and paralegal placement
- Employment agencies specializing primarily in attorney placement
- Bar association meetings open to the public
- Legal secretaries who may have leads
- Legal administrators who may have leads
- Local attorneys who have written articles in bar journals
- Stories in legal newspapers on recent large cases that are in litigation or are about to go into litigation (page 88)
- Local and national politicians who represent your area
- Service companies and consulting firms (page 46)

14. Job Interview Checklist

1. _____ Exact location of interview
2. _____ Time of arrival
3. _____ Professional appearance in dress
4. _____ Extra copies of résumé
5. _____ Extra copies of writing samples
6. _____ Copies of your transcripts
7. _____ Name of person(s) who will conduct interview
8. _____ Background research on the firm or company so that you know the kind of law it practices, why it is considering hiring paralegals, etc.
9. _____ Role-playing of job interview in advance with a friend
10. _____ Preparation for difficult questions that might be asked, such as why you left your last job so soon after starting it
11. Preparation of questions that you will ask regarding:
    _____ Responsibilities of position
    _____ Skills needed for the position
    _____ Methods of supervision

_____ Office's prior experience with paralegals
_____ Career ladder for paralegals
_____ Relationship between paralegals, secretaries, and other clerical staff
_____ Client contact
_____ Opportunities for growth
_____ Methods of evaluating paralegals
_____ Continuing education
_____ Billable hours expected of paralegals
_____ Availability of systems
_____ Working conditions (typing, photocopying, office, etc.)
_____ Travel
_____ Overtime
_____ Computers and other equipment use
_____ Compensation and fringe benefits (see Exhibit 2.14)
12. _____ Follow-up letter

15. Job Interview—Analysis Sheet

Write out the following information *after* each job interview that you have.

1. Date of interview
2. Name, address, and phone number of firm or company where you interviewed
3. Name(s) and phone number(s) of interviewer(s)
4. Kind of position that was open
5. Date you sent the follow-up letter
6. What you need to do next (send list of references, send writing samples, provide missing information that you did not have with you during the interview, etc.)
7. Your impressions of the interview (how you think you did, what surprised you, what you would do differently the next time you have an interview)
8. Notes on why you were not offered the job
9. Notes on why you turned down the job offered

16. Record Keeping

You need a system to keep track of the steps taken to date. See Exhibit 2.17 (Record Keeping and the Job Search). In addition, keep a calendar where you record important future dates, such as when you must make follow-up calls, when the local paralegal association meets, etc.

Section F
YOUR SECOND JOB

If you examine want ads for paralegals (p. 82), you will find that most prospective employers want paralegals with experience. The market for such individuals is excellent. But if you are *new* to the field, you are caught in the dilemma of not being able to find a job without experience (full-time or temporary) and not being able to get experience without a job. How do you handle this classic Catch-22 predicament?

● You work even harder to compile an impressive résumé. You make sure that you have collected a substantial writing-sample file. Such writing samples are often the closest equivalent to prior job experience available to you.

> My "advice is to get your foot in the door of a law firm doing *anything* necessary to obtain practical experience."
>
> —Cheryl Weaver-Meister (November 1995)

Exhibit 2.17 Record Keeping and the Job Search

PERSON/OFFICE CONTACTED	
HOW CONTACTED (PHONE, LETTER)	
DATE OF CONTACT	
ADDRESS	
NOTES ON THE CONTACT	
DATE FURTHER CONTACT NEEDED	
DATE RÉSUMÉ SENT/DELIVERED	
DATE WRITING SAMPLE SENT/DELIVERED	
DATE OF INTERVIEW	
NOTES ON INTERVIEW	
DATE THANK-YOU NOTE SENT	
DATE FURTHER CONTACT NEEDED	

(Fill out one card per contact; file alphabetically.)

- When you talk to other paralegals, you seek specific advice on how to present yourself as an applicant for your first job.
- You consider doing some volunteer work as a way to acquire experience for your résumé. Legal service offices (page 43) and public interest law firms (page 45) often encourage volunteer (i.e., pro bono) work. A recent law school graduate struggling to start a practice may be another option.
- Contact four or five law firms and offer to perform "runner" services for them at low or no cost, e.g., delivery of documents, filing, service of process.
- You may have to reassess what you will accept for your first job. Perhaps you can eventually turn the first job into a more acceptable position. You may simply use it to gain the experience necessary for landing a better second job.

Once you have had several years of experience and have demonstrated your competence, you will find many more employment options available to you. You will find it substantially easier to negotiate salary and articulate your skills in a job interview. You can also consider other kinds of employment where your legal training, skills, expertise, and experience are valuable. It is not uncommon for a paralegal to be recruited by former or active clients of a first employer. Numerous business contacts are made in the course of a job; these contacts could turn into new careers. In Exhibit 2.18 you will find a list of

Exhibit 2.18   Positions for Experienced Paralegals

- Paralegal supervisor
- Law office administrator (legal administrator)
- Law firm marketing administrator
- Paralegal consultant
- Freelance/independent paralegal
- Law librarian/assistant
- Paralegal teacher
- Paralegal school administrator
- Placement officer
- Bar association attorney referral coordinator
- Court administrator
- Court clerk
- Sales representative for legal publisher/vendor
- Investigator
- Customs inspector
- Compliance and enforcement inspector
- Occupational safety and health inspector
- Lobbyist
- Legislative assistant
- Real estate management consultant
- Real estate specialist
- Real estate portfolio manager
- Land acquisitions supervisor
- Title examiner
- Independent title abstractor
- Abstractor
- Systems analyst
- Computer analyst
- Computer sales representative
- Bank research associate
- Trust officer (Trust administrator)
- Trust associate
- Assistant loan administrator
- Fiduciary accountant
- Financial analyst/planner

- Investment analyst
- Assistant estate administrator
- Enrolled agent
- Equal employment opportunity specialist
- Employee benefit specialist/consultant
- Pension specialist
- Pension administrator
- Compensation planner
- Corporate trademark specialist
- Corporate manager
- Securities analyst
- Securities compliance officer
- Insurance adjustor
- Actuarial associate
- Claims examiner
- Claims coordinator
- Director of risk management
- Environmental specialist
- Editor for a legal or business publisher
- Recruiter, legal employment agency
- Personnel director
- Administrative law judge
- Arbitrator
- Mediator
- Internal security inspector
- Evidence technician
- Demonstrative evidence specialist
- Fingerprint technician
- Polygraph examiner
- Probation officer
- Parole officer
- Corrections officer
- Politician
- Etc.

some of the types of positions that paralegals have taken after they demonstrated their ability and acquired legal experience.

In short, you face a different market once you have acquired a record of experience and accomplishment. You are in greater demand in law firms and businesses. Furthermore, your legal skills are readily transferable to numerous law-related positions.

Chapter Summary

Someone once said that finding a job is a job in itself. This is especially true in the current market. You will need determination to find what you want. The first step is to become informed about where paralegals work and what they do at those locations. The first part of this chapter was designed to provide you with this information. The major employers of paralegals are private law firms, the government, legal service offices, corporations, and other businesses. While other settings also exist, these are the largest. After examining these settings, we looked at approximately forty-five specialties such as bankruptcy and criminal law. Our focus was the identification of paralegal functions in the specialties and a paralegal perspective of what life is like in each. For the specialties where most paralegals work—corporate law, estates, family law, litigation, real estate, and tort law—quotations from job ads identified traits and skills employers want.

In the second half of the chapter, we turned to strategies for finding employment. The strategies addressed the following questions: When should you begin the search? How do you compile a job hunting notebook? How do you organize an employment workshop? How do you locate working paralegals in order to obtain leads to employment? How do you arrange an informational interview? How can you use local paralegal associations as a resource? How do you locate potential employers? How do you do background research on potential employers? What should your résumé contain? What is an effective cover letter? What kinds of writing samples should you prepare, and when should you start preparing them? How should you prepare for a job interview? What kinds of questions should you anticipate? What kinds of questions should you ask? How can you organize all of the contacts, events, and pieces of paper that are involved in a comprehensive job search?

Finally, we examined alternative career opportunities for paralegals, particularly for those who have gained paralegal experience on the job.

KEY TERMS

private law firm, 39
Paralegal Specialist, 40
General Schedule (GS), 40
Office of Personnel
    Management, 42
indigents, 43
pro bono, 44
corporate counsel, 44
special interest groups, 45
group legal services, 45
legal insurance, 45

public defenders, 45
assigned counsel, 45
freelance paralegals, 45
service companies, 46
conflicts specialist, 58
legalman, 66
land technician, 68
landmen, 68
public benefits, 69
tort, 72
PI, 72

job bank, 78
informational interview, 79
networking, 81
blind ad, 83
staffing agency, 86
*Martindale-Hubbell Law
    Directory*, 86
CLE, 87
Internet, 89
World Wide Web, 89
chronological résumé, 94

functional résumé, 94
parallelism, 95
cover letter, 98
group interview, 102
open-ended question, 103
closed-ended question, 103
hypothetical question, 104
conflict of interest, 109

Appendix 2.A   Employment in Selected Large Law Firms and Corporations

Most of the employers listed in this chart are law firms. The exceptions are the entries with business notations after their names (e.g., "Inc.," "Corp.," "Co."). Long law firm names have been shortened to the first two to three names of the firm. (Commas are not used between names.) After each employer, you will find one or two numbers separated by a slash (/). The first number is the number of attorneys in that office. The number after the slash is the number of paralegals in that office. If the latter information is not available, the single number refers to attorneys. This is useful to know because, in general, an office with a relatively large number of attorneys will often employ a proportionately large number of paralegals. The list is selective and is not meant to indicate the largest offices in any particular city. To obtain the address and phone numbers of these offices, check standard phone directories (white and yellow pages) and legal directories such as *Martindale-Hubbell Law Directory* (see photo on page 87) or *West's Legal Directory* online (see Exhibit 2.7 in chapter 2). When you call the office, ask if there is a paralegal manager or coordinator you could speak to about employment opportunities. Otherwise, ask for the personnel department.

ALABAMA
Birmingham
  Balch Bingham: 50
  Bradley Arant Rose: 127/22
  Burr Forman: 105/35
  Johnson Barton Proctor: 43/6
  Lange Simpson Robinson: 58
  Maynard Cooper Gale: 90/14
  Sirote Permutt: 98/27
  Torchmark Corp.: 25
Mobile
  Hand Arendall Bedsole: 48
Montgomery
  HB Daniels Corp.: 60

ARIZONA
Phoenix
  Beus Gilbert Morrill: 32/8
  Brown Bain: 75/20
  Bryan Cave: 29/12
  Fennemore Craig: 104/14
  Gallagher Kennedy: 79/10
  Jennings Strouss Salmon: 65/10
  Lewis Roca: 108/28
  Morrison Hecker: 30
  O'Connor Cavanagh: 120/27
  Quarles Brady: 40/7
  Snell Wilmer: 139/34
  Squire Sanders Dempsey: 39/9
  Steptoe Johnson: 25/5
  Streich Lang: 91/21
  Teilborg Sanders: 47/12
Tucson
  Snell Wilmer: 28/4

ARKANSAS
Little Rock
  Friday Eldredge Clark: 77
  Rose Law Firm: 49/3
  Wright Lindsey Jennings: 57

CALIFORNIA
Bakersfield
  Borton Petrini Conron: 97
Beverly Hills
  Litton Industries Inc.: 46
  Rosenfeld Meyer Susman: 55
Burbank
  Walt Disney Co.: 117
Calabasas
  Lockheed Corp.: 50
Century City
  Gibson Dunn Crutcher: 27
  Loeb Loeb: 70
  O'Melveny Myers: 56/7
Costa Mesa
  Latham Watkins: 57/14
  Paul Hastings Janofsky: 36/7
  Robins Kaplan Miller: 17/9
  Rutan Tucker: 97/7
Cupertino
  Apple Computer Inc.: 50
Fresno
  Baker Manock Jensen: 45/10
  McCormick Barstow Sheppard: 60
Glendale
  Knapp Peterson Clarke: 63
Irvine
  Berger Kahn Shafton: 39
  Bryan Cave: 21/6
  Gibson Dunn Crutcher: 77/11
  Morrison Foerster: 38/4
  Palmieri Tyler Wiener: 38/7
  Snell Wilmer: 33/7
Long Beach
  Keesal Young Logan: 56/9
Los Angeles
  Adams Duque Hazeline: 57/5
  ARCO: 90

Arter Hadden: 56
Atlantic Richfield Co.: 111
Baker Hostetler: 66/11
Brobeck Phleger Harrison: 71/12
Buchalter Nemer Fields: 72/18
Fulbright Jaworski: 41/4
Gibson Dunn Crutcher: 218/27
Graham James: 108/20
Greenberg Glusker Fields: 86/12
Hill Wynne Troop: 104
Irell Manella: 120/22
Jeffer Mangels Butler: 81/12
Jones Day Reavis: 86/18
Katten Muchin Zavis: 64/6
Kirkland Ellis: 35/12
Knobbe Martens Olson: 70/18
Latham Watkins: 201/27
Lewis D'Amato Brisbois: 101
Loeb Loeb: 158/21
Manatt Phelps Philips: 162/22
McDermott Will Emery: 56/7
McKenna Cuneo: 54/2
Mitchell Silberberg Knupp: 122/20
Morgan Lewis Bockius: 81/12
Morrison Foerster: 96/14
Munger Tolles Olson: 98/24
Musick Peeler Garrett: 80/13
Nossaman Gunther Knox: 50/20
Occidental Petroleum Corp.: 102
O'Melveny Myers: 223/70
Orrick Herrington Sutcliff: 39/11
Paul Hastings Janofsky: 178/15
Pillsbury Madison Sutro: 129/16
Sheppard Mullin Richter: 137/16
Sidley Austin: 95/14
Skadden Arps Slate: 94/13
Sonnenschein Nath: 56/8
Times Mirror Co.: 30

Tuttle Taylor: 49/6
Unocol Corp.: 48
Menlo Park
Weil Gotshal Manges: 22/8
Mountain View
Sun Microsystems Inc.: 50
Newport Beach
Irell Manella: 23
Knobbe Martens Olson: 46
McDermott Will Emery: 21/6
O'Melveny Myers: 56/15
Sheppard Mullin Richter: 27/3
Stradling Yocca Carlson: 77
Oakland
Larson Burham: 73/9
Crosby Heafey Roach: 152/31
Palo Alto
Brobeck Phleger Harrison: 75/15
Cooley Godward Castro: 142/49
Fenwick West: 140/39
Gray Cary Ware: 112/26
Heller Ehrman White: 51/16
Hewlett-Packard Co.: 116
Morrison Foerster: 61/14
Wilson Sonsini Goodrich: 300/110
Redwood City
Ropers Majeski Kohn: 70
Riverside
Best Best Krieger: 63/18
Sacramento
Diepenbrock Wulff Plant: 50/8
Downey Brand Seymour: 64/8
Kronick Moskovitz Tiedemann:
60/16
McDonough Holland Allen: 65/14
Orrick Herrington Sutcliffe: 29/9
San Diego
Ault Deuprey Jones: 52
Baker McKenzie: 31
Brobeck Phleger Harrison: 35/5
Cooley Godward Castro: 26/10
Duckor Spradling: 30
Edwards White Sooy: 33
Gray Cary Ware: 116/22
Higgs Fletcher Mack: 46
Hillyer Irwin: 35
Latham Watkins: 57/11
Lewis D'Amato Brisbois: 34
Littler Mendelson Fastiff: 28/2
Luce Forward Hamilton: 149/19

McInnis Fitzgerald Rees: 55
Milberg Weiss Bershad: 48
Neil Dymott Perkins: 31
Pillsbury Madison Sutro: 33/7
Procopio Cory Hargraves: 38
Seltzer Caplan Wilkins: 57/21
Sheppard Mullin Richter: 37/6
Wingert Grebing Anello: 27
San Francisco
Baker McKenzie: 47
BankAmerica Corp.: 175
Brobeck Phleger Harrison: 383/68
Bronson Bronson McKinnon: 87/14
Chevron Corp.: 150
Cooley Godward Castro: 74/20
Farella Braun Martel: 80/21
Folger Levin: 42/13
Gibson Dunn Crutcher: 40/6
Gordon Rees: 110
Graham James: 75/15
Hancock Rothert Bunshoft: 89/49
Hanson Bridgett Marcus: 83/16
Heller Ehrman White: 162/54
Howard Rice Nemerovski: 103/22
Jackson Tufts Cole: 41/13
Landels Ripley Diamond: 66/18
Latham Watkins: 59/12
Lillick Charles: 71/8
Littler Mendelson Fastiff: 75/6
Long Levit: 60
McCutchen Doyle Brown: 147/24
Morrison Foerster: 198/60
Murphy Weir Butler: 36/8
O'Melveny Myers: 41/8
Orrik Herrington Sutcliffe: 120/27
Pacific Gas & Electric Co.: 80
Pacific Telesis Group: 87
Paul Hastings Janofsky: 54/5
Pillsbury Madison Sutro: 254/46
Sedwick Detert Moran: 102
Sheppard Mullin Richter: 37/6
Sonnenschein Nath: 54/5
Steefel Levitt Weiss: 57/12
Thelen Marrin Johnson: 115/24
Townsend Townsend: 53/13
Transamerica Corp.: 50
UnionBanCal Corp.: 32
Wells Fargo Co.: 60
San Jose
Jackson Tufts Cole: 18/5

Littler Mendelson Fastiff: 32/2
Ropers Majeski Kohn: 30
Skjerven Morrill MacPherson: 57/12
Santa Clara
Intel Corp.: 50
Santa Monica
Bryan Cave: 28/6
Haight Brown Bonesteel: 139
Seal Beach
Rockwell International Corp.: 52
COLORADO
Englewood
U.S. West, Inc.: 77
Denver
Ballard Spahr Andrews: 29/4
Davis Graham Stubbs: 84/15
Faegre Benson: 32/5
Gibson Dunn Crutcher: 33/7
Gorsuch Kirgis: 55/11
Holland Hart: 129/16
Holme Roberts Owen: 127/31
Kutak Rock: 41/5
Leboeuf Lamb Green: 28/4
Morrison Foerster: 19/6
Moye Giles O'Keefe: 31/3
Parcel Mauro Hultin: 62
Rothgerber Appel Powers: 52/8
Sherman Howard: 97/24
CONNECTICUT
Bridgeport
Pullman Comley: 60
Zeldes Needle Cooper: 29/5
Danbury
Union Carbide Corp.: 40
Fairfield
General Electric Co.: 424
Hartford
Aetna Life and Casualty Co.: 120
Cummings Lockwood: 27
Day Berry Howard: 133/36
Hallorin Sage: 55
Hebb Gitlin: 60/17
ITT Hartford Group Inc.: 57
Murtha Cullina Richter: 68/16
Pepe Hazard: 61/10
Robinson Cole: 102/15
Schatz Schatz Ribicoff: 66
Shipman Goodwin: 94/28
United Technologies Corp.: 24/5
Updike Kelly Spellacy: 49/6

Appendix 2.A   **Employment in Selected Large Law Firms and Corporations —continued**

New Haven
  Bergman Horowitz Reynolds: 28/9
  Tyler Cooper Alcorn: 71/14
  Wiggin Dana: 106/31
Stamford
  Cummings Lockwood: 84/13
  Day Berry Howard: 43/10
  GTE Corp.: 120
  Kelley Drye Warren: 36/6
  Paul Hastings Janofsky: 35/4
  Pitney Bowes Inc.: 21
  Robinson Cole: 25
  Winthrop Stimson Putnam: 21/2
  Xerox Corp.: 141

DELAWARE
Wilmington
  Columbia Gas System Inc.: 51
  Duane Morris Heckschter: 21/3
  E. I. du Pont de Nemours Co.: 241
  Morris James Hitchens: 41/16
  Morris Nichols Arsht: 64/13
  Potter Anderson Corroon: 56/17
  Prickett Jones Elliott: 45
  Richards Layton Finger: 84/18
  Skadden Arps Slate: 43/15
  Young Conaway Stargatt: 58/21

DISTRICT OF COLUMBIA
  Akin Gump Strauss: 246/73
  Arent Fox Kintner: 196/39
  Arnold Porter: 263/74
  Arter Hadden: 55
  Baker Hostetler: 66/11
  Bryan Cave: 67/8
  Cleary Gottlieb Steen: 69/13
  Covington Burling: 296/82
  Crowell Moring: 212/62
  Dewey Ballantine: 60/19
  Dickstein Shapiro Morin: 175/25
  Dow Lohnes Albertson: 113/24
  Epstein Becker Green: 63/5
  Federal Natl Mortgage Assn.: 63
  Finnegan Henderson: 153/51
  Foley Lardner: 76/20
  Fried Frank Harris: 105/14
  Fulbright Jaworski: 72/21
  Hogan Hartson: 434/50
  Holland Knight: 90/14
  Howrey Simon: 280/56
  Hunton Williams: 66/11
  Jones Day Reavis: 176/43

King Spalding: 64/19
Kirkland Ellis: 86/12
Kirkpatrick Lockhart: 108/32
Latham Watkins: 89/17
Marriott International Inc.: 60
McDermott Will Emery: 128/26
McKenna Cuneo: 121/13
Miller Chevalier: 93/16
Morgan Lewis Bockius: 214/37
Morrison Foerster: 64/15
O'Melveny Myers: 61/17
Patton Boggs: 140/26
Paul Hastings Janofsky: 49/9
Piper Marbury: 87/12
Reed Smith Swaw: 94/9
Seyfarth Shaw Fairweather: 52/4
Shaw Pitman Potts: 252/36
Sidley Austin: 118/19
Skadden Arps Slate: 150/45
Squire Sanders Dempsey: 47/6
Steptoe Johnson: 213/36
Sutherland Asbill Brennan: 111/20
Swidler Berlin: 138/28
Venable Baetjer Howard: 71/7
Verner Liipfert Bernhard: 143/15
Vinson Elkins: 60/9
Weil Gotshal Manges: 41/7
Wiley Rein Fielding: 177/41
Wilke Farr Gallagher: 50/9
Wilmer Cutler Pickering: 188/82
Williams Connolly: 136
Winston Strawn: 110/6

FLORIDA
Boca Raton
  Proskauer Rose Goetz: 15/4
  W. R. Grace & Co.: 80
Ft. Lauderdale
  Becker Poliakoff: 37
  Ruden McClosky: 88/22
  Holland Knight: 34/6
  Tripp Scott Conklin: 31/26
Jacksonville
  Barnett Banks Inc.: 19
  Foley Lardner: 40/5
  Holland Knight: 37/15
  Leboeuf Lamb Greene: 21/4
  Mahoney Adams Criser: 50/10
  Rogers Towers Bailey: 35/7
Lakeland
  Holland Knight: 24/5

Melbourne
  Harris Corp.: 34
Miami
  Adoro Zeder: 50
  Fowler White Burnett: 46/15
  Greenberg Traurig: 136/22
  Gunster Yoakley Valdes: 30/6
  Kenney Nachwalter: 20/7
  Holland Night: 84/16
  McDermott Will Emery: 20/5
  Mershon Sawyer Johnson: 50
  Morgan Lewis Bockius: 38/6
  Popham Haik Schnobrich: 30/11
  Rubin Baum Levin: 26/5
  Ruden Barnett McClosky: 24
  Shutts Bowen: 66/14
  Stearns Weaver Miller: 54/9
  Steel Hector Davis: 119/22
  Walton Lantaff Schroeder: 40
  Weil Gotshal Manges: 20/5
  White Case: 33/5
  Wicker Smith Tutan: 25/10
Orlando
  Akerman Senterfitt Eidson: 53
  Baker Hostetler: 44/13
  Broad Cassel: 27
  Foley Lardner: 50/5
  Holland Knight: 27/5
  Lowndes Drosdick Doster: 70
  Maguire Voorhis Wells: 61
  Rumberger Kirk Caldwell: 35
Tampa
  Annis Mitchell Cockry: 47/11
  Bush Ross Gardner: 27/3
  Carlton Fields Ward: 89/17
  Foley Lardner: 21/6
  Fowler White Gillen: 139/35
  Holland Knight: 67/14
  MacFarlane Ausley Ferguson: 62
  Shumaker Loop Kendrick: 23/4
  Trenam Kemker Scharf: 55/9
West Palm Beach
  Gunster Yoakley Valdes: 117/27
  Honigman Miller Schwartz: 12/6
  Quarles Brady: 15/6
  Steel Hector Davis: 35/7

GEORGIA
Atlanta
  Alston Bird: 297/39
  Arnall Golden Gregory: 87/21

Appendix 2.A   Employment in Selected Large Law Firms and Corporations —continued

BellSouth Corp.: 140
Coca-Cola Co.: 139
Dow Lohnes Albertson: 21/5
Drew Eckl Farnam: 78/25
Fisher Phillips: 73
Georgia Pacific Corp.: 45
Holland Knight: 53/11
Hunton Williams: 61/14
Jones Day Reavis: 86/16
Kilpatrick Cody: 74/48
King Spalding: 241/63
Long Aldridge Norman: 102/23
Nelson Mullins Riley: 49
Paul Hastings Janofsky: 72/16
Powell Goldstein Frazer: 153/26
Smith Gambrell Russell: 110/15
Swift Currie McGhee: 65/14
Sutherland Asbill Brennan: 120/23
Troutman Sanders: 190/34

HAWAII
Honolulu
  Ashford Wriston: 39/7
  Cades Schutte Fleming: 71/20
  Carlsmith Ball Wichman: 50/13
  Cronin Fried Sekiya: 16/6
  Goodsill Anderson Quinn: 95/16
  McCorriston Miho Miller: 42/10

IDAHO
Boise
  Boise Cascade Corp.: 16
  Holland Hart: 13/4

ILLINOIS
Abbott Park
  Abbott Laboratories: 54
Bloomington
  State Farm Mutual: 76
Chicago
  Altheimer Gray: 172/22
  Ameritech Corp.: 69
  Amoco Corp.: 181
  Arnstein Lehr: 70/11
  Baker McKenzie: 161/22
  Bell Boyd Lloyd: 159/19
  Cassidy Schade Gloor: 67
  Chapman Cutler: 166/10
  Clausen Miller Gorman: 101
  D'Ancona Pflaum: 78/8
  First Chicago NBD Corp.: 100
  FMC Corp.: 40
  Foley Lardner: 46/7

Gardner Carton Douglas: 180/22
Goldberg Kohn Bell: 52/8
Hinshaw Culbertson: 330/47
Holleb Coff: 131/24
Hopkins Sutter: 132/19
Jenner Block: 321/52
Johnson Bell: 84
Jones Day Reavis: 105/15
Katten Muchin Zavis: 270/38
Keck Mahin Cate: 173/46
Kirkland Ellis: 300/62
Latham Watkins: 73/12
Lord Bissell Brook: 253/38
Mayer Brown Platt: 407/64
McDermott Will Emery: 262/37
Neal Gerber Eisenberg: 91
Peterson Ross: 81/13
Pretzel Stouffer: 80/12
Quaker Oats Co.: 22
Querrey Harrow: 98/4
Rooks Pitts Poust: 87/13
Ross Hardies: 126/12
Rudnick Wolfe: 211/40
Sachnoff Weaver: 79
Schiff Hardin Waite: 187/25
Sears Roebuck and Co.: 69
Seyfarth Shaw Fairweather: 195/11
Shefsky Froelich Devine: 40/11
Sidley Austin: 378/97
Skadden Arps Slate: 98/23
Sonnenschein Nath: 207/24
Vedder Price Kaufman: 142/19
Wildman Harrold Allen: 161/21
Willian Brinks Hofer: 94/10
Williams Montgomery: 80/3
Winston Strawn: 286/67
Deerfield
  Baxter International Inc.: 148
  Premark International Inc.: 22
Moline
  Deere & Co.: 25
Northbrook
  Allstate Corp.: 97
Oakbrook
  McDonald's Corp.: 61
  WMX Technologies: 98
Peoria
  Caterpillar Inc.: 56
  Heyl Royster: 36/7
Prospect Heights

Household International Inc.: 34
Schaumburg
  Motorola Inc.: 140

INDIANA
Fort Wayne
  Baker Daniels: 40/7
  Barnes Thornburg: 14/3
  Lincoln National Corp.: 45
Indianapolis
  Baker Daniels: 142/24
  Barnes Thornburg: 122/21
  Bingham Summers Welsh: 63/5
  Bose McKinney Evans: 64/10
  Eli Lilly and Co.: 70
  Ice Miller Donadio: 188/29
  Locke Reynolds Boyd: 82/16
  McHale Cook Welch: 33/2
South Bend
  Baker Daniels: 17/3
  Barnes Thornburg: 44/5

IOWA
Des Moines
  Davis Hockenberg Wine: 59/9
  Nymaster Goode McLaughlin: 64/5

KANSAS
Overland Park
  Blackwell Sanders Matheny: 28
  Bryan Cave: 91/18
  Shook Hardy Bacon: 19
  Wallace Saunders Austin: 50
Wichita
  Foulston Siefkin: 65
  Koch Industries Inc.: 47

KENTUCKY
Ashland
  Ashland Oil Co.: 87
Lexington
  Landrum Shouse: 43
  Stites Harbison: 45/9
  Wyatt Tarrant Combs: 42
Louisville
  Boehl Stopher Graves: 40/26
  Brown Todd Heyburn: 93/38
  Greenebaum Doll McDonald: 74/12
  Providian Corp.: 28
  Stites Harbison: 67/21
  Wyatt Tarrant Combs: 93/8

LOUISIANA
Baton Rouge

Appendix 2.A   Employment in Selected Large Law Firms and Corporations —continued

Adams Reese: 18
Kean Miller Hawthorne: 58
Phelps Dunbar: 22
New Orleans
Adams Reese: 92
Chaffe McCall Phillips: 62/14
Deutsch Kerrigan Stiles: 55
Jones Walker Waechter: 117/30
Lemie Kelleher: 58
Liskow Lewis: 58
McDermott International Inc.: 52
McGlinchey Stafford Lang: 84
Phelps Dunbar: 93/31
Stone Pigman Walther: 74/16
Shreveport
Cook Yancey King: 32/15

MAINE
Bangor
Eaton Peabody Bradford: 28/9
Portland
Ater Wynne Hewitt: 44
Bernstein Shur Sawyer: 53
Drummond Woodsum: 34/6
Pierce Atwood: 79/11
Preti Flaherty Beliveau: 46
UNUM Corp.: 40
Verrill Dana: 56/6

MARYLAND
Baltimore
Ballard Spahr Andrews: 28
Gebhardt Smith: 27/8
Goodell Devries Leech: 40/15
Gordon Feinblatt Rothman: 75/25
Hogan Hartson: 26
McGuire Woods Battle: 24/4
Miles Stockbridge: 102/16
Ober Kaler Grimes: 91/21
Piper Marbury: 157/29
Semmes Bowen Semmes: 102
Smith Somerville Case: 69/11
Tydings Rosenberg: 48/13
USG&G Corp.: 135
Venable Baetjer Howard: 132/14
Weinberg Green: 77/10
Whiteford Taylor Preston: 124/26
Bethesda
Martin Marietta Corp.: 90
Rockville
Shulman Rogers Gandal: 50
Silver Spring

Linowes Blocher: 44
Townson
Venable Baetjer Howard: 20

MASSACHUSETTS
Boston
Bank of Boston Corp.: 60
Brigham Dana Gould: 225/20
Brown Rudnick Freed: 85/14
Burns Levinson: 107
Choate Hall Stewart: 166/14
Day Berry Howard: 55/9
Edwards Angell: 34
Fish Richardson: 52/9
Fleet Financial Group Inc.: 50
Foley Hoag Eliot: 151/24
Gillette Co.: 35
Goldstein Manello: 55
Goodwin Procter Hoar: 302/44
Goulston Storrs: 106/27
Hale Dorr: 229/63
Hill Barlow: 100/24
Hinckley Allen Snyder: 100/36
Hutchins Wheeler Dittmar: 94/16
Kirkpatrick Lockhart: 36/4
McDermott Will Emery: 39/6
Mintz Levin Cohn: 182/52
Morrison Mahoney Miller: 135
Nutter McClennen Fish: 110/15
Palmer Dodge: 157/26
Parker Coulter Daley: 57
Peabody Arnold: 93/27
Peabody Brown: 88/16
Posternak Blankstein Lund: 50
Ropes Gray: 297/43
Sherburne Powers: 63/11
Skadden Arps Slate: 31/7
State Street Boston Corp.: 48
Sullivan Worcester: 117/19
Testa Hurwitz Thibeault: 174/23
Warner Stackpole: 61
Lexington
Raytheon Co.: 39
Maynard
Digital Equipment Corp.: 129
Springfield
Buckley Richardson Gelinas: 34/8
Mass Mutual Life Ins. Co.: 46
Worcester
Bowditch Dewey: 43/18
Mirich O'Connell Demallie: 44/16

MICHIGAN
Benton Harbor
Whirlpoorl Corp.: 30
Bloomfield Hills
Dickinson Wright Moon: 45/6
Dykema Gossett: 43/5
Howard Howard: 55
Miller Canfield Paddock: 22/10
Dearborn
Ford Motor Co.: 290/59
Detroit
Bodman Longley Dahling: 56/10
Bowman Brooke: 23/17
Butzel Long: 89/14
Clark Hill: 116/20
Dickinson Wright Moon: 230/40
Dykema Gossett: 123/24
General Motors Corp.: 389
Honigman Miller Schwartz: 156/28
Jaffe Raitt Heuer: 77/8
Kitch Drutchas Wagner: 79
Miller Canfield Paddock: 112/19
Pepper Hamilton Scheetz: 31/5
Plunkett Cooney: 82
Farmington Hills
Kohn Secrest Wardle: 50
Grand Rapids
Law Weathers Richards: 33/5
Mika Meyers Beckett: 35/5
Miller Johnson Snell: 74/14
Smith Haughey Rice: 56
Varnum Riddering Schmidt: 108/19
Warner Norcross Judd: 134/20
Highland Park
Chrysler Corp.: 61
Kalamazoo
Miller Canfield Paddock: 27/4
Upjohn Co.: 33
Lansing
Dickinson Wright Moon: 25/4
Foster Swift Collins: 65/12
Midland
Dow Chemical Co.: 171
Dow Corning Corp.: 38
Southfield
Sommers Schwartz Silver: 77
Sullivan Ward Bone: 50
Troy
Harness Dickey Pierce: 46

Appendix 2.A   Employment in Selected Large Law Firms and Corporations —continued

MINNESOTA
Bloomington
  Larkin Hoffman Daly: 77
Minneapolis
  Banc One Corp.: 100
  Best Flanagan: 48/7
  Bowman Brooke: 33/13
  Briggs Morgan: 125/24
  Doherty Rumble Butler: 50/15
  Dorsey Whitney: 270/43
  Faegre Benson: 223/33
  First Bank System Inc.: 30
  Fredrikson Byron: 122/19
  General Mills Inc.: 17
  Gray Plant Mooty: 110/26
  Honeywell Inc.: 50
  Kinney Lange: 26/5
  Leonard Street Deinard: 128/29
  Linquist Vennum: 99/12
  Maslon Edelman Borman: 57/15
  Meagher Geer: 68
  Merchant Gould: 83/16
  Moss Barnett: 55
  Oppenheimer Wolff: 137/24
  Popham Haik Schnobrich: 120/34
  Rider Bennett Egan: 85
  Robins Kaplan Miller: 133/48
  Shatz Paquin Lockridge: 36/8
  Zell Larson: 76
St. Paul
  Briggs Morgan: 66
  Doherty Rumble Butler: 108/17
  Minn. Mining Mfg. Co. (3M): 148
  St. Paul Cos. Inc.: 300
  Winthrop Weinstine: 55

MISSISSIPPI
Jackson
  Butler Snow O'Mara: 65
  Watkins Ludlam Stennis: 52/17

MISSOURI
Kansas City
  Armstrong Teasdale Schlafly: 26
  Blackwell Sanders: 172/35
  Bryan Cave: 91/18
  Gage Tucker: 63
  Hillix Brewer Hoffhaus: 33/11
  Husch Eppenberger: 31/11
  Lathrop Norquist: 77/10
  Lewis Rice Fingersh: 32
  Morrison Hecker: 84

  Posinelli White Vardeman: 88/28
  Shook Hardy Bacon: 200/41
  Shughart Thomson Kilroy: 99
  Smith Gill Fisher: 62/14
  Spencer Fane Britt: 68
  Sprint Corp.: 71
  Stinson Mag Fizzell: 105/14
  Watson Marshall: 62
St. Louis
  Anheuser-Busch Companies: 45
  Armstrong Teasdale: 134/18
  Boatmen's Bancshares Inc.: 23
  Brown James: 50
  Bryan Cave: 176/26
  Coburn Croft: 79/26
  Emerson Electric Co.: 24
  Evans Dixon: 79
  Gallop Johnson Neuman: 74/13
  Greensfelder Hemker Gale: 88
  Husch Eppenberger: 82/19
  Lewis Rice Fingersh: 101/14
  Mallinckrodt Group Inc.: 25
  McDonnell Douglas Corp.: 50
  Monsanto Co.: 90
  Peper Martin Jensen: 75/13
  Ralston Purina Co.: 40
  Sonnenschein Nath: 40/7
  Stolar Partnership: 42/7
  Thompson Coburn: 210/44

NEBRASKA
Omaha
  Baird Holm McEachen: 50/2
  Kutak Rock: 98/10
  McGrath North Mullin: 66

NEVADA
Las Vegas
  Lionel Sawyer Collins: 47/11
Reno
  Lionel Sawyer Collins: 18/3

NEW HAMPSHIRE
Concord
  Orr Reno: 40/7
Manchester
  Divine Millimet Branch: 59/22
  McLane Graf Raulerson: 44/17
  Sheehan Phinney Bass: 60
  Wiggin Nourie: 46/15

NEW JERSEY
Basking Ridge
  AT&T: 385

Camden
  Campbell Soup Co.: 22
Hackensack
  Cole Schotz Meisel: 74/15
  Harwood Lloyd: 47
Haddonfield
  Archer Greiner: 75/19
Islin
  Hanson Industries: 40
Livingston
  Morgan Melhuish Monaghan: 56
Madison
  Schering-Plough Corp.: 46
Middletown
  Giordana Halleran Ciesla: 65
Morris Plains
  Warner-Lambert Co.: 46
Morristown
  Allied-Signal Inc.: 75
  McElroy Deutsch Mulvaney: 55
  Pitney Hardin Kipp: 153/33
  Porzio Bromberg Newman: 44/33
  Riker Danzig Scherer: 151/33
  Shanley Fisher: 106/25
Newark
  Carpenter Bennett Morrissey: 80
  Crummy Del Deo Dolan: 107/20
  Leboeuf Lamb Greene: 26/8
  McCarter English: 192/50
  Prudential Insurance Co.: 202
  Robinson St. John Wayne: 66
  Sills Cummis Zuckerman: 135/25
  Wilson Elser Moskowitz: 27
New Brunswick
  Johnson Johnson: 52
Park Ridge
  Sony Corp. of America: 46
Parsippany
  BASF Corp.: 30
Princeton
  Dechert Price Rhoads: 24/1
  Drinker Biddle Reath: 37/15
  Stark Stark: 60
  Summit Bancorp.: 24
Roseland
  Brach Eichler Rosenberg: 55
  Connel Foley Geiser: 73
  Grotta Glassman Hoffman: 52
  Hannoch Weisman: 81/17
  Lowenstein Sandler Kohl: 131/36

Appendix 2.A   Employment in Selected Large Law Firms and Corporations —continued

Wolff Samson: 61/4
Secaucus
Waters McPherson McNeill: 54
Short Hills
Budd Larner Gross: 65/14
Somerville
Hoechst Celanese Corp.: 54
Norris McLaughlin Marcus: 57/11
Wayne
American Cyanamid Co.: 38
Wayne Camp Corp.: 13
Whitehouse Station
Merck & Co.: 90
Woodbridge
Greenbaum Rowe Smith: 70/14
Wilentz Goldman Spitzer: 115/42
Woodcliff Lake
Ingersoll-Rand Co.: 18
NEW MEXICO
Albuquerque
Hunkle Cox Eaton: 55
Miller Stratvert Torgerson: 48
Modrall Sperling Roehl: 57/16
Rodey Dickason Sloan: 62/19
NEW YORK
Albany
Cooper Erving Savage: 23/12
Whiteman Osterman Hanna: 51/6
Armonk
IBM Corp.: 424
Bethpage
Grumman Corp.: 22
Binghamton
Hinman Howard Kattell: 50
Brooklyn Heights
Cullen Dykman: 49/54
Buffalo
Damon Morey: 70/17
Hodgson Russ Andrews: 109/33
Jaeckle Fleischmann Mugel: 63/10
Phillips Lytle Hitchcock: 88/24
Saperston Day: 60/30
Corning
Corning Inc.: 22
New York City
American Express Co.: 85
American Intl Group Inc.: 53
American Home Products: 90
Anderson Kill Olick: 143/67
Arnold Porter: 59/8

Baker McKenzie: 67/13
Bankers Trust New York Corp.: 40
Bank of New York Co. Inc.: 45
Battle Fowler: 101
Bear Stearns Cos. Inc.: 37
Borden Inc.: 23
Bristol-Myers Squibb Co.: 93
Brown Wood: 218/33
Bryan Cave: 39/8
Cadwalader Wickersham: 230/27
Cahill Gordon Reindel: 204/29
Carter Ledyard Milburn: 80/7
Chadbourne Parke: 229/43
Chase Manhattan Corp.: 220
Chemical Bank: 93
Citicorp/Citybank, NA: 280
Cleary Gottlieb Steen: 278/55
Colgate-Palmolive Co.: 70
Consolidated Edison Co.: 72
Coudert Brothers: 116/16
Cravath Swaine Moore: 323/112
Curtis Mallet-Prevost: 154/12
Darby Darby: 44/19
Davis Polk Wardwell: 390/74
Davis Scott Weber: 37/12
Debevoise Plimpton: 295/58
Dewey Ballantine: 267/51
Donovan Leisure Newton: 94/21
Emmet Marvin Martin: 64/17
Epstein Becker Green: 85
Equitable Life . . . of U.S.: 50
Fish Neave: 117/26
Fitzpatrick Cella Harper: 69/25
Fried Frank Harris: 289/103
Fulbright Jaworski: 80/11
Gibson Dunn Crutcher: 97/9
Haight Gardner Poor: 71/11
Hawkins Delafield Wood: 88/4
Haythe Curley: 61/11
Herzfeld Rubin: 82
Hunton Williams: 53/15
Hughes Hubbard Reed: 165/26
Jackson Lewis Schnitzler: 34/14
Jones Day Reavis: 110/17
J. P. Morgan & Co.: 85
Kaye Scholer Fieman: 250/21
Kelley Drye Warren: 163/21
Kenyon Kenyon: 88/30
Kirkland Ellis: 60/14
Kramer Levin Nafalis: 149/35

Kronish Lieb Weiner: 71/13
ITT Corp.: 133
Latham Watkins: 126/19
LeBoeuf Lamb Green: 221/68
Lehman Bros. Holdings Inc.: 37
Loeb Loeb: 62/10
Lorel Corp.: 28
Mayer Brown Platt: 104/17
McDermott Will Emery: 61/8
Mendes Mount: 143
Merrill Lynch & Co. Inc.: 220
Metropolitan Life Ins. Co.: 39
Milbank Tweed Hadley: 243/66
Morgan Finnegan: 91/21
Morgan Lewis Bockius: 198/47
Morgan Stanley Co.: 71
Morrison Foerster: 55/8
Mudge Rose Guthrie: 171/43
New York Life Insurance Co.: 61
O'Melveny Myers: 110/32
Orrick Herrington Sutcliffe: 135/26
PaineWebber Group Inc.: 76
Parker Chapin Flattau: 119/20
Patterson Belknap Webb: 138
Paul Hastings Janofsky: 77/7
Paul Weiss Rifkind: 295/60
Pennie Edmonds: 81/24
Pfizer Inc.: 100
Philip Morris Companies: 120
Port Authority of NY/NJ: 81
Proskauer Rose Goetz: 340/81
Reboul MacMurray Hewitt: 61/11
Reid Priest: 135/19
Reliance GroupHoldings Inc.: 150
Republic New York Corp.: 17
Richards O'Neil: 79/15
RJR Nabisco Holdings Corp.: 44
Robinson Silverman Pearce: 107
Rogers Wells: 304/62
Rosenman Colin: 226/25
Schulte Roth Zabel: 178/45
Seward Kiseel: 75/17
Shearman Sterling: 426/67
Shereff Friedman Hoffman: 58/8
Sidley Austin: 69/13
Siemens Corp.: 51
Simpson Tacher Bartlett: 406/107
Skadden Arps Slate: 574/170
Solomon Inc.: 42
Strook Strook Lavan: 215/50

Sullivan Cromwell: 317/57
Tenzer Greenblatt: 83/17
Thacher Proffitt Wood: 161/24
Time Warner Inc.: 127
Travelers Corp.: 497
Viacom International Inc.: 160
Wachtell Lipton Rosen: 142/39
Walter Conston Alexander: 60/17
Weil Gotshal Manges: 376/77
White Case: 282/61
Whitman Breed Abbott: 149/30
Willke Farr Gallagher: 299/66
Wilson Elser Moskowitz: 209
Winston Strawn: 97/18
Winthrop Stimson Putnam: 184/26
Pleasantville
  Reader's Digest Assn Inc.: 23
Purchase
  International Paper Co.: 33
  PepsiCo Inc.: 70
Rochester
  Eastman Kodak Co.: 130
  Harris Beach Wilcox: 92/29
  Harter Secrest Emery: 85/16
  Nixon Hargrave Devans: 127/52
  Phillips Lytle Hitchcock: 23/18
Syracuse
  Bond Schoeneck King: 112/21
  Hancock Estabrook: 62/5
  Hiscock Barclay: 47
Uniondale
  Rivkin Radler Kremer: 142/28
White Plains
  NYNEX Corp.: 121
  Texaco Inc.: 185

NORTH CAROLINA
Charlotte
  Belle Seltzer Park: 40
  First Union Corp.: 61
  Kennedy Covington Lobdell: 95/19
  Moor Van Allen: 79/19
  NationsBank Corp.: 115
  Parker Poe Adams: 84/14
  Robinson Bradshaw Hinson: 74/15
  Smith Helms Mulliss: 58/15
  Womble Carlyle Sandridge: 39/7
Greensboro
  Smith Helms Mulliss: 67/17
Raleigh
  Hunton Williams: 37/9

Maupin Taylor Ellis: 55/18
Poyner Spruill: 56/25
Smith Anderson Blount: 54
Smith Helms Mulliss: 22/8
Womble Carlyle Sandridge: 40/16
Winston-Salem
  Petree Stockton: 125/40
  Wachovia Corp.: 17
  Womble Carlyle Sandridge: 110/41

OHIO
Akron
  B. F. Goodrich Co.: 30
  Brouse McDowell: 57/10
  Buckinghap Doolittle: 7/17
  Goodyear Tire & Rubber Co.: 37
  Roetzel & Andress: 55
Cincinnati
  Chiquita Brands Intn Inc.: 40
  Dinsmore Shohl: 164/41
  Frost Jacobs: 130/32
  Graydon Head Ritchey: 50
  Keating Muethling Klekamp: 65/17
  Proctor & Gamble Co.: 175/13
  Strauss Troy: 41/6
  Taft Stettinius Hollister: 132/25
  Thompson Hine Flory: 68/8
  Vorys Sater Seymour: 32
Cleveland
  Arter Hadden: 89/13
  Baker Hostetler: 147/14
  Benesch Friedlander: 96/14
  Calfee Halter Griswold: 152/15
  Eaton Corp.: 34
  Hahn Loeser Parks: 77/16
  Jones Day Reavis: 222/66
  KeyCorp: 66
  McDonald Hopkins Burke: 58/14
  National City Corp.: 65
  Squire Sanders Dempsey: 147/22
  Thompson Hine Flory: 156/24
  TRW Inc.: 45
  Ulmer Berne: 66/9
  Weston Hurd Fallon: 52/8
Columbus
  Amer. Electrical Power Corp: 50
  Arter Hadden: 43
  Baker Hostetler: 69/8
  Banc One Corp.: 100
  Bricker Eckler: 105/20
  Emens Kegler Brown: 67/16

Jones Day Reavis: 56/8
Porter Wright Morris: 147/19
Schottenstein Zox Dunn: 62/6
Squire Sanders Dempsey: 65/13
Thompson Hine Flory: 40/9
Vorys Sater Seymour: 282/51
Dayton
  Porter Wright Morris: 19/4
  Thompson Hine Flory: 51/10
Toledo
  Dana Corp.: 14
  Fuller Henry: 52
  Shumaker Loop Kendrick: 66/19

OKLAHOMA
Bartlesville
  Phillips Petroleum Co.: 67
Oklahoma City
  Crowe Dunlevy: 77/20
  McAfee Taft: 60
  Kerr-McGee Corp.: 27
Tulsa
  Citgo Petroleum Corp.: 11
  Crowe Dunlevy: 22/6
  Gable Gotwals: 40/16
  Hall Estill Hardwick: 58

OREGON
Portland
  Bogle Gates: 24/5
  Bullivant Houser Bailey: 61/22
  Davis Wright Tremaine: 67/11
  Heller Ehrman White: 71/15
  Herschner Hunter Moulton: 26/4
  Lane Powell Spears: 84/30
  Miller Nash Wiener: 94/19
  Perkins Coie: 27/4
  Schwabe Williamson Wyatt: 92/12
  Stoel Rives: 144/31
  Tonkin Torp Galen: 51/7
  U.S. Bancorp.: 29

PENNSYLVANIA
Allentown
  Air Products/Chemicals Inc.: 28
Bethlehem
  Bethlehem Steel Corp.: 21
  Union Pacific Corp: 60
Blue Bell
  Unisys Corp.: 70
Collegeville
  Rhone-Poulenc Rorer, Inc.: 32
Harrisburg

Appendix 2.A   Employment in Selected Large Law Firms and Corporations —continued

Buchanan Ingersoll: 21
McNees Wallace Nurick: 66/13
Lancaster
Barley Snyder Senft: 40
Philadelphia
Ballard Spahr Andrews: 183/38
Blank Rome Comisky: 224/39
CIGNA Corp.: 475
Clark Ladner Fortenbaigh: 83/17
Cohen Shapiro Polisher: 60/23
Cozen O'Connor: 143/49
Dechert Price Rhoads: 225/52
Dilworth Paxson Kalish: 82
Drinker Biddle Reath: 156/29
Duane Morris Heckscher: 155/31
Rox Rothchild O'Brien: 86
Harvey Pennington Herting: 57
Hoyle Morris Kerr: 51/9
Klehr Harrison Harvey: 70/8
LaBrum Doak: 68
Margolis Edelstein Scherlis: 96
Marshall Dennehey Warner: 98/5
Meisirov Gelman Jaffe: 71/16
Morgan Lewis Bockius: 206/50
Montgomery McCracken: 144/20
Obermayer Rebmann: 89/17
Pepper Hamilton Scheetz: 158/46
Post Schell: 97/17
Reed Smith Swaw: 80/20
Rohm & Hass Co.: 33
Saul Ewing Remick: 158/26
Schnader Harrison Segal: 140/34
Stradley Ronon Stevens: 119/20
Sun Co. Inc.: 45
White Williams: 140/21
Wolf Block Schorr: 160/21
Pittsburgh
Aluminum Co. of America: 41
Buchanan Ingersoll: 243/33
Cohen Gigsby: 70
Dickie McCamey Chilcote: 120
Doepken Keevican Weiss: 55/5
Eckert Seamans Cherin: 104/27
Kirkpatrick Lockhart: 195/69
H. J. Heinz Co.: 20
Jones Day Reavis Pogue: 43/17
Klett Lieber Rooney: 62/9
Mellon Bank Corp.: 53
Miles Inc.: 40
PNC Bank Corporation: 736

PPG Industries Inc.: 33
Reed Smith Swaw: 166/27
Thorp Reed Armstrong: 77/25
USX Corp.: 103
Westinghouse Electric Corp.: 100
Reading
Stevens Lee: 44
RHODE ISLAND
Providence
Edwards Angell: 83
Hickley Allen Snyder: 70
Textron Inc.: 75
SOUTH CAROLINA
Columbia
McNair Sanford: 89
Nelson Mullins Riley: 102
Nexen Pruet Jacobs: 78
Sinkler Boyd: 35
Turner Padget Graham: 31/8
Greenville
Haynsworth Baldwin Johnson: 22/5
Haynsworth Marion McKay: 59
Leatherwood Walker Todd: 44/12
Nelson Mullins Riley: 21
Ogletree Deakins Nash: 41/14
TENNESSEE
Chattanooga
Baker Donelson Bearman: 27
Leitner Warner Moffitt: 40
Miller Martin: 66
Memphis
Baker Donelson Bearman: 71
Nashville
Baker Donelson Bearman: 41
Bass Berry Sims: 95/28
Boult Cummings Conners: 69/13
Farris Warfield Kanaday: 34/6
First American Corp.: 98
Harwell Howard Hyne: 28/15
Waller Lansden Dortch: 75/11
Wyatt Tarrant Combs: 20
TEXAS
Austin
Baker Botts: 33/7
Bickerstaff Heath Smiley: 38/10
Brown McCarroll Oaks: 108/38
Clark Thomas Winters: 75/25
Fulbright Jaworski: 38/15
Graves Dougherty Hearon: 45/7
Jenkins Gilchrist: 31/5

McGinnis Lochridge Kilgore: 57
Small Craig Werkenthin: 50
Dallas
Akin Gump Strauss: 111/19
American Airlines Inc.: 28
Andrews Kurth: 36/9
Baker Botts: 92/27
Bickel Brewer: 35/7
Carrington Coleman: 84/16
Cowles Thompson: 83/20
Dresser Industries Inc.: 28
Fulbright Jaworski: 70/20
Haynes Boone: 145/32
Gardere Wynne: 182/38
Gibson Dunn Crutcher: 54/8
Hughes Luce: 113/20
Jackson Walker: 104/13
Jenkins Gilchrist: 154/34
Jones Day Reavis: 136/27
Kimberly-Clark Corp.: 46
Liddell Sapp Zivley: 37/8
Locke Purnell Rain: 162/25
Munsch Hardt Kopf: 50/18
Strasburger Price: 164/48
Texas Instruments, Inc.: 75
Thompson Coe Cousins: 53/16
Thompson Knight: 189/37
Vial Hamilton Koch: 110/34
Vinson Elkins: 77/18
Weil Gotschal Manges: 43/16
Winstead Sechrest Minick: 113/16
Worsham Forsythe: 45/4
El Paso
Kemp Smith Duncan: 52/12
Ft. Worth
Cantey Hanger: 86/15
Haynes Boone: 24/3
Kelly Hart Hallman: 70/8
Houston
Akin Gump Strauss: 59/15
Andrews Kurth: 145/23
Arnold White Durkee: 127/32
Baker Botts: 213/50
Baker Hostetler: 31/5
Baker Hughes Inc.: 20
Beirne Maynard Parsons: 45/16
Bracewell Patterson: 149/27
Butler Binion: 66
Chamberlain Hrdlicka White: 55/13
Coastal Corp.: 80

Compaq Computer Corp.: 16
Cooper Industries Inc.: 37
Enron Corp.: 112
Fulbright Jaworski: 283/57
Gardere Wynne Sewell: 64/12
Haynes Boone: 36/6
Hutcheson Grundy: 50/11
Jackson Walker: 49/12
Liddle Sapp Zivley: 105/15
Mayer Brown Platt: 38/8
Mayor Day Caldwell: 95/31
Pennzoil Co.: 22
Porter Hedges: 51/7
Sheinfield Maley Kay: 40/10
Shell Oil Co.: 100
Tenneco Inc.: 80
Vinson Elkins: 341/93
Weil Gotshal Manges: 54/9
Winstead Sechrest Minick: 43
Irving
  Exxon Corp.: 470
Plano
  Electronic Data Sys. Inc.: 75
San Antonio
  Akin Gump Strauss: 63/22
  Ball Weed: 30/12
  Cox Smith: 56/7
  Fulbright Jaworski: 39/10
  Matthews Branscomb: 55
  SBC Communications: 106
  Thornton Summers Biechlin: 30

UTAH
Salt Lake City
  Holme Roberts Owen: 19/1
  Jones Waldo Holbrook: 48/4
  Kimball Parr Waddoups: 50
  Parsons Behle Latimer: 96/18
  Ray Quinney Nebeker: 70
  Van Cott Bagley Cornwall: 78/12

VERMONT
Burlington
  Downs Rachlin Martin: 28/7
  Gravel Shea: 19/3

VIRGINIA
Alexandria
  Burnes Doane Swecker: 53
Charlottesville
  McGuire Woods Battle: 26/11
Falls Church

General Dynamic Corp.: 20
  Hazel Thomas: 39/7
Fairfax
  Hazel Thomas: 44
  Hunton Williams: 29
  Mobil Corp.: 170
McLean
  Hogan Hartson: 21
  Hunton Williams: 36/4
  McGuire Woods Battle: 50/13
  Venable Baetjer Howard: 23
  Watt Tieder Hoffar: 51/7
Norfolk
  Kaufman Canoles: 61/20
  McGuire Woods Battle: 23/6
  Wilcox Savage: 57/11
Richmond
  Christian Barton: 49/7
  CSX Corp.: 49
  Hunton Williams: 197/79
  Mays Valentine: 102/25
  McGuire Woods Battle: 215/79
  Reynolds Metals Co.: 26
  Sands Anderson Marks: 45/13
  Williams Mullen Christian: 85/21
  Wright Robinson McCammon: 35
Roanoke
  Gentry Locke Rakes: 49/17
  Woods Rogers Hazlegrove: 67/22
Tysons Corner
  McGuire Woods Battle: 50/13
Virginia Beach
  Huff Poole Mahoney: 25/14

WASHINGTON STATE
Bellevue
  Perkins Coie: 28
Seattle
  Boeing Co.: 73
  Bogle Gates: 139/40
  Bullivant Houser Bailey: 26/7
  Davis Wright Tremaine: 125/25
  Foster Pepper Shefelman: 122/32
  Garvey Schubert Barer: 56/10
  Graham James: 76/12
  Heisell Fetterman Martin: 54/28
  Heller Ehrman White: 71/15
  Hills Clark Martin: 32/7
  Karr Tuttle Campbell: 49/17
  Lane Powell Spears: 140/76

  Mundt Macgregor Hoppel: 16/7
  Perkins Coie: 208/55
  Preston Gates Ellis: 133/31
  Reed McClure: 49/12
  Riddell Williams Bullitt: 77/13
  Safeco Corp.: 88
  Short Cressman Burgess: 39/5
  Stoel Rives Boley: 58/9
  Williams Kastner Gibbs: 66/18
Spokane
  Lukins Annis: 37/16
Tacoma
  Gordon Thomas Honeywell: 57
  Weyerhaeuser Co.: 25

WEST VIRGINIA
Charleston
  Bowles Rice McDavid: 62
  Jackson Kelly: 89/35
  Robinson McElwee: 58
  Spilman Thomas Battle: 38/9
Clarksburg
  Steptoe Johnson: 47

WISCONSIN
Madison
  Foley Lardner: 52/12
  Michael Best Friedrich: 35/5
  Quarles Brady: 25/5
Milwaukee
  Davis Kuelthau: 53/7
  Firstar Corp.: 20
  Foley Lardner: 214/29
  Godfrey Cahn: 93/24
  Hinshaw Culbertson: 28
  Johnson Controls Inc.: 50
  Michael Best Friedrich: 135/14
  Quarles Brady: 188/25
  Reinhart Boerner: 130/22
  Whyte Hirschboeck Dudek: 94/13

Sources: *West's Legal Directory;* National Law Journal, *The NLJ 250 Largest Law Firms,* October 9, 1995; National Law Journal, *The NLJ List Who Represents Financial America,* June 17, 1996; National Association of Legal Placement, *Directory of Legal Employers: The Lawyer's Almanac 1996* (Aspen Law & Business, 1996); *San Diego Commerce,* May 24, 1995; *Martindale-Hubbell Law Directory* (1996); *The Incredible Shrinking Law Firm,* 13 California Lawyer 55 (November 1993); *PIC's National Law Network* (Spring 1996); and independent checking.

Appendix 2.B   Summary Chart—Survey of State Government Job Classifications for Paralegals

GOVERNMENT	POSITION	RESPONSIBILITIES	QUALIFICATIONS	SALARY
Alabama Personnel Dept. 64 N. Union St. Montgomery, AL 36130 334-242-3389	Legal Assistant 10/22/82 (11503)	● Perform legal research ● Draft pleadings ● Interview witnesses in preparation for trial ● Conduct routine investigations ● Assist attorney at depositions ● Digest laws and cases ● Write draft of Attorney General opinions ● Perform office administrative duties	Certificate from accredited college with minimum of 30 semester hours or 50 quarter hours in Legal Assistant Studies with courses in investigation, legal bibliography, evidence, criminal procedure, civil litigation and trial preparation, court management, and paralegalism	$19,180–$29,172 per year

Other positions to check in Alabama: Docket Clerk (11501); Legal Opinions Clerk (11505); Contract Clerk (119.267-018); Legal Investigator (119.267-022); Title Examiner (119.287-010); Appeals Referee (119.267-014).

GOVERNMENT	POSITION	RESPONSIBILITIES	QUALIFICATIONS	SALARY
Alaska Department of Administration Division of Personnel Pouch C P.O. Box 110201 Juneau, AK 99811 907-465-4430	Paralegal Assistant I 4/1/84 (7105-13)	● Interview clients ● Obtain statements and affidavits ● Conduct investigations ● Perform legal research ● Coordinate witness scheduling ● Represent clients at hearings	Certificate from a state paralegal training program OR Associate of Arts program with a major in paralegal, criminal justice, or law studies; or a bachelor's degree in social studies or behavioral sciences OR 3 years of experience as legal secretary, court clerk, etc.	$30,432–$41,460 per year

Other positions to check in Alaska: Paralegal Assistant II (7106-16); Investigator II (7767); Latent Fingerprint Examiner (7756).

GOVERNMENT	POSITION	RESPONSIBILITIES	QUALIFICATIONS	SALARY
American Samoa Department of Human Resources American Samoa Government Pago Pago, AS 96799 684-633-4489 684-633-4485	Legal Assistant I (E2-09-7524)	● Conduct routine investigations ● Perform legal research ● Review citations for traffic court cases ● Interview witnesses ● Present traffic cases in court ● Prepare orders to show cause	Bachelor's degree with a major in police science, corrections, or a related field	$9,317–$15,167 per year

Other positions to check in American Samoa: Legal Assistant II (E2-10-7525); Legal Assistant III (E2-11-7526); Paralegal (12-13-7552).

continued

Appendix 2.B Summary Chart—Survey of State Government Job Classifications for Paralegals—continued

GOVERNMENT	POSITION	RESPONSIBILITIES	QUALIFICATIONS	SALARY
Arizona Dept. of Administration Human Resources Division 1831 West Jefferson St. Phoenix, AZ 85007 602-542-5482	Legal Assistant I 7/22/88 (32201)	• Perform legal research • Write drafts of briefs • Write correspondence • Provide general assistance to attorney	4 years of full-time paralegal experience OR Associate's degree in paralegal studies OR Associate's degree in any area PLUS paralegal certification through an accredited program	$20,902–$32,687 per year

Other positions to check in Arizona: Legal Assistant II (32202); Legal Assistant III (32203); Legal Assistant Project Specialist (32204); Process Server (32206).

Arkansas Office of Personnel Management P.O. Box 3278, 1509 West 7th St. Little Rock, AR 72203 501-682-1507 501-682-5094	Legal Assistant 7/1/77 7/1/79-R (R177)	• Perform legal research • Check court files to inform attorneys of status of cases • Maintain law library • Prepare summaries of documents • File documents in court	The formal education equivalent of 1 year of law school OR 1 year of paralegal experience (Other job-related education and/or experience may be substituted for all or part of the requirements.)	$15,662–$28,444 per year
California State Personnel Board 801 Capitol Mall P.O. Box 944201 Sacramento, CA 95814 916-653-1042 916-631-1705 ALSO: Dept. of Personnel Administration 1115 11th St., 1st Fl. Sacramento, CA 95814 916-322-5193	Legal Assistant 3/13/75 6/12/90 (JY66, 1820)	• Assist in reviewing legal documents to determine if they comply with the law • Analyze proposed legislation • Digest and index opinions, testimony, depositions, and other trial documents • Perform research of legislative history • Assist in drafting complaints and other pleadings • Help answer inquiries on legal requirements • Perform routine legal research	6 units of paralegal or undergraduate legal studies (3 of which are in legal research) AND 2 years of experience in state gov't in legal clerical position or 1 year with other law-related duties such as an investigator OR 3 years as a law clerk or legal secretary in a law office (Post–high school education can substitute for some of the experience requirement. 2 years of paralegal education can substitute for 1 year of experience.) *Applicants must sit for an examination.*	$2,515–$3,027 per month

continued

Appendix 2.B	Summary Chart—Survey of State Government Job Classifications for Paralegals—continued			
GOVERNMENT	**POSITION**	**RESPONSIBILITIES**	**QUALIFICATIONS**	**SALARY**
California—continued	Legal Analyst 7/2/81; 6/12/96 (JY62, 5237)	● Investigate and analyze facts ● Coordinate witnesses ● Draft interrogatories ● Draft pleadings ● Summarize discovery documents	2 years of gov't experience as a legal assistant AND 6 units of paralegal or other legal courses (3 of which are in legal research) OR 2 years of experience as a paralegal elsewhere AND 12 units of paralegal or other legal courses OR equivalent to graduation from college	$2,853–$3,430 per month
Colorado Dept. of Personnel General Support Services State Centennial Bldg. 1525 Sherman St. Denver, CO 80203 303-866-2321 303-866-3221	Legal Assistant I 9/1/93 (H5E1XX)	● Conduct legal research ● Take notes at depositions ● Conduct interviews ● Identify legal issues ● Review documents for legal sufficiency ● Monitor status of cases ● Provide information on legal procedures	Bachelor's degree and certificate from approved paralegal studies program	$2,294 per month

Other position to check in Colorado: Legal Assistant II (H5E2XX), who functions at a more advanced level than the Legal Assistant I.

Connecticut Personnel Div. Dept. of Administration Services 165 Capital Ave. Hartford, CT 06106 203-566-3081	Paralegal Specialist 1 5/25/93 (6140)(1090A; S.G.AR.21)	● Act as liaison between legal and clerical staff ● Perform legal research ● Assist in drafting legal documents ● Maintain tickler systems ● Present written and oral argument at administrative hearings ● Maintain records	2 years of experience working for a lawyer OR A designated number of college courses in law or paralegal studies (Substitutions are allowed.)	$30,983–$37,280 per year

Other positions to check in Connecticut: Paralegal Specialist 2 (6141, 1090A; S.G.AR.18); Legal Office Administrator (5373, 9389c, MP 18).

Delaware State Personnel Office Townsend Bldg.	Legal Assistant 7/86 (12846)	● Review documents to assess consistency with law	Enough education and/or experience to demonstrate competence in research,	$22,503–$28,129 per year

continued

Appendix 2.B — Summary Chart—Survey of State Government Job Classifications for Paralegals—continued

GOVERNMENT	POSITION	RESPONSIBILITIES	QUALIFICATIONS	SALARY
Delaware—continued P.O. Box 1401 Dover, DE 19903 302-739-4195		• Summarize cases • Draft pleadings, deeds, and other documents • Interview clients and witnesses • Assist in investigations • File documents in court	drafting, filing, interviewing, record keeping, and communication (oral and written)	

Other positions to check in Delaware: License Investigator (Dept. of Administrative Services); Clerk of Court I (Family Court) (12311); Law Library Assistant.

GOVERNMENT	POSITION	RESPONSIBILITIES	QUALIFICATIONS	SALARY
District of Columbia D.C. Personnel Office 441 4th St. NW Wash. D.C. 20001 202-727-6406	Paralegal Specialist	• Similar to Paralegal Specialist positions in the federal government. (See page 40.)		
Florida Dept. of Administration Division of Personnel Management Services 4050 Esplanade Way Tallahassee, FL 32399 904-488-5823	Paralegal Specialist 1/1/84 (7703)	• Take affidavits from victims and witnesses • Perform legal research • Maintain case files and tickler system • Perform notary functions • Prepare case summaries • Draft pleadings	Completion of legal assistant (or related legal) training course OR Bachelor's degree with major in allied legal services OR 4 years of experience as a paralegal or legal secretary	$1,387–$2,244 per month

Other positions to check in Florida: Appeals Coordinator/Clerk (Public Employees Relations Commission) (7704); Legal Trainee (7706)

GOVERNMENT	POSITION	RESPONSIBILITIES	QUALIFICATIONS	SALARY

Georgia
State Merit System of
    Personnel
    Administration
200 Piedmont Ave. SE
Atlanta, GA 30334
404-656-2705
	Legal Assistant
	1/1/81
	(44330)
		• Perform legal research
		• Review litigation documents
		• Summarize law
		• Develop forms and procedures
			2 years of legal experience involving legal research, interpreting laws, or relevant administrative responsibilities	$21,408–$38,646 per year

Other positions to check in Georgia: Law Clerk (44340)—requires a law degree OR two years of legal assistant experience; Paralegal (nonmerit position in State Law Department); Research Assistant (nonmerit position in State Law Department).

GOVERNMENT	POSITION	RESPONSIBILITIES	QUALIFICATIONS	SALARY
Guam Department of Administration Division of Personnel	Paralegal I 3/86 (2.810)	• Perform legal research • Index public laws • Prepare updates to administrative laws	3 years of experience working with laws and procedures OR	$24,656 per year

continued

Appendix 2.B   Summary Chart—Survey of State Government Job Classifications for Paralegals—continued

GOVERNMENT	POSITION	RESPONSIBILITIES	QUALIFICATIONS	SALARY
Guam—continued P.O. Box 884 Agana, GU 96910 671-477-6788		• Draft bills and simple pleadings • Compile laws by subject matter • Interview clients and witnesses	A bachelor's degree OR Completion of a course leading to certification as a paralegal OR Equivalent experience and training	
Other positions to check in Guam: Paralegal II (2.811); Legal Clerk I (2.805).				
Hawaii Dept. of Human Resources Development 235 S. Beretania St. Honolulu, HI 96813 808-587-1100	Legal Assistant II 4/15/83 (2.141)	• Act as conduit between attorneys and client, e.g., provide legal information • Perform legal research • Summarize laws • Collect and evaluate evidence for trial • Perform cite checks • Index depositions	4 years of legal experience OR Graduation from an accredited legal assistant training program	$27,828–$39,624 per year
Other position to check in Hawaii: Legal Assistant III (2.142).				
Idaho Personnel Commission 700 West State St. Boise, ID 83720 208-334-2263	Legal Assistant 3/3/95 (05910)	• Identify legal issues • Perform legal research • Draft legal documents • Help design computer database for cases • Answer inquiries	Good knowledge of legal research method, the court system, court procedures, and legal ethics. Experience interpreting and analyzing laws, preparing legal documents, tracking documents on a computer database, etc.	$12.09–$17.78 per hour
Illinois Department of Central Management Services Bureau of Personnel 500 Stratton Office Bldg. Springfield, IL 62706 217-782-3379	Paralegal Assistant 2/25/94 (1887, 30860) (RC-062-12)	• Write legal memoranda and other documents for attorneys • Analyze hearing transcripts • Excerpt data from transcripts • Prepare statistical reports	Knowledge and skill equivalent to four years of college and knowledge and skills relevant to job responsibilities Completion of 4 years of college with coursework in areas such as prelegal, medical, English, and statistics OR Equivalent training and experience	$1,885–$2,484 per month

continued

Appendix 2.B Summary Chart—Survey of State Government Job Classifications for Paralegals—continued

GOVERNMENT	POSITION	RESPONSIBILITIES	QUALIFICATIONS	SALARY
Illinois—continued				
Other position to check in Illinois: Legal Research Assistant (1888) (23350) (MC-02) (RC-028-13).				
Indiana State Personnel Dept. 402 W. Washington St. IGCS, Rm. W161 Indianapolis, IN 46204 317-232-3059	Legal Assistant 3/7/90 (22015/1VA5)	• Perform legal research • Verify citations to be used in memos and decisions • Maintain files • Schedule hearings • Respond to requests for subpoenas • Supervise clerical staff • Respond to inquiries from attorneys on current hearings • Set up hearing sites • Provide follow-up questions to attorneys at depositions • Prepare budget	3 years of full-time paralegal experience in law office. Accredited college training in paralegal studies, political science, business administration, pre-law, or a related area can substitute for 2 years of experience.	$698–$1,049 biweekly
Iowa Department of Personnel Grimes State Office Building E. 14th St. & Grand Ave. Des Moines, IA 50319 515-281-3351	Paralegal (Office of Attorney General) 10/30/87 (45004)	• Represent the state at license revocation hearings • Write administrative appeal briefs • Resolve appeals not needing a hearing • Initiate suggestions to improve hearing procedures	2-year paralegal degree	$976–$1,217 biweekly
Other positions to check in Iowa: Paralegal (95004, Dept. of Personnel); Administrative Assistant I (00708)				
Kansas Dept. of Administration Div. of Personnel Services Landon State Office Bldg. 2 North & J St. Topeka, KS 66612 913-296-4278	Legal Assistant 6/94 (D3 4093)	• Perform legal research • Schedule witnesses • Draft pleadings and discovery documents • Compile administrative transcripts • Conduct investigations • Maintain law library • Prepare trial notebook	Completion of a Legal Assistant training program of at least 60 semester hours.	$10.43–$13.97 per hour
Kentucky Dept. of Personnel 200 Fair Oaks Lane	Paralegal 12/1/85 (9856)	• Conduct analytical research • Investigate cases	Bachelor's degree in paralegal science OR	$1,427–$2,745 per month *continued*

Appendix 2.B	Summary Chart—Survey of State Government Job Classifications for Paralegals—continued

GOVERNMENT	POSITION	RESPONSIBILITIES	QUALIFICATIONS	SALARY
Kentucky—Continued Frankfort, KY 40601 502-564-4460		• Interview complainants and witnesses • Draft documents • Provide general assistance to attorneys in litigation	Post-baccalaureate certificate in paralegal studies OR Bachelor's degree with a minor in paralegal studies OR Completion of a 2-year program in paralegal studies (Paralegal experience can substitute for some of the education.)	

Other positions to check in Kentucky: Paralegal Senior (9857); Paralegal Chief (9858); Law Clerk (9801).

Louisiana Dept. of Civil Service P.O. Box 94111 Capitol Station Baton Rouge, LA 70804 504-342-8083	Paralegal Assistant 6/7/93 (113470) (C1 PA)	• Perform legal research • Draft pleadings • Interview potential trial witnesses • Compose briefs and memoranda • Collect delinquent payments • Index legal opinions • Maintain law library	Completion of a paralegal/legal assistant studies program at a 4-year college, at a junior college, or at an otherwise approved school	$1,504–$2,347 per month

Other position to check in Louisiana: Legal Research Assistant (70490).

Maine Bureau of Human Resources State Office Bldg. 4 State House Station Augusta, ME 04333 207-287-3761	Paralegal Assistant (0016) (CFA8015101) (0994)	• Summarize documents that affect land titles • Perform legal research • Assist attorney at hearings • Conduct investigations	4 years of college and 1 year of paralegal experience OR Graduation from an approved paralegal course (Relevant experience may substitute for education requirement.)	$10.12–$13.55 per hour

Other positions to check in Maine: Legal Researcher (0018, 02045, 0979, 20E); Law Clerk (secretarial position with paralegal duties) (0061, 41255, 202.362-014, 0380, 0880, 18R); Workers Compensation Assistant (036900).

Maryland Department of Personnel State Office Bldg. #1 301 W. Preston St. Baltimore, MD 21201 410-767-4715	Legal Assistant I (12/1/81) 0589	• Perform legal research • Conduct investigations • File pleadings • Prepare affidavits • Maintain docket file • Coordinate employee activities	High school diploma or certificate and 4 years of experience as a clerk or secretary in a law office (One year of paralegal education can substitute for two years of experience.)	$19,128–$24,801 per year

continued

A p p e n d i x 2 . B	Summary Chart—Survey of State Government Job Classifications for Paralegals—continued			
GOVERNMENT	**POSITION**	**RESPONSIBILITIES**	**QUALIFICATIONS**	**SALARY**
Maryland—continued				
Other positions to check in Maryland: Legal Assistant (209, 13); Legal Assistant II (1292); Para-Legal I (e.g., Howard County Office of State's Attorney)				
Massachusetts Department of Personnel Administration One Ashburton Pl. Boston, MA 02108 617-727-1556 617-727-3777	Paralegal Specialist 5/11/88 (10-R39) (Group 31)	● Answer inquiries on agency rules ● Analyze statutes ● Digest the law ● Prepare briefs and answers to interrogatories ● Interview parties ● Evaluate evidence ● Develop case tracking systems ● Schedule appointments	2 years of experience in legal research or legal assistant work. (An associate's degree or a higher degree with a major in paralegal studies can be substituted for the required experience.)	$28,956– $38,653 per year
Michigan Dept. of Civil Service Capitol Commons Center 400 South Pine St. P.O. Box 30002 Lansing, MI 48909 517-373-3020	Paralegal 8 10/93 (8020403)	● Perform legal research ● Conduct investigations ● Draft legal documents ● Prepare interrogatories ● Digest and index laws ● Serve and file legal papers	Associate's degree in a paralegal program OR Equivalent combination of experience and education to perform the job	$12.11– $14.65 per hour
Other positions to check in Michigan: Paralegal 9 (8020404); Paralegal E10 (8020405); Paralegal 11 (8031106). Note: The Legal Assistant 1 position requires a law degree.				
Minnesota Dept. of Employee Relations 200 Centennial Bldg. 658 Cedar St. St. Paul, MN 55101 612-296-8366	Legal Technician 2/75, 3/76, 11/92 (001541)	● Perform legal research ● Prepare legal documents ● Collect documents for attorney	Completion of paralegal training program OR 2 years of varied paralegal experience OR 1 year of law school	$22,905– $31,863 per year
Other positions to check in Minnesota: Legal Technician-Farm Real Estate (Dept. of Agriculture); Legal Text Edit Specialist (001936, 206).				
Mississippi State Personnel Board 301 N. Lamar St. Jackson, MS 39201 601-359-2704	Paralegal Specialist 7/83; 11/92 (1848-PR 188-269, D)	● Interpret and explain laws to staff ● Assist in preparing legal documents ● Review reports ● Assist in referring cases for prosecution	Bachelor's degree in paralegal studies or a related field and 1 year of legal experience OR High school or GED plus 5 years related experience	$17,323 per year

continued

A p p e n d i x 2 . B	**Summary Chart—Survey of State Government Job Classifications for Paralegals—continued**			
GOVERNMENT	**POSITION**	**RESPONSIBILITIES**	**QUALIFICATIONS**	**SALARY**
Mississippi—continued		• Train and supervise staff in research • Perform research	(of which 1 year is *directly* related)	

Other position to check in Mississippi: Legal Clerk I (1962-PR 081-162, B) (clerical position with paralegal duties).

Missouri Office of Administration Division of Personnel P.O. Box 388 Jefferson City, MO 65102 314-751-4162	Paralegal or legal assistant positions are not found under the Missouri Merit System. Individual agencies not covered by the Merit System, however, may have such positions.			
Montana Dept. of Administration Personnel Division Mitchell Bldg., Rm. 130 125 Roberts P.O. Box 200127 Helena, MT 59620 406-444-3871	Paralegal Assistant I 1/80 (119004)	• Perform legal research • Compile citations and references; check cites • Assemble exhibits • Explain laws • Arrange interviews and depositions • File pleadings • Supervise clerical staff	Associate's degree in paralegal studies plus 1 year of related experience in a legal setting. (Incumbents need to possess thorough knowledge of legal research, law libraries, legal forms and procedures, administrative law, litigation, etc.)	Grade 11 $22,775– $26,646 per year

Other positions to check in Montana: Paralegal Assistant II (119005); Agency Legal Services Investigator (168155).

Nebraska State Personnel Division Dept. of Administrative Services P.O. Box 94905 Lincoln, NE 68509 402-471-2075	Legal Aide I 5/1/78 (C318131)	• Perform legal research • Proofread legal material • Help draft regulations • Help maintain hearing room tapes and films	Any combination of training and/or experience that will enable the applicant to possess the required knowledge, ability, and skills	$15,504– $21,706 per year

Other position to check in Nebraska: Legal Aide II (C318132).

Nevada Department of Personnel 209 E. Musser St. Capitol Complex Carson City, NV 89710 702-687-4050 800-992-0900	Legal Assistant 7/1/89; 2/15/91 (2.155)	• Digest information in files • Explain status of case to clients or to the public • Offer advice on procedures • Interview clients and witnesses • Schedule depositions • Organize and prepare exhibits	3 years of experience as a legal secretary (or 1 year as a legal secretary I in Nevada State service) <u>OR</u> Completion of 1 year of a 2-year paralegal course plus 1 year of legal secretary experience or completion of classes in typing and office management <u>OR</u>	$18,803– $25,136 per year

continued

Appendix 2.B **Summary Chart—Survey of State Government Job Classifications for Paralegals—continued**

GOVERNMENT	POSITION	RESPONSIBILITIES	QUALIFICATIONS	SALARY
Nevada—continued			Any equivalent combination of education and experience that demonstrates possession of entry-level knowledge, skills, and abilities	

Other positions to check in Nevada: Legal Assistant II (2.159); Legal Research Assistant (7.750).

GOVERNMENT	POSITION	RESPONSIBILITIES	QUALIFICATIONS	SALARY
New Hampshire Division of Personnel State House Annex 25 Capitol St. Concord, NH 03301 603-271-3261	Paralegal I 2/4/76; 10/25/91 7-5-5 (6793-15)	• Maintain docket control and file organization • Conduct investigations • Review complaints of alleged violations • Help assess credibility of potential witnesses • Examine legal documents to ensure compliance with law	2 years of experience in law or a related field <u>AND</u> An associate's degree <u>OR</u> A paralegal certificate from a certified paralegal program (Substitutions are allowed.)	$21,762–$25,662 per year

Other positions to check in New Hampshire: Paralegal II (6792-18); Legal Coordinator and Contracts Monitor (5668-22); Legal Research Assistant (5676-23); Legal Research Aide I (5670-16); Legal Research Aide II (5671-18); Legal Aide (5660-14).

GOVERNMENT	POSITION	RESPONSIBILITIES	QUALIFICATIONS	SALARY
New Jersey Department of Personnel 3 Station Plaza, CN317 44 S. Clinton Ave. Trenton, NJ 08625 609-292-4144	Paralegal Technician 2/9/95 (G17-37208)	• Help perform legal research • Coordinate case calendar • Prepare court statistics	Completion of an approved course of paralegal training <u>AND</u> 2 years of experience as a paralegal responsible for reviewing and analyzing legal documents	$25,939–$36,327 per year

Other positions to check in New Jersey: Legal Services Assistant I (A18-72743); Paralegal Technician Assistant (A13-30459); Paralegal Technician, Law and Public Safety (A17-30461); Paralegal Technician, Casino Control Commission (X17-98648); Research Analyst (A18-03171); Research Analyst—Civil Service (A18-03171); Supervising Research Analyst—Div. of Youth and Fam. Services (A28-03184B).

GOVERNMENT	POSITION	RESPONSIBILITIES	QUALIFICATIONS	SALARY
New Mexico State Personnel Office 810 W. San Mateo Rd. Santa Fe, NM 87503 505-827-8120	Legal Assistant 1 8/29/79; 7/26/92 (SPB-1330)	• Provide help in legal research • Prepare affidavits and exhibits • Serve legal papers • Prepare and maintain records • Handle routine legal correspondence	Education and legal experience equaling 4 years. The experience can be gained as a paralegal. An associate's degree in paralegal studies can substitute for 3 years of experience.	$14,891–$24,760 per year

Other position to check in New Mexico: Legal Assistant II (1331).

continued

Appendix 2.B   Summary Chart—Survey of State Government Job Classifications for Paralegals—continued

GOVERNMENT	POSITION	RESPONSIBILITIES	QUALIFICATIONS	SALARY
New York Dept. of Civil Service State Campus, Bldg. 1 1220 Washington Ave. Albany, NY 12239 518-457-3701 518-457-9374	Legal Assistant I 2/10/84 (26-880)	● Compile and organize documentation ● Help prepare legal documents and forms ● Respond to inquiries and complaints ● Maintain files ● Monitor legislation ● Perform legal research	Associate's degree in paralegal studies OR Completion of general practice legal specialty training of 150 or more classroom hours leading to a certificate AND *Passing a test* on law, procedure, interviewing, and legal research	$28,225 per year
Other positions to check in New York: Legal Assistant Trainee I (00-107); Legal Assistant II (26-881).				
North Carolina Office of State Personnel 116 West Jones St. Raleigh, NC 27603 919-733-7108	Paralegal I 6/82 (NC 1422) (INCAC 8G.0402)	● Draft legal instruments ● Prepare routine opinions on agency ● Handle complaints and inquiries from the public ● Administer the law office ● Perform legal research	Graduation from a certified paralegal school and 1 year of paralegal experience	$24,090– $39,321 per year
Other positions to check in North Carolina: Paralegal II (NC 1423); Paralegal III (NC 1424).				
North Dakota Central Personnel Division Office of Management & Budget 600 E. Boulevard Ave., 14th Fl. Bismarck, ND 58505 701-328-3290	Legal Assistant I 4/87; 12/91 (0701)	● Draft legal documents ● Maintain case files ● Answer letters seeking information on laws ● Maintain law library ● File documents in court ● Assist attorneys in litigation	Completion of 2 years of college in legal or pre-law studies AND 2 years of experience in legal research analysis	$1,356– $2,161 per month
Other position to check in North Dakota: Legal Assistant II (0702).				
Ohio Dept. of Administrative Services Div. of Personnel 30 E. Broad Street Columbus, OH 43266 614-466-3455	Paralegal/Legal Assistant 3/95 (6381)	● Perform legal research ● Review corporate filings ● Prepare responses to legal inquiries ● Prepare case summaries ● Negotiate settlements ● File documents in court ● Schedule hearings	Completion of paralegal certification program OR Other evidence showing you have the legal knowledge and skills required OR Completion of 1 year of law school	$11.29– $13.25 per hour

continued

Appendix 2.B   Summary Chart—Survey of State Government Job Classifications for Paralegals—continued

GOVERNMENT	POSITION	RESPONSIBILITIES	QUALIFICATIONS	SALARY
Ohio—continued				
Other positions to check in Ohio: Hearing Assistant (63821); Hearing Officer (63831).				
Oklahoma Office of Personnel Management 2101 N. Lincoln Blvd. Oklahoma City, OK 73105 405-521-2177 800-522-8122	Legal Research Assistant 7/1/81; 7/1/93 (K101 FC: K10)	• Perform legal research • Conduct investigations • Assist attorneys in litigation • File pleadings • Maintain law library	Completion of approved legal research assistant program OR Completion of bachelor's degree in legal studies OR Completion of 18 semester hours of law school	$21,723–$28,554 per year
Other positions to check in Oklahoma: Legal Assistant I; Legal Assistant II (Office of the Municipal Counselor, Oklahoma City).				
Oregon Dept. of Admin. Services Personnel & Labor Relations Div. 155 Cottage St. N.E. Salem, OR 97310 503-378-3020	Paralegal Specialist 4/90; 11/91 (1526) (1622G)	• Organize complex facts • Communicate with experts • Analyze cases • Assist attorneys in litigation • Arrange for case settlements • Answer interrogatories	3 years of experience in a technical or professional field like real estate or accounting AND 2 years of subparalegal experience as a legal secretary or in an administrative job in court, OR a 1-year certificate program in paralegal studies OR An equivalent combination of training and experience	$2,372–$3,154 per month
Other positions to check in Oregon: Paralegal 1 (1523); Paralegal 2 (1524); Paralegal 3 (1525); Investigator (C1031); Special Investigator (X 1032); Legal Assistant (C0680).				
Pennsylvania Office of Administration Bureau of Personnel 514 Finance Bldg. Harrisburg, PA 17105 717-787-5545	Legal Assistant 1 6/89 (07010)	• Review work of field personnel for possible legal implications • Summarize cases • Review files • Prepare reports	3 years of progressively responsible clerical, auditing, enforcement, or investigative experience OR Any equivalent combination of experience and training	$21,223–$31,668 per year
Other positions to check in Pennsylvania: Legal Assistant 2 (07020); Legal Assistant Supervisor (07030); Legal Assistant Manager (07040).				

continued

A p p e n d i x 2 . B   **Summary Chart—Survey of State Government Job Classifications for Paralegals—continued**

GOVERNMENT	POSITION	RESPONSIBILITIES	QUALIFICATIONS	SALARY
Rhode Island Office of Personnel Administration 1 Capitol Hill Providence, RI 02908 401-277-2160	Paralegal Aide 11/24/85 (02461300)	• Perform legal research • Conduct investigations • Answer questions by interpreting laws • Assist in litigation • Maintain files	Completion of an approved paralegal training program OR Para-professional experience in an extensive legal service program	$21,810–$23,691 per year
South Carolina Budget and Control Board Division of Budget and Analyses Office of Human Resources 1201 Main St. Columbia, SC 29201 803-737-0900	Administrative Assistant 7/96 (AA75) [The Paralegal Assistant classification was combined with about 30 other job titles to create the Administrative Assistant position.]	• Help perform legal research • Draft legal documents • Proofread legal documents	A high school diploma and work experience that is directly related to the area of employment (The employing agency may impose other requirements.)	$19,259–$35,629 per year
South Dakota Bureau of Personnel 500 E. Capitol Pierre, SD 57501 605-773-3148	Legal Assistant 8/93 (11205)	• Conduct legal research • Perform investigations • Summarize discovery documents • Draft correspondence and pleadings • Index trial materials • Act as client liaison • Attend depositions, hearings, and trials	An equivalent combination of education and experience will be used to qualify applicants. Graduation from a college or university with an associate's degree in paralegal studies or a related field.	$18,928–$28,371 per year
Tennessee Dept. of Personnel 505 Deaderick St. Nashville, TN 37243 615-741-2958	Legal Assistant 7/1/84; 8/1/92 (02350)	• Help attorney prepare for trial • Summarize laws and regulations • Maintain law library • Answer routine inquiries on laws and regulations	Associate's degree in paralegal studies, bachelor's degree in paralegal studies, or 1 year of law school OR High school graduation (or equivalent) or 2 years of full-time experience in researching legal issues and documenting findings to assist in building case files, settling legal disputes, and/or providing legal counsel to clients	$1,339–$2,145 per month

continued

Appendix 2.B Summary Chart—Survey of State Government Job Classifications for Paralegals—continued

GOVERNMENT	POSITION	RESPONSIBILITIES	QUALIFICATIONS	SALARY
Texas State Auditor's Office P.O. Box 12067 419 Reagan State Office Bldg. 206 East 9th St. Ste. 1900 Austin, TX 78711 512-479-4700	Legal Assistant I 9/1/89 (3570)	• Perform legal research • Check citations and references • Schedule meetings and depositions • Screen calls for attorneys • Help prepare legal documents • File pleadings in court	Graduation from a 4-year college or university with major coursework in law or a related field AND Should have some experience in paralegal work	$22,032–$27,744 per year

Other positions to check in Texas: Legal Assistant II (3572); Legal Assistant III (3574); Administrative Technician II (Office of Attorney General).

GOVERNMENT	POSITION	RESPONSIBILITIES	QUALIFICATIONS	SALARY
Utah Department of Human Resources Management 2120 State Office Bldg. Salt Lake City, UT 84114 801-538-3080	Paralegal I 1/29/94 (85305)	• Perform directed legal research • Conduct investigations • Maintain document control in litigation • Draft routine legal documents	High school diploma or equivalent AND Certificate of paralegal studies from an accredited institution AND 1 year of paid experience performing the duties of the position	$10.39–$15.61 per hour

Other positions to check in Utah: Paralegal II (85306); Legal Assistant—Unemployment Insurance (85010).

GOVERNMENT	POSITION	RESPONSIBILITIES	QUALIFICATIONS	SALARY
Vermont Agency of Administration Dept. of Personnel 110 State St., Drawer 20 Montpelier, VT 05620 802-828-3491	Paralegal Technician I 8/11/89; 5/17/93 (081800) (CLS 18)	• Assist attorneys in litigation • Conduct investigations • Interview parties • Perform legal research • Audit records • Interpret laws • Draft briefs and legal documents • Advise parties of their rights	High school diploma AND 4 years of experience at or above senior clerical level, including 1 year of investigatory, analytical, research, or paralegal duties (30 college credits in legal or paralegal studies can substitute for general experience requirement; a JD degree is considered qualifying.)	$22,444–$35,464 per year

Other position to check in Vermont: State Investigator—Civil Rights.

continued

Appendix 2.B Summary Chart—Survey of State Government Job Classifications for Paralegals—continued

GOVERNMENT	POSITION	RESPONSIBILITIES	QUALIFICATIONS	SALARY
Virginia Dept. of Personnel and Training 101 N. 14th St. Richmond, VA 23219 804-225-2131	Legal Assistant 11/1/83; 1/1/88 (21521)	• Perform legal research • Keep track of cases • Prepare witnesses for trial • Manage law library • Prepare exhibits of physical evidence	Graduation from high school or equivalent. Paralegal coursework or training preferred. AND Experience in judicial and quasi-judicial systems and in the application of legal principles (Equivalent training and experience can be substituted.)	$20,976—$32,027 per year (For northern Virginia: $22,931–$35,012 per year)
Washington D.C. (See District of Columbia)				
Washington State Department of Personnel 521 Capitol Way S. P.O. Box 47500 Olympia, WA 98504 206-586-0194	Paralegal 1 9/14/79; 7/10/87 (46610)	• Organize litigation files • Enter data into computer databases • Conduct investigations • Prepare responses to interrogatories • Prepare deposition questions • Prepare trial notebook • Negotiate claims	2 years of experience as paralegal OR Graduation from 2-year paralegal course OR 4-year college degree plus 9-month paralegal program or 1 year of paralegal experience OR 3 years of legal secretarial experience plus 30 quarter hours of paralegal college courses	$26,148–$33,192 per year
Other positions to check in Washington: Paralegal 2 (46620); Paralegal 3 (46630).				
West Virginia Division of Personnel 1900 Kanawha Blvd. East Charleston, WV 25305 304-558-3950	Paralegal 10/16/90; 6/22/93 (9500)	• Perform legal research • Summarize evidence • Supervise clerical staff • Maintain case calendar of attorneys • Compose routine correspondence • Monitor pending legislation	Completion of an approved paralegal assistant training program OR 2 years of paid experience in a legal setting performing legal research, reading and interpreting laws, and preparing legal documents under attorney supervision	$17,256–$28,104 per year
Other positions to check in West Virginia: Child Advocate Legal Assistant (9501); Lead Paralegal (9502).				

continued

Appendix 2.B	Summary Chart—Survey of State Government Job Classifications for Paralegals—continued			
GOVERNMENT	**POSITION**	**RESPONSIBILITIES**	**QUALIFICATIONS**	**SALARY**
Wisconsin Dept. of Employment Relations 137 East Wilson St. P.O. Box 7855 Madison, WI 53707 608-266-9820	Legal Assistant 5/15/94 (19202)	● Help an attorney prepare for trial ● Collect and compile data ● Conduct preliminary witness interviews ● Perform legal research ● Provide information to public ● Draft routine legal documents ● Represent the agency at administrative hearings	The qualifications required will be determined on a position-by-position basis at the time of recruitment. Hiring will be based on an analysis of the education, training, work, or other life experiences that provide reasonable assurance that the knowledge and skills required for the position have been acquired.	$10.66–$14.96 per hour

Other positions to check in Wisconsin: Legal Assistant Entry (19201); Legal Assistant—Confidential (19211; 19212).

| **Wyoming**
Personnel Management Division
Department of Administration and Information
2001 Capitol Ave.
Cheyenne, WY 82002
307-777-6713 | Paralegal
6/91; 4/94
(LR37) | ● Perform legal research
● Help establish form files
● Help attorneys prepare for trial
● Help in discovery
● Draft pleadings
● Perform docket control and file maintenance duties | Any combination of training and experience equivalent to an associate degree in paralegal studies or pre-law | $1,460–$2,131 per month |

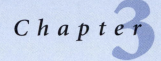

Chapter 3

ON-THE-JOB REALITIES: ASSERTIVENESS TRAINING FOR PARALEGALS

► *Chapter Outline*

Section A
THE IDEAL

The practice of law is not for the faint of heart. In this chapter we will explore some of the major techniques needed to survive and thrive in the practice of law. Before doing so, we pause to examine the ideal.

What is a "perfect" paralegal job? Perhaps it is impossible to describe perfection in its fullest sense, but if we made the attempt, what would the description contain? Exhibit 3.1 presents such an attempt: it tries to identify seventy-five factors of an ideal paralegal job environment. The factors are not of equal importance, and some of them overlap. Nor would every paralegal agree that all seventy-five are needed. In general, however, these are the factors (not necessarily listed in order of priority) that must be considered according to many working paralegals.

Assignment 3.1

(a) Which of the seventy-five factors in Exhibit 3.1 do you think are *not* important for job satisfaction? Why?

(b) Select what you feel are the fifteen most important factors. Write out your list and make a copy. Indicate whether you have ever had any law office work experience as a secretary, a paralegal, etc.

(c) Give the copy of your list to a person in the class whom your instructor will designate as the statistician. The latter will collect all the copies from the students and make the following tabulations: (1) which factors received the most votes on the "top fifteen" list by the students who have had prior law office experience; (2) which received the most votes from the other students.

In class, discuss the results of these tabulations. Are there significant differences in the opinions of the two groups? Can you explain the differences or similarities?

We move now to the *reality* of paralegal employment. The seventy-five factors obviously do not exist in every paralegal job. To be candid, some paralegals are quite dissatisfied with their job. As of the late 1970s and early 1980s:

- Paralegal turnover was high; the average length of a paralegal's first job was two to three years.
- Approximately 25 percent of working paralegals indicated that they did not plan to remain in the paralegal career.

Today the statistics are *not* as discouraging. Nevertheless, as you enter the career, it is important that you understand some of the danger signals of discontent. This understanding is our goal in this chapter. While our focus will be on *problems*, do not get the impression that gloom is the order of the day. A large majority of paralegals express substantial satisfaction with their work and career. Though even these paralegals point to areas that need improvement, they will tell you that they find their work stimulating and even fascinating at times. Most paralegals are satisfied with the career they have chosen. These are not the paralegals, however, that this chapter is primarily about.

It should also be pointed out that many of the problems we will be discussing are not peculiar to paralegalism. Sexism, for example, and the hassles of worker coexistence are

Exhibit 3.1   Seventy-Five Factors That Affect Paralegal Job Satisfaction

1. Your pay is satisfactory.
2. You receive satisfactory bonuses.
3. Your fringe benefits are satisfactory (e.g., health plan, life insurance, pension; see Exhibit 2.14 in chapter 2).
4. Your compensation is fair in relation to that of attorneys, other paralegals, and secretaries.
5. You are part of the professional staff in that you do *not* receive overtime pay for the extra hours you work.
6. You are part of the administrative staff in that you *do* receive overtime pay for the extra hours you work.
7. You are given financial support and time off to participate in activities of paralegal associations.
8. You are given financial support and time off to attend training sessions outside the office at paralegal schools, paralegal associations, bar associations, etc.
9. Adequate supplies are readily available.
10. Your hours are satisfactory.
11. You have your own office.
12. You have adequate access to secretarial help.
13. You have adequate access to word processing and other computer equipment.
14. You have your own business card.
15. You are challenged by your job.
16. You like your job.
17. Your privacy is respected.
18. No sexism or racism exists.
19. People in the office share the same basic values.
20. The office has high standards of performance; there are many good role models.
21. You are respected.
22. You are not taken advantage of.
23. You are not unduly pressured to meet a billable-hour quota.
24. You are not unduly pressured to work evenings or weekends.
25. You are encouraged to develop new skills.
26. Your paralegal training is being used by the office.
27. You have meaningful client contact.
28. Your name is in the office directory.
29. You do not feel isolated; there are few or no "attorney only" social events.
30. The office politics are manageable.
31. The secretaries, clerks, and other support personnel understand your job and accept your role in the office.
32. Your supervisors are not afraid of delegating tasks to paralegals.
33. The attorneys in the office understand your job and accept your role.
34. You are not in competition with anyone else in the office.
35. You have good rapport with other paralegals in the office.
36. You respect others in the office.
37. The office functions as a team; employees are not obsessed with a niche or territory that they are protecting.
38. People in the office are willing to compromise on personnel methods and procedures.
39. The office follows high standards of ethics and moral responsibility.
40. There is a career ladder in the office for paralegals.
41. You are not constantly being relegated to someone else's deadline; it is recognized that you have deadlines of your own to which others must be sensitive.
42. People in the office know how to listen; employees do not simply *talk at* everyone else.
43. You feel you are making a contribution to the office.
44. You have the feeling that your office is offering a social service; it is not "just a business."
45. There is an adequate flow of communication in the office; you know what is going on because the office makes it known. The grapevine is not the main source of information.
46. There is a clear line of authority; you know who your supervisors are.
47. The importance of profit is never emphasized at the expense of people's lives.
48. At all times, you know which people you can go to for help and you are encouraged to seek this help.
49. You are adequately supervised by attorneys and other senior personnel.
50. You are encouraged to do self-evaluations, which are given serious consideration.
51. You are regularly evaluated in a constructive manner.
52. You are given credit for the contributions you make.
53. The roof does not cave in if you disagree with your supervisors.
54. If you make a mistake, it's not the end of the world.
55. You attend regular staff meetings.
56. You are allowed to participate in office training programs for new attorneys.
57. You attend strategy meetings for cases to which you

Exhibit 3.1   Seventy-Five Factors That Affect Paralegal Job Satisfaction —continued

are assigned.

58. You are not constantly being asked why you don't become an attorney.

59. There is low turnover in your office; people feel comfortable enough about the office to make a long-term commitment to it.

60. You are not the first paralegal in the office; the office has had experience working with paralegals.

61. You are not constantly interrupted with new assignments, new priorities, new crises; you are not the dumping ground for everyone else's problems.

62. You are kept busy all the time without feeling overburdened; "the time flies by."

63. You are permitted to see the end product of your work, for example, you occasionally have contact with a case from beginning to completion.

64. You are encouraged to make use of the law library.

65. Office manuals or procedure guides are available on many assignments.

66. A personnel manual clearly spells out critical employee policies.

67. You are encouraged to give your opinion on law office management issues.

68. You are encouraged to give your opinion on case strategy.

69. You have some independence; there are opportunities to work alone in the office.

70. You are given authority.

71. You are encouraged to make decisions within your competence, and someone will back you up on these decisions.

72. There is reasonable variety in your assignments.

73. You are given a reasonable amount of time to complete your assignments.

74. You are not given assignments beyond your present capacity.

75. You are given reasonable time and training to learn new areas.

Source: Sheila Swanson, 14 At Issue 8 (San Francisco Ass'n of Legal Assistants, January 1987)

---

certainly not unique to the law office. Indeed, this chapter is probably as much about human nature as it is about the paralegal career.

Some of the discussion will be directed at attorneys and what they must do to solve a particular employment problem. Yet a major concern of this chapter is what the *paralegal* can do to overcome difficulties, even those that appear to be beyond the control of the paralegal. According to Beth King, president of the Oregon Legal Assistant Association:

> Job satisfaction is one of life's most important assets. As such, it is something we should cherish and cultivate. We may blame a lack of job satisfaction on our employer or those with whom we work. In truth, satisfaction with our jobs lies within our control.[1]

Section B
THE BIG THREE EMPLOYMENT PROBLEMS

Three problems are mentioned most frequently: inadequate opportunity for advancement, inadequate compensation, and underutilization. Throughout the chapter we will be addressing these and related concerns. Again, every paralegal does not experience them, and they are becoming less common as the paralegal field continues to grow. But they are part of the early history of paralegalism and have not been totally resolved today.

INADEQUATE OPPORTUNITY FOR ADVANCEMENT

Once paralegals have become successful on the job, they need opportunities for internal advancement. Some large law offices have begun to create **career-ladder** structures,

---

[1]King, *President's Message,* 10 Newsletter 1 (Oregon Legal Assistant Ass'n, February 1987).

as we saw in chapter 1. In smaller offices, however, there is seldom a "next step" in the development of one's career. In a recent survey of all paralegals in Oregon, 85 percent of the paralegals responding to the survey said that their firm or company had not developed a career path for paralegals.[2] Too often, a paralegal has no place to go other than to another paralegal job or to law school. Since experienced paralegals are in great demand (as evidenced by the vast majority of want ads seeking paralegals with specific experience), moving to another job has become attractive for some paralegals. Yet most paralegals would prefer to remain where they are. Meaningful career ladders within a law office would help a lot.

INADEQUATE COMPENSATION

Some paralegals are not satisfied with their compensation. When used effectively, they can be a **profit center** primarily because of the paralegal fees that attorneys charge clients; yet some paralegals are dissatisfied with the pay and fringe benefits that they receive. The consequences to the law office can be unfortunate. A candid bar association article on ways to make paralegals more profitable gives employers the following advice:

> Hire the level of experience you need and pay accordingly. There are very few bargains in the paralegal job market. If you do find people at a bargain salary, be aware that you stand the risk of losing them to a higher paying position after you have trained them.[3]

Not all employers follow this advice, however.

UNDERUTILIZATION

Unfortunately, the following description of a paralegal's job does *not* apply to every paralegal in the country:

> Attorney Ron Bliss of Bradbury, Bliss & Riordan did not hire his legal assistant to do a few narrow, limited tasks. "She does everything that she's capable of doing."[4]

The paralegal at this firm does not feel underutilized. Some paralegals, however, complain they have skills that are not being used. The result is mounting frustration. A paralegal should not be stuck doing the same task over and over. Yet this does occur, particularly in law offices handling very large cases where there may be thousands of documents that must be identified, read, organized, stamped, coded, indexed, digested, etc. In extreme situations, paralegals have referred to such offices as "sweatshops."[5] A few law offices *expect* their paralegals to become bored with relatively tedious tasks and then move on. While many offices are starting to use part-time paralegals or independent paralegals for such tasks, a fair number of full-time paralegals find themselves in the middle of document avalanches.

This problem of *underutilization* is most acute in larger law firms where the practice of law is often compartmentalized into specialty areas (such as litigation, corporate law, real estate) with little crossover among the specialties. The more specialized the supervising attorney, the more specialized his or her paralegal will probably be. And it is within the specialties—particularly the litigation specialty—that paralegals are more likely to find themselves performing the same tasks over and over. It must be emphasized, however,

---

[2]Michaelis, *The Legal Assistant Profession, Part II,* 13 Paragram 10 (Oregon Legal Assistants Ass'n, May 1991).
[3]Wesemann, *Ten Ways to Make Paralegals More Profitable,* 134 Pittsburgh Legal Journal 20 (April 1986).
[4]Johnson, *Attorneys and the Use of Legal Assistants,* AALA News (Alaska Ass'n of Legal Assistants, August 1987).
[5]Fenn, *Letters to the Editor,* 10 National Paralegal Reporter 6 (Nat'l Federation of Paralegal Associations, June 1986).

that this is not universally so. There are many paralegals in the so-called "megafirms" who have fascinating and challenging careers.

When underutilization does exist, regardless of the size of the law office, the problem cannot be solved unless attorneys are willing to delegate meaningful tasks to paralegals. Paralegals also have a role in bringing about change. Here is the advice of two experienced paralegals:

> It is frustrating to beginning paralegals to be assigned "menial tasks"; however, we cannot run until we have learned to walk. Therefore, even assignments that seem menial must be done well. Once we prove ourselves in small assignments, large assignments will follow, as will increased responsibility and job satisfaction.[6]

> It is common today in any group of paralegals to find a vast disparity in job responsibility. It is equally common to find a vast difference in job duties among paralegals from the same firm. This is not good, but it happens. Don't despair. Sometimes this occurs because entry-level paralegals must pay their dues (much like their predecessors) before they secure the really challenging assignments. You must accept these mundane responsibilities and demonstrate your willingness to complete the task to the best of your ability. Once you are perceived as a team player and a professional, you will receive the meaty assignments you prepared for during your paralegal education or training.[7]

Of course, from the perspective of the client, *every* task of the office is important; incompetence in performing even menial tasks can have devastating consequences for the outcome of a case.

While underutilization is a problem for many paralegals, the opposite problem of *over*utilization also exists. Some paralegals, particularly in smaller law firms, are given tremendous amounts of responsibility. The constant pressure and tension can be extreme. One paralegal, who loves her job, describes her life this way:

> I am trusted to the extent that I have nightmares about what I may have forgotten to do. I generally work ten to twelve hours a day, five days a week, and another five hours on Saturday. I have children who want to know why I am home so early if I come in the door at seven.[8]

Another paralegal, who was once a litigation specialist, commented, "I miss the pressure. I miss being overworked."[9] For most paralegals, however, such an environment can become overwhelming. In addition to covering techniques to combat underutilization, we also need to explore ways to handle work overloads.

Section C
COMMUNICATION

There is nothing leisurely about the practice of law, particularly in a litigation practice where most paralegals work. The atmosphere can be highly charged because of the high stakes and egos involved. In such an environment, communication can easily break down.

Here is a case in point. A senior partner thinks he has told his paralegal to take care of an important filing. In actuality, all he told the paralegal to do was to *draft* the necessary docu-

---

[6]*Paralegal Pride: Is There Such a Thing?*, 10 Precedent (Indiana Paralegal Ass'n, April 1987).
[7]Sova, *Bridging the Gap from Student to Professional*, 7 Legal Professional 47 (January/February 1990).
[8]Slate, *Mousebites*, 9 Newsletter 3 (Dallas Ass'n of Legal Assistants, March 1985).
[9]Frank, *Paralegal Burnout*, 70 American Bar Association Journal 30 (December 1984).

Source: Sheila Swanson, 14 At Issue 8 (San Francisco Ass'n of Legal Assistants, January 1987)

ments to make the filing. The paralegal drafts the documents and puts them in the senior partner's in-box for his review. The filing deadline is missed. The senior partner blames his paralegal. The worst part of this scenario is that the paralegal is never told what happened or that she is being blamed. Perhaps the senior partner wishes to avoid a confrontation; perhaps he fears being told that the problem is not only his responsibility, but also his fault. In any event, the paralegal's reputation is smeared among the professional staff.[10]

In a case such as this, trying to establish the truth—what actually happened—can sometimes be fruitless. People may simply be in no mood for "explanations."

The need, of course, is to *prevent* miscommunication. Be aware of the standard factors that contribute to communication problems:

- Distractions
- Physical impairment (e.g., hearing difficulty, defective eyeglasses)
- Time pressures
- Work overload
- Embarrassment over asking for clarification
- Personality conflicts
- Equipment breakdown
- Etc.

You can take specific steps to help avoid miscommunication. For example, you can keep an assignment notebook, diary, or daily journal in which you write down precisely what you are asked to do. You can repeat an assignment back to your supervisor immediately after receiving it. For lengthy or complex assignments, you could send your supervisor a brief note in which you confirm what you have been asked to do and when it is due.

---

[10]Sgarlat, *The Scape Goat Phenomenon,* 6 The Journal 10 (Sacramento Ass'n of Legal Assistants, June 1986).

Perhaps most important of all is to have a constant awareness of the potential for miscommunication in a busy law office. The danger can be quite high. If you are constantly aware of the danger, you'll be in a better position to help avoid it. It's a little like crossing the street. The busier the intersection, the more caution you must use to avoid an accident. Most law offices are very busy intersections.

Section D
EXPECTATIONS

A fair amount of paralegal frustration on the job is due to unrealistic expectations about the career in general and about a particular job. Frustration is mainly generated by surprise: "I never thought the job would be like this!"

One of the objectives of this book is to provide you with information that will help prevent this surprise. You need a candid account of what you might find. Chapter 2 outlined steps on doing background research on a potential employer *before* you accept a job, such as talking with paralegals who have worked or who still work at the office. Following these steps, whenever possible, should give you an accurate picture of what lies ahead if you take the job.

In a seller's market where there are more applicants than jobs, you may be so anxious to obtain a job that you will overlook its potential negative aspects. This is unfortunate. It is essential that you walk into a job, or any situation, with open eyes. Not only will accurate information help reduce any frustration that may eventually develop, but the information will also be the foundation for corrective steps you can begin taking as soon as possible.

You need a lot of information. In the best of all possible worlds, you would have information relevant to each of the seventy-five factors listed in Exhibit 3.1 that affect potential job satisfaction. (At a minimum, you would like information on the fifteen factors that you identified as most important in Assignment 3.1.) Of course, there are limitations on what you can learn now. Furthermore, even the information you receive can at best be a guide to your own prediction of how these factors might apply to you as an individual once you are on the job. This should not deter you, however, from going after whatever information is available about the paralegal field in your area and about particular prospective employers.

Whether the information you gather is extensive or minimal, however, the healthiest attitude is to expect the unexpected. Be prepared for surprises about what supervisors think you are capable of doing, the level and quantity of assignments you are given, how secretaries and other paralegals in the office respond to you, who in the office will become the major influences on your growth and success as a paralegal, etc. This is not to say that everything you encounter will be a surprise. But it may not be a bad idea to proceed as if it will be. In short, be careful of your preconceptions about what is going to happen. Don't let them block the challenges waiting for you.

Section E
THE ENVIRONMENT OF A LAW OFFICE

When you walk into a law office, some of your first impressions might be as follows:

- The office is very formal and organized.
- The people here know what they are doing and are set in their ways.

These impressions can be very misleading. A law office is in a state of perpetual *becoming*. The environment is always changing. New people are added, new clients come in, old clients are lost, new ways of doing things are developed, personality conflicts arise—numerous factors interact to produce an office that is in constant transition. Furthermore, *you* go through a process of change along with everyone else as the office continues to grow. On the surface, the office may appear to be a model of stability, but underneath all the layers of order and permanence, there is a *live* office that is in motion.

The consequences of this reality for the new paralegal are twofold:

- Do not be deceived by appearances.
- Recognize your own responsibility and *power* to help create the environment in which you are working.

If you become dissatisfied with your job, avoid being passive or defeatist. Everyone else in the office is trying to mold the environment to his or her own needs. Join the club! You may not succeed the first time. You may not succeed the fifth time. You may not even be aware of when your advocacy for yourself is having an impact. *Yet you must assert yourself and do so regularly.* Change usually does *not* occur within the timetable of the person trying to bring about the change. Occasionally, you will get the impression that everyone is resisting what you feel is right. You must be prepared to lose on some points. But you must stick with it. The person who wins is often the person who outlasts the others. The losers are those who demand instant success—whether or not there is justice behind their positions.

Three things must happen before change can occur:

- You convince yourself that you have the power to create change.
- Your mind generates ten to fifteen ways of creating the change.
- You have the stamina and perspective to live through the unsuccessful attempts until you finally hit upon the strategy that produces the change.

What kind of changes are we talking about? They could involve any of the following:

- Salary
- Workload/billable hour expectations
- Secretarial help
- Career ladders
- In-house training
- Equipment needs
- How the office treats clients
- How the office treats vendors
- Office procedures
- Ethical irregularities
- Etc.

If you are the type of person who wants every possible change made in every area in need of change, and you want all the changes made *now,* you may not have the temperament needed to survive and thrive in a busy law office. Change is possible, and you can play a major role in creating it as long as you are not impatient and you keep looking for new ways to try to bring it about.

Section F
OFFICE POLITICS

Few people like **office politics.** Most of us want to work where office politics does not exist. If this is not possible, our instinct is to blame others. We do what is right; others play politics.

These attitudes are illusions and interfere with your chances of bringing about change. Whenever two people work together, politics is involved. When fifty people work together,

> "It is difficult to explain to outsiders the pressures of a law firm environment. Client demands are never ending, equipment failures send staff into a frenzy, messengers run throughout the city like maniacs, paralegals pore through documents to find 'the one' to save the day or hour, receptionists cannot find various personnel because they did not check in or out, the accounting [department] is complaining about time and billing, and priorities change every minute."
>
> —Mary Ryan, Human Resources Consultant

politics is the order of the day. The "people you work with become your second family, complete with squabbles and jealousies. It is not possible to completely avoid confrontations or politics."[11] People often disagree about minor and major matters. As a result, conscious or unconscious *negotiation* becomes the mechanism by which things get done. Bargaining takes place all the time. More to the point, bargaining in the context of egos takes place all the time. There is simply no alternative to this process.

If there is harmony in an office, it is because people are engaged in *effective* office politics. People are trading what others want. Disharmony usually results from the fact that people are not responding to each other's needs. A cardinal principle of human relations is that you cannot get anyone to do anything well until you have found a way of making them happy or at least satisfied about doing it. Coercion and management-by-might have within them the seeds of their own defeat. They may work for a while, but at great cost. People generally want to do their jobs well, but this will not happen unless they strive hard to help *other* people do *their* jobs well.

The following dimensions of office politics may at first appear to be unpleasant to some paralegals:

- You must make sure that the decision-makers in the office learn about your work.
- You must make sure that everyone in the office with whom you work has a good opinion of you.

Such behavior is distasteful to some who say good work should speak for itself and be its own reward. Why make a campaign about it?

Unfortunately, there is a danger, particularly in a large firm, of the paralegal getting lost in the shuffle. The remedy is to be constantly looking for ways to sell yourself without appearing to do so. This goes against the grain of many paralegals. They don't like to sell themselves, especially after they have been at an office for a while. They want to settle in and not be obsessed with getting ahead. Yet you can't have it both ways. You can't complain about conditions of employment and refuse to assert your most valuable asset— yourself. This means establishing credibility and making sure that people know your worth.

> Blow your own horn: let the attorney know how you saved the client thousands of dollars, how you found the hard-to-locate witness, how you organized a huge file in mere hours, how the information you gathered helped win the case, etc. (Attorneys do this all the time.) Make sure your colleagues know of your special areas of expertise. For example, perhaps you are a good photographer, know everything there is to know about stocks and bonds, or speak several languages. (One paralegal I know dabbles in handwriting analysis; her firm found out and now she is a 'handwriting expert.') Show an interest in other matters your firm is handling. Compliment an attorney with whom you are not presently working when you hear he/she won in court, closed a complicated big dollar deal, negotiated brilliantly, etc. . . . Be a real team player.[12]

> Ignoring, or worse, denying the ever-present politics of legal environments can be hazardous to your employment. You must be in-tune with the un-spoken; listen to your intuition and the grapevine. Stay out of gossip groups, keeping your ears open and your mouth shut. Watch how the attorneys interact with each other. Monitor power plays and coalitions. Make an effort to understand each of the attorneys you work with on an individual basis, and by that I mean: writing style, organizational preferences, demeanor. *You* must adapt to each attorney. . . . Strategize yourself when possible: work with other attorneys in your firm, or with outside

---

[11]McLaverty, *Office Politics and Communication*, 24 WALS State Journal 50 (January 1990).
[12]Chernowsky, *Toward Greater Visibility*, 15 Reporter (Los Angeles Paralegal Ass'n, August 1986).

co-counsel; assist baby lawyers without a demeaning attitude. (Remember that baby lawyers grow up to be associates and associates grow up to be partners.) Enlist help within and without your firm—usually persons you have no control over. You must appeal to them and win them over to help you. But be genuine! Everyone can spot a fake.[13]

What do you think of the following advice from another successful paralegal? "Set your goals and aim for them. Open your mouth and let people know that you're headed up. Search out greater responsibility. Work your tail off—and let everyone know about it."[14] Too extreme? Too risky? People really don't get ahead this way? You don't have to advertise talent because it will eventually be discovered without self-promotion? Maybe. Talk with successful and satisfied paralegals around you. Make inquiries. Take a long look at people you respect in a competitive environment. Try to assess whether their abilities might have gone untapped without a healthy, effective, measured dose of self-assertiveness.

Section G
SELF-ASSESSMENT AND EMPLOYER EVALUATIONS

None of the techniques and strategies discussed in this chapter can ever be a substitute for your own competence as a paralegal. The techniques and strategies are designed to combat unrecognized and unrewarded competence.

Are you competent? To answer this question, you must evaluate yourself and receive the evaluations of others. Here are some suggestions for making both kinds of evaluations more meaningful, now and on the job.

- Carefully read the evaluation form in Exhibit 3.2.[15] First, note the standards used to earn a "Superior" rating and a "Very Good" rating in the eight categories being evaluated. These standards should be the day-to-day employment goals of every paralegal. Second, apply the form *now* to your present job or to any of your prior jobs, regardless of the kind of work involved. What ratings would you give yourself in the eight categories? What ratings do you think your supervisor would give you? (If you have never worked in a law office, simply substitute the word *supervisor* every time the word *attorney* is used in the form.)
- When you become a paralegal, the ideal will be for you and your supervisor to design an evaluation form *together*. The goal is to have a form that is specifically geared to the tasks you perform in the office. Even if the office already has an evaluation form, think about ways to adapt it more closely to you as an individual. Make notes on what you would like to see in such a form. Discuss it with your supervisor. Your initiative in this regard will be much appreciated, especially if you make clear that your goal is to use the evaluation to improve communication and to find ways to increase your skills and productivity.
- Start preparing for your evaluation on the first day of your employment *and* on the day after your last evaluation. Do not wait until a few days before the evaluation itself.[16]

---

[13]Michele Boerder, *Four Pointers to Professionalism*, 14 DALA Newsletter 3 (Dallas Ass'n of Legal Assistants, December 1990).

[14]Oder, *Paralegal Upward Mobility*, 6 National Paralegal Reporter 6 (Nat'l Federation of Paralegal Associations, Fall/Winter, 1981); Los Angeles Paralegal Ass'n, *Reporter* (September 1981).

[15]Reprinted with the permission of Heller, Ehrman, White & McAuliffe, San Francisco, California.

[16]Wojt, *Making the Most of Your Performance Review*, 38 The Docket 22 (April/May 1990).

Exhibit 3.2   Legal Assistant Evaluation Form

Personal and Confidential

Legal Assistant _____ Hire Date _____

Review Period _____ Department _____

Evaluating Attorney _____

A. CONTACT. Indicate the contact you have had with the legal assistant during the review period.

_____ *Substantial.* Regular, daily, or weekly contact. (Included in most attorney briefing/strategy meetings.)

_____ *Occasional.* Specific assignments and routine maintenance work requiring occasional personal instruction.

_____ *Infrequent.* Limited contact.

B. WORK PERFORMED. Describe the work performed by the legal assistant for you, listing some examples. Specify the degree of difficulty and expertise required.

_____

_____

_____

_____

_____

C. PERFORMANCE EVALUATION. Evaluate the legal assistant in each of the following areas. Check the blank to the left of the rating description that best summarizes the legal assistant's performance. Use the space on the back of the last page for additional comments.

1. Work Product. (Consider the legal assistant's ability to understand what is required and to provide a work product that is both thorough and complete. Consider the speed and efficiency with which the work product is returned.)

_____ *Superior.* In most cases, needs little instruction. Takes initiative in asking questions if aspects of the task are unclear. Is resourceful in developing more efficient ways to complete projects. Demonstrates ability to consider factors not indicated by attorney that make the work product more useful.

_____ *Very good.* Needs instruction once or twice. Legal assistant completes task thoroughly and keeps attorney informed as to work progress.

_____ *Good.* Sometimes needs to do a task several times before he or she feels comfortable. Substantial attorney supervision is necessary during first attempts at a project. Once legal assistant is comfortable with the job requirements, he or she does a thorough and complete work product.

_____ *Marginal.* Has difficulty understanding what kind of work product is required. Sometimes does an incomplete job and takes more time than should be needed.

_____ *Unacceptable.* Seldom masters what is required, and hence cannot do a thorough and complete work product.

_____ *No opportunity to form an opinion.*

2. Efficient Management of Workload. (Consider the volume of work produced and the efficient use of time in order to meet deadlines.)

_____ *Superior.* Highly efficient. Completes all assignments successfully, on time, and without prompting.

_____ *Very good.* Efficient. Most assignments completed successfully. Rarely misses deadlines.

_____ *Good.* Basically efficient. Assignments are generally completed successfully within a reasonable amount of time.

| Exhibit 3.2 | Legal Assistant Evaluation Form
—continued |

_____ *Marginal.* Needs to improve efficiency. Assignments sometimes go uncompleted. Needs substantial attorney supervision.

_____ *Unacceptable.* Inefficient. Deadlines are rarely met. Assignments often uncompleted.

_____ *No opportunity to form an opinion.*

3. **Ability to Work Well under Pressure.** (Consider the ability of the legal assistant to make sound judgments and to organize work under pressure.)

_____ *Superior.* Nearly always works well under pressure. Maintains organization and control over assignments; continues to make sound judgments.

_____ *Very good.* In most cases works well under pressure; rarely makes unsound judgments or becomes disorganized.

_____ *Good.* Generally works fairly well under pressure; sometimes makes judgments that are not carefully considered or becomes slightly disorganized.

_____ *Marginal.* Frequently fails to work well under pressure. Tends to become disorganized and to exercise poor judgment.

_____ *Unacceptable.* Rarely works well under pressure. Allows pressure to interfere with effective management of assignments, and often uses poor judgment.

_____ *No opportunity to form an opinion.*

4. **Analytical Skill.** (Consider the legal assistant's ability to digest and analyze the facts of a particular case or assignment and the thoroughness of performing factual research.)

_____ *Superior.* Is exceptionally thorough in gathering facts and quick to master the facts. Depth of understanding is evidenced by a high-quality work product.

_____ *Very good.* Is thorough in gathering information. Masters facts quickly and uses them well in preparation of work product.

_____ *Good.* Generally thorough in gathering information. Masters facts over an acceptable period of time. Sometimes needs attorney direction in developing the information required for work product.

_____ *Marginal.* Sometimes misses essential information during factual investigation. Knowledge of facts is incomplete. Needs substantial attorney direction in order to analyze facts correctly.

_____ *Unacceptable.* Often misses essential information during factual investigation. Knowledge of facts is seriously deficient. Work product needs substantial revision in order to insure completeness. Sometimes careless in presentation of facts to attorney.

_____ *No opportunity to form an opinion.*

5. **Professionalism.** (Consider the extent to which the legal assistant is personally involved in his or her work; the extent to which he or she takes the job requirements seriously; and the extent to which he or she demonstrates responsibility for high-quality work in all instances.)

_____ *Superior.* Exhibits exceptionally high level of personal involvement in assignments and is extremely responsible. Takes initiative.

_____ *Very good.* Highly involved in assignments. Demonstrates strong commitment to his or her work. Very dependable.

_____ *Good.* Generally dependable and involved in assignments. Demonstrates average commitment to his or her work.

_____ *Marginal.* Frequently appears to lack interest in assignments. Needs substantial follow-up by attorney as to both deadlines and quality of work.

Exhibit 3.2 Legal Assistant Evaluation Form —continued

_____ *Unacceptable.* Unwilling to assume the necessary responsibility.

_____ *No opportunity to form an opinion.*

6. **Ability to Work Independently.** (Consider the legal assistant's ability to exercise good judgment by making well-reasoned choices and then to maintain necessary communication with attorney.)

_____ *Superior.* Considers all options and makes good decisions. Always keeps attorney well informed.

_____ *Very good.* In most cases makes good decisions. Occasionally needs attorney assistance in defining options. Keeps attorney well informed.

_____ *Good.* Usually considers options before making a decision. May not recognize the need to request attorney assistance in defining options.

_____ *Marginal.* Has difficulty making well-reasoned choices after options are defined. Fails to cover necessary material with attorney and does not readily call upon attorney for assistance or explanation.

_____ *Unacceptable.* Is not able to make reasonable choices after options are defined. Rarely keeps attorney informed and lacks understanding as to appropriate area of legal assistant work as defined by attorney.

_____ *No opportunity to form an opinion.*

7. **Quality of Written Work.** (Consider the ability of the legal assistant to express himself or herself in a clear, precise language; thoroughness; organization; accuracy and neatness; grammar.)

_____ *Superior.* Exceptionally clear, precise, and thorough work that is neat and free from errors.

_____ *Very good.* In most cases, precise, clear, and thorough.

_____ *Good.* Generally acceptable but occasionally needs improvement.

_____ *Marginal.* Frequently lacking in one or more respects.

_____ *Unacceptable.* Work product is almost always lacking in one or more respects.

_____ *No opportunity to form an opinion.*

8. **Outside Contact.** (Consider the extent to which the legal assistant is required to work with persons outside the firm, such as co-counsel, clients, state and federal agencies, state and federal court personnel.)

_____ *Superior.* Consistently demonstrates ability to readily gain the cooperation and confidence the assignment requires. Establishes excellent working relationships.

_____ *Very good.* Generally gains cooperation and confidence. Establishes cooperation and confidence.

_____ *Good.* Needs occasional assistance but is able to gain the necessary cooperation and confidence.

_____ *Marginal.* Unable to handle outside assignments without substantial attorney assistance. Has difficulty developing necessary confidence and cooperation.

_____ *Unacceptable.* No understanding of what is required in order to gain necessary cooperation and confidence. Complaints received with regard to legal assistant's behavior.

_____ *No opportunity to form an opinion.*

COMMENTS. On the back of this form, space is provided to allow for elaboration of any of the ratings checked under the preceding categories. You are encouraged to provide additional comments on the legal assistant's performance: strengths, weaknesses, and suggestions for improvement.

- When you work on large projects, ask for a "project evaluation" at the conclusion of the project. This evaluation should be in *addition* to any regularly scheduled evaluations you receive.
- Before a regularly scheduled evaluation, write a **pre-evaluation memo** and submit it to your supervisor. The memo should list the major cases or projects you have worked on since the last evaluation, your functions on each, names of your supervisors and co-workers on each, special accomplishments, events showing initiative (such as weekend work), written or oral quotations from individuals commenting on your work, etc.[17]
- Before an evaluation, review the criteria by which you will be evaluated, if available.
- Before an evaluation, review your job description. If your duties have been slowly changing, rewrite your job description to reflect these changes. Submit the revision to your supervisor for approval.
- If this is your first formal evaluation by a particular supervisor, try to talk with others in the office who have been evaluated by this supervisor before. Find out what you might expect from this person.
- After an evaluation, set some *measurable* goals. Do not simply pledge that you will "work harder." Establish goals that are much more concrete. For example:
  - "Before January, attend a bar-association seminar or a paralegal-association conference covering an aspect of my job."
  - "For the next ten weeks, spend a minimum of ten minutes a day studying paragraph structure in grammar/writing books."
  - "Once a month for the next six months, go to lunch with a paralegal whose professionalism I respect in order to brainstorm techniques for improvement."
  - "Within five weeks, reread the word-processing software manual from cover to cover."

  Note that each of these goals can be placed on a calendar. You can determine whether each has been met. Of course, you should also commit yourself to broader goals, like learning how to digest interrogatories or improving your research skills. Yet be sure to include more objective, short-term, self-measurable goals as well.
- If you receive a negative evaluation, ask for a follow-up evaluation *before* your next regularly scheduled evaluation in order to determine whether you have made any progress on what was considered negative.
- Suppose you work in an office that does not have regularly scheduled performance evaluations. It uses little or no formal written evaluations. Employees are evaluated, but not on an organized, consistent, written basis. You need to become an advocate for a more structured system of evaluation. You will be successful if you can convince your supervisor of two things: structured evaluations have value and will not take too much of the supervisor's time. To save time, use other evaluations such as the one in Exhibit 3.2. Design your own evaluation form, as suggested earlier. Ask a busy supervisor to give you a brief oral evaluation, making sure that your strengths and weaknesses are covered. Take detailed notes. Then write out your notes in the form of a memo. Give it to the supervisor and ask if it accurately reflects what the supervisor said.
- When your supervisor sees that you are not threatened by criticism and that you are not defensive when you receive it, you will be more likely to receive constructive criticism. It is better to have something negative said directly to you than to have it whispered behind your back. Here are some suggestions on taking criticism:[18]

---

[17]In some offices, the employee will be asked to fill out a *self*-evaluation form before any formal evaluations by a supervisor take place.

[18]Barbara Middleton, *Taking Criticism,* 7 Newsletter 25 (Texas Legal Assistant Division, November 1991).

- Listen to all comments without trying to influence or criticize the critic.
- Be sure you understand the complaint.
- Admit when you are wrong; it's a sign of strength.
- Agree with the truth.
- Admit that you don't know.
- Ask for clarification.
- Ask for instructions or advice; be teachable.
- Think of ways you can put the advice into action.

We will have more to say about evaluations later when we discuss ways to support a request for a salary increase.

Section H
CHARACTERISTICS OF SOME ATTORNEYS

The personality of a particular attorney has a great deal to do with the effectiveness of a paralegal-attorney working relationship. Many paralegals speak in glowing terms about their attorney-supervisor. Not only is the attorney easy to work with, but also he or she provides a challenging environment within which the paralegal can grow. Other attorneys, however, fall short of this standard; they do not function well as the leader of a team. According to two experts on the practice of law, a number of characteristics common to many attorneys do not encourage effective team-building:[19]

Autonomy. Attorneys are less likely to collaborate than people in other occupations. Often they adhere to their preferred approach even when another is equally desirable.

Critical. The successful attorney is highly critical. Typically, the focus of the attorney is on what is wrong with an idea. The merits of the idea are often ignored.

Competitive. Like the very nature of the legal system, the attorney is competitive and adversarial. In policy questions and in personal relationships, progress and truth are achieved through varying degrees of confrontation.

It may not be easy to work with attorneys who fit these characteristics. The key to survival is assertiveness. According to one expert, "attorneys prefer to work with assertive paralegals who are competent and knowledgeable. If you are not assertive with attorneys, they will lose confidence in you, and you may find yourself burdened with problems [including] . . . boring work, poor raises, and poor working conditions."[20]

Thus far in the chapter, we have referred to the importance of initiative and assertiveness several times. We now turn to a closer examination of this topic.

Section I
ASSERTIVE/NONASSERTIVE/AGGRESSIVE BEHAVIOR

Of the three behaviors discussed here, nonassertive behavior is the easiest to define. It is passiveness or undue silence. A nonassertive person rarely, if ever, complains to a person causing or contributing to a problem.

---

[19]Allen & Williams, *Team-Building Frenzy Reaches Law Firms*, The National Law Journal 20 (December 17, 1990).

[20]Wagner, *Tips and Traps for the New Paralegal*, 8 Legal Assistant Today 78, 82 (March/April 1991).

Aggressive behavior is at the other extreme; it is constant complaining. An aggressive person is a negative person who cannot express dissatisfaction without depressing someone else. Aggressive people may be right in many of the things they are saying, but they are so unpleasant that supervisors and co-workers seldom listen to them.

In between these two extremes is **assertive** behavior. Assertive people:

- are competent and display competence.
- are prepared.
- show initiative (do not always wait to be told what to do).
- act like they belong in the office.
- are always willing to learn.
- respect the competence of others.
- are problem-solvers.
- know that one of the best ways to help others solve problems is to provide them with options.
- appreciate the value of timing ("now" is not always the best time to resolve a problem).
- act like professionals.
- do not shy away from office politics.
- know the difference between griping and negotiating.
- understand the necessity of compromise.
- know the difference between little concerns and major ones (do not treat every problem as a crisis).
- know when and how to lose gracefully.
- advocate with resolve, not fanfare.
- are self-assured enough to give credit to subordinates.
- are willing to help others do their job well.
- are secure enough to be able to say *no*.
- are not offensive.
- can express an opinion without putting someone down.

Assertive paralegals make themselves known. The backbone of assertiveness is competence—you know that you are capable. The trump card of assertiveness is timing—you watch for the right moment to come forward. The foundation of assertiveness is preparation—you have collected all the facts that support your position.

Suppose, for example, you feel that you are not earning what you are worth. What do you do? You can take one of a number of approaches:

Nonassertive

You hope that things will get better, but you don't want to rock the boat. After all, your salary isn't *that* bad; it could be worse. You talk with fellow paralegals about your salary, and you are very frank with your aunt when the two of you talk on the phone about your work. But there's no sense in trying to get the firm to pay you more. The firm probably doesn't earn that much. And Mr. Smith, the head of the firm, is very pleasant to work with. Money isn't that important. Maybe next year will be better.

Aggressive

Three weeks after you begin your job, you tell your supervisor that your salary is ridiculous. "With inflation, how do you expect me to live on this salary?" When your supervisor is not responsive, you send a memo to all the attorneys in the firm demanding that "something be done about paralegal salaries." When you walk the corridors of the firm, you are always visibly angry.

Assertive

- You prepare a fact sheet of paralegal salaries in your area after you talk with paralegals at other firms and examine salary surveys conducted by local and national paralegal associations, such as the following:
  - *National Utilization and Compensation Survey Report* published by the National Association of Legal Assistants
  - *Compensation and Benefits Report* published by the National Federation of Paralegal Associations
  - *Legal Assistant Managers and Legal Assistant Compensation* published by the Legal Assistant Management Association
- You make sure that your supervisors have evaluated you regularly in writing. You summarize these evaluations and add them to the fact sheet.
- You make a list of the various projects you have worked on. You highlight special projects, like helping design part of the office manual or training a new paralegal or attorney.
- You make sure that the decision-makers in the firm know who you are and what you have accomplished.
- You add up your billable hours over a designated period. The total is added to the fact sheet.
- You make note of every nonbillable task you performed that freed an attorney to devote more of his or her time to billable tasks.
- You discuss strategies for seeking a raise with other paralegals in the firm, with other paralegals in the area, and perhaps with some attorneys in the firm with whom you have developed considerable rapport.
- When others make a favorable comment about your work, you ask them to put it in writing so that it can go into your personnel file.
- You select the right time to meet with your supervisor. You decide to wait until the supervisor is not hassled with a difficult case.
- You may adopt a two-part strategy: you first ask for a meeting with your supervisor to discuss ways of increasing your contribution and productivity. At a follow-up meeting, you raise the question of a salary increase.
- Months before you ask for a raise, you ask your supervisor to identify those factors that will be taken into consideration in evaluating your overall performance and in recommending a salary level. In the months that follow, you make sure that you organize your efforts and your notes in accordance with the criteria the supervisor initially identified.
- You let your supervisor know what increase you are requesting, phrasing it as a range rather than as a single rigid figure.
- If you are unsuccessful in obtaining the amount you are seeking, you have a fall-back position ready—for example, you seek a performance bonus in lieu of a raise; additional insurance, educational tuition, or other fringe benefits; perhaps a different office setting; or flex time.

If you ask successful paralegals their secret of success (see Exhibit 3.3), one message will come through loud and clear: *Seize the initiative.* No one is going to hand you anything simply because you are smart or because you have a certificate. You must prove yourself. You must be assertive.

Exhibit 3.3   Taking the Initiative: Recommendations of Successful Paralegals

Tami Coyne:

I have heard this tired refrain many times: "I am a hard worker and just don't get the recognition or the responsibility I deserve." This attitude gets you nowhere. If you believe that it is up to your employer to pick you out of the crowd and reward you just because you do your job, you will be sorely disappointed. In order to advance as a paralegal, you must prove that you are capable of taking on greater responsibility by performing your present duties exceptionally well. Show your initiative by anticipating the next stage of any assignment and completing it before you are asked to do it. Do not wait for recognition or feedback. You must be the one to initiate a feedback discussion after you have completed an assignment.[21]

Renee Sova:

Volunteer to draft the next document. Say, "I can do that; will you let me try?" Patience is a virtue. If the lawyer doesn't accommodate your first request, keep asking. Upon receiving and ultimately completing the assignment, there is nothing wrong with asking: "What could I have done differently to make it better?" This shows you truly care about your work product. Always do more than is expected. Few professionals became successful [by leaving] their careers to fate.[22]

Laurie Roselle:

If you feel like a second-class citizen, that's the way you will be treated—and that's how you should be treated. However, if you want respect in this profession, you must command it. To command this respect, you must be an intelligent professional willing to take on responsibility without having to be asked. Find ways to make yourself even more valuable than you already appear to be. Don't sit and complain about the way things are. Take charge and change them.[23]

Chere Estrin:

Be assertive. Take an attorney to lunch![24]

Carol Musick:

Stay current on file status. Don't wait to be told to do something. Attorneys don't have time to spoon feed their paralegals. Stay current and find out "what comes next" on your own initiative.[25]

Marian Johnson:

The greatest key to success is something no one can give you—a good attitude! Enthusiasm has nothing to do with noise; it has more to do with motivation. It deals with our attitude. An attitude is something you can do something about. I can choose to be enthusiastic or I can choose not to be. Excitement is infectious. It's sort of like a case of the measles. You can't infect someone unless you have the real thing![26]

---

[21]Coyne, *Strategies for Paralegal Career Development,* Nat'l Paralegal Reporter 20 (NFPA, Winter 1990).

[22]Sova, *Bridging the Gap from Student to Professional,* 7 Legal Professional 47 (January/February 1990).

[23]Roselle, *I Don't Get No Respect!,* 9 Nat'l Paralegal Reporter 2 (NFPA, November/December 1984).

[24]Estrin, *10 Easy Steps to Leveraging Your Career,* 10 TALA Newsletter 7 (Toledo Ass'n of Legal Assistants, October 1989).

[25]Musick, *Productivity,* 5 FWPA Newsletter 3 (Fort Worth Paralegal Ass'n, May 1987).

[26]Johnson, President's Message, *Newsletter* 1 (Arizona Paralegal Ass'n, July 1988).

Section J
KEEPING A DIARY AND A CAREER DEVELOPMENT FILE

Keep a *daily diary* or journal in which you record:

- the assignments you are given.
- the dates the assignments are given and the due dates for completion.
- the dates when the assignments are actually completed.
- favorable and unfavorable comments (written or oral) that have been made about your work.
- total billable hours per day attributable to your work.
- total nonbillable hours devoted to assigned tasks.
- the dates when you work evenings and weekends.
- the dates when you work on something at home.
- the dates you were late, absent, or had to leave early.
- the dates when you came in early or worked through lunch hour.
- the names of any clients you referred to the firm.
- the amount of time you spent doing your own typing or photocopying.
- the time you spend in courses, seminars, or other ventures to improve your skills.

You need to have the facts of your employment at your command. The diary is your personal record; you keep it to yourself for use as needed. Not only will the facts be valuable when you are making an argument for a raise, they also might be essential when misunderstandings arise about what you have or have not done.

The diary may be burdensome for you at first, and you may not make use of it for a while. It is worth the burden and the wait. A law firm respects someone who has the facts, particularly with dates!

In addition, start a *career development file* that contains everything that is relevant to your employment and growth as a paralegal. It should include:

- *Résumés.* A copy of every résumé you have written, including a current one that you should update every two or three months.
- *Job history.* A record of the dates you were hired in previous and current jobs; who hired you; who supervised you; a copy of your job descriptions; starting salary; amounts and dates of raises, bonuses, and other benefits received; the dates and reasons you left.
- *Work accomplishments.* A copy of every written evaluation; letters received from clients commenting on your work; verbal comments made about your work by supervisors that you later wrote down.
- *Professional activities.* Evidence of your involvement with paralegal associations; attendance at conferences, seminars, and classes (including names of major teachers, copies of syllabi, etc.); speaking engagements; articles you have written for paralegal newsletters; significant events at church or other community groups.
- *Conflict-of-interest data.* A list of the cases on which you worked, including the exact names of all clients, opposing parties, and opposing attorneys; a brief description of your role in each case; the dates of your involvement in these cases. (These data may be needed when you seek employment with another law office that wants to avoid being disqualified from a case because of your involvement with a particular party at a prior job. See page 282).

Now you are ready. If the job you are waiting for opens up, you have almost everything ready to present to the prospective employer; or you are armed and ready to sit down with management to show you deserve the raise you have been so patiently waiting for; or you are prepared to show your supervisor you are ready to take on that new case that just came into the firm.[27]

Section K
THE "SWOOSE SYNDROME"

Is a paralegal part of the clerical staff or part of the professional staff? In most offices, the answer is both. If someone is part swan and part goose, he or she is experiencing the **swoose syndrome.**[28] A paralegal has also been referred to as a "tweener": one who performs both clerical and attorney tasks and hence falls somewhere in be*tween* these two employment categories.[29]

A cynic once said: "The person who asked a simple question and received a simple answer did not ask a lawyer." The question "Is a paralegal a professional?" is a simple question. The answer is *yes* in some respects and *no* in others. Exhibit 3.4 presents some of the main differences that exist between professional and clerical employees. The factors listed in the exhibit do not apply to every office, but they give a general idea of the distinctions that often exist. Later in chapter 4 we will discuss the controversial question of whether paralegals are entitled to overtime compensation. In general, professionals do not receive overtime; their extra efforts are recognized by the office in the form of a bonus.

"Good morning Mr. Davis. Here is the deposition summary I worked on till midnight, plus your coffee and danish."

---

[27]Kunz, *Personal Management File,* WDALA Summons (Western Dakota Ass'n of Legal Assistants, August 1990).

[28]Brandom, *Comments on Educating the Attorney to Employ, Utilize and Retain Legal Assistants,* 5 Facts & Findings 1, 10 (NALA, January/February 1979).

[29]Zavalney, *The Price of Success,* 6 Texas Lawyer 10, 11 (January 21, 1991).

Exhibit 3.4   Factors Affecting Professional vs. Clerical Status

FACTORS THAT TEND TO INDICATE A PARALEGAL HAS PROFESSIONAL STATUS	FACTORS THAT TEND TO INDICATE A PARALEGAL HAS CLERICAL STATUS
1. Does not do typing for anyone else	1. Does typing for others
2. Only occasionally types own material	2. Often types own material
3. Has own office	3. Does not have own office
4. Has own computer (used primarily for database management)	4. Has own computer (but used primarily for word processing)
5. Does not do own photocopying	5. Photocopies for others
6. Has secretarial help	6. Does not have secretarial help
7. Has a business card	7. Does not have a business card
8. Has name printed on letterhead of firm	8. Does not have name printed on letterhead
9. Is paid a bonus rather than overtime	9. Is usually paid overtime rather than given a bonus
10. Is paid a salary comparable to new attorneys	10. Is paid a salary comparable to that of secretaries and other clerical staff
11. Always attends strategy meetings on cases	11. Never or only occasionally attends strategy meetings on cases
12. Is given financial support and time off to attend association meetings and training sessions.	12. Rarely is given financial support or time off to attend association meetings and training sessions
13. Can become an associate member of a bar association	13. Is not eligible to become an associate member of a bar association
14. Clients can be separately billed for time	14. Clients cannot be separately billed for time; services are part of overhead

Section L
PARALEGAL CLE

Elsewhere in this book we have stressed the reality that your legal education never ends. There is always something to learn. This is true for attorneys, and it is certainly true for paralegals. Education after employment is referred to as **CLE**—continuing legal education. CLE is offered mainly by bar associations and by paralegal associations. It usually consists of relatively short seminars that take place on a workday afternoon at a downtown hotel or over a two- or three-day weekend in another city. CLE is often significantly different from the paralegal education you initially received. Since CLE occurs while you are employed, you are able to select seminars that directly and immediately relate to your day-to-day job responsibilities. Here is an example of this reality from Felicia Garant, a paralegal in Maine:

I had an experience where I attended a half-day title insurance seminar and passed around a memo to attorneys in my section of the firm summarizing what I had learned there. A few minutes after I circulated the memo, an attorney flew out of his office exclaiming, "There's a new law on this subject?" He asked me to help him get a copy of the law since he had a case at that time that would be directly affected. You are the attorney's extra pair of eyes and ears, and you may pick up something at these seminars which will be new to the attorney. Your attendance at seminars, educating yourself, then passing the information on to the attorney

"I'm headed out for a show tonight, and tomorrow I'll be at the golf tournament. I know the report is due tomorrow. I'll ask Helen, my paralegal, to do the report. She needs something to do."

not only increases your qualifications as a legal assistant, but also makes you a valuable employee.[30]

Often, but not always, the employer is willing to pay all or part of your expenses in attending such seminars and to give you time off if they occur during work hours. (See Exhibit 2.14 in chapter 2 for an overview of fringe benefits some paralegals receive.) Even if your employer refuses to pay for them, you should go on your own time and at your own expense. Few things are more important to the professional development of a paralegal than CLE.

Some paralegal associations have begun to *require* a paralegal to attend a designated number of CLE hours per year as a condition of renewing voting membership in the association. In chapter 4 we will discuss the certification programs of the National Association of Legal Assistants (NALA) and the National Federation of Paralegal Associations (NFPA). Once you pass their national certification exams you need to attend a required number of CLE hours to maintain your certification status. (See Exhibit 4.8 in chapter 4.)

Of course, CLE is not a requirement to *be* a paralegal in any state. The situation is different for attorneys in those states that require a designated number of CLE hours per year as a condition of being able to practice law.

Section M
RESPONSIBILITIES OF SUPERVISORS

What is a good attorney supervisor? The checklist in Exhibit 3.5 lists the factors that constitute effective supervision. You might cautiously consider showing this checklist to your supervisors so that they might evaluate themselves as supervisors. Do not do this, however, until you are well established in your job. Considerable tact is needed when suggesting that a supervisor might be less than perfect.

---

[30]Garant, *Speech to USM Paralegal Program Graduates,* Newsletter 3 (Maine Ass'n of Paralegals, April 1990).

Exhibit 3.5 Checklist for Effective Supervision of Paralegals

(Grade each factor on a scale of 1 to 5 with a 5 indicating that the supervisor is excellent in this factor and 1 indicating an unsatisfactory rating.)

FACTOR	RATING (on a scale of 1–5)
a. You give clear instructions to the paralegal on assignments.	a. _____
b. You do not overburden the paralegal with assignments. Before you give a new assignment, you determine what the paralegal already has to do. If the demands on a paralegal are great, you consider alternatives such as hiring temporary paralegal help.	b. _____
c. You provide reasonable deadlines on assignments, with adequate time built in for review and redrafting where appropriate.	c. _____
d. You take affirmative steps to inquire about the paralegal's progress on assignments to determine if you should offer more guidance or if deadline extensions are needed. You do not simply wait for the paralegal to come to you with problems.	d. _____
e. You provide adequate training for each assignment given. You take the time to make sure the paralegal can perform the task.	e. _____
f. You are not afraid to delegate tasks to the paralegal.	f. _____
g. You delegate meaningful tasks, not just the drudgery. Also, you do not ask the paralegal to do personal errands for you.	g. _____
h. You make sure that the paralegal has some variety in his or her work.	h. _____
i. You are supportive when the paralegal makes a mistake; your corrective suggestions for the future are constructive.	i. _____
j. You permit paralegals to experience the end product of cases on which they are working—for example, you give them a copy of the finished product, or you invite them to your court presentation.	j. _____
k. You include the paralegal in strategy meetings on cases.	k. _____
l. You encourage the paralegal to use the law library in order to increase his or her knowledge and to appreciate the legal context of a case.	l. _____
m. You use the paralegal's skills and regularly look for ways the paralegal can increase his or her skills.	m. _____
n. You encourage paralegals to give their opinion on cases and on office policy.	n. _____
o. You design systems with instructions, checklists, forms, etc. for the performance of tasks involving paralegals.	o. _____
p. You encourage the paralegal to help you write these systems.	p. _____
q. You regularly evaluate the paralegal, informally and in writing.	q. _____
r. You encourage the paralegal to help you design a relevant paralegal evaluation form.	r. _____
s. You encourage the paralegal to evaluate you as a supervisor.	s. _____
t. You give credit to the paralegal where credit is due.	t. _____
u. You make sure others in the firm know about the contribution of the paralegal.	u. _____
v. You lobby with other attorneys who do not use paralegals or do not appreciate their value in order to change their attitude.	v. _____
w. You make yourself aware of any tension that may exist among paralegals, secretaries, and other staff members in the office in order to help end the tension.	w. _____
x. You back the paralegal's reasonable requests on salary and working conditions.	x. _____
y. You introduce your clients to the paralegal, explain the latter's role, and express your confidence in your employee.	y. _____
z. You do not pressure the paralegal about producing a quota of billable hours.	z. _____

E x h i b i t 3 . 5	**Checklist for Effective Supervision of Paralegals—continued**

(Grade each factor on a scale of 1 to 5 with a 5 indicating that the supervisor is excellent in this factor and 1 indicating an unsatisfactory rating.)

FACTOR	RATING (on a scale of 1–5)
aa. You make sure the paralegal has suitable office space, supplies, secretarial support, access to word processing, etc.	aa. _____
bb. When changes are made in office procedures that affect paralegals, you let them know in advance so that they can make suggestions about the changes.	bb. _____
cc. You support the paralegal's need for financial help and time off to attend outside training programs (CLE).	cc. _____
dd. You support the paralegal's need for financial help and time off to participate in the activities of paralegal associations.	dd. _____
ee. You recognize that the paralegal, like any employee, will need reasonable time off to attend to pressing personal matters.	ee. _____
ff. You consider letting the paralegal have reasonable time off to do some **pro bono** work (e.g., time donated to poverty law offices or public interest law firms).	ff. _____
gg. You don't assume that the paralegal is happy about his or her job simply because you have no complaints and the paralegal hasn't expressed dissatisfaction; you take the initiative to find out what is on the paralegal's mind.	gg. _____
hh. You treat the paralegal as an individual.	hh. _____
ii. You treat the paralegal as a professional.	ii. _____

S e c t i o n   N
RELATIONSHIP WITH SECRETARIES

At one time many secretaries, particularly those in smaller law offices, resented the hiring of paralegals. This friction arose for a number of reasons:

Historically, the legal secretary was "queen" of her territory. The more competent she was, the more control she had over her immediate environment—how the office looked, how the work was done, how the clients were handled, and for that matter, how the lawyer was trained. The longer she worked with one lawyer, the more responsibility she was given, and the better she got at her job. In the office of the sole practitioner, the practice could go on smoothly even if the lawyer was in court or out of town. She was just about as indispensable as one person could be. There was a relationship of mutual trust and respect between the legal secretary and the lawyer that was practically impenetrable. Then along came the legal assistant, intruding on the legal secretary's territory, doing many of the things that the legal secretary had been doing for years. To add insult to injury, the legal secretary was expected to perform secretarial work for the legal assistant![31]

Treat your secretary well. Do not convey the attitude that you think you are more important than she is. Secretaries have vast and underrated power to make or break you at the firm.

—Nancy Pulsifer, "Unwritten Rules," *How to Survive in a Law Firm* 39 (Wiley, 1993)

---

[31] *The Legal Assistant and the Legal Secretary: Friend or Foe*, 8 The Journal 4 (Sacramento Ass'n of Legal Assistants, April 1988).

Fortunately, this problem is less prevalent today, even in smaller law offices. But the paralegal still needs to be sensitive to the needs of the secretary, particularly the veteran secretary who was a valuable fixture in the office long before the paralegal arrived.[32]

When you start working with legal secretaries, consider the following recommendations for a smooth working relationship:[33]

- Give the secretary accurate, detailed instructions along with a reasonable timetable for completion.
- Make sure your written instructions are legible.
- Avoid waiting until the last minute to assign work that you know about beforehand.
- Don't pawn off undesirable chores that are rightly yours.
- Limit interruptions.
- Make yourself available to discuss problems or questions that arise during the performance of a task.
- Provide all the tools necessary to complete a job.
- Look for ways to recognize the contribution of secretaries. (The Rhode Island Paralegal Association, for example, conducts an annual secretary-appreciation luncheon.) "Remember that a pat on the back is just a few vertebrae removed from a kick in the pants, but miles ahead in results."[34]
- A cheerful demeanor can go a long way toward making your relationship more pleasant. Treat your secretary the way you wish to be treated, and don't forget basic courtesies, such as saying "good morning" and "have a nice evening."

Paralegals sometimes complain that attorneys do not treat paralegals with respect. How ironic that an insensitive paralegal could become subject to this same criticism.

Section O
SEXUAL HARASSMENT

There are two kinds of sexual harassment on the job:

Quid Pro Quo Harassment
Submission to or rejection of unwelcome sexual conduct by an individual is used as the basis for employment decisions affecting that individual, such as promotion or other job-related benefits.

Hostile Environment Harassment
Pervasive unwelcome sexual conduct or sex-based ridicule unreasonably interferes with an individual's job performance or creates an intimidating, hostile, or offensive working environment, even if it leads to no tangible or economic job consequences. The work environment is significantly pervaded by sexual commentary, dirty jokes, offensive pic-

---

[32]The largest organization of legal secretaries is **NALS,** the National Association of Legal Secretaries (see Appendix B for address). It administers the Professional Legal Secretary (PLS) exam. Passing the exam entitles the secretary to use the designation **Certified PLS** after his or her name. Many legal secretaries do not consider themselves significantly different from paralegals. In fact, a very large number of NALS members call themselves paralegals or legal assistants. One of the major *paralegal* associations, the National Association of Legal Assistants (NALA), was originally formed as a breakaway group from NALS.

[33]Rosen, *Effective Delegation,* 13 Update 8 (Cleveland Ass'n of Legal Assistants, June/July 1990).

[34]Guinn, *Personnel Management Techniques,* 8 Legal Assistant Today 56, 58 (March/April 1991).

tures, or generalized sexual conduct even if there is no direct trading of sexual favors for employment benefits.[35]

———

Studies indicate that the harassment can come from a superior, a colleague, or a client of the law office. See Exhibit 3.6. Here are some concrete examples:

The paralegal . . . told of one incident in which a partner placed his hand on her knee and asked if she had thought about her future with the firm. "Harassment of women lawyers is only the tip of the iceberg," according to the paralegal. "The support staff has it much, much worse."[36]

Recently a female paralegal began working with an insecure male lawyer who was a first year associate at the firm. He started "making the moves" on her by constantly asking if she was dating anyone. One day he called her in his office, closed the door, dialed a number on the phone, and handed the receiver to the paralegal. "What I heard was an obscene recording. I laughed, opened the door, and left." She did not believe in pursuing office relationships. Resentment developed when they began working on the same case together. He falsely accused the paralegal of lying and of not completing assignments on time. He made derogatory comments to her co-workers. When she confided in a female lawyer at the firm, she was

Exhibit 3.6	Incidents of Sexual Harassment in Law Offices		
PERCENTAGE OF RESPONDENTS WHO REPORT HAVING EXPERIENCED VARIOUS TYPES OF SEXUAL HARASSMENT ON THE JOB			
Incident	**By Superior**	**By Colleague**	**By Client**
Unwanted sexual teasing, jokes, remarks, or questions	36	30	32
Unwanted pressure for dates	8	6	10
Unwanted letters, telephone calls, or materials of a sexual nature	4	3	4
Unwanted sexual looks or gestures	21	11	16
Unwanted deliberate touching, leaning over, cornering, or pinching	14	6	9
Unwanted pressure for sex	6	3	4
Unwanted pressure for sex in return for promotions or business	1	0	1
Actual or attempted rape or assault	1	0	0

Source: *National Law Journal/West Publishing Company Survey on Women and Law,* National Law Journal S2 (December 11, 1989).

———

[35]Wapner, *Sexual Harassment in the Law Firm,* 16 Law Practice Management 42, 43 (September 1990); Smith, *Sexual Harassment Discussed at Litigation Sectional,* MALA Advance 19 (Minnesota Ass'n of Legal Assistants, Summer, 1989); 29 CFR § 1604.11(a)(2) and (a)(3); 47 Federal Register 74,676 (November 10, 1980).

[36]Goldberg, *Law's "Dirty Little Secret,"* 76 ABA Journal 34 (October 1990).

told that the associate acts that way with all the women at the firm, that the paralegal supervisor and the associate are very good friends, and that the partner in charge "sticks to this associate like glue" and does not want to be bothered by "petty personnel problems."[37]

When something of this nature happens, make detailed notes on who said and did what. Do this immediately after the incident. Should you do anything more? A passive response would be to ignore the problem and hope that it will go away. Another response would be to blame yourself. Phyllis Schlafly told the Senate Labor and Human Resources Committee that "Men hardly ever ask sexual favors of women from whom the certain response is *no*."[38] It is highly unlikely, however, that blaming yourself is either correct or productive.

For isolated and less serious problems, all that may be needed is a firm comment to the offender such as:

Mr. Smith, you know that I respect your ability and authority in the firm. But I want you to know that I do not appreciate the comment you made at that meeting about women. I did not think it was appropriate or professional.

Unfortunately, this approach may be inadequate when the problem becomes more complicated and persists. Clearly, all possible internal avenues for resolving the problem should be attempted. Hopefully, *somebody* in a position of responsibility will lend a sympathetic ear. Local paralegal associations should be a source of ideas and support. Speak with officers of the association. Go to general meetings. Ask for advice. It is highly likely that you will find others who have had similar experiences and who can provide concrete suggestions.

If all else fails, you have a powerful weapon at your disposal: the law. Harassment on the basis of sex is a violation of Title VII of the Civil Rights Act. The federal **Equal Employment Opportunity Commission** (EEOC) as well as state departments of civil rights are available to enforce the law.

It is not enough for a law office to announce that any sexual harassment in the office is forbidden. The employer must *actively* combat such harassment by informing employees of their right to raise (and telling them how to raise) the issue of harassment under Title VII, establishing a written policy against harassment and distributing it throughout the office, investigating all allegations of harassment promptly, and developing appropriate sanctions for actual harassment. An office that ignores the problem or that adopts an attitude that "men will be men" could be subject to liability.

In 1994, the legal community was shocked by a jury award of $6.9 million in punitive damages against the world's largest law firm, Baker & McKenzie, because of sexual harassment by one of its partners against his legal secretary. With other damages, the award came to $7.1 million. One of the jurors later said that the punitive award was based on 10 percent of the 1,700-member law firm's capital. The court later reduced the award to about $3.5 million. The partner dumped candy in the front pocket of the secretary's blouse and fondled her breast. At a luncheon, he grabbed her hips and asked her repeatedly, "What is the wildest thing you have done?" The jury found that the firm was negligent in the way it responded to her allegations against the partner. It was not enough for the firm to transfer the employee to another attorney when she complained of his behavior. The court was not persuaded by the argument that the partner simply had an "overactive imagination." After the trial, her attorney said that the case should substantially affect

---

[37]Nat'l Federation of Paralegal Associations, *Harassment: Personnel Problem or Worse?* 9 Nat'l Paralegal Reporter 7 (February 1985).

[38]Baca, *Speech to Nat'l Capital Area Paralegal Ass'n* (April 29, 1981).

law firms across the country. And the chairman of Baker & McKenzie's executive committee said the firm will handle any future complaints of sexual harassment from its employees very differently.[39]

Section P
WORKING WITH SYSTEMS

Some paralegal employment problems are attributed to the fact that the firm has not carefully examined how paralegals can be effectively used in the office. Paralegals should be part of an attorney-paralegal-secretary team. The difficulty, however, is that the office may not have done the necessary planning to design the *system* that the team will execute.

A system is simply an organized way of accomplishing a task. All participants are supposed to perform those functions that they are capable of handling and for which they are not overtrained. Here is how many systems are created:

- Select the task that is to be systematized. It will usually be a task that the office performs regularly, such as incorporating a business, probating an estate, filing for divorce, engaging in discovery. (According to some studies, attorneys perform over 75 percent of their tasks more than once.)
- Carefully study the task to identify its various components. What are the pieces that must always be performed? What facts must always be obtained? What letters must always be sent? What forms must always be prepared?
- Prepare a systems or procedural manual containing a description of the task, instructions or checklists of things to be done, standardized letters, pleadings, forms and other documents that are customarily used for that task. The manual might be placed in a three-ring notebook and/or on a computer.
- Place photocopies of statutes, court rules, or other laws frequently used to perform the task in a special section of the manual, often in the appendix.
- Delegate the performance of the components of the task to various members of the team.

It takes considerable sophistication to *design* a system. Even more sophistication is sometimes needed to *implement* the system and make it work. The participants must believe in the system and ideally have had a role in its design if it requires changes in their work habits. Many attorneys are notoriously resistant to change, particularly if they believe that the system fails to recognize the role of professional judgment. If you have been doing something the same way for fifteen years, you tend to be suspicious of suggestions that more efficient ways are possible. Furthermore, in the transition from blueprint to operation, the system may have to be modified to work out the "bugs." In short, a precondition for success is a willingness and a determination of the participants to make the new system work.

When paralegals walk into an office for the first time, they may confront a number of situations:

- There are no systems; everybody practices law in their own individualistic way.
- There is talk of systemization, but no one has yet done any serious design work.
- An ineffective system is in place.

---

[39]R. Thompson, *Legal Secretary Awarded Record $7.1 Million in Sexual Harassment*, 12 Legal Assistant Today 14 (November/December 1995).

- A system is in place, but the participants do not believe in it.
- A system exists on paper, but no one has expended the time and energy to make the system work.

All these environments can make life difficult for the paralegal. A disorganized office can be very frustrating.

One of the most valuable things a paralegal can do is to observe an effective system in place. One or more may exist in other parts of the firm where you work. It may be possible for you to visit other firms in the area. Formbooks, manuals, and legal periodical literature on law office management describe systems, but these descriptions are no substitute for seeing the real thing.

Don't be reluctant to try to design your own system. You might want to begin with a system for a portion of one of your tasks. Start out on a small scale by writing instructions or checklists for functions that you regularly perform. Write the system so that a new paralegal would be able to read it and know what to do. Here is an example of how a project led to the creation of a system:

> Diedre Wilton's organizational skills were really put to the test during a recent assignment which required her to file fictitious business name statements for a client in every county in California. "Almost every county had a different form!" lamented Diedre. "And I had to arrange for publication in fifty-eight different newspapers." She is creating an extensive file on the project so that . . . when the filings come up for renewal, the next person won't have to start from scratch.[40]

Supervisors will be *very* impressed by such efforts to create systems. A paralegal with this much initiative will soon become a prized member of the office.

Section Q
CAREER LADDERS

In the early days of the paralegal movement, a common complaint among paralegals was the absence of career ladders. Once a paralegal demonstrates competence by making a significant contribution to the office, what comes next? Higher salaries, a better office, more variety in assignments—these are all helpful, but they are not the same as *promotion*. Yet what can a paralegal be promoted to? The only next step was lawyerdom. But going to law school is a rather drastic step. Taking this step means, of course, leaving the field of paralegalism entirely. Hence, in those early days, the only way up was out!

Although some progress has been made in developing career ladders, the progress has been primarily limited to law offices that employ relatively large numbers of paralegals. Most of the paralegals in small offices still have no career ladder. For this and related reasons, surveys show that between 10 and 15 percent of working paralegals today say that they intend to go to law school—eventually.

Yet other paralegals resent the following question put to them by attorneys: "So when are you going to law school?" or "Why don't you become an attorney?" Here is another example of this mentality:

> One day I accompanied an attorney to a deposition, at the request of our client. When we arrived at the opposing counsel's office, the attorney I was working with introduced me as the

---

[40]*Paralegal Profile,* 12 Points & Authorities 9 (San Joaquin Ass'n of Legal Assistants, March 1991).

paralegal working on the case. The opposing counsel responded with, "Oh, so you're an aspiring attorney." "No," I responded, "I'm an aspiring paralegal."[41]

These paralegals see paralegalism as an end in itself, not necessarily as a stepping-stone to becoming an attorney. Attorneys are not always asked, "When are you going to become a judge?" And nurses do not constantly hear, "When are you going to become a doctor?" Paralegals deserve the same respect. Many wish that they could stop having to answer "the law-school question."

The solution, of course, is the creation of meaningful career ladders for paralegals within a particular law office. As indicated, the larger law offices have responded. The Legal Assistants Management Association (LAMA), for example, has defined six different levels within the world of the legal assistant:

legal assistant clerk

legal assistant

senior legal assistant

supervising legal assistant

case manager

legal assistant manager

These levels were defined in chapter 1 (see Exhibit 1.2). Under this tiered structure, the lowest position is called the legal assistant clerk. Not all offices, however, use this terminology. An office might call the position *case clerk, document clerk,* or some similar term.

It must be emphasized again, however, that this kind of career ladder does *not* apply to all law offices. Many paralegals begin work in a law office as a paralegal or legal assistant and end their work there with the same title. If they want to experience a different level of work, they must try to obtain a job at another office that employs more paralegals and is enlightened enough to have instituted a meaningful career ladder.

Section R
YOUR NEXT JOB

It is extremely important to remember that throughout your current employment, you will be creating a record for your *next* job. While it is possible that you will remain in one position for your entire paralegal career, the likelihood is that you will one day be employed at another law firm, corporation, or other law office. You should assume that everyone in a position of authority where you now work will one day be called by a prospective employer who will ask a series of questions about you:

- What kind of a worker were you?
- How did you get along with coworkers?
- Did you show initiative?
- Did you function well under pressure? etc.

The legal profession is conservative by nature. Attorneys like to stay with winners; they are often reluctant to take chances. The most attractive candidate for a paralegal job is

---

[41]Burdett, *Rodney Dangerfield: You're Not Alone,* 12 Nat'l Paralegal Reporter 12 (Nat'l Federation of Paralegal Associations, Spring 1988).

someone who has been successful at a previous paralegal job. Attorneys are hesitant to hire people who have run into difficulty at an earlier job—even if it was not their fault. Hence, *treat all supervisors in the office as potential references.*

Section S
PARALEGAL ASSOCIATIONS AND NETWORKING

"I discovered first hand the value of networking. Attorneys, legal assistants, and legal secretaries alike are all part of this maze we call our legal system. When we develop contacts, exchange ideas and information, reach out for help or lend a hand to someone else, we are creating a map for ourselves and others to navigate that infrastructure more effectively. Networking enables us to expand and diversify our profession as well as our individual goals and aspirations."

—Deborah Worthington, Paralegal, Dallas, 1996

Your greatest ally in confronting any of the on-the-job problems discussed in this chapter is the paralegal association at the local and national level. (See Appendix B). Not only are the associations a source of excellent information about paralegal practice in your area and across the nation, but they are also a potential gold mine of ideas and strategies. It is probably impossible for you to have a problem on the job that has not been experienced by numerous other paralegals within an association. Tap into this resource as soon as possible. You can learn a great deal by listening to the problems of others and finding out how they tried to solve them. What worked? Why? What didn't work? Why not? What is the next thing that should be tried? Answers to such questions will be readily available to you through the paralegal associations. (To begin your contact with them now, use the forms at the end of the index of this book.)

The national paralegal associations are now on-line. For example, on the Internet (see chapters 11 and 13), the World Wide Web address of the National Federation of Paralegal Associations is *http://www.paralegals.org.* There are "list serve" lists and discussion groups that you can easily join if you are on-line. Here are the list services that are free to members of the associations that are part of the National Federation of Paralegal Associations:

bankruptcy@paralegals.org	paralegals@paralegals.org
corporatelaw@paralegals.org	laborlaw@paralegals.org
education@paralegals.org	litigation@paralegals.org
familylaw@paralegals.org	realestatelaw@paralegals.org
freelance@paralegals.org	students@paralegals.org

Paralegals can use forums such as these to talk about issues that concern them. Within seconds, you are able to send out your questions to hundreds and potentially thousands of members of a group. For example, you might type in questions such as the following:

```
I'm a paralegal in a law firm that has 75 attorneys and 10 paralegals.
With rare exceptions, the firm has never helped paralegals pay fees to
attend paralegal association meetings. I'd be interested in hearing whether
other paralegals have had this problem and how they have handled it.

Our Illinois office has a client that incorporated one of its branches
in Montana in 1957. I need to find out what the filing fees were in
1957. I was just handed this assignment, and as usual, the attorney
needs it yesterday. Anybody got any ideas?

Does anyone have a copy of the 1976 report of the New York State Bar
Association, Committee on Professional Ethics? I think the name of the
report is Guidelines for the Utilization of Lawyers of the Services of
Legal Assistants. My fax number is 619-456-0268.
```

Within an hour or two, you might get scores of replies filled with ideas, suggestions, greetings, and irrelevancies. It is a wonderful new resource for reaching other paralegals.

The key is **networking,** which is the process of establishing a large number of social and professional contacts with people, making notes on what they do and how to reach them, and organizing these notes so that you can renew the contacts in the future as the need arises. In short, networking means establishing contacts that may be helpful to you now or in the future. For a paralegal, the most natural and fruitful networking arenas are the local and national paralegal associations you can join.

Assignment 3.2

Examine the following fact situations. For each situation:

- Identify the problem or problems that you see.
- What strategies do you think would be helpful in resolving the problem or problems? Why?
- What strategies do you think would be counterproductive? Why?
- What do you think could have been done to prevent the problem or problems from occurring in the first place? How could they have been avoided?
- In your responses, specify what you think would be assertive, nonassertive, and aggressive behavior.

(a) Tom has been a paralegal at a firm for three years. His paralegal training in school was in drafting, legal research, investigation, etc. For the entire three years, however, he has been collating and digesting numerous documents in a big antitrust case. It is a very important case, and the firm is reluctant to take him off it due to his familiarity with these documents. The problem, however, is that Tom is becoming bored. He is satisfied with his pay but dreads coming to work each day. He tried to explain this to his supervisor, but he was simply told how important he was to the case. The supervisor said, "If you decide to leave the firm, I hope you will give us six months' lead time so that you can train a replacement." This made Tom all the more depressed since he does not want to leave.

(b) Ellen is a probate paralegal at a firm. She has worked there two years. At a recent paralegal association meeting, she discovered that other probate paralegals in the city with the same experience are making at least $4,000 more per year than she is. She wants to talk with her supervisor about this, but is not sure if this is the right time. The last three months have been difficult for her. She has missed work a lot due to illness. She also recently began work on a new complex case. She is struggling to keep up with the new work involved in the case and must constantly ask her supervisor for help. The supervisor appears to be irritated with her progress on the case. Her next scheduled salary review is ten months away.

(c) Jim, Janet, Brenda, Helen, and Pat are paralegals at a law firm. They are all unhappy about their job: low pay, long hours, sexism, menial tasks, etc. On a number of occasions they have met with the senior partners in the firm to discuss ways of improving their situation. Minor changes were made, but the problems persist. They are approached by a local union about joining the union.

(d) Fran is a paralegal in a firm where she works for the senior partner—the most powerful person in the firm. Fran receives excellent pay and fringe benefits. She loves her work. Other paralegals in the firm, however, resent her because their benefits are much lower and they receive assignments that they dislike.

(e) Same situation as in (d) above. Fran's supervisor, the senior partner, is currently going through a divorce, and the strain on him has been enormous. One consequence of this is that Fran's workload is increasing. More of his work is being shifted to her. He is extremely sensitive to any criticism about the way he practices law, so Fran is reluctant to talk with him about the extra work—particularly when he is under so much pressure due to the divorce. Yet Fran is worried about her ability to do her job competently in view of the increased work. She hopes that things will get back to normal when the divorce is over.

(f) Mary works in a law firm that charges clients $225 an hour for attorney time and $75 an hour for paralegal time. She and another paralegal, Fred, are working with an attorney on a large case. She sees all of the time sheets that the three of them submit to the firm's accounting office. She suspects that the attorney is **padding** his time sheets by overstating the number of hours he works on the case. For example, he lists thirty hours for a four-day period when he was in court every day on another case. Furthermore, Fred's time is being billed at the full $75-an-hour rate even though he spends about 80 percent of his time typing correspondence, filing, and performing other clerical duties.

(g) Tom has been a paralegal at the firm for six years. He works for three attorneys. One day he is told by a memo from the office administrator that an outside consultant has been hired to study Tom's job in order to find ways "to increase productivity." The letter instructs Tom to spend the next two days permitting the consultant to follow him around and ask questions about what he does. Tom is furious.

(h) Mary has been a paralegal at the firm for two years. She works for one attorney, Mr. Getty. One day a client calls Mary and says, "I'm sending you another copy of the form that Mr. Getty said you lost." This is news to Mary. She works with the client's file every day and knows that she has never lost anything. She pauses, trying to think of what to say to this client over the phone before hanging up.

(i) Veronica works for a law firm where none of the supervisors give formal evaluations of the paralegals. The supervisors feel that formal evaluations would be too time-consuming and too general to be helpful. They are also afraid that they might be sued for making negative comments about employees. Veronica has received yearly raises, and according to her supervisor, this is the best indication of what the firm thinks of her. Veronica is unhappy, however, with the feedback she has gotten about her work.

(j) How would you handle the fact situation involving sexual harassment (questions about dating, obscene recording, etc.) presented on page 175? Assume the paralegal does not want to quit and is afraid that she will lose her job if she institutes legal action.

Assignment 3.3

Karen considers herself a quiet, nonaggressive person. She has two job offers: (a) a large law firm (seventy-five attorneys and twenty-two paralegals) and (b) a one-attorney/one-secretary office. She likes the type of work both offices do. The pay and benefits in both offices are roughly the same. How would you advise Karen on which job to take?

Assignment 3.4

According to Douglas McGregor in *The Human Side of Enterprise* (1960), there are two basic views of human behavior at work. "Theory X" says that a person has a natural dislike of work and will avoid it whenever possible. "Theory Y" says that physical and mental work are as natural to a person as any other activity. Under theory Y, workers do not naturally shy away from responsibility.

- Describe a law office using paralegals that is managed under theory X. How would it function? How would the office handle paralegal problems?
- Describe a law office using paralegals that subscribes to theory Y. How would it function? How would the office handle paralegal problems?
- Which theory do you think is correct?
- Which theory describes you?

🏛 *Assignment 3.5*

What needs does a paralegal or any worker have? What is our "hierarchy of needs"? Rearrange the following needs so that you think they reflect the conscious or unconscious priorities of most human beings: the need to be fulfilled; the need to be respected; the need to eat, sleep, and be clothed; the need to be safe; the need to be admired; the need to belong; the need to have self-worth. See Maslow, A., *Motivation and Personality* (1970).

Chapter Summary

A major theme of chapter 3 is the critical importance of paralegal initiative. Every occupation has its problems. This chapter covered problems in the paralegal arena and how initiative is a primary vehicle for resolving them. After listing seventy-five factors that influence job satisfaction, we turned to some of the major on-the-job difficulties that some paralegals face. The following topics were examined: the need for career ladders, the adequacy of compensation, the inability of some attorneys to use paralegals effectively, the breakdown of communication in the hectic environment of a law practice, the lack of realistic expectations of what it means to work with attorneys, the characteristics of some attorneys that do not make them good supervisors, the inevitability of office politics, the central role of self-evaluation and employer evaluation, the question of professional status, the tensions that might exist in the attorney-paralegal-secretary relationship, and finally the problem of sexual harassment.

While initiative cannot solve all of the problems that may exist, it appears to be a central ingredient in the success of competent paralegals. Such paralegals take advantage of opportunities for continuing legal education; they know how to work with—and to help create—systems; they know what it means to be prepared; and they understand the value of networking, particularly through paralegal associations.

KEY TERMS

career ladder, 152
profit center, 153
office politics, 157
pre-evaluation memo, 163
assertive, 165

swoose syndrome, 169
CLE, 170
pro bono, 173
NALS, 174
Certified PLS, 174

quid pro quo harassment, 174
hostile environment harassment, 174

Equal Employment Opportunity Commission, 176
networking, 180
padding, 182

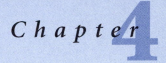
THE REGULATION
OF PARALEGALS

► *Chapter Outline*

Section A
KINDS OF REGULATION

The activities of paralegals could be regulated in seven important ways:

- Laws on the unauthorized practice of law and on the *authorized* practice of law by nonattorneys
- State licensing
- Regulation of education
- Self-regulation
- Fair Labor Standards Act
- Tort law (e.g., the negligence liability of paralegals and of attorneys who employ them)
- Ethical rules

The first six of these methods of regulation are covered in this chapter. Ethics will be examined in the next chapter. As we explore these methods, you should keep in mind the terminology of regulation outlined in Exhibit 4.1.

What do we mean when we say that a paralegal or legal assistant is "certified"? It can have different meanings. For example:

- You have successfully completed a short or long training program that offers a "certificate" to each graduate; every graduate is "certified." As indicated in Exhibit 4.1, however, some prefer the word "certificated" when the certificate comes from a school or training program.
- You have met the qualifications for membership in a nongovernmental agency, which now recognizes that you have done so; every member is "certified."
- You have passed the national CLA (Certified Legal Assistant) examination of NALA (the National Association of Legal Assistants) or PACE (Paralegal Advanced Competency Exam), the national examination of NFPA (the National Federation of Paralegal Associations); or the state-specific examination in California, Florida, Louisiana, or Texas; a person who passes any of these tests is "certified."

In short, "certified" does not have a legal definition that everyone uses for all occasions. The word could mean that you have completed training, are part of an organization, or have passed a test.

Section B
UNAUTHORIZED AND AUTHORIZED PRACTICE OF LAW

1. DEFINING THE PRACTICE OF LAW

Every state has laws on the **unauthorized practice of law,** which simply means the performance of services that constitute the **practice of law** by someone not authorized to provide such services. In many states it is a *crime* to practice law illegally. It is not a crime to represent yourself, but you risk going to jail if you practice law on behalf of someone else. Why such a harsh penalty? Legal problems often involve complicated, serious issues. A great deal can be lost if citizens do not receive competent legal assistance. To protect the public, the state has established a system of licensing attorneys to provide this assistance and to punish anyone who tries to provide it without the license.

> Legal Assistant regulation is on the horizon in one form or another, [and possibly in many forms]. It is imperative that we approach the regulation "can of worms" from an informed and knowledgeable vantage point, and that we participate in the formative process.
>
> —Gail White Nicholson, Vice-President, Greenville Association of Legal Assistants, 1991

Exhibit 4.1   The Terminology of Regulation

Regulation is any governmental or nongovernmental method of controlling conduct.

Accreditation is the process by which an organization evaluates and recognizes a program of study (or an institution) as meeting specified qualifications or standards.

Approval means the recognition that comes from accreditation, certification, licensure, or registration. As we will see, the American Bar Association uses the word "approval" as a substitute for "accreditation" of paralegal education programs.

Certification is the process by which a nongovernmental organization grants recognition to a person who has met qualifications set by that organization. It is a voluntary process; not having certification usually does not affect the right of the person to engage in a particular career. Three of the most common qualifications for certification are:

- Graduating from a school or training program, and/or
- Passing a standard examination, and/or
- Completing a designated period of work experience.

Once certification has been bestowed by one or a combination of these methods, the individual is said to have been **certified.** If the certification comes from a school or training program, some prefer to say that the person has been **certificated.** (Occasionally, a government agency will have what it calls a certification program. This program may be similar to those described above, or it may in fact be a license program.)

Code is any set of rules that regulates conduct.

Ethics are rules that embody standards of behavior to which members of an organization are expected to conform.

Guideline is suggested conduct that will help an applicant obtain accreditation, certification, licensure, registration, or approval.

Licensure is the process by which an agency of government grants permission to persons meeting specified qualifications to engage in an occupation and often to use a particular title. This permission is a license. The qualifications seek to ensure that the person has at least the minimum competency needed for the protection of the public. Licensure is one of the more drastic methods of controlling entry into a career.

Limited licensure (also called **specialty licensure**) is the process by which an agency of government grants permission to persons meeting specified qualifications to engage in designated activities that are customarily (but not always exclusively) performed by another category of license holder. (If, in the future, paralegals are granted a limited license in a particular state, they will be authorized to sell designated services—now part of the attorney monopoly—directly to the public in that state.)

Registration or **enrollment** is the process by which individuals or institutions list their names on a roster kept by an agency of government or by a nongovernmental organization. There may or may not be qualifications that must be met before one can go on the list.

But what is the *practice of law?* Unfortunately, there is no clear definition. (See Appendix F for how your state handles the definition.) The American Bar Association says:

[I]t is neither necessary nor desirable to attempt the formulation of a single, specific definition of what constitutes the practice of law. Functionally, the practice of law relates to the rendition of services for others that call for the professional judgment of a lawyer. The essence of the professional judgment of a lawyer is his educated ability to relate the general body and philosophy of law to a specific legal problem of a client. EC 3-5, *ABA Model Code of Professional Responsibility* (1981).

Hence the practice of law is performing services that require the professional judgment of an attorney on a person's specific legal problem. Professional judgment is often called for in three main kinds of activities:

● Representing someone in court or in an administrative agency proceeding;
● Drafting legal documents for someone; and
● Giving someone legal advice.

The third category—giving legal advice—usually takes place while performing the other two activities, although legal advice can also be given independently of them. The essence of the practice of law is performing any of the three activities to help a particular person resolve a specific legal problem.

Suppose that you write a self-help book on how to sue your landlord. The book lists all the laws, provides all the forms, and gives precise guidelines on how to use the laws and the forms. Are you practicing law? No, because you are not addressing the *specific* legal problem of a *specific* person. It is not the practice of law to sell law books or similar materials to the general public even if a member of the public uses them for his or her specific legal problem. Now suppose that you open an office in which you sell the book and even type the forms for customers. Practice of law? No, *unless you provide individual help in filling out the forms.* You can type the forms so long as the customer does all the thinking about what goes in the forms! So too:

● It is proper for a nonattorney to charge citizens a fee to type legal forms in order to obtain a divorce. But it is the unauthorized practice of law to provide personal assistance on how to fill out the forms.
● It is proper for a nonattorney to charge citizens a fee to type their will or trust. But it is the unauthorized practice of law to provide personal assistance on what should go in the will or trust.[1]

For years, attorneys have complained that large numbers of individuals were crossing the line by providing this kind of personal assistance. Bar associations often asked the state to prosecute many of them. Yet some charged that the attorneys were less interested in protecting the public than in preserving their own monopoly over the practice of law. Perhaps the most famous recent case involving this controversy was that of Rosemary Furman and the Florida bar.

Rosemary Furman: Folk Hero?

Rosemary Furman, a former legal secretary, believes that you should be able to solve simple legal problems without hiring an attorney. Hence she established the Northside Secretarial Service in Jacksonville, Florida. She compiled and sold packets of legal forms (for $50) on divorce, name changes, and adoptions. The price *included her personal assistance in filling out and filing the forms.* The Florida Bar Association and the Florida courts moved against her with a vengeance for practicing law illegally. She was convicted and sentenced to 30 days in jail. She never served the sentence, however.

Widespread support for Ms. Furman developed. Her case soon became a cause célèbre for those seeking increased

---

[1] The same distinction applies to preparing documents to be filed in bankruptcy court. Congress calls such an individual a **bankruptcy petition preparer.** This is a person, other than an attorney or an employee of an attorney, who prepares for compensation a bankruptcy petition or other document for filing by a debtor in a United States Bankruptcy Court or a United States District Court. These individuals can type the documents; if they do much more, they are subject to substantial fines. 11 U.S.C. § 111. See also *In re Bachmann,* 113 Bankruptcy Reporter 769 (S.D. Fla. 1990).

access to the legal system for the poor and the middle class.[2] Many were outraged at the legal profession and the judiciary for their treatment of Ms. Furman.

The CBS program *60 Minutes* did a story that was favorable to her cause. Other national media, including *Newsweek,* covered the case. Warner Brothers considered doing a docudrama on the story. Rosemary Furman struck a responsive chord when she claimed that for every $50 she earned, an attorney lost $500. An editorial in the *Gainesville Sun* said, "Throw Rosemary Furman in jail? Surely not after the woman forced the Florida bar and the judiciary to confront its responsibility to the poor. Anything less than a 'thank you' note would indeed show genuine vindictiveness on the part of the legal profession" (Nov. 4, 1984). There were, however, other views. An editorial in *USA Today* said that what she was doing was illegal. "If she can give legal advice, so can charlatans, frauds, and rip-off artists" (February 2, 1984).

The events in the Rosemary Furman story are as follows:

- 1978 & 1979: The Florida Bar Association takes Rosemary Furman to court, alleging that she is practicing law without a license.
- 1979: The Florida Supreme Court rules against her. She is enjoined from engaging in the unauthorized practice of law.

---

[2]Peoples & Wertz, *Update: Unauthorized Practice of Law,* 9 Nat'l Paralegal Reporter 1 (Nat'l Federation of Paralegal Associations, February 1985).

- 1982: The Florida Bar Association again brings a complaint against her business, alleging that she was continuing the unauthorized practice of law.
- 1983: Duval County Circuit Judge A. C. Soud, Jr., finds her in contempt of court for violating the 1979 order. The judge makes this decision in a nonjury hearing. She is then ordered to serve 30 days in jail.
- 1984: The United States Supreme Court refuses to hear the case. This has the effect of allowing the state jail sentence to stand. The Court is not persuaded by her argument that she should have been granted a jury trial of her peers rather than have been judged solely by a profession (attorneys and judges) that was biased against her.
- Her attorneys ask the Florida Supreme Court to vacate the jail sentence if she agrees to close her business.
- The Florida Bar Association tells the Florida Supreme Court that the jail term is a fitting punishment and should be served.
- November 13, 1984: The Florida Supreme Court orders her to serve the jail sentence for practicing law without a license. (451 So. 2d 808)
- November 27, 1984: Rosemary Furman is granted clemency from the 30-day jail term by Florida Governor Bob Graham and his Clemency Board. She does not have to go to jail.
- Furman and her attorneys announce that they will work on a constitutional amendment defining the

practice of law to make it easier for citizens to avoid dependency on attorneys in civil cases. Says Ms. Furman, "I have only begun to fight."

This case has had an impact in Florida and elsewhere in the country. Recently, for example, Florida made a dramatic change in the definition of unauthorized practice of law. Under this definition, it "shall not constitute the unauthorized practice of law for nonlawyers to engage in limited oral communications to assist individuals in a completion of legal forms approved by the Supreme Court of Florida. Oral communications by nonlawyers are restricted to those communications reasonably necessary to elicit factual information to complete the form(s) and inform the individual how to file such form(s)."[3] Later in this chapter, we will discuss the even more dramatic concept of *limited licensing* for paralegals, which is being considered in a number of states. Some have referred to these developments as "the long shadow of Rosemary Furman."

---

[3]Rule 10-1.1(b), *Rules Regulating the Florida Bar.* See also *The Florida Bar,* 591 So. 2d 594 (Fla. 1991) and *Florida Bar News* 12 (August 1, 1989).

🏛 *A s s i g n m e n t   4 . 1*

(a) Define the practice of law in your state. Quote from your state code, court rules, or other official authority that is available. (See Appendix F.)
(b) Would Rosemary Furman have been prosecuted for the unauthorized practice of law in your state today? Why or why not?

The Furman case involved direct competition with attorneys. More indirect competition comes from people engaged in law-related activities, such as accountants, claims adjusters, real estate agents, life insurance agents, and officers of trust departments of banks. For years, bar associations complained about such activities. In many instances, they challenged the activities in court as the unauthorized practice of law. The problem was so pervasive that some bar associations negotiated a **statement of principles** (sometimes called a treaty) with these occupations in an attempt to identify boundary lines and methods of resolving difficulties. Most of these treaties, however, have been ineffective in defining the kinds of law-related activities that can and cannot be performed by nonattorneys. A tremendous amount of effort and money is needed to negotiate, monitor, and enforce the treaties. The resources are simply not available. Furthermore, there is a concern that such efforts by attorneys to restrain competition might violate the antitrust laws, as we will see later in the chapter.

Some practitioners of law-related occupations have gone directly to the legislature to seek enactment of statutes that authorize what would otherwise be the unauthorized practice of law. In many instances, they have been successful. For example:

Code of Georgia, § 15-19-52. . . . Furthermore, a title insurance company may prepare such papers as it thinks proper or necessary in connection with a title which it proposes to insure, in order, in its opinion, for it to be willing to insure the title, where no charge is made by it for such papers.

Utah Code Ann. § 61-2-20. (1) Principal brokers and associate brokers may fill out any documents associated with the closing of a real estate transaction.

The effect of such statutes is to allow members of designated occupations to perform certain legal tasks that are intimately related to their work without having to hire attorneys or without forcing their clients to hire them.

2. AUTHORIZED PRACTICE OF LAW

Examine the following phrase closely: unauthorized practice of law by nonattorneys. If there is such a thing as the *un*authorized practice of law, then, by implication, there must be an *authorized* practice of law. And indeed there is. The treaties and statutes discussed above are examples of this. There are also other areas where nonattorneys are given a special authorization to practice law. Occasionally, attempts are made to call what they do something other than the practice of law, but as we will see, these attempts conflict with reality since the nonattorneys are doing what attorneys usually do, although often in a limited sense. Why has there been an erosion, however limited, in attorney monopoly over the practice of law? Why does the authorized practice of law by nonattorneys exist?

Some members of the public view attorneys as fighters, people who will pursue an issue to the bitter end. While the client for whom an attorney is doing battle may view this trait favorably, many feel that an attorney's aggressive inclinations can be counterproductive. Administrative agencies, for example, are often suspicious of the involvement of attorneys. They are viewed as combatants who want to turn every agency decision into an adversarial proceeding. Agencies often see courtroom gymnastics and gimmicks as the attorney's primary mode of operation. The attorney is argumentative to a fault.

This image of the attorney as someone who complicates matters is best summed up by an old accountants' joke that taxation becomes more and more complex in direct proportion to attempts by attorneys to *simplify* the tax law. Whether or not this view of attorneys is correct, it has accounted for some erosion of the legal profession's monopoly over the practice of law.

The unavailability of attorneys has also contributed to this result. A vast segment of our population has legal complaints that are never touched by attorneys. This is due, in part, to the fact that most of these complaints do not involve enough money to attract attorneys. Yet many attorneys in this country are unemployed or underemployed. The logical solution would appear to be for attorneys to lower the cost of their services to meet the demand. This has not happened to any significant extent. Hence the pressure for alternatives continues.

We now turn to a fuller exploration of these themes under the following headings:

a. Court "representation" by nonattorneys
b. Attempted restrictions on the activities of the "jailhouse lawyer" and the broader policy considerations raised by such restrictions
c. Agency representation by nonattorneys

(a) Court Representation

In the vast majority of courts in this country, only attorneys can represent someone in a judicial proceeding. There are, however, some limited—but dramatic—exceptions.

In Maryland, a nonattorney employee of a nonprofit legal service office can represent tenants in a summary ejectment proceeding in the District Court of Maryland! A special Lay Advocacy Program oversees this form of court advocacy by nonattorneys.[4] Another extraordinary example exists in North Dakota where lay advocates assist women who are petitioners seeking protective orders in domestic violence cases. Some judges "encourage and allow" the lay advocate "to conduct direct and cross-examination of witnesses and make statements to the court." A proposal has been made to formalize this activity by creating a new position called a Certified Domestic Violence Advocate. Under this

---

[4]*Lay Advocacy Program Defends Indigent Tenants*, 6 Bar Bulletin 3 (Maryland Bar Ass'n, January 1991). Annotated Code of Maryland §10-101 (1991 Supp).

proposal, the following activities of this nonattorney would *not* be considered the unauthorized practice of law: helping a petitioner fill out printed forms, sitting with the petitioner during court proceedings, and making written or oral statements to the court.[5]

In some lower courts in the country, particularly in the West, parties can have nonattorneys represent them. Examples include Justice of the Peace Courts, Magistrates Courts, and Small Claims Courts. It is relatively rare, however, for parties to have *any* representation in such courts.

When a business is sued, some states allow a nonattorney employee of the business to represent it in court. An example is the Conciliation Court, which is a Small Claims Court, in Minnesota:

> **Minnesota Statutes Annotated, § 491A.02.** A corporation, partnership, limited liability company, sole proprietorship, or association may be represented in Conciliation Court by an officer, manager, or partner or may appoint a natural person who is an employee to appear on its behalf to settle a claim in Conciliation Court. This representation does not constitute the unauthorized practice of law. . . .

Similarly, in the District of Columbia, a corporation can have one of its nonattorney employees appear for it in court in a landlord-tenant action.[6] If the other side files an answer or a counterclaim, however, the corporation must be represented by an attorney.

As we learned in chapter 2, Tribal Courts on Indian reservations have jurisdiction over designated civil and criminal matters involving Native Americans. In many of these courts, both parties are represented by nonattorney advocates.

Government employees occasionally act in a representative or semi-representative capacity in court proceedings, even though they are not attorneys. In North Carolina cases involving the termination of parental rights, for example, the United States Supreme Court has noted the role of nonattorneys:

> In fact, . . . the North Carolina Departments of Social Services are themselves sometimes represented at termination hearings by social workers instead of by lawyers.[7]

It is well known that attorneys are forced to waste a good deal of pretrial time traveling to court and waiting around simply to give documents to the judge and to set dates for the various stages of pretrial and trial proceedings. Another problem is that an attorney may have to be in two different courtrooms at the same time. For example, an early morning hearing may be unexpectedly extended, preventing the attorney from appearing at a previously scheduled mid-morning proceeding in another courtroom on a different case. In such situations, wouldn't it be helpful if the attorney's paralegal could "appear" in court for the limited purpose of delivering papers to the judge, asking for a new date, or presenting some other message? *In most states, such activity is strictly prohibited.*

On August 16, 1982, a Kentucky paralegal learned about this prohibition in a dramatic way. Her attorney was involved in a trial at the Jefferson Circuit Court. He asked the paralegal to go to another courtroom during "Motion Hour," where attorneys make motions and schedule future proceedings on a case. He told her to ask for a hearing date on another case that he had pending. She did so. When the case was called during "Motion Hour," she rose, identified herself as the attorney's paralegal, and gave the message to the judge, asking for the hearing date. Opposing counsel was outraged. He verbally assaulted the paralegal in the courtroom and filed a motion to hold the paralegal and her attorney in

---

[5] *Role of Lay Advocates in Domestic Violence Proceedings,* 15 Note Pad 1 (State Bar Ass'n of North Dakota, April 5, 1991).

[6] Rule 49, Unauthorized Practice of Law (D.C. Court of Appeals), *Bar Report,* (August/September 1993).

[7] *Lassiter v. Dept. of Social Services,* 452 U.S. 18, 29, 101 S. Ct. 2153, 2161, 68 L. Ed. 2d 640, 651 (1981).

contempt of court for the unauthorized practice of law. When a hearing was later held on this motion, members of a local paralegal association packed the courtroom. Tensions were high. When the judge eventually *denied* the motion, after a hearing on the matter, the audience broke out into loud applause. "Apparently the judge concluded that [the paralegal] had rendered no service involving legal knowledge or advice, but had merely transmitted to the court [the attorney's] message regarding disposition of the motion, that is, she had been performing a function that was administrative, not legal in nature."[8]

About twenty years earlier, a celebrated Illinois opinion, *People v. Alexander,*[9] took a position similar to this Kentucky court. In this opinion, the defendant was an unlicensed law clerk (a student studying to become an attorney) who appeared before the court to state that his employing attorney could not be present in court at the moment because he was trying a case elsewhere. On behalf of his employer, the law clerk requested a continuance. The defendant's actions were challenged. It was argued that *any* appearance by nonattorneys before a court in which they give information as to the availability of counsel or the status of litigation constitutes the unauthorized practice of law. The Illinois court took the unique position that this was not the practice of law. The reasoning of the court is presented in the following excerpt from the opinion:

People v. Alexander
Appellate Court of Illinois, First District
53 Ill. App. 2d 299, 202 N.E.2d 841 (1964)

. . .

In the case of *People ex rel. Illinois State Bar Ass'n v. People's Stock Yards State Bank,* 344 Ill. 462, at page 476, 176 N.E. 901, at page 907, wherein a bank was prosecuted for the unauthorized practice of law, the following quotation is relied upon:

"According to the generally understood definition of the practice of law in this country, it embraces the preparation of pleadings, and other papers incident to actions and special proceedings, and the management of such actions and proceedings on behalf of clients before judges and courts * * *."

Since this statement relates to the appearance and management of proceedings in court on behalf of a client, we do not believe it can be applied to a situation where a clerk hired by a law firm presents information to the court on behalf of his employer.

We agree with the trial judge that clerks should not be permitted to make motions or participate in other proceedings which can be considered as "managing" the litigation. However, if apprising the court of an employer's engagement or inability to be present constitutes the mak-

ing of a motion, we must hold that clerks may make such motions for continuances without being guilty of the unauthorized practice of law. Certainly with the large volume of cases appearing on the trial calls these days, it is imperative that this practice be followed.

In *Toth v. Samuel Phillipson & Co.,* 250 Ill. App. 247 (1928) the court said at page 250:

"It is well known in this county where numerous trial courts are sitting at the same time the exigencies of such a situation require that trial attorneys be represented by their clerical force to respond to some of the calls, and that the court acts upon their response the same as if the attorneys of record themselves appeared in person."

After that opinion was handed down, the number of judges was substantially increased in the former Circuit and Superior Courts and the problem of answering court calls has at least doubled. We cannot add to the heavy burden of lawyers who in addition to responding to trial calls must answer pre-trial calls and motion calls—all held in the morning—by insisting that a lawyer must personally appear to present to a court a motion for a continuance on grounds of engagement or inability to appear because of illness or other unexpected circumstances. To reduce the backlog, trial lawyers should be kept busy actually trying lawsuits and not answering court calls.

---

[8]Winter, *No Contempt in Kentucky,* 7 Nat'l Paralegal Reporter 8 (Nat'l Federation of Paralegal Associations, Winter 1982).
[9]53 Ill. App. 2d 299, 202 N.E.2d 841 (1964).

It must be emphasized that most states would *not* agree with Kentucky and Illinois. Most states would prohibit nonattorneys from doing what was authorized by the two courts in these two states. Fortunately, however, at least a few additional states have begun to move in the direction of a minority view.

The Allen County Bar Association of Indiana, for example, has taken the bold move of permitting paralegals to perform what hitherto had been considered attorney functions in court. A paralegal is authorized:

- To "take" default judgments
- To "set" pretrial conferences, uncontested divorces, and all other hearing dates
- To "file" stipulations or motions for dismissal
- Etc.

The paralegal, however, must perform these tasks with court personnel other than judges; nonattorneys cannot communicate directly with judges.

The vast majority of attorneys in the country would be amazed to learn what is going on in Allen County. Once the shock subsides, however, these attorneys will probably see the wisdom and common sense of what Allen County has done and begin to think of ways to try it themselves.

The rules of the Allen County program are as follows:

Paralegal Rules of Practice
Allen County Bar Association (Indiana)

1. Generally, a legal assistant employee shall be limited to the performance of tasks which do not require the exercising of legal discretion or judgment that affects the legal right of any person.

2. All persons employed as legal assistants shall be registered [see Exhibit 4.2] by their employer law firm with the Allen County Circuit and Superior Court Administrator and the Clerk of the Allen Superior and Circuit Courts. Said law firm shall, by affidavit, state that it shall be bound and liable for the actions of its legal assistant employee, and that any and all actions or statements made by such personnel shall be strictly and completely supervised by his employer member of the Bar. All documents the legal assistant presents or files must contain the attorney's signature, either as an attorney for the petitioning party, or a statement affixed indicating that the documents were prepared by said attorney. Each law firm shall certify in writing that the legal assistant employee is qualified in each field in which they will act with the Courts (probate, dissolution of marriage, collection, etc.). A copy of such statement and certification shall be given to such legal assistant and shall be carried by such person whenever activity with the Court is pursued by such person. . . .

3. Such employee shall be limited to the following acts:
   (a) Such employee may take default judgments upon the filing of an affidavit in each case stating the amount of damages and that proper service was obtained sworn to by affidavit.
   (b) Such employee shall have authority to set Pre-Trial Conferences, Uncontested Divorces, and all other hearing dates.
   (c) Such employee shall have authority to obtain trust account deposits at the Allen County Clerk's Office but only in the name of his employer firm.
   (d) Such employee shall have authority to file stipulations or motions for dismissal.
   (e) Such an employee shall have the authority to do all filing of documents and papers with the Clerk of the Allen Superior Courts and Circuit Court where such documents and papers are not to be given to anyone authorized to affix a judge's signature or issue Court orders.
   (f) Notwithstanding the limitations of subparagraph (e) above, such employee shall have the authority to obtain from the law clerk the signature stamp of the judge on non-discretionary standard orders and notices, such as notice of hearing, and orders to appear and to answer interrogatories on the filing of a Verified Motion for Proceedings Supplemental.

Note: Standard orders which depart from the usual format, restraining orders, suit and support orders, bench warrants, and body attachments must be secured by an attorney.

(g) Such employee is not to negotiate with opposing litigants within the Courthouse nor confer with a judge on legal matters. Matters requiring communications with a judge, require an attorney.

(h) Where circumstances permit, attorneys shall take precedence over such employees in dealings with courts and clerks.

E x h i b i t 4 . 2   **Allen County Circuit and Superior Court Certification of Legal Assistants**

Statement of Certification

This is to certify that _____
is employed by the law firm of _____.
Said law firm binds itself and takes full responsibility and liability for the actions of its legal assistant employee above-named and that any and all actions or statements made by such personnel shall be strictly and completely supervised by a member of the Bar of the State of Indiana. This is to certify that the above-mentioned legal assistant is qualified to assist an attorney in the _____ area of law.

LAW FIRM OF: _____

BY: _____

STATE OF INDIANA, COUNTY OF ALLEN, SS:

Subscribed and sworn to before me, a Notary Public in and for said County and State, this _____ day _____ , 19 _____.

_____
Notary Public

Note again that the Allen County program does not allow the paralegal to talk directly with a judge in performing the authorized tasks. ("Matters requiring communications with a judge, require an attorney.") Why such a restriction? Wouldn't it make sense to allow paralegal-judge communication on some procedural matters that are of a routine nature? *No,* would be the response of most bar associations.

Yes, however, is the refreshing response of several county bar associations in the state of Washington. Under the sponsorship of the Seattle–King County Bar Association and the Tacoma–Pierce County Bar Association, paralegals are allowed to "present" certain orders to judges. The orders must be those that the parties have already agreed on, or must be **ex parte** (which means involving one party only). In presenting such orders to a judge, the paralegal must obviously deal directly with—and perhaps even communicate with—a judge! The prohibition on communicating with a judge in Allen County, Indiana, does not exist in these two counties of Washington State.

(b) The Jailhouse Lawyer

A **jailhouse lawyer** is a nonattorney who helps other prisoners with their legal problems. Jailhouse lawyers clearly practice law, often for fees in the form of cigarettes, cash, etc. Some prisons attempted to prevent jailhouse lawyers from providing this legal assistance even though the prisons provided no meaningful alternatives to such assistance. This prohibition was struck down, however, by the United States Supreme Court in *Johnson v. Avery* in 1969. The basis of the opinion was that without the jailhouse lawyer, prisoners may not have access to the courts. The concurring opinion of Justice Douglas has become one of the most widely quoted and influential statements in the field of paralegalism.

Case

Johnson v. Avery

Supreme Court of the United States, 1969.
393 U.S. 483, 89 S. Ct. 747, 21 L. Ed. 2d 718

. . .

Mr. Justice DOUGLAS, concurring.

While I join the opinion of the Court [in striking down the prohibition on the activities of jailhouse lawyers] I add a few words in emphasis of the important thesis of the case.

The increasing complexities of our governmental apparatus at both the local and the federal levels have made it difficult for a person to process a claim or even to make a complaint. Social security is a virtual maze; the hierarchy that governs urban housing is often so intricate that it takes an expert to know what agency has jurisdiction over a particular complaint; the office to call or official to see for noise abatement, for a broken sewer line, or a fallen tree is a mystery to many in our metropolitan areas.

A person who has a claim assertable in faraway Washington, D.C., is even more helpless, as evidenced by the increasing tendency of constituents to rely on their congressional delegation to identify, press, and process their claims.

We think of claims as grist for the mill of the lawyers. But it is becoming abundantly clear that more and more of the effort in ferreting out the basis of claims and the agencies responsible for them and in preparing the almost endless paperwork for their prosecution is work for laymen. There are not enough lawyers to manage or supervise all of these affairs; and much of the basic work done requires no special legal talent. *Yet there is a closed-shop philosophy in the legal profession that cuts down drastically active roles for laymen. . . . That traditional, closed-shop attitude is utterly out of place in the modern world where claims pile high and much of the work of tracing*

and pursuing them requires the patience and wisdom of a layman rather than the legal skills of a member of the bar. [Emphasis added.]

"If poverty lawyers are overwhelmed, some of the work can be delegated to sub-professionals. New York law permits senior law students to practice law under certain supervised conditions. Approval must first be granted by the appellate division. A rung or two lower on the legal profession's ladder are laymen legal technicians, comparable to nurses and lab assistants in the medical profession. Large law firms employ them, and there seems to be no reason why they cannot be used in legal services programs to relieve attorneys for more professional tasks." Samore, *Legal Services for the Poor*, 32 Albany L.Rev. 509, 515–516 (1968).

The plight of a man in prison may in these respects be even more acute than the plight of a person on the outside. He may need collateral proceedings to test the legality of his detention or relief against management of the parole system or against defective detainers lodged against him which create burdens in the nature of his incarceration status. He may have grievances of a civil nature against those outside the prison. His imprisonment may give his wife grounds for divorce and be a factor in determining the custody of his children; and he may have pressing social security, workmen's compensation, or veterans' claims.

While the demand for legal counsel in prison is heavy, the supply is light. For private matters of a civil nature, legal counsel for the indigent in prison is almost nonexistent. Even for criminal proceedings, it is sparse. While a few States have post-conviction statutes providing such counsel, most States do not. Some States like California do appoint counsel to represent the indigent prisoner in his collateral hearings, once he succeeds in making out a prima facie case. But as a result, counsel is not on hand for preparation of the papers or for the initial decision that the prisoner's claim has substance.

Notes

1. "Jailhouse lawyers, or **writ writers,** as they are sometimes called, have always been part of prison society. But in recent years their numbers as well as the amount of litigation they generate, has increased substantially. In 1985, prisoners filed 33,400 petitions in federal and state courts, . . ." One jailhouse lawyer at Soledad prison "devotes 16 hours a day to his legal work, subscribes to dozens of legal publications (at a cost of $1,800 a year), and files a steady stream of lawsuits." Suing "has become almost a national pastime. Prisoners act no differently from other citizens in a litigious society." Kroll, *Counsel Behind Bars: Jailhouse Lawyers . . .* , 7 California Lawyer 34 (June 1987).

2. The *Johnson* opinion stressed that the prison provided *no* alternative to the jailhouse lawyer. If alternatives had been available, the inmate would not be allowed to practice law. In *Williams v. U.S. Dep't of Justice,* 433 F.2d 958 (5th Cir. 1970), the court held that the presence of law students in the prison could be an alternative, but only if it were demonstrated that the students were meeting the need for inmate legal services. If the inmates had to wait a considerable period of time, for example, before they could be interviewed by the law students, then no adequate alternative would exist and the jailhouse lawyer could not be prevented from helping other inmates.

3. In *Gilmore v. Lynch,* 319 F. Supp. 105 (N.D. Cal. 1970), affirmed by the United States Supreme Court in *Younger v. Gilmore,* 404 U.S. 15 (1971), the court held that California either had to satisfy the legal needs of its prisoners or expand the prison law library to include a more comprehensive collection of law books. See also *Bounds v. Smith,* p. 199.

4. Finally, the right of an inmate to assist other inmates in legal matters does *not* extend to representing an inmate in court. *Guajardo v. Luna,* 432 F.2d 1324 (5th Cir. 1970). Nor can a nonattorney represent an inmate in court even if this nonattorney is not

Jailhouse lawyer, Fernando Jackson, Soledad Prison, California

an inmate himself or herself. This latter point was decided by the United States Supreme Court in *Hackin v. Arizona*, 389 U.S. 143 (1967).

5. How far can the rationale of *Johnson* be extended? Suppose, for example, it is demonstrated that many claimants before state administrative agencies are not receiving legal services because they cannot afford attorneys. Would the *Johnson* opinion permit paralegal representation before such agencies even if the latter prohibited it? What is the difference between an inmate's right to have access to the courts and *anyone's* right to complain to an agency? How do you think Justice Douglas would handle the case if it came before him?

"Although the *Johnson* case is admittedly narrow in scope, it does nevertheless, give aid and comfort to the view that whenever lawyers are unavailable for whatever reason, society will sanction alternative systems for the delivery of legal services. The paramount consideration will not be ethics nor the exclusivity of the right to practice law, but rather it will be the facilitation of access routes to the grievance machinery set up for the resolution of claims. If lawyers are not available to assist the citizenry with these claims, then the question arises as to whether skilled nonlawyers represent a viable alternative. The inevitability of this question becomes clear when we listen to the statistics on the demand for the services of a lawyer. Estimates have been made to the effect that if every lawyer devoted full time to the legal needs of the poor, there would still be a significant shortage of lawyers for the poor. If the legal needs of the middle class are added, the shortage of legal services becomes overwhelming." Statsky, W. and Lang, P., *The Legal Paraprofessional as Advocate and Assistant: Roles, Training Concepts and Materials,* 49–50 (1971). See also Statsky, W., *Inmate Involvement in Prison Legal Services: Roles and Training Options for the Inmate as Paralegal* (American Bar Association, Commission on Correctional Facilities and Services, Resource Center on Correctional Law and Legal Services, 1974).

Two other important Supreme Court cases involving nonattorneys in prison need to be considered: the *Procunier* case and the *Bounds* case:

Case
Procunier v. Martinez
Supreme Court of the United States, 1974.
416 U.S. 396, 94 S. Ct. 1800, 40 L. Ed. 2d 244

. . .

The District Court also enjoined continued enforcement of Administrative Rule MV-IV-02, which provides in pertinent part:

"Investigators for an attorney-of-record will be confined to not more than two. Such investigators must be licensed by the State or must be members of the State Bar. Designation must be made in writing by the Attorney."

By restricting access to prisoners to members of the bar and licensed private investigators, this regulation imposed an absolute ban on the use by attorneys of law students and legal paraprofessionals to interview inmate clients. In fact attorneys could not even delegate to such persons the task of obtaining prisoners' signatures on legal documents. The District Court reasoned that this rule constituted an unjustifiable restriction on the right of access to the courts. We agree.

The constitutional guarantee of due process of law has as a corollary the requirement that prisoners be afforded access to the courts in order to challenge unlawful convictions and to seek redress for violations of their constitutional rights. This means that inmates must have a reasonable opportunity to seek and receive the assistance of attorneys. Regulations and practices that unjustifiably obstruct the availability of professional representation or other aspects of the right of access to the courts are invalid.

Ex parte Hull, 312 U.S. 546, 61 S. Ct. 640, 85 L. Ed. 1034 (1941).

The District Court found that the rule restricting attorney-client interviews to members of the bar and licensed private investigators inhibited adequate professional representation of indigent inmates. The remoteness of many California penal institutions makes a personal visit [by attorneys] to an inmate client a time-consuming undertaking. The court reasoned that the ban against the use of law students or other paraprofessionals for attorney-client interviews would deter some lawyers from representing prisoners who could not afford to pay for their traveling time or that of licensed private investigators. And those lawyers who agreed to do so would waste time that might be employed more efficaciously in working on the inmates' legal problems. Allowing law students and paraprofessionals to interview inmates might well reduce the cost of legal representation for prisoners. The District Court therefore concluded that the regulation imposed a substantial burden on the right of access to the courts.

Case

Bounds v. Smith

Supreme Court of the United States, 1977
430 U.S. 817, 97 S. Ct. 1491, 52 L. Ed. 2d 72

[In this opinion the Supreme Court is again concerned with the need of prisoners to have access to the courts and the use of nonlawyers in helping to obtain that access. The Court held that prisons must assist inmates in the preparation and filing of meaningful legal papers by providing the inmates with adequate law libraries or adequate assistance from persons trained in the law. The Court rejected the claim that nonlawyer inmates were ill-equipped to use the "tools of the trade of the legal profession." In the Court's experience, nonlawyer petitioners are capable of using law books to file cases raising claims that are "serious and legitimate" whether or not such petitioners win the cases. In outlining the options available to a prison, the Court specifically referred to paralegals:]

It should be noted that while adequate law libraries are one constitutionally acceptable method to assure meaningful access to the courts, our decision here, . . . , does not foreclose alternative means to achieve that goal. Nearly half the States and the District of Columbia provide some degree of professional or quasi-professional legal assistance to prisoners. . . . Such programs take many imaginative forms and may have a number of advantages over libraries alone. Among the alternatives are the training of inmates as para-legal assistants to work under lawyers' supervision, the use of paraprofessionals and law students, either as volunteers or in formal clinical programs, the organization of volunteer attorneys through bar associations or other groups, the hiring of lawyers on a part-time consultant basis, and the use of full-time staff attorneys, working either in new prison legal assistance organizations or as part of public defender or legal services offices.

🏛 Assignment 4.2

Linda Mookely is an attorney who represents fifty inmates on a consolidated case in the state court. The inmates are in fourteen different institutions throughout the state. Linda asks the director of the state prison system to allow her paralegal, Mark Smith, to interview all fifty inmates at a central location. The director responds as follows:

- He refuses to transport the inmates to one location. The inmates would have to be interviewed at the institutions where they are currently living.
- He refuses to let anyone into any institution unless the individual either has a law degree *or* has been through the prison's two-week orientation program totaling twenty hours in the evening at the state capital. The orientation program gives an overview of the prison

system and covers general techniques for helping inmates with different kinds of social and mental problems.

Mark Smith has not taken the orientation program, and it would be very inconvenient for him to do so since he lives 150 miles from the capital. How would *Johnson, Procunier,* or *Bounds* apply to this problem?

(c) Agency Representation

A considerable number of administrative agencies will permit a paralegal or other nonattorney to represent clients at the agency. These individuals are usually called agents, practitioners, or representatives. They engage in informal advocacy for their clients at the agency or formal advocacy, including representation at an **adversarial** administrative hearing. (A proceeding is adversarial if another side appears in the controversy, whether or not the other side is represented. If no other side is present in the matter before the agency, the proceeding is considered nonadversarial.) Often the issues before the agency are economic, statistical, or scientific, but legal issues are also involved. It is clear that in conducting an adversarial hearing before an agency, the nonattorney can be practicing law in a manner that is remarkably similar to an attorney's representation of a client in court. Our study of this phenomenon will begin with federal administrative agencies, and then we will cover state agencies.

Nonattorney Practice before Federal Administrative Agencies. Congress has passed a statute, the **Administrative Procedure Act,** that governs procedures before *federal* administrative agencies such as the Federal Trade Commission. The Act gives each federal agency the power to decide for itself whether only attorneys can represent clients before it:

> **Administrative Procedure Act 5 U.S.C.A. § 555 (1967).** (b) A person compelled to appear in person before an agency is entitled to be accompanied, represented, and advised by counsel or, if permitted by the agency, by other qualified representative. . . .

See Appendix E on the extent of nonattorney representation in federal agencies.

When an agency decides to use this power to permit nonattorney representation, it can simply allow anyone to act as the agent or representative of another before the agency, or it can establish qualifications or standards of admission to practice before it. If the agency takes the latter course, its qualifications or standards could include a specialized test to demonstrate competency in the subject matter regulated by the agency, minimum educational or experience requirements, registration or enrollment on the agency's approved roster of representatives, and an agreement to abide by designated ethical rules of practice—a violation of which could result in suspension and "disbarment."

The United States Patent Office has established criteria for individuals to practice (as **registered agents**) before this agency by drafting and filing applications for patents, searching legal opinions on patentability, etc.[10] In 1982, approximately 12,000 registered agents had met these criteria at the agency. Of this number, about 1,900 (or 15.8 percent) were nonattorneys. At the former Interstate Commerce Commission, close to 10,000 nonattorney **practitioners** were authorized to represent clients at ICC proceedings that often involved issues such as rate increases and service extensions for railroads and other transportation carriers.[11] Perhaps the largest use of nonattorneys in federal agencies is at

---

[10]37 C.F.R. § 1.341–1.348 (1983).
[11]49 C.F.R. § 1103.1–1103.5 (1983).

the Internal Revenue Service within the Treasury Department.[12] Any certified public accountant is authorized to practice before the IRS. The American Institute of Certified Public Accountants has more than 190,000 members, most of whom are not attorneys.[13] In addition, the IRS has enrolled, i.e., registered, thousands of nonattorneys to represent taxpayers at all administrative proceedings within the IRS. These individuals, called **enrolled agents,** charge clients fees for their services. (Once a dispute goes to court, however, an attorney must take over.) To become an enrolled agent, an individual must either pass a written IRS examination or prove that he or she once worked at the IRS for five years interpreting and applying tax laws. In most states there are organizations of enrolled agents; the major national organization is the National Association of Enrolled Agents.

While many federal agencies allow nonattorney representation, relatively few nonattorneys actually use the authority they have. A study by the American Bar Association of thirty-three federal administrative agencies reached the following conclusion: "We found that the overwhelming majority of agencies studied permit nonlawyer representation in both adversarial and nonadversarial proceedings. However, most of them seem to encounter lay practice very infrequently (in less than 5% of adjudications), while only a few encounter lay practice as often as lawyer practice. Thus, although universally permitted, lay practice before federal agencies rarely occurs."[14]

One agency where nonattorney representation is fairly high (about 15 percent) is the Social Security Administration (SSA). Paralegals are frequently appointed by clients (see Exhibit 4.3) to represent them before the agency. Here is what the SSA says about the role of representatives:

What A Representative May Do

We [SSA] will work directly with your appointed representative unless he or she asks us to work directly with you. Your representative may:

- get information from your Social Security file;
- give us evidence or information to support your claim;
- come with you, or for you, to any interview, conference, or hearing you have with us;
- request a reconsideration, hearing, or Appeals council review; and
- help you and your witnesses prepare for a hearing and question any witnesses.

In 1993, a study compared the success of clients at hearings based on who represented them. The results were as follows:

- 72.6 percent of clients represented by attorneys were successful.
- 69.8 percent of clients represented by nonattorneys were successful.
- 52.7 percent of clients who represented themselves were successful.[15]

Attorneys and paralegals can charge fees for their services in representing clients before the SSA, but the agency must specifically approve the fee. This is not to say, however, that attorneys and paralegals are treated alike. If an attorney successfully represents a claimant, the agency will deduct up to 25 percent of the claimant's award, which will be paid directly

---

[12]31 C.F.R. §§ 10.3–10.75 (1983); 20 U.S.C. § 1242 (1975).

[13]Rose, *Representation by Non-Lawyers in Federal Administrative Agency Proceedings* (Administrative Conference of the United States, 1984); Vom Baur, *The Practice of Non-Lawyers before Administrative Agencies,* 15 Federal Bar Journal 99 (1955).

[14]ABA Standing Committee on Lawyers' Responsibility for Client Protection, *Report of 1984 Survey of Nonlawyer Practice before Federal Administrative Agencies* (October 19, 1984).

[15]Social Security Administration, Office of Hearings and Appeals, Office of Policy Planning and Evaluation, *Highlights for Fiscal Year 1993,* Tables 1, 2 (November 30, 1993).

Exhibit 4.3 Appointment of Representative

Social Security Administration

Please read the back of the last copy before you complete this form.

Form Approved
OMB No. 0960-0527

Name (Claimant) (**Print or Type**)	Social Security Number
Wage Earner (If Different)	Social Security Number

Part I   APPOINTMENT OF REPRESENTATIVE

I appoint this person, _____ ,

(Name and Address)

to act as my representative in connection with my claim(s) or asserted right(s) under:

☐ Title II
   (RSDI)

☐ Title XVI
   (SSI)

☐ Title IV FMSHA
   (Black Lung)

☐ Title XVIII
   (Medicare Coverage)

This person may, entirely in my place, make any request or give any notice; give or draw out evidence or information; get information; and receive any notice in connection with my pending claim(s) or asserted right(s).

☐ I am appointing, or I now have, more than one representative. My main representative
   is _____ .
              (Name of Principal Representative)

Signature (Claimant)	Address
Telephone Number (with Area Code) ( )	Date

Part II   ACCEPTANCE OF APPOINTMENT

I, _____ , hereby accept the above appointment. I certify that I have not been suspended or prohibited from practice before the Social Security Administration; that I am not disqualified from representing the claimant as a current or former officer or employee of the United States; and that I will not charge or collect any fee for the representation, even if a third party will pay the fee, unless it has been approved in accordance with the laws and rules referred to on the reverse side of the representative's copy of this form. If I decide not to charge or collect a fee for the representation, I will notify the Social Security Administration. (Completion of Part III satisfies this requirement.)

☐ I am an attorney.   ☐ I am not an attorney.   (Check one.)

Signature (Representative)	Address
Telephone Number (with Area Code) ( )	Date

Part III (Optional)   WAIVER OF FEE

I waive my right to charge and collect a fee under sections 206 and 1631(d)(2) of the Social Security Act. I release my client (the claimant) from any obligations, contractual or otherwise, which may be owed to me for services I have provided in connection with my client's claim(s) or asserted right(s).

Signature (Representative)	Date

Part IV (Optional)   ATTORNEY'S WAIVER OF DIRECT PAYMENT

I waive only my right to direct payment of a fee from the withheld past-due retirement, survivors, disability insurance or black lung benefits of my client (the claimant). I do not waive my right to request fee approval and to collect a fee directly from my client or a third party.

Signature (Attorney Representative)	Date

Form SSA-1696-U4 (9-94)
Destroy prior editions

(**See Important Information on Reverse**)

FILE COPY

to the attorney to cover fees. On the other hand, if a paralegal successfully represents a claimant, the paralegal must collect the fee directly from the client, since the SSA will not deduct anything from the award in such cases.[16]

Nonattorney Practice before State Administrative Agencies.

At the *state* level, there is often a similar system for authorizing nonattorneys to provide representation at many state administrative agencies. The state agencies most likely to allow nonattorney representation are those handling unemployment insurance, worker's compensation, public health and public assistance benefits, employment discrimination, and real estate assessments.[17] In New York, a 1993 survey found that 70 percent of New York state agencies and 63 percent of New York City agencies permitted some form of nonlawyer representation.[18]

Of course, the organized bar has never been happy that federal and state administration agencies have given this special authorization to nonattorneys. Since there are state statutes on who can practice law (and often criminal penalties for nonattorneys who practice law in violation of these statutes), how can an administrative agency allow a nonattorney to engage in activity that is clearly the practice of law? The answer to this question is somewhat different for federal and state agencies.

If the agency permitting nonattorney representation is a *federal* agency (for example, the United States Patent Office, the Internal Revenue Service, and the Social Security Administration), its authorization takes precedence over any *state* laws on the practice of law that would prohibit it. This principle was established in the United States Supreme Court case of *Sperry v. State of Florida ex rel. the Florida Bar.*[19] The case involved a nonattorney who was authorized to represent clients before the United States Patent Office. The Florida Bar claimed that the nonattorney was violating the state practice-of-law statute. The Supreme Court ruled that the **Supremacy Clause** of the United States Constitution gave federal laws supremacy over conflicting state laws. The Court also said:

> Examination of the development of practice before the Patent Office and its governmental regulation reveals that: (1) nonlawyers have practiced before the Office from its inception, with the express approval of the Patent Office and to the knowledge of Congress; (2) during prolonged congressional study of unethical practices before the Patent Office, the right of nonlawyer agents to practice before the Office went unquestioned, and there was no suggestion that abuses might be curbed by state regulation; (3) despite protests of the bar, Congress in enacting the Administrative Procedure Act refused to limit the right to practice before the administrative agencies to lawyers; and (4) the Patent Office has defended the value of nonlawyer practitioners while taking steps to protect the interests which a State has in prohibiting unauthorized practice of law. We find implicit in this history congressional (and administrative) recognition that registration in the Patent Office confers a right to practice before the Office without regard to whether the State within which the practice is conducted would otherwise prohibit such conduct.
>
> Moreover, the extent to which specialized lay practitioners should be allowed to practice before some 40-odd federal administrative agencies, including the Patent Office, received continuing attention both in and out of Congress during the period prior to 1952. The Attorney General's Committee on Administrative Procedure which, in 1941, studied the need for

---

[16]42 U.S.C. § 406 (1975).

[17]American Bar Association, Commission on Nonlawyer Practice, *Nonlawyer Activities in Law-Related Situations,* 146 (1995).

[18]New York County Lawyers' Association, Committee on Legal Assistants, *Committee Report* (October 14, 1993).

[19]373 U.S. 379, 387, 83 S. Ct. 1322, 1327, 10 L. Ed. 2d 428 (1963).

procedural reform in the administrative agencies, reported that "[e]specially among lawyers' organizations there has been manifest a sentiment in recent years that only members of the bar should be admitted to practice before administrative agencies. The Committee doubts that a sweeping interdiction of nonlawyer practitioners would be wise. . . ."

Suppose, however, that a *state* agency permits nonattorney representation. Can this be challenged by the bar? The issue may depend on who has the *power* to regulate the practice of law in a particular state. If the state legislature has this power, then the agency authorization of nonattorney representation is valid, since the agency is under the jurisdiction and control of the legislature. So long as the nonattorney representation is based on a statute of the legislature, it is valid. If, however, the state *judiciary* has the power to control the practice of law in a state, then the courts may be able to invalidate any nonattorney representation that is authorized by the agency.

Nonattorneys who have the authority to provide representation at an administrative agency may do so as independent paralegals or as full-time employees of attorneys. The following ethical opinion from California involves the latter—a paralegal employee of a law firm. The opinion discusses some of the issues that are involved when the law firm wants its paralegal to use the special authorization for nonattorney representation at a particular administrative agency—the Workers' Compensation Appeals Board. Later in chapter 5 we will examine the ethical issues involved in this opinion in greater depth.

Formal Opinion 1988–103
State Bar Committee on Professional Responsibility and Conduct (California)

Issue

May a law firm, having advised its clients of its intention to do so, delegate authority to a paralegal employee to make appearances at Workers' Compensation Appeals Board hearings and to file petitions, motions or other material?

Digest

A law firm may delegate such authority, provided that the paralegal employee is adequately supervised.

Authorities Interpreted

Rules 3-101, 3-103 and 6-101 of the Rules of Professional Conduct of the State Bar of California.

* * *

Issue

A client has contracted for the services of a law firm for representation in a matter pending before the Workers' Compensation Appeals Board (hereinafter "WCAB"). The law firm employs and intends to utilize the services of the paralegal in connection with the proceedings pending

before the WCAB to make appearances, file petitions and present motions.

The client has consented to the law firm utilizing the services of the paralegal, after being informed as to the potential consequences of representation by a person of presumably lesser qualification and skill than may be reasonably expected of an attorney. In addition, the status of the employee as a paralegal rather than an attorney will be fully disclosed at all proceedings at which the paralegal appears and on all documents which the paralegal prepares.

Discussion

It is unlawful for any person to practice law in this state without active membership in the State Bar of California. (Bus. & Prof. Code, ¶6125) The practice of law includes the performing of services in any matter pending in a court or administrative proceeding throughout its various stages, as well as the rendering of legal advice and counsel in the preparation of legal instruments and contracts by which legal rights are secured. (cf. *Smallberg v. State Bar* (1931) 212 Cal. 113.)

It has been held that the representation of claimants before the Industrial Accident Commission (predecessor to the WCAB) constitutes the performance of legal services. (*Bland v. Reed* (1968) 261 Cal. App. 2d 445, 448.) However, the representation by a nonattorney of an applicant before the WCAB is expressly authorized by Labor Code 5501 and 5700 as follows:

> The application may be filed with the appeals board by any party in interest, his attorney, or other representative authorized in writing . . . ,
>
> . . . Either party may be present at any hearing, in person, by attorney, or by any other agent, and may present testimony pertinent under the pleading.

Thus, the principal issue is whether an attorney may hire a nonattorney to engage in conduct on behalf of the attorney's client which the employee is authorized to perform independently, but which, if performed by the attorney, would constitute the practice of law.

It is the opinion of the Committee that because the client has been informed about, and has consented to the involvement of the paralegal, no violation occurs with respect to dishonesty or deceit. (See Bus. & Prof. Code, ¶6106, 6128, subd.(a).) In addition, if the status of the employee as a paralegal rather than attorney is fully disclosed at all proceedings at which the paralegal appears and on all documents which the paralegal prepares, no violation of the prohibition on an attorney lending his or her name to be used as an attorney by a person not licensed to practice law will occur. (See Bus. & Prof. Code, ¶6105.)

In addition, because Labor Code sections 5501 and 5700 expressly authorize nonattorneys to represent applicants before the WCAB, the proposed arrangements would not constitute a violation of Rule of Professional Conduct 3-101(A), which provides as follows:

> A member of the State Bar shall not aid any person, association, or corporation in the *unauthorized* practice of law. (Emphasis added.)

Further, there is no indication that the facts presented that the relationship between the paralegal and the law firm would constitute a partnership in violation of Rule of Professional Conduct 3-103, which provides as follows:

> A member of the State Bar shall not form a partnership with a person not licensed to practice law if any of the activities of the partnership consist of the practice of law.

The pivotal consideration is that the client contracted for the services of the law firm, rather than a paralegal, for representation. However, since the safeguards mentioned above have been taken to avoid misleading or deceiving the client or any one else regarding the status of the paralegal, the Committee finds no ethical insufficiency inherent in the participation of paralegals.

A lawyer or law firm contemplating entering into such an arrangement should remember that an attorney stands in a fiduciary relationship with the client. (*Krusesky v. Baugh* (1982) 138 Cal. App. 3d 562, 567.) When acting as a fiduciary, the law imposes upon a member the strictest duty of prudent conduct as well as an obligation to perform his or her duties to the best of the attorney's ability. (*Clark v. State Bar* (1952) 39 Cal. 2d 161, 167; and cf. Bus. & Prof. Code, ¶6067; Rule of Professional Conduct 6-101(A). However, an attorney does not have to bear the entire burden of attending to every detail of the practice, but may be justified in relying to some extent on nonattorney employees. (*Moore v. State Bar* (1964) 62 Cal. 2d 74, 80; *Vaughn v. State Bar* (1972) 6 Cal. 3d 847, 857.)

The attorney who delegates responsibilities to his or her employees must keep in mind that he or she, as the attorney, has the duty to adequately supervise the employee. In fact, the attorney will be subject to discipline if the lawyer fails to adequately supervise the employee. (*Chefsky v. State Bar* (1984) 36 Cal. 3d 116, 123; *Palomo v. State Bar* (1984) 36 Cal. 3d 785; *Gassman v. State Bar* (1976) 18 Cal. 3d 125.)

What constitutes adequate supervision will, of course, depend on a number of factors, including, but not limited to, the complexity of the client matter, the level of experience of the paralegal and the facts of the particular case.

It is the opinion of the Committee that, even though the paralegal will be providing substantive legal services to the client, adequate supervision under these unique facts does not require the attorney to ensure that the paralegal performs the services in accordance with the level of competence that would be expected of the attorney under rule 6-101.

So long as the paralegal is adequately supervised and the law firm does not mislead the client that the services will be performed in accordance with the attorney level of competence or that an attorney will be handling the matter, the Committee does not believe the attorney would be in violation of the Rules of Professional Conduct.

This opinion is issued by the Standing Committee on Professional Responsibility and Conduct of the State Bar of California. It is advisory only. It is not binding upon the courts, the State Bar of California, its Board of Governors, or any persons or tribunals charged with regulatory responsibility or any member of the State Bar.

▥ *Assignment 4.3*

Make a list of every state and local administrative agency in your state. Have a class discussion in which students identify as many state and local agencies as they can. Then divide the total number of agencies by the number of students in the class so that each student will be assigned the same number of agencies. For your agencies, find out whether nonattorneys can represent citizens. What are the requirements, if any, to provide this representation informally (e.g., calling or writing the agency on behalf of someone else) or formally (e.g., representing someone else at an agency hearing)? Check your state statutes. Check the regulations of the agency. If possible, call the agency to ask what its policy is and whether it can refer you to any statutes or regulations on the policy.

▥ *Assignment 4.4*

Paul is a nonattorney who works at the Quaker Draft Counseling Center. One of the clients of the center is Dan Diamond. Paul says the following to Mr. Diamond:

You don't have anything to worry about. The law says that you cannot be drafted until you have had an administrative hearing on your case. I will represent you at that hearing. If you are drafted before that hearing, I will immediately draft a habeas corpus petition that can be filed at the United States District Court.

Any problems with Paul's conduct?

Section C
LICENSING OF PARALEGALS

Many occupations (electricians, brokers, nurses, etc.) are licensed by the government. To date, *no* federal, state, or local government has imposed a licensing requirement on traditional paralegals. Proposals for licensing have been made in some legislatures, but none has been enacted into law. For paralegals who work under the supervision of attorneys, licensing is arguably unnecessary, since the public is protected by this supervision. But what about the relatively small number of independent paralegals who work directly with the public without attorney supervision? Many have argued that there *is* a need to license them in order to protect the public. The phrase *limited licensing* refers to a government authorization to perform a designated number of activities that are now part of the attorney monopoly (see Exhibit 4.1). While no limited licensing proposal has yet been enacted into law, the likelihood of passage is very real in spite of substantial attorney opposition. Before covering limited licensing, let's examine efforts to enact broad-based licensing schemes covering all activities of all paralegals.

BROAD-BASED LICENSING

A number of states have proposed legislation to license all paralegals. Many of these proposals confuse the word *certification* with *licensure*. Certification is usually a statement by a *non*governmental organization that a person has met certain qualifications. Licensure, on the other hand, is a permission or authorization *by a government* to engage in a certain activity. (See Exhibit 4.1.)

In 1977, for example, the Michigan legislature gave serious consideration to passing the Legal Assistant Act to "regulate the practice of legal assistants." Under this proposal, a nine-member commission would be created to establish the requirements for the "certification" of legal assistants. Even though the proposal uses the word *certification,* it was a licensure program, since it would establish the qualifications to engage in a particular occupation. If this legislation had been enacted, a person could not be a legal assistant in Michigan without passing a statewide examination and having the educational credentials identified by the commission.

This plan was *not* adopted in Michigan. Such licensing schemes are usually vigorously opposed by paralegal associations as being premature, unnecessary, and unduly restrictive. A commonly voiced fear is that the license might limit what paralegals are now authorized to do without a license, and that some competent paralegals who now work in law offices might not fit within rigid eligibility criteria that might be established for the license. The organized bar is also opposed to broad-based licensing. The following excerpts from bar association reports give some of the reasons why:

North Carolina Bar, *Report of Special Committee on Paralegals* 3 (1980)

Several states have considered the possibility of adopting a licensing statute for paralegals, but none has done so. Licensing itself is subject to great public and legislative concern at present. So long as the work accomplished by non-lawyers for lawyers is properly supervised and reviewed by a licensed and responsible attorney, there would seem to be no need for a further echelon of licensing for the public's protection. Furthermore, licensing might be more dangerous than helpful to the public. The apparent stamp of approval of a license possibly could give the impression to the public that a person having such a license is qualified to deal directly with and give legal advice to the public. Although the Committee would not attempt to close the door on licensing of paralegals in the future if circumstances change and if, for example, the use of independent, non-lawyer employee paralegals were to become widespread, present conditions, at least, do not call for any program of licensing for paralegals.

Illinois State Bar Association, *Report on the Joint Study Committee on Attorney Assistants* 6 (6/21/77)

Our Joint Committee arose because there was a suggestion that attorney assistants be licensed. After due consideration we recommend no program of licensure or certification of attorney assistants or other lay personnel.

We are opposed to licensure because the standards on which licensure are to be based are difficult or impossible to formulate. Furthermore, we have started with a premise that precedes this conclusion; to wit: no delegation of any task to an attorney assistant shall diminish the responsibility of the attorney for the services rendered. We believe that any program which purports to say who is "licensed" and who is "not licensed" creates a standard which will diminish the attorney's responsibility. It furthermore may exclude from useful and desirable employment people who, under the supervision and control of an attorney, may perform useful tasks but who may not meet the standards of licensure involved.

We are further opposed to licensure because of the danger that it poses to the public. If a group of persons appears to be authorized to perform tasks directly for the public, without the intervening control of an attorney, it would be humanly inevitable that many of the licensed persons would try to deal directly with the public. We think these risks would be substantially increased by licensure.

⚏ *A s s i g n m e n t   4 . 5*

How would you characterize the opposition to licensure expressed in the above excerpts from the bar reports? Do you think there is a conflict of interest in attorneys making these judgments about paralegal control? Explain.

LIMITED LICENSING

As we saw earlier, some independent, or freelance, paralegals have their own businesses, through which they sell their services to attorneys. A larger number work directly for the public without attorney supervision. For example, a paralegal might sell divorce forms and type them for clients. This is not the illegal practice of law, so long as no legal advice is given in the process. One of the reasons Rosemary Furman got into trouble was that she gave such advice along with the forms she typed; hence she was charged with the unauthorized practice of law by the Florida bar.

Some have argued that the law that led to the prosecution of people like Rosemary Furman should be changed. Why not grant them a limited license (sometimes called a specialty license) to practice law? Remarkably, a suggestion to this effect was actually made by a Commission of the American Bar Association! The ABA does not favor broad-based licensing of all paralegals. In a 1986 report, however, an ABA Commission on Professionalism cautiously suggested—on page 52 of the report—that there be "limited licensing of paralegals" and "paraprofessionals" to perform certain functions such as handling some real estate closings, drafting simple wills, and performing certain tax work. The report argued that such a proposal could help reduce the cost of legal services:

> No doubt, many wills and real estate closings require the services of a lawyer. However, it can no longer be claimed that lawyers have the exclusive possession of the esoteric knowledge required and are therefore the only ones able to advise clients on any matter concerning the law.[20]

This remarkable proposal caused quite a stir. Many refer to the controversy it created as the **page 52 debate.** For years, many attorneys were suspicious of paralegalism because of a fear that paralegals might eventually be licensed and compete with attorneys. Then along comes a report of an ABA Commission that recommends licensing! Yet it must be remembered that neither the report nor the Commission speaks for the entire ABA. In fact, the proposal in the report "drew the ire" of other ABA members *and was never given serious consideration by the ABA as a whole.*

In 1995, the ABA took a different approach. It established a Commission on Nonlawyer Practice to conduct hearings throughout the country. Its goal was "to determine the implications of nonlawyer practice for society, the client and the legal profession." The Commission studied four categories of nonlawyers:

- **Self-Represented Person** A person who represents him or herself, with or without assistance from someone else. The self-represented person acts **pro se,** which means appearing or representing oneself. A pro se litigant, for example, will argue his or her own case in court. This person is proceeding **in properia persona**—in one's own proper person. (The abbreviation is **pro per.**)

---

[20]*In the Spirit of Public Service: A Blueprint for Rekindling of Lawyer Professionalism,* 52 (ABA, Comm'n on Professionalism, 1986). See 112 F.R.D. 243 (1986)—The Federal Rules Decisions reporter.

- **Document Preparer**　A person who assists someone in the preparation of forms and documents using information provided by a self-represented person. No advice or substantive information is provided on which forms or documents to use, how to fill them out, or where to file them. The document preparer (also called a **scrivener** or professional copyist) does little more than type.
- **Paralegal**　A person who performs substantive work or provides advice to a client under the supervision of an attorney or for which an attorney is accountable. A paralegal (also called a legal assistant) is an employee of attorneys or is retained by attorneys as an independent contractor. The Commission refers to this category as the *traditional paralegal* because an attorney has control and responsibility over the paralegal's work product.
- **Legal Technician**　A person who provides advice or other substantive legal work to the public without attorney supervision and for which no attorney is accountable.

For two years the Commission studied these individuals, particularly the document preparer and legal technician. It heard the testimony of hundreds of witnesses and received thousands of pages of written testimony. The diversity of points of view presented to the Commission was enormous:

> Many suggestions received passionate support and were then opposed with equal vehemence. Experienced lawyers and nonlawyers often testified to diametrically opposed perceptions of consumer needs, risks of harm, nonlawyer capabilities and deficiencies, and the potential economies or effectiveness of any chosen regulatory approach.[21]

Throughout the country, the final report of the Commission was eagerly awaited. Supporters of limited licensing were hoping that the report would endorse some form of limited licensing. Some attorneys, however, feared that the Commission would move in this direction. At a meeting of bar association leaders, John Bracton, the former president of the New York State Bar Association said, "I will tell you that, unanimously, we reacted in horror to the idea that somehow the ABA might sanction an increase in nonlawyer practice."[22]

When the Commission issued its final report, however, no dramatic recommendations were made. (See Exhibit 4.4.) There was nothing comparable to the "page 52" debate that emerged from the 1986 report. The Commission made relatively lukewarm recommendations about expanding the role of the traditional paralegal (recommendation 2) and of nonattorneys in state administrative agencies (recommendation 3). But in many states this expansion had been underway for years with relatively little controversy. What everyone wanted to know was whether the Commission was going to conclude that the time was ripe for limited licensing.

Its answer to this volatile question was *maybe*. Rather than make a recommendation one way or another, the Commission said that each state should decide the question for itself (recommendation 6). The main contribution of the Commission was to suggest guidelines or criteria that a state should use in deciding whether the state's current regulation of nonattorney activity was sufficient and, if not, what further regulation was needed, including the option of allowing limited licensing of legal technicians.

First of all, the Commission believes a state should ask whether nonattorneys are posing risks to the public. If "there is no serious risk to the consumer even when the

---

[21]American Bar Association, Commission on Nonlawyer Practice, *Nonlawyer Activity in Law-Related Situations*, 175 (1995).

[22]Mike France, *Bar Chiefs Protect the Guild*, The National Law Journal, p. A1, A28 (August 7, 1995).

> *E x h i b i t 4 . 4*   **Recommendations of the ABA Commission on Non-Lawyer Practice (*Nonlawyer Activity in Law-Related Situations, 1995*)**
>
> **Recommendation 1.** The American Bar Association, state, local and specialty bar associations, the practicing bar, courts, law schools, and the federal and state governments should continue to develop and finance new and improved ways to provide access to justice to help the public meet its legal and law-related needs.
>
> **Recommendation 2.** The range of activities of traditional paralegals should be expanded with lawyers remaining accountable for their activity.
>
> **Recommendation 3.** States should consider allowing nonlawyer representation of individuals in state administrative agency proceedings. Nonlawyer representatives should be subject to the agencies' standards of practice and discipline.
>
> **Recommendation 4.** The American Bar Association should examine its ethics rules, policies and standards to ensure that they promote the delivery of affordable, competent services and access to justice.
>
> **Recommendation 5.** The activities of nonlawyers who provide assistance, advice and representation authorized by statute, court rule or agency regulation should be continued subject to review by the entity under whose authority the services are performed.
>
> **Recommendation 6.** With regard to the activities of all other nonlawyers [e.g., the legal technician], states should adopt an analytical approach in assessing whether and how to regulate varied forms of nonlawyer activity that exist or are emerging in their respective jurisdictions. Criteria for this analysis should include:
>
> **(a)** whether the nonlawyer activity poses a serious risk to the consumer's life, health, safety, or economic well-being,
>
> **(b)** whether potential customers have the knowledge needed to properly evaluate the qualifications of nonlawyers offering the services, and
>
> **(c)** whether the net effect of regulating the activities will be a benefit to the public (i.e., would the benefits of regulation to the public outweigh any likely negative consequences of regulation?).
>
> The highest courts should take the lead in examining specific nonlawyer activities within their jurisdictions with the active support and participation of the bar and the public.

nonlawyer's service is poor, then a state may conclude that the activity should be unregulated."[23] The same conclusion might be reached if the state thinks the public is sufficiently able to judge for itself whether a legal technician is qualified to offer his or her services.

Establishing a regulatory scheme is an expensive and often politically explosive undertaking. This is true whether the regulation seeks to ban an activity or to grant someone a limited license to perform it. A state must decide whether the resulting uproar is justified by the amount of risk the public might suffer without the regulatory scheme. For example, a state might reach the following conclusions about the landlord-tenant legal problems of the public:

- There is a serious shortage of help on these problems.
- It is not economical for attorneys to handle many of these cases.
- Legal technicians can help meet the demand for legal services in this area.

---

[23]ABA, *Nonlawyer Activity,* supra note 21 at p. 177.

- But serious harm can result if a consumer receives erroneous legal services in a landlord-tenant case.
- Because of the complexity of some landlord-tenant problems, the public may not be able to judge which legal technicians are qualified to work on them.
- A limited licensing program can be established that meets these concerns. The program would institute standards for training legal technicians, testing them, requiring them to carry liability insurance, disciplining them for unethical behavior, etc.

On the other hand, the state might conclude that the benefits of allowing legal technicians to work in this area are outweighed by the cost of setting up the elaborate licensing scheme that would be needed to make sure the public is protected from the substantial harm that can result from incompetent landlord-tenant legal services. Hence the state would reject a program of limited licensing for these kinds of legal problems. This is the kind of analysis the Commission says each state must undertake for all areas of nonattorney activity. (See recommendation 6 in Exhibit 4.4.)

The reaction to the Commission's report was mixed. Many welcomed the positive comments the report made about the important role paralegals have played in the delivery of legal services. Others, however, were critical of the Commission for being so tepid. For example, Merle Isgett, President of the National Federation of Paralegal Associations and a member of the Commission, said it was a "cop out" for the Commission to send the big issues like limited licensing back to the states instead of making forthright proposals for change. "We should have laid out the rules for state Supreme Courts to adopt. That's what the ABA does. All this says is that states should look at it."[24] "It's going to be put on some shelf somewhere and collect a lot of dust."[25] It remains to be seen whether this prediction is accurate.

Prior to the work of the ABA Commission, there were a number of attempts in several states to pass limited licensing laws, but *none were successful.* Here is an overview of some of these attempts:

California: The state bar created a Commission on Legal Technicians to study whether independent paralegals can help meet the public's "overwhelming unmet need" for legal services. The Commission's answer was *yes,* and it recommended that the California Supreme Court authorize *licensed independent paralegals* to practice law in three areas: bankruptcy law, family law, and landlord-tenant law. They could open offices and give advice, but they could not represent anyone in court. To earn this limited license, an applicant would have to pass a written examination and meet minimum levels of education or experience.[26] The plan was never adopted.

Arizona: An Arizona State Bar Task Force on the Unauthorized Practice of Law recommended that the state license *Non-Lawyer Legal Technicians* (NLLTs) to prepare living wills, applications for name changes, documents for real estate transfers, incorporations, uncontested divorces, etc. To become an NLLT, an applicant would have to meet educational requirements, pass an examination, be subject to a formal discipline

---

[24]Mark Curriden, *The ABA Nonlawyer Practice Report,* 13 Legal Assistant Today 89 (November/December 1995).

[25]Mark Curriden, *The ABA Has Spoken: Will the Nonlawyer Practice Report Make a Difference?* 14 Legal Assistant Today 62 (January/February 1996).

[26]A more radical California plan was proposed by **HALT** (Help Abolish Legal Tyranny), a national organization that combats the attorney monopoly over the practice of law. The HALT plan would have allowed nonattorneys to practice in fourteen areas of law.

Demonstration in front of the California State Bar Association on the issue of limited licensing.

process, and offer proof of financial responsibility. This proposal was rejected by the Arizona legislature.

Oregon: The Oregon Bar Association recommended that *Limited Law Advisors* (LLAs) be licensed to work on landlord-tenant cases, name changes, wills for estates under $300,000, etc. An LLA could give legal advice, but would not be allowed to represent someone in court. The state legislature has not acted on this proposal.

Florida: A report by the Special Committee on Non-Lawyer Practice of the Florida Bar recommended the limited licensing of *independent paralegals.* The state bar's board of governors rejected the recommendation.

Minnesota: The state legislature passed a law requiring the state supreme court to study the feasibility of licensing independent *specialized legal assistants.* A committee of the court recommended against doing so. Licensing would require the creation of a new regulatory system and be too costly. Instead, the committee recommended that a *registration* scheme be established for freelance paralegals who would work under the supervision of attorneys. A *registered legal assistant* would be permitted to perform expanded duties in the areas of landlord-tenant cases, simple wills, uncontested probate proceedings, etc. He or she would have to meet specified education requirements. The Supreme Court accepted the committee's recommendations. The state legislature, however, has not acted on the proposal.

Illinois: An Independent Licensing Act was introduced in the Illinois legislature to license *independent paralegals* to draft wills, conduct real estate closings, etc. The origin of this act is quite interesting. A paralegal student designed a regulation plan as part of a class assignment. When the student went to work for an Illinois state legislator, the plan eventually became the basis of the licensing plan that was actually introduced in the legislature! It was not enacted, however.

These proposals generated considerable controversy. The two national paralegal associations—National Association of Legal Assistants (NALA) and National Federation of Paralegal Associations (NFPA)—took very different positions on limited licensing.

For example, NALA *opposed* the California proposal for a number of reasons. First, the proposal did not provide sufficient guidelines to determine the kinds of cases an independent paralegal would be competent to handle. Many legal cases presented by clients are complex at the outset or become complex as they unfold. Such cases require the attention of an attorney. Independent paralegals are not in the best position to determine when a case is beyond their skills. Second, the licensing of independent paralegals could eventually lead to a climate in which *traditional* paralegals and legal assistants who work for attorneys would have to become licensed. Third, the licensing of independent paralegals would lead to open warfare with attorneys and to public disillusionment with the legal system. "For all practical purposes," the independent paralegals covered by the California proposal, "will become direct and fierce competitors of . . . lawyers who will not look kindly upon these untrained 'mini-lawyers.' It is only a matter of time . . . [until] the inevitable will occur; the public will have a bad experience working with one of these untrained, inadequately educated non-lawyers and it will become further disillusioned with the legal system. Thus the results will further blacken the public's image of lawyers and the law profession."[27] Finally, NALA objects to the use of the word *paralegal* for anyone who does not work under the supervision of an attorney.

The National Federation of Paralegal Associations has taken a radically different position. The NFPA has written a Model Act for Paralegal Licensure to be called the State Licensed Paralegal Act. The proposal establishes a seven-member State Board of Paralegal Practice to be appointed by the governor. Only two of the members can be attorneys. The Board would regulate the field of paralegal practice through a two-tier licensing scheme: an entry-level paralegal license, and a specialty paralegal license that is practice-specific.

Paralegal License (Entry-Level)

To be eligible for a *paralegal license,* an applicant must:

- be eighteen years of age or older;
- be of good moral character;
- meet specified minimum educational requirements in general and legal specialty courses; and
- pass a "proficiency-based" legal knowledge examination that includes ethics, general legal topics, and topics that are **state-specific,** i.e., covering the law of one state.

The paralegal license would automatically expire every two years. It could be renewed upon proof of meeting specified CLE (continuing legal education) requirements.

Specialty Paralegal License

To be eligible to become a *specialty licensed paralegal,* an applicant must:

- have had an entry-level paralegal license for a minimum of four years, and
- pass a specialty examination that will "test in a satisfactory manner the qualifications of the applicant to specialize in the legal area" for which the specialty license is sought.

To date, no state has adopted this model act.

---

[27]National Ass'n of Legal Assistants, *Statement to . . . State Bar of California* (1991).

As we have seen, there are attorneys who intensely oppose any form of limited licensing. A former president of the State Bar of California said, "It's like letting nurses do brain surgery." Scoffing at the notion that it is possible to carve out tasks that do not require the attention of an attorney, a judge commented, "You never know if you have a simple case until an expert looks at it. It's like a pain in the side. Only an expert can tell whether it should be treated with aspirin or by surgery."[28] Here are some other comments from attorneys: "This is the worst thing since the plague!" They think "just about everybody should be able to practice law. I guess they think everybody should be able to slice open a belly and remove an appendix." "I cannot think of anything that would be more injurious to the public." This is an idea "whose time has not yet come." "This is potentially the most fractious and controversial issue ever confronted" by the bar association. So far, such opposition has been successful since none of the limited license proposals have been enacted into law.

A much more modest form of limited licensing has been enacted into law in the state of Washington, however. A totally new category of worker has been created in the real estate industry, the **Limited Practice Officer** (LPO), also referred to as a Closing Certified Officer. This individual is a nonattorney with the authority "to select, prepare and complete legal documents incident to the closing of real estate and personal property transactions."[29] The state supreme court has created a Limited Practice Board to which applicants apply for "admission" to become an LPO. (See Exhibit 4.5.) The Board approves the form of the documents that the LPO can "select, prepare, and complete" in a closing, e.g., deeds, promissory notes, guaranties, deeds of trust, reconveyances, mortgages, satisfactions, security agreements, releases, Uniform Commercial Code documents, assignments, contracts, real estate excise tax affidavits, and bills of sale. As in the system for regulating attorneys, an LPO applicant must demonstrate "good moral character" and pass a combined essay and multiple-choice examination on the law. Once certified, LPOs can be disciplined for violating their authority. They must provide proof of financial responsibility by such means as purchasing a liability insurance policy ("errors and omissions insurance coverage") or showing that coverage exists under a bond taken out by their employer. By the end of 1993, approximately 1,700 LPOs existed in the state.

🏛 *A s s i g n m e n t   4 . 6*

Do you agree with NALA's position on limited licensing, or that of NFPA? Why?

What are the chances of a licensing requirement becoming law? Even though proposals for broad-based licensing continue to appear, passage is unlikely in view of widespread opposition from attorneys and paralegals. *Limited* licensing, on the other hand, may eventually become a reality, in spite of the position of NALA and of many bar associations. The LPO program in Washington represents a small crack in the door.

It is becoming increasingly difficult for attorneys to oppose limited licensing on the basis of the need to protect the public. A system now exists for identifying and punishing unscrupulous and incompetent attorneys; a similar system could be designed to regulate independent paralegals or legal technicians. And, of course, no one is proposing the equivalent of allowing nondoctors to perform brain surgery. The proposals for limited licensing simply try to identify services that do not require all of the skills of an attorney.

---

[28]Judge William Hogoboom, quoted in Harry Krause, *Family Law,* 3d ed., p. 734 (West Pub. Co. 1990).
[29]Washington Supreme Court Rule 12(a).

Exhibit 4.5 **Application for Admission to Limited Practice as a Limited Practice Officer in the State of Washington under the Admission to Practice Rule 12**

To the Washington State Limited Practice Board:
I hereby apply for a limited license to practice law in the State of Washington as a limited practice officer under the Admission to Practice Rule 12.

Applicant's Name in Full _____
                            Last   First   Middle

Applicant's Date of Birth _____
                            Month   Day   Year

Applicant's Business Address _____
                                          Address

                            _____
                            City   State   Zip Code

Applicant's Business Phone _(___)_____
                            Area Code   Number

Applicant's Home Address _____
                                          Address

                            _____
                            City   State   Zip Code

Applicant's Home Tel. No. _(___)_____
                            Area Code   Number

Applicant's Social Security Number _____

Please list:
Employers/Supervisors   **From**   **To**   **Telephone Number**
(Past five years) Attach separate
sheet if needed.

Perhaps the most compelling argument for limited licensing is the fact that attorneys have priced themselves out of the market. Recent studies continue to document a vast unmet need for legal services in our society. Attorneys, however, point to the reforms that have made legal services more accessible at a lower cost. See Exhibit 4.6. Yet, in spite of these reforms and in spite of the dramatic increase in the number of attorneys coming out of our law schools, the unmet need for legal services among the poor and middle class continues to grow. Here, for example, are some of the conclusions of legal-needs studies covering two large states:

Each year in Illinois, by conservative estimates, 300,000 low-income families face approximately 1,000,000 civil legal problems for which they do not receive legal help.[30]

---

[30]Illinois State Bar Association and Chicago Bar Association, *Illinois Legal Needs Study* 5 (1989).

Exhibit 4.6 Reforms in the Practice of Law Designed to Increase the Number of People Receiving Legal Services

- *Pro bono work. Pro bono publico* means for the public good. **Pro bono work** refers to work performed free of charge. Many law firms and corporations give their attorneys time off to provide free legal services to the poor.
- *Simplified forms.* Some bar associations have helped create legal forms that are relatively easy for the public to use without the assistance of an attorney.
- *Prepaid legal services.* Some companies and unions have developed legal insurance plans that enable participants to pay a set amount each month for designated legal services that might be needed while the participant is in the program. These are called **prepaid legal service** plans.
- *Attorney advertising.* Advertising has arguably made the public more aware of legal services and more inclined to use such services.
- *Publicly funded legal services.* The bar associations have consistently supported increased funding by the government for organizations such as legal service offices and legal aid societies that provide free legal services to the poor.
- *Traditional paralegals.* The increased use of paralegals by attorneys can lead to lower client costs since the billing rate for paralegal time is considerably lower than the billing rate for most attorneys.

The poor in New York face nearly 3,000,000 civil legal problems per year without legal help. Not more than 14% of their overall need for legal assistance is being met.[31]

The statistics are even more alarming if the legal needs of the middle class are included. In light of these numbers, critics are calling for drastic reform.

In areas such as divorce and bankruptcy, an increasingly large underground network of nonattorneys is providing low-cost legal services to citizens. Why not bring these nonattorneys out into the open? Subject them to testing and other license requirements to help insure competence and honesty. While many attorneys see this cure as worse than the disease, others are more receptive to the idea.

Each state must make its own determination of whether limited licensing should be adopted. It is quite possible that one or two states will take the plunge in the near future and enact limited licensing. Will your state do so? Keep in mind that even if it does, it will probably affect very *few* paralegals in your state. The likelihood is that the requirement will apply only to those paralegals who do not work for attorneys. This means that the vast majority of paralegals in the state who work for attorneys would continue as they are—with no license requirement. It is true that some paralegals favor limited licensing for traditional paralegals who work under the supervision of attorneys in order to expand what they are allowed to do for attorneys. But any movement toward such expansion is considerably weaker than the current momentum toward licensing independents.

When a licensing proposal—or a proposal for any kind of paralegal regulation—comes before the legislature, here are some of the steps that should be taken immediately:

---

[31]New York State Bar Association, *New York Legal Needs Study: Draft Final Report,* 196 (1989).

What to Do When the Legislature Proposes Legislation to Regulate Paralegals

(In general, see also *How to Monitor Proposed Legislation,* p. 637.)

1. Obtain a copy of the proposed legislation or bill as soon as possible. If you know the name of the legislator sponsoring the bill, write or call him or her directly. Otherwise contact the office of the Speaker of the House, Speaker of the Assembly, President of the Senate, etc. Ask how you can locate the proposed bill. For a list of phone numbers to your state legislature see Appendix J, State Resources.

2. Find out the exact technical status of the bill. Has it been formally introduced? Has it been assigned to a committee? What is the next scheduled formal event on the bill?

3. Immediately inform the sponsoring legislator(s) and the relevant committee(s) that you want an opportunity to comment on the bill. Find out if hearings are going to be scheduled on the bill. Make known your interest in participating in such hearings. Your goal is to slow the process down so that the bill is not rushed into enactment. Be particularly alert to the possibility that the paralegal bill may be buried in proposed legislation on a large number of related or unrelated topics. Again, there is a real danger that the bill will get through relatively unnoticed.

4. Determine why the paralegal bill is being proposed. What is the *public* reason given for the proposal of the bill? More important, what is the underlying *real* reason for the proposal? Perhaps some special interest or small group (real estate agents, for instance) is seeking a special privilege in a law-related field. Yet the language of the bill they are proposing may be so broad that paralegals will be adversely affected.

5. Alert your local paralegal association. It needs to be mobilized in order to express an organized position on the bill. Contact the major national paralegal associations: NFPA and NALA (see Appendix B). Do they know about the proposed legislation? Have they taken a position? They need to be activated.

6. If your local bar association has a paralegal committee, seek its support.

7. Launch a letter-writing campaign. Make sure that large numbers of paralegals in the area know about the bill and know how to express their opinion to the legislature.

8. Ask local paralegal schools to take a position.

Keep in mind that we are talking about mandatory *licensing* by the state, not voluntary *certification* by entities such as paralegal associations. The certification debate will be covered later in the chapter.

A s s i g n m e n t   4 . 7

(a) Do you favor broad-based licensing for every paralegal? Limited licensing? Will licensing advance or restrict the development of paralegalism?

(b) If all attorneys in the country drastically cut their fees, would there be a need for paralegal licensing?

(c) Paralegals who work for attorneys (traditional paralegals) cannot perform some tasks, such as taking the deposition of a witness. Should there be limited licensing to authorize such tasks?

Assignment 4.8

Evaluate the following observation: "The emerging professions and the more established professions have frequently sought greater regulation of their occupational group. They are often motivated, despite the obligatory language on protection of the public interest, to do so in efforts to establish their 'territorial imperative' or to establish barriers to entry into the profession and thereby enhance their economic self-interest." Should paralegals establish such barriers on who can become a paralegal? Sapadin, *A Comparison of the Growth and Development of the Physician Assistant and the Legal Assistant,* in Journal of the American Association for Paralegal Education: Retrospective 1983, 142 (1983).

Section D
BAR ASSOCIATION CONTROL OF PARALEGAL EDUCATION

Since the early 1970s, the American Bar Association has been "approving" paralegal training programs based on a recommendation made by its standing Committee on Legal Assistants, all of whose members are attorneys. There is no requirement that a school be ABA-approved in order to train paralegals. In fact, most training programs are not so approved. The approval process is voluntary, and the majority of programs have decided *not* to apply for approval. A program must meet state government accreditation standards, but it does not have to seek the approval of the ABA or of any other bar association.

The ABA approval process has been controversial from its inception. Those who oppose total attorney control of paralegalism feel that the bar associations are inappropriate mechanisms to regulate training institutions. Since a major goal of attorneys is to increase their profits by employing paralegals, critics argue that it is a conflict of interest for attorneys to control the field totally. When regulatory decisions must be made on matters such as the approval of schools, whose interest would the attorneys be protecting in making these decisions? The interest of the paralegals? The interest of the public? Or the profit interest of the attorney-regulators?

The ABA has been somewhat sensitive to this criticism and, as we will see, at one time considered withdrawing from the approval process. In recent years, challenges have been made to the monopoly that bar associations exercise over the practice of law. In 1975, the United States Supreme Court sent shock waves throughout the legal profession when the Court ruled in the *Goldfarb* case that attorneys were no longer exempt from the *antitrust* laws, and that some minimum fee schedules are a violation of these laws.[32] In 1979, an antitrust charge was brought against the ABA on the ground that its paralegal-school approval process was designed to eliminate competition from, and restrict entry into, the market for recruitment, training, and placement of paralegals. The ABA won this case.[33] Despite the victory, the ABA remains vulnerable to future challenge. A dramatic event occurred in 1995 when the Antitrust Division of the United States Justice Department filed a civil lawsuit alleging that the ABA used its power as the *law school* accrediting agency to limit competition. The ABA and the Justice Department eventually

---

[32] *Goldfarb v. Virginia State Bar,* 421 U.S. 773 (1975).
[33] *Paralegal Institute, Inc. v. American Bar Association,* 475 F. Supp. 1123 (E.D.N.Y. 1979).

settled this antitrust case when the ABA agreed to withdraw some of the requirements it imposed on law schools seeking ABA accreditation. Clearly, the ABA does not want similar antitrust challenges filed against it because of its regulatory role in the approval of paralegal education.

Note that the ABA uses the word "approval" rather than accreditation in describing its process of exercising a measure of control over educational institutions. Yet the process meets the accepted definition of accreditation presented in Exhibit 4.1 at the beginning of this chapter. The use of the more euphemistic word "approval" may be an indication that the ABA is itself not sure whether it should be in the business of regulating paralegal education. Indeed, in 1981, the House of Delegates of the ABA instructed its Committee on Legal Assistants to terminate ABA involvement in the approval process. However, some schools that had already received approval objected. As a result, the Committee proposed and the House of Delegates accepted an alternative system of approving schools.

The alternative was the creation of an ABA Approval Commission to implement the approval process. The final decision on approval of individual schools is still left in the hands of the ABA. The Commission makes its recommendations to the Committee on Legal Assistants, which in turn makes it recommendations to the House of Delegates of the ABA. The major difference between the Committee and the Commission is that the latter must contain nonattorney members. There are eleven members of the Commission, all of whom are appointed by the president of the ABA on advice from the Committee:

- Three attorneys (one of whom has taught in a paralegal program)
- One attorney who represents the ABA Committee on Legal Assistants
- One paralegal nominated by the National Federation of Paralegal Associations (NFPA)
- One paralegal nominated by the National Association of Legal Assistants (NALA)
- Two representatives nominated by the American Association for Paralegal Education (AAfPE)
- One representative nominated by the Association of Legal Administrators (ALA)
- One nonlegal educator
- One representative of the general public

The ABA does not view the Commission as a permanent institution. The plan is to phase it out over a period of years and to replace it with an *independent* accrediting body that is equally broad based. It is unclear, however, whether this replacement is feasible. It depends on the willingness of paralegal schools to submit themselves to this still-voluntary approval process. Furthermore, an independent body would be very expensive to run. Its revenues would come from fees paid by the schools that apply for approval and for renewals of approval. If large numbers of schools continue to bypass a national accrediting or approval entity, the process will lose both the political and the financial support it needs. Since there is no realistic hope that an independent accrediting body will be formed, the ABA will probably continue its approval program indefinitely.

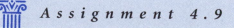

Assignment 4.9

Who should control accreditation? Are there too many attorneys on the ABA Approval Commission? Too few paralegals? Could there be *too many paralegals* on such a body? Do you favor an independent accrediting entity? Who should run it? Should it be voluntary?

Only one thing is sure: change is on the horizon. The legal profession can no longer feel secure in its privileged position, as the following speech demonstrates.

The Legal Profession: A Bow to the Past—a Glimpse of the Future
by J. Sims

[Mr. Sims was the Deputy Assistant Attorney General in the Antitrust Division of the United States Department of Justice. The following are excerpts from a speech he delivered before a conference of the Federation of Insurance Counsel in Arizona.]

Today, in Los Angeles, legal services are being advertised on television. That fact alone gives us some idea of how much change has come to the legal profession in the last few years.

That change has not always come easy, but the fact that it has come so far, so fast, tells us quite a bit about what will happen in the future. We lawyers as a group have grumbled and argued, fought and yelled, struggled and been confused—but there are now lawyers advertising on television. Even a casual observer cannot fail to appreciate the significance of this change.

Competition, slowly but surely, is coming to the legal profession. This opening of traditional doors, the breaking of traditional barriers is the result of many forces—the number of new lawyers, the awakening of consumerism, the growing realization that the complexity of our society requires legal assistance in more and more areas. But one contributing factor has been antitrust litigation and the Department of Justice. . . .

[T]he Supreme Court fired the shot heard 'round the bar [o]n June 16, 1975. [I]n a unanimous decision [*Goldfarb v. Virginia State Bar*, 421 U.S. 773 (1975)], the Court held that the minimum fee schedule challenged by the Goldfarbs violated Section 1 of the Sherman Act. This decision broke the dam and released the flood of change that we see engulfing the profession today. For better or worse, the Goldfarbs had set in motion a series of events that were to change the character of the legal profession forever.

The Court decided several things in *Goldfarb*, but the most important was that the legal profession was subject to the antitrust laws—there was no "professional exemption." The response to *Goldfarb* was fascinating. A large number of private suits were filed challenging various aspects of bar regulation. . . .

[An] area sure to be controversial in the future is unauthorized practice. There is already at least one antitrust challenge, against the Virginia State Bar, seeking to prohibit the bar from promulgating unauthorized practice opinions. This case, which involves title insurance, is a direct challenge to the extraordinary power that the legal profession now has—in most states—to define the limits of its own monopoly. It would be strange indeed for a state to hand over to, say its steel industry, not only the power to regulate entry into the industry and the conduct of those within it, but also the power to define what the industry was. In many states, that is exactly the power the organized bar now has, and that power is being challenged as inconsistent with the antitrust laws.

The heart of this challenge is that lawyers shouldn't be deciding what is the practice of law—defining the scope of the legal monopoly. The papers filed in that case . . . indicate that the objection is not to such a decision being made; the objection is to the State's delegation of that power to the [legal] profession.

In fact, of course, the principle behind this lawsuit could be expanded not only to other subject matter areas, but also to arrangements between the organized bar and other professions which have as their basic result the division of commercial responsibilities.

For example, the American Bar Association has entered into "statements of principles" with respect to the practice of law with a variety of other professions and occupations ranging from accountants to claim adjusters, publishers, social workers, and even professional engineers [page 190]. These documents generally set forth the joint views of the professions as to which activities fall within the practice of law and which activities are proper for members of the other profession. They nearly all provide that each profession will advise its clients to seek out members of the other profession in appropriate circumstances.

As a general rule, two competitors may not agree with each other to allocate markets, or bids, or even functions; if they do, they violate the antitrust laws. At the least, this traditional antitrust principle raises some questions about the legal effect of such "statements of principles." . . .

[T]he efforts of the bar to limit the scope of paralegal responsibilities and, in some jurisdictions, to seek a certification requirement for paralegals are seen by many as simply another effort to preserve and protect the legal services monopoly. Many believe that non-lawyers could perform many tasks reserved today for people with law degrees. . . .

A s s i g n m e n t   4 . 1 0

What are the implications of Mr. Sims's remarks on the role of bar associations in regulating paralegal education?

S e c t i o n   E
SHOULD PARALEGALS BECOME PART OF BAR ASSOCIATIONS?

At present, no paralegals are full members of any bar association. In recent years, how-ever, a number of state and local bar associations have invited paralegals to join their organizations in various capacities. The association might allow the paralegals in:

- as associate members of the entire association, including its committees and sections;
- as associate members of committees or sections only;
- as affiliate members of the entire association, including its committees and sections;
- as affiliate members of committees or sections only; or
- as full members of special legal assistant divisions.

The most active example of a division is the Legal Assistant Division of the State Bar of Texas. It has over 2,300 members who pay an annual membership fee of $50. In some of the associations, paralegals are allowed to vote on issues within the section, committee, or division of which they are members. But they cannot vote on general bar association issues. Most bar associations, however, do *not* have any categories for paralegal member-ship. The Louisiana State Bar Association, for example, voted in 1989 *not* to offer associ-ate membership to paralegals because "the occupation of paralegals has not been suffi-ciently defined so as to provide guidance as to who is a trained and qualified paralegal, and who is not."[34]

A s s i g n m e n t   4 . 1 1

Does the state, city, or county bar association where you live have a membership category for paralegals? If so, what are the eligibility requirements for membership and what are the benefits of membership?

What about the major national bar association—the American Bar Association (ABA)? For a long time, many argued that paralegals should become affiliated with the ABA in some way. In 1982 the ABA Committee on Legal Assistants proposed that the ABA cre-ate a new category of membership for paralegals. The National Association of Legal Assis-tants (NALA) warmly endorsed the proposal, while the National Federation of Paralegal Associations (NFPA) opposed it. Initially, the House of Delegates of the ABA rejected the proposal of the Committee on the ground that the addition of this nonattorney

---

[34]Landers, *Louisiana State Bar Association Decides Against Associate Membership for Paralegals,* 4 The Advocate (Louisiana State Paralegal Ass'n, August 1989).

membership category would further "dilute" the primary attorney category. Eventually, however, this objection was overcome. The House of Delegates agreed to accept a *legal assistant associate* category of membership. (For an application form, see Exhibit 4.7.) An

Legal Assistant Associate** Persons who, although not members of the legal profession, are qualified through education, training, or work experience, are employed or retained by a lawyer, law office, governmental agency, or other entity in a capacity or function which involves the performance, under the direction and supervision of an attorney, of specifically delegated substantive legal work, which work, for the most part, requires a sufficient knowledge of legal concepts such that, absent that legal assistant, the attorney would perform the task.

**An ABA member who supervises you <u>MUST</u> sign your application (attorney attestation).

Exhibit 4.7 ABA Associate Membership Application

ASSOCIATE APPLICATION
American Bar Association

Please Tell Us About Yourself *(required)*

_____
Name *(for membership roster and certificate, please print*

_____
Title

_____
Firm, agency or organization

_____
Mailing address

_____
City   State/Country   Zip

This address is my
❏ Business   ❏ Home   ❏ Both

Choose Your Associate Category

Legal Assistant Associate . ❏ $100.00

• Persons qualified through education, training or work experience who perform specifically delegated legal work which requires sufficient knowledge of legal concepts and which otherwise would be performed by an attorney in absence of a legal assistant.

I verify that the above applicant for Legal Assistant Associate does or has performed for me in the capacity which meets the requirements described above and that I am a current ABA member.

Supervising Attorney's Signature

_____
                              (required)

ABA ID# _____
                              (required)

( )_____   ( )_____
Business phone   Home phone
( )_____
Fax number

Social Security Number (optional)
☐☐☐-☐☐-☐☐☐☐

Birthdate ☐-☐-☐ ❏ Male ❏ Female
          mo dy yr

_____
Education-Institution

_____
Types of Degree or Certificate

Privileges of Associates

1. Attend meetings of the Association, including sessions of the House of Delegates and the Assembly, and to enjoy any floor privileges, extended to nonmembers.

2. Receive Association publications that are regularly provided to all members of the Association.

3. Be appointed to any Committee or Commission of the Association for which nonmembers are eligible for appointment.

4. Receive benefits available to ABA members, with the exception of the insurance programs provided through the American Bar Endowment and the American Bar Insurance.

5. Affiliate with one or more of the Sections, Divisions and Forums of their choice, upon application and payment of the annual Section, Division and Forum rates then in effect.

ABA member who supervises the legal assistant must sign the latter's application for associate membership. As of 1991, there were 1,200 Legal Assistant Associates in the ABA.

As indicated, not all paralegals endorsed the concept of associate or affiliate membership in bar associations when the idea was first proposed. Here are some typical comments in opposition:

> I haven't been able to understand why paralegals would want to become second class members of an organization that represents the interests of another profession. [Some paralegals view associate membership] as a positive development, while the very idea is enough to raise the blood pressure of other paralegals.[35]

> [It is] in the public interest that the allied legal professions remain autonomous. [It is] necessary and advisable that paralegals retain primary control in the development of the paralegal profession.[36]

> It is a recognized and uncontested fact that the purpose of any bar association is to promote and protect attorneys and their practice of law, rather than legal assistants. Further, associate members do not participate in the administrative and substantial legal decisions which are made by the Bar Association, e.g., no vote on dues, by-laws, budget or substantive issues of membership requirements. [Avoiding membership in a bar association may] eliminate possible conflicts of interest on issues where attorneys and legal assistants hold differing perspectives and opinions regarding the future of legal practice.[37]

Those who viewed paralegals as an autonomous, self-directed profession tended to disagree with the effort to join bar associations in any form. Yet this point of view is *not* shared by the majority of paralegals today. The momentum is toward more and more bar associations creating membership categories for paralegals. And when this option is made available, many paralegals take advantage of it for a number of reasons. It looks good on a résumé. It fosters a positive relationship between paralegals and attorneys. Employers often pay all or part of the paralegal's membership fee. Bar association meetings can be an excellent place for networking. Members receive newsletters and announcements, thus keeping them better informed about developments in the legal community. Etc. This perspective is best summed up in the following comment made by a paralegal before the ABA created the associate membership category:

> It is time our profession stopped being paranoid about ABA Associate Membership and open our eyes to opportunities presented to us. [We should not be spending time] dreaming up reasons to reject a chance for growth and improved relations within the established legal community. No guarantees have been given to assure us that associate membership would be beneficial, but why close *any* doors opened to us? If just a few paralegals would like to take advantage of this opportunity, why slam the door in their faces? The spirit of cooperation and teamwork within the legal community are the key reasons to encourage associate membership.[38]

---

[35]Whelen, *An Opinion: Bar Association's Paralegal Non-Voting Membership,* 15 At Issue 9 (San Francisco Ass'n of Legal Assistants, May 1987).

[36]*NFPA Findings,* 8 The Journal 3 (Sacramento Ass'n of Legal Assistants, January 1986).

[37]Heller, *Legal Assistant Associate Membership in the ABA,* 14 On Point 1, 14 (Nat'l Capital Area Paralegal Ass'n, August 1988).

[38]Anderson, *ABA Associate Membership: A Different Perspective,* 3 Findings and Conclusions 7 (Washington Ass'n of Legal Assistants, August 1987).

Assignment 4.12

(a) Should paralegals become a formal part of bar associations? What effect do you think associate membership would have on existing paralegal associations? Strengthen them? Destroy them? Is it healthy or unhealthy for paralegals to organize themselves as independent entities? Is it healthy or unhealthy for them to be able to challenge the organized bar? What is the conflict-of-interest argument against associate membership? Do you agree with this argument?

(b) Under the ABA associate membership category (see Exhibit 4.7), what kinds of paralegals are excluded from membership? Is such exclusion a good idea?

(c) Should a paralegal association allow *attorneys* to become full members of its association? Associate members? Why or why not?

(d) Should a paralegal association allow *secretaries* to become full members of its association? Associate members? Why or why not?

(e) Should a paralegal association allow *paralegal managers* (e.g., nonattorney senior paralegals) to become full members of its association? Associate members? Why or why not?

(f) To become an associate or affiliate member of a bar association, the applicant usually must obtain the signed statement of an attorney-employer asserting or attesting certain facts about the applicant—for instance, that he or she is a paralegal who works for the attorney. The statement is called an **attorney attestation.** For example, to obtain affiliate membership in the State Bar of Michigan, the attorney must "hereby attest" that the applicant "is employed by me and is recognized as a legal assistant (paralegal) and that he/she, under the supervision and direction of a lawyer, performs the services" specified elsewhere on the application. Some *paralegal* associations require the same kind of attorney attestation as a condition of allowing paralegals to join the paralegal association. Do you think attorney attestation is a good idea for associate/affiliate membership in a bar association? For full membership in a paralegal association?

Section F
SELF-REGULATION BY PARALEGALS: THE CERTIFICATION DEBATE

A number of times in this book we have examined the impact of the two major national associations of paralegals:

- National Federation of Paralegal Associations (NFPA): An association of associations; its membership consists of state and local paralegal associations.
- National Association of Legal Assistants (NALA): An association of individuals, plus a number of state and local paralegal associations, and several student paralegal associations.

Appendix B contains a list of state and local paralegal associations, with a notation of whether they are part of NFPA, part of NALA, or unaffiliated.

NALA is *not* a member of NFPA, and vice versa. In fact, the two groups take very different positions on a number of issues, two of the most important being limited licensing of independent paralegals and certification of all paralegals. Earlier in this chapter we examined the clash of views on limited licensing. We turn now to the older and perhaps more intense debate over certification.

As we saw in Exhibit 4.1 at the beginning of this chapter, *certification* is the process by which a nongovernmental organization grants recognition to a person who has met the qualifications set by that organization. To date, two national organizations and four state organizations have established such a process.

In 1976, NALA created the first major certification exam for paralegals—the **Certified Legal Assistant (CLA)** exam. Twenty years later in 1996, NFPA launched its own certification exam—the **Paralegal Advanced Certification Exam (PACE)** consisting of two parts or "tiers." CLA and PACE are summarized in Exhibit 4.8. There are some major differences between them. For example, the CLA exam is an entry-level exam; PACE isn't. It is possible to take the CLA exam without any paralegal work experience (see "Eligibility to

Exhibit 4.8	**National Certification Examinations for Paralegals: CLA and PACE**	
Name of Exam	Certified Legal Assistant Program	PACE: Paralegal Advanced Certification Exam
Sponsor	National Association of Legal Assistants (see address in Appendix B)	National Federation of Paralegal Associations (see address in Appendix B)
Credential	CLA (Certified Legal Assistant). There are two ways you could sign your name: Sam Smith, CLA Sam Smith, Certified Legal Assistant	PACE Registered Paralegal or RP. There are several ways you could sign your name: Sam Smith, PACE Registered Paralegal Same Smith, RP Sam Smith, RP Immigration Coordinator
Required for Employment?	No. The test is voluntary, although some employers may be impressed by a job applicant who is a CLA.	No. The test is voluntary, although some employers may be impressed by a job applicant who is PACE Accredited.
Cost	$250 ($225 if NALA member)	$225
Date Exam Began	1976	1996
Can You Take the Exam Immediately upon Graduating from School?	Yes, if you apply under Category 1. You do not need experience as a paralegal. The CLA exam is an entry-level exam. If you apply under Categories 2 or 3, however, you need paralegal experience to take the exam.	No. You must have a minimum of 2 years of experience as a paralegal. PACE is not an entry-level exam.
Eligibility to Take Exam	Requirements to take the CLA exam. You do *not* have to be a member of NALA to take the exam. An applicant must fit within one of the following three categories: • **Category 1:** You are a graduate from a legal assistant program that grants an associate degree, or grants a postbaccalaureate certificate, or has a minimum of	There are two tiers to PACE: I and II. Requirements to take the Tier I exam: **(a)** You have a bachelor's degree, *and* **(b)** You completed a paralegal program at an accredited school, *and* **(c)** You have a minimum of 2 years work experience. (You must file an Affidavit of Work Experience to meet this requirement.)

Exhibit 4.8	National Certification Examinations for Paralegals: CLA and PACE—continued	
Eligibility to Take Exam —continued	60 semester (or equivalent quarter) hours, at least 15 of which are substantive legal courses, or is ABA approved. ● **Category 2:** You have a bachelor's degree in any field, plus 1 year of experience as a legal assistant. ● **Category 3:** You have a high school diploma or equivalent, plus 7 years of experience as a legal assistant, plus 20 hours of CLE (continuing legal education). (You must file an "Attestation" from your employer stating that you meet this work requirement.)	(A grandparenting provision waives the three conditions and allows one to take the exam with at least 4 years of paralegal experience.) The requirements to take the Tier II exam are outlined below.
Where Given	The exam is given three times a year at locations throughout the country.	The exam is given at one of the 200 Sylvan Learning Centers throughout the country. The Centers are open for testing six days a week during which you can take the exam.
Length of Exam	12 hours over 2 days	4 hours (taken entirely on a computer) in 1 day
Is the Exam State-Specific?	No. The exam is national in scope. It does not test on the law of any particular state.	Not at the present time. Today the exam is national in scope. In the future, "state-specific modules will be developed as the need arises."
Topics Tested	(a) verbal and written communication skills, (b) judgment and analytical ability, (c) ethics, (d) human relations and interviewing, (e) legal terminology, (f) legal research, and (g) the American legal system, and (h) any 4 of the following 8 areas (you select the 4): administrative law, bankruptcy, contracts, business organizations, criminal law, litigation, probate/estate planning, and real estate.	(a) administration of client legal matters (e.g., conducting a conflict check): 23% of the test, (b) development of client legal matters (e.g., interviewing prospective clients): 30%, (c) factual and legal research (e.g., validating and updating legal research): 22%, (d) factual and legal writing (e.g., drafting legal documents): 20.5%, and (e) office administration (e.g., developing and maintaining a billing system): 4.5%.
Format of Examination	Objective questions (e.g., true/false, multiple choice, matching). Some essay and short answer questions. Examples of Objective Questions: [1] True or False: Federal statutes are printed in codified form in Federal Reporter, 3d. [2] The Model Penal Code was drafted by (a) ABA, (b) American Law Institute, (c) Congress, (d) None of the above [3] "The appellate brief is poorly written, sloppy, and should have been shortened." This sentence: (a) violates parallelism, (b) has too many commas,	All objective questions: 200 multiple-choice questions. Examples: [1] A letter sent to the defendant's insurer that summarizes the plaintiff's damages, lost wages, medical treatment, and medical bills and requests monetary compensation is commonly known as: (a) a statement of damages, (b) a demand letter, (c) a memorandum of law, (d) an opinion letter. [2] Which one of the following kinds of deeds offers the most protection to the

Exhibit 4.8	National Certification Examinations for Paralegals: CLA and PACE—continued	
Format of Examination —continued	(c) contains the passive voice, (d) a & b, (e) a & c (f) a, b, & c. Answers: [1] False, [2] (b), [3] (e).	buyer? (a) Quitclaim, (b) Warranty, (c) Trustee, (d) Survivorship [3] Which federal statute enables any citizen, upon proper request, to obtain documents from a federal agency? (a) Open Records Act, (b) Freedom of Information Act, (c) Administrative Communication Act, (d) Privileged Information Act. Answers: [1] (b), [2] (b), [3] (b).
Passing Score	Total points possible: 500 Number needed to pass: 350	Total points possible: 700 Number needed to pass: 550 (Scoring for PACE will be on a scale score like the SAT. The range will be from 300–700.)
Continuing Legal Education (CLE) Requirements	The CLA credential must be renewed every five years by attending a designated number of CLE hours during this period.	PACE ACCREDITED paralegals must complete 12 hours of CLE every 2 years. (At least 1 of the 12 must be in ethics.)
Statistics	Approximately 5% of all working paralegals nationwide are CLAs. Number who have taken CLA exam: 17,553. Number passed: over 7,800. Almost half of all CLAs are in Florida and Texas.	No statistics available yet.
Study Manual	*CLA Review Manual* (NALA & West Publishing Co.)	*PACE Study Manual* (NFPA)
Additional Certification	NALA also offers a specialty certification: CLAS (Certified Legal Assistant Specialist). To be eligible to take this 4-hour CLAS exam, an applicant must already be a CLA. The cost is $115 ($100 for NALA members). A separate CLAS test is given in each of the following areas: bankruptcy, intellectual property, civil litigation, probate/estate planning, corporate/business law, criminal law, real estate. There are 626 CLASs in the country as of May 1996.	There is a TIER II exam. To be eligible to take the TIER II PACE exam, an applicant must have: **(a)** successfully passed the TIER I exam *and* **(b)** have a minimum of 4 years work experience. (There is a grandparenting provision available.) The Tier II exam covers specialty areas of the law.

Take Exam"—Category 1—in Exhibit 4.8). No one can take either Tier I or Tier II of the PACE exam, however, without a minimum of two years of paralegal experience (for Tier I) and four years (for Tier II).

It is important to note that certification is *not* required for employment. Certification is voluntary. A person can be a paralegal in any state without taking any of the certification exams that exist.

The NFPA has always opposed the CLA exam of NALA, largely because the NFPA believes that there is no need for entry-level certification. At times the opposition has been bitter. For example, the NFPA points out that only a small percentage of paralegals in the country have the CLA certification (about 5 percent) and that most of them are concentrated in a few states. The NFPA also cites surveys showing that paralegals who are CLAs have *lower* salaries than paralegals who are not CLAs, while NALA counters with surveys that show the opposite.

Both NALA and the NFPA have separate, *advanced* certification exams covering specialty areas of the law:

NALA: Once a person has passed the CLA exam, he or she can take the **Certified Legal Assistant Specialist (CLAS)** exam in areas such as bankruptcy and real estate. See the last entry in Exhibit 4.8 ("Additional Certification"). Paralegal experience in the specialty is *not* required to take a CLAS test, although most paralegals who take this test have such experience.

NFPA: Once a person has passed Tier I of PACE and has four years of paralegal work experience, he or she can sit for Tier II of PACE. Tier II will also be in specialty areas of the law.

Four states have their own *state-specific* certification exam: California, Florida, Texas, and Louisiana (see Exhibit 4.9):

- CAS (California Advanced Specialist)
- CFLA (Certified Florida Legal Assistant)
- Board Certified Legal Assistant, [name of specialty], Texas Board of Legal Specialization
- LCP (Louisiana Certified Paralegal)

Like the national certification exams, the state exams are voluntary. Those of California, Florida, and Louisiana are entry-level. Texas certification, however, is advanced. You need a minimum of five years of experience to sit for the Texas exam.

Several years ago the American Bar Association studied the question of certification. Some suggested that the ABA should certify individual paralegals. It declined the invitation, taking the position that certification should be undertaken by a national body that includes paralegals, attorneys, educators, and members of the general public. Furthermore, the ABA favored specialty certification, *not* entry-level certification. It felt that the benefits of entry-level certification of minimal competence would *not* be worth the time, expense, and effort to implement the program.[39]

Nevertheless, the momentum toward certification continues. Paralegals want to control their own future, and many see certification as a practical way to accomplish this goal. Certification will remain controversial, however. The debates will include all of the following:

- Whether enough paralegals are interested in pursuing certification. (The numbers applying to date have been relatively modest, especially since very few prospective employers seem to limit their search to individuals who have passed certification exams.)
- Whether certification should be entry-level, specialty, or both.
- Whether certification will stifle creativity in paralegal schools because they will be pressured to "teach only the exam."

---

[39]ABA Standing Committee on Legal Assistants, *Position Paper on the Question of Legal Assistant Licensure or Certification,* 5 Legal Assistant Today 167 (1986).

Exhibit 4.9	State-Specific Certification Programs: Testing the Law and Procedure of a Particular State			
	CALIFORNIA	**FLORIDA**	**TEXAS**	**LOUISIANA**
Name of Exam	California Advanced Specialty Program	Certified Florida Legal Assistant Exam	Legal Assistant Specialty Certification Exam	Louisiana Certified Paralegal Exam
Sponsors	California Alliance of Paralegal Associations in cooperation with National Association of Legal Assistants	Florida Legal Assistants, Inc.	Texas Board of Legal Specialization	Louisiana State Paralegal Association
Credential	CAS (Californai Advanced Specialist) (For example, John Jones, CAS)	CFLA (Certified Florida Legal Assistant) (For example, Patricia Evans, CFLA)	Board Certified Legal Assistant [name of specialty] Texas Board of Legal Specialization (For example, Mary Smith, Board Certified Legal Assistant, Family Law, Texas Board of Legal Specialization)	LCP (Louisiana Certified Paralegal) (For example, Edward Duffy, LCP)
Required for Employment?	No. The test is voluntary	No. The test is voluntary.	No. The test is voluntary.	No. The test is voluntary.
Cost	$150	$95 ($75 for members of Florida Legal Assistants, Inc.)	$150	$175 for members of the Louisiana State Paralegal Association ($195 for nonmembers)
Date Started	1995	1983	1994	1996
Eligibility to Take Exam	You have already passed the CLA exam of NALA	You have already passed the CLA exam of NALA.	(a) 5 years experience as a legal assistant, *and* (b) at least 50% of your functions in the last 3 years has been in the specialty area for which certification is being sought, *and* (c) a bachelor's degree in any	No prerequisites, but within 3 years of passing the LCP exam, you must take and pass the CLA exam of NALA.

Exhibit 4.9	State-Specific Certification Programs: Testing the Law and Procedure of a Particular State—continued			
	CALIFORNIA	**FLORIDA**	**TEXAS**	**LOUISIANA**
Eligibility to Take Exam —continued			field, *or* completion of a legal assistant program meeting specified criteria, *or* completion of an ABA-approved program, *or* passing the CLA exam of NALA, *and* **(d)** a minimum of 30 hours of CLE (continuing legal education) in the specialty within the last 3 years.	
Topics Tested	Advanced knowledge and proficiency in specialty areas of California law. The level of testing will require substantial experience in the specialty areas. There are three areas: civil litigation, business organizations and business law, and real estate.	Part I: ethics, general Florida law. Part II: you select 6 questions from the Florida substantive law of contracts, corporate law, business law, civil litigation, criminal law, estate/probate law, and real estate law.	Texas civil trial law, Texas family law, Texas personal injury (tort) law (other areas to be added).	General Louisiana law, Louisiana civil procedure, Louisiana ethics. You choose 4 areas from the following: business organizations, contracts, criminal law, evidence, family law, property, torts, and wills/probate/trusts.
Length of Exam	4 hours	4 hours	4 hours	10½ hours over 2 days
Passing Score	70%	70%	A curve method (Norm Reference Testing) is used to calculate the pass/fail results.	70%
Continuing Legal Education (CLE) Requirements	20 hours of CLE every 5 years	30 hours of CLE on Florida law over 5 years	75 hours of CLE over 5 years	2.5 units every 5 years in Louisiana substantive and procedural law; 0.5 unit in ethics.

- Whether voluntary certification programs will be confused with mandatory licensing programs. (Will the public think that a certified paralegal is a licensed one?)
- Whether the eligibility requirements to take the certification exam are so high that they will discourage people from entering the profession.

🏛 *A s s i g n m e n t   4 . 1 3*

(a) Do you favor the certification of paralegals? Why or why not?
(b) If certification exists, should it be entry-level, specialty, or both? Why?
(c) Who should control certification? Paralegals? Attorneys? The government? Why?

🏛 *A s s i g n m e n t   4 . 1 4*

When a new local paralegal association is formed, it is often lobbied by NALA and the NFPA to become a part of one of these national organizations. The local association will usually make one of three decisions: affiliate with NALA, affiliate with the NFPA, or remain unaffiliated. If you were a member of a local association faced with the decision of whether to join NALA, NFPA, or stay unaffiliated, what would your vote be? Why?

🏛 *A s s i g n m e n t   4 . 1 5*

Is it a good idea to have two national associations? Why or why not?

Throughout this book the importance of paralegal associations has been stressed. They have had a major impact on the development of paralegalism. Many state and local bar associations as well as the ABA have felt the effect of organized paralegal advocacy through the associations.

As soon as possible, you should join a paralegal association. Find out if the association allows students to become members. (See the forms at the end of this book after the index.) If an association does not exist in your area, you should form one and decide whether you want to become part of the National Federation of Paralegal Associations or the National Association of Legal Assistants. The paralegal association is your main voice in the continued development of the field. Join one now and become an active member. In addition to the educational benefits of membership and the job placement services that many associations provide, you will experience the satisfaction of helping shape your career in the years to come. Attorneys and the bar associations should not be the sole mechanism for controlling paralegals.

Section G
FAIR LABOR STANDARDS ACT

Yes, I am paid overtime. I am paid at time and a half rate. I agree with being paid overtime. If the attorney asks me to work additional long hours and weekends, then yes I do believe I should be compensated for yielding my free time for work. This does not make me any less of a professional. My professionalism will show through my work product.[40]

My firm doesn't pay paralegals overtime, and I don't want to be classified as a person eligible for overtime. For one thing, people paid overtime are non-professionals, and I don't think of myself as a non-professional. I feel that my salary, salary increases, and bonuses reflect a degree of compensation for the extra hours I work.[41]

One of the "hot topics" in the field is GOD: the Great Overtime Debate. "The mere mention of the subject of overtime in any group of working legal assistants is guaranteed to spark a prolonged session of horror-story telling."[42] The topic is so controversial that one paralegal association recently established a hotline to answer questions confidentially. Some paralegals have filed—and won—lawsuits against their employers for failure to pay *overtime compensation* for hours worked beyond forty hours in a week.

There is a definite body of law that determines whether overtime compensation must be paid; the issue is not dependent on the preferences of individual paralegals. The governing law is the federal **Fair Labor Standards Act,**[43] which is enforced by the Wage and Hour Division of the U.S. Department of Labor. Under the Act, overtime compensation must be paid to employees unless they fall within one of the three "white collar" exemptions. Exempt employees are those who work in a professional, administrative, or executive capacity.[44]

Some paralegals are clearly part of management. They are the paralegal supervisors, legal assistant managers, paralegal directors, etc. who are often members of an organization such as the Legal Assistant Management Association. These individuals are exempt employees; they are not entitled to overtime compensation. What about the other 99 percent of paralegals in the country?

The question of whether they are exempt does not have a definitive answer for two reasons. First, paralegals are relatively new to the employment world. As we saw in chapter 1, they did not emerge as a separately identifiable category of employment until the late

---

[40] *The Member Connection,* 14 Facts & Findings 7 (NALA, June 1988).

[41] *The Membership Responds,* 9 The ParaGraph (Georgia Ass'n of Legal Assistants, September/October 1987).

[42] Acosta, *Let's Talk About Overtime!,* 10 Ka Leo O' H.A.L.A. 6 (Hawaii Ass'n of Legal Assistants, August/September 1987).

[43] 29 U.S.C.A. §§ 201 *et seq.* (1976).

[44] The Professional Employee Exemption:

- Primary duty consists of work requiring knowledge of an advanced type in a field customarily acquired by a prolonged course of specialized intellectual instruction and study. (Such course of study means at least a baccalaureate degree or equivalent.)
- Work requires the consistent exercise of judgment and discretion.
- Work is predominantly intellectual and varied in character, as opposed to routine, mental or physical work.

The Administrative Employee Exemption:

- The employee's primary duty consists of work related to management policies or general business operations.
- The employee regularly exercises discretion and independent judgment.

The Executive Employee Exemption:

- The employee's primary duty consists of the management of the enterprise.
- The employee regularly supervises two or more other employees. 29 C.F.R. part 541 (1983).

1960s and early 1970s. Consequently, there is not a great deal of employment law specifically governing them. Second, and most important, what paralegals do varies tremendously. Some paralegals exercise considerable independence. Others perform repetitive tasks requiring very little discretion. Hence the answer to the question of whether paralegals are entitled to overtime compensation is hardly profound: some are and some aren't.

The Department of Labor would agree that paralegal managers (e.g., members of the Legal Assistant Management Association) are exempt. As to most other paralegals, however, the Department has consistently taken the position that they are *not* exempt and hence are entitled to overtime compensation. A major reason for this position is the ethical obligation of attorneys to supervise a paralegal's work. Someone requiring such supervision, argues the Department, could not be exercising the degree of discretion and independent judgment that would fit within any of the exemptions.

This position was challenged in the 1994 federal trial court case of *Reich v. Page & Addison.*[45] Page & Addison is a Texas law firm that employed twenty-three paralegals over a three-year period and did not pay them overtime compensation. When one left, she sued for back pay, claiming the firm was wrong in treating its paralegals as exempt. Most of the paralegals who remained at the firm disagreed with her. They did *not* want overtime compensation; they preferred to be treated as part of the exempt staff. Nevertheless, the Department of Labor investigated and concluded that none of the paralegals were exempt. The case then went to the United States District Court in Texas. Here is part of the judge's instruction to the jury:

> To prove this exemption is applicable, the Defendant [the Page & Addison law firm] must prove plainly and unmistakably that: 1) the employee's primary duty 2) requires the exercise of discretion and independent judgment 3) in the performance of office or non-manual field work. . . . "Discretion and independent judgment" involve the comparison and evaluation of possible courses of conduct and acting or making a decision after the various possibilities have been considered. An employee exercises discretion and independent judgment if that employee has the authority or power to make an independent choice, free from immediate direction and supervision and with respect to matters of significance. An employee who merely applies his knowledge in following prescribed procedures or determining which procedures to follow is not exercising discretion and independent judgment. The discretion and independent judgment exercised must be real and substantial, that is, they must be exercised with respect to matters of consequence. The fact that an employee's work is subject to approval and possible rejection by a supervisory employee does not mean that the employee does not exercise discretion and independent judgment. . . . The employee's job title is of little or no assistance in determining the employee's exempt or non-exempt status.

Note that the Court said that someone can be exempt even if he or she is supervised by someone else. Hence a paralegal can be exempt even if an attorney has an ethical duty to supervise the work of that paralegal. The key is whether the paralegal acts "free from *immediate direction and supervision* and with respect to matters of significance" (emphasis added).

The jury came to the conclusion that the paralegals at Page & Addison *did* exercise discretion and independent judgment. Therefore they were exempt and not entitled to overtime compensation. This was a fairly dramatic conclusion. It was the first time a court had addressed the question so directly.

---

[45]1994 WL 143208 (U.S. District Court, Northern District, Texas). WL refers to WESTLAW (see chapters 11 and 13).

Is the issue now settled? No. "[F]ar from providing any clearcut direction, the case has only fueled the controversy about overtime pay for paralegals."[46] A 1995 national salary survey showed that 58 percent of paralegals were treated as exempt by their employers, while 42 percent were treated as nonexempt. The trend is toward classifying more and more paralegals as exempt, but there is still a great deal of diversity on the issue. Differences can be found even within a particular law firm. An example is Page & Addison, the law firm that won the case in *Reich v. Page & Addison.* After the case was over, the firm set up a three-tiered system of paralegals: junior paralegal, paralegal, and senior paralegal. The firm treats its junior position, for starting paralegals, as nonexempt. "The paralegal position, for experienced paralegals who work independently, is exempt from overtime, as is the senior paralegal position, designed for legal assistants who supervise others."[47] The Department of Labor decided not to appeal *Reich v. Page & Addison,* which, as indicated, was a trial court case. Hence we don't have the benefit of a higher court's view of the issue. This will change as the law in this area continues to evolve. In the meantime, the Department of Labor is free to investigate other law firms to determine whether *their* paralegals are exempt. In spite of *Reich v. Page & Addison,* the Department is inclined to the view that paralegals are not exempt.

Assignment 4.16

(a) If you had a choice, would you want to receive overtime compensation as an entry-level paralegal?

(b) Surveys have shown that between 20 and 40 percent of *nonexempt* paralegals today do *not* receive overtime compensation. Can you explain this fact?

Section H
TORT LIABILITY OF PARALEGALS

Thus far we have discussed a number of ways that paralegal activities are or could be regulated:

- Criminal liability for violating the statutes on the unauthorized practice of law
- Special authorization rules on practice before administrative agencies and other tribunals
- Licensing
- Bar rules on paralegal education
- Self-regulation
- Labor laws

Finally, we come to **tort liability,** which is another method by which society defines what is and is not permissible. A tort is a private wrong or injury other than a breach of contract or the commission of a crime, although some breaches of contract and crimes can also constitute torts.

---

[46]Shari Caudron, *Overtime Pay,* 13 Legal Assistant Today 50, 53 (January/February 1996).
[47]Id. at pp. 51, 55.

Two questions need to be kept in mind. First, when are paralegal employees *personally liable* for their torts? Second, when are employers *vicariously liable* for the torts of their paralegal employees? (As we will see, **vicarious liability** simply means being liable because of what someone else has done or failed to do.) The short answer to the first question is: *always.* The short answer to the second question is: *when the wrongdoing by the paralegal was within the scope of employment.* After covering both questions, we will then examine the separate question of when malpractice insurance will pay for such liability.

Several different kinds of wrongdoing are possible. The paralegal might commit:

- The tort of negligence
- An intentional tort, such as battery.
- An act that is both a crime (such as embezzlement) *and* an intentional tort (such as conversion).

A client who is injured by any of these torts can sue the paralegal in the same manner that a patient in a hospital can sue a nurse. Paralegals are not relieved of liability simply because they work for, and function under the supervision of, an attorney. Every citizen is *personally* liable for the torts he or she commits. The same is true of criminal liability.

Next we turn to the employers of paralegals. Are they *also* liable for wrongdoing committed by their paralegals? Assume that the supervising attorneys did nothing wrong themselves. For example, the attorney did not commit the tort or crime as an active participant with the paralegal, or the attorney was not careless in selecting and training the paralegal. Our question is: Can an attorney be liable to a client solely because of the wrongdoing of a paralegal? As we noted, such *vicarious liability* exists when one person is liable solely because of what someone else has done or failed to do. The answer to our question is found in the doctrine of **respondeat superior,** which makes employers responsible for the torts of their employees or agents when the wrongdoing occurs within the **scope of employment.**[48]

Hence, if a paralegal commits a tort within the scope of employment, the client can sue the paralegal or the attorney, or both. This does not mean that the client recovers twice; there can be only one recovery for a tort. The client is simply given a choice in bringing the suit. In most cases, the primary target of the client will be the employer, who is the so-called **deep pocket,** meaning the one who has resources from which a judgment can be satisfied.

Finally, we need to examine what is meant by "scope of employment." Not every wrongdoing of a paralegal is within the scope of employment simply because it is employment related. The test is as follows: Paralegals act within the scope of employment when they are furthering the business of their employer, which for our purposes is the practice of law. Slandering a client for failure to pay a law firm bill certainly furthers the business of the law firm. But the opposite is probably true when a paralegal has an argument with a client over a football game and punches the client during their accidental evening meeting at a bar. In the latter example, the client could not sue the paralegal's employer for the intentional tort of battery under the doctrine of respondeat superior, because the battery was not committed while furthering the business of the employer. Only the paralegal would be liable for the tort under such circumstances.

---

[48]We are talking here of vicarious *civil* liability, or more specifically, the tort liability of employers because of the torts committed by their employees. Employers are not subject to vicarious *criminal* liability. If a paralegal commits a crime on the job, only the paralegal goes to jail (unless the employer actually participated in the crime).

The most common tort committed by attorneys is **negligence.** This tort occurs when a client is injured because of a failure to use the ordinary skill, knowledge, and diligence normally possessed and used, under similar circumstances, by a member of the profession in good standing. In short, the tort is committed by failure to exercise the reasonable care expected of an attorney. An attorney is not an insurer, however. Every mistake will not lead to negligence liability even if it causes harm to the client. The harm must be due to an *unreasonable* mistake, such as forgetting to file an action in court before the statute of limitations runs out.

When a *paralegal* commits negligence for which the attorney becomes liable under respondeat superior, the same standard applies. Since the work product of the paralegal blends into the work product of the supervising attorney, the attorney becomes as fully responsible for what the paralegal did as if the attorney had committed the negligence. Unreasonableness is measured by what a reasonable attorney would have done, not by what a reasonable paralegal would have done.

There have not been many tort cases in which paralegals have been sued for wrongdoing in a law office. Yet as paralegals become more prominent in the practice of law, more are expected to be named as defendants. Michael Martz, General Counsel of the Mississippi Bar Association, makes the unsettling point that the prominence of paralegalism means there will be more suits against them. "As paralegals become more and more professional and proficient, they . . . will become better targets for disgruntled clients looking for someone to sue."[49] The most common kinds of cases involving paralegals have occurred when the paralegal was a notary and improperly notarized signatures under pressure from the supervising attorney.

⚖ Assignment 4.17

Mary Smith is a paralegal at the XYZ law firm. One of her tasks is to file a document in court. She negligently forgets to do so. As a result, the client has a default judgment entered against her. What options are available to the client?

⚖ Assignment 4.18

In this assignment you will need to use the *American Digest System.* For information on this digest and its use, see pages 524 and 594 in chapter 11. If you do not have access to this digest, answer questions (a) and (b) below using a regional digest (which covers the opinions of courts in a cluster of states) or a state digest (which covers the opinions of courts in a single state).

Using the *American Digest System,* give citations to and brief summaries of the topics listed in (a) and (b) below. Start with the Descriptive Word Index volumes of the most recent Decennial. After you check the appropriate key numbers (page 523) in that Decennial, check those key numbers in all the General Digest volumes that follow the most recent Decennial. Then check for case law in at least three other recent Decennials. Once you obtain citations to case law in the digest paragraphs, you do not have to go to the reporters to read the full text of the opinions. Simply give the citations you find and brief summaries of the cases as they are printed in the digest paragraphs.

---

[49]Michael Martz, *Ethics, Does a Paralegal Need Insurance?* The Assistant, p. 13 (Mississippi Ass'n of Legal Assistants, Fall 1993).

(a) Cases, if any, dealing with the negligence of attorneys in the hiring and supervision of legal secretaries, law clerks, investigators, and paralegals. (If there are many, select any five cases.)

(b) Cases, if any, dealing with the negligence of doctors and/or hospitals in the hiring and supervision of nurses, paramedics, and other medical technicians. (If there are many, select any five cases.)

Section I
Malpractice Insurance

Legal **malpractice** generally refers to wrongful conduct by an attorney for which an injured party (the attorney's client) can receive damages. Just as doctors purchase malpractice insurance against suits by their patients, so too attorneys can buy such insurance to cover suits against them by their clients for alleged errors and omissions. (See Exhibit 4.10.) We need to examine how paralegals fit into this picture.

Until the 1940s, not many attorneys bought malpractice insurance because suits by clients were relatively rare. Today, the picture has changed radically; cautious attorneys do not practice law without such insurance against their own malpractice. "Statistically, the new attorney will be subjected to three claims before finishing a legal career."[50] Hence, very few attorneys are willing to **go bare**—that is, practice without insurance. This change has been due to a number of factors. As the practice of law becomes more complex, the likelihood of error increases. Furthermore, the public is becoming more aware of its right to sue. In spite of disclaimers by attorneys that they are not guaranteeing any results, client expectations tend to be high, and hence clients are more likely to blame their attorney for an unfavorable result. And attorneys are increasingly willing to sue each other. In fact, some attorneys have developed a legal malpractice specialty in which they take clients who want to sue other attorneys. As malpractice awards against attorneys continue to rise (see Exhibit 4.11), the market for malpractice insurance has dramatically increased. And so has the cost. In some cities, the premium for insurance can be between $5,000 and $15,000 per year per attorney.

Two kinds of professional liability insurance policies cover attorney malpractice: occurrence policies and claims-made policies. An **occurrence policy** covers all occurrences (such as negligent error or omission) during the period the policy is in effect, even if the claim on such an occurrence is not actually filed until after the policy expires. Insurance companies are reluctant to write such policies because of the length of time it sometimes takes to uncover the existence of the negligent error or omission. Here's an example: An attorney makes a careless mistake in drafting a will that is not discovered until the person who hired the attorney dies many years later. Under an occurrence policy, the attorney is protected if the mistake occurred while the policy was in effect, even if the actual claim was not filed in court until after the policy terminated. The most common kind of policy sold by insurance companies today is the **claims-made policy** under which coverage is limited to claims actually filed (made) during the period in which the policy is in effect.[51]

---

[50]R. Mallen & J. Smith, *Legal Malpractice*, 3rd ed., 2 (1989).

[51]It is possible for a claims-made policy to cover a negligent error or omission that took place *before* the effective date of the policy, but most companies exclude coverage for prepolicy claims that the attorney knows about or could have reasonably foreseen at the time the policy is applied for.

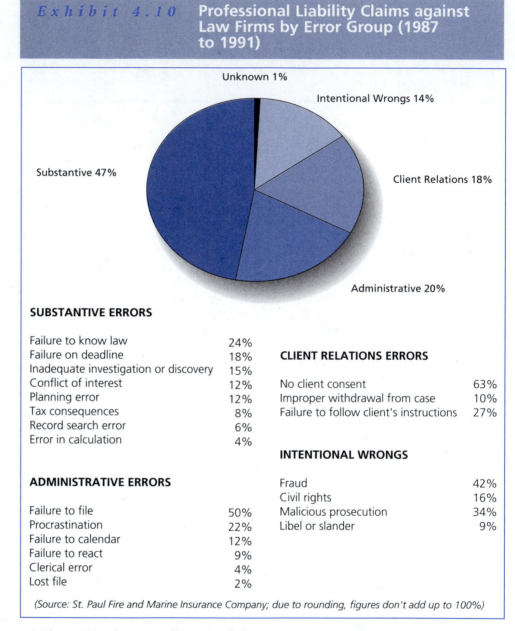

Exhibit 4.10 — Professional Liability Claims against Law Firms by Error Group (1987 to 1991)

Unknown 1%
Intentional Wrongs 14%
Substantive 47%
Client Relations 18%
Administrative 20%

SUBSTANTIVE ERRORS

Failure to know law	24%
Failure on deadline	18%
Inadequate investigation or discovery	15%
Conflict of interest	12%
Planning error	12%
Tax consequences	8%
Record search error	6%
Error in calculation	4%

CLIENT RELATIONS ERRORS

No client consent	63%
Improper withdrawal from case	10%
Failure to follow client's instructions	27%

INTENTIONAL WRONGS

Fraud	42%
Civil rights	16%
Malicious prosecution	34%
Libel or slander	9%

ADMINISTRATIVE ERRORS

Failure to file	50%
Procrastination	22%
Failure to calendar	12%
Failure to react	9%
Clerical error	4%
Lost file	2%

(Source: St. Paul Fire and Marine Insurance Company; due to rounding, figures don't add up to 100%)

Malpractice policies usually cover all the attorneys *and* the nonattorney employees of the law office. One policy, for example, defines the individuals covered—"the insured"—as follows:

> The insured includes the firm, all lawyers within the firm, and all non-lawyer employees, as well as former partners, officers, directors and employees solely while they acted on behalf of the insured firm.[52]

Such inclusion of employees is not always automatic, however. The policies of some insurance companies do not include paralegals or secretaries unless the law firm specifically

---

[52]Home Insurance Companies, Professional Liability Insurance.

Exhibit 4.11	Malpractice Liability Claims against Attorneys

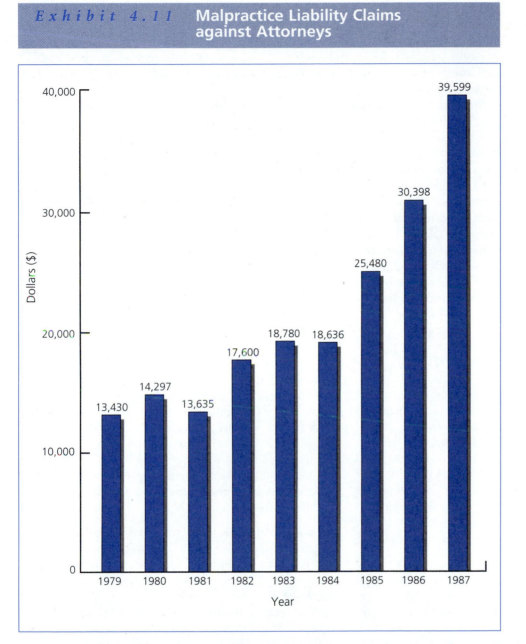

Source: St. Paul Fire & Marine Insurance Company.

In 1979 the average claim paid, including all expenses, was $13,430. By 1987 this amount had risen 295 percent to a new average of $39,599.

requests coverage for them and pays an additional premium for their inclusion. Paralegals should therefore ask their employers if their malpractice policy explicitly covers paralegals.

What about freelance or independent paralegals who sell their services to attorneys? Although they may not be considered employees of the firm, they will usually be covered under the firm's policy in the same manner as full-time, in-house paralegal employees.

So long as the employing attorney supervises and is responsible for the conduct of the paralegal, the malpractice policy usually provides coverage. In the language of one widely used policy, coverage is provided for "any other person for whose acts, errors or omissions the insured is legally responsible,"[53] which would include freelance paralegals. A sophisticated freelance paralegal would make sure that this is so before undertaking work for an attorney.

Some freelance paralegals have explored the possibility of obtaining their own malpractice insurance policies. To date, most traditional insurance companies have not made such policies available, although there are exceptions. Complete Equity Markets, Inc., for example, offers "Paralegals Professional Indemnity Insurance" as a claims-made policy. For approximately $1,800 a year, a paralegal can purchase $250,000 worth of malpractice insurance. Also, the National Federation of Paralegal Associations has endorsed a claims-made policy that covers freelance paralegals as well as employed paralegals (for those who work for firms that do not have policies). It is called the Paralegal/Legal Assistant Professional Liability Program. Since most paralegals work for an attorney and are already covered under the attorney's policy, few paralegals have purchased their own policy. Yet if paralegals are eventually granted a form of limited license that authorizes them to sell their services directly to the public, separate paralegal malpractice policies will become common and may even be mandated as a condition of receiving the license.[54]

Chapter Summary

Criminal prosecution may result from violating statutes on the unauthorized practice of law. In general, they prohibit nonattorneys from appearing for another in a representative capacity, drafting most legal documents, and giving legal advice. Nonattorneys can sell forms and other legal materials but cannot give individual help in using them.

There are some major exceptions to the prohibitions on nonattorney conduct. In a very limited number of circumstances, nonattorneys are authorized to do what would otherwise constitute the unauthorized practice of law. For example:

- In most states, a real estate broker can draft sales contracts.
- Several specialized courts allow nonattorneys to represent clients in court, although this is rare.
- A few states allow paralegals to "appear" in court to request a continuance or a new date for the next hearing in a case.

- An inmate can "practice law" in prison—for example, he or she can draft court documents for and give legal advice to another inmate if the prison does not offer adequate alternative methods of providing inmates with legal services.
- Many administrative agencies, particularly at the federal level, allow nonattorneys to represent clients before the agencies.

A number of states have considered broad-based licensing (which would cover all activities of all paralegals), and limited licensing (which would cover specified activities of those paralegals, often called legal technicians, who are not supervised by attorneys). To date, neither kind of licensing has been enacted. Relatively soon, however, a limited-license requirement will probably be enacted in one or two states. While this would be a dramatic event, it would affect very few paralegals, since limited licensing would probably not apply to paralegals who work for attorneys.

---

[53]American Home Assurance Company, Lawyers Professional Liability Policy.

[54]As we saw earlier, most Enrolled Agents are nonlawyers who are authorized to provide certain tax services to the public. The National Association of Enrolled Agents offers a "Professional Liability Insurance Plan" through the St. Paul Fire and Marine Insurance Company. The Association's brochure says, "You can now secure protection against an unexpected lawsuit or penalty for damages arising from services you provide as an Enrolled Agent." Attorneys are not eligible to purchase this insurance.

All paralegal schools in the country must be licensed by their state. There is no requirement that they be accredited by the bar association. The American Bar Association, however, has an "approval" process whereby a school can be approved by the ABA.

A number of bar associations allow paralegals to become associate or affiliate members. For example, the American Bar Association has a membership category called Legal Assistant Associate.

There are two national certification programs. NALA offers an entry-level CLA (Certified Legal Assistant) exam and an advanced CLAS (Certified Legal Assistant Specialist) exam. NFPA offers Tiers I and II of PACE (Paralegal Advanced Certification Exam), both of which require paralegal work experience to take. Four states have state-specific certification exams: California, Florida, Louisiana, and Texas.

The Fair Labor Standards Act requires employers to pay overtime compensation to employees unless the latter are exempt. Paralegal managers are exempt. The United States Department of Labor believes that all other paralegals are not exempt, although a recent trial court case in Texas came to the opposite conclusion. Exemption depends in part on the extent to which the paralegal exercises discretion and independent judgment on the job.

If a paralegal commits a tort, such as negligence, he or she is personally liable to the defendant. Under the theory of respondeat superior, the supervising attorney is also liable for the wrong committed by the paralegal if it occurred within the scope of employment. Most attorneys have a claims-made malpractice insurance policy that covers their employees.

KEY TERMS

unauthorized practice of law, 186
practice of law, 186
regulation, 187
accreditation, 187
approval, 187
certification, 187
certified, 187
certificated, 187
code, 187
ethics, 187
guideline, 187
licensure, 187
limited licensure, 187
specialty licensure, 187
registration, 187

enrollment, 187
bankruptcy petition preparer, 188
statement of principles, 190
ex parte, 195
jailhouse lawyer, 195
writ writer, 197
adversarial, 200
Administrative Procedure Act, 200
registered agents, 200
practitioners, 200
enrolled agents, 201
Supremacy Clause, 203
page 52 debate, 208
self-represented person, 208

pro se, 208
in propria persona, 208
pro per, 208
document preparer, 209
scrivener, 209
legal technician, 209
HALT, 211
state-specific, 213
Limited Practice Officer, 214
pro bono work, 216
prepaid legal service, 216
attorney attestation, 224
Certified Legal Assistant (CLA), 225
Paralegal Advanced Certification Exam

(PACE), 225
Certified Legal Assistant Specialist (CLAS), 228
Fair Labor Standards Act, 232
tort liability, 234
vicarious liability, 235
respondeat superior, 235
scope of employment, 235
deep pocket, 235
negligence, 236
malpractice, 237
go bare, 237
occurrence policy, 237
claims-made policy, 237

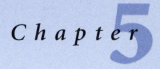
ATTORNEY ETHICS AND PARALEGAL ETHICS

► *Chapter Outline*

Section A
THE TEN COMMANDMENTS OF AN ETHICAL CONSERVATIVE

As you know from the media, the legal profession is under attack. The general public does not have a favorable opinion of attorneys. Elsewhere in this book, we examine some of the reasons for this hostility. Here in chapter 5, we confront one of the main reasons: the perception that attorneys are not very ethical, or, more cynically, the perception that attorneys are ethical only when it doesn't cost them anything.

The organized bar has responded to this problem in different ways. Every law school is now required to offer a required course in legal ethics. Many state bar associations require practicing attorneys to attend annual continuing education courses or seminars on ethical themes. And state disciplinary bodies have hired more attorneys (and paralegals) to investigate claims of ethical violations by practicing attorneys.

Of course, attorneys are not the only individuals under attack for ethical misconduct. Some commentators claim that the problem is rampant throughout society. Our focus here, however, is the legal profession.

As paralegals, you are about to enter a very special arena. You will meet many different kinds of attorneys: those whose ethical behavior is beyond reproach, those who engage in blatantly unethical behavior, and those who walk a thin line between ethical and unethical behavior. Which of these categories of attorneys will one day be your employers and supervisors? The short answer, of course, is that you don't know. The central question then becomes, how do you prepare yourself for any work environment?

We begin with the ideal: when it comes to ethics, *you should be a conservative*. The paramount question must always be, "What is the right thing to do?" Answering this question will not always be easy, particularly when you may have to make a choice between your ethics and your job. (See Section E of this chapter.) What is an ethical conservative? He or she is a follower of the Ten Commandments outlined in Exhibit 5.1. Study—indeed, memorize—these commandments as soon as possible.

Section B
ENFORCING ETHICS

1. ETHICS AND SANCTIONS

Ethics are rules that embody standards of behavior to which members of an organization must conform. The organization is often an association of individuals in the same occupation—for example, attorneys, paralegals, stockbrokers, or accountants. The ethical rules of some organizations are enforced by **sanctions.** A sanction is any penalty or punishment imposed for unacceptable conduct.[1] Other organizations, however, have ethical rules that are not tied to any system of enforcement.

All of the major national paralegal associations have adopted ethical rules, as we will see later in Exhibit 5.5. *None* are enforced by meaningful sanctions, however. A paralegal association might occasionally throw someone out of the association because of misconduct, but it is highly unlikely that the expulsion would interfere with his or her ability to

---

[1]Another meaning of the word *sanction* is to give formal approval. Example: the fee was paid once the court *sanctioned* the payment.

> ### Exhibit 5.1   Paralegal Ethics: The Ten Commandments of an Ethical Conservative
>
> 1. If what you are asked to do doesn't feel right, don't proceed until it does. Adhere to rigorous standards of professional ethics, even if those standards are higher than those followed by attorneys, paralegals, and others around you.
> 2. Study the ethical rules governing attorneys, including those on the ethical use of paralegals by attorneys. Read the rules. Re-read them. Attend seminars on ethics conducted by bar associations and paralegal associations. If you understand when attorneys are vulnerable to charges of unprofessional conduct, you will be better able to assist them in avoiding such charges.
> 3. Assume that people outside your office do not have a clear understanding of what a paralegal or legal assistant is. Make sure that everyone with whom you come in contact (clients, prospective clients, attorneys, court officials, agency officials, the public) understands that you are not an attorney.
> 4. Never tell anyone who is not working on a case anything about that case. This includes your co-workers, your spouse, your best friend, and your mother!
> 5. Know what legal advice is. When you are asked questions that call for legal advice, refuse to be coaxed into providing it, no matter how innocent the question appears to be, no matter how clear it is that you know the correct answer, and no matter how confident your supervisor is that you can handle such questions on your own.
> 6. Never make contact with an opposing party in a legal dispute, or with anyone closely associated with that party, unless you have the permission of your supervising attorney and of the attorney for the opposing party, if the latter has one.
> 7. Disclose your inexperience. Let your supervisor know if all or part of an assignment is new to you and that you may need additional training and supervision to undertake it competently.
> 8. Don't sign your name to anything if you are not certain that what you are signing is 100 percent accurate and that the law allows a paralegal to sign it. If you are asked to witness someone's signature, be sure that the document you are witnessing is signed in your presence.
> 9. Never pad your time sheets. Insist that what you submit be 100 percent accurate.
> 10. Know the common rationalizations for misrepresentation and other unethical conduct:
>   - It's always done.
>   - The other side does it.
>   - The cause of our client is just.
>   - If I don't do it, I will jeopardize my job.
>
>   Promise yourself that you will not allow any of these rationalizations to entice you to participate in unethical conduct.

work as a paralegal—unless the misconduct is so serious that others in the legal community eventually find out about it.

Attorneys, on the other hand, *are* subject to enforceable ethical rules that can affect whether they are allowed to continue practicing law. Attorney ethics are backed by sanctions. These rules attempt to govern everything an attorney does in the practice of law from adding clients to withdrawing from representing clients.

One of the things an attorney does is employ paralegals. Hence, there are rules on how an attorney can use a paralegal ethically. Unethical use of paralegals by an attorney can subject the attorney to sanctions. We will spend considerable time in this chapter examining this reality.

2. ATTORNEY CODES

In most states, the regulation of attorneys is primarily under the control of the highest court in the state (often called the Supreme Court), which determines when an attorney can be granted a license to practice law and under what conditions the license will be taken away or suspended because of unethical conduct. Since the state legislature may also exert some regulatory authority over attorneys, a dispute occasionally arises over which branch of government can control a particular aspect of the practice of law. The judiciary often wins this dispute and becomes the final authority. In practice, however, the judicial branch and the legislative branch usually share regulatory jurisdiction over the practice of law, with the dominant branch being the judiciary. The day-to-day functions of regulation, however, are delegated to an entity such as a state bar association and a disciplinary board or grievance commission.

There are four kinds of bar associations:

- National (for example, American Bar Association, Association of Trial Lawyers of America, Hispanic National Bar Association)
- State (for example, Illinois State Bar Association, State Bar of Montana)
- Local (for example, Boston Bar Association, New York County Bar Association, San Diego County Bar Association)
- Specialty (for example, Academy of Matrimonial Attorneys, Association of Trial Lawyers of America, Association of the Customs Bar)

All national, local, and specialty bar associations are voluntary; no attorney is required to be a member. The majority of *state* bar associations in the country, however, are *integrated*, which simply means that membership is required as a condition of practicing law in the state. (**Integrated bar associations** are also referred to as *mandatory* or *unified* bar associations. See Exhibit 5.2.) There is a state bar association in every state. Most, but not all, are integrated.

Under the general supervision of the state's highest court, the state bar association has a large role in regulating most aspects of the practice of law. For example, dues charged by integrated bar associations are used to fund the state's system of enforcing ethical rules. States that do not have integrated bar associations often have a **registration** requirement. Each attorney in the state registers to practice law and pays a registration fee that is used to fund that state's system of enforcing the ethical rules. Even in these states, the state bar association has a great influence over the regulation of attorneys. Given this dominant role of bar associations, the method of regulating attorneys in America is essentially that of self-regulation: attorneys regulating attorneys.[2]

There is no national set of ethical rules that applies to every state. Each state can adopt its own state code to regulate the attorneys in that state. The state code may have different names such as code of ethics, canons of ethics, code of professional responsibility, model rules. In fact, however, the rules that the states have adopted are quite similar. The reason for this similarity is the influence of the American Bar Association.

---

[2]This is so even in states that allow nonattorneys to serve on boards or commissions that regulate an aspect of the legal profession.

Exhibit 5.2   States with Integrated Bar Associations (1991)

Alabama	Idaho	Montana	North Dakota	Utah
Alaska	Kentucky	Nebraska	Oklahoma	Virginia
Arizona	Louisiana	Nevada	Oregon	Washington
California	Michigan	New Hampshire	South Carolina	West Virginia
Florida	Mississippi	New Mexico	South Dakota	Wisconsin
Georgia	Missouri	North Carolina	Texas	Wyoming

The American Bar Association is a voluntary national bar association; no attorney must belong to it. Yet approximately 55 percent of the attorneys in America do belong to the ABA. It publishes ethical rules but does *not* discipline attorneys for unethical conduct. The role of the ABA in this area is to write ethical rules and to *propose* to the individual states that they be accepted. A state is free to adopt, modify, or reject the rules. The current recommendation of the ABA is found in a document called the *Model Rules of Professional Conduct.* This document has been very influential throughout the country. Many states adopted it with relatively minor changes. The *Model Rules* is a revision of the ABA's *Model Code of Professional Responsibility,* which a number of states still follow.

Exhibit 5.3 presents an overview of the major ethical codes governing attorney conduct. The most important ones include provisions that are directly relevant to paralegals and other nonattorneys who work for attorneys. (See the last column of Exhibit 5.3.) Later in the chapter, we will be examining these provisions more closely.

3. ACCUSATION OF UNETHICAL CONDUCT

When an attorney is charged with unethical conduct, the case is investigated by a disciplinary body appointed by the state's highest court. The name for this body differs from state to state, e.g., the Grievance Commission, the Attorney Registration and

E x h i b i t 5 . 3		**Ethical Codes Governing Attorney Conduct**			
NAME OF DOCUMENT	**DATE**	**AUTHOR**	**STATUS**	**STRUCTURE**	**RELEVANCE TO PARALEGALS**
Model Rules of Professional Conduct	1983	American Bar Association	Current. It replaces the *Model Code* (see below). The *Model Rules* is not binding since no attorney is required to be a member of the ABA. It is a set of rules recommended to the states. Thirty-eight states have adopted it in whole or with changes.	There are eight main rules in the *Model Rules*. All of the rules are followed by interpretative comments.	Rule 5.3 of the *Model Rules* covers the ethical use of paralegals by attorneys. (For the text of Rule 5.3, see page 290 later in this chapter.)
Model Code of Professional Responsibility	1969	American Bar Association	An earlier code of the ABA that was recommended to the states. (Now replaced by the *Model Rules*.) Some states never adopted the *Model Rules*. They continue to follow their version of the *Model Code*.	There are nine main canons in the *Model Code*. Within each canon are Disciplinary Rules (DR), which are mandatory statements or rules, and Ethical Considerations (EC), which are behavioral guidelines.	DR 3-101 of the *Model Code* covers the unauthorized practice of law. EC 3-6 of the *Model Code* covers the proper delegation of tasks to paralegals. (See page 289 later in this chapter.)
State Codes	Varies	Highest state court in the state. In addition, the state legislature may also pass statutes governing attorney ethics.	This is the code that is binding on every practicing attorney in the state. Most states have based their code on the ABA *Model Rules*. Some, however, still follow their version of the ABA *Model Code*.	Varies. If based on the ABA *Model Rules* or *Model Code,* the state code will be similar in structure to the ABA document.	Varies. May have Rule 5.3 (if the state code is based on the *Model Rules*) or may have DR 3-101 and EC 3-6 (if based on the *Model Code*).
Special Codes	Varies	A separate city, state, regional, or national bar association	These special bar associations often have their own code of ethics. For example, the code of the American Academy of Matrimonial Lawyers is called the *Bounds of Advocacy/Standards of Conduct*.	Varies	Seldom specifically refer to paralegals.

Disciplinary Commission, the Committee on Professional Conduct, the Board of Professional Responsibility.

A hearing is held to determine whether unethical conduct was committed by the accused attorney. The commission, committee, or board then makes its recommendation to the state's highest court, which makes the final determination of whether to accept this

Exhibit 5.4   Attorney Sanctions for Unethical Conduct

Disbarment:

The termination of the right to practice law. The disbarment can be permanent or temporary. If it's temporary, the attorney will be allowed to apply for readmission after a designated period.

Suspension:

The removal of an attorney from the practice of law for a specified minimum period, after which the attorney can apply for reinstatement. An *interim suspension* is a temporary suspension pending the imposition of final discipline. The attorney may be required to notify clients of the suspension.

Reprimand:

A public declaration that the attorney's conduct was improper. This does not affect his or her right to practice. A reprimand is also called a *censure,* a *public censure,* or a *public reproval.*

Admonition:

A nonpublic declaration that the attorney's conduct was improper. An admonition is the mildest form of punishment that can be imposed. It does not affect the attorney's right to practice. An admonition is also known as a *private reprimand* or a *private reproval.*

Probation:

Allowing the attorney to continue to practice but under specified conditions, such as submitting to periodic audits of client funds controlled by the attorney or making restitution to a client whose funds were wrongly taken by the attorney. He or she may also be asked to take or retake the Professional Responsibility Exam.

recommendation. A number of sanctions can be imposed by the court. As you can see from Exhibit 5.4, they can range from relatively mild slaps on the wrist (reprimand, admonition)[3] to expulsion from the legal profession itself (permanent disbarment).

4. PARALEGAL CODES AND GUIDELINES

Thus far we have been discussing attorney codes of ethics. Can a *paralegal* be sanctioned for violating these codes? Not directly. The codes apply to attorneys only.[4] Since paralegals cannot join a bar association as full members, they cannot be sanctioned by a bar association or by any other entity set up to monitor attorney conduct. Serious paralegal wrongdoing, however, can lead to severe consequences: the paralegals might be fired by their employer, they might be sued for negligence, they might face criminal prosecution, their supervising attorney might face ethical charges because of the paralegal wrongdoing, etc. But the paralegals themselves cannot be punished for unethical conduct by the entity that regulates attorneys.

Now we turn to **paralegal codes.** These are sets of rules and guidelines devoted exclusively to issues of paralegal ethics. There are two kinds of paralegal codes: those written by attorneys and those written by paralegals. See Exhibit 5.5 for an overview of both.

---

[3]For minor infractions, Florida allows attorneys to attend a one-day ethics school on professional responsibility skills. *Ethics School Continues to Assist Errant Lawyers,* Florida Bar News, 21 (August 1, 1995).

[4]Remarkably, there is one jurisdiction—the District of Columbia—that allows a nonattorney to become a full owner/partner of a law firm! This individual must agree to abide by the ethical code that governs attorneys. In D.C., therefore, the ethical rules governing attorneys *do* apply to a nonattorney who has become a partner. Very few, however, have done so. The first was an accountant.

Exhibit 5.5 Paralegal Codes and Guidelines

NAME OF DOCUMENT	DATE	AUTHOR	COMMENTS
A. Those Written by Attorneys			
Model Guidelines for the Utilization of Legal Assistant Services	1991	American Bar Association	A series of ethical guidelines recommended by the ABA for adoption by the states on the ethical use of paralegals by attorneys. States are free to adopt, amend, or reject these guidelines.
State Codes and Guidelines	Varies	State Bar Association	Seventeen states have adopted rules and guidelines on ethically practicing law with paralegals. (See Appendix F.)
B. Those Written by Paralegals			
Model Code of Ethics and Professional Responsibility	1993	National Federation of Paralegal Associations	This *Model Code* is a revision of NFPA's earlier ethics document called the *Affirmation of Responsibility* (1977). NFPA recommends the adoption of its *Model Code* by the member associations of NFPA.
Code of Ethics and Professional Responsibility	1975 1995	National Association of Legal Assistants	All members of NALA must agree to abide by its *Code of Ethics.*
Model Standards and Guidelines for Utilization of Legal Assistants	1991	National Association of Legal Assistants	The goal of the *Model Standards* is to act as an informational and educational resource for attorneys and bar associations. Many of the guidelines in the *Model Standards* elaborate on NALA's *Code of Ethics.*
Special Codes	Varies	Local, state, or regional paralegal association	Other paralegal associations have written ethical codes to govern their membership. For example, the *Code of Ethics* of the California Association of Freelance Paralegals; the *Code of Ethics and Professional Responsibility* of the Houston Legal Assistants Association

Codes Written by Attorneys

The ABA has issued the *Model Guidelines for the Utilization of Legal Assistant Services.* Like the ABA's *Model Rules* and *Model Code* (see Exhibit 5.3), the *Model Guidelines* are recommendations to the states. The ABA itself does not discipline anyone for violating the *Model Guidelines.* (Later in this chapter, you will find a discussion of every guideline or rule contained in the *Model Guidelines.*) To date, seventeen states have their own state paralegal codes that are similar to the *Model Guidelines.* Most were adopted by the state bar association or by the committee of the bar association that covers paralegals. The *Model Guidelines* and the state paralegal codes are primarily directed to attorneys who use paralegals in their practice. Hence, if there are violations by paralegals, it is the supervising attorney who may be subject to sanctions by the state entity that regulates attorney ethics. (For a summary of state guidelines for your state, see Appendix F.)

Codes Written by Paralegals

The two national paralegal associations, NFPA and NALA, have also written paralegal codes. They are listed in the first column of Exhibit 5.5 and reprinted in full in Section D of this chapter. As indicated earlier, these codes are not enforced by meaningful sanctions. The associations might terminate a paralegal's membership in the association for ethical improprieties, but this is rarely done. The associations simply do not have the resources or clout to implement a system of enforcement.

This does not mean, however, that the paralegal codes are unimportant. Their main value is to reinforce the critical importance of ethics in the practice of law. Paralegals are on the front line. *One of their primary responsibilities is to help an attorney avoid being charged with unethical conduct.* A recent seminar conducted by the Los Angeles Paralegal Association was entitled "Law Firm Ethics: How to Keep Your Attorneys off '60 Minutes'!" Hence, the paralegal must be intimately familiar with ethical rules. Our goal in this chapter is to provide you with that familiarity.

Section C
ETHICAL RULES

We turn now to an overview of specific ethical rules that apply to attorneys. The overview is based on the ABA's *Model Rules of Professional Conduct.* (See Exhibit 5.3.) The rule numbers used in the discussion (such as Rule 1.5) refer to the *Model Rules.* Since not all states have adopted the *Model Rules,* we will occasionally refer to the ABA's *Model Code of Professional Responsibility,* which some states still follow.

Where appropriate, the discussion will include a *paralegal perspective* based on the ABA's *Model Guidelines* and the other paralegal codes mentioned in Exhibit 5.5. In Appendix F of the book, you will also find a state-by-state breakdown of important ethical rules.

One final note before we begin: Most ethics charges are brought by disgruntled clients who claim to have been harmed by the attorney's alleged unethical behavior. For example, the client's case was dismissed because the attorney carelessly forgot to file a pleading in court. We need to emphasize, however, that a person who initiates a charge of unethical conduct does *not* have to prove he or she suffered actual harm thereby. Suppose, for example, an attorney represents a client with whom the attorney has a clear conflict of interest. The attorney should never have taken the case. Representing the client in the case is unethical even if the attorney wins the case for the client! Proof of harm is not necessary to establish a violation of the ethical rules, although such harm is usually present.

1. COMPETENCE

An attorney shall provide competent representation to a client. Model Rule 1.1

A **competent** attorney is one who uses the *knowledge* and *skill* that are reasonably necessary to represent a particular client. What is reasonably necessary depends on the complexity of the case. A great deal of knowledge and skill, for example, will be needed when representing a corporate client accused of complicated antitrust violations.

How do attorneys obtain this knowledge and skill? They draw on the general principles of legal analysis and legal research learned in law school. But more importantly, they take the time needed to *prepare* themselves. They spend time in the law library. They talk with their colleagues. In some instances, they formally associate themselves with more experienced attorneys in the area. Attorneys who fail to take these steps are acting unethically if their failure means that they do not have the knowledge and skill reasonably necessary to represent a particular client.

Some attorneys have so many clients that they could not possibly give proper attention to each. Always looking for more lucrative work, they run the risk of neglecting the clients they already have. As a consequence, they might miss court dates or other filing deadlines, lose documents, fail to determine what law governs a client's case, etc. Such an attorney is practicing law "from the hip"—incompetently and unethically.

> Example: Mary Henderson, Esq. has a large criminal law practice. She agrees to probate the estate of a client's deceased son. She has never handled such a case before. Five years go by. No progress is made in determining who is entitled to receive the estate. If some minimal legal research had been done, Henderson would have been able to close the case within six months of taking it.

Henderson has probably acted unethically. The failure to do basic research on a case is a sign of incompetence. The need for such research is clear in view of the fact that she has never handled a probate case before. Either she must take the time to find out how to probate the estate, or she must contact another attorney with probate experience and arrange to work with this attorney on the case. Not doing either is unethical.

The vast majority of graduates of law schools need considerable on-the-job study and guidance before they are ready to handle cases of any complexity. A law school education gives new attorneys a good theoretical understanding of the law. This is different from the *practical* knowledge and skill needed to work on real cases. Many law schools have **clinical education** programs in which students receive credit for working on actual cases under the supervision of attorneys. For example, the school might operate its own tax clinic for senior citizens or might assign students to work several hours a week on different kinds of cases at a local legal aid office. While these clinical programs provide practical experience, they are not a major part of the law school curriculum of every law school. Most new attorneys (including those with clinical experience), therefore, are quite nervous when they face their first client on their first job. The nervousness is based on the fact that they are acutely aware of how much they *don't* know. This doesn't necessarily mean they are incompetent to practice law. It simply means they must take the time to prepare themselves and to draw on the assistance of others where needed.

CLE (**continuing legal education**) is another vehicle used by attorneys to achieve competence. Most states require attorneys to participate in a designated number of hours of CLE per year as a condition of maintaining their license to practice law. These CLE sessions are designed to keep busy practicing attorneys current in their areas of practice. The sessions are often conducted by a CLE institute affiliated with the bar association. Throughout the year, and particularly during bar conventions, attorneys have the opportunity to attend relatively short CLE sessions, e.g., an afternoon.

If an attorney is incompetent, he or she can be sanctioned for being unethical. In addition, the incompetence may have other consequences as well. The client might try to sue the attorney for negligence in a legal malpractice case. (Such suits were discussed in chapter 4.) If the client is a criminal defendant who was convicted, he or she may try to appeal the conviction on the ground that the attorney's incompetence amounted to a denial of the effective "Assistance of Counsel" guaranteed by the Sixth Amendment of the U.S. Constitution.

Paralegal Perspective:

● "An attorney who utilizes a legal assistant's services is responsible for determining that the legal assistant is competent to perform the tasks assigned, based on the legal assistant's education, training, and experience . . . ."[5] While the attorney has this supervisory responsibility, paralegals also have a responsibility to maintain their own competence.

- If you are given assignments that are beyond your knowledge and skill, let your supervisor know. Either you must be given training with close supervision, or you must be given other assignments. A "lawyer should explain to the legal assistant that the legal assistant has a duty to inform the lawyer of any assignment which the legal assistant regards as beyond his capability."[6]

- Be careful of the attorney who has so much confidence in your competence that he or she uses your work product with little or no checking. This is extremely dangerous, particularly for paralegals who work for very busy attorneys. The danger is that you will make a mistake that will not be caught until damage is done to the client. No matter how much experience you develop in an area of the law, unique problems often arise. Unless someone is reviewing your work, how will you know whether you have missed one of these problems? Your ego will appreciate the confidence your supervisor expresses in you by delegating so much responsibility, but the attorney still has an ethical obligation to supervise your work. Your competence is not a substitute for this supervision.

- After you complete an assignment, look for an opportunity to ask your supervisor how you could have improved your performance on the assignment. Do not wait for a year-end evaluation to learn what you can do to become a more competent paralegal.

- Find out which attorneys, administrators, paralegals, and secretaries in the office have a reputation for explaining things well. Spend time with such individuals even if you do not work with them on a daily basis. Take them to lunch. Find time to sit with them on a coffee break. Ask lots of questions. Let them know you respect high-quality work and appreciate anything they can tell you to help you increase your competence.

- Invest in CLE (continuing legal education). Take the initiative in continuing your training after your formal education is over. Do not wait for someone to suggest further training. Ask if you can attend CLE sessions for attorneys in the areas of law that are relevant to your case assignments. (Check the local bar association journal for CLE ads.) National and local paralegal associations also have afternoon and weekend CLE programs you need to explore. (Check the newsletters of paralegal associations.) Find the time to attend, even if you must pay for them yourself. Because the law is changing so rapidly, CLE is an important way to maintain competence.

- Review the section in chapter 4 on malpractice insurance. No matter how competent you are, you could be a defendant in a negligence suit brought against a law firm by a disgruntled client. Before you are hired by a firm, find out if the firm has a malpractice policy, whether it covers paralegal employees, whether certain kinds of errors are excluded, and whether you need to obtain your own professional liability insurance.

2. DILIGENCE/UNWARRANTED DELAY

An attorney shall act with reasonable diligence and promptness in representing a client. Model Rule 1.3

An attorney must make reasonable efforts to expedite litigation. Model Rule 3.2

---

[5]American Bar Association, *Model Guidelines for the Utilization of Legal Assistant Services,* Comment to Guideline 1 (1991). See Exhibit 5.5. [Hereinafter cited as ABA *Model Guidelines.*]
[6]Section 20–110, Committee Commentary, *New Mexico Rules Governing the Practice of Law* (Judicial Pamphlet 16).

Angry clients often complain that attorneys take forever to complete a case and keep clients in the dark about what is happening. "He never answers my calls." "It took months to file the case in court." "She keeps telling me that everything is fine, but nothing ever gets done." Such complaints do not necessarily indicate unethical behavior by the attorney. Events may be beyond the control of the attorney. For example, the court calendar is crowded or the other side is not responding. Yet this does not excuse a lack of regular communication with clients to keep them reasonably informed about the status of their case.

Other explanations for a lack of diligence and promptness, however, are more serious:

- The attorney is disorganized. The law office has not developed adequate systems to process cases. The delays are due to careless mistakes and a lack of skill.
- The attorney is taking many more cases than the office can handle. Additional personnel should be hired to do the needed work, or new cases should not be accepted.

Often the failure to use reasonable diligence and promptness causes harm to the client. For example, the attorney neglects to file a suit before the statute of limitations has run against the client. Unreasonable procrastination, however, can be unethical even if such harm does not result.

Another problem is the attorney who intentionally causes numerous delays in an effort to try to wear the other side down. It is unethical to engage in such dilatory practices. Attorneys must use reasonable efforts to expedite litigation, consistent with protecting the interests of their clients.

Paralegal Perspective:

- An overloaded attorney probably works with an overloaded paralegal. Successful paralegals often take the initiative by asking for additional work. But reason must prevail. If you have more work than you can handle, you must let your supervisor know. Otherwise, you might find yourself contributing to the problem of undue procrastination.
- Learn everything you can about office systems. Find out how they are created. (See chapter 3.) After you have gained some experience in the office, you should start designing systems on your own initiative. Effective office systems substantially reduce the risk of unethical delays in client representation.
- When a busy attorney is in court or cannot be disturbed because of pressing work on another case, someone in the office should be available to communicate with clients who want to know the status of their case. In many offices, the paralegal is in a position to provide this information. The role is delicate, however, since in addition to asking about the status of their case, clients often ask questions that call for legal advice. Giving such advice may constitute the unauthorized practice of law. Later we will examine in greater depth the temptations and pressures on a paralegal to give legal advice.

3. FEES

An attorney's fee shall be reasonable. Model Rule 1.5(a)

There is no absolute standard to determine when a fee is excessive and therefore unreasonable. A number of factors must be considered: the amount of time and labor involved, the complexity of the case, the experience and reputation of the attorney, the customary fee in the locality for the same kind of case, etc.

Examples: In 1979, a court ruled that $500 an hour was excessive in a simple battery case involving a guilty plea and no unusual issues. In 1984, a court ruled that a fee of $22,500 was excessive in an uncomplicated real estate case involving very little time. The case was settled through the efforts of someone other than the attorney.

The basis of the fee should be communicated to the client before or soon after the attorney starts to work on the case. This is often done in the contract hiring the attorney called a **retainer**.[7] (See Exhibit 8.1 in chapter 8 for an example of a retainer. Kinds of fees are also discussed in greater detail in chapter 14.)

In Exhibit 5.3, we outlined the major attorney codes of ethics. Many bar associations write formal and informal opinions that interpret sections of their code. Attorneys can submit questions to the bar's ethics committee.[8] The questions selected are sometimes published as formal or informal opinions so that the entire legal community can benefit from the bar's interpretive advice. Recently, in Formal Ethics Opinion 93-379, the American Bar Association addressed its rule on fees (Model Rule 1.5) and some of the serious charges made against billing practices of attorneys:

Formal Ethics Opinion 93-379
American Bar Association, 1993

It is a common perception that pressures on lawyers to bill a minimum number of hours and on law firms to maintain or improve profits may have led some lawyers to engage in problematic billing practices. . . . The Committee has decided to address several practices that are the subject of frequent inquiry, with the goal of helping the profession adhere to its ethical obligations to its clients despite economic pressures.

The first set of practices involves billing more than one client for the same hours spent. In one illustrative situation, a lawyer finds it possible to schedule court appearances for three clients on the same day. He spends a total of four hours at the courthouse, the amount of time he would have spent on behalf of each client had it not been for the fortuitous circumstance that all three cases were scheduled on the same day. May he bill each of the three clients, who otherwise understand that they will be billed on the basis of time spent, for the four hours he spent on them collectively?

In another scenario, a lawyer is flying cross-country to attend a deposition on behalf of one client, expending travel time she would ordinarily bill to that client. If she decides not to watch the movie or read her novel, but to work instead on drafting a motion for another client, may she charge both clients, each of whom agreed to hourly billing, for the time during which she was traveling on behalf of one and drafting a document on behalf of the other?

A third situation involves research on a particular topic for one client that later turns out to be relevant to an inquiry from a second client. May the firm bill the second client, who agreed to be charged on the basis of time spent on his case, the same amount for the recycled work product that it charged the first client? . . .

At the outset of the representation the lawyer should make disclosure of the basis for the fee and any other charges to the client. This is a two-fold duty, including not only an explanation at the beginning of engagement of the basis on which fees and other charges will be billed, but also a sufficient explanation in the statement so that the client may reasonably be expected to understand what fees and other charges the client is actually being billed. . . .

In addressing the hypotheticals regarding (a) simultaneous appearance on behalf of three clients, (b) the airplane flight on behalf of one client while working on another client's matters and (c) recycled work product, it is helpful to consider these questions, not from the perspective of what a client could be forced to pay, but rather from the perspective of what the lawyer actually earned. A lawyer who spends four hours of time on behalf of three clients has not earned twelve billable hours. A lawyer who flies for six hours for one client, while working for five hours on behalf of another, has not earned eleven billable hours. A

---

[7]Another meaning of the word *retainer* is the amount of money (or other property) paid by the client as a deposit or advance against future attorney fees, expenses such as travel, and costs such as court filing fees.
[8]No actual names or other identifying information is given in the question in order to protect client confidentiality.

lawyer who is able to reuse old work product has not re-earned the hours previously billed and compensated when the work product was first generated. Rather than looking to profit from the fortuity of coincidental scheduling, the desire to get work done rather than watch a movie, or the luck of being asked the identical question twice, the lawyer who has agreed to bill solely on the basis of time spent is obliged to pass the benefits of these economies on to the client. The practice of billing several clients for the same time or work product, since it results in the earning of an unreasonable fee, therefore is contrary to the mandate of . . . Model Rule 1.5.

Moreover, continuous toil on or overstaffing a project for the purpose of churning out hours is also not properly considered "earning" one's fees. . . . A lawyer should take as much time as is reasonably required to complete a project, and should certainly never be motivated by anything other than the best interests of the client when determining how to staff or how much time to spend on any particular project.

It goes without saying that a lawyer who has undertaken to bill on an hourly basis is never justified in charging a client for hours not actually expended.

At one time, bar associations published a list of "recommended fees" that should be charged for designated kinds of services. These **minimum-fee schedules** have now been prohibited by the United States Supreme Court. They constitute illegal price fixing by the bar in violation of the antitrust laws.

Contingent fees can sometimes present ethical problems. A contingent fee is a fee that is dependent on the outcome of the case.

Example: An attorney signs a retainer to represent a client in an automobile negligence case. If the jury awards the client damages, the attorney will receive 30 percent of the award. If the client loses the case, the attorney receives no fee.

This is a contingent fee since it is dependent on the outcome of the negligence case.

The benefit of a contingent fee is that it provides an incentive for an attorney to take the case of a client who does not have funds to pay hourly fees to an attorney while the case is pending. But contingent fees are not ethical in every case, even if the amount to be received by the successful attorney is otherwise reasonable. A contingent fee in a criminal case, and in most divorce cases, for example, is unethical.

Example: Gabe Farrell is a client of Sam Grondon, Esq. in a criminal case where Gabe is charged with murder. Gabe agrees to pay Grondon $100,000 if he is found innocent. Grondon will receive nothing if Gabe is convicted of any crime.

This fee agreement is unethical. Contingent fees are not allowed in criminal cases. Note the pressures on Grondon. He arguably has no incentive to try to negotiate a guilty plea to a lesser charge, e.g., manslaughter, since such a plea would mean a conviction and, hence, no fee. In such a situation, the attorney's own personal interest (obtaining the $100,000) could conflict with the interest of the client (receiving a lesser penalty through a negotiated plea). Similar pressures can arise in family law cases.

Example: To obtain a divorce from his wife, a client hires an attorney. The fee is $25,000 if the divorce is granted.

As the case develops, suppose a glimmer of hope arises that the husband and wife might reconcile. Here again, the attorney's interest (obtaining the $25,000) could conflict with the interest of the client (reconciling). This might lead the attorney to discourage the reconciliation or to set up roadblocks to it. Reconciliation obviously removes the possibility of the contingency—obtaining the divorce—from occurring. In family law cases, therefore, contingent fees are unethical if the fee is dependent on securing a divorce, on the amount of alimony obtained, on the amount of support obtained, or on the amount of a property settlement in lieu of alimony or support. Model Rule 1.5(d). This is so even if the terms of the contingent fee are otherwise reasonable.[9]

One final theme should be covered: **fee splitting.** The splitting or division of a fee refers to a single client bill covering the fee of two or more attorneys who are not in the same firm.

> Example: John Jones, Esq. is hired by a singer who is charging her record company with copyright infringement and breach of contract. Jones calls in Randy Smith, Esq., a specialist in copyright law from another firm. Both work on the case. They share (split) the fees paid by the singer, who receives one bill for the work of both attorneys even though they work for different law firms.

The attorneys are splitting or dividing the fee between them.[10] This arrangement is proper under certain conditions. For example, the total fee must be reasonable, and the client must be told about the participation of all the attorneys and not object.

Suppose, however, that the attorney splits the fee with a nonattorney.

> Example: Frank Martin is a freelance investigator. He refers accident victims to a law firm. For every client he refers to the firm, he receives 25 percent of the fee collected by the firm.

> Example: Helen Gregson is a chiropractor. She refers medical malpractice cases to a law firm, which compensates her for each referral.

These are improper divisions of fees with nonattorneys—even if the amount of the division is reasonable and the clients brought in by Martin or Gregson consent to their receiving a part of the fee. An attorney cannot share with a nonattorney a portion of a fee *paid by particular clients.* The rationale behind this prohibition is that the nonattorney might exercise some control over the attorney and thereby jeopardize the attorney's independent judgment.

For the same reason, an attorney cannot form a partnership with a nonattorney if any of the activities of the partnership consist of the practice of law. If the office practices law as a corporation, a nonattorney cannot own any interest in the company or be a director or officer.[11]

When a client has a serious dispute with an attorney over a fee, the client will sometimes dismiss the attorney and ask for a return of the client's file, which may contain many documents such as correspondence, complaints, other pleadings, exhibits, and reports of experts. This file is the property of the client and must be surrendered by the attorney when the client requests it even if there are unpaid bills for fees and costs. If the attorney has a claim for payment, the remedy is to sue the client for breach of contract; it is unethical for the attorney to hold the file hostage to ensure payment. The attorney can copy the file before turning it over, but at the attorney's own expense.[12]

---

[9]In some states, an exception exists in cases to collect *past due* child support payments. A contingent fee in such cases might be allowed so long as the divorce is already final. South Dakota Bar Association, *Ethics Opinion 95-8.*

[10]An attorney who refers a case to another attorney receives what is called a **referral fee** or **forwarding fee** from the latter.

[11]C. Wolfram, *Modern Legal Ethics,* §9.2.4 (1986). In the District of Columbia, however, where nonattorneys *are* allowed to be owner-partners in law firms, nonattorneys can obviously share legal fees with attorneys. See footnote 4.

[12]See chapter 14 for a discussion of the separate issue of how long an attorney must store a client's files after the case is over, whether or not the attorney's bills are paid.

Paralegal Perspective:

- An attorney or law firm may include paralegals and other nonattorney employees in a compensation or retirement plan, even though the plan is based in whole or in part on a profit-sharing arrangement. Model Rule 5.4(a)(3).

  Example: Frank is a paralegal at a law firm. The firm has a retirement plan under which the firm contributes a portion of its profits into the plan. Frank is a member of this retirement plan.

  The firm is not acting unethically. In most states, paralegals can receive compensation and retirement benefits that are based on the fees received by the firm so long as they are not receiving all or part of *particular* legal fees. "The linchpin of the prohibition [against splitting fees with a legal assistant] seems to be the advance agreement of the lawyer to 'split' a fee based on a pre-existing contingent arrangement. There is no general prohibition against a lawyer who enjoys a particularly profitable period recognizing the contribution of the legal assistant to that profitability with a discretionary bonus. Likewise, a lawyer engaged in a particularly profitable specialty of legal practice is not prohibited from compensating the legal assistant who aids materially in that practice more handsomely than the compensation generally awarded to legal assistants in that geographic area who work in law practices that are less lucrative. Indeed, any effort to fix a compensation level for legal assistants and prohibit greater compensation would appear to violate the federal antitrust laws."[13]

- A related restriction in many states is that an attorney cannot give a paralegal any compensation for referring business to the attorney. "It appears clear that a legal assistant may not be compensated on a contingent basis for a particular case or paid for 'signing up' clients for a legal practice."[14]

- Attorneys must not allow their paralegals to accept cases, to reject cases, or to "set fees." The responsibility "for establishing the amount of a fee to be charged for a legal service" may not be delegated to a paralegal.[15]

- "A lawyer may include a charge for the work performed by a legal assistant in setting a charge for legal services."[16] As we saw in chapter 1, most attorneys bill clients for paralegal time. Paralegals record their time on time sheets that become the basis of bills sent to clients. The amount that an attorney bills for paralegal time must be reasonable. Reasonableness is determined by a number of factors, such as the experience of the paralegal, the nature of the tasks the paralegal undertakes, and the market rate for paralegals in the area. Many retainers state the amount a client will be charged for a paralegal's time. (See Exhibit 8.1 in chapter 8.) The fact that the client agrees to a fee, however, does not prove that the fee is reasonable. Factors such as experience and market rate must still be used to determine whether the fee is reasonable. Furthermore, the fees must be for the performance of paralegal tasks. It is unethical to claim such fees for time the paralegal spent performing clerical duties such as photocopying. (See Appendix F for summaries of court cases in which attorneys were criticized for trying to bill paralegal rates for secretarial tasks performed by paralegals.)

---

[13] ABA *Model Guidelines,* Comment to Guideline 9. See footnote 5.
[14] Ibid.
[15] ABA *Model Guidelines,* Guideline 3(b). See footnote 5.
[16] ABA *Model Guidelines,* Guideline 8. See footnote 5.

In some cases, the losing side can be forced to pay the attorney fees of the winning party in litigation. In addition to attorney fees, paralegal fees must also be paid. The same guidelines apply: the paralegal fees must be reasonable and cannot cover nonparalegal tasks. Some states ask attorneys to submit an affidavit to support the amount claimed for the paralegal's time. The affidavit must give a detailed statement of the time and services rendered by the paralegal, a summary of the paralegal's qualifications, etc.

- Your time records should be contemporaneous, that is, made at approximately the same time as the events you are recording. Try to avoid recording time long after you perform tasks that require time records.
- Avoid **double billing.** It is fraudulent to charge a client twice for the same service.

> Example: Charles is a litigation paralegal in a law firm. One of his tasks is to digest (i.e., summarize) a deposition. The firm bills the client twenty hours for this task at the paralegal's rate ($65 per hour). The firm also bills the client ten hours of Attorney Bedford's time for digesting the same deposition at the attorney's rate ($150 per hour).

The client is being double billed, a grossly unethical practice. It would be proper for an attorney to charge a client for time spent *supervising* a paralegal's work, but not for *performing* the work of the paralegal. The related offense of **padding** is also fraudulent. It occurs when you add hours to your time sheet that were not in fact spent on the client's case.

> Example: It takes Charles, the litigation paralegal, twelve hours to digest a deposition. His time sheets, however, say he spent twenty hours on the task.

Padding is a serious problem in the practice of law:

> [It] occurs most typically when attorneys are under the gun to bill a large number of hours. Everyone knows of lawyers who begin work at 8:00, leave the office at 6:00 and yet bill 10 hours a day—a feat that utterly amazes me. Whether it be eating lunch, talking to a spouse, working with support staff, reading advance sheets or just taking a break, some portion of every day is spent on non-billable matters. [A young associate at a medium-sized midwestern firm says] padding or fabrication of entries is encouraged, or at the very least tolerated, at his firm, and many others, to judge from his friends' experiences. The pressure to pad is intense.[17]

Unfortunately, paralegals can find themselves under a similar pressure, which, of course, must be resisted.

> One of the most common temptations that can corrupt a paralegal's ethics is to inflate billable hours, since there is often immense pressure in law firms to bill high hours for job security and upward mobility. Such "creative billing" is not humorous; it's both morally wrong and illegal. It's also fraudulent and a plain and simple case of theft.[18]

When you are employed as a paralegal, will you face such pressure? Yes, or at least very probably, if you work in an office where income is generated through fees. The office wants high billings to increase its income. The paralegal wants high billings to demonstrate to the office that he or she is financially valuable to the office. This does

---

[17]Doe, *Billing: Is "Padding" Widespread?* 76 American Bar Ass'n Journal 42 (December 1990).
[18]Smith, *AAfPE National Conference Highlights*, 8 Legal Assistant Today 103 (January/February 1991).

not mean that everyone submits fraudulent time sheets and billings. But the pressure to do so is real.

A veteran paralegal recently made the following dramatic and troublesome comments about this problem:

> The economic benefits [of using paralegals] to the client are receiving greater attention. From my experience, however, there has been more abuse than benefit. The client is billed for a task traditionally performed by a secretary, doublebilled for redoing a task because it was poorly delegated and is being billed at an attorney's rate for "routine tasks" which can be best handled by a qualified paralegal.[19]

---

[19]C. Paddelford, President of the Sacramento Association of Legal Assistants, 7 RECAP 2 (California Alliance of Paralegal Associations, Fall 1992).

Brown v. Hammond

810 F. Supp. 644
United States District Court, Eastern District,
Pennsylvania, 1993

WALDMAN, District Judge.

Plaintiff is a former employee of defendant attorney and his law firm. She is suing for wrongful discharge after having "blown the whistle" on the defendants' allegedly improper billing practices. Jurisdiction is based on diversity of citizenship.* Defendants have moved to dismiss the complaint for failure to state a claim upon which relief can be granted, pursuant to Fed.R.Civ.P. [Federal Rule of Civil Procedure] 12(b)(6).

I. LEGAL STANDARD

The purpose of a Rule 12(b)(6) motion is to test the legal sufficiency of a complaint. See *Sturm v. Clark*, 835 F.2d 1009, 1111 (3d Cir. 1987). In deciding a motion to dismiss for failure to state a claim, the court must "accept as true all the allegations in the complaint and all reasonable inferences that can be drawn therefrom, and view them in the light most favorable to the non-moving party." See *Rocks v. Philadelphia*, 868 F.2d 644, 645 (3d Cir. 1989). Dismissal is not appropriate unless it clearly appears that plaintiff can prove no set of facts in support of his claim which could entitle him to relief. See *Hishon v. King & Spalding*, 467 U.S. 69, 73, 104 S. Ct. 2229, 2232, 81 L. Ed. 2d 59 (1984). . . . A complaint may be dismissed when the facts pled and the reasonable inferences drawn therefrom are legally insufficient to support the relief sought. . . .

---

*Plaintiff is a citizen of Texas, and defendants are citizens of Pennsylvania. The amount in controversy exceeds $50,000.

II. FACTS

The pertinent factual allegations in the light most favorable to plaintiff are as follows. From November 4, 1990 to April 4, 1991, plaintiff was employed by defendants at-will as a paralegal and secretary. The time she spent on client matters was billed to clients as "attorney's time" without any notice to such clients that the work was done by a non-lawyer. Her supervisors directed her at times to bill her work directly as attorney's time despite her protests that the practice was improper. She then informed various authorities and affected clients of this practice. Plaintiff does not allege that she had any responsibility for overseeing the firm's billing practices.

Defendants responded by imposing new work rules with respect to hours of employment which applied only to and discriminated against plaintiff. She was subsequently terminated.

In count I, plaintiff asserts that she was terminated in violation of public policy for reporting the wrongful actions of defendants. In count II, she asserts that she was terminated in violation of public policy for refusing to perform wrongful actions. . . .

III. DISCUSSION

It is well established under Pennsylvania law that "absent a statutory or contractual provision to the contrary . . . either party [may] terminate an employment relationship for any or no reason." *Geary v. United States Steel Corp.*, 456 Pa. 171, 175–176, 319 A.2d 174 (1974). An employer may determine, without any fair hearing to an at-will employee, that the employer simply wishes to be rid of him. *Darlington v. General Electric*, 350 Pa. Super. 183, 210, 504 A.2d 306 (1986). An employer's right to terminate an at-will employee has been characterized as "virtually absolute." *O'Neill v. ARA Services, Inc.*, 457 F. Supp. 182, 186 (E.D. Pa. 1978).

Pennsylvania law does recognize, however, a nonstatutory cause of action for wrongful discharge from employment-at-will, but only in the quite narrow and limited circumstance where the discharge violates a significant and recognized public policy. *Borse v. Piece Goods Shop,* 963 F.2d 611, 617 (3d Cir. 1992); *Geary,* supra; *Darlington,* supra. Such a public policy must be "clearly mandated" and of a type that "strikes at the heart of a citizen's social right, duties and responsibilities." *Novosel v. Nationwide Insurance Co.,* 721 F.2d 894, 899 (3d Cir. 1983). *Geary* signals a "narrow rather than expansive interpretation of the public policy exception." *Bruffett v. Warner Communications, Inc.,* 692 F.2d 910, 918 (3d Cir. 1982). Public policy exceptions "have been recognized in only the most limited of circumstances." *Clay v. Advanced Computer Applications, Inc.,* 522 Pa. 86, 89, 559 A.2d 917 (1989).

While courts generally look to constitutional or legislative pronouncements, some courts have found an expression of significant public policy in professional codes of ethics. See *Paralegal v. Lawyer,* 783 F. Supp. 230, 232 (E.D. Pa. 1992); *Cisco v. United Parcel Services,* 328 Pa. Super. 300, 476 A.2d 1340 (1984). . . .

The court in [the] *Paralegal* [v. Lawyer case] found that the Pennsylvania Rules of Professional Conduct as adopted by the Pennsylvania Supreme Court pursuant to state constitutional powers, Pa. Const. art. 5, § 10(c), could provide the basis for a public policy exception to the at-will employment rule. See *Paralegal [v. Lawyer],* 783 F. Supp. at 232 (finding public policy against falsifying material facts and evidence from rules 3.3(a)(1), 3.4(a), and 3.4(b)). In that case, a paralegal whose employer was being investigated by the state bar was terminated after she learned that the attorney-employer had created a false record to exculpate himself and so informed the lawyer who was representing the employer in disciplinary proceedings.

Taking plaintiff's allegations as true, defendants would appear to have violated the Pennsylvania Rules of Professional Conduct by misrepresenting to clients who had performed work for which they were paying or by effectively permitting the unauthorized practice of law by a non-lawyer. See Rule 1.5 (regulating fees); Rule 5.5(a) (prohibiting aiding non-lawyers in unauthorized practice of law); Rule 7.1 (prohibiting false or misleading communications about lawyer's services); 8.4(c) (defining "professional misconduct" to include dishonesty, fraud, deceit or misrepresentation).

Based upon pertinent precedent and persuasive authority, the court must distinguish between gratuitous disclo-sure of improper employer conduct and disclosures by persons responsible for reporting such conduct or for protecting the public interest in the pertinent area. See *Smith v. Calgon Carbon Corp.,* 917 F.2d 1338, 1345 (3d Cir. 1990), cert. denied, 111 S. Ct. 1597, 113 L. Ed. 2d 660 (1991) (discharged chemical company employee not responsible for reporting improper emissions or spills); *Field v. Philadelphia Electric Co.,* 388 Pa. Super. 400, 565 A.2d 1170 (1989) (nuclear safety expert discharged for making statutorily required report to federal agency). See also *Hays v. Beverly Enters.,* 766 F. Supp. 350 (W.D. Pa.), aff'd, 952 F.2d 1392 (3d Cir. 1991) (physician's duty does not extend to plaintiff nurse); *Gaiardo v. Ethyl Corp.,* 697 F. Supp. 1377 (M.D. Pa. 1986), aff'd, 835 F.2d 479 (3d Cir. 1987) (plaintiff not supervisor or responsible for quality control).

The court concludes that plaintiff's termination for gratuitously alerting others about defendants' improper billing practice does not violate the type of significant, clearly mandated public policy required to satisfy the new narrow exception to Pennsylvania's rigid at-will employment doctrine.

By her own characterization what plaintiff did was to "blow the whistle" on wrongful conduct by her employer. The Pennsylvania Whistleblower Law, 43 Pa. C.S.A. [Consolidated Statutes Annotated] § 1421 et seq., protects from retaliatory adverse employment action employees of public bodies or entities receiving public appropriations who report wrongdoing.* That Law, which excludes from its protection wholly private employment, has been found not to codify any previously existing legal right or privilege and held not to constitute an expression of clearly mandated public policy in the context of private at-will employment.† See *Smith,* 917 F.2d at 1346; *Cohen v. Salick Health Care, Inc.,* 772 F. Supp. 1521, 1531 (E.D. Pa. 1991) (employee discharged for alerting employer's prospective contractee of inflated financial projections); *Wagner v. General Electric Co.,* 760 F. Supp. 1146, 1155 (E.D. Pa. 1991) (employee discharged after expressing criticism of employer's product to customers).

---

*While the Whistleblower Law protects covered employees who report impropriety to outside authorities, it does not authorize such employees to voice complaints directly to clients of a public or publicly funded entity.

†Because of the special nature of the attorney-client relationship, an attorney's misrepresentation about the source, quality, nature or cost of work performed is arguably more reprehensible than such misrepresentation to clients and customers by other suppliers of goods and services. It is not, however, sufficiently different in kind therefrom to satisfy the narrow public policy exception to Pennsylvania's stringent at-will employment doctrine.

On the other hand, courts are less reluctant to discern important public policy considerations where persons are discharged for refusing to violate the law themselves. See *Smith*, 917 F.2d at 1344; *Woodson v. AMF Leisureland Centers, Inc.*, 842 F.2d 699 (3d Cir. 1988) (refusal to sell liquor to intoxicated patron); *Shaw v. Russell Trucking Line, Inc.*, 542 F. Supp. 776, 779 (W.D. Pa. 1982) (refusal to haul loads over legal weight); *McNulty v. Borden, Inc.*, 474 F. Supp. 1111 (E.D. Pa. 1979) (refusal to engage in anti-trust violations). No employee should be forced to choose between his or her livelihood and engaging in fraud or other criminal conduct. To the extent that plaintiff appears to allege that she was also terminated for refusing herself to engage directly in fradulent billing, her action may proceed. . . .

An appropriate order will be entered.

ORDER

AND NOW, this 12th day of January, 1992, upon consideration of defendants' Motion to Dismiss Plaintiff's Complaint, consistent with the accompanying memorandum, IT IS HEREBY ORDERED that said Motion is GRANTED in part and DENIED in part in that [count I] of plaintiff's complaint [is] DISMISSED.

Assignment 5.1

(a) Who won this case? What happens next? In the next proceeding in the case, what does the paralegal have to prove?

(b) Do you think a paralegal has an obligation to report unethical conduct? Should there be a "snitch rule"? If so, to whom should the report be made? See the discussion later in the chapter (p. 287) on an attorney's duty to report misconduct. Should paralegals have a similar duty?

4. CRIME OR FRAUD BY AN ATTORNEY

An attorney must not engage in criminal or fraudulent conduct. Model Rule 8.4

Sadly, there are attorneys who are charged with criminal conduct, such as theft of client funds, securities fraud, falsifying official documents, or tax fraud. Since such conduct obviously affects the attorney's fitness to practice law, sanctions for unethical conduct can be imposed in addition to prosecution in a criminal court. Once an attorney is convicted of a serious crime in court, a separate disciplinary proceeding is often instituted to suspend or disbar the attorney for unethical conduct growing out of the same incident.

Paralegal Perspective:

● Value your integrity above all else. A paralegal in Oklahoma offers the following advice: "Insist on the highest standards for yourself and for your employer. One small ethical breach can lead to a series of compromises with enormous" disciplinary and "legal malpractice consequences."[20]

● If your supervisor is charged with criminal conduct, the chances are good that you will be questioned by prosecutors, and you might become a suspect yourself.

---

[20]Tulsa Ass'n of Legal Assistants, *Hints for Helping Your Attorney Avoid Legal Malpractice*, TALA Times (August 1989).

- In the highly charged, competitive environment of a law office, some attorneys may be willing to violate the law in the interest of winning. Be sensitive to the overt and subtle pressure on you to participate in such violations. If you are subjected to this pressure, talk with other paralegals who have encountered this problem. Don't sit in silence. If there is no one in the office with whom you can frankly discuss the elimination of these pressures, you must consider quitting. (See Section E of this chapter.)
- Paralegals who are also notaries are sometimes asked by their supervisors to notarize documents that should *not* be notarized. In fact, paralegals "are most often named as defendants for false notarization of a signature."[21]

    Assume that a law office is sued and the paralegal is named as one of the defendants. If the plaintiff wins, who pays the judgment? As we saw in chapter 4, the office may have a malpractice insurance liability policy that will pay judgments against it and its employees. These policies often exclude intentional acts of misconduct, however. (False notarization is usually an intentional act.) Hence, the losing defendants—including the paralegal—must pay the judgments out of their personal pockets. In short, be extremely cautious of what you are asked to sign. The same is true of documents you are asked to witness even if no formal notarization is involved. Don't sign a clause saying you witnessed something being performed or executed (called an **attestation clause**) unless you *actually* witness it.

- At some law firms, employees have succumbed to the temptation of using a "hot tip" that crosses their path in a corporate takeover case.[22] Assume that Company X is planning to merge with Company Y. The news is not yet public. When it does become public, the value of the stock in Company X is expected to rise dramatically. You work at a law firm that represents Company X, and you find out about the planned merger while at work. If you buy stock in Company X before the announcement of the merger, you would benefit from the increased value of the stock that would result after the announcement. This might be an illegal use of inside information, called **insider trading.** In a dramatic recent case, a paralegal who worked at a securities law firm in Boston was charged with insider trading by the Securities and Exchange Commission (SEC). While working on a case involving a proposed merger, she learned certain information, which she gave to outside investors who used it to make illegal profits in the stock market. The story made national news. One headline read, "SEC Says Boston Paralegal Gave Tip Worth $823,471." Soon after the incident, she was fired. All employees of law firms must be extremely careful. Innocently buying stock as a personal investment could turn into a nightmare. One attorney "recommends that any paralegal who would like to buy or sell securities should check first with a corporate attorney in the firm to see if the firm represents the issuer or a company negotiating with the issuer. If it does, an accusation of 'insider trading' might later be made."[23] The same caution applies when a member of the paralegal's immediate family buys or sells such securities.

- Another problem area is the use of so-called **pirated software.** Many businesses buy or lease one copy of computer software and then copy it so that other employees in the office can use it on other terminals. If the software manufacturer has not authorized such copying as part of the original purchase or lease agreement, the copying is illegal and can subject violators to criminal penalties and civil damages.

---

[21]Race, *Malpractice Maladies*, Paradigm 12 (Baltimore Ass'n of Legal Assistants, July/August 1989).
[22]Milford, *Law Firms Expected to Take Steps to Avert Insider Trading Scandals*, The News Journal D3 (October 16, 1989).
[23]Shays, *Ethics for the Paralegal*, Postscript 15 (Manhattan Paralegal Ass'n, August/September 1989).

- In all aspects of your career as a paralegal, adopt the motto, "If it doesn't feel right, it probably isn't." (See the first "commandment" in Exhibit 5.1 at the beginning of this chapter.)

5. CRIME OR FRAUD BY A CLIENT

An attorney shall not counsel a client to engage in conduct the attorney knows is criminal or fraudulent. Model Rule 1.2(d)

The client hires the attorney and controls the purpose of the attorney-client relationship. Furthermore, the client is entitled to know the legal consequences of any action he or she is contemplating. This does not mean, however, that the attorney must do whatever the client wants.

> Example: The president of a corporation hires Leo Richards, Esq. to advise the company on how to dump toxic waste into a local river.

Note that the president has not asked Richards *if* the dumping is legal. It would be perfectly ethical for Richards to answer such a question. In the example, the president asks *how* to dump. If Richards feels that the dumping can legally take place, he can so advise the president. Suppose, however, that it is clear to Richards that the dumping would violate the federal or state criminal code. Under such circumstances, it would be unethical for Richards to advise the president on how to proceed with the dumping. The same would be true if the president wanted help in filing an environmental statement that misrepresented the intentions of the company. Such an application would be fraudulent, and an attorney must not help someone commit what the attorney knows is fraudulent conduct.

When attorneys are later charged with unethical conduct in such cases, their defense is often that they did not know the conduct proposed by the client was criminal or fraudulent. This defense can be successful. If the law applicable to the client's case is unclear, an attorney can make a good-faith effort to find a legal way for the client to achieve his or her objective. The point at which the attorney crosses the ethical line is when he or she *knows* the client is trying to accomplish something criminal or fraudulent.

Paralegal Perspective:

- An attorney will rarely tell paralegals or other staff members that he or she knows the office is helping a client do something criminal or fraudulent. But you might learn that this is so, particularly if there is a close, trusting relationship between you and your supervising attorney. You must let this attorney or some other authority in the office know you do not feel comfortable working on such a case.

6. FRIVOLOUS LEGAL POSITIONS

An attorney must not bring a frivolous claim or assert a frivolous defense. Model Rule 3.1

We often say that we have an **adversarial system** of justice. This means that our method of resolving a legal dispute is to have opposing sides fight it out before an impartial decision maker. We believe that truth and fairness are more likely to emerge when each side has an equal chance to present its case forcefully. Within this system, a client has a right to hire an attorney who is a vigorous advocate. Otherwise there could be an imbalance in the arguments presented to the decision maker.

But there are limits on how vigorous an advocate can be. It is unethical, for example, for an attorney to assert **frivolous positions** as claims or defenses. There are two major tests for determining when a legal position is frivolous: the good-faith test and the intentional-injury test.

First, a position is frivolous if the attorney is unable to make a good-faith argument that existing law supports the position, or the attorney is unable to make a good-faith argument that existing law should be changed or reversed to support the position. A position is not necessarily frivolous simply because the attorney thinks the client will probably lose. The key is whether there is a good-faith argument to support the position. If the attorney can think of absolutely no rational support for the position, it is frivolous. Since the law is often unclear, it is difficult to establish that an attorney is acting unethically under the test of good faith.

Second, a position is frivolous if the client's primary purpose in having the position asserted is to harass or maliciously injure someone.

Paralegal Perspective:

● In the heat of controversy, tempers can run high. Attorneys do not always exhibit the detachment expected of professionals. They may so thoroughly identify with the interests of their clients that they lose perspective. Paralegals working for such attorneys may get caught up in the same fever, particularly if there is a close attorney-paralegal working relationship on a high-stakes case that has lasted a considerable time. The momentum is to do whatever it takes to win. While this atmosphere can be exhilarating, it can also create an environment where less and less attention is paid to the niceties of ethics.

7. SAFEKEEPING PROPERTY

An attorney shall hold client property separate from the attorney's own property. Model Rule 1.15

A law office often receives client funds or funds of others connected with the client's case—for example, attorneys receive money in settlement of a case, or as trustees or escrow agents. Such funds should be held in separate accounts, with complete records kept on each. The attorney should not **commingle** (i.e., mix) law firm funds with client funds. It is unethical to place everything in one account. This is so even if the firm maintains accurate records on what amounts in the single account belong to which clients and what amounts belong to the firm. In a commingled account, the danger is too great that client funds will be used for nonclient purposes.

It is also improper for an office to misuse funds on retainer. Clients sometimes deposit funds with an office to cover future fees and expenses. The office should not draw on these fees before they are earned or use the funds for expenses not yet incurred. This is so even if the funds were never commingled when deposited by the client.

Paralegal Perspective:

● Use great care whenever your responsibility involves client funds, such as receiving funds from clients, opening bank accounts, depositing funds in the proper account at a bank, and making entries in law firm records on such funds. It should be fairly obvious to you whether an attorney is violating the rule on commingling funds. It may be less clear whether the attorney is improperly using client funds for unauthorized purposes. Attorneys have been known to "borrow" money from client accounts and then return the money before anyone discovers what was done. They might pay the account interest while using the money. Elaborate bookkeeping and accounting gimmicks might be used to disguise what is going on. Such conduct is unethical even if the attorney pays interest and eventually returns all the funds. In addition, the attorney may eventually be charged with theft or criminal fraud. Of course, anyone who knowingly assists the attorney could be subject to the same consequences.

8. FALSE STATEMENTS AND FAILURE TO DISCLOSE

An attorney shall not knowingly:
(1) make a false statement of material fact or law to a tribunal,
(2) fail to disclose a material fact to a tribunal when disclosure is necessary to avoid assisting a client commit a criminal or fraudulent act,
(3) fail to tell a tribunal about laws or other authority directly against the position of the attorney's client if this law or authority is not disclosed by opposing counsel, or
(4) offer evidence that the attorney knows is false. Model Rule 3.3(a)

One of the reasons the general public holds the legal profession in low esteem is the perception that attorneys seldom comply with the above rules. Our adversarial system does not always encourage the participants to cooperate in court proceedings. In fact, quite the opposite is often true. In extreme cases, attorneys have been known to lie to the court, to offer knowingly false evidence, etc. Under Model Rule 3.3(a), such conduct is unethical.

Subsection (3) of Model Rule 3.3(a) is particularly startling.

Example: Karen Singer and Bill Carew are attorneys who are opposing each other in a bitter trial involving a large sum of money. Singer is smarter than Carew. Singer knows about a very damaging but obscure case that goes against her client. But because of sloppy research, Carew does not know about it. Singer never mentions the case, and it never comes up during the trial.

It is certainly understandable why Singer does not want to say anything about the case. She does not want to help her opponent. But she must pay a price for her silence. She is subject to sanctions for a violation of her ethical obligation of disclosure under Model Rule 3.3(a)(3).

Another controversial part of Model Rule 3.3(a) is subsection (2) requiring disclosures that involve criminal or fraudulent acts. Since this raises issues of confidentiality, we will discuss such disclosures later when we cover confidentiality.

Paralegal Perspective:

- Be aware that an attorney who justifies the use of deception in one case will probably repeat such deceptions in the future on other cases. To excuse the deception, the attorney will often refer to the necessity of protecting the client or to the alleged evilness of the other side. Deceptions are unethical despite such justifications. (See the tenth "commandment" in Exhibit 5.1.)
- Chances are also good that employees of such an attorney will be pressured into participating in deception—for example, give a false date to a court clerk, help a client lie (commit perjury) on the witness stand, help an attorney alter a document to be introduced into evidence, or improperly notarize a document.
- Do not compromise your integrity no matter how much you believe in the cause of the client, no matter how much you detest the tactics of the opposing side, no matter

how much you like the attorney for whom you work, and no matter how important this job is to you.

9. WITHDRAWAL

An attorney must withdraw from a case: if continuing would result in a violation of ethical rules or other laws, if the client discharges the attorney, or if the attorney's physical or mental condition materially impairs his or her ability to represent the client. Model Rule 1.16(a)

Attorneys are not required to take every case. Furthermore, once they begin a case, they are not obligated to stay with the client until the case is over. If, however, the case has already begun in court after the attorney has filed a notice of appearance, **withdrawal** is usually improper without the permission of the court.

In some circumstances, an attorney *must* withdraw from a case that has begun:

- Representation of the client would violate ethical rules—for example, the attorney discovers that he or she has a conflict of interest with the client that cannot be **cured** (i.e., corrected or overcome) even with the consent of the client.
- Representation of the client would violate the law—for example, the client insists that the attorney provide advice on how to defraud the Internal Revenue Service.
- The client fires the attorney. An attorney is an agent of the client. Clients are always free to dismiss their agents.
- The attorney's physical or mental health has deteriorated to the point where the attorney's ability to represent the client has been materially impaired. This may be due to alcohol or drug abuse, marital problems, etc.

These are examples of when the attorney *must* withdraw from the case. There may be other circumstances that do not require withdrawal, but are serious enough to give the attorney the option of withdrawing without being charged with unethically walking away from the client. This option exists, for example, if the client insists on an objective that the attorney considers repugnant (such as pursuing litigation solely to harass someone) or imprudent (such as refiling a motion the attorney feels is an obvious waste of time and likely to incur the anger of the court). Model Rule 1.16(b)(3).

Once an attorney withdraws, it is important that he or she send the client a **disengagement letter** (also called a **declination letter**). It formally notifies the client that the attorney will no longer be representing the client. The letter confirms the termination of the attorney-client relationship. It should provide the reason for the withdrawal, a summary of the scope of the representation that was attempted, and a statement of the disposition of funds, if any, remaining in the client's account.[24]

Paralegal Perspective:

- When you have a close working relationship with an attorney, particularly in a small law office, you become aware of his or her professional strengths and personal weaknesses. Bar associations around the country are becoming increasingly concerned about the **impaired attorney**, someone who's not functioning properly due to substance abuse or similar problems. A paralegal with such an attorney for a supervisor is obviously in a predicament. Seemingly small problems have the potential of turn-

---

[24]If the attorney decides *not* to represent someone, the attorney should send a **letter of nonengagement**, which explicitly tells a prospective client that the attorney will not be representing him or her.

ing into a crisis. If it is not practical to discuss the situation directly with the attorney involved, you need to seek the advice of others in the firm.

10. CONFIDENTIALITY OF INFORMATION

An attorney must not reveal information relating to the representation of a client unless (a) the client consents to the disclosure or (b) the attorney reasonably believes the disclosure is necessary to prevent a client from committing a criminal act that is likely to result in imminent death or substantial bodily harm. Model Rule 1.6

Information is confidential if others do not have a right to receive it. When access to information is restricted in this way, the information is considered **privileged.** While our primary focus in this section is on the ethical dimensions of confidentiality, we also need to examine confidentiality in the related contexts of the attorney-client privilege and the attorney work-product rule.

Ethics and Confidentiality

The ethical obligation to maintain **confidentiality** applies to all or almost all information that relates to the representation of a client, whatever its source. A recent court said, "virtually any information relating to a case should be considered confidential . . . even unprivileged client information." *Phoenix Founders, Inc. v. Marshall,* 887 S.W.2d 831, 834 (Tex. 1994). Note also that the obligation is broader than so-called secrets or matters explicitly communicated in confidence. Confidentiality has been breached in each of the following examples:

At a party, an attorney tells an acquaintance from another town that the law firm is representing Jacob Anderson, whose employer is trying to force him to retire.

At a bar association conference, an attorney tells an old law school classmate that a client named Brenda Steck is considering a suit against her brother over the ownership of property left by their deceased mother.

A legal secretary carelessly leaves a client's file open on his desk where a stranger (e.g., another client) can read parts of it.

The rule on confidentiality is designed to encourage clients to discuss their case fully and frankly with their attorney, including embarrassing and legally damaging information. Arguably, a client would be reluctant to be open with an attorney if he or she had to worry about whether the attorney might reveal the information to others. The rule on confidentiality makes it unethical for attorneys to do so.

Of course, a client can always **consent** to an attorney's disclosure about the client—*if* the client is properly consulted about the proposed disclosure in advance. Furthermore, sometimes the client implicitly authorizes disclosures because of the nature of his or her case. In a dispute over alimony, for example, the attorney would obviously have to disclose certain financial information about the client to a court or to opposing counsel during the settlement negotiations.

Disclosure can also be ethically permissible in cases involving future criminal conduct.

Example: An attorney represents a husband in a bitter divorce action against his wife. During a meeting at the law firm, the husband shows the attorney a gun and says he is going to use it to kill his wife later the same day.

Can the attorney tell the police what the husband said? Yes. It is not unethical for an attorney to reveal information about a crime if the attorney reasonably believes that disclosure is necessary to prevent the client from committing a criminal act that could lead to someone's imminent death or substantial bodily harm.

Finally, some disclosures can be proper in suits between attorney and client. Suppose, for example, the attorney later sues the client for nonpayment of a fee, or the client sues the attorney for malpractice. In such proceedings, an attorney can reveal information about the client if the attorney reasonably believes disclosure is necessary to present a claim against the client or to defend against the client's claim.

Attorney-Client Privilege

The **attorney-client privilege rule** serves a similar function as the ethical rule on confidentiality. The two doctrines overlap. The attorney-client privilege is an *evidentiary* rule that applies to judicial and other proceedings in which an attorney may be called as a witness or otherwise required to produce evidence concerning a client. Under the attorney-client privilege, the attorney can refuse to disclose communications with his or her client if the purpose of the communication was to facilitate the provision of legal services for the client. The privilege also applies to paralegals and other employees of an attorney with respect to the same kind of communication—those whose purpose was to facilitate legal services.

Who May Not Testify without Consent
Colorado Revised Statutes § 13-90-107 (1)(b) (1996)

An attorney shall not be examined without the consent of his client as to any communication made by the client to him or [as to] his advice given thereon in the course of professional employment; nor shall an attorney's secretary, paralegal, legal assistant, stenographer, or clerk be examined without the consent of his employer concerning any fact, the knowledge of which he has acquired in such capacity.

The *ethical* rule on confidentiality tells us when sanctions can be imposed on attorneys when they (or their employees) disclose confidential client information to anyone outside the law office. The *attorney-client privilege* tells us when attorneys (or their employees) can refuse to answers questions pertaining to confidential client information.

Attorney Work-Product Rule

Suppose that, while working on a client's case, an attorney prepares a memorandum or other in-house document that does *not* contain any confidential communications. The memorandum or document, therefore, is *not* protected by the attorney-client privilege. Can the other side force the attorney to provide a copy of the memorandum or document? Are they **discoverable,** meaning that an opposing party can obtain information about it during discovery at the pretrial stage of a lawsuit? This question leads us to the **attorney work-product rule.**

Under this rule, the *work product* of an attorney is considered confidential. Work product consists of any notes, working papers, memoranda, or similar documents and tangible things prepared by the attorney in anticipation of litigation. An example is an attorney's interoffice memorandum that lays out his or her strategy in litigating a case. Attorneys do not have to disclose their work product to the other side. It is not discoverable.[25] To the extent that such documents are not discoverable, they are privileged. (The work-product rule is sometimes referred to as the work-product privilege.)

Inadvertent Disclosure of Confidential Material

The great fear of law office personnel is that the wrong person will obtain material that should be protected by ethics, by the attorney-client privilege, or by the work-product rule. This can have devastating consequences. For example, if a stranger overhears a confidential communication by a client to the attorney or to the attorney's paralegal, a court might rule that the attorney-client privilege has been waived. At a recent paralegal conference, a speaker told a stunned audience that a paralegal in her firm accidentally "faxed" a strategy memo on a current case to the opposing attorney! The paralegal punched in the wrong phone number on the fax machine!

Paralegal Perspective:

- Attorneys must instruct their paralegals and other nonattorney assistants on the obligation not to disclose information relating to the representation of a client. "It is the responsibility of a lawyer to take reasonable measures to ensure that all client confidences are preserved by a legal assistant."[26] When you are hired, the firm may ask you to sign a formal **confidentiality agreement** in which you promise not to divulge client information to anyone who is not working on the client's case. The agreement is simply a device to stress the importance of confidentiality. You, of course, are bound to maintain confidentiality even if your employer does not ask you to sign such an agreement.

- As we shall see later, the two major national paralegal associations also stress the ethical obligation of confidentiality in their own ethical codes (see Exhibit 5.5):
  - "A legal assistant must protect the confidences of a client and must not violate any rule or statute now in effect or hereafter enacted controlling the doctrine of privileged communications between a client and an attorney." Canon VII. National Association of Legal Assistants, *Code of Ethics and Professional Responsibility.*
  - "A paralegal shall preserve all confidential information provided by the client or acquired from other sources before, during, and after the course of the professional relationship." " 'Confidential information' denotes information relating to a client, whatever its source, which is not public knowledge nor available to the public." Canon 5. National Federation of Paralegal Associations, *Model Code of Ethics and Professional Responsibility.*

- Paralegals face *many* temptations to violate confidentiality. For example, a paralegal inadvertently reveals confidential information:
  - while networking with other paralegals at a paralegal association meeting;
  - during animated conversation with another paralegal at a restaurant or on an elevator;
  - after returning home from work during casual discussions with a relative, spouse, or roommate about interesting cases at the office.

  Some paralegals make the mistake of thinking that the rule applies only to damaging or embarrassing information or that the rule simply means you should not reveal things to the other side in the dispute. Not so. The rule is much broader. Virtually all

---

[25]An exception exists if the "party seeking discovery has substantial need of the materials in the preparation of his case" and is unable to obtain them without undue hardship by other means. This test is rarely met. Federal Rule of Civil Procedure 26(b)(3).

[26]ABA *Model Guidelines,* Guideline 6. See footnote 5.

information relating to the representation of a client must not be revealed to *anyone* who is not working on the case in the office.

- In Missouri, the obligation of silence is even broader. The paralegal must not disclose information—"confidential or otherwise"—relating to the representation of the client.[27] In Texas, confidential information includes both privileged information and unprivileged client information. An attorney must "instruct the legal assistant that all information concerning representation of a client (indeed even the fact of representation, if not a matter of public record) must be kept strictly confidential."[28] In Philadelphia, paralegals are warned that it is "not always easy to recognize what information about your firm's clients or office is confidential. Moreover, a client of your office might be offended to learn that a . . . firm employee has discussed the client's business in public, even if the information mentioned is public knowledge. The easiest rule is to consider *all* work of the office to be confidential: do not discuss the business of your office or your firm's clients with any outsider, no matter how close a friend, at any time, unless you are specifically authorized by a lawyer to do so."[29] Under guidelines such as these, there is very little that paralegals can tell someone about their work!

- During the war, sailors were told that "loose lips sink ships." The same applies to law firms. One law firm makes the following statement to all its paralegals, "Throughout your employment, you will have access to information that must at all times be held in strictest confidence. Even the seemingly insignificant fact that the firm is involved in a particular matter falls within the orbit of confidential information. Unless you have attorney permission, do not disclose documents or contents of documents to anyone, including firm employees who do not need this information to do their work."[30]

- If you attend a meeting on a case outside the law office, ask your supervisor whether you should take notes or prepare a follow-up memorandum on the meeting. Let the supervisor decide whether your notes or the memo might be discoverable.[31]

- Be *very* careful when you talk with clients in the presence of third persons. Overheard conversations might constitute a waiver of the attorney-client privilege. Cellular phones can sometimes cause problems. The signal in mobile communications is transmitted by frequency over airwaves. Therefore, outsiders can listen to conversations with relative ease. If you are on a cellular phone with a client, warn him or her that confidential information should not be discussed.[32]

- Do not listen to messages on a phone answering machine when others in the room can hear the messages as well. Clients often leave messages that contain confidential information. When using speaker phones, intercoms, or paging systems, don't broadcast confidential information. Assume that many people will be hearing you on these public systems and that most of them are not entitled to hear what you are saying.

- Make sure your door is closed when discussing a client's case.

---

[27]*Guidelines for Practicing with Paralegals,* Missouri Bar Ass'n (1987).

[28]State Bar of Texas, *General Guidelines for the Utilization of the Services of Legal Assistants by Attorneys* (1981). Rule 1.01, Texas Disciplinary Rules of Professional Conduct (1990).

[29]*Professional Responsibility for Nonlawyers,* Professional Responsibility Committee of the Philadelphia Bar Ass'n (1989) (emphasis added).

[30]*Orientation Handbook for Paralegals* 2 (Lane, Powell, Moses & Miller, 1984).

[31]Daniels, *Privileged Information for Paralegals,* 17 At Issue 15 (San Francisco Ass'n of Legal Assistants, November 1990).

[32]Betty Reinert, *Cyberspacing Around Cowtown,* 13 Cowtown Paralegal Reporter 10 (March/April 1995).

- When working on your computer, try to position the monitor so that others cannot read the screen, especially when you need to leave your desk. Some computers have a program that automatically makes the screen go dark after a designated period of time when there is no typing. The screen then reappears when you continue typing. Find out if your office can have this program installed on your computer.
- Use a shredding machine when throwing away papers containing confidential information.
- Use a stamp marked *privileged* on protected documents.
- During a job interview, do not use writing samples that contain confidential information, such as the position of a particular client at a law office where you worked or volunteered in the past. Before using such samples, obtain the consent of your former supervisor. If the interviewer asks you about cases you worked on, don't reveal anything confidential. Your lack of professionalism in carelessly referring to confidential information during the interview will probably destroy your chances of getting the job. What about the identity of clients you worked for in prior jobs? As we will see later, prospective employers *will* need this information. It will help them determine whether hiring you could disqualify the office from representing a particular client because your prior work presents a conflict of interest as to that client.

11. CONFLICT OF INTEREST

An attorney should avoid a conflict of interest with his or her client.

Three words strike dread into the heart of a practicing attorney: **conflict of interest.** Why? Because if it exists, it can lead to the disqualification of the attorney (and his or her entire law firm) from representing the particular client with whom the conflict exists— even if the attorney is in the middle of the representation of this client! A conflict of interest means serving two masters. More precisely:

> Conflict of interest is the presence of divided loyalty that actually or potentially places a person at a disadvantage even though this person is owed undivided loyalty.

Note that the conflict does not have to lead to actual harm; all that is needed is the *potential* for harm or disadvantage.

Conflicts of interest are not limited to law. They can exist in many settings:

> Example: Bill Davenport is a salesman who does part-time work selling the same type of product manufactured by two competing companies.

Davenport has a conflict of interest. How can he serve two masters with the same loyalty? Normally, a company expects the undivided loyalty of people who work for it. How can Davenport apportion his customers between the two companies? There is an obvious danger that he will favor one over the other. The fact that he may try to be fair in his treatment of both companies does not eliminate the conflict of interest. A *potential* certainly exists that one of the companies will be disadvantaged. It may be that both companies are aware of the problem and are not worried. This does not mean that there is no conflict of interest; it simply means that the affected parties have consented to take the risks involved in the conflict.

Let's look at another example of how widespread these conflicts can be:

> Example: Frank Jones is the head of the personnel department of a large company. Ten people apply for a job, one of whom is Frank's cousin.

Frank has a conflict of interest. He has loyalty to his company (pressuring him to hire the best person for the job) and a loyalty to his cousin (pressuring him to help a relative). There is a potential that the company will be disadvantaged, since Frank's cousin may not be the best qualified for the job. The conflict exists even if the cousin *is* the best qualified, and even if Frank does *not* hire his cousin for the job, and even if the company *knows* about the relationship but still wants Frank to make the hiring decision. For conflict of interest to exist, all you need is the potential for disadvantage due to *divided loyalties;* you do not have to show that harm or disadvantage actually resulted.

In legal settings, conflict of interest is a major concern. To understand why, we need to examine the following topics:

(a) Business transactions with a client
(b) Loans to a client
(c) Gifts from a client
(d) Sex with a client
(e) Personal bias
(f) Multiple representation
(g) Former client/present adversary
(h) Law firm disqualification
(i) Switching jobs and "the Chinese wall"
(j) Conflicts checks

As we examine each of these topics, one of our central concerns will be whether the independence of the attorney's professional judgment is compromised in any way because of conflicting interests.

(a) Business Transactions with a Client

Attorneys sell professional legal advice and representation. When they go beyond such services and enter a business transaction with the client, a conflict of interest can arise.

> Example: Janet Bruno, Esq. is Len Oliver's attorney. Oliver owns an auto repair business for which Bruno has done legal work. Oliver sells Bruno a 30 percent interest in the repair business. Bruno continues as Oliver's attorney.

Serious conflict-of-interest problems may exist here. Assume that the business runs into difficulties and Oliver considers bankruptcy. He goes to Bruno for legal advice on bankruptcy law. Bruno has dual concerns: to give Oliver competent legal advice and to protect *her own* 30 percent interest in the business. Bankruptcy may be good for Oliver but disastrous for Bruno's investment. How can an attorney give a client independent professional advice when the advice may go against the attorney's own interest? Bruno's concern for her investment creates the potential that Oliver will be placed at a disadvantage. Divided loyalties exist.

This is not to say, however, that it is always unethical for an attorney to enter a business transaction with a client. If certain strict conditions are met, it can be proper.

> *An attorney shall not enter a business transaction with a client, unless:*
> *(i) the terms of the business transaction are fair and reasonable to the client and are fully disclosed to the client in understandable language in writing, and*
> *(ii) the client is given reasonable opportunity to seek advice on the transaction from another attorney who is not involved with the transaction or the parties, and*
> *(iii) the client consents to the business transaction in writing.* Model Rule 1.8(a)

In our example, Oliver must be given the chance to consult with an attorney other than Bruno on letting Bruno buy a 30 percent interest in the business. Bruno would have to give Oliver a clear, written explanation of their business relationship. And the relationship must be fair and reasonable to Oliver.

(b) Loans to a Client

An attorney, like all service providers, wants to be paid. Often a client does not have the resources to pay until *after* the case is over.

Example: Harry Maxell, Esq. is Bob Smith's attorney in a negligence action in which Smith is seeking damages for serious injuries caused by the defendant. Since the accident, Smith has been out of work and on welfare. While the case is pending, Maxell agrees to lend Smith living expenses and court-filing fees.

A debtor-creditor relationship now exists between Smith and Maxell in addition to their attorney-client relationship. The loan covering *living expenses* creates a conflict of interest. Suppose that the defendant in the negligence case makes an offer to settle the case with Smith. Should he accept the offer? There is a danger that Maxell's advice on this will be colored by the fact that he has a financial interest in Smith—he wants to have his loan repaid. The amount of the offer to settle may not be enough to cover the loan. Should he advise Smith to accept the offer? Accepting the offer may be in Smith's interest but not in Maxell's own interest. Such divided loyalty is an unethical conflict of interest. Model Rule 1.8(e).

The loan covering *litigation expenses,* such as filing fees and other court costs, is treated differently. Such loans can be ethical. In our example, Maxell's loan to cover the cost of the filing fees is proper.

(c) Gifts from a Client

Clients sometimes make gifts to their attorneys or to the spouse or relative of their attorneys. Such gifts rarely create ethical problems except when a document must be prepared to complete the gift.

Example: William Stanton, Esq. has been the family attorney of the Tarkinton family for years. At Christmas, Mrs. Tarkinton gives Stanton a television set and tells him to change her will so that Stanton's ten-year-old daughter would receive funds for a free college education.

If a document is needed to carry out the gift, it is unethical for the attorney to prepare that document. Its preparation would create a conflict of interest. In our example, the gift of money for college involves a document—Mrs. Tarkinton's will. Note the conflict. It would be in Mrs. Tarkinton's interest to have the will written so that the executor of her will retained considerable flexibility when questions arise on how much to pay for the college education. (For example, is there to be a maximum amount? Is room and board included?) And flexibility is needed on the effect of contingencies, such as a delay or an interruption in going to college. (What happens if the daughter does not go to college until after she marries and raises her own children?) Other questions could arise as well. Stanton, of course, would want the will drafted so that his daughter received the most money possible; he does not want any contingencies in the will that might threaten receipt of the funds. It is in his interest to prepare the will so that Mrs. Tarkinton's executor has very little flexibility.

Because of this conflict, an attorney cannot prepare a document such as a will, trust, or contract that results in any substantial gift from a client to the attorney or to the attorney's children, spouse, parents, or siblings. If a client wants to make such a gift, *another* attorney must prepare the document.[33] There is, however, one exception. If the client-

---

[33]This other attorney should not be a member of the same law firm. Later we will discuss the related topic of imputed disqualification.

donor is *related* to the person receiving the gift, the attorney can prepare the document. Model Rule 1.8(c).

There does not appear to be any ethical problem in taking the gift of the television set from Mrs. Tarkinton. No documents are involved.

Paralegal Perspective:

- Can a paralegal accept a gift from a client, e.g., a Christmas present, a trip, or other bonus from a client who just won a big judgment? First of all, never consider accepting gifts from clients unless your supervising attorney approves. Considerations of which you are unaware may make the gift inappropriate. Suppose, however, it is approved, but the gift involves the preparation of a document, which the attorney prepares. Though technically not the same as the attorney preparing the document for a gift to his or her spouse or children, the similarities certainly create an appearance of impropriety. The attorney will probably want to prepare the document to achieve the maximum advantage for his or her employee. This may not be in the best interest of the client—the giver of the gift.

(d) Sex with a Client

One of the more dramatic examples of a conflict of interest is the attorney who develops a romantic relationship with a current client, particularly a sexual relationship. Clients often come to an attorney when they are most vulnerable. Under such circumstances, it is unconscionable for the attorney to take advantage of this vulnerability. An attorney with a physical or emotional interest in a client will be looking for ways to increase that interest and to inspire a reciprocal interest from the client. Needless to say, this may not be what the client needs. But the attorney's own need could well cloud his or her ability to put the client's welfare first. The only way to maintain professional independence is for attorneys—and their paralegals and other employees as well—to avoid these kinds of relationships with current clients. When the case is over and they cease being clients, such relationships are less likely to constitute a conflict of interest.

Only a few states, however, specifically mention this subject in their code of ethics. Bar associations have been very reluctant to recommend a total ban on sex with current clients. In Florida, for example, there is a prohibition only if it can be shown that the sexual conduct "exploits the lawyer-client relationship." Rule 4-8.4.

(e) Personal Bias

Do you think the attorneys in the following cases have a conflict of interest?

- A homosexual attorney represents a parent seeking to deny custody to the other parent because the latter is gay.
- An attorney, who believes abortion is immoral, works on a case where the client is Planned Parenthood.
- An attorney, whose father was murdered ten years ago, represents a client charged with murdering his wife.
- An attorney, who is opposed to the death penalty, is the prosecutor on a case where the state has asked for the death penalty.

These attorneys have a **bias,** which is a predisposition to think and perhaps to act in a certain way. It is a prejudice. The opposite of bias is objectivity or **disinterestedness.**

In our adversarial system, as indicated earlier, clients are entitled to vigorous representation within the bounds of law and ethics. If an attorney or paralegal has strong personal feelings that go against what a client is trying to accomplish, there is a likelihood—not a guarantee—that the feelings will interfere with the ability to provide that representation. If there is interference, it is unethical to continue. (We will return to the topic of bias in chapter 8 on interviewing.)

(f) Multiple Representation

Rarely can a client receive independent professional counsel and vigorous representation in a case of **multiple representation** (also referred to as **common representation**), where the same attorney represents both sides in a dispute.

> Example: Tom and Henry have an automobile accident. Tom wants to sue Henry for negligence. Both Tom and Henry ask Mary Franklin, Esq. to represent them in the dispute.

Franklin has a conflict of interest. How can she give her undivided loyalty to both sides? Tom needs to prove that Henry was negligent; Henry needs to prove that he was not negligent, and perhaps that Tom was negligent himself. How can Franklin vigorously argue that Henry was negligent and at the same time vigorously argue that Henry was not negligent? How can she act independently for two different people who are at odds with each other? Since Tom and Henry have **adverse interests,** she cannot give each her independent professional judgment. (Adverse interests are simply opposing purposes or claims.) The difficulty is not solved by Franklin's commitment to be fair and objective in giving her advice to the parties. Her role as attorney is to be a partisan advocate for the client. It is impossible for Franklin to play this role for two clients engaged in a dispute where they have adverse interests. An obvious conflict of interest would exist. In *every* state, it would be unethical for Franklin to represent Tom and Henry in this case.

Furthermore, client consent would *not* be a defense to the charge of unethical conduct. Even if Tom and Henry agree to allow Franklin to represent both of them, it would be unethical for her to do so. The presence of adverse interests between the parties makes it unethical for an attorney to represent both sides with or without their consent.

Suppose, however, that the two sides do *not* have adverse interests. Certain cases must go before a court even though the parties are in agreement about everything.

> Example: Jim and Mary Smith are separated, and both want a divorce. They have been married only a few months. There are no children and no marital assets to divide. George Davidson, Esq. is an attorney that Jim and Mary know and trust. They decide to ask Davidson to represent both of them in the divorce.

Can Davidson ethically represent both sides here? A few states *will* allow him to do so, on the theory that there is not much of a conflict between the parties. Jim and Mary want the divorce, there is no custody battle, and there is no property to fight over. All they need is a court to decree that their marriage is legally over. Hence the potential for harm caused by multiple representation in such a case is almost nonexistent. Other states, however, disagree. They frown on multiple representation in so-called "friendly divorces" of this kind.

There is no absolute ban on all multiple representation in the Model Rules, although such representation is certainly discouraged:

> *An attorney shall not represent a client if the representation of that client will be directly adverse to another client, unless*
> *(i) the attorney reasonably believes the representation will not adversely affect the relationship with the other client, and*
> *(ii) both clients consent after consultation about the risks of the multiple representation.*
> Model Rule 1.7

In the Smith example, both conditions can probably be met. Such a divorce is little more than a paper procedure since there is no real dispute between the parties. Hence Davidson would be reasonable in believing that his representation of Jim would not adversely affect Mary, and vice versa. Davidson can represent both sides so long as Jim and Mary consent to the multiple representation after Davidson explains what risks might be involved.

Nevertheless, attorneys are urged *not* to engage in multiple representation even if it is ethically proper to do so under the standards listed above. The case may have been "friendly" at the outset, but years later, when everything turns sour, one of the parties inevitably attacks the attorney for having had a conflict of interest. Cautious attorneys *always* avoid multiple representation.

(g) Former Client/Present Adversary

As indicated earlier, clients are encouraged to be very open with their attorney since the latter needs to know favorable and unfavorable information about the client in order to evaluate the legal implications of the case. The more trust that exists between them, the more frank the client will usually be. Assume that such a relationship exists and that the case is eventually resolved. Months later, another legal dispute arises between the same parties, but this time the attorney represents the other side!

Example: Helen Kline, Esq. represented Paul Andrews in his breach-of-contract suit against Richard Morelli, a truck distributor. Andrews claimed that Morelli failed to deliver five trucks that Andrews ordered. A court ruled in favor of Morelli. Now, a year later, Andrews wants to sue Morelli for slander. After accidentally meeting at a conference, they started discussing the truck suit. Morelli allegedly called Andrews a liar and a thief. In the slander suit, Andrews hires Michael Manna, Esq. to represent him. Morelli hires Helen Kline, Esq.

A former client is now an adversary. Kline once represented Andrews; she is now representing a client (Morelli) who is an adversary of Andrews. Without the consent of the former client (Andrews), it is unethical for Kline to switch sides and represent Morelli against him. Model Rule 1.9(a). Consent is needed *when the second case is the same as the first one or when the two are substantially related.* The slander suit is substantially related to the breach-of-contract suit, since they both grew out of the original truck incident.

If the cases are the same or are substantially related, the likelihood is strong that the attorney will use information learned in the first case to the detriment of the former client in the second case. Kline undoubtedly found out a good deal about Andrews when she represented him in the breach-of-contract case. She would now be in a position to use that information *against* him while representing Morelli in the slander case.

Kline had a **duty of loyalty** when she represented Andrews. This duty does not end once the case is over and the attorney fees are paid. The duty continues if the same case arises again or if a substantially related case arises later—even if the attorney no longer represents the client. A conflict of interest exists when Kline subsequently acquires a new client who goes against Andrews in the same case or in a substantially related case. This, of course, is what happened in our example. Her duty of undivided loyalty to the second client would clash with her *continuing* duty of undivided loyalty to the former client in the original case.

Suppose, however, that an attorney *can* take the second case against a former client because the second case is totally unrelated to the first. There is still an ethical obligation to refrain from using any information relating to the representation in the first case to the disadvantage of the former client in the second case. There is no ethical ban on taking the case, but if the office has any information relating to the first case, that information cannot be used against the former client in the second case. While this duty might exist, it is not easy to enforce. Think of how difficult it might be to prove that the attorney in the second case used information obtained solely from the first case.

(h) Law Firm Disqualification

If an attorney is disqualified from representing a client because of a conflict of interest, every attorney in the *same law firm* is also disqualified unless the client being protected by this rule consents to the representation.

> Example: Two years ago, John Farrell, Esq. of the law firm of Smith & Smith represented the stepfather in a custody dispute with the child's grandmother. The stepfather won the case, but the grandmother was awarded limited visitation rights. The grandmother now wants to sue the stepfather for failure to abide by the visitation order. John Farrell no longer represents the stepfather. The grandmother asks John Farrell to represent her. He declines because of a conflict of interest, but sends her to his law partner, Diane Williams, Esq., down the corridor at Smith & Smith.

The *stepfather* would have to consent to the representation of the grandmother by Williams. There would certainly be a conflict of interest if John Farrell tried to represent the grandmother against the stepfather. The custody dispute and the visitation dispute are substantially related. Once one attorney in a firm is disqualified because of a conflict of interest, every other attorney in that firm is also disqualified. This is known as **imputed disqualification** or **vicarious disqualification.** The entire firm is treated as one attorney. The disqualification of any one **tainted** attorney in the office contaminates the entire firm. Farrell's partner (Williams) is disqualified because Farrell, the tainted attorney, would be disqualified. Model Rule 1.10. Someone is tainted (also called **infected**) if he or she brings a conflict of interest to a law office, which thereby becomes **contaminated.**

(i) Switching Jobs and "the Chinese Wall"

Finally, we need to consider the conflict-of-interest problems that can arise from changing jobs. We just saw that there can be an imputed disqualification of an entire law firm because one of the attorneys in the firm has a conflict of interest with a client. If that attorney now goes to work for a *new* firm, can there be an imputed disqualification of the new firm because of the same conflict of interest?

> Example: Kevin Carlson, Esq. works at Darby & Darby. He represents Ajax, Inc. in its contract suit against World Systems, Inc. The latter is represented by Polk, Young & West. Carlson quits his job at Darby & Darby and takes a job at Polk, Young & West.

While Carlson was at Darby & Darby, he obviously acquired confidential information about Ajax. Clearly, he cannot now represent World Systems in the contract litigation against Ajax. Blatant side-switching of this kind is highly unethical. But what about other attorneys at Polk, Young & West? Is the *entire* firm contaminated and hence disqualified from continuing to represent World Systems because of the hiring of Carlson? If other attorneys at Polk, Young & West are allowed to continue representing World Systems against Ajax, there would be pressures on Carlson to tell these attorneys what he knows about Ajax. Must Polk, Young & West, therefore, withdraw from the case?

The same question can be asked about **tainted paralegals** and other nonattorney employees who switch jobs:

> Example: Ted Warren is a paralegal who works for Mary Winter, Esq. Winter represents Apple, Inc., in the case of *Apple, Inc. v. IBM, Inc.* Ted has substantial paralegal responsibilities

on this case. While the case is still going on, Ted switches jobs. He goes to work for Quinton & Oran, which represents IBM in the litigation with Apple.

Ted is tainted. He brings a conflict of interest to the firm of Quinton & Oran. While Ted worked for Mary Winter, he obviously acquired confidential information about Apple. There are pressures on him to tell the attorneys at Quinton & Oran what he knows about Apple so that they can use the information to the advantage of their client, IBM, in the litigation against Apple. Is the entire firm of Quinton & Oran, therefore, contaminated so that it must now withdraw from the case?

There are two main ways that contaminated law offices *try* to avoid imputed disqualification due to tainted attorneys or tainted paralegals whose job switching creates a conflict of interest: consent and screening.

Consent   The cleanest way a contaminated law office can avoid imputed disqualification is to try to obtain the consent of the party who has the most to lose—the party whose confidentiality is in jeopardy. In most cases, the consent of this person will avoid disqualification.

In our example of the tainted attorney: Kevin Carlson, Esq. once represented Ajax at Darby & Darby in the litigation against World Systems. Carlson now works for Polk, Young & West, which represents World Systems. Ajax could be asked to consent to the continued representation of World Systems by Polk, Young & West even though Carlson now works for Polk, Young & West.

In our example of the tainted paralegal: Ted Warren once worked for the law office of Mary Winter, Esq. who represents Apple in the litigation against IBM. Warren now works for Quinton & Oran, which represents IBM. Apple could be asked to consent to the continued representation of IBM by Quinton & Oran even though Warren now works for Quinton & Oran.

It is unlikely that clients will give their consent in such situations. Their current attorney will probably advise them that the risks are too great that the tainted employee will share (or has already shared) confidential information with the new employer. This is true even if the new employer swears that no such information was shared and promises that it will screen the tainted employee (see discussion of the Chinese Wall below) from the ongoing litigation.

Screening   The contaminated law office will often try to avoid imputed disqualification by screening the tainted employee from the case in question. As we will see, however, it is not always successful. The screening is known as a **Chinese Wall** (sometimes called an **ethical wall** or a **cone of silence**) that is built around the tainted employee who brought the conflict of interest into the office. He or she becomes the **quarantined** employee. The components of the Chinese Wall are outlined in Exhibit 5.6.

We said that consent is a clear way to avoid imputed disqualification. What about screening? Can it avoid disqualification if consent cannot be obtained? In this discussion we are assuming that the tainted employee has not already communicated confidential information to the new employer. If this has happened, screening will not prevent disqualification. Hence, in our examples, if Kevin Carlson tells attorneys at Polk, Young & West anything significant he knows about Ajax, Inc., the Polk firm will be disqualified from continuing to represent World Systems, Inc. If Ted Warren tells attorneys at Quinton & Oran anything significant he knows about Apple, Inc., the Quinton firm will be disqualified from continuing to represent IBM, Inc. Screening will never prevent disqualification if the damage has already been done by improper disclosures from the tainted employee. The purpose of the screening is to *prevent* such disclosures.

Exhibit 5.6   Components of a Chinese Wall

The following are the most effective steps a law office can take to screen a tainted employee (e.g., attorney, paralegal, investigator, secretary) who brings a conflict of interest to the office. The goal is to avoid imputed disqualification by isolating the employee from the case in which he or she has the conflict of interest.

1. The screening begins as soon as the tainted employee arrives at the office.
2. The tainted employee signs a statement promising not to discuss what he or she knows about the case with anyone in the office.
3. Those working on the case in the office promise not to discuss it with, or in the presence of, the tainted employee.
4. There is a written policy notifying everyone in the office that the screening mechanisms are in place and that violations will result in sanctions.
5. If there are several attorneys working in the office, the tainted employee will not be assigned to work with the attorney handling the case in question.
6. Others not working on the case in the office are told that if they learn anything about the case, they must not discuss it with the tainted employee.
7. The tainted employee works in an area that is physically segregated from work on the case in the office. This area is designed to avoid inadvertent access to the case file.
8. The file in the case is locked in cabinets or other storage facilities so that the tainted employee will have no access to the file.
9. Colored labels or "flags" are placed on each document in the file to indicate it is off limits to the tainted employee. For example, a sticker might say, "ACCESS RESTRICTED."
10. If any office files are located on a central computer system to which everyone has access, either the file in question is removed and placed in a separate database to which the tainted employee does not have access and/or the tainted employee is not given the password that grants a user access to the restricted file in the central system.
11. The tainted employee will not directly earn any profit from, participate in the fees of, or obtain any other financial gain from the case.

Suppose that there have been no disclosures. The office discovers that one of its employees is tainted. It then offers to quarantine this employee by building a Chinese Wall around him or her. Will this prevent disqualification in the absence of consent? Not all states answer this question in the same way, and the answer may differ if the tainted employee is an attorney as opposed to a paralegal or other nonattorney.

Tainted Attorneys   In some states, a Chinese Wall will *not* avoid imputed disqualification. These states doubt that the tainted attorney will be able to resist the pressure to disclose what he or she knows in spite of the screening mechanisms of the wall. "Whether the screen is breached will be virtually impossible to ascertain from outside the firm."[34]

Other states, however, do not automatically impose the extreme sanction of disqualification. These states consider three main factors in deciding whether to disqualify. First,

---

[34]C. Wolfram, *Modern Legal Ethics* §7.6.4 (1986).

how soon did the office erect the wall around the tainted attorney? Courts like to see the wall in place at the outset of the employment transfer. They are more suspicious if the wall was not built until the other side (i.e., the former employer of the tainted attorney) raised the conflict-of-interest objection. Second, how effective was the wall in preventing the tainted attorney from having contact with the case at the new firm? Courts like to see comprehensive screening devices that are scrupulously enforced. (See Exhibit 5.6.) And third, how involved was the tainted attorney in the case while at the previous firm? If the involvement was relatively minor, the court is less likely to be concerned.

Tainted Paralegals   Courts are more sympathetic to tainted paralegals—so long as they have not actually revealed confidential information to their new employer and are effectively quarantined by a Chinese Wall. Here are some of the major developments in this area:

- In *Phoenix Founders, Inc. v. Marshall,* 887 S.W.2d 831 (Tex. 1994), a paralegal worked on a case at one firm and then switched jobs to work for opposing counsel on the same case. The court said that if a paralegal does any work on a case, there is a conclusive presumption that he or she obtained "confidences and secrets" about that case. There is also a presumption that the paralegal shared this information with her new firm, *but this presumption is not conclusive;* it can be rebutted by showing that the new firm took "sufficient precautions . . . to guard against any disclosure of confidences" through a Chinese Wall. At the new firm, "the newly-hired paralegal should be cautioned not to disclose any information relating to the representation of a client of the former employer. The paralegal should also be instructed not to work on any matter on which the paralegal worked during the prior employment, or regarding which the paralegal has information relating to the former employer's representation. Additionally, the firm should take other reasonable steps to ensure that the paralegal does not work in connection with matters on which the paralegal worked during the prior employment." In some circumstances, however, disqualification will always be required unless the former client consents to allow the paralegal to continue working at the new firm: "(1) when information relating to the representation of an adverse client has in fact been disclosed, or (2) when screening would be ineffective or the nonlawyer necessarily would be required to work on the other side of a matter that is the same as or substantially related to a matter on which the nonlawyer has previously worked. . . ." In effect, there will be disqualification if there is proof the paralegal made actual disclosures of confidential information to the new firm, or if there is little chance the screening of the Chinese Wall would be effective.[35]
- What's it like to work behind a Chinese Wall? Calling it a "deadly cone of silence," a Los Angeles paralegal recently described the experience of being quarantined this way: "I was a problem. . . . I was put behind an ethical wall, and could hardly walk anywhere in the firm without having to shut my eyes and ears or look the other direction."[36]

---

[35]The court said we need to determine "whether the practical effect of formal screening has been achieved." To make this determination, several factors should be considered. They include "the substantiality of the relationship between the matter on which the paralegal worked at the old firm and the matter she worked on at the new firm; the time elapsing between the matters; the size of the firm; the number of individuals presumed to have confidential information; the nature of their involvement in the former matter; and the timing and features of any measures taken to reduce the danger of disclosure." 887 S.W.2d at 836.
[36]Susan L. Order, *Beware of Deadly Cone of Silence,* 18 Precedents 25 (San Diego Ass'n of Legal Assistants, July/August 1994).

- Many paralegals change jobs frequently. The market for experienced paralegals is outstanding. Bar associations realize that an overly strict disqualification rule could severely hamper the job prospects for such paralegals. In *Informal Opinion 88-1526,* the American Bar Association said:

  > It is important that nonlawyer employees have as much mobility in employment opportunity as possible consistent with the protection of clients' interests. To so limit employment opportunities that some nonlawyers trained to work with law firms might be required to leave the careers for which they are trained would disserve clients as well as the legal profession. Accordingly, any restrictions on the nonlawyer's employment should be held to the minimum necessary to protect confidentiality of client information.

  While such statements are comforting, the reality is that tainted paralegals are in a very vulnerable position. Many contaminated offices *terminate* the tainted paralegal who caused the contamination. Rather than take the risk that a Chinese Wall built around this paralegal will be judged too little and too late, the office will take the safer course and let the paralegal go.

- In a recent dramatic case, a contaminated paralegal caused a San Francisco law firm to be disqualified from representing nine clients in asbestos litigation involving millions of dollars. The sole reason for the disqualification was that the firm hired a paralegal who had once worked for a law firm that represented the opponents in the asbestos litigation. Soon after the controversy arose, the disqualified firm laid off the tainted paralegal who brought this conflict to the firm. He was devastated when he found out that he was being let go. "I was flabbergasted, totally flabbergasted." He has not been able to find work since.[37] The case was widely reported throughout the legal community. A front-page story in the *Los Angeles Daily Journal* said that it "could force firms to conduct lengthy investigations of paralegals and other staffers before hiring them."[38]

- One law firm makes the following statement to all its paralegals, "If you or a temporary legal assistant working under your supervision were formerly employed by opposing counsel, this could be the basis for a motion to disqualify" this law firm. "So also could personal relationships such as kinship with the opposing party or attorney or dating an attorney from another firm. Make your attorney aware of such connections."[39]

- If you have worked (or volunteered) for an attorney in the past in *any* capacity (as a paralegal, as an investigator, as a secretary, etc.), you should make a list of all the clients and cases with which you were involved. When you apply for a new job, your list will be relevant to whether the law firm will be subject to disqualification if you are hired. You must be careful with the list, however. Do not attach it to your résumé and randomly send it around town! Until employment discussions have become serious, do not show it to the prospective employer. Furthermore, try to notify prior attorneys with whom you have worked that you are applying for a position at a law firm where its "conflicts check" on you must include knowing what cases you worked

---

[37]Motamedi, *Landmark Ethics Case Takes Toll on Paralegal's Career, Family,* 7 Legal Assistant Today 39 (May/June 1990). *In re Complex Asbestos Litigation,* 232 Cal. App. 3d 572, 283 Cal. Rptr. 732 (Cal. Ct. App. 1991).

[38]M. Hall, *S.F. Decision on Paralegal Conflict May Plague Firms,* 102 Los Angeles Daily Journal 1, col. 2 (September 25, 1989).

[39]Orientation Handbook for Paralegals 3 (Lane, Powell, Moses & Miller, 1984).

on with previous attorneys. Giving them this notice is not always practical and may not be required. Yet it is a safe procedure to follow whenever possible.

● Freelance paralegals who work for more than one law office on a part-time basis are particularly vulnerable to conflict-of-interest charges. For example, in a large litigation involving many parties, two opposing attorneys might unknowingly use the same freelance paralegal to work on different aspects of the same case, or might use two different employees of this freelance paralegal. Another example is the freelance paralegal who worked on an earlier case for a client and now works on a different but similar case in which that client is the opponent. The California Association of Freelance Paralegals has attempted to address this problem in Article 11 of its proposed Code of Ethics: "A freelance paralegal shall avoid conflicts of interest relating to client matters. The freelance paralegal shall not accept any case adverse to the client of {an attorney who hires the paralegal] if the latter case bears a substantial connection to the earlier one or if there is a possibility that the two cases are substantially related, regardless of whether confidences were in fact imparted to the freelance paralegal by the attorney or the attorney's client in the earlier case."[40] There are practical problems with such rules. It is not always easy to determine whether two cases are "adverse" or bear a "substantial connection" with each other. If there is doubt, it is in the economic self-interest of the freelance paralegal *not* to tell the attorney since he or she will most likely refuse to hire the paralegal rather than take the risk of later disqualification because of contamination injected into the case by this paralegal. Finally, conducting a conflicts check could be somewhat difficult for a busy, experienced freelance paralegal who has worked for scores of attorneys and hundreds of clients over the years. In spite of these practical problems, it has been held that attorneys can ethically use the services of independent paralegals. See *In re Opinion No. 24*, 128 N.J. 114, 607 A.2d 962 (1992). Adequate supervision is required, however. The attorney cannot simply turn over work and be available to answer questions. At a minimum, the attorney must make inquiries about the independent paralegal's prior client casework for other attorneys in order to determine whether there are any conflicts.

(j) Conflicts Checks

A prospective client walks in the door or someone makes a referral of a prospective client. How does the office determine whether any of its attorneys, paralegals, or other nonattorney employees have a conflict of interest with this prospect? A **conflicts check** must be undertaken. To perform this check, the office needs a comprehensive database containing information such as the following about every former and present client of the office:

● Names of clients (plus any aliases or earlier names before marriage)
● Names of spouses of clients
● Names of children of clients
● Names of key employees of clients (including the chief executive officers and directors of corporate clients)
● Names of major shareholders in companies in which the client has an interest
● Names of parent and subsidiary corporations affiliated with the client, plus their chief executive officers and directors
● Names of members of small associations the client controls or is a member of [41]

---

[40]California Ass'n of Freelance Paralegals, "CAFP's Proposed Code of Ethics," Article 11, *Freelancer* 9 (July/August 1991).
[41]David Vangagriff, *Computing Your Conflicts*, 10 The Compleat Lawyer 42 (Fall 1993).

It is often an arduous job to find and check this information to determine whether any possible conflict exists. Some offices have hired paralegals to go through the office's computer files to try to identify conflict problems that must be addressed by senior attorneys in the office. (These paralegals are sometimes called **conflict specialists.**) Unfortunately, however, many offices perform conflicts checks carelessly or not at all.

Similar information is needed when the office is thinking about hiring a new attorney or paralegal from another office (called a **lateral hire**). To determine whether they might contaminate the office, the names of the parties in their prior casework must be checked against the office's current and prospective clients.

When a law office applies for malpractice insurance, the insurance carrier will often inquire about the system the office uses for conflicts checks. See Exhibit 5.7 for examples of questions asked by one of the major liability insurance companies.

Some categories of information are sometimes difficult for the office to obtain. For example:

- Whether an employee in the office holds stock in the company of the adversary of a prospective client
- Whether a spouse, relative, or intimate friend of an employee in the office is employed by or holds stock in the company of the adversary of a prospective client
- Whether an employee in the office is related to or has had a romantic relationship with the adversary of a prospective client

---

Exhibit 5.7 **Questions on Malpractice Insurance Application about Conflict-of-Interest Avoidance**

ADMINISTRATIVE SYSTEMS AND PROCEDURES—CONFLICT OF INTEREST

	Yes	No
22. Do you have a written internal control system for maintaining client lists and identifying actual or potential conflicts of interest?	☐	☐
23. How does the firm maintain its conflict of interest avoidance system? ☐ Oral/Memory ☐ Single Index Files ☐ Multiple Index Files ☐ Computer		
24. Have the firm members disclosed in writing, all actual conflicts of interest and conflicts they reasonably believe may exist as a result of their role as director, officer, partner, employee or fiduciary of an entity or individual other than the applicant firm?	☐	☐
25. Do firm members disclose to their clients, in writing, all actual conflicts of interest and conflicts they reasonably believe may exist?	☐	☐
26. Upon disclosure of actual or potential conflicts, do firm members always obtain written consent to perform ongoing legal services?	☐	☐
27. Has the firm acquired, merged with or terminated a formal business relationship with another firm within the last three years?	☐	☐
28. Does the firm's conflict of interest avoidance system include attorney-client relationships established by predecessor firms, merged firms and acquired firms?	☐	☐

Source: The St. Paul Companies, Professional Liability Application for Lawyers.

- Whether an employee in the office is related to or has had a romantic relationship with anyone in the law office that represents the adversary of a prospective client

To discover this kind of information, the office usually must rely on its employees to come forward and reveal such connections.

12. COMMUNICATION WITH THE OTHER SIDE

In representing a client, an attorney shall not communicate with a party on the other side about the subject of the case if the attorney knows that the party is represented by another attorney. The latter attorney must consent to such a communication. Model Rule 4.2

If the other side is not represented, an attorney must not give him or her the impression that the attorney is uninvolved. The attorney should not give this person advice other than the advice to obtain his or her own attorney. Model Rule 4.3

The ethical concern here is that an attorney will take unfair advantage of the other side.

Example: Dan and Theresa Kline have just separated and are thinking about a divorce. Each claims the marital home. Theresa hires Thomas Farlington, Esq. to represent her. Farlington calls Dan to ask him if he is interested in settling the case.

It is unethical for Farlington to contact Dan about the case if Farlington knows that Dan has his own attorney. Farlington must talk with Dan's attorney. Only the latter can give Farlington permission to communicate with Dan. If Dan does not have an attorney, Farlington can talk with Dan, but he must not allow Dan to be misled about Farlington's role. Farlington works for the other side; he is not *disinterested*. Dan must be made to understand this fact. The only advice Farlington can give Dan in such a situation is to seek his own attorney.

Paralegal Perspective:

- The ethical restrictions on communicating with the other side apply to the employees of an attorney as well as to the attorney. "The lawyer's obligation is to ensure that the legal assistants do not communicate directly with parties known to be represented by an attorney, without that attorney's consent, on the subject of such representation."[42] You must avoid improper communication with the other side. If the other side is a business or some other large organization, do not talk with anyone there unless your supervisor tells you that it is ethical to do so. Never call the other side and pretend you are someone else in order to obtain information.
- If your office allows you to talk with someone who is not represented by an attorney, you cannot give this person any advice other than the advice to secure his or her own attorney.

13. SOLICITATION

In person or on the phone, an attorney may not solicit employment from a prospective client with whom the attorney has no family or prior professional relationship when a significant motive for doing so is the attorney's monetary gain.[43] Model Rule 7.3

---

[42]Section 20-104, Committee Commentary, *New Mexico Rules Governing the Practice of Law* (Judicial Pamphlet 16).
[43]The prohibition in Rule 7.3 applies to *live* telephone conversations in which the attorney seeks to be hired. For example, an attorney cannot call an accident victim to offer legal services.

People in distress are sometimes so distraught that they are not in a position to evaluate their need for legal services. They should not be subjected to pressures from an attorney who shows up wanting to be hired, particularly if the attorney is not a relative or has never represented them in the past.[44] Such in-person **solicitation** is unethical.

Example: Rachael Winters, Esq. stands outside the police station and gives a business card to any individual being arrested. The card says that Winters is an attorney specializing in criminal cases.

Winters is obviously looking for prospective clients. Doing so in this manner is referred to as **ambulance chasing,** which is a pejorative term for aggressively tracking down anyone who probably has a legal problem in order to drum up business. There is no indication that Winters is related to any of the people going into the police station or that she has any prior professional relationship with them (for example, they are *not* former clients). Winters appears to have one goal: finding a source of fees. Hence her conduct is unethical. Direct, in-person, one-on-one solicitation of clients in this way is not allowed. The concern is that an attorney who approaches strangers in trouble may exert undue influence on them. This is less likely to occur if the solicitation comes in the mail or through a prerecorded phone message, even though it is directed at individuals known to need legal services.

Example: An attorney obtains the names of homeowners facing foreclosure and sends them the following letter: "It has come to my attention that your home is being foreclosed on. Federal law may allow you to stop your creditors and give you more time to pay. Call my office for legal help."

While critics claim that such solicitation constitutes "ambulance chasing by mail," the technique is ethical in most states as long as it is truthful and not misleading.[45] *In-person* (i.e., face-to-face) solicitation, however, is treated differently because of the obvious pressure that it imposes. It is "easier to throw out unwanted mail than an uninvited guest."[46]

Although truthful direct-mail solicitations cannot be prohibited, they can be regulated by the state. For example, the state may require the attorney to print the phrase "Advertising Material" on the outside of the envelope and may prohibit all solicitations to victims and their relatives for thirty days following the accident or disaster for which the attorney is offering legal services.

Paralegal Perspective:

● An unscrupulous attorney may try to use a paralegal to solicit clients for the office.

Example: Bill Hill is a senior citizen who lives at a home for senior citizens. Andrew Vickers, Esq. hires Bill as his "paralegal." His sole job is to contact other seniors with legal problems and to refer them to Vickers.

Andrew Vickers is engaging in unethical solicitation through Bill Hill. Attorneys cannot hire a paralegal to try to accomplish what they cannot do themselves. Nor can

---

[44]Furthermore, the improper solicitation of clients and promotion of litigation constitutes the crime of **barratry** in some states. For example, in 1990 three attorneys and an employee of a law firm were indicted in Texas on charges that they illegally sought clients at hospitals and funeral homes after twenty-one students were killed and sixty-nine were injured in a school bus accident. *4 Said to Have Used Bus Crash to Get Business for Law Firm,* New York Times 8, col. 5 (April 7, 1990).

[45]*Shapero v. Kentucky Bar Ass'n,* 486 U.S. 466, 108 S. Ct. 1916, 100 L. Ed. 2d 475 (1988).

[46]Metzner, *Strategies That Break the Rules,* National Law Journal, 16 (July 15, 1991).

they use a **runner**[47]—an employee or independent contractor who contacts personal-injury victims or other potential clients in order to solicit business for an attorney.
- See also the related topic of splitting fees with nonattorneys discussed earlier under *fees*.

14. ADVERTISING

An attorney may advertise services on radio, on TV, in the newspaper, or through other public media as long as the ad is neither false nor misleading and does not constitute improper in-person solicitation. Model Rule 7.2

At one time, almost all forms of advertising by attorneys were prohibited. Traditional attorneys considered advertising to be highly offensive to the dignity of the profession. In 1977, however, the United States Supreme Court stunned the legal profession by holding that truthful advertising cannot be completely banned.[48] The First Amendment protects such advertising. Furthermore, advertising does not pose the same danger as in-person solicitation by an attorney. A recipient of advertising is generally under very little pressure to buy the advertised product—in this case, an attorney's services. Hence attorneys can ethically use truthful, nonmisleading advertising to the general public in order to generate business.

Studies have shown that over one-third of all attorneys in the country engage in some form of advertising. Most of it consists of listings in the Yellow Pages. The use of other marketing tools is also on the rise. More than $89 million was spent on television advertising in 1989, for example.[49] Former Chief Justice Warren Burger commented that some attorney ads "would make a used-car dealer blush with shame." Proponents of attorney advertising, however, claim that it has made legal services more accessible to the public and has provided the public with a better basis for choosing among available attorneys.

15. REPORTING PROFESSIONAL MISCONDUCT

Attorneys with knowledge that another attorney has committed a serious violation of the ethical rules must report this attorney to the appropriate disciplinary body. Model Rule 8.3

Attorneys may pay a price for remaining silent when they become aware of unethical conduct. The failure of an attorney to report another attorney may mean that both attorneys can be disciplined for unethical behavior. This is known as the "rat rule," the "snitch rule," or more euphemistically, the "whistle-blower rule." Not every ethical violation must be reported, however. The ethical violation must raise a substantial question of the attorney's honesty, trustworthiness, or fitness to practice law.

Paralegal Perspective:

- Suppose that a paralegal observes his or her supervising attorney commit fraud, steal from client funds, or use perjured testimony. Clearly, the paralegal has an obligation to avoid participating in such conduct. Such assistance could subject the paralegal to criminal and civil penalties. The problem is real since sooner or later unethical attorneys will probably ask or pressure their paralegals to participate in the unethical conduct.

---

[47]Also called a **capper** if the person uses fraud or deception in the solicitation.
[48]*Bates v. State Bar of Arizona*, 433 U.S. 350, 97 S. Ct. 2691, 53 L. Ed. 2d 810 (1977).
[49]Hornsby, *The Complex Evolution of Attorney Ad Regs*, Nat'l Law Journal S4 (August 6, 1990).

But is the paralegal under an ethical obligation to report the offending attorney to the bar association or other disciplinary body? The National Federation of Paralegal Associations (NFPA) thinks so. In its *Model Code of Ethics and Professional Responsibility* (printed later in the chapter, p. 305), the obligation is stated as follows in EC-3.2:

> A paralegal shall advise the proper authority of any action of another legal professional which clearly demonstrates fraud, deceit, dishonesty, or misrepresentation. EC-3.2

As pointed out earlier, ethical rules written by paralegals are not binding in the sense that they affect the paralegal's right to work as a paralegal. A paralegal who violates EC-3.2 by failing to report his or her attorney to the bar association cannot be suspended or fired from his or her job. He or she might be kicked out of the paralegal association that has adopted NFPA's *Model Code,* but it is highly unlikely that this will affect his or her employment prospects.

What then should a conscientious paralegal do? Here are some guidelines. First and foremost, don't participate directly or indirectly in the unethical conduct. Second, consult with fellow paralegals in the office and in your local paralegal association. Without naming names and without breaching client confidentiality, find out how others have handled similar predicaments on the job. Third, go to a senior officer at the firm, e.g., a partner, and let him or her know that the conduct you have observed is troubling you. You may need to confront the offending attorney him- or herself. Whomever you approach, be sure to have your facts straight! What appears to you to be an ethical violation may simply be aggressive or zealous advocacy that is on the edge but still within the bounds of propriety.

Should you go to the bar association or to a law enforcement agency? This is obviously a very tough question. The answer may depend on whether you have exhausted available routes within the office to resolve the matter to your satisfaction and, more importantly, whether you think this is the only way to prevent serious harm to a client. (See also An Ethical Dilemma: Your Ethics or Your Job! on p. 310.)

If you do report an attorney in your office and you are fired or retaliated against in some other way, do you have any recourse? Review the case of *Brown v. Hammond* earlier in the chapter (p. 260).

16. APPEARANCE OF IMPROPRIETY

How would you feel if you were told that, even though you have not violated any rule, you are still going to be punished because what you did *appeared* to be improper? That would be the effect of an obligation to avoid even the appearance of impropriety. In some states it is unethical for attorneys to engage in such appearances.[50] The ABA Model Rules, however, does not list appearance of impropriety as an independent basis for determining unethical conduct. To be disciplined in states that have adopted the Model Rules, an attorney must violate one of the specific ethical rules. Yet even in these states, conservative attorneys are as worried about apparent impropriety as they are about specific, actual impropriety.

---

[50]See Canon 9 of the *ABA Code of Professional Responsibility* (1969). "A lawyer should avoid even the appearance of professional impropriety." (See Exhibit 5.3.)

17. UNAUTHORIZED PRACTICE OF LAW

An attorney shall not assist a nonattorney in the unauthorized practice of law. Rule 5.5(b)

In chapter 4, we saw that it is a crime in many states for a nonattorney to engage in the **unauthorized practice of law.** Our main focus in chapter 4 was the nonattorney who works for an office other than a traditional law office. An example would be an independent paralegal who owns a do-it-yourself divorce office that sells kits and typing services. Now our focus is the nonattorney who works under the supervision of an attorney in a law office. We want to explore the ways in which attorneys might be charged with unethically assisting *their own paralegals* in engaging in the unauthorized practice of law. For example, an attorney might allow a paralegal to give legal advice, to conduct depositions, or to sign court documents. These areas will be discussed below along with an overview of other major ethical issues involving paralegals.

18. PARALEGALS

We turn now to a more direct treatment of when attorneys can be disciplined for the unethical use of paralegals. We will cover the following topics:

(a) Paralegals, the ABA Model Code, and the ABA Model Rules (see Exhibit 5.3)
(b) Misrepresentation of paralegal identity or status
(c) Doing what only attorneys can do
(d) Absentee, shoulder, and environmental supervision

(a) Paralegals, the ABA Model Code, and the ABA Model Rules

The first major statement by the American Bar Association on the ethical use of paralegals by attorneys came in its *Model Code of Professional Responsibility:*

DR 3-101(A): A lawyer shall not aid a nonlawyer in the unauthorized practice of law.

EC 3-6: A lawyer often delegates tasks to clerks, secretaries, and other lay persons. Such delegation is proper if the lawyer maintains a direct relationship with his client, supervises the delegated work, and has complete professional responsibility for the work product. This delegation enables a lawyer to render legal services more economically and efficiently.[51]

A 1967 opinion elaborated on these standards:

Formal Opinion 316
American Bar Association, 1967

A lawyer can employ lay secretaries, lay investigators, lay detectives, lay researchers, accountants, lay scriveners, non-lawyer draftsmen or non-lawyer researchers. In fact, he may employ non-lawyers to do any task for him except counsel clients about law matters, engage directly in the practice of law, appear in court or appear in formal proceedings as part of the judicial process, so long as it is he who takes the work and vouches for it to the client and becomes responsible for it to the client. In other words, we do not limit the kind of assistance that a lawyer can acquire in any way to persons who are admitted to the Bar, so long as the non-lawyers do not do things that lawyers may not do or do the things that lawyers only may do.

---

[51]See Exhibit 5.3 on the meaning of DR and EC in the ABA *Model Code.*

From these documents we learn that an attorney can hire a paralegal and is responsible for what the paralegal does. There are two levels of this responsibility: civil liability for malpractice and ethical liability for violation of ethical rules. In chapter 4, we discussed civil liability for malpractice under the topic of respondeat superior and negligence. Here in chapter 5 our primary focus is on ethical violations by attorneys based on what their paralegals do or fail to do.

> Example: The law firm of Adams & Adams represents Harold Thompson in his negligence suit against Parker Co. At the firm, Elaine Stanton, Esq. works on the case with Peter Vons, a paralegal whom she supervises. Peter neglects to file an important pleading in court, and carelessly gives confidential information about Thompson to the attorney representing Parker. All of this causes Thompson great damage.

Stanton is fully responsible to the client, Thompson, who might decide to bring a malpractice suit in court against her. She cannot hide behind the fact that her paralegal was at fault. (See the discussion of malpractice liability and respondeat superior in chapter 4. See also Appendix F for examples of attorney negligence in supervising staff.)

What about ethics? Can Stanton be reprimanded, suspended, or disbarred because of what her paralegal did? Responsibility to a client for malpractice often raises separate issues from responsibility to a bar association (or other disciplinary body) for unethical conduct. The two kinds of responsibility can be closely interrelated because the same alleged wrongdoing can be involved in the malpractice suit and in the disciplinary case. Yet the two proceedings are separate and should be examined separately.

In 1983, the ABA replaced the *Model Code of Professional Responsibility* with its *Model Rules of Professional Conduct*. The *Model Rules* are more helpful in telling us when attorneys are subject to ethical sanctions because of their paralegals. This is done in **Model Rule 5.3,** covering paralegals. All attorneys in the law firm are not treated the same in Rule 5.3. As you read this rule, note that different standards of ethical responsibility are imposed on the following three categories of attorneys:

- A partner in the firm—see section (a)
- An attorney in the firm with direct supervisory authority over the paralegal—see section (b)
- Any attorney in the firm—see section (c)

Model Rules of Professional Conduct Rule 5.3. Responsibilities Regarding Nonlawyer Assistants
American Bar Association, 1983

With respect to a nonlawyer employed or retained by or associated with a lawyer:

(a) a partner in a law firm shall make reasonable efforts to ensure that the firm has in effect measures giving reasonable assurance that the person's conduct is compatible with the professional obligations of the lawyer;

(b) a lawyer having direct supervisory authority over the nonlawyer shall make reasonable efforts to ensure that the person's conduct is compatible with the professional obligations of the lawyer; and

(c) a lawyer shall be responsible for conduct of such a person that would be a violation of the Rules of Professional Conduct if engaged in by a lawyer if:

(1) the lawyer orders or ratifies the conduct involved; or

(2) the lawyer is a partner in the law firm in which the person is employed, or has direct supervisory authority over the person, and knows of the conduct at a time when its consequences can be

avoided or mitigated but fails to take reasonable remedial action.

Comment:

Lawyers generally employ assistants in their practice, including secretaries, investigators, law student interns, and paraprofessionals. Such assistants, whether employees or independent contractors, act for the lawyer in rendition of the lawyer's professional services. A lawyer should give such assistants appropriate instruction and supervision concerning the ethical aspects of their employment, particularly regarding the obligation not to disclose information relating to representation of the client, and should be responsible for their work product. The measures employed in supervising nonlawyers should take account of the fact that they do not have legal training and are not subject to professional discipline.

Let us analyze Rule 5.3 by applying it to Elaine Stanton, Esq. in our example. First of all, under 5.3(c)(1), *any* attorney in the firm who "orders" the paralegal to commit the wrongdoing in question is ethically responsible for that conduct. The same is true if the attorney "ratifies" (that is, approves or endorses) the wrongdoing after the paralegal commits it. There is no indication in the example that Stanton or any other attorney in the firm told Peter not to file the pleading in court, or told him to give confidential information about Thompson to the other side. Nor is there any indication that an attorney approved of (ratified) Peter's conduct after it occurred.[52] Therefore, Rule 5.3(c)(1) does not apply.

We need to know whether Stanton is a partner in the firm. If so, she has an ethical obligation under 5.3(a) to "make reasonable efforts to ensure that the firm has in effect measures giving reasonable assurance" that the paralegal's conduct "is compatible with the professional obligations of the lawyer." Hence a partner cannot completely ignore office paralegals in the hope that someone else in the firm is monitoring them. Reasonable steps must be taken by *every partner* to establish a system of safeguards. Here are some examples:

- Make sure that all paralegals in the firm are aware of the ethical rules governing attorneys in the state. Have all paralegals sign a statement that they have read the rules.
- Make sure that all paralegals in the firm are aware of the importance of deadlines in the practice of law and of the necessity of using manual or computer date-reminder (tickler) techniques.

In the example, Peter Vons is supervised by Elaine Stanton, Esq. Hence she is an attorney with "direct supervisory authority" over Peter. Rule 5.3(b) governs the conduct of such attorneys. This section requires her to "make reasonable efforts to ensure" that the paralegal's conduct "is compatible with the professional obligations of the lawyer."

Assume that Stanton is charged with a violation of Rule 5.3(b) because her paralegal, Peter, failed to file an important pleading in court and disclosed confidential information about a client. At Stanton's disciplinary hearing, she would be asked a large number of questions about how she supervised Peter. For example:

- How do you assign tasks to Peter?
- How do you know if he is capable of handling an assignment?
- How often do you meet with him after you give him an assignment?

---

[52]By Peter's conduct, we mean both what he did (disclose confidential information) and what he failed to do (file the papers in court).

- How do you know if he is having difficulty completing an assignment?
- Has he made mistakes in the past? If so, how have you handled them?

Peter might be called as a witness in her disciplinary hearing and be interrogated extensively. For example:

- How were you trained as a paralegal?
- What kinds of assignments have you handled in your paralegal career?
- How long have you worked for Elaine Stanton?
- How does she evaluate your work?
- What do you do if you have a question on an assignment but she is not available in the office?
- Why didn't you file the court document on time?
- Describe the circumstances under which you revealed confidential information to the opponent in the Thompson case.

The purpose of asking all these questions of Stanton and of Peter would be to find out if Stanton made "reasonable efforts" to ensure that Peter did not violate ethical standards. Note that attorney supervisors do *not* have to guarantee that a paralegal will act ethically. They simply have to "make reasonable efforts" that this will occur. The above questions are relevant to whether Stanton exerted such efforts with respect to Peter.

Another basis of ethical liability is Rule 5.3(c)(2). Both a partner and a supervisory attorney can be subject to discipline if they knew about the paralegal's misconduct yet failed to take reasonable corrective steps at a time when such steps would have avoided or minimized ("mitigated") the damage. At their disciplinary hearing, a partner and/or a supervising attorney would be asked such questions as:

- When did you first find out that Peter did not file the court document?
- What did you do at that time? Why didn't you act sooner?
- When did you first find out that Peter spoke to the opposing attorney?
- What did you do at that time? Why didn't you act sooner?

Peter, too, might be asked questions at the hearing relevant to when his supervising attorney (Stanton) or any partner in the firm found out about what he had done—and what they did when they found out.

(b) Misrepresentation of Paralegal Identity or Status

"It is the lawyer's responsibility to take reasonable measures to ensure that clients, courts, and other lawyers are aware that a legal assistant, whose services are utilized by the lawyer in performing legal services, is not licensed to practice law."[53] A person who comes into contact with paralegals must not think they are attorneys. To learn how to avoid a misrepresentation of status, intentionally or accidentally, the following issues need to be examined:

- Titles
- Disclosure of status
- Business cards
- Letterhead
- Signature on correspondence
- Advertisements, announcement cards, signs, lists, and directories
- Name on court documents

---

[53]ABA *Model Guidelines*, Guideline 4. See Exhibit 5.5 and footnote 5.

What Title Can Be Used?

There are no ethical problems with the titles *paralegal* or *legal assistant*. No one is likely to think that persons with such titles are attorneys. Some bar associations prefer titles that are even more explicit in communicating nonattorney status—for example, *lawyer's assistant* and *nonattorney assistant*. Yet, they are seldom used because of the widespread acceptance and clarity of the titles *paralegal* and *legal assistant*. Some years ago, the Philadelphia Bar Association[54] said that the titles *paralegal* and *legal assistant* should be given only to employees who possessed "the requisite training and education." No state, however, is this explicit in stating who can use the titles—at least not yet.

It is unethical to call a paralegal an "associate" or to refer to a paralegal as being "associated" with a law firm. The title, "paralegal associate," for example, should not be used. The common understanding is that an associate is an attorney. In Iowa, similar problems exist with the title, "Certified Legal Assistant," as we shall see shortly. (See Exhibit 5.9).

Note on Disbarred or Suspended Attorney as Paralegal

When attorneys have been disbarred or suspended from the practice of law for ethical improprieties, they may try to continue to work in the law as paralegals for attorneys willing to hire them. Some states will not allow this because it shows disrespect for the court that disciplined the attorney and because of the high likelihood that the individual will engage in the unauthorized practice of law by going beyond paralegal duties. Other states are more lenient but might impose other restrictions, such as not allowing a disbarred or suspended attorney to have any client contact while working as a paralegal.

Should Paralegals Disclose Their Nonattorney Status to Clients, Attorneys, Government Officials, and the General Public?

Yes, this disclosure is necessary. The more troublesome questions are: What kind of disclosure should you make and when must you make it? Compare the following communications by a paralegal:

- "I work with Ward Brown at Brown & Tams."
- "I am a paralegal."
- "I am a legal assistant."
- "I am not an attorney."

The fourth statement is the clearest expression of nonattorney status. The first is totally unacceptable since you have said nothing about your status. For most contacts, the second and third statements will be ethically sufficient to overcome any misunderstanding about your nonattorney status. Yet some members of the public may be confused about what a paralegal or legal assistant is. Hence the only foolproof communication in all circumstances is the fourth. If you use any of the first three, you should *also* use the fourth.

In some states, the disclosure of nonattorney status is necessary only if a client, an attorney, a government official, or a member of the public is unaware of this status. Other states say that the paralegal should always disclose his or her nonattorney status at the outset of the contact. Furthermore, the failure to provide an oral clarification of status is *not* cured simply by handing over a business card that says you are a paralegal or a legal assistant. If there is any possibility of doubt, use the magic words, "I am not an attorney."

Do not assume that a person with whom you come in contact for the first time knows you are not an attorney; the safest course is to assume the opposite!

May a Paralegal Have a Business Card?

Every state allows paralegals to have their own *business cards* as long as their nonattorney status is clear. (See Exhibit 5.8. For other

---

[54]Throughout this discussion, there will be references to the opinions of specific bar associations. For a summary of these opinions and their citations, see Appendix F.

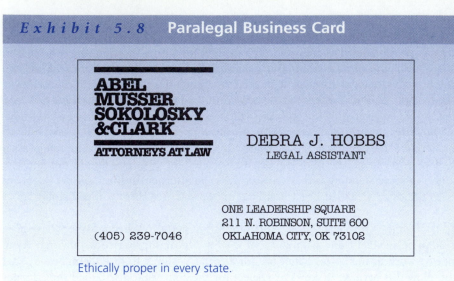

Exhibit 5.8 Paralegal Business Card

ABEL MUSSER SOKOLOSKY &CLARK
ATTORNEYS AT LAW

DEBRA J. HOBBS
LEGAL ASSISTANT

ONE LEADERSHIP SQUARE
211 N. ROBINSON, SUITE 600
OKLAHOMA CITY, OK 73102

(405) 239-7046

Ethically proper in every state.

examples of business cards, see Appendix G.) At one time, some states wanted the word "nonlawyer" used along with the paralegal's office title. This is rarely required today.

Since paralegals are not allowed to solicit business for their employer, the card may not be used for this purpose. The primary focus of the card must be to identify the paralegal rather than the attorney for whom the paralegal works. Finally, there must be nothing false or misleading printed on the card. In most states, a paralegal who is a *Certified Legal Assistant (CLA)* can include this fact on his or her card. In Iowa, however, this is not permitted, as we will see when we discuss signatures on correspondence. The concern in Iowa is that the CLA designation is too confusing. (See Exhibit 5.9.)

May the Letterhead of Law Firm Stationery Print the Name of a Paralegal? States differ in their answer to this question, although most now agree that nonattorneys' names

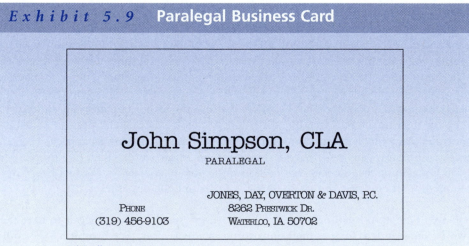

Exhibit 5.9 Paralegal Business Card

John Simpson, CLA
PARALEGAL

JONES, DAY, OVERTON & DAVIS, P.C.
8262 PRESTWICK DR.
WATERLOO, IA 50702

PHONE
(319) 456-9103

Ethically proper in every state *except* Iowa.

Exhibit 5.10   **Attorney Letterhead That Prints Paralegal Names**

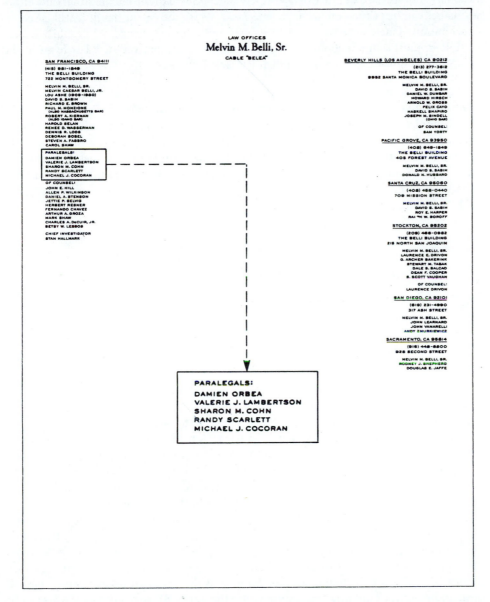

can be printed on *law firm letterhead* if their title is also printed so that their nonattorney status is clear. (See Exhibit 5.10.) Before 1977, almost all states did *not* allow attorney stationery to print the names of nonattorney employees. The concern was that the letterhead would be used as a form of advertising by packing it with names and titles to make the office look impressive. This concern evaporated in 1977, however, when the Supreme Court held that all forms of attorney advertising could not be banned.[55] After this date, most states withdrew their objection to the printing of paralegal names on attorney letter-

---

[55]See footnote 48 above.

head as long as no one would be misled into thinking that the paralegals were attorneys. In Michigan, it was recommended, but not required, that attorneys and nonattorneys be printed on different sides of the stationery to "enhance the clarification that the paraprofessional is not licensed to practice law." A few states adhere to the old view that only attorney names can be printed on law firm letterhead. Yet, to the extent that it is still based on a prohibition of attorney advertising, this view is subject to challenge. While ethically permissible in most states, it should be pointed out, however, that very few law firms in the country print nonattorney names on their law firm letterhead.

May a Paralegal Write and Sign Letters on Attorney Stationery?   There is never an ethical problem with a paralegal writing a letter that will be reviewed and signed by an attorney. Suppose, however, that the attorney wants the paralegal to sign his or her own name to the letter. Most states will permit this if certain conditions are met. For example, a title must be used that indicates the signer's nonattorney status, and the letter must not give legal advice.

The following formats are proper:

Sincerely,	Sincerely,	Sincerely,
Leonard Smith	Pauline Jones	Jill Strauss
Paralegal	Legal Assistant	Legal Assistant for the Firm

The following formats, however, pose difficulties:

Sincerely,	Sincerely,	Sincerely,
William Davis	John Simpson, CLA	Mary Page
		Certified Legal Assistant

The first format is ethically improper. The lack of a title could mislead the reader into thinking that William Davis is an attorney. In most states, using the designations "CLA" or "Certified Legal Assistant" is also proper. (See chapter 4 for a discussion of the CLA program.) In Iowa, however, they cannot be used. "A reader might think that CLA was a legal degree"; and if "Certified Legal Assistant" is used, "the public might be misled about his or her nonlawyer status." Hence, the second and third formats just shown cannot be used in Iowa. Presumably this also applies to a business card with the CLA designation. (See Exhibit 5.9.) This is an extreme view and is unlikely to be followed elsewhere.

In most states, there are no limitations on the persons to whom a paralegal can send letters. Yet, in a few states (such as New Jersey), only an attorney can sign a letter to a client, to an opposing attorney, or to a court. A very minor exception to this rule would be "a purely routine request to a court clerk for a docket sheet." A paralegal can sign such a letter. This also is an extreme position. So long as the paralegal's nonattorney status is clear, and so long as an attorney is supervising the paralegal, restrictions on who can be the recipient of a paralegal-signed letter make little sense. Most states impose no such restrictions.

May an Attorney Print the Name of a Paralegal in an Advertisement, an Announcement Card, a Door Sign, an Outdoor Sign, a Law Directory or Law List, an Office Directory, or a Telephone Directory?   Attorneys communicate to the public and to each other through advertisements, law directories or lists (that print the names of practicing attorneys), office directories, general telephone directories, door signs, outdoor signs, and announcement cards (that announce that the firm has moved, opened a new branch, merged with another firm, taken on a new partner, etc.). It is relatively rare that an attorney will want to print the name of his or her paralegal in one of these vehicles of communication. In a small city or town, however, a solo practitioner or small law firm might want to do so. While several states will not allow attorneys to do this, most states that have addressed the issue say it is ethically permissible if nothing false or misleading is said about the paralegal and the latter's nonattorney status is clear.

May an Attorney Print the Name of a Paralegal on a Court Document?   Formal documents that are required in litigation, such as appellate briefs, memoranda supporting a motion, complaints, or other pleadings, must be signed by an attorney representing a party in the dispute. With rare exceptions, the document cannot be signed by a nonattorney, no matter how minor the formal document may be. In most states, a paralegal can sign a letter on a routine matter to a clerk or other nonjudge, but formal litigation documents require an attorney's signature.

Suppose, however, that the attorney wishes to print on a document the name of a paralegal who worked on the document *in addition to* the attorney's name and signature. The attorney may simply want to give a measure of recognition to the efforts of this paralegal. Most states permit this as long as there is no misunderstanding as to the paralegal's nonattorney status, and no attempt is made to substitute a nonattorney's signature for an attorney's signature.

Occasionally, a court opinion will recognize the contribution of a paralegal. Before the opinion begins, the court lists the names of the attorneys who represented the parties. The name of a paralegal might be included with these attorneys. Here, for example, is the list of attorneys that includes the name of a paralegal (Becky Strickland) in the case of *United States v. Cooke,* 625 F.2d 19 (4th Cir. 1980):

> Thomas J. Keith, Winston-Salem, N.C., for appellant.
> David B. Smith, Asst. U.S. Atty. (H. M. Michaux, Jr., U.S. Atty., Durham, N.C., Becky M. Strickland, Paralegal Specialist on brief), for appellee.
> Before HALL and PHILLIPS, Circuit Judges, and HOFFMAN, Senior District Judge.

(c) Doing What Only Attorneys Can Do

There are limitations on what attorneys can ask their paralegals to do. We just examined one such limitation: paralegals should never be asked to sign court documents. The failure to abide by these limits might subject the attorney to a charge of unethically assisting a nonattorney to engage in the unauthorized practice of law. The areas we need to examine are as follows:

- Legal advice
- Nonlegal advice
- Drafting documents
- Real estate closings
- Depositions
- Executions of wills
- Settlement negotiations
- Court appearances
- Counsel's table
- Administrative hearings

May a Paralegal Give Legal Advice?   Unfortunately, it is not easy to define legal advice or the practice of law. According to the American Bar Association:

It is neither necessary nor desirable to attempt the formulation of a single, specific definition of what constitutes the practice of law. Functionally, the practice of law relates to the rendition of services for others that call for the professional judgment of a lawyer. The essence of the professional judgment of the lawyer is his educated ability to relate the general body and philosophy of law to a specific legal problem of a client. . . . Where this professional judgment is not involved, non-lawyers, such as court clerks, police officers, abstracters, and many governmental employees, may engage in occupations that require a special knowledge of law in certain areas. But the services of a lawyer are essential in the public interest whenever the exercise of *professional judgment* is required.[56]

(See Appendix F for the definition of the practice of law in your state.) The major way that an attorney communicates this professional judgment is through *legal advice.* According to the ABA, it occurs when "the general body and philosophy of law" is related or applied "to a specific legal problem." You are giving legal advice when you tell a particular person how the law might affect a particular legal problem or how to achieve a particular legal result that solves or avoids such a problem. Such advice from a paralegal is the unauthorized practice of law, whether or not you charge for the advice, and whether or not your advice is correct.

Compare the following sets of statements:

General Information about the Law	Information about the Law as Applied to a Specific Person
"The Superior Court is located at 1223 Via Barranca."	"Your case must be heard in the Superior Court, which is located at 1223 Via Barranca."
"There are several different kinds of bankruptcy."	There are several different kinds of bankruptcy, but you should file under Chapter 13."
"The failure to pay child support will lead to prosecution."	"Your failure to pay child support will lead to prosecution."

Arguably, the statements in the second column constitute legal advice; general information about the law has been related or applied to a particular legal problem of a particular person. The legal questions or problems addressed are: What court can hear (has jurisdiction over) *your* case? What kind of bankruptcy should *you* file? Can *you* be prosecuted for not paying child support?

The statements in the first column do not appear to focus on any particular person's legal problem. Hence such statements do not constitute legal advice, at least not explicitly. But we need to examine some of these statements more closely. When you tell someone that there are "several different kinds of bankruptcy," are you, by implication, telling that person that he or she should consider, and may qualify for, at least one of the kinds of bankruptcy? When you tell someone that the "failure to pay child support will lead to prosecution," are you, by implication, telling that person that his or her failure to pay child support will lead to his or her prosecution? The moment there is a focus on a particular person's legal problem, you are in the realm of legal advice. This focus can be express or implied. Whenever *any* statement about the law is made, you must ask yourself two questions:

- Am I trying to relate legal information to any particular person's legal problem? (If so, I am giving express legal advice.)

---

[56]EC 3-5, ABA *Model Code of Professional Responsibility* (1981).

- Could a person reasonably interpret what I am saying as relating legal information to a particular person's legal problem even if this is not my intent? (If so, I am giving implied legal advice.)

Great care is sometimes needed to avoid giving legal advice.

A number of circumstances increase the likelihood that statements can reasonably be interpreted as giving implied legal advice. For example:

- The statement is made by someone who works in the law, such as an attorney, paralegal, or legal secretary.
- The statement is made by someone who has helped the person with his or her legal problems in the past.
- The statement is made by someone who knows that the person has a current legal problem.
- The person is distressed about his or her current legal problem.

Under such circumstances, the person is likely to interpret *any* statement about the law as being relevant to his or her particular legal problem.

A number of paralegals have pointed out how easy it is to fall into the trap of giving legal advice:

> Legal assistants should be alert to all casual questions [since your answers] might be interpreted as legal advice.[57]

> Most of us are aware of the obvious, but we need to keep in mind that sometimes the most innocent comment could be construed as legal advice.[58]

> A . . . typical scenario, particularly in a small law office where legal assistants have a great deal of direct client contact, is that the clients themselves will coax you to answer questions about the procedures involved in their cases, and lead you into areas where you would be giving them legal advice. Sometimes this is done innocently—because the attorney is unavailable and they are genuinely unaware of the difference between what you can do for them and what their legal counsel [must] do. . . . They will press you for projections, strategy, applicable precedents—in short, legal advice. Sometimes you are placed in situations where you are not adequately supervised and your own expertise may be such that you know more about the specialized area of law than the attorney does anyway. . . . We have all walked the thin line between assisting in the provision of legal services and actually practicing law.[59]

When a paralegal gives legal advice in these circumstances, he or she is engaged in the unauthorized practice of law. An attorney who permits this to occur, or who fails to take the preventive steps required by Model Rule 5.3, is aiding the paralegal in the unauthorized practice of law—and hence is acting unethically.

The consequences can be extremely serious. In addition to the sanctions described in Exhibit 5.4, insurance problems may exist. Suppose a client sues and alleges that the firm's paralegal gave legal advice. Will the firm's malpractice insurance policy cover this suit? No, according to the General Counsel of the Mississippi Bar Association. "No available insurance policy will cover judgments resulting from a civil suit brought by an angry client based on the theory that a paralegal gave the client legal advice. In fact, if the paralegal gives legal advice, the predominant rule is that coverage is void for such

---

[57]King, *Ethics and the Legal Assistant,* 10 ParaGram 2 (Oregon Legal Assistants Ass'n, August 1987).
[58]DALA Newsletter 2 (Dallas Ass'n of Legal Assistants, December 1990).
[59]Spiegel, *How to Avoid the Unauthorized Practice of Law,* 8 The Journal 8–10 (Sacramento Ass'n of Legal Assistants, February 1986).

act. Therefore, the paralegal is warned not to give the client advice (even if the paralegal knows the answer) even though it may be an emergency situation. Why? Giving legal advice constitutes the unauthorized practice of law, and the unauthorized practice of law is not covered."[60]

There are a number of situations, however, in which a paralegal *can* give legal advice. First, a paralegal can tell a client precisely what the attorney tells the paralegal to say, even if the message constitutes legal advice. The paralegal, however, cannot elaborate on or explain this kind of message from the attorney. Paralegals "may be authorized to communicate legal advice so long as they do not interpret or expand on that advice."[61] Second, the paralegal may be working in an area of the law where nonattorneys are authorized to represent clients, such as social security hearings. (See chapter 4.) In such areas, the authorization includes the right to give legal advice.

May a Paralegal Give a Client Nonlegal Advice?

Yes. An attorney may allow a paralegal to render specialized advice on scientific or technical topics. For example, a qualified paralegal can give accounting advice or financial advice. The danger is that the nonlegal advice might also contain legal advice or that the client might reasonably interpret the nonlegal advice as legal advice.

May a Paralegal Draft Legal Documents?

Yes. A paralegal can draft any legal document as long as an attorney supervises and reviews the work of the paralegal. Some ethical opinions say that the document must lose its separate identity as the work of a paralegal and must leave the office as the work product of an attorney. In West Virginia, for example, "anything delegated to a nonattorney must lose its separate identity and be merged in the service of the lawyer." The key point is that an attorney must stand behind and be responsible for the document.

May a Paralegal Attend a Real Estate Closing?

The sale of property is finalized at an event called a real estate closing. Many of the events at the closing are formalities, such as signing and exchanging papers. Occasionally, however, some of these events turn into more substantive matters where negotiation, legal interpretation, and legal advice are involved.

In most states, paralegals are allowed to attend closings in order to assist their attorney-supervisor. The real question is whether they can attend *alone* and conduct the closing themselves. Chicago has one of the most liberal rules. There, paralegals can conduct the closing without the attorney-supervisor being present if no legal advice is given, if all the documents have been prepared in advance, if the attorney-supervisor is available by telephone to provide help, and if the other attorney consents. In some states, additional conditions must be met before allowing paralegals to act on their own. For example, the closing must take place in the attorney-supervisor's law office with the attorney readily accessible to answer legal questions. It must be noted, however, that this is a minority position. Most states would say that it is unethical for an attorney to allow a paralegal to conduct a real estate closing alone regardless of where the closing is held.

May a Paralegal Conduct a Deposition?

No. Paralegals can schedule depositions, can assist in preparing a witness who will be deposed (called the deponent), can take notes

---

[60]Michael Martz, *Ethics: Does a Legal Assistant Need Insurance?* The Assistant, p. 13 (Mississippi Ass'n of Legal Assistants, Fall 1993).
[61]ABA *Model Guidelines,* Comment to Guideline 3. See footnote 5.

at the deposition, and can summarize deposition transcripts, but they cannot conduct the deposition. Asking and objecting to deposition questions are attorney-only functions.

May a Paralegal Supervise the Execution of a Will?   In Connecticut, the execution of a will must be supervised by an attorney. A paralegal can act as a witness to the execution, but an attorney must direct the procedure. Most other states would probably agree, although few have addressed this question.

May a Paralegal Negotiate a Settlement?   A few states allow a paralegal to negotiate with a nonattorney employee of an insurance company, such as a claims adjuster, as long as the paralegal is supervised by an attorney. Most states, however, limit the paralegal's role to exchanging messages from the supervising attorney and do not allow any actual give-and-take negotiating by the paralegal.

May a Paralegal Make a Court Appearance?   In the vast majority of courts, a paralegal cannot perform even minor functions in a courtroom, such as asking a judge to schedule a hearing date for an attorney. As we saw in chapter 4, very few exceptions to this rule exist. Only attorneys can act in a representative capacity before a judge. There are, however, a small number of specialized courts, like the small claims court of some states, where you do not have to be an attorney to represent parties. This exception, however, is rare. And, as mentioned earlier, a paralegal should not sign a formal court document that is filed in litigation.

May a Paralegal Sit at Counsel's Table during a Trial?   In many courts, only attorneys can sit at counsel's table during a trial. Yet, in some courts a paralegal is allowed to sit with the attorneys if permission of the presiding judge is obtained. The paralegal does not take an active role in the trial. He or she provides general assistance (e.g., note taking, organizing trial documents) for the attorney. While at the table, the paralegal is sometimes said to be sitting in the **second chair.** This phrase, however, is more accurately used to refer to another attorney who assists the lead attorney who is the "first chair." When a nonattorney such as a paralegal is allowed to sit at counsel's table, it might be more accurate to refer to him or her as being in the "third chair."

May a Paralegal Represent Clients at Administrative Hearings?   Yes, when this is authorized at the particular state or federal administrative agency. (See chapter 4, Appendix E, and Appendix F.)

(d) Absentee Supervision, Shoulder Supervision, and Environmental Supervision

It is difficult to overestimate the importance of attorney supervision in the arena of ethics. Almost every ethical opinion involving paralegals (and almost every attorney malpractice opinion involving paralegals) stresses the need for effective supervision. The justification for the very existence of perhaps 95 percent of paralegal activity is this supervision. Indeed, one of the main reasons many argue that paralegal licensing is not necessary is the protective cover of attorney supervision.

What is meant by supervision? The extremes are easy to identify. *Absentee supervision* refers to the attorney who is either never around or seldom available. Once tasks are assigned, paralegals are on their own. At the other extreme is *shoulder supervision,* practiced by attorneys who are afraid to delegate. When they do get up enough courage to delegate something, they constantly look over the shoulder of the paralegal, who is rarely left alone for more than two-minute intervals. Such attorneys suffer from *delegatitis,* the inordinate fear of letting anyone do anything for them.

Both kinds of supervision are misguided. If you work for an attorney who practices absentee supervision, disaster is just around the corner. You may feel flattered by the confidence placed in you; you may enjoy the challenge of independence; you may be highly compensated because of your success. But you are working in an office that is traveling 130 miles per hour in a 50 miles per hour zone. Any feeling of safety in such an office is illusory. Shoulder supervision, on the other hand, provides safety at the expense of practicality. Perpetual step-by-step surveillance will ultimately defeat the economy and efficiency motives that originally led the office to hire paralegals.

Perhaps the most effective kind of supervision is *"environmental supervision,"* or what might be called *holistic supervision.* It is far broader in its reach than the immediate task delegated to a paralegal. It addresses the essential question: What kind of environment will lead to a high-quality paralegal work product without sacrificing economy or ethics? The components of this kind of supervision are outlined in Exhibit 5.11. Environmental supervision requires *hiring* the right people, *training* those people, *assigning* appropriate tasks, *providing* the needed resources, *monitoring* the progress, *reviewing* the end product, and *rewarding* competence.

Unfortunately, most law offices do *not* practice environmental supervision as outlined in Exhibit 5.11. The chart represents the ideal. Yet you need to know what the ideal is so that you can advocate for the conditions that will help bring it about.

Thus far, our discussion on supervision has focused on the traditional paralegal who works full time in the office of an attorney. We also need to consider the freelance paralegal who works part-time for one attorney or for several attorneys in different law firms. Very often this freelance or independent paralegal works in his or her own office. (See chapters 1 and 4, and Appendix M.) How can attorneys fulfill their ethical obligation to supervise such paralegals?

> Example: Gail Patterson has her own freelance business. She offers paralegal services to attorneys who hire her for short-term projects, which she performs in her own office.

Arguably, attorneys who hire Gail often do not provide the same kind of supervision that they can provide to a full-time paralegal who works in their office. We saw earlier that Model Rule 5.3(c)(2) says that an attorney has the responsibility to take steps to avoid the consequences of an ethical violation by a paralegal and, if a violation occurs, to mitigate the consequences. Suppose that Gail commits an ethical impropriety—for example, she reveals confidential communications. Since she works in her own office, the attorney who hired her may not learn about this impropriety in time to avoid or mitigate its consequences. Conflict of interest is another potential problem. Gail works for many different attorneys and hence many different clients of those attorneys. It is possible that she could accept work from two attorneys who are engaged in litigation against each other without either attorney knowing that the other has hired Gail on the same case. (See the earlier discussion of this problem on page 283.)

What kind of supervision is needed to prevent such problems? There is no clear answer to this question. It is not enough that the attorney vouches for, and takes responsibility for, the final product submitted by the freelance paralegal. Ongoing supervision is also needed under Model Rule 5.3. Not many states, however, have addressed this area of ethics. In the future, we will probably see the creation of new standards to govern this kind of paralegal.

E x h i b i t   5 . 1 1   "Environmental Supervision": The Ethical Ideal

1. Before paralegals are hired, the office undertakes a study of its practice in order to identify what tasks paralegals should perform and what levels of ability will be required to perform those tasks.

2. As part of the interview process, the office conducts background checks on applicants for paralegal jobs in order to insure that competent people are hired who already have the needed skills or who are trainable so that they can acquire these skills on the job.

3. A program of orientation and training is created to introduce paralegals to the office and to prepare them for the tasks ahead.

4. Before the paralegal is hired, the office conducts a "conflicts check" to determine whether he or she might have a conflict of interest with any current client of the office. These conflicts might result from the paralegal's prior legal work as well as from his or her family and business connections with anyone who might oppose current clients.

5. Paralegals are given a copy of the ethical rules governing attorneys in the state. In addition to reading these rules, they are given training on the meaning of the rules.

6. Paralegals are told what to do if they feel that an ethical problem exists. Lines of authority are identified if the paralegal needs to discuss the matter with someone other than, or in addition to, his or her immediate supervisor.

7. The office does not assume that every attorney knows how to supervise paralegals. Paralegals are assigned to attorneys who have the required supervisory sensitivity and skill. Furthermore, the office is always looking for ways to increase this sensitivity and skill.

8. An attorney reviews all paralegal work. While paralegals may be given discretion and asked to exercise judgment in the tasks assigned, this discretion and judgment are always subjected to attorney review.

9. No task is assigned that is beyond the capacity of the paralegal. Specialized instruction always accompanies tasks the paralegal has not performed before.

10. Once a task is assigned, the paralegal is told where to receive assistance if the immediate supervisor is not available. This lack of availability, however, is relatively rare.

11. For tasks that the office performs on a recurring basis, there are manuals, office procedures, checklists, or other written material available to the paralegal to explain how the tasks are performed and where samples or models can be found. If such *systems* material does not currently exist, the office has realistic plans to create such material.

12. To cut down on misunderstanding, every paralegal assignment includes the following information:
    - A *specific due date.* ("Get to this when you can" is unacceptable and unfair.)
    - A *priority assessment.* ("Should everything else be dropped while I do this assignment?")
    - A *context.* ("How does this assignment fit into the broader picture of the case?") and
    - A *financial perspective.* ("Is this billable time?")

13. At reasonable times before the due date of selected assignments, the supervisor monitors the progress of the paralegal to insure that the work is being done professionally and accurately.

14. A team atmosphere exists at the office among the attorneys, paralegals, secretaries, and other employees. Everyone knows each other's functions, pressures, and potential as resources. A paralegal never feels isolated.

15. Evaluations of paralegal performance are constructive. Both the supervisor and paralegal act on the assumption that there will always be a need and opportunity for further learning.

16. The office sends the paralegal to training seminars conducted by paralegal associations and bar associations to maintain and to increase the paralegal's skills.

17. The office knows that an unhappy employee is prone to error. Hence the office makes sure that the work setting of the paralegal encourages personal growth and productivity. This includes matters of compensation, benefits, work space, equipment, and advancement.

Section D
ETHICAL CODES OF THE PARALEGAL ASSOCIATIONS

As indicated at the beginning of this chapter, there are no binding ethical rules published by paralegal associations. Yet the two major national associations—the National Federation of Paralegal Associations (NFPA) and the National Association of Legal Assistants (NALA)—have written ethical codes that you should know about. See Exhibit 5.5 for an overview of the structure and functions of their codes.

Model Code of Ethics and Professional Responsibility
National Federation of Paralegal Associations, 1993

PREAMBLE

The National Federation of Paralegal Associations, Inc. ("NFPA") is a professional organization comprised of paralegal associations and individual paralegals throughout the United States. Members of NFPA have varying types of backgrounds, experience, education, and job responsibilities which reflect the diversity of the paralegal profession. NFPA promotes the growth, development and recognition of the paralegal profession as an integral partner in the delivery of legal services.

NFPA recognizes that the creation of guidelines and standards for professional conduct are important for the development and expansion of the paralegal profession. In May 1993, NFPA adopted this Model Code of Ethics and Professional Responsibility ("Model Code") to delineate the principles for ethics and conduct to which every paralegal should aspire. The Model Code expresses NFPA's commitment to increasing the quality and efficiency of legal services and recognizes the profession's responsibilities to the public, the legal community, and colleagues.

Paralegals perform many different functions, and these functions differ greatly among practice areas. In addition, each jurisdiction has its own unique legal authority and practices governing ethical conduct and professional responsibilities.

It is essential that each paralegal strive for personal and professional excellence and encourage the professional development of other paralegals as well as those entering the profession. Participation in professional associations intended to advance the quality and standards of the legal profession is of particular importance. Paralegals should possess integrity, professional skill and dedication to the improvement of the legal system and should strive to expand the paralegal role in the delivery of legal services.

CANON 1

A paralegal* shall achieve and maintain a high level of competence.

EC-1.1 A paralegal shall achieve competency through education, training, and work experience.

EC-1.2 A paralegal shall participate in continuing education to keep informed of current legal, technical and general developments.

EC-1.3 A paralegal shall perform all assignments promptly and efficiently.

CANON 2

A paralegal shall maintain a high level of personal and professional integrity.

EC-2.1 A paralegal shall not engage in any ex parte† communications involving the courts or any other adjudicatory body in an attempt to exert undue influence or to obtain advantage for the benefit of only one party.

EC-2.2 A paralegal shall not communicate, or cause another to communicate, with a party the paralegal knows to be represented by a lawyer in a pending matter without the prior consent of the lawyer representing such other party.

***"Paralegal"** is synonymous with **"Legal Assistant"** and is defined as a person qualified through education, training, or work experience to perform substantive legal work that requires knowledge of legal concepts and is customarily, but not exclusively performed by a lawyer. This person may be retained or employed by a lawyer, law office, governmental agency or other entity or may be authorized by administrative, statutory or court authority to perform this work.

†**"Ex Parte"** denotes actions or communications conducted at the instance and for the benefit of one party only, and without notice to, or contestation by, any person adversely interested.

EC-2.3 A paralegal shall ensure that all timekeeping and billing records prepared by the paralegal are thorough, accurate, and honest.

EC-2.4 A paralegal shall be scrupulous, thorough and honest in the identification and maintenance of all funds, securities, and other assets of a client and shall provide accurate accountings as appropriate.

EC-2.5 A paralegal shall advise the proper authority of any dishonest or fraudulent acts by any person pertaining to the handling of the funds, securities or other assets of a client.

CANON 3

A paralegal shall maintain a high standard of professional conduct.

EC-3.1 A paralegal shall refrain from engaging in any conduct that offends the dignity and decorum of proceedings before a court or other adjudicatory body and shall be respectful of all rules and procedures.

EC-3.2 A paralegal shall advise the proper authority of any action of another legal professional which clearly demonstrates fraud, deceit, dishonesty, or misrepresentation.

EC-3.3 A paralegal shall avoid impropriety and the appearance of impropriety.

CANON 4

A paralegal shall serve the public interest by contributing to the delivery of quality legal services and the improvement of the legal system.

EC-4.1 A paralegal shall be sensitive to the legal needs of the public and shall promote the development and implementation of programs that address those needs.

EC-4.2 A paralegal shall support bona fide efforts to meet the need for legal services by those unable to pay reasonable or customary fees; for example, participation in pro bono projects and volunteer work.

EC-4.3 A paralegal shall support efforts to improve the legal system and shall assist in making changes.

CANON 5

A paralegal shall preserve all confidential information provided by the client or acquired from other sources before, during, and after the course of the professional relationship.

EC-5.1 A paralegal shall be aware of and abide by all legal authority governing confidential information.

EC-5.2 A paralegal shall not use confidential information to the disadvantage of the client.

EC-5.3 A paralegal shall not use confidential information to the advantage of the paralegal or of a third person.

EC-5.4 A paralegal may reveal confidential information only after full disclosure and with the client's written consent; or, when required by law or court order; or, when necessary to prevent the client from committing an act which could result in death or serious bodily harm.

EC-5.5 A paralegal shall keep those individuals responsible for the legal representation of a client fully informed of any confidential information the paralegal may have pertaining to that client.

EC-5.6 A paralegal shall not engage in any indiscreet communications concerning clients.

CANON 6

A paralegal's title shall be fully disclosed.††

EC-6.1 A paralegal's title shall clearly indicate the individual's status and shall be disclosed in all business and professional communications to avoid misunderstandings and misconceptions about the paralegal's role and responsibilities.

EC-6.2 A paralegal's title shall be included if the paralegal's name appears on business cards, letterhead, brochures, directories, and advertisements.

CANON 7

A paralegal shall not engage in the unauthorized practice of law.

EC-7.1 A paralegal shall comply with the applicable legal authority governing the unauthorized practice of law.

CANON 8

A paralegal shall avoid conflicts of interest and shall disclose any possible conflict to the employer or client, as well as to the prospective employers or clients.

EC-8.1 A paralegal shall act within the bounds of the law, solely for the benefit of the client, and shall be free of compromising influences and loyalties. Neither the paralegal's personal or business interest, nor those of

---

"Confidential Information" denotes information relating to a client, whatever its source, which is not public knowledge nor available to the public. (**"Non-Confidential Information"** would generally include the name of the client and the identity of the matter for which the paralegal provided services.)

††**"Disclose"** denotes communication of information reasonably sufficient to permit identification of the significance of the matter in question.

other clients or third persons, should compromise the paralegal's professional judgment and loyalty to the client.

EC-8.2   A paralegal shall avoid conflicts of interest which may arise from previous assignments whether for a present or past employer or client.

EC-8.3   A paralegal shall avoid conflicts of interest which may arise from family relationships and from personal and business interests.

EC-8.4   A paralegal shall create and maintain an effective recordkeeping system that identifies clients, matters, and parties with which the paralegal has worked, to be able to determine whether an actual or potential conflict of interest exists.

EC-8.5   A paralegal shall reveal sufficient non-confidential information about a client or former client to reasonably ascertain if an actual or potential conflict of interest exists.

EC-8.6   A paralegal shall not participate in or conduct work on any matter where a conflict of interest has been identified.

EC-8.7   In matters where a conflict of interest has been identified and the client consents to continued representation, a paralegal shall comply fully with the implementation and maintenance of an Ethical Wall.***

*****"Ethical Wall"** refers to the screening method implemented in order to protect a client from a conflict of interest. An Ethical Wall generally includes, but is not limited to, the following elements: (1) prohibit the paralegal from having any connection with the matter; (2) ban discussions with or the transfer of documents to or from the paralegal; (3) restrict access to files; and (4) educate all members of the firm, corporation or entity as to the separation of the paralegal (both organizationally and physically) from the pending matter. For more information regarding the Ethical Wall, see the NFPA publication entitled "The Ethical Wall—Its Application to Paralegals."

Code of Ethics and Professional Responsibility
National Association of Legal Assistants, 1975, 1995

Preamble

A legal assistant must adhere strictly to the accepted standards of legal ethics and to the general principles of proper conduct. The performance of the duties of the legal assistant shall be governed by specific canons as defined herein so that justice will be served and goals of the profession attained.

The canons of ethics set forth hereafter are adopted by the National Association of Legal Assistants, Inc., as a general guide intended to aid legal assistants and attorneys. The enumeration of these rules does not mean there are not others of equal importance although not specifically mentioned. Court rules, agency rules and statutes must be taken into consideration when interpreting the canons.

Definition

Legal assistants, also known as paralegals, are a distinguishable group of persons who assist attorneys in the delivery of legal services. Through formal education, training, and experience, legal assistants have knowledge and expertise regarding the legal system and substantive and procedural law which qualify them to do work of a legal nature under the supervision of an attorney.

Canon I

A legal assistant must not perform any of the duties that attorneys only may perform nor take any actions that attorneys may not take.

Canon II

A legal assistant may perform any task which is properly delegated and supervised by an attorney, as long as the attorney is ultimately responsible to the client, maintains a direct relationship with the client, and assumes professional responsibility for the work product.

Canon III

A legal assistant must not:

a. engage in, encourage, or contribute to any act which could constitute the unauthorized practice of law; and

b. establish attorney-client relationships, set fees, give legal opinions or advice or represent a client before a court or agency unless so authorized by that court or agency; and

c. engage in conduct or take any action which would assist or involve the attorney in a violation of professional ethics or give the appearance of professional impropriety.

Canon IV

A legal assistant must use discretion and professional judgment commensurate with knowledge and experience but must not render independent legal judgment in place of an attorney. The services of an attorney are essential in the public interest whenever such legal judgment is required.

Canon V

A legal assistant must disclose his or her status as a legal assistant at the outset of any professional relationship with a client, attorney, a court or administrative agency or personnel thereof, or a member of the general pubic. A legal assistant must act prudently in determining the extent to which a client may be assisted without the presence of an attorney.

Canon VI

A legal assistant must strive to maintain integrity and a high degree of competency through education and training with respect to professional responsibility, local rules and practice, and through continuing education in sub-

stantive areas of law to better assist the legal profession in fulfilling its duty to provide legal service.

Canon VII

A legal assistant must protect the confidences of a client and must not violate any rule or statute now in effect or hereafter enacted controlling the doctrine of privileged communications between a client and an attorney.

Canon VIII

A legal assistant must do all other things incidental, necessary, or expedient for the attainment of the ethics and responsibilities as defined by statute or rule of court.

Canon IX

A legal assistant's conduct is guided by bar associations' codes of professional responsibility and rules of professional conduct.

Model Standards and Guidelines for Utilization of Legal Assistants
National Association of Legal Assistants, 1991

INTRODUCTION

[These] Guidelines represent a statement of how the legal assistant may function in the law office. The Guidelines are not intended to be a comprehensive or exhaustive list of the proper duties of a legal assistant. Rather, they are designed as guides to what may or may not be proper conduct for the legal assistant. In formulating the Guidelines, the reasoning and rules of law in many reported decisions of disciplinary cases and unauthorized practice of law cases have been analyzed and considered. In addition, the provisions of the American Bar Association's Model Code of Professional Responsibility and the Model Rules of Professional Conduct, as well as the ethical promulgations of various state courts and bar associations have been considered in development of the Guidelines.

While the Guidelines may not have universal application, they do form a sound basis for the legal assistant and the supervising attorney to follow in the operation of a law office. The Model will serve as a definitive and well-reasoned guide to those considering voluntary standards and guidelines for legal assistants. If regulation is to be

imposed in a given jurisdiction the Model may serve as a comprehensive resource document.

I PREAMBLE

Proper utilization of the services of legal assistants affects the efficient delivery of legal services. Legal assistants and the legal profession should be assured that some measures exist for identifying the legal assistants and their role in assisting attorneys in the delivery of legal services. Therefore, the National Association of Legal Assistants, Inc., hereby adopts these Model Standards and Guidelines as an educational document for the benefit of legal assistants and the legal profession.

COMMENT

The three most frequently raised questions concerning legal assistants are (1) How do you define a legal assistant; (2) Who is qualified to be identified as a legal assistant; and (3) What duties may a legal assistant perform? The definition [presented below] answers the first question insofar as legal assistants serving attorneys are concerned. The Model sets forth minimum education, training, and experience through standards which will assure that one denominated as a legal assistant has the qualifications to be held out to the public in that capacity. The Guidelines identify those acts which the reported cases hold to be proscribed and give examples of services which the legal assistant may perform under the supervision of an attorney. . . .

The NALA Guidelines constitute a statement relating to services performed by non-lawyer employees as approved by court decisions and other sources of authority. The purpose of the Guidelines is not to place limitations or restrictions on the legal profession. Rather, the Guidelines are intended to outline for the legal profession an acceptable course of conduct. By voluntary recognition and utilization of the Model Standards and Guidelines the legal profession will avoid many problems.

II DEFINITION

Legal assistants* are a distinguishable group of persons who assist attorneys in the delivery of legal services. Through formal education, training, and experience, legal assistants have knowledge and expertise regarding the legal system and substantive and procedural law which qualify them to do work of a legal nature under the supervision of an attorney.

COMMENT

This definition has been used to foster a distinction between a legal assistant as one working under the direct supervision of an attorney and a broader class of paralegals who perform tasks of similar nature, but not necessarily under the supervision of an attorney. In applying the standards and guidelines it is important to remember that they in turn were developed to apply to the legal assistant as defined therein.

III STANDARDS

A legal assistant should meet certain minimum qualifications. The following standards may be used to determine an individual's qualifications as a legal assistant:

1. Successful completion of the Certified Legal Assistant certifying ("CLA") examination of the National Association of Legal Assistants, Inc.;
2. Graduation from an ABA approved program of study for legal assistants;
3. Graduation from a course of study for legal assistants which is institutionally accredited but not ABA approved, and which requires not less than the equivalent of 60 semester hours of classroom study;
4. Graduation from a course of study for legal assistants, other than those set forth in (2) and (3) above,

plus not less than six months of in-house training as a legal assistant;
5. A baccalaureate degree in any field, plus not less than six months in-house training as a legal assistant;
6. A minimum of three years of law-related experience under the supervision of an attorney, including at least six months of in-house training as a legal assistant; or
7. Two years of in-house training as a legal assistant.

For purposes of these Standards, "in-house training as a legal assistant" means attorney education of the employee concerning legal assistant duties and these Guidelines. In addition to review and analysis of assignments the legal assistant should receive a reasonable amount of instruction directly related to the duties and obligations of the legal assistant.

COMMENT

The Standards set forth suggested minimum qualifications for a legal assistant. These minimum qualifications as adopted recognize legal related work backgrounds and formal education backgrounds, both of which should provide the legal assistant with a broad base in exposure to and knowledge of the legal professioin. This background is necessary to assure the public and the legal profession that the one being identified as a legal assistant is qualified.

The Certified Legal Assistant ("CLA") examination offered by NALA is the only voluntary nationwide certification program for legal assistants. The "CLA" designation is a statement to the legal profession and the public that the legal assistant has met the high levels of knowledge and professionalism required by NALA's certification program. Continuing education requirements, which all certified legal assistants must meet, assure that high standards are maintained. Certification through NALA is available to any legal assistant meeting the educational and experience requirements.

IV GUIDELINES

These guidelines relating to standards of performance and professional responsibility are intended to aid legal assistants and attorneys. The responsibility rests with an attorney who employs legal assistants to educate them with respect to the duties they are assigned and to supervise the manner in which such duties are accomplished.

COMMENT

In general, a legal assistant is allowed to perform any task which is properly delegated and supervised by an

---

*Within this occupational category some individuals are known as paralegals.

attorney, so long as **the attorney is ultimately responsible to the client and assumes complete professional responsibility for the work product. . . .**

V

Legal assistants should:

1. Disclose their status as legal assistants at the outset of any professional relationship with a client, other attorneys, a court or administrative agency or personnel thereof, or members of the general public;
2. Preserve the confidences and secrets of all clients; and
3. Understand the attorney's Code of Professional Responsibility and these guidelines in order to avoid any action which would involve the attorney in a violation of that Code, or give the appearance of professional impropriety.

COMMENT

Routine early disclosure of the legal assistant's status when dealing with persons outside the attorney's office is necessary to assure that there will be no misunderstanding as to the responsibilities and role of the legal assistant. Disclosure may be made in any way that avoids confusion. If the person dealing with the legal assistant already knows of his or her status, further disclosure is unnecessary. If at any time in written or in oral communication the legal assistant becomes aware that the other person may believe the legal asistant is an attorney, it should be made clear that the legal assistant is not an attorney.

The attorney should exercise care that the legal assistant preserves and refrains from using any confidence or secrets of a client, and should instruct the legal assistant not to disclose or use any such confidences or secrets. . . .

The ultimate responsibility for compliance with approved standards of professional conduct rests with the supervising attorney. . . . However, the legal assistant should understand what he may or may not do. The burden rests upon the attorney who employs a legal assistant to educate the latter with respect to the duties which may be assigned and then to supervise the manner in which the legal assistant carries out such duties. However, this does not relieve the legal assistant from an independent obligation to refrain from illegal conduct. Additionally, and notwithstanding that the Code is not binding upon non-lawyers, the very nature of a legal assistant's employment imposes an obligation not to engage in conduct which would involve the supervising attorney in a violation of the Code. NALA has adopted the ABA Code as a part of its Code of Ethics.

VI

Legal assistants should not:

1. Establish attorney-client relationships, set legal fees, give legal opinions or advice, or represent a client before a court; nor
2. Engage in, encourage, or contribute to any act which could constitute the unauthorized practice of law. . . .

VII

Legal assistants may perform services for an attorney in the representation of a client, provided:

1. The services performed by the legal assistant do not require the exercise of independent professional legal judgment;
2. The attorney maintains a direct relationship with the client and maintains control of all client matters;
3. The attorney supervises the legal assistant;
4. The attorney remains professionally responsible for all work on behalf of the client, including any actions taken or not taken by the legal assistant in connection therewith; and
5. The services performed supplement, merge with and become the attorney's work product. . . .

VIII

In the supervision of a legal assistant, consideration should be given to:

1. Designating work assignments that correspond to the legal assistants' abilities, knowledge, training and experience.
2. Educating and training the legal assistant with respect to professional responsibility, local rules and practices, and firm policies;
3. Monitoring the work and professional conduct of the legal assistant to ensure that the work is substantively correct and timely performed;
4. Providing continuing education for the legal assistant in substantive matters through courses, institutes, workshops, seminars and in-house training; and
5. Encouraging and supporting membership and active participation in professional organizations. . . .

IX

Except as otherwise provided by statute, court rule or decision, administrative rule or regulation, or the attorney's Code of Professional Responsibility; and within the preceding parameters and proscriptions, a legal assistant may perform any function delegated by an attorney, including but not limited to the following:

1. Conduct client interviews and maintain general contact with the client after the establishment of the attorney-client relationship, so long as the client is aware of the status and function of the legal assistant, and the client contact is under the supervision of the attorney.
2. Locate and interview witnesses, so long as the witnesses are aware of the status and function of the legal assistant.
3. Conduct investigations and statistical and documentary research for review by the attorney.
4. Conduct legal research for review by the attorney.
5. Draft legal documents for review by the attorney.
6. Draft correspondence and pleadings for review by and signature of the attorney.
7. Summarize depositions, interrogatories, and testimony for review by the attorney.
8. Attend executions of wills, real estate closings, depositions, court or administrative hearings and trials with the attorney.
9. Author and sign letters provided the legal assistant's status is clearly indicated and the correspondence does not contain independent legal opinions or legal advice.

COMMENT

The United States Supreme Court has recognized the variety of tasks being performed by legal assistants and has noted that use of legal assistants encourages cost effective delivery of legal services, *Missouri v. Jenkins,* 491 U.S. 274, 109 S. Ct. 2463, 2471, n. 10 (1989). In Jenkins, the court further held that legal assistant time should be included in compensation for attorney fee awards at the prevailing practice in the relevant community to bill legal assistant time. . . .

The Guidelines were developed from generally accepted practices. Each supervising attorney must be aware of the specific rules, decisions and statutes applicable to legal assistants within his jurisdiction.

Section E
AN ETHICAL DILEMMA: YOUR ETHICS OR YOUR JOB!

Throughout this chapter we have stressed the importance of maintaining your integrity through knowledge of and compliance with ethical rules. There may be times, however, when this is much easier said than done. Consider the following situations:

- You are not sure whether an ethical violation is being committed. Nor is anyone else in the office sure. Like so many areas of the law, ethical issues can be complex.
- You are sure that an ethical violation exists, and the violator is your supervisor!
- You are sure that an ethical violation exists, and the violators are everyone else in the office!

You face a potential dilemma (1) if no one seems to care about the ethical problem or, worse, (2) if your supervising attorney is the one committing the ethical impropriety or (3) if the entire office appears to be participating in the impropriety. People do not like to be told that they are unethical. Rather than acknowledge the fault and mend their ways, they may turn on the accuser, the one raising the fuss about ethics. Once the issue is raised, it may be very difficult to continue working in the office.

You need someone to talk to. In the best of all worlds, it will be someone in the same office. If this is not practical, consider contacting a teacher whom you trust. Paralegal associations are also an excellent source of information and support. A leader in one paralegal association offers the following advice:

I would suggest that if the canons, discipline rules, affirmations, and codes of ethics do not supply you with a clear-cut answer to any ethical question you may have, you should draw upon the network that you have in being a member of this association. Getting the personal input of other paralegals who may have been faced with similar situations, or who have a greater knowledge through experience of our professional responsibilities, may greatly assist you in working your way through a difficult ethical situation.[62]

Of course, you must be careful not to violate client confidentiality during discussions with someone outside the office. Never mention actual client names or any specific information pertaining to a case. You can talk in hypothetical terms. For example, "an attorney working on a bankruptcy case asks a paralegal to. . . ." Once you present data in this sterilized fashion, you can then ask for guidance on the ethical implications of the data.

If handled delicately, most ethical problems that bother you can be resolved without compromising anyone's integrity or job. Yet the practice of law is not substantially different from other fields of endeavor. There will be times when the clash between principle and the dollar cannot be resolved to everyone's satisfaction. You may indeed have to make a choice between your ethics and your job.

Section F
DOING RESEARCH ON AN ETHICAL ISSUE

1. At a law library, ask where the following two items are kept:

    ● The code or rules of ethics governing the attorneys in your state (see Exhibit 5.3)
    ● The ethical opinions that interpret the code or rules

2. Contact your state bar association. Ask what committee or other body has jurisdiction over ethics. Contact it to find out if it has published any opinions, guidelines, or other materials on paralegals. Also ask if there is a special committee on paralegals. If so, find out what it has said about paralegals.

3. Do the same for any other bar associations in your area, such as city or county bar associations.

4. At a law library, ask where the following two items are kept:

    ● The ABA's *Model Rules of Professional Conduct*
    ● The ethical opinions that interpret these *Model Rules* as well as the earlier *Model Code of Professional Responsibility* of the ABA

5. Examine the *ABA/BNA Lawyers' Manual on Professional Conduct.* This is a loose-leaf book containing current information on ABA ethics and the ethical rules of every state.

6. Other material to check in the library:

    ● C. Wolfram, *Modern Legal Ethics* (1986)
    ● G. Hazard and W. Hodes, *The Law of Lawyering: A Handbook on the Model Rules of Professional Conduct,* 2d ed (1992)
    ● *National Reporter on Legal Ethics and Professional Responsibility* (1982–   )
    ● *The Georgetown Journal of Legal Ethics* (periodical)
    ● *Lawyers' Liability Review* (newsletter)

7. Computer research in either WESTLAW or LEXIS will enable you to do legal research on the law of ethics in your state. (See chapters 11 and 13.) Here, for example, is a

---

[62]Harper, *Ethical Considerations for Legal Assistants,* Compendium (Orange County Paralegal Ass'n, April 1987).

query (question) you could use to ask WESTLAW to find cases in your state in which a paralegal was charged with the unauthorized practice of law:

paralegal "legal assistant" /p "unauthorized practice"

After you instructed WESTLAW to turn to the database containing the court opinions of your state, you would type this query at the keyboard in order to find out if any such cases exist. For many states, there are separate databases devoted to ethics.

8. Another way to find court opinions on ethics in your state is to go to the digest covering the courts in your state. Use its index to find cases on ethical issues.

Assignment 5.2

(a) What is the name of the code of ethics that governs attorneys in your state?

(b) To what body or agency does a client initially make a charge of unethical conduct against his or her attorney in your state?

(c) List the steps required to discipline an attorney for unethical conduct in your state. Begin with the complaint stage and conclude with the court that makes the final decision. Draw a flow chart that lists these steps.

Assignment 5.3

Paul Emerson is an attorney who works at the firm of Rayburn & Rayburn. One of the firm's clients is Designs Unlimited, Inc. (DU), a clothing manufacturer. Emerson provides corporate advice to DU. Recently, Emerson made a mistake in interpreting a new securities law. As a consequence, DU had to postpone the issuance of a stock option for six months. Has Paul acted unethically?

Assignment 5.4

(a) Three individuals in Connecticut hire a large New York law firm to represent them in a proxy fight in which they are seeking control of a Connecticut bank. They lose the proxy fight. The firm then sends these individuals a $358,827 bill for 895 hours of work over a one-month period. Is this bill unethical? What further facts would you like to have to help you answer this question?

(b) Victor Adams and Len Patterson are full partners in the law firm of Adams, Patterson & Kelly. A client contacts Patterson to represent him on a negligence case. Patterson refers the case to Victor Adams, who does most of the work. (Under an agreement between them, Patterson will receive 40 percent and Adams will receive 60 percent of any fee paid by this client.) Patterson does not tell the client about the involvement of Adams in the case. Any ethical problems?

(c) An attorney establishes a bonus plan for her paralegals. A bonus will be given to those paralegals who bill a specified number of hours in excess of a stated minimum. The amount of the bonus will depend on the amount billed and collected. Any ethical problems?

Assignment 5.5

Mary works in a law firm that charges clients $225 an hour for attorney time and $75 an hour for paralegal time. She and another paralegal, Fred, are working with an attorney on a large case. She sees all of the time sheets that the three of them submit to the firm's accounting office. She suspects that the attorney is padding his time sheets by overstating the number of hours he works on the case. For example, he lists thirty hours for a four-day period when he was in court every day on another case. Furthermore, Fred's time is being billed at the full $75-an-hour rate even though he spends about 80 percent of his time typing correspondence, filing, and performing other clerical duties. Mary also suspects that her attorney is billing out Mary's time at the attorney rate rather than the paralegal rate normally charged clients for her time. Any ethical problems? What should Mary do?

Assignment 5.6

Smith is an attorney who works at the firm of Johnson & Johnson. He represents Ralph Grant, who is seeking a divorce from his wife, Amy Grant. In their first meeting, Smith learns that Ralph is an experienced carpenter but is out of work and has very little money. Smith's fee is $150 an hour. Since Ralph has no money and has been having trouble finding work, Smith tells Ralph that he won't have to pay the fee if the court does not grant him the divorce. One day while Smith is working on another case involving Helen Oberlin, he learns that Helen is looking for a carpenter. Smith recommends Ralph to Helen, and she hires him for a small job. Six months pass. The divorce case is dropped when the Grants reconcile. In the meantime, Helen Oberlin is very dissatisfied with Ralph's carpentry work for her; she claims he didn't do the work he contracted to do. She wants to know what she can do about it. She tries to call Smith at Johnson & Johnson but is told that Smith does not work there anymore. Another attorney, Georgia Quinton, Esq. helps Helen. Any ethical problems?

Assignment 5.7

John Jones is a paralegal working at the XYZ law firm. The firm is handling a large class action involving potentially thousands of plaintiffs. John has been instructed to screen the potential plaintiffs in the class. John tells those he screens out (using criteria provided by the firm) in writing or verbally that "unfortunately, our firm will not be able to represent you." Any ethical problems?

Assignment 5.8

A paralegal quits the firm of Smith & Smith. When she leaves, she takes client documents she prepared while at the firm. The documents contain confidential client information. The paralegal is showing these documents to potential employers as writing samples.

(a) What is the ethical liability of attorneys at Smith & Smith under Model Rule 5.3?

(b) What is the ethical liability of attorneys at law firms where she is seeking employment under 5.3?

(c) What is the paralegal's liability?

Assignment 5.9

(a) Mary Smith is a paralegal at the ABC law firm. She has been working on the case of Jessica Randolph, a client of the office. Mary talks with Ms. Randolph often. Mary receives a subpoena from the attorney of the party that is suing Ms. Randolph. On the witness stand, Mary is asked by this attorney what Ms. Randolph told her at the ABC law office about a particular business transaction related to the suit. Randolph's attorney (Mary's supervisor) objects to the question. What result?

(b) Before Helen became a paralegal for the firm of Harris & Derkson, she was a chemist for a large corporation. Harris & Derkson is a patent law firm where Helen's technical expertise in chemistry is invaluable. Helen's next-door neighbor is an inventor. On a number of occasions, he discussed the chemical makeup of his inventions with Helen. Now the government has charged the neighbor with stealing official secrets to prepare one of these inventions. Harris & Derkson represent the neighbor on this case. Helen also works directly on the case for the firm. In a prosecution of the neighbor, Helen is called as a witness and is asked to reveal the substance of all her conversations with the neighbor concerning the invention in question. Does Helen have to answer?

Assignment 5.10

Bob and Patricia Fannan are separated, and they both want a divorce. They would like to have a joint-custody arrangement in which their son would spend time with each parent during the year. The only marital property is a house, which they agree should be sold, with each to get one-half of the proceeds. Mary Franklin, Esq. is an attorney whom Bob and Patricia know and trust. They decide to ask Franklin to represent both of them in the divorce. Any ethical problems?

Assignment 5.11

George is a religious conservative. He works for a law firm that represents Adult Features, Inc., which distributes X-rated videos. The client is fighting an injunction sought by the police against its business. George is asked by his supervisor to do some research on the case. Any ethical problems?

Assignment 5.12

Peter is a paralegal at Smith & Smith. One of the cases he works on is *Carter v. Horton.* Carter is the client of Smith & Smith. Peter does some investigation and scheduling of discovery for the case. Horton is represented by Unger, Oberdorf & Simon. The Unger firm offers Peter a job working in its law library and in its computer department on database management. He takes the job. While at the Unger firm, Peter can see all the documents in the *Carter v. Horton* case. At lunch a week after Peter joined the firm, he tells one of the Unger attorneys (Jack Dolan) about an investigation he conducted while working for Smith & Smith on the *Carter* case. (Jack is not one of the Unger attorneys working on *Carter v. Horton.*) Two weeks after Peter was hired, the Unger firm decides to set up a Chinese Wall around Peter. He is told not to discuss *Carter v. Horton* with any Unger employee, all Unger employees are told not to discuss the case with Peter, the files are kept away from Peter, etc. The wall is rigidly enforced. Nevertheless, Smith & Smith makes a motion to disqualify Unger, Oberdorf & Simon from continuing to represent Horton in the *Carter v. Horton* case. Should this motion be granted?

Assignment 5.13

Alice is a freelance paralegal with a specialty in probate law. One of the firms she has worked for is Davis, Ritter & Boggs. Her most recent assignment for this firm has been to identify the assets of Mary Steck, who died six months ago. One of Mary's assets is a 75 percent ownership share in the Domain Corporation. Alice learns a great deal about this company, including the fact that four months ago it had difficulty meeting its payroll and expects to have similar difficulties in the coming year.

Alice's freelance business has continued to grow because of her excellent reputation. She decides to hire an employee with a different specialty so that her office can begin to take different kinds of cases from attorneys. She hires Bob, a paralegal with four years of litigation experience. The firm of Jackson & Jackson hires Alice to digest a series of long deposition documents in the case of *Glendale Bank v. Ajax Tire Co.* Jackson & Jackson represents Glendale Bank. Peterson, Zuckerman & Morgan represents Ajax Tire Co. Alice assigns Bob to this case. Ajax Tire Co. is a wholly owned subsidiary of the Domain Corporation. Glendale Bank is suing Ajax Tire Co. for fraud in misrepresenting its financial worth when Ajax Tire Co. applied for and obtained a loan from Glendale Bank.

Any ethical problems?

Assignment 5.14

Assume that you owned a successful freelance business in which you provided paralegal services to over 150 attorneys all over the state. How should your files be organized in order to avoid a conflict of interest?

Assignment 5.15

Joan is a paralegal who works for the XYZ law firm, which is representing Goff in a suit against Barnard, who is represented by the ABC law firm. Joan calls Barnard and says, "Is this the first time that you have ever been sued?" Barnard answers, "Yes it is. Is there anything else that you would like to know?" Joan says *no* and the conversation ends. Any ethical problems?

Assignment 5.16

Mary is a paralegal who is a senior citizen. She works at the XYZ legal service office. One day she goes to a senior citizens center and says the following:

All of you should know about and take advantage of the XYZ legal service office where I work. Let me give you just one example why. Down at the office there is an attorney named Armanda Morris. She is an expert on insurance company cases. Some of you may have had trouble with insurance companies that say one thing and do another. Our office is available to serve you.

Any ethical problems?

Assignment 5.17

(a) What restrictions exist on advertising by attorneys in your state? Give an example of an ad on TV or in the newspaper that would be unethical. On researching an ethical issue, see Section F.

(b) In *Bates v. State Bar of Arizona,* 433 U.S. 350 (1977), the United States Supreme Court held that a state could not prohibit all forms of lawyer advertising. Has *Bates* been cited by state courts in your state on the advertising issue? If so, what impact has the case had in your state? To find out, shepardize *Bates.* The specific techniques of Shepardizing a case are found in Checklist 4a, page 609.

Assignment 5.18

Mary Jackson is a paralegal at Rollins & Rollins. She is supervised by Ian Gregory. Mary is stealing money from the funds of one of the firm's clients. The only attorney who knows about this is Dan Roberts, Esq., who is not a partner at the firm and who does not supervise Mary. Dan says and does nothing about Mary's actions. What ethical obligations does Dan have under Model Rule 5.3?

Assignment 5.19

John Smith is a paralegal who works for the firm of Beard, Butler, and Clark. John's immediate supervisor is Viola Butler, Esq. With the full knowledge and blessing of Viola Butler, John

Smith sends a letter to a client of the firm (Mary Anders). Has Viola Butler acted unethically in permitting John to send out this letter? The letter is as follows:

Law Offices of
Beard, Butler, and Clark
310 High St.
Maincity, Ohio 45238
512-663-9410

Attorneys at Law   *Paralegal*

Ronald Beard   **John Smith**
Viola Butler
Wilma Clark

                                                                    May 14, 1997

Mary Anders
621 S. Randolph Ave.
Maincity, Ohio 45238

Dear Ms. Anders:

  Viola Butler, the attorney in charge of your case, has asked
me to let you know that next month's hearing has been post-
poned. We will let you know the new date as soon as possible.
If you have any questions don't hesitate to call me.

                                             Sincerely,

                                             John Smith
                                             Legal Intern

JS:wps

Assignment 5.20

Under what circumstances, if any, would it be appropriate for you to refer to a client of the office where you work as "my client"?

Assignment 5.21

John Jones is a paralegal who works for an attorney named Linda Sunders. Linda is away from the office one day and telephones John, who is at the office. She dictates a one-line letter to a client of the office. The letter reads, "I advise you to sue." Linda asks John to sign the letter for her. The bottom of the letter reads as follows:

Linda Sunders
by John Jones

Any ethical problems?

Assignment 5.22

Mary is a paralegal who works at the XYZ law firm. She specializes in real estate matters at the firm. Mary attends a real estate closing in which her role consists of exchanging documents and acknowledging the receipt of documents. Are there ethical problems in allowing her to do so? Answer this question on the basis of the following variations:

(a) The closing takes place at the XYZ law firm.

(b) The closing takes place at a bank.

(c) Mary's supervising attorney is not present at the closing.

(d) Mary's supervising attorney is present at the closing.

(e) Mary's supervising attorney is present at the closing except for thirty minutes, during which time Mary continued to exchange documents and acknowledge the receipt of documents.

(f) During the closing, the attorney for the other party says to Mary, "I don't know why my client should have to pay that charge." Mary responds: "In this state that charge is always paid in this way."

Assignment 5.23

John is a paralegal who works for the XYZ law firm, which is representing a client against the Today Insurance Company. The Company employs paralegals who work under the Company's general counsel. One of these paralegals is Mary. In an effort to settle the case, Mary calls John and says, "We offer you $200.00." John says, "We'll let you know." Any ethical problems?

Assignment 5.24

John Smith is a paralegal who works for Beard, Butler, and Clark. He sends out the following letter. Any ethical problems?

> **John Smith**
> **Paralegal**
> **310 High St.**
> **Maincity, Ohio 45238**
> **512-663-9410**
>
> June 1, 1997
>
> State Unemployment Board
> 1216 Southern Ave.
> Maincity, Ohio 45238
>
> Dear Gentlepeople:
>
> I work for Beard, Butler, and Clark, which represents Mary Anders, who has a claim before your agency. A hearing originally scheduled for June 8, 1997, has been postponed. We request that the hearing be held at the earliest time possible after the 8th.
>
> Sincerely,
>
> John Smith
>
> JS:wps

🏛 *Assignment 5 . 25*

In Section C of chapter 2, there is a long list of tasks that paralegals have performed and comments by paralegals working in the specialties covered. Identify any three tasks or paralegal comments that *might* pose ethical problems or problems of unauthorized practice. Explain why.

🏛 *Assignment 5.26*

(a) Examine NFPA's *Model Code of Ethics,* NALA's *Code of Ethics,* and NALA's *Model Standards and Guidelines* printed in Section D of the chapter. Make a list of the similarities and differences among all three documents.

(b) Draft one paralegal code of ethics based solely on all three documents. Combine them all into one code. (Don't include comments or footnotes.) Where there are language differences on the same topic, adopt the language you think would be best for the paralegal field. If a topic is covered in one document but not in another, include it if you think inclusion would be best for the paralegal field.

🏛 *Assignment 5 . 27*

Draft your own paralegal code as a class project. Use any of the material in chapter 5 as a resource. First, have a meeting in which you make a list of all the issues that you think should be covered in the code. Divide up the issues by the number of students in the class so that every student has roughly the same number of issues. Each student should draft a proposed rule on each of the issues to which he or she is assigned. Accompany each rule with a brief commentary on why you think the rule should be as stated. Draft alternative versions of the proposed rule if different versions are possible and you want to give the class the chance to examine all of them. The class then meets to vote on each of the proposed rules. Students will make presentations on the proposed rules they have drafted. If the class is not happy with the way in which a particular proposed rule was drafted by a student, the latter will redraft the rule for later consideration by the class. One member of the class should be designated the "code reporter," who records the rules accepted by the class by majority vote.

After you have completed the code, you should consider inviting attorneys from the local bar association to your class in order to discuss your proposed code. Do the same with officials of the closest paralegal association in your area.

C h a p t e r   S u m m a r y

Ethics are the standards of behavior to which members of an organization must conform. Begin your paralegal career by committing yourself to become an ethical conservative.

Attorneys are regulated primarily by the highest court in the state, often with the extensive involvement of the state bar association. Since paralegals cannot practice law and cannot become full members of a bar association, they can-

not be punished by the bar association for a violation of the ethical rules governing attorneys. The American Bar Association is a voluntary association; no attorney must be a member. The ABA publishes ethical rules that the states are free to adopt, modify, or reject.

The current rules of the ABA are found in its *Model Rules of Professional Conduct.* These ethical rules require attorneys to be competent, to act with reasonable diligence and promptness, to charge fees that are reasonable, to avoid conduct that is criminal and fraudulent, to avoid asserting claims and defenses that are frivolous, to safeguard the property of clients, to avoid making false statements of law and fact to a tribunal, to withdraw from a case for appropriate reasons, to maintain the confidentiality of client information, to avoid conflicts of interest, to avoid improper communications with an opponent, to avoid improper solicitation of clients, to avoid improper advertising, to report serious professional misconduct of other attorneys, to avoid assisting nonattorneys to engage in the unauthorized practice of law, and to supervise paralegal employees appropriately.

Ethical opinions or guidelines exist in almost every state on the proper use of a paralegal by an attorney. All states agree that the title used for this employee must not mislead anyone about his or her nonattorney status, and that the employee must disclose his or her nonattorney status when necessary to avoid misunderstanding. Rules also exist on other aspects of the attorney-paralegal relationship, but not all states agree on what these rules should be. The following apply in most states:

Under attorney approval and supervision, paralegals in most states:

- can have their own business card
- can have their name printed on the law firm letterhead
- can sign law firm correspondence
- can give nonlegal advice
- can draft legal documents
- can attend a real estate closing
- can represent clients at agency hearings if authorized by the agency

With few exceptions, paralegals in most states:

- cannot give legal advice
- cannot conduct a deposition
- cannot sign formal court documents
- cannot supervise the execution of a will
- cannot make an appearance in court

Separate ethical rules and guidelines have been adopted by the National Association of Legal Assistants and by the National Federation of Paralegal Associations.

KEY TERMS

ethics, 244
sanctions, 244
integrated bar association, 246
registration, 246
disbarment, 249
suspension, 249
reprimand, 249
admonition, 249
probation, 249
paralegal codes, 249
competent, 251
clinical education, 252
continuing legal education, 252
retainer, 255
minimum-fee schedule, 256
contingent fees, 256
fee splitting, 257
referral fee, 257

forwarding fee, 257
double billing, 259
padding, 259
attestation clause, 263
insider trading, 263
pirated software, 263
adversarial system, 264
frivolous positions, 265
commingle, 265
withdrawal, 267
cured, 267
disengagement letter, 267
declination letter, 267
letter of nonengagement, 267
impaired attorney, 267
privileged, 268
confidentiality, 268
consent, 268
attorney-client privilege

rule, 269
discoverable, 269
attorney work-product rule, 269
confidentiality agreement, 270
conflict of interest, 272
bias, 275
disinterestedness, 275
multiple representation, 276
common representation, 276
adverse interests, 276
duty of loyalty, 277
imputed disqualification, 278
vicarious disqualification, 278
tainted, 278
infected, 278

contaminated, 278
tainted paralegals, 278
Chinese Wall, 279
ethical wall, 279
cone of silence, 279
quarantined, 279
conflicts check, 283
conflict specialists, 284
lateral hire, 284
solicitation, 286
ambulance chasing, 286
barratry, 286
runner, 287
capper, 287
unauthorized practice of law, 289
Model Rule 5.3, 290
second chair, 301

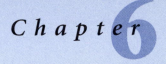
INTRODUCTION TO THE LEGAL SYSTEM

► *Chapter Outline*

Section A
FEDERALISM, CHECKS AND BALANCES, AND PARALEGALS

What are the components of our legal system and what kind of laws do they produce? These are our concerns in this chapter as we continue to explore the role of the paralegal.

Our legal system is really *three* systems consisting of three levels of government. They are the federal government (called the U.S. government), fifty state governments,[1] and a large variety of local governments (called counties, cities, and townships).

One of the most important characteristics of our legal system is the division of powers between the federal government and the state governments. Only the federal government, for example, has the power to declare war, whereas only a state government has the power to issue a marriage license or a divorce decree. The term **federalism** refers to the division of powers between the federal government and the state governments. Federalism simply means that we live in a society where some powers are exercised by the federal government, others by the state governments, and still others by both the federal and the state governments.

Within the federal, state, and local levels of government, there are three *branches:* one that makes laws (**legislative branch**), one that carries out laws (**executive branch**), and one that interprets laws and resolves disputes that arise under them (**judicial branch**). The categories of law that these three branches of government write are outlined in Exhibit 6.1.

Exhibit 6.1   Kinds of Laws

CATEGORY	DEFINITION	WHO WRITES THIS KIND OF LAW?
(a) **Opinion**	A court's written explanation of how it applied the law to the facts before it to resolve a legal dispute. Also called a **case.**	Courts—usually appellate courts.
(b) **Statute**	A law that declares, commands, or prohibits something. Also called **legislation.** (An **act** is the official document that contains the statute.)	The legislature. Some states also allow a direct vote of the people by referendum.
(c) **Constitution**	The fundamental law that creates the branches of government and identifies basic rights and obligations.	Varies. Often a combination of the legislature and a vote of the people. Another option might be a constitutional convention.
(d) **Administrative Regulation**	A law designed to explain or carry out the statutes and executive orders that govern an administrative agency. Also called an **administrative rule.**	Administrative agency.
(e) **Administrative Decision**	A resolution of a controversy between a party and an administrative agency involving the application of the regulations, statutes, or executive orders that govern the agency. Also called an **administrative ruling.**	Administrative agency.

---

[1]Plus the District of Columbia, which has a special status but in some respects is treated as a state.

Exhibit 6.1	**Kinds of Laws—continued**	
CATEGORY	**DEFINITION**	**WHO WRITES THIS KIND OF LAW?**
(f) **Charter**	The fundamental law of a municipality or other local unit of government authorizing it to perform designated governmental functions.	Varies. The state legislature often writes charter provisions for cities in the state.
(g) **Ordinance**	A law that declares, commands, or prohibits something. (Same as a statute, but at the local level.)	The local legislature (e.g., City Council, County Commission).
(h) **Rules of Court**	The procedural laws that govern the mechanics of litigation before a particular court. Also called **court rules.**	Varies. The legislature and/or the highest court in the jurisdiction.
(i) **Executive Order**	A law issued by the chief executive pursuant to specific statutory authority or to the executive's inherent authority to direct the operation of governmental agencies.	President (for U.S. government); Governor (for state government); Mayor (for local government).
(j) **Treaty**	An international agreement between two or more foreign governments.	The President makes treaties by and with the consent of the U.S. Senate.
(k) **Opinion of the Attorney General**	Formal legal advice given by the chief law officer of the government to another government official or agency. (Technically, this is *not* a category of law, but it is often relied on as a source of law.)	Attorney General.

Federal Government

Legislative branch: The Congress

Executive branch: The President and the federal administrative agencies (see the chart in Appendix D.)

Judicial branch: The U.S. Supreme Court, the U.S. Courts of Appeal, the U.S. District Courts, and other federal courts (see Exhibits 6.3 and 6.4)

State Government

Legislative branch: The state legislature

Executive branch: The governor and the state administrative agencies

Judicial branch: The state courts (see Exhibit 6.2)

Local Government

Legislative branch: The City Council or County Commission

Executive branch: The Mayor or County Commissioner and the local administrative agencies

Judicial branch: The local courts (many local courts, however, are considered part of the state judiciary)

In addition to the division of power between the federal and state levels of government, there is also a division of power among the three branches—legislative, executive, and judicial—within each level. This division is called the system of **checks and balances** and is designed to prevent any one branch from becoming too powerful. The system allocates governmental powers among the three branches. One branch is allowed to block or check what another branch wants to do so that a balance of powers is maintained among the branches. Let's look at an example.

The legislative branch has the primary responsibility for writing the law. By majority vote, the legislature creates what are called *statutes* (see Exhibit 6.1). But there are significant checks on this power. First of all, the chief executive must give final approval to a proposed law before it can become a statute. He or she can reject (i.e., veto) the proposed law. The legislature, however, has another power that operates as a countercheck on the chief executive's power to veto proposed laws. The legislature can nullify (i.e., override) the chief executive's veto by a two-thirds vote. These are some of the ways that the legislative and executive branches check each other.

The judiciary branch has a similar function. Courts can check the legislative and executive branches through the power of **judicial review.** This is the power to refuse to enforce a law because it is in conflict with the *constitution.* In turn, the judicial branch can be checked by the other branches. For example, the legislature controls the budget of the courts, and the chief executive often nominates the persons who will be judges.

The result of all these checks and counterchecks is a *balance* of power among the three branches so that no one branch becomes too powerful.

How do paralegals fit within these levels and branches of government? First of all, many paralegals are civil service employees of government, particularly in federal, state, and local administrative agencies (see Appendix 2.B in chapter 2). To a more limited extent, paralegals are also employees of legislatures and courts. Second, paralegals help attorneys solve the legal problems of clients by applying the different kinds of law outlined in Exhibit 6.1 to the facts presented by client cases. A single client case can involve the laws of different levels and branches of government.

For example:

Linda Thompson applies for unemployment compensation benefits after being terminated from her job. Her former employer says the termination was due to a slowdown in business at the company. Linda believes she was let go because she is a woman and because she is HIV positive. You are a paralegal working for Sims & Sims, which represents her. Your supervisor may ask you to undertake a variety of tasks: interviewing, investigation, research, analysis, drafting, law office administration, etc. A central focus of everything the attorney and paralegal do on such a case is the application of laws to the facts of the case. The laws are written by different branches of government at the different levels of government. Here are some examples of laws that might apply to Linda Thompson's case:

• The Fourteenth Amendment of the United States Constitution guaranteeing equal protection of the law.

• Federal statutes on civil rights, sex discrimination, disability discrimination, evidence and civil procedure in federal courts, etc.

• Opinions of federal courts on civil rights, sex discrimination, disability discrimination, civil procedure in federal courts, etc.

• Administrative regulations on sex discrimination of the U.S. Equal Employment Opportunity Commission and other federal administrative agencies.

• The Equal Rights Amendment of the state constitution prohibiting sex discrimination.

• State statutes on unemployment compensation, civil rights, sex discrimination, evidence and civil procedure in state courts, etc.

• State court opinions on unemployment compensation, civil rights, sex discrimination, evidence and civil procedure in state courts, etc.

• Administrative regulations on unemployment compensation of the State Unemployment Compensation Commission.

These, then, are the major laws and institutions involved in the practice of law. We can say that our legal system is an organized method of resolving legal disputes and achieving justice through the enforcement and interpretation of laws written by different levels and branches of government. To participate, paralegals need to have a basic understanding of the essential components of this process.

Assignment 6.1

Find a recent article in your local general newspaper that meets the following criteria: (a) it refers to more than one kind of law listed in Exhibit 6.1, and (b) it refers to more than one level of government. Since the article will have no formal citations to laws, do the best you can to guess what kinds of law and levels of government are involved. Clip out the article. In the margin, next to each reference to a law, place the appropriate abbreviation: FO (if you think the reference is to a federal court opinion); SO (if you think the reference is to a state court opinion); FS (federal statute); SS (state statute); FC (United States Constitution); SC (state constitution); FAR (administrative regulation of a federal agency); SAR (administrative regulation of a state agency). Make up your own abbreviations for any other kind of law listed in Exhibit 6.1. If the article refers to the same law more than once, make a margin note only the first time the law is mentioned. (We'll have an informal contest to see which student can find the article with the most different kinds of laws involving more than one level of government.)

Section B
COMMON LAW AND OUR ADVERSARIAL SYSTEM

Before examining the components of our judicial system, we need to understand two of its critical characteristics. First of all, the system is based on the **common law.** This phrase has at least four meanings, the last of which will be our primary concern in this book:

- At the broadest level, common law simply means case law—court opinions—as opposed to statutory law. In this sense, all case law develops and is part of the common law.

- Common law also refers to the legal system of England and America. Its counterpart is the **civil law system** of many Western European countries other than England (e.g., France). The origin of civil law includes the jurisprudence of the Roman Empire set forth in the Code of Justinian. (Louisiana is unique in that, unlike the remaining forty-nine common law states, its state law is in large measure based on the civil law— the Code Napoléon.) While there is overlap between the two systems, common law systems generally place greater reliance on case law, whereas civil law systems tend to place greater emphasis on code or statutory law.

- More narrowly, common law refers to all of the case law *and* statutory law in England and in the American colonies before the American Revolution. The phrase **at common law** often refers to this colonial period.

- The most prevalent definition of common law is judge-made law in the absence of controlling statutory law or other higher law. As we shall see, statutes are superior in authority to the common law. Indeed, statutes are often passed with the express purpose of changing the common law in a particular area. Such statutes are referred to as **statutes in derogation of the common law.** Another meaning of the phrase "at common law," therefore, is judge-made law that exists until changed by statute.

Courts are sometimes confronted with disputes for which there is no applicable law. There may be no constitutional provisions, statutes, or administrative regulations governing the dispute. When this occurs, the court will apply—and if necessary, create—common law to resolve the controversy. Here common law is used in the fourth sense given above. That is, it is made by judges to compensate for the lack of statutory and other law applicable to the case at hand. In creating the common law, the court relies primarily on the unwritten customs and values of the community from time immemorial. Very often these customs and values are described and enforced in old opinions that are heavily cited by modern courts in the continuing process of developing the common law.

The second critical characteristic of our judicial system is that it is **adversarial.** An adversarial system is a form of head-to-head combat. If a dispute arises, you get everyone in the same room and have them fight it out—in the open. This approach is based on the theory that justice and truth have a greater chance of being achieved when the parties to a controversy appear (on their own or through a representative or advocate) before a neutral judge to present their conflicting positions. We don't expect the judge to control the case by calling and questioning the witnesses. By and large, we leave this to the parties and their representatives. More specifically, an adversarial system assumes the following:

- The decision maker is neutral and relatively passive; he or she has the responsibility of deciding the case.
- The parties themselves develop and present the evidence on which the decision will be based.
- The proceeding is concentrated, uninterrupted, and otherwise designed to emphasize the clash of opposing evidence and argument presented by the parties.
- The parties have an equal opportunity to present and argue their case to the decision maker.[2]

These are the ideal circumstances under which our adversarial system operates. Unfortunately, the system is often criticized for failing to live up to the ideal.

Section C
JUDICIAL SYSTEMS

The lifeblood of a court is its jurisdiction in relationship to other courts. After examining the nature of jurisdiction, our goal here will be to identify the major courts that exist and to explore how they are interrelated.

1. JURISDICTION

There are fifty state court systems and one main federal court system. Each court within a system is identified by its **jurisdiction.** The word *jurisdiction* has three meanings.

---

[2]William Burnham, *Introduction to the Legal System of the United States,* 83 (1995).

First, the word is often used to refer to the geographic area over which a particular court has authority. A state trial court, for example, has **geographic jurisdiction** to hear cases arising in a specific county or district of the state. A state supreme court, in contrast, has geographic jurisdiction to hear appeals in cases arising anywhere in the state. Thus a state supreme court will often say "in this jurisdiction" when referring to its authority in its own state. The phrase has the same meaning as "in this state."

Second, jurisdiction refers to the power of a court over a defendant to adjudicate a dispute against the defendant. **Adjudication** is the process by which a court (or administrative agency) resolves a legal dispute through litigation. For the court to have the power to order the defendant to do anything (or to refrain from doing something), the court must have **personal jurisdiction** over the defendant. This is also called **in personam jurisdiction.** How does a court acquire such jurisdiction? One requirement is to give proper notice to the defendant that a suit based on the dispute has been filed against him or her. This is done through what is called **service of process.**

Third, jurisdiction means the power that a court must have over the subject matter or over the particular kind of dispute that has been brought before it. Some of the more common classifications of **subject-matter jurisdiction** are:

- Limited jurisdiction
- General jurisdiction
- Exclusive jurisdiction
- Concurrent jurisdiction
- Original jurisdiction
- Appellate jurisdiction

a. Limited Jurisdiction

A court of **limited** (or special) subject-matter **jurisdiction** can hear only certain kinds of cases. A criminal court is not allowed to take a noncriminal case, and a small claims court is authorized to hear only cases in which the plaintiff claims a relatively small amount of money as damages from the defendant. (The maximum amount a small claims court can award is set by statute.)

b. General Jurisdiction

A court of **general jurisdiction** can, with some exceptions, hear any kind of case. A state court of general jurisdiction can handle any case that raises **state questions** (i.e., questions arising from or based on the state constitution, state statutes, state regulations, or state common law); a federal court of general jurisdiction can handle any case that raises **federal questions** (i.e., questions arising from or based on the federal constitution, federal statutes, federal regulations, or other federal laws).[3]

c. Exclusive Jurisdiction

A court of **exclusive jurisdiction** is the only court that can handle a certain kind of case. For example, a Juvenile Court may have exclusive jurisdiction over all cases involving children under a certain age who are charged with acts of delinquency. If this kind of case is brought in another court, there could be a challenge on the ground that the court lacked jurisdiction over the case.

d. Concurrent Jurisdiction

Sometimes two courts have jurisdiction over a case; the case could be brought in either court. In such a situation, both courts are said to have **concurrent jurisdiction** over the

[3]In this context, the word *federal* means United States. The United States government is the federal government, the United States courts are the federal courts, etc.

case. For example, a Family Court and a County Court may have jurisdiction to enforce a child-support order.

e. Original Jurisdiction

A court of **original jurisdiction** is the first court to hear a case. It is also called a trial court or a **court of first instance.** In addition, it is a court of limited jurisdiction (if it can try only certain kinds of cases), or of general jurisdiction (if it can try cases involving any subject matter), or of exclusive jurisdiction (if the trial can take place only in that court), or of concurrent jurisdiction (if the trial can take place either in that court or in another kind of court).

f. Appellate Jurisdiction

A court with **appellate jurisdiction** can hear appeals from lower tribunals. An **appeal** is a review or reexamination of what a lower court or agency has done to determine if there was any error. Sometimes a party who is dissatisfied with a lower court ruling can appeal as a matter of right to the appellate court (the court must hear the appeal); in other kinds of cases, the appellate court has discretion as to whether it will hear the appeal.

2. STATE COURT SYSTEMS

First we examine jurisdiction in our state courts. See Exhibit 6.2.

a. Courts of Original Jurisdiction

A state will have one or more levels or tiers of trial courts (courts of original jurisdiction). These courts hear the dispute, determine the facts of the case, and make the initial determination or ruling. In addition, they may sometimes have the power to review cases that were initially decided by an administrative agency.

The most common arrangement is a two-tier system of trial courts. At the lower level are courts of limited or special jurisdiction, the so-called **inferior courts.** Local courts, such as city courts, county courts, small claims courts, or justice of the peace courts, often fall into this category. These courts may have original jurisdiction over relatively minor cases, such as violations of local ordinances and lawsuits involving small sums of money. Also included in this category are special courts that are limited to specific matters, such as surrogate courts or probate courts that hear matters involving the estates of deceased or mentally incompetent persons.

Immediately above the trial courts of limited jurisdiction are the trial courts of general jurisdiction, which usually handle more serious cases, such as lawsuits involving large sums of money. The name given to the trial courts at this second level varies greatly from state to state. They are known as superior courts, courts of common pleas, district courts, or circuit courts. New York is especially confusing. There, the trial court of general jurisdiction is called the *supreme court,* a label reserved in most states for the court of final appeals, the highest court in the system.

Not all states have a two-tier trial system. Some states have only one court of original jurisdiction. Moreover, the individual levels may be segmented into divisions. A court of general jurisdiction, for example, may be broken up into specialized divisions such as landlord-tenant, family, juvenile, and criminal divisions.

b. Courts of Appeals

The primary function of courts of appeals (also called **appellate courts**) is to **review** decisions made by lower courts in order to correct **errors of law.**[4] That is, they look to see

---

[4]As we saw earlier, the phrase *judicial review* refers to the power of a court to refuse to enforce a law because it is in conflict with the constitution.

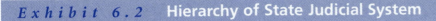

| *E x h i b i t   6 . 2* | **Hierarchy of State Judicial System** |

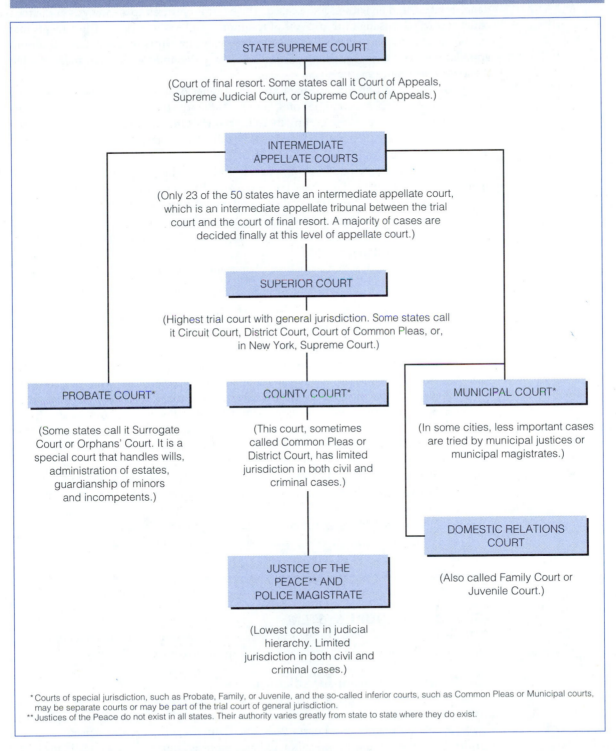

STATE SUPREME COURT

(Court of final resort. Some states call it Court of Appeals,
Supreme Judicial Court, or Supreme Court of Appeals.)

INTERMEDIATE APPELLATE COURTS

(Only 23 of the 50 states have an intermediate appellate court,
which is an intermediate appellate tribunal between the trial
court and the court of final resort. A majority of cases are
decided finally at this level of appellate court.)

SUPERIOR COURT

(Highest trial court with general jurisdiction. Some states call
it Circuit Court, District Court, Court of Common Pleas, or,
in New York, Supreme Court.)

PROBATE COURT*

(Some states call it Surrogate
Court or Orphans' Court. It is a
special court that handles wills,
administration of estates,
guardianship of minors
and incompetents.)

COUNTY COURT*

(This court, sometimes
called Common Pleas or
District Court, has limited
jurisdiction in both civil and
criminal cases.)

MUNICIPAL COURT*

(In some cities, less important cases
are tried by municipal justices or
municipal magistrates.)

DOMESTIC RELATIONS COURT

(Also called Family Court or
Juvenile Court.)

JUSTICE OF THE PEACE AND POLICE MAGISTRATE**

(Lowest courts in judicial
hierarchy. Limited
jurisdiction in both civil and
criminal cases.)

* Courts of special jurisdiction, such as Probate, Family, or Juvenile, and the so-called inferior courts, such as Common Pleas or Municipal courts,
may be separate courts or may be part of the trial court of general jurisdiction.
** Justices of the Peace do not exist in all states. Their authority varies greatly from state to state where they do exist.

Source: *Law and the Courts,* 20 (American Bar Association, 1974).

if the lower court correctly interpreted and applied the law to the facts of the dispute. In this review process, appellate courts do not make their own findings of fact. No new evidence is taken, and no witnesses are called. The court limits itself to an analysis of the **trial court record** (consisting of transcripts of testimony, copies of the various documents that were filed, etc.) to determine if that lower court made any errors of law. Attorneys submit **appellate briefs** containing their arguments on the correctness or incorrectness of what the lower court did.

An appellate court often consists of an odd number of justices, e.g., five, seven, nine, eleven, fifteen. This helps avoid tie votes. Some of these courts hear cases in smaller groups of judges, usually three. These groups are called **panels.** Once a panel renders its decision, the parties often have the right to petition to the full court to hear the case **en banc,** meaning with the entire membership of the court.

Many states have only one level of appellate court to which trial court judgments are appealed. About half the states have two levels of appellate courts. The first level is the court of middle appeals, sometimes called an **intermediate appellate court.** The decisions of this court can in turn be reviewed by a second-level appellate court, the court of final appeals. This latter court, often known as the **supreme court,** is the **court of final resort,** the highest state court in the state.

Exhibit 6.2 on page 329 shows the lines of appeal in many state court systems.

📜 *A s s i g n m e n t* 6 . 2

(a) Redraw Exhibit 6.2 so that your chart includes all the state courts of your state. Identify each level of state court in your state using Exhibit 6.2 as a guide. Give the complete name of each court you include and a one-sentence description of its subject-matter jurisdiction. Draw the lines of appeal among these courts. To find out what state courts exist in your state, check your state statutory code and your state constitution. This is the only way to obtain current information about your state court system. You may come across a chart written by someone else, but it may not reflect recent changes in the structure and names of your state courts.

(b) Select any state trial court of general jurisdiction in your state. State its name, address, and phone number. Also state the name, phone number, and fax number of the chief clerk of this court.

(c) Give the name, address, and phone number of the court to which decisions of the trial court you selected are appealed. Also state the name, phone number, and fax number of the chief clerk of this appellate court.

3. FEDERAL COURT SYSTEM

The federal court system, like the state systems, consists of two basic kinds of courts: courts of original jurisdiction (trial courts) and appellate courts. See Exhibit 6.3.

a. Courts of Original Jurisdiction

The basic federal court at the trial level is the **United States District Court.** There are districts throughout the country, at least one for every state, the District of Columbia, Guam, the Virgin Islands, and Puerto Rico. The District Courts exercise general, original jurisdiction over most federal litigation and also serve as courts of review for many cases initially decided by federal administrative agencies.

Exhibit 6.3   **Hierarchy of Federal Judicial System**

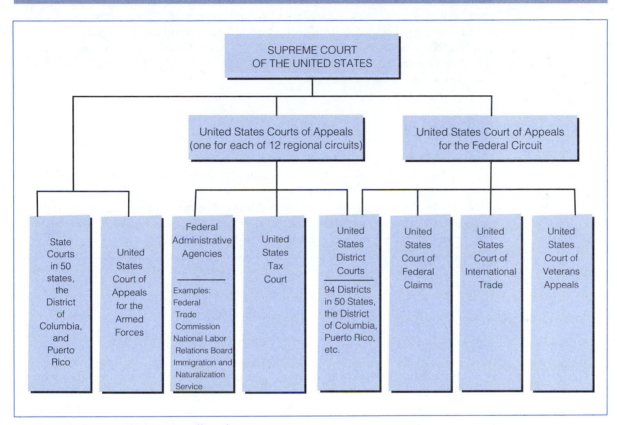

Source: United States Administrative Office of Courts.

In addition to the District Courts, several federal courts, such as the United States Court of Federal Claims, exercise original, limited jurisdiction over specialized cases.

b. Court of Appeals

The federal system, like almost half of the fifty state judicial systems, has two levels of appellate courts: middle appeals and final appeals. The primary court at the middle level is the **United States Court of Appeals.** These courts are divided into twelve geographic circuits, eleven of them made up of groupings of various states and territories, with a twelfth for the District of Columbia. Their primary function is to review the decisions of the federal courts of original jurisdiction, primarily the District Courts. In addition, decisions of certain federal agencies, notably the National Labor Relations Board, are reviewed directly by a Court of Appeals without first going to a District Court. Finally, there is a specialized Court of Appeals called the Court of Appeals for the Federal Circuit. This court reviews (a) decisions from the United States Court of Federal Claims, the United States Court of International Trade, and the United States Court of Veterans Appeals, and (b) some decisions of the District Courts where the United States government is a defendant.[5]

---

[5]The United States Court of Appeal for the Federal Circuit also reviews cases from other special tribunals such as the United States Patent and Trademark Office, the Board of Contract Appeals, and the International Trade Commission.

The federal court of final appeals is, of course, the **United States Supreme Court,** which provides the final review of the decisions of all federal courts and agencies. The Supreme Court may also review certain decisions of the state courts when these decisions raise questions involving the United States Constitution, a federal statute, or other federal law.

Exhibit 6.4 illustrates the division of the federal court system into twelve geographic circuits. Each circuit has its own United States Court of Appeals. The United States District Courts exist within these circuits.

Assignment 6.3

(a) What is the complete name of the federal trial court that covers where you live? Give its address and phone number. Also, state the name, phone number, and fax number of the chief clerk of this court.

(b) What is the name of the United States Court of Appeals to which decisions of your federal trial court are appealed? Give its address and phone number. Also, state the name, phone number, and fax number of the chief clerk of this appellate court.

Section D
ADMINISTRATIVE AGENCIES

An **administrative agency** is a unit of government whose primary mission is to carry out—or administer—the statutes of the legislature and the executive orders of the chief of the executive branch of government. At the federal level, the chief is the president; at the state level, it is the governor; and at most local levels, it is the mayor. As we will see in a moment, many agencies also have rule-making and dispute-resolution responsibilities.

Administrative agencies can have a wide variety of names. Here are some examples:

- Fire Department
- Board of Licenses and Occupations
- Civil Service Commission
- Agency for International Development
- Department of Defense
- Office of Management and Budget
- Legal Services Corporation
- Bureau of Taxation
- Internal Revenue Service
- Division of Child Support and Enforcement
- Social Security Administration

Certain types of agencies exist at all three levels of government. For example, there is a separate tax collection agency in each of the federal, state, and local governments. Other agencies, however, are unique to one of the levels. For example, only the federal government has a Department of Defense (DOD) and a Central Intelligence Agency (CIA). Nothing comparable exists at the state and local levels of government. The latter have police departments and the highway patrol, but their role is significantly different from the DOD and CIA.

For a list of some of the most important federal agencies, see Appendix D.

There are three main kinds of administrative agencies:

- *Executive department agencies*
- *Independent regulatory agencies*
- *Quasi-independent regulatory agencies*

Exhibit 6.4 United States Courts of Appeals and United States District Courts

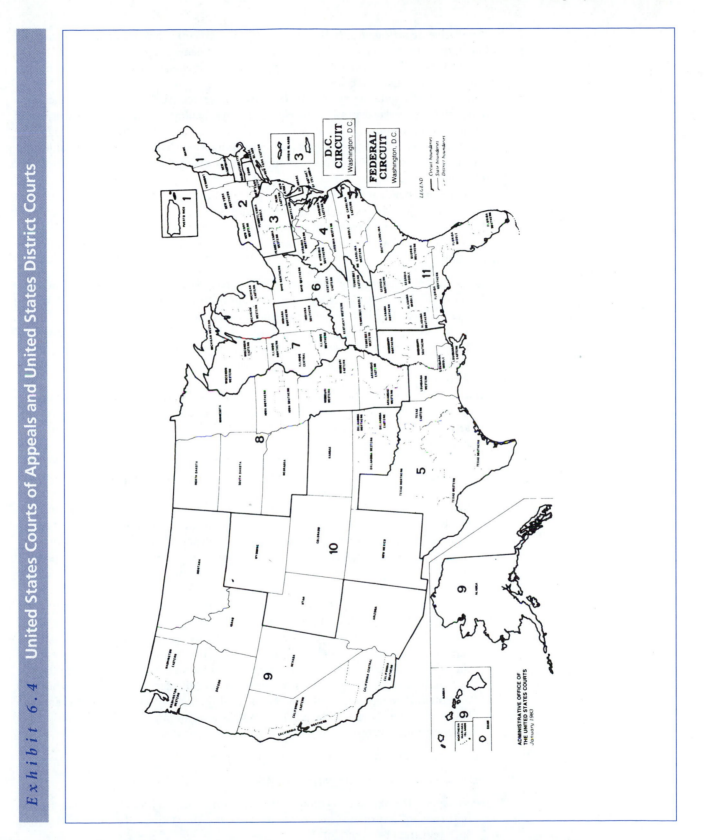

Executive department agencies exist within the executive branch of the government, often at the cabinet level. Examples include the Department of Agriculture and the Department of Labor. These agencies are answerable to the chief executive, who usually has the power to dismiss those in charge of them.

Independent regulatory agencies exist outside the executive department and, therefore, outside the day-to-day control of the chief executive. Examples include the Securities and Exchange Commission and the Public Utilities Commission. Their function is usually to regulate an aspect of society—often a particular industry such as securities and public utilities. To insulate these agencies from politics, those in charge usually cannot be removed at the whim of the chief executive.

A **quasi-independent regulatory agency** is a hybrid agency, often with characteristics of the two kinds just described. It has more independence than an executive department agency, yet it might exist within the executive department.

Most administrative agencies have three functions: execution, rule making, and dispute resolution:

- *Execution.* The primary function of the agency is to carry out (i.e., execute) the statutes governing the agency and the administrative regulations created by the agency itself. This is the agency's executive function.
- *Rule Making.* The agency often has the authority to write rules and regulations. (See Exhibit 6.1 for a definition of administrative regulation.) In so doing, the agency is "making law" like a legislature. Indeed, such laws are often referred to as **quasi-legislation.**
- *Dispute Resolution.* The agency has the authority to interpret the statutes and regulations that govern it. Furthermore, it often has the authority to resolve disputes that arise over the application of such laws. It will hold administrative hearings and issue decisions. (See Exhibit 6.1 for a definition of administrative decision.) In this sense the agency is acting like a court when the latter resolves (i.e., adjudicates) disputes. The dispute-resolution power of the agency is therefore called a **quasi-judicial power.** The phrase **quasi-adjudication** refers to the process by which agencies act like courts in interpreting laws and resolving disputes. An agency exercises its quasi-judicial power at several levels. At the first level is a *hearing,* which is similar to a trial in a court of original jurisdiction. The presiding agency official—known variously as **hearing examiner, trial examiner,** or **administrative law judge**—will, like the judge in a trial court, take testimony of witnesses and other evidence, determine the facts of the case, and apply the law to those facts in order to render a decision. In many agencies, the findings of fact and the decision of the hearing officer constitute only a recommendation to the director, commissioner, secretary, or other high official who will make the decision at this level. Like the courts, many agencies then provide a second, "appellate" level where a body such as a board or commission reviews the decision of the hearing examiner (or other official) to correct errors. After the parties to the dispute have used all these avenues of redress within the agency, they have **exhausted administrative remedies** and may then appeal the final administrative decision to a court. (Later in chapter 10 we will take a closer look at the dispute-resolution [quasi-adjudication] function of an agency.)

Here is an example of an agency using all three powers:

Securities and Exchange Commission (SEC)

- *Execution.* The SEC accepts filings of registration statements containing financial data on issuers of securities. This is done to carry out the statutes of Congress requiring such registration.

- *Rule Making.* The SEC writes regulations that provide greater detail on what the registration statements must contain.
- *Dispute Resolution.* The SEC holds a hearing to decide whether a corporation has violated the registration requirements laid out in the statutes and administrative regulations. The end product of the hearing is often an administrative decision.

Assignment 6.4

Give the name, address, phone number, fax number, and function (stated briefly) of:
(a) Three federal agencies with offices in your state.
(b) Five state agencies in your state.
(c) Five city or county agencies with offices in your city or county.

Section E
THE LEGISLATIVE PROCESS

The legislative process consists of the steps that a bill must go through before it becomes a statute. (A **bill** is simply a proposed statute.) Exhibit 6.5 outlines these steps for the federal legislature—Congress. The chart in Exhibit 6.5 assumes that the same idea for a bill is introduced simultaneously in both chambers of Congress, the House of Representatives and the Senate. It is, of course, also possible for a bill to be introduced in one chamber, go through all the steps for passage in that chamber, and *then* be introduced in the other chamber. The conference committee step outlined in the chart occurs only when both chambers have enacted their own version of the bill.

Congress is **bicameral,** meaning that it consists of two chambers, the House of Representatives and the Senate. In some state legislatures, the chambers have different names, such as the Assembly and the House of Delegates. Legislatures with only one chamber are called **unicameral.** Very few state legislatures are unicameral. Local legislatures, however, such as city councils, are often unicameral.

The process of enactment can involve six major stages:

- Proposal
- Initial committee consideration
- Floor debate
- Conference committee consideration
- Floor debate
- Response of the chief executive

The **legislative history** of a statute is what occurs at each of these stages.

(a) *Proposal.* The idea for a statute can come from many sources. The chief executive of the government (for example, the president or governor) may initiate the process by sending the legislature a message stating the reasons for a proposed law. Frequently, an administrative agency has made a study of a problem, which is the impetus for the proposal. The agency will usually be the entity with responsibility for administering the proposal if it is enacted into law.

The bar association might prepare a report to the legislature calling for the new legislation. The legislature or chief executive may have established a special commission to study the need for changes in the law and to propose changes where

Exhibit 6.5 **The Legislative History of a Federal Statute—How a Bill Becomes a Law**

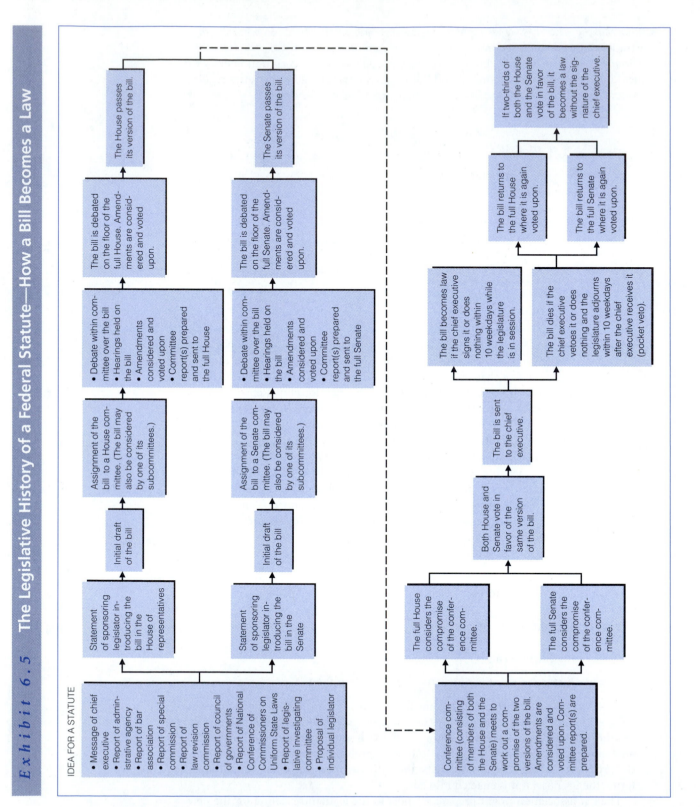

IDEA FOR A STATUTE

• Message of chief executive
• Report of administrative agency
• Report of bar association
• Report of special commission
• Report of law revision commission
• Report of council of governments
• Report of National Conference of Commissioners on Uniform State Laws
• Report of legislative investigating committee
• Proposal of individual legislator

Statement of sponsoring legislator introducing the bill in the House of representatives

Initial draft of the bill

Assignment of the bill to a House committee. (The bill may also be considered by one of its subcommittees.)

• Debate within committee over the bill
• Hearings held on the bill
• Amendments considered and voted upon
• Committee report(s) prepared and sent to the full House

The bill is debated on the floor of the full House. Amendments are considered and voted upon.

The House passes its version of the bill.

Statement of sponsoring legislator introducing the bill in the Senate

Initial draft of the bill

Assignment of the bill to a Senate committee. (The bill may also be considered by one of its subcommittees.)

• Debate within committee over the bill
• Hearings held on the bill
• Amendments considered and voted upon
• Committee report(s) prepared and sent to the full Senate

The bill is debated on the floor of the full Senate. Amendments are considered and voted upon.

The Senate passes its version of the bill.

Conference committee (consisting of members of both the House and the Senate) meets to work out a compromise of the two versions of the bill. Amendments are considered and voted upon. Committee report(s) are prepared.

The full House considers the compromise of the conference committee.

The full Senate considers the compromise of the conference committee.

Both House and Senate vote in favor of the same version of the bill.

The bill is sent to the chief executive.

The bill becomes law if the chief executive signs it or does nothing within 10 weekdays while the legislature is in session.

The bill dies if the chief executive vetoes it or does nothing and the legislature adjourns within 10 weekdays after the chief executive receives it (pocket veto).

The bill returns to the full House where it is again voted upon.

The bill returns to the full Senate where it is again voted upon.

If two-thirds of both the House and the Senate vote in favor of the bill, it becomes a law without the signature of the chief executive.

appropriate. The commission might consist of members of the legislature and out-side experts. Some states have ongoing law revision commissions that frequently make proposals for legislation. In many areas a council of governments made up of neighboring governments studies problems and proposes legislative changes. The National Conference of Commissioners on Uniform State Laws is an organization with members from each state. The conference makes proposals to the state legisla-tures for the enactment of **uniform state laws** where it deems uniformity to be desirable.

Finally, the idea for the legislation may be generated within the legislature itself. One or both houses may have established an investigating committee to examine a particular problem and propose legislation where needed. Individual legislators can also propose bills. Can private citizens propose a bill? Usually not. They must con-vince an individual legislator to introduce or sponsor their idea for a bill.

(b) *Initial Committee Consideration.* When a member of the legislature introduces a bill, he or she usually accompanies it with a statement on why the bill should be enacted. As bills are introduced, they are assigned a consecutive number (S 250 is the 250th bill introduced in the Senate during the current session; HR 1753 is the 1753rd bill introduced in the House of Representatives during the current session).

Once the bill is introduced, it follows a similar procedure in each chamber. The bill is sent to the committee with responsibility over the subject matter of the bill—for example, a bill to change the criminal law might go to the Judiciary Committee. The initial draft of the bill might be considered by this committee and by one of its subcommittees. Hearings are held. Citizens and public officials give testimony for or against the bill. In some legislatures this testimony is transcribed so that a word-for-word record is available. Legislators often propose amendments to the bill, which are voted on by the committee. The committee then issues a report summarizing why the bill is needed and what its major provisions are. If there is disagreement on the committee, a minority report is often prepared.

(c) *Floor Debate.* The bill with its accompanying report(s) then goes to the floor of the chamber of which the committee is a part. The bill is debated by the full chamber. During the debate, which will usually be recorded or transcribed, members ask questions about the meaning of certain provisions in the bill: what is covered and what is not. Amendments are often made from the floor and voted upon.

(d) *Conference Committee Consideration.* Since both chambers act independently of each other in considering the bill, it is rare that they both produce exactly the same bill. Inevitably, the amendment process leads to different versions of the proposed law. To resolve these differences, a *conference committee* is established, consisting of key members of both chambers, such as the chairpersons of the committees that ini-tially considered the bill or the members who first introduced or sponsored the bill. A compromise is attempted in the conference committee. Amendments are consid-ered and a final report of the conference committee is issued. Dissenting members of the committee might prepare a minority report. The majority report summarizes the major terms of the compromise and explains why it should be enacted by each chamber.

(e) *Floor Debate.* The conference committee compromise then goes back to the floor of each chamber where more debate, explanations, and amendments are considered. Again, everything is recorded or transcribed. If both chambers pass the same version of the bill, usually by a majority vote, it goes to the chief executive.

(f) *Response of Chief Executive.* There are three main ways for the bill to become law after it reaches the chief executive. First, he or she can sign it. Second, the chief executive can do nothing. If the legislature stays in session for at least ten weekdays after he or she receives it, the bill automatically becomes law—without requiring a signature. Third, if the chief executive rejects or **vetoes** the bill, it can still become law if both chambers of the legislature **override** the veto by a two-thirds vote.

There are two main ways for the chief executive to reject a bill. First, he or she can explicitly veto the bill and send it back to the legislature, often with a statement of the reasons for the rejection. Second, he or she can do nothing. If the legislature adjourns within ten weekdays after the chief executive receives it, the bill automatically dies. This is known as a **pocket veto.**

Assignment 6.5

(a) Redraw Exhibit 6.5 so that your chart includes the steps needed for a bill to become a statute in your state legislature.

(b) Give the name, address, phone number, and fax number of the chief legislator of both chambers of your legislature, e.g., Speaker of the House, President of the Senate. (If your state legislature is unicameral [Nebraska], answer these questions for the one chamber that exists.)

(c) What is the full name of the legislative committee in each chamber (e.g., Judiciary Committee) with primary authority to consider laws that directly affect your state courts such as procedural laws that govern the conduct of litigation? Give the name, political party, phone number, and fax number of the current chairperson of each of these committees.

(d) What is the name of the *local* legislature in your city or county? Give the name, address, phone number, and fax number of the chief legislator of this body. (If you have both a city and a county legislature, answer this question for both.)

Chapter Summary

Our legal system consists of three levels of government (federal, state, and local) and three branches of government (executive, legislative, and judicial) within each level. Federalism is the division of powers between the federal or national government and the state governments. To keep any one branch from becoming too powerful, our system imposes checks and balances among all three branches.

There are ten main categories of laws: opinions, statutes, constitutions, administrative regulations, administrative decisions, charters, ordinances, rules of court, executive orders, and treaties. (In a special category are opinions of the attorney general.) These laws are written by one of the three branches of government (legislative, executive, and judicial) that exist within the three levels of government (federal, state, and local).

Ours is a common law legal system. The common law is judge-made law in the absence of controlling statutory law or other higher law. The method of resolving legal disputes is adversarial. The opposing sides go before a neutral decision maker who listens to the arguments of each side before rendering a decision.

An understanding of jurisdiction is key to understanding our judicial system. Two of the main kinds of jurisdiction are geographic jurisdiction, which specifies an area of the country over which a court can exercise its power, and subject-matter jurisdiction, which specifies the kinds of cases over which a court can exercise its power. There are six main kinds of subject-matter jurisdiction: limited, general, exclusive, concurrent, original, and appellate. Another important kind of jurisdiction is personal jurisdiction, which gives the court the power to order a defendant to do something or to refrain from doing something. Courts of original jurisdiction are the trial courts. There may be two levels of trial courts within a judicial system. There may also be two levels of courts with appellate jurisdiction.

There are three kinds of administrative agencies: executive department agencies, independent regulatory agencies, and quasi-independent regulatory agencies. Agencies serve three main functions: to carry out statutes and executive orders, to write rules and regulations, and to resolve disputes that arise under laws for which the agency has responsibility.

The federal legislature (Congress) and most state legislatures are bicameral; that is, they consist of two chambers. For a bill to become a statute, it must go through approximately six stages. First, the bill is proposed, and then introduced into one of the chambers of the legislature. It may be introduced into the other chamber simultaneously or at a later date. Second, a committee of each chamber gives the bill initial consideration. If the committee votes in favor of the bill, it goes to the next stage. Third, all of the members of one of the chambers debate and vote on the bill, and then all of the members of the other chamber debate and vote on the bill. Fourth, a conference committee made up of members of both chambers considers the bill. The role of this committee is to try to reconcile any differences in the two versions of the bill passed by each chamber. Fifth, the bill goes back to the full membership of each chamber for a vote on what the conference committee produced. Sixth, the chief executive signs or vetoes the bill. If he or she vetoes the bill, it can still become a statute if two-thirds of each chamber vote to override the chief executive. The legislative history of a statute consists of what happens during these six stages.

KEY TERMS

federalism, 322
legislative branch, 322
executive branch, 322
judicial branch, 322
opinion, 322
case, 322
statute, 322
legislation, 322
act, 322
constitution, 322
administrative regulation, 322
administrative rule, 322
administrative decision, 322
administrative ruling, 322
charter, 323
ordinance, 323
rules of court, 323
executive order, 323
treaty, 323
opinion of the attorney general, 323
checks and balances, 324

judicial review, 324
common law, 325
civil law system, 325
at common law, 325
statutes in derogation of the common law, 326
adversarial, 326
jurisdiction, 326
geographic jurisdiction, 327
adjudication, 327
personal jurisdiction, 327
in personam jurisdiction, 327
service of process, 327
subject-matter jurisdiction, 327
limited jurisdiction, 327
general jurisdiction, 327
state questions, 327
federal questions, 327
exclusive jurisdiction, 327
concurrent jurisdiction, 327
original jurisdiction, 328

court of first instance, 328
appellate jurisdiction, 328
appeal, 328
inferior courts, 328
appellate courts, 328
review, 328
errors of law, 328
trial court record, 330
appellate briefs, 330
panels, 330
en banc, 330
intermediate appellate court, 330
supreme court, 330
court of final resort, 330
United States District Court, 330
United States Court of Appeals, 331
United States Supreme Court, 332
administrative agency, 332
executive department

agencies, 334
independent regulatory agencies, 334
quasi-independent regulatory agency, 334
quasi-legislation, 334
quasi–judicial power, 334
quasi-adjudication, 334
hearing examiner, 334
trial examiner, 334
administrative law judge, 334
exhausted administrative remedies, 334
bill, 335
bicameral, 335
unicameral, 335
legislative history, 335
uniform state laws, 337
vetoes, 338
override, 338
pocket veto, 338

Part **II**

THE SKILLS
OF A PARALEGAL

➤ *Contents*

Chapter 7

INTRODUCTION TO LEGAL ANALYSIS

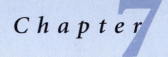

Chapter Outline

Section A
THE STRUCTURE OF LEGAL ANALYSIS

Legal analysis is at the heart of the practice of law. It is the application of rules of law to facts in order to answer a legal question or issue. The goal is to solve a legal dispute, to prevent such a dispute from arising, or to prevent the dispute from getting worse.

Paralegals need to study legal analysis for two main reasons. First, many paralegals are given assignments that in varying degrees call for legal analysis. Secondly, and perhaps more importantly, since attorneys talk the language of legal analysis all the time (issues, rules, elements, briefing, reasoning, etc.), a paralegal who knows the basics of legal analysis will be better equipped to understand and communicate with attorneys.

There is a basic structure to legal analysis, as demonstrated in the following relatively simple example:

RULE +	FACTS +	ISSUE +	CONNECTION (rule and facts) =	CONCLUSION
§ 10. "Any business within the city must apply for and obtain a license to do business within the city limits."	Bill and his neighbors in the city have formed a food co-op through which members buy their food collectively from a wholesale company. All funds received by the co-op go for expenses and the purchase of more food to sell.	Is a food co-op a "business" within the meaning of § 10 requiring a license "to do business"?	The city argues that the co-op is a business in the city. The co-op concedes that it is in the city but argues that it does not "do business," since the co-op does not earn a profit.	The co-op has the better argument. § 10 was not intended to cover nonprofit ventures. Hence, the co-op does not have to have a license.

Note the components of the process:

- You start with a specific rule, such as a statute or regulation. You quote the relevant language exactly.
- You state the major facts.
- You phrase the legal issue in terms of specific language in the rule and specific facts that raise a question or controversy.
- You draw the *connection* between specific language in the rule and specific facts. The substance of the analysis *is* this connection. Another term for connection is **application**—applying the rules to the facts.
- You reach a conclusion based on the above steps.

The following is a more detailed statement of the analysis referred to as the "connection" in the above chart:

§ 10 provides as follows:

"Any business within the city must apply for and obtain a license to do business within the city limits."

There are two main elements to § 10:

1. Any business
2. Within the city

When the facts fit within these two elements, the entity in question must apply for and obtain a license to do business. The consequence of the rule is the need to be licensed. This consequence is mandated once both elements exist.

1. *Any Business.* The city claims that the co-op is a business. It does not matter to the city that the co-op does not earn profits in the traditional sense. According to the city, the co-op members are "selling" goods to each other. A business is any entity that engages in any form of selling.

   The co-op, on the other hand, argues that § 10 was not intended to cover co-ops. A business is an enterprise that makes a profit over and above expenses. Nothing of this kind occurs in the co-op. Everything taken in by the co-op goes out in the form of food purchases and expenses. Hence, the co-op is not a business and does not have to have a license.

2. *Within the City.* There is no dispute between the parties on this element. The city and the co-op agree that the co-op operates within the city limits. The only dispute in this case concerns whether the co-op is a business.

If you had included legal research data on the meaning of § 10, the analysis might *also* have contained:

- A discussion of court opinions, if any, that interpret § 10
- A discussion of administrative regulations, if any, that implement § 10
- A discussion of the legislative history, if available, of § 10
- A discussion of secondary authority, if any, that interprets § 10, such as legal periodical literature and legal treatises
- A discussion of constitutional provisions, if any, that affect the applicability of § 10

The analysis, the facts, the issues, etc., are often presented in the format of a **memorandum of law,** which will be examined in greater detail in chapter 12 on Legal Writing.

In law schools, many future attorneys are taught **IRAC,** an acronym that stands for Issue, Rule, Application, and Conclusion:

Issue: Identify the legal issue to be resolved.

Rule: State the rule of law that is the center of the issue.

Application: Apply the rule of law to the relevant facts.

Conclusion: State the conclusion of how the rule of law applies to the facts.

If the problem involves more than one rule of law, each is "IRAC-ed" in the same manner. Note that IRAC provides essentially the same structure for legal analysis as the chart presented above. There is no magic way to do legal analysis. What is important is covering the essentials, which are rules, facts, issues, connections (or applications), and conclusions.

We turn now to three skills that are important in legal analysis: the element-identification skill, the issue-statement skill, and the definitions skill.

Section B
The Element-Identification Skill

All rules have consequences. There are rules that impose punishments, require payments, establish norms of behavior, make declarations of policy, institute procedures, etc. How do you determine when a rule applies so that its consequences must be followed? The answer is: When *all* of the **elements** of that rule apply. In our example on § 10, note that the analysis proceeded through a discussion of the elements of § 10. An element is a component or portion of a rule that is a precondition of the applicability of the entire rule. If you can show that all of the elements of a rule apply to a fact situation, then the rule itself—and its consequence—applies to the fact situation. The failure of any one of the elements to apply means that the entire rule cannot apply.

The elements of § 10 were relatively short (business; within the city). This is not always so. How long should an element be? This question has no absolute answer. The two main criteria to keep in mind are these: (1) each element must be a precondition to the consequence of the entire rule, and (2) you should be able to discuss each element separately with relative ease.

Let us examine some additional examples:

§ 971.22. Change of place of trial. The defendant may move for a change of the place of trial on the ground that an impartial trial cannot be had in the county. The motion shall be made at the time of arraignment.

Step one is to break the rule into its elements. The effect or consequence of the rule is to change the place of the trial. Ask yourself what must happen before this consequence will follow. What conditions or preconditions must exist before the result will occur? The answer will provide you with the elements of the rule:

1. Defendant
2. May move for a change of the place of trial
3. On the ground that an impartial trial cannot be had in the county
4. The motion must be made at the time of the arraignment

Hence, there are four elements to § 971.22. All four must exist before the place of the trial will be moved.

Suppose you are analyzing the following rule found in a statute:

§ 25-403. A pharmacist must not sell prescription drugs to a minor.

As with almost all rules, this one is not already broken down into elements. You must identify the elements on your own. Ask yourself what conditions must exist before § 25-403 applies. Your answer will consist of its elements:

1. Pharmacist
2. Must not sell
3. Prescription drugs
4. To a minor

No violation exists unless all four elements of the statute are established. If, for example, a pharmacist sells simple aspirin (a nonprescription drug) to a minor, he or she has not violated the statute. The third element cannot be established. Hence, no violation, since one of the elements (preconditions) cannot be met.

For a number of reasons, rules such as statutes and regulations can be difficult to break into elements. For example, the rule may be long or may contain:

- Lists
- Alternatives
- Exceptions or provisos

Nevertheless, the same process is used. You must take the time to dissect the rule into its component elements. Examine the following rule as we try to identify its elements.

§ 5. While representing a client in connection with contemplated or pending litigation, a lawyer shall not advance or guarantee financial assistance to his client, except that a lawyer may advance or guarantee court costs, expenses of investigation, expenses of medical examination, and costs of obtaining and presenting evidence provided the client remains ultimately liable for such expenses.

Elements of § 5:

1. A lawyer
2. Representing a client in connection with contemplated litigation or in connection with pending litigation
3. Shall not advance financial assistance to his client or guarantee financial assistance to his client, except that the following is proper:

   a. lawyer advances or guarantees court costs, or
   b. lawyer advances or guarantees expenses of investigation, or
   c. lawyer advances or guarantees expenses of medical examination, or
   d. lawyer advances or guarantees costs of obtaining and presenting evidence

   as long as the client remains ultimately liable for all expenses ("a"–"d").

When an element is stated in the alternative, list all the alternatives within the same element. Alternatives related to one element should be kept within the phrasing of that element. The same is true of exception or proviso clauses. State them within the relevant element, since they are intimately related to the applicability of that element.

In the above example, the most complicated element is the third—(3). It contains lists, alternatives, an exception, and a proviso. But they all relate to the same point—the propriety of financial assistance. None of the subdivisions of the third element should be stated as a separate element. Sometimes you must do some unraveling of a rule in order to identify its elements. This certainly had to be done with the third element of § 5. Do not be afraid to pick the rule apart in order to cluster its thoughts around unified themes that should stand alone as elements. Diagram the rule for yourself as you examine it.

If more than one rule is involved in a statute, regulation, constitutional provision, charter, ordinance, etc., treat one rule at a time. Each rule should have its own elements, and, when appropriate, each element should be subdivided into its separate components, as in the third element of § 5.

Once you have broken the rule down into its elements, you have the structure of the analysis in front of you. Each element becomes a separate section of your analysis. You discuss one element at a time, concentrating on those that pose the greatest difficulties.

Element identification has many benefits in the law, as demonstrated in Exhibit 7.1.

To a very large extent, as you can see in Exhibit 7.1, legal analysis proceeds by *element analysis.* A major characteristic of sloppy legal analysis is that it does not clearly take the reader (or listener) through the important elements of rules that must be analyzed.

Exhibit 7.1   The Benefits of Element Identification

- *Identifying Issues.* Once you identify the elements of a rule, the next step is to find the *elements* that are most likely to be in contention. These elements become the basis of legal issues (as we shall see in the next section).
- *Drafting a Complaint.* When drafting a legal complaint, you often organize your factual allegations around the *elements* of each important rule in the controversy. (The most important rule is called the **cause of action,** which is a legally acceptable reason for suing someone; negligence is an example.)
- *Drafting an Answer.* When drafting an answer to a complaint, you often state your defenses by alleging facts that support the *elements* of each defense. (Many **defenses,** such as the statute of limitation, are nothing more than rules designed to defeat the claims of another.)
- *Organizing an Interview of a Client.* One of the goals of interviewing a client is to obtain information on facts relevant to each of the *elements* of the potential causes of action and defenses in the case. Element analysis, therefore, helps you organize the interview and give it direction.
- *Organizing an Investigation.* One of the goals of investigation is to obtain information on facts relevant to each of the *elements* of the potential causes of action and defenses in the case. Element analysis, therefore, helps you organize the investigation and give it direction.
- *Conducting a Deposition.* During a deposition, many of the questions are designed to determine what facts the other side may be able to prove that support the *elements* of the potential causes of action and defenses in the case.
- *Organizing a Memorandum of Law.* One of the purposes of a memorandum of law is to tell the reader what rules might apply to the case, what *elements* of these rules might be in contention, and what strategy should be undertaken as a result of this analysis.
- *Organizing an Examination Answer.* Many essay examinations in school are organized around the key *elements* of the rules that should be analyzed.
- *Charging a Jury.* When a judge charges (that is, instructs) a jury, he or she will go over each of the *elements* of the causes of action and defenses in the case in order to tell the jury what standard to use to determine whether facts in support of those elements have been sufficiently proven during the trial.

Assignment 7.1

Break the following rules into their elements:

(a) § 200. Parties to a child custody dispute shall attempt mediation before filing for a custody order from the court.

(b) § 75(b). A lawyer shall not enter into a business transaction with a client if they have differing interests therein and if the client expects the lawyer to exercise his professional judgment therein for the protection of the client.

(c) § 38. A person or agency suing or being sued in an official public capacity is not required to execute a bond as a condition for relief under this section unless required by the court in its discretion.

(d) § 1.2. A lawyer may not permit his legal assistant to represent a client in litigation or other adversary proceedings or to perform otherwise prohibited functions unless authorized by statute, court rule or decision, administrative rule or regulation or customary practice.

(e) § 179(a)(7). If at any time it is determined that application of best available control technology by 1988 will not assure protection of public water supplies, agricultural and industrial uses, and the protection and propagation of fish, shellfish and wildlife, and allow recreational activities in and on the water, additional effluent limitations must be established to assure attainment or maintenance of water quality. In setting such limitations, EPA must consider the relationship of the economic and social costs of their achievement, including any economic or social dislocation in the affected community or communities, the social and economic benefits to be obtained, and determine whether or not such effluent limitations can be implemented with available technology or other alternative control strategies.

Section C
THE ISSUE-STATEMENT SKILL

After you have broken a rule into its elements, the next step is to identify the **element in contention.** That element then becomes the basis of a **legal issue.** An element is in contention when you can predict that the other side in the controversy will probably not agree with your interpretation of that element and/or with whether the facts support that element. If a rule has five elements and you anticipate disagreement over all of them, phrase five separate issues. If, however, only one of the five elements will probably be in contention, phrase only one issue. There is no need to waste time over elements that will most likely not be the basis of disagreement.

Legal issues are often phrased in *shorthand* such as "Does § 34 apply?" "Can a van be burglarized?" A more *comprehensive* phrasing of a legal issue would consist of:

● A brief quote from the element in contention, and
● Several of the important facts relevant to that contention

For example, suppose that you are analyzing the following rule and facts:

§ 92. The operator of any vehicle riding on a sidewalk shall be fined $100.

Facts: Fred rides his ten-speed bicycle on the sidewalk. He is charged with violating § 92.

The element breakdown and issue statement would be as follows:

Elements of § 92:

1. Operator
2. Any vehicle
3. Riding
4. On a sidewalk

Issue: Is a ten-speed bicycle a "vehicle" under § 92?

The parties will probably agree that Fred rode his bicycle on a sidewalk and that Fred was the operator of his bicycle. The first, third, and fourth elements, therefore, should not be be made into legal issues. The only disagreement will be over the second element. Hence, it is the basis of an issue. Note the quotation marks around the element in contention (vehicle) and the inclusion of an important fact that is relevant to this contention (it was a ten-speed bicycle).

Assignment 7.2

Provide a comprehensive phrasing of the legal issue or issues in each of the following situations:

(a) *Facts:* Harry Franklin works for the XYZ Agency. In one of the Agency's personnel files is a notation that Paul Drake, another Agency employee, was once arrested for fraud. Harry obtains this information from this file and tells his wife about it. (She also knows Paul.) Harry is unaware that Paul has told at least three other employees about his fraud arrest.

Regulation: 20(d). It shall be unlawful for any employee of the XYZ Agency to divulge confidential material in any file of the Agency.

(b) *Facts:* Jones has a swimming pool in his backyard. The pool is intended for use by the Jones family members and guests who are present when an adult is there to supervise. One hot summer night, a neighbor's child opens an unlocked door of a fence that surrounds the Jones's yard and goes into the pool. (There is no separate fence around the pool.) The child knows that he should not be there without an adult. No one else is at the pool. The child drowns.

Statute: § 77. Property owners are liable for the foreseeable harm that occurs on their property.

(c) *Facts:* Dr. Carla Jones is the family physician of the Richardson family. After an appointment with Mary Richardson, age 16, Dr. Jones prescribes birth control pills. Mary tells Dr. Jones that she can't afford the pills and does not want her parents to know she is taking them. Dr. Jones says she will give her a supply of the pills at no cost in exchange for an afternoon of office clerical work at Dr. Jones's office.

Statute: § 25-403. A pharmacist must not sell prescription drugs to a minor. (See page 346.)

Section D
THE DEFINITIONS SKILL

Language can frequently be defined broadly or narrowly. Assume that Jim meets a friend in a parking lot and says to him, "You can use my car." Jim is quite upset, however, when the friend returns five months later after driving the car through about twenty states. The friend asserts that he did nothing more than "use" the car. The question becomes: What is the definition of "use"?

Broad Definition: Use means to operate or employ something for any purpose and for any length of time.

Narrow Definition: Use means to operate or employ something for a reasonable purpose within a reasonable time.

The same dynamic is found when interpreting ambiguous language within elements in contention. Recall the bicycle example discussed in the preceding section:

§ 92. The operator of any vehicle riding on a sidewalk shall be fined $100.

Facts: Fred rides his ten-speed bicycle on the sidewalk. He is charged with violating § 92.

Issue: Is a ten-speed bicycle a "vehicle" under § 92?

This controversy may well turn on whether "vehicle" should be defined broadly or narrowly. Fred will argue that it should be interpreted narrowly, whereas the government will argue for a broad definition:

Broad Definition: Vehicle means any method of transportation.
Narrow Definition: Vehicle means any motorized method of transportation.

Whenever you have an element in contention that contains ambiguous language, you should put yourself in the shoes of each person in the controversy and try to identify what definition of the language each would propose. Think of a broad and a narrow definition, and state which side would argue which definition.

To help resolve a definition dispute, you would undertake some legal research—for example, you would try to find cases interpreting "vehicle" under § 92 and trace the legislative history of § 92. Often, however, you will *not* find the answer in the library. The precise question may never have arisen before. This is particularly true of recent statutes and regulations.

Assignment 7.3

In each of the following problems, identify any ambiguous language in elements in contention. Give broad and narrow definitions of this language and state which side would argue which definition. Do not do any legal research.

(a) *Facts:* Alice Anderson is nine months pregnant. A police officer gives her a ticket for driving in a car-pool lane in violation of § 101. The officer said he gave her the ticket because she was alone in the car at the time.

Regulation: § 101. Car-pool lanes can be used only by cars in which there is at least one passenger in the car with the driver.

(b) *Facts:* Mary is arrested for violating § 55. She is charged as a felon. She forced open the lock on the driver's side of a van at 5 P.M. Mary didn't know that the door on the passenger side was unlocked. She went into the back of the van and fell asleep on the floor. The police arrested her after waking her up at 9 P.M. The owner of the van claims that a $20 bill is missing. Mary had a $20 bill on her, but she said it was her own.

Statute: § 55. A person who breaks and enters a dwelling at night for the purpose of stealing property therein shall be charged as a felon.

Assignment 7.4

Analyze the problem in the following situations. Do not do any legal research. Simply use the facts and rules you are given. Be sure to include in your analysis what you have learned about elements, issues, and definitions.

(a) Susan is arrested for carrying a dangerous weapon. While in a hardware store, she got into an argument with another customer. She picked up a hammer from the counter and told the other customer to get out of her way. The customer did so and Susan put the hammer back. She was later arrested and charged with violating § 402(b), which provides: "It is unlawful for anyone to carry a dangerous weapon."

(b) It is against the law in your state "to practice law without a license" (§39). Fred is charged with violating this law. He told a neighbor that a certain parking ticket received by the neighbor could be ignored since the police officer was incorrect in issuing the ticket. In gratitude, the neighbor buys Fred a drink. (Assume that what Fred told the neighbor about the ticket was accurate and that Fred is *not* an attorney.)

(c) Ted and Ann are married. Ted is a carpenter and Ann is a lawyer. They buy an old building that Ted will repair for Ann's use as a law office. Ted asks Ann to handle the legal aspects of the purchase of the building. She does so. Soon after the purchase, they decide to obtain a divorce. Ted asks Ann if she will draw up the divorce papers. She does so. Ted completes the repair work on the building for which Ann pays him a set amount. Has Ann violated § 75(b) stated in problem (b) on page 348 in Assignment 7.1, above?

Section E
BRIEFING COURT OPINIONS

The word *brief* has several meanings.

First, to **brief** a court opinion is to summarize its major components (e.g., key facts, issues, reasoning, disposition). Such a brief is your own summary of the opinion for later use. Second, a **trial brief** is an attorney's set of notes on how he or she will conduct the trial. The notes (often placed in a **trial notebook**) will be on the opening statement, witnesses, exhibits, direct and cross-examination, closing argument, etc. This trial brief is sometimes called a trial manual or trial book. Third, the **appellate brief** is the formal written argument to a court of appeals on why a lower court's decision should be affirmed, modified, or reversed. The focus of the appellate brief is on the claimed errors made "below." An appellate brief is submitted to the appellate court and to the other side.

Here our concern is the first meaning of the word brief—a summarization of the ten essential components of a court opinion. (See Exhibit 7.2 on page 356.) Before we examine these components, we will study an opinion as it might appear in a library reporter volume.

The circled numbers are explained after the opinion.

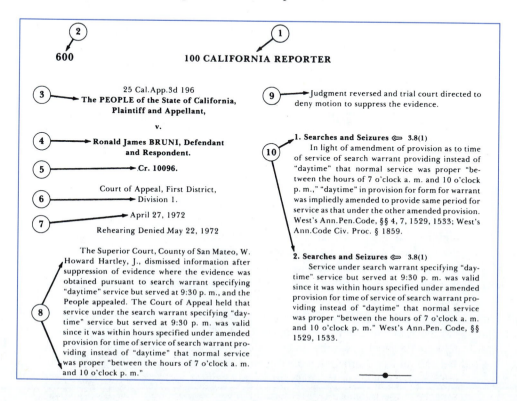

100 CALIFORNIA REPORTER

600

25 Cal.App.3d 196
**The PEOPLE of the State of California,
Plaintiff and Appellant,**

v.

**Ronald James BRUNI, Defendant
and Respondent.**

Cr. 10096.

Court of Appeal, First District,
Division 1.

April 27, 1972

Rehearing Denied May 22, 1972

The Superior Court, County of San Mateo, W. Howard Hartley, J., dismissed information after suppression of evidence where the evidence was obtained pursuant to search warrant specifying "daytime" service but served at 9:30 p. m., and the People appealed. The Court of Appeal held that service under the search warrant specifying "daytime" service but served at 9:30 p. m. was valid since it was within hours specified under amended provision for time of service of search warrant providing instead of "daytime" that normal service was proper "between the hours of 7 o'clock a. m. and 10 o'clock p. m."

Judgment reversed and trial court directed to deny motion to suppress the evidence.

1. Searches and Seizures ⟺ 3.8(1)
In light of amendment of provision as to time of service of search warrant providing instead of "daytime" that normal service was proper "between the hours of 7 o'clock a. m. and 10 o'clock p. m.," "daytime" in provision for form for warrant was impliedly amended to provide same period for service as that under the other amended provision. West's Ann.Pen.Code, §§ 4, 7, 1529, 1533; West's Ann.Code Civ. Proc. § 1859.

2. Searches and Seizures ⟺ 3.8(1)
Service under search warrant specifying "daytime" service but served at 9:30 p. m. was valid since it was within hours specified under amended provision for time of service of search warrant providing instead of "daytime" that normal service was proper "between the hours of 7 o'clock a. m. and 10 o'clock p. m." West's Ann.Pen. Code, §§ 1529, 1533.

Evelle J. Younger, Atty. Gen. of California, Edward P. O'Brien, Robert R. Granucci, Deputy Attys. Gen., San Francisco, for appellant. (11)

William F. DeLucchi, Regalado & Lindquist, Redwood City, for respondent.

Smith, Judge. (12)

The People appeal from a judgment dismissing an Information after suppression of evidence, (13) where the evidence was obtained pursuant to a search warrant specifying "daytime" service, but (14) which was served at 9:30 p. m. at night.

In 1970, section 1533 of the Penal Code was amended to eliminate the provision for "daytime" service for normal service of a search warrant. Instead of "daytime," the statute now specifies normal service as proper "between the hours of 7 (15) o'clock a. m. and 10 o'clock p. m." Apparently by oversight, the Legislature neglected to also amend the mandatory provisions under section 1529 of the Penal Code, which continues to require "daytime" service. An inconsistency exists as to the mandatory requirements of search warrants unless section 1529 of the Penal Code is read as having been amended by implication when section 1533 of the Penal Code was expressly amended. Otherwise, the only warrant an issuing magistrate could authorize, without possibly violating one or the other statute, would be one for unlimited service at any hour of day or night upon a showing of good cause. Nothing suggests that this was the legislative intent.

The provisions of the Penal Code "are to be construed according to the fair import of their terms, with a view to effect its objects and to pro- (16) mote justice." (Pen.Code. § 4.) "In the construction of a statute the intention of the Legislature... is to be pursued, if possible; and when a (18) general and particular provision are inconsistent, the latter is paramount to the former." (Code (16) Civ.Proc., § 1859.)

[1] Under the definition in Section 7 of the (10a) Penal Code, daytime is defined as "the period between sunrise and sunset." This general provision is clearly inconsistent with the particular provision relating to service of search warrants between the hours of 7 o'clock a. m. and 10 o'clock p. m. estab- (18) lished under the amendment of section 1533 of the Penal Code. Under the general rules of statutory construction, we interpret "daytime" in the particular provisions of section 1529 of the Penal Code

as having been impliedly amended to provide the (19) same period for service as that under amended section 1533 of the Penal Code.

(18) "...'where the language of a statute is reasonably susceptible of two constructions, one of which in application will render it reasonable, fair and harmonious with its manifest purpose, and another which will be productive of absurd consequences, the former construction will be adopted.' (citation); and 'if certain provisions are repugnant, effect should be given to those which best comport with the end to be accomplished and render the statute effective, rather than nugatory.'" (Dept. of (17) Motor Vehicles of California v. Indus. Acc. Com. (1939) 14 Cal.2d 189, 195, 93 P.2d 131, 134.)

(10a)
(19) [2] We hold that the People are correct in their assertion that service was valid since it was within the hours specified under amended section 1533 of the Penal Code. See Tidwell v. Superior Court (1971) 17 Cal.App.3d 780, 786-787, 95 Cal.Rptr. 213. (17)

This court has always been scrupulous in demanding a high standard for the admission of evidence pursuant to warrants. Our ruling today does not violate this standard. The integrity of our trial system in large measure depends upon the integrity of the evidence admitted at trial. The case before us deals with the timing of serving a warrant. If the case had involved other aspects of the war- (21) rant such as its specificity, our result would probably have been different.

The judgment is reversed, and the trial court is directed to deny the motion to suppress the (20) evidence.

Jones, Judge (Concurring in result only). (22)

Thomas, Judge (Dissenting). (23)

If the California legislature intended to amend section 1529 of the Penal Code, it should have done so expressly. It is not the function of the judiciary to amend the statutes passed by the legislature. The public has a right to rely on the written language of statutes; in fact, we frequently admonish the citizenry if they ignore that language. For the courts to alter the language after the fact not only infringes upon the right of the legislature to be the sole entity under our system that can enact and amend legislation, but also is a signal to the public and to government officials that they can no longer trust the law as validly passed by the legislative branch. Both results are intolerable.

I would affirm the judgment below.

---

① The *California Reporter* is an unofficial reporter of state opinions in California. The "100" indicates the volume number of the reporter.

② The *Bruni* case begins on page 600. The citation of this case is *People v. Bruni,* 25 Cal. App. 3d 196, 100 Cal. Rptr. 600 (1972). The official cite is given at the top of the first column above the word PEOPLE. (We will cover citations in chapter 11.)

③ When the *People* or the state brings an action, it is often a criminal case. This is an appellate court decision. Trial court decisions are appealed to the appellate court. The **appellant** is the party bringing the appeal because of dissatisfaction with the ruling or decision of the lower court. The state of California brought the case as the plaintiff and prosecutor in the lower court (Superior Court, County of San Mateo) and is now the appellant in the higher court (Court of Appeal, First District, Division 1).

④ Bruni was the defendant in the lower court since he was being sued or, in this case, charged with a crime. The appeal is taken against him by the People (appellant), because the lower court ruling was favorable to Bruni, to the dissatisfaction of the People. The party against whom a case is brought on appeal is called the **respondent.** Another word for respondent is **appellee.**

⑤ "Cr. 10096" refers to the *docket,* or calendar number of the case. "Cr." stands for *criminal.* (Docket numbers are not used in the citation of reported cases. See number 7 below.)

⑥ Make careful note of the name of the court writing the opinion. As soon as possible, you must learn the hierarchy of state courts in your state. (See Exhibit 6.2 in chapter 6.) In many states, there are three levels of courts: trial level, middle appeals level, and supreme level. (Most cases are appealed from the trial court to the middle appeals level, and then to the supreme level.) Here, we know from the title of the court (Court of Appeal) that it is an appellate court. It is not the supreme court, because in California the highest court is the California Supreme Court.

The name of the court is significant because of legal authority. If the court is the highest or supreme court of the state, then the case would be applicable throughout the state. A middle appeals court case, on the other hand, applies only in the area of the state over which it has jurisdiction. When you see that the case was written by a trial or middle appeals court, you are immediately put on notice that you must check to determine whether the case was ever appealed subsequent to the date of the case. The main system for checking is called **shepardizing** (see Checklist 4a in chapter 11).

⑦ When a reported case is being cited, only the year (here, 1972) is used, not the month or day (April 27). (If the case has not yet been reported, the month, day, and year are used— along with the docket number.) Sometimes, the text of the reported opinion will also give you the date of the hearing or rehearing as well as the date of the decision. The year of the decision is still the critical one for citation purposes.

⑧ Here the editors provide the reader with a summary of what the case says. The court did not write this summary; the editors did. It, therefore, is not an official statement of the law. It is merely an aid to the reader, who can quickly read this summary to determine whether the case covers relevant areas of law. This summary paragraph is often called the **syllabus.**

⑨ Here continues the unofficial summary, providing the reader with what procedurally must happen as a result of the April 27 case.

⑩ These are editor's **headnotes,** which are small paragraph summaries of portions of the case. When the editors first read the case, they decide how many major topics or issues are covered in the case. Each of these topics is summarized in a headnote, all of which are then given consecutive numbers, here 1 and 2. These numbers correspond with the bracketed numbers [1] and [2] in the case itself. (See ⑩ₐ.) If, for example, you wanted to read the portion of the case that was summarized in the second headnote of the case, you would go to the text of the case that begins with the bracketed [2].

The headnotes also have a **key number,** which consists of a topic and a number, here "Searches and Seizures ☞ 3.8(1)." Each headnote will also be printed in the **digests** of West Publishing Company. Digests are volumes that contain nothing but the headnotes of court opinions. You can find out what other courts have said about the same or similar points by going to the digest volumes, looking up the key number of a headnote (e.g., Searches and Seizures ☞ 3.8(1)), and reading summary paragraphs from many court cases such as our case, *People v. Bruni.*

Caution is needed in reading the syllabus and headnotes of opinions. As indicated earlier, they are not written by the court and therefore should never be relied on or quoted. They are merely preliminary guides to what is in an opinion. To understand the opinion, you must carefully study the language of the opinion itself through the process called *briefing.*

⑪ Here are the attorneys who represented the appellant and respondent on appeal. Note that the attorney general's office represented the People. The attorney general or the district attorney's office represents the state in criminal cases.

⑫ The opinion begins with the name of the judge who wrote the opinion, Judge Smith. In this spot you will sometimes find the words *The Court, Per Curiam Opinion,* or *Memorandum Opinion,* which simply means that the court decided not to mention the name of the individual judge who wrote the opinion for the court, usually a short opinion covering a relatively minor issue.

⑬ In reading or briefing a case, make note of the history of the litigation to date. The lower court rendered a judgment dismissing the information (similar to an indictment) against Bruni after certain evidence was suppressed and declared inadmissible. (This is the prior proceeding.) The People have now appealed the judgment. (This is the present proceeding.)

If the words *information* or *suppression* are new to you, look them up in a legal dictionary before proceeding. Do this for every new word.

⑭ It is critical to state the facts of the case accurately. Here the facts are relatively simple: A search warrant that said "daytime" service was served at 9:30 P.M., and evidence was taken pursuant to this search warrant. Defendant objected to the admission of this evidence at trial. In most cases, the facts are not this simple. The facts may be given at the beginning of the case, or they may be scattered throughout the case. If you confront the latter situation, you must carefully read the entire case to piece the facts together. Ultimately, your goal is to identify the **key facts** of the opinion. A key fact is simply one that was very important to the result or holding of the court.

⑮ The next critical stage of reading a case is to state the issue (or issues) that the court was deciding in the case. When phrasing an issue, you should make specific reference to the language of the rule in controversy (e.g., a statute) along with important facts that raise this controversy. The issue in *Bruni* is as follows: When § 1533 was amended to allow service up to 10:00 P.M., did the legislature impliedly also amend § 1529, which continues to require "daytime" service, so that evidence obtained pursuant to a warrant served at 9:30 P.M. can be admitted into evidence?

⑯ The court refers to other statutes to support the conclusion it will reach. Note the interrelationship of the statutory sections. One statute is interpreted by interpreting other statutes. Section 4 of the Penal Code ("Pen. Code") says that the sections of the Penal Code are to be interpreted ("construed") rationally in order to carry out their purpose or objective and to promote justice. Section 1859 of the Code of Civil Procedure ("Code Civ. Proc.") says that when a general and a particular section are inconsistent, the latter is preferred.

The interrelationship of the statutes in this case is as follows:

- Section 1529 of the Penal Code says "daytime."
- Section 7 of the Penal Code defines daytime as sunrise to sunset.
- Section 1533 of the Penal Code, as amended, says between 7:00 A.M. and 10:00 P.M.
- Section 4 of the Penal Code and § 1859 of the Code of Civil Procedure provide principles of interpreting statutes that are inconsistent.

⑰ In the same manner, a court will refer to other cases to support its ruling. In this way, the court argues that the other cases are **precedents** for the case before the court. The court in *People v. Bruni* is saying that *Dept. of Motor Vehicles of California v. Indus. Acc. Com.* and *Tidwell v. Superior Court* are precedents for its own ruling. Precedent is important because of the principle of **stare decisis,** which means that courts should decide similar cases in the same way unless there is good reason to do otherwise.

⑱ Here is the **reasoning** of the court to support its ruling: If there is a general statute (such as § 1529) and a specific statute (such as § 1533) that are inconsistent, the latter is paramount and is preferred. Hence the legislature probably intended to amend the more general statute—§ 1529—when it amended § 1533.

⑲ The result, or **holding,** of the court's deliberation of the issue must then be identified. The holding is that § 1529 was impliedly amended to authorize service up to 10:00 P.M. The holding is also called the court's ruling.

⑳ The procedural consequences of the court's resolution of the issue are then usually stated, as here, toward the very end of the case. The judgment of the lower court is reversed. The lower court cannot continue to suppress (i.e., declare inadmissible) the evidence seized at the 9:30 P.M. search. This is the **disposition** of the case.

An appeals court could take a number of positions with respect to a lower court's decision. It could affirm it; modify it (reverse it only in part); **remand** the case (send it back to the lower court) with instructions on how to proceed or how to retry the case, etc.

㉑ In theory, a judge must be very precise in defining the issue before the court—and in resolving only that issue. The judge should not say more than *must* be said to decide the case. This theory, however, is sometimes not observed. Judges will go off on tangents, giving long dissertations or speeches through their opinions. As indicated, this can make your job more difficult; you must wade through all the words to identify (1) the key facts, (2) the precise issues, (3) the precise holding, and (4) the precise reasoning.

The worst tangent that a judge can stray into is called **dictum.** Dictum is a judge's or court's view of what the law is, or might be, on facts that are *not* before the court. Judge Smith indicated that the result of the case might be different if the warrant were not specific, e.g., if it did not name the individual to be searched or what the investigator was looking for. This was not the situation in the *Bruni* case; therefore, Judge Smith's commentary or speculation is dictum.

㉒ On any court there may be several judges. They do not always agree on what should be done in a case. The majority controls. In *Bruni,* Judge Smith wrote the **majority opinion.** A **concurring opinion** is one that votes for the result reached by the majority but for different reasons. In *Bruni,* Judge Jones concurred but specified that he accepted only the result of Judge Smith's opinion. Normally, judges in such situations will write an opinion indicating their own point of view. Judge Jones did not choose to write an opinion. He simply let it be known that he did not necessarily agree with everything Judge Smith said; all he agreed with was the conclusion that the warrant was validly served. To reach this result, Judge Jones might have used different reasoning, relied on different cases as precedent, etc.

㉓ A **dissenting opinion** disagrees with part or with all of the opinion of the majority. Dissenting opinions are sometimes heated. Of course, the dissenter's opinion is not controlling. It is often valuable to read, however, in order to determine what the dissenter thinks that the majority decided.

We turn now to the ten components found in the brief of a court opinion (Exhibit 7.2) followed by a ten-part brief of *Bruni* that conforms to the guidelines of briefing presented in Exhibit 7.2.

Exhibit 7.2   Brief of a Court Opinion

I. CITATION
Where can the case be found? Provide a full *citation* to the case you are briefing, e.g., the volume number of the reporter, the abbreviation of the reporter, the page on which the case begins, the date of decision.

II. PARTIES
Who are the *parties*? Identify the lead parties, their relationship to each other, their litigation status when the case began (e.g., defendant), and their litigation status now (e.g., appellant).

III. OBJECTIVES OF PARTIES
When the litigation began, what were the parties seeking? State the ultimate objectives of the parties in terms of the end result they want from the litigation. At this point, do not focus on tactical or procedural objectives.

Exhibit 7.2   Brief of a Court Opinion—continued

IV. THEORIES OF THE LITIGATION

What legal theories are the parties using? At the trial level of a civil case, state the cause of action and the main defense. In a criminal case, state what the prosecution was for and the response of the defendant. If the case is now on appeal, briefly state the main theory of each party. Where relevant, always refer to specific rules.

V. HISTORY OF THE LITIGATION

What happened below—what are the prior proceeding(s)? For each *prior proceeding*, briefly state the nature of the proceeding, the party initiating it, the name of the court or agency involved, and the result of the proceeding. For the *present proceeding*, briefly state the nature of the proceeding, who initiated it, and the name of the court or agency involved.

VI. FACTS

What are the facts of the case? Specifically, state the facts that were very important or key to the holding(s) reached by this court.

VII. ISSUE(S)

What are the questions of law now before the court? Provide a comprehensive statement of each *issue* by making specific reference to the language of the rule in controversy (e.g., a statute) along with important facts that raise this controversy.

VIII. HOLDING(S)

What are this court's answers to the issues? If you have stated each issue comprehensively, its holding will be a simple YES or NO response.

IX. REASONING

Why did the court answer the issues the way it did? State the reasons for each holding.

X. DISPOSITION

What order did this court enter as a result of its holding(s)? State the procedural consequences of the court's resolution of the issue(s).

Brief of *People v. Bruni*

CITATION:	*People v. Bruni*, 25 Cal. App. 3d 196, 100 Cal. Rptr. 600 (1972).
PARTIES:	People of California/prosecution/plaintiff below/appellant here
	v.
	Bruni/accused/defendant below/respondent here
OBJECTIVES OF PARTIES:	The People want to convict and punish Bruni for criminal conduct. Bruni wants to avoid conviction and punishment.
THEORIES of the LITIGATION:	1. TRIAL: The People sought to prosecute Bruni for the alleged commission of a crime. (The opinion does not tell us which crime. The legal theory that justifies the bringing of the prosecution is the alleged commission of a crime.) Since Bruni is resisting the prosecution, we can assume that the basis and theory of his case is simply that he did not commit the crime. At the trial this was probably his main defense. 2. APPEAL: Bruni says that the state violated § 1529 when the search warrant was served at 9:30 P.M. The People say § 1529 was impliedly amended by § 1533, which allows service up to 10:00 P.M.
HISTORY of LITIGATION Prior Proceeding:	1. TRIAL: A criminal prosecution was brought by the People (the state) in the Superior Court (San Mateo). RESULT: Judgment for Bruni dismissing the information after the court granted a motion to suppress the evidence obtained from the search warrant.

Present Proceeding: 2. APPEAL: The People now appeal the dismissal of the information to the Court of Appeals (First District).

FACTS: A search warrant that said "daytime" service was served at 9:30 P.M. Evidence was obtained during this search, which the People unsuccessfully attempted to introduce during the trial.

ISSUE: When § 1533 was amended to allow service up to 10:00 P.M., did the legislature impliedly also amend § 1529 which continues to require "daytime" service, so that evidence obtained pursuant to a warrant served at 9:30 P.M. can be admitted into evidence?

HOLDING: YES.

REASONING: If there is a general statute (such as § 1529) and a specific statute (such as § 1533) that are inconsistent, the latter is paramount and is preferred. Hence the legislature probably intended to amend the more general statute—§ 1529—when it amended § 1533.

DISPOSITION: The trial court's judgment dismissing the information is reversed. When the trial resumes, the court must deny the motion to suppress the evidence based on the time of the service.

At the end of your brief, you should consider adding some notes that cover the following topics:

- What has happened to the case since it was decided? Has it been overruled? Has it been expanded or restricted by later cases? You can find this out by shepardizing the case.
- Summary of concurring opinions, if any.
- Summary of dissenting opinions, if any.
- Interesting dictum in the majority opinion, if any.
- Your own feelings about the opinion. Was it correctly decided? Why or why not?

🏛 *A s s i g n m e n t   7 . 5*

Prepare a ten-part brief of each of the following three opinions:

(a) *United States v. Kovel* printed below.
(b) *Quinn v. Lum* printed below. (You do not need to give the citation of this opinion. It is an actual opinion, but was not reported in a traditional reporter.)
(c) *Brown v. Hammond* on page 260 in chapter 5.

United States v. Kovel

United States Court of Appeals
Second Circuit, 1961, 296 F.2d 918

FRIENDLY, Circuit Judge.

This appeal from a sentence for criminal contempt for refusing to answer a question asked in the course of an inquiry by a grand jury raises an important issue as to the application of the attorney-client privilege to a non-lawyer employed by a law firm.

Kovel is a former Internal Revenue agent having accounting skills. Since 1943 he has been employed by Kamerman & Kamerman, a law firm specializing in tax law. A grand jury in the Southern District of New York was investigating alleged Federal income tax violations by Hopps, a client of the law firm; Kovel was subpoenaed to appear on September 6, 1961. The law firm advised the Assistant United States Attorney that since Kovel was an employee under the direct supervision of the partners, Kovel could not disclose any communications by the client or the result of any work done for the client, unless the latter consented; the Assistant answered that the attorney-client privilege did not apply to one who was not an attorney.

On September 7, the grand jury appeared before Judge Cashin. The Assistant United States Attorney informed the judge that Kovel had refused to answer "several questions . . . on the grounds of attorney-client privilege"; he proffered "respectable authority . . . that an accountant, even if he is retained or employed by a firm of attorneys, cannot take the privilege." The judge answered "You don't have to give me any authority on that." A court reporter testified that Kovel, after an initial claim of privilege had admitted receiving a statement of Hopps' assets and liabilities, but that, when asked "what was the purpose of your receiving that," had declined to answer on the ground of privilege "Because the communication was received with a purpose, as stated by the client"; later questions and answers indicated the communication was a letter addressed to Kovel. After verifying that Kovel was not a lawyer, the judge directed him to answer, saying "You have no privilege as such." The reporter then read another question Kovel had refused to answer, "Did you ever discuss with Mr. Hopps or give Mr. Hopps any information with regard to treatment for capital gains purposes of the Atlantic Beverage Corporation sale by him?" The judge again directed Kovel to answer reaffirming "There is no privilege—You are entitled to no privilege, as I understand the law."

Later on September 7, they and Kovel's employer, Jerome Kamerman, now acting as his counsel, appeared again before Judge Cashin. The Assistant told the judge that Kovel had "refused to answer some of the questions which you had directed him to answer." A reporter reread so much of the transcript heretofore summarized as contained the first two refusals. The judge offered Kovel another opportunity to answer, reiterating the view, "There is no privilege to this man at all." Counsel referred to New York Civil Practice Act, § 353, which we quote in the margin.*

Counsel reiterated that an employee "who sits with the client of the law firm . . . occupies the same status . . . as a clerk or stenographer or any other lawyer . . ."; the judge was equally clear that the privilege was never "extended beyond the attorney." The court held [Kovel] in contempt, sentenced him to a year's imprisonment, ordered immediate commitment and denied bail. Later in the day, the grand jury having indicted, Kovel was released until September 12, at which time, without opposition from the Government, I granted bail pending determination of this appeal.

Here the parties continue to take generally the same positions as below—Kovel, that his status as an employee of a law firm automatically made all communications to him from clients privileged; the Government, that under no circumstances could there be privilege with respect to communications to an accountant. The New York County Lawyers' Association as *amicus curiae* has filed a brief generally supporting appellant's position.

Decision under what circumstances, if any, the attorney-client privilege may include a communication to a non-lawyer by the lawyer's client is the resultant of two conflicting forces. One is the general teaching that "The investigation of truth and the enforcement of testimonial duty demand the restriction, not the expansion, of these privileges," 8 Wigmore, *Evidence* (McNaughton Rev. 1961), § 2192, p. 73. The other is the more particular lesson "That as, by reason of the complexity and difficulty of our law, litigation can only be properly conducted by professional men, it is absolutely necessary that a man . . . should have recourse to the assistance of professional lawyers, and . . . it is equally necessary . . . that he should be able to place unrestricted and unbounded confidence in the professional agent, and that the communications he so makes to him should be kept secret . . . ," Jessel, M. R. in *Anderson v. Bank*, 2 Ch.D. 644, 649 (1876). Nothing in the policy of the privilege suggests that attorneys, simply by placing accountants, scientists or investigators on their payrolls and maintaining them in their offices, should be able to invest all communications by clients to such persons with a privilege the law has not seen fit to extend when the latter are operating under their own steam. On the other hand, in contrast to the Tudor times when the privilege was first recognized, the complexities of modern existence prevent attorneys from effectively handling clients' affairs without the help of others; few lawyers could now practice without the assistance of secretaries, file clerks, telephone operators, messengers, clerks not yet admitted to the bar, and

---

*"An attorney or counselor at law shall not disclose, or be allowed to disclose, a communication, made by his client to him, or his advice given thereon, in the course of his professional employment, nor shall any clerk, stenographer or other person employed by such attorney or counselor . . . disclose, or be allowed to disclose any such communication or advice."

aides of other sorts. "The assistance of these agents being indispensable to his work and the communications of the client being often necessarily committed to them by the attorney or by the client himself, the privilege must include all the persons who act as the attorney's agents." 8 Wigmore, *Evidence,* § 2301; Annot., 53 A.L.R. 369 (1928).

Indeed, the Government does not here dispute that the privilege covers communications to non-lawyer employees with "a menial or ministerial responsibility that involves relating communications *to an attorney.*" We cannot regard the privilege as confined to "menial or ministerial" employees. Thus, we can see no significant difference between a case where the attorney sends a client speaking a foreign language to an interpreter to make a literal translation of the client's story; a second where the attorney, himself having some little knowledge of the foreign tongue, has a more knowledgeable non-lawyer employee in the room to help out; a third where someone to perform that same function has been brought along by the client; and a fourth where the attorney, ignorant of the foreign language, sends the client to a non-lawyer proficient in it, with instructions to interview the client on the attorney's behalf and then render its own summary of the situation, perhaps drawing on his own knowledge in the process, so that the attorney can give the client proper legal advice. All four cases meet every element of Wigmore's famous formulation, § 2292, "(1) Where legal advice of any kind is sought (2) from a professional legal advisor in his capacity as such, (3) the communications relating to that purpose, (4) made in confidence (5) by the client, (6) are at his instance permanently protected (7) from disclosure by himself or by the legal advisor, (8) except the protection be waived," . . . § 2301 of Wigmore would clearly recognize the privilege in the first case and the Government goes along to that extent; § 2301 would also recognize the privilege in the second case and § 2301 in the third unless the circumstances negated confidentiality. We find no valid policy reason for a different result in the fourth case, and we do not read Wigmore as thinking there is. Laymen consulting lawyers should not be expected to anticipate niceties perceptible only to judges—and not even to all of them.

This analogy of the client speaking a foreign language is by no means irrelevant to the appeal at hand. Accounting concepts are a foreign language to some lawyers in almost all cases, and to almost all lawyers in some cases. Hence the presence of an accountant, whether hired by the lawyer or by the client, while the client is relating a complicated tax story to the lawyer, ought not destroy the privilege, any more than would that of the linguist in the second or third variations of the foreign language theme discussed above; the presence of the accountant is necessary, or at least highly useful, for the effective consultation between the client and the lawyer which the privilege is designed to permit. By the same token, if the lawyer has directed the client, either in the specific case or generally, to tell his story in the first instance to an accountant engaged by the lawyer, who is then to interpret it so that the lawyer may better give legal advice, communications by the client reasonably related to that purpose ought fall within the privilege; there can be no more virtue in requiring the lawyer to sit by while the client pursues these possibly tedious preliminary conversations with the accountant than in insisting on the lawyer's physical presence while the client dictates a statement to the lawyer's secretary or is interviewed by a clerk not yet admitted to practice. What is vital to the privilege is that the communication be made *in confidence* for the purpose of obtaining *legal* advice *from the lawyer.* If what is sought is not legal advice but only accounting service, or if the advice sought is the accountant's rather than the lawyer's, no privilege exists. We recognize this draws what may seem to some a rather arbitrary line between a case where the client communicates first to his own accountant (no privilege as to such communications, even though he later consults his lawyers on the same matter, *Gariepy v. United States,* 189 F.2d 459, 463 (6th Cir. 1951)),‡ and others, where the client in the first instance consults a lawyer who retains an accountant as a listening post, or consults the lawyer with his own accountant present. But that is the inevitable consequence of having to reconcile the absence of a privilege for accountants and the effective operation of the privilege of client and lawyer under conditions where the lawyer needs outside help. We realize also that the line we have drawn will not be so easy to apply as the simpler positions urged on us by the parties—the district judges will scarcely be able to leave the decision of such cases to computers; but the distinction has to be made if the privilege is neither to be unduly expanded nor to become a trap.

The judgment is vacated and the cause remanded for further proceedings consistent with this opinion.

---

‡We do not deal in this opinion with the question under what circumstances, if any, such communications could be deemed privileged on the basis that they were being made to the accountant as the client's agent for the purpose of subsequent communication by the accountant to the lawyer; communications by the client's agent to the attorney are privileged, 8 Wigmore, *Evidence,* § 2317-1.

Quinn v. Lum and Cronin, Fried, Sekiya & Kekina

Civ. No. 81284
Hawaii Court of Appeals

On January 25, 1984, Richard K. Quinn, Attorney at Law, a Law Corporation, filed suit against Rogerlene Lum, a member of the Hawaii Association of Legal Assistants (HALA) and formerly legal secretary with the Quinn firm, for injunctive relief based on the allegation that Mrs. Lum possesses confidential client information from her work as Quinn's legal secretary, which information would be transmitted to the co-defendant, Mrs. Lum's new employer, Cronin, Fried, Sekiya & Kekina, Attorneys at Law, if she were to begin her employment with the Cronin firm as a legal assistant.

On or about January 3, 1984 Mrs. Lum notified Quinn that she had accepted a position as a paralegal with the Cronin firm. Quinn subsequently discussed and corresponded with Mr. Cronin regarding the hiring of Mrs. Lum, who was scheduled to begin work with the Cronin firm on January 30, 1984. Mr. Cronin repeatedly refused Quinn's request that she not be hired by the Cronin firm.

On January 26, a hearing on the application for a temporary restraining order was heard by Judge Philip T. Chun of the Circuit Court of the First Circuit, State of Hawaii. The application was denied.

Quinn alleges in the pleadings filed with the Court in Civil No. 81284 that Mrs. Lum's employment with the Quinn firm from December 1, 1982 to January 17, 1984, and as Mr. Quinn's secretary from April 25, 1983 to January 17, 1984, included attendance at the firm's case review committee meetings. Confidential discussions occurred concerning case evaluation, settlement evaluation, strategy and tactics between Quinn, his associates, and their clients.

Cronin et al. are attorneys of record for the plaintiffs in *Firme v. Honolulu Medical Group and Ronald P. Peroff, M.D.* Quinn's firm represents the defendants. The case was set for trial on March 19, 1984. According to exhibits attached to the records filed in the instant case, Mr. Cronin recognized the *Firme* situation and agreed that Mrs. Lum would not be involved in the *Firme* case in her new employment, nor would his firm "[ever] seek to obtain any information from her concerning cases with which she was involved while in [Quinn's] office, nor would we have her work on any while here." Mr. Cronin goes on to say in his January 24 letter to Quinn that Quinn should consult with his clients

in the *Firme* case as to whether Quinn's "attempt . . . to stop Mrs. Lum from working for [the Cronin firm] is with their approval."

Quinn also alleges that while his firm is known in the Honolulu legal community as one which represents hospitals, doctors and other health care providers, the Cronin firm is known as a plaintiff medical malpractice firm. Quinn lists in several pleadings that on more than one occasion, these firms found themselves adversaries in the same cases.

[Quinn contends] that this action was brought not to "bar Lum from working as a legal secretary or even as a paralegal, since that would be ludicrous given the size of Hawaii's legal community." In fact, Quinn states he would have "no objection to Lum's working for any other law firm in Hawaii other than one which specializes in medical malpractice plaintiffs' work, like [Cronin's]."

A subsequent hearing on the original complaint for injunctive relief was then held in Judge Ronald Moon's court on February 6. Plaintiff's motion for a preliminary injunction that would bar such employment "for at least two years" was denied, with the judge noting *Quinn v. Lum* as a case of first impression.

The Court explained its decision in light of the standards to be met before a preliminary injunction could be issued, as dealt with in depth by Mrs. Lum's attorney, David L. Fairbanks, who is also the current President of the Hawaii State Bar Association.

The standards which must be met in order to obtain a preliminary injunction, as listed by Judge Moon, follow:

1. The Court did not feel there was a substantial likelihood that plaintiff would prevail on the merits. If an injunction were to be issued, it would:

    "[E]ssentially prevent a paralegal or legal secretary, [or] attorney from joining any law firm that may have had some case in the past, . . . cases pending at the present time, or potential cases which may be worked on in the future" (Transcript of the Hearing, page 82).

2. The evidence is lacking regarding irreparable damage to Richard Quinn's clients.

3. The public interest would not be served by issuing such an injunction.

When an attorney enters practice in the State of Hawaii, he or she agrees to abide and be governed by the Hawaii Code of Professional Responsibility. This code does not attempt to govern the ethical actions of the non-attorneys. While Canon 37 of the American Bar Association's Code of Professional Responsibility, adopted pre-1971, states that a lawyer's employees have the same duty to preserve client confidences as the lawyer, this Canon is not included in the Hawaii code. Compliance, therefore, with the same rules of ethics guiding the Hawaii attorney is currently left to the discretion—and conscience—of the non-attorney.

If an attorney in Hawaii breaches the Code of Professional Responsibility, the office of Disciplinary Counsel may choose to investigate the matter and may pass the matter on to the Disciplinary Board and possibly, to the Hawaii Supreme Court for adjudication.

If an employee of a law office becomes suspect of some breach of ethics or acts of omission, the employing attorney becomes responsible for the employee's deeds. For example, if a legal secretary fails to file the complaint the day the Statute of Limitations expires thinking the next day would suffice, it is the attorney who is responsible to the client. The attorney can fire the secretary "for cause" but the attorney, nevertheless, stands responsible. It appears the only way for an attorney to further censor the employee directly is via a civil suit for tortious damages.

Whether a permanent injunction can or will be granted has yet to be seen in this case. What is clear is that neither the office of Disciplinary Counsel nor the Hawaii Supreme Court would or could become involved; they have no jurisdiction over the non-attorney working in a law office.

Section F
APPLYING COURT OPINIONS

As we have seen, a court opinion interprets one or more rules of law that are applied to the fact situation before the court. There are two main kinds of rules of law that are interpreted and applied in this way:

- Enacted law
- Common law

Enacted law consists of *constitutional provisions* (created by constitutional convention, legislative approval, and sometimes by vote of the electorate), *statutes* (created by the legislature), *administrative regulations* (created by agencies), *ordinances* (created by city councils and county boards), etc. (See Exhibit 6.1 in chapter 6.) **Common law** is judge-made law created by the courts when there is no controlling enacted law that governs the controversy before the court. For example, most of the law on negligence was initially created as common law by the courts because the legislature had not provided any statutes in this area. If, however, such statutes did exist, the courts would have to apply them. Since statutes are superior in authority to common law, new statutes can always change common law. Statutes that bring about such change are called **statutes in derogation of the common law.**

The starting point in your analysis is a set of facts presented to you by a client or by your instructor for a school assignment. The goal is to apply the court opinion to this set of facts. The opinion reached a certain result, called a holding or ruling. The conclusion of your legal analysis of the opinion will be your assessment of whether this holding applies to the set of facts presented to you. How do you reach this assessment?

- First, you *compare* the *rule* that was interpreted and applied in the opinion with the rule that you have uncovered through legal research as potentially applicable.
- Second, you *compare* the *facts* given to you by the client or by your instructor with the key facts in the opinion.

RULE COMPARISON

Suppose your client is charged with a violation of § 23(b) of the state code on the payment of certain taxes. One of your first steps is to go to the law library and find § 23(b). You want to know whether § 23(b) applies to your client. After a preliminary analysis of this statute on your own, you search for court opinions that interpreted and applied § 23(b). You would not try to find opinions that interpreted housing or pollution statutes. You focus on opinions that cover the *same* rule involved in the case of the client—here, § 23(b). This is also true of the common law. If the client has a negligence case, for example, you search for opinions that interpret the law of negligence.

Rule comparison in the analysis of opinions, therefore, is fairly simple. The general principle is: you compare the rule involved in your client's case (or school assignment) with the rule interpreted and applied in the opinion, and you proceed only if the rule is exactly the same. While there are some exceptions, this principle will be sufficient to guide you most of the time.

FACT COMPARISON

Here is the heart of the analysis. Before the holding of an opinion can apply, you must demonstrate that the key facts of the opinion are substantially the same as the facts in the client's case (or school assignment). If the facts are exactly the same or almost exactly the same, the opinion is said to be **on all fours** with your facts. If so, then you will have little difficulty convincing someone that the holding of the opinion applies to your facts. It is rare, however, that you will find an opinion on all fours. Consequently, careful analysis of *factual similarities and differences* must be made. In general, if the facts are substantially similar, the ruling applies; if they are substantially different, it does not.

You must make a determination of what the *key facts* are in the opinion, since it is these facts alone that are the basis of the comparison. As indicated earlier, a key fact is a very important fact—a fact that was crucial to the conclusion or holding of the court. In a divorce opinion, for example, it will probably not be key that a plaintiff was thirty-three years old. The court would have reached the same result if the plaintiff was thirty-two or thirty-four. Age may have been irrelevant or of very minor importance to the holding. What *may* have been key is that the plaintiff beat his wife, since without this fact the court may not have reached the conclusion that the ground of cruelty existed. You carefully comb the opinion to read what the judge said about the various facts. Did the court emphasize certain facts? Repeat them? Label them as crucial or important? These are the kinds of questions you must ask yourself to determine which facts in the opinion were key.

Let us assume that you have been able to identify the key facts of opinion. Your next concern is *comparing* these facts and the facts of your own problem. For example:

Your Facts

Client sees an ad in the paper announcing a sale at a local store. He goes to the back of the store and falls into a pit. There was a little sign that said *danger* near the pit. The client wants to sue the store owner, J. Jackson, for negligence in failing to use reasonable care in preventing his injury. The law office assigns a paralegal to research the case. The paralegal finds the case of *Smith v. Apex Co.* and wants to argue that it applies.

The Opinion: *Smith v. Apex Co.*

This case involved a man (Smith) who is looking for an address. He is walking down the street. He decides to walk into an office building to ask someone for directions. While coming down the corridor, he slips and falls on a wet floor. There was a small sign in the corridor that said *wet floor,* which Smith saw. Smith sued the owner of the building (Apex Co.) for negligence. The court held that the owner was negligent for failure to exercise reasonable care for the safety of users of the building. The cite of the opinion is *Smith v. Apex Co.,* 223 Mass. 578, 78 N.E.2d 422 (1980).

First, identify all factual similarities:

- The client was in a public place (a store). Smith was also in a public place (an office building).
- Both situations involved some kind of warning (the *danger* sign and the *wet floor* sign).
- The warning in both situations was not conspicuous (the *danger* sign was "little"; the *wet floor* sign was "small").

Next, identify all factual differences:

- The client was in a store, whereas Smith was in an office building.
- The client's case involved a hole or pit, whereas *Smith v. Apex Co.* involved a slippery surface.
- The client was there about a possible purchase, whereas Smith was looking for directions and therefore not trying to transact any business in the office building.

Next, identify any factual gaps:

- Smith saw the *wet floor* sign, but we do not know whether the client saw the *danger* sign.

Ninety percent of your legal analysis is complete if you have been able to make the above identifications. Many students do a sloppy job at this level. They do not carefully pick apart the facts in order to identify similarities, differences, and gaps.

Once you have done this properly, you make your final arguments about the opinion:

- If you want the holding in the opinion to apply, you emphasize the similarities between your facts and the key facts in the opinion. If any of your facts differ from a fact in the opinion, you try to point out that this is not significant since the latter was not a key fact in the opinion.
- If you do not want the holding in the opinion to apply, you emphasize the differences between your facts and the key facts in the opinion. If any of your facts is similar to a fact in the opinion, you try to point out that this is not significant since there is still a dissimilarity with at least one of the key facts in the opinion.

Factual gaps sometimes pose a problem. If the factual gap is in the facts of your client's case, you simply go back to the client and ask him or her about the fact. In the above case, for example, the paralegal asks the client whether he saw the "danger" sign. Suppose, however, that the factual gap is in the opinion itself. Assume that your client was running when he fell into the pit, but that the opinion does not tell you whether Smith was running, walking, etc. You obviously cannot go to Smith or to the judge who wrote the opinion and ask. You must make a guess of what the judge would have done in the opinion if Smith was running at the time he slipped on the corridor floor. You may decide that it would have changed the result or that this additional fact would have made no difference to the ruling reached.

We turn now to an overview of how *Smith v. Apex Co.* would be applied to the client's case in a memorandum of law. The latter is simply a written analysis of a legal problem. In chapter 12 we will discuss the components of a memorandum of law in greater detail. For now, we concentrate on only three components: legal issue, facts, and analysis.

The client's case and the *Smith* opinion involve exactly the same rule—the law of negligence. Assume that the part of this rule that is in contention (the *element* in *contention*) between the client and the store owner, J. Jackson, is the requirement that "reasonable care" be used.

Issue: Did the store use "reasonable care" for the safety of users of the store when the only warning of a pit in the store was a small *danger* sign near the pit?

Facts: The client saw an ad in the newspaper announcing a sale. He went to the back of the store and fell into a pit. There was a small sign that said *danger* near the pit.

Analysis: An opinion on point is *Smith v. Apex Co.*, 233 Mass. 578, 78 N.E.2d 422 (1980). In this opinion, the holding of the court was that the owner of an office building was liable for negligence when Smith slipped on a wet corridor floor in the building. There was a small *wet floor* sign in the corridor. This opinion is substantially similar to our own client's case. Both were in public buildings where owners can expect people to be present. In both situations, the warning was insufficient. The *wet floor* sign in the opinion was "small." The *danger* sign in our situation was "little." Because of all these important similarities, it can be argued that the holding in *Smith v. Apex Co.* applies.

It is true that in the opinion the judge pointed out that Smith saw the sign. Our facts do not state whether the client saw the *danger* sign in the store. This should not make any difference, however, since the judge in the opinion would probably have reached the same result if Smith had not seen the *wet floor* sign. In fact, the case would probably have been stronger for Smith if he did *not* see the sign. The building was dangerous in spite of the fact that users of the building such as Smith could see the sign. Obviously, the danger would be considered even greater if such users could not see the sign. We should find out from our client whether he saw the *danger* sign, but I do not think that it will make any difference in the applicability of the holding in *Smith v. Apex Co.*

The store owner will try to argue that the opinion does not apply. The argument might be that a pit is not as dangerous as a wet floor, since a pit is more conspicuous than a wet floor and hence not as hazardous. A user is more likely to notice a hole in the floor than to know whether a floor is slippery enough to fall on. Our client could respond by pointing out that the pit was in the back of the store where it may not have been very noticeable. Furthermore, the wet floor in the opinion was apparently conspicuous (Smith saw the *wet floor* sign), yet in the opinion the judge still found the defendant liable.

🏛 *Assignment 7.6*

In the following situations, point out any factual similarities, differences, and gaps between the client facts and the facts of the opinion.

(a) *Client Facts:* Jim is driving his car 30 m.p.h. on a dirt road at night. He suddenly sneezes and jerks the steering wheel slightly, causing the car to move to the right and run into Bill's fence. Bill sues Jim for negligence.
Opinion: A pedestrian brings a negligence action against Mary. Mary is driving her motorcycle on a clear day. A page of a newspaper unexpectedly flies into Mary's face. Since she cannot see where she is going, she runs into a pedestrian crossing the street. The court finds for Mary, ruling that she did not act unreasonably in causing the accident.

(b) *Client Facts:* Helen is the mother of David, age four. The state is trying to take David away from Helen on the ground that Helen has neglected David. Helen lives alone with

David. She works part-time and leaves David with a neighbor. Helen's job occasionally requires her to travel. Once she was away for a month. During this period, David was sometimes left alone, since the neighbor had to spend several days at the hospital. When David was discovered alone, the state began proceedings to remove David on the ground of neglect.

Opinion: The state charged Bob Thompson with the neglect of his twins, aged ten. The state wishes to place the twins in a foster home. Bob is partially blind. One day he accidentally tripped and fell on one of the twins, causing severe injuries to the child. Bob lives alone with the twins but refuses to hire anyone to help him run the home. The court ruled that Bob did not neglect his children.

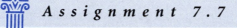

Assignment 7.7

(a) Before Helen became a paralegal for the firm of Harris & Derkson, she was a chemist for a large corporation. Harris & Derkson is a patent law firm where Helen's technical expertise in chemistry is invaluable. Helen's next-door neighbor is an inventor. On a number of occasions, he discussed the chemical makeup of his inventions with Helen. The neighbor is being charged by the government with stealing official secrets in order to prepare one of these inventions. Harris & Derkson represents the neighbor on this case. Helen also works directly on the case for the firm. In a prosecution of the neighbor, Helen is called as a witness and is asked to reveal the substance of all her conversations with the neighbor concerning the invention in question. Does Helen have to answer? Apply *United States v. Kovel* to this question. Do not do any legal research. Limit yourself to the application of this one opinion based on the guidelines of this section. For the text of *Kovel,* see Assignment 7.5 on page 358.

(b) Salem is a factory town of 500 inhabitants in Hawaii. The factory employs 95 percent of the workers in the town. The town has only two private attorneys: Ann Grote and Timothy Farrell. Forty of the employees have decided to sue the factory over a wage dispute. Ann Grote represents all these employees. She works alone except for her only employee, Bob Davis, a paralegal. In this litigation, the factory is represented by Timothy Farrell who has no employees—no secretaries and no paralegals. Grote and Farrell are young attorneys who have just begun their practices. Their only clients are the forty employees and the factory, respectively. The litigation has become quite complicated. Several months before the case is scheduled to go to trial, Farrell offers Davis a job as a paralegal at double the salary he is earning with Grote. He accepts the offer. Grote goes to court seeking a preliminary injunction against Davis and Farrell, which would bar them from entering this employment relationship. Apply *Quinn v. Lum and Cronin, Fried, Sekiya & Kekina* to the facts of the case of *Grote v. Davis and Farrell.* Do not do any legal research. Limit yourself to the application of this one opinion based on the guidelines of this section. For the text of *Quinn,* see Assignment 7.5 above.

(c) Anthony Bay is a paralegal who works for Iverson, Kelley, and Winters in Philadelphia. He is an at-will employee. His supervising attorney is Grace Swenson. One day Bay notices that Swenson deposited a client settlement check in the general law firm account. Bay calls the bar association disciplinary committee and charges Swenson with commingling funds unethically. Bay is fired for disloyalty. In the meantime, the bar investigates the charge of commingling and finds that the charge is accurate. Swenson is eventually disciplined. Can Bay sue Swenson and Iverson, Kelley, and Winters for wrongful dismissal? Apply *Brown v. Hammond* to answer this question. Do not do any legal research. Limit yourself to the application of this one opinion based on the guidelines of this section. For the text of *Brown,* see page 260 in chapter 5.

Chapter Summary

Legal analysis is the process of connecting a rule of law to a set of facts in order to determine how that rule might apply to a particular situation. The goal of the process is to solve a legal dispute or to prevent one from arising. The structure of legal analysis is always the same: a rule and facts lead to a legal issue, which is generally phrased as a question. That question is answered by drawing a connection between the language of the rule and the facts, producing a conclusion.

An important skill in legal analysis is the ability to break a rule down into its elements. An element is simply a component or portion of a rule that is a precondition of the applicability of the entire rule. If all the elements apply to a fact situation, then the rule applies to the fact situation. If any one element does not apply, then the rule does not apply. A legal issue is often phrased to ask whether one of the elements applies to the facts. (This element is sometimes referred to as the element in contention or the element in controversy.) The answer may depend on whether the element is to be interpreted broadly or narrowly.

To brief an opinion means to identify its ten major components: citation, parties, objectives of the parties, theories of the litigation, history of the litigation, facts, issues, holdings, reasoning, and disposition. In addition, it is often essential to determine the subsequent history of the opinion. There are two main steps in applying an opinion to a set of facts from a client's case. First, you compare the rule (which will either be an enacted law or a common law) that was interpreted in the opinion with the rule you are considering in the client's case. With limited exceptions, the opinion cannot apply unless these two rules are the same. Second, you compare the key facts in the opinion with the facts of the client's case. In general, the opinion will apply if these facts are the same or are substantially similar.

KEY TERMS

legal analysis, 344
application, 344
memorandum of law, 345
IRAC, 345
elements, 346
cause of action, 348
defenses, 348
element in contention, 349
legal issue, 349
brief, 352

trial brief, 352
trial notebook, 352
appellate brief, 352
appellant, 353
respondent, 354
appellee, 354
shepardizing, 354
syllabus, 354
headnotes, 354
key number, 354

digests, 354
key facts, 355
precedents, 355
stare decisis, 355
reasoning, 355
holding, 356
disposition, 356
remand, 356
dictum, 356
majority opinion, 356

concurring opinion, 356
dissenting opinion, 356
enacted law, 362
common law, 362
statute in derogation of the
    common law, 362
rule comparison, 363
fact comparison, 363
on all fours, 363

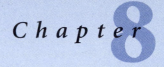

Chapter 8

LEGAL INTERVIEWING

> ► *Chapter Outline*

Section   A
CLIENT RELATIONS IN AN ERA OF LAWYER BASHING

Before beginning our study of interviewing, we need to examine some preliminary matters that often influence client relationships today.

You may be working with many clients who are hiring an attorney for the first time. Their image of the legal profession is often heavily influenced by the portrayal of attorneys in the media. Lately, the media have been very negative about attorneys. In a steady stream of commercials, cartoons, and jokes, attorneys have been held up to public ridicule. Indeed, there has been so much unfavorable publicity that many bar associations have accused the media of lawyer bashing and have urged their members to take affirmative steps to improve the image of the profession.

This may be the environment in which a paralegal comes into contact with clients. How they perceive you matters a great deal. The way you dress, how you communicate, and how you perform your job can reinforce the negativism or help reverse it. Whether you are interviewing the client or closing the client's case file, it is extremely important that you project yourself as a professional. There is no better way to combat negative stereotypes of attorneys than for everyone in the office to maintain a high level of integrity and competence.

You should act on the assumption that every large or small task you perform on a client's case is of critical importance. Even if you have only a small role in a particular client's case, you should assume that how you perform your role will help determine whether the client is satisfied with the services rendered by the entire office and whether he or she will readily recommend the office to relatives, friends, and business associates. This is particularly important since about 40 percent of a law office's new business comes from referrals and recommendations of satisfied clients.[1]

Admittedly, you can't single-handedly correct the public's perception of attorneys. It is due to forces beyond your control. Attorneys sometimes take unpopular cases such as defending people charged with committing heinous crimes. When interviewed on TV or radio, these attorneys seldom generate much sympathy when they suggest that the accused is the victim. Attorneys are frequently injected into the middle of bitter disputes where they become lightning rods for underlying and overt hostility. Opponents often accuse the other attorney of causing the hostility or of setting up roadblocks to resolution in order to increase fees. While you can't eliminate these perceptions, you can perform your job in such a way that the client feels his or her case is the most important case you are working on, and that you are doing everything possible to help the office keep costs to a minimum. This kind of professionalism will go a long way toward correcting public misconceptions about the practice of law.

Section   B
HIRING THE FIRM

First things first. Before or during the first interview, the law office and the prospective client must decide whether to establish an attorney-client relationship. This is normally done by a contract called the **retainer.** It hires—or retains—the attorney. (See Exhibit 8.1.) The word *retainer* also refers to an amount of money (or other property)

---

[1] Brent Roper, *Practical Law Office Management* 121 (1995).

Exhibit 8.1   Sample Retainer

_____ , 19____

ATTORNEY-CLIENT FEE CONTRACT

This ATTORNEY-CLIENT FEE CONTRACT ("Contract") is entered into by and between _____ ("Client") and _____ ("Attorney").

1. CONDITIONS. This Contract will not take effect, and Attorney will have no obligation to provide legal services, until Client returns a signed copy of this Contract and pays the deposit called for under paragraph 3.

2. SCOPE AND DUTIES. Client hires Attorney to provide legal services in connection with _____ . Attorney shall provide those legal services reasonably required to represent Client, and shall take reasonable steps to keep Client informed of progress and to respond to Client's inquiries. Client shall be truthful with Attorney, cooperate with Attorney, keep Attorney informed of developments, abide by this Contract, pay Attorney's bills on time, and keep Attorney advised of Client's address, telephone number, and whereabouts.

3. DEPOSIT. Client shall deposit $_____ by _____ . The sum will be deposited in a trust account, to be used to pay:

____ Costs and expenses only.

____ Costs and expenses and fees for legal services.

Client hereby authorizes Attorney to withdraw sums from the trust account to pay the costs or fees or both that Client incurs. Any unused deposit at the conclusion of Attorney's services will be refunded.

4. LEGAL FEES. Client agrees to pay for legal services at the following rates:

partners—$_____ an hour; associates—$_____ an hour; paralegals—$_____ an hour; law clerks—$_____ an hour; and for other personnel as follows:

If services to Client require extensive word processing work for documents in excess of 15 pages, Client will be charged $_____ a page.

Attorneys and paralegals charge in minimum units of 0.2 hours.

5. COSTS AND EXPENSES. In addition to paying legal fees, Client shall reimburse Attorney for all costs and expenses incurred by Attorney, including, but not limited to, process servers' fees, fees fixed by law or assessed by courts or other agencies, court reporters' fees, long-distance telephone calls, messenger and other delivery fees, postage, in-office photocopying at $_____ a page, parking, mileage at $_____ a mile, investigation expenses, consultants' fees, expert witness fees, and other similar items. Client authorizes Attorney to incur all reasonable costs and to hire any investigators, consultants, or expert witnesses reasonably necessary in Attorney's judgment, unless one or both of the clauses below are initialed by Client and Attorney.

____ Attorney shall obtain Client's consent before incurring any cost in excess of $_____.

____ Attorney shall obtain Client's consent before retaining outside investigators, consultants, or expert witnesses.

6. STATEMENTS. Attorney shall send Client periodic statements for fees and costs incurred. Client shall pay Attorney's statements within _____ days after each statement's date. Client may request a statement at intervals of no less than 30 days. Upon Client's request, Attorney will provide a statement within 10 days.

7. LIEN. Client hereby grants Attorney a lien on any and all claims or causes of action that are the subject of Attorney's representation under this Contract. Attorney's lien will be for any sums due and owing to Attorney at the conclusion of Attorney's services. The lien will attach to any recovery Client may obtain, whether by arbitration award, judgment, settlement, or other means.

8. DISCHARGE AND WITHDRAWAL. Client may discharge Attorney at any time. Attorney may withdraw with Client's consent or for good cause. Good cause includes Client's breach of this Contract, Client's refusal to cooperate with Attorney or to follow Attorney's advice on a material matter, or any other fact or circumstance that would render Attorney's continuing representation unlawful or unethical.

9. CONCLUSION OF SERVICES. When Attorney's services conclude, all unpaid charges shall become immediately due and payable. After Attorney's services conclude, Attorney will, upon Client's request, deliver Client's file to Client, along with any Client funds or property in Attorney's possession.

E x h i b i t   8 . 1   **Sample Retainer—continued**

10. DISCLAIMER OF GUARANTEE. Nothing in this Contract and nothing in Attorney's statements to Client will be construed as a promise or guarantee about the outcome of Client's matter. Attorney makes no such promises or guarantees. Attorney's comments about the outcome of Client's matter are expressions of opinion only.

11. EFFECTIVE DATE. This Contract will take effect when Client has performed the conditions stated in paragraph 1, but its effective date will be retroactive to the date Attorney first provided services. The date at the beginning of this Contract is for reference only. Even if this Contract does not take effect, Client will be obligated to pay Attorney the reasonable value of any services Attorney may have performed for Client.

"Attorney"

By: _____

"Client"

_____

Source: Pamela I. Everett, *Fundamentals of Law Office Management,* 196–7 (1994).

paid by the client as a deposit or advance against future attorney fees, expenses such as travel, and costs such as court filing fees.

Suppose, however, the attorney decides *not* to accept the case. This may happen for a number of different reasons. There may be a conflict of interest because the law office once represented the opponent of the prospective client (see chapter 5). The attorney may feel that the case lacks merit because there is no legal justification for what the client wants to accomplish. More commonly, the attorney will refuse to take the case for economic reasons. The client may not be able to afford the anticipated legal fees, and the party the client wants to sue may not have enough cash or other resources to pay a winning judgment. (Such an opponent is said to lack a **deep pocket.**) Whatever the reason, it is very important for the office to document its rejection of a prospective client by sending him or her a letter explicitly stating that the office will not be representing him or her. The document is called a **letter of nonengagement.** Its purpose is to avoid any misunderstandings if the person later claims to have been confused about whether the office had agreed to take the case.

Section C
THE CONTEXT OF INTERVIEWING IN LITIGATION

There are three main kinds of legal interviews:

- The initial client interview
- The follow-up client interview
- The investigation field interview of someone other than the client

In the **initial client interview,** the attorney-client relationship is established and legal problems are identified as the fact collection process begins. Follow-up interviews occur after the initial interview. The client is asked about additional facts and is consulted on a variety of matters that require his or her attention, consent, and participation. The field interview is conducted during investigation; the interviewer seeks out a great diversity of people for a wide range of purposes. Investigation will be examined in the next chapter. Here our focus will be the initial client interview.

Paralegal interviewing a client.

Interviewing is among the most important skills used in a law office. Since it appears to be relatively easy to engage in interviewing (all you need is a person to interview and some time), it is commonly assumed that legal interviewing, like good conversation, requires little more than intelligence and a pleasing personality. This misconception often leads to incomplete and sloppy interviewing. Legal interviewing is much more than conversation, although they are similar in that both involve building a relationship and exchanging information. In legal interviewing, however, the goal is to help solve a client's problem. To do this, the interviewer must establish a relationship with the client that is warm, trusting, professional, and goal-oriented.

Paralegals in different settings have varied duties and authority. In a private law office, an attorney will usually conduct the initial interview and may assign the paralegal the task of gathering detailed information from the client on a specific topic. For example, a paralegal may be asked to help a bankruptcy client obtain details on debts and financial entanglements by listing them all on a worksheet. On the other hand, in a government agency or in a government-funded legal service office, the paralegal's interviewing responsibilities can be extensive. For example, a paralegal might conduct the initial interview with a client and remain the primary office contact for the client throughout the resolution of the case.

The initial client interview is critical because it sets the foundation for the entire litigation process. (See Exhibit 8.2.) The facts obtained from this interview are further pursued through field *investigation;* subsequent or *follow-up client interviews* are often needed to clarify new facts and pursue leads uncovered during investigation; the laws governing the facts are *researched* in the law library; the facts and the governing law are informally

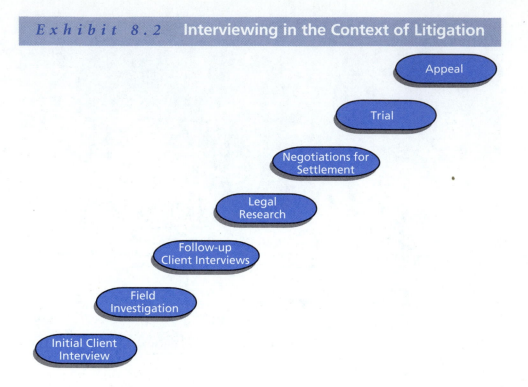

Exhibit 8.2   Interviewing in the Context of Litigation

argued between counsel for the parties in an effort to *settle* the case through *negotiation;* if there is no settlement, a *trial* is held in which the facts are formally established; finally, the process ends with an *appeal.* Everything begins with the facts obtained through the initial client interview. A poor job done at this stage can have major negative consequences throughout the remaining steps of the litigation process.

Section D
The Format of an Intake Memo

Before analyzing the interviewing process, we should look briefly at one of the end products of the interview—the **intake memo.** This is the document the paralegal writes on the basis of notes taken at the interview. The intake memo goes first to the supervisor and then into a newly opened case file on the client. The memo often has five parts:

1. *Heading.* The heading provides the following information at the top of the first page:

   - The name of the person who wrote the memo (you)
   - The supervisor in charge of the case to whom the memo is addressed
   - The date the memo was written
   - The date the interview was conducted
   - The name of the case
   - The office file number of the case
   - The kind of case (general area of the law)
   - The notation **RE,** which means concerning or in reference to. After RE, you state the general subject matter of the memo.

2. *Personal Data.*

   - Name of the client
   - Home address
   - Phone numbers where the client can be reached
   - Age of client
   - Marital status
   - Place of employment of the client
   - Etc.

3. *Statement of the Assignment.* The first paragraph of the memo should state the precise objective the paralegal was given in conducting the interview. It is a more detailed statement of what was listed under RE in the heading.

4. *Body of the Memo.* Here the facts are presented in a coherent, readable manner according to a number of possible organizational principles:

   - A chronological listing of the facts so that the events are unfolded as a story with a beginning, middle, and end
   - A categorizing of the facts according to the major topics or issues of the case, each with its own subject heading under which the relevant facts are placed
   - Any other format called for by the supervisor

5. *Conclusion.* Here a number of things could be included:

   - A brief summary of the major facts listed in the body of the memo
   - The paralegal's impressions of the client, such as
     - how knowledgeable the client appeared to be
     - how believable the client appeared to be
   - A list of the next steps, for example:
     - What further facts should be sought through investigation
     - What legal research should be undertaken
     - Any other recommendations on what should be done on the case based on what was learned during the interview
   - A list of anything the paralegal told the client to do, for example:
     - Bring in specified documents relevant to the case
     - Check on further facts and call back
     - Return for another interview

   Exhibit 8.3 shows a sample of the introductory parts of an intake memo.

Section E
WHAT FACTS DO YOU SEEK?
GUIDES TO THE FORMULATION OF QUESTIONS

Unless the paralegal knows what to accomplish in an interview, valuable time will be wasted. For example, suppose a client is being interviewed concerning legally sufficient reasons (called **grounds**) for a divorce. The paralegal does not simply write down *all* the facts about the marriage and the client's problems in it. The facts must be clustered or arranged in categories that are relevant to grounds for divorce. Unless the paralegal has this objective in mind before and during the interview, he or she may end up with a

---

> ### *Exhibit 8.3* Beginning of an Intake Memo
>
> ### Intake Memo
>
> **To:** Ann Fuller, Supervisor
> **From:** Jim Smith, Paralegal
> **Date of Memo:** March 13, 1996
> **Date of Interview:** March 12, 1996
>
> **Case:** John Myers vs. Betsy Myers
> **File Number:** 96-102
> **Kind of Case:** Child Custody
> **Re:** Intake Interview of John Myers
>
> **Personal Data:**
> **Name of Client:** John Myers
> **Address:** 34 Main Street, Salem, Massachusetts 01970
> **Phone:** 966-3954 (H) 297-9700 (x 301) (W)
> **Age:** 37
> **Marital Status:** Married but separated from his wife, Betsy Myers
> **Employment:** ABC Construction Co., 2064 South Street, Salem, Massachusetts 02127
>
> You asked me to conduct a comprehensive intake interview of John Myers, our client, in order to obtain a listing of his assets and the facts surrounding his relationship with his children.
>
> A. ASSETS
> John Myers owns . . .

confusing collection of facts and have to conduct a second interview to go over matters that should have been covered initially. This does not mean that the paralegal cannot talk about anything other than what is directly related to the objective, but it does mean that each interview must have a definite *focus*.

There are six major ways a paralegal can achieve focus in the formulation of questions to be asked of a client:

- Instructions of the supervisor for the interview
- Checklists
- Legal analysis
- "Fact particularization"
- Common sense
- Flexibility

These methods are designed to help you avoid all the following examples of an *ineffective* interview:

- You fail to seek the information that the supervisor wanted you to obtain.
- You miss major relevant facts.
- You fail to obtain sufficient detail on the major relevant facts.
- You fail to ask questions about the extent to which the client was sure *or unsure* about the major facts given you.
- You fail to pursue leads the client provides about other relevant themes or topics that may not have been part of the supervisor's explicit instructions or may not have been within the scope of your initial questions.

INSTRUCTIONS OF THE SUPERVISOR FOR THE INTERVIEW

The instructions of the supervisor control what you do in the interview. You may be asked to do a limited interview or a comprehensive one. Be sure to write down what the

> **"If you don't know where you're going, when you get there you'll be lost."**
> **—Yogi Berra**

supervisor wants from the interview. One concern that frequently arises is the amount of detail desired. Attorneys like facts. During three years of law school, they were constantly asked by their law professors, "What are the facts?" The likelihood is that the attorney for whom you work will want considerable detail from the interview. Even if you are told to limit yourself to obtaining the basic facts from the client, you may find that the supervisor wants a lot of detail about those basic facts. When in doubt, the safest course is to be detailed in your questioning. If possible, try to sit in on an interview conducted by your supervisor to observe his or her method of questioning and the amount of detail sought. Also, examine some closed case files that contain intake memos. Ask the supervisor if any of these memos is exemplary, and if so, why. Once you have a model, it can be very useful as a guide.

CHECKLISTS

The office where you work may have checklists that are used in conducting interviews. For some kinds of cases, such as probate or estate matters, the checklists may be extensive. If such checklists are not available, you should consider writing your own for the kinds of cases in which you acquire experience.

Caution is needed in using checklists:

- You should find out why individual questions were inserted in the checklist.
- You should be flexible enough to ask relevant questions that may not be on the checklist.

A checklist must be viewed as a guide that should be adjusted to adapt to the case and client in front of you, rather than as a rigid formula from which there can never be deviation.

LEGAL ANALYSIS

Extensive **legal analysis** does not take place while the interview is being conducted. Yet *some* legal analysis may be needed to conduct an intelligent interview. (See chapter 7 for an overview of legal analysis.)

Most of the questions you ask in the interview must be **legally relevant,** which means that the office needs the answer to determine whether a particular legal principle governs. At least a general understanding of legal analysis is needed to be able to apply the concept of legal relevance intelligently. It could be dangerous for the paralegal to be asking questions by rote, even if checklists are used. The question-and-answer process is a little like a tennis match—you go where the ball is hit or it passes you by.

Suppose that you are interviewing a client on an unemployment compensation claim. The state denied the claim because the client is allegedly not "available for work." You cannot conduct a competent interview unless you know the legal meaning of this phrase. From this understanding you can formulate questions that are legally relevant to the issue of whether the client has been and is "available for work." You will ask obvious questions such as:

Where have you applied for work?

Were you turned down, and if so, why?

Did you turn down any work, and if so, why?

What is your present health?

Suppose that during the interview, the client tells you the following:

There were some ads in the paper for jobs in the next town, but I didn't want to travel that far.

You must decide whether to pursue this matter by inquiring about the distance to the town, whether public transportation is available, the cost of such transportation, whether the client owns a car, etc. Again, legal analysis can be helpful. Does "available for work" mean available in the same area? Is one *un*available for work because of a refusal to make efforts to travel to an otherwise available job in another area? Questions such as these must go through your mind as you decide whether to seek more details about the ads for work in the other town. These are questions of legal analysis. *You must be thinking while questioning.* Some instant mental analysis should be going on all the time. This does not mean you must know the answer to every legal question that comes to mind while interviewing the client. But you must know something about the law and must be flexible enough to think about questions that should be generated by unexpected facts provided by the client.

When in doubt about whether to pursue a line of questions, check with your supervisor. If he or she is not available, the safest course is to pursue it. As you acquire additional interviewing experience in particular areas of the law, you will be better equipped to know what to do. Yet you will never know everything. There will always be fact situations that you have never encountered before. Legal analysis will help you handle such situations.

FACT PARTICULARIZATION

Fact particularization is one of the most important concepts in this book. To *particularize a fact* means to ask an extensive series of questions about that fact in order to explore its uniqueness. Fact assessment is critical to the practice of law; fact particularization (FP) is critical to the identification of the facts that must be assessed. FP is a fact-collection technique. It is the process of viewing every person, thing, or event as unique—different from every other person, thing, or event. Every important fact a client tells you in an interview should be particularized. You do this by asking a large number of follow-up questions once you have targeted the fact you want to explore. (See Exhibit 8.4.)

Example: You are working on an automobile negligence case. Two cars collide on a two-lane street. They were driven by Smith and Jones. Jones is a client of your law office. One of the facts in the file is that, according to Jones, Smith's car "veered into Jones's lane moments before the collision." Your job is to *obtain a much more detailed picture of what happened.* This is done by elaborating on the facts already collected. Using FP, you ask the following commonsense questions: who, what, where, how, when, and why.

- What does Jones mean by veering into the other lane?
- How much veering was done? An inch? A foot? The entire car came into the other lane? How much of an angle was there?

E x h i b i t   8 . 4   Fact Particularization

You *particularize* a fact you already have:
1. by assuming that what you know about this fact is woefully inadequate,
2. by assuming that there is more than one version of this fact, and
3. by asking a large number of basic who, what, where, how, when, and why questions about the fact, which, if answered, will provide as comprehensive a picture of that fact as is possible at this time.

- Who saw this happen? According to Jones, Smith's car veered. Did Jones see this happen himself? Who else saw it, if anyone? Any passengers in Jones's car? Any passengers in Smith's car? Were there any bystanders? Has the neighborhood been checked for witnesses, e.g., people who live or work in the area, people who frequently sit on public benches in the area?
- Were the police called after the accident? If so, who was the officer? Was a report made? If so, what does it say, if anything, about the car veering into the other lane? Where is this report? How can you obtain a copy?
- How fast was Jones's car going at the time of the veering? Who would be able to substantiate the speed? Who might have different views of how fast Jones was going?
- How fast was Smith's car going at the time of the veering? Who would be able to substantiate the speed? Who might have different views of how fast Smith was going?
- Have there been other accidents in the area? If so, how similar have they been to this one?
- What was the condition of the road at the time Smith started to veer? At the time of the collision?
- What was the weather at the time?
- How was visibility?
- What kind of a road is it? Straight? Curved at the area of the collision? Any inclines? Any hills that will affect speed and visibility?
- What kind of area is it? Residential? Commercial?
- Is there anything in the area that would distract drivers, e.g., potholes?
- Where is the nearest traffic light, stop sign, or other traffic signal? How, if at all, did they affect traffic at the time of the accident?
- What is the speed limit of the area?
- What kind of car was Smith driving? Were there any mechanical problems with the car? Would these problems help cause the veering? What prior accidents has Smith had, if any?
- What kind of car was Jones driving? Were there any mechanical problems with the car? What prior accidents has Jones had, if any?
- Etc.

FP can be a guide for the attorney and paralegal in formulating questions that need to be asked in different settings:

- In a client interview (our focus in this chapter)
- In investigations (see chapter 9)
- In drafting interrogatories (see chapter 10)
- In preparing for a deposition (see chapter 10)
- In examining witnesses on the stand during a hearing (see chapters 10 and 15)

In legal interviewing, the starting point for the FP process is an important fact that the client has told you during the interview. Here are additional examples: "I tried to find work"; "the car hit me from the rear"; "the pain was unbearable"; "the company was falling apart"; "he told me I would get the ranch when he died"; "he fired me because I am a woman"; etc. Then you ask the client eight categories of questions about the fact being particularized. (See Exhibit 8.5.)

The eight categories are not mutually exclusive, and all eight categories are not necessarily applicable to every fact that you will be particularizing. The questions need not be asked in any particular order so long as you are comprehensive in your search for factual

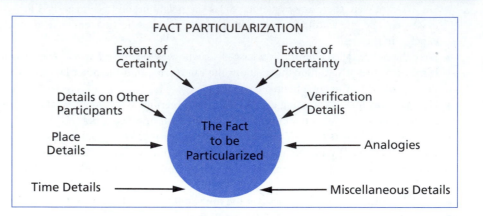

Exhibit 8.5 **The Categories of Fact Particularization**

detail. The point of FP is simply to get the wheels of your mind rolling so that you will think of a large number of questions and avoid conducting a superficial interview.

Time Details

When did the fact occur or happen? Find out the precise date and time. The interviewer should be scrupulous about all dates and times. If more than one event is involved, ask questions about the dates and times of each. If the client is not sure, ask questions to help jog the memory and ask the client to check his or her records or to contact other individuals who might know. Do not be satisfied with an answer such as, "It happened about two months ago." If this is what the client says, record it in your notes, but then probe further. Show the client a calendar and ask about other events going on at the same time in an effort to help him or her be more precise.

Place and Environment Details

Be equally scrupulous about geography. Where did the event occur? Where was the thing or object in question? Where was the client at the time? Ask the client to describe the surroundings. Ask questions with such care that you obtain a verbal photograph of the scene. If relevant, ask the client to approximate distances between important objects or persons. You might want to have the client draw a diagram, or you can draw a diagram on the basis of what you are told and ask the client if the drawing is accurate. Ask questions about the weather or about lighting conditions. You want to know as much as you can about the environment or whatever the client could observe about the environment through the senses of touch, sight, hearing, and smell.

Details on Other Participants

Who else was involved? Ask questions about who they were, their roles, their age, appearance, etc., if relevant. Where were they at the time? When did they act? Why did they act? Why did they fail to act? Could you have anticipated what they did or failed to do? Why or why not? Have they ever acted or failed to act in this way before? Ask questions designed to obtain a detailed picture of who these other participants were and their precise relationship to the fact being particularized.

Extent of Certainty/Uncertainty

Everything the client tells you can be placed somewhere on the spectrum of certainty:

Absolutely Certain	Substantially Certain	Fairly Certain	Have a Vague Certainty	Unsure	Do Not Know

It would be a big mistake, for example, to record that the client said a letter was received two weeks ago when in fact the client said. "I think it came two weeks ago." Do not turn uncertainty into certainty by sloppy listening and sloppy recording in your intake memo of what the client said. Of course, it may be possible for a client to be uncertain about a fact initially but then become more certain of it with the help of your questioning. If so, record this transition by saying, "The client was first unsure of who else was present, but then said she was fairly certain that Fred was there."

Explain to the client right at the beginning how critical it is for you to obtain accurate information. Encourage the client to say, "I'm not sure" when that's the case. It is important that the client be relaxed and unthreatened. It would not be wise for you to keep asking, "Are you sure?" after every fact the client tells you. Yet you must find out where on the spectrum of certainty a fact falls. Temper your probe with tact and sensitivity.

Verification Details

The fact that the client tells you something happened is *some* evidence that it happened. Verification data are *additional* evidence that supports what the client has said. Always pursue such verification details. Ask yourself how you would establish the truth of what the client has said if the client suddenly disappeared and you had to rely exclusively on other sources. Inquire about documents (such as letters or check stubs) that support the client's statements. Inquire about other people who might be available to testify to the same subject. Ask the client questions that will lead you to such verification details. This approach does not mean that you do not trust the client, or that you think the client is lying. It is simply a good practice to view a fact from many perspectives. You are always seeking the strongest case possible. This calls for questioning about verification details.

Analogies

Some facts that you are particularizing (e.g., "the pain was unbearable"; "I was careful"; "it looked awful"; "I was scared") are difficult to pin down. In the interview, you should ask the client to explain such statements. Sometimes it is helpful to ask the client to use **analogies** to describe what is meant. An analogy is simply explaining something by comparing it to something else. For example, you ask the client:

What would you compare it to?

Was it similar to anything you have ever seen before?

Have you observed anyone else do the same thing?

Have you ever been in a similar situation?

Did it feel like a dentist's drill?

You ask the client to compare the fact to something else. Then you ask about the similarities and differences. Through a series of directed questions you are encouraging the client to analogize the fact he or she is describing to some other fact. This is done in a further attempt to obtain as comprehensive a picture as possible of what the client is saying.

Miscellaneous Details

Here you simply ask about any details that were not covered in the previous categories of questions. Include questions on anything else that might help in particularizing the fact under examination.

Class Exercise 8.A

In this exercise, FP will be role-played in class. One student will be selected to play the role of the client and another, the role of the paralegal interviewer. The rest of the class will observe and fill out the FP Score Card on the interview.

Instructions to Interviewer. You will not be conducting a complete interview from beginning to end. You will be trying to particularize a certain fact that's given to you. Go through all the categories of FP described above. Use any order of questioning that you want. Probe for comprehensiveness. Your instructor will select one of the following facts, which will be used as the basis of the interview:

(a) "I was hit in the jaw by Mary."
(b) "He neglects his children."
(c) "I have not been promoted because I am a woman."

Your opening question to the client will be, "What happened?" The client will make one of the three statements above. You then use the process of FP to particularize this statement.

Instructions to Client. The interviewer will ask you what happened. Simply make one of the three statements above as selected by the instructor. Then the interviewer will ask you a large number of questions about the statements. Make up the answers—ad lib your responses. Do not, however, volunteer any information. Answer only the questions asked.

Instructions to Class. Observe the interview. Use the following score card to assess how well you think the interviewer particularized the fact.

FP Score Card

Precision in obtaining time details	5 4 3 2 1	Sloppiness in obtaining time details
Precision in obtaining place details	5 4 3 2 1	Sloppiness in obtaining place details
Precision in obtaining details on other participants	5 4 3 2 1	Sloppiness in obtaining details on other participants
Precision in finding out where the client's statements fall on the spectrum of certainty	5 4 3 2 1	Sloppiness in finding out where the client's statements fall on the spectrum of certainty
Precision in seeking verification details	5 4 3 2 1	Sloppiness in seeking verification details
Effectiveness in using analogies to obtain greater detail	5 4 3 2 1	Ineffectiveness in using analogies to obtain greater detail

Precision in obtaining miscellaneous details	⌞_⌞_⌞_⌞_⌞⌟ 5 4 3 2 1	Sloppiness in obtaining miscellaneous details

Following the interview, put a check on the appropriate number for each of the above categories of assessment. A "5" score means you thought the interview was very precise or effective in fulfilling the goal of FP. A "1" score means the opposite. Also, make notes of questions you think the interviewer *should have asked.* These questions, and your scores, will be discussed in class after the interview.

COMMON SENSE

Common sense is another major guide to determining what questions to ask, achieving comprehensiveness, and giving the interview a focus. Though law is full of legalisms and technicalities, good judgment and common sense are still at the core of the practice of law. It is common sense, for example, to organize an interview by having the client tell the relevant events chronologically in the form of a story with a beginning, middle, and end. It is common sense to follow up on a topic the client mentions with further questioning even though you had not anticipated the topic. If the client says something you do not understand, common sense dictates that you ask what the client means before continuing with the interview. At times, it may be common sense to stop the interview for a moment to obtain further guidance from your supervisor.

FLEXIBILITY

In the previous discussion, the importance of flexibility was mentioned a number of times. You must be prepared to expect the unexpected and you must be relaxed. Although you lead the interview and give it direction, you must be ready to go where the interview takes you. It would be potentially disastrous for you to block out topics that arise simply because they were not part of your game plan in conducting the interview or are not on your checklist. As with so many areas of the law, you may not know what you are looking for until you find it. In interviewing a client about incorporating a business, for example, you may stumble across a lead from something the client says that could involve fraud or criminal prosecution on a matter unrelated to the incorporation. Don't block this out. Pursue what appears to be reasonably related to the law office's relationship with the client. Check with your supervisor. Again, let common sense be your guide. Flexibility is one of the foundations of common sense.

Section F
WHAT DOES THE CLIENT WANT?

A number of points can be made about many clients, particularly new ones:

- They are not sure what they want.
- They change their minds about what they want.
- They are not aware of their legal and nonlegal options.
- The legal problem they tell you about involves other legal problems that they are not aware of and that even you may not be aware of at the outset.

Suppose a client walks into the office and says, "I want a divorce." The following observations *might* be possible about the client:

1. The client has an incorrect understanding of what a divorce is.
2. The client says she wants a divorce because she thinks this is the only legal remedy available to solve her problem.
3. If the client knew that other options existed (e.g., annulment, judicial separation, a restraining order, a support order) she would consider them.
4. What really troubles the client is that her husband beats the kids; a divorce is the only way she thinks she can stop it.
5. The client does not want a divorce. She is being pressured by her husband to institute divorce proceedings. He threatened her with violence if she refuses.
6. The client consciously or unconsciously wants and needs an opportunity to tell someone how badly the world is treating her, and if given this opportunity, she may not want to terminate the marriage.
7. If the client knew more about marriage or family counseling, she would consider using it before taking the drastic step of going to a law office for a divorce.

If any of these observations is correct, think of how damaging it would be for someone in the law office to take out the standard divorce forms and quickly fill them out immediately after the client says, "I want a divorce." This response would not be appropriate without first probing beneath the statement to determine what in fact is on the client's mind. Some clients who speak only of divorces and separation agreements are receptive to and even anxious for reconciliation. The danger exists that the client might be steered in the direction of a divorce because no other options are presented to her, because no one takes the time to help her express the ideas, intentions, and desires that are lurking beneath the seemingly clear statement, "I want a divorce."

This is not to say that you must psychoanalyze every client or that you must always distrust what the client tells you initially. It is rather a recognition of the fact that *most people are confused about the law and make requests based on misinformation about what courses of action are available to solve problems.* Common sense tells us to avoid taking all statements at face value. People under emotional distress need to be treated with sensitivity. We should not expect them to be able to express their intentions with clarity all the time in view of the emotions involved and the sometimes complicated nature of the law.

Assignment 8.1

During an interview, the client makes the following statements. What areas do you think need to be probed to make sure the office does not misunderstand what the client wants?

(a) I want to institutionalize my sick father.
(b) I want my boss arrested for assaulting me.
(c) I want to file for bankruptcy.

Section G
ASSESSING YOUR OWN BIASES

You need to be aware of how your personal feelings might affect your work on the case. Such feelings are the foundation of **bias,** which is an inclination or tendency to think and perhaps to act in a certain way. How would you answer the following question: "Am I objective enough that I can assist a person even though I have a personal distaste for what that person wants to do or what that person has done?" Many of us would quickly answer "yes" to this question. We all like to feel that we are levelheaded and not susceptible to letting our prejudices interfere with the job we are asked to accomplish. Most of us, however, have difficulty ignoring our personal likes and dislikes.

Assignment 8.2

The following fact situations involve aspects of domestic relations cases. To what extent might an individual be hampered in delivering legal services because of personal reactions toward the client? Identify potential bias.

(a) Mr. Smith, the client of your office, is being sued by his estranged wife for custody of their two small children. Mr. and Mrs. Smith live separately, but Mr. Smith has had custody of the children during most of their lives while Mrs. Smith has been in the hospital. Mrs. Smith has charged that Mr. Smith often yells at the children, leaves them with neighbors and day care centers for most of the day, and is an alcoholic. Your investigation reveals that Mrs. Smith will probably be able to prove all these allegations in court.

(b) Mrs. Jones is being sued by Mr. Jones for divorce on the ground of adultery. Mrs. Jones is the client of your office. Thus far your investigation has revealed that there is considerable doubt over whether Mrs. Jones did in fact commit adultery. During a recent conversation with Mrs. Jones, however, she tells you that she is a prostitute.

(c) Jane Anderson is seeking an abortion. She is not married. The father of the child wants to prevent her from having the abortion. Jane comes to your office for legal help. She wants to know what her rights are. You belong to a church that believes abortion is murder. You are assigned to work on the case.

(d) Tom Donaldson is a client of your office. His former wife claims that he has failed to pay court-ordered alimony payments and that the payments should be increased substantially because of her needs and his recently improved financial status. Your job is to help Tom collect a large volume of records concerning his past alimony payments and his present financial worth. You are the only person in the office who is available to do this record gathering. It is clear, however, that Tom does not like you. On a number of occasions, he has indirectly questioned your ability.

Having analyzed the fact situations in Assignment 8.2, do you still feel the same about your assessment of your own **objectivity**? Clearly, we cannot simply wish our personal feelings away or pretend that they do not exist. Nor are there any absolute rules or techniques that apply to every situation you will be asked to handle. Nor are the following admonitions very helpful: "Be objective," "be dispassionate," "don't get personally involved," "control your feelings." Such admonitions are too general, and when viewed in the abstract, they may appear not to be needed, since we want to believe that we are always objective, dispassionate, detached, and in control.

We must recognize that there are facts and circumstances that arouse our emotions and tempt us to impose our own value judgments. Perhaps if we know where we are vulnerable, we will be in a better position to prevent our reactions from interfering with our work. It is not desirable for you to be totally dispassionate and removed. A paralegal who is cold, unfeeling, and incapable of empathy is not much better than a paralegal who self-righteously scolds a client. It is clearly not improper for a paralegal to express sympathy, surprise, and perhaps even shock at what unfolds from the client's life story. If these feelings are genuine and if they would be normal reactions to the situation at a given moment, then they should be expressed. The problem is *how to draw the line* between expressing these feelings and reacting so judgmentally that you interfere with your ability to communicate with the client now and in the future. Again, there are no absolute guidelines. As you gain experience in the art of dealing with people, you will hopefully develop styles and techniques that will enable you to avoid going over that line. The starting point in this development is to recognize how easy it is to go over the line.

Some paralegals apply what is called the "stomach test." If your gut tells you that your personal feelings about the case are so intense that you may not be able to do a quality job for the client, you need to take action.[2] Talk with your supervisor. You may have some misunderstandings about the case that your supervisor can clear up. You may be able to limit your role in the case or be reassigned to other cases. Without breaching client confidentiality, contact your local paralegal association to try to talk with other paralegals who have handled similar situations. They may be able to give you some guidance.

Attorneys often take unpopular cases involving clients who have said or done things that run the gamut from being politically incorrect to being socially reprehensible. As professionals, attorneys are committed to the principle that *everyone* is entitled to representation. Paralegals need to have this same commitment. But attorneys and paralegals are human beings. No one can treat every case identically. In the final analysis, you need to ask yourself whether your bias is so strong that it might interfere with your ability to give the needs of the client 100 percent of your energy and skill. If such interference is likely, you have an obligation not to work on the case. As we saw in chapter 5, the failure to recognize the presence of this kind of bias can have ethical implications. It is unethical for you to be working on a case to which you cannot devote 100 percent of your professional skills.

🏛 *A s s i g n m e n t   8 . 3*

Think about your past and present contacts with people who have irritated you the most. Make a specific list of what bothered you about these people. Suppose that you are working in a law office where a client did one of the things on your list. Could you handle such a case?

S e c t i o n   H
COMMUNICATION SKILLS

INTRODUCTION

You've probably been interviewed hundreds of times in your life. You may also have interviewed others frequently. The next assignment and the class exercise that follows it are designed to identify what you now know about interviewing in general.

---

[2]Shari Caudron, *Crisis of Conscience*, 12 Legal Assistant Today 73, 75 (September/October 1994).

Assignment 8.4

Write down your answers to the following questions. When you have finished this chapter, come back to what you have written and ask yourself whether your perspective has changed.

(a) List some of the times you have interviewed someone. List some of the times you have been interviewed by someone.

(b) Describe what you feel are the central ingredients of a good interview in any setting.

(c) Describe a bad interview. From your experience, what are some of the worst mistakes an interviewer can make?

(d) Describe what you think are some of your strong and weak points as an interviewer. What can you do to improve?

In the following exercise, you will observe an interview role-played in class. After watching this interview, you will be asked to deduce some principles of communication involved in interviewing.

Class Exercise 8.B

In this exercise, two students will role-play a legal interview in front of the class. The rest of the class will observe the interview and comment on it.

Instructions to Client. You will role-play the part of a client. A month ago you sprained your back while lifting a computer and carrying it from one room to another. You are an accountant. When you came to work that day, you found the computer on your desk. It did not belong there, and you did not know how it got there. You decided to move it to another desk. That was when you sprained your back.

You have come to the law office for legal advice. You have already seen an attorney in this office who has agreed to take your case. An interviewer has been assigned to conduct an interview with you to obtain a complete picture of what happened. This interview will now be role-played in front of the class.

The basic facts involve the computer, as indicated above. You can make up all other facts to answer the interviewer's questions. Make up the name of the company for which you work, the details surrounding the accident, etc. You can create *any* set of facts as long as your answers are reasonably consistent with the basic facts given to you above.

Instructions to Interviewer. You will play the role of the interviewer in the case involving the sprained back. You are a paralegal in the office. All you know about the case thus far is that the office has agreed to represent the client and you have been assigned to interview the client for detailed information about the client and about the accident. Start off by introducing yourself and stating the purpose of the interview. Then proceed to the questions. Take notes on the client's answers.

You do not need to know any law in order to conduct the interview. Let common sense be your guide. Your goal is to compile a comprehensive picture of the facts as this client is able to convey them. Consult the material on fact particularization (FP) as you prepare and formulate questions. Be sure to listen carefully to the answers so that you can ask appropriate questions that seek more details on the facts contained in the answers.

The class will observe you to assess the manner and content of the interview. A good deal of constructive criticism may develop from the class discussion. As you listen to the criticism, try to be as objective as you can. It is difficult to conduct a comprehensive interview and probably impossible to conduct one flawlessly. For every question that you ask, there may be twenty observations on how you could have asked it differently. Hence, try not to take the comments personally.

Instructions to Class. You will be watching the interview involving the sprained back. You have two tasks:

1. Fill out a LICS (Legal Interview Communications Score) form. After the interview, take a moment to score the interview according to the LICS form that follows. The teacher will ask you to state the total score you gave the interview or to submit this score to someone who will calculate the average score from all students' scores.

2. Identify as many dos and don'ts of interviewing as you can. If you were writing a law office manual on *How to Interview,* what would you include? What guidance would you give an interviewer on taking notes during the interview, asking follow-up questions, maintaining eye contact with the client, etc.? After you observe the interview, discuss specific suggestions on what an interviewer should or should not do. Ideas will also come to mind while you are filling out the LICS form.

Legal Interviewing Communications Score (LICS)

How to Score:

You will be observing the role-playing of a legal interview and evaluating the interviewer on a 100-point scale. These 100 points will be earned in the four categories listed below. The score is not based on scientific data. It is a rough approximation of someone's oral communication skills in a legal interview. A score is interpreted as follows:

90–100 Points: Outstanding Interviewer
80–89 Points: Good Interviewer
60–79 Points: Fair Interviewer
0–59 Points: A Lot More Work Needs to Be Done

(Of course, the LICS does *not* assess the interviewer's ability to *write* an intake memorandum of law for the file. See Exhibit 8.3 and the discussion of the intake memo at the beginning of this chapter on page 374.)

Category I: Factual Detail

On a scale of 0–80, how would you score the interviewer's performance in asking enough questions to obtain factual comprehensiveness? How well was FP performed?

(An 80 score means the interviewer was extremely sensitive to detail in his or her questions. A low score means that the interviewer stayed with the surface facts, with little or no probing for the who-what-where-why-when-how details. The more facts you think the interviewer did *not* obtain, the lower the score should be.)

Category I Score:

Category II: Control

On a scale of 0–10, how would you score the interviewer's performance in controlling the interview and in giving it direction?
(A 10 score means the interviewer demonstrated an excellent sense of control and direction. A low score means the interviewer rambled from question to question or let the client ramble from topic to topic.)

Category II Score:

Legal Interviewing Communications Score (LICS)—continued

Category III: Earning the Confidence of the Client

On a scale of 0–5 how would you score the interviewer's performance in gaining the trust of the client and in setting him or her at ease?

(A 5 score means the interviewer appeared to do an excellent job of gaining the trust and confidence of the client. A low score means the client seemed to be suspicious of the interviewer and probably doubted his or her professional competence. The more the interviewer made the client feel that he or she was genuinely concerned about the client, the higher the score. The more the client obtained the impression that the interviewer was "just doing a job," the lower the score.)

Category III Score: ☐

Category IV: Role Identification

On a scale of 0–5, how well did the interviewer explain his or her role and the purpose of the interview?

(A 5 score means the interviewer took time to explain clearly what his or her job was in the office and what he or she hoped to accomplish in the interview. A low score means the interviewer gave little or no explanation at all or mumbled an explanation without being sensitive to whether the client understood.)

Category IV Score: ☐

Total Score: ☐

ANALYSIS OF A LEGAL INTERVIEW

Introduction

We will now examine portions of a hypothetical interview[3] involving Sam Donnelly, who walks into the law office of Day & Day seeking legal assistance. Last month he was a passenger in a car that collided with a truck.

Our goal in this analysis is to identify guidelines that can help you conduct competent interviews. In particular, we want to increase your sensitivity to the large variety of factors that affect the quality of the communication between a client and an interviewer. Earlier in the chapter, we discussed fact particularization as an important technique in achieving factual comprehensiveness in the interview. Here our focus will be the broader context of interviewing and communication.

Assume that Mr. Donnelly is in the office of William Fenton, Esq., one of the partners of Day & Day. During their meeting, the law firm agrees to represent Mr. Donnelly. The arrangement is confirmed in the *retainer* that Mr. Donnelly signs. (See Exhibit 8.1 for a sample retainer.) At the conclusion of the meeting, Mr. Fenton calls his paralegal, Jane Collins. He asks her to come to his office so that he can introduce her to Mr. Donnelly.

Attorney: *[As the paralegal walks into Mr. Fenton's office, he says: . . .]* Mr. Donnelly, I want to introduce you to Jane Collins who will be working with me throughout the case. I have asked her to schedule an appointment with you to do a comprehensive interview that will cover the facts you and I began to discuss today. Jane will be an additional contact for you throughout the case. If at any time you can't reach me, let

---

[3]The word **hypothetical** means not actual or real, but presented for purposes of discussion or analysis.

Jane know what concerns, questions, or needs you have. I will be reviewing all of Jane's work and will be meeting with her regularly. Jane is a trained paralegal. She is not an attorney and therefore can't give legal advice, but she can do many things to help me represent you.

Client: Nice to meet you.

Paralegal: *[Jane walks over to where Mr. Donnelly is sitting and, with a smile, extends her hand to offer a firm handshake.]* I'm very pleased to meet you, Mr. Donnelly. I look forward to working with you on the case. Let me give you one of my cards so that you'll know how to reach me.

Client: Thank you.

Attorney: I've already explained to Mr. Donnelly that you will be doing an in-depth interview with him on the case.

Paralegal: Yes. . . . When would be a good time for me to call you to set up an appointment for the interview, Mr. Donnelly?

It is extremely important to note that the supervising attorney, Mr. Fenton, has taken the initiative to introduce the client to the paralegal. This sets the tone for the client-paralegal relationship. Many clients have little more than a general understanding of what a paralegal is. Here, the introduction by the supervising attorney is very specific in identifying Jane as a nonattorney who has been trained to help attorneys represent clients. She will also act as a liaison between the attorney and the client.

Note also the manner in which the paralegal treats the client. She walks toward the client to greet him with a firm handshake and a smile. She tells the client that she looks forward to working with him. She gives him her business card. (This is often appreciated since the client is probably meeting several new faces during the first few visits to a law office.) She's very deferential to the client in asking when she can call him for an appointment. These are signs of a paralegal who is a professional and who is willing to go out of her way to make the client feel important. Throughout the remainder of the chapter, we will see other techniques paralegals can use to set clients at ease.

Preparing for the Interview

How do you get ready for an interview? Exhibit 8.6 lists some of the major steps you should take to prepare. The list assumes that this is one of the first legal interviews you have conducted.

In addition to the suggestions in Exhibit 8.6, try to observe someone interview a client. Find out if anyone else in the office will be conducting an interview soon. If so, ask permission to sit in. Watching others interview can be very instructive. Another way to prepare is to read some intake memos or other reports written after interviews in other cases. They can be found in the open or closed files of other clients. Pay particular attention to the amount and kind of information obtained in those cases.

Your mental attitude in preparing for the interview is very important. You need to approach each interview as if it is going to be a totally new experience for you. It is very dangerous for you to think that you know what the client is going to say, no matter how many times you have worked on a particular kind of case before. The danger is that you won't be listening carefully to what the client is saying. An interviewer who has an I've-heard-it-all-before attitude may block out what is unique about the facts of *this* client's case.

The hallmark of the *professional* is to view every client, every problem, and every incident as different and potentially unique. ("There's never been one like this before.") A professional interviewer, therefore, keeps probing for more facts to try to show that this case is not like all the rest. The goal of the professional is to find out what makes this case stand out. The trademark of the *bureaucrat,* on the other hand, is to see the similarities in clients, problems, and incidents. ("These cases are a dime a dozen.") The bureaucrat clusters things together into coherent groupings and patterns so that time can be saved and efficiency achieved. The bureaucrat feels that chaos could result if we viewed everything as potentially unique. An interviewer who has a bureaucratic attitude usually does not spend much time probing for facts; his or her goal is to fit this case into a category of similar cases handled in the past.

We all have within us professional and bureaucratic tendencies that are sometimes at war with each other.[4] Our bureaucratic self is very practical; our professional self can be a bit extreme in its search for uniqueness. When conducting legal interviews, however, or engaging in any task in the representation of a client, our goal is to try within reason to let our professional selves dominate.

Environment

You need to consider the impact of the physical setting or environment in which you conduct the interview. It will usually take place in the office of the interviewer. If this

---

Exhibit 8.6   **Preparing for an Interview**

- Schedule the interview during a time when you will not be rushed or constantly interrupted.
- Schedule the interview at a location that will be private and convenient for the client.
- Call or write the client in advance to confirm the date and place of the interview. Give an estimate of how long the interview will take. If the directions are complex, offer to send or fax a map (hand-drawn if necessary). Remind the client of anything you want him or her to bring to the interview, e.g., insurance policies, copies of tax returns.
- Anticipate and prepare for the client's comfort, e.g., a comfortable chair, a pad and pencil in case the client wants to take notes, a supply of tissues. Also, know where you can quickly get fresh water or coffee after offering them to the client early in the interview.
- If the office has already opened a file on the client, read everything in it before the interview. Bring any documents in the file that you may want to question the client about or have the client review during the interview.
- Have a final brief meeting with your supervisor to make sure you understand the goals of the interview.
- Find out if the office has any checklists you should use in asking questions. If none exist, prepare an outline of about a dozen major questions you will ask the client. You will have many more questions in the interview, but you can use this outline as a guide.
- Spend a little time in the law library doing some general background research in the area of the law involved in the client's case to obtain an overview of some of the major terminology and legal issues. This overview will suggest additional questions you will want to cover during the interview.
- Prepare any forms you may want the client to sign during the interview, e.g., consent to release medical information, authorization to obtain employment history records.
- Have your own supplies ready for note taking. Some interviewers recommend using different colored pens so that you can switch colors when the client is telling you something you want to give particular emphasis in your notes.[5]
- Walk into the interview with the attitude that the client will be telling you a story that you have never heard before. Don't assume you know what the client is going to say even if you have handled many cases of this kind before.

---

[4]William P. Statsky & Philip C. Lang, *The Legal Paraprofessional as Advocate and Assistant: Roles, Training Concepts and Materials* (Center on Social Welfare Policy and Law, 1971).
[5]Denise Clemens, *Client Interviewing,* 11 California Paralegal Magazine 12, 13 (October/December 1991).

office is not private enough, however, try to reserve the conference room or borrow an available office from someone else if it would be more private than your own. In our example, let us assume that Jane Collins's office is suitable for her interview with Sam Donnelly.

[There is a knock at Jane Collins's door. She gets up from her chair, goes over to the door, opens it, and says, as she extends her hand. . . .]

Paralegal: Hello, Mr. Donnelly. I'm Jane Collins, Mr. Fenton's paralegal. It's good to see you again. Won't you come in? . . . Did you have any trouble finding the office?

Client: No, I had to use the bus, but it worked out fine.

Paralegal: Let me take your coat for you. Please have a seat. *[The paralegal points the client toward a chair on the opposite side of the desk from where she sits. They face each other.]*

Note the seating arrangement the paralegal selects as illustrated in diagram A. "I" stands for interviewer and "C" stands for client.

Diagram A

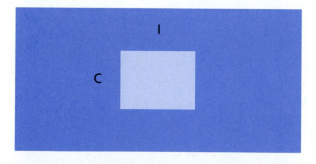

A number of other seating arrangements could have been used:

Diagram B

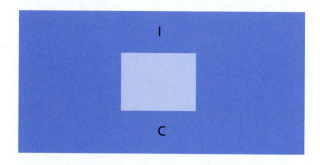

Diagram C

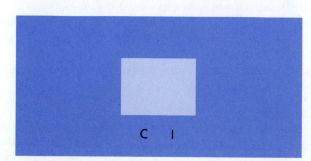

Diagram D

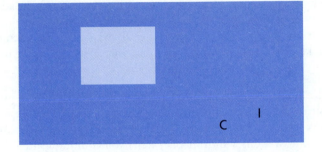

The chairs can be arranged so that the interviewer and the client sit on opposite sides of a desk (diagram A), diagonally across a desk (diagram B), on the same side of a desk (diagram C), or in another part of the room away from the desk altogether (diagram D). Seating arrangements are usually made at the convenience of the "owner" of the office. Rarely is enough thought given to how a particular arrangement may help or hurt the flow of communication. Sometimes the seating arrangement will create an austere and official atmosphere; other settings may be close and warm.

Of the four seating arrangements diagrammed above, which do you think would be most effective? Which would you feel most comfortable with? Which do you think the client would be most comfortable with? A number of factors can help you answer these questions. First, there is probably no single seating arrangement that will be perfect for all situations. The interviewer must be flexible enough to experiment with different arrangements. For most legal interviews, you will be taking extensive notes as the client answers your questions. If you are going to make any notes about the client that you may not want him or her to see (e.g., "appears reluctant to answer"), you will want to select a seating arrangement that does not allow the client to read what you are writing.

To some extent, seating arrangements can be a reflection of your personality. How do you want to project yourself? As an authority figure? If so, you might be inclined toward the seating arrangement in diagram A. Do you, on the other hand, want the client to feel closer to you and not to have the impression that you are hiding behind a desk? Do you think it would ever be wise to change a seating arrangement in the middle of an interview? If a particular arrangement is used for the initial interview, do you think a different arrangement might ever be appropriate for follow-up interviews with the same client? When clients look up, do you want them to be looking straight at you (diagram A) or do you think that it might be more comfortable for them to be able to face in other directions (diagram B) without appearing to scatter their attention?[6]

Of course, an office is much more than an arrangement of desks and chairs. Describe the potential benefits or disadvantages of the following:

- Numerous posters on the wall display political slogans, e.g., "Down with the Republicans!" or "Pro choice IS Pro Family."
- A copy of the latest issue of the Rush Limbaugh Newsletter is on the desk.
- The desk is cluttered with papers, books, and half-eaten food.
- A sign on the wall says, "Don't even think of smoking here."

You want the office to help you project a professional image of yourself. A messy desk usually suggests the opposite. Be careful about explicit messages around the room. Your

---

[6]See also White, *Architectural Suggestions for a Law Office Building,* 9 Practical Lawyer 66 (No. 8, 1956).

political views may clash with those of the client. Don't broadcast your politics by having partisan literature on the walls or the desk. What do you think of the no-smoking sign? Courtesy would suggest a more friendly way of letting clients know that they shouldn't smoke in your room, e.g., a sign that says, "Thank you for not smoking."

Getting Started

Note that the paralegal, Jane Collins, went to the door to greet the client. Suppose that, instead, she had remained in her chair and called, "Come in," in a loud voice. Do you think it makes any difference whether the interviewer walks over to the client? When you walk into a room with someone, aren't you communicating the message "Come share my room with me"? If, on the other hand, you are seated at your desk and call the visitor in, isn't the message to the visitor likely to be "This is my room; I control it; you have my permission to enter"? While this is not necessarily an inappropriate message, it is not as friendly and warm as going to the door to escort the client in.

Notice, however, that the paralegal apparently did *not* go out to the front entrance of the law firm to greet the client. Here is what may have happened: the client came to the front door, was greeted by a receptionist, was told to wait in the reception area, and was then given directions to find the paralegal's office on his own. If this is what happened, it was a mistake. The paralegal should have left instructions with the receptionist to call her when the client arrived, and the paralegal then should have gone out to the reception area to greet the client and personally walk him back to her office. This would be the most courteous approach. Furthermore, you don't want clients roaming around offices—even if they know the way. A wandering client may overhear confidential conversations between other members of the firm or see open files of other clients on the desks of secretaries. It is unethical for the law firm to allow someone to know *anything* about the cases of other clients. This danger is minimized if the paralegal escorts the client from the front door to her office.

Note that the paralegal reintroduced herself to the client: "Hello, Mr. Donnelly. I'm Jane Collins, Mr. Fenton's paralegal. It's good to see you again." She doesn't expect the client to remember who she is. It's a sign of courtesy to reintroduce yourself at the beginning of a second meeting. And never call a client by his or her first name unless expressly invited to do so by the client.

Paralegal: Thank you for coming in today, Mr. Donnelly. Are you ready for today's session?

Client: Ready as I can be.

Paralegal: Good. . . . How have you been?

Client: Not bad considering all this mess. I can't believe all this is happening.

Paralegal: Being involved in an accident can be very upsetting. It must be very hard for you. . . . Our office has handled cases like this before. While no one can predict how a case will turn out, you can rest assured that we will be doing everything possible to help lessen the burden on you.

Client: Thank you.

Paralegal: Let me ask you, Mr. Donnelly, is there anything that you want to cover now before we begin?

Client: This letter came in the mail this morning. It looks like the truck company has its lawyers on the case.

Paralegal: [She takes the letter from Mr. Donnelly and spends a few moments reading it.] This is a letter from the attorney representing the truck company seeking information from you. They obviously don't know yet that we represent you. Once they know you are represented, it is improper for them to contact you directly. They need to go through your attorney. I'll let Mr. Fenton know about this letter right away.

Why don't I photocopy it before you leave so that you can keep a copy for your records. After Mr. Fenton sees this, we'll let you know if there is anything you need to do about the letter. For now, let us take care of it.

———

Early on, the paralegal thanked the client: "Thank you for coming in today." Throughout the case, the office may ask the client to do many things such as come to meetings, sign documents, and collect information. Each time, you should express appreciation for doing what was asked. Never expect the client to thank *you*, although this may occur. You don't want the client to get the impression that you are doing the client a favor. The reverse is always true. Hence, constantly be appreciative.

Soon after inviting the client in, the paralegal asked, "Did you have any trouble finding the office?" And a little later, "How have you been?" It is a good idea to begin the interview at a personal level with some small talk about the weather, how the client is doing, or a recent sports event the client might know something about. This helps put the client at ease. The client may still be a bit nervous about the accident or whatever led to the conflict and the involvement of attorneys. Being a little lighthearted and personal for a few moments at the beginning of the interview may help break the ice.

When clients are particularly stressed or overwhelmed, you need to provide reassurance that the office will be actively working on the case and that the situation is manageable. The paralegal did that here when she told the client the office has handled similar cases in the past and would be doing everything possible to help lessen the burden on him. Comments such as these should help reassure the client. Of course, many clients want to be told they are going to win their cases. Avoid making any statement that could be interpreted as a promise or guarantee of success. Otherwise, the office could be sued for **breach of contract** if the case is not successful. Instead of telling a client, "You've got a great case," say something like the following: "There is no way of telling how a case will turn out. You've got a lot of good points in your favor, and we're going to work as hard as we can for you."

The paralegal also told the client, "Being involved in an accident can be very upsetting. It must be very hard for you." Here the paralegal is expressing understanding and empathy for the client's predicament. This is extremely important. The comment tells the client that the paralegal is *listening* to what the client is saying. Mr. Donnelly refers to the "mess" he is in and says, "I can't believe all this is happening." Rather than ignore this comment, the paralegal lets the client know that she has heard what he said. This is comforting for clients. On the other hand, you don't want to be patronizing or condescending. A comment such as "You poor fellow" would fall into this category.

Interviewers often learn a large number of highly personal facts about the client's life. Think of how you would feel if you were revealing such facts about yourself to a stranger. Think of how you would want this person to react to what you are revealing. At such a vulnerable time, clients need understanding and compassion. This doesn't mean that you should lose your objectivity. As indicated earlier, if it would be natural for you to express an emotion in response to what a client tells you, express the emotion. For example, "I'm very sorry to hear that" or "I can understand why you'd be angry." At the same time, you need to have an appropriate professional distance from the emotions and drama of the client's story.

Of course, never be judgmental of the client. Don't ask the client, "Why did you do that?" if your tone is one of suspicion or disbelief. Clients should not feel that they are required to justify their actions or inactions to you. This obviously would not encourage open communication between interviewer and client.

Also important was the paralegal's question, "is there anything that you want to cover now before we begin?" Early in the interview, find out if the client has any immediate concerns or questions on his mind. This should be done not only as a matter of courtesy, but also as a technique to make sure the client has your undivided attention. On the way into the law office, the client may have been thinking of several things he wants to ask about. He may be worried that he will forget them. Or, he may be a little embarrassed about asking his questions. Give the client a chance to express anything on his mind at the outset before you begin your barrage of questions. In our example, this technique worked. Mr. Donnelly did have something on his mind—the letter he received from opposing counsel.

> Paralegal: Our goal today is to obtain a comprehensive statement of the facts of the accident. It will take at least an hour, maybe a little more. As Mr. Fenton told you, I'm not an attorney. I'll be able to help on the case in many ways, but I won't be able to give you legal advice. That will have to come from Mr. Fenton. If anything comes up today that calls for legal advice, I'll bring it to Mr. Fenton's attention so that we can get you the response you need. Since I work for an attorney, you should know that everything you tell me is protected by the attorney-client privilege.
>
> Client: Fine.
>
> Paralegal: Before we begin, Mr. Donnelly, you mentioned that you had to take the bus in. Is there a problem with your car? It wasn't involved in the accident with the truck, was it?
>
> Client: No, no. . . . I let my brother borrow my car today.
>
> Paralegal: All right. . . . I want to start by getting an overview of what happened on the day of the accident. Then we'll go back and fill in the details. I'll be taking detailed notes to make sure that I remember everything you say. . . . OK, what happened that day?

This is the second meeting between the paralegal and Mr. Donnelly. Although the supervising attorney, Mr. Fenton, told Mr. Donnelly that Jane Collins was not an attorney, it is a good idea for the paralegal to reinforce this point herself. Paralegals who have a lot of contact with clients are often pressured by clients to give legal advice. Making it clear at the outset that this is inappropriate can cut down on this pressure, although unfortunately, it will not eliminate it.

The paralegal also told the client that what he tells her "is protected by the attorney-client privilege." The client needs to know this, but *not* in this way. The phrase "attorney-client privilege" is legal **jargon.** It is technical language that does not have an everyday meaning. Avoid jargon unless the client needs to know it and you explain it in language the client can understand. When you use jargon or confusing terms, don't interpret the client's lack of questions to mean that the client understands the jargon. Don't wait for the client to ask you to explain unfamiliar terms. Take the initiative to provide explanations. In our example, it probably would have been sufficient to tell Mr. Donnelly that what he tells her will be confidential rather than using the more technical phrase, attorney-client privilege.

Another useful technique for beginning an interview is to briefly state the major goal of the interview—here, to obtain a comprehensive statement of the facts of the accident. Give the client an overview of what you hope to accomplish and how long it may take.

Let the client know you will be taking notes so you will have an accurate record of what he says during the interview. As indicated earlier, the document that contains the detailed report of the interviewer is often called the *intake memo* (see Exhibit 8.3). Others in the office working on the case need to be able to read and rely on this report since they all can't interview the client.

Occasionally, your supervisor will want you to tape-record the interview. Be sure the client consents to the recording. At the beginning of the interview, say, "This is Jane Collins, a paralegal in the law office of Day & Day. Today's date is March 13, 1997. I am in our law office with Mr. Samuel Donnelly. Mr. Donnelly, have you agreed to have this interview tape-recorded?" The latter question and answer will help disprove any allegations that you secretly recorded the interview.

A good interviewer is always listening for clues to other legal or relevant nonlegal problems. There is always a danger that an interviewer will block out anything that doesn't fit within the topics scheduled for discussion. In our example, the paralegal said to Mr. Donnelly, "you mentioned that you had to take the bus in. Is there a problem with your car?" While the car apparently has nothing to do with the case, it was worth inquiring into. Suppose, for example, the client is not driving because of injury to his eyes caused by an eye doctor. Or perhaps the client has had a contract dispute with an auto mechanic. It is a good idea to listen for suggestions or clues to other problems provided by a client. If you do not want to cover the matter immediately, make a note to raise it later in the interview at a more appropriate or convenient time.

The major techniques and guidelines for beginning an interview are summarized in Exhibit 8.7.

Exhibit 8.7   Beginning the Interview

- Introduce yourself by name and title. If this is your second meeting with the client, reintroduce yourself.
- Do not call a client by his or her first name unless expressly invited to do so by the client.
- Express appreciation each time the client does something the office asks, e.g., come in for an interview, read and sign a document.
- Make sure the client understands you are not an attorney and cannot give legal advice.
- Start at a personal level (e.g., with some small talk) rather than launching right into the task at hand.
- Review the goals of the interview with the client (based on the assignment from your supervisor), and provide an estimate of how long the interview might take.
- Make the client feel that his or her case is special. Avoid giving the impression that you're engaged in anything boring or routine.
- Never tell a client how busy you are. It suggests to the client that he is bothering you and gives the impression that the office may be disorganized.
- Express understanding and empathy for the client's predicament without being condescending.
- Don't be judgmental.
- Make sure the client understands that what he or she tells you is confidential.
- Find out if there are immediate concerns that the client wants to raise.
- Avoid legal jargon unless the client needs to become familiar with the jargon and you provide clear definitions and explanations.
- Let the client know you will be taking notes, and why.
- Listen for clues to other legal and relevant nonlegal problems that the office should know about.

> ## E x h i b i t 8 . 7   Beginning the Interview—continued
>
> - Begin new topics with open-ended questions. (See the discussion below on the kinds of questions an interviewer can ask.)
> - Spend the first few minutes getting an overview/outline of the entire event or transaction. Then go back to obtain the details. (See the discussion on kinds of questions.)
> - Encourage the client to give you the facts chronologically as a story with a beginning, middle, and end. If more than one event is involved in the case, cover them separately in the same chronological way. Then go into how the events are interconnected. (See the discussion on kinds of questions.)
> - If the client appears overwhelmed or unusually distressed, try to provide reassurance by letting him or her know that the office is actively working on the case and is doing everything it can. Do not, however, promise results.

Kinds of Questions

One of the early questions the paralegal asked the client was, "what happened that day?" This is known as an **open-ended question.** It is a broad, relatively unstructured question that cannot be answered in one or two words. An open-ended question gives the client more control over the kind and amount of information to be provided in response. It also gives the interviewer an opportunity to size up the ability of the client to organize his or her thoughts in order to present a coherent response. Here are some other examples of open-ended questions: "What brings you in today?" "What led to the crisis at the bank?" One of the most frequently used categories of open-ended questions is the **overview question,** which asks for a summary of something such as an important event. For example, "What happened during your first year in college?" or Jane Collins's question, "what happened that day?" An open-ended *request* (e.g., "Tell me about the problem") invites the same kind of broad response, but is phrased as a request rather than as a question.

Open-ended questions (or requests) invite the person questioned to give a long and potentially rambling answer. Hence they should not be overused. These questions are often most effective when beginning a new topic in the interview.

At the opposite extreme is the **closed-ended question,** which is a narrowly structured question that often can be answered in one or two words. Examples: "How old are you?" "What time did the accident occur?" "Did you receive the letter?" Closed-ended questions give the interviewer more control over the interview since they let the client know precisely what information is sought.

If the facts of a case are relatively complex, you should consider spending the first few minutes asking overview questions in order to obtain an outline of the entire event or transaction, and then going back to obtain the details. Once you have the big picture, you will be better able to see connections among the individual facts. The paralegal in our example took this approach when she said, "I want to start by getting an overview of what happened on the day of the accident. Then we'll go back and fill in the details." She then followed this up with the open-ended overview question, "what happened that day?"

Both the request for an overview and the detailed questioning should be designed to get the client to tell the events of the case *chronologically*. The case may have many confusing aspects. The client may be inclined to talk about four or five things simultaneously—the accident, the hospitalization, the events leading up to the accident, the deceitfulness of the other side, etc. The best way to conduct an orderly interview is to help the client structure the case as a *story* with a beginning, middle, and end. Hence you should be regularly asking **chronological questions** such as "What happened next?" or "What did you do then?" If the client says something substantially out of chronological sequence, politely say, "Could we get to that in a moment? First I want you to finish telling me what happened after . . . ." While you want to see the interconnections among the various events of the case, the discussion may become tangled and confusing unless you cover one topic at a time in the same methodical manner. In most instances, the most methodical way of getting at the facts is chronologically.

In general, you should avoid asking **leading questions** in which the answer is suggested in the question. For example, "You didn't return the call, did you?" "You've forgotten everything that occurred during the meeting?" The danger of a leading question is that a nervous client or witness will simply give you the answer you appear to want. Leading questions might sometimes be useful when trying to challenge something that a hostile witness is saying, but this should not be the case with your own client. If a client is having difficulty remembering something (e.g., the weather on a particular day), a leading question might help jog the memory (e.g., "Was it raining that day?"). If a client needs constant prodding through leading questions, however, you may have reason to doubt the client's entire story.

Another category is the **corroborative question,** which seeks to verify (or corroborate) facts beyond the word of the client or witness. For example, "Were there any passengers in the car who will back that up?"

Be careful about asking too many questions at the same time; they might confuse the client. A **multiple-choice question** asks the client to choose between options presented by the interviewer. For example, "Did you personally have any reason to believe that the account was inaccurate, or did you rely on your accountant to find out that additional data should have been obtained?" The client might not remember both options and simply respond to the last part of the question. Break compound or multiple questions into individual questions unless the choices are very limited and call for brief answers. Asking "Was it a car or a truck in the other lane?" is not confusing even though it is a multiple-choice question.

See Exhibit 8.8 for an overview of the major kinds of questions an interviewer can ask.

E x h i b i t 8 . 8   **Kinds of Questions**

Here are some of the major categories of questions, some of which overlap:
- *Open-Ended Questions.* Those that are broad and relatively unstructured, allowing the client or witness to express what is on his or her mind. They cannot be answered by one or two words. Examples: "What can we do for you today?" "Tell me what happened on the day of the accident?" "What kind of a marriage did you have?"
- *Closed-Ended Questions.* Those that narrowly focus the attention of the client or witness and call for a very brief answer, often yes or no. Examples: "Are you seeking a divorce?" "Were you wearing your glasses when you saw the accident?" "Did your husband ever hit you?"
- *Overview Questions.* Those that seek a summary of a major event. Examples: "Would you first give me a general picture of what happened?" "What are the major incidents that led to the dismissal?" "Could you start me off by giving a brief description of what happened at the party before the shooting?"
- *Chronological Questions.* Those designed to get the client or witness to tell the story of what happened chronologically—step by step. Examples: "Then what happened?" "What did he say after he saw the accident?" "What happened next?"
- *Leading Questions.* Those in which the answer is suggested in the question. Examples: "Where was the fender dented?" "The car wasn't damaged when you received it, was it?" "You were traveling 75 m.p.h.?"

Exhibit 8 . 8   **Kinds of Questions—continued**

- *Corroborative Questions.* Those designed to verify (or corroborate) facts by seeking information beyond the word of the client or witness. Examples: "Who else saw the accident?" "Were you the only one who complained?" "Do you have receipts?"
- *Multiple-Choice Questions.* Those that ask the client or witness to choose between options presented by the interviewer. Examples: "Was the car red or blue?" "Did you accept the offer, reject it, or ask for more time to consider?"

Attentive Listening

Studies have shown that clients rate "evidence of concern" as being more significant than the results they obtain from a law office.[7] This is a remarkable conclusion. Of course, clients want to win their cases. Yet they are also desperate for a sympathetic ear. Being involved in a legal dispute is often traumatic for them. In addition to being treated competently as a plaintiff or defendant, clients want a law office that is genuinely concerned about them as persons.

One of the best ways to demonstrate concern is through **attentive listening.** This simply means that you take affirmative steps to let the client know that you have heard what he or she has said and that you consider every meeting with the client important. Exhibit 8.9 summarizes some of the major techniques of attentive listening.

Experienced paralegals often handle the same kind of case over and over. Clients, however, want to feel that their case deserves and will get *individual* attention; they do not want their cases handled in an assembly-line or mass-production manner. While they like having experienced attorneys and paralegals working for them, they are particularly pleased when they feel that the office is treating their case as special.

Comprehensiveness

A major goal of most legal interviews is to achieve factual comprehensiveness; you want to obtain as many relevant facts as the client is able to give. The most important technique in accomplishing this goal is *fact particularization* discussed earlier in the chapter. (See Exhibits 8.4 and 8.5.) Also important are *corroborative questions* that ask about documents or other individuals who can support the version of the facts the client is relating. (See Exhibit 8.8.)

Most clients want to tell you about the facts that support their case. You need to encourage them to tell you negative as well as positive facts. Tell them how important it is for the attorney to know *all* the facts. The attorney for the other side may find out about negative facts. Indeed, one of the preoccupations of the other side is to find the facts that will hurt the client. The client's attorney must know all the facts in advance so that he or she can prepare a response when these facts come out.

Clients are often opinionated. Probe beneath the opinions to obtain the underlying facts. If a client says, "He's a liar," or "The road is dangerous," probe beneath these opinions to get at the underlying facts that led the client to reach these opinions. Again, fact particularization will help you uncover them.

Earlier we said that checklists of questions can be helpful in preparing for an interview. Be careful in using checklists, however. Although they can provide guidance on what to

---

[7]H. Freeman & H. Weihofen, *Clinical Law Training, Interviewing and Counseling* 13 (1972).

Exhibit 8.9   **Attentive Listening**

- Make it obvious to the client that he or she has your full attention. If you know that there might be an interruption during the interview, alert the client and apologize in advance.
- Occasionally lean forward toward the client as he or she speaks.
- Avoid being fidgety or appearing nervous.
- Take notes. This is an obvious sign that you think what the client is saying is important.
- Maintain eye contact whenever you are not taking notes.
- As the client speaks, give frequent *yes* nods. Also, say "ah hum" or "I see" when the client momentarily pauses while answering your questions. This will let the client know you are following what he or she is saying.
- Periodically let the client know he or she is providing useful information. Make comments such as "That could be very important" or "I'm glad you recall the event in such detail."
- In addition to listening to the words of the client, "listen" to the feelings the client is expressing through gestures and other body language. Words are not the only way a client lets you know that he or she is anxious, suspicious, worried, or in pain.
- At appropriate times, restate a feeling the client is trying to describe, e.g., "The stress you were under must have been overwhelming." You may want to do this in the form of a question, e.g., "You were really angry when you found out, weren't you?"
- Occasionally read something from your notes out loud to the client and ask if you have correctly recorded what he or she has said. At other times, paraphrase what the client says in your own words to encourage the client to provide further clarification or to confirm that you have understood what the client has said. ("Let me see if I understand what you've said. . . .") This reinforces the value of precision in the practice of law as well as letting the client know how important this interview is.
- While a client is answering a question, try to avoid interrupting unless he or she is rambling and you need clarification before the client moves to another point.
- Ask spontaneous questions that occur to you while listening to an answer of the client. This helps demonstrate you are not trying to fit the client's answers into your preconceived notions about the case. Rather, you are following the client's train of thought.
- Refer back to what the client said earlier, e.g., "When we were discussing the purchase, you said that your father wanted his brother to manage the property. Could you tell me what you meant?"
- Never express impatience, no matter how frustrated you are at the client's failure to answer what you feel is an easy question.
- Don't finish the client's sentences for him or her no matter how certain you are of what the client is trying to say. Finishing someone's sentences demonstrates your impatience and is condescending.

cover in the interview, you must be flexible enough to deviate from the checklist when relevant topics come up that are not on the checklist. Use any checklist (whether written by others or prepared on your own) as no more than a starting point. Suppose, for example, you are interviewing a client about his financial assets. You are working from a checklist of questions on wages, real estate holdings, stocks, bonds, etc. During the interview, the client happens to mention an ailing grandparent who is very fond of the client. This suggests the possibility of another possible asset: inheritance. Suppose, however, the checklist contains no questions about future inheritances. Common sense (one of the guides to formulating questions discussed earlier in the chapter) should tell you to ask whether the client thinks he might be a beneficiary in someone's will.

Take accurate notes on the facts the client gives you. Recall that one of the components of fact particularization is to record the extent of the certainty/uncertainty a client expresses about a fact. Suppose the client tells you, "I'm not sure" how fast an approaching car was going, but then says it was "about 50 mph." Your final report based on your notes should say:

> When I asked the client how fast the other car was going, he said he was "not sure." Then he estimated "about 50 mph."

This lets the supervising attorney know that the client may be vulnerable as a witness in court if questioned about the matter of speed. An interviewer does not achieve the desired factual comprehensiveness unless he or she asks about and records the extent to which the client is certain or uncertain about the facts conveyed.

The techniques for obtaining factual comprehensiveness are summarized in Exhibit 8.10.

Ethical Concerns

Paralegal: *[Telephone rings.]* Excuse me, Mr. Donnelly. "Yes, hello. How are you? . . . No, the Jackson case has been resolved. Mr. Jackson decided not to go through with his suit after McDonald's made its offer. . . . You're welcome." Sorry, Mr. Donnelly, let's get back to the . . . .

A legal interview must be conducted competently *and ethically*. Unfortunately, there are more than a few opportunities for an interviewer to run afoul of ethical rules.

Mr. Donnelly has just heard the paralegal discuss the Jackson case on the phone. This is a violation of the paralegal's ethical obligation to preserve the confidence of a client. Even though Mr. Donnelly may not have understood anything about the Jackson and McDonald case, he was not entitled to hear what he heard. He should not even know that Jackson or McDonald is a client of Day & Day. Revealing information about a client is a breach of confidentiality, whether it is done intentionally or carelessly. Mr. Donnelly may now have the impression that the paralegal will be as careless about discussing *his case* in front of strangers.

Client: A friend of mine told me that if another car rams into you and commits a clear traffic violation, their negligence is automatic. Is that true?
Paralegal: I'll take that question up with Mr. Fenton and get back to you. All legal questions like that need to be dealt with by an attorney.

Another major ethical danger that can arise during an interview is giving legal advice. As we saw in chapter 5, legal advice consists of applying laws or legal principles to the

---

Exhibit 8.10   Achieving Factual Comprehensiveness

- Apply the technique of fact particularization to all the major facts the client tells you and that you need to cover. (See Exhibits 8.4 and 8.5).
- Ask corroborative questions. (See Exhibit 8.8.)
- Encourage the client to tell you about negative facts.
- Probe beneath client opinions to obtain the underlying facts.
- Follow available checklists of questions, but be prepared to ask questions not on the checklist if they pertain to relevant topics that come up during the interview.
- Ask questions to determine the extent to which the client is certain or uncertain about an event.

facts of a particular client's case. The more contact a paralegal has with clients, the greater the likelihood the paralegal will be asked to give legal advice. This is especially true during legal interviews. Clients are often hungry for answers. Mr. Donnelly is no exception. He asked the paralegal whether a traffic violation makes one's negligence "automatic." Even general questions about the law could be interpreted as questions that call for legal advice. Mr. Donnelly is probably trying to understand how the courts will handle his case.

Suppose the paralegal knows the correct answer. Think of how tempting it would be for her to answer the question. It takes a lot of will power for her to refrain from answering. She wants to appear intelligent. We all want to show off what we know. Be conservative, however, about ethics. (See Exhibit 5.1 in chapter 5 on the Ten Commandments of an Ethical Conservative.) When in doubt, avoid giving an answer. The paralegal told Mr. Donnelly that she would "get back" to him after consulting with Mr. Fenton. This is better than coldly saying, "I'm not allowed to answer that question." When she said, "All legal questions like that need to be dealt with by an attorney," she is also helping to train the client about the limitations inherent in the paralegal's role. This may cut down on pressures in the future from Mr. Donnelly's attempts to ask her for legal advice.

Some of the major areas of ethical concern are summarized in Exhibit 8.11.

Ending the Interview

The interview is over when you have accomplished the objectives of the interview or when the client is not able to provide you with any additional information. The client may need to check some of his records at home or contact a family member or business associate in order to answer some of your questions. While much of the missing data can be communicated on the phone or through the mail, don't be reluctant to reschedule the interview if needed.

Give the client the opportunity to raise anything that *he* thinks should have been covered. For example, you could say, "Before we end today's session, let me ask you if there is anything you think we haven't covered or haven't covered enough." If the client raises anything, you may want to take some additional time now to go over the client's areas of concern, or you may have to tell the client that you'll get back to him on when you'll be

---

E x h i b i t 8 . 1 1   **Avoiding Ethical Problems during Interviews**

- If you cannot avoid phone interruptions or visits by others to your office during the interview, be sure that you do not discuss the facts of other clients' cases. Excuse yourself and leave the room if you must discuss anything about other cases.
- While talking to the client, do not have open files of other clients on the desk.
- Do not let the client wander in the corridors of the office, e.g., to go to the coffeepot. You do not want the client to overhear conversations about other cases among attorneys, paralegals, secretaries, or other employees.
- Make sure the client understands you are not an attorney.
- Resist pressures from the client to give legal advice. When in doubt, don't answer. Refer the matter to your supervising attorney.
- If the client says anything during the interview that suggests the possibility of a conflict of interest (e.g., the client tells you that the opposing side's spouse once was represented by your law firm), stop the interview and check with your supervisor about whether you should continue.
- Never discuss fees with a client.

able to go over those concerns. The important point is to find out how the client feels about what was discussed during the interview and to respond to any of his concerns.

Often the client needs to sign documents that authorize the office to obtain confidential information about the client, e.g., a consent to release medical information. Be sure to explain the document clearly to the client and give him some time to read through what he is being asked to sign. Don't simply hand the client a document and say, "I'll need your signature on this form that will allow us to get your medical records." Here is a more appropriate approach:

> Paralegal: *[Handing the document to him.]* Mr. Donnelly, I want you to take a look at this document. It's a consent to release medical information. We'll use it to ask doctors, hospitals, or other medical providers to give us information about your medical condition. Would you please take a moment to read through it and let me know if you have any questions about it. If not, there's a space at the end of the document for your signature.
>
> Client: OK.
>
> Paralegal: Once you sign it, I'll keep the original and get you a copy for your records.

The client will want to know what's going to happen next—after the interview. Remind the client of any scheduled appointments, e.g., doctor visits, depositions. If there are none, simply tell the client that you will be preparing a report for the attorney on the case and that the office will be getting back to the client. Also, summarize anything you asked the client to do during the interview, e.g., call you to provide the exact address of a former employer.

Begin preparing a draft of your intake memorandum soon after the interview is over while the data and your notes are fresh in your mind. (See Exhibit 8.3.) Do this even if you need to obtain additional facts to include in your memorandum by follow-up interviewing or investigation. Modern word processing makes it relatively easy to make additions to documents. (See chapter 13.) Don't wait until you have all the facts before you start writing.

Also, make a notation in the client's file that you conducted the interview, even before you complete the intake memo. Someone else in the office working on the case (e.g., supervising attorney, law clerk, secretary) should be able to pick up the file and tell what has been done to date.

For a summary of these and similar steps you need to take at the end of an interview, see Exhibit 8.12.

Personality Observations

After conducting an interview, you should formulate some preliminary observations about the client's personality. Here is how one attorney described this aspect of the interview:

> "Assess the client's personality" and whether you think the office "can work with this person." "Watch for red flags or danger signals, including the client who is emotionally distraught or vengeful; is inconsistent with the story or avoids answering questions; has unrealistic objectives; suggests use of improper influence or other unethical or illegal conduct; rambles, wanders off the subject, or constantly interrupts you"; tells the office "how to run the case; has already discharged or filed disciplinary complaints against other lawyers; has a personality disorder; or is flirtatious."[8]

---

[8] *The Initial Interview,* 12 Family Advocate 6 (Winter 1990).

E x h i b i t   8 . 1 2   **Ending the Interview**

- Ask the client to sign any standard forms needed by the office, e.g., consent to release medical information, authorization to obtain employment history records.
- Ask the client if there is anything else on his or her mind that he or she would like to raise before the interview is concluded.
- Let the client know precisely what the next step will be in the office's representation of the client, e.g., the attorney will call the client, the paralegal will schedule a medical examination of the client.
- Remind the client how to reach you. Have additional copies of your business card on the desk.
- Thank the client for the interview.
- Start preparing a draft of your intake memorandum.
- In the client's file, make a brief note of the fact that you conducted the interview. Include the date and time of the interview.

In your intake memorandum to your supervisor, include your observations and assessments relevant to concerns such as these.

Improving Your Interviewing Skills

There are many ways you can improve your interviewing skills. They are summarized in Exhibit 8.13. Be a perpetual student of the law. Always be inquisitive. Never be totally comfortable with any of your skills. One of the fascinating aspects of the practice of law is the availability of infinite opportunities to grow and improve.

E x h i b i t   8 . 1 3   **Improving Your Interviewing Skills**

- There is a good deal of literature on legal interviewing. Check legal periodicals and legal treatises. Ask a law librarian for leads to such literature. See also Checklists #6 and #8 in chapter 11.
- Try to attend seminars that cover legal interviewing, e.g., CLE (Continuing Legal Education) seminars for attorneys conducted by bar associations or CLE seminars conducted by paralegal associations.
- Ask someone in the office you respect to observe you interview a client and then give you a critique. (You will need the advance permission of the client for this person to sit in.)
- Ask someone in the office you respect to read your intake memorandum and critique it. An experienced interviewer will be able to see if there are any gaps in what you covered in your memorandum.
- Try to sit in when others in the office are interviewing clients. Read their memorandum on the interview and ask them questions about their interviewing techniques.
- Ask attorneys and other paralegals about their interviewing experiences even if you can't watch them conduct an interview.

Class Exercise 8.C

Form a circle of chairs with a single chair in the middle. The student sitting in the middle will play the role of the client. The students in the circle (numbering about ten) will be the interviewers, in rotation. The instructor will ask one of the students to begin the interview. As this student runs into difficulty during the interview, the student to his or her right picks up the interview, tries to resolve the difficulty in his or her own way, and then proceeds with the interview. If *this* student cannot resolve the difficulty, the student to his or her right tries, and so on. The objective is to identify as many diverse ways of handling difficulties as possible in a relatively short period. No interviewer should have the floor for more than a minute or two at any one time. The student playing the role of the client is given specific instructions about how to play the role—that is, sometimes he or she is asked to be shy; other times, demanding. The client should not overdo the role, however. He or she should respond naturally within the role assigned. Here are four sets of instructions to attempt this "interview in rotation."

(a) The interviewer greets the client and says, "I am a paralegal." The client is confused about what a paralegal is. The interviewer explains. The client is insistent upon a comprehensive definition that he or she can understand.

(b) The client comes to the law office because he or she is being sued for negligent driving. The interviewer asks the client if he or she must wear eyeglasses to drive. The answer is *yes.* The interviewer then asks if he or she was wearing eyeglasses during the accident. The client is very reluctant to answer. (In fact, the client was not wearing glasses at the time.) The client does not appear to want to talk about this subject. The interviewer persists.

(c) The client is being sued by a local store for $750.00 in grocery bills. The client has a poor memory and the interviewer must think of ways to help him or her remember. The client wants to cooperate but is having trouble remembering.

(d) The client wants to sue an auto mechanic. The client gives many opinions, conclusions, and judgments (such as: "The mechanic is a crook," "I was their best customer," "The work done was awful.") The interviewer is having difficulty encouraging the client to state the facts underlying the opinions. The client insists on stating conclusions.

After each exercise, the class should discuss principles, guidelines, and techniques of interviewing.

Class Exercise 8.D

Below are two additional role-playing exercises to be conducted in class.

(a) The instructor asks the class if anyone was involved, in any way, in a recent automobile accident. If someone says *yes,* this student is interviewed by another class member whose job is to obtain as complete a picture as possible of what happened. At the outset the interviewer knows nothing other than that some kind of an automobile accident occurred.

(b) The instructor asks the class if anyone has recently had trouble with any government agency (like the post office or sanitation department). If someone says *yes,* this student is interviewed by another class member whose job is to obtain as complete a picture as possible of what happened. The interviewer at the outset knows nothing other than the fact that the person being interviewed has had some difficulty with a government agency.

⌖ *Class Exercise 8.E*

When an office represents a debtor, one of the paralegal's major responsibilities may be to interview the client in order to write a comprehensive report on the client's assets and liabilities. Assume that your supervising attorney has instructed you to conduct a comprehensive interview of the client in order to write such a report. Assets are everything the client *owns* or has an interest in. Liabilities are everything *owed;* they are debts. These are the only definitions you need; you do not need any technical knowledge of law to conduct this interview. All you need is common sense in the formulation of questions.

Your instructor will role-play the client in front of the room. It will be a collective interview. Everyone will ask questions, but you will each write individual reports on the interview based on your own notes. Raise your hand to be recognized. Be sure to ask follow-up questions when needed for factual clarity and comprehensiveness. You can repeat the questions of other students if you think you might elicit a more detailed response. Any question is fair game as long as it is directly or indirectly calculated to uncover assets or liabilities. There may be information the client does not have at this time, such as bank account numbers. Help the client determine how such information can be obtained later. In your notes, state that you asked for information that the client didn't have and state what the client said he or she would do to obtain the information. To achieve comprehensiveness, you must obtain factual detail. This means that you go after names, addresses, phone numbers, dates, relevant surrounding circumstances, verification data, etc. In short, we want fact particularization. Take detailed notes on the questions asked by every student (not just your own) and the answers provided in response. You will have to write your report based on your own notes.

The heading of your report will be as follows:

Inter-Office Memorandum

To: [name of your instructor]
From: [your name]
Date: [date you prepared the report]
RE: Comprehensive Interview of

_____

Case File Number: _____

(Make up the case file number.) The first paragraph of your report should state what your supervisor has asked you to do in the report. Simply state what the assignment is. Organization of the data from your notes is up to you. Use whatever format you think will most clearly communicate what you learned from the client in the interview.

● *Chapter Summary*

Projecting competence and professionalism is an essential ingredient in performing any task on behalf of a client. The retainer establishes the attorney-client relationship. If the office decides not to represent the prospective client, it should send him or her a letter of nonengagement. In the initial client interview, the attorney-client relationship is established and legal problems are identified.

Interviewing is conversation for the purpose of obtaining information. In a law office, legal interviewing is designed to obtain facts that are relevant to the identification and eventual resolution of a legal problem. These facts are often reported in a document called an intake memo. Six major guides exist to the kinds of questions that should be asked during a legal interview. The most important is the instructions of the supervisor on the goals of the interview. Other guides include preprinted checklists for certain kinds of interviews, legal analysis to help you focus on relevance, "fact particularization" as a device to achieve comprehensiveness, and finally, common sense and flexibility to help you remain alert and responsive as the interview unfolds.

Determining what the client wants often takes probing and presentation of options. Otherwise the office might fail to identify client objectives. Most of us are not fully aware of how our prejudices affect our performance. Detecting interviewer bias may not be easy since it is sometimes difficult to separate our personal feelings from the client's objectives.

The supervising attorney helps set the tone for an effective interview by introducing the client to the paralegal and explaining the latter's role. The professional interviewer strives to uncover facts that make the case of each client unique. There are many ways to prepare for an interview such as scheduling the interview at a convenient time, reading everything in the file, having supplies available, and preparing initial questions. The seating arrangement should facilitate communication. The walls, desk, and overall appearance of the office should project a professional image. Go out to greet the client when he or she arrives at the reception desk.

Always be appreciative of what the client does. Some small talk at the beginning of the interview can help decrease client tension. Avoid making any promises of what the office can accomplish. Express empathy without being condescending or losing objectivity. Find out if there are any immediate concerns on the client's mind. Avoid legal jargon unless the client needs to know about it and clear explanations are given. Briefly restate the purpose of the interview for the client. Let the client know why you are taking notes. Listen for clues to other problems the office should know about.

The following are the major kinds of questions an interviewer can ask (some of which overlap): open-ended, overview, closed-ended, chronological, leading, corroborative, and multiple-choice. One of the most important ways of building a relationship with the client is through attentive listening techniques such as maintaining eye contact and repeating back what the client has told you. Factual comprehensiveness is achieved through fact particularization, corroborative questions, probing, etc. The interviewer must be alert to potential ethical problems such as breach of confidentiality and giving legal advice.

At the conclusion of the interview, ask the client to read and sign needed forms, find out if the client has any concerns not addressed during the interview, tell the client what next steps are planned, and make sure the client knows how to reach you. As soon as possible, make a note to the file that you conducted the interview. Begin writing the report or intake memo soon after the interview, making note of any personality characteristics relevant to working with the client that you observed. To improve your interviewing technique, read literature and attend CLE seminars on interviewing, seek the critique of others, try to observe others interview, etc.

KEY TERMS

retainer, 370
deep pocket, 372
letter of nonengagement, 372
initial client interview, 372
intake memo, 374
RE, 374

grounds, 375
legal analysis, 377
legally relevant, 377
fact particularization, 378
analogies, 381
bias, 384
objectivity, 385

hypothetical, 389
breach of contract, 395
jargon, 396
open-ended question, 398
overview question, 398
closed-ended question, 398
chronological question, 399

leading question, 399
corroborative question, 399
multiple-choice question, 399
attentive listening, 400

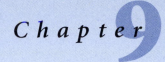

Chapter 9

INVESTIGATION IN A LAW OFFICE

→ *Chapter Outline*

Section A

THE NATURE AND CONTEXT OF INVESTIGATION

Legal investigation is the process of gathering additional facts and verifying presently known facts in order to advise a client about solving or avoiding a legal problem. "Paralegals are often called upon by attorneys to track down important information that is relevant to a real estate transaction, a corporate transaction, a case that is in litigation or a case where litigation is anticipated."[1] Lana Clark, a litigation paralegal says, "[m]any of us have been approached by our attorneys at the last minute to interview a witness and 'Find out what he knows.' "[2] For some cases, a law firm might use an outside licensed private investigator. More often, however, the firm will turn to one of its own employees, usually a paralegal, for the investigation assignment.[3]

In chapter 8 on legal interviewing, we examined six major guides to fact gathering:

- Instructions of the supervisor
- Checklists
- Legal analysis
- Fact Particularization (FP)
- Common sense
- Flexibility

You should review these guides now since they are equally applicable to investigation. Fact Particularization (FP) is especially important.

We begin our study of legal investigation with some general observations about its nature and context:

1. *Investigative techniques are often very individualistic.* Styles, mannerisms, and approaches to investigation are often highly personal. Through a sometimes arduous process of trial and error, the investigator develops effective techniques. While some of these techniques come from the suggestions of fellow investigators, most are acquired from on-the-job experience.

2. *It is impossible to overemphasize the importance of hustle, imagination, and flexibility.* If there is one characteristic that singles out the effective investigator, it is a willingness to dig. While many investigation assignments may be relatively easy (e.g., photograph the ceiling of a bathroom that a tenant claims is falling down), most assignments are open-ended with an extensive range of options and possible conclusions. The answer is not always there for the asking. For such assignments, investigators must be prepared to identify and pursue leads, be unorthodox, and let their feelings, hunches, and intuition lead where they will. In short, the formal principles of investigation must give way to hustle, imagination, and flexibility.

   Good investigators are always in pursuit. They are on the offensive and don't wait for the facts to come to them. They know that legwork is required. They know that

---

[1] Massachusetts Paralegal Association, *Fact Finding for the Legal Assistant* (MCLE Seminar 1993).

[2] Lana Clark, *Developing a Strategy for Witness Interviews,* 10 Legal Assistant Today 65 (January/February 1993).

[3] See the discussion later in the chapter on whether paralegals who conduct investigations must have an investigator's license (page 436).

50 percent of their leads will turn out to be dead ends. They are not frightened by roadblocks and therefore do not freeze at the first hurdle. They know that there are no perfect ways of obtaining information. They know that they must take a stab at possibilities and that it takes persistent thinking and imagination to come up with leads. At the same time, good investigators are not fools. They do not pursue blind alleys. After being on the job for a while, they have developed "a feel" for whether a possibility or lead is reasonable. They have been able to develop this feel because, when they first started investigating, they had an open mind and were not afraid to try things out.

3. *Investigators may not know what they are looking for until they find it.* As with legal interviewing and legal research, good investigation may sometimes have a life of its own in terms of what it uncovers. There are two kinds of investigation assignments: the closed-ended assignment (where the end product is carefully defined in advance, such as the photograph assignment mentioned in the tenant case), and the open-ended assignment (where the investigator begins with only the general contours of a problem and is asked to fill in the facts). An example of an open-ended assignment is to find out as much as possible about the case of a client charged with burglary. In the open-ended assignment (and in some closed-ended ones), investigators are walking into the unknown. They may have no idea what they will uncover. In the burglary assignment, suppose the investigator sets out to focus on whatever is relevant to the burglary charge and in the process discovers that an embezzlement was involved, as yet unknown to the police. The investigator had no idea that she would find this until she found it. Suppose the law firm has a client who is charging his employer with racial discrimination, and in the process of working on the case, the investigator discovers that this employee had a managerial job at the company and that several of the workers under him have complained that *he* practiced sex discrimination against them. The investigator had no idea that she would uncover this until it was uncovered. In short, an open mind is key when undertaking an assignment.

4. *Investigation and interviewing are closely related.* The interviewer conducting the initial client interview has two responsibilities: to help identify legal problems and to obtain from the client as many relevant facts on those problems as possible. The starting point for the investigator is the report or intake memo (see Exhibit 8.3 in chapter 8) prepared by the interviewer on what the client said. The investigation needs may be clear from this report, or they may become clear only after the investigator and his or her supervisor have defined them more precisely.

The investigator should approach the interview report with a healthy skepticism. Thus far, all the office may know is what the client has said. The perspective of the office is therefore narrow. Without necessarily distrusting the client's word, the investigator's job is to verify the facts given during the interview and to determine whether new facts exist that were unknown or improperly identified during the interview. The interview report should not be taken at face value. New facts may be revealed or old facts may for the first time be seen in a context that gives them an unexpected meaning. The investigator must approach a case almost as if the office knows nothing about it or as if what the office knows is invalid. By adopting this attitude, the investigator will be able to give the case an entirely different direction when the product of the investigation warrants it.

5. *The investigator must be guided by goals and priorities.* It is one thing to say that the investigator must be open-minded enough to be receptive to the unexpected. It is quite another to say that the investigator should start in a void. The starting point

is a set of instructions from the supervisor. How clear a supervisor is about an investigation assignment may vary with each assignment. For example:

- Supervisors may have a very definite idea of what they want.
- Supervisors may think they know what they want but are not sure.
- Whatever conception supervisors have about what they want, they are not effective in explaining it to the investigator.
- Supervisors have no idea what they want other than a desire to obtain as many facts about the case as possible.

The first responsibility of the investigator is to establish communication with the supervisor. With as much clarity as possible, determine what the supervisor wants to accomplish through the investigation.

6. *Investigation, negotiation, and trial are closely related.* There are two ultimate questions that should guide the investigator's inquiry into every fact being investigated:

- How will this fact assist or hurt the office in attempting to settle or negotiate the case without a trial?
- How will this fact assist or hurt the office in presenting the client's case at trial?

A large percentage of legal claims never go to full trial; they are negotiated in advance. Opposing counsel hold a number of bargaining sessions in which they attempt to hammer out a settlement acceptable to their clients. Very often they discuss the law that they think will be applicable if the case goes to trial. Even more often they present each other with the facts that they think they will be able to establish at trial. Here the investigator's report becomes invaluable. As a result of this report, the attorney should be able to suggest a wide range of facts that could be used at trial ("we have reason to believe . . ." or "we are now pursuing leads that would tend to establish that . . ." etc.). The attorney's bargaining leverage is immeasurably increased by a thorough investigation report.

If negotiations do not produce a settlement, the investigator's report can help the attorney in a number of ways:

- Determining whether to go to trial
- Deciding what witnesses to call
- Choosing questions to ask of witnesses
- Deciding how to **impeach** (i.e., contradict or attack the credibility of) opposing witnesses
- Determining what tangible or physical evidence to introduce
- Deciding how to attack the tangible or physical evidence the other side will introduce

The investigator should be familiar with the standard, pretrial **discovery devices:** depositions, interrogatories, requests for admissions, medical examination reports, etc. (See chapter 10.) A **deposition** is a pretrial question-and-answer session conducted outside court, usually in the office of one of the attorneys. The attorney asks questions of the other party (or of a witness of the other party) in order to obtain facts that will assist in preparing for trial. Depositions are often transcribed so that typed copies of the session are available. **Interrogatories** are used for the same purpose, but differ in that the questions and answers are usually submitted in writing rather than in person. An interrogatory is simply a question submitted by one party to another. A **request for admission** is a statement of fact submitted by one party to another. The latter is asked to admit or deny the statement. Statements that are admitted do not have to be proven at trial. A request for a medical examination will be granted by the judge when medical issues are relevant to the trial.

Investigators can be of assistance during this discovery stage by helping the attorney decide what questions to ask in a deposition or in an interrogatory, what admissions to request, whether to ask for a medical examination, etc.

After the discovery devices have been used, the investigator should carefully study all the facts these devices disclose in order to:

- cross-check or verify these facts, and
- look for new leads (names, addresses, incidents) that could be the subject of future investigation.

7. *It is important to distinguish between absolute proof of a fact and some evidence of a fact.* Investigators must not confuse their role with that of a judge or jury in deciding truth or falsity. The function of investigators is to identify reasonable options or fact possibilities. To be sure, they can speculate on whether a judge or jury would ever believe a fact to be true. But the presence or absence of absolute proof is not the test that should guide them in their investigations. The tests that an investigator should apply in determining whether to pursue a fact possibility are:

- Am I reasonable in assuming that a particular fact will help establish the case of the client? Am I reasonable in assuming that if I gather enough evidence on such a fact, a judge, jury, or hearing officer *might* accept it as true?
- Am I reasonable in assuming that a particular fact will help to challenge or discredit the case of the opposing party? Am I reasonable in assuming that if I gather enough evidence on such a fact (evidence that will challenge or discredit the case of the other side) a judge, jury, or hearing officer *might* accept it as true?

It is important to be able to approach the case from the perspective of the opponent, even to the point of assuming that you work for the other side! What facts will the opponent go after to establish its case? What is the likelihood that such facts will be accepted? Again, do not confuse proof with evidence.

8. *The investigator must know some law.* Investigators do not have to be experts in every area of the law or in any particular area of the law in order to perform their job. For their field work to have a focus, however, they must have at least a general understanding of evidence, civil procedure, and the areas of the law governing the facts of the client's case. They must know, for example, what *hearsay* and *relevance* mean. They must understand basic procedural steps in litigation in order to see where fact gathering can be used and how it is often used in different ways at different steps in the litigation process. Some substantive law is also needed. In a divorce case, for example, the investigator must know what the grounds for divorce are in the state. The same kind of basic information is needed for every area of the law involved or potentially involved in the client's case. Such knowledge can be obtained:

- In paralegal courses or seminars
- Through brief explanations from the supervisor
- By talking to experienced attorneys and paralegals whenever they have time to give you an overview of the relevant law
- By reading a chapter in a legal treatise or a section in a legal encyclopedia that provides an overview of the relevant law. (See chapter 11.)

9. *The investigator must know the territory.* When you are on the job as an investigator, it is important to begin acquiring a detailed knowledge of the makeup of the city, town, or state where you will be working. Such knowledge should include:

- The political structure of the area: Who is in power? Who is the opposition? In what direction is the political structure headed?
- The social and cultural structure of the area: Are there racial problems? Are there ethnic groupings that are diffused or unified? Are there different value systems at play?
- The contacts that are productive: If you want something done at city hall, whom do you see? Does the director of a particular agency have any control over the staff? What agencies have "real services" available? What court clerk is most helpful?

It is usually very difficult for the investigator to acquire this knowledge in any way other than going out into the field and obtaining it through experience. Others can provide guidance, and often will. In the final analysis, however, you will probably discover that what others say is biased or incomplete. You must establish your own network of contacts and sources of information. First and foremost, you must establish your credibility in the community. People must get to know and trust you. Simply announcing yourself as an investigator (or presenting a printed card indicating title and affiliation) will not be enough to win instant cooperation from the community. You must *earn* this cooperation. If you gain a reputation as arrogant, dishonest, opportunistic or insensitive, you will quickly find that few people want to deal with you. An investigator could be in no worse predicament.

Often the best way to learn about an area and begin establishing contacts is by being casual and unassuming. Have you ever noticed that insurance agents often spend time talking about the weather, sports, politics, the high cost of housing, etc., *before* coming to their sales pitch? Their intent is to relax you, to find out what interests you, to show you that they are human. Then they hit you with the benefits of buying their insurance. The investigator can use this approach not only in establishing contacts at agencies and in the community generally, but also in dealing with prospective witnesses on specific cases.

Section B
FACT ANALYSIS: ORGANIZING THE OPTIONS

The process of structuring or organizing fact options may initially appear to be complex and cumbersome. But the process can become second nature to you once you understand it, try it out, evaluate it, modify it, and find it helpful. It is, of course, perfectly proper to adopt any process that you find effective. Whatever method you use, you need to develop the *discipline* of fact analysis as soon as possible.

A number of fundamental characteristics of facts should be kept in mind:

- Events take place.
- Events mean different things to different people.
- Different people, therefore, have different versions of events.
- Inconsistent versions of the same event do not necessarily indicate fraud or lying.
- Although someone's version may claim to be the total picture, it probably will contain only a piece of the picture.
- In giving a version of an event, people usually mix statements of *why* the event occurred with statements of *what* occurred.
- Whenever it is claimed that an event occurred in a certain way, one can logically expect that certain signs, indications, or traces (evidence) of the event can be found.

Given these truisms, the investigator should analyze the facts along the lines indicated in Exhibit 9.1. It is possible for a single client's case to have numerous individual facts that

---

E x h i b i t 9 . 1 **Fact Analysis in Investigation**

Starting Point:

All the facts you currently have on the case.

Procedure:

- Arrange the facts chronologically.
- Place a number before each fact that must be established in a legal proceeding.

State the Following Versions of Each Fact:

Version I: The client's
Version II: The opponent's (as revealed to you or as assumed)
Version III: A witness's
Version IV: Another witness's
Version V: Any other reasonable version (e.g., from your own deductions)

As to Each Version:

- State precisely (with quotes if possible) what the version is.
- State the evidence or indications that tend to support the version according to persons presenting the version.
- State the evidence or indications that tend to contradict this version.
- Determine how you will verify or corroborate the evidence or indications.

---

are in dispute. Furthermore, facts can change, or people's versions of facts can change in the middle of a case. Each new or modified fact demands the same comprehensive process of fact analysis that is outlined in Exhibit 9.1.

Obtaining different versions of a fact may be difficult because the differences may not be clear on the surface. Of course, every fact will not necessarily have multiple versions. It is recommended, however, that you assume there will be more than one version until you have demonstrated otherwise to yourself. Undoubtedly, you will have to do some probing to uncover the versions that exist. Better to do so now than to be confronted with a surprise at trial or at an agency hearing.

People will not always be willing to share their accounts or versions of facts with you. If you are not successful in convincing them to tell their story, you may have to make assumptions of what their story is *likely* to be and then check out these assumptions.

S e c t i o n C
DISTORTIONS IN INVESTIGATION

Investigators are not mere newspaper reporters or photographers who simply report what they see, hear, or otherwise experience. You have a much more dynamic role. In a very significant sense, you sometimes have the power of influencing what someone else says about the facts. This can have both positive and negative consequences.

At its worst, this can mean that you are not listening to the person or that you are asking questions in such a manner that you are putting words into the person's mouth. The primary technique that can bring about this result is the **leading question.** A leading question is one that contains (or suggests) the answer in the statement of the question. For example, "You were in Baltimore at the time, isn't that correct?" "You earn over $200 a week?" "Would it be correct to say that when you drove up to the curb, you didn't see the light?" (For more on the different kinds that can be asked, see Exhibit 8.8 in chapter 8.)

Questions can intentionally or unintentionally manipulate someone's answer by including a premise that has yet to be established. It takes an alert person to say to such questions, "I can't answer your question (or it is invalid) because it assumes another fact that I haven't agreed to." In the following examples of questions and answers, the person responding to the question refuses to be trapped by the form of the question:

Q: How much did it cost you to have your car repaired after the accident?
A: It's not my car and it wasn't an accident; your client deliberately ran into the car that I borrowed.

Q: Have you stopped beating your wife?
A: I never beat my wife!

Q: Can you tell me what you saw?
A: I didn't see anything; my brother was there and he told me what happened.

The last leading question containing the unestablished premise can be highly detrimental. Suppose the question and answer went as follows:

Q: Can you tell me what you saw?
A: The car was going about 70 MPH.

In fact, the person answering the question did not see this himself; his brother told him that a car was traveling at this speed. There are a number of reasons why this person may have failed to tell the investigator that he didn't see anything first-hand:

- Perhaps he did not hear the word "saw" in the investigator's question.
- He may have wanted the investigator to think that he saw something himself; he may want to feel important by conveying the impression that he is special because he has special information.
- He may have felt that correcting the investigator's false assumption was not important; he may have thought that the investigator was more interested in *what* happened than in *who* saw what happened.

Whatever the reason, the investigator has carelessly put himself or herself in the position of missing a potentially critical fact, namely that the person is talking from hearsay. Before asking what the person "saw," the investigator should ask, "Were you there?" and if so, "Did you see anything?"

Also, be careful about the way you phrase a question. "Research indicates the wording of questions to witnesses significantly affects their recall. For example, more uncertain or 'don't know' responses are given if a witness is asked about an indefinite item (e.g., 'Did you see *a* knife?') than occurs when the question contains a definite article ('Did you see *the* knife?')."[4]

---

[4]A. Daniel Yarmey, *The Psychology of Eyewitness Testimony* 9 (Free Press, 1979), citing E. Loftus et al., *Powerful Eyewitness Testimony,* Trial Magazine 64–66 (April 1988).

Communication is often blurred when the questioner concentrates on some themes to the exclusion of others. If you do not ask questions about certain matters, intentionally or otherwise, you are likely to end up with a distorted picture of a person's version of the facts. For example, assume that Smith and Jones have an automobile collision. The investigator, working for the attorney who represents Jones, finds a witness who says that she saw the accident. The investigator asks her to describe what she saw, but fails, however, to ask her where she was at the time she saw the collision. In fact, she was sitting in a park more than two blocks away and could only see the collision through some shrubbery. The investigator didn't ask questions to uncover this information; it wasn't volunteered. The investigator, therefore, walks away with a potentially distorted idea of how much light this individual can shed on what took place. This is similar to the distortion that can result from the use of questions that contain an unestablished premise.

Yet, in some instances, these techniques may have beneficial results. First of all, a leading question can help jar someone's memory, making the person better able to recall the facts. If, however, this individual constantly needs leading questions in order to remember, you have strong reason to suspect that, rather than being merely shy, inarticulate, or in need of a push now and then, the person knows little or nothing.

Suppose that the witness being questioned is uncooperative or has a version of the facts that is damaging to the client of the investigator's office. It may be that the techniques described in this section as normally improper can be used to challenge a version of the facts. A leading question with an unestablished premise, for example, may catch an individual off guard and give the investigator reasonable cause to believe that the person is not telling the truth. Here's how Bryon Keith describes his use of leading statements or questions:

> A technique I've found very successful is to ask a question I feel will evoke a factual answer. For example, I would ask Mr. John Doe, "Mr. Doe, you claim that you are a witness to the accident when, in fact, I understand you were not in a position to see everything that happened." Often, the person will respond with a defensive answer similar to, "I was in a position to see everything," and then continue to tell me their location and what they saw.[5]

Suppose that the person being questioned is not hostile but is neutral, or seemingly so. The way such individuals are questioned may help them emphasize certain facts as opposed to others. Once witnesses have committed themselves to a version of the facts, either completely on their own or with some subtle help from the questioner, there is a good chance that they will stick by this version because they do not want to appear to be vague, uncertain, or inconsistent later. An investigator who takes such a course of action must be extremely careful, however. You are taking certain risks, not because your conduct is illegal or unethical, but because a witness who needs subtle pressuring to state a version of the facts in a certain way is probably going to be a weak witness at trial or at an agency hearing. On cross-examination, the witness may fall apart.

Section D
SOURCES OF EVIDENCE/SOURCES OF LEADS

Evidence is anything used to prove or disprove a fact. **Testimonial evidence** is what someone says. **Tangible evidence** (also called physical evidence) is what can be seen or

---

[5]Bryon Keith, *Dealing Smartly with Different Witnesses,* The Legal Investigator 38 (November 1991).

Exhibit 9.2 Checklist of the Standard Sources of Evidence and Leads

- Statements of the client
- Documents the client brings or can obtain
- Information from attorneys involved with the case in the past
- Interrogatories, depositions, other discovery devices; letters requesting information
- Pleadings (such as complaints) filed thus far in the case
- Newspaper accounts; interviews with news reporters
- Notices in the media requesting information
- General records of municipal, state, and federal administrative agencies
- Business records (such as canceled receipts)
- Employment records, including job applications
- Photographs
- Hospital records
- Informers or the "town gossip"
- Surveillance of the scene
- Reports from the police and other law enforcement agencies (see Exhibit 9.3)
- Fingerprints
- School records
- Military records
- Information that may be voluntarily or involuntarily provided by the attorney for the other side
- Use of alias
- Bureau of vital statistics and missing persons

- Court records
- Worker's Compensation records
- Office of politicians
- Records of Better Business Bureaus and consumer groups
- Telephone book
- Boat register
- *Polk Directory*
- *Reverse Directory*
- Accounts of eyewitnesses
- Hearsay accounts
- Automobile register (DMV)
- County assessor (for real property)
- Tax assessor's offices
- County election records
- Post office (record of forwarding addresses)
- Object to be traced (such as an auto)
- Credit bureaus
- Reports of investigative agencies written in the past
- Resources of public library
- Associations (trade, professional, etc.)
- *Who's Who* directories
- Insurance Company Clearing House
- Standard and Poor's *Register of Directors and Executives*
- Telling your problem to a more experienced investigator and asking for other leads
- Shots in the dark

touched. A *lead* is simply a path to potentially admissible evidence. Of course, evidence is often its own lead to other evidence.

Exhibit 9.2 provides a partial checklist of some of the standard sources of evidence and leads at the investigator's disposal. (The list is not presented in order of priority.)

Section E
GAINING ACCESS TO RECORDS

Often the simplest way to obtain a record or other information is to ask for it. See, for example, the sample letter requesting information in Exhibit 12.1 in chapter 12. Gaining access to some records, however, can sometimes be difficult. There are four categories of records:

1. Those already in the possession of the client or of an individual willing to turn them over to you on request
2. Those in the possession of a governmental agency or of a private organization and available to anyone in the public (for example, see Exhibit 9.3)

Exhibit 9.3   **Request for Copy of Peace Officer's Accident Report**

REQUEST FOR COPY OF PEACE OFFICER'S ACCIDENT REPORT
(PLEASE SUBMIT IN DUPLICATE)

Statistical Services
Texas Department of Public Safety
P.O. Box 15999
Austin, Texas 78761–5999

Date of Request _____

Claim or Policy No. _____

Enclosed is a (check)(money order) payable to the Texas Department of Public Safety in the amount of $ _____
for (check service desired):
☐ Copy of Peace Officer's Accident Report - $4.00 each
☐ Certified Copy of Peace Officer's Accident Report - $8.00 each
for the accident listed below:

Please provide as accurate and complete information as possible.

ACCIDENT DATE _____
           MONTH   DAY   YEAR

ACCIDENT LOCATION _____ _____ _____
                        COUNTY   CITY   STREET OR HIGHWAY

WAS ANYONE
KILLED IN THE ACCIDENT? _____ If So, Name of one Deceased _____

INVESTIGATING AGENCY AND/OR OFFICER'S NAME (IF KNOWN) _____

| | DRIVER INFORMATION (If Available) | | |
DRIVER'S FULL NAME	DATE OF BIRTH	TEXAS DRIVER LICENSE NO.	ADDRESS
1. _____			
2. _____			
3. _____			

Texas Statutes allow the investigating officer 10 days in which to submit his report.
Requests should not be submitted until at least 10 days after the accident date to allow time for receipt of the report.

The Law also provides that if an officer's report is not on file when a request for a copy of such report is received, a certification to that effect will be provided in lieu of the copy and the fee shall be retained for the certification.

Mail To _____

Mail Address _____

City _____ State _____ Zip _____

Requested by _____ Phone # _____

> ### Exhibit 9.4   Guidelines for Gaining Access to Records
>
> 1. Write, phone, or visit the organization and ask for the record.
> 2. Have the client write, phone, or visit and ask for it.
> 3. Draft a letter for the client to sign that asks for it.
> 4. Have the client sign a form stating that he or she gives you authority to see any records that pertain to him or her and that he or she specifically waives any right to confidentiality with respect to such records.
> 5. Find out if one of the opposing parties has the record, and if so, ask his or her attorney to send you a copy.
> 6. Find out if others have it (such as a relative of the client or a co-defendant in this or a prior court case) and ask them if they will provide you with a copy.
> 7. For records available generally to the public, find out where these records are and go use them.
> 8. If you meet resistance (fourth category of records), make a basic fairness pitch to the organization as to why you need the records.
> 9. Find out (by legal research) if there are any statutes, regulations, or cases that arguably provide the client with the right of access to records kept by government agencies—for example, through the **Freedom of Information Act** (FOIA) of Congress covering federal agencies. (See Exhibit 9.5.) Many states have their own FOIA for state agencies.
> 10. If the person who initially turns down the request for access is a line officer, appeal the decision formally or informally to his or her supervisor, and up the chain of command to the person with final authority.
> 11. Solicit the intervention of a politician or some other respectable and independent person in trying to gain access.
> 12. Let the organization know that your office is considering (or is preparing) a suit to establish a right to the record (when this is so).

3. Those in the possession of a governmental agency or of a private organization and available only to the client or to the individual who is the subject of the records
4. Those in the possession of a governmental agency or of a private organization and claimed to be confidential except for in-house staff

Obviously, there should be no difficulty in gaining access to the first category of records unless they have been misplaced or lost, in which event the person who once had possession would ask the source of the records to provide another copy. As to records in the latter three categories, the checklist in Exhibit 9.4 should provide some guidelines on gaining access.

Section F
EVALUATING TESTIMONIAL AND PHYSICAL EVIDENCE

At all times, you must make value judgments on the usefulness of the evidence that you come across. A number of specific criteria can be used to assist you in assessing the worth of what you have. The checklists in Exhibits 9.6 (page 422) and 9.7 (page 423) may be helpful in determining this worth.

Exhibit 9.5   Sample FOIA Letter

Agency Head or FOIA Officer
Title
Name of Government Agency
Address of Agency
City, State, Zip

Re: Freedom of Information Act (FOIA) Request.

Dear _____ :

Under the provisions of the Freedom of Information Act, 5 U.S.C. 552, I am requesting access to (identify the records as clearly and specifically as possible).

If there are any fees for searching for, or copying, the records I have requested, please inform me before you fill the request. (Or: . . . please supply the records without informing me if the fees do not exceed $ _____.)

[Optional] As you know, the FOIA permits you to reduce or waive fees when the release of the information is considered as "primarily benefiting the public." I believe that this request fits that category and I therefore ask that you waive any fees.

[Optional] I am requesting this information (state the reason for your request if you think it will assist you in obtaining the information.)

If all or any part of this request is denied, please cite the specific exemption(s) that you think justifies your refusal to release the information, and inform me of the appeal procedures available to me under the law.

I would appreciate your handling this request as quickly as possible, and I look forward to hearing from you within 10 days, as the law stipulates.

Sincerely,

Signature
Name
Address
City, State, Zip

Source: U.S. Congress. House. Committee on Government Operations. *A Citizen's Guide on How to Use the Freedom of Information Act and the Privacy Act Requesting Government Documents,* 95th Congress, 1st sess. (1977).

Section G
INTERVIEWING WITNESSES

Francis Ritter, a seasoned investigator, tells us that there are six parts to every conversation: three for the speaker and three for the listener. For the *speaker* they are:
- what he or she wants to say
- what the speaker actually says, and
- what the speaker thinks he or she said.

The *listener* deals with:
- what he or she wants to hear,
- what the listener actually heard,
- what the listener thinks he or she heard.[6]

---

[6]Francis Ritter, *The Art of Hearing Between the Lines,* The Legal Investigator 9 (February 1992).

Exhibit 9.6 Checklist on the Validity of Testimonial Evidence

CHECKLIST TO USE IF THE WITNESS IS SPEAKING FROM FIRST-HAND (EYEWITNESS) INFORMATION

- How long ago did it happen?
- How good is the memory of this witness?
- How far from the event was the witness at the time?
- How good is the sight of the witness?
- What time of day was it and would this affect vision?
- What was the weather at the time and would this affect vision?
- Was there a lot of commotion at the time and would this affect vision or ability to remember?
- What was the witness doing immediately before the incident?
- How old is the witness?
- What was the last grade of school he or she completed?
- What is the witness's employment background?
- What is the reputation of the witness in the community for truthfulness?
- Was the witness ever convicted of a crime? Are any criminal charges now pending against him or her?
- Is the witness an expert on anything?
- What are the qualifications of the witness?
- Is the witness related to, an employee of, or friendly with either side in the litigation? Would it be to this person's benefit, in any way, to see either side win?
- Does any direct evidence exist to corroborate what this witness is saying?
- Does any hearsay evidence exist to corroborate it?
- Is the witness willing to sign a statement covering what he or she tells the investigator? Is he or she willing to say it in court?
- Is the witness defensive when asked about what he or she knows?
- Are there any inconsistencies in what the witness is saying?
- How does the witness react when confronted with the inconsistencies? Defensively?
- Are there any gaps in what the witness is saying?
- Does the witness appear to exaggerate?
- Does the witness appear to be hiding or holding anything back?

CHECKLIST TO USE IF THE WITNESS IS SPEAKING FROM SECOND-HAND (HEARSAY) INFORMATION

- How well does the witness remember what was told to him or her by the other person (the declarant) or what the witness heard him or her say to someone else?
- How is the witness sure that it is exact?
- Is the declarant now available to confirm or deny this hearsay account of the witness? If not, why not?
- Under what conditions did the declarant allegedly make the statement (for example, was declarant ill)?
- Is there other hearsay testimony that will help corroborate this hearsay?
- Does any direct evidence exist to corroborate this hearsay?
- How old is the witness? How old is the declarant?
- What are the educational and employment backgrounds of both?
- What is their reputation in the community for truthfulness?
- Was either ever convicted of a crime? Are any criminal charges pending against either?
- Is either an expert on anything?
- What are their qualifications?
- Is the witness or the declarant related to, an employee of, or friendly with either side in the litigation? Would it be to the benefit of the witness or the declarant to see either side win?
- Is the witness willing to sign a statement covering what he or she tells the investigator? Is he or she willing to say it in court?
- Is the witness defensive when asked about what he or she was told by the declarant or what he or she heard the declarant say to someone else?
- Are there any inconsistencies in what the witness is saying?
- How does the witness react when confronted with the inconsistencies? Defensively?
- Are there any gaps in what the witness is saying?
- Does the witness appear to exaggerate?
- Does the witness appear to be hiding or holding anything back?

The following guidelines apply to all witness interviews:

1. *Know what image you are projecting of yourself.* In the minds of many people, an investigator is often involved in serious and dangerous undertakings. How would you react if a stranger introduced himself or herself to you as an investigator? Since

| *E x h i b i t   9 . 7* | **Checklist on the Validity of Physical (Tangible) Evidence** |

CHECKLIST FOR WRITTEN MATERIAL	**CHECKLIST FOR NONWRITTEN MATERIAL**
• Who wrote it? • Under what circumstances was it written? • Is the original available? If not, why not? • Is a copy available? • Who is available to testify that the copy is in fact an accurate copy of the original? • Is the author of the written material available to testify on what he or she wrote? If not, why not? • Is there any hearsay testimony available to corroborate the authenticity of the writing? • Is there any other physical evidence available to corroborate the authenticity of the writing? • What hearsay or direct evidence is available to corroborate or contradict what is said in the writing? • Can you obtain sample handwriting specimens of the alleged author?	• Who found it and under what circumstances? • Where was it found? • Why would it be where it was found? Was it unusual to find it there? • Who is available to identify it? • What identifying characteristics does it have? • Who owns it? Who used it? • Who owned it in the past? Who used it in the past? Who has had possession? • Who made it? • What is its purpose? • Does it require laboratory analysis? • Can you take it with you? • Can you photograph it? • Is it stolen? • Is there any public record available to trace its history? • What facts does it tend to establish? • Was it planted where it was found as a decoy?

this would cause many people to be guarded and suspicious, you may not want to call yourself an investigator. You may want to say, "My name is _____ , I work for (name of law office) and we are trying to get information on _____ ." On the other hand, you may find that you are most effective when you are direct and straightforward.

Can you think of different people who would respond more readily to certain images of investigators? The following is a partial list of some of the images that an investigator could be projecting by dress, mannerisms, approach, and language:

- A professional
- Someone who is just doing a job
- Someone who is emotionally involved in what he or she is doing
- A neutral bystander
- A friend
- A manipulator or opportunist
- A salesperson
- A wise person
- An innocent and shy person

You must be aware of (a) your own need to project yourself in a certain way, (b) the way in which you think you are projecting yourself, (c) the way in which the person to whom you are talking perceives you, and (d) the effect that all this is having on what you are trying to accomplish.

Here is how one paralegal, Janet Jackson, describes her approach:

[The] basic techniques are to approach the person as a friend, make him or her feel comfortable talking, and gain his or her trust. One simple way of doing this is using the principle that people respond to their names. I address the contact by name several times throughout the interview. I also use a friendly, soft, nonthreatening, inquisitive tone of voice. The first few moments . . . are always the most difficult and the most important. Usually in these few moments the contact makes the decision whether to talk. So, a strong opening is needed. I plan, write out, and practice my opening so I can deliver it smoothly and quickly in a friendly, confident voice. . . . I say, "Hello, Mr. Jones, my name is Janet Jackson and I work for the law firm of X, Y & Z. We have been retained by the T. Company to represent them in a lawsuit brought against them by Mr. John Smith. I would like to ask you a few questions about the lawsuit. . . ." I then identify myself as a legal assistant and explain that I am collecting information. Often I have found that saying that I am a legal assistant, not an attorney, causes people to relax and let down their guard.[7]

2. *There are five kinds of witnesses: hostile, skeptical, friendly, disinterested or neutral, and a combination of the above.* Hostile witnesses want your client to lose; they will try to set up roadblocks in your way. Skeptical witnesses are not sure who you are or what you want in spite of your explanation of your role. They are guarded and unsure whether they want to become involved. Friendly witnesses want your client to win and will cooperate fully. **Disinterested** or neutral witnesses don't care who wins. They have information that they are usually willing to tell anyone who asks.

If the hostile witness is the opposing party who has retained counsel, it is unethical for the investigator to talk directly with this person without going through his or her counsel (see chapter 5). If the hostile witness is not a party but is closely associated with a party, you should check with your supervisor on how, if at all, to approach such a witness.

To complicate matters, it must be acknowledged that witnesses are seldom totally hostile, skeptical, friendly, or neutral. At different times during the investigation interview, and at different times throughout the various stages of the case, they may shift from one attitude to another. While it may be helpful to determine the general category witnesses fit into, it would be more realistic to view any witness as an individual in a state of flux in terms of what he or she is capable of saying and what he or she wants to say.

3. *The investigator must have the trust of the witness.* You have the sometimes difficult threshold problem of sizing up the witness from whom you are trying to obtain information. Here are some of the states of mind that witnesses could have:

- They want to feel important.
- They want to be "congratulated" for knowing anything, however insignificant, about the case.
- They want absolute assurance from you that they won't get into trouble by talking to you. They shy away from talk of courts, lawyers, and law.
- They are willing to talk only after you have given full assurance that you will never reveal the source of the information they give you.
- They are willing to talk to you only in the presence of their friends.
- If they know your client, they want to be told that you are trying to keep the client out of trouble.
- They want the chance to meet you first and then have you go away so they can decide whether they want to talk to you again.

---

[7]Janet Jackson, *Interviewing Witnesses,* At Issue 1 (San Francisco Ass'n of Legal Assistants, April 1994).

- They are not willing to talk to you until you fulfill some of their needs—for example, listen to their troubles; act in a fatherly or motherly manner; play subtle, seductive games; etc.

In short, the investigator must gain the trust of individuals by assessing their needs and by knowing when they are ready to tell you what they know. If you take out your notebook immediately upon introducing yourself, you are probably too insensitive to establish the communication that's needed.

4. *The investigator must assess how well the witness would do under direct and cross-examination.* As witnesses talk, ask yourself a number of questions:

- Would they be willing to testify in court? Whatever the answer to this question is now, are they likely to change their minds later?
- Would they be effective on the witness stand?
- Do they know what they are talking about?
- Do they have a reputation for integrity and truthfulness in the community?
- Are they defensive?
- Would they know how to say "I'm not sure" or "I don't understand the question," as opposed to giving an answer for the sake of giving an answer (e.g., to avoid being embarrassed)?
- When they talk, are they internally consistent?
- Do they know how to listen as well as talk?
- Do they understand the distinction between right and wrong, truth and lying?

Section H
SPECIAL INVESTIGATIVE PROBLEMS: SOME STARTING POINTS

JUDGMENT COLLECTION

The person who wins a money judgment in court is called the **judgment creditor.** Unfortunately, collecting that judgment can be a difficult undertaking. An investigator may be asked to assist the law firm in ascertaining the financial assets of a particular individual or corporation against whom the judgment was obtained, called the **judgment debtor.**

One of the best starting points for such an investigation is government records. The following is a partial list of records available from the county clerk or court office:

- Real property records (check grantee and grantor indexes)
- Real and personal property tax assessments
- Filings made under the Uniform Commercial Code
- Federal tax liens
- Court dockets—to determine whether the judgment debtor has been a plaintiff or defendant in prior litigation (check the abstract-of-judgment index)
- Inheritance records—to determine whether the judgment debtor has inherited money or other property (determined by checking records of the surrogate's court or probate court, which handles inheritance and trust cases)

Such records could reveal a good deal of information on the financial status of the party under investigation. You might find out whether he or she owns or has an interest in valuable personal or business property. Even though tax records often undervalue the property being taxed, they are some indication of a person's wealth. Another indication is the existence of past suits against the party. If a party has been sued in the past, someone made a determination that he or she probably had a **deep pocket** at that time, meaning sufficient assets to satisfy a judgment.

For corporations that are judgment debtors, check the records of state and federal government agencies (such as the Secretary of State and the Securities and Exchange Commission) with whom the corporation must file periodic reports or disclosures on its activities and finances. You should also check with people who have done business with the corporation (customers or other creditors) as well as with its competitors in the field. These records and contacts could provide good leads.

A great deal of this information is now on-line so that it can be searched through computers. Here, for example, are some of the databases that can be searched on WESTLAW:

Asset Locator (ASSET). Identifies major property holdings of a person or business including real estate, stocks, aircraft, watercraft, business equipment, and inventory.

Sleuth (SLEUTH). Identifies relationships between people and businesses by searching public records (corporate and limited partnership filings, state and county UCC and lien filings, sales and use tax information, and county assumed or fictitious name filings) in selected states and counties.

Business Finder® (BF). Provides abstracts based on business listings compiled from the yellow pages of nearly 5,000 telephone directories.

Executive Affiliation® (EA). Provides abstracts from selected state corporate and limited partnership filings, as well as business listings compiled from the yellow pages of nearly 5,000 telephone directories.

Dun & Bradstreet Business Records Plus (DUNBR). Provides information on a company's history, operations, and financial performance as well as intracompany relationships for 11 million companies worldwide.

Combined Corporate & Limited Partnership Records (ALLCORP). Provides abstracts of corporate, limited partnership, and limited liability company filing information.

UCC Filings, Liens & Judgments (UCC). Provides abstracts of UCC documents filed with state and selected county authorities, federal and state tax liens, attachment liens, and judgment liens.

County Records (COU). Provides abstracts of public information such as county-level UCC filings, lien filings, deeds, general execution dockets, assumed names, trade names, judgments, lis pendens, and other local court records.

Bankruptcy Records (BKR). Provides abstracts of filings in U.S. bankruptcy courts. Includes business filings in all 50 states and personal filings in selected states.

Lawsuits (LS). Provides abstracts of civil lawsuits filed in selected state and local courts.

Real Property Records, Liens & Judgments (RLJ). Provides abstracts of federal, state, and county real property liens and judgments in selected counties.

TRW REDI Real Property Data–Combined States Records (TRW-PROP). Provides abstracts of real property tax records from county assessors in selected counties.

Dow Jones–All Plus Wires (ALLNEWS-PLUS). Provides documents from all wires, newspapers, magazines, journals, newsletters, and transcripts as provided by Dow Jones & Company, Inc.

MISSING PERSONS

An investigator may be asked to locate a missing heir, a relative of a client, a person who must be served with process in connection with current litigation, etc. A missing person is generally not difficult to locate—unless this person does not want to be found.

John Lehe, a legal investigator, suggests that you begin with the easily available resources: telephone books, directory assistance operators, and cross-reference directories. "In contacting directory assistance operators, ask for telephone numbers for anyone with the same last name on the street of the last-known address. It is possible for relatives to live on the same street and they may be able to provide the [missing person's] current address or place of employment."[8] Local neighborhood libraries often have a telephone reference section that should be checked. Find out if they have any old telephone directories available.

Your local library may have a cross-reference directory (sometimes called a reverse or criss-cross directory). If all you have is the address of a person, you may be able to use this resource to find out who lives at that address, plus his or her surrounding neighbors.

Try sending a registered letter to the person's last-known address, "return receipt requested," which asks the post office to send you back a notice with the signature of the person who signed to receive the letter.

Several programs on the World Wide Web provide access to addresses nationally. For example:

```
http://www.switchboard.com
```

More sophisticated on-line search databases are available on LEXIS and WESTLAW. An example is "People Finder" on WESTLAW, which allows you to search a network of public information and records containing more than 146 million names, 92 million households, 71 million telephone numbers, 40 million death certificates, and 160 million Social Security numbers. People Finder obtains this information from the U.S. Census Bureau, change-of-address files of the U.S. Postal Service, voter registration records, telephone directories, publishers' mailing lists, county or city tax assessor rolls, credit bureau information, etc.

The Social Security Administration will not give you personal information on recipients. Knowing the person's number, however, might provide a clue. The first three digits of a social security number indicate the state in which the card was issued.[9] For example:

545–573 California	010–034 Massachusetts	540–544 Oregon
602–626 California	362–386 Michigan	159–211 Pennsylvania
261–267 Florida	468–477 Minnesota	449–467 Texas
589–595 Florida	135–158 New Jersey	627–645 Texas
318–361 Illinois	050–134 New York	387–399 Wisconsin
212–220 Maryland	268–302 Ohio	

People who "disappear" sometimes return to the state where they grew up—often the state where they obtained their social security card.

Other possible sources of information:

- Relatives and friends
- Former landlord, neighbors, mail carrier, and local merchants in the area of the last-known address
- Professional associations such as unions and other job-related groups (people often retain membership in local chapters as they move around the country)
- Local credit bureau
- Police department, hospitals

---

[8]John Lehe, *Techniques for Locating Missing Parties,* 11 Legal Assistant Today 80, 81 (January/February 1994).
[9]Id. at pp. 82-3.

- References listed on employment applications
- Naturalization certificate, marriage record, driver's license, car registration
- Newspaper indexes (central and university libraries often keep such indexes; check obituary columns, local interest stories, etc.)

BACKGROUND INVESTIGATIONS

Exhibit 9.8 presents a form used by a large investigative firm for its general background investigations on individuals. The first part of the form seeks information regarding identification of the subject. The antecedent data cover prior history.

Exhibit 9.8   **Background Investigations**

Identification of Subject

1. Complete Name _____ Age _____ SS# _____ Marital Status _____
   Spouse's Name; Pertinent Info _____
   _____

   Children's Names and Ages _____
   _____
   _____

2. Current Residence Address and Type of Neighborhood _____
   _____
   _____

   How Long at Present Address—Prior Residence Info _____
   _____
   _____

3. Business Affiliation and Address, Position, Type of Bus. _____
   _____
   _____
   _____

Antecedent History

1. Place & Date of Birth _____
   Parents' Names & Occupations _____
   _____

   Where Did They Spend Their Youth? _____
   _____

2. Education—Where, Which Schools, Dates of Attendance
   _____
   _____

   Degree? What Kind? _____Any Other Info Pertaining to Scholastic Achievement, Extracurric.
   Activities _____
   _____
   _____

3. First Employer, to Present—F/T or P/T, Position or Title, Job Description, Exact Dates of Employment, Type of Company
   _____
   _____
   _____

Exhibit 9.8 **Background Investigations—continued**

4. Relationship with Peers, Supervisors, Subordinates—Where Do Subj.'s Abilities Lie? Any Outside Activities? Reputation for Honesty, Trustworthiness, Integrity? Does Subj. Work Well under Pressure? Anything Derogatory? If So, What Are Details? Reasons for Leaving? Would They Rehire? Salaries? Health? Reliability? Job Understanding? Willingness to Accept Responsibility? _____

_____

_____

_____

_____

_____

_____

If Self-Employed—What Was the Nature of the Business? With Whom Did Subj. Deal? Corp. Name?

_____

Date & Place of Incorporation _____

Who Were Partners, If Any? _____

What % of Stock Did Subj. Own? _____ Was Business Successful? _____ What Happened to It? _____

_____

If Sold, to Whom? _____

Any Subsid. or Affiliates? _____

_____

5. What Is Subj.'s Character or Personality Like? Did Informer Know Subj. Personally?

_____

Hobbies? _____

Family Life? _____

Even-Tempered? _____ Loner or Joiner? _____

Introverted, Extroverted? _____ Written or Oral Abilities? _____

Does Informer Know Anyone Else Who Knows Subj.? _____

_____

6. Credit Information _____

_____

_____

7. Subj.'s Involvement in Litigation _____ Civil _____ Criminal _____ Bankruptcy _____

State _____ Federal _____ Local _____

_____

_____

8. Banking—Financial: Bank _____

Types of Accounts—Average Bal. _____

How Long Did Subj. Have Accounts? _____ Any Company Accounts? _____

_____

Is Subj. Personally Known to Officers of the Bank? _____ Any Borrowing? _____

Secured or Unsecured? _____ If Secured, by What? _____

Do They Have Financial Statement on the Subj.? _____

What Is Net Worth of Subj.? _____ Other Assets? Real Estate _____

Stocks _____

Equity in Subj.'s Co., etc. _____

AUTOMOBILE ACCIDENTS

Auto Accident Analysis
by Dale W. Felton
27 Trial Magazine 60 (February 1991)[10]

Accidents don't just happen. Except in instances of mechanical failure or acts of God, vehicle collisions occur because of driver negligence. If a collision is properly investigated and analyzed, who was at fault can usually be determined. If the analysis reveals the defendant was negligent, demonstrative evidence can be used to show jurors how the defendant's negligence caused the collision.

Every law office handling vehicle-accident cases would benefit from learning effective methods of investigation and accident analysis. Many of these cases could be settled if insurance adjusters were shown definitive or scientific facts demonstrating that fault lies with the insured and not with the plaintiff. Insurance adjusters—like jurors—are receptive to scientific analysis of liability. . . .

An analysis of negligence should not be attempted without first conducting a thorough investigation. It is important to investigate as quickly as possible. Accident scenes change, and witnesses move. Of course, you often do not get a case until months after the accident occurred. Even then, the investigation should be started immediately. Bits of evidence and many helpful facts may still be available.

Reports

Begin the investigation by getting a complete statement of facts from the client. Then, get a police report of the collision. This report will include the officer's estimate of the damage to each vehicle as well as the location of the damage. Often the report will list names, addresses, and telephone numbers of the witnesses and usually the statements that each party gave to the officer at the scene. The report will also show who was ticketed and why. Reports often include a sketch of the accident scene as well as the officer's analysis of the factors contributing to the collision.

Sometimes, however, these drawings may be inaccurate. The officer's analysis of contributing factors may not make sense. In fact, in most instances where an insurance company denies liability, it is because an investigating officer indicated that the plaintiff was in some way at fault. Here

the law office must prove that the police officer's analysis was not correct.

In serious collisions, investigating police officers will often keep notes, take photographs, and make a scale drawing of the scene. You can obtain these by subpoena.

After obtaining a police report, take witness statements, being careful that each statement includes all facts the witness knows. The vehicles involved and the accident scene should be photographed as soon as possible because vehicles may be repaired quickly and accident scenes may change due to construction, resurfacing, installation of traffic control devices, etc. A full investigation also includes taking appropriate measurements and determining the point of impact from physical evidence at the scene, the police report, and the witness statements.

Photographs

Law offices should own and know how to use a 35mm camera, even if they employ full-time investigators or photographers. Many times, if you wait for someone else to take a photograph, the accident scene will have changed.

Know what photographs you need and make sure that the proper ones are taken. The only way to be sure to get the *right* photograph is to ensure that plenty are taken. The late Axel Hanson, one of the greatest investigators who ever lived, once said that he took 211 photographs of a vehicle involved in a fatality, and *one* proved to be the key to liability.

Photographers should move around the vehicle in a circle, taking photographs "every five minutes on the hands of a clock." Photographers should also take close-ups of damaged areas and use a flash to ensure that shadows do not obscure these areas.

Photographers should take shots from beneath the damaged part of the vehicle, an area that will often reveal the severity of the impact. Photographs taken while focusing straight down on the damaged area are needed because they will reveal the angle of impact. Photographers should carry ladders or, if they are allowed to, stand on the vehicle itself to get these shots. Downward shots of the vehicles involved in a collision can be matched to illustrate the angle at which the vehicles collided.

The photographer should also take pictures of any internal damage to the vehicle, including the speedometer and seats. In a rear-end collision the seats will often be bent

---

[10]Reprinted with permission of Trial (February 1991) © copyright The Ass'n of Trial Lawyers of America.

backward or broken off at the frames. Jurors can readily understand that an impact strong enough to break seats would be severe enough to injure a human being.

A 50mm lens best approximates the view as seen by the human eye. To illustrate what each driver saw, photographers should work from as far back as 1,000 feet from the point of collision. (If drivers did not travel 1,000 feet on the road in question before impact, photos should be taken starting from the point where each driver entered the roadway.) Photographs should be taken every 100 feet until 300 feet from the collision site; then every 50 feet until 100 feet from the point of impact; then every 25 feet to the point of impact. Only in this way can photographs show what the driver of each vehicle could see when approaching the collision site.

In photographing a crash scene, the photographer should obtain the same types of vehicles that were in the actual accident from a used-car lot or car dealership. Measurements should be made to determine driver's-eye height. Photographers can set tripods at this height to take approach shots. If a bus or truck is involved, it will be necessary to measure driver's-eye height in the same type of vehicle. In these instances, photographers must use ladders to get eye-height shots of what the drivers could see as they approached the collision site. A foot or two can make a world of difference in what a driver can see. These photographs should show any obstructions to a driver's view.

Photographs should also be taken of all road signs, not only to show their wording but also to show their location. At the point of impact, photos should be taken of gouge marks, scrapes, and any other damage the vehicles caused to the road surface or surrounding area. Both distance and close-up shots should be taken to pinpoint the damage. For close-up shots, it is often advisable to include a ruler or a pencil in order to indicate the scale.

Light Bulbs

Examining the light bulbs near a vehicle's damaged area will reveal whether they were operating at the time of the crash. During a collision, a heated light filament will stretch or break, while an inoperative cool filament will not. A bulb with a stretched or broken filament can easily be compared with a new bulb to show whether the bulb in question was functioning at the time of the collision. This principle applies to tail lights; brake lights; to turn indicators (front, back, or side); and to headlights.

The person examining the vehicles should *always* consider whether lighting could have been a factor in the col-

lision and, if so, examine the appropriate bulbs. For example, in all rear-end collisions at night, tail lights are a factor. Brake lights and turn signals may be factors day or night. If bulbs figured in the crash, they should be removed by an investigator and retained. It may be many months before the plaintiff's lawyer learns that the defendant is claiming that the plaintiff did not have the appropriate lights on or failed to give a turn signal.

Photographers should document the removal of bulbs, which should be placed in a padded, labeled box. It is important to indicate the vehicle they came from, their location on the vehicle, the person who removed them, and the date and time of removal. In *Golleher v. Herrera*, the court ruled that to introduce expert testimony concerning whether a vehicle's light bulb was functioning at the time of a collision, not only must the bulb be put into evidence but there must also be testimony that the bulb was the one that came from a particular location on one vehicle in the collision. 651 S.W.2d 329, 333–34 (Tex. Ct. App. 1983).

Skid Marks

Careful measurements of all skid marks at the scene are essential.* Before measuring them, the investigator should ensure that the skid marks were laid down in the collision in question. To avoid measuring the wrong marks, it is best to have someone who can definitely identify the marks—the client, a witness, or an ambulance driver—at the scene for the investigation. Of course, this also applies for measuring gouges, scrapes, and other physical damage at the accident site. Formulas can be used to determine the minimum speed of the vehicle before the driver applied the brakes.

Straight-skid speed formula. Often a vehicle traveling at a high rate of speed leaves only a few feet of skid marks because the brakes were not applied until the instant before impact. In those instances, determining the speed from skid marks may not be possible. But where skid marks were laid down over a long distance, the straight-skid speed formula may reveal that the colliding vehicle was traveling at excessive speed.

Yaw mark formula. A yaw mark is left on a road surface by the sideward motion of a tire when the driver turned the wheel sharply, usually to avoid a collision or to take a curve at excessive speed. A yaw mark will reveal

---

*J. Baker, *Traffic Accident Investigation Manual* 216–27 (1975).

the speed at the time the vehicle made the mark. A yaw mark should not be confused with a skid mark. It is a scuff mark made while the tire is rotating. It is easily identified by striations left on the roadway by the tire sidewall.

Flip-vault formula. If an object was thrown from either vehicle because of the impact, the investigator can calculate the minimum speed of the colliding vehicle if the exact point of impact of the vehicles and the exact point where the item first contacted the ground are known. The calculation is done using the flip-vault formula. Therefore, when examining the scene, the investigator should look for anything that may have been thrown from either vehicle.

For example, if a toolbox was thrown from the back of a truck and it can be determined exactly where it hit the ground, applying the flip-vault formula can determine the speed of the colliding vehicle at impact. In one case, a screwdriver with the driver's name taped to the handle was thrown from the colliding vehicle, and the screwdriver stuck blade-first into the ground many feet away from where the vehicles collided. The investigator applied the flip-vault formula to determine speed.

Fall formula. Investigators can use the fall formula to determine the speed of a vehicle that ran off an embankment. The investigator must measure the horizontal distance that the vehicle traveled before hitting the ground and then measure the vertical distance that the vehicle dropped. This formula can be helpful in proving whether a vehicle that went off an embankment was speeding.

Drag Factor

Investigators cannot determine speed from skid marks or yaw marks unless they know the drag factor of the roadway. The drag factor is the coefficient-of-friction, plus or minus grade. It is that percentage of the weight of an object that is required to push or pull it along a surface. The grade takes into account whether or not the object was going uphill or downhill.

To determine speed from skid marks, investigators must measure the drag factor accurately. Many books and other publications give drag-factor ranges for dry concrete, wet concrete, dry asphalt, wet asphalt, gravel, and ice.[‡] These ranges are best used only to get a general idea of what

might be expected for each surface. The drag factor can vary greatly, even on the same roadway. Speed from skid marks or a yaw mark can only be determined by conducting a drag-factor test at the specific point where the marks were made. Just as important, the test must be conducted in the same direction that the vehicle was traveling to take into account the plus or minus grade.

Measurements and Scale Drawings

In examining a collision scene, the investigator should take all measurements relative to a fixed reference point located close to the point of impact like a telephone pole or a corner of a building. The best method is to use a north-south, east-west grid and locate each distance measured north, south, east, or west of the reference point. Using this method, investigators can make an infinite number of measurements and plot each point on a scale drawing of the scene. Triangulation could also be used in measuring a scene, but it requires many times the number of measurements and is much more time-consuming. However, where the roadway is curved, roadway edges are uneven, or an object some distance off the roadway must be pinpointed, triangulation is the only method that will work. The grid method is simplest for most situations.

Besides the obvious distances that must be measured—such as the width of each roadway and the location of all traffic signs—the exact locations of any buildings or obstructions to clear view between the vehicles should be precisely determined.

A 1:20 scale is one scale to use for drawings in almost all these cases. The drawing helps in performing a time and distance analysis, as well as in seeing the entire collision process on paper. Along with minimum speed calculations, a scale drawing of the accident scene can be persuasive when presented to an insurance adjuster. If the case does not settle, a scale drawing can be used to prove a plaintiff's case at trial.

Time and Distance Analysis

Once the investigation is complete and a scale drawing made, the collision can be analyzed.

Time and distance must be taken into account in every collision or vehicle-pedestrian accident. Every moving mass is traveling at a certain speed that converts to either miles per hour or feet per second. To determine the feet per second a vehicle was traveling, multiply miles per hour times 1.47. If you convert miles per hour to feet per second, you can work backward from the point of impact and place the vehicles at the various points on the scale drawing for

---

[‡]L. Fricke, *Traffic Accident Reconstruction* 62–14 (1990); "How to Use the Traffic Template and Calculator," Traffic Institute, Northwestern University, at 19 (1984); R. Rivers, *Traffic Accident Investigators' Handbook* 157 (1980).

each second or even one-tenth of a second before the collision occurred. With the scale drawing and the locations of each vehicle at different intervals before impact, you can see the view each driver had of the scene and of each other, determine to what extent speed of each driver was a factor, and determine what action or actions could have been taken by either driver to avoid a collision.

Of course, the miles-per-hour figure may come from the testimony of the driver. In many instances, a defendant driver will say in deposition that the vehicle was going at a slower rate of speed than it actually was. The statement may hurt the defense because at the lower speed the defendant would have had more time to see plaintiff's vehicle and come to a stop or turn in order to avoid a collision.

Time and distance can also be used to refute contributory negligence on the part of the plaintiff. For example, where the defendant pulled out in front of the plaintiff or made a left turn into the plaintiff's path, time and distance calculations can be used to show that the legal speed at which the plaintiff was traveling did not allow stopping before colliding with the defendant. In many instances, taking into account the judicially accepted three-quarters-of-a-second reaction time will show that the plaintiff did not even have time to apply the brakes.

A time and distance analysis is especially helpful in pedestrian cases. Pedestrians have a normal walking speed of about three miles per hour. At this speed it takes several seconds to walk just a few steps. It can usually be shown that in those several seconds the driver had more than ample time to avoid striking the pedestrian.

The flip-vault formula can also be applied in pedestrian cases. If the point of impact and the point where a pedestrian hit the ground after impact are known, the speed of the striking vehicle can be determined. Often, doing a time and distance analysis and applying the flip-vault formula will clearly demonstrate a driver's fault.

Determining Negligence (See Examples on page 434.)

In Example 1, the driver(s) was traveling at a speed that was safe for the circumstances (an uncontrolled intersection ahead with a view obstruction on the right). The driver looked to the right and as soon as an approaching vehicle (T) was observed, applied the brakes and yielded the right-of-way.

In Example 2, the driver was traveling at a speed too great for existing conditions. At 35 miles per hour, even though the driver maintained a proper lookout and saw the approaching vehicle, he could not stop in time to avoid colliding with it.

In Example 3, the driver was traveling at a safe speed but was not looking to see if a vehicle was approaching from the right. By the time she saw the approaching vehicle, it was too late. Failure to keep a proper lookout was the cause of the collision.

In Example 4, the driver was traveling at a speed that was safe for conditions and kept a proper lookout. However, he chose the wrong evasive tactic. The driver tried to turn left in front of the approaching vehicle rather than apply the brakes and yield the right-of-way to the vehicle.

In Example 5, the driver was traveling at a safe speed, kept a proper lookout, but did nothing to avoid the collision. She simply failed to apply the brakes.

Example 6 shows a combination of errors. The driver was traveling at a greater speed than existing conditions permitted and failed to keep a proper lookout.

A similar analysis on your scale drawing will clearly illustrate to an insurance adjuster, a defense lawyer, and—if those two are hardheaded—a jury, precisely what the defendant did wrong. After seeing and understanding this type of accident analysis, jurors are less likely to fall for the defendant who testifies, "I don't know where he came from. He just came out of nowhere."

What about a rear-end collision? Where the rear-ended vehicle is stopped, the colliding driver may have been negligent in speed, lookout, or brakes application. But what about a rear-end collision that occurs as two cars are traveling down a roadway at about the same speed and the first car has to stop for some unexpected reason?

Alleging that speed caused the collision is faulty, because the first driver was traveling at the same rate of speed as the second. If the second driver testifies that the instant he saw the first driver's brake lights come on he slammed on his brakes, he is probably telling the truth. Usually this type of rear-end collision is not the result of negligent speed, lookout, or brakes application. It is the result of following too closely.

Analysis Works

Accident analysis really works, but it will not work unless law offices put their best efforts into it. If they ensure that a proper investigation is done and perform an accident analysis in each case, the results will be rewarding.

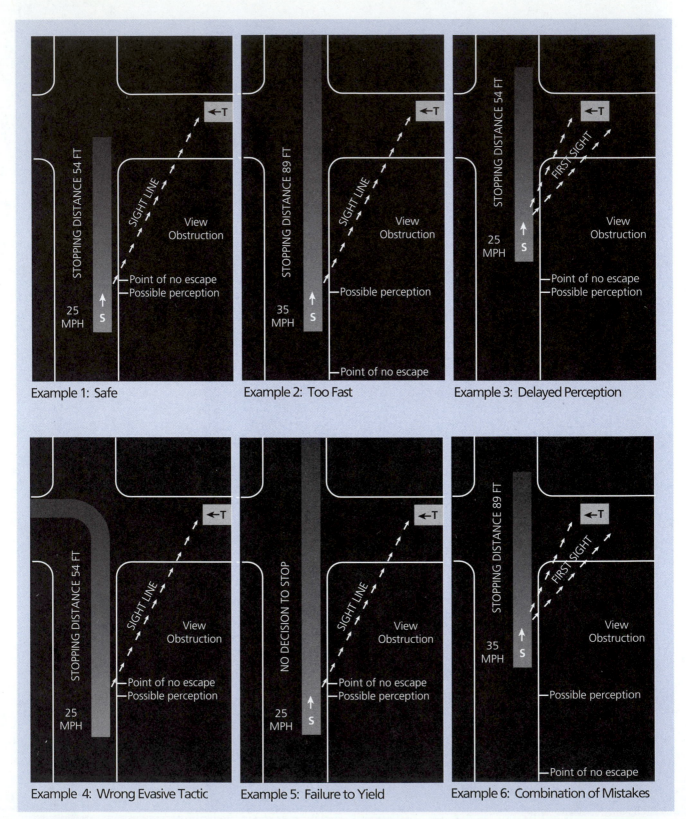

Example 1: Safe

Example 2: Too Fast

Example 3: Delayed Perception

Example 4: Wrong Evasive Tactic

Example 5: Failure to Yield

Example 6: Combination of Mistakes

Assignment 9.1

Which of the following statements do you agree or disagree with? Why? How would you modify the statements you disagree with to reflect your own view?

(a) Investigation is a separate profession.

(b) There is a great difference between investigation conducted by the police and that conducted by a paralegal working for a law office.

(c) An investigator is an advocate.

(d) It is impossible for the investigator to keep from showing his or her own personal biases while in the field investigating.

(e) There is often a need for a separate investigation to verify the work of another investigation.

(f) A good investigator will probably be unable to describe why he or she is effective. There are too many intangibles involved.

(g) It is a good idea for an investigator to specialize in one area of the law, such as automobile negligence cases.

(h) If someone is willing to talk to and cooperate with an investigator, there is reason to suspect that this person has a bias.

Assignment 9.2

If you were Tom in each of the following situations, what specific things would you do to deal with the situation?

(a) On September 1, Tom decides that he wants to enter a community college. School opens in five days. There are only two colleges that still allow time for registration. Both are about the same distance from his home, and he can afford both. Tom's problem is that he doesn't know enough about either college to make a decision. He works full-time from 9 to 6 and *must* continue to work right up to the first day of school in order to be able to finance his education.

(b) Tom teaches a second-grade class. It is the end of the school day on Friday and the bus is in front of the school ready to take his class home. If the students are not out in time for the bus, it will leave without them. It is 2:50 P.M., and the bus is scheduled to leave at 3:05 P.M. Tom discovers that his briefcase is missing from the top of his desk.

(c) Tom is the father of two teenagers, Ed and Bill. He comes home one day and finds a small package of marijuana in the front hall. He immediately suspects that Ed or Bill left it there. He turns around and goes out to look for them.

(d) Tom's son, Bill, has been accused of using abusive language in front of his teacher. Tom calls the teacher, who refuses to talk about it. The teacher refers Tom to the principal. The principal refuses to talk about it and refers Tom to the assistant superintendent at the central office.

(e) Tom's sister is ill. She received a letter from a local merchant where she often buys goods on credit. The letter informs her that she owes $122.00 and that unless she pays within a week "legal proceedings will be instituted" against her. She calls Tom and tells him that she paid the bill by sending $122.00 in cash last week. She asks Tom to help her.

(f) Tom works for a local legal service office. The office has a client who wants to sue her landlord because the kitchen roof is falling down. Tom is assigned to the case.

(g) Sam owes Tom $50,000. When Tom asks for his money, Sam tells him that he is broke. Tom suspects differently.

(h) Tom's uncle once lived in Boston. After spending two years in the army, he started traveling across the country; he has not been heard from for five years. Tom wants to locate his uncle.

(i) A welfare department has told a client that it is going to terminate public assistance because the client's boyfriend is supporting her and her family. The client denies this. Tom is assigned to the case.

(j) A client has been to the office seeking help in obtaining custody of his children from their mother (to whom he is not married). He claims that she is not taking proper care of the children. Tom is assigned to the case.

🏛 *A s s i g n m e n t   9 . 3*

How would you find the following information?

(a) The average life span of a lobster.

(b) The maiden name of the wife of the first governor in your state's history.

(c) The assessed property tax value of the tallest commercial building in your city in 1980.

(d) The number of vehicles using diesel fuel that drove in or through the state last month.

(e) The salary of the air traffic controller with the most seniority on duty on the day last year when the nearest airport experienced the largest rainfall of the year.

Note on the Need for a License

In some states, investigators must be licensed. What about paralegals who are assigned investigation tasks by their supervising attorneys? A literal reading of the licensing statute might lead to the conclusion that such paralegals must be licensed along with traditional, self-employed private investigators. Often, however, the legislature will make an exception to the licensing requirement for employees of attorneys who engage in investigation under the attorney's supervision. Paralegal associations have been successful in seeking these exemptions for paralegals. The main opposition to such exemptions has come from organizations of private investigators, who allegedly seek to impose roadblocks to paralegal investigation in order to secure more business for themselves.

Section I
EVIDENCE AND INVESTIGATION

There is a close relationship between investigation and the law of evidence. One of the aims of investigation is to uncover and verify facts that will eventually be *admissible* in court. Admissibility is determined by the law of evidence. When attorneys are negotiating a case to try to reach a settlement in order to avoid a trial, they frequently talk (and argue) about the admissibility of the facts in the event that a trial does occur.

Evidence in General

Evidence is anything used to prove or disprove a fact.

Admissible evidence is evidence that the judge will permit the jury to consider. Admissible evidence does not mean that the evidence is true. It simply means that there are no valid objections to keep the evidence out. The jury is free to conclude that it does not believe the evidence that the judge ruled admissible.

Direct evidence is evidence (usually from personal observation or knowledge) that tends to establish a fact (or to disprove a fact) without the need for an inference.

Circumstantial evidence is evidence of one fact from which another fact can be inferred.

Example: The police officer says, "I saw skid marks at the scene of the accident." This statement is:

Direct evidence	● that the police officer spoke these words.
	● that skid marks were at the scene of the accident.
Circumstantial evidence	● that the driver of the car was speeding (this is the inference that can be drawn from the officer's statement).

Examples of *direct* evidence that someone was speeding would be an admission by the driver that he or she was speeding, radar results, testimony of people who saw the car being driven, etc.

Investigation Guideline:
Direct evidence is preferred over circumstantial, although both kinds of evidence may be admissible. It is important that you are able to identify the inference in the circumstantial evidence. Then try to find direct evidence of whatever was inferred.

Relevance

Relevant evidence is evidence that reasonably tends to make the existence of a fact more probable or less probable than it would be without that evidence. Relevancy is a very broad concept. It simply means that the evidence *may* be helpful in determining the truth or falsity of a fact involved in a trial. The test of relevancy is common sense and logic. If, for example, you want to know whether a walkway is dangerous, it is relevant that people have slipped on this walkway in the immediate past. Prior accidents under the same conditions make it more reasonable for someone to conclude that there is danger.

All relevant evidence is not necessarily admissible evidence, however. It would be highly relevant, for example, to know that the defendant told his attorney he was driving 80 m.p.h. at the time of the accident, yet the attorney-client privilege would make such a statement inadmissible. Also, relevant evidence is not necessarily conclusive evidence. The jury will usually be free to reject relevant evidence it does not believe. Relevancy is simply a *tendency* of evidence to establish or disestablish a fact. It may be a very weak tendency. Prior accidents may be relevant to show danger, but the jury may still conclude, in the light of all the evidence, that there was no danger.

Investigation Guideline:
Let common sense be your main guide in pursuing relevant evidence. So long as there is some logical connection between the fact you are pursuing and a fact that must be established at trial, you are on the right track.

🏛 *A s s i g n m e n t   9 . 4*

Examine the following four situations. Discuss the relevance of each item of evidence being introduced.

(a) Mrs. Phillips is being sued by a department store for the cost of a gas refrigerator. Mrs. Phillips claims that she never ordered and never received a refrigerator from the store.

The attorney for Mrs. Phillips wants to introduce two letters: (1) a letter from Mrs. Phillips's landlord stating that her kitchen is not equipped to handle gas appliances and (2) a letter from another merchant stating that Mrs. Phillips bought an electric refrigerator from him a year ago.

(b) Phil Smith has been charged with burglary in Detroit on December 16, 1996. His attorney tries to introduce testimony into evidence that on December 7, 8, 11, 15, and 22, 1996, the defendant was in Florida.

(c) Al Neuman is suing Sam Snow for negligence in operating his motor vehicle. Al's attorney tries to introduce into evidence the fact that Snow currently has pending against him four other automobile negligence cases in other courts.

(d) Jim is on trial for the rape of Sandra. Jim's attorney wants to introduce into evidence (1) the fact that Sandra subscribes to *Cosmopolitan* magazine, (2) the fact that Sandra is a member of AA, and (3) the fact that Sandra is the mother of Jim's child, who was born three years ago when they were dating. They separated in bitterness five months after the birth and never married.

Competence of Witnesses

A witness is competent to testify if the witness:

- understands the obligation to tell the truth.
- has the ability to communicate.
- has knowledge of the topic of his or her testimony.

Children or mentally ill persons are not automatically disqualified. They are competent to testify if the judge is satisfied that the above criteria are met.

The competence of a witness must be carefully distinguished from the credibility of the witness. **Competency** is simply a ticket into the trial. **Credibility** goes to the *weight* of the evidence. This weight is assessed by the trier of fact—usually the jury. Competence goes to whether that witness will be allowed to testify at all, a decision made by the judge. The jury may decide that everything said by a competent witness has little weight and therefore is unworthy of belief.

Lay Opinion Evidence

An **opinion** is an inference from a fact. For example, after you watch George stagger down the street and smell alcohol on his breath, you come to the conclusion that he is drunk. The conclusion is the inference. The facts are the observation of staggering and the smell of alcohol on his breath. Technically, a lay witness should not give opinion evidence. He or she must state the facts and let the trier of fact form the opinions. (Under certain circumstances, expert witnesses *are* allowed to give opinions on technical subjects not within the understanding of the average layperson.) The problem with the lay opinion rule, however, is that it is sometimes difficult to express oneself without using opinions, as when a witness says it was a sunny day or the noise was loud. Courts are therefore lenient in permitting opinion testimony by lay witnesses when the witness is talking from his or her own observations and it would be awkward for the witness not to express the opinion. If people regularly use opinions when discussing the topic in question, it will be permitted.

Investigation Guideline:
Know when a person is stating an opinion. Even though an opinion may be admissible, you should assume that it will *not* be admissible. Pursue all of the underlying facts that support

the inference in the opinion. In the event that the person is not allowed to testify by using the opinion, be prepared by having admissible evidence of the underlying facts the person relied on for the opinion.

🏛 *A s s i g n m e n t   9 . 5*

Make a list of the questions that you would ask in order to uncover the underlying facts that formed the basis of the following opinions:

(a) He was insane.

(b) She couldn't see.

(c) It was cold out.

(d) He was traveling very fast.

Hearsay

Hearsay is testimony in court, or written evidence, of a statement made out of court when the statement is offered to show the truth of matters asserted in the statement and thus relies for its value on the credibility of the out-of-court asserter.[11] If evidence is hearsay, it is inadmissible unless one of the exceptions to the hearsay rule applies.

Example:

Sam, a witness in court, says, "Fred told me on Elm Street that he was speeding."

Note the four conditions for the presence of hearsay:

Testimony in court	The witness, Sam, is on the stand.
Statement made out of court	The statement by Fred was made on Elm Street, not in court.
Offered to assert the truth of the matter in the statement	Assume that the purpose of the attorney questioning Sam is to show that Fred was speeding—that is, that the statement is true.
The value of the statement depends on the credibility of the out-of-court asserter	Fred is the out-of-court asserter. The value of the statement depends on how believable or credible *Fred* is.

If the statement is not offered to prove the truth of the matters asserted in the statement, it is not hearsay. Suppose, for example, that the attorney wants to prove that Fred was alive immediately after the accident—that death was not instantaneous. The above statement would be admitted to prove that Fred actually said something, in other words, that Fred was alive enough to make a statement. If the testimony of the witness is offered to prove simply that the words were spoken by Fred rather than to prove that Fred was speeding, then the statement is not hearsay. The testimony that "Fred told me on Elm Street that he was speeding" would therefore be admissible. The jury would have to be cautioned to examine the testimony for the limited purpose for which it is offered and not to consider it evidence that Fred was speeding.

Conduct intended as a substitute for words can also be hearsay. For example, the witness is asked, "What did Fred say when you asked him if he was speeding?" The witness

---

[11]E. Cleary, ed., McCormick's *Handbook of the Law of Evidence* 584 (1972).

answers, "He nodded his head yes." This testimony is hearsay if it is offered to prove that Fred was speeding. Conduct—nodding the head—was intended as a substitute for words.

Investigation Guideline:
Know when hearsay exists so that you can try to find alternative, nonhearsay evidence to prove the truth of the assertions made in the hearsay.

🏛 *A s s i g n m e n t   9 . 6*

Is hearsay evidence involved in the following situations? Examine the four conditions of hearsay in each.

(a) Tom is suing Jim for negligence. On the witness stand, Tom says, "Jim was speeding at the time he hit me."

(b) Tom is suing Jim for negligence. While Tom is on the stand, his attorney introduces into evidence a mechanic's bill showing that the repair of the car cost $178.

(c) Mary and George were passengers in Tom's car at the time of the collision with Jim. George testifies that just before the collision, Mary shouted, "Look out for that car going through the red light!"

(d) He told me he was God.

There are a number of exceptions to the hearsay rule that have the effect of making evidence admissible even though it fulfills all the conditions of hearsay. Here are some examples:

1. *Admission by Party-Opponent.* An **admission by a party-opponent** is an earlier statement by a party that is now offered in court by an opponent. Example: Mary sues Sam for negligence. While Mary is presenting her case, she introduces a statement that Sam made to Paul in which Sam said, "I screwed up big time." This statement is admissible as an admission by a party-opponent—Sam. (Note, however, that many states and the federal rules declare such statements by party-opponents to be admissible because they are nonhearsay rather than as an exception to the hearsay rule.)

2. *Statement against Self-Interest.* A **statement against self-interest** is an out-of-court statement, made by a nonparty (who is now unavailable as a witness), that was against the financial interest of the declarant at the time it was made. Example: A nonparty tells a friend at a ball game, "I still owe the bank the money."

3. *Dying Declaration.* A **dying declaration** is an out-of-court statement concerning the causes or circumstances of death made by a person whose death is imminent. Example: Tom dies two minutes after he was hit over the head. Seconds before he dies, he says, "Linda did it." Some courts limit the dying-declaration exception to criminal cases. Other states would also allow it to be used in a civil case, such as in a civil battery or wrongful death case against Linda.

4. *Excited Utterance.* An **excited utterance** is an out-of-court statement relating to a startling event or condition made while the declarant was under the stress of excitement caused by the event or condition. Example: Fred says, "I heard John say, 'Oh my God, the truck just hit a child.' "

5. *Statement of Present Sense Impression.* A **statement of present sense impression** is an out-of-court statement describing or explaining an event or condition made while the declarant was perceiving the event or condition or immediately thereafter. Example: Janice says, "As the car turned the corner, a bystander turned to me and said, 'That car will never make it.' "

6. *Statement of Existing Physical or Mental Condition.* A **statement of existing physical or mental condition** is an out-of-court statement of a then-existing physical or mental condition. Example: Bob says, "A second before Sheila fell, she said to me, 'I feel dizzy.' "

7. *Declaration of State of Mind.* A **declaration of state of mind** is an out-of-court statement made about the person's present state of mind. Example: Len says, "The manager said she knew about the broken railing and would try to fix it."

8. *Business Record.* A **business record** is a record kept in the course of a regularly conducted business activity. This also applies to nonprofit organizations such as universities. Example: A hospital record containing a description of a patient's condition upon entering the emergency room.

🏛 *A s s i g n m e n t 9 . 7*

Smith is being sued for assaulting Jones, who later died. Smith is on the stand when the following exchange occurs.

Counsel for Smith: "Did you strike the decedent, Jones?"
Smith: "Yes."
Counsel for Smith: "Did Jones say anything to you before you struck him?"
Smith: "Yes, he told me that he was going to kill me."
Counsel for Jones's estate: "Objection, your honor, on the grounds of hearsay. Smith cannot give testimony on what the decedent said since the decedent is obviously not subject to cross-examination."

(a) Is Jones's statement hearsay?
(b) If so, is it admissible?

Privilege

A **privilege** in the law of evidence is the right to refuse to testify or the right to prevent someone else from testifying on a matter.

1. *Privilege against Self-Incrimination.* Under the **privilege against self-incrimination,** an accused person cannot be compelled to testify in a criminal proceeding or to answer questions that directly or indirectly connect the accused to the commission of a crime, i.e., incriminating questions.

2. *Attorney-Client Privilege.* Under the **attorney-client privilege,** a client and an attorney can refuse to disclose any communications between them whose purpose was to facilitate the provision of legal services for that client. The attorney cannot disclose the communication without the permission of the client.

3. *Doctor-Patient Privilege.* Under the **doctor-patient privilege,** a patient and doctor can refuse to disclose any confidential (private) communications between them that relate to medical care. The doctor cannot disclose the communication without the permission of the patient.

4. *Clergy-Penitent Privilege.* Under the **clergy-penitent privilege,** a penitent and a member of the clergy can refuse to disclose any confidential (private) communications between them that relate to spiritual counseling or consultation. The minister, priest, or rabbi cannot disclose the communication without the permission of the penitent.

5. *Marital Communications.* A husband and wife can refuse to disclose confidential (private) communications between them during the marriage. One spouse can also prevent the other from making such disclosures. Both spouses must agree to the disclosure. The **marital communications privilege** does not apply, however, to litigation between spouses, e.g., divorce litigation.

6. *Government Information.* Some information collected by the government about citizens is confidential and privileged. Examples include adoption records and tax records. The privilege would not prevent use of the information to prosecute the citizen in connection with the citizen's duty to provide accurate information. It would, however, prevent third parties from gaining access to the confidential information.

Investigation Guideline:

When a privilege applies, look for alternative, nonprivileged sources of obtaining the information protected by the privilege.

Best Evidence Rule

To prove the contents of a private (nonofficial) writing, you should produce the original writing unless it is unavailable through no fault of the person now seeking to introduce a copy of the original, e.g., it was destroyed in a storm.

Authentication

Authentication is evidence that a writing (or other physical item) is genuine and that it is what it purports to be—for example, the testimony of witnesses who saw the document being prepared.

Parol Evidence Rule

Oral evidence cannot be introduced to alter or contradict the contents of a written document if the parties intended the written document to be a complete statement of the agreement.

Section J
Taking a Witness Statement

There are four major kinds of **witness statements**:

1. Handwritten statement
2. Recorded statement in question-and-answer format (on audio or video tape)
3. Responses to a questionnaire that is mailed to the witness to answer
4. A statement taken in question-and-answer format with court reporters

The most common kind of statement is the first, which we shall consider here.

In a handwritten statement, the investigator writes down what the witness says, or the witness writes out the statement himself or herself. There is no formal structure to which the written statement must conform. The major requirements for the statement are clarity and accuracy.

Here is how one paralegal explains the process to the witness:

"What I'd like to do today is take a written statement from you. After we talk about what you recall about the accident, I'd like to write it down, then have you review it, verifying with your signature that this statement is indeed what you have said about the matter."[12]

From whom should you take a witness statement? "Many people feel that a witness can only be someone who has actually viewed the event or occurrence. Obviously, this is not true. Quite often the so-called **occurrence witness** cannot offer as significant a contribution in testimony as the **pre-occurrence witness** or **post-occurrence witness.** An alert, intelligent post-occurrence witness can shed a great deal of light upon the matter in dispute by testifying as to physical facts such as positions of cars or skid marks. He could also testify as to statements made immediately after the occurrence by a party to the lawsuit. The pre-occurrence witness can testify as to the condition of premises or machinery immediately before the accident. Therefore, the paralegal should be interested in interviewing witnesses who can set the stage for the scene of the accident, in addition to those who actually witnessed the occurrence."[13]

Suppose that a person says he or she knows nothing. Should a "witness" statement be taken of this person? Some recommend that you *should* take a "negative statement" to discourage this person from coming back later to claim "remembered information." Here's an example of such a statement:

"I was not at xxx address on xxx date and did not see a traffic accident at the time. I did not see anything happen at xxx location. I did not hear anything. I talked to no one about this accident nor did I hear anyone say anything about it."[14]

A written statement should begin by identifying (1) the witness (name, address, place of work, names of relatives, and other identifying data that may be helpful in locating the witness later); (2) the date and place of the taking of the statement; and (3) the name of the person to whom the statement is being made. See the example of a witness statement in Exhibit 9.9.

Then comes the body of the statement, in which the witness provides information about the event or occurrence in question (an accident that was observed, what the witness did

---

Exhibit 9.9   Witness Statement

Statement of Patricia Wood

I am Patricia Wood. I am 42 years old and live at 3416 34th Street, N.W., Nashua, New Hampshire 03060. I work at the Deming Chemical Plant at Region Circle, Nashua. My home phone is 966-3954. My work phone is 297-9700 X301. I am married to John Wood. We have two children, Jessica (fourteen years old) and Gabriel (eleven years old). I am making this statement to Rose Thompson, a paralegal at Fields, Smith and Farrell. This statement is being given on March 13, 1996 at my home, 3416 34th Street, NW.

On February 15, 1996, I was standing on the corner of . . . .

---

[12]K. Wilkoff, *Writing Witness Statements That Win Cases,* 12 Legal Assistant Today 51, 52 (September/October 1994).

[13]Yetta Blair, *Interviewing Witnesses and Securing Their Signed Written Statements,* 14 Points and Authorities 10 (San Joaquin Ass'n of Legal Assistants, May 1992).

[14]Kathryn Andrews, *Interviews and Statements* 10 (Oregon Legal Assistant Ass'n, October 1988).

and saw just before a fire, where the witness was on a certain date, etc.). Be sure that the statement includes facts relevant to the ability of the witness to observe, e.g., amount of light available, weather conditions, obstructions. This lends credibility to the statement. It is often useful to have the witness present the facts in chronological order, particularly when many facts are involved in the statement.

At the end of the statement, the witness should say that he or she is making the statement of his or her own free will, without any pressure or coercion from anyone. The witness then signs the statement. The signature goes on the last page. Each of the other pages is also signed or initialed. If others have watched the witness make and sign the statement, they should also sign an **attestation clause,** which simply states that they observed the witness sign the statement.

Before the witness signs, he or she should read the entire statement and make any corrections that need to be made. Each correction should be initialed by the witness. Each page should be numbered with the total number of pages indicated each time. For example, if there are four pages, the page numbers would be "1 of 4," "2 of 4," "3 of 4," and "4 of 4." Each of these page numbers should be initialed and dated by the witness. The investigator should not try to correct any spelling or grammatical mistakes made by the witness. The statement should exist exactly as the witness spoke or wrote it. Just before the signature of the witness at the end of the statement, the witness should say (in writing), "I have read all _____ pages of this statement, and the facts within it are accurate to the best of my knowledge." The witness should also write the date next to his or her signature.

Investigators sometimes use various tricks of the trade to achieve a desired effect. For example, if the investigator is writing out the statement as the witness speaks, the investigator may *intentionally* make an error of fact. When the witness reads over the statement, the investigator makes sure that the witness catches the error and initials the correction. This becomes added evidence that the witness carefully read the statement. The witness might later try to claim that he or she did not read the statement. The initialed correction helps rebut this position.

Another trick of the trade is to try to make sure that every page of the witness statement (other than the last) ends in the middle of a sentence or somewhere before the period. This is to rebut a later allegation that someone improperly added pages to the witness statement after it was signed. The allegation is somewhat difficult to support if the bottom line of one page contains a sentence that is continued at the top of the next page.

Witness statements are generally not admitted into evidence at the trial. They might be admissible to help the attorney demonstrate that the pretrial statement of the witness is inconsistent with the testimony of this witness during the trial itself. The main value of witness statements is thoroughness and accuracy in case preparation. Trials can occur years after the events that led to litigation. Witnesses may disappear or forget. Witness statements taken soon after the event can sometimes be helpful in tracking down witnesses and in helping them recall the details of the event.

🏛 *A s s i g n m e n t   9 . 8*

Select any member of the class and take a witness statement from this person. The statement should concern an accident of any kind (e.g., a minor mishap at home, a highway collision) in which the witness was a participant or an observer. (The witness, however, should not be a party to any litigation growing out of the accident.) You write out the statement from what the witness says in response to your questions. Do not submit a statement handwritten by the witness except for his or her signature, initials, etc. Assume that you (the investigator-paralegal) work for the law firm of Davis and Davis, which represents someone else involved in the accident.

Section K
THE SETTLEMENT WORK-UP

One of the end products of investigation is the **settlement work-up,** which is a summary of the major facts obtained through investigation, client interviewing, answers to interrogatories, deposition testimony, etc. The work-up, in one form or another, is used in negotiation with the other side or with the other side's liability insurance company in an effort to obtain a favorable settlement in lieu of trial.

Exhibit 9.10 shows a memo containing data for a proposed settlement work-up.[15] Note its precision and attention to detail. Excellent FP (fact particularization, see Exhibit 8.5 in chapter 8) had to be used as the basis of this report.

Exhibit 9.10   Settlement Work-Up

Interoffice Memorandum

To: Mary Jones, Esq.
From: Katherine Webb, Paralegal
Date: October 12, 1975
Re: Joseph Smith vs. Dan Lamb
    Case Summary—Settlement Work-Up

I. Facts of Accident:
The accident occurred on September 6, 1973, in Orange, California. Joseph Smith was driving westbound on Chapman Avenue, stopped to make a left turn into a parking lot, and was rear-ended by the one-half-ton panel truck driven by Dan Lamb.

The defendant driver, Mr. Lamb, was cited for violation of Vehicle Code Sections 21703 and 22350, following too close, and at an unsafe speed for conditions.

II. Injuries:
Severe cervical and lumbar sprain, superimposed over pre-existing, albeit asymptomatic, spondylolisthesis of pars inter-articulus at L5-S1, with possible herniated nucleus pulposus either at or about the level of the spondylolisthesis; and contusion of right knee.

Please see attached medical reports for further details.

III. Medical Treatment:
Mr. Smith felt an almost immediate onset of pain in his head, neck, back, and right knee after the accident and believes that he may have lost consciousness momentarily. He was assisted from his car and taken by ambulance to the St. Joseph Hospital emergency room, where he was initially seen by his regular internist, Raymond Ross, M.D.

Dr. Ross obtained orthopedic consultation with Brian A. Ewald, M.D., who reviewed the multiple X-rays taken in the emergency room and found them negative for fracture. Lumbar spine X-rays did reveal evidence of a spondylolisthesis

---

[15]Prepared by Katherine Webb, Legal Assistant at Cartwright, Sucherman, Slobodin & Fowler, Inc., San Francisco, California.

Exhibit 9.10 Settlement Work-Up—continued

defect at the pars interarticulus of L5, but this was not felt to represent acute injury. Dr. Ewald had Mr. Smith admitted to St. Joseph Hospital on the same day for further evaluation and observation.

On admission to the hospital, Mr. Smith was placed on complete bed rest, with a cervical collar and medication for pain. On September 10, neurological consultation was obtained with Michael H. Sukoff, M.D., who, although he did not find any significant objective neurological abnormality, felt that there might be a herniated disc at L4-L5, with possible contusion of the nerve roots.

Drs. Ewald and Sukoff followed Mr. Smith's progress throughout the remainder of his hospitalization. He was continued on bed rest, physiotherapy, and medication, and fitted with a lumbosacral support. He was ultimately ambulated with crutches and was discharged from the hospital on September 25, 1973, with instructions to continue to rest and wear his cervical collar and back brace.

On discharge from the hospital, Mr. Smith was taken by ambulance to the Sky Palm Motel in Orange, where his wife and children had been staying during his hospitalization. Arrangements were made for home physiotherapy and rental of a hospital bed, and Mr. Smith was taken by ambulance on the following day to his residence at the Riviera Country Club in Pacific Palisades.

After returning home, Mr. Smith continued to suffer from headaches, neck pain, and severe pain in his lower back, with some radiation into both legs, especially the right. He was totally confined to bed for at least two months following the accident, where he was cared for by his wife. Daily physical therapy was administered by Beatrice Tasker, R.P.T.

Mr. Smith continued to receive periodic outpatient care with Dr. Ewald. By the end of December 1973, Mr. Smith was able to discontinue the use of his cervical collar and was able to walk, with difficulty, without crutches. At the time of his office visit with Dr. Ewald on December 21, he was noted to be having moderate neck discomfort, with increasingly severe low back pain. At the time, Dr. Ewald placed Mr. Smith on a gradually increasing set of Williams exercises and advised him to begin swimming as much as possible.

Mr. Smith continued to be followed periodically by Dr. Ewald through March 1974, with gradual improvement noted. However, Mr. Smith continued to spend the majority of his time confined to his home and often to bed, using a cane whenever he went out. In addition, he suffered periodic severe flareups of low back pain, which would render him totally disabled and would necessitate total bed rest for several days at a time.

During this period of time, Mr. Smith also experienced headaches and blurred vision, for which Dr. Ewald referred him to Robert N. Dunphy, M.D. Dr. Dunphy advised that the symptoms were probably secondary to his other injuries and would most likely subside with time.

On April 1, 1974, Mr. Smith consulted Dr. Ewald with complaints of increased back pain following an automobile ride to San Diego. Dr. Ewald's examination at that time revealed bilateral lumbar muscle spasm, with markedly decreased range of motion. Due to his concern about the extremely prolonged lumbar symptoms, and suspecting a possible central herniated nucleus pulposus, Dr. Ewald recommended that Mr. Smith undergo lumbar myelography. This was performed on an inpatient basis at St. Joseph Hospital on April 4, 1974, and reported to be within normal limits.

Mr. Smith continued conservative treatment with Dr. Ewald through February 1974, following the prescribed program of rest, medication, exercise, and daily physiotherapy administered by his wife. He was able to graduate out of his lumbosacral support by approximately October 1974, resuming use of the garment when he experienced severe flareups of low back pain.

In his medical report dated January 2, 1975, Dr. Ewald stated that he expected a gradual resolution of lumbar symptomatology with time. However, in his subsequent report, dated January 10, 1975, Dr. Ewald noted that since his original report, Mr. Smith had suffered multiple repetitive episodes of low back pain, secondary to almost any increase of activity. At an office visit on February 25, Mr. Smith was reported to have localized his discomfort extremely well to the L5-S1 level, and range of motion was found to have decreased to approximately 75%. Since his examination in February, Dr. Ewald has discussed at length with both Mr. Smith and his wife the possibility of surgical intervention, consisting of lumbar stabilization (fusion) at the L5-S1 level, secondary to the spondylolisthesis present at that level. Dr. Ewald has advised them of the risks, complications, and alternatives with regard to consideration of surgical stabilization, noting that surgery would be followed by a 6-to-9-month period of rehabilitation, and further warning that even if the surgical procedure is carried out, there is no guarantee that Mr. Smith will be alleviated of all of his symptomatology.

As stated in Dr. Ewald's medical report dated March 10, 1975, Mr. Smith is himself beginning to lean toward definite consideration with regard to surgery, although he is presently continuing with conservative management.

Exhibit 9.10   Settlement Work-Up—continued

Dr. Ewald recommends that in the event Mr. Smith does choose to undergo surgery, a repeat myelogram should be performed in order to rule out, as much as possible, the presence of a herniated nucleus pulposus either above or at the level of the spondylolisthesis.

IV. Residual Complaints

Mr. Smith states that his neck injury has now largely resolved, although he does experience occasional neck pain and headaches. However, he continues to suffer from constant, severe pain in his low back, with some radiation of pain and numbness in the right leg.

Mr. Smith notes that his low back pain is worse with cold weather and aggravated by prolonged sitting, walking, driving, or nearly any form of activity. He finds that he must rest frequently and continues to follow a daily regimen of swimming, Williams exercises, pain medication, and physiotherapy administered by his wife. He has also resumed the use of his lumbosacral brace.

Mr. Smith was an extremely active person prior to the accident, accustomed to working 12 to 16 hours per day and engaging in active sports such as tennis. Since the accident, he has had to sell his business and restrict all activities to a minimum, because he has found that any increase in activity will trigger a flareup of low back pain so severe that he is totally incapacitated for several days at a time.

As stated by Dr. Ewald, Mr. Smith is now seriously considering the possibility of surgical stabilization, despite the risks and complications involved. He has always viewed surgery as a last resort but is now beginning to realize that it may be his only alternative in view of his prolonged pain and disability. However, he currently intends to delay any definite decision until after the summer, during which time he intends to increase his swimming activity and see if he can gain any relief from his symptomatology.

V. Specials

(Copies of supporting documentation attached hereto.)

A. Medical:

1. Southland Ambulance Service (9/6/73)	$ 37.00
2. St. Joseph Hospital (9/6–9/25/73)	2,046.29
3. Raymond R. Ross, M.D. (Emergency Room, 9/6/73)	25.00
4. Brian A. Ewald, M.D. (9/6/73–4/28/75)	604.00
5. Michael H. Sukoff, M.D. (9/10–9/22/75)	140.00
6. Wind Ambulance Service (9/25/73)	39.50
7. Wind Ambulance Service (9/26/73)	89.00
8. Beatrice Tasker, R.P.T. (9/21–10/22/73)	825.00
9. Abbey Rents (Rental of hospital bed and trapeze bar, 9/25–11/25/73)	222.00
10. Allied Medical & Surgical Co. (Purchase of cane, 1/10/73)	10.45
11. Rice Clinical Laboratories (2/1/74)	4.00
12. Robert N. Dunphy, M.D. (2/1–4/15/74)	95.00
13. St. Joseph Hospital (X-rays and lab tests, 2/9/74)	156.00
14. St. Joseph Hospital (Inpatient myelography, 4/23–4/24/74)	251.60
15. Medication	357.70
Total Medical Expenses	$4,902.54

B. Miscellaneous Family Expenses

(During plaintiff's hospitalization, 9/6–9/25/75.)

1. Sky Palm Motel (Lodging for wife and children)	$1,050.50
2. Taxicab (9/6/73)	2.45
Total Miscellaneous Expenses	$1,052.95

C. Wage Loss

At the time of the accident, Mr. Smith was employed as president and co-owner, with Mr. George Frost, of the Inter Science Institute, Inc., a medical laboratory in Los Angeles. As stated in the attached verification from Mr. Mamikunian, Mr. Smith was earning an annual salary of $48,000.00, plus automobile, expenses, and fringe benefits.

Exhibit 9.10   Settlement Work-Up—continued

In a telephone conversation with Mr. Frost on May 6, 1975, he advised me that the Inter Science Institute had grossed $512,000.00 in 1973 and $700,000.00 in 1974. He further confirmed that prior to the accident of September 6, 1973, both he and Mr. Frost had been approached on at least two to three different occasions by companies, including Revlon and a Canadian firm, offering substantial sums of money for purchase of the business. On the basis of the foregoing, both Mr. Smith and Mr. Frost place a conservative estimate of the value of the business at $2,000,000.00.

Due to injuries sustained in the subject accident, Mr. Smith was unable to return to work or perform the necessary executive and managerial functions required in his position as president and part owner of the business. As a result, on or about October 26, 1973, while still totally incapacitated by his injuries, Mr. Smith was forced to sell his 50% stock interest in the Inter Science Institute for a total sum of $300,000.00.

On the basis of the prior estimated value of the business at $2,000,000.00, *Mr. Smith sustained a loss of $700,000.00 in the sale of his one-half interest in Inter Science Institute, Inc., in addition to the loss of an annual salary of $48,000.00, plus automobile, expenses, and fringe benefits.*

Even if one were to assume that the sale of his interest in the business was reasonable value, Mr. Smith has sustained a loss in salary only in the sum of *$84,000.00* to date, based on an annual salary of $48,000.00 up to October 12, 1975.

🏛 **A s s i g n m e n t   9 . 9**

Assume that the settlement work-up in Exhibit 9.10 is not successful. The case must now go to trial. Prepare a report for the litigator of all the evidence that should be collected and considered for use at the trial.

(a) List all possible witnesses your side (representing Joseph Smith) might call and give a summary of what their testimony is likely to be.

(b) List all possible witnesses the other side (representing Dan Lamb) might call and give a summary of what their testimony is likely to be.

(c) List all possible physical evidence your side should consider using and give a summary of what each item might establish.

(d) List all possible physical evidence the other side is likely to consider using and give a summary of what each item might establish.

(e) What further facts do you think need to be investigated?

Chapter Summary

The goal of investigation is to obtain new facts and to verify facts already known by the office. It is a highly individualistic skill where determination, imagination, resourcefulness, and openness are critical. A good investigator has a healthy suspicion of preconceived notions of what the facts are when this might interfere with uncovering the unexpected. In the search for the facts, the investigator is concerned with truth in the context of the evidence that will be needed to establish that truth in court. But the standard that guides the search is not absolute truth or proof; the guideline of the investigator is to pursue whatever degree of evidence (large or small) is reasonably available.

People often have different perspectives on what did or did not happen, particularly in regard to emotionally charged events. When different versions of facts exist, the investigator must seek them out.

Competent investigation requires a knowledge of the standard sources of information; an ability to use the techniques of gaining access to records, and an ability to evaluate the trustworthiness of both testimonial and physical evidence.

Investigators must be aware of the image they project of themselves, be prepared for witnesses with differing levels of factual knowledge, be ready for witnesses who are unwilling to cooperate, and be able to gain the trust of witnesses.

The law of evidence is an important part of the investigator's arsenal. This should include an understanding of the following: admissible evidence, the distinction between direct evidence and circumstantial evidence, the nature of relevance, when a witness is competent to give testimony and to state an opinion, the nature of hearsay, and the major exceptions that allow hearsay to be admitted. Investigators need to understand the effect of the privilege against self-incrimination, the attorney-client privilege, the doctor-patient privilege, the clergy-penitent privilege, the privilege for marital communications, and the confidentiality of some government information. They must also understand the best evidence rule, the authentication of evidence, and the parol evidence rule.

Two important documents that are the products of competent investigation are a witness statement, which is taken to preserve the testimony of an important witness, and a settlement work-up, which is an advocacy document that compiles and organizes facts in an effort to encourage a favorable settlement.

KEY TERMS

legal investigation, 410
impeach, 412
discovery devices, 412
deposition, 412
interrogatories, 412
request for admission, 412
leading question, 416
evidence, 417
testimonial evidence, 417
tangible evidence, 417
Freedom of Information
   Act, 420
disinterested, 424
judgment creditor, 425
judgment debtor, 425

deep pocket, 426
admissible evidence, 436
direct evidence, 437
circumstantial evidence, 437
relevant evidence, 437
competency, 438
credibility, 438
opinion, 438
hearsay, 439
admission by party-
   opponent, 440
statement against self-
   interest, 440
dying declaration, 440
excited utterance, 440

statement of present sense
   impression, 441
statement of existing
   physical or mental
   condition, 441
declaration of state of
   mind, 441
business record, 441
privilege, 441
privilege against self-
   incrimination, 441
attorney-client
   privilege, 441
doctor-patient privilege, 441

clergy-penitent
   privilege, 442
marital communications
   privilege, 442
best evidence rule, 442
authentication, 442
parol evidence rule, 442
witness statements, 442
occurrence witness, 443
pre-occurrence witness, 443
post-occurrence
   witness, 443
attestation clause, 444
settlement work-up, 445

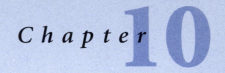
LITIGATION ASSISTANTSHIP

► *Chapter Outline*

Section A
OVERVIEW OF LITIGATION

America is a **litigious** society. This means that we have a tendency to sue people. We engage in **litigation**—a lot. In 1991 over 93 million new cases were filed in state courts, and 253,500 new cases were filed in federal courts.[1]

Litigation is the formal process of resolving legal controversies through special tribunals established for this purpose. The main tribunals are courts and administrative agencies acting in their **quasi-judicial** capacity.[2] Paralegals can perform many functions in assisting attorneys who are litigating cases. Before studying what these functions are, read the following overview of litigation, which will provide a context for understanding the roles of the attorney and paralegal. The overview is presented in the form of a story—the litigation woes of Michael Brown, who finds himself embroiled in a civil trial, a criminal trial, and an administrative dispute. At the end of the story, you will find most of this overview in outline form in Exhibits 10.2 and 10.3. (See pages 471–474.)

A **civil dispute** consists of (a) one private party suing another private party, or (b) a private party suing the government, or (c) the government suing a private party for a matter other than the commission of a crime. A **criminal dispute** is a suit brought by the government for the alleged commission of a crime.

THE LEGAL ODYSSEY OF MICHAEL BROWN: AN ANATOMY OF THE LITIGATION PROCESS

Michael Brown is a truck driver for the Best Bread Company. Several years ago, as Brown was walking home from work, Harold Clay, an old friend from the past, stopped and offered him a ride. They had not seen each other since Clay had moved cross-country a number of years ago. They carried on an excited conversation as Clay drove. After a few blocks, a car driven by George Miller, a resident of a neighboring state, ran through a red light and struck Clay's car. All three individuals were seriously injured and were taken to a local hospital. Clay died two weeks later from injuries received in the crash.

Several days after the accident, Brown's boss, Frank Best, wrote Brown a letter. In it, Best said he had learned that the police had found about half an ounce of heroin under the front passenger seat of Clay's car and were planning to charge Brown with possession of narcotics with intent to distribute. Best also stated that several thefts had occurred at the company warehouse recently, and that he now suspected Brown of having been involved in them. For these reasons, he decided to fire Brown, effective immediately.

At least three different legal disputes involving Brown could arise out of this fact situation:

1. A dispute among Brown, Miller, and Clay's estate regarding civil liability for the accident.
2. A dispute between Brown and the government regarding the criminal drug charge.
3. A dispute among Brown, the Best Bread Company, and the State Unemployment Compensation Board concerning Brown's entitlement to unemployment compensation benefits.

---

[1] Randall Samborn, *In Courts: Caseloads Still Rise,* National Law Journal 10 (July 5, 1993).
[2] *Quasi-judicial* means like or similar to a court. When an administrative agency holds a hearing to resolve a dispute, it is acting quasi-judicially. See chapter 6.

Each of these disputes could lead to a number of court decisions. The third dispute might involve an administrative decision, possibly followed by one or more court decisions, all concerning Brown's claim for unemployment compensation.

1. Civil Liability

Brown suffered substantial injury as a result of the crash. From whom could he collect *damages?* Who was *liable* for the accident? Was Miller at fault? Clay? Was each of them *jointly* and *severally* liable?

Damages: An award of money (paid by the wrongdoer) to compensate the person who has been harmed.

Liable: Legally responsible.

Joint and several liability: When two or more persons are jointly and severally liable, they are legally responsible, together and individually. Each wrongdoer is individually responsible for the entire judgment. The person who has been wronged can collect from one of them or from all of them until his or her court-awarded damages are paid.

Brown hired Brenda Davis, Esq., to represent him. Once Brown signed the *retainer,* Davis would later enter an *appearance* and become the *attorney of record.*

Retainer: The contract that formally establishes the attorney-client relationship. It states the nature and cost of the services to be rendered. (Retainer also refers to an amount of money or other property paid by the client as a deposit or advance against future fees, expenses, and costs of representation.)

Appearance: Going to court to act on behalf of a party to the litigation. The attorney usually appears by filing a *notice of appearance* in court, which is often accomplished through a *praecipe.* A praecipe is a formal request to the court (usually made through the court clerk) that something be done. Here the request is that the attorney become the attorney of record.

Attorney of record: An attorney of record is the attorney who has filed a notice of appearance (through a praecipe or other means) and who is formally mentioned in court records as the official attorney of the party. Once this occurs, the attorney often cannot withdraw from the case without court permission.

The attorney explained that a number of factors had to be considered before deciding on the *forum* in which to sue Miller and Clay's *estate.* Brown might be able to bring the suit in a number of places: (a) in a state trial court where Brown lives, (b) in a state trial court where Miller lives, (c) in a state trial court where Clay's estate is located, (d) in the federal trial court sitting in Brown's state, (e) in the federal trial court sitting in Miller's state, or (f) in the federal trial court sitting in the state where Clay's estate is located. The reason Brown could sue in a federal court is the existence of *diversity of citizenship.* Davis advised Brown to sue in federal court. The suit would be brought in the U.S. District Court sitting in Brown's own state, since this would be the most convenient *venue* for Brown.

Forum: The court where the case is to be tried.

Estate: All the property left by a decedent (one who has died), from which any obligations or debts of the decedent must be paid.

Diversity of citizenship: A kind of jurisdiction giving a federal court the power to hear a case based upon the fact that (a) the parties to the litigation are citizens of different states, and (b) the amount of money involved exceeds the amount specified by federal statute.

Venue: The place of the trial. In most judicial systems, there is more than one trial court. For example, there may be one for each county or district. The selection of a particular trial court within a judicial system is referred to as a *choice of venue.*

Having decided on a court, Davis was ready to begin the lawsuit. She instructed her paralegal, Ted Alexander, to prepare the first draft of the *complaint,* naming Brown as the *plaintiff* and *stating a cause of action* for negligence against Miller and Clay's estate as *codefendants.* The complaint was the first *pleading* of the case. In the complaint, Davis stated the facts she felt constituted a cause of action for negligence. Some of the factual *allegations* were based on Brown's personal knowledge, while others were based on *information and belief.* The prayer for relief in the complaint contained an *ad damnum* clause that asked for $100,000. When she finished drafting the complaint, Davis signed the pleading, attached a written demand for a *jury trial,* and *filed* both documents with the clerk of the court.

> **Complaint:** A pleading (see definition below) filed by the plaintiff that tries to state a claim or *cause of action* (see definition below) against the defendant.
>
> **Plaintiff:** The party initiating the lawsuit.
>
> **Cause of action:** Facts that give a party the right to judicial relief. A legally acceptable reason for suing.
>
> **Stating a cause of action:** Including in a *pleading* (see definition below) facts that, if proved at trial, would entitle the party to the judicial relief sought (assuming the other party does not plead and prove any defenses that would defeat the effort).
>
> **Codefendants:** More than one defendant sued in the same civil case. More than one defendant prosecuted in the same criminal case.
>
> **Pleading:** A formal document that contains allegations and/or responses of the parties in a trial. The major pleadings are the complaint and answer.
>
> **Allegation:** A claimed fact; a fact that a party will try to prove at trial.
>
> **Information and belief:** A standard legal term used to indicate that the allegation is not based on the firsthand knowledge of the person making the allegation but that the person, nevertheless, believes in good faith that the allegation is true.
>
> **Ad damnum:** A statement in the complaint in which the plaintiff asks for a specified sum of money as damages. (See prayer for relief in Exhibit 10.12 later in the chapter.)
>
> **Jury trial:** A jury is a group of citizens who will decide the issues or questions of fact at the trial. The judge decides the issues or questions of law. If there is no jury at the trial, then the judge decides both the questions of law and the questions of fact.
>
> **Filed:** To deposit a pleading, motion, or other formal document with a court clerk or other court official. Often what is filed thereby becomes a public record.

Service of process came next. It was accomplished when a copy of the complaint, along with the *summons,* was served on both Miller and on the legal representative of Clay's estate. Davis did not serve these parties herself. She used a *process server,* who then had to file with the court an *affidavit* of service indicating the circumstances under which service was achieved. Service was made before the *statute of limitations* on the negligence cause of action had run out. Once the defendants were properly served, the court acquired *in personam jurisdiction* over them.

> **Service of process:** *Process* is the means used by the court to acquire or exercise its power or jurisdiction over a person. *Service of process* is the formal notification given to a defendant that a suit has been initiated against him or her and that he or she must respond to it. (The words *summons* and *process* are often used interchangeably.) The most common method of service of process is to place the complaint and summons in the hands of the defendant.
>
> **Summons:** The formal notice from the court ordering the defendant to appear and answer the plaintiff's allegations. The summons is *served* on the defendant.
>
> **Process server:** A person who charges a fee for serving process.

Affidavit: A written statement of fact in which a person (called the *affiant*) swears that the facts in the statement are true.

Statute of limitations: The law establishing the period within which the lawsuit must be commenced. If it is not brought within that time, it can never be brought; it is *barred.*

In personam jurisdiction: The power of the court over the person of the defendant obtained in part by proper service of process. (It is also called **personal jurisdiction.**)

Both Miller and Clay's estate filed *motions to dismiss* for *failure to state a cause of action.* The motions were denied by the court.

Motion to dismiss: A request that the court decide that a party may not further litigate a claim—that is, that the claim be dropped.

Failure to state a cause of action: Failure of the plaintiff to allege enough facts in the complaint. Even if the plaintiff proved all the facts alleged in the complaint, the facts would not establish a cause of action entitling the plaintiff to recover against the defendant. The motion to dismiss for failure to state a cause of action is sometimes referred to as (a) a *demurrer* or (b) a *failure to state a claim upon which relief can be granted.*

Because the case had been filed in a federal court, the *procedural law* governing the case would be found in the *Federal Rules of Civil Procedure.* (The *substantive law* of the case would be the state law of negligence.) According to the Federal Rules of Civil Procedure, Miller and Clay's estate were each required to file an *answer* to Brown's complaint within twenty days. Miller filed his answer almost immediately. Since Clay was dead and unable to tell his attorney what had happened at the accident, the attorney for the estate had some difficulty preparing an answer and was unable to file it within the twenty days. To avoid a *default judgment* against the estate, the attorney filed a *motion* asking for an extension of thirty days within which to file the answer. The motion was granted by the court, and the answer was filed within the new deadline.

Procedural law: The technical rules setting forth the steps required to resolve a dispute in court or in an administrative agency.

Federal Rules of Civil Procedure (FRCP): The technical rules governing the manner in which civil cases are brought in and progress through the federal trial courts.

Substantive law: The rights and duties imposed by law (such as the duty to use reasonable care) other than procedural rights and duties.

Answer: The pleading that responds to or answers allegations of the complaint.

Default judgment: An order of the court deciding the case in favor of the plaintiff because the defendant failed to appear or to file an answer before the deadline.

Motion: A request made to the court, such as a motion to dismiss. The party making the motion is called the *movant.* The verb is *move,* as in "I move that the court permit the demonstration," or, "I move that the case be dismissed."

The answer filed on behalf of Clay's estate denied all allegations of negligence and raised an *affirmative defense* of contributory negligence against Brown on the theory that if Clay had been partially responsible for the collision, it was because Brown had distracted him through his conversation in the car. Finally, the answer of Clay's estate raised a *cross-claim* against the codefendant Miller, alleging that the accident had been caused solely by Miller's negligence. The estate asked $1,000,000 in damages.

Defense: A response to a claim of the other party, setting forth reason(s) why the claim should be denied. The defense may be as simple as a flat denial of the other party's factual allegations or may involve entirely new factual allegations. (In the latter situation, the defense is an *affirmative defense.*)

Affirmative defense: A defense that is based on new factual allegations by the defendant not contained in the plaintiff's allegations.

Cross-claim: Usually, a claim by one codefendant against another codefendant.

Miller's answer also raised the defense of contributory negligence against Brown and stated a cross-claim against Clay's estate, alleging that the accident had been caused solely by the negligence of Clay, or of Clay and Brown together. On this same theory (that Brown together with Clay had negligently caused the accident), Miller's answer also stated a *counterclaim* against Brown. Miller sought $50,000 from Brown and $50,000 against Clay's estate as damages.

Counterclaim: A claim or a cause of action against the plaintiff stated in the defendant's answer.

For a time, Miller and his attorney considered filing a *third-party complaint* against his own insurance company since the company would be liable for any judgment against him. They decided against this strategy since they did not want to let the jury know that Miller was insured. If the jury knew this fact, it might be more inclined to reach a verdict in favor of the plaintiff and for a high amount of damages. The strategy was also unnecessary because there was no indication that Miller's insurer would *contest* its obligation to compensate Miller (within the policy limits of his insurance) for any damages that he might have to pay Brown or Clay's estate in the event that the trial resulted in an *adverse judgment* against him.

Third-party complaint: A complaint filed by the defendant against a third party (that is, a person not presently a party to the lawsuit). This complaint alleges that the third party is or may be liable for all or part of the damages that the plaintiff may win from the defendant.

Contest: To challenge.

Adverse judgment: A judgment or decision against you.

At this point, five claims had been filed by the parties. A sixth, Miller's third-party claim against his insurer, had been considered but ultimately had not been filed. These claims and their relationship to each other are illustrated in Exhibit 10.1.

Exhibit 10.1   Diagram of the Claims in the Brown/Miller/Clay's Estate Litigation

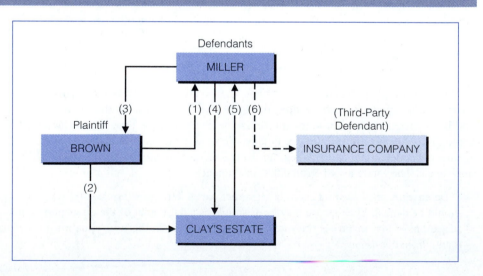

1. Plaintiff Brown's complaint for negligence against Miller and
2. against Clay's Estate, as codefendants
3. Defendant Miller's counterclaim for negligence against plaintiff, Brown
4. Defendant Miller's cross-claim for negligence against his codefendant, the Estate
5. Defendant Estate's cross-claim for negligence against its codefendant, Miller
6. Third-party complaint that defendant Miller considered but ultimately decided *not* to file against his insurance company

Once the pleadings were filed, all three parties began to seek *discovery*. Each attorney first served *written interrogatories* on the opposing parties. These were followed by *depositions* and *requests for admissions*. Miller refused to answer several questions during his deposition in his attorney's office. As a result, Brown's attorney had to file a discovery motion, seeking an *order* from the court compelling Miller to answer. A *hearing* was subsequently held on the motion, and after listening to arguments by all of the attorneys, the judge granted the motion in full, ordering Miller to answer the questions. Faced with the court's order, Miller answered the remaining questions.

Each party then filed a *motion for summary judgment.* The judge denied these motions, and the case was ready for trial.

> **Discovery:** The pretrial devices that can be used by one party to obtain facts and information about the case from the other party in order to assist in preparing for trial. The major discovery devices are *written interrogatories, deposition, production of documents and things, physical or mental examination,* and *request for admissions.* (For an overview of all these devices, see Exhibit 10.4 later in the chapter on page 477.)

> **Written interrogatories:** A discovery device consisting of written questions about the case submitted by one party to the other party. The answers to the interrogatories are usually given under oath—that is, the person answering the questions signs a sworn statement that the answers are true.

> **Deposition:** A discovery device by which one party asks questions of the other party or of a witness for the other party. The person who is *deposed* is called the *deponent.* The deposition is conducted under oath outside the courtroom, usually in one of the attorney's offices. A recording or transcript—a word-for-word account—is made of the deposition. (Most depositions consist of *oral* questions and answers. A deposition can be written, however.)

> **Requests for admissions:** Written statements of fact concerning the case whose truth must be accepted or denied by an adverse party to whom they are submitted by another party. Those statements that are admitted will be treated by the court as having been established and need not be proven at trial.

> **Order:** An official command by the court requiring, allowing, or forbidding some act to be done.

> **Hearing:** A proceeding in which the judge or presiding officer examines some aspect of the dispute. An *adversary hearing* exists when both parties are present at the hearing to argue their respective positions. An *ex parte hearing* exists when only one party is present at the hearing. Hearings occur in court as well as in administrative agencies.

> **Motion for a summary judgment:** A request by a party that a decision be reached on the basis of the pleadings alone without going through an entire trial. A summary judgment is normally allowed only when there is no dispute between the parties as to any of the material or significant facts. Summary judgment can be granted on the entire case or on some of the claims raised within it. The word *summary* means done relatively quickly and informally without going through an entire adversary hearing or an entire trial.

As the trial date neared, each of the attorneys received a notice asking them to appear before a *magistrate* for a *pretrial conference.* On the appointed day, the attorneys met with the magistrate to prepare the case for trial. During the conference, the magistrate, with the help of the attorneys, prepared a pretrial statement for the trial judge on the case. It contained a statement of the facts that had been *stipulated* by the attorneys and the facts that were still *in issue*. It also listed the *tangible evidence* and witnesses that each attorney intended to *introduce* at the trial.

Magistrate: A judicial officer having some but not all of the powers of a judge. In the federal trial courts (the U.S. District Courts), the magistrate may conduct many of the preliminary or pretrial proceedings in both civil and criminal cases.

Pretrial conference: A meeting between the judge (or magistrate) and the attorneys to go over preliminary matters before the trial begins. At this conference, the presiding officer often encourages the parties to settle the dispute on their own in order to avoid a trial.

Stipulated: Agreed to. A *stipulation* of fact will not be *contested* or disputed. Hence, no evidence need be presented as to the truth or falsity of that fact at trial.

In issue: In question. A *question* or issue *of fact* means that the truth or falsity of that fact must be established at the trial. A question or issue *of law* means that the judge must rule on what the law is or how the law applies to the facts.

Tangible evidence: Physical evidence; evidence that can be seen or touched, such as letters, photographs, or skeletons. **Testimonial evidence** is evidence of what someone says, such as the statements made by anyone sitting in the witness box.

Introduce evidence: To place evidence formally before the court so that it will become part of the record for consideration by the judge and jury.

After some delay, the case was finally *set for trial*. All of the parties and their attorneys assembled in the courtroom. The judge entered, took the bench, and ordered the *bailiff* to summon a *jury panel* for the trial. Once the potential or prospective jurors were seated in the courtroom, *voir dire* began. Several jurors were *challenged for cause* and dismissed— one because she worked for the insurance company that had issued the policy on Miller's car. The position as to this prospective juror was that she might be *biased*. Several other jurors were dismissed as a result of *peremptory challenges*. A panel of twelve jurors plus two *alternates* was eventually selected and seated in the jury box.

Set for trial: To schedule a date when the trial is to begin.

Bailiff: A court employee who keeps order in the courtroom and renders general administrative assistance to the judge.

Jury panel: A group of citizens who have been called to jury duty. From this group, juries for particular trials are selected.

Voir dire: The oral examination of prospective jurors by the attorneys, by the judge, or by both the attorneys and the judge for the purpose of selecting a jury.

Challenge for cause: A request from a party to a judge that a prospective juror *not* be allowed to become a member of this jury because of specified causes or reasons.

Bias: A predisposition to think and perhaps to act in a certain way. Unfairly leaning in favor of or against someone. The potential for unfairness because of prior knowledge or involvement leading to possible preconceptions and a lack of open-mindedness.

Peremptory challenge: A request from a party to a judge asking that a prospective juror *not* be allowed to become a member of this jury without stating a reason for this request. Both sides are allowed a limited number of peremptory challenges, but they will be granted as many challenges for cause as they can establish.

Alternate: An extra juror who will take the place of a regular juror if one becomes incapacitated during the trial.

When the jury was seated, Brown's attorney rose and told the judge that she wished to invoke the *rule on witnesses*. The judge nodded to the bailiff, who then led all of the witnesses (except for the parties themselves) out of the courtroom. Brown's attorney then began the trial with her *opening statement* to the jury. When she finished, Miller's attorney also delivered an opening statement. The attorney for Clay's estate, however, decided to reserve his opening statement until it was time for him to present the estate's case.

Rule on witnesses: A rule that requires certain witnesses to be removed from the courtroom until it is time for their individual testimony so that they will not be able to hear each other's testimony.

Opening statement: A speech or presentation made by each attorney to the jury summarizing the facts the attorney intends to try to prove during the trial.

Brown's attorney, whose client had the *burden of proof,* called her first witness, a ten-year-old boy who had seen the accident. Miller's attorney immediately rose and requested a *bench conference.* When all the attorneys had gathered around the bench, he stated that he *objected* to the witness on the basis of *competency.* The judge then *excused the jury* temporarily while he conducted a brief *examination* of the witness. The judge *overruled* the objection upon being satisfied that the boy was old enough to understand the obligation to tell the truth and had the ability to communicate what he knew.

Burden of proof: The responsibility of proving a fact at the trial. Generally, the party making the factual allegation has the burden of proof as to that allegation.

Bench conference: A discussion between the judge and the attorneys held at the judge's bench so that the jury cannot hear what is being said.

Objection: A formal challenge usually directed at the evidence that the other side is trying to pursue or introduce.

Competency: Legal capacity to testify.

Excused the jury: Asked the jury to leave the room.

Examination: Questioning, asking questions of.

Overrule: Deny. (The word *overrule* is also used when a court repudiates the holding of a prior opinion written by the same court.)

The jury was brought back into the courtroom, and Brown's attorney began her *direct examination.* After a few questions, Miller's attorney again objected, this time on the *ground* that the child's answer had been *hearsay.* The judge *sustained* the objection and, after instructing the jury to disregard the boy's answer, ordered it *stricken from the record.* Brown's attorney continued her examination of the witness for a few minutes before announcing that she had no further questions. The attorney for the estate then rose to conduct a brief *cross-examination* of the boy. He was followed by Miller's attorney, whose cross-examination was also brief. There was no *redirect examination.*

Direct examination: Questioning the witness first. Normally, the attorney who *calls* the witness to the stand conducts the direct examination.

Ground: Reason.

Hearsay: Testimony in court (or written evidence) on a statement asserted or made by someone else out of court when the statement is being offered to establish the truth of the statement, and thus its value is based on the credibility of the out-of-court asserter.

Sustain: To affirm the validity of.

Strike from the record: To remove the testimony or evidence from the written record or *transcript* of the trial.

Cross-examination: Questioning the witness after the other side has completed the direct examination. Generally, the person conducting the cross-examination must limit himself or herself to the topics or subject matters raised during the direct examination of this witness by the other side.

Redirect examination: Questioning the witness after the cross-examination. The attorney who conducted the direct examination conducts the redirect examination.

Brown's attorney, Davis, called several other witnesses who had seen the accident occur. Each witness was examined and cross-examined in much the same fashion as the boy had been. Davis was about to call her fourth witness, Dr. Hadley, when the judge announced a brief recess for lunch. The judge admonished the jury not to discuss the case with anyone, even among themselves, and ordered everyone to be back in the courtroom by 2:00 P.M.

Dr. Hadley was called to the stand immediately after the lunch recess. Brown's attorney began her direct examination with a series of questions about the doctor's medical training and experience in order to *qualify* him as an *expert witness.* She then moved that Dr. Hadley be recognized as an expert witness. The *court,* with no objections by either defense counsel, granted the motion.

Qualify: To present evidence of a person's education and experience sufficient to convince the court that the witness has expertise in a particular area.

Expert witness: A witness who has been *qualified* as an expert and who, therefore, will be allowed to give his or her expert opinion to assist the jury in understanding technical subjects not within the understanding of the average lay person.

Court: Here refers to the judge trying the case.

Brown's attorney then asked the doctor to testify as to the nature and extent of the injuries that the plaintiff, Brown, had suffered as a result of the accident. In addition to multiple cuts and bruises, the doctor stated that Brown had suffered a broken knee. The knee, in the doctor's opinion, had been permanently injured, and Brown would continue to suffer periodic pain and stiffness due to the injury. To show the expense that these injuries had cost Brown,

An attorney examines an expert witness during a trial.

the attorney produced the original copies of the bills that the doctor had sent to Brown. She handed the bills to the *clerk,* who marked them as plaintiff's *exhibit* number one. After allowing defense counsel to inspect the bills, Brown's attorney handed them to the doctor, who promptly identified them. The attorney then *moved the bills into evidence* and turned the witness over to defense counsel for cross-examination.

> **Clerk:** The court employee who assists judges with record keeping at the trial and other administrative duties.
>
> **Exhibit:** An item of physical or tangible evidence offered to the court for inspection.
>
> **Move . . . into evidence:** To request that the items be formally declared *admissible*. This is not the same as declaring them to be true. Admissible means that the items will be admitted simply for consideration as to their truth or falsity.

It was late in the afternoon when Brown's attorney finished with her final witness, Brown himself. The judge did not want to recess for the day, however, until the attorneys for the defendants completed their cross-examination of Brown. After about an hour, all the defense attorneys completed their questioning of Brown, and Brown's attorney *rested her case.* The judge *adjourned* the trial until the following morning.

> **Rest one's case:** To announce formally that you have concluded the presentation of evidence (through the introduction of tangible evidence, through direct examination of your own witnesses, etc.). While the other side presents its case, however, you will be entitled to cross-examine its witnesses.
>
> **Adjourn:** To halt the proceedings temporarily.

On the following morning, the attorney for Clay's estate advised the judge that he had a preliminary matter to bring up before the jury was brought into the courtroom. He then proceeded to make a motion for a *directed verdict* in favor of the estate on Brown's claim of negligence. Miller's attorney made a similar motion on behalf of his client. The judge listened to arguments by the attorneys and then stated his decision. As to defendant Miller, the motion was denied because the plaintiff had introduced sufficient evidence to make out a *prima facie case* of negligence that should go to the jury. As to the estate, the judge would neither grant nor deny the motion but would *take it under advisement.*

> **Directed verdict:** An order by the court that the jury reach a verdict for the party making the motion for a directed verdict on the ground that the other side, which has just rested its case, has failed to produce enough convincing evidence to establish a cause of action.
>
> **Prima facie case:** The party's evidence, if believed by the jury, would be legally sufficient to support a verdict in favor of that party—that is, the party has introduced evidence that, if believed, would include all the facts necessary to establish a cause of action. If the plaintiff *fails* to establish a prima facie case, the judge will decide the case in favor of the defendant without any further proceedings. If the judge finds that there *is* a prima facie case, the defendant will be allowed an opportunity to produce contrary evidence. The case will then go to the jury to decide which version of the facts meets the *standard of proof* (see definition below).
>
> **Take under advisement:** To delay ruling on the motion until another time.

The jury was summoned into the courtroom and seated in the jury box for the second day of the trial. The attorney for the estate began his case by making an opening statement to the jury, reserved from the previous day. He then proceeded to call his witnesses. He had only a few witnesses and was able to conclude his case just before noon, at which time he introduced Clay's death certificate into evidence. The judge then declared a recess for lunch.

Miller's attorney began to present his case in the afternoon, and by late afternoon he too had rested his case. The judge dismissed the jury until the following morning and told the attorneys to be prepared for *closing arguments* at that time. He also asked them to submit any *jury instructions* they would like to request, so that he could review them. Brown's attorney requested an instruction that the codefendants had to overcome a *presumption* of negligence against them. The judge denied this request. Finally, he announced that he had decided to deny the estate's earlier motion for a directed verdict.

> **Closing argument:** The final statements by the attorneys summarizing the evidence they think they have established and the evidence they think the other side has failed to establish.
>
> **Jury instructions:** A statement of the guidelines and law given to the jury by the judge for use in deciding the issues of fact. The instructions to the jury are also referred to as the *charge* to the jury. The attorneys are usually allowed to submit proposed instructions for consideration by the judge.
>
> **Presumption:** An assumption that a certain fact is true. A *rebuttable* presumption is an assumption that can be overcome or changed if the other side introduces enough facts to overcome it. If the other side does not rebut the presumption, then the assumption stands. A *nonrebuttable* presumption cannot be overcome no matter how convincing the evidence of the other side against the assumption.

Closing arguments began late the following morning. Each attorney carefully reviewed the evidence for the jury and argued for a *verdict* in favor of his or her client. Following a brief recess for lunch, the judge thanked the alternate jurors for their time and dismissed them. He then began to instruct the remaining twelve jurors as to the law they were to follow in finding the facts and in reaching a verdict. He said that they, as jurors, were the finders of fact and were to base their decision solely upon the testimony and exhibits introduced during the trial. He explained the concept of burden of proof and stated which party had to carry this burden as to each of the various *elements* of negligence. Each element had to be proved by a *preponderance of the evidence*. This was the *standard of proof* for this kind of case. Finally, he described the manner in which they should compute the amount of damages, if any, suffered by the parties. The jury was then led out of the courtroom to deliberate on its verdict. The judge retired to his chambers, and the attorneys settled back with their clients to wait.

> **Verdict:** The final conclusion of the jury.
>
> **Elements:** Here, the components of a cause of action. (An element is a component or portion of a rule that is a precondition of the applicability of the entire rule.)
>
> **Preponderance of the evidence:** A standard of proof (used in many civil suits) that is met when a party's evidence on a fact indicates that it is "more likely than not" that the fact is as the party alleges it to be.
>
> **Standard of proof:** A statement of how convincing a version of a fact must be before the trier of facts (usually the jury) can accept it as true. The main standards of proof are proof *beyond a reasonable doubt* (in criminal cases only), proof *by clear and convincing evidence*, and proof by *preponderance of the evidence*.

After about an hour, the judge received a note from the foreman of the jury, asking that the jury be allowed to view several of the exhibits. The items requested consisted largely of the various medical bills allegedly incurred by Brown and Clay. The attorneys for Brown and for the estate took this as a good sign—the jury had probably decided the case against Miller and was now trying to compute damages.

A second note arrived in another hour, announcing that the jury had reached a verdict. The bailiff summoned everyone back to the courtroom, and the jury came in a few minutes later. At the clerk's request, the foreman rose to read the verdict. On Brown's original complaint against Miller for negligence, the jury found for Brown and against Miller, awarding Brown $30,000 in damages. However, on Brown's complaint against Clay's estate (the codefendant), the jury decided in favor of the estate, finding that Clay had not been negligent. The jury found for the estate on its cross-claim against its codefendant, Miller, awarding $750,000 in damages to the estate. Finally, the jury found against Miller on his own cross-claim against the estate, as well as on his counterclaim against Brown. The judge entered a judgment against Miller in the amounts awarded by the jury. After denying a motion by Miller for a *judgment notwithstanding the verdict*, he thanked the jurors and dismissed them.

> **Judgment:** The final conclusion of a court. The judgment will resolve the legal dispute before the court or will indicate what further proceedings are needed to resolve it. Many judgments order the losing party to do something (such as pay damages) or to refrain from doing something. A *declaratory judgment* establishes the rights and obligations of the parties, but it does not order the parties to do or refrain from doing anything.

> **Judgment notwithstanding the verdict:** A judgment by the trial judge that is contrary to the verdict reached by the jury, in effect, overruling the jury. (Also referred to as *a judgment n.o.v.*)

Miller's attorney immediately made a *motion for a new trial*, arguing several possible grounds. When this motion was denied by the trial judge, he moved for a reduction of the verdict on the grounds that the amounts awarded were excessive. This motion was also denied, and the attorney announced his intention to *appeal*. The judge did, however, grant Miller a *stay* of the judgment, conditioned upon his filing a *timely notice of appeal* and posting the appropriate *bond*.

> **Motion for a new trial:** A request that the judge set aside the judgment and order a new trial on the basis that the trial was improper or unfair due to specified prejudicial errors that occurred.

> **Appeal:** To ask a court of *appellate jurisdiction* (a higher court within the same judicial system as the trial court) to *review* or examine the decision of the lower court on the basis that the lower court made some errors of law in conducting the trial.

> **Stay:** To delay enforcement or *execution* of the court's judgment.

> **Timely:** On time, according to the time specified by law.

> **Notice of appeal:** A document announcing an intention to appeal, which is filed with the appellate court and served on the opposing party.

> **Bond:** A sum of money deposited with the court to insure compliance with some requirement.

Miller asked his attorney what the $30,000 verdict against him meant. Since Brown had originally sued for $100,000, could Brown later sue Miller again for the rest of the amount he claimed? The attorney explained that, because of the stay granted by the judge, Miller would not have to pay anything until a decision on appeal had been reached. Furthermore, Brown could not sue Miller again on the same cause of action, because Brown had received a *judgment on the merits* which would be *res judicata* and would *bar* any later suit on the same negligence cause of action. The same would be true of a later negligence action by Clay's estate against Miller.

> **Judgment on the merits:** A decision on the substance of the claims raised. Normally, a judgment of dismissal based solely on some procedural error is not a judgment on the merits. A judgment that is not on the merits results in a *dismissal without prejudice*. A party who

has received a judgment on the merits cannot bring the same suit again. A party whose case has been dismissed without prejudice can bring the same suit again so long as the procedural errors are corrected (i.e., cured) in the later action.

Res judicata: The legal doctrine that a judgment on the merits will prevent the same parties from relitigating the same cause of action on the same facts; the parties have already had their day in court.

Bar: Prevent or stop.

Miller's attorney filed his notice of appeal with the United States Court of Appeals and posted bond the following week. As attorney for the *appellant,* it was also his duty to see to it that the *record,* including *transcripts* and copies of exhibits, was transmitted to the Court of Appeals and that the case was *docketed* by the clerk of that court. Miller's attorney then had forty days in which to draft and file his *appellate brief* with the Court of Appeals. He served copies of the brief on the attorneys for the *appellees,* Brown and Clay's estate, who in turn filed their briefs concerning the *issues on appeal.*

Appellant: The party initiating the appeal; the party who is complaining of error(s) made by the lower court.

Record: The official collection of all the trial pleadings, exhibits, orders, and word-for-word testimony that took place during the trial.

Transcript: The word-for-word typed record of everything that was said during the trial. The court reporter types this transcription, which is paid for by the parties requesting it.

Docket: The court's official calendar of pending cases. Once all the necessary papers have been filed, the appeal is "docketed" by the clerk—that is, placed on the court's official calendar.

Appellate brief: A party's written argument covering the issues on appeal relating to claimed errors that occurred during the trial. The brief is filed in the appeals court and served on opposing parties.

Appellee: The party against whom the appeal is brought (also called the *respondent*). Generally, the appellee is satisfied with what the trial court did and wishes the appellate court to approve of or *affirm* the trial court's judgment.

Issues on appeal: The claimed errors of law committed by the trial judge below. The appellate court does not retry the case. No witnesses are called, and no testimony is taken by the appellate court. The court examines the record and determines whether errors of law were committed by the trial judge.

Several months passed before the attorneys finally received a notice from the clerk of the Court of Appeals that the appeal had been scheduled for *oral argument* before a three-judge *panel* of the court. The arguments were heard a few weeks later. Six months after oral argument, the attorneys received the decision of the court in its written *opinion.* By a vote of two to one (one judge *dissenting*), the court *affirmed* the judgments against Miller. The only error that the majority found was the admission of certain testimony offered through Brown's expert witness. However, because Miller's attorney had not objected to this testimony at trial, the opinion stated, he had *waived* this defect.

Oral argument: A verbal presentation made by the attorneys before the appellate court, during which positions on the validity or invalidity of what the trial judge did are presented.

Panel: The group of judges, usually three, who decide a case. (For other meanings of *panel,* see the glossary at the end of the book.)

Opinion: A court's written explanation of how it applied the law to the facts to resolve a legal dispute. One case can contain several opinions: a majority opinion, a concurring opinion (see the definition that follows), and a dissenting opinion. Opinions are often collected in official and unofficial *reporters.*

Dissent: Disagree with the decision (the result and the reasons) of the *majority* on the court. If a judge agrees with the result reached by the majority but disagrees with reasons the majority used to support that result, the judge would cast a *concurring* vote and might write a separate concurring opinion.

Affirm: To agree with or uphold the lower court judgment. If the appellate court *remanded* the case, it would be sending it back to the lower court with instructions to correct the irregularities specified in the appellate opinion. If the appellate court *reversed* the court below, it would have changed the result reached below.

Waive: To lose a right or privilege because of an explicit rejection of it or a failure to claim it at the appropriate time. Here the court is referring to the rule that failure to object during trial is an implied waiver of the right to complain about the alleged error on appeal.

Miller, undaunted, *petitioned* for a *rehearing* by the court *en banc.* The petition was denied. Miller then discussed the possibility of further appeal with his attorney. The attorney explained that Miller could, if he desired, try to appeal to the United States Supreme Court. He cautioned Miller, however, that he could not *appeal as a matter of right* in this case, but would be limited to a petition for a *writ of certiorari.* He advised Miller that it was extremely unlikely that the Supreme Court would grant the petition and that it probably would not be worth the expense. Miller agreed, and no further appeal was attempted. Shortly thereafter the Court of Appeals issued its *mandate,* and the case was returned to the District Court, where Miller, through his insurance company, *satisfied* the judgment.

Petition: To make a formal request; similar to a motion. (The word *petition* is sometimes synonymous with the word *complaint,* the plaintiff's pleading that attempts to state a cause of action.)

Rehearing: A second hearing by a court to reconsider the decision it made after an earlier hearing.

En banc: By the entire court. The *panel* of judges that heard the first appeal may have consisted of only three judges, yet the number of judges on the full court may be much larger.

Appeal as a matter of right: An appeal in which the appellate court has no discretion on whether to hear the appeal and thus is *required* to review the decision below.

Writ of certiorari: An order by an appellate court requiring a lower court to certify the record of a lower court proceeding and to send it up to the appellate court, which has decided to accept an appeal of the proceeding. The writ is used in a case in which the appellate court has discretion to accept or reject the appeal. If the writ is denied, the court refuses to hear the appeal, and, in effect, the judgment below stands unchanged. If the writ is granted, the lower court "sends up" the record and the appeal proceeds.

Mandate: The order of the court. Here the mandate of the appellate court was to affirm the trial court's judgment.

Satisfy: To comply with a legal obligation, here to pay the judgment award.

2. Criminal Liability

Brown was involved in a second legal dispute at the same time the negligence suit was under way. In addition to suing Clay's estate and Miller, Brown was defending himself in a criminal *prosecution* for possession of narcotics.

Prosecution: The bringing and processing of legal proceedings against someone; usually a criminal proceeding, but the word includes civil proceedings as well. Prosecution also refers to the attorney representing the government in a criminal case.

As Brown was leaving the hospital after having recovered from his injury, he was met at the door by two police officers. The officers produced a *warrant* and advised Brown that he was under arrest. After he was read his rights, he was taken to the police station.

> **Warrant:** An order from a judicial officer authorizing an act such as the arrest of an individual or the search of property.

The following morning Brown was taken before a judge for his *initial appearance*. The judge advised Brown that he had been charged with a *felony,* "possession of narcotics with intent to distribute." He then advised Brown of his rights, including his right to be represented by an attorney. Since Brown was unemployed and without adequate funds to pay an attorney, the judge asked him if he would like the court to appoint an attorney to handle the case. Brown said yes. An attorney was *assigned* to represent Brown. The judge, at the attorney's request, then agreed to give Brown a chance to confer with his new attorney before continuing the hearing.

> **Initial appearance:** The first court appearance by the accused during which the court (a) informs him or her of the charges, (b) makes a decision on bail, and (c) determines the date of the next court proceeding.
>
> **Felony:** A crime punishable by a sentence of one year or more. A *misdemeanor* is a crime punishable by a sentence of less than a year.
>
> **Assigned:** Appointed. Assigned counsel is an attorney appointed by the court to represent an individual who is *indigent,* which means lacking funds to hire an attorney. If the attorney is a government employee handling criminal cases, he or she is often called a *public defender.*

When the case was recalled, Brown and his court-appointed attorney again approached the bench and stood before the judge. The attorney handed the clerk a praecipe formally entering his name as attorney of record for Brown and advised the judge that he was prepared to discuss the matter of *bail.* He proceeded to describe for the judge the details of Brown's background—his education, employment record, length of residence in the city, etc. He concluded by asking that he be released on his own *personal recognizance.* The prosecutor was then given an opportunity to speak. He recommended a high *bond,* pointing out that the defendant was unemployed and had no close relatives in the area. These facts, he argued, coupled with the serious nature of a felony charge, indicated a very real risk that the defendant might try to flee. The judge nevertheless agreed to release Brown on his personal recognizance and set a date for a *preliminary hearing* the following week.

> **Bail:** A sum of money or other property deposited with the court in order to insure that the defendant will reappear in court at designated times.
>
> **Personal recognizance:** The defendant's sworn promise that he or she will return to court at the designated times. No bail money is required.
>
> **Bail bond:** A written obligation to pay a sum of money to the court if the defendant fails to appear at designated times.
>
> **Preliminary hearing:** A hearing during which the state is required to produce sufficient evidence to establish that there is *probable cause* (see definition below) to believe that the defendant committed the crimes charged.

The only witness at the preliminary hearing was the police officer who had been at the scene of the accident. The officer testified that when he helped pull Brown out of the car, he noticed a small paper sack sticking out from under the passenger's side of the front seat. Several glassine envelopes containing a white powdery substance, the officer said, had spilled out of the sack. The substance, totaling about one-half ounce, was tested and proved to be 80 percent pure heroin. Brown's attorney cross-examined the officer briefly, but little additional information came out. The judge found that there was *probable cause* to hold the defendant and ordered the case *bound over* for *grand jury* action. He continued Brown's release on personal recognizance.

Probable cause: A reasonable basis to believe that the defendant is guilty of the crime(s) charged.

Bound over: Submitted.

Grand jury: A special jury whose duty is to hear evidence of felonies presented by the prosecutor to determine whether there is sufficient evidence to return an *indictment* (see definition below) against the defendant and cause him or her to stand trial on the charges.

Shortly after the preliminary hearing, Brown's attorney went to the prosecutor to see if he could work out an informal disposition of the charge. He tried to convince the prosecutor to enter a *nolle prosequi* on the charge, explaining that Brown had simply been offered a ride home and was not aware that the heroin was in the car. The prosecutor was unwilling to drop the charge. However, he was willing to "nolle" the felony charge of possession with intent to distribute if Brown would agree to *plead* guilty to the lesser offense of simple possession of a dangerous drug, a misdemeanor. The attorney said he would speak to his client about it.

Nolle prosequi: A statement by the prosecutor that he or she is unwilling to prosecute the case. The charges, in effect, are dropped.

Plead: To deliver a formal statement or response. In a criminal case, to *plead* means to admit or deny the charges made by the prosecutor.

He spoke to Brown that same afternoon, told him about the *plea bargaining* session, and advised him of the prosecutor's offer. Brown was not interested. He felt he was innocent and was unwilling to plead guilty, even to a misdemeanor.

Plea bargaining: Negotiation between the prosecution and the defense attorney during which an attempt is made to reach a compromise in lieu of a criminal trial. Generally, the defendant agrees to plead guilty to a lesser charge in return for the state's willingness to drop a more serious charge.

Several weeks went by before Brown's attorney was notified that the grand jury had returned an *indictment* against his client. The next step would be the *arraignment* on the following Monday. On this date, Brown and his attorney appeared before the judge, and Brown was formally notified of the indictment. He entered a plea of not guilty to the charge. The judge set a trial date about two-and-one-half months away and again agreed to continue Brown's release on personal recognizance.

Indictment: A formal document issued by a grand jury accusing the defendant of a crime. (If the state has no grand jury, the accusation is often contained in a document called an *information.*)

Arraignment: A court proceeding in which the defendant is formally charged with a crime and enters a plea. Arrangements are then made for the next proceeding.

The day for the trial arrived, and both sides (Brown's attorney and the prosecutor) announced that they were ready. Voir dire was held, and a jury was *impaneled.* The trial itself was relatively uneventful, lasting less than a day. The prosecutor, following a brief opening statement, presented only two witnesses: the police officer who had been at the scene, and an expert from the police lab who identified the substance as heroin. He then rested his case. Brown's attorney then made his opening statement and presented his only witness, Brown himself. The jury listened attentively as Brown, on direct examination, explained the events leading up to the accident and his subsequent arrest. Not only had he been unaware of the heroin, he testified, but he had never even seen it, since he had been knocked unconscious by the accident and had not revived until he was in the ambulance. Brown had a previous conviction for shoplifting, and the prosecutor on cross-examination attempted to use this conviction to *impeach* Brown's testimony. Brown's attorney successfully objected, arguing that the conviction, which had occurred eight years previously, was too remote to be *relevant*. The judge agreed and prohibited any mention of the prior conviction. After a few more questions, the prosecutor concluded his cross-examination, and the defense rested its case.

> **Impaneled:** Selected, sworn in, and seated.
>
> **Impeach:** To attack or discredit by introducing evidence that the testimony of the witness is not credible (believable).
>
> **Relevant:** Tending to prove or disprove a fact in issue.

Both sides presented their closing arguments following the lunch recess. The judge then instructed the jury; he described the elements of the offense and explained that the burden of proof in a criminal case is on the *government*. That burden, he continued, is to prove each element of the offense *beyond a reasonable doubt*. The jury took less than forty-five minutes to reach its verdict. All parties quickly reassembled in the courtroom to hear the foreman announce the verdict *acquitting* Brown of the offense. A *poll* of the jury, requested by the prosecutor, confirmed the result, and the judge advised Brown that he was free to go.

> **Government:** Here, the prosecutor.
>
> **Beyond a reasonable doubt:** The standard of proof required for conviction in a criminal case. If any reasonable doubt exists as to any element of the crime, the defendant cannot be convicted. Reasonable doubt is such doubt as would cause prudent persons to hesitate before acting in matters of importance to themselves.
>
> **Acquit:** Find not guilty; absolve of guilt.
>
> **Poll:** To question jurors individually in open court as to whether each agrees with the verdict announced by the foreman.

Generally, criminal cases in which the defendant is acquitted may not be appealed by the prosecutor. Hence, in this case, there was no appeal of the trial judgment. If a defendant is convicted, he or she is sentenced. A convicted defendant *does* have the right to appeal.

3. Administrative Dispute

The day after his indictment on the felony charge, Brown went down to the state unemployment office to apply for benefits. After being interviewed by a clerk, he filled out an application form. The clerk told Brown that he would receive a letter in about a week notifying him of the agency's initial determination of his eligibility. If he were eligible, his benefits would start in about ten days.

Brown received the letter a few days later. It advised him that, although he was otherwise eligible for benefits, a routine check with his former employer had disclosed that he had been fired for misconduct. For this reason, the letter stated, he would be deemed disqualified for a nine-week period. Moreover, the benefits due for those nine weeks would be deducted from the total amount he would otherwise have been entitled to. If he wished to appeal this decision, the letter went on, he could request an *administrative hearing* within ten days.

> **Administrative hearing:** A proceeding at an administrative agency presided over by a hearing officer (called a *hearing examiner*, an *administrative law judge*, a *referee*, etc.) to resolve a controversy. The hearing is usually conducted less formally than a court hearing or trial.

Brown felt that he needed some legal advice, but he was still out of work and broke. (The lawsuit in the civil action had not been filed yet—it would be well over a year before the case would be tried, appealed, and the judgment award actually paid.) Brown therefore decided to obtain help from the local legal aid office. He explained his problem to a receptionist and was introduced to the paralegal who would be handling his case. The paralegal, an expert in unemployment compensation law, discussed the case with Brown and agreed to represent Brown at the hearing. He helped Brown fill out a form requesting a hearing and promised to let him know as soon as the date was set. Brown left and the paralegal, after consulting with his supervisor, began to research and draft a *memorandum* to submit to the *hearing examiner* on Brown's behalf.

Memorandum: Here, a written presentation of a party's arguments on facts and legal issues in the case.

Hearing examiner: A person who presides over the hearing and makes findings of fact and rulings of law, or who recommends such findings and rulings to someone else in the agency who will make the final decision.

The hearing, held ten days later, lasted about an hour and a half. The only witnesses were Brown and his former boss, Frank Best. Best told the examiner about Brown's arrest and about the thefts from the warehouse. Taken together, he argued, these events made it impossible for him to trust Brown on the job any longer. Brown, in turn, denied any participation in the thefts and maintained his innocence on the drug charge. (Brown had not yet been acquitted of the felony.) The hearing examiner, at the close of the proceedings, thanked the parties and promised a decision within a few days.

The hearing examiner's decision arrived shortly thereafter in a document labeled *Proposed Findings and Rulings*. The last paragraph contained the examiner's recommended decision. The hearing examiner agreed with Brown that his boss's mere suspicion that Brown was involved in the thefts was not enough to justify a finding of misconduct. However, the decision went on, the pending criminal charges for a drug-related offense did provide the employer with good cause to fire Brown, since drug involvement could affect his ability to operate a truck safely. The paragraph concluded by recommending a finding of misconduct and the imposition of a nine-week penalty period.

Proposed findings and rulings: Recommended conclusions presented to someone else in the agency who will make the final decision.

A second letter arrived ten days later giving the *administrative decision* of the agency. The letter, signed by the director of the local agency, adopted the recommended decision of the hearing examiner. This decision, the letter concluded, could be appealed within fifteen days to the State Unemployment Compensation *Board of Appeals*. Brown immediately appealed.

Administrative decision: A resolution of a controversy between a party and an administrative agency involving the application of the regulations, statutes, or executive orders that govern the agency. In this case, the decision refers to a determination by a superior of the hearing examiner adopting, modifying, or rejecting the recommended decision of the hearing examiner.

Board of Appeals: A nonjudicial administrative tribunal that reviews the decision made by the hearing officer or by the head of the agency.

Copies of the hearing transcript along with memoranda from both sides were filed with the Board of Appeals. The Board, exercising its *discretion,* refused to allow oral arguments before it and reversed the decision reached *below*. It issued a short written decision stating that, while Best may have had cause to be suspicious of Brown, there wasn't sufficient evidence of actual misconduct on Brown's part. The Board, in this final administrative decision, ordered the local office to begin paying benefits immediately, including back benefits to cover the period since Brown had first applied.

Discretion: The power to choose among various courses of conduct based solely on one's reasoned judgment or preference.

Below: The lower tribunal that heard the case before the appeal was brought.

Best decided to appeal this administrative decision in a state court. He was allowed to do so since he had *exhausted* his *administrative remedies.* He filed a complaint in the county court seeking review of the Board's decision. He submitted the entire record from the proceedings below and asked the court for a *trial de novo.* Brown, now represented by an attorney from the legal aid office, filed his answer and immediately made a motion for summary judgment. The court, upon a review of the record and the pleadings, granted the motion and affirmed the judgment of the Board of Appeals. Best, after discussing the case at length with his attorney, decided against a further appeal of the case to the state court of appeals.

Exhausting administrative remedies: Pursuing *all* available methods of resolving a dispute within the administrative agency before asking a court to review what the agency did. A court generally will not allow a party to appeal an administrative decision until administrative remedies are exhausted.

Trial de novo: A totally new fact-finding hearing.

Many of the steps described in the litigation woes of Michael Brown, which you have just read, are outlined in Exhibit 10.2 (overview of civil litigation) and in Exhibit 10.3 (overview of criminal litigation).

S e c t i o n B
ALTERNATIVE DISPUTE RESOLUTION (ADR)

As you can see, litigation can be an involved and costly process. If the parties cannot resolve the dispute on their own, an increasingly popular option is alternative dispute resolution (**ADR**). Many disputants try it before resorting to traditional litigation. In some kinds of cases, e.g., medical malpractice, disputants may be required to try ADR before being allowed to have a court trial. ADR may take several forms:

Arbitration: Both sides agree to submit their dispute to a neutral third party who will listen to the evidence and make a decision. They can also agree on whether the decision of the arbitrator will be binding or advisory. The arbitrator is usually a professional arbitrator hired through organizations such as the American Arbitration Association. An arbitration proceeding is not as formal as a court trial. Generally, the decision of an arbitrator is not appealable to a court. If a party is dissatisfied, he or she must go to court and start all over again rather than appeal a particular arbitration decision.

Rent-a-Judge: This is actually another form of arbitration. A retired judge is hired by both sides to listen to the evidence and to make a decision, which has no more or less validity than any other arbitrator's decision.

Mediation: Both sides agree to submit their dispute to a neutral third party who will help the disputants reach a negotiated settlement on their own. The mediator does not render a decision, although sometimes he or she may make suggestions or recommendations.

Exhibit 10.2   Overview of Civil Litigation

(Possible proceedings where administrative decisions, court rulings, and opinions could be written. The events and their sequence presented below are examples only.)

EVENT	DEFINITIONS	DECISIONS, RULINGS, AND OPINIONS
I. Agency Stage 1. Someone protests an action taken by the *administrative agency* 2. *Agency hearing* 3. *Intra-agency appeal* to a commission, board of appeals, director, or secretary within the agency. (If no agency is involved, the litigation begins in court at the pretrial stage.)	*Administrative agency:* a governmental body whose primary function is to carry out or administer statutes passed by the legislature *Agency hearing:* a proceeding, similar to a trial, in which the hearing examiner of the agency listens to evidence and legal arguments before deciding the case *Intra-agency appeal:* a review within the agency of an earlier decision to determine if that decision was correct	A mid-level agency official (e.g., hearing examiner), writes a *recommended decision.* The commission, board of appeals, director, or secretary issues an *administrative decision.*
II. Pretrial Stage 4. Plaintiff files a *complaint* 5. Clerk issues a *summons* 6. *Service of process* on defendant 7. Defendant files an *answer* 8. *Discovery* by *written interrogatories* 9. *Discovery* by *deposition* 10. Pretrial *motions* 11. *Settlement* efforts 12. *Voir dire*	*Complaint:* a pleading in which the plaintiff states claim(s) against defendant *Summons:* a court notice requiring the defendant to appear and answer the complaint *Service of process:* a formal notification to a defendant that a suit has been instituted against him or her and that he or she must respond to it *Answer:* a pleading in which the defendant gives a response to the plaintiff's complaint *Discovery:* methods by which one party obtains information from the other party about the litigation before trial *Written interrogatories:* a method of discovery through written questions submitted by one party to another before trial *Deposition:* a method of discovery in which parties and their prospective witnesses are questioned before trial *Motion:* a formal request to the court, such as a motion to dismiss *Settlement:* a resolution of the dispute, making the trial unnecessary *Voir dire:* selection of the jury (not all cases are tried by a jury)	The trial court often makes rulings concerning these events but rarely writes an opinion on any of the rulings. Occasionally, a party may be allowed to appeal a pretrial ruling to an appeals court, which may write an opinion affirming, modifying, or reversing the ruling. Such an appeal is called an *interlocutory* appeal. It takes place before the trial court reaches a final judgment.

Exhibit 10.2   Overview of Civil Litigation—continued

EVENT	DEFINITIONS	DECISIONS, RULINGS, AND OPINIONS

III. Trial Stage
13. *Opening statement* of plaintiff
14. *Opening statement* of defendant
15. Plaintiff presents its case:
  (a) *evidence* introduced
  (b) *direct examination*
  (c) *cross-examination*
16. *Motions* to dismiss
17. Defendant presents its case:
  (a) *evidence* introduced
  (b) *direct examination*
  (c) *cross-examination*
18. Closing arguments to jury by attorneys
19. *Charge* to jury
20. *Verdict* of jury
21. *Judgment* of court
	Opening statement: a summary of the facts the attorney will try to prove during the trial
	Evidence: that which is offered to help prove or disprove a fact involved in the dispute
	Direct examination: questioning by an attorney of his or her own witness
	Cross-examination: questioning of a witness by an attorney for the other side
	Charge: the judge's instructions to the jury on how it should go about reaching its verdict
	Verdict: the results of the jury's deliberation
	Judgment: the final conclusion of a court
		The trial court often makes rulings concerning these events, but rarely writes an opinion on any of the rulings.
		After the trial, the trial court delivers its judgment. Usually, *no opinion* (explaining the judgment) is written.
		Several trial courts, however, such as federal trial courts (U.S. District Courts) and New York State trial courts, do sometimes write opinions.

IV. Appeal Stage 22. Filing of *notice of appeal* 23. Filing of *appellant's appellate brief* 24. Filing of *appellee's appellate brief* 25. Filing of appellant's reply brief 26. Oral argument by attorneys 27. Judgment of court	*Notice of appeal:* a statement of the intention to seek a review of the trial court's judgment *Appellant:* the party bringing the appeal because of dissatisfaction with the trial court's judgment *Appellee:* the party against whom the appeal is brought *Appellate brief:* a party's written argument covering the issues on appeal relating to claimed errors that occurred during the trial	An opinion of the middle appeals court (intermediate appellate court) is often written. This opinion of the middle appeals court might be further appealed to the highest court, in which event another opinion could be written. [Note that in some states there is no middle appeals court; the appeal goes directly from the trial court to the highest state court. See Exhibit 6.2 in chapter 6.]

Med-Arb: First, mediation is tried. If it is not successful, the proceeding becomes an arbitration, and the mediator switches roles. He or she then makes a decision as an arbitrator.

Neighborhood Justice Center (NJC): In many localities, an NJC exists to offer mediation and arbitration services for disputes involving ongoing relationships in the community, such as between landlord and tenant or among neighbors. The NJC could be sponsored by the government, a foundation, or an existing community organization.

Summary Jury Trial: The parties use an advisory jury, which often comes from the regular pool of jurors in the county. The attorneys present their evidence to this jury in an abbreviated format. The jury deliberates and renders a nonbinding advisory verdict. Attorneys then question the jurors on the strengths and weaknesses of each side's pre-

(continued on page 474)

Exhibit 10.3   Overview of Criminal Litigation

(Possible proceedings where court rulings, and opinions could be written. The events and their sequence presented below are examples only.)

EVENT	DEFINITIONS	RULINGS AND OPINIONS
I. Pretrial Stage 1. *Arrest* 2. *Initial appearance* before a judge or a magistrate 3. *Preliminary hearing* 4. Indictment by grand jury 5. *Arraignment* 6. Limited pretrial discovery 7. Pretrial motions 8. *Voir dire*	*Arrest:* to take someone into custody in order to bring him or her before the proper authorities *Initial appearance:* the first court appearance by the accused during which the court (a) informs him or her of the charges, (b) makes a decision on bail, and (c) determines the date of the next court proceeding *Preliminary hearing:* a court proceeding during which a decision is made as to whether there is probable cause to believe that the accused committed the crime(s) charged *Indictment:* a formal charge issued by the grand jury accusing the defendant of a crime. (If no grand jury is involved in the case, the accusation is contained in a document called an *information.*) *Arraignment:* a court proceeding in which the defendant is formally charged with the crime and enters a plea. Arrangements are then made for the trial. *Voir dire:* selection of the jury (not all cases are tried by a jury)	The trial court often makes rulings concerning these events, but rarely writes an opinion on any of the rulings. Occasionally, a party may be allowed to appeal a pretrial ruling immediately to an appeals court, which may write an opinion affirming, modifying, or reversing the ruling. This interlocutory appeal takes place before the trial court reaches a final judgment.
II. Trial Stage 9. *Opening statements* of attorneys 10. Government presents its case against the defendant: (a) *evidence* introduced (b) *direct examination* (c) *cross-examination* 11. Motions to dismiss 12. Defendant presents its case: (a) *evidence* introduced (b) *direct examination* (c) *cross-examination*	*Opening statements:* a summary of the facts the attorney will try to prove during the trial *Evidence:* that which is offered to help prove or disprove a fact involved in the dispute *Direct examination:* questioning by an attorney of his or her own witness *Cross-examination:* questioning of a witness by an attorney for the other side *Charge:* the judge's instructions to the jury on how it should go about reaching its verdict	The trial court often makes rulings concerning these events, but rarely writes an opinion on any of the rulings. After the trial, the trial court delivers its judgment. Usually, no opinion (explaining the judgment) is written. Several trial courts, however, such as federal trial courts (U.S. District Courts) and New York State trial courts, do sometimes write opinions.

Exhibit 10.3	Overview of Criminal Litigation—continued	
EVENT	**DEFINITIONS**	**RULINGS AND OPINIONS**
13. Closing arguments to jury by attorneys 14. *Charge* to jury 15. *Verdict* to jury 16. *Judgment* of court, including the sentence if defendant is convicted	*Verdict:* the results of the jury's deliberation *Judgment:* the final conclusion of a court	

III. Appeal Stage

17. Filing of *notice of appeal* 18. Filing of *appellant's appellate brief* 19. Filing of *appellee's appellate brief* 20. Filing of appellant's reply brief 21. Oral argument by attorneys 22. Judgment of court	*Notice of appeal:* a statement of the intention to seek a review of the trial court's judgment. *Appellant:* the party bringing the appeal because of dissatisfaction with the trial court's judgment *Appellee:* the party against whom the appeal is brought *Appellate brief:* a party's written argument covering the issues on appeal relating to claimed errors that occurred during the trial	An opinion in the middle appeals court (intermediate appellate court) will often be written. This opinion in the middle appeals court might be appealed to the highest court, in which event another opinion could be written. [Note that in some states, there is no middle court; the appeal goes directly from the trial court to the highest state court. See Exhibit 6.2 in chapter 6.]

sentation. The parties use all of this information in deciding whether they should settle and, if so, for what.

Paralegals have many roles in assisting attorneys who have cases in ADR. For example, a paralegal can organize files, schedule discovery and ADR itself, conduct investigations, summarize or digest data from discovery, help prepare the client for ADR, and assist the attorney during the ADR proceeding in much the same fashion as paralegals assist attorneys during regular trials.

In addition, some paralegals have become arbitrators and mediators themselves. In most states, you do not have to be an attorney to conduct arbitration or mediation. Service companies are available that offer arbitration and mediation services to parties involved in disputes. A few of these companies hire people with paralegal training and experience to be arbitrators or mediators.

Section C
LITIGATION ASSISTANTSHIP: PRETRIAL STAGE

For a list of paralegal functions in litigation, see the overview in chapter 2, page 47. The following are some of the most important paralegal functions at the *pretrial* state:

1. Service of process and court filings
2. Data retrieval
3. Digesting and indexing

4. Calendar control and scheduling
5. Drafting interrogatories and answers to interrogatories
6. Drafting pleadings
7. Drafting the settlement work-up
8. Preparation of trial notebook
9. Interviewing
10. Investigation
11. Legal research

The remainder of this chapter will cover most of these tasks, particularly those at the beginning of the list. Some are also discussed in chapter 8 on interviewing, chapter 9 on investigation, chapter 11 on legal research, chapter 13 on computers in the law, and chapter 14 on law office administration.

1. SERVICE OF PROCESS AND COURT FILINGS

The lawsuit begins with service of process—the delivery of the complaint and summons to the defendant. This is often done in person, although there are circumstances when the law allows substituted service such as by registered mail. In addition, witnesses are often served with a **subpoena,** which is a command to appear at a certain time and place to give testimony. A paralegal may be asked to serve process or to serve a subpoena. Alternatively, the law firm may decide to hire a service company that is a professional process server. If so, a paralegal may have the responsibility of hiring and supervising the company.

Completing a service yourself takes preparation and care. You have to know the local rules on how to serve someone properly. In addition, you need to anticipate the kinds of difficulty you might encounter "on the street." Here is how David Busch describes his first service assignment:

"I was given a subpoena to serve on a lady for a hearing the next day. I rushed to the courthouse to pick up the subpoena and immediately proceeded to the address given to me by the attorney. I spent over an hour looking for the address when I realized that it was a bad address. I frantically found a pay phone and called the lawyer." He was in court. His secretary "gave me a work address. I rushed to the work address to find out that she was on vacation for two weeks beginning yesterday. . . . This was frustrating. This was my first service and I could not even find the lady." I realized that process serving is not as easy as handing someone a copy of a lawsuit.[3]

Filing documents in court also requires careful preparation:

There are few things more frustrating to the legal assistant than getting something to the courthouse for filing, often on the very last day it is due, and having it returned, not filed, because of a technical error or oversight. Since the legal assistant is the "last checkpoint" for pleadings and other documents being sent to the courthouse, it falls on him or her to ensure those documents are complete and acceptable.

This observation is from litigation paralegal Erin Schlemme, who recommends the following basic steps for successful filings:[4]

- Know the correct address of the court where the filing must be made.
- Phone in advance to determine the exact hours when the clerk's office will be open to accept filings.

> "Litigation can be a fickle animal! The paralegal must be prepared to do whatever, whenever—at a moment's notice."
>
> —Kai Hollinger, Paralegal Supervisor, 1995

---

[3]David Busch, *A Job and an Adventure,* 12 AAPLA Advocate 3 (Alamo Area Professional Legal Assistants, October/November 1993).
[4]Erin Schlemme, *Courthouse Etiquette,* 11 The TALA Times 4 (Tulsa Ass'n of Legal Assistants, February 1993).

- Place the correct court number on what you are filing (this may be the docket number or a special computer coding number provided by the court's file management system).
- Use the correct format including the proper size of paper, content of the cover sheet, etc.
- Have the correct fees (know whether the clerk can accept a personal check or will accept only cash or a law firm check).
- Obtain an official statement indicating that you have made the filing, e.g., a dated receipt or a copy of what you have filed that has the clerk's court stamp on it.

Similar care is needed when filing in courts that allow facsimile filing. Under this method, pleadings are "faxed" directly to the court, eliminating the need to go to the court yourself or to hire a delivery service. The special procedures instituted by the court to use this method of filing must be scrupulously followed.

2. DATA RETRIEVAL

Finding or retrieving data from a file can sometimes be a difficult task. As soon as a lawsuit starts, letters, memoranda, affidavits, and other documents are collected at a rather fast pace. The filing problems presented by this volume of documents can be substantial. A usable index system should exist to let everyone know what is in a file. Even with a good index, however, portions of an active file may be scattered throughout the office on the desks of different people working on the case.

Several basic guidelines should be part of the paralegal's standard practice when engaged in any data retrieval assignment:

- Have a comprehensive knowledge of the office's filing system. Be sure you know who in the office already has this knowledge so that they can be consulted. Is there an index system? Is there a cross-index system? Are file summaries available?
- Have a comprehensive knowledge of the different stages of litigation and the most common documents involved in each stage.
- If possible, find out who wrote the document that contains the data you are trying to retrieve. Ask him or her for leads.
- Determine whether the data you are seeking may be found in more than one document and, if so, look for each document.
- Recognize that data in a document may be contradicted by other data in other documents. To determine the most current status of data, start examining the most recent documents in the file and work back.

Computerization, as we will see in chapter 13, has dramatically changed the way law offices store, manage, and retrieve data from the large number of files that a case often generates. Entire documents can be placed into a computer database by typing them word by word or by "scanning" them in through a photocopy-type machine that can "lift" text from a sheet of paper directly into a computer database. Once the documents are in the computer, searching for data can be relatively easy. For example, you can ask the computer to locate every document in which the phrase "back pain" is found. A well-designed computer database can answer such a question in seconds.

3. DIGESTING AND INDEXING

As litigation assistants, paralegals perform a large number of tasks during pretrial discovery. For an overview of these tasks, see Exhibit 10.4.

Exhibit 10.4   Paralegal Roles during Pretrial Discovery

DISCOVERY DEVICE	WHO MUST SUBMIT TO DEVICE?	ROLE OF LITIGATION ASSISTANT
1. Written interrogatories A series of written questions is sent by one party to the other. (See Federal Rule of Civil Procedure #33.)	Parties only. Nonparty witnesses do not have to answer and cannot send interrogatories.	a. Prepare a draft of the interrogatories. b. Prepare a draft of answers to interrogatories received from the other side. c. Read all pleadings, interview reports, and investigation reports as background for the drafting tasks listed in (a) and (b) above. d. Arrange conference with client to go over questions and answers. e. Draft a motion to compel a response to interrogatories. f. Draft a motion to have matters not answered be deemed admitted. g. Index and digest interrogatories and answers for office file. h. Enter due dates in office tickler to serve as reminders.
2. Oral deposition A deposition is a question-and-answer session usually conducted in the office of one of the attorneys. (See Federal Rule of Civil Procedure #30.)	A deposition can be taken of a party to the suit. It is also possible to take the deposition of a nonparty witness. The party being *deposed* (i.e., asked questions) is called the *deponent.*	a. Schedule time and place for the deposition. b. Prepare **subpoena duces tecum,** which is a command that specific documents or other items be produced. Here it asks the deponent to bring something to the deposition. c. Prepare a list of suggested questions for attorney to ask deponent. d. Arrange for scheduling and payment of stenographer or reporter. e. Order transcript of deposition. f. Read all pleadings, interview reports, investigation reports, and prior answers to interrogatories, if any, in order to prepare indexes, digests, and draft questions (see (c) above) for the attorney. g. Take notes at the deposition. h. Prepare motion to force compliance by other side. i. Prepare motion to have matters not answered deemed admitted. j. Read transcript of deposition to index it, digest it, compare it to interrogatory answers, look for inconsistencies, etc. k. Make entries in office tickler on due dates.

Exhibit 10.4 **Paralegal Roles during Pretrial Discovery—continued**

DISCOVERY DEVICE	WHO MUST SUBMIT TO DEVICE?	ROLE OF LITIGATION ASSISTANT
3. Written deposition Same as oral deposition, except that both attorneys are not present. The attorneys prepare the questions on behalf of their clients who are the deponents. But the questions are asked by a stenographer or reporter. (See Federal Rule of Civil Procedure #31.)	Same as oral deposition.	Same as oral deposition.
4. Production of documents and things; entry on land for inspection and other purposes A party wants to inspect, test, or copy documents (e.g., photos, drawings) or other tangible things, or go upon land to inspect, photograph, or measure. If a party has made a statement about the case, e.g., to the insurance adjuster, this discovery device may be a way to obtain a copy of the statement. (See Federal Rule of Civil Procedure #34.)	This device is directed at parties only. The party must be in possession or control of the document, thing, or land in question. If you want a *non-party* to turn over documents and other materials, you can seek a deposition of this non-party and use a *subpoena duces tecum* to specify what should be brought to the deposition.	**a.** Prepare a draft of a request for production of documents, things, etc. specifying what you want to copy, inspect, or test, and when you want to do so. **b.** Arrange who will do the inspecting, copying, etc., payment of costs involved, etc. **c.** Draft a motion to compel the inspection, copying, etc. **d.** File, digest, and index the report(s) based on the inspection, copying, etc. **e.** Enter scheduled dates for inspection, copying, etc. in the officer tickler.
5. Physical or mental examination The person to be examined is given the name and address of the doctor who will conduct the physical or mental exam. All parties, including the person examined, are given a copy of the doctor's report. (See Federal Rules of Civil Procedure #35.)	Limited to parties only and to persons under the control of parties e.g., the child of a party. (In a few courts, the employees of a party can also be forced to undergo a physical or mental examination.)	**a.** Schedule doctor's appointment and payment. **b.** Enter appointment date in office tickler. **c.** Prepare court motion to order the examination. **d.** Prepare court motion to have matters relevant to the examination be deemed admitted for failure to submit to examination.

E x h i b i t 1 0 . 4	**Paralegal Roles during Pretrial Discovery—continued**	
DISCOVERY DEVICE	**WHO MUST SUBMIT TO DEVICE?**	**ROLE OF LITIGATION ASSISTANT**
6. Request for admissions One party sends the other statements of fact and asks that the truth of the statements be admitted so that the requesting party does not have to prove the facts at trial. A similar request may be made to admit the genuineness of certain documents or other things. The responding party must either agree to the admission or disagree, with reasons why he or she is denying the request for admission. (See Federal Rule of Civil Procedure #36.)	Limited to parties only.	**a.** Read everything in the file (interview and investigation reports, interrogatory answers, deposition transcript, etc.) in order to prepare a list of facts the other side will be requested to admit. **b.** File, index, and digest the responses from the other side in the office file. **c.** Enter due dates in office tickler.

Perhaps one of the most frequently performed discovery tasks is digesting or summarizing discovery documents, particularly depositions. Here is how Dana Nikolewski describes a recent experience with this seemingly never-ending task:

It's Thursday and I'm on page 20 of a 300-page deposition, which I really should have finished summarizing last week. The phone rings and I relish the thought of this brief interruption, until I recognize the voice on the other end as none other than our local courier announcing the arrival of 200 more depositions which I know need to be summarized ASAP.[5]

Litigation paralegals do indeed spend a good deal of time digesting. Occasionally, you will see a want ad for paralegals to digest depositions full-time. Such individuals are sometimes called **depo summarizers.** While all paralegals do not perform the task full-time, the experience of Dana Nikolewski is not unusual.

To **digest** a document, you summarize it according to a given organizational principle. To **index** a document, you state where certain topics are covered in the document. The complexity of the task depends on the complexity of the case and the volume of paper generated before and during discovery.

Some of the basic objectives of digesting and indexing include:

- Creating order out of what might be hundreds or thousands of pages of data
- Providing ready access to selected topics in these pages once the summaries are correlated by subject matter

---

[5]Dana Nikolewski, *Just Call Me Dorothy,* 13 Newsletter 5 (Dallas Ass'n of Legal Assistants, April 1989).

- Providing a way of comparing testimony, verifying facts, spotting inconsistencies, and identifying evidentiary holes that need to be filled by further interviewing, investigation, and discovery
- Assisting the attorney in organizing the trial, particularly by suggesting questions to be used in the direct and cross-examination of witnesses on the stand. Such strategy considerations will often go into the attorney's *trial notebook* (see discussion below), which you may be asked to help prepare.

The starting point in *indexing* any document is to find out what topics in the document your supervisor wants you to index, such as leg injuries, wage history, medical payments, or tax assessments. Every time these topics appear in the document, you note the page number so that someone else can find these topics easily in that document. For an example of an index of a deposition, see Exhibit 10.5.

Exhibit 10.5 **Deposition Index**

INDEX OF DEPOSITION OF IAN SMITH
3/13/97

TOPIC	PAGES IN DEPOSITION
Leg injuries	2, 24, 33, 35, 45
Medical payments	1, 7, 19
Tax assessments	40, 43, 50
Wage history	1, 2, 4, 7, 25, 29

The method of *digesting* or summarizing data is also fairly simple. Suppose, for example, the following material comes from page 65 of the transcript of a deposition of Mr. Smith:

```
Line
1. Q. Could you tell me please exactly how long after the accident
2.    you first felt the pain in your leg?
3. A. Well, it's hard to say precisely because everything happened
4.    so fast and my head was spinning from. . . .
5. Q. Was it an hour, a day, a week?
6. A. Oh no, it wasn't that long. I'd say the pain started
7.    about ten minutes after the collision.
```

The above transcript testimony could be digested into:

> Began feeling pain in leg about 10 min. after collision: page 65, lines 1–7

Your supervisor might want you to present this digest in three columns in what is called a **page/line format.** For example:

PAGE/LINE	SUMMARY	TOPIC
65:1–7	Began feeling pain in leg about 10 min. after collision	Injury, Leg Pain

As you can see, considerable space can be saved by eliminating the question-and-answer format and focusing directly on the information sought. Such summaries could be placed on small file cards under the heading "Injury" or on summary sheets that are categorized by such headings. Alternatively, the summaries can be entered into computer programs. (An example of such a program is called SUMMATION II.) You can then collate all statements made by the same witness on a particular topic. You can compare what this same deposition witness said about a particular topic in his or her answers to interrogatories. You can compare what other witnesses have said about the same topic. The possibilities are endless once you have prepared careful, readable summaries.

Before examining some of the major kinds of digesting that are used in a law office, read the general guidelines on digesting in Exhibit 10.6.

Exhibit 10.6   Guidelines for Digesting Discovery Documents

1. Obtain clear instructions from your supervisor. What precisely have you been asked to do? What have you expressly or by implication been told not to do? It is a good idea to write down the supervisor's instructions. If you have never worked with a particular supervisor before, show him or her your work soon after you begin the assignment to make sure you have understood the instructions.

2. Know the difference between paraphrasing testimony and quoting testimony. To **paraphrase** is to phrase the testimony partly or entirely in your own words. To quote is to use the exact words of the witness even though you may leave out part of what the witness said. Supervisors may not want you to do any paraphrasing. They may want to do their own paraphrasing. Again, you need to know precisely what is expected.

3. Do not "editorialize," i.e., inject your personal comments. For example, do not say that the response of a witness whose testimony you are digesting is "unbelievable."

4. Know the case inside and out. You cannot digest something you do not understand. You must have a general understanding of the causes of action and the defenses so that you can grasp the context of the testimony. Read the client file, including interview and investigation reports, pleadings, interrogatory answers, other discovery documents, etc.

5. The answers given in a deposition often ramble. (The same may be true of some interrogatory answers.) Given this reality, act on the assumption that the same topic is covered in more than one place in the discovery document. Look for this diversity and record it in your summary by pointing out *each* time the same topic is mentioned.

6. Don't expect the answers to be consistent—even from the same witness. Do not consciously or unconsciously try to help the witness by blocking out potential inconsistencies. If on page 45 the witness said she saw a "car" but on page 104 said she saw a "van," do not blot out the distinction by saying she saw a "motor vehicle," or by failing to mention both. The danger of doing this is more serious than you think, particularly when you are reading hundreds of pages and are getting a little red in the eyes.

7. Always think in terms of categories as you summarize. Place your summaries into categories. The categories may be as broad as the name of a given witness. Other categories include:

   - Background information
   - Education
   - Past employment
   - Present employment
   - Medical history
   - Insurance
   - Prior claims
   - Pre-accident facts
   - Accident facts
   - Post-accident facts
   - Medical injuries from this accident
   - Damage to property
   - Prior statements made

   Your supervisor will usually tell you what categories or topics to use in organizing your summaries. If not, use your common sense and create your own.

8. Each summary should include the specific document you used (e.g., deposition), the page, and, if possible, the lines on the page that are the basis of the summary.

Exhibit 10.6   Guidelines for Digesting Discovery Documents—continued

9. Find out if the law firm has an office manual that gives you instructions on digesting. If not, check closed case files for samples of the kind of digesting and indexing that the firm has done in the past. Ask your supervisor if you should use such samples as models.
10. Prepare summaries of your summaries whenever you have an extensive digesting assignment that requires the examination of numerous documents for numerous topics.
11. Update the summaries. After you finish your digest, more facts may become known through further investigation and discovery. Supplement your earlier summary reports by adding the new data.
12. Keep a list (or know where to find a list) of every piece of paper in a file. Some digesting/indexing assignments will require you to examine everything in the file.

There are two major kinds of summaries:

- *Digest by person*
- *Digest by subject matter*

Digest by Person

In a **digest by person,** you focus on a particular witness, such as the person questioned in a deposition. Your instructions may be to provide a page-by-page summary of what the witness said. If so, you simply go through the entire document and summarize everything (see Exhibit 10.7). Include a table of contents at the beginning of the report you prepare that provides the summary (see Exhibit 10.8).

Exhibit 10.7   Digest by Person

PAGE/LINE	SUMMARY	TOPIC
1:1–35	John R. Smith, 12 Main St. Buffalo N.Y. 14202; 456-9103.	Personal Data
1:36–40	Mechanic, XYZ Factory, 3/13/73; became supervisor 3/87.	Employment
2:1–28	Met plaintiff 7/31/81 at factory; was plaintiff's superior; trained plaintiff to operate equipment.	Relationship to Plaintiff
2:29–47	Was working on date of accident (9/1/90); saw plank fall on plaintiff.	Accident

---

Exhibit 10.8   Table of Contents for Digest by Person

DIGEST OF DEPOSITION OF JOHN R. SMITH

CASE: Jones v. XYZ Factory
DEPONENT: John R. Smith, supervisor of plaintiff
DATE OF DEPOSITION: 2/24/91
DATE SUMMARY PREPARED: 5/16/91
SUMMARY PREPARED BY: George Henderson, Paralegal

OFFICE FILE NUMBER: 90-341
COURT DOCKET NUMBER: Civ. 2357-1
ATTORNEY ON CASE: Linda Stout

Exhibit 10.8	**Table of Contents for Digest by Person—continued**

TABLE OF CONTENTS

Topic	Pages in Deposition
Background Information	1–4, 9
Smith's Knowledge of Accident	2–3, 5, 7–10
Company Report Filed by Smith	23
Smith's Instructions to Plaintiff Just Before Accident	15–17

Digest by Subject Matter

In a **digest by subject matter,** you are asked to focus on a particular topic only. For example:

- Everything the witness said about the dismissal
- Everything that all the witnesses said about the condition of the car after the accident
- Everything that all the witnesses said about events after 6 P.M. on 5/30/95
- All statements made to the police after the accident
- All references to the meeting of 7/23/96

The subject-matter or topic can be limited to a particular discovery document, such as a deposition, or it can cover a large number of documents:

- The complaint
- The answer
- Interrogatory answers
- Deposition transcript
- Responses to requests for admission
- Reports obtained via a motion to produce documents or other things
- Medical examination reports
- Other investigation reports
- Etc.

Hence, one digest summary can pull together everything on a particular topic from all of the above sources so that comparisons, correlations, and commentaries can be made.

If the case involves a large number of events (e.g., arising out of a relatively complex personal injury or business dispute), the office may also want a **time-line summary** in which you present the sequence of events in careful chronological fashion. For example:

- 3/13/96. John Farrell (JF) notifies London Car Rental (LCR) about defect in steering wheel.
- 3/14/96. JF returns vehicle to LCR. Given replacement truck.
- 3/15/96. Accident occurs on Rt. 52 outside Portsmouth, OH.
- Etc.

4. CALENDAR CONTROL AND SCHEDULING

The central focus of calendar control is the office **tickler system,** which is used to record important dates and to remind everyone to take appropriate action on these dates. Attorneys need constant reminders of due dates, particularly when they are working on more than one case, or when more than one attorney is working on a single case. Here are some examples of tasks and events about which attorneys need to be "tickled": client meetings, filing complaint before the running of the statute of limitations, sending demand to insurance company, requesting a jury trial, filing interrogatories, responding to interrogatories, filing requests for production of documents, responding to requests for

"The words a paralegal should never, ever be heard saying are, 'Oh, was that today?' " Being on top of due dates should be "second nature" to a paralegal.

—Christofer French, Denver, 1996

production of documents, conducting depositions, filing pretrial motions, appearing at hearings on pretrial motions, conducting settlement negotiations, etc.

Scheduling is often a secretarial responsibility, although in complex cases, paralegals can become involved. Arrangements must be made for expert witnesses to prepare reports and to give deposition and trial testimony; timely notifications of discovery events must be made; medical examinations must be arranged, etc.

5. DRAFTING INTERROGATORIES AND ANSWERS TO INTERROGATORIES

Here are some sample interrogatories used in a personal injury case:

Sample Interrogatories Covering Injuries and Damages

6. State the name of each person for whom you claim damages for personal injuries.
7. Describe in detail all injuries and symptoms, whether physical, mental, or emotional, experienced since the occurrence and claimed to have been caused, aggravated, or otherwise contributed to by it.
8. As to each medical practitioner who has examined or treated any of the persons named in your answer to Interrogatory 6, above, for any of the injuries or symptoms described, state:
   (a) The name, address, and specialty of each medical practitioner;
   (b) The date of each examination or treatment;
   (c) The physical, mental, or emotional condition for which each examination or treatment was performed.
9. Has any person named in your answers to Interrogatory 6, above, been hospitalized since the occurrence? _____ If so, state:
   (a) The name and location of each hospital in which each was confined;
   (b) The dates of each hospitalization;
   (c) The conditions treated during each hospitalization;
   (d) The nature of the treatment rendered during each hospitalization.

10. Have any diagnostic studies, tests, or procedures been performed since the accident? _____ If so, state:
    (a) The nature thereof;
    (b) The name, address, and occupation of the person performing same;
    (c) The place where performed, and, if in a clinic, laboratory, or hospital, the name and address thereof;
    (d) The name and present or last-known address of each party now in possession or control of any records prepared in connection with each study, test, or procedure.
11. Is any person named in your answer to Interrogatory 6, above, still under the care of any medical practitioner? _____ If so, state:
    (a) The name and address of each practitioner;
    (b) The nature of each condition for which care is being rendered;
    (c) Which of the conditions are related to the accident.
12. State as to each item of medical expense attributable to the accident:
    (a) The amount;
    (b) The name and address of the person or organization paid or owed therefor;
    (c) The date of each item of expense (attach copies of itemized bills).

Considerable skill is required in drafting and replying to or answering interrogatories. The tasks have opposite objectives: in drafting interrogatories, you want to obtain as much information as possible from the other side, while in responding to interrogatories you usually want to say as little as possible without be untruthful. Exhibits 10.9 and 10.10 present guidelines on drafting and answering interrogatories.

Exhibit 10.9   Guidelines on Drafting Interrogatories

1. Be sure that your office tickler system states when the interrogatories must be filed.
2. Obtain general and specific instructions from your supervisor on the questions to be asked in the interrogatories.
3. Read all the documents on the case that have been prepared thus far (such as the client interview report [intake memo], field investigation report, complaint, and answer).
4. Look at drafts of other interrogatories that have been used in other cases that are similar to your case. Determine whether courts in your area have approved any standard-form interrogatories.
5. Recognize the need to adapt interrogatories from the files of other clients to the peculiar needs of your case.
6. Start out with requests for basic data (name, address, age, occupation, etc.) from the person who will be answering the interrogatories—the respondent.
7. Try to avoid questions that call for simple *yes/no* answers unless you also ask questions about the factual basis for such answers.
8. Try to avoid questions that call for an opinion from the respondent unless the opinion is relevant or might provide leads to other facts.
9. Phrase the questions so as to elicit facts.
10. Know what facts will be necessary to establish your client's case, and ask specific questions focusing on those facts. Know the elements of the causes of action and defenses in the case. Ask questions designed to uncover facts for each element.
11. As to each fact, ask questions calculated to elicit the respondent's ability to comment on the fact. (How far away was he or she? Does he or she wear glasses? etc.)
12. Phrase the fact questions so that the respondent will have to indicate clearly whether he or she is talking from firsthand knowledge or hearsay.

Exhibit 10.10   Guidelines on Responding to Interrogatories

1. Be sure that your office tickler system states when the answers are due.
2. Obtain general and specific instructions from your supervisor on drafting the answers.
3. Check all the facts in proposed answers with the facts asserted in available documents (such as the client interview report [intake memo], field investigation report, complaint, and answer).
4. Do not volunteer information beyond the confines of the question unless necessary to clarify a position (when, for example, a simple answer would be damagingly misleading without the clarification).
5. When an answer to a question is not known, say so.
6. Preface most answers by saying "to the best of my knowledge" or "as far as I can recall" in order to provide some leeway if the answer later proves to be incorrect.
7. Recognize that the other side will try to use the answers against you. For example, opposing counsel may try to get the client to say something on cross-examination that will contradict the answers given by the client in the interrogatories.

Exhibit 10.10 **Guidelines on Responding to Interrogatories—continued**

8. Recognize the kinds of improper questions that a party does not have to answer. For example:
- Clearly irrelevant questions that are not likely to lead to admissible evidence
- Unduly repetitive or burdensome questions
- Questions inquiring into **attorney work product,** e.g., questions that ask for the attorney's strategy or that ask for copies of legal memoranda.
- Questions that expressly or implicitly call for a violation of the attorney-client privilege, e.g., "what did your attorney tell you?"

9. Prepare supplemental answers to prior answers where new facts are obtained after the interrogatories were answered and filed.

6. DRAFTING PLEADINGS

The major pleadings in litigation are the complaint, answer, reply, and counterclaim. Very often you will use standard forms as the starting point in drafting pleadings. Closely examine the guidelines in Exhibit 10.11 on using standard forms.

Here, we will concentrate on drafting a complaint through an examination of its basic structure:

- Caption
- Designation of the pleading
- Statement of jurisdiction
- Body
- Prayer for relief
- Subscription
- Verification

Not all complaints follow this format. You need to check the requirements in the statutes and court rules that govern the structure for complaints in the court where you are filing the action. Exhibit 10.12 presents a sample complaint[6] that follows the basic structure listed above. (See page 488.)

Caption

A **caption** is the heading of a complaint. It should contain the name of the court, the names of the parties, and the number assigned to the case by the court.

Designation of the Pleading

The title of the pleadings should be clearly stated at the top. The pleading for our example in Exhibit 10.12 is a Complaint for Negligence. (See page 488.)

Statement of Jurisdiction

Not all state courts require a statement of the court's **subject-matter jurisdiction**—its power or authority to hear this kind of case. A complaint filed in federal court, however, usually contains a statement of the U.S. District Court's subject-matter jurisdiction.

For purposes of determining **venue**—the place of the trial—the complaint may also have to allege the residence of the parties, where the accident or wrong allegedly occurred, etc.

---

[6]Adapted from MacDonald, Pick, DeWitt, & Volz, *Wisconsin Practice Methods,* 2d ed., § 1530, page 239 (West, 1959).

Exhibit 10.11   How to Avoid Abusing a Standard Form

1. A standard form is an example of the document or instrument that you need to draft, such as a pleading, contract, or other agreement.

2. Standard forms are found in a number of places—for example, in formbooks, in manuals, in practice texts, in some statutory codes, and in some court rules.

3. Most standard forms are written by private attorneys. Occasionally, however, a standard form will be written by the legislature or by the court as the suggested or required format to use.

4. Considerable care must be exercised in the use of a standard form. Such forms can be deceptive in that they appear to require little more than filling in the blanks. The intelligent use of these forms usually requires much more.

5. The cardinal rule is: *adapt* the form to the particulars of the client's case.

6. Do not be afraid of changing the printed language in the form if you have a good reason. Whenever you make such a change, bring it to your supervisor for approval.

7. You should never use a standard form unless and until you have satisfied yourself that you know the meaning of *every* word and phrase on the form. This includes **boilerplate,** which is standard language often used in the same kind of document. The great temptation of most form users is to ignore what they do not understand because the form has been used so often in the past without any apparent difficulty. Do not give in to this temptation. Find out what everything means by:
   - Using a legal dictionary
   - Asking your supervisor
   - Asking other knowledgeable people
   - Doing other legal research

8. You need to know whether the entire form or any part of it has ever been litigated in court. To find this out, do some legal research in the area of the law relevant to the form.

9. Once you have found a form that appears useful, look around for another form that attempts to serve the same purpose. Analyze the different or alternative forms available. Which one is preferable? Why? The important point is: keep questioning the validity of the form. Be very skeptical about the use of any form.

10. Do not leave any blank spaces on the form. If a question does not apply, make a notation to indicate this, such as N.A.

11. If the form was written for another state, be sure that the form can be adapted and is adapted to the law of your state. Often, however, an out-of-state form is simply unadaptable to your state because of the differences in the laws of the two states.

12. Occasionally, you may go to an old case file to find a document that might be used as a model for a similar document that you need to draft on a current case. All the above cautions apply to the adaptation of documents from closed case files.

Body

The claims of the plaintiff are presented in the *body* of the complaint. A claim is a cause of action. Every separate cause of action being used by the plaintiff should be stated in a separate "count," e.g., Count I, Count II, or simply as First Cause of Action, Second Cause of Action, etc. The paragraphs should be consecutively numbered. Each paragraph should contain a single fact or a closely related grouping of facts.

Exhibit 10.12   Structure of Complaint

Caption

STATE OF _____ COUNTY OF _____
_____ COURT
John Doe, Plaintiff

v.   Civil Action No. _____

Richard Roe, Defendant

Designation of Pleading →

COMPLAINT FOR NEGLIGENCE

Statement of Jurisdiction →

Plaintiff alleges that:

1. The jurisdiction of this court is based on section _____, title _____ of the [State] Code.

2. Plaintiff is a plumber, residing at 107 Main Street in the City of _____, _____ County, State of _____ .

3. Upon information and belief, defendant is a traveling salesman, residing at 5747 Broadway Street in the City of Chicago, Cook County, Illinois.

4. On or about the second day of January, 1989 an automobile driven by defendant, on Highway 18 in the vicinity of Verona, _____, struck an automobile being driven by the plaintiff on said highway.

Body

5. Defendant was negligent in the operation of said automobile at the aforesaid time and place as to:
   a. Speed,
   b. Lookout,
   c. Management and control.

6. As a result of said negligence of defendant, his automobile struck plaintiff's automobile and caused the following damage:
   a. Plaintiff was subjected to great pain and suffering.
   b. Plaintiff necessarily incurred medical and hospital expense.
   c. Plaintiff suffered a loss of income.
   d. Plaintiff's automobile was damaged.

Prayer for Relief →

Wherefore plaintiff demands judgment in the amount of one hundred thousand dollars ($100,000), together with the costs and disbursements of this action.

_____
Plaintiff's Attorney
1 Main Street

_____ , _____

Subscription →

State of _____
                                                      ss
County of _____

John Doe, being first duly sworn on oath according to law, deposes and says that he has read the foregoing complaint and that the matters stated therein are true to the best of his knowledge, information, and belief.

_____
John Doe

Verification

Subscribed and sworn to before me on this_____ day of _____, 19 _____ .

_____
Notary Public

My commission expires:

With what factual detail must the complaint state the cause of action? There are two main schools of thought on this question: fact pleading versus notice pleading.

1. *Fact Pleading.* In **fact pleading,** there must be a statement of the *ultimate facts* that set forth the cause of action. Not every detail that the plaintiff intends to try to prove at trial is pleaded. The complaint need not contain a catalog of the evidence that the plaintiff will eventually introduce at the trial. Only the ultimate facts are pleaded. There is, however, no satisfactory definition of an ultimate fact. Generally, it is one that is essential to the establishment of an element of a cause of action.

   The complaint must *not* state conclusions of law, such as "Jones assaulted Smith" or "Jones violated section 23 of the state code." The problem, however, is that it is as difficult to define a conclusion of law as it is to define an ultimate fact. Some statements are mixed statements of fact and law—for example, "Jones negligently drove his car into . . . ." As a matter of common sense and practicality, if the conclusion of law (here, "negligently") is also a convenient way of stating facts, it will be permitted.

   The only reliable guide for a pleader is to determine what the prior decisions of the courts in the state have concluded are proper and improper statements of fact in a complaint.

2. *Notice Pleading.* In federal courts under the Federal Rules of Civil Procedure and in states that have adopted the lead of the federal courts, the goal of the complaint is to say enough to notify or inform the defendant of the nature of the claims against him or her. This is the essence of **notice pleading.** There is no requirement that ultimate facts be alleged. The plaintiff must simply provide a "short and plain statement of the claim showing the pleader is entitled to relief."

   It is not improper to fail to plead an ultimate fact. The critical point is that the complaint will not be thrown out if it *fails* to plead an ultimate fact or if it *includes* conclusions of law—as long as the complaint gives adequate notice of the nature of the claim. The technicalities of pleading facts, conclusions of law, etc. are unimportant in notice pleading.

   Notice pleading does not necessarily require a different kind of pleading from fact pleading; notice pleading is simply more liberal or tolerant in what is acceptable.

When the plaintiff lacks personal knowledge of a fact being alleged, the fact should be stated **"upon information and belief"** as in the third paragraph of Exhibit 10.12.

There are times when the law requires specificity in the pleading. For example, allegations of fraud must be stated with specificity or particularity. Also, when special damages are required in defamation cases, the facts must be pleaded with some specificity.

Prayer for Relief

In the **prayer for relief,** the complaint asks for a specific amount of damages, or for some other form of relief such as an injunction against a nuisance. (If the prayer asks for damages, the clause requesting it is called the *ad damnum* clause.) In the event that the defendant fails to appear and answer the complaint, a default judgment is entered against the defendant. The relief given the plaintiff in a default judgment cannot exceed what the plaintiff asked for in the prayer for relief.

Subscription

The **subscription** is the signature of the attorney who prepared the complaint and who represents the plaintiff. If the plaintiff wrote the complaint and is acting as his or her own attorney in the case, the plaintiff signs.

Verification

A **verification** is an affidavit that is submitted with the pleading. It is signed by a party on whose behalf the pleading was prepared, who swears that he or she has read the pleading and that it is true to the best of his or her knowledge, information, and belief. (Not all states require that complaints be verified.)

7. DRAFTING THE SETTLEMENT WORK-UP

Throughout the pretrial stage of litigation, the opposing attorneys often engage in efforts to negotiate a settlement of the case in order to avoid a trial. One of the formal documents the parties sometimes use during negotiations is the **settlement work-up,** also called a settlement brochure. It contains a summary of the major facts in the case presented in a manner designed to encourage the other side (or its liability insurance company) to settle the case. Paralegals often have a large role in helping draft this document. For a sample settlement work-up, see Exhibit 9.10 in chapter 9.

8. PREPARATION OF TRIAL NOTEBOOK

A **trial notebook,** also called a trial book, is a collection of documents, arguments, and strategies that an attorney plans to use during a trial. It is often organized in a loose-leaf binder for easy use by the attorney. The notebook becomes the attorney's checklist for conducting the trial.

Not all trial notebooks are organized the same way. Litigation assistant Pam Robtoy cautions us that "Just as each attorney has different preferences on how they want you to perform different tasks, each notebook you organize will be different, depending on which attorney will be utilizing the notebook and the particular requirements of the case. For example, a trial notebook for a medical malpractice case would likely contain a section for medical research regarding the surgical procedure, medication, etc. that is the focus of the case."[7] A trial notebook for a breach-of-contract case would not.

Many trial notebooks contain the following sections:[8]

- Table of Contents
- Things to Do
- Trial Schedule/Deadlines
- Trial Team (addresses, phone numbers)
- Case Outline
- Statement of Facts
- Pleadings
- Trial Briefs/Trial Memoranda (submitted to the court)
- Law
- Outline of Liability
- Our Exhibits
- Opposition Exhibits
- Our Witnesses
- Opposition Witnesses
- Witness Statements
- Requests for Production and Responses

---

[7]Pam Robtoy, *Preparing Trial Notebooks,* 14 Legal Paraphernalia 5 (St. Louis Ass'n of Legal Assistants, July/August 1994).

[8]Hollins, *Assignment: Trial Prep,* 2 California Paralegal 30 (April/June 1990); Feder, *Translating Professional Competence into Performance Competence,* 15 Legal Economics 44 (April 1989).

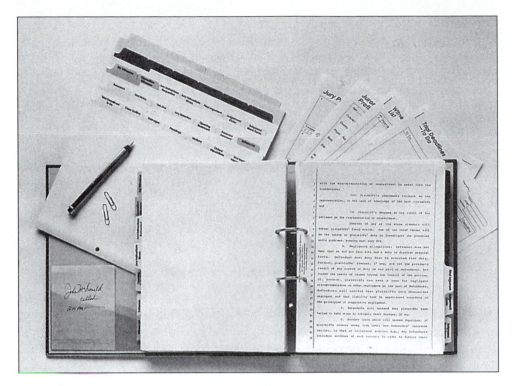

LawFiles Trial Notebook. Courtesy of Bindertek, Sausalito, California.

- Requests for Admission and Responses
- Direct Examination Outline of Questions
- Anticipated Cross-Examination Questions
- Outline of Damages
- Motions
- Deposition Index and Outlines
- Voir Dire Questions
- Juror Information
- Jury Chart
- Records
- Opening Statements
- Plaintiff Testimony
- Jury Instructions Requests
- Defendant Testimony
- Final Arguments

It's often the paralegal's job to collect the material that will go into the notebook, organize it, keep it current, and help make it useful to the attorney as a vehicle for trial preparation and trial management. Specifically, the paralegal might:

- Prepare summaries of deposition testimony.
- Prepare a list of all parties and witnesses plus people who are expected to be mentioned during testimony; index this list to the rest of the trial notebook.
- Prepare sample questions to ask witnesses, particularly when needed to lay the foundation for evidence to be introduced.

- Prepare a summary description or log of all the exhibits to be used.
- Prepare an abstract of the contents of every document.
- State the location of documents and exhibits that will not be contained in the trial notebook itself.
- Cross-index material on particular witnesses or on legal theories.
- Summarize all information known about each juror from voir dire.
- Prepare end tabs for each section of the notebook.
- Color-code different kinds of documents and information, such as using blue sheets for citations to authorities supporting claims and yellow sheets for deposition testimony and other statements of the opposing party.

Section D
LITIGATION ASSISTANTSHIP: TRIAL STAGE

The role of paralegals at trials depends, in part, on the involvement that they have had with the case up to trial. If the involvement has been minimal, then they may not have much to do to assist the attorney at trial. If, on the other hand, they have been working closely with the attorney on the case all along, their role at trial could include a number of tasks:

- Monitoring all the files, documents, and evidence that the attorney will need to plan and to replan strategy as outlined in the trial notebook
- Helping design trial exhibits. (See Exhibit 10.13 for an example.)

Exhibit 10.13   Trial Graphic Designed by a Paralegal

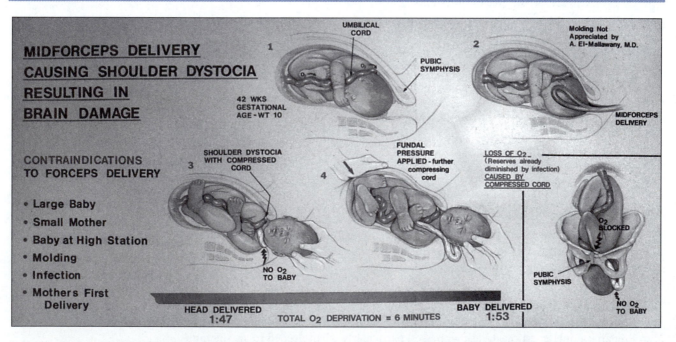

Illustration created by paralegal Kathleen Young, Litigation Visuals, Inc., that helped win a $3.9 million verdict. "Illustrations really do help the jury know where they are going in calculating damages." 11 *Legal Assistant Today* 28 (November/December, 1993).

- Doing some spot legal research on issues that come up during the trial that require an answer fairly quickly
- Preparing preliminary drafts of certain motions and other documents that are required during the course of the trial
- Assuring the presence of witnesses; assisting the attorney in preparing them for direct examination and in anticipating what may be asked of them on cross-examination
- Taking notes on the testimony of certain witnesses. The attorney may be able to use these notes in preparing for other segments of the trial. A typed transcript of the testimony may not be available until after the trial.
- Making suggestions to the attorney on what questions to ask a witness based on the paralegal's close following of what has happened thus far in the trial, and based on his or her involvement with the documents and files prepared during the pretrial stage.

See p. 301 on the role of the paralegal sitting "second chair" (or "third chair") during the trial.

If the office is about to begin a very important and potentially complex trial, it may decide to conduct a **shadow trial** first. A shadow trial is a mock (i.e., pretend) trial designed to give the participants "stand-up" practice and feedback. For example, the office might hire some strangers to play the roles of jurors and conduct part of the trial in front of them. Attorneys in the office would be assigned the roles of opposing counsel. "Jury" deliberations would take place in front of everyone. After the trial, there would be a freewheeling discussion of the strengths and weaknesses of the case. In effect, the shadow trial acts as a kind of focus group in preparation for the real trial. (Since actual opposing attorneys and witnesses are not involved, a mock trial is different from the summary jury trial discussed earlier under ADR—alternative dispute resolution.) Litigation paralegals often have a large role in helping organize shadow trials, e.g., hiring the jurors, holding an orientation session for them before the proceedings, acting as a nonvoting juror to keep the deliberations moving along and on track.

Section E
LITIGATION ASSISTANTSHIP: APPEAL STAGE

After the trial, the losing attorney plans appeal strategies. He or she must review all of the documents and testimony in the trial in order to identify grounds for an appeal. The paralegal may be asked to go back over the record and do the following:

- Make a list of every time I objected to something during the trial. Include the page number where my objection is found, a brief summary of what my objection was, and the ruling of the judge on my objection.
- Make a list of every time opposing counsel made reference to a particular topic, such as the plaintiff's prior involvement in other litigation.
- Make a list of every time the judge asked questions of witnesses.

Other paralegal tasks can include:

- Researching the legislative history of relevant statutes
- Shepardizing cases and conducting cite checking
- Reading over appellate briefs to cross-check the accuracy of quoted testimony from the typed transcript of the trial
- Monitoring the typing, printing, and filing of appellate briefs

> "You might have a stress attack before you walk into a courtroom for a big trial. Are all of the exhibits in order? Did you remember extra exhibit stickers? Will you be able to find that one piece of paper out of a thousand when the attorney" wants it during the trial?
>
> —Barbara J. Howell, Litigation Paralegal, Houston, 1996

Section F
LITIGATION ASSISTANTSHIP: ENFORCEMENT STAGE

If a money judgment was awarded to the client, considerable work may be required in collecting it from the **judgment debtor,** the party obligated by the court to pay the judgment. (The person who won the judgment and must be paid is the **judgment creditor.**) The paralegal can arrange for the sheriff to begin **execution,** which is the process of carrying out or enforcing a judgment. The judgment debtor may be ordered by the court to submit to an examination of what his or her assets are. Investigation work will probably be required to determine what assets exist, where they are, and how they might be reached. In some cases, the attorney may be able to petition the court for a contempt order against the judgment debtor for noncompliance. The paralegal can help by assembling the factual basis to support this charge and in drafting some of the court papers involved.

Chapter Summary

Civil litigation begins with the filing of a complaint, to which the defendant responds with an answer. In these pleadings, the parties state their causes of action and defenses. The next major event is discovery, which can include interrogatories, depositions, requests for admissions, etc. If motions for summary judgment are denied, the trial proceeds. After voir dire and opening statements to the jury, the party with the burden of proof puts on its case through the introduction of evidence and the direct examination of witnesses. The latter can be cross-examined by the other party. When the first party rests, the other goes through the same steps. A motion for a directed verdict will be granted (thus ending the case), if there was a failure to establish a prima facie case. After closing statements to the jury and the instructions of the judge, the case goes to the jury. Its verdict (if accepted by the court) becomes the basis of the court's judgment.

If dissatisfied with the judgment, the appellant files a notice of appeal and an appellate brief. The appellee also files an appellate brief. After oral argument, the appellate court affirms, modifies, or reverses the judgment of the lower court. A further appeal to a higher appellate court might also be possible.

Criminal litigation often begins with an arrest warrant, followed by an initial appearance. Once the decision on bail is made, the prosecution proceeds to the preliminary hearing to determine whether probable cause exists. If so, the grand jury will then determine whether to issue an indictment. The arraignment is next. If plea bargaining is unsuccessful, the case goes to trial, where guilt must be established beyond a reasonable doubt. The criminal trial then proceeds in a manner similar to a civil trial: voir dire, opening statements, etc. The appeal process is also similar: notice of appeal, appellate briefs, etc.

In an administrative hearing, a hearing examiner makes a decision on the dispute within the agency. His or her decision will usually be in the form of a recommendation to a higher official or body within the agency. When a party has exhausted administrative remedies, he or she can appeal the agency's decision to a court.

Alternatives to litigation can include arbitration, rent-a-judge, mediation, med-arb, neighborhood justice centers, and summary jury trial.

Among the roles fulfilled by paralegals during litigation are the following: serving and filing documents, retrieving and organizing data from the files, indexing and digesting discovery documents, maintaining the calendar, drafting interrogatories and answers to interrogatories, drafting complaints and other pleadings, helping prepare the trial notebook, providing assistance as needed during the trial, retrieving and digesting facts in preparation for appeal, and providing general assistance in collecting a judgment.

KEY TERMS

litigious, 452
litigation, 452
quasi-judicial, 452
civil dispute, 452
criminal dispute, 452
damages, 453
liable, 453
joint and several liability, 453
retainer, 453
appearance, 453
attorney of record, 453
forum, 453
estate, 453
diversity of citizenship, 453
venue, 453
complaint, 454
plaintiff, 454
cause of action, 454
stating a cause of
   action, 454
codefendant, 454
pleading, 454
allegation, 454
information and belief, 454
ad damnum, 454
jury trial, 454
filed, 454
service of process, 454
summons, 454
process server, 454
affidavit, 455
statute of limitations, 455
in personam jurisdiction, 455
personal jurisdiction, 455
motion to dismiss, 455
failure to state a cause of
   action, 455
procedural law, 455
Federal Rules of Civil
   Procedure (FRCP), 455
substantive law, 455
answer, 455
default judgment, 455
motion, 455
defense, 455
affirmative defense, 456
cross-claim, 456

counterclaim, 456
thirty-party complaint, 456
contest, 456
adverse judgment, 456
discovery, 457
written interrogatories, 457
deposition, 457
requests for admissions, 457
order, 457
hearing, 457
motion for summary
   judgment, 457
magistrate, 458
pretrial conference, 458
stipulated, 458
in issue, 458
tangible evidence, 458
testimonial evidence, 458
introduce evidence, 458
set for trial, 458
bailiff, 458
jury panel, 458
voir dire, 458
challenge for cause, 458
bias, 458
peremptory challenge, 458
alternate, 458
rule on witnesses, 459
opening statement, 459
burden of proof, 459
bench conference, 459
objection, 459
competency, 459
excuse the jury, 459
examination, 459
overrule, 459
direct examination, 459
ground, 459
hearsay, 459
sustain, 459
strike from the record, 459
cross-examination, 459
redirect examination, 460
qualify (a witness), 460
expert witness, 460
court, 460
clerk, 461

exhibit, 461
move into evidence, 461
rest one's case, 461
adjourn, 461
directed verdict, 461
prima facie case, 461
take under advisement, 461
closing argument, 462
jury instructions, 462
presumption, 462
verdict, 462
elements, 462
preponderance of the
   evidence, 462
standard of proof, 462
judgment, 463
judgment not withstanding
   the verdict, 463
motion for a new trial, 463
appeal, 463
stay, 463
timely, 463
notice of appeal, 463
bond, 463
judgment on the merits, 463
res judicata, 464
bar, 464
appellant, 464
record, 464
transcript, 464
docket, 464
appellate brief, 464
appellee, 464
issues on appeal, 464
oral argument, 464
panel, 464
opinion, 464
dissent, 465
affirm, 465
waive, 465
petition, 465
rehearing, 465
en banc, 465
appeal as a matter of
   right, 465
writ of certiorari, 465
mandate, 465

satisfy, 465
prosecution, 465
warrant, 466
initial appearance, 466
felony, 466
assigned, 466
bail, 466
personal recognizance, 466
bail bond, 466
preliminary hearing, 466
probable cause, 467
bound over, 467
grand jury, 467
nolle prosequi, 467
plead, 467
plea bargaining, 467
indictment, 467
arraignment, 467
impaneled, 468
impeach, 468
relevant, 468
government, 468
beyond a reasonable
   doubt, 468
acquit, 468
poll, 468
administrative hearing, 468
memorandum, 469
hearing examiner, 469
proposed findings and
   rulings, 469
administrative decision, 469
board of appeals, 469
discretion, 470
below, 470
exhausting administrative
   remedies, 470
trial de novo, 470
ADR, 470
arbitration, 470
rent-a-judge, 470
mediation, 470
med-arb, 472
Neighborhood Justice
   Center (NJC), 472
summary jury trial, 472
subpoena, 475

KEY TERMS—continued

subpoena duces tecum, 477
depo summarizers, 479
digest, 479
index, 479
page/line format, 480
paraphrase, 481
digest by person, 482
digest by subject matter, 483

time-line summary, 483
tickler system, 483
attorney work product, 486
caption, 486
subject-matter
    jurisdiction, 486
venue, 486
boilerplate, 487

fact pleading, 489
notice pleading, 489
upon information and
    belief, 489
prayer for relief, 489
subscription, 489
verification, 490
settlement work-up, 490

trial notebook, 490
shadow trial, 493
judgment debtor, 494
judgment creditor, 494
execution, 494

LEGAL RESEARCH

Chapter Outline—continued

Section A
INTRODUCTION

This chapter does not cover every aspect of legal research, nor does it treat every conceivable legal resource that could be used in a law library. Rather, the chapter examines the major components of legal research with the objective of identifying effective starting points.

A paralegal in the law library

A great deal of information is provided in the pages that follow. You should first read the chapter through quickly to obtain an overview and to begin seeing where some concepts are covered in more than one place. The second time you read the chapter, you should begin collecting the terminology called for in Assignments 11.1 and 11.2. The best way to avoid becoming overwhelmed is to start feeling comfortable with terminology as soon as possible.

When you walk into a law library, your first impression is likely to be one of awe. You are confronted with row upon row of books, most of which seem unapproachable; they do not invite browsing. To be able to use the law library, your first responsibility as a legal researcher is to break down any psychological barrier that you may have with respect to the books and other resources in it. This is done not only by learning the techniques of research but also by understanding the limitations of the law library.

A major misunderstanding about the law library is that it contains the answer to every legal question. In many instances, legal problems have no definitive answers. The researcher often operates on the basis of "educated guesses" of what the answer is. To be sure, your guess is supported by what you uncover through legal research in the law library. The end product, however, is only the researcher's opinion of what the law is, rather than the absolute answer. No one will know for sure what the "right" or final answer is until the matter is litigated in court. If the problem is never litigated, then the "right" answer will be whatever the parties accept among themselves through negotiation or settlement. The researcher will not know what answer carries the day for the client until the negotiation process is over.

Many simple problems, however, can be answered by basic (easy) legal research. If someone wants to know, for example, the name of the government agency in charge of incorporating a business or the maximum number of weeks one can receive unemployment compensation, finding the answer is not difficult if the researcher knows what books or other resources to go to and how to use their indexes or other points of access. Many legal research problems, however, are not this simple.

Perhaps the healthiest way to approach the law library is to view it not so much as a source of answers but as a storehouse of ambiguities that are waiting to be identified, clarified, manipulated, and applied to the facts of a client's case. You may have heard the story of a client who walked into a law office and asked to see a one-armed attorney. When asked why he required an attorney meeting such specifications, he replied that he was tired of presenting problems to attorneys and having them constantly tell him that "on the one hand" he should do this but "on the other hand" he should do that; he hungered for an attorney who would give him an answer. This concern is well taken. A client is entitled to an answer, to clear guidance. At the same time (or, on the other hand), part of the attorney's job is to identify alternatives or options and to weigh the benefits and liabilities of each particular course of action. Good attorneys are so inclined because they understand that our legal system is infested with unknowns and ambiguities. Good legal researchers also have this understanding. They are not frightened by ambiguities; they thrive on them.

Section B
ORGANIZATION OF THE CHAPTER

This chapter has two main parts. The second half covers checklists and strategies for finding the ten main categories of law that might be needed to resolve a legal issue that has arisen out of the facts of a client's problem. The ten categories of law are:

opinions	charters
statutes	ordinances
constitutions	rules of court
administrative regulations	executive orders
administrative decisions	treaties

For definitions of these categories (plus a special eleventh category—the opinions of the attorney general), see Exhibit 6.1 in chapter 6.

Before we learn how to find these categories of law, we need to do two things: cover some of the *basics* needed to perform any research task, and study the major *research resources.* These will be our goals in the first half of the chapter.

Basics

The basics include the following topics:

- Terminology of legal research
- Kinds of legal authority
- Citation of legal authority
- Indexes

Once we have grasped these fundamentals, we turn to the research resources.

Research Resources

The major research resources we will use to find the law needed to resolve a legal issue are as follows:

card catalogs	legal periodicals
digests	legal encyclopedias
annotations	treatises
Shepard's	phone and mail
loose-leaf services	computers

Our approach in this chapter, therefore, will be as follows: first, we will cover the basics and the research resources; then, we will use this material to find the ten major categories of law.

Section C
THE IMPORTANCE OF LEGAL RESEARCH

You will eventually forget most of the law that you learn in school. If you do not forget most of it, you should! No one can know all of the law at any given time, even in a specialty. Furthermore, the law is always changing. Nothing is more dangerous than someone with out-of-date "knowledge" of the law. Law cannot be practiced on the basis of the rules learned in school, since those rules may no longer be valid by the time you try to use them in actual cases. Thousands of courts, legislatures, and administrative agencies spend considerable time writing new laws and changing or adapting old ones.

The law library and the techniques of legal research are the indispensable tickets of admission to current law. School teaches you to think. *You teach yourself the law through the skill of legal research.* Every time you walk into a law library, you are your own professor. You must accept nothing less than to become an expert on the topic of your research, no matter how narrow the topic. The purpose of the law library is to enable you to become an expert on the current law of your topic. Do not fall into the trap of thinking that you must be an expert in an area of the law to research it properly. The reverse is true. A major way for you to become an expert in an area is by discovering on your own what the law library can teach you about that area.

Never be reluctant to undertake legal research on a topic simply because you know very little about the topic. Knowing very little is often the healthiest starting point for the researcher! Preconceptions about the law can sometimes lead you away from avenues in the library that you should be traveling.

Becoming an expert through comprehensive legal research does not necessarily mean that you will know everything. Experts are not people who simply know the answers; they also know how to *formulate the questions that remain unanswered even after comprehensive legal research.* An expert is someone who can say:

This is what the current law says, and these are the questions that the law has not yet resolved.

Of course, you cannot know what is unresolved until you know what is resolved. The law library will help tell you both.

Section D
FRUSTRATION AND LEGAL RESEARCH

You are in the position of the king who sadly discovered that there is no royal road to geometry. If he wanted to learn geometry, he had to struggle through it like everyone else. Legal research is a struggle and will remain so for the rest of your career. The struggle will eventually become manageable and even enjoyable and exciting—but there is no way to avoid the struggle no matter how many shortcuts you learn. The amount of material in a law library is simply too massive for legal research to be otherwise, and the material is growing every day with new laws, new formats for law books, new technology, and new publishers offering new services that must be mastered.

Unfortunately, many cannot handle the pressure that the law library sometimes seems to donate in abundance. Too many attorneys, for example, stay away from the library and consequently practice law "from the hip." Such attorneys need to be sure that they have extensive malpractice insurance!

Legal research will be difficult for you at the beginning, but with experience in the law library, the difficulties will become manageable. The most important advice you can receive is *stick with it*. Spend a lot of time in the library. Be inquisitive. Ask a lot of questions of fellow students, teachers, librarians, attorneys, paralegals, legal secretaries, etc. Be constantly on the alert for tips and techniques. Take strange books from the shelf and try to figure out what they contain, what they try to do, how they are used, and how they duplicate or complement other law books that are not strange to you. Do not wait to be taught how to use sets of books that are new to you. Strike out on your own.

The coming of computer technology to legal research is of some help, but computers cannot eliminate your need to learn the basics. The struggle does not disappear if you are lucky enough to study or work where computers are available. Intelligent use of computers requires an understanding of the fundamental techniques of legal research.

At this stage of your career, most of the frustration will center on the question of how to *begin* your legal research of a topic. Once you overcome this frustration, the concern will then become how to *end* your legal research. After locating a great deal of material, you will worry about when to stop. In this chapter, our major focus will be the techniques of beginning. Techniques of stopping are more troublesome for the conscientious researcher. It is not always easy to determine whether you have found everything that you should find. Although guidelines do exist and will be examined, a great deal of experience with legal research is required before you can make the judgment that you have found everything available on a given topic. Don't be too hard on yourself. The techniques will come with time and practice. You will not learn everything now; you can only begin the learning that must continue throughout your career.

Keep the following "laws" of legal research in mind:

1. *The only books that will be missing from a shelf are those that you need to use immediately.*
2. *A vast amount of information on law books and research techniques exists, most of which you will forget soon after learning.*
3. *Each time you forget something, relearning it will take half the time it previously took.*
4. *When you have relearned something for the fourth time, you own it.*

At times you will walk away from a set of law books that you have used and wonder what you have just done—even if you obtained an answer from the books. At times you will go back to a set of books that you have used in the past and draw a blank on what the books are and how to use them again. These occurrences are natural. You will forget and you will forget again. Stay with it. Be willing to relearn. You cannot master a set of books after using them only a few times. Learning legal research is a little like learning to play a musical instrument: a seat is waiting for you in the orchestra, but you must practice. A royal road does not exist.

Section E
FLEXIBILITY IN LEGAL RESEARCH

Researchers have reached an enviable plateau when they understand the following paradox: You sometimes do not know what you are looking for until you find it. Since simple answers are rare, researchers are constantly confronted with frustration and ambiguity. As they pursue avenues and leads, they invariably come upon new avenues and thoughts that never occurred to them initially. An entirely new approach to the problem may be uncovered that radically changes their initial perceptions. They reached this stage not because they consciously sought it out but because they were flexible and open-minded enough to be receptive to new approaches and perceptions. This phenomenon is by no means peculiar to legal research. Take the situation of the woman in need of transportation. She sets herself to the task of determining the most economical way to *buy* a good car. In her search, she stumbles upon the practice of leasing cars. After studying this option, she concludes that leasing is the most sensible resolution of her transportation problem. She did not know what she was looking for—a car *leasing* deal—until she found it. Compare this situation with that of a client who comes into a law office for advice on how to write a will so that a certain amount of money will pass to designated individuals upon death. The attorney asks you to do some legal research in the area of wills. While in the law library studying the law of wills, you see reference to life insurance policies as a substitute for wills in passing cash to beneficiaries at death. You bring this to the attention of the attorney, who decides that this option is indeed worth pursuing. You did not know what you were looking for—a will substitute—until you found it.

Section F
THE TERMINOLOGY OF LEGAL RESEARCH

This section contains two lists. The first is a list of essential research terms that you need to understand before you start doing any legal research (see Exhibit 11.1 and Assignment 11.1). The second is a more comprehensive list of terms that you need to understand by the time you finish studying legal research (see Exhibit 11.2 and Assignment 11.2). All of the terms in the essentials list (Exhibit 11.1) are also in the comprehensive list (Exhibit 11.2).

Exhibit 11.1 The Terminology of Legal Research: The Essentials

1. act (512)
2. administrative decision (640)
3. administrative regulation (640)
4. advance sheet (for reporters) (512)
5. annotation (513)
6. authority (547)
7. bill (514)
8. *Bluebook: A Uniform System of Citation* (515)
9. citation (521)
10. common law (626)
11. constitution (638)
12. cumulative (522)
13. dicta, dictum (551)
14. digests (for reporters) (522)
15. executive order (323)
16. headnote (520)
17. key number (523)

18. legal encyclopedia (532)
19. legal periodical (533)
20. legal treatise (534)
21. legislative history (634)
22. LEXIS (534)
23. loose-leaf service (534)
24. notes of decisions (627)
25. opinion (516)
26. Opinion of the Attorney General (323)
27. ordinance (323)
28. parallel cite (521)
29. pocket part (536)
30. reporter (516)
31. rules of court (537)
32. Shepardize (538)
33. statutory code (542)
34. WESTLAW (545)

Exhibit 11.2 The Terminology of Legal Research: A Comprehensive Checklist

1. act (512)
2. administrative code (513)
3. administrative decision (640)
4. administrative regulation (640)
5. advance sheet (for reporters) (512)
6. advance sheet (for Shepard's) (512)
7. *A.L.R. Blue Book of Supplemental Decisions* (515)
8. *ALR Digest to 3d, 4th, 5th, Federal* (598)
9. A.L.R. First, A.L.R.2d, A.L.R.3d, A.L.R.4th, A.L.R.5th, A.L.R. Fed (513)
10. *ALR Index* (598)
11. *ALR2d Digest* (598)
12. *A.L.R.2d Later Case Service* (600)
13. American Digest System (524)
14. *American Jurisprudence 2d (Am. Jur. 2d)* (514)

15. American Law Institute (537)
16. amicus curiae brief (515)
17. annotated statutory code (514)
18. annotated reporter (513)
19. annotation (513)
20. annotation, superseded (600)
21. annotation, supplemented (600)
22. Annotation History Table (600)
23. appellant (353)
24. appellate brief (515)
25. appellate court (328)
26. appellee (354)
27. *Atlantic Digest* (514)
28. *Atlantic 2d (A.2d)* (519)
29. authority (547)

Exhibit 11.2   The Terminology of Legal Research: A Comprehensive Checklist—continued

30. authority, mandatory (548)
31. authority, persuasive (548)
32. authority, primary (547)
33. authority, secondary (547)
34. *Auto-Cite* (625)
35. bill (514)
36. *Bluebook: A Uniform System of Citation* (515)
37. *Blue and White Book* (515)
38. brief of a case (515)
39. *California Reporter (Cal. Rptr.)* (515)
40. CALR (623)
41. CARTWHEEL (583)
42. case (516)
43. casebook (516)
44. case on point (549)
45. *CCH U.S. Supreme Court Bulletin* (517)
46. CD-ROM (520)
47. *Century Digest* (524)
48. certiorari (566)
49. charter (323)
50. citation (521)
51. citator (521)
52. cite checking (577)
53. cited material (Shepard's) (604)
54. citing material (Shepard's) (604)
55. code, codify (521)
56. *Code of Federal Regulations (C.F.R.)* (521)
57. common law (626)
58. concurring opinion (356)
59. *Congressional Record* (522)
60. constitution (638)
61. *Corpus Juris Secundum* (C.J.S.) (522)
62. cumulative (522)
63. *Current Law Index* (522)
64. *Decennial Digest* (524)
65. depository library (507)
66. Descriptive Word Index (DWI) (595)
67. DIALOG (624)
68. dicta, dictum (551)
69. digests (for reporters) (522)
70. digests (for A.L.R. annotations) (598)
71. docket number (566)
72. enacted law (548)
73. et al. (565)
74. et seq. (613)
75. executive order (323)

76. *Federal Digest* (524)
77. *Federal Practice Digest 2d* (525)
78. *Federal Practice Digest 3d* (525)
79. *Federal Practice Digest 4th* (525)
80. *Federal Supplement (F. Supp.)* (517)
81. *Federal Register* (528)
82. *Federal Reporter 2d (F.2d)* (517)
83. *Federal Reporter 3d (F.3d)* (517)
84. *Federal Rules Decisions (F.R.D.)* (517)
85. *General Digest* (524)
86. headnote (520)
87. hornbook (530)
88. *Index Medicus* (620)
89. *Index to Legal Periodicals* (ILP) (617)
90. In re (566)
91. *Insta-Cite* (706)
92. Internet (530)
93. Interstate compact (532)
94. key number (523)
95. law review (533)
96. *Lawyers' Edition (L. Ed.)* (516)
97. legal dictionary (532)
98. legal encyclopedia (532)
99. legal newspaper (533)
100. legal periodical (533)
101. legal thesaurus (534)
102. *LegalTrac* (534)
103. legal treatise (534)
104. legislative history (634)
105. LEXIS (534)
106. loose-leaf service (534)
107. majority opinion (356)
108. *Maroon Book* (576)
109. *Martindale-Hubbell Law Directory* (535)
110. memorandum opinion (355)
111. *Military Justice Reporter* (517)
112. *Modern Federal Practice Digest* (524)
113. National Reporter System (518)
114. *National Reporter Blue Book* (515)
115. *New York Supplement (N.Y.S.)* (536)
116. nominative reporter (566)
117. *North Eastern 2d (N.E.2d)* (519)
118. *North Western Digest* (536)
119. *North Western 2d (N.W.2d)* (519)
120. notes of decisions (627)

continued

E x h i b i t 1 1 . 2   **The Terminology of Legal Research: A Comprehensive Checklist—continued**

121. nutshell (536)
122. official reporter (516)
123. on all fours (625)
124. opinion (516)
125. Opinion of the Attorney General (323)
126. ordinance (323)
127. overrule (550)
128. *Pacific 2d (P.2d)* (519)
129. *Pacific Digest* (536)
130. parallel cite (521)
131. Parallel Table of Authorities and Rules (in *C.F.R.*) (641)
132. per curiam (355)
133. *Permanent A.L.R. Digest* (598)
134. pinpoint cite (567)
135. pocket part (536)
136. Popular Name Table (633)
137. public domain citation (521)
138. Public Law (PL) (628)
139. record (537)
140. regional digest (525)
141. remand (356)
142. reporter (516)
143. respondent (354)
144. Restatements (537)
145. rules of court (537)
146. series (537)
147. session law (610)
148. Shepardize (538)
149. slip law (539)
150. slip opinion (539)
151. *South Eastern Digest* (539)
152. *South Eastern 2d (S.E.2d)* (519)
153. *Southern 2d (So. 2d)* (519)

154. *South Western 2d (S.W.2d)* (519)
155. squib (523)
156. stare decisis (550)
157. star paging (516)
158. statute, private (544)
159. statute, public (544)
160. *Statutes at Large (Stat.)* (542)
161. statutory code (542)
162. *Supreme Court Reporter (S. Ct.)* (542)
163. syllabus (in reporters) (606)
164. syllabus (in Shepard's) (606)
165. Table of Authorities (672)
166. Table of Courts and Circuits (in *A.L.R.*) (599)
167. Table of Jurisdictions Represented (in *A.L.R.*) (599)
168. Table of Laws, Rules, and Regulations (in *A.L.R.*) (599)
169. Total Client-Service Library (543)
170. treaty (323)
171. unofficial reporter (516)
172. *U.S. Code (U.S.C.)* (542)
173. *U.S. Code Annotated (U.S.C.A.)* (542)
174. *U.S. Code Service (U.S.C.S.)* (542)
175. *U.S. Code Congressional and Administrative News (U.S.C.C.A.N.)* (544)
176. U.S. Court of Appeals (331)
177. U.S. District Court (330)
178. *U.S. Law Week (U.S.L.W.)* (544)
179. *U.S. Reports (U.S.)* (516)
180. *U.S. Statutes at Large (Stat.)* (544)
181. *U.S. Supreme Court Digest* (L. Ed.) (525)
182. *U.S. Supreme Court Digest* (West) (525)
183. WESTLAW (545)
184. World Wide Web (530)
185. *Words and Phrases* (545)

Assignment 11.1 should be done now. Assignment 11.2 should be completed by the end of the course.

Both lists contain page numbers in parentheses that will direct you to pages in the book where the term is discussed.

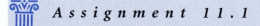

A s s i g n m e n t 1 1 . 1

For each of the words and phrases in Exhibit 11.1, prepare a three-by-five-inch index card on which you include the following information:

● The word or phrase

- The pages in this text where the word or phrase is discussed (begin with the page number given in parentheses, then add other page numbers as the word or phrase is discussed elsewhere in the text)
- The definition or function of the word or phrase
- Other information about the word or phrase that you obtain as you use the law library
- Comments by your instructor in class about any of the words and phrases

Some words and phrases will call for more than one card. You should strive, however, to keep the information on the cards brief. Place the cards in alphabetical order. The cards will become your own file system on legal research that you can use as a study guide for the course and as a reference tool when you do legal research in the library. Be sure to add cards for new words and phrases that you come across in class and in the library.

See also Assignment 11.12 for other data that you can add to your cards.

Assignment 11.2

Do Assignment 11.1 for the list in Exhibit 11.2. Turn in this assignment when you complete your study of legal research.

Section G
FINDING LAW LIBRARIES

The availability of law libraries depends to a large degree on the area where you live, study, or work. Rural areas, for example, have fewer possibilities than larger cities or capitals.

Twelve different law library possibilities are listed below. Find out which ones exist in your area. You may need permission to use some of them. (This is certainly true of a private law firm's library.) Find out where the nearest **depository library** is located. This is a public or private library that receives free federal government publications to which it must admit the general public. If a private law school or university is a depository library, it must allow you to use the publications it receives free, but you may be denied access to the rest of the library's collection. (For the names and phone numbers of depository libraries in your state, see Appendix H.)

Locations of Law Libraries

- Law school library
- General university library (may have a law section)
- Law library of a bar association
- State law library (in the state capital and perhaps in branch offices in counties throughout the state)
- Local public library (may have a small law section)
- Law library of the legislature or city council
- Law library of the city solicitor or corporation counsel
- Law library of the district attorney or local prosecutor
- Law library of the public defender
- Law library of a federal, state, or local administrative agency (particularly in the office of the agency's general counsel)

- Law library of a court
- Law library of a private law firm

You may need some ingenuity to locate these libraries and to gain access to them. Try more than one avenue of entry. Do not become discouraged when the first person you contact tells you that the library is for members or private use only. Some students adopt the strategy of walking into a library—particularly a library supported by public funds—and acting as if they belong. Rather than asking for permission, they wait for someone to stop them or to question their right to be there. Other students take the wiser course of seeking permission in advance. Yet, even here, some creativity is needed in the way that you ask for permission. The bold question, "Can I use your library?" may be less effective than an approach such as, "Would it be possible for me to use a few of your law books for a short period of time for some important research that I must do?"

There is one other law library that you need to consider: your own. It is not too soon for you to start collecting your own law books, beginning with your course books on law. But never buy a practice book or manual without checking with at least two attorneys or paralegals on the *practical* value of the book. Ask them how often they consult the book. It is not necessarily wise to purchase a book simply because it treats an area of the law you need to know something about. Also, be prepared for sticker shock when you find out what many of these books cost.

Once you gain access to a law library, you may face another problem. Some library employees resent spending a great deal of time answering students' questions. At a recent conference of the American Association of Law Libraries, an entire session was devoted to the theme of student paralegal requests for assistance that "can take a tremendous amount of the law librarian's time and energy." Even if an employee at the desk is willing to give you all the time you need, the *supervisor* of that employee may be opposed to the attention you are getting. Use your common sense in such situations. Keep your requests to a minimum, particularly if other students are seeking the same kind of help. Before you ask a question, reread the textbook. Many questions can be answered on your own.

Section H
A GLOSSARY OF LEGAL MATERIALS

We begin with an overview of the major research terms and legal materials that we will encounter throughout the chapter. The overview is presented in the form of a glossary. Later in the chapter our focus will be on how to *use* the materials summarized in this glossary. Here our intent is simply to *introduce* them to you. At the end of the glossary (on page 545), Exhibit 11.6 will diagram many of the materials covered in the glossary and elsewhere in the chapter.

A law library contains four main kinds of legal materials that serve the following functions:

- Materials that contain the *full text* of a category of law
- Materials that can be used to *locate* that category of law
- Materials that can be used to help *explain* that category of law
- Materials that can be used to help *determine the current validity* of that category of law

Some materials cover more than one category of law and serve more than one of these four functions. The chart in Exhibit 11.3 presents a catalog of research materials according to their function.

A final word of caution before we begin the glossary: The same word or phrase can often have a different meaning depending on the context in which it is used. *Supreme Court,* for

(cont. on page 512.)

Exhibit 11.3 A Catalog of Research Materials

Kind of Law	Materials That Contain the Full Text of This Kind of Law	Materials That Can Be Used to Locate This Kind of Law	Materials That Can Be Used to Help Explain This Kind of Law	Materials That Can Be Used to Help Determine the Current Validity of This Kind of Law

(a) Opinions	Reports
	Reporters
	A.L.R., A.L.R.2d,
	  A.L.R.3d,
	  A.L.R.4th,
	  A.L.R.5th,
	  A.L.R. Fed.
	Legal newspapers
	Loose-leaf services
	Slip opinion
	Advance sheets
	CD-ROM
	WESTLAW
	LEXIS
	Internet
		Digests
		Annotations in
		  A.L.R., A.L.R.2d,
		  A.L.R.3d,
		  A.L.R.4th,
		  A.L.R. 5th,
		  A.L.R. Fed.
		Shepard's
		Legal periodicals
		Legal encyclopedias
		Legal treatises
		Loose-leaf services
		Words and Phrases
			Legal periodicals
			Legal encyclopedias
			Legal treatises
			Legal newsletters
			Annotations in
			  A.L.R., A.L.R.2d,
			  A.L.R.3d,
			  A.L.R.4th,
			  A.L.R.5th,
			  A.L.R. Fed.
			Loose-leaf services
				Shepard's
				Insta-Cite
				Auto-Cite

(b) Statutes	Statutory Code
	Statutes at Large
	Session Laws
	Compilations
	Consolidated Laws
	Slip Laws
	Acts & Resolves
	Laws
	CD-ROM
	WESTLAW
	LEXIS
	Internet
		Index volumes of
		  statutory code
		Loose-leaf services
		Footnote references
		  in other materials
		  such as periodicals,
		  encyclopedias,
		  and treatises
			Legal periodicals
			Legal encyclopedias
			Legal treatises
			Legal newsletters
			Annotations in
			  A.L.R., A.L.R.2d,
			  A.L.R.3d,
			  A.L.R.4th,
			  A.L.R.5th,
			  A.L.R. Fed.
			Loose-leaf services
				Shepard's

(c) Constitutions	Statutory Code
	Separate volumes
	  containing the
	  constitution
	CD-ROM
	WESTLAW
	LEXIS
	Internet
		Index volumes of
		  statutory code
		Loose-leaf services
		Footnote references
		  in other materials
			Legal periodicals
			Legal encyclopedias
			Legal treatises
			Legal newsletters
			Annotations in
			  A.L.R., A.L.R.2d,
			  A.L.R.3d,
			  A.L.R.4th,
			  A.L.R.5th,
			  A.L.R. Fed.
			Loose-leaf services
				Shepard's

continued

Exhibit 11.3   A Catalog of Research Materials—continued

Kind of Law	Materials That Contain the Full Text of This Kind of Law	Materials That Can Be Used to Locate This Kind of Law	Materials That Can Be Used to Help Explain This Kind of Law	Materials That Can Be Used to Help Determine the Current Validity of This Kind of Law
(d) Administrative Regulations	Administrative Code Separate volumes containing the regulations of certain agencies Loose-leaf services CD-ROM WESTLAW LEXIS Internet	Index volumes of the administrative code Loose-leaf services Footnote references in other materials	Legal periodicals Legal treatises Legal newsletters Annotations in A.L.R., A.L.R.2d, A.L.R.3d, A.L.R.4th, A.L.R.5th, A.L.R. Fed. Loose-leaf services	Shepard's (for some agencies) List of Sections Affected (for federal agencies)
(e) Administrative Decisions	Separate volumes of decisions of some agencies Loose-leaf services WESTLAW LEXIS Internet	Loose-leaf services Index to (or digest volumes for) the decisions Footnote references in other materials	Legal periodicals Legal treatises Legal newsletters Annotations in A.L.R., A.L.R.2d, A.L.R.3d, A.L.R.4th, A.L.R.5th, A.L.R. Fed. Loose-leaf services	Shepard's (for some agencies)
(f) Charters	Separate volumes containing the charter Municipal Code State session laws Official journal Legal newspaper Internet	Index volumes to the charter or municipal code Footnote references in other materials	Legal periodicals Legal treatises Annotations in A.L.R., A.L.R.2d, A.L.R.3d, A.L.R.4th, A.L.R.5th, A.L.R. Fed.	Shepard's
(g) Ordinances	Municipal Code Official journal Legal newspaper Internet	Index volumes of municipal code Footnote references in other materials	Legal periodicals Legal treatises Annotations in A.L.R., A.L.R.2d, A.L.R.3d, A.L.R.4th, A.L.R.5th, A.L.R. Fed.	Shepard's
(h) Rules of Court	Separate rules volumes Statutory code	Index to separate rules volumes Index to statutory code	Practice manuals Legal periodicals Legal treatises	Shepard's

Exhibit 11.3   A Catalog of Research Materials—continued

Kind of Law	Materials That Contain the Full Text of This Kind of Law	Materials That Can Be Used to Locate This Kind of Law	Materials That Can Be Used to Help Explain This Kind of Law	Materials That Can Be Used to Help Determine the Current Validity of This Kind of Law
(h) Rules of Court —continued	Practice manuals CD-ROM WESTLAW LEXIS Internet	Index to practice manuals Footnote references in other materials	Legal newsletters Annotations in A.L.R., A.L.R.2d, A.L.R.3d, A.L.R.4th, A.L.R.5th, A.L.R. Fed. Legal encyclopedias Loose-leaf services	
(i) Executive Orders	Federal Register Code of Federal Regulations U.S. Code Congressional and Administrative News U.S.C./U.S.C.A./ U.S.C.S. WESTLAW LEXIS Internet	Index volumes to the sets of books listed in the second column Footnote references in other materials	Legal periodicals Legal treatises Legal newsletters Annotations in A.L.R., A.L.R.2d, A.L.R.3d, A.L.R.4th, A.L.R.5th, A.L.R. Fed. Loose-leaf services	Shepard's
(j) Treaties	Statutes at Large (up to 1949) United States Treaties and Other International Agreements Department of State Bulletin International Legal Materials United Nations Treaty Series	Index within the volumes listed in second column World Treaty Index Current Treaty Index Footnote references in other materials	Legal periodicals Legal treatises Legal newsletters Annotations in A.L.R., A.L.R.2d, A.L.R.3d, A.L.R.4th, A.L.R.5th, A.L.R. Fed. Legal encyclopedias Loose-leaf services	Shepard's U.S. Code Service (Notes to Uncodified Laws and Treaties)
(k) Opinions of the Attorney General	Separate volumes containing these opinions WESTLAW LEXIS Internet	Digests Footnote references in other materials		

example, refers to the *highest* court in our federal judicial system as well as to the *trial* court in New York State; and the word *opinion* can refer to the judicial decisions of courts and to the administrative decisions of agencies. Although standard definitions are generally used, you should be prepared to find variations.

Assignment 11.3

Throughout the glossary, there are photos of law books and pamphlets. Make a list of every photo. (Do not include photos of machines or pages from books.) In a law library, try to find as many of the items on your list as possible. You will not be able to find everything. The library (or libraries) you are using may simply not carry a book you are seeking. Some library materials are thrown away when they are reprinted in another format (e.g., *advance sheets* are thrown away when the bound *reporter* volumes come out). Next to each item on your list:

(a) State the name and address of the law library you used to try to find the item.

(b) State whether you found the item *exactly* as pictured in the photograph, e.g., the same volume number.

(c) If you were not able to find the item exactly as pictured, state how close you were able to come, e.g., you were able to find a different volume number from the same set of books.

Example of a pamphlet containing session laws

Act; Acts and Resolves

An **act** is the official document that contains the statute passed by the legislature. *Acts and Resolves* is the set of books that contain all the acts of the legislature. They are also sometimes called Session Laws, Statutes, Statutes at Large, Laws, etc. A major characteristic of all of these books is that the statutes in them are printed chronologically as they are passed. They are not classified or organized by subject matter, unlike a statutory code. *See* Code (page 521).

Administrative Code

An **administrative code** is a collection of the regulations of one or more agencies. The regulations in a code are organized by subject matter. Generally, the regulations of state and local administrative agencies are poorly organized and difficult to obtain. Not so for the federal agencies. *See* Code of Federal Regulations.

Advance Sheet

An **advance sheet** is a pamphlet printed before (in advance of) a bound volume, or a thicker pamphlet, that will consolidate the material in several of the earlier advance sheets. When the bound volume or thicker pamphlet comes out, the advance sheet is thrown away. There are two kinds of advance sheets in the law library: an advance sheet for reporters (containing the full text of court opinions) and an advance sheet for Shepard's (containing the updating data of volumes called *Shepard's Citations*). We will cover these law books in detail later in the chapter. For now our concern is to introduce you to the concept of an advance sheet.

Advance sheet for a reporter (here the *Supreme Court Reporter*). The advance sheet contains the full text of court opinions that will later be printed in a bound *Supreme Court Reporter* volume.

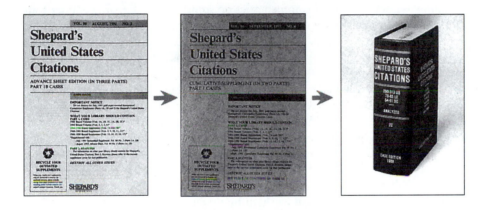

Advance sheet supplements for Shepard's (here the *Shepard's United States Citations*). The first photo is the advance sheet, which is later printed in a thicker pamphlet (the middle photo), and finally in a bound volume (third photo).

A.L.R., A.L.R.2d, A.L.R.3d, A.L.R.4th, A.L.R.5th, A.L.R. Fed.

- A.L.R.1st: *American Law Reports*, First Series
- A.L.R.2d: *American Law Reports*, Second Series
- A.L.R.3d: *American Law Reports*, Third Series
- A.L.R.4th: *American Law Reports*, Fourth Series
- A.L.R.5th: *American Law Reports*, Fifth Series
- A.L.R. Fed.: *American Law Reports*, Federal Series.

These sets of books contain the complete text of *selected* court opinions followed by extensive commentary or research papers on issues within the opinions selected. These research papers are called **annotations.** The sets of books are therefore called **annotated reporters,** because they print the full text of opinions plus commentary on them. They are published by Lawyers Co-operative Publishing Company (Lawyers Co-op.). As we shall see later, annotations are excellent case finders. (While the abbreviation, A.L.R., sometimes refers to the First Series only, more commonly it refers to all six sets collectively.) Recently, many annotations were placed **online** so that they can now be found and read on a computer screen. Something is online when it is connected to a host computer system or information service—usually through the telephone lines. The computer systems that provide this online access to A.L.R. are WESTLAW and LEXIS.

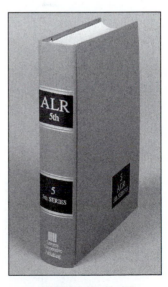

Example of a volume of **American Law Reports, Fifth Series**

American Digest System

The American Digest System is a multivolume set of digests that summarizes case law from every state and federal court. It includes three separate digests: *Century Digest, Decennial Digests, General Digest. See* Digests (page 522, page 594).

American Jurisprudence 2d (Am. Jur. 2d)

Am. Jur. 2d is a national **legal encyclopedia** published by Lawyers Co-op. (It is the second edition of Am. Jur. First.) A legal encyclopedia is a multivolume set of books that summarizes almost every major legal topic. Topics are covered alphabetically, as in most encyclopedias. Am. Jur. 2d is particularly useful (a) as background reading before beginning legal research in a new area of law, and (b) as a case finder because of its extensive footnotes to court opinions, and (c) as a point of reference to other publications of Lawyers Co-op. The main competitor of Am. Jur. 2d is *Corpus Juris Secundum.*

Example of a volume of **American Jurisprudence 2d**

Annotation

An *annotation* is a set of notes or commentaries on something. The main volumes containing annotations are the six sets of *American Law Reports:* A.L.R., A.L.R.2d, A.L.R.3d, A.L.R.4th, A.L.R.5th, and A.L.R. Fed. The annotations are research papers that are based on selected court opinions in these volumes. When you are asked to "find out if there are any annotations," you are being sent to A.L.R., A.L.R.2d, etc.

The verb is **annotated.** If materials are annotated, they contain notes or commentaries. An **annotated statutory code** prints statutes by subject matter and includes research references such as notes of court opinions that have interpreted the statutes. The abbreviation for annotated is "Ann." (e.g., Del. Code Ann. for Delaware Code Annotated), or "A." (e.g., U.S.C.A. for United States Code Annotated). An *annotated reporter* prints court opinions along with notes or commentaries. An *annotated bibliography* (page 646) contains a list of references along with a brief comment on each reference.

With rare exceptions, annotations are written by private publishers and authors. They are not official documents of courts, legislatures, or agencies.

Atlantic Digest

A digest that summarizes state court opinions in the *Atlantic Reporter. See* Exhibit 11.5. *See also* Digests (page 527).

Atlantic Reporter 2d (A.2d)

A regional reporter that prints the full text of state court opinions in the Atlantic region of the country. *See* Exhibit 11.4. *See also* Cases (page 519).

Ballentine's Law Dictionary

See Legal Dictionary (page 532).

Bill

A **bill** is a proposed statute (one that has not yet been enacted into law). If the bill becomes law, it is printed in a small booklet or pamphlet called a **slip law.**

Example of a bill introduced in the House of Representatives of Congress

Black's Law Dictionary

See Legal dictionary (page 532).

Blue Book

The phrase **blue book** (or *bluebook*) usually refers to one of the three following books or sets of books:

- *Bluebook: A Uniform System of Citation*
- *National Reporter Blue Book*
- *A.L.R. Blue Book of Supplemental Decisions*

Bluebook: A Uniform System of Citation. A small blue pamphlet published by the law reviews of several law schools. The pamphlet covers the "rules" of citation form. It is considered by many to be the bible of citation form.

National Reporter Blue Book. A set of books published by West Publishing Company that will enable you to find a parallel cite (an additional reference) to a court opinion. The *National Reporter Blue Book* covers every state. Some states have a *Blue and White Book,* which provides parallel cites for one state only.

The *A.L.R. Blue Book of Supplemental Decisions* will enable you to update the annotations found in *A.L.R. First Series. See* page 600.

Brief

The word *brief* means a summary or outline of an argument. In the law, the word is used in four main senses. First, a brief is a document submitted to an appellate court in which a party asks the court to approve, modify, or reverse what a lower court has done. Such briefs are called **appellate briefs.** If a nonparty receives permission to submit an appellate brief, it is called an **amicus curiae** (or friend-of-the-court) **brief.** (It is possible to locate appellate briefs in some large law libraries and online through LEXIS and WESTLAW.) Second, a brief is a document submitted to a trial court in support of a particular position, e.g., a brief in support of a motion to dismiss. Third, a brief is a summary of the main components of a single court opinion including the key facts, the issues, the holdings, the reasoning, etc. When you *brief a case,* you are providing such a summary. (See Exhibit 7.2 in chapter 7). Fourth, a *trial brief* is an attorney's personal set of notes on how to conduct a trial.

Bulletin

A bulletin is a publication issued on an ongoing or periodic basis (such as the *Internal Revenue Bulletin*).

California Reporter (Cal. Rptr.)

A court reporter containing selected California cases. *See* Cases (page 518).

Front cover of an appellate brief submitted to the U.S. Supreme Court

Example of a casebook

Casebook

A **casebook** is a law school textbook. It consists mainly of a collection of edited court opinions and other materials relating to a particular area of the law, e.g., Lockhart, Kamisar, Choper, and Shiffrin, *Constitutional Law: Cases, Comments, Questions.*

Cases

A **case** is a dispute that has been litigated in court or that is now in litigation. The word is sometimes used interchangeably with the word **opinion,** although the latter word is more often used to mean the court's written explanation for reaching a particular result. The full text of cases is found in volumes called **reports** or **reporters.** An **official reporter** is published under the authority of the government and is often printed by the government itself. An **unofficial reporter** is printed by a private or commercial publishing company (such as West) without special authority from the government.

We will now examine the reporters containing opinions of the federal courts. Then we look at the reporters for state courts.

Federal Court Opinions   The opinions of the United States Supreme Court are printed in an official reporter, *United States Reports* (abbreviated "U.S."), and in several unofficial reporters: the *Supreme Court Reporter* published by West (abbreviated "S. Ct.") and *United States Supreme Court Reports, Lawyers' Edition,* published by Lawyers Co-op. (abbreviated "L. Ed.").

The three major reporters containing opinions of the United States Supreme Court

When an opinion is printed in the *United States Reports,* it will also be printed word-for-word in S. Ct. and in L. Ed., the unofficial reporters—but not necessarily on the same page numbers. Suppose that you are reading an opinion in an unofficial reporter and you want to quote from it. The standard practice is to give the reference or citation to the quote as it appears in the *official* reporter. Suppose, however, that the latter is not available in your library, but one of the unofficial reporters is. How do you quote a page number in an official reporter when all you have available is an unofficial reporter? You use a technique called **star paging.** While you are reading a page in an unofficial reporter, you will find a notation of some kind provided by the printer (an asterisk, a star, or a special indentation) plus a page number, usually in bold black print. The latter is a reference to a page number of the same case in the official reporter. Star paging therefore enables you to determine on what pages the same court language can be found in official and unofficial reporters.

Two loose-leaf services (page 534) also print the text of all U.S. Supreme Court opinions:

- *United States Law Week* (U.S.L.W.) published by Bureau of National Affairs (BNA)

- *United States Supreme Court Bulletin* (S. Ct. Bull.) published by Commerce Clearing House. (CCH)

It is also possible to read U.S. Supreme Court opinions in electronic formats. They are all available online from the main computer services, LEXIS and WESTLAW. Increasingly, the opinions are becoming available on the **Internet,** a special network of networks to which millions of individual computer users have access (see page 530). Finally, West and Lawyer's Co-op publish U.S. Supreme Court opinions on **CD-ROM,** an optical information-storage system (see page 520).

Federal Reporter, Third Series (F.3d). Currently contains the full text of the opinions written by the United States Courts of Appeals. (For a photo of F.2d on ultrafiche, see page 535.)

We now turn to reporters for the *lower* federal courts, primarily the U.S. Courts of Appeals and the U.S. District Courts. (For an overview of these courts in the federal judicial system, see the maps in Exhibits 6.3 and 6.4 in Chapter 6.) Two major reporters contain the full text of opinions from these lower federal courts:

- *Federal Reporter* (abbreviated "F.")
- *Federal Reporter, Second Series* (abbreviated "F.2d")
- *Federal Reporter, Third Series* (abbreviated "F.3d")
- *Federal Supplement* (abbreviated "F. Supp.")

The first set of reporters (F., F.2d, F.3d) primarily contains opinions written by the U.S. Courts of Appeals. The second set of reporters (F. Supp.) primarily contains opinions written by the U.S. District Courts. Both sets are unofficial reporters published by West. The reporters do *not* contain every opinion written by the courts that they cover. The courts decide which opinions are sufficiently important to submit to West for publication.

In addition to F., F.2d, F.3d, and F. Supp., West publishes several specialty or topical reporters that also cover federal courts. For example:

Federal Rules Decisions (F.R.D.)
- Contains opinions of the U.S. District Courts on the Federal Rules of Civil and Criminal Procedure, and also
- Contains articles, speeches, and conference reports on federal procedural issues

Military Justice Reporter (M.J.)
- Contains opinions of the United States Court of Military Appeals and the Courts of Military Review for the Army, Navy-Marine, Air Force, and Coast Guard

Federal Supplement (F. Supp.) Currently contains the full text of the opinions written by the United States District Courts.

Bankruptcy Reporter (B.R.)
- Contains opinions of the United States Bankruptcy Courts and selected bankruptcy opinions of other federal courts

Federal Claims Reporter
- Contains opinions of the United States Court of Federal Claims (formerly called the United States Claims Court)

West's Veterans Appeals Reporter
- Contains opinions of the United States Court of Veterans Appeals and of federal courts hearing appeals from this court.

In addition to these bound reporters, the opinions of lower federal courts are available online through LEXIS and WESTLAW. Many may also be accessible on the Internet.

State Court Opinions   At one time, all states had official reports containing the opinions of their highest state courts. A large number of states, however, have discontinued their official reports. For such states, the unofficial reporters are the main or only source where you can find the opinions of their state courts.

Example of an official state reports volume

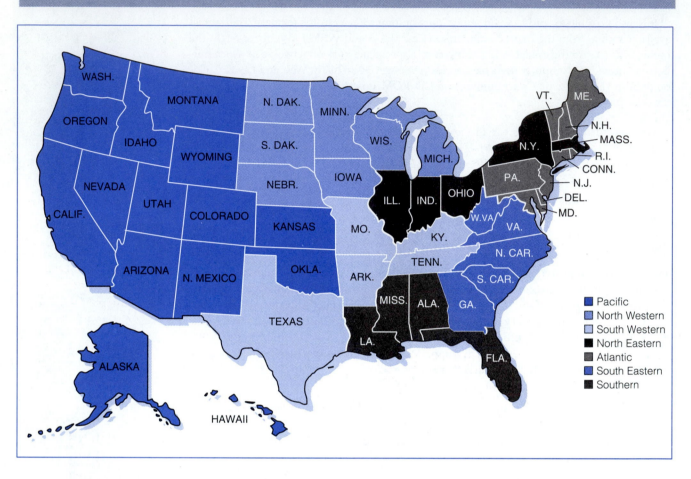

Exhibit 11.4

National Reporter System

Legend:
- Pacific
- North Western
- South Western
- North Eastern
- Atlantic
- South Eastern
- Southern

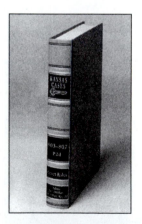

A volume of **Kansas Cases** (a special edition state reporter) containing all the Kansas opinions printed in *Pacific Reporter, 2d*

The major publisher of unofficial state reports is West Publishing Company through its *National Reporter System*. There are seven **regional reporters** in the System. (West's other reporters are also part of the National Reporter System.) For a photo of each regional reporter, see page 519.

The seven regional reporters and the states they cover can be seen on the map in Exhibit 11.4.

If a law office subscribes to a regional reporter covering its own state, the office is also receiving opinions of other states in the same region. These other opinions may be of little practical value to the office. West therefore publishes special state editions for many of the states. These **special edition state reporters** (sometimes called *offprint reporters*) contain only the opinions of an individual state that are also printed in the regional reporter. For example, the opinions of the highest court in Kansas are printed in the *Pacific Reporter*. A Kansas attorney who does not want to subscribe to the *Pacific Reporter* can subscribe to the special edition Kansas reporter, called *Kansas Cases*.

Finally, West publishes three separate reporters for New York, California, and Illinois:

- New York Supplement (N.Y.S.)
- California Reporter (Cal. Rptr.)
- Illinois Decisions (Ill. Dec.)

Each contains the opinions of the highest court in the state as well as selected opinions of its lower courts.

The Seven Regional Reporters in the National Reporter System

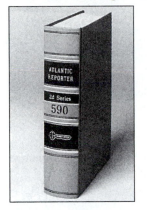

Atlantic Reporter (A.), Atlantic Reporter, Second Series (A.2d). The opinions of the highest state court and some intermediate appellate courts in the following states: Conn., Del., D.C., Me., Md., N.H., N.J., Pa., R.I., Vt.

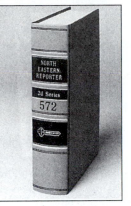

North Eastern Reporter (N.E.), North Eastern Reporter, Second Series (N.E.2d). The opinions of the highest state court and some intermediate appellate courts in the following states: Ill., Ind., Mass., N.Y., Ohio.

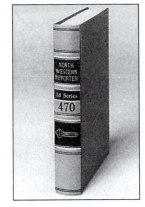

North Western Reporter (N.W.), North Western Reporter, Second Series (N.W.2d). The opinions of the highest state court and some intermediate appellate courts in the following states: Iowa, Mich., Minn., Neb., N.D., S.D., Wis.

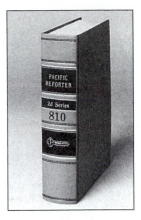

Pacific Reporter (P.), Pacific Reporter, Second Series (P.2d). The opinions of the highest state court and some intermediate appellate courts in the following states: Alaska, Ariz., Cal., Colo., Haw., Idaho, Kan., Mont., Nev., N.M., Okla., Or., Utah, Wash., Wyo.

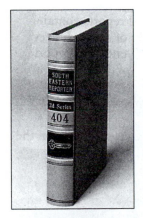

South Eastern Reporter (S.E.), South Eastern Reporter, Second Series (S.E.2d). The opinions of the highest state court and some intermediate appellate courts in the following states: Ga., N.C., S.C., Va., W.Va.

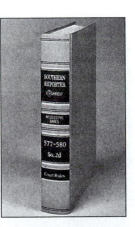

Southern Reporter (So.), Southern Reporter, Second Series (So. 2d). The opinions of the highest state court and some intermediate appellate courts in the following states: Ala., Fla., La., Miss.

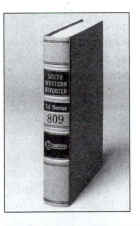

South Western Reporter (S.W.), South Western Reporter, Second Series (S.W.2d). The opinions of the highest state courts and some intermediate appellate courts in the following states: Ark., Ky., Mo., Tenn., Tex.

Major Characteristics of West Reporters

- The reporters contain the full text of court opinions.
- The opinions are arranged in roughly chronological order according to the date of the decision; they are not arranged by subject matter. A murder case, for example, could follow a tax case.
- The reporters have advance sheets that come out before the bound volumes.
- A Table of Cases appears at the beginning of each reporter volume.
- Many reporters have a Table of Statutes Construed, listing the statutes interpreted within an individual reporter volume.
- There is *no* traditional subject-matter index in any reporter volume (the main index to the opinions in reporters is the separate set of books called *digests*).
- Each opinion is summarized in a series of small paragraphs called **headnotes.** They are written by West editors, not by the court. Headnotes are eventually printed in at least five places: first, just before the opinion begins; second, at the beginning of the advance sheet containing the opinion; third, at the end of the bound reporter volume containing the opinion; fourth, in West digests (As we will see later, it is this feature of digests that enables them to become indexes to court opinions.); fifth, in WESTLAW.

Where else is the full text of state court opinions found?

- On **ultrafiche,** which is a single sheet of film containing material that has been reduced by a factor of 100 or more. West publishes an ultrafiche edition of the National Reporter System. *See* Microforms (page 535).
- Online through LEXIS and WESTLAW.
- Online on the Internet (for some state courts).
- On CD-ROM (for some state courts).

CD-ROM

CD-ROM ("compact disk read-only memory") is an optical information-storage system that operates much like a compact disk sold in music stores. Through your computer sys-

CD-ROM products of West Publishing Company

tem, you gain access to the vast amount of information stored on the disk. Up to 60 large volumes of law books can be stored on one disk! Users cannot add any information to the disk; they can only read the information on it through their computer screen or monitor. (Hence the phrase *read only.*) Unlike more traditional computer-assisted research systems, you do not need a modem (see chapter 13) to use CD-ROM.

Century Digest

The *Century Digest* is one of the three digests within the American Digest System. The other two are the *Decennial Digest* and the *General Digest. See* Digests (page 522) and the photo on page 524.

Citation

A **citation** (also called a *cite*) is a reference to any material printed on paper or stored in a computer database, e.g., an opinion, statute, law review article, treatise, or treaty. The citation is the "address" where you can locate and read the material. Most citations are to printed materials; such citations consist of information such as volume number, page number, and date. As we will see later in the chapter, there are citation guidelines for citing different kinds of legal materials. The major publication containing these guidelines is *The Bluebook: A Uniform System of Citation,* which we saw earlier. A **parallel cite** is an additional reference to the *same* material. If, for example, there are two parallel cites to an opinion, you will be able to find the same opinion—word-for-word—in two different reporters.

A new development in the arena of citations is the **public domain citation.** This is a citation that is medium-neutral, which means that the references in the citation are not to traditional volume and page numbers of commercial publishers. As we will see later, courts assign numbering systems that go into the public domain citation.

Citator

A **citator** is a book containing lists of citations that serve two functions: first and foremost, to help you assess the current validity of a case, statute, or other law; and secondarily, to provide you with leads to additional laws. Citators often provide other features as well; e.g., they might give you a parallel citation. The major citator in legal research is Shepard's. The columns of Shepard's contain nothing but citations that are relevant to whatever you are "shepardizing" (pages 538, 602). There are also citators on computer systems, such as Insta-Cite (found on WESTLAW) and Auto-Cite (found on LEXIS).

Code

A **code** is a collection of laws or rules classified by subject matter regardless of when they were enacted. To **codify** something means to rearrange it by subject matter. *Uncod*ified material is arranged chronologically by date of enactment; *codified* material is arranged by subject matter or topic regardless of when passed or enacted. When statutes are first passed by the legislature, they are placed in uncodified books called Session Laws, Acts and Resolves, Statutes at Large, etc. Most of these statutes are later codified into statutory codes. *See* Statutory Code. Administrative regulations are also often codified. *See* Administrative Code.

Code of Federal Regulations (C.F.R.)

The C.F.R. is a set of pamphlets containing many of the regulations of federal agencies. *See* Administrative Code. The C.F.R. is also published on WESTLAW and LEXIS.

Code of Federal Regulations

Congressional Record

The *Congressional Record* is an official collection of the day-to-day happenings of Congress. It is one source of legislative history (page 634) for federal statutes. It also contains many relatively trivial items that are relevant only to the districts of individual legislators.

Corpus Juris Secundum (C.J.S.)

Corpus Juris Secundum

Corpus Juris Secundum (C.J.S.) is a national legal encyclopedia published by West. (It is the second edition of *Corpus Juris.*) This set of books summarizes almost every major legal topic. Topics are covered alphabetically, as in most encyclopedias. C.J.S. is particularly useful (a) as background reading before beginning legal research in a new area of law, (b) as a case finder because of the extensive footnotes to court opinions, and (c) as a point of reference to other publications of West. The main competitor of C.J.S. is *American Jurisprudence 2d.*

Cumulative

Cumulative means that which repeats earlier material and consolidates it with new material. A cumulative supplement, for example, is a pamphlet or volume that repeats, updates, and consolidates all earlier pamphlets or volumes. Because of the repetition, the earlier pamphlets or volumes can be thrown away. Similarly, pocket parts (containing supplemental material at the end of a book) are often cumulative. When the most recent pocket part comes out, the old one can be thrown away. Here is an example of a cumulative pocket part in a statutory code:

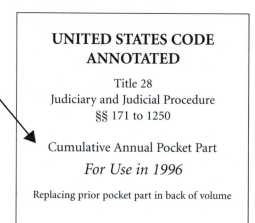

Current Law Index

Current Law Index (CLI) is the most comprehensive general index to legal periodical literature available. (The other major one is the *Index to Legal Periodicals.*) The CLI comes out in three versions: a paper version (consisting of pamphlets and bound volumes), a CD-ROM version called *LegalTrac*), and an online version (called *Legal Resource Index*). The online version is available on WESTLAW and LEXIS. *See* Legal Periodical (page 533).

Decennial Digest

The *Decennial Digest* is one of the three digests within the American Digest System. The other two are the *Century Digest* and the *General Digest. See* Digests.

Digests

Our goals in this section are to define **digest,** to identify the major digests, and to explain the relationship between digests and reporters. Later in the chapter, we will cover the techniques of using digests in research (page 592).

Digests are volumes containing small-paragraph summaries of court opinions organized by subject matter. (These summaries are sometimes called **abstracts** or **squibs**.) The primary purpose of digests is to summarize—to digest—case law. For this reason, digests serve as excellent case finders. The major publisher of digests is West. Its **key number system** is the organizational principle used to classify the millions of small-paragraph summaries in the digests. Here is how this principle works. West divides all of law into a large number of general topics such as Arson, Infants, Marriage, Negligence, and Obscenity. Each of these general topics is further classified into subtopics, and each subtopic is then assigned a number. The phrase *key number* refers to two things: the general topic and the number of the subtopic. Examine the following examples of subtopics under the general topic of Negligence:

NEGLIGENCE

🗝 22. Dangerous instrumentalities and operations

🗝 28. Care required in general

🗝 32(2.9). Deliverymen and haulers

The second key number in this example is referred to as "Negligence 28." (It is *not* referred to as "28 Care required in general.") The key number must include the general topic. You usually do not have to state what the subtopic is; giving the general topic and the number is enough. If a supervisor asks you to check Negligence 28 in a West digest, you simply go to the N volume of the digest where you will check number 28 under Negligence.

Once you find a key number (consisting of a general topic and a number) that is relevant to your research problem, you will find summaries of court opinions under that key number. For example, the following excerpt from a digest contains opinions that are summarized (or digested) under key number Obscenity 1, and key number Obscenity 2:

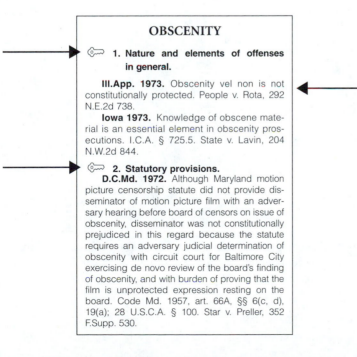

OBSCENITY

🗝 **1. Nature and elements of offenses in general.**

Ill.App. 1973. Obscenity vel non is not constitutionally protected. People v. Rota, 292 N.E.2d 738.

Iowa 1973. Knowledge of obscene material is an essential element in obscenity prosecutions. I.C.A. § 725.5. State v. Lavin, 204 N.W.2d 844.

🗝 **2. Statutory provisions.**

D.C.Md. 1972. Although Maryland motion picture censorship statute did not provide disseminator of motion picture film with an adversary hearing before board of censors on issue of obscenity, disseminator was not constitutionally prejudiced in this regard because the statute requires an adversary judicial determination of obscenity with circuit court for Baltimore City exercising de novo review of the board's finding of obscenity, and with burden of proving that the film is unprotected expression resting on the board. Code Md. 1957, art. 66A, §§ 6(c, d), 19(a); 28 U.S.C.A. § 100. Star v. Preller, 352 F.Supp. 530.

Beneath each summary paragraph is a citation to the case being summarized. For example, see the citation for *People v. Rota* in the first paragraph listed.

Where do these summary paragraphs come from? They come from the *headnotes* of court opinions in West reporters. As we saw earlier, a headnote is a summary of a portion of the opinion that is printed before the opinion begins.

We now turn to an overview of the following four kinds of West digests:

- A national digest covering most state and federal courts
- Federal digests covering only federal courts
- Regional digests covering the courts found in the regional reporters
- Digests of individual courts or states

National Digest   West publishes one national digest: the American Digest System. This massive set (containing over 100 volumes) gives you small-paragraph summaries of the court opinions of most appellate state and federal courts and some lower state and federal courts. The American Digest System has three main units:

- *Century Digest,* covering summaries of opinions written between 1658 and 1896.
- *Decennial Digests,* covering summaries of opinions written during ten-year periods starting in 1897. The more recent Decennials are printed in two parts. Part 1 of the Tenth Decennial, for example, covers the period from 1986 to 1991. Part 2 covers 1991 to 1996. (Prior to the Ninth Decennial, all of the Decennial Digests were issued in one part only—covering the entire ten years.)
- *General Digests,* covering summaries of opinions written since the last Decennial was published. The General Digest volumes are kept on the shelf only until they are eventually consolidated (cumulated) into the next Decennial Digest. When the latter arrives, all of the General Digest volumes are thrown away.

Here are examples of volumes from each of the three units of the American Digest System:

 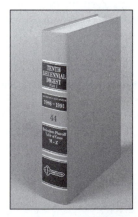

Example of a **Century Digest** volume

Example of a **Decennial Digest** volume

Example of a **General Digest** volume

Federal Digests Covering Only Federal Courts   West publishes five large digests that cover the three main federal courts: the U.S. Supreme Court, the U.S. Courts of Appeals, and the U.S. District Courts. The five digests are:

- *Federal Digest*
- *Modern Federal Practice Digest*

- *Federal Practice Digest* 2d
- *Federal Practice Digest* 3d
- *Federal Practice Digest* 4th

The last digest listed—*Federal Practice Digest 4th*—is the most important because it covers the most recent period; it digests federal cases from 1975 to the present. The other four cover earlier time periods and are therefore used less frequently.

Finally, West publishes a number of special digests that cover specific federal courts or specific topics of federal law:

- *West's Bankruptcy Digest*
- *West's Military Justice Digest*
- *West's Federal Claims Digest*
- *West's Education Law Digest*
- *United States Supreme Court Digest* (West)

**Federal Practice
Digest 4th.**

The *United States Supreme Court Digest* (West) covers opinions of the United States Supreme Court only. A competing digest is the *United States Supreme Court Digest, Lawyers Edition* published by Lawyers Co-op. Since it is not a West digest, it does not use the key number system to classify the small-paragraph summaries in it. It has its own headnote system.

**United States
Supreme Court
Digest.** Published by
West.

**United States
Supreme Court
Digest, L. Ed.** Pub-
lished by Lawyers
Co-op.

Pacific Digest, one of
the regional digests.

Regional Digests   A **regional digest** contains small-paragraph summaries of those court opinions that are printed in its corresponding regional reporter. The opinions in the *Pacific Reporter*, for example, are digested in the *Pacific Digest*. As we shall see in Exhibit 11.5, only four of the seven regional reporters have corresponding regional digests. Those digests are *Atlantic Digest*, *North Western Digest*, *Pacific Digest*, and *South Eastern Digest*. (Regional digests for the other three regions either do not exist or have been discontinued.)

Digests of Individual States   An individual state digest contains small-paragraph summaries of the opinions of the state courts within that state, as well as the opinions of the federal courts that are relevant to that state. The following are examples of state digests:

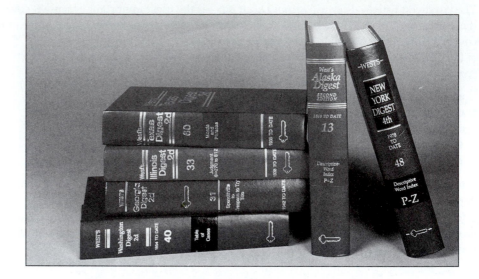

To summarize, examine Exhibit 11.5 where you will find a list of reporters, the names of the courts whose full opinions are currently printed in those reporters, and the names of the digests that give small-paragraph summaries of those opinions.

Exhibit 11.5	**Reporters and Digests: A Checklist**	
NAME OF REPORTER	**THE COURTS WHOSE OPINIONS ARE CURRENTLY PRINTED IN FULL IN THIS REPORTER**	**THE DIGESTS THAT CONTAIN SMALL-PARAGRAPH SUMMARIES OF THE OPINIONS IN THIS REPORTER**
United States Reports (U.S.) Supreme Court Reporter (S.Ct.) United States Supreme Court Reports, Lawyers Edition (L.Ed.) United States Law Week (U.S.L.W.) United States Supreme Court Bulletin (CCH)	United States Supreme Court	American Digest System United States Supreme Court Digest (West) United States Supreme Court Digest, L.Ed. Federal Digest Modern Federal Practice Digest Federal Practice Digest, 2d Federal Practice Digest, 3d Federal Practice Digest, 4th Individual state digests (for Supreme Court cases relevant to that state)

Exhibit 11.5	Reporters and Digests: A Checklist— continued	
NAME OF REPORTER	**THE COURTS WHOSE OPINIONS ARE CURRENTLY PRINTED IN FULL IN THIS REPORTER**	**THE DIGESTS THAT CONTAIN SMALL-PARAGRAPH SUMMARIES OF THE OPINIONS IN THIS REPORTER**
Federal Reporter, 2d (F.2d) Federal Reporter, 3d (F.3d)	United States Courts of Appeals	American Digest System Federal Digest Modern Federal Practice Digest Federal Practice Digest, 2d Federal Practice Digest, 3d Federal Practice Digest, 4th Individual state digests (for federal cases relevant to that state)
Federal Supplement (F. Supp.)	United States District Courts	American Digest System Federal Digest Modern Federal Practice Digest Federal Practice Digest, 2d Federal Practice Digest, 3d Federal Practice Digest, 4th Individual state digests (for federal cases relevant to that state)
Atlantic Reporter 2d (A.2d)	The highest state court and some intermediate appellate courts in Conn., Del., D.C., Me., Md., N.H., N.J., Pa., R.I., Vt.	American Digest System Atlantic Digest Individual state digests for Conn., D.C., Me., Md., N.H., N.J., Pa., R.I., Vt.
North Eastern Reporter 2d (N.E.2d)	The highest state court and some intermediate appellate courts in Ill., Ind., Mass., N.Y., Ohio	American Digest System Individual state digests for Ill., Ind., Mass., N.Y., Ohio (There is *no* North Eastern Digest)
North Western Reporter 2d (N.W.2d)	The highest state court and some intermediate appellate courts in Iowa, Mich., Minn., Neb., N.D., S.D., Wis.	American Digest System North Western Digest Individual state digests for Iowa, Mich., Minn., Neb., N.D., S.D., Wis.

continued

Exhibit 11.5	Reporters and Digests: A Checklist—continued	
NAME OF REPORTER	**THE COURTS WHOSE OPINIONS ARE CURRENTLY PRINTED IN FULL IN THIS REPORTER**	**THE DIGESTS THAT CONTAIN SMALL-PARAGRAPH SUMMARIES OF THE OPINIONS IN THIS REPORTER**
Pacific Reporter, 2d (P.2d)	The highest state court and some intermediate appellate courts in Alaska, Ariz., Cal., Colo., Haw., Idaho, Kan., Mont., Nev., N.M., Okla., Or., Utah., Wash., Wyo.	American Digest System Pacific Digest Individual state digests for Alaska, Ariz., Cal., Colo., Haw., Idaho, Kan., Mont., N.M., Okla., Or., Wash., Wyo.
South Eastern Reporter, 2d (S.E.2d)	The highest state court and some intermediate appellate courts in Ga., N.C., S.C., Va., W.Va.	American Digest System South Eastern Digest Individual state digests for Ga., N.C., S.C., Va., W.Va.
Southern Reporter, 2d (So. 2d)	The highest state court and some intermediate appellate courts in Ala., Fla., La., Miss.	American Digest System Individual state digests for Ala., Fla., La., Miss. (There is *no* Southern Digest)
South Western Reporter, 2d (S.W.2d)	The highest state court and some intermediate appellate courts in Ark., Ky., Mo., Tenn., Tex.	American Digest System Individual state digests for Ark., Ky., Mo., Tenn., Tex. (There is *no* South Western Digest)

Federal Cases

Federal Cases is the name of the reporter that contains very early opinions of the federal courts (up to 1880) before F., F.2d, F.3d, and F. Supp. came into existence.

Federal Practice Digest 2d; Federal Practice Digest 3d; Federal Practice Digest 4th

See Digests (page 527).

Federal Register (Fed. Reg.)

The *Federal Register* is a daily publication of the federal government that prints proposed regulations of the federal administrative agencies; executive orders and other executive documents; and news from federal agencies, such as announcements inviting applications for federal grants. Many of the proposed regulations that are adopted by the federal agencies are later printed in the *Code of Federal Regulations* (C.F.R.).

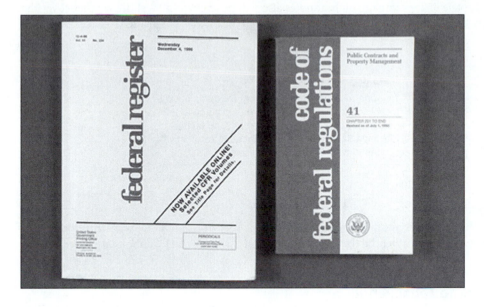

Examples of the **Federal Register** and the **Code of Federal Regulations.** The C.F.R. prints regulations in force that were first proposed in the Fed. Reg.

Federal Reporter 2d; Federal Reporter 3d

A reporter currently containing opinions of the United States Courts of Appeals. *See* photo on page 517.

Federal Rules Decisions (F.R.D.)

A reporter containing opinions of United States District Courts on issues of civil and criminal procedure, plus articles and speeches on federal procedural issues. *See* Cases.

Federal Supplement (F. Supp.)

A reporter containing opinions of the United States District Courts. *See* photo on page 517.

Formbook

A **formbook** is a legal treatise in the form of a manual. A **legal treatise** is a book written by a private individual (or by a public official writing as a private citizen) that provides an overview, summary, or commentary on a legal topic. Manuals often contain summaries of the law, checklists, sample forms, etc. A formbook (also called a *practice manual* or *handbook*) is a single-volume or multivolume how-to-do-it text.

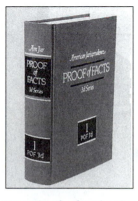

General Digest

The *General Digest* is one of three digests within the American Digest System. The other two are the *Century Digest* and the *Decennial Digest*. *See* Digests and the photo on page 524.

Headnote

A *headnote* is a small-paragraph summary of a portion of an opinion, printed just before the opinion begins. It is written by the publisher of the reporter, not by the court. In West reporters, each headnote is numbered consecutively and is assigned a *key number,* which

Example of a formbook

consists of a general topic and a number. See the following example of a single headnote on libel and slander. For a sample page from a reporter that shows several headnotes, see chapter 7, page 352. Eventually, all headnotes also will be printed in West digests that cover that reporter. See Exhibit 11.5. For other places where headnotes are printed, see page 593.

---

3. Libel and Slander ⚷ **28**

One may not escape liability for defamation by showing that he was merely repeating defamatory language used by another person, and he may not escape liability by falsely attributing to others the ideas to which he gives expression.

Examples of hornbooks

Hornbook

A **hornbook** is another kind of *legal treatise.* (*See* Formbook above.) Hornbooks summarize the law but tend to be less practical than formbooks. Hornbooks are more popular with law students than with practitioners.

Index to Legal Periodicals

Index to Legal Periodicals is one of the two major general indexes to legal periodical literature. (The other is the *Current Law Index.*) The ILP is available in three versions: paper (consisting of pamphlets and bound volumes), CD-ROM, and online. *See* Legal Periodical (page 533).

Internet

The **Internet** is a special network of networks to which millions of individual computer users all over the world have access. It is not run or controlled by any single government or organization. A *network* is a group of computers connected by telephone lines, fiber optic cables, satellites, or other systems. The members of the network can communicate with each other to share information that is placed on the network. Vast quantities of data are available on the networks of the Internet, including legal information. Examples include court opinions, statutes, administrative regulations, treaties, court addresses, and directories of attorneys. Here, for example, is the online "site" where you can find New Jersey statutes, bills, names of state legislators, the current legislative calendar, etc.:

`http://www.njleg.state.nj.us`

At the federal level, a number of major Internet sites provide laws and information from and about Congress, federal courts, and federal administrative agencies. For example:

`http://thomas.loc.gov/`
`http://www.fedworld.gov/`

(We will cover such sites in greater detail later in chapter 13.) There is no charge for most of this information once you have paid for the computer equipment and start-up connections that are needed. Since the Internet is essentially unregulated, however, data found there do not have the same kind of assurance of accuracy as would the same data printed in bound volumes and in the more traditional research computer databases such as LEXIS and WESTLAW. This may change, however, as the Internet continues to grow.

One of the best ways to find information on the Internet is through the **World Wide Web.** The Web allows you to gain access to other data through *hypertext,* which is a method

Examples of Internet sites on federal laws

Thomas
`http://thomas.loc.gov/`

Fedworld
`http://www.fedworld.gov/`

of displaying and linking together information that is located in different places on the Internet. For example, if you are in a document that contains the court opinions of your state, you may be able to "click" the phrase *state statutes* to switch to another document or site that contains the information on the statutes of your state.

Here, for example, is a recent announcement on a resource that is available on the Internet, the Legal Explorer:

> We invite you to take a look at our "recently updated Legal Explorer web site (URL: http://www.ll.georgetown.edu). The Georgetown University Legal Explorer contains links to many sources of law and law-related information. Some of these links are accessed by clicking on buttons for the following areas: Federal, State and Territorial, and Foreign and International. State and Territorial coverage is provided through a clickable map of the United States whose links lead to separate pages for each of the states and territories. These pages cover the law and government of each state or territory. Additional links are provided to sites relating to state and local government. The links for Federal and Foreign and International coverage are not quite as comprehensive yet, but new links are being added on a daily basis. The Library also maintains databases of the opinions of the U.S. Court of Appeals for the District of Columbia Circuit and the U.S. Court of Appeals for the Federal Circuit. The opinions of both are downloaded nightly and are reformatted for viewing and for downloading in WP5.1, Word 2 and ASCII formats. The opinions of all of the U.S. Courts of Appeals are available both from a clickable map and from the Federal Judicial page on the Legal Explorer. The Legal Explorer continually grows and evolves. [W]e invite you to visit it."

Interstate Compact

An **interstate compact** is an agreement between two or more states governing a problem of mutual concern, such as the resolution of a boundary dispute. The compact is passed by the legislature of each state and is therefore part of the statutes of the states involved. Congress must give its approval. Hence, the compact also becomes part of the statutes of Congress.

Legal Dictionary

A **legal dictionary** contains definitions of words and phrases used in the law. Examples include *Black's Law Dictionary* (West), *Ballentine's Law Dictionary* (Lawyers Co-op), and *West's Legal Thesaurus/Dictionary* (West). The major multivolume legal dictionary is *Words and Phrases* from West. The definitions in this set consist of thousands of excerpts from court opinions that have treated the word or phrase. Hence, this massive dictionary can also serve as an excellent case finder.

Black's Law Dictionary

Legal Encyclopedia

A **legal encyclopedia** is a multivolume set of books that summarizes almost every major legal topic. It is valuable (a) as background reading for a research topic that is new to you, and (b) as a case finder (due to its extensive footnotes). The two competing national encyclopedias are *American Jurisprudence 2d,* published by Lawyers Co-op, and *Corpus Juris Secundum,* published by West. (For photos of these two encyclopedias, see pages 514 and 522.) A number of states have their own encyclopedias covering the law of that state, e.g. *Florida Jurisprudence* and *Michigan Law and Practice.*

Legal Newsletter

Many private companies and public-interest groups publish **legal newsletters** that provide practical guidelines and current developments in very specific areas of the law. Exam-

ples: *Corporate Counsellor, Daily Tax Report, AIDS Policy & Law, Matrimonial Strategist.*
Printed weekly or monthly, they are often quite expensive even though they tend to be relatively brief.

Legal Newspaper

There are two kinds of **legal newspapers:** local and national. Local legal newspapers are usually published daily. They print court calendars, dockets, the full text of selected opinions of local courts, information on new court rules, job announcements, etc. Most large cities have their own legal newspaper. Examples: *New York Law Journal, Daily Washington Law Reporter, San Francisco Daily Journal.* There are several national legal newspapers such as the weekly *National Law Journal.* They cover more than one state on topics such as law firm mergers and dissolutions, salary surveys, careers of prominent attorneys, trends in federal areas of the law, etc.

Example of a national legal newspaper

Legal Periodical

There are three main kinds of **legal periodicals:** academic, commercial, and bar association. They are first published as small pamphlets and are later bound by most libraries. (1) Academic legal periodicals (often called **law reviews** or **law journals**) are published by law schools, and hence are scholarly in nature. Law students are selected to do some of the writing and all of the editing for these periodicals. (It is a mark of considerable distinction for a student to be *on law review.*) Most academic legal periodicals are general in scope, covering a wide variety of legal topics. Others are considered special-interest or specialized periodicals since they focus on specific subjects such as women's rights and environmental law. (2) Commercial legal periodicals are published by private companies. They tend to be more practice-oriented, specialized, and expensive than the academic legal periodicals. (3) Bar association periodicals are published by national, state, and local bar associations. Their focus is on practical articles and features of interest to the membership.

Examples of academic legal periodicals:

As we shall see later, there are two major general indexes to legal periodical literature:

- *Index to Legal Periodicals* (ILP)
- *Current Law Index* (CLI)

These indexes are available in different versions: paper (consisting of pamphlets and bound volumes), CD-ROM, and online. (One of the most popular is *Legal Trac*, the CD-ROM version of CLI.) In addition to these general indexes, there are special indexes to legal periodical literature on topics such as tax law.

Legal Thesaurus

A **legal thesaurus** provides word alternatives for words used in legal writing. The thesaurus may also be helpful in forming queries for computer-assisted legal research (page 707). Two examples: Burton's *Legal Thesaurus,* 2d ed. (Macmillan, 1992), and Statsky's *Legal Thesaurus/Dictionary: A Resource for the Writer and Legal Researcher* (West, 1985).

LegalTrac

LegalTrac is a major general index to legal periodical literature. It is the CD-ROM version of the *Current Law Index,* the most comprehensive general index to legal periodical literature available. (See page 619.)

Legal Treatise

A *legal treatise* (not to be confused with treaty) is any book written by a private individual (or by a public official writing as a private citizen) that provides an overview, summary, or commentary on a legal topic. The treatise will usually attempt to give an extensive treatment of that topic. Hornbooks and formbooks are also treatises. Some treatises are designed primarily as study aids for students. (*See* Nutshell, page 536.) Treatises are printed in several formats, such as single volume, multivolume, and loose-leaf.

Legislation

Legislation is the process of making statutory law by the legislature. The word *legislation* also refers to the statutes themselves.

LEXIS

LEXIS is a legal research computer system owned by the Reed Elsevier company. (See page 625.)

Loose-Leaf Service

Most law books come in one of three forms:

- Pamphlet
- Hardcover bound volume
- Loose-leaf

A **loose-leaf** text or **service** is a three-ring (or post) binder containing pages that can easily be inserted or taken out. As new material is written covering the subject matter of the loose-leaf text, it is placed in the binder, often replacing the pages that the new material has changed or otherwise supplemented. Since this kind of updating can sometimes occur as often as once a week, loose-leaf services frequently contain the most current material available in print.

Some loose-leaf services are legal treatises, others are reporters, and others are combination treatise-reporters. There are few areas of the law that are *not* covered by one or more loose-leaf services. Examples of such services include *Environmental Reporter, Tax Management, Employment Practices Guide, Standard Federal Tax Reports, United States Law Week, Criminal Law Reporter, Family Law Reporter, Media Law Reporter, Sexual Law Reporter, Labor Relations Reporter.*

Example of a loose-leaf service

While some loose-leaf services do little more than print the most current opinions in their specialty, most have a variety of features:

- The full text plus summaries of court opinions in the area of the specialty
- The full text plus summaries of administrative regulations and decisions in the area of the specialty (some of which may not be available elsewhere)
- Summaries of the major statutory provisions of the specialty
- Suggestions on how to practice in the specialty

The major publishers of loose-leaf services are Commerce Clearing House (CCH), Bureau of National Affairs (BNA); Clark Boardman Callaghan; Warren, Gorham & Lamont; and Matthew Bender.

Martindale-Hubbell Law Directory

The *Martindale-Hubbell Law Directory* is a multivolume set of books that serves three major functions by providing:

- An alphabetical listing of attorneys and law firms by state and city—this is the **law directory,** which is the main component of the set; for some firms, the listing includes paralegals and other nonattorney personnel (see page 87 in chapter 2)
- Short summaries of the law of all fifty states (in its separate Digest volume)
- Short summaries of the law of many foreign countries (in its separate Digest volume)

The *Martindale-Hubbell Law Directory* is also available on the Internet at the following site:

```
http://www.martindale.com
```

Martindale-Hubbell Law Directory

Microforms

Microforms are images or photographs that have been reduced in size. Among the materials stored on microforms are pages from reporters, codes, treatises, periodicals, etc. Vast amounts of material can be stored in this way. An entire volume of a 1,000-page law book can fit on a single plastic card! Special machines (*reader-printers* and *fiche readers*) magnify the material so that it can be read. Several kinds of microforms are available. (a) *Microfilm* stores the material on film reels or cassettes. (b) *Microfiche* stores the material on single sheets of film. (c) *Ultrafiche* is microfiche with a considerably greater storage capacity—providing a reduction factor of 100 or more.

Example of West's ultrafiche, containing a volume of the *Federal Reporter 2d*

New York Supplement (N.Y.S.)

A reporter containing New York cases. *See* Cases (page 518).

North Eastern Reporter 2d (N.E.2d)

A regional reporter that prints the full text of state court opinions in the North East region of the country. See Exhibit 11.4. *See also* Cases (page 519).

North Western Digest

A digest that summarizes state court opinions printed in the *North Western Reporter*. *See* Exhibit 11.5. *See also* Digests (page 527).

North Western Reporter 2d (N.W.2d)

A regional reporter that prints the full text of state court opinions in the North West region of the country. See Exhibit 11.4. *See also* Cases (page 519).

Nutshell

A **nutshell** is a legal treatise written in pamphlet form. It summarizes a topic that is often covered in a law school course. Nutshells, therefore, are primarily used as study aids by law students. They are published by West.

Pacific Digest

A digest that summarizes state court opinions printed in the *Pacific Reporter*. *See* Exhibit 11.5. *See also* Digests (page 528).

Pacific Reporter 2d (P.2d)

A regional reporter that prints the full text of state court opinions in the Western region of the country. See Exhibit 11.4. *See also* Cases (page 519).

Pocket Part

A **pocket part** is a small pamphlet addition placed in a special pocket built into the inside cover of a bound volume (usually the back cover). The purpose of the pocket part is to update the material in the bound volume.

Examples of nutshells

Example of a law book with a pocket part

Record

When referring to a trial, the **record** is the official collection of what happened during the trial. It includes a word-for-word transcript of, what was said, the pleadings, all the exhibits, etc. *See also* Congressional Record (page 522).

Regional Digest

A digest that summarizes cases in a regional reporter. *See* Exhibit 11.5 and Digests (page 525).

Restatements

Restatements are scholarly legal treatises published by the **American Law Institute** (ALI) that attempt to formulate (that is, restate) the existing law of a given area. Occasionally, the Restatements also state what the ALI thinks the law *ought* to be.

Examples of Restatements:

Restatement of Agency	*Restatement of Property*
Restatement of Conflicts of Law	*Restatement of Restitution*
Restatement of Contracts	*Restatement of Security*
Restatement of Foreign	*Restatement of Torts*
Relations Law	*Restatement of Trusts*
Restatement of Judgments	

Example of a Restatement

Since the Restatements are written by a private organization (ALI) rather than by an official government entity, they are not laws. But because of their scholarly content, they have great prestige in the courts; judges frequently rely on them in their opinions. One of the reasons this is so is the elaborate procedure the ALI follows before issuing one of its Restatements. First, a renowned scholar in the field prepares an initial draft of the Restatement. This draft is reviewed by a committee of Advisors consisting of other scholars and specialists in the field. A special Council of the ALI then reviews and revises the draft. This leads to a *tentative draft* that is considered by the ALI at one of its annual meetings. After further editing and revision, the final version is approved by the ALI.

Rules of Court

Rules of court, also called **court rules,** are the laws of procedure that govern the conduct of litigation before a particular court. They are often found in the statutory code and in separate volumes or pamphlets.

Series

An **edition** is a revision of an earlier version of a book or set of books. The word **series,** on the other hand, refers to a new numbering order for new volumes within the *same* set of books. Reporters, for example, come in series. Federal Reporter, First Series (F.) has 300 volumes. After volume 300 was printed, the publisher decided to start a new series of the same set of books—Federal Reporter, Second Series (F.2d). The first volume of F.2d is volume 1. F.2d has 999 volumes. After volume 999 was printed, the publisher decided to start a new series of the same set of books—Federal Reporter, Third Series (F.3d). After a large number of F.3d volumes are printed, we will undoubtedly see an F.4th, which will begin again with volume 1. There is no consistent number of volumes that a publisher will print before deciding to start a new series for a set of books.

Examples of rules of court volumes

Session Law

Session laws are an uncodified printing of statutes. The statutes are listed chronologically rather than by subject matter. *See* Act; Acts and Resolves (page 512).

Shepard's

Our goal here is to provide a brief overview of Shepard's and sheparzing by identifying the major sets of Shepard's volumes that exist. Later in the chapter, we will learn how to use Shepard's—how to **shepardize**. (See page 602.)

```
        ˙          – 327 –          ⊏
      ⅄n89        ICT§2.16       622F2dᵈ₁.
                                 492FS⁹774
                   – 365 –
      – 946 –       Cir. 4          – 485 –
       Cir. 9    623F2dᵈ¹²891       W V⁞
     23F2dᵈ561      Cir. 5       268Sℝ⅀3(
                 623F2dᵈ¹⁰359
      – 953 –    623F2dᵈ¹¹359       – 5⌐
       Cir. 4    623F2dᵈ¹²359         ⊏
     ⎧24F2dᵈ510  623F2dᵈ¹³359      613P2⁞
                 623F2dᵈ¹⁴359
      – 995 –    623F2dᵈ¹⁵359        – ⌐
       Cir. 7    623F2dᵈ¹⁶359         ⊏
     491FS⁴970   f623F2dᵈ³360      4BR
    e491FS¹²972  f623F2dᵈ⁷360
                 623F2dᵈ¹⁰397        –
      – 1010 –   623F2dᵈ¹¹397
        DC       j623F2d403       492⁞
     412A2d35    f623F2d
                      [¹⁰1088
   3  – 1202 –   f623F2d
        Cir. 2        [¹²1089    ⁄
   –  d490FS⁹1218 f624F2dᵈ¹³539
                 f624F2dᵈ¹⁰554
  242  – 1209 –  f624F2dᵈ¹¹55⌐
        Kan      f624F2dᵈ¹²5⌐
  ⎰–   615P2d135 f624F2dᵈ¹¹
  ꝫ              f624F2⎺
```

Excerpt from a page in a Shepard's volume

Shepard's Citations are citators (page 521). To *shepardize* an item means to use the volumes of Shepard's to collect the research references provided for that item. The references differ depending on what you are shepardizing. If, for example, you are shepardizing a case, you will be given the parallel cite (if one exists) for this case, the history of the case (such as appeals within the same litigation), other cases that have interpreted or mentioned the case you are shepardizing, legal periodical literature on the case, etc. If you are shepardizing a statute, you may be given the session law cite for the statute, amendments, repeals or additions to the statute, court opinions that have interpreted the statute, legal periodical literature on the statute, etc.

What can you shepardize? Here is a partial list:

- Court opinions
- Statutes
- Constitutions
- Some administrative regulations
- Some administrative decisions
- Ordinances
- Charters

- Rules of court
- Some executive orders
- Some treaties
- Patents, trademarks, copyrights
- Restatements
- Some legal periodical literature

As we shall see later, the items in this list constitute the *cited material*—that which you are shepardizing. When you go to the references to these cited materials in the volumes of Shepard's, you will be given a variety of other references on the cited materials, such as cases that have interpreted statutes, annotations that mention the statutes, and cases that have overruled prior cases. These other references are called the *citing material*. (See page 604.)

On pages 539–541, there is an overview of some of the major items that can be shepardized with the appropriate sets of Shepard's that you would use to shepardize them.

Shepard's Citations are also available online through WESTLAW and LEXIS.

An Overview of Major Items That Can Be Shepardized

Assume that you want to shepardize an opinion of the United States Supreme Court:

Supreme Court Reporter

Here is the set of Shepard's you use to shepardize an opinion of the United States Supreme Court:

Shepard's United States Citations, Case Edition

Assume that you want to shepardize opinions found in *Federal Reporter, 2d:*

Federal Reporter, 2d (F.2d)

Here is the set of Shepard's you use to shepardize an F.2d opinion:

Shepard's Federal Citations

Assume that you want to shepardize opinions found in Federal Supplement:

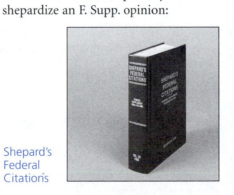

Federal Supplement (F. Supp.)

Here is the set of Shepard's you use to shepardize an F. Supp. opinion:

Shepard's Federal Citations

Assume that you want to shepardize a federal statute of Congress: a statute found in U.S.C.A. (*United States Code Annotated*) or in U.S.C.S. (*United States Code Service*) or in U.S.C. (*United States Code*):

Here is the set of Shepard's that you use to shepardize a federal statute:

Shepard's United States Citations, Statute Edition

Assume that you want to shepardize a regulation of a federal agency found in C.F.R. *(Code of Federal Regulations)*:

Here is the set of Shepard's that will enable you to shepardize a regulation in C.F.R.:

Shepard's Code of Federal Regulations Citations

Assume that you want to shepardize opinions found within the following regional reporters:

    Atlantic Reporter 2d
    Pacific Reporter 2d
    South Western Reporter 2d
    South Eastern Reporter 2d
    North Eastern Reporter 2d

At the right are the sets of Shepard's that you use to shepardize the opinions in these regional reporters.

Assume that you want to shepardize the following:

A Rhode Island court opinion

A Rhode Island statute

A Rhode Island constitutional provision

A New Hampshire court opinion

A New Hampshire statute

A New Hampshire constitutional provision

Here are the sets of Shepard's that you would use:

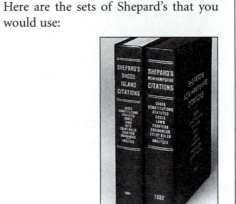

Note: Every state has its own set of Shepard's similar to Shepard's Rhode Island Citations and Shepard's New Hampshire Citations above.

Slip Law

A **slip law** is a single act passed by the legislature. It is printed separately, often in a small pamphlet. It is the first official publication of the act. All slip laws are later printed chronologically in volumes that may be called Session Laws, Acts, Statutes at Large, etc. Finally, if the slip law is a public law or statute, it is also printed in a **statutory code,** where the arrangement is by subject matter.

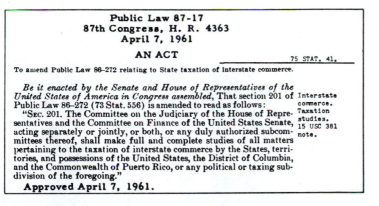

Example of a slip law

Slip Opinion

When a court first announces a decision, it is usually published in what is called a **slip opinion** or slip decision. It contains a single case in pamphlet form. The slip opinions are later printed in advance sheets for reporters, which in turn become bound reporters.

South Eastern Digest

A digest that summarizes state court opinions printed in the *South Eastern Reporter. See* Exhibit 11.4. *See also* Digests (page 528).

South Eastern Reporter 2d (S.E.2d)

A regional reporter that prints the full text of state court opinions in the South East region of the country. See Exhibit 11.4. *See also* Cases (page 519).

Southern Reporter 2d (So. 2d)

A regional reporter that prints the full text of state court opinions in several Southern states. See Exhibit 11.4. *See also* Cases (page 519).

South Western Reporter 2d (S.W.2d)

A regional reporter that prints the full text of state court opinions in the South West region of the country. See Exhibit 11.4. *See also* Cases (page 519).

Statutes at Large

An uncodified printing of statutes. *See* Act; Acts and Resolves. *See also* United States Statutes at Large.

Statutory Code

A *statutory code* is a collection of the statutes of the legislature organized by subject matter. For example, the statutes on murder are together, the statutes on probate are together, etc. Statutory codes are often annotated, meaning that notes or commentaries accompany the full text of the statutes. The notes might include summaries of cases (often called *notes of decisions*) that have interpreted the statute and information on the legislative history of the statute such as the dates of earlier amendments. Statutes are published in printed volumes and online through WESTLAW and LEXIS.

The three major *federal* statutory codes are:

U.S.C.—United States Code (published by the U.S. Government Printing Office) (official)
U.S.C.A.—United States Code Annotated (published by West) (unofficial)
U.S.C.S.—United States Code Service (published by Lawyers Co-op) (unofficial)

Example of a *state* statutory code

The three major federal statutory codes

Supreme Court Reporter (S. Ct.)

An unofficial reporter that prints every opinion of the United States Supreme Court. It is published by West. *See* Cases and photos on pages 516 and 540.

Total Client-Service Library

The *Total Client-Service Library* is the system by which Lawyers Co-op refers you to many of the books and materials it publishes. If, for example, you are reading an annotation in A.L.R., A.L.R.2d, A.L.R.3d, A.L.R.4th, A.L.R.5th, or A.L.R. Fed, you may be referred to other Lawyers Co-op books on the same subject matter, such as *American Jurisprudence 2d,* U.S.C.S. (United States Code Service), *Am Jur Pleading and Practice Forms,* etc. Note that the following example also refers you to the Auto-Cite computer service of Lawyers Co-op.

Total Client-Service Library® References

The following references may be of related or collateral interest to a user of this annotation.

Annotations

See the related annotations listed in the body of the annotation.

Encyclopedias and Texts

43 Am Jur 2d, Insurance §§ 621, 622

Practice Aids

14 Am Jur Pl & Pr Forms (Rev), Insurance Forms 641–645, 652–657
7 Am Jur Proof of Facts 3d 1, Injuries from Drugs
29 Am Jur Proof of Facts 2d 223, Unintentional Barbiturate Overdose
12 Am Jur Trials 549, Actions on Life Insurance Policies

Digests and Indexes

L Ed Digest, Insurance §§ 201, 202
ALR Digest, Insurance §§ 108.6, 651.5, 653, 672–674, 680, 687, 692, 694
ALR Index, Accident or Accidental; Barbiturates; Cocaine; Drugs and Narcotics; Foreseeability; Health and Accident Insurance; Heroin; Insurance and Insurance Companies; Life Insurance; Morphine; Overdose

Auto-Cite®

Cases and annotations referred to herein can be further researched through the Auto-Cite® computer-assisted research service. Use Auto-Cite to check citations for form, parallel references, prior and later history, and annotation references.

Ultrafiche

See Microforms.

United States Code (U.S.C.)

The official code containing federal statutes. *See* Statutory Code.

United States Code Annotated (U.S.C.A.)

An unofficial code containing federal statutes. *See* Statutory Code.

United States Code Congressional and Administrative News (U.S.C.C.A.N.)

U.S.C.C.A.N., published by West, will enable you to:

- Obtain the complete text of public laws or statutes of Congress before they are published in U.S.C./U.S.C.A./U.S.C.S.
- Obtain the complete text of some congressional committee reports (important for legislative history)
- Translate a Statute at Large cite into a U.S.C./U.S.C.A./U.S.C.S. cite (through Table 2)
- Obtain leads to the legislative history of federal statutes (primarily through Table 4)

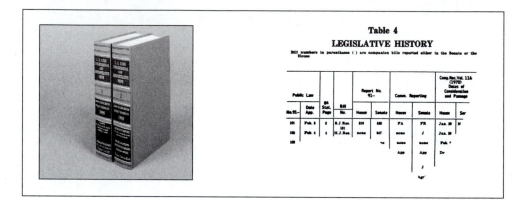

- Obtain the complete text of some federal agency regulations (duplicating what is found in the *Federal Register—Fed. Reg.* and in the *Code of Federal Regulations—C.F.R.*)
- Obtain the complete text of executive orders and other executive documents
- Obtain the complete text of all current United States Statutes at Large (*see* below)

United States Code Service (U.S.C.S.)

An unofficial code containing federal statutes. *See* Statutory Code.

United States Law Week (U.S.L.W.)

U.S.L.W. is a loose-leaf service published by the Bureau of National Affairs (BNA) that prints the full text of every United States Supreme Court case on a weekly basis. It also prints other data on cases in the Supreme Court and summarizes important cases from other courts.

United States Reports (U.S.)

An official reporter that prints every opinion of the United States Supreme Court. *See* Cases.

United States Statutes at Large (Stat.)

The United States Statutes at Large (Stat.) contains the full text of every public law or statute and every private law or statute of Congress. (A private law or private statute applies to specifically named individuals or to groups and has little or no permanence or general interest, unlike a public law or public statute.) The statutes within Stat. are printed chronologically. All current statutes at large are now also printed in *U.S. Code Congressional and Administrative News* as well as in separate Stat. volumes. (The public laws of general interest are later codified and printed in each of the three sets of codified federal statutes: U.S.C., U.S.C.A., U.S.C.S.)

United States Supreme Court Reports, L. Ed.

An unofficial reporter that prints every opinion of the United States Supreme Court. *See* Cases.

WESTLAW

WESTLAW is a legal research computer system owned by West Publishing Company. (See page 624).

Words and Phrases

A multivolume legal dictionary. Most of the definitions in this dictionary are quotations from court opinions. *See* Legal Dictionary.

Multivolume legal dictionary

For a summary of many of the glossary entries we have been examining, see Exhibit 11.6.

Exhibit 11.6	Major Legal Reference Materials: An Outline	
BOOKS OF LAW	*Federal Statutes*	U.S. Statutes at Large U.S. Code U.S. Code Annotated U.S. Code Service
	State Statutes	Session Laws State Statutory Codes
	Federal Court Opinions	
	U.S. Supreme Court	U.S. Reports Lawyers' Edition Supreme Court Reporter U.S. Law Week U.S. Supreme Court Bulletin (CCH)
	U.S. Courts of Appeals	Federal Reporter 3d
	U.S. District Courts	Federal Supplement
	State Court Opinions	
	Regional Reporters of the National Reporter System	Atlantic Reporter 2d North Eastern Reporter 2d North Western Reporter 2d Pacific Reporter 2d South Eastern Reporter 2d Southern Reporter 2d South Western Reporter 2d

Exhibit 11.6 Major Legal Reference Materials: An Outline—continued

Others . . . .
- Official state reporters
- Special edition state reporters

- Within statutory code

Federal & State Constitutions . . . . .

Federal Administrative Regulations . . . .
- Federal Register
- Code of Federal Regulations

State Administrative Regulations . . . .
- State Register
- State administrative code
- Municipal Code

BOOKS OF SEARCH AND/OR INTERPRETATION

Digests . . . .
- American Digest System
  - Century Digest
  - Decennial Digests
  - General Digests
- U.S. Supreme Court Digests
- Regional Digests
- Individual State Digests
- Federal Digest
- Modern Federal Practice Digest
- Federal Practice Digest 2d
- Federal Practice Digest 3d
- Federal Practice Digest 4th
- Bankruptcy Digest
- Military Justice Digest
- Federal Claims Court Digest
- Education Law Digest

Legal Encyclopedias . . . .
- American Jurisprudence 2d
- Corpus Juris Secundum

Legal Periodicals . . . .
- Index to Legal Periodicals
- Current Law Index
- Legal Resource Index
- LegalTrac

Annotations . . . .
- American Law Reports
- American Law Reports 2d
- American Law Reports 3d
- American Law Reports 4th
- American Law Reports 5th
- American Law Reports Fed.

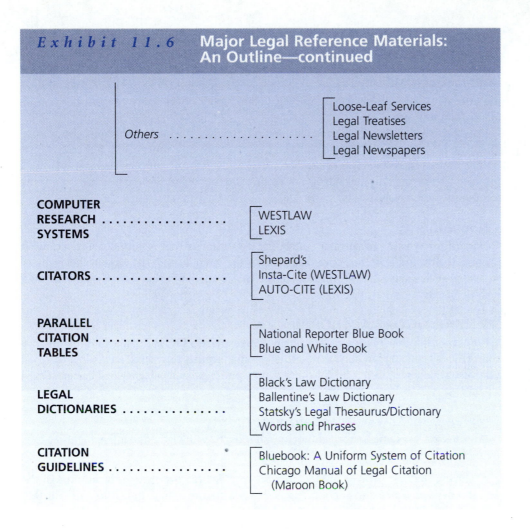

Exhibit 11.6   Major Legal Reference Materials: An Outline—continued

Others ....
- Loose-Leaf Services
- Legal Treatises
- Legal Newsletters
- Legal Newspapers

COMPUTER RESEARCH SYSTEMS ....
- WESTLAW
- LEXIS

CITATORS ....
- Shepard's
- Insta-Cite (WESTLAW)
- AUTO-CITE (LEXIS)

PARALLEL CITATION TABLES ....
- National Reporter Blue Book
- Blue and White Book

LEGAL DICTIONARIES ....
- Black's Law Dictionary
- Ballentine's Law Dictionary
- Statsky's Legal Thesaurus/Dictionary
- Words and Phrases

CITATION GUIDELINES ....
- Bluebook: A Uniform System of Citation
- Chicago Manual of Legal Citation (Maroon Book)

Section I
AUTHORITY IN RESEARCH AND WRITING

1. INTRODUCTION

Authority is anything that a court can rely on in reaching its decision.

Primary and Secondary Authority

Primary authority is any *law* that the court can rely on in reaching its decision. Examples include statutes, administrative regulations, constitutional provisions, executive orders, charters, ordinances, treaties, and other court opinions (see Exhibit 6.1 in chapter 6).

Secondary authority is any *nonlaw* that the court can rely on in reaching its decision. Examples include legal and nonlegal periodical literature, legal and nonlegal encyclopedias, legal and nonlegal dictionaries, legal and nonlegal treatises. (See Exhibit 11.7 later in this section on page 552.)

Mandatory Authority and Persuasive Authority

Mandatory authority is whatever the court *must* rely on in reaching its decision. Only primary authority—such as another court opinion, a statute, or a constitutional provision—can be mandatory authority. A court is never required to rely on secondary authority, such as a legal periodical article or legal encyclopedia. Secondary authority cannot be mandatory authority.

Persuasive authority is whatever the court relies on when it is not required to do so. There are two main kinds of persuasive authority: (a) a prior court opinion that the court is not required to follow but does so because it finds the opinion persuasive, and (b) any secondary authority that the court is not required to follow but does so because it finds the secondary authority persuasive.

Nonauthority

Nonauthority is (a) any primary or secondary authority that is not on point because it is not relevant and does not cover the facts of the client's case, (b) any invalid primary authority, such as an unconstitutional statute, or (c) any book that is solely a finding aid, such as *Shepard's Citations* or digests.

2. MANDATORY AUTHORITY

Courts *must* follow mandatory authority. There are two broad categories of mandatory authority: (a) **enacted law** such as a statute, a constitutional provision, an ordinance, or an administrative regulation,[1] and (b) other court opinions. Each category will be considered separately.

(a) Enacted Law as Mandatory Authority

Any enacted law is mandatory authority and must be followed if the following three tests are met:

- The enacted law is being applied in a geographic area over which the authors of the law have power or jurisdiction (e.g., a Florida statute being applied to an event that occurred in the state of Florida).
- It was the intention of the authors of the enacted law (e.g., the legislature that wrote the statute) to cover the facts that are currently before the court.
- The application of this enacted law to these facts does not violate some other law that is superior in authority (e.g., the statute does not violate the constitution).

If an enacted law such as a state statute meets these tests, it is mandatory authority in every state court in the state. Suppose that Smith is arrested in Florida for burglarizing a Florida house and is prosecuted in a Florida state court. Assume that § 14 of the Florida Code provides, "It shall be a felony to break and enter a dwelling for the purpose of stealing property therein." Section 14 is mandatory authority for the court as long as it is clear that the statute is being applied in a geographic area over which the Florida legislature has power, the Florida legislature intended the statute to cover this kind of situation, and the statute does not violate a higher law—the constitution. Suppose, however, that Smith was arrested for breaking into a car. Is a car a "dwelling" for purposes of § 14? Did the legislature intend to include motor vehicles within the meaning of "dwelling"? Would it depend on whether the owner ever slept in the car? These are questions of **legislative intent.** If the

---

[1] *Enacted law* is law that is not produced through litigation or adjudication. The most common enacted laws are the statutes of legislatures.

statute was not intended to cover these facts, it is not applicable; it cannot be mandatory authority.

Even if the enacted law was intended to cover the facts before the court, it is not mandatory authority if it violates some higher law. The authors of an administrative regulation, for example, may intend to cover a particular individual's activities, but if this regulation is inconsistent with the statute that the regulation is supposed to be carrying out, the regulation is not mandatory authority; it is invalid. Similarly, a statute may clearly cover a given set of facts but be invalid because the statute is unconstitutional. For example, a statute that prohibits marriage between the races is clearly intended to prevent interracial marriage, but the statute is not mandatory authority because it is in violation of the constitution.

State enacted law (e.g., a state statute, a state administrative regulation) is usually mandatory only in the state that enacted that law. Suppose, however, that a state court is considering a *federal* enacted law.

Federal enacted law (e.g., the United States Constitution, a federal statute, a federal administrative regulation) can sometimes be mandatory authority in *state* courts. The United States Constitution is the highest authority in the country. If a provision of this Constitution applies, it controls over any state law to the contrary. Federal statutes and the regulations of federal administrative agencies are also superior in authority to state laws in those areas entrusted to the federal government by the United States Constitution, such as interstate commerce, patents, bankruptcy, or foreign affairs. Federal statutes and regulations in these areas are mandatory authority in state courts.

(b) Court Opinions as Mandatory Authority

When is a court *required* to follow a court opinion? Two conditions must be met:

- The opinion is *on point,* that is, it must be *analogous.*
- The opinion was written by a higher court. It was written by a court that is superior to the court currently considering the applicability of the opinion.

In general, something is **on point** when it is relevant or covers the facts of your research problem, and something is **analogous** when it is similar, although there are differences. More specifically, in legal research, a court opinion is on point and analogous when there is a sufficient similarity between the key facts of the opinion and the facts of the client's case, *and* between the rule of law (e.g., statute, common-law principle) that was interpreted and applied in the opinion and the rule of law that must be interpreted and applied in the client's case. If the opinion is not on point or analogous because this similarity does not exist, the opinion cannot be mandatory authority; it is nonauthority.

The second condition for the existence of mandatory authority requires us to examine the relationship between the court that wrote the opinion and the court that is currently considering that opinion. We will briefly cover six variations:

1. The highest court in the judicial system is considering an opinion written by a lower court in the same judicial system.
2. A lower court is considering an opinion written by the highest court in the same judicial system.
3. A court is considering an opinion written in the past by the same court.
4. A court in one state is considering an opinion written by a court from another state.
5. A state court is considering an opinion written by a federal court.
6. A federal court is considering an opinion written by a state court.

In each of these six situations, a court is attempting to determine whether a prior opinion is binding in the litigation currently before the court. Assume that each opinion *is* analogous: The facts currently before the court are similar to the important or key facts in the opinion under consideration, and the rules of law are also the same or similar.

1. **The highest court is considering an opinion written by a lower court in the same judicial system.**

   A higher court is never required to follow an opinion written by a lower court in the same judicial system, whether or not the opinion is analogous. The California Supreme Court, for example, does not have to follow an opinion written by a California Superior Court, one of the lower courts in the California judicial system. Similarly, the United States Supreme Court does not have to follow an opinion written by a United States District Court, the trial court in the federal judicial system. If the opinion is analogous, it can only be persuasive authority; the higher court can follow it if it chooses to do so.

2. **A lower court is considering an opinion written by the highest court in the same judicial system.**

   An opinion written by the highest court in a judicial system *is* mandatory on every lower court in the same judicial system—if that opinion is analogous. An analogous opinion by the Supreme Court of Montana, for example, must be followed by every lower state court in Montana.

3. **A court is considering an opinion written in the past by the same court.**

   Does a court have to follow its *own* prior opinions? If, for example, the Florida Supreme Court wrote an opinion in 1970, is that opinion mandatory authority for the Florida Supreme Court in 1997 if the opinion is analogous? No. A court is always free to **overrule** and in effect invalidate its own prior opinions. This, however, rarely happens. A court is reluctant to change prior opinions unless there are good reasons to do so. This reluctance is known as **stare decisis.**

   Suppose that the opinion was written by an intermediate or middle appeals court. (See Exhibits 6.2 and 6.3 in chapter 6.) Does that same court have to follow this opinion later if the opinion is analogous? No. *Any* court can later overrule itself and reach a holding that differs from the holding it reached in the earlier opinion as long as there is no opinion in existence written by a higher court that is contrary to the result the court now wants to reach.

4. **A state court is considering an opinion written by a state court in another state.**

   A state court, generally, does not have to follow an opinion written by a state court in another state no matter how similar or analogous the opinion is. An Idaho court, for example, does not have to follow an opinion written by a Texas court.

   There are two main exceptions to the principle that an opinion of one state is not mandatory authority in another state. The first involves conflicts of law and the second, full faith and credit:

   • **Conflicts of Law.** Suppose that an accident occurs in New York, but the negligence suit based on this accident is brought in an Ohio state court. Assume that the Ohio court has **subject-matter jurisdiction** over the dispute (meaning that the court has the power to hear this kind of dispute), and **personal jurisdiction** over the parties (meaning that the court has the power to render a decision that would bind these particular parties). What negligence law does the Ohio court apply? Ohio negligence law or New York negligence law? The negligence law of the two states may differ in significant respects. This is a conflicts-of-law problem, which arises whenever there is an inconsistency between the laws of two different, co-equal legal systems such as two states. Under the principles of the conflicts of law, a court of one state may be required to apply the law of another state. For example, the law to be applied may be the law of the state where the injury occurred or the law of the state that is at the center of the dispute. If this state is New York, then the Ohio court will apply New York negligence law. Analogous opinions of New York courts on the law of negligence will be mandatory authority in the Ohio court.

- **Full Faith and Credit.** The United States Constitution provides that "Full Faith and Credit shall be given in each State to the public Acts, Records, and judicial Proceedings of every other State." art. IV, § 1. Suppose that Richards sues Davis for breach of contract in Delaware. Davis wins. Richards cannot go to another state and bring a breach-of-contract suit against Davis arising out of the same facts. If the Delaware court had proper jurisdiction (subject matter and personal) when it rendered its judgment, the Delaware opinion must be given full faith and credit in every other state. The case cannot be relitigated. The Delaware opinion is mandatory authority in every other state.

5 and 6. *A state court is considering an opinion written by a federal court and vice versa.*

The general rule is that state courts have the final say on what the state law is, and federal courts have the final say on what the federal law is. State courts do *not* have to follow opinions written by federal courts *unless* the issue before the state court involves a federal question—one arising out of the United States Constitution or out of a statute of Congress. Federal courts do not have to follow state court opinions *except to the extent that* the federal court needs to know what the state law is on a given topic, and the state court opinions provide this information. When does a federal court need to know what the state law is on a given topic? Mainly in *diversity of citizenship* cases where the case before the federal court raises a state question rather than a federal question arising under the United States Constitution or statute of Congress. In a proper diversity case,[2] a federal court will apply state law to resolve the controversy. In such cases, state court opinions will be mandatory authority in the federal court.

3. COURT OPINIONS AS PERSUASIVE AUTHORITY

Review the two conditions mentioned earlier on when an opinion is mandatory authority: The opinion must be analogous, or on point, *and* it must have been written by a court that is superior to the court currently considering that opinion. If *both* these tests are not met, either the opinion is nonauthority, or it might be *persuasive authority*.

Assume that the holding in the *X v. Y* opinion is not analogous to the legal issues currently being considered by a court in the *A v. B* litigation. Assume also that *X v. Y* contains some **dictum** that has relevance or some bearing on the issues before the *A v. B* court. By definition, the dictum cannot be part of the *X v. Y* holding, since dictum is a statement by a judge that was not necessary to resolve the narrow legal issues before the court. Dictum, therefore, can never be mandatory authority. The *A v. B* court is not *required* to follow the *X v. Y* dictum. The *A v. B* court, however, has the discretion to adopt or reject the *X v. Y* dictum, since it does relate to the issues before the *A v. B* court. If the court does adopt the dictum, it has become persuasive authority.

Suppose that you are reading an opinion that *is* analogous, or on point, but is not mandatory because of one of the following:

- It was written by an inferior court and is now being considered by a court within the same judicial system that is superior to the court that wrote the opinion; or

---

[2]The amount in controversy must exceed $50,000 and the parties must be citizens of different states. 28 U.S.C.A. § 1332(a) (1993).

● It was written by a court from a judicial system that is different from the judicial system where the court considering that opinion sits. (Assume that there are no conflict-of-interest or full-faith-and-credit issues.)

If either of these two situations exists, the court, as we have seen, does *not* have to follow the opinion; it is not mandatory authority. If, however, the opinion is analogous or on point, the court would be free to adopt it as persuasive authority.

A number of factors go into a court's determination of whether a prior opinion is persuasive enough to adopt. A judge is usually interested in knowing how many other courts have adopted the result of this opinion. Is there a "majority rule" or school of thought that has developed around that result? Has the opinion been frequently cited with approval? How well reasoned is the opinion? These considerations will help a judge decide whether to adopt an opinion as persuasive. Finally, it is human nature for judges to gravitate toward those opinions that are most in tune with their personal philosophies and biases—although preferences on this basis are never acknowledged.

4. SECONDARY AUTHORITY AS PERSUASIVE AUTHORITY

Secondary authority such as a legal treatise or a legal periodical article is not the law itself. It is *not* written by the legislature, a court, an agency, a city council, etc. Secondary authority can never be mandatory authority; it can only be persuasive. The chart in Exhibit 11.7 provides an overview of the major kinds of secondary authority that a court could decide to rely on in reaching its conclusion.

Exhibit 11.7   Categories of Secondary Authority

KIND	CONTENTS	EXAMPLES
1a. Legal Encyclopedias	Summaries of the law, organized by topic	*Corpus Juris Secundum* *American Jurisprudence 2d*
1b. Nonlegal Encyclopedias	Summaries of many topics on science, the arts, history, etc.	*Encyclopedia Britannica*
2a. Legal Dictionaries	Definitions of legal terms taken almost exclusively from court opinions	*Words and Phrases*
2b. Legal Dictionaries	Definitions of legal terms that come from a variety of sources	*Black's Law Dictionary* *Ballentine's Law Dictionary* West's *Legal Thesaurus/Dictionary*
2c. Nonlegal Dictionaries	Definitions of all words in general use	*Webster's Dictionary*
3a. Legal Periodicals (academic)	Pamphlets (often later bound) containing articles on a variety of legal topics	*Harvard Law Review* *Utah Law Review* *Yale Journal of Law and Feminism*

Exhibit 11.7   Categories of Secondary Authority—continued

KIND	CONTENTS	EXAMPLES
3b. Legal Periodicals (commercial)	Pamphlets (later often bound) containing articles on a variety of legal topics	*Case and Comment* *Practical Lawyer*
3c. Legal Periodicals (bar association)	Pamphlets (often later bound) containing articles on a variety of legal topics	*American Bar Association Journal* *California Lawyer* *Colorado Lawyer*
3d. Nonlegal Periodicals	Pamphlets (often later bound) containing articles on a variety of mainly nonlegal topics	*Newsweek* *Foreign Affairs*
4a. Legal Treatises	Summaries of and commentaries on areas of the law	*McCormick on Evidence* Johnstone and Hopson, *Lawyers and Their Work* *Restatement of the Law of Torts*
4b. Nonlegal Treatises	Summaries of and commentaries on a variety of mainly nonlegal topics	Samuelson, *Economics*
5. Formbooks, Manuals, Practice Books	Same as legal treatises with a greater emphasis on the "how-to-do-it" practical dimensions of the law	Dellheim, *Massachusetts Practice* Moore's *Federal Practice* *Am Jur Pleading and Practice Forms Annotated*
6. Loose-Leaf Services	Collections of materials in three-ring binders covering current law in designated areas	*State Tax Guide* (CCH) *Labor Relations Reporter* (BNA)
7a. Legal Newspapers	Daily or weekly information relevant to practice	*Daily Washington Law Reporter* *National Law Journal*
7b. Nonlegal Newspapers	General circulation newspapers	*New York Times* *Detroit Free Press*
8. Legal Newsletters	Weekly, biweekly, or monthly information on a specific area of the law	*Washington Tax Review* *AIDS Policy & Law*

Some secondary authorities quote from the law itself; that is, they quote primary authority. For example, here is a quotation from page 54 of a legal treatise called *Administrative Law and Process,* by Richard J. Pierce, which quotes from § 1(20) of the United States Code (U.S.C.):

> The government had contended that the standards used . . . contained the same type of vague phrases that had been used [in 15 U.S.C. § 1(20)] to authorize . . . the Interstate Commerce Commission (ICC) to allow railroads to operate as the "public convenience and necessity may require." Richard J. Pierce, *Administrative Law and Process,* 54 (1985).

If you want to quote § 1(20) in your memorandum or other writing, do not do it through a quote in a secondary authority such as this legal treatise. Go directly to the current United States Code (U.S.C.) and quote from § 1(20) itself. Do not rely on Pierce's quote from § 1(20). You may *also* want to cite Pierce's observation on and quote from § 1(20), but not as a substitute for a direct quote. As a general rule, *you should never use someone else's quotation of the law.* Quote *directly* from the primary authority. Use the secondary authority to bolster your arguments on the interpretation of the primary authority. This is one of the main functions of secondary authority: to help you persuade a court to adopt a certain interpretation of primary authority. You are on very dangerous ground when you use secondary authority as a substitute for primary authority.

Secondary authority frequently paraphrases or summarizes primary authority (e.g., a legal treatise or encyclopedia summarizes the law on a particular topic). You will be *very* tempted to use such summaries in your own writing. Generally, secondary authority is clearly written and quotable. It provides summaries of the law that often seem to fit very nicely into what you are trying to say. There are serious dangers, however, in relying on quotes containing these summaries. While there are circumstances in which the summaries can be used (with appropriate citation to avoid the charge of **plagiarism**), you need to be aware of the five major dangers of doing so:

- The excerpts are secondary authority, and the goal of your writing is to use primary authority to support your arguments.
- The excerpts may contain summaries of several court opinions; these opinions should be *individually* analyzed before you use any of them in your writing.
- The excerpts may be based on opinions from different states, and your legal writing must focus on the law of the state in which the client is litigating the case.
- The excerpts may contain summaries of opinions written by federal courts, and your case may be in a state court where there are no federal issues.
- The excerpts may contain summaries of opinions on state issues written by state courts, and your case may be in a federal court where there are no state issues.

In short, too much reliance on such excerpts from secondary authority amounts to laziness in legal research and analysis. It is sometimes difficult to find and apply primary authority. If someone else at least appears to have done all the work for you in secondary authority, why not use it? The answers to this question are the five dangers just mentioned.

Even if you never use secondary authority in your writing, it may still be of value to you. For example, the footnotes in a treatise, encyclopedia, or periodical might give you leads to the primary authority that you need to find and analyze. Furthermore, if you are doing research in an area of the law that is new to you, some background reading in a legal treatise, encyclopedia, or periodical often provides an excellent introduction to the area as we will see in Exhibit 11.14 later in the chapter. Armed with some basic definitions and a general understanding, you will be better equipped to launch your research and analysis into the specific issues before you.

Suppose you want to *use* an excerpt from a secondary authority *in your legal writing*. You may, for example, want to quote from a treatise to bolster your argument on the interpretation of a statute or other primary authority. As such, you are asking the court to accept the secondary authority as persuasive authority. What steps are necessary to do so properly? What is the proper *foundation* for the use of secondary authority in legal writing? Exhibit 11.8 presents this foundation.

Many well-written and comprehensively researched legal memoranda and appellate briefs make very few references to secondary authority. Experienced advocates know that judges are suspicious of secondary authority. It is true that some secondary authorities are highly respected, such as *Prosser on Torts* or any of the *Restatements* of the American Law Institute. Yet even these must be used with caution. The preoccupation of a court is on primary authority. Before you use secondary authority in your writing, you must be sure that (a) the secondary authority is not used as a substitute for the primary authority; (b) the secondary authority is not unduly repetitive of the primary authority; (c) the secondary authority will be helpful to the court in adopting an interpretation of primary authority, particularly when there is not a great deal of primary authority on point; (d) you discuss the secondary authority after you have presented the primary authority; and (e) the foundation for the use of secondary authority (see Exhibit 11.8) can be demonstrated if needed.

Suppose you find a quote in a legal treatise that not only does not contradict any law within the jurisdiction where the client is in litigation, but also concisely states the law that does exist. In this instance, the treatise quote is, in effect, an accurate summary of the law. While you are on much safer ground in using such a quote, you should provide some indication in your legal writing that such a parallel exists between the law and the treatise quote. At the very least, you should state in your writing that the quote from the secondary authority is consistent with the law of the jurisdiction and be prepared to back up this statement if it is later challenged or questioned by anyone.

Finally, you may find statements in secondary authority that neither contradict nor summarize the law of your jurisdiction. The issue being discussed in the secondary authority may simply have never arisen in your jurisdiction. Such issues are called issues of **first impression**. Again, you are on relatively safe ground in using such discussions in your legal

---

Exhibit 11.8   **The Foundation for Using a Quote from a Legal Treatise or any Other Secondary Authority in Your Legal Writing as Possible Persuasive Authority**

1. The quote from the legal treatise (or other secondary authority) is not a substitute for a direct quote from the court opinion, statute, or other primary authority. When you need to tell the reader what the primary authority says, you do not do so solely through secondary authority.

2. The quote from the legal treatise (or other secondary authority) that you want to use does not contradict case law, statutory law, or any other primary authority that exists in the jurisdiction where the client is in litigation. Stated more simply, there is no contrary mandatory authority.

3. If the quote from the legal treatise (or other secondary authority) *does* contradict case law, statutory law, or any other primary authority, you cannot use the quote unless you satisfy yourself:
   - that the court (before which the client is in litigation) has the power to change the law that contradicts what the legal treatise (or other secondary authority) says and, in effect, to adopt a new interpretation of the law in the jurisdiction; and
   - that there is a reasonable likelihood that a court with such power is inclined to change the law.

writing. In fact, the use of secondary authority is usually most effective when it treats issues that have not yet been resolved in your jurisdiction. Courts are often quite receptive to adopting secondary authority as persuasive authority when novel questions or issues are involved.

Assignment 11.4

Are the following statements true or false? Explain why you think any of the statements are false.

(a) All primary authority is mandatory authority, since primary authority consists of statutes, constitutional provisions, or other laws.

(b) Secondary authority can be mandatory authority.

(c) An invalid state statute can be persuasive authority if a court decides to follow it even though it does not have to.

(d) A federal administrative regulation can be mandatory authority in a state court.

(e) An opinion of the United States District Court can be mandatory authority for the United States Supreme Court.

(f) Since dictum is a comment by the court that was not necessary to resolve the issues before the court, dictum is nonauthority.

(g) An opinion in one state cannot be mandatory authority in the court of another state.

(h) A federal court can overrule an opinion of a state court.

(i) If your library does not have a copy of the statute you need to cite, you can cite the language of the statute that is printed in a scholarly analysis of the statute in a law review article.

(j) A dissenting opinion can be persuasive authority.

Assignment 11.5

Mary Franklin is pregnant. The father, Bob Vinson, disappears before the baby is born. Mary agrees to let a Missouri couple adopt the baby. Bob was never notified of the adoption. When he finds out, he seeks to have the adoption nullified so that he can have full custody of the child.

Assume that each of the following authorities is relevant to the issue of whether Bob Vinson can invalidate the adoption, and that you want to cite all of them in your memorandum of law. In what order would you cite them if you wanted to cite the most controlling first? Place them in ascending order of importance, starting with the most important.

(a) An administrative regulation of a Missouri agency

(b) A statute of the Missouri legislature

(c) A statute of Congress

(d) A *Harvard Law Review* article on parental consent to adoption

(e) An opinion of the highest state court in Missouri interpreting a statute of the Missouri legislature

(f) A provision of the Missouri Constitution

(g) A legal treatise written by a Missouri judge on adoption

(h) An opinion of the highest state court in New York

(i) An provision of the United States Constitution

Section J
CITATION FORM

A *citation,* or *cite,* is a reference to any written material. The cite gives you the "address" where you can go in the library to find whatever is cited.

Are there any consistent rules on citation form? If you pick up different law books and examine the citations of similar material within them, you will notice great variety in citation form. You will find that people abbreviate things differently, do not include the information in the same order in the cite, use parentheses differently, use punctuation within the cite differently, include different amounts of information in the same kind of cite, etc. There does not appear to be any consistency. Yet, in spite of this diversity and confusion, you are often scolded by supervisors for failing to use "proper citation form." What, you may well ask, is "proper"?

Start by checking the rules of court or statutes governing the court that will have jurisdiction over the problem you are researching. They may or may not contain *official citation rules.* If such rules exist, they must obviously be followed no matter what any other citation guide book may say. These are, in effect, citation *laws.*

Suppose, however, that there are no official citation laws in your state or that such laws do not cover the citation question that you have. In such circumstances, *ask your supervisor what citation form you should use.* You will probably be told, "Use the Bluebook." This is a reference to *The Bluebook: A Uniform System of Citation,* which we looked at earlier (page 515). It is a small blue pamphlet (although in earlier editions, white covers were used). The Bluebook is published by a group of law students on the law reviews of their law schools.

Caution is needed in using the Bluebook. It is a highly technical and sometimes difficult-to-use pamphlet because it packs so much information into a relatively small space. Primary users of the Bluebook are law schools that typeset their law reviews by using professional printers. What about those of us who use regular typewriters or word processors and do not typeset what we produce? While the Bluebook does cover many of our citation needs, keep in mind that we are not the main audience of the Bluebook. Also, be aware that many courts do *not* follow the Bluebook even if there are no court rules on citation form for their courts. Judges often simply use their own "system" of citation without necessarily being consistent.

GENERAL CITATION GUIDELINES

1. Find out if there are citation laws in the rules of court or in statutes.
2. Ask your supervisor if he or she has any special instructions on citation form.
3. Consult the Bluebook.
4. Consult the specific citation guidelines presented below (I–VII). Most of these rules are based on the Bluebook.
5. Remember that the *functional* purpose of a citation is to enable readers to locate your citation in a library. You must give enough information in the cite to fulfill this purpose. Courtesy to the reader in providing this help is as important as compliance with the niceties of citation form.
6. Often a private publisher of a book will tell you how to cite the book. ("Cite this book as. . . .") Ignore this instruction! Instead, follow guidelines 1–5 above.
7. When in doubt about whether to include something in a citation after carefully following guidelines 1–5 above, resolve the doubt by including it in the cite.

SPECIFIC CITATION GUIDELINES

Use the citation formats on the following pages unless General Citation Guidelines 1–2 above tell you otherwise:

    I. Citing Opinions
   II. Citing Constitutions and Charters
  III. Citing Federal Statutes
  IV. Citing State Statutes
   V. Citing Administrative Regulations
  VI. Citing Documents of Legislative History
 VII. Citing Secondary Authority

I. Citing Opinions

First let's look at the components of a typical citation of an opinion. See Exhibit 11.9. Not all opinions are cited in the same way, however. The citation format that you use

Exhibit 11.9 Components of a Typical Citation of an Opinion

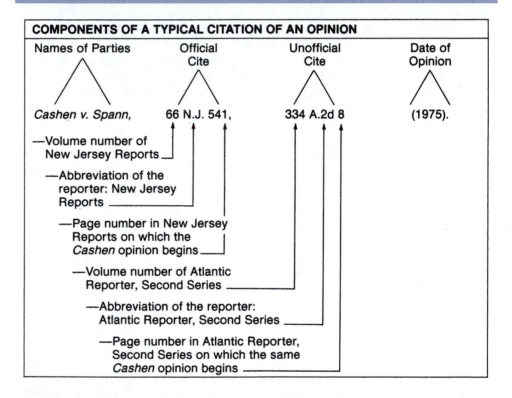

depends on the kind of court that wrote the opinion. Before examining the guidelines that explain these differences, here is an overview:

Example A: Format of a Citation to an Opinion of the Highest Federal Court (the United States Supreme Court):

> *Taglianetti v. United States*, 394 U.S. 316 (1969).

Example B: Format of a Citation to an Opinion of a Federal Middle Appeals Court (the United States Court of Appeals for the Second Circuit):

> *Sterling Nat'l Bank & Trust Co. of N.Y. v. Fidelity Mortgage Investors,* 510 F.2d 870 (2d Cir. 1975).

Example C: Format of a Citation to an Opinion of a Federal Trial Court (the United States District Court, Western District in Wisconsin):

> *Stone v. Schmidt,* 398 F. Supp. 768 (W.D. Wis. 1975).

Example D: Format of a Citation to an Opinion of the Highest State Court (New Jersey Supreme Court):

> *Petlin Associates, Inc. v. Township of Dover,* 64 N.J. 327, 316 A.2d 1 (1974).

Example E: Format of a Citation to an Opinion of a Lower State Court (Connecticut Superior Court, Appellate Session):

> *Huckabee v. Stevens,* 32 Conn. Supp. 511, 338 A.2d 512 (Super. Ct. 1975).

Example F: Format of a Citation to an Administrative Decision (National Labor Relations Board):

> *Standard Dry Wall Products, Inc.,* 91 N.L.R.B. 544 (1950).

Example G: Format of a Citation to an Opinion of the Attorney General:

> 40 Op. Att'y Gen. 423 (1945).

Example H: Format of a Public Domain Citation

> *Jenkins v. Patterson,* 1997 Wis. Ct. App. 45, ¶ 157, 612 N.W.2d 1043.

Guidelines for Citing Opinions:

1. The names of the parties in a case should be *italicized* (if your printer has this capacity) or <u>underlined</u> (i.e., underscored). If you are able to use italics, an example would be as follows:

   Steck v. Farrell, 479 F.2d 1129 (7th Cir. 1990).

   If you cannot italicize the names of the parties, underline (underscroe) them:

   <u>Steck v. Farrell</u>, 479 F.2d 1129 (7th Cir. 1990).

2. You will note that some of the citations in the above boxed examples have *parallel cites* (see Examples D and E) and some do not. Before examining the rules of providing parallel cites and the techniques of finding such cites, some basics need to be covered.
3. The same opinion can be printed in more than one reporter. A parallel cite is a reference to an *additional* reporter where the same opinion (word-for-word) can be found. In Example D, the *Petlin* opinion can be found in New Jersey Reports (abbreviated "N.J.") and in Atlantic Reporter 2d ("A.2d").

4. Do not confuse (a) the parallel cite with (b) the *same case on appeal*. Examine the following three citations:

- *Smith v. Jones,* 24 Mass. 101, 19 N.E.2d 370 (1920).
- *Jones v. Smith,* 26 Mass. 228, 21 N.E.2d 1017 (1922).
- *Smith v. Jones,* 125 F.2d 177 (1st Cir. 1925).

Assume that these three opinions involve the same litigation—the same parties and the same issues. The case went up on appeal three times: twice to the Massachusetts Supreme Judicial Court and once to the United States Court of Appeals for the Second Circuit. The first two opinions have parallel cites. For example, the first opinion is printed in both Massachusetts Reports (24 Mass. 101) and in North Eastern Reporter, 2d (19 N.E.2d 370). The third opinion has no parallel cite. *Smith v. Jones, Jones v. Smith,* and *Smith v. Jones* are citations to the "same case on appeal." They are *not* parallel cites to each other. While the same litigation is involved, the citations are to three distinct opinions, two of which have parallel cites.

5. There are six main techniques of finding a parallel cite:

- Shepardize the case in the standard sets of *Shepard's Citations,* such as *Shepard's United States Citations* (see photo on page 539). The first cite in parentheses is the parallel cite. If you find no cite in parentheses, it means (a) that no parallel cite exists, (b) that the reporter containing the parallel cite has not been printed yet, or (c) that the parallel cite was given in one of the earlier volumes of Shepard's and was not repeated in the volume you are examining.

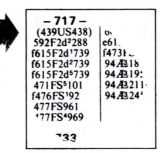

Using *Shepard's Citations* to find a parallel cite. The parallel cite to the case that begins on page **-717-** is (439 US 438).

- Use the *Shepard's Case Names Citator.* Shepard's also has a separate set of citators called Case Name Citators. Their sole function is to give you parallel cites. Court opinions are listed alphabetically by party names along with the parallel cites.

Wil-Win	ILLINOIS CASE NAMES CITATOR	
Wilson v. Parker 132 Ill App 2d 5, 269 NE2d 523 (1971)	**Wilson v. Reeves Red-E-Mix Concrete Products** 29 Ill App 3d 448. 330 NE2d 521 (1975)	
Wilson v. Peters 343 Ill App 354, 99 NE2d 150 (1951)	**Wilson & Tavridges Inc. v. Industrial Commission** 32 Ill 2d 355, 204 NE2d 446 (1965)	
Wilson, Ranson v. 335 Ill App 7, 80 NE2d 381 (1948)	**Wilson Enterprises Inc., Thakkar v.** 120 Ill App 3d 878, 76 Ill Dec 331, 458 NE2d 985 (1983)	

Using *Shepard's Case Names Citator* to find a parallel cite. The parallel cites of *Wilson v Peters* are 343 Ill App 354 and 99 NE2d 150.

- Go to the *National Reporter Blue Book,* a set of books published by West. (See photo on page 515.) The *National Reporter Blue Book* will also tell you which official reporters have been discontinued. If your state has a *Blue and White Book,* you can also use it to try to find a parallel cite.

● Check the top of the caption. Go to the reporter that contains the opinion. At the beginning of the opinion, there is a **caption** giving the names of the parties, the court, etc. See if there is a parallel cite at the top of this caption. (This technique does not always work, but it is worth a try.)

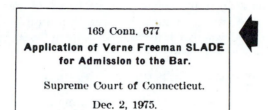

169 Conn. 677

**Application of Verne Freeman SLADE
for Admission to the Bar.**

Supreme Court of Connecticut.

Dec. 2, 1975.

Finding a parallel cite by checking the top of the caption

● Check the Table of Cases in a digest. Go to every digest that gives small-paragraph summaries of court opinions for the court that wrote the opinion, e.g., the American Digest System. Go to the Table of Cases in these digests. See if there is a parallel cite for your case. In the following excerpt from a digest table of cases, you find two cites for *Ames v. State Bar*—106 Cal. Rptr. 489 and 506 P.2d 625:

```
        ..an Tre..
     corp, TexCiv.
     App  &  E  79
     Costs 260(4);  S  es 181(11).           Te
 Ames v. State Bar 106 CalRptr 489,          E
     506 P2d 625—Atty & C 32, 58, 125;   anc
     Const Law 230(2), 287.              Archer
 Amherst, Town of, v. Cadorette, N.H.        Const
     300 A2d 327.   See Town of Am-          ry 39.
     herst v. Cadorette.                  Archuleta
 Ammerman v. Bestline Products, Inc,         F2d 33—
     DCWis, 352 FSupp 1077—Courts 263        392.
     (6);  nd Civ Proc           15.      Argonaut
 Amr-                                         SE2d
```

Finding a parallel cite by checking the Table of Cases in digests

● Use WESTLAW and LEXIS. When you call up your case on either of the two main online research computer systems, WESTLAW and LEXIS, you are always given existing parallel cites.

6. When do you provide a parallel cite? To answer this question, we will focus first on state court cases. Assume that you are writing something in the law library. If you want to cite a case, should you provide the official cite of the case in a state reporter along with its unofficial cite in the regional reporter? (An unofficial cite is a cite to an *unofficial reporter*. For a definition of the latter, see page 516.) When do you need to give a paralle cite of a state court case? Unfortunately, this simple question does not have a simple answer. According to the Bluebook, the answer depends on three factors: (a) whether a parallel cite exists, (b) the kind of writing you are preparing, and (c) who publishes the unofficial reporter that is the basis for the unofficial cite.

(a) *The existence of a parallel cite.*

Of course, you cannot give a parallel cite if one does not exist. Several reasons may account for the absence of a parallel cite. First, it may not exist because the *official reporter* has been discontinued.[3] Second, the official reporter may not have been

---

[3]You can find out if an official reporter has been discontinued by consulting the *National Reporter Blue Book* or the *Blue and White Book*. See page 515.

published yet. (Official reporters are sometimes printed as much as a year after the printing of the unofficial reporter.) If the official reporter has been discontinued or has not been printed yet, all you have is the unofficial cite in a regional reporter. If so, here are the guidelines to follow:

Suppose, for example, that you want to cite the case of *Nace v. Nace* decided by the Supreme Court of Arizona. Assume that because the case is so recent, the official cite is not available. All you have is the unofficial cite in the Pacific Reporter, 2d (P.2d). Here is how you would cite this case:

Nace v. Nace, 790 P.2d 48 (Ariz. 1998).

Note the abbreviation *Ariz.* just before the date in the parentheses. This is an abbreviation of the court that wrote the case. When the abbreviation is the abbreviation of the state itself, you know that the case was written by the highest state court in the state. If you did not provide this abbreviation, someone looking at the cite would not know what court wrote it. The general rule is to provide an abbreviation of the court that wrote the case if its identity is not clear by looking at the abbreviation of any of the reporters in the cite. The reporter in this cite is Pacific Reporter 2d (P.2d). Looking at the cite of this reporter certainly does not tell you what court wrote *Nace.* (Many states are covered in P.2d. See Exhibit 11.4.) Hence, you must abbreviate the court in the parentheses before the date.

Suppose, however, that the official cite of the *Nace* case *was* available and you wanted to provide it. Here is how you would cite the case:

Nace v. Nace, 162 Ariz. 411, 790 P.2d 48 (1998).

Note that there is no need to include the abbreviation of the court that wrote the case in the parentheses before the date. When the abbreviation of a reporter is the abbreviation of a state, you can assume that the case was written by the highest state court in that state. Hence, there is no need to abbreviate the court in the parentheses with the date. You can tell by looking at the abbreviation of the official reporter (162 Ariz. 411) that the highest state court in Arizona wrote the case since *Ariz.* is the abbreviation of the state.

(b) *The kind of writing you are preparing.*

What are you preparing? A memo? An appellate brief? Who is the audience? Your supervisor? A court? Answers to such questions will provide us with the next important guideline on when to provide a parallel cite.

In a document to be submitted to a state court (such as an appellate brief), all citations to cases decided by courts of that state must include a citation to the official state reporter (if available) in addition to the unofficial regional reporter. Only these cases require a parallel cite. Consequently, the following case citations *never* require a parallel cite:

- Citations to cases written by a state court that you want to use in a document that will be submitted to a court in a different state
- Citations to cases written by a state court that you want to use in a document that will not be submitted to any court

In these two instances, the cite to the unofficial regional reporter is sufficient.

Assume that during your research, you come across the *Lausier* case whose full cite is as follows:

Lausier v. Pescinski, 67 Wis. 2d 4, 226 N.W.2d 180 (1975)

This case was written by the highest state court in Wisconsin. You can tell this because *Wis.* is the abbreviation of the state. Under the above guidelines, if you are preparing an appellate brief to be submitted to a state court in New York or in Hawaii, here is how you cite *Lausier* in your brief:

Lausier v. Pescinski, 226 N.W.2d 180 (Wis. 1975)

If, however, you are preparing an appellate brief to be submitted to a state court in Wisconsin, here is how you cite it in your brief:

Lausier v. Pescinski, 67 Wis. 2d 4, 226 N.W.2d 180 (1975)

If the document you are preparing is not going to be submitted to any court, here is how you would cite this case in your document:

Lausier v. Pescinski, 226 N.W.2d 180 (Wis. 1975)

Again, the only time you provide a parallel cite is when the document you are preparing is to be submitted to a state court, and the case you are citing was decided by a state court in the same state.

(c)   *Where the unofficial cite is published.*

Our examples thus far have assumed that the unofficial cite was one of the seven regional reporters (Atlantic, North Eastern, North Western, Pacific, South Eastern, Southern, and South Western. See Exhibit 11.4). Suppose, however, that the case is published in a different unofficial source, e.g., a loose-leaf service, a reporter of Lawyers Co-op such as A.L.R.5th, or a database in WESTLAW or LEXIS. Do you ever cite one of these unofficial sources? No—unless the cite to the regional reporter does not exist. The only unofficial cite to use is the regional reporter except when it is unavailable.

It must be pointed out that everyone does *not* agree with the above Bluebook guidelines on when to provide a parallel cite to a state court opinion. The better rule is as follows: If parallel cites to an official state reporter and to an unofficial regional reporter exist, *always* provide both as a courtesy to the reader. If the cite to the regional reporter does not exist, cite other unofficial sources such as a loose-leaf service. If, however, your supervisor insists that you follow the Bluebook, use the above guidelines.

🏛 *A s s i g n m e n t   1 1 . 6*

Here are two citations to the same case:

(a) *Velletri v. Lussier,* 88 R.I. 352, 148 A.2d 360 (1959)
(b) *Velletri v. Lussier,* 148 A.2d 360 (R.I. 1959)

Assume that you wanted to cite the *Velletri* case in the following documents. According to the Bluebook, which citation would you use and why?

(1) A memorandum submitted to a Rhode Island Superior Court in support of a motion to dismiss.
(2) A law review article.
(3) An appellate brief to be submitted to the United States Supreme Court.
(4) An interoffice memorandum prepared by a paralegal for the paralegal's supervisor who is preparing an appellate brief that will be submitted to the Rhode Island Supreme Court.

7. Loose-leaf services often provide the most current legal material available. Some services send out opinions within a week of their issuance by the court. As indicated above, however, do *not* include the citation to the loose-leaf service *unless* the citation to the regional reporter is not available at the time.

8. Court opinions are found in traditional library volumes (reporters) and on *computerized legal research services.* Some opinions, however, are found only *online* in these services. An example is *Bucknum v. Bucknum,* which was decided on February 19, 1991, by the Minnesota Court of Appeals. Its docket number is No. C6-90-1798. This opinion is found on WESTLAW and on LEXIS but not in a traditional library reporter volume. Here is how the case is cited in WESTLAW and LEXIS, respectively:

Bucknum v. Bucknum, 1991 WL 17881 (Minn. App.).
Bucknum v. Bucknum, 1991 Minn. App. LEXIS 145.

The number 17881 is an internal WESTLAW number, and 145 is an internal LEXIS number.

The Bluebook does *not* follow these citation formats. The Bluebook has its own format for citing cases found in WESTLAW and LEXIS:

Bucknum v. Bucknum, No. C6–90–1798, 1991 WL 17881 (Minn. App. Feb. 19, 1991).
Bucknum v. Bucknum, No. C6–90–1798, 1991 Minn. App. LEXIS 145 (Feb. 19, 1991).

Note that in these Bluebook cites, the docket number and the WESTLAW/LEXIS cite are given, along with the full date of the decision in parentheses at the end.

When do you cite a case in WESTLAW or LEXIS? Only when the case is not available in traditional library volumes such as reporters.

9. There is some disagreement as to whether parallel cites are needed for opinions of the U.S. Supreme Court. The Bluebook says you should never provide a parallel cite for such opinions if you have the official cite ("U.S."), even if the parallel cites in "S. Ct." and "L. Ed." are also available. (See Example A.) The better view, however, is to give all three cites when they are available.

10. When parallel cites are to be cited, always place the official cite first before the unofficial cite. (See Examples D and E.)

11. There is never a parallel cite for Federal Reporter 2d cases (F.2d) (see Example B) or for Federal Reporter 3d cases (F.3d). Abbreviate the circuit in parentheses at the end of the cite before the year. 2d Cir. means the opinion was decided by the U.S. Court of Appeals for the Second Circuit. D.C. Cir. would mean the case was decided by the U.S. Court of Appeals for the District of Columbia Circuit. (For a map of all the circuits, see Exhibit 6.4 in chapter 6.) The caption of the opinion will tell you which circuit court wrote the opinion.

12. There is never a parallel cite for Federal Supplement cases (F. Supp.). (See Example C.) Abbreviate the U.S. District Court in parentheses at the end of the cite before the year. W.D. Wis. means the opinion was written by the United States District Court, Western District, sitting in Wisconsin. The caption of the opinion will tell you which U.S. District Court wrote the opinion.

13. In Example D, the parentheses at the end of the cite to the *Petlin* case contain the date of the decision, but nothing more. As stated earlier, there is no need to indicate the name of the court in the parentheses if the identity of the court is otherwise clear from the abbreviation of a reporter in the cite. In Example D, the *Petlin* case was written by the highest court (the Supreme Court) in the state of New Jersey. You know this by examining the abbreviation of the official reporter in the cite (64 N.J. 327). When the abbreviation of the reporter (here, N.J.) is the abbreviation of the state, you can assume that the case was written by the highest court in that state.

Suppose, however, that you did not have this official reporter cite. If all you had was the unofficial Atlantic 2d cite (316 A.2d 1), you would cite the case as follows:

Petlin Associates, Inc. v. Township of Dover, 316 A.2d 1 (N.J. 1974).

By looking at the abbreviation of the reporter (A.2d), you cannot tell which court wrote this case. Therefore, you must abbreviate the name of the court in the parentheses before the date. Using the abbreviation of the state alone (N.J.) tells you that it was the highest state court in the state.

14. In Example E, "Super. Ct." appears before the date in the parentheses. This is the abbreviation of the Connecticut Superior Court, which wrote the case. This abbreviation is necessary because you cannot tell which court wrote it by examining the abbreviation of any of the reporters in the cite. Neither "Conn. Supp." nor "A.2d" tells you. Note also that it is not necessary to tell the reader in the parentheses that this court is in Connecticut because it is clear from the abbreviation of the reporter (32 Conn. Supp. 511) that it is a Connecticut case.

15. Include only the last name of parties who are people. For example, if the parties are listed as "Frank Taylor v. Mary Smith" in the caption, your cite should list them as *Taylor v. Smith.*

16. If a party is a business, use the full name of the business, but abbreviate words such as Corporation (Corp.), Incorporated (Inc.), Company (Co.), Limited (Ltd.), and Brothers (Bros.). If, for example, a party is listed in the caption as "John J. Dover, Incorporated," your cite would read *John J. Dover, Inc.* (If, however, John J. Dover was a party suing or being sued as a human person rather than as a business, your cite would simply list this party as *Dover.*)

17. When the United States is a party, do not use the abbreviation "U.S." Spell it out. See Example A.

18. Assume that Maine is a party. Your cite should say "State" (rather than "State of Maine" or "Maine") *if and only if* the opinion was written by a Maine state court. Suppose, however, that Maine is a party in a case written by an Ohio court. In such a case, use "Maine" (not "State of Maine" or "State") in your cite as the name of this party. This same guideline applies for the words "Commonwealth" and "People." These words are used alone in a cite only if the court that wrote the opinion you are citing is in the same state referred to by the words "Commonwealth" and "People." Example: You are citing an opinion of the California Supreme Court, whose caption describes the parties as follows:

People of California v. Gabriel S. Farrell

Your cite of this opinion would be *People v. Farrell.*

19. When an opinion consolidates more than one litigation, it is referred to as a *consolidated litigation.* A supreme court, for example, may use one opinion to resolve similar issues raised in several different lower court cases. The caption of such an opinion will probably list all the parties from these different lower court cases. For example, the caption might say: *A v. B; C v. D; E v. F.* When you cite this opinion, include only the *first* set of parties listed in the caption—here, *A v. B.* If the caption says **et al.** (and others) after the name of a party, do not include the phrase *et al.* in your cite.

20. Often the court will tell you the **litigation status** of the parties, such as plaintiff, defendant, appellant, or appellee. Do not include this information in your cite.

21. Titles of individual parties (such as administrator or secretary) should be omitted from your cite. One exception is the Commissioner of Internal Revenue. Cite this party simply as "Commissioner"—for example, *Jackson v. Commissioner.*

22. Include the phrase **in re** (meaning "in the matter of") in your cite—for example, *In re Jones.*

23. Include the year of the decision at the end of the cite in parentheses. If more than one date is given in the caption of the opinion, use the year from the date the opinion was decided.

24. Do not include the **docket number** of the case in the cite unless the case is not printed in a traditional reporter (see guideline 8), or unless the case is still pending. (The docket number is the number assigned to a case by the court.)

25. Once an opinion is written, the disappointed party often appeals. Your citation should alert the reader about important events on appeal. Here is an example:

Herbert v. Lando, 568 F.2d 974 (2d Cir. 1977), *rev'd* 444 U.S. 111 (1979).

It would obviously be important to let the reader know that the *Herbert* case was reversed *(rev'd)* on appeal. In addition, you would want to include whether the case was affirmed *(aff'd)* on appeal, and whether an appellate court accepted certiorari *(cert. granted),* or denied certiorari *(cert. denied).* (Certiorari refers to the **writ of certiorari.** This is an order by an appellate court requiring a lower court to certify the record of a lower court proceeding and to send the record "up" to the appellate court, which has decided to accept the appeal.) For older cases, a reader would usually not be interested in knowing whether an appellate court accepted or denied certiorari. Hence this information is included in your cite only if the case you are citing is less than two years old. If, however, you feel it is important for the reader to have this kind of information on the subsequent history of older cases, include it in the citation.

26. The reporter volumes that contain current opinions are conveniently arranged by volume number. All the volumes of the same set have the same name, e.g., Atlantic Reporter 2d. At one time, however, life was not this simple. Volumes of opinions were identified by the name of the individual person who had responsibility for compiling the opinions written by the judges. These individuals were called reporters. "7 Cush. 430," for example, refers to an opinion found on page 430 of volume 7 of Massachusetts cases when Mr. Cushing was the official reporter. When he ended his employment, Mr. Gray took over, and the cite of an opinion in the volume immediately after "7 Cush." was "1 Gray." By simply looking at the cover of the volume, you *cannot* tell what court's opinions are inside unless you happen to be familiar with the names of these individuals and the courts for which they worked. These volumes are called **nominative reporters** because they are identified by the name of the individual person who compiled the opinions for the court.

27. Assume that all you know are the names of the parties and the name of the court that wrote the opinion. How do you obtain the full cite so that you can find and read the opinion?

    ● Go to every digest that covers that reporter. See Exhibit 11.5. Check the table of cases in the digests.

    ● Call the court clerk for the court that wrote the opinion. If it is a recent case, the clerk may be able to send you a copy. Occasionally, the clerk will give you the cite of the case. (It will help if you can tell the clerk the docket number of the case.)

    ● Go to the reporter volumes that cover the court that wrote the opinion. Since you do not have a volume number, you cannot go directly to the volume that has the opinion. If you can *approximate* the date of the case, however, you can check the table of cases in each reporter volume that probably covers that year. You may have to check the table of cases in ten to fifteen volumes before achieving success. The opinions are printed in the reporters in roughly chronological order.

- If you have access to WESTLAW or LEXIS, simply enter the name of the case in the appropriate database. In WESTLAW, for example, if you are looking for the full cite of the *Miranda* case, you would type "Miranda" as a title (ti) search in the Supreme Court database (sct). This would give you the U.S. cite, the S. Ct. cite, and the L. Ed. 2d cite of *Miranda* (plus the full cite of every other case before the Supreme Court in which "Miranda" was one of the parties).

28. If you are quoting from specific language in an opinion, your citation must include both the number of the page on which the opinion begins *and* the number of the page on which the quoted language begins. (The same is true when you are quoting from legal periodical literature.) This makes the citation a **pinpoint cite** (also called a *jump cite*). A pinpoint cite is a reference to a specific page number in an opinion in addition to the page number where the opinion begins. (In some documents the pinpoint cite is to a specific paragraph number in the document.) The "pinpointed" number goes immediately after the page number on which the opinion begins, separated by a comma. Assume that you want to quote from an opinion that has a parallel cite. Hence your quote will be found in the opinion printed in both reporters, but on different page numbers. A pinpoint cite of this opinion would state the page number in each reporter where the opinion begins *plus* the page number in each reporter on which your quote is found. In the following example, the *Bridgeton* case begins on page 17 of Maryland Reports ("Md.") and on page 376 of the Atlantic Reporter 2d ("A.2d"). The quote from the *Bridgeton* case, however, is found on page 20 and on page 379 of these reporters:

Example

"Even though laches may not apply, one must use reasonable promptness when availing himself of judicial protection." *Bridgeton Educ. Ass'n v. Bd. of Educ.*, 147 Md. 17, 20, 334 A.2d 376, 379 (1975).

29. Example H at the beginning of this section (see page 559) is an example of a *public domain citation*. This will be discussed after Assignment 11.8 when we have concluded our coverage of the traditional citation formats (see page 576).

II. Citing Constitutions and Charters

Constitutions and charters are cited to (a) the abbreviated name of the constitution or charter, (b) the article, and (c) the section.

Example

U.S. Const. art. I, § 9.
N.M. Const. art. IV, § 7.

In citing constitutions and charters currently in force, the date of enactment should *not* be given.

III. Citing Federal Statutes

1. All federal statutes of Congress are collected in chronological order of passage as session laws in the *United States Statutes at Large* (abbreviated "Stat."). If the statute is of general public interest, it is also printed in *each* of three codes:

- United States Code (U.S.C.)
- United States Code Annotated (U.S.C.A.)—West Publishing Co.
- United States Code Service (U.S.C.S.)—Lawyers Co-op.

The preferred citation format is to U.S.C., which is the *official code.*

Example

42 U.S.C. § 3412(a)(1970).
or
Narcotic Rehabilitation Act of 1966, 42 U.S.C. § 3412(a)(1970).

While it is not necessary to give the **popular name** of the statute (as in the second version of the above example), citing the popular name when known is often helpful.

2. A new edition of the U.S.C. comes out every six years. The date you use in citing a statute in U.S.C. is the date of the edition you are using unless your statute is found in one of the annual Supplements to the U.S.C., which come out in between editions. If your statute is in a Supplement, you cite the volume and year of this Supplement. Suppose your statute is found in the sixth Supplement published in 1983. Your cite would be as follows:

29 U.S.C. § 169 (Supp. VI 1983).

The date you use in citing a statute in U.S.C. is not the year the statute was enacted or passed by the legislature. Nor is it the year the statute became effective. The date you use is the date of the edition of the code or of the Supplement year.

3. Although citation to U.S.C. is preferred, it is not uncommon to find citations to the other codes: U.S.C.A. and U.S.C.S. (There is never a need, however, to cite more than one of the three codes.) The format is as follows:

29 U.S.C.A. § 169 (West 1983).
29 U.S.C.S. § 169 (Law. Co-op. 1982).

In parentheses before the date, include the name of the publisher. Use the year that appears on the title page of the volume, or its latest copyright year, in this order of preference. If your statute is in one of the annual pocket parts of either of these two codes, include "Supp." and give the year of the pocket part—for example: (West Supp. 1998).

4. There is one instance in which you *must* cite to the *United States Statutes at Large* (Stat.) rather than to U.S.C. The rule is as follows: Cite to the statute in Statutes at Large if (a) there is a difference in the language of the statute between Stat. and U.S.C. and (b) the statute in U.S.C. is in a title that has *not* been enacted into positive law by Congress.

It is highly unlikely that you will find a difference in language between Stat. and U.S.C. Yet the conscientious researcher must check this out before relying on any statutory language.

All the statutes in U.S.C. fall within one of fifty titles—for example, title 11 on Bankruptcy, title 39 on the Postal Service. If Congress goes through all the statutes in a particular title and formally declares that all of them are valid and accurate, then that title has been enacted into positive law. You can rely exclusively on the language of such statutes even if the language is different from the statute as it originally appeared in Statutes at Large. At the beginning of the first volume of U.S.C., you will be told which titles of the U.S.C. have been enacted into positive law.

5. A Statute at Large cite, when needed, should include (a) the name of the statute if one exists; if one does not exist, include "Act of" and give the full date of enactment—month, day, and year, (b) the Public Law number of the statute or its chapter number, (c) the section of the statute you are citing, (d) the volume number of the Statutes at Large used, (e) the abbreviation "Stat.", (f) the page number on which your statute is

found in the Stat. volume, (g) in parentheses, the year the statute was enacted or passed by the legislature. Do not include the year, however, if you used the "Act of" option referred to in (a).

Example

Narcotic Addict Rehabilitation Act, Pub. L. No. 80–793, § 9, 80 Stat. 1444 (1966).

Note again that the year in parentheses at the end of the cite is the year the statute was passed. Guideline 2 above said that you do not use the date of enactment when citing a statute in U.S.C. The rule is different when giving a Stat. cite.

This example referred you to section number 9 of this Public Law (Pub. L.). The statute might also have several title numbers. If so, § 9 would be found within one of these titles. Assume, for example, that § 9 is in title III of the Public Law. It is important to remember that these section and title numbers are found in the original *session law* edition of the statute. When this statute is later printed in U.S.C. (assuming it is a public law of general interest), it will *not* go into § 9 of the third title. The U.S.C. has its own title and section number scheme. (For example, title III, § 9 of the above statute might be found in title 45, § 1075(b) of the U.S.C.) This can be very frustrating for the researcher new to the law. If you are reading a statute in its original session or Public Law form, you will not be able to find this statute under the same title and section number in U.S.C. You must *translate* the Public Law or Stat. cite into a U.S.C. cite. Phrased another way, you must translate the session law cite into a code cite. Later, we will see that this is done by using one of two tables: Table III in a special Tables volume of U.S.C./U.S.C.A./U.S.C.S., or Table 2 in U.S. Code Congressional and Administrative News (U.S.C.C.A.N.).

6. Of course, if the statute is a private law that is deemed to be of no general public interest, it will not be printed in the U.S.C. or the U.S.C.A. or the U.S.C.S. It will be found only in Statutes at Large.

7. The Internal Revenue Code (I.R.C.) is within the U.S.C. Hence, you use guideline 1 above in citing a tax statute.

Example

26 U.S.C. § 1278 (1976).

There is, however, *another* option that is considered acceptable:

Example

I.R.C. § 1278 (1976).

8. There is a special format for citing Federal Rules of Civil Procedure, Federal Rules of Criminal Procedure, Federal Rules of Appellate Procedure, and the Federal Rules of Evidence.

Examples

Fed. R. Civ. P. 15
Fed. R. Crim. P. 23
Fed. R. App. P. 3
Fed. R. Evid. 310

IV. Citing State Statutes

1. Like federal statutes, the statutes of the various states are compiled in two kinds of collections: state *codes* (arranged by subject matter) and *session laws* (arranged in chronological order of enactment).

2. Citations to state codes vary from state to state. In Exhibit 11.10, there are examples of standard Bluebook citation formats. Use these as guides unless local rules of court dictate otherwise. The year at the end of the cite should be the year that appears on the spine of the volume, or the year that appears on the title page, or the latest copyright year—in this order of preference.

E x h i b i t   1 1 . 1 0   State Statutory Code Citations

Examples of State Statutory Code Citations that Comply with the Bluebook

Alabama:	Ala. Code § 37–10–3 (1977).
Alaska:	Alaska Stat. § 22.10.110 (1962).
Arizona:	Ariz. Rev. Stat. Ann. § 44–1621 (1956).
Arkansas:	Ark. Code Ann. § 20–316 (Michie 1968).
California:	Cal. Prob. Code § 585 (West 1956). Cal. Prob. Code § 585 (Deering 1956).
Colorado:	Colo. Rev. Stat. Ann. § 32–7–131 (West 1971). Colo. Rev. Stat. § 32-7-131 (1971).
Connecticut:	Conn. Gen. Stat. § 34–29 (1989). Conn. Gen. Stat. Ann. § 53a–135 (West 1972).
Delaware:	Del. Code Ann. tit. 18, § 2926 (1974).
District of Columbia:	D.C. Code Ann. § 16–2307 (1981).
Florida:	Fla. Stat. ch. 2.314 (1986). Fla. Stat. Ann. ch. 6.341 (Harrison 1985).
Georgia:	Ga. Code Ann. § 110–118 (Michie 1973). Ga. Code Ann. § 22–1414 (Harrison 1977).
Hawaii:	Haw. Rev. Stat. § 431:19–107 (1988).
Idaho:	Idaho Code § 18–3615 (1987).
Illinois:	Ill. Rev. Stat. ch. 85, para. 8–103 (1985). Ill. Ann. Stat. ch. 40, para. 501 (Smith-Hurd 1980).
Indiana:	Ind. Code § 9–8–1–13 (1976). Ind. Code Ann. § 9–8–1–13 (Burns 1983). Ind. Code Ann. § 9–8–1–13 (West 1979).
Iowa:	Iowa Code § 455.92 (1958). Iowa Code Ann. § 98.14 (West 1984).
Kansas:	Kan. Stat. Ann. § 38–1506 (1986). Kan. Corp. Code Ann. § 17–6303 (Vernon 1975).
Kentucky:	Ky. Rev. Stat. Ann. § 208.060 (Baldwin 1988). Ky. Rev. Stat. Ann. § 44.072 (Michie/Bobbs-Merrill 1986).
Louisiana:	La. Rev. Stat. Ann. § 15:452 (West 1981). La. Code Civ. Proc. Ann. art. 3132 (West 1961).
Maine:	Me. Rev. Stat. Ann. tit. 36, § 1760 (West 1964).
Maryland:	Md. Fam. Law Code Ann. § 7–106 (1984). Md. Ann. Code art. 78, § 70 (1957).
Massachusetts:	Mass. Gen. L. ch. 106, § 2–318 (1984).

Exhibit 11.10   State Statutory Code Citations—continued

Examples of State Statutory Code Citations that Comply with the Bluebook

Massachusetts: —continued	Mass. Gen. Laws Ann. ch. 156, § 37 (West 1970). Mass. Ann. Laws ch. 123, § 15 (Law. Co-op. 1988).
Michigan:	Mich. Comp. Laws § 550.1402 (1980). Mich. Comp. Laws Ann. § 211.27 (West 1986). Mich. Stat. Ann. § 28.1070 (Callaghan 1987).
Minnesota:	Minn. Stat. § 336.1–101 (1988). Minn. Stat. Ann. § 104.08 (West 1987).
Mississippi:	Miss. Code Ann. § 19–13–57 (1972).
Missouri:	Mo. Rev. Stat. § 545.010 (1986). Mo. Ann. Stat. § 334.540 (Vernon 1989).
Montana:	Mont. Code Ann. § 37–5–313 (1989).
Nebraska:	Neb. Rev. Stat. § 44–406 (1983).
Nevada:	Nev. Rev. Stat. § 463.150 (1987). Nev. Rev. Stat. Ann. § 679B.180 (Michie 1986).
New Hampshire:	N.H. Rev. Stat. Ann. § 318:25 (1984).
New Jersey:	N.J. Rev. Stat. § 40:62–127 (1961). N.J. Stat. Ann. § 14A:5–20 (West 1969).
New Mexico:	N.M. Stat. Ann. § 31–6–2 (Michie 1978).
New York:	N.Y. Penal Law § 155.05 (McKinney 1988). N.Y. Town Law § 265 (Consol. 1978).
North Carolina:	N.C. Gen. Stat. § 15A–1321 (1988).
North Dakota:	N.D. Cent. Code § 23–12–11 (1989).
Ohio:	Ohio Rev. Code Ann. § 2935.03 (Anderson 1987). Ohio Rev. Code Ann. § 2305.131 (Baldwin 1975).
Oklahoma:	Okla. Stat. tit. 42, § 130 (1979). Okla Stat. Ann. tit. 21, § 491 (West 1983).
Oregon:	Or. Rev. Stat. § 450.870 (1987).
Pennsylvania:	1 Pa. Cons. Stat. § 1991 (1972). 18 Pa. Cons. Stat. Ann. § 3301 (1983). Pa. Stat. Ann. tit. 24, § 7–708 (1949).
Puerto Rico:	P.R. Laws Ann. tit. 7, § 299 (1985).
Rhode Island:	R.I. Gen. Laws § 34–1–2 (1956).
South Carolina:	S.C. Code Ann. § 16–23–10 (Law. Co-op. 1976).
South Dakota:	S.D. Codified Laws Ann. § 15–6–54(c) (1984).
Tennessee:	Tenn. Code Ann. § 33–1–204 (1984).
Texas:	Tex. Penal Code Ann. § 19.06 (West 1989). Tex. Rev. Civ. Stat. Ann. art. 5336 (West 1962).
Utah:	Utah Code Ann. § 41–3–8 (1953).
Vermont:	Vt. Stat. Ann. tit. 19, § 708 (1987).

continued

Exhibit 11.10   State Statutory Code Citations—
continued

Examples of State Statutory Code Citations that Comply with the Bluebook

Virginia:	Va. Code Ann. § 18.2–265.3 (Michie 1950).
Washington:	Wash. Rev. Code § 7.48A.010 (1987).
	Wash. Rev. Code Ann. § 11.17.110 (West 1967).
West Virginia:	W. Va. Code § 23–1–17 (1985).
Wisconsin:	Wis. Stat. § 52.28 (1967).
	Wis. Stat. Ann. § 341.55 (West 1971).
Wyoming:	Wyo. Stat. § 26–18–113 (1977).

V. Citing Administrative Regulations

1. Federal administrative regulations are published in the *Federal Register* (Fed. Reg.). Many of these regulations are later codified by subject matter in the *Code of Federal Regulations* (C.F.R.).
2. Federal regulations that appear in the *Code of Federal Regulations* are cited to (a) the title number in which the regulation appears, (b) the abbreviated name of the code— C.F.R., (c) the number of the particular section to which you are referring, and (d) the date of the code edition that you are using.

Example

29 C.F.R. § 102.60(a) (1975).

3. Federal regulations that have not yet been codified into the *Code of Federal Regulations* are cited to the *Federal Register* using (a) the volume in which the regulation appears, (b) the abbreviation "Fed. Reg.", (c) the page on which the regulation appears, and (d) the year of the *Federal Register* you are using.

Example

27 Fed. Reg. 2,092 (1962).

VI. Citing the Documents of Legislative History

1. The main documents of legislative history (page 634) are bills, reports and hearings of congressional committees, transcripts of floor debates, etc.
2. Bills are cited by reference to (a) the number assigned to the bill by the House of Representatives or Senate, (b) the number of the Congress during which the bill was introduced, and the year of the bill.

Examples

H.R. 3055, 94th Cong. (1976).
S. 1422, 101st Cong. (1989).

3.   Reports of congressional committees are cited by reference to (a) the number of the report, (b) the number of the Congress during which the report was published, (c) the number of the page to which you are referring, and (d) the year in which the

If the report is also printed in the set of books called, *United States Code Congressional and Administrative News* (U.S.C.C.A.N.), include the volume number of U.S.C.C.A.N. (which will be a year) and the page number in U.S.C.C.A.N. where the report begins.

Examples

H.R. Rep. No. 92–238, at 4 (1979)
S. Rep. No. 92–415, at 6 (1971), *reprinted in* 1971 U.S.C.C.A.N. 647, 682.

4. Hearings held by congressional committees are cited by reference to (a) the title of the hearing, (b) the number of the Congress during which the hearing was held, (c) the number of the page in the published transcript to which you are referring, and (d) the year in which the hearing was held.

Example

Hearings on S. 631 Before the Subcomm. on Labor of the Senate Comm. on Labor and Public Welfare, 92d Cong. 315 (1971).

5. The *Congressional Record* is issued on a daily basis and later collected into bound volumes. The *bound* volumes are cited by referring to (a) the number of the volume in which the item appears, (b) the abbreviation *Cong. Rec.*, (c) the number of the page on which the item appears, and (d) the year. The *daily* volumes are cited in the same manner except that (a) the page number should be preceded by the letter "H" or "S" to indicate whether the item appeared in the House pages or the Senate pages of the volume, (b) the date should include the exact day, month, and year, and (c) the phrase "daily ed." should go before the date.

Examples

Bound volumes:
103 Cong. Rec. 2889 (1975).
Daily volumes:
122 Cong. Rec. S2395 (daily ed. Feb. 26, 1976).
132 Cong. Rec. H1385 (daily ed. Mar. 13, 1990).

VII. Citing Secondary Authority

1. Legal treatises and other books are cited to (a) the number of the volume being referred to (if part of a set), (b) the full name of the author, (c) the full title of the book as it appears on the title page, (d) the number of the section or page to which you are referring, (e) the edition of the book, if other than the first, and (f) the date of publication. The title of the book should be italicized or underscored. The name of the publisher is almost never given.

Examples

6 Melvin M. Belli, *Modern Trials* § 289 (1963).
George Osborne, *Handbook on the Law of Mortgages* 370 (2d ed. 1970).

2. Law review *articles* are cited by reference to (a) the full name of the author, (b) the title of the article, (c) the number of the volume in which the article appears, (d) the abbreviated name of the law review, (e) the number of the page on which the article begins, and (f) the year of publication. The title of the article should be italicized or underscored.

Examples

Robert Catz & Susan Robinson, *Due Process and Creditor's Remedies,*
28 Rutgers L. Rev. 541 (1975).
William P. Statsky, *The Education of Legal Paraprofessionals: Myths,
Realities, and Opportunities,* 24 Vand. L. Rev. 1083 (1971).

If you are referring to a specific page in an article, you need a *pinpoint cite* that will
give that page number in full in the citation. The page number you are pinpointing
goes immediately after the page number on which the article begins. Suppose, for
example, that you were quoting from page 550 of the above Rutgers Law Review article. The cite would be:

Robert Catz & Susan Robinson, *Due Process and Creditor's Remedies,*
28 Rutgers L. Rev. 541, 550 (1975).

3. Law review *notes* and *comments* written by law students are cited in the same manner
   as the law review articles (see guideline 2) except that the word *Note, Comment,* or
   Special Project is placed after the author's name just before the title.
4. Legal encyclopedias are cited by reference to (a) the number of the volume, (b) the
   abbreviated name of the encyclopedia, (c) the subject heading to which you are referring—in italics or underscored, (d) the number of the section to which you are referring, and (e) the date of publication of the volume you are citing.

Examples

83 C.J.S. *Subscriptions* § 3 (1953).
77 Am. Jur. 2d *Vendor and Purchaser* § 73 (1975).

5. *Restatements of the Law* published by the American Law Institute are cited by reference to (a) the title of the Restatement, (b) the edition being referred to (if other than
   the first edition), (c) the number of the section being referred to, and (d) the date of
   publication.

Example

Restatement (Second) of Agency § 37 (1957).

6. Annotations in A.L.R., A.L.R.2d, A.L.R.3d, A.L.R.4th, A.L.R.5th, and A.L.R. Fed. are cited
   by (a) the full name of the author, if available, (b) the word, "Annotation," (c) the title of
   the annotation—in italics or underscored, (d) the volume number, (e) the abbreviation of
   the A.L.R. unit, (f) the page number where the annotation begins, and (g) the date of the
   volume.

Example

James J. Watson, Annotation, *Attorney's Fees: Cost of Services Provided by Paralegals or the
Like as Compensable Element in Award in State Court,* 73 A.L.R.4th 938 (1989).

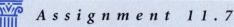 **A s s i g n m e n t   1 1 . 7**

Each of the following citations has one or more things wrong with it. Describe the errors
and gaps in format. For example, a parallel cite is missing or something is abbreviated incorrectly. You do not have to go to the library to check any of these cites. Simply use the guidelines presented above.

(a) <u>Smith v. Jones,</u> 135 Mass. 37, 67 N.E. 2d 316, 320 (1954). First assume that you are citing this case in a motion submitted to a state trial court in Massachusetts. Then assume that you are citing it in a memorandum submitted to the United States District Court sitting in Boston.

(b) <u>Paul Matthews v. Edward Foley, Inc.</u>, 779 F. 2d 729 (W.D.N.Y., 1979). First assume that you are citing this case in a motion submitted to the United States District Court sitting in Manhattan. Then assume that you are citing it in an appellate brief submitted to the highest state court in New York.

(c) <u>Jackson v. Jackson,</u> 219 F.Supp. 1276, 37 N.E. 2d 84 (1980). First assume that you are citing this case in a motion submitted to a state trial court in California. Then assume that you are citing it in a law review article.

(d) <u>Davis v. Thompson</u>, et al, 336 P. 2d 691, 210 N.M. 432 (1976). First assume that you are citing this case in a motion submitted to a state appellate court in Florida. Then assume that you are citing it in an appellate brief submitted to the New Mexico Supreme Court.

(e) <u>Washington Tire Company v. Jones</u>, 36 N.J.Super. 222, 351 A. 2d 541 (1976). First assume that you are citing this case in a news story for a paralegal newsletter published by a New Jersey paralegal association. Then assume that you are citing it in a memorandum submitted to the New Jersey Supreme Court.

(f) <u>State of New Hampshire v. Atkinson</u>, 117 N.H. 830, 228 A. 2d 222 (N.H.Super., 1978). First assume that you are citing this case in an appellate brief submitted to the New Hampshire Supreme Court. Then assume that you are citing it in an appellate brief submitted to the Ohio Supreme Court.

(g) <u>Richardson v. U.S.</u>, 229 U.S. 220 (1975).

(h) American Law Institute, <u>Restatement of Torts</u> (2d ed 1976).

(i) U.S.Const. Art. III (1797).

(j) Smith, F., Products Liability (3rd ed. 1985).

(k) 42 USC 288 (1970).

(l) 17 U.S.C.A. 519 (1970).

(m) 40 Fed. Reg. § 277 (1976).

Assignment 11.8

(a) For your state, check the state code and rules of court of the highest state court in the state to find out whether any special citation rules must be followed in documents submitted to the courts. If so, redo Assignment 11.7 by stating which, if any, of the citations in (a) to (m) would have to be changed if they had to conform to these special citation rules.

(b) Find any court opinion written by the highest state court in your state. Locate this opinion by using the regional reporter for your state. (See Exhibits 11.4 and 11.5.) Pick an opinion that is at least ten pages long.

  (i) Write down every citation in this opinion (up to a maximum of twenty-five).

  (ii) State whether these citations conform to the Bluebook citation rules outlined here in this section of Chapter 11. Point out any differences.

  (iii) State whether these citations conform to the special citation rules, if any, you identified in answering question (a) above. Point out any differences.

Note on the Maroon Book

For years, many have criticized *The Bluebook: A Uniform System of Citation*. People find its citation rules too arbitrary and the book itself difficult to use. In 1989, a major challenger to the Bluebook appeared: *The University of Chicago Manual of Legal Citation*, also known as the Maroon Book because of the color of its cover. Whereas the Bluebook tries to include citation rules for almost every situation, the Maroon Book adopts a substantially different point of view. Because "it is neither possible nor desirable to write a particular rule for every sort of citation problem that might arise," the citation rules in the Maroon Book "leave a fair amount of discretion to practitioners, authors, and editors." To a devotee of the Bluebook, such discretion is very distasteful. It is too early to tell what impact the Maroon Book will have on the world of citation. Because the Bluebook is so firmly entrenched, it is unlikely that a competitor will replace it any time soon.

Note on Public Domain or Generic Citation

The vast majority of citations to cases contain volume and page numbers, e.g., *Smith v. Smith,* 300 N.E.2d 202 (N.Y. 1996). In this example, the volume number is to a particular reporter—volume 303 of the North Eastern Reporter, Second Series. The case begins on page 202. Critics have argued that we need to get ready for the paperless law library when all or most legal materials, particularly primary authority, will be available online through computers. When this time comes, we should be able to cite cases and other documents without referring to volume and page numbers. Indeed, proposals have been advanced for what is called a **generic citation** system—one that gives references to documents without using traditional volume and page numbers.

The system has different names. It is referred to as **electronic citation** because the references are to online documents. It is also called a **public domain citation** system when it refers you to free materials that are not dependent on the volumes of commercial companies such as West, the publisher of the widely used National Reporter System (see Exhibit 11.4). Something is *in the public domain* when it is free and open to anyone who wants it. The format of traditional case citations is dependent on volume and page numbers. A generic or public domain citation system is referred to as "medium neutral," "format neutral" or "vendor neutral" (the vendor being the seller/publisher of reporter volumes).

The essence of a generic citation system is sequential opinion and paragraph numbering. When a court writes an opinion, it will assign a sequential number to it (perhaps similar to a docket number) and then a sequential number to every paragraph: ¶ 1, ¶ 2, ¶ 3, ¶ 4, etc. If, for example, you wanted to quote a sentence that appeared in the eighty-ninth paragraph of *Davis v. Cardiff,* the citation might be:

Davis v. Cardiff, 1996 Wis. Ct. App. 234, ¶ 89.

This would refer you to the 89th paragraph in *Davis v. Cardiff,* which was the 234th opinion issued in 1996 by the Wisconsin Court of Appeals. If researchers wanted to check this citation, they would go online. For example, they might go to the site on the Internet that contains opinions of Wisconsin state courts, find opinion no. 234, and quickly "click" to ¶ 89. (As we saw earlier, a citation that refers a reader to a particular page or paragraph within an opinion is called a *pinpoint cite.*)

A few states have already adopted generic citation systems like this. Such systems do *not* replace the traditional volume/page citation system, however. At least not yet. Comprehensive law libraries will continue to add traditional reporter volumes to their shelves. But an alternative is slowly emerging. In the meantime, if a state has adopted an official public domain citation system, use it, but also include a traditional reporter cite where available. For example:

Stevens v. State, 1996 S.D. 1, ¶ 217, 402 N.W.2d 327.

S e c t i o n   K
CITE CHECKING

When an assignment involves **cite checking,** you are given a document written by someone else and asked to check the citations provided by the author of the document. The assignment is quite common in law firms, particularly when the document to be checked is an appellate brief. Students on law review in law school also do extensive cite checking on the work of fellow students and outside authors.

While our focus in this section will be the writing of others, the guidelines discussed here are in large measure equally applicable to your own writing.

GUIDELINES FOR CITE CHECKING

1. The first step is to obtain clear instructions from your supervisor on the scope of the assignment. Should you do a "light check" or a comprehensive one? Should you focus solely on citation form, or should you determine the accuracy of all quotes used by the writer of the document? On citation form, what rules should you use? The Bluebook?

   ───────────

The following guidelines assume that you have been asked to undertake a comprehensive check.

2. Make sure that you have a *copy* of the document on which you can make comments. Avoid using the original.

3. If the pages of the document already have pencil or pen markings made by others (or by the author who made last-minute insertions), use a pencil or pen that is a different color from all other markings on the pages. In this way it will be clear to any reader which corrections, notations, or other comments are your own. If you find that you do not have enough room to write in the margins of the pages, use separate sheets of paper. You can increase the size of the margins by photocopying the document on a machine that will reduce the size of what is copied.

4. If the document will be submitted to a court, be sure that you are using the official citation rules, if any, that must be followed for all citations in documents submitted to that court.

5. Before you begin, try to find a model. By going through the old case files of the office, you may be able to locate a prior document, such as an old appellate brief, that you can use as a general guide. Ask your supervisor to direct you to such a document. While it may not cover all the difficulties you will encounter in your own document, you will at least have a general guide approved by your supervisor.

6. Check the citation form of *every* cite in the document written by the author of that document. This includes any cites in the body of the text, the footnotes, the appendix material, and the introductory pages of the document, such as the Table of Authorities (page 672) at the beginning of a brief.

7. For longer documents, you need to develop your own system for ensuring the completeness of your checking. For example, you might want to circle every cite that you have checked and found to be accurate, and place a small box around (or a question mark next to) every cite that is giving you difficulties. You will want to spend more time with the latter, seeking help from colleagues and your supervisor.

8. When you find errors in the form of the citation, make the corrections in the margin of the pages where they are found.

9. For some errors, you will not be able to make the corrections without obtaining additional information, such as a missing date or a missing parallel cite. If you can obtain this data by going to the relevant library books (or available online resources), do so. Otherwise make a notation in the margin of what is missing or what still needs correction.

10. Consistency in citation format is extremely important. On page 2 of the document, for example, the author may use one citation format, but on page 10, he or she may use a completely different format for the same kind of legal material. You need to point out this inconsistency, and make the consistency corrections that are called for.

11. Often your document will quote from cases, statutes, or other legal materials. Check the accuracy of these quotations. Go to the material being quoted, find the quote, and check it against the document line by line, word by word, and punctuation mark by punctuation mark. Be scrupulous about the accuracy of quotations.

12. Shepardize anything that can be shepardized, such as cases and statutes. Here are some examples of what you need to determine through shepardizing:

   • Whether any of the cited cases have been overruled or reversed
   • Whether any of the cited statutes have been repealed or amended by the legislature, or have been invalidated by a court

13. Check the accuracy of all **supra** references.

   The word *supra* means "above" or "earlier." It refers to something already mentioned (and cited) in the document you are cite checking. For example, assume that footnote 8 on page 23 of the document contains the following cite:

   [8]Robert G. Danna, *Family Law* 119 (1992).

   The particular reference is to page 119 of Danna's book. Now assume that ten pages later—in footnote 17—the document again refers to Danna's book, this time to page 35. You do *not* have to repeat the full citation of the book as follows:

   [17]Robert G. Danna, *Family Law* 35 (1992).

   Instead, a *short form* of the cite is usually appropriate:

   [17]Danna, *supra* note 8 at 35.

   This means that the full cite of Danna's book was already given earlier *(supra)* in the document in footnote 8. There is no need to repeat the full cite. The cite checker must simply go to footnote 8 and make sure that the full cite of the book is provided there.

   Finally, assume that Danna's book was cited in full in the body of the text of the document rather than in a footnote. A later *footnote* reference to the same book would be as follows:

   [17]Danna, *supra*, at 35.

   The accuracy of this reference is checked in the same way: make sure that the full cite of Danna's book is in fact provided earlier in the body of the document.

   Infra means "below" or "later" and refers to something that will come later in the document. In the same manner as you checked the *supra* references, you must determine whether the *infra* references are accurate.

14. Check the accuracy of all of *short form case citations*.

   Assume that the document you are cite checking gives the following reference early in the document:

   Sierra Club v. Sigler, 695 F.2d 957, 980 (5th Cir. 1983).

The cite is to page 980 of the *Sierra Club* case, which begins on page 957 of the Federal Reporter, Second Series. Now assume that the author wants to refer to page 962 of the same case later in the document. Generally, there is no need to repeat the entire citation. The following short form may be used:

Sierra Club, 695 F.2d at 962.

To check the accuracy of this cite, you must go back in the document to make sure that *Sierra Club* has already been cited in full.

You do *not* use *supra* when citing a case more than once in the same document. *Supra* can be used for many items such as treatises and periodicals. With rare exceptions, however, you do not use it in citations to court opinions.

Cite-Checking Software

Computer companies have developed two kinds of cite-checking software. First, there is *format* software that tells you whether a particular citation conforms to *The Bluebook: A Uniform System of Citation.* The developers placed the entire Bluebook into the program so that it can recognize discrepancies between the rules of the Bluebook and citations that are typed into the computer. In addition to pointing out citation errors, the program will refer you to specific rules in the Bluebook that have been violated. Two examples of such software are The Electronic Bluebook and CiteRite. The second kind of cite-checking software provides *validation* data on citations. You will be told, for example, whether a particular court opinion has been overruled and whether a particular statute has been repealed. Two examples of such software are WESTcheck, used in conjunction with WESTLAW, and CheckCite, used in conjunction with LEXIS. Unlike the format cite-checking software, the validation programs are online and hence are used through a modem.

Section L
COMPONENTS OF MANY LAW BOOKS

Many law books are similar in structure. To be sure, some books, such as *Shepard's Citations,* are unique. In the main, however, the texts follow a pattern. The following components are contained in many:

1. *Outside Cover.* On the outside cover, you will find the title of the book, the author(s) or editor(s), the name of the publisher (usually at the bottom), the edition of the book (if more than one edition has been printed), and the volume number (if the book is part of a set or series of books). After glancing at the outside cover, you should ask yourself the following questions:

   - Is it a book *containing* law (written primarily by a court, a legislature, or an administrative agency), or is it a book *about* the law (written by a scholar who is commenting on the law)? Is the book a combination of both?
   - Is this book the most current available? Look at the books on the shelf in the area where you found the book that you are examining. Is there a replacement volume for your book? Is there a later edition of the book? Check your book in the card catalog to see if other editions are mentioned.

2. *Publisher's Page.* The first few pages of the book often include a page or pages about the publisher. The page may list other law books published by the same company.
3. *Title Page.* The **title page** repeats most of the information contained on the outside cover: title, author, editor, publisher. It also contains the date of publication.

4. *Copyright Page.* The **copyright page** (often immediately behind the title page) has a copyright mark © plus a date or several dates. The most recent date listed indicates the timeliness of the material in the volume. Given the great flux in the law, it is very important to determine how old the text is. If the book has a pocket part (see item 14 below), it has been updated to the date on the pocket part.

COPYRIGHT © 1979, 1983, 1989, 1994 WEST PUBLISHING CO.

COPYRIGHT © 1997

By

WEST PUBLISHING CO.

The dates on this copyright page indicate that the material in the book is current up to 1997, the latest copyright date. Caution, however, is needed in reaching this conclusion. Publishers like to have their books appear to be as current as possible. A book with a 1997 copyright date may in fact have been published *at the beginning* of 1997 or *at the very end* of 1996! A 1997 date does not necessarily mean that you are current up to December of that year. We will return to this concern later when we discuss pocket parts.

5. *Foreword or Preface.* Under such headings, you may find some basic information about the book, particularly material on how the book was prepared and guidance on how to use it.

6. *Summary Table of Contents.* On one or two pages, you may find the main topics treated in the book.

7. *Detailed Table of Contents.* When provided, the detailed table of contents can be very extensive. The major headings of the summary table of contents are repeated, and detailed subheadings and sub-subheadings are listed. Use this table as an additional index to the book.

8. *Table of Cases.* The **table of cases** lists, alphabetically, every case that is printed or referred to in the text, with the page(s) where the case is found or discussed. This table is sometimes printed at the end of the book.

9. *Table of Statutes.* The **table of statutes** gives the page numbers where every statute is interpreted or referred to in the text. This table is sometimes printed at the end of the book.

10. *List of Abbreviations.* The abbreviation list, if provided, is critical. A reader who is unfamiliar with law books should check this list immediately. It may be the only

History of Case	
a (affirmed)	Same case affirmed on appeal.
cc (connected case)	Different case from case cited but arising out of same subject matter or intimately connected therewith.
D (dismissed)	Appeal from same case dismissed.
m (modified)	Same case modified on appeal.
r (reversed)	Same case reversed on appeal.
s (same case)	Same case as case cited.
S (superseded)	Substitution for former opinion.
v (vacated)	Same case vacated.
US cert den	Certiorari denied by U. S. Supreme Court.
US cert dis	Certiorari dismissed by U. S. Supreme Court.
US reh den	Rehearing denied by U. S. Supreme Court.
US reh dis	Rehearing dismissed by U. S. Supreme Court.
Treatment of Case	
c (criticised)	Soundness of decision or reasoning in cited case criticised for reasons given.
d (distinguished)	Case at bar different either in law or fact from case cited for reasons given.
e (explained)	Statement of import of decisions in cited case. Not merely a restatement of the facts.
f (followed)	Cited as controlling
h (harmonized)	Apparent inconsistency explained and shown not to exist.
j (dissenting opinion)	Citation in dissenting opinion.
L (limited)	Refusal to extend decision of cited case beyond precise issues involved.
o (overruled)	Ruling in cited case expressly overruled.
p (parallel)	Citing case substantially alike or on all fours with cited case in its law or facts.
q (questioned)	Soundness of decision or reasoning in cited case questioned.

Example of abbreviations used by Shepard's

place in the book that spells out the abbreviations used in the body of the text. In *Shepard's Citations,* for example, abbreviations are found in the first few pages of the bound volumes and in most of its pamphlets (see bottom of page 580.)

11. *Statutory History Table.* Some texts, particularly statutory codes, may include a **statutory history table** that lists every statute cited in the book and indicates whether it has been repealed or whether it has a new section number and title. The legislature may have changed the entire name of the statutory chapter (from Prison Law to Correction Law, for instance) and renumbered all the sections. Without this table, the researcher can become lost. In the example below, note that former Prison Law sections 10–20 are now found in Correction Law sections 600–610. You may find a citation to a Prison Law section in a book that was published before the state changed to Correction Law sections. When you go to look up the Prison Law section, you will find nothing unless you have a way to translate the section into a Correction Law section. The *statutory history table* will be one way to do it.

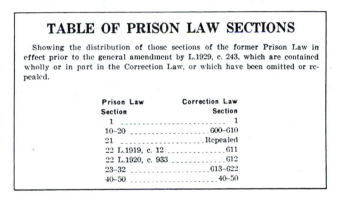

Example of a statutory history table

12. *Body of the Text.* The fundamental characteristic of the body of many legal texts is that it is arranged according to units such as parts, subparts, divisions, subdivisions, chapters, subchapters, sections, subsections, etc. Often each unit covers a similar subject matter and is numbered or lettered in sequence. You should thumb through the entire book to obtain a feel for the numbering and classification system used by the author or editor.

13. *Footnotes.* Footnotes are very important in law books; researchers place great emphasis on them. They often give extensive citations to cases and other cross-references, and hence can be an excellent lead to additional law.

14. *Pocket Parts and Other Updating Features.* A unique and indispensable feature of many law books is the *pocket part.* It is a small booklet addition to the text, usually placed at the very end of the text in a specially devised pocket built into the inside of the rear cover. (See page 536.) The pocket part is published after the book is printed and is designed to bring the book up-to-date with the latest developments in the field covered by the book. Of course, a pocket part can also grow out of date. Normally, it is replaced once a year. On the front cover of the pocket-part booklet, there is a date telling you what period is covered. The title page (see item 3 above) may say that the last edition of the book was published in 1990, but the front page of the pocket part may say "for use during 1996–1997." Again, however, use caution in interpreting these dates. The publisher may have prepared this pocket part at the end of 1996 or at the beginning of 1997. You cannot assume that the material in the pocket part is current up to December of 1997.

Normally, the organization of the pocket part exactly parallels the organization of the main text. For example, to find out if there has been anything new in the area covered by chapter 7, part 2, section 714 of the main text, you go to chapter 7, part 2, section 714 of the pocket part. If you find nothing there, then nothing new has happened. If changes or additions have occurred, they will be found there.

Pocket parts are *cumulative* in that, whenever a pocket part is replaced by another pocket part, everything in the early pocket part is consolidated into the most recent one. The earlier pocket part is thrown away.

Not all law books have pocket parts. For an overview, see Exhibit 11.11.

Exhibit 11.11   Pocket Parts

LAW BOOKS THAT ALWAYS OR OFTEN HAVE POCKET PARTS:	LAW BOOOKS THAT NEVER HAVE POCKET PARTS:
• State Statutory Codes (e.g., *Georgia Code Annotated*)	• Shepard's (e.g., *Shepard's Federal Citations*)
• Unofficial Federal Codes (e.g., *U.S.C.A.* and *U.S.C.S.*)	• American Digest System (*Century Digest, Decennial Digests, & General Digests*)
• Annotated Reporters (e.g., *A.L.R.3d*)	• Loose-leaf Services (e.g., *United States Law Week*)
• Legal Encyclopedias (e.g., *C.J.S.* and *Am. Jur. 2d*)	• West Reporters (e.g., regional reporters, S. Ct., F.2d, F. Supp.)
• State Digests (e.g., *Illinois Digest 2d*)	• Session Laws (e.g., *United States Statutes at Large*)
• Regional Digests (e.g., *Pacific Digest*)	• Legal Periodicals (e.g., *Boston College Law Review*)
• Federal Digests (e.g., *Federal Practice Digest 4th*)	• Legal Newspapers (e.g., *San Francisco Daily Journal*)
• Legal Treatises written for practitioners (e.g., C.Z. Nothstein, *Toxic Torts*)	• Legal Newsletters (e.g., *The Guardian*)

How is new material added to law books without pocket parts—the ones listed in the second column of Exhibit 11.11? Shepard's is kept current by advance sheets (p. 512) and supplemental pamphlets; the American Digest System by adding *General Digest* volumes, which are thrown away when the next *Decennial Digest* is published; loose-leaf services by inserting pages with new material into the binders and removing pages with outdated material. For the other items in the second column of Exhibit 11.11—West reporters, session laws, etc.—new material is added simply by adding new volumes or issues.

Some sets of books use a variety of methods to bring them up to date: pocket parts, supplement pamphlets, supplement volumes, reissued volumes, revised volumes, etc.

15. *Appendix.* The text may include one or more appendixes at the end. Normally, they include tables, charts, or the entire text of statutes or regulations, portions of which are discussed in the body of the book.

16. *Glossary.* The book may include a glossary, which is a dictionary that defines a selected number of words used in the body of the book.

17. *Bibliography.* A brief or extended bibliography of the field covered by the book may be included at the end of each chapter or at the end of the book.

18. *Index.* The index is a critical part of the book. Unfortunately, some books either have no index or do a sloppy job of indexing. The index is arranged alphabetically and should refer the reader to the page number(s) or to the section number(s) where topics are treated in the body of the text. The index is found at the end of the book. If there are many volumes in the set, you may find more than one index. For example, there may be a *general index* for the entire set and a series of smaller indexes covering individual volumes.

S e c t i o n   M
THE CARTWHEEL

Most people think that using an *index* is a relatively easy task—until they start trying to use indexes of law books! These indexes are often poorly written because they are not comprehensive. To be comprehensive, an index might have to be as long as the text it is indexing. Hence, publishers are reluctant to include such indexes.

Because of this reality, one of the most important skills in legal research is the creative use of indexes in law books. When you master this skill, 70 percent of the research battle is won. The **CARTWHEEL** is a word-association technique designed to assist you in acquiring the skill. (See Exhibit 11.12.)

The objective of the CARTWHEEL can be simply stated: to develop the habit of phrasing every word involved in the client's problem *fifteen to twenty different ways!* When you go to the index (or to the table of contents) of a law book, you naturally begin looking up the words and phrases that you think should lead you to the relevant material in the book. If you do not find anything relevant to your problem, two conclusions are possible:

- There is nothing relevant in the law book.
- You looked up the wrong words in the index and table of contents.

While the first conclusion is sometimes accurate, nine times out of ten, the second conclusion is the reason you fail to find material that is relevant to the client's problem. The solution is to be able to phrase a word in as many different ways and in as many different contexts as possible. Hence, the CARTWHEEL.

Suppose the client's problem involved, among other things, a wedding. The first step would be to look up the word *wedding* in the index of any law book you are examining. Assume that you are not successful with this word, either because the word is not in the index or because the page or section references do not lead you to relevant material in the body of the book. The next step is to think of as many different phrasings and contexts of the word *wedding* as possible. This is where the eighteen steps of the CARTWHEEL can be useful.

If you applied the steps of the CARTWHEEL to the word "wedding," here are some of the words and phrases that you would check:

1. *Broader words:* celebration, ceremony, rite, ritual, formality, festivity, etc.
2. *Narrower words:* civil wedding, church wedding, golden wedding, proxy wedding, sham wedding, shotgun marriage, etc.
3. *Synonyms:* marriage ceremony, nuptial, etc.

Exhibit 11.12   The CARTWHEEL: Using the Index of Law Books

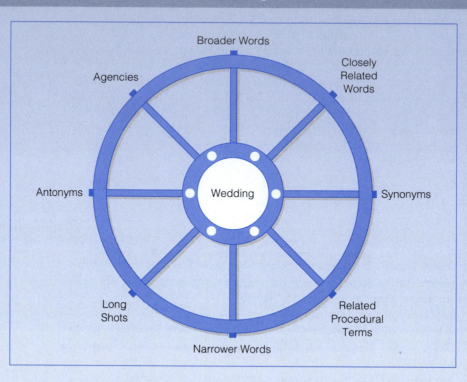

1. Identify all the *major words* from the facts of the client's problem, e.g., wedding (most of these facts can be obtained from the intake memorandum written following the initial interview with the client). Place each word or small set of words in the center of the CARTWHEEL.
2. In the index, look up all of these words.
3. Identify the *broader categories* of the major words.
4. In the index, look up all of these broader categories.
5. Identify the *narrower* categories of the major words.
6. In the index, look up all of these narrower categories.
7. Identify all *synonyms* of the major words.
8. In the index, look up all of these synonyms.
9. Identify all of the *antonyms* of the major words.
10. In the index, look up all of these antonyms.
11. Identify all words that are *closely related* to the major words.
12. In the index, look up all of these closely related words.
13. Identify all *procedural* terms related to the major words.
14. In the index, look up all of these procedural terms.
15. Identify all *agencies,* if any, that might have some connection to the major words.
16. In the index, look up all of these agencies.
17. Identify all *long shots.*
18. In the index, look up all of these long shots.

Note: The above categories are not mutually exclusive.

4. *Antonyms:* alienation, annulment, divorce, separation, legal separation, judicial separation, etc.

5. *Closely related words:* license, blood test, contract, minister, matrimony, marital, conjugal, domestic, husband, wife, bride, anniversary, custom, children, premarital, spouse, relationship, family, home, consummation, cohabitation, sexual relations, betrothal, wedlock, oath, community property, name change, domicile, residence, etc.

6. *Procedural terms:* action, suit, statute of limitations, complaint, discovery, defense, petition, jurisdiction, court, superior court, county court, etc.

7. *Agencies:* Bureau of Vital Statistics, County Clerk, Department of Social Services, License Bureau, Secretary of State, Justice of the Peace, etc.

8. *Long shots:* dowry, common law, single, blood relationship, fraud, religion, illegitimate, remarriage, antenuptial, alimony, bigamy, pregnancy, gifts, chastity, impotence, incest, virginity, support, custody, consent, paternity, etc.

If the CARTWHEEL can generate this many words and phrases from a starting point of just one word (wedding), potentially thousands more can be generated when you subject all of the important words from the client's case to the CARTWHEEL. Do you check them all in the index volume of every code, digest, encyclopedia, practice manual, and treatise? No. You can't spend your entire legal career in the law library working on one case! Common sense will tell you when you are on the right track and when you are needlessly duplicating your efforts. You may get lucky and find what you are after in a few minutes. For most important tasks in any line of work (or play), however, being comprehensive is usually time-consuming.

As indicated in Exhibit 11.12, the categories may overlap; they are not mutually exclusive. There are two reasons for checking antonyms: they might cover your topic, or they might give you a cross-reference to your topic. It is not significant whether you place a word in one category or another so long as the word comes to your mind as you comb through the index and table of contents. The CARTWHEEL is, in effect, a *word-association game* that should become second nature to you with practice. Perhaps some of the word selections seem a bit far-fetched. You will not know for sure, however, whether a word is fruitful until you try it. Be imaginative, and take some risks.

Assignment 11.9

CARTWHEEL the following words or phrases:
(a) Paralegal
(b) Woman
(c) Rat bite
(d) Rear-end collision
(e) Monopoly

Indexes and tables of contents are often organized into *headings, subheadings, sub-subheadings* and perhaps even sub-sub-subheadings. In the following excerpt from an index, "Burden of proof" is a sub-subheading of "Accidents" and a subheading of "Unavoidable accident or casualty." The latter is a subheading of "Accidents," which is the main heading of the index entry. If you were looking for law on burden of proof, you might be out of luck unless you *first* thought of looking up "accidents" and "unavoidable accident."

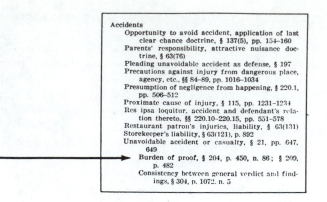

Accidents
  Opportunity to avoid accident, application of last
    clear chance doctrine, § 137(5), pp. 154–160
  Parents' responsibility, attractive nuisance doc-
    trine, § 63(76)
  Pleading unavoidable accident as defense, § 197
  Precautions against injury from dangerous place,
    agency, etc., §§ 84–89, pp. 1016–1034
  Presumption of negligence from happening, § 220.1,
    pp. 506–512
  Proximate cause of injury, § 115, pp. 1231–1234
  Res ipsa loquitur, accident and defendant's rela-
    tion thereto, §§ 220.10–220.15, pp. 551–578
  Restaurant patron's injuries, liability, § 63(131)
  Storekeeper's liability, § 63(121), p. 892
  Unavoidable accident or casualty, § 21, pp. 647,
    649
    Burden of proof, § 204, p. 450, n. 86; § 209,
      p. 482
    Consistency between general verdict and find-
      ings, § 304, p. 1072, n. 5

Suppose that you identify the following words to check in an index:

minor	sale
explosion	warranty
car	damage

The index may have no separate heading for "minor," but "minor" may be a subheading under "sale." If so, you would not find "minor" unless you first thought of checking "sale." Under each of the above six words, you should be alert to the possibility that the other five words may be subheadings for that word. Hence the process of pursuing these six words in an index (or table of contents) would be as follows: (The word in bold letters is checked first and then the five words *under it* are checked to see if any of them are subheadings.)

Car	Damage	Explosion	Minor	Sale	Warranty
damage	car	car	car	car	car
explosion	explosion	damage	damage	damage	damage
minor	minor	minor	explosion	explosion	explosion
sale	sale	sale	sale	minor	minor
warranty	warranty	warranty	warranty	warranty	sale

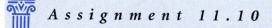 Assignment 11.10

One way to gain an appreciation for the use of indexes is to write one of your own. When you write an index for this assignment, be sure to use headings, subheadings, sub-subheadings, etc. in each index.

(a) Write a comprehensive index of your present job or the last job that you had.

(b) Pick one area of the law that you have covered in class or read about. Write your own comprehensive index on what you have learned.

(c) Write a comprehensive index of the following statute:

§ 132. Amount of force. The use of force against another for the purpose of effecting the arrest or recapture of the other, or of maintaining custody of him, is not privileged if the means employed are in excess of those which are reasonably believed to be necessary.

Assignment 11.11

Examine the index from a legal encyclopedia in Exhibit 11.13. It is an excerpt from the heading of "Evidence." "Death" is the subheading of "Evidence." What sub-subheadings or sub-sub-subheadings of "Evidence" would you check to try to find material on the following:

(a) Introducing a death certificate into evidence.

(b) The weight that a court will give to the personal conclusions of a witness.

(c) Introducing the last words of a decedent into evidence.

(d) A statement by the person who died disclaiming ownership of land around which he or she had placed a fence.

Exhibit 11.13   Excerpt from Index

EVIDENCE

Dealers,
  Securities, judicial notice, § 29, p. 890
Value,
  Household goods, opinion evidence, § 546(121), p. 479, n. 95
  Property, § 546(115), p. 430
    Opinion evidence, § 546(122), p. 483
Death,
  Autopsy, generally, ante
  Best evidence rule, § 803, p. 136
  Book entries,
    Entrant, proof of handwriting, § 693, p. 942
    Supplemental testimony respecting entries by clerks and third persons, § 693, p. 939
    Supporting entries by deceased persons by oath of personal representative, § 684, p. 910
  Clerk or employee making book entries, § 692
  Copy of record, certification by state registrar, § 664, p. 865, n. 69
  Declaration against interest, death of declarant, § 218, p. 604
  Declarations, § 227, p. 624
    Death of declarant as essential to admission, § 230
  Dying declarations, generally, post
  Experiments, object or purpose, § 588(1)
  Former evidence, death of witness, § 392
  General reputation, § 1048
  Hearsay, § 227, p. 624
    Death certificates, § 194, pp. 561, 562; § 766, p. 66
    Death of declarant, § 205
    Impossibility of obtaining other evidence, § 204
  Letters, § 703, p. 976
  Maps and diagrams of scenes of occurrence, § 730(1), p. 1045
  Memorandum, § 696, p. 955
  Mortality tables, generally, post
  Newspaper announcement, § 227, p. 625
  Opinion evidence,
    Animals, § 546(68)
    Cause and effect, § 546(11), p. 129
    Effect on human body, § 546(97), p. 374
    Fixing time, § 546(91), n. 16
  Owners, admissions, § 327
    Personal property, § 334
  Parol or extrinsic evidence, rule excluding, action to recover for, § 861, p. 230
  Photographs, personal appearance or identity, § 710
  Presumptions, ancient original public records, official making, § 746, p. 37
  Prima facie evidence, record of, § 644
  Private documents, recitals, § 677
  Public records and documents, registers of, § 623
  Reputation, § 227, p. 626
  Res gestae, statements, § 410, p. 991
  Rumor, § 227, p. 625
  Self-serving declarations, effect of death of declarant, § 216, p. 591
  Services, value, opinion evidence in death action, § 546(124), p. 489, n. 96
  Statements, weight of evidence, § 266
  Value of service rendered by claimant, opinion evidence, § 546(125), p. 493, n. 41

Death—Continued
  Witness, unsworn statements, circumstances tending to disparage testimony, § 268
  Wrongful death,
    Admissions, husband and wife, § 363
    Admissions of decedent, privity, § 322, n. 96.5
    Declarations against interest, § 218, p. 607
    Loss of life, value, opinion evidence, § 546(121), p. 473, n. 54
    Municipal claim, evidence of registry, § 680, n. 21
    Value of decedent's services, opinion evidence, § 546(124), p. 489, n. 96
Death certificates,
  Certified copies, § 651, p. 851
    Officer as making, § 664, p. 865, n. 69
    Prima facie evidence, § 773
  Church register, competency, § 727
  Conclusiveness, § 766, p. 64
  Expert testimony, supporting opinion, § 570
  Foreign countries, authenticated copies, § 675, p. 885
  Hearsay, § 194, pp. 561, 562; § 766, p. 66
  Kinship, § 696, p. 949, n. 2
  Official document, § 638, pp. 823, 824
  Prima facie case or evidence, post
Debate, judicial notice, United States congress, § 43, p. 995
Debs, judicial notice, § 67, p. 56, n. 17
Debtor and creditor, admissions, § 336
Debts. Indebtedness, generally, post
Decay,
  Judicial notice, vegetable matter, § 88
  Opinion evidence, buildings, § 546(73), p. 290
Decedents' estates,
  Judicial admissions, claim statements, § 310
  Judicial records, inferences from, § 765
  Official documents, reports and inventories of representatives, § 638, p. 818
  Value, opinion evidence, § 546(121), p. 478
Deceit. Fraud, generally, post
Decisions, judicial notice, sister states, § 18, p. 861
Declaration against interest, §§ 217–224, pp. 600–615
  Absence of declared from jurisdiction, § 218, p. 604
  Account, § 224
  Admissions, distinguished, § 217, p. 603
  Adverse character, § 222
  Affirmative proof as being best evidence obtainable, § 218, p. 604
  Apparent interest, § 219, p. 608
  Assured, § 219, p. 611
  Best evidence obtainable, necessity of, § 218, p. 604
  Boundaries, § 219, p. 611
  Coexisting, self-serving interest, § 221
  Contract, § 224
  Criminal prosecution, statement subjecting declarant to, § 219, p. 608
  Death action, § 218, p. 607
  Death of declarant, § 218, p. 605
  Dedication to public use, § 219, p. 611
  Deeds, § 224
  Disparagement of title § 219, p. 611
  Distinctions, § 217, p. 603
  Enrollment of vessel, § 224

Section N
THE FIRST LEVEL OF LEGAL RESEARCH: BACKGROUND

There are three interrelated levels of researching a problem:

Background Research. Provides you with a general understanding of the area of law involved in your research problem.

Specific Fact Research. Provides you with primary and secondary authority that covers the specific facts of your research problem.

Validation Research. Provides you with information on the current validity of all the primary authority you intend to use in your research memorandum on the problem.

At times all three levels of research go on simultaneously. If you are new to legal research, however, it is recommended that you approach your research problem in the three stages just listed. Our concern in this chapter is the first level: background research. See Exhibit 11.14. The other two levels are covered throughout the remainder of this chapter.

Exhibit 11.14   Techniques for Doing Background Research on a Topic

1. Legal Dictionaries

Have access to a *legal dictionary* throughout your research. For example:

> *Black's Law Dictionary*
> *Ballentine's Law Dictionary*
> *Oran's Law Dictionary*
> Statsky's *Legal Thesaurus/Dictionary*

Look up the meaning of all important terms that you come across in your research. These dictionaries are starting points only. Eventually you want to find primary authority that defines these terms.

2. Legal Encyclopedias

Find discussions of your topic in the major national *legal encyclopedias:*

> *American Jurisprudence 2d*
> *Corpus Juris Secundum*

Also check encyclopedias, if any, that cover only your state. Use the CARTWHEEL to help you use their indexes.

3. Legal Treatises

Find discussions of your topic in *legal treatises.* Go to your card catalog or computer index in the library. Use the CARTWHEEL to help you locate treatises such as hornbooks, handbooks, formbooks, practice manuals, scholarly studies, etc. Many of these books will have *KF call numbers.* Use the CARTWHEEL to help you use the indexes of these books.

4. Annotations

Find discussions of your topic in the *annotations* of A.L.R., A.L.R.2d, A.L.R.3d, A.L.R.4th, A.L.R.5th, and A.L.R. Fed. Use the CARTWHEEL to help you find these discussions through indexes such as the *Index to Annotations.*

E x h i b i t   1 1 . 1 4   **Techniques for Doing Background Research on a Topic—continued**

5. Legal Periodical Literature

Find discussions of your topic in *legal periodical* literature. The three main indexes to such literature are:

> *Index to Legal Periodicals* (ILP)
> *Current Law Index* (CLI)
> *LegalTrac* (the CD-ROM version of CLI)

Use the CARTWHEEL to help you use these indexes to locate legal periodical literature on your topic.

6. Agency Reports/Brochures

If your research involves an administrative agency, call or write the agency. Find out what agency reports, brochures, or newsletters are available to the public. Such literature often provides useful background information.

7. Committee Reports

Many research projects involve one or more statutes. Before statutes are passed, committees of the legislature often write reports that comment on and summarize the legislation. (See Exhibit 6.5 in chapter 6.) In addition to being good sources of legislative history on the statute, the reports are excellent background reading. If practical, contact both houses of the legislature to find out which committees acted on the statute. If the statute is fairly recent, they may be able to send you copies of the **committee reports** or tell you where to obtain them. If you live near the library of the legislature, you may be able to find committee reports there. The committee reports of many recent federal statutes are printed in *U.S. Code Congressional and Administrative News* (U.S.C.C.A.N.).

8. Reports/Studies of Special Interest Groups

There are *special interest* groups for almost every area of the law, e.g., unions, bar associations, environmental associations, tax associations, insurance and other business associations. They often have position papers and studies that they might be willing to send you. Although one-sided, such literature should not be ignored.

9. Martindale-Hubbell Digest

The *Digest* volume of *Martindale-Hubbell Law Directory* provides concise summaries of the law of the fifty states and many foreign countries. (See page 535.)

Our assumption here is that you are researching a topic that is totally new to you. Spend an hour or two (depending on the complexity of the area) doing some reading in law books that will provide you with an overview—a general understanding of the area. This will help you identify the major terminology, the major agencies involved, if any, and some of the major issues. Of course, while doing this background research, you will probably *also* come up with leads that will be helpful in the second and third levels of research.

All this background research will be in *secondary authority*—legal dictionaries, legal encyclopedias, legal treatises, legal periodical literature, etc. Use these materials for the limited purposes of (1) background reading and (2) providing leads to *primary authority*—particularly through footnotes. You will not have time to use all of the nine techniques of background research presented in Exhibit 11.14. Usually, one or two of the techniques is sufficient for the limited purpose of providing an overview and getting you started.

Can you ever use (e.g., quote from) secondary authority in your writing? Review page 554 on the five major dangers of relying on secondary authority. In particular, see Exhibit

11.8 on the foundation for using secondary authority in legal writing as possible persuasive authority.

Section O
Checklists for Using Ten Major Search Resources

We have said that the main objective of legal research is to locate mandatory primary authority. There are three levels of government—federal, state, and local. Exhibit 11.15 presents an overview of their primary authority.

Exhibit 11.15 Kinds of Primary Authority		
FEDERAL LEVEL OF GOVERNMENT	**STATE LEVEL OF GOVERNMENT**	**LOCAL LEVEL OF GOVERNMENT (CITY, COUNTY, ETC.)**
U.S. Constitution	State constitution	Charter
Statutes of Congress	State statutes	Local ordinances
Federal court opinions	State court opinions	Local court opinions
Federal administrative regulations	State administrative regulations	Local administrative regulations
Federal administrative decisions	State administrative decisions	Local administrative decisions
Federal rules of court	State rules of court	Local rules of court
Executive orders of the president	Executive orders of the governor	Executive orders of the mayor
Opinions of the U.S. attorney general	Opinions of the state attorney general	Opinions of the corporation counsel
Treaties		

Later in this chapter, we examine methods of finding most of these kinds of primary authority. Throughout our examination, you will be referred back to the ten checklists for the major finding tools presented here. These ten findings tools (or search resources) are often useful for locating more than one kind of primary authority. Hence they are presented together here.

Many of the ten search resources are also helpful in doing background research in the secondary sources. Indeed, some of the search resources *are* secondary sources themselves. Finally, some of the search resources are helpful in doing the third level of research—validation research, particularly via Shepard's.

In short, the following ten search resources are the foundation of legal research itself:

1. Card catalog
2. Digests
3. Annotations
4. Shepard's
5. Loose-leaf services
6. Legal periodical literature
7. Legal encyclopedias
8. Legal treatises
9. Phone and mail
10. Computers

"A good paralegal doesn't know all the answers; a good paralegal knows where to find all the answers."

—Terry Florian, Paralegal, McDonough, Holland & Allen

1. CARD CATALOG

A well-organized card catalog is one of the researcher's best friends. If the law library has not switched over to a completely computerized catalog, you need to learn some of the basics of the manual card catalog. Most law libraries use the *Library of Congress (LC) classification system.* Under this system, many law books have **KF call numbers.** Here is an example of a card from a card catalog:

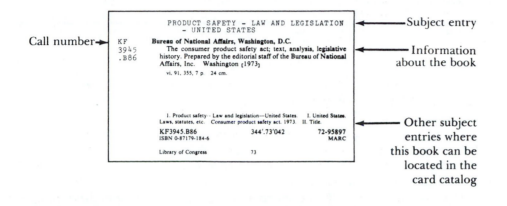

Call number →

KF 3945 .B86

PRODUCT SAFETY – LAW AND LEGISLATION – UNITED STATES

Bureau of National Affairs, Washington, D.C.
    The consumer product safety act; text, analysis, legislative history. Prepared by the editorial staff of the Bureau of National Affairs, Inc. Washington ₍1973₎
        vi, 91, 355, 7 p. 24 cm.

1. Product safety.- Law and legislation—United States.   I. United States. Laws, statutes, etc. Consumer product safety act. 1973. II. Title.

KF3945.B86   344′.73′042   72-95897
ISBN 0-87179-184-6   MARC

Library of Congress   73

→ Subject entry

→ Information about the book

→ Other subject entries where this book can be located in the card catalog

---

Checklist #1   Checklist for Using the Card Catalog

1. Find out if your law library has more than one card catalog. Is there a catalog with entries by subject matter and another with entries by author? Are there different catalogs for different topics or areas of the law? Has the library computerized its catalog? If so, be sure to use any "HELP" keys or online tutorials that are available to teach you how to conduct searches on the computer. (The remainder of this checklist covers the noncomputerized card catalog.)

2. Find out if the library has any descriptive literature on how to use the catalog.

3. Pull out a tray from the catalog at random. Thumb through the KF cards in this tray. Put a paper clip on an example of each kind of card that appears to be organized differently or that contains different kinds of information. Pick any three of these cards. Try to figure out why the cards are different. If you can't, ask a staff member of the library to briefly explain the differences.

4. Be sure you understand the card information that tells you where the books are located in the library. Some books may be on reserve, in special rooms, or in other buildings.

5. Select several KF cards at random, particularly on books housed in different locations within the same building. Try to find these books. Ask for help if you cannot locate them.

6. Now try the reverse process. Select at random three different kinds of books from the library shelves (not the same books you looked at in #5 above). Take these books to the card catalog and try to find their cards. Your goal is to become as proficient in the structure and use of the card catalog as possible. Steps #3–6 are designed to help you achieve this goal before you experience the pressure of actual research.

7. Ask a staff member what kinds of research material, if any, are *not* cataloged, such as microfilm, ultrafiche, appellate briefs, or old exams.

8. Ask a staff member what special lists of law books, if any, are in the library, such as a list of legal periodicals or a list of reserve books.

9. Ask a staff member to explain the difference between the library's card catalog and *Kardex.* (The latter is the place where many libraries keep records of current serial publications that come into the library every day.) If the library does not use Kardex, ask what it uses instead.

10. When using any card catalog, the CARTWHEEL will help you think of words and phrases to check.

11. Never antagonize the employees of a law library! You are going to need all the help you can get! Do not abuse their availability. Do not ask any questions until you first try to find the answer on your own.

☰ *A s s i g n m e n t 1 1 . 1 2*

Assignment 11.2 at the beginning of this chapter asked you to organize a system of three-by-five-inch index cards for each of the legal research words and phrases listed there. For each card with the name of a law book on it, find out where the book or set of books is located in a law library near you. Obtain this information from the card catalog or other library list, and enter it on the index cards.

2. DIGESTS

We have already examined the major *digests* and the names of reporters whose opinions are summarized (in small paragraphs) in the digests. You should review this material now. See Exhibit 11.5 on page 526.

Our focus here is on the digests of West, which are organized by the *key number system*. (For a description of this system see page 523.) Lawyers Co-operative Publishing Company also has digests for Supreme Court opinions and for its annotations in A.L.R., A.L.R.2d, etc., which are organized differently.

The beauty of the West digests is that once you know how to use one of the digests, you know how to use them all. To demonstrate this, we begin by following the journey of a court opinion from the time it arrives at West. (See Exhibit 11.16.)

E x h i b i t 1 1 . 1 6   Journey of a Court Opinion

JOURNEY OF A STATE COURT OPINION, e.g., CALIFORNIA	JOURNEY OF A FEDERAL COURT OPINION, e.g., A U.S. COURT OF APPEALS
1. The California Supreme Court sends a copy of its opinion to West Publishing Company in Minnesota.	1. The U.S. Court of Appeals sends a copy of its opinion to West Publishing Company in Minnesota.
2. West editors write brief paragraph *headnotes* for the opinion. Each headnote is a summary of a portion of the opinion.	2. West editors write brief paragraph *headnotes* for the opinion. Each headnote is a summary of a portion of the opinion.
3. The headnotes are printed at the beginning of the full text of the opinion in the reporter—here, the *Pacific Reporter 2d* (P.2d). The editors assign each of these headnotes a key number, which consists of a topic and a number, e.g., Criminal Law ☞ 1064(5).	3. The headnotes are printed at the beginning of the full text of the opinion in the reporter—here, the *Federal Reporter 3d* (F.3d). The editors assign each of these headnotes a key number, which consists of a topic and a number, e.g., Appeal and Error ☞ 1216.
4. In addition to being printed at the beginning of the opinion in P.2d, the headnotes will *also* be printed at the beginning of the advance sheet for P.2d that contains the opinion, and in the back of the bound P.2d volume that contains the opinion.	4. In addition to being printed at the beginning of the opinion in F.3d, the headnotes will *also* be printed at the beginning of the advance sheet for F.3d that contains the opinion, and in the back of the bound F.3d volume that contains the opinion.

E x h i b i t   1 1 . 1 6 **Journey of a Court Opinion—continued**

JOURNEY OF A STATE COURT OPINION, e.g., CALIFORNIA	**JOURNEY OF A FEDERAL COURT OPINION, e.g., A U.S. COURT OF APPEALS**

5. This headnote is *also* printed in the appropriate digests of West. The above example will go in the "C" volume of these digests where "Criminal Law" is covered. The headnote will be placed under key number 1064(5) of Criminal Law along with summaries of other opinions on the same or similar areas of law. In what digests will such headnotes from a recent California opinion be printed? The list follows:

- All headnotes of P.2d cases go into the *American Digest System*. First, the headnote goes into a *General Digest* volume. After a ten-year period (in two five-year intervals), all the *General Digests* are thrown away, with the material in them printed in the next *Decennial Digest*.
- All headnotes of P.2d cases are *also* printed in its regional digest—the *Pacific Digest*.
- All headnotes of California cases in P.2d are *also* printed in the individual state digest—the *California Digest*.

6. Hence, the headnote from the California opinion will be printed:

- at the beginning of the opinion in P.2d.
- at the beginning of the P.2d advance sheet containing the opinion.
- at the end of the bound P.2d volume containing the opinion.
- in the *American Digest System* (first in the *General Digest* and then in the *Decennial Digest*).
- in the regional digest—*Pacific Digest*.

5. This headnote is *also* printed in the appropriate digests of West. The above example will go in the "A" volume of these digests where "Appeal and Error" is covered. The headnote will be placed under key number 1216 of Appeal and Error along with summaries of other opinions on the same or similar areas of law. In what digests will such headnotes from a recent F.3d opinion be printed? The list follows:

- All headnotes of F.3d cases go into the *American Digest System*. First, the headnote goes into a *General Digest* volume. After a ten-year period (in two five-year intervals), all the *General Digests* are thrown away with the material in them printed in the next *Decennial Digest*.
- All headnotes of F.3d cases are *also* printed in the most current federal digest—the *Federal Practice Digest 4th*.
- If our F.3d case dealt with a particular state, the headnotes of the F.3d case will *also* be printed in the individual state digest of that state.

6. Hence, the headnote from the opinion of the U.S. Court of Appeals will be printed:

- at the beginning of the opinion in F.3d.
- at the beginning of the F.3d advance sheet containing the opinion.
- at the end of the bound F.3d volume containing the opinion.
- in the *American Digest System* (first in the *General Digest* and then in the *Decennial Digest*).

continued

E x h i b i t 1 1 . 1 6	**Journey of a Court Opinion— continued**

JOURNEY OF A STATE COURT OPINION, e.g., CALIFORNIA	**JOURNEY OF A FEDERAL COURT OPINION, e.g., A U.S. COURT OF APPEALS**
• in the individual state digest— *California Digest*. In all the above digests, the headnote will be printed in the "C" volume for Criminal Law under number 1064(5) along with headnotes from other opinions on the same or similar area of the law.	• in the *Federal Practice Digest 4th.* • in a state digest if the F.3d case dealt with a particular state. In all the above digests, the headnote will be printed in the "A" volume for Appeal and Error under number 1216 along with headnotes from other opinions on the same or similar area of the law.
7. Finally, West publishes all of these opinions and headnotes on WESTLAW, its computer research system.	**7.** Finally, West publishes all of these opinions and headnotes on WESTLAW, its computer research system.

Keep the following points in mind about Exhibit 11.16:

- The state court opinions printed in West's reporters from the other forty-nine states go through the process or journey outlined in the *first* column of Exhibit 11.16 for California. Of course, different states have their own reporters and digests (see Exhibit 11.5), but the process is the same.
- All U.S. District Court opinions printed in *Federal Supplement* (F. Supp.) go through the process or journey outlined in the *second* column of Exhibit 11.16.
- All U.S. Supreme Court opinions printed in *Supreme Court Reporter* (S. Ct.) go through the process or journey outlined in the *second* column of Exhibit 11.16. (For additional digests that summarize all U.S. Supreme Court opinions, see Exhibit 11.5.)

Assume that you are doing research on the right of a citizen to speak in a public park. You find that West's digests cover this subject under the following key number:

Constitutional Law ☞ 211

West publishes about sixty digests—state, federal, and national. You can go to the "C" volume of *any* of these sixty digests, turn to "Constitutional Law" and look for number "211" under it. Do you want only Idaho case law? If so, go to Constitutional Law ☞ 211 in the *Idaho Digest*. Do you want only case law from the states in the western United States? If so, go to Constitutional Law ☞ 211 in the *Pacific Digest*. Do you want only current federal case law? If so, go to Constitutional Law ☞ 211 in the *Federal Practice Digest 4th*. Do you want only U.S. Supreme Court cases? If so, go to Constitutional Law ☞ 211 in the *U.S. Supreme Court Digest* (West).

Do you want the case law of *every* court in the country? If so, trace Constitutional Law ☞ 211 through the three units of the American Digest System:

- Go to Constitutional Law ☞ 211 in every *General Digest* volume.
- Go to Constitutional Law ☞ 211 in every *Decennial Digest*.
- Go to the equivalent number for Constitutional Law ☞ 211 in the *Century Digest*.

To **trace a key number** through the *American Digest System* means to find out what case law, if any, is summarized under its topic and number in every unit of the American Digest System. (For the *Century Digest*, you will need an equivalent number, since there are no key numbers in the *Century Digest*. See step 8 in checklist #2.)

One final point: The headnotes and digests we are discussing are written by a private publishing company—West. You never quote headnotes or digests in your legal writing. They cannot be authority—primary or secondary. They are mere leads to case law.

Checklist #2   Checklist for Using the Digests of West

1. Locate the right digests for your research problem. This is determined by identifying the kind of case law you want to find. State? Federal? Both? Review pages 524 ff. on the American Digest System, the four regional digests, the five major federal digests, the two digests for U.S. Supreme Court cases (only one of which is a West digest), the individual state digests, etc. You must know what kind of case law is summarized in each of these digests. See the chart in Exhibit 11.5.

2. Find a key number to cover your research problem. There are thousands of topics and subtopics in West's digests. How do you find the ones relevant to your research problem? There are eight techniques:

• Descriptive Word Index (DWI). Every digest has a **DWI.** Use the CARTWHEEL to help you locate key topics in the DWI.

• Table of Contents. There are approximately 400 main topics (e.g., Constitutional Law, Criminal Law), which are scattered throughout the volumes of the digest you are using. At the beginning of each main topic, you will find a table of contents. If you can find one of these main topics in the general area of your research, you then use its table of contents to locate specific key numbers. These tables of contents have different names: "Scope Note," "Analysis," or "Subjects Included." Use the CARTWHEEL to help you locate key numbers in them.

• Headnote in West Reporter. Suppose that you already have an opinion on point. You are reading its full text in a West reporter. Go to the most relevant headnotes at the beginning of this opinion. (For example, see the search and seizure headnotes at the beginning of the *Bruni* opinion on page 352 of chapter 7.) Each headnote has a key number. Use this key number to go to any of the digests to try to find *more* case law under that number.

• Table of Cases in the Digests. Suppose again that you already have an opinion on point. You are reading its full text in a reporter. Go to the table of cases in the American Digest System or in any other digest that covers the reporter your opinion is in. Look up the name of the case in this table of cases. There you will find out what key numbers that case is digested under in the digest. Go to those key numbers in the body of the digest to find that case summarized along with *other* cases under the same key numbers. (Note: the table of cases in some West digests is called *Plaintiff-Defendant Table* or *Defendant-Plaintiff Table*, depending on which party's name comes first. The Defendant-Plaintiff Table is useful if you happen to know only the name of the defendant or if you want many cases where the same party was sued, e.g., General Motors. Defendant-Plaintiff Tables usually refer you back to the Plaintiff-Defendant Table, where the key numbers are listed.)

• Library References in a West Statutory Code. After West prints the full text of statutes in the statutory codes it publishes, it also provides research references, such as Historical Note, Cross References, Library References, and Notes of Decisions. The Library References give you key numbers on topics covered in the statutes. For an example, see page 629 containing an excerpt from a statutory code (§ 146). After the text of the statute, there are Library References to two key numbers: Prisons 13, and Reformatories 7. Hence, a West statutory code has given you a lead to a key number, which you can take to any of the West digests to find case law.

• Library References in West's *Corpus Juris Secundum* (C.J.S.). As we have seen, C.J.S. is a legal encyclopedia that summarizes almost every area of the law. In addition, it often provides "Library References" to key numbers on the topics summarized in the encyclopedia. Hence, a West encyclopedia has given you a lead

continued

to a key number, which you can take to any of the West digests to find case law.

- Key Number References That Are Part of Annotations in *Recent* Volumes of A.L.R.5th and A.L.R. Fed. (There are *no* key number references in earlier volumes of A.L.R. 5th and A.L.R. Fed. Nor are there any in A.L.R. First, A.L.R.2d, A.L.R.3d, and A.L.R.4th.)
- WESTLAW. As we will see in chapter 13, one of the searches you can make on WESTLAW is a digest field search, which will give you almost instant access to the millions of headnotes printed in West digests.

3. Assume that while using the Descriptive Word Index (DWI) in any of the digests, you come across a key number that appears to be relevant to your research problem. But when you go to check that number in the body of the digest, you find no case law, and the phrase "See Scope Note for Analysis." The DWI has, in effect, led you to nonexistent case law! The editors are telling you that there are no cases digested under this key number *at this time*. Go to the table of contents for the main topic you are in (see step #2 above). Check the Scope Note there to see if you can find a more productive key number. Or, go to a different digest to see if you will have more luck with your original key number.

4. The West editors occasionally add new topics and numbers to the key number system. Hence, you may find topics and numbers in later digest volumes that are not in earlier digest volumes.

5. The first key number under most topics and subtopics is often labeled "In General." This is obviously a broad category. Many researchers make the mistake of overlooking it in their quest for more specific topic headings. Go after more specific key numbers, but do not neglect this general one.

6. The West digests obviously duplicate each other in some respects. The American Digest System, for example, contains everything that is in all the other digests. A regional digest will duplicate everything found in the individual state digests covered in that region. (See the chart in Exhibit 11.5.) It is wise, nevertheless, to check more than one digest. Some digests may be more up-to-date than others in your library. You may miss something in one digest that you will catch in another.

7. Be sure you know all the units of the most comprehensive digest—the American Digest System: *Century Digest, Decennial Digests, General Digest.* These units are distinguished solely by the period of time covered by each unit. Know what these periods of time are: *Century Digest* (1658–1896), *Decennial Digest* (ten-year periods), *General Digest* (the period since the last *Decennial Digest* was printed).

8. At the time the *Century Digest* was printed, West had not invented the key number system. Hence, topics are listed in the *Century Digest* by *section* numbers rather than by key numbers. Assume that you started your research in the *Century Digest.* You located a relevant section number and you now want to trace this number through the *Decennial Digests* and *General Digests.* To do this, you need a corresponding *key* number. There is a parallel table in volume 21 of the First Decennial that will tell you the corresponding *key* number for any *section* number in the *Century Digest.* Suppose, however, that you started your research in the *Decennial Digests* or the *General Digests.* You have a key number and now want to find its corresponding section number in the *Century Digest.* In the First and Second Decennial, there is a "see" reference under the *key* number that will tell you the corresponding *section* number in the *Century Digest.*

9. Tricks of the trade are also needed in using the *General Digest,* which covers the most recent period since the last *Decennial Digest* was printed. When the current ten-year period is over, all the *General Digest* will be thrown away. The material in them will be consolidated or cumulated into the next *Decennial Digest* (which is issued in two parts beginning with the Ninth Decennial). When you go to use the *General Digest,* there may be twenty to thirty bound volumes on the shelf. To be thorough in tracing a key number in the *General Digests,* you must check *all* these bound volumes. There is, however, one shortcut. Look for the *Table of Key Numbers* within the *General Digests.* This table tells you which *General Digests* contain anything under the key number you are searching. You do not have to check the other *General Digests.*

3. ANNOTATIONS

An annotation is a set of notes or commentary on something. It is, in effect, a research paper. The most extensive *annotations* are those of the Lawyers Co-operative Publishing Company in the following six sets of books:

A.L.R.   A.L.R.4th
American Law Reports, First   *American Law Reports, Fourth*
A.L.R.2d   A.L.R.5th
American Law Reports, Second   *American Law Reports, Fifth*
A.L.R.3d   A.L.R. Fed.
American Law Reports, Third   *American Law Reports, Federal*

All six sets are reporters in that they print opinions in full. They are *annotated reporters* in that notes or commentaries are provided with each opinion in the form of an annotation. Unlike West reporters, these A.L.R. reporters contain only a small number of opinions. The editors select opinions raising novel or interesting issues, which then become the basis of an annotation. The following is an example of an annotation found on page 1015, volume 91 of A.L.R.3d:

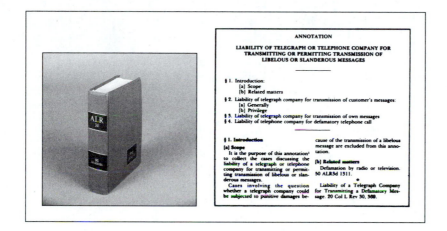

One of the joys of legal research is to find an annotation on point. A wealth of information is contained in annotations, such as a comprehensive, state-by-state survey of law on an issue. A single annotation often contains hundreds of citations to court opinions. Picture yourself having the capacity to hire your own team of researchers to go out and spend weeks finding just about everything there is on a particular point of law. While none of us is likely to have this luxury, we do have a close equivalent in the form of annotations in the six sets of *American Law Reports*. They are a gold mine of research references. Since there are hundreds of volumes in these six sets, the chances are very good that you will find an annotation that is *on point*, i.e., that covers the facts of our research problem.

Most of the references in the annotations are to case law. Their primary service, therefore, is to act as a case finder. Because of this, the annotation system of Lawyers Co-op is the major competitor of the other massive case finders—the digests of West. It is to our advantage that each system claims to do a better job than the other. Their competition has led to a rich source of material at our disposal.

The annotations cover both federal and state law. A.L.R. First, A.L.R.2d, and most of A.L.R.3d cover both state and federal law. The later volumes of A.L.R.3d and all of A.L.R.4th and 5th cover mainly state law. A.L.R. Fed. covers only federal law. The annotations in these six sets do not follow any particular order. There may be an annotation on zoning, for example, followed by an annotation on defective wheels on baby carriages. The annotations in A.L.R. First and A.L.R.2d are older than the annotations in the other sets, but this is not significant because all of the annotations can be updated.

We turn now to the two major concerns of the researcher:

- How do you find an annotation on point?
- How do you update an annotation that you have found?

As you will see, it is much easier to find and update annotations in A.L.R.3d, A.L.R.4th, A.L.R.5th, and A.L.R. Fed. than in the earlier A.L.R. First and A.L.R.2d.

(a) Finding an Annotation on Point

The major ways of *finding* annotations on point are outlined in Exhibit 11.17. These methods are most useful when you are at the very beginning of your search and have no leads. As you can see in Exhibit 11.17, the six sets of A.L.R.s do not have the same index system: the multivolume *ALR Index* covers all of the sets (except for A.L.R. First), a Quick

Exhibit 11.17	**Finding Annotations When You Have No Leads**		
INDEX SYSTEMS FOR A.L.R. FIRST	**INDEX SYSTEMS FOR A.L.R.2d**	**INDEX SYSTEMS FOR A.L.R.3d, A.L.R.4th, A.L.R.5th**	**INDEX SYSTEMS FOR A.L.R. FED.**
• *ALR First Series Quick Index* • *Permanent ALR Digest*	• *ALR Index* • LEXIS • *ALR2d Digest*	• *ALR Index* • *ALR Quick Index 3d, 4th, 5th* • LEXIS • WESTLAW • *ALR Digest to 3d, 4th, 5th, Federal*	• *ALR Index* • *ALR Federal Quick Index* • LEXIS • WESTLAW • *ALR Digest to 3d, 4th, 5th, Federal*

Index volume covers all of the sets (except for A.L.R.2d), a LEXIS search will lead you to annotations in all the sets (except for A.L.R. First), and a WESTLAW search will lead you to annotations in all sets (except for A.L.R. First and A.L.R. 2d). Finally, all six sets have digests that provide summaries of the annotations in them. Although more awkward to use, these digests can serve as indexes to the annotations in all the sets.

Exhibit 11.18 tells you what to do if you are further along in your research and already have an opinion (state or federal), a statute (state or federal), or a regulation (federal) that is on point, or potentially on point. Use the methods listed in the second column of Exhibit 11.18 to try to find any annotations that discuss or mention that opinion, statute, or regulation.

In the next section, we will see that annotations are one of the "citing materials" in Shepard's. This simply means that the annotations have discussed or mentioned whatever you are shepardizing. Hence, if you shepardize the items in the first column of Exhibit 11.18,

Exhibit 11.18	Finding Annotations When You Aleady Have a Lead
IF YOU ALREADY HAVE A CITATION TO:	**USE THE FOLLOWING METHODS OF FINDING ANNOTATIONS THAT MENTION THAT CITATION:**
A State Court Opinion	• Shepardize the opinion. • Check Auto-Cite (on LEXIS).
A Federal Court Opinion	• Shepardize the opinion. • Check Auto-Cite (on LEXIS).
A State Statute	• Shepardize the statute.
A Federal Statute	• Shepardize the statute. • Check the "Table of Laws, Rules, and Regulations" in the last volume of *ALR Index*.
A Federal Regulation	• Shepardize the regulation. • Check the "Table of Laws, Rules, and Regulations" in the last volume of *ALR Index*.

you will be led to all annotations, if any, that have mentioned that item. If you have access to Auto-Cite (available on LEXIS), this computer service will tell you what annotations have mentioned your federal or state court opinion. Finally, use the *"Table of Laws, Rules, and Regulations"* to find annotations on a federal statute (in U.S.C., U.S.C.A., or U.S.C.S.) or on a federal administrative regulation (in C.F.R.). This excellent table is located in the last volume of the *ALR Index*. (See end of Exhibit 11.18.)

As indicated earlier, some of the annotations in the six sets are very long and comprehensive. How do you find the law of a *particular* state or court within an annotation without having to read the entire annotation? At the beginning of annotations in A.L.R.3d and A.L.R.4th, you will find a *"Table of Jurisdictions Represented,"* which will direct you to specific sections of the annotation that cover the law of your state. At the beginning of annotations in A.L.R. Fed., there is a *"Table of Courts and Circuits,"* which will direct you to sections of the annotation dealing with certain federal courts. In addition to these tables, there will usually be other indexes or tables of contents at the beginning of the annotations.

TABLE OF JURISDICTIONS REPRESENTED
Consult POCKET PART in this volume for later cases

US: §§ 2[b]. 3. 4[a]. 5[b]. 6[a]. 7[a]. 10[b]
Ala: §§ 2[b]. 4[a]. 6[a]. 7[a]. 8. 10[b]
Cal: §§ 4[a. b]. 7[a. b]. 10[b]. 11
Fla: §§ 5[a]
Ga: §§ 3. 4[b]. 5[b]. 6[b]. 10[a]
Ill: §§ 4[b]. 5[a. b]. 6[a. b]. 10[a]
Ind: §§ 4[a]. 5[b]. 6[a]. 7[a. b]. 8. 9. 10[b]
Iowa: §§ 7[a]. 8
Ky: §§ 3. 4[a]. 5[b]
La: §§ 5[b]. 7[a. b]
Me: §§ 5[b]. 7[a]. 10[b]
Md: §§ 4[b]
Mich: §§ 4[a]. 10[b]
Miss: §§ 4[a]
Mo: §§ 4[a]. 6[a]. 10[b]
NH: §§ 3. 4[b]
NC: §§ 7[a]
Ohio: §§ 4[a]. 6[a]. 7[a. b]. 10[b]
Or: §§ 4[a]. 10[b]
Pa: §§ 4[a]. 7[a]. 10[b]
Tenn: §§ 4[a]. 5[b]. 6[a]
Tex: §§ 4[a]. 7[a]. 10[b]
Vt: §§ 9
Wash: §§ 6[a]. 7[a]. 8
Wis: §§ 7[a]. 8. 10[b]. 11

TABLE OF COURTS AND CIRCUITS
Consult POCKET PART in this volume for later cases and statutory changes

Sup Ct: §§ 2[a]. 3[a]. 5. b. 14
First Cir: §§ 5[b]. 6[b]. 15[b]. 16[a]. 18[a]
Second Cir: §§ 2[b]. 3[a. b]. 5[a]. 12[a]. 16[a]. 18[a]
Third Cir: §§ 3[a]. 5[a]. 7. 11[b]. 12[b]. 13[a]. 15[b]
Fourth Cir: §§ 2[b]. 3[a]. 4[b]. 5[a. b]. 8. 9. 10[b]. 12[a. b]. 13[b]. 14. 15[a. b]. 16[a]. 17. 18[a]
Fifth Cir: §§ 3[a]. 5[a. b]. 8. 10[a]. 11[a. b]. 13[a]. 15[a]. 16[b]. 18[b]
Sixth Cir: §§ 5[b]. 6[b]. 10[a. b]. 12[a. b]. 13[a]. 15[b]
Seventh Cir: §§ 2[a. b]. 4[b]. 5[b]. 10[b]. 15[b]
Eighth Cir: §§ 3[a]. 4[a. b]. 5[a. b]. 6[a]. 12[a]. 13[a]. 15[b]. 16[a]. 17. 19
Ninth Cir: §§ 2[a. b]. 3[a]. 4[a]. 5. a. 6[b]. 7. 8. 10[a. b]. 11[a. b]. 12[a. b]. 13[a. b]. 15[a. b]. 16[b]. 17. 18[a. b]
Tenth Cir: §§ 2[b]. 3[a]. 5[a. b]. 6[a. b]. 9. 11[a. b]. 12[a]. 14. 17. 18[b]
Dist Col Cir: §§ 3[b]. 5[b]. 6[b]. 10[a. b]
Ct Ct: § 16[a]

The table at the beginning of annotations in A.L.R.5th is called *"Jurisdictional Table of Cited Statutes and Cases."* The state-by-state breakdown in the table includes full citations to the statutes and cases discussed in the annotation.

(b) Updating an Annotation

Suppose that you have found an annotation on point. It has led you to very useful law. This annotation, however, may be ten, twenty, thirty, or more years old. How do you update this annotation to find the most current law on the points covered in the annotation? Of course, any opinion or statute found within the annotation can be shepardized as a technique of finding more law. But our focus here is the updating systems within A.L.R. itself. Exhibit 11.19 outlines these systems.

E x h i b i t 1 1 . 1 9	**How to Update an Annotation**	
UPDATING AN ANNOTATION IN A.L.R FIRST	**UPDATING AN ANNOTATION IN A.L.R.2d**	**UPDATING AN ANNOTATION IN A.L.R.3d, A.L.R.4th, A.L.R.5th, AND A.L.R. FED.**
• *A.L.R. Blue Book of Supplemental Decisions*	• *A.L.R.2d Later Case Service*	• Pocket part of volume containing the annotation
• "Annotation History Table" in the last volume of *ALR Index*	• "Annotation History Table" in the last volume of *ALR Index*	• "Annotation History Table" in the last volume of *ALR Index*
	• 1-800-225-7488	• 1-800-225-7488

Note: Any case you find in an annotation can also be updated by shepardizing that case.

If the annotation you want updated is in A.L.R. First, start with the *A.L.R. Blue Book of Supplemental Decisions.* (Check each volume of this *Blue Book.*) If the annotation you want updated is in A.L.R.2d, start with the *A.L.R.2d Later Case Service.* (Check the volume that covers your annotation, plus the pocket part of this volume of the *Later Case Service.*) If the annotation you want updated is in A.L.R.3d, or in A.L.R.4th, or in A.L.R.5th, or in A.L.R. Fed., you check the *pocket part* of the volume containing the annotation.

There are no pocket parts to the volumes of A.L.R. First and A.L.R.2d. Hence you need the *Blue Book* and *Later Case Service* in order to perform needed updating. Thankfully, the volumes of A.L.R.3d, A.L.R.4th, A.L.R.5th, and A.L.R. Fed. *do* have pocket parts that can be used to update annotations in them. The existence of these pocket parts makes it much easier to update annotations in A.L.R.3d, A.L.R.4th, A.L.R.5th, and A.L.R. Fed. than to update annotations in A.L.R. First or A.L.R.2d.

A toll-free number is available for obtaining additional updating information on the annotations in A.L.R.2d, A.L.R.3d, A.L.R.4th, A.L.R.5th, and A.L.R. Fed. Any member of the public can use this number; you do not have to be a subscriber. Currently, the number is 1-800-225-7488. It is called the *Latest Case Service Hotline.*

One final updating feature must be covered: the *Annotation History Table.* Note that Exhibit 11.19 lists this table as a further method of updating annotations in all six sets of A.L.R. The law in some annotations may become so outdated that it is replaced by another annotation. The outdated annotation is called a **superseded annotation,** which should no longer be read. If, however, an annotation is substantially updated but not totally replaced by another annotation, the older annotation is called a **supplemented annotation,** which can be read along with the newer annotation. There are two ways to find out which annotations have been superseded or supplemented. Check the "Annotation History Table" found in the last volume of the *ALR Index*. Another way to find out is to check the standard method for updating annotations in A.L.R. First (the *Blue Book*), in A.L.R.2d *(Later Case Service)*, in A.L.R.3d (pocket parts), in A.L.R.4th (pocket parts), in A.L.R.5th (pocket parts), and in A.L.R. Fed. (pocket parts).

Note on Another Annotated Reporter of Lawyers Co-op   Lawyers Co-op publishes *United States Supreme Court Reports, Lawyers' Edition* (abbreviated L. Ed.). This is also an annotated reporter in that it prints the full text of opinions (those of the U.S. Supreme Court) with annotations on issues within some of these opinions. (See photo of this reporter on page 516.)

Checklist #3   **Checklist for Finding and Updating Annotations in A.L.R., A.L.R.2d, A.L.R.3d, A.L.R.4th, A.L.R.5th, and A.L.R. Fed.**

1. Your goal is to use the six sets to find annotations on your research problem. The annotations are extensive research papers on numerous points of law.
2. The most current annotations available are in A.L.R.3d, in A.L.R.4th, in A.L.R.5th, and in A.L.R. Fed. Start with these sets. Then try to find annotations in A.L.R.2d and in A.L.R. First. Use the CARTWHEEL to help you locate annotations in the following index resources:
   (a) To find annotations in A.L.R.3d, in A.L.R.4th, and in A.L.R.5th:
   * Use *ALR Index*.
   * Use *ALR Quick Index 3d, 4th, 5th.*
   * Use LEXIS or WESTLAW.
   * Use *ALR Digest to 3d, 4th, 5th, Federal.*
   (b) To find annotations in A.L.R. Fed.:
   * Use *ALR Index*.
   * Use *ALR Federal Quick Index.*
   * Use LEXIS or WESTLAW.
   * Use *ALR Digest to 3d, 4th, 5th, Federal.*
   (c) To find annotations in A.L.R.2d:
   * Use *ALR Index*.
   * Use LEXIS or WESTLAW.
   * Use *ALR2d Digest.*
   (d) To find annotations in A.L.R. First:
   * Use *ALR First Series Quick Index.*
   * Use *Permanent ALR Digest.*
3. If you have already found a particular law (see list below) and you want to know if there is an annotation that mentions that law, check the following resources:
   (a) If you already have a federal opinion or a state opinion:
   * Shepardize that opinion.
   * Check Auto-Cite (in LEXIS).
   (b) If you already have a state statute:
   * Shepardize that statute.
   (c) If you already have a federal statute:
   * Shepardize that statute.
   * Check the "Table of Laws, Rules, and Regulations" in the last volume of *ALR Index*.
   (d) If you already have a federal administrative regulation:
   * Shepardize that regulation.
   * Check the "Table of Laws, Rules, and Regulations" in the last volume of *ALR Index*.
4. Use the tables or other indexes at the beginning of the annotation to help you locate specific sections of the annotation. (Before you spend much time with the annotation, however, check the "Annotation History Table" to determine if it has been superseded or supplemented by another annotation. See step 5 below.)
5. Update all annotations that are on point.
   (a) To update an annotation in A.L.R. First:
   * Check the *A.L.R. Blue Book of Supplemental Decisions.*
   * Check the "Annotation History Table" in the last volume of *ALR Index*.
   (b) To update an annotation in A.L.R.2d:
   * Check the *A.L.R.2d Later Case Service.*
   * Check the "Annotation History Table" in the last volume of *ALR Index*.
   * Call 1-800-225-7488.

continued

(c) To update an annotation in A.L.R.3d, in A.L.R.4th, in A.L.R.5th, or in A.L.R. Fed.:
- Check the pocket part.
- Check the "Annotation History Table" in the last volume of *ALR Index*.
- Call 1-800-225-7488.

6. Within the six sets of annotations, Lawyers Co-op will give you lists of its other publications (e.g., Am.Jur.2d) that cover the same or similar topics in its annotations. As we saw earlier, the main vehicle used to provide these leads is the list called Total Client-Service Library References. (See page 543.)

4. SHEPARD'S

There have been four great research inventions in the law:

- The key number system of the West digests
- The annotations in A.L.R., A.L.R.2d, A.L.R.3d, A.L.R.4th, A.L.R.5th, and A.L.R. Fed
- *CALR* (Computer Assisted Legal Research), particularly WESTLAW and LEXIS
- Shepard's

The first three are extensively used as case finders. While Shepard's is not primarily designed to be a case finder, it can serve this function, along with other functions, as we shall now see.

Before we examine Shepard's and the techniques of *shepardizing*, you should review the material starting on page 538 covering the kinds of Shepard's volumes that exist, the material on page 560 covering the use of Shepard's as one of the six techniques of finding a parallel cite, and the material on page 512 describing an *advance sheet* for Shepard's.

Shepard's is a *citator*, which means that it contains lists of citations that help you assess the current validity of a law and that gives you leads to more laws. We will examine Shepard's through the following topics:

(a) The units of a set of Shepard's
(b) Determining whether you have a complete set of Shepard's
(c) The distinction between *cited material* and *citing material*
(d) Abbreviations in Shepard's
(e) Shepardizing a case (court opinion)
(f) Shepardizing a statute
(g) Shepardizing a regulation

We will limit ourselves to shepardizing cases, statutes, and regulations. Knowing how to shepardize these items, however, will go a long way toward equipping you to shepardize other items as well (such as constitutions, administrative decisions, charters, and rules of court).

(a) The Units of a Set of Shepard's

By "set of Shepard's" we mean the group of volumes of Shepard's that cover whatever you are trying to shepardize. Every set of Shepard's includes two main units: (a) *hardcover* red volumes and (b) white, gold, blue, gray, yellow, or red *pamphlet* supplements. The hardcover volumes and the pamphlet supplements are sometimes broken into parts, e.g., Part 1, Part 2. The white pamphlet is the advance sheet (page 513) that is later thrown away and cumulated (or consolidated) into a larger pamphlet. Eventually, all the pamphlets are thrown away and cumulated into hardcover red volumes. The pamphlet supplements contain the most current shepardizing material.

(b) Determining Whether You Have a Complete Set of Shepard's

You should not try to shepardize anything until you are satisfied that the set of Shepard's on the shelf in front of you is complete. As we saw above, Shepard's comes in sets, e.g., the set of Shepards for United States statutes, the set for New Mexico laws. You need a complete set in order to shepardize. To determine whether you have a complete set, go through the following steps:

1. Pick up the most recently dated pamphlet supplement—usually the advance sheet—that the library has received for that set of Shepard's (see photo on page 513). The date is at the top of the supplement. What you find on the shelf, however, may *not* be the most recent; someone else may be using it or it may have been misshelved. To determine the most recent Shepard's supplement received by the library, check the computer catalog. Type in the name of the set of Shepard's. Among the information provided, the computer should tell you the most recent supplement received by the library. (If not, ask a librarian how you can determine what is the most recent.)

2. Once you are satisfied that you have the most recent unit, find the following statement on the front cover: WHAT YOUR LIBRARY SHOULD CONTAIN. This will tell you what is a complete set of Shepard's for the set you are using. Go down the list and make sure everything you are told should be on the shelf is indeed there. (The last entry on the list should be the pamphlet supplement that contains the list you are reading.)

3. Some sets of Shepard's have an even more recent supplement called Shepard's EXPRESS Citations. If one exists for the set you are using, you need to check it as well.

Assume, for example, that today's date is September 1995. You want to shepardize a Washington State case and a Washington State statute. You go to *Shepard's Washington Citations.* On the front cover of a September 1995 advance sheet for this set of Shepard's, you find the following:

WHAT YOUR LIBRARY SHOULD CONTAIN

1994 Bound Volume, Cases* (Parts 1–3)
1994 Bound Volume, Statutes* (Parts 1, 2)
*Supplemented with:
   –*October, 1994 Annual Cumulativbe Supplement Vol. 87
    No. 2*
   –*Sept., 1995 Cumulative Supplement Vol. 88 No. 3*
   –*Sept., 1995 Advance Sheet–Express Update Vol. 88
    No. 3A*

DESTROY ALL OTHER ISSUES

SEE TABLE OF CONTENTS ON PAGE III

To be complete, therefore, the following units of *Shepard's Washington Citations* should be on the shelf:

- a 1994 bound volume of *Shepard's Washington Citations* covering cases (Part 1); *and*
- a 1994 bound volume of *Shepard's Washington Citations* covering cases (Part 2); *and*

- a 1994 bound volume of *Shepard's Washington Citations* covering cases (Part 3); *and*
- a 1994 bound volume of *Shepard's Washington Citations* covering statutes (Part 1); *and*
- a 1994 bound volume of *Shepard's Washington Citations* covering statutes (Part 2); *and*
- an October 1994 Annual Cumulative Supplement of *Shepard's Washington Citations*, Vol. 87, No. 2; *and*
- a September 1995 Cumulative Supplement of *Shepard's Washington Citations*, Vol. 88, No. 3; *and*
- a September 1995 Advance Sheet–Express Update of *Shepard's Washington Citations*, Vol. 88, No. 3A

The last item on the list is always the pamphlet that contains the list you are reading. Hence, the above list is found on the September 1995 Advance Sheet pamphlet of *Shepard's Washington Citations,* Vol. 88, No. 3A.

Occasionally, the list can become quite involved. For example, you may find two lists on the pamphlet. One list tells you what should be on the shelf before a certain bound Shepard's volume is received by the library, and a second list tells you what should be on the shelf after that bound volume is received by the library. Yet the same process is followed. Carefully go through the list (or lists) one unit at a time, checking to see if what the list says should be on the shelf is there.

(c) The Distinction between "Cited Material" and "Citing Material"

- **Cited material** is whatever you are shepardizing, such as a case, statute, or regulation.
- **Citing material** is whatever mentions or discusses the cited material, such as another case, a legal periodical article, an annotation in A.L.R., etc.

Suppose you are shepardizing the case found in 75 F.2d 107 (a case that begins on page 107 of volume 75 of Federal Reporter 2d). While reading through the columns of Shepard's, you find the following cite: f56 S.E.2d 46. The *cited* material is 75 F.2d 107. The *citing* material is 56 S.E.2d 46, which followed (f) or agreed with the decision in 75 F.2d 107.

Suppose you are shepardizing a statute: 22 U.S.C. § 55.8 (section 55.8 of title 22 of the United States Code). While reading through the columns of Shepard's, you find the following cite: 309 U.S. 45. The *cited* material is 22 U.S.C. § 55.8. The *citing* material is 309 U.S. 45, which interpreted or mentioned 22 U.S.C. § 55.8.

Shepard's always indicates the cited material by the black bold print along the top of every page of Shepard's and by the black bold print numbers that are the volume or section numbers of the cited material. In the following excerpt, the cited material is 404 P.2d 460. The citing material follows the number **460:**

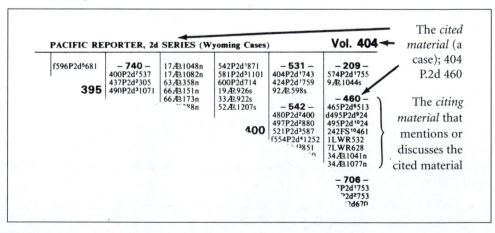

In the following excerpt, the cited material is a statute: § 37–31 of the Wyoming Statutes. The citing material is indicated beneath § **37–31.**

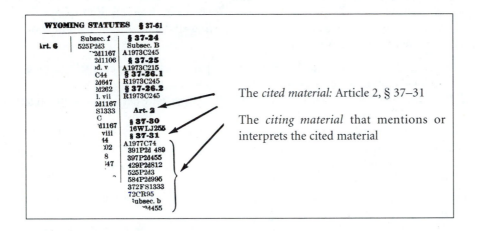

The *cited material:* Article 2, § 37–31

The *citing material* that mentions or interprets the cited material

(d) Abbreviation in Shepard's

Shepard's packs a tremendous amount of information (the cites) into every one of its pages. Each page contains up to eight columns of cites for the cited and the citing materials. For the sake of economy, Shepard's uses many abbreviations that are peculiar to Shepard's. For example:

FS   → means Federal Supplement

A3 → means American Law Reports 3d

* → means that a regulation of a particular year was discussed

Δ → means that a regulation was discussed without mentioning the year of the regulation

Most researchers do not know the meaning of every abbreviation and signal used by Shepard's. *But you must know where to find their meaning.* There are two places to go:

- The abbreviations tables at the beginning of most units of Shepard's (for an example, see page 580).
- The preface or explanation pages found at the beginning of most units of Shepard's.

Many researchers neglect the latter. Buried within the preface or explanation pages may be an interpretation of an abbreviation or symbol that is not covered in the abbreviation tables.

(e) Shepardizing a Case (Court Opinion)

Almost every reporter has a corresponding set of Shepard's, which will enable you to shepardize cases in that reporter (page 541). For example, if the case you want to shepardize is 193 Mass. 364, you go to the set of Shepard's that covers cases in Massachusetts Reports—*Shepard's Massachusetts Citations.* If the case you want to shepardize is 402 F.2d 1064, you go to the Shepard's that covers F.2d cases—*Shepard's Federal Citations.*

Of course, many cases have *parallel cites*—the case is found word-for-word in more than one reporter. You can shepardize most cases with parallel cites through *either* reporter. Assume you want to shepardize the following case:

Welch v. Swasey, 193 Mass. 364, 79 N.E. 745 (1907).

This case is found in two reporters: *Massachusetts Reports* and *North Eastern Reporter*. Hence, you can shepardize the case and obtain similar citing material from two different sets of Shepard's: *Shepard's Massachusetts Citations* and *Shepard's Northeastern Citations*. A thorough researcher will shepardize his or her case by using *both* sets of Shepard's.

To shepardize a *case* means to obtain the following six kinds of information about the cited case (the case you are shepardizing):

1. The parallel cite of the case. The first entry in parenthesis is the parallel cite. (See page 560 for the reasons why you may find no parallel cite here.)
2. The history of the case. Here you will find all cases that are part of the same litigation, e.g., appeals, reversals.
3. Citing cases that have analyzed or mentioned the cited case—for example, followed it, distinguished it, or just mentioned it.
4. Citing legal periodical literature (law review articles, case notes, etc.) that has analyzed or mentioned the cited case.
5. Citing annotations in A.L.R., A.L.R.2d, A.L.R.3d, A.L.R.4th, A.L.R.5th, or A.L.R. Fed. that have analyzed or mentioned the cited case.
6. Citing opinions of the attorney general that have analyzed or mentioned the cited case.

The great value of Shepard's as a case finder comes through items 3 to 5. If a *citing case* mentions or discusses the cited case, the two cases probably deal with similar facts and law. All citing cases, therefore, are potential leads to more case law on point. Similarly, a citing legal periodical article or annotation will probably discuss a variety of cases in addition to the cited case. Hence again, you are led to more case law through Shepard's.

Items 2 and 3 above also enable you to do validation research (page 644). They help you determine if the cited case is still good law. Has it been reversed? Has it been discussed with approval by citing cases? Has it been ignored by other courts?

One final point before examining an excerpt from a Shepard's page. Recall that cases in reporters are broken down into headnotes at the beginning of the case (page 529). These headnotes are written by a private publisher such as West. Shepard's calls these headnotes of the case the **syllabus** of the case—small-paragraph summaries of portions of the case found at the beginning of the case.[4]

A case can involve many issues, only a few of which may be relevant to your research problem. Is it possible to narrow your shepardizing to those parts of the case that are most relevant to your research problem? Yes. It is possible to shepardize a portion of a case through its *headnote* or *syllabus numbers*. In effect, you are *shepardizing the headnote!* How is this done?

- Every headnote or syllabus paragraph of the *cited* case has a consecutive number: 1, 2, 3, 4, etc.
- When the editors of Shepard's come across a *citing* case that deals with only one of the headnotes or syllabus paragraphs of the *cited* case, they include the number of this headnote or syllabus paragraph as part of the reference to the *citing* case in the columns of Shepard's.
- The number is printed as a small raised, or elevated, number—called a small superior figure—within the reference to the *citing* case.[5]

---

[4]There are two main meanings of the word *syllablus*. First, it refers to the one-paragraph summary of an entire case printed at the beginning of the case below the caption. For an example, see the *Bruni* case in chapter 7 (page 352). Second, it is the name that Shepard's uses for the headnotes of a case.
[5]A raised or elevated figure is called a *superscript* character in the language of printing.

Be careful. It is easy to become confused. The superior figure refers to the headnote or syllabus number of the *cited* case, not the citing case.

For example, assume again that you are shepardizing *Welch v. Swasey,* 193 Mass. 364. In the columns of Shepard's you find the following:

f193Mas⁸476

The *citing* case is 193 Mass. 476. This case follows (agrees with) the *cited* case of: *Welch v. Swasey,* 193 Mass. 364. Note the raised number 8—the superior figure. This 8 refers to the eighth headnote or syllabus of the *cited* case, *Welch v. Swasey.* The *citing* case dealt with that portion of *Welch* that was summarized in the eighth headnote or syllabus of the *Welch* case. Again, do not make the mistake of thinking that the small raised number refers to a headnote or syllabus in the citing case. It refers to a headnote or syllabus number of the *cited* case.

We now look at a sample or specimen page from *Shepard's Massachusetts Citations* (see Exhibit 11.20), where we will begin to shepardize *Welch v. Swasey,* 193 Mass. 364. Read the oval inserts on this specimen page now—before carefully studying the following comments.

Let us assume that in your legal research you have located the case of *Welch v. Swasey,* reported in volume 193 of Massachusetts Reports at page 364. This again is the cited case that we want to shepardize.

The specimen page contains a reproduction of page 726 in the 1967 Case Edition of *Shepard's Massachusetts Citations.* Note the number of the volume of reports, "Vol. 193," in the upper left corner of the page.

Find our page number in bold print "—**364**—" in the third column. (See the arrow.) This is the initial page of our cited case under consideration. Following this page number you will find the citations (79NE745), (118AS523), (23Lns1160), indicating that the same case is also reported in 79 *North Eastern Reporter* 745, 118 *American State Reports* 523, and 23 *Lawyers Reports Annotated, New Series* 1160. These are parallel citations. As indicated earlier, abbreviations are explained at the beginning of Shepard's volumes.

Next comes the history of the cited case. On appeal to the United States Supreme Court, our cited case was affirmed "a" in 214US91 (also printed in 53LE923 and in 29SC567). Also, the cited case has been followed "f" and distinguished "d" in subsequent cases of the Massachusetts and federal courts.

In the citation f242 Mas⁶34 (see top of next column), the small superior figure ⁶ before the citing page number 34 indicates that the principle of law brought out in the sixth paragraph of the syllabus (i.e., of the headnotes) of 193 Mass. 364 has been followed in 242 Mass. 34.

This case has also been cited in several legal periodicals: *Harvard Law Review* "HLR," *Boston University Law Review* "BUR," and *Massachusetts Law Quarterly* "MQ." These constitute citing legal periodical materials or references.

The citations appearing in annotations of the *American Law Reports* are grouped together after the legal periodical citing references.

By examining the same volume and page number of the cited case in the other bound volumes and supplement pamphlets of *Shepard's Massachusetts Citations,* more citing material for this case will be found. Your goal is to obtain all the citing material available in Shepard's, up to the current date.

Recently, Shepard's added a new feature to its case citations. Beneath the page number of the cited case, Shepard's now spells out the name of the cited case and its year of decision. Assume, for example, that you wanted to shepardize the case of *Greer v. Northwestern*

Exhibit 11.20 Excerpt from Shepard's Page (Cases)

SPECIMEN PAGE—Shepard's Massachusetts Citations, Case Edition, 1967

Vol. 193 **MASSACHUSETTS REPORTS**

Callout annotations (in rounded boxes):

- Followed with reference to paragraph six of syllabus
- Cited by lower federal court
- Cited in Boston University Law Review
- Cited in Harvard Law Review
- Cited in Massachusetts Law Quarterly
- Cited in annotations of Annotated Reports System
- Same case reported in Northeastern Reporter, American State Reports and Lawyers Reports Annotated, New Series
- Affirmed by United States Supreme Court
- Distinguished with reference to paragraph eight of syllabus

For later citations see any subsequent bound supplement or volume, the current issue of the periodically published paper-covered cumulative supplement and any current issue of the advance sheet.

National Insurance Co., 109 Wash.2d 191 (1987). If you went to *Shepard's Washington Citations*, here is what you might find:

Vol. 109	**WASHINGTON REPORTS, 2d SERIES**

70TxL604
17PcL249
17PcL269
AE§ 1.13

—191—

Greer v
Northwestern
National
Insurance Co.
1987

(743P2d1244)
s 36WAp330
j 109Wsh2d745
111Wsh2d³456
112Wsh2d²11
113Wsh2d⁵94
50WAp³572
54WAp¹339

Name of the case you are
sheardizing—the cited case

Note that the name of the cited case is spelled out beneath its opening page number—191.

Checklist #4a   Checklist for Shepardizing a Case

1. You have a case you want to shepardize. In what reporter is this case found? Go to the set of Shepard's in the library that covers this reporter. (See page 538.)
2. If the case you want to shepardize has a *parallel cite* that you already have, find out if the library has a set of Shepard's for the other reporter volumes in which the case is also printed. You may be able to shepardize the case through more than one set of Shepard's. A thorough researcher will shepardize a case through all available sets of Shepard's. (There are sets of Shepard's for the individual state official reports and for all the reporters of West's unofficial National Reporter System. See page 519.)
3. Know whether you have a complete set of Shepard's in front of you by reading the "What Your Library Should Contain" list on the most recent pamphlet of that set.
4. The general rule is that you must check the cite of the case you are shepardizing (the cited case) in *every* unit of a set of Shepard's. With experience you will learn, however, that it is possible to bypass some of the units of the set. There may be information on the front cover of one of the Shepard's volumes, for example, that will tell you that the date or volume number of the reporter

containing your cited case will not be covered in that Shepard's volume. You can bypass it and move on to other units of the set.
5. In checking all the units of Shepard's, it is recommended that you work *backward* by examining the most recent Shepard's pamphlets first so that you obtain the latest history of the case and citing materials first.
6. Suppose that in one of the units of a set of Shepard's, you find nothing listed for the cited case. This could mean one of three things:
   (a) You are in the wrong set of Shepard's.
   (b) You are in the right set of Shepard's, but the Shepard's unit you are examining does not cover the particular volume of the reporter that contains your cited case. (See #4 above.)
   (c) You are in the right set of Shepard's. The silence in Shepard's about your cited case means that since the time of the printing of the last unit of Shepard's for that set, nothing has happened to the case—there is nothing for Shepard's to tell you.
7. Know the six kinds of information that you can try to obtain when shepardizing a case: parallel cites, history of the cited case, citing cases, citing legal periodical lit-

Checklist #4a   Checklist for Sheparizing a Case—continued

erature, citing annotations, and citing opinions of the attorney general.

8. The page number listed for every citing case is the page on which the cit*ed* case is mentioned. It is not the page on which the cit*ing* case begins.

9. Use the abbreviations tables and the preface pages at the beginning of most units of Shepard's—and use them often.

10. A small "n" to the right of the page number of citing material (e.g., 23ALR198n) means the cited case is

mentioned within an annotation. A small "s" to the right of the page number of citing material (e.g., 23ALR198s) means the cited case is mentioned in a supplement to (or pocket part of) the annotation.

11. You can also shepardize a case online through either WESTLAW or LEXIS. For a photograph of a WESTLAW screen containing Shepard's, see Exhibit 13.12 in chapter 13.

(f) Sheparizing a Statute

You shepardize a *statute* to try to find the following seven kinds of information:

1. A parallel cite of the statute (found in parentheses immediately after the section number of the statute). The parallel cite (if given) is to the *session law* edition of the statute (see the discussion that follows).

2. The history of the statute in the legislature, such as amendments, added sections, repealed sections, renumbered sections, etc.

3. The history of the statute in the courts, such as citing cases that have analyzed or mentioned the statute, declared it unconstitutional, etc.

4. Citing administrative decisions, such as agency decisions that have analyzed or mentioned the statute

5. Citing legal periodical literature, such as law review articles that have analyzed or mentioned the statute

6. Citing annotations in A.L.R., A.L.R.2d, A.L.R.3d, A.L.R.4th, A.L.R.5th, and A.L.R. Fed. that have analyzed or mentioned the statute

7. Citing opinions of the attorney general that have analyzed or mentioned the statute

When a statute is passed by the legislature, it comes out as a slip law (page 541) and then is printed in volumes called Session Laws, Laws, Acts, Acts and Resolves, Statutes at Large, etc. (For convenience, all these items will be referred to below as session laws.) Session laws are arranged chronologically by year—the statutes are not arranged by subject matter in the session law volumes. Finally, many (but not all) of the session laws are later printed in statutory codes. They are *codified*, which means that they *are* organized by subject matter rather than chronologically. As indicated earlier, not all session laws are codified. The statute may not be considered of sufficient general interest to be codified. If codification has occurred, there will be two cites for the same statute. Here are examples of session law and codified cites of a state statute (Ohio) and of a federal statute.

Session Law Cite of a Statute	Codified Cite of the Same Statute
1975 Ohio Laws, C. 508 ⟵————————⟶	Ohio Rev. Code Ann. § 45 (1978)
87 Stat. 297 (1965) ⟵————————⟶	34 U.S.C. § 18(c) (1970)

Notice the totally different numbering system in the codified and session law cites—yet they are the same statutes. Section 45 of the Ohio Revised Code Annotated is found word-for-word in Chapter (C.)508 of the 1975 session laws of Ohio. And section 18(c) of title 34 of the United States Code is found word-for-word in volume 87 of Statutes at Large (Stat.)

on page 297. Notice also the different years for the same statute. The year in the **session law cite** is the year the legislature passed the statute. The year in the **codified cite,** however, is usually the year of the edition of the code.

Now the question becomes: When do you shepardize a statute through its session law cite and when do you shepardize through its codified cite?

There are two instances when you *must* shepardize the statute through its session law cite:

- If the statute will never be codified because it is not of general public interest, or,
- If the statute has not yet been codified because it is so recent (codification will come later).

If the statute *has* been codified, you must shepardize it through its latest codified cite. But suppose you know only the session law cite of the statute. How do you find its codified cite? Go to the current code that should contain your statute. Look for special tables at the beginning or end of the code. For federal statutes in the United States Code, for example, there is a *Tables volume* in which you will find Table III. It will enable you to translate a session law cite into a codified law cite (page 634). (A Tables volume also exists for U.S.C.A. and for U.S.C.S.)

Shepard's has its own abbreviation system for session laws. Suppose that you are shepardizing Kan. Stat. Ann. § 123 (1973)—a codified cite. Section 123 is the cited statute—what you are shepardizing. In the Shepard's columns for Kansas statutes, you might find:

Section 123
(1970C6)
A1972C23
Rp1975C45

The parallel cite in parentheses is 1970C6, which means Chapter 6 of the 1970 Session Laws of the state of Kansas. The mention of a year in Shepard's for statutes usually refers to the session laws for that year. (You find the meaning of "C" by checking the abbreviations tables at the beginning of the Shepard's volume.)

Immediately beneath the parentheses in the above example for section 123 (the cited statute), you find two other references to session laws:

A1972C23   This means that in Chapter 23 of the 1972 Session Laws of Kansas, there was an amendment to section 123 (which is what "A" means according to Shepard's abbreviations tables).

Rp1975C45   This means that in Chapter 45 of the 1975 Session Laws of Kansas, section 123 was repealed in part (which is what "Rp" means according to Shepard's abbreviations tables).

You will note that Shepard's does *not* tell you what the amendment was, nor what was repealed in part. How do you find this out? Two ways. First, you go to the actual session laws, if your library has them. Second, you go to the cited statute (§ 123) in the codified collection of the statutes (here the Kansas Statutes Annotated). At the bottom of the statute in the code, there may be historical or legislative history notes that will summarize amendments, repeals, etc. (Also check the same kind of notes for the cited statute in the pocket part of the code volume you are using.)

Other citing material given in Shepard's for a statute is less complicated. For example, there are cites to citing cases, citing legal periodical articles, etc., that follow a very similar pattern to the citing material for cases you are shepardizing (see Checklist #4a on shepardizing a case).

Assume that you want to shepardize a federal statute—in the United States Code (U.S.C.). As with the shepardizing of every statute, you must shepardize through the most current edition of the code. A new edition of the U.S.C. comes out every six years, e.g., 1970 Edition, 1976 Edition. In between editions, the U.S.C. is supplemented by annual Supplement volumes, e.g., Supplement 1971, Supplement 1972 (also referred to as Supplement II, Supplement III, etc.). Shepardize your statute through the latest code edition *and* through any of the Supplement years indicated at the top of the pages used to shepardize a federal statute in *Shepard's United States Citations, Statute Edition* (page 540).

Assume that the most current code edition is the 1970 edition and that the latest Supplement year is 1972. You want to shepardize 18 USC § 700 (1970). You trace this cite through all the units of *Shepard's United States Citations, Statute Edition*. Exhibit 11.21 shows an excerpt containing one column from a page in one of these units.

Exhibit 11.21 Excerpt from a Shepard's Page (Federal Statutes)

```
United
States
Code, 1970
Edition
and
Supple-
ment, 1972
TITLE 18
§ 700

Ad82St291    1
C302FS1112   2

394US604
22LE592
89SC1372
445F2d226
462F2d96
479F2d1177   3
313FS49
317FS138
322FS593
324FS1278
343FS165

41 A3 3504n  5

Subsec. a
C454F2d972
C462F2d96
445F2d226
479F2d1179
324FS1278
Subsec. b    6
C462F2d96
445F2d226
Subsec. c
394US598
22LE588
89SC1360
322FS585
```

Citations to section § 700 of Title 18 of the United States Code, 1970 Edition and the 1972 Supplement are shown in the boxed excerpt at the left.

Citations for each cited statutory provision are grouped as follows:

1. Amendments, repeals, etc. by acts of Congress
2. Citing cases of the United States Supreme Court and the lower federal courts analyzed as to constitutionality or validity
3. Other citing cases
4. Citing legal periodical literature (none in this excerpt)
5. Citing annotations
6. Citing material for specific subdivisions of the statute

For the purpose of illustration only, this grouping has been indicated by brackets. Note again that as yet there is no citing material in group four.

The first citation shown indicates that section 700 of Title 18 was added "Ad" by an act of Congress printed in 82 United States Statutes at Large "St" at page 291. This section is next shown to have been held constitutional "C" by a lower federal court in a case reported in 302 Federal Supplement "FS" 1112 and to have been cited in several cases before the lower federal courts and the United States Supreme Court. The section was also cited in an annotation "n" of the American Law Reports, Third Series "A3".

Citing references to specific subdivisions of the section are then shown. Subsection (Subsec) "a" of section 700, for example, was held constitutional (C) in two lower federal court cases reported in 454 F.2d 972 and 462 F.2d 96.

Checklist #4b Checklist for Shepardizing a Statute

1. Go to the set of Shepard's that will enable you to shepardize your statute. For federal statutes, it is *Shepard's* *United States Citations, Statute Edition*. For state statutes, go to the set of Shepard's for your state. This

Checklist #4b   Checklist for Shepardizing a Statute—continued

set of Shepard's may cover both state cases and state statutes in the same units or in different case and statute editions of the set.

2. If the statute has been codified, shepardize it through its latest codified cite. If all you have is the session law cite of the statute, translate it into a codified cite by using the tables in the current code. For federal statutes, go to Table III of the Tables volume of U.S.C./U.S.C.A./U.S.C.S. (page 634).

3. If the statute has not been codified, you can shepardize it through its session law cite.

4. Know whether you have a complete set of Shepard's in front of you by reading the "What Your Library Should Contain" list on the most recent pamphlet of that set.

5. Check your cite in *every* unit of Shepard's. It is recommended that you work *backward* by examining the most recent Shepard's pamphlets first so that you obtain the latest history and citing material first.

6. At the top of a Shepard's page, and in its columns, look for your statute by the name of the code, year, article, chapter, title, or section. Repeat this for every unit of Shepard's.

7. Know the seven kinds of information you can try to obtain by shepardizing a statute: parallel cite (not always given), history of the statute in the legislature, history of the statute in the courts, citing administrative decisions, citing legal periodical literature, citing annotations, citing opinions of the attorney general.

8. The history of the statute in the legislature will give you the citing material in session law form, e.g., A1980C45. This refers to an amendment (A) printed in the 1980 Laws of the legislature, Chapter (C) 45. Another example: A34St.654. This refers to an amendment (A) printed in volume 34, page 654, of the Statutes at Large. If you want to locate these session laws, find out if your library keeps the session laws. Also, check the historical note after the statute in the statutory code (page 628).

9. The notation **et seq** means "and following" (et sequens). The citing material may be analyzing more than one statutory section.

10. Find the meaning of abbreviations used by Shepard's in its tables and preface material at the beginning of most of the units of the set of Shepard's.

11. If your state code has gone through revisions or renumberings, read the early pages in the statutory code and in the Shepard's volumes to try to obtain an explanation of what has happened. This information may be of considerable help to you in interpreting the data provided in the Shepard's units for your state code.

12. You can also shepardize a federal statute (and many state statutes) online through either WESTLAW or LEXIS.

(g) Shepardizing a Regulation

You cannot shepardize administrative regulations of state agencies. No sets of Shepard's cover state regulations. Until recently, the same was true of most federal regulations. Today, however, it is possible to shepardize federal regulations in the Code of Federal Regulations (C.F.R.). This is done through *Shepard's Code of Federal Regulations Citations*. (See page 540.) It will also allow you to shepardize presidential proclamations, executive orders, and reorganization plans.

To shepardize a C.F.R. regulation means to obtain the following three kinds of information about the *cited regulation* (the regulation you are shepardizing):

1. The history of the regulation in the courts—for example, citing cases that have invalidated or otherwise discussed the cited regulation.

2. Citing legal periodical literature that has analyzed or mentioned the cited regulation.

3. Citing annotations in A.L.R., A.L.R.2d, A.L.R.3d, A.L.R.4th, A.L.R.5th, and A.L.R. Fed. that have analyzed or mentioned the cited regulation.

The C.F.R. comes out in a new edition every year. All the changes that have occurred during the year are incorporated in the new yearly edition. Two kinds of changes can be made:

- Those changes made *by the agency* itself, e.g., amendments, repeals, renumbering—this is the history of the regulation in the agency.
- Those changes forced on the agency *by the courts,* e.g., declaring a section of the regulation invalid—this is part of the history of the regulation in the courts.

Unfortunately, Shepard's will give you only the history of the regulation *in the courts* (plus references to the regulation in legal periodical literature and in annotations). The columns of Shepard's will *not* give you the history of the regulation in the agency. (As we will see later on page 641, to obtain the latter, you must check elsewhere, e.g., the *"CFR Parts Affected"* tables in the Federal Register.) The main value of the Shepard's for C.F.R. is that it will lead you to what *the courts* have said about the regulation (plus the periodical and annotation references).

When sheparding through the Shepard's C.F.R. Citations, the cited material, of course, is the federal regulation—which we refer to as the cited regulation. Shepard's provides two categories of *citing* material:

- Citing cases, periodicals, and annotations that refer to the cited regulation *by year,* that is, by C.F.R. edition.
- Citing cases, periodicals, and annotations that refer to the cited regulation *without* specifying the year or edition of the regulation in the C.F.R.

To indicate the first kind of citing material, Shepard's gives you a small elevated *asterisk* just before a given year. If, for example, the cited regulation you were sheparding is 12 C.F.R. § 218.111(j) (1965), you might find the following:

§ 218.111(j)
420F2d90*1965

The citing material is a citing case—420 F.2d 90. The small asterisk means that this case specifically identified the year of the cited regulation—1965. This year is *not* the year of the citing case. It is the year of the cited regulation. We are not given the year of the citing case.

Now let us examine the second kind of citing material mentioned above. There may be citing material that mentions the regulation but does *not* tell us the specific year or edition of that regulation. Shepard's uses a *triangle* in such situations. If, for example, the cited regulation you were sheparding is 12 C.F.R. § 9.18(a)(3) (1962), you might find the following:

§9.18(a)(3)
274FS628△1967

The citing material is a citing case—274 F. Supp. 628. The small triangle means that the citing case did not refer to the year or edition of section 9.18(a)(3). When this occurs, the year next to the triangle is the year of the citing case and *not* the year of the cited regulation. The citing case of 274 F. Supp. 628 was decided in 1967. For other examples, see Exhibit 11.22.

Checklist #4c Checklist for Sheparding a Federal Regulation

1. Go to *Shepard's Code of Federal Regulations Citations.* (For a photo, see page 540.)
2. Know whether you have a complete set of Shepard's in front of you by reading the "What Your Library Should Contain" list on the most recent pamphlet in that set.
3. Shepardize your regulation through every unit of this set of Shepard's.

Checklist #4c   Checklist for Sheparizing a Federal Regulation—continued

4. Know the three kinds of information you can obtain when sheparizing a federal regulation: history of the regulation in the courts, citing legal periodical literature, and citing annotations.

5. An asterisk or a triangle will appear next to the year of all citing material: the citing cases, the citing periodical literature, and the citing annotations.

   (a) The asterisk means that the citing material referred to the specific year of the cited regulation. Hence the year is the year of the cited regulation, not of the citing material.

   (b) The triangle means that the citing material did not refer to the specific year of the cited regulation. Hence the year is the year of the citing material, not of the cited regulation.

6. The set of Shepard's for C.F.R. does not directly tell you what amendments, revisions, or other changes were made *by the agencies* to the regulations. You are told only what *the courts* have said about the regulations. (To find out what the agencies have done to the regulations, you must check sources such as the "CFR Parts Affected" tables in the *Federal Register.*)

7. Check the meaning of abbreviations in the tables and preface at the beginning of most of the Shepard's units.

8. All regulations in C.F.R. are based on statutes of Congress. As we will see later, you can find out what statutes in U.S.C. are the authority for particular regulations in C.F.R. by checking the "authority" reference under many of the regulations in C.F.R. Once you know the statute that is the basis for the regulation, you might want to sheparize that statute for more law in the area. (See Checklist 4b on sheparizing a statute.)

Exhibit 11.22   Excerpts from a Shepard's Page (C.F.R.)

Code of Federal Regulations

```
CFR
TITLE
42
§53.111
323F2d965 △1963
458F2d1117 △1972
551F2d333 *1972
Va559F2d973 △1977
327FS113 △1971
359FS911 *1973          1
Vp373FS551 △1974
373FS559 △1974
409FS711 △1976
Up453FS410 *1973
453FS680 *1976
Mass
382NE1043 *1977
NY                      2
413S2d88 △1979
Ore
582P2d48 *1976
88YLJ277 *1977          3
11ALRF684n △1972        4
```

Shepard's Code of Federal Regulation Citations gives citations to the Code of Federal Regulations and to Presidential Proclamations, Executive Orders, and Reorganization Plans as cited by the United States Supreme Court, by the lower federal courts, and by state courts in cases reported in any unit of the National Reporter System, and in annotations of American Law Reports. In addition, citations appearing in articles in legal periodicals are shown.

If the citing material mentioned the year of the cited CFR regulation, that year is preceded by the symbol *. When you find a year preceded by the symbol △, the year is the date of the citing material.

Citations to each provision of the Code of Federal Regulations are grouped as follows:

1. Citing federal cases
2. Citing state cases
3. Citing legal periodical literature
4. Citing annotations

In the above example, the 1973 CFR edition of section 53.111 was held unconstitutional in part "Up" by a case reported in 453 Federal Supplement "FS" 410. Also a 1974 case held § 53.111 void or invalid in part "Vp." A 1977 case determined that § 53.111 was valid, "Va."

Section 53.111 has also been cited by the courts of Massachusetts, New York, and Oregon. There is a citing legal periodical, 88 Yale Law Journal "YLJ" 277, and a citing annotation "n," 11 American Law Reports, Federal "ALRF" 684.

Inserting pages into a loose-leaf service

5. LOOSE-LEAF SERVICES

Loose-leaf services are law books with a three-ring (or post) binder structure. (See another photo on page 534.) Additions to these services are made frequently—monthly or sooner. The major publishers of the services are Commerce Clearing House (CCH); Bureau of National Affairs (BNA); Clark Boardman Callaghan; Warren, Gorman & Lamont; and Matthew Bender. They cover numerous areas of the law, such as criminal law, taxes, corporate law, and unions. You should assume that one or more loose-leaf services exist for the topic of your research problem until you prove otherwise to yourself. The contents of loose-leaf services often include the following:

- Recent court opinions or summaries of opinions
- Relevant legislation—usually explained in some detail
- Administrative regulations and decisions, or summaries of them (some of this material may not be readily available elsewhere)
- References to relevant studies and reports
- Practice tips

In short, the loose-leaf services are extremely valuable. Unfortunately, however, they are sometimes awkward to use. Occasionally, library users of the loose-leaf services misfile pages that they take out for photocopying.

The loose-leaf books do not have a standard format. You may find the following, for example:

- One volume or multivolume
- Organization by page number, organization by section number, organization by paragraph number, or a combination of these
- Different colored pages to indicate more recent material
- Indexes at the end, in the middle, or at the beginning of the volumes
- Bound volumes that accompany the three-ring volumes
- Transfer binders that contain current material

You should approach the structure of each loose-leaf service as a small puzzle sitting on the shelf waiting to be put together.

Checklist #5   Checklist for Finding and Using Loose-Leaf Services

1. Divide your research problem into its major topics, such as family law, tax law, antitrust law, etc. Assume that one or more loose-leaf services exist for these topics until you demonstrate otherwise to yourself.

2. Find out where the loose-leaf services are located in your library. Are they all together? Are they located in certain subject areas? Does the library have a separate list of them?

3. Check the card catalog. Look for subject heading cards on your topics to see if loose-leaf services are mentioned. Check the names of the major publishers of loose-leaf services—Bureau of National Affairs and

Commerce Clearing House. (See Checklist #1 on using the card catalog.)

4. Ask library staff members if they know of loose-leaf services on the major topics of your research.

5. Call other law libraries in your area. Ask the staff members there if they know of loose-leaf services on the major topics of your research. See if they can identify loose-leaf services that you have not yet found.

6. Speak to experts in the area of the law, e.g., professors. (See Checklist #9.) Ask them about loose-leaf services.

7. Once you have a loose-leaf service in front of you, you must figure out how to use it:

Checklist #5 **Checklist for Finding and Using Loose-Leaf Services —continued**

(a) Read any preface or explanatory material in the front of the volumes of the loose-leaf service.

(b) Ask library staff members to give you some help.

(c) Ask attorneys or paralegals who are experts in the area if they can give you a brief demonstration of its use.

(d) Ask a fellow student who is familiar with the service.

(e) Read any pamphlets or promotional literature by the publishers on using their loose-leaf services.

For each loose-leaf service, you need to know the following:

• What it contains and what it does not contain
• How it is indexed
• How it is supplemented
• What its special features are
• How many volumes or units it has and the inter-relationship among them

You obtain this information through techniques (a) to (e) above.

8. In your research memo, you rarely cite a loose-leaf service unless the material you found there does not exist elsewhere. Use the loose-leaf service mainly as background research (see Exhibit 11.14) and as a search tool for leads to find primary authority, such as cases, statutes, and regulations.

6. LEGAL PERIODICAL LITERATURE

Legal periodical literature consists of the following:

● Lead articles and comments written by individuals who have extensively researched a topic
● **Case notes** that summarize and comment on important court opinions
● Book reviews.

There are three major publishers of periodicals: academic institutions including almost all of the nation's law schools (where the students running the periodicals have the prestige of being "on law review"), commercial companies, and bar associations. Legal periodicals are either general, covering a wide variety of legal topics, e.g., *Harvard Law Review,* or specialized, e.g., *Family Law Journal.* (See Exhibit 11.7.) The large number of legal periodicals that exist provide researchers with a rich source of material.

How can you locate legal periodical literature on point? What index systems will allow you to gain access to the hundreds of legal periodicals and the tens of thousands of articles, comments, case notes, book reviews, and other material in them? Two major general index systems exist:

● *Index to Legal Periodicals* (ILP) published by H.W. Wilson Co.
● *Current Law Index* (CLI) published by Information Access Corporation

Of the two, the CLI is more comprehensive because it indexes more legal periodicals. Both are available in three different versions: a paper version (consisting of pamphlets and bound volumes), a CD-ROM version, and an online version. Few law libraries subscribe to all the legal periodicals indexed in the ILP and the CLI. Hence you may be obtaining leads to periodicals that your library does not have. If so, check other libraries in the area.

In addition to these general indexes, ILP and CLI, there are special indexes to legal periodical literature on topics such as tax law.

Examples of the paper versions of the *Index to Legal Periodicals* (ILP) and the *Current Law Index* (CLI). Both are also available online and on CD-ROM.

(a) Index to Legal Periodicals (ILP)

- The ILP first comes out in pamphlets that are later consolidated (i.e., cumulated) into bound volumes.
- You must check each ILP pamphlet and each ILP bound volume for whatever years you want.
- The ILP regularly adds new periodicals to be indexed.
- Every ILP pamphlet and bound volume has four indexes:
  (1) A *Subject and Author Index*
  (2) A *Table of Cases* commented on
  (3) A *Table of Statutes* commented on (added recently)
  (4) A *Book Review Index*
- Abbreviation tables appear at the beginning of every pamphlet and bound volume.
- The Subject and Author Index in the ILP is easy to use. You simply go to the topic on which you are seeking periodical literature. If you have the name of an author and want to know if he or she has written anything on the topic of your research, you simply check that author's last name in this index.[6]
- Toward the end of every ILP pamphlet and bound volume is a Table of Cases. Suppose that elsewhere in your research you come across an important case, and you now want to know if that case was ever commented on (i.e., noted) in the legal periodicals. Go to the ILP pamphlet or bound volume that covers the year of the case and check the Table of Cases.
- The Table of Statutes serves the same function for statutes. This table will tell you where you can find periodical literature commenting on certain statutes.
- At the end of every pamphlet and bound ILP volume is a Book Review Index. If you are looking for a review of a law book you have come across elsewhere in your research, go to the ILP pamphlet or bound volume that covers the year of publication of the book for which you are seeking reviews.

---

[6]Prior to 1983, the entries under an author's name had to be cross-referenced to the "subject" portions of the index. Today, there are full bibliographic entries under both topics and author names.

- The ILP is also available:
  - **(1)** On WILSONLINE, the publisher's online research system
  - **(2)** On WILSONDISC, a CD-ROM system
  - **(3)** On WESTLAW
  - **(4)** On LEXIS

(b) Current Law Index (CLI)

The CLI indexes substantially more periodicals than the ILP. In fact, one of the reasons the CLI was created was the unwillingness of the publisher of the ILP to expand the number and kind of periodicals it indexed.

- The CLI first comes out in pamphlets that are later consolidated (i.e., cumulated) into bound volumes.
- You must check each CLI pamphlet and each annual CLI issue for the years you want.
- There are four indexes within each CLI unit:
  - A Subject Index
  - An Author-Title Index
  - A Table of Cases
  - A Table of Statutes
- Abbreviation tables appear at the beginning of every CLI unit.
- The Subject Index gives full citations to periodicals under a topic and under an author's name.
- Book reviews are included under the Author-Title Index along with cites to periodical literature by the authors.
- The Table of Cases is valuable if you already know the name of a case located elsewhere in your research. To find out if that case was commented on, check the Table of Cases in the CLI unit that covers the year of the case.
- The Table of Statutes is equally valuable. If you already have the name of a statute from your other research (such as Atomic Energy Act; California Fair Employment Practices Act), look for the name of that statute in the Table of Statutes for the CLI unit that covers the approximate time the statute was passed.
- The CLI began in 1980; it does not index periodicals prior to this date. The ILP must be used for the period before 1980.

Legal Resource Index (LRI)   The *Legal Resource Index* (LRI) is the online version[7] of the *Current Law Index*. The LRI is available on WESTLAW and LEXIS.

LegalTrac   *LegalTrac* is the CD-ROM version of the *Current Law Index*.

Other Index Systems

A number of other periodical index systems exist:

- Index to Federal Tax Articles
- Index to Foreign Legal Periodicals
- Index to Canadian Legal Periodical Literature
- Jones-Chipman Index to Legal Periodical Literature (covering periodical literature up to 1937 only)

---

[7]The LRI is also available on a special microfilm reader. However, due to the popularity of the CD-ROM version of the CLI *(LegalTrac)*, many libraries do not have this microfilm version.

- Index Medicus (covers medical periodicals—usually available only in medical libraries)
- MEDLINE (a computer search system for medical periodicals—available mainly in medical libraries)

Checklist #6	Checklist for Finding Legal Periodical Literature

1. Use legal periodical literature mainly for background research and for leads to primary authority, particularly through the extensive footnotes in this literature. (See Exhibit 11.14.)
2. There are two major general index systems: *Index to Legal Periodicals* (ILP) and *Current Law Index* (CLI). Subsequent guidelines in this checklist cover the paper versions of ILP and CLI. (There are also CD-ROM versions and online versions, which are considerably easier to use. One of the most popular is *LegalTrac*, the CD-ROM version of CLI.)
3. The CARTWHEEL will help you locate material in ILP and CLI.
4. Both ILP and CLI also contain separate indexes. You should become familiar with all these internal index features.
5. Start with the subject headings index within ILP and CLI.
6. Identify the name and date of every important case that you have found in your research thus far. Go to the Table of Cases in ILP and in CLI to find out if any periodical literature has commented on that case. (Go to the ILP and CLI units that would cover the year the case was decided. To be safe, also check their units for two years after the date of the case.)
7. If you are researching a statute, find out if any periodical literature has commented on the statute. This is done in two ways:
   (a) Check the Table of Statutes in ILP and CLI.
   (b) Break your statute down into its major topics. Check these topics in the Subject Indexes of ILP and CLI to see if any periodical literature on these topics discusses your statute.
8. If you have the name of an author who is known for writing on a particular topic, you can also check for literature written by that author under his or her name in ILP and CLI.
9. Ask library staff members if the library has any other indexes to legal periodical literature, particularly in specialty areas of the law.
10. It is possible to shepardize some legal periodical literature. If you want to know whether the periodical article, note, or comment was ever mentioned in a court opinion, go to *Shepard's Law Review Citations*.
11. It is possible to search for legal periodical literature online in WESTLAW, LEXIS, and WILSONLINE.

7. LEGAL ENCYCLOPEDIAS

The major multivolume *legal encyclopedias* are *Corpus Juris Secundum* (C.J.S.), a dark blue set published by West, and *American Jurisprudence 2d* (Am. Jur. 2d), a green set published by Lawyers Co-op. In many law libraries, they are the most frequently used volumes on the shelf because they are easy to use and are comprehensive. If you know how to use a general encyclopedia, you know how to use a legal encyclopedia. The volumes contain hundreds of alphabetically arranged topics on almost every area of the law. For each topic, you are given explanations of the basic principles of law, and extensive footnote references supporting these principles. The vast majority of the references are to cases, although for certain topics such as federal taxation, there are references to statutes as well. Legal encyclopedias have two main values. They are excellent as background research in a new area of the law. (See Exhibit 11.14.) They are also valuable as leads to primary authority, particularly case law. In addition to the national legal encyclopedias, some states have state-specific encyclopedias devoted to the law of one state, e.g., *Florida Jurisprudence*.

For a sample page from C.J.S., see Exhibit 11.23. Every section begins with a summary of that section in black bold print. The phrase **black letter law** has come to mean any summary or overview that contains basic principles of law.

E x h i b i t   1 1 . 2 3   **Excerpt from a Page in *Corpus Juris Secundum***

§§ 22–23 BURGLARY

c. Use of Instrument, Explosives, or Torch

In order to constitute burglary, entry need not be made by any part of accused's body, but entry may be made by an instrument, where the instrument is inserted for the purpose of committing a felony.

In order to constitute a burglary, it is not necessary that entry be made by any part of the body; it may be by an instrument,[5] as in a case where a hook or other instrument is put in with intent to take out goods, or a pistol or a gun with intent to kill.[6] It is necessary, however, that the instrument shall be put within the structure, and that it shall be inserted for the immediate purpose of committing the felony or aiding in its commission, and not merely for the purpose of making an opening to admit the hand or body, or, in other words, for the sole purpose of breaking.

A statute making it an offense to break and enter a building with intent to commit a crime, and defining "enter" as including insertion into the building of any instrument held in defendant's hand and intended to be used to detach or remove property, does not require that the offender intend the detachment or removal of property to occur at the moment of insertion only, and the intended detachment or removal relates to a later time as well. . . .

5. Cal.—People v. Walters, 57 Cal.Rptr. 484, 249 C.A.2d 547. Del.—Bailey v. State, 231 A.2d 469.
Me.—State v. Liberty, 280 A.2d 805.
N.J.—**Corpus Juris Secundum quoted in** State v. O'Leary, 107 A.2d 13, 16, 31 N.J.Super 411.
N.M.—State v. Tixier, 551 P.2d 987, 89 N.M. 297.
Or.—Terminal News Stands v. General Cas. Co., 278 P.2d 158, 203 Or. 54.

Tenn.—State v. Crow, 517 S.W.2d 753.
Tex.—Tanner v. State, Cr., 473 S.W.2d 936.
Wyo.—Mirich v. State, 593 P.2d 590.
6. N.J.—**Corpus Juris Secundum quoted in** State v. O'Leary, 107 A.2d 13, 16, 31 N.J.Super. 411.
Pa.—Commonwealth v. Stefanczyk, 77 Pa.Super. 27.
Tex.—Stroud v. State, 60 S.W.2d 439, 124 Tex.Cr. 56.

At the end of both C.J.S. and Am. Jur. 2d is a huge *general index*. There are also extensive topic indexes within individual volumes.

C h e c k l i s t   # 7   **Checklist for Using Legal Encyclopedias**

1. Use the two national legal encyclopedias (Am. Jur. 2d and C.J.S.) for the following purposes:
   (a) As background research for areas of the law that are new to you
   (b) For leads in their extensive footnotes to primary authority, such as cases and statutes.
2. Both legal encyclopedias have multivolume general indexes at the end of their sets. Use the CARTWHEEL to help you locate material in them. In addition to these general indexes, Am. Jur. 2d and C.J.S. have separate indexes in many of the individual volumes.
3. Neither Am. Jur. 2d nor C.J.S. includes a table of cases.
4. C.J.S. does not have a table of statutes. Am. Jur. 2d, however, has a separate volume called *Table of Statutes, Rules, and Regulations Cited*. Check this table if you
continued

have found a relevant statute, regulation, or rule of court from your other research that you want to find discussed in Am. Jur. 2d.

5. Am. Jur. 2d is published by Lawyers Co-op. C.J.S. is published by West. Within these legal encyclopedias, the publishers provide library references to other research books that they publish. In Am. Jur. 2d, for example, Lawyers Co-op will refer you to annotations in A.L.R.,

A.L.R.2d, A.L.R.3d, A.L.R.4th, A.L.R.5th, and A.L.R. Fed. In C.J.S., West will refer you to its key number digests.

6. Find out if your library has a *local* encyclopedia that is limited to the law of your state. States with such encyclopedias include California, Florida, Kentucky, Illinois, Maryland, Michigan, New York, Ohio, Pennsylvania, and Texas.

8. LEGAL TREATISES

A *legal treatise* is any book written by private individuals (or by public officials writing in a private capacity) on a topic of law. Some treatises are scholarly while others are more practice oriented. The latter are often called *hornbooks, handbooks, formbooks,* and *practice manuals.* Treatises give overview summaries of the law, plus references to primary authority. There are single-volume treatises such as *Prosser on Torts,* as well as multivolume treatises such as *Moore's Federal Practice, Collier on Bankruptcy,* etc.

1. Always look for legal treatises on the topics of your research problem. Assume, until you prove otherwise to yourself, that three or four such treatises exist and are relevant to your problem.

2. Treatises are useful for background research, and for leads to primary authority. See Exhibit 11.14.

3. Many treatises are updated by pocket parts, supplemental volumes, and page inserts if the treatise has a three-ring (or post) binder structure.

4. Start your search for treatises in the card catalog (see Checklist #1 on using the catalog) or in the library's computer catalog system.

5. Check with experts in the area of law in which you are interested, e.g., teachers, for recommendations on treatises you should examine. See Checklist #9.

6. If your library has open stacks, find the treatise section (with KF call numbers, for example). Locate the areas containing treatises on your topic. Browse through the shelves in these areas of the stacks to try to find additional treatises. (Some treatises that you need, however, may be on reserve rather than in the open stacks.)

7. Once you have found a treatise, check that author's name in the Index to Legal Periodicals (ILP) or the Current Law Index (CLI) to try to find periodical literature on the same topic by this author. You can also use these indexes to see if there are any book reviews on the treatises. (See Checklist #6 on finding legal periodical literature.)

9. PHONE AND MAIL—CONTACT THE EXPERTS

Don't be reluctant to call experts on the topics of your research. If you can get through to them and if you adopt a sufficiently humble attitude, they may give you leads to important laws and may even discuss the facts of your research problem. Many experts are quite willing to help you free of charge, as long as you are respectful and do not give the impression that you want more than a few moments of their time. You do not ask to come over to spend an afternoon!

Checklist #9   Checklist for Doing Phone and Mail Research

1. Your goal is to contact someone who is an expert in the area of your research problem. You want to try to talk with him or her briefly on the phone. (You can try to contact experts through the mail, but this route is seldom as successful as phone contact.)

2. Do not try to contact an expert until you have first done a substantial amount of research on your own. For instance, you should have already checked the major cases, statutes, regulations, treatises, legal periodical literature, annotations, etc., that are readily available in the library.

3. Prepare the questions you want to ask the expert. Make them short and to the point. For example, "Do you know of any recent case law on the liability of a municipality for . . .?" "Could you give me any leads to literature on the doctrine of promissory estoppel as it applies to . . .?" "Do you know anyone I could contact who has done empirical research on the new EPA regulations?" "Do you know of anyone currently litigating § 307?" Do *not* recite all the facts of the research problem to the expert and say, "What should I do?" If the expert wants more facts from you, let him or her ask you for them. You must create the impression that you want no more than a few moments of the expert's time. If the experts want to give your request more attention, they will let you know.

4. Introduce yourself as a student doing research on a problem. State how you got their name (see the next guideline) and then state how grateful you would be if you could ask them a "quick question."

5. Your introductory comments should state how you came across their name and learned of their expertise. For example, say "I read your law review article on . . . ." "I saw your name as an attorney of record in the case of . . . ." "Mr./Ms. _____ told me you were an expert in this area and recommended that I contact you."

6. Where do you find these experts? A number of possibilities exist:

   (a) *Special interest groups and associations*
       Contact attorneys within groups and associations such as unions, environmental groups, and business associations. Ask your librarian for lists of such groups and associations, for example, the *Encyclopedia of Associations.*

   (b) *Government agencies*
       Contact the law departments of the government agencies that would be involved in the area of your research.

   (c) *Specialty libraries*
       Ask your librarian for lists of libraries, such as the *Directory of Special Libraries and Information Centers.*

   (d) *Law professors*
       Ask a librarian if the library has the *AALS Law Teacher's Directory,* which lists teachers by name and specialty across the country.

   (e) *Attorneys of Record*
       If you have found a recent court opinion on point, the names of the attorneys for the case are printed at the beginning of the opinion (see page 353). Try to obtain the phone number and address of the attorneys in *West's Legal Directory* (available on WESTLAW) or in the *Martindale-Hubbell Law Directory.* These attorneys may be willing to send you a copy of appellate briefs on the case. Also ask them about any ongoing litigation in the courts.

       Often you are permitted to go to the court clerk's office and examine pleadings, appellate briefs, etc., on pending cases. All of these documents will give the names and addresses of the attorneys of record who prepared them. Finally, don't forget to check the closed case files of your own office for prior research that has already been done in the same area as your problem.

   (f) *Authors of legal periodical literature and of treatises*
       Try to contact the author of a treatise or law review article that is relevant to your research. The author's business address can often be found in sources such as the *AALS Law Teacher's Directory, West's Legal Directory, Martindale-Hubbell,* etc.

10. COMPUTERS

If you have access to any of the computerized legal research services, ask for a demonstration on how to operate the computer from the librarian or from the company that produces the computer. **CALR** (Computer Assisted Legal Research) is becoming more and more common and essential. The major legal research computer services are WESTLAW and LEXIS.

WESTLAW® by West Publishing Company

WESTLAW contains a great deal of material. Here are some examples: federal court opinions; state court opinions; United States Code; state statutes; the Code of Federal Regulations; administrative decisions; treatises published by West, Commerce Clearing House, Bureau of National Affairs, and other publishers; legal periodical literature; a *West's Legal Directory* containing the addresses of attorneys throughout the United States; annotations in A.L.R.3d, A.L.R.4th, A.L.R.5th, and A.L.R. Fed.; nonlegal data from Dow Jones and DIALOG. (DIALOG provides access to information on business, energy, biotechnology, engineering, electronics, medicine, the social sciences and humanities, current news, etc.) You can check the current validity of cases and statutes by using Insta-Cite, QuickCite, Shepard's Preview, and Shepard's online—without leaving the computer. There are also special databases in many areas, such as international law, professional responsibility (ethics), taxation, securities, medicine, etc. Other special databases that can be of unique value to litigators contain the names and addresses of experts in the fields of science, engineering, economics, etc. There are also bankruptcy records, information on deeds and other data recorded in counties throughout the country, abstracts of tax records, etc. Each day more material is added to WESTLAW.

Terminal using WESTLAW.

LEXIS® by Reed Elsevier

LEXIS is also a massive source of online data. Examples include federal and state court opinions; federal and state statutes; Code of Federal Regulations; administrative decisions; treatises, *Martindale-Hubbell Law Directory*; annotations in A.L.R.2d, A.L.R.3d, A.L.R.4th, A.L.R.5th, A.L.R. Fed., and in Lawyers' Edition 2d; legal periodical literature; special libraries on taxation, labor law, insurance, and international law; public records such as deed transfers; treatises published by Commerce Clearing House and the Bureau of National Affairs; nonlegal databases covering medicine, patents, current news, etc.; validation data through Shepard's and Auto-Cite, etc. (Auto-Cite is an online citator that provides parallel citations, the history of litigation involved in an opinion, references to other opinions that affect the validity of the opinion you are checking, etc.) As with WESTLAW, materials are added to LEXIS regularly.

In chapter 13 when we discuss databases in general, we will examine WESTLAW and LEXIS in greater detail. In particular, we will cover the critical skill of formulating a **query**, or research question, to ask WESTLAW and LEXIS.

Section P
FINDING CASE LAW

In chapter 7, we covered the structure of a court opinion, the briefing of an opinion, and the application of an opinion to a set of facts. Here our focus is on *finding* these opinions in the library—finding case law.

> "There is a high that comes with finding that case **on all fours**—the one that just makes your brief smoke—there's nothing like that sense of triumph."
>
> —James Clay, Paralegal Huffman, Arrington, Kihle, Goberino & Dunn
>
> [A case is "on all fours'" when its facts are exactly the same or almost the same as the facts of your client's case.]

In searching for case law, you will probably find yourself in one or more of the following situations:

- You already have one opinion on point (or close to being on point) and you want to find additional ones.
- You are looking for opinions interpreting a statute, constitution, charter, ordinance, court rule, or regulation that you already have.
- You are starting from square one. You want to find case law when you do *not* have a case, statute, or other law to begin with. You may be looking for opinions containing **common law** (judge-made law in the absence of controlling statutory or constitutional law), and you have no such opinions to begin with.

The following search techniques are not necessarily listed in the order in which they should be tried. Your goal is to know how to use all of them. In practice, you can vary the order.

First, a reminder about doing the first level of legal research: background research. You should review the checklist for background research presented in Exhibit 11.14. While doing this research, you will probably come across laws that will be of help to you on the specific facts of your problem (which is the second level of research). If so, you may already have some case law and now want to find more.

TECHNIQUES FOR FINDING CASE LAW WHEN YOU ALREADY HAVE ONE CASE ON POINT

1. *Shepardize the case that you have.* (See Checklist #4a on shepardizing cases, page 609.) In the columns of Shepard's, look for cases that have mentioned your case. Such cases will probably cover similar topics.

2. *Shepardize cases cited by the case you have.* Almost every court opinion discusses or at least refers to other opinions. Is this true of the case you already have? If so, shepardize every case your case cites that might be relevant to your research. (See Checklist #4a on shepardizing cases.)

3. *Use the West digests.* There are two ways to do this:
   (a) Go to the Table of Cases in all the digests covering the court that wrote the case you already have, such as the Table of Cases in the American Digest System. The Table of Cases will tell you what key numbers your case is digested under in the main volumes of the digest. Find your case digested under those key numbers. Once you have done so, you will probably be able to find other case law under the same key numbers.
   (b) Go to the West reporter that contains the full text of the case you already have. At the beginning of this case in the reporter, find the headnotes and their key numbers. Take the key numbers that are relevant to your problem into any of West's digests to find more case law.

(See Checklist #2 on using digests, page 595.)

4. *Find an annotation.* First identify the main topics or issues in the case you already have. Look up these topics in the *ALR Index* and in the other index systems for finding annotations in A.L.R., A.L.R.2d, A.L.R.3d, A.L.R.4th, A.L.R.5th, and A.L.R. Fed. (For a description of these annotation index systems, see Exhibit 11.17 and Checklist #3.) Another way to try to find annotations is by shepardizing the case you have. Annotations are among the *citing materials* of Shepard's. (See Checklist #4a on shepardizing cases, page 609.) Once you find an annotation, you will be given extensive citations to more case law. (See Checklist #3 on finding annotations.)

5. *Find a discussion of your case in the legal periodicals.* Go to the Table of Cases in the *Index of Legal Periodicals* (ILP) and the *Current Law Index* (CLI). There you will be told if your case was analyzed (noted) in the periodicals. If so, the discussion may give you additional case law on the same topic. (See Checklist #6 on finding legal periodical literature, page 620.)

6. *Go to Words and Phrases.* Identify the major words or phrases that are dealt with in the case you have. Check the definition of those words and phrases in the multi-volume legal dictionary called *Words and Phrases*. (See photo on page 545.) By so doing you will be led to other cases defining the same words or phrases.

Now let us assume that you already have a statute and you want case law interpreting that statute. The techniques for doing so (many of which are the same when seeking case law interpreting constitutions, regulations, etc.) are as follows:

Techniques for Finding Case Law Interpreting a Statute

1. *Shepardize the statute that you have.* (See Checklist #4b on shepardizing statutes, page 612.) In the columns of Shepard's, look for cases that have mentioned your statute.

2. *Examine your statute in the statutory code.* At the end of your statute in the statutory code, there are paragraph summaries of cases (often called **Notes of Decisions**) that have interpreted your statute. (See Exhibit 11.24 in the next section, page 629.) Look for these summaries in the bound volume of the code, in the pocket part of this volume, and in any supplemental pamphlets at the end of the code. (For federal statutes, the codes to check are U.S.C.A. and U.S.C.S. The U.S.C. will not have such case summaries.)

3. *Find an annotation on your statute.* To find out if there is an annotation in A.L.R, A.L.R.2d, etc. that mentions your statute, shepardize that statute. Such annotations are among the citing materials of Shepard's. (Also, check the *Table of Laws, Rules, and Regulations* in the last volume of the *ALR Index*. See Exhibit 11.18.) Such annotations will probably lead you to more case law on the statute.

4. *Find legal periodical literature on your statute.* Law review articles on statutes, for example, often cite cases

that interpret the statutes. There are three ways to find such articles:

   (a) Shepardize the statute. (See technique 1 above.) Citing material for a statute includes citing legal periodical literature.

   (b) Check the Table of Statutes in the *Index to Legal Periodicals* (ILP) and in the *Current Law Index* (CLI).

   (c) Go to the Subject Indexes in ILP and CLI, and check the topics of your statute.

5. *Go to loose-leaf services on your statute.* Find out if there is a loose-leaf service on the subject matter of your statute. Such services often give extensive cites to cases on the statute. (See Checklist #5 on loose-leaf services, page 616.)

6. *Go to legal treatises on your statute.* Most major statutes have treatises on them that contain extensive cites to cases on the statute. (See Checklist #8 on legal treatises, page 622.)

7. *Shepardize any cases you found through techniques 1–6 above.* You may be led to additional case law on the statute.

Finally, we assume that you are starting from scratch. You are looking for case law and you do not have a starting case or statute with which to begin. You may be looking for common law or for cases interpreting statutes that you have not found yet.

Techniques for Finding Case Law When You Do Not Have a Case or Statute to Begin With

1. *West digests.* In the Descriptive Word Indexes (DWI) of the West digests, try to find key numbers on the topics of your research. (See Checklist #2 on using the West digests, page 595.)

2. *Annotations.* Try to locate annotations on the topics of your research through the index systems for A.L.R.,

A.L.R.2d, A.L.R.3d, A.L.R.4th, A.L.R.5th, and A.L.R. Fed. (See Exhibit 11.17 and Checklist #3 on finding annotations, page 601.)

3. *Legal treatises.* Try to find treatises on the topics of your research in the card catalog. (See Checklist #8 on finding treatises, page 622.)

Techniques for Finding Case Law When You Do Not Have a Case or Statute to Begin With—continued

4. *Loose-leaf services.* Find out if there are loose-leaf services on the topics of your research. (See Checklist #5 on finding loose-leaf services, page 616.)

5. *Legal periodical literature.* Try to find legal periodical literature on the topics of your research in the Subject Indexes of ILP and CLI. (See Checklist #6 on finding legal periodical literature, page 620.)

6. *Legal encyclopedias.* Go to the indexes for Am. Jur. 2d and C.J.S. Try to find discussions in these legal encyclopedias on the topics of your research. (See Checklist #7 on using legal encyclopedias, page 621.)

7. *Computers* (page 623).

8. *Phone and mail research.* Find an expert. (See Checklist #9 on doing phone and mail research, page 622.)

9. *Words and Phrases.* Identify all the major words or phrases from the facts of your research problem. Look up these words or phrases in the multivolume legal dictionary, *Words and Phrases,* which gives case law definitions.

10. *Sheparizing.* If techniques 1–9 lead you to any case law, shepardize what you have found in order to look for more cases. (See Checklist #4a on shepardizing a case, page 609.)

Section Q
READING AND FINDING STATUTES

READING STATUTES

In Exhibit 11.24, there is an excerpt from a New York statutory code. It is an *annotated code,* which simply means that the statutes are organized by subject matter (rather than chronologically), and that a variety of research references are provided along with the text of the statutes. Here is an explanation of the circled numbers in this excerpt:

① This is the section number of the statute. The mark "§" before "146" means section.

② This is a heading summarizing the main topic of the statute. Section 146 covers who can visit state prisons in New York. This summarization was written by the private publishing company, not by the New York state legislature.

③ Here is the body of the statute written by the legislature.

④ At the end of a statutory section, you will often find a reference to *session laws* (page 610), using abbreviations such as L. (laws), P.L. (Public Law), Stat. (Statutes at Large), etc. Here you are told that in the Laws (L) of 1962, chapter (c) 37, § 3, this statute was amended. The Laws referred to are the session laws. See the Historical Note ⑥ below for a further treatment of this amendment.

⑤ The amendment to § 146 was effective (*eff.*) on February 20, 1962. The amendment may have been passed by the legislature on an earlier date, but the date on which it became the law of New York was February 20, 1962.

⑥ The **Historical Note** provides the reader with some of the legislative history (page 634) of § 146. First, the reader is again told that § 146 was amended in 1962. Note that early in the body of the statute, there is a reference to the title "commissioner of general services." The 1962 amendment simply changed the title from "superintendent of standards and purchase" to "commissioner of general services."

⑦ Also, part of the Historical Note is the *Derivation* section. This tells the reader that the topic of § 146 of the Corrections Law was once contained in § 160 of the Prison Law, which dates back to 1847. In 1929 there was another amendment. The Historical Note was written by the private publisher, not by the New York state legislature.

E x h i b i t 1 1 . 2 4 **Excerpt from a Statutory Code (New York State)**

① ②

§ 146. Persons authorized to visit prisons

The following persons shall be authorized to visit at pleasure all state prisons: The governor and lieutenant-governor, commissioner of general services, secretary of state, comptroller and attorney-general, members of the commission of correction, members of the legislature, judges of the court of appeals, supreme court and county judges, district attorneys and every minister of the gospel having charge of a congregation in the town wherein any such prison is situated. No other person not otherwise authorized by law shall be permitted to enter a state prison except under such regulations as the commissioner of correction shall prescribe. The provisions of this section shall not apply to such portion of a prison in which prisoners under sentence of death are confined. **③**

⑤

As amended L.1962, c. 37, § 3, eff. Feb. 20, 1962.

④

Historical Note **⑥**

L.1962, c. 37, § 3, eff. Feb. 20, 1962, substituted "commissioner of general services" for "superintendent of standards and purchase". **⑦**

Derivation. Prior to the general amendment of this chapter by L.1929,

c. 243, the subject matter of this section was contained in former Prison Law, § 160; originally derived from R.S., pt. 4, c. 3, tit. 3, § 159, as amended L.1847, c. 460.

Cross References **⑧**

Promoting prison contraband, see Penal Law, §§ 205.20, 205.25.

Library References **⑨**

Prisons ☞13.
Reformatories ☞7.

C.J.S. Prisons §§ 18, 19.
C.J.S. Reformatories §§ 10, 11.

⑩

Notes of Decisions

I. Attorneys

Warden of maximum security prison was justified in requiring that interviews of prisoners by attorney be conducted in presence of guard in room, in view of fact that attorney, who sought to interview 34 inmates in a day and a half, had shown no retainer agreements and had not stated purpose of consultations. Kahn v. La Vallee, 1961, 12 A.D.2d 832, 209 N.Y.S.2d 591.

Supreme court did not have jurisdiction of petition by prisoner to compel prison warden to provide facilities in prison which would not interfere with alleged violation of rights of prisoner to confer in pri-

vate with his attorney. Mummiani v. La Vallee, 1959, 21 Misc.2d 437, 199 N.Y.S.2d 263, affirmed 12 A.D.2d 832, 209 N.Y.S.2d 591.

Right of prisoners to confer with counsel after conviction is not absolute but is subject to such regulations as commissioner of correction may prescribe, and prisoners were not entitled to confer with their attorney privately within sight, but outside of hearing of a prison guard, when warden insisted on having a guard present in order to insure against any impropriety or infraction of prison rules and regulations during interview. Id.

⑧ The *Cross References* refer the reader to other statutes that cover topics related to § 146.

⑨ The *Library References* refer the reader to other texts that address the topic of the statute. On the left-hand side, there are two *key numbers* (Prisons 13 and Reformatories 7) that can be used to find more case law in the digests of West Publishing Company. In the right column, the library reference is to specific sections of C.J.S. *(Corpus Juris Secundum)*, a West legal encyclopedia.

⑩ The most important research resource in an annotated code is the *Notes of Decisions*. It includes a series of paragraphs that briefly summarize every court decision that has interpreted or applied § 146. Of course, the decisions cover cases decided before the code volume containing § 146 was published. For later decisions, the reader must look to the *pocket part* of this code volume, and to any supplemental pamphlets that have been added to the code. The first decision that you are given is *Kahn v. La Vallee*. Next is *Mummiani v. La Vallee*. At the end of the final paragraph, you will find **Id.,** which means that the paragraph refers to the case cited in the immediately preceding paragraph, the *Mummiani* case. (In addition to using the Notes of Decisions, another way to find later decisions is to shepardize § 146. See Checklist #4b on shepardizing a statute, page 612.)

With this perspective of what a statute in an annotated code looks like, we turn to some general guidelines on understanding statutes:

1. *The organization of a statutory code is often highly fragmented because it contains a large number of units and subunits.* A statutory code can contain anywhere from 5 to 150 volumes. If you are unfamiliar with a code, you should examine the first few pages of the first volume. There you will usually find the subject matter arrangement of all the volumes, e.g., "agency," "corrections," "corporations."

   An individual subject in a code may be further broken down into titles, parts, articles, or chapters, which are then broken down into sections and subsections. Here is an example of a possible categorization for the state of "X":

   X State Code Annotated
   Title 1. Corporate Law
   Chapter 1. Forming a Corporation
   Section 1. Choosing a Corporate Name
   Subsection 1(a). Where to File the Name Application
   Subsection 1(b). Displaying the Name Certificate
   Subsection 1(c). Changing the Corporate Name
   Section 2 . . . .
   Chapter 2 . . . .
   Etc.

   Of course, each state may adopt its own classification terminology. What is called a chapter in one state may be called a title in another.

   You also need to be sensitive to the internal context of a particular statutory section. A section is often a sub-sub-subunit of larger units.

   Example: Examine § 1183 in Exhibit 11.25.
   Note that § 1183 is within Part II, which is within Subchapter II, which is within Chapter 12, which is within Title 8.

   As indicated earlier, a legislature may completely revise its labeling system (page 581). What was once "Prison Law," for example, may now fall under the topic heading of "Correction Law." What was once section 73(b) of "Corporations Law" may now be

Exhibit 11.25 **Sections, Parts, Subchapters, Chapters, and Titles in a Statutory Code**

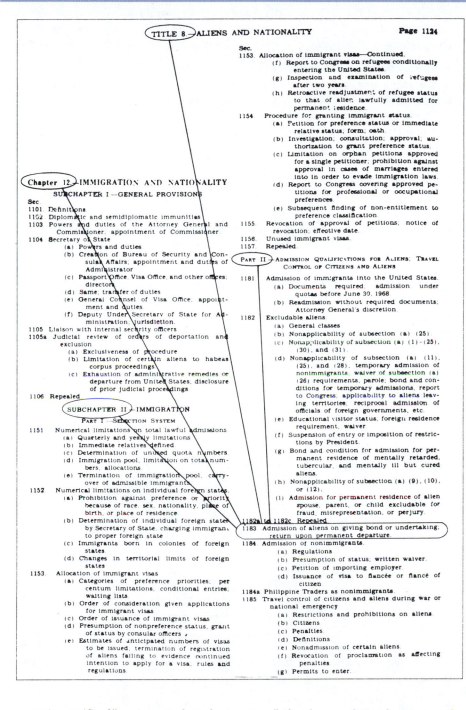

section 13(f) of "Business and Professions Law." If such a reordering has occurred, you should be able to find out about it either in a transfer table at the beginning of one of the code volumes or in the Historical Note at the bottom of the section.

2. *Statutes on administrative agencies often follow a common sequence.* A large number of statutes in a code cover administrative agencies. In fact, statutes are carried out mainly by administrative agencies. The agency may be a grant-making or service agency (such as the Social Security Administration) or a regulatory agency (such as the Federal Power Commission or the State Utilities Commission). Statutes that cover administrative agencies are sometimes organized in the following sequence:

- The agency is created and named.
- The major words and phrases used in this cluster of statutes are defined.
- The administrators of the agency are given titles and powers.
- The budgetary process of the agency is specified.
- The method by which the public first comes into contact with the agency is established, such as applying for the benefits or services of the agency.
- The way in which the agency must act when a citizen complains about the agency's actions is established.
- How the agency must go about terminating a citizen from its services is established.
- The way in which a citizen can appeal to a court, if not satisfied with the way the agency handled his or her complaint, is established.

3. *All statutes must be based on some provision in the Constitution that gives the legislature the power to pass the statute.* Legislatures have no power to legislate without constitutional authorization. The authorization may be the general constitutional provision vesting all legislative powers in the legislature, or, more often, it will be a specific constitutional provision such as the authority to raise revenue for designated purposes.

4. *Check to see if a statutory unit has a definition section.* At the beginning of a cluster of statutes, look for a definition section. If it exists, the section will define a number of words used in the remaining sections of the unit. Here is an example of such a definition section:

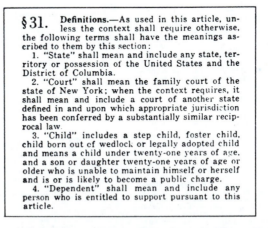

§ 31. **Definitions.**—As used in this article, unless the context shall require otherwise, the following terms shall have the meanings ascribed to them by this section:

1. "State" shall mean and include any state, territory or possession of the United States and the District of Columbia.

2. "Court" shall mean the family court of the state of New York; when the context requires, it shall mean and include a court of another state defined in and upon which appropriate jurisdiction has been conferred by a substantially similar reciprocal law.

3. "Child" includes a step child, foster child, child born out of wedlock or legally adopted child and means a child under twenty-one years of age, and a son or daughter twenty-one years of age or older who is unable to maintain himself or herself and is or is likely to become a public charge.

4. "Dependent" shall mean and include any person who is entitled to support pursuant to this article.

5. *Statutes should be briefed.* A "brief" of a statute consists of answers to the following questions:

(a) What is the citation of the statute? (On citing statutes, see Exhibit 11.10.)
(b) What are the *elements* of the statute? (See Exhibit 7.1 in chapter 7 on element identification.)

(c) To whom is the statute addressed? Who is the audience? (Everyone? The director of an administrative agency? Citizens who want to apply for a permit? Etc.)

(d) What condition(s) make the statute operative? (Often a statute will have "when" or "if" clauses that specify condition(s) for the applicability of the statute.)

(e) Is the statute mandatory or discretionary? A **mandatory statute** requires that something happen or be done ("must", "shall"). A **discretionary statute** permits something to occur, but does not impose it ("may", "can").

(f) What is the internal statutory context of the statute? To what other statutes, if any, does your statute refer?

(g) What is the effective date of the statute?

(h) Has the statute been amended in the past? (Check the Historical Notes that follow the statute. Briefly summarize major changes.)

(i) Has the statute been declared valid or invalid by the courts? (Check Notes of Decisions following the statute and shepardize the statute.)

(j) Do administrative regulations exist that interpret and carry out the statute? (On finding regulations based on statutes, see page 641. Give citations to any such regulations.)

6. *Statutory language tends to be unclear.* Seldom, if ever, is it absolutely clear what a statute means or how it applies to a given set of facts. For this reason, statutory language regularly requires close scrutiny and interpretation.

7. *Statutes are to be read line by line, pronoun by pronoun, punctuation mark by punctuation mark.* Statutes cannot be speed read. They should be read with the same care that you would use if you were translating a foreign language to English. Sentences sometimes appear endless. Occasionally so many qualifications and exceptions are built into a statute that it appears incomprehensible. Don't despair. The key is perseverance and a willingness to tackle the statute slowly, piece by piece—through its elements.

FINDING STATUTES

Techniques for Finding Statutes

1. Go to the statutory code in which you are interested. Some states have more than one statutory code. (See Exhibit 11.10.) For federal statutes, there are the *United States Code* (U.S.C.), the *United States Code Annotated* (U.S.C.A.), and the *United States Code Service* (U.S.C.S.). Know how to use all available statutory codes that cover the same set of statutes. While they contain the same statutes, the index and research features may differ.

2. Read the explanation or preface pages at the beginning of the first volume of the statutory code. Also read the comparable pages at the beginning of the Shepard's volumes that will enable you to shepardize statutes in that code. These pages can be very helpful in explaining the structure of the code, particularly if there have been new editions, revisions, or renumberings.

3. Most statutory codes have general indexes at the end of the set as well as individual indexes for separate volumes. Use the CARTWHEEL to help you use these indexes. Also check any tables of contents that exist. Some statutes have popular names, such as the Civil Rights Act of 1964. If you know the popular name of a statute, you can find it in the statutory code through a **Popular Name Table** that often exists within the code itself.

4. While reading one statute in the code, you may be given a cross-reference to another statute within the same code. Check out these cross-references.

5. Loose-leaf services. Find out if there is a loose-leaf service on the topic of your research. Such services will give extensive references to applicable statutes. (See *continued*

Techniques for Finding Statutes—continued

Checklist #5 on finding and using loose-leaf services, page 616.)

6. Legal treatises. Find out if there are legal treatises on the topics of your research. Such treatises will often give extensive references to applicable statutes. (See Checklist #8 on finding and using legal treatises, page 622.)

7. Legal periodical literature. Consult the *Index to Legal Periodicals* (ILP) and the *Current Law Index* (CLI). Use these indexes to locate periodical literature on the topics of your research. This literature will often give extensive references to applicable statutes. (See Checklist #6 on finding legal periodical literature, page 620.)

8. Annotations. Use the available index systems for A.L.R., A.L.R.2d, A.L.R.3d, A.L.R.4th, A.L.R.5th, and A.L.R. Fed. to help you locate annotations. Annotations will sometimes refer you to statutes—particularly in A.L.R. Fed. for federal statutes. (See Exhibit 11.17 and Checklist #3 on finding and updating annotations, page 601.)

9. Legal encyclopedias. Occasionally, legal encyclopedias such as Am. Jur. 2d and C.J.S. will summarize important statutes in the text and refer you to important statutes in the footnotes. (See Checklist #7 for using legal encyclopedias, page 621.)

10. Computers. (See page 623.)

11. Phone and mail research. Try to find an expert. (See Checklist #9 on doing phone and mail research, page 623.)

12. For every federal statute that you find, determine whether there are federal regulations on that statute. To

find out, check the "Parallel Table of Authorities and Rules" in the *C.F.R. Index and Finding Aids* volume.

13. Shepardize any statute that you locate through techniques 1–11 above. (See Checklist #4b on shepardizing a statute, page 612.)

14. Check the legislative history of important statutes (page 634).

15. Also update any statute that you find in the statutory code by checking the pocket part of the volume you are using, supplementary pamphlets, bound supplement volumes, etc.

16. Occasionally, in your research you will come across a statute that is cited in its *session law* form (page 610). To find this statute in the statutory code, you must translate the session law cite into the codified cite. This is done by trying to find transfer tables in the statutory code. For federal statutes, a session law or Statute at Large cite is translated into a U.S.C./U.S.C.A./U.S.C.S. cite by:

  (a) Checking Table III in the Tables volume of U.S.C./U.S.C.A./U.S.C.S.

  (b) Checking Table 2 in *U.S. Code Congressional and Administrative News* (U.S.C.C.A.N.)

Some session laws, however, are never printed in the statutory code. Hence there is no codified cite for such statutes. You must go directly to the session laws in the library—if the library has them. (For federal statutes, the session laws are in *United States Statutes at Large*, page 544.) It is also possible to shepardize session laws that are not codified, page 611.

Section R
LEGISLATIVE HISTORY

In chapter 6, we examined the six stages of the legislative process through which a bill becomes law. (See Exhibit 6.5.) The documents and events of this process constitute the **legislative history** of a statute. Here we consider two themes:

- Why researchers search for legislative history
- Finding legislative history

1. WHY SEARCH FOR LEGISLATIVE HISTORY: ADVOCACY OBJECTIVES

Problem: In 1975 the state legislature enacts the Liquor Control Act. Section 33 of this Act provides that "Liquor shall not be sold on Sunday or on any day on which a local, state, or federal election is being held." The Fairfax Country Club claims that § 33 does not apply to the sale of liquor on Sunday or on election day *by membership clubs;* it applies only to bars that provide service to any customers that come in off the street. The question, therefore, is whether the legislature intended to include membership clubs within the restrictions of § 33. The state liquor board says that it did. The Fairfax Country Club argues that it did not.

How can the legislative history of § 33 help resolve this controversy? An advocate has two objectives while researching the legislative history of a statute:

- To determine whether the specific facts currently in controversy were ever discussed by the legislature while it was considering the proposed statute, and
- To identify the broad or narrow purpose that prompted the legislature to enact the statute and to assess whether this purpose sheds any light on the specific facts currently in controversy

For example, when the legislature was considering § 33, was there any mention of country or membership clubs in the governor's message, in committee reports, in floor debates, etc.? If so, what was said about them? What was said about the purpose of § 33? Why was it enacted? What evil or mischief was it designed to combat? Was the legislature opposed to liquor on moral grounds? Did it want to reduce rowdyism that comes from the overuse of liquor? Did it want to encourage citizens to go to church on Sunday and to vote on election day? Were complaints made to the legislature about the use of liquor by certain groups in the community? If so, what groups? Answers to such questions might be helpful in formulating arguments on the meaning and scope of § 33. The advocate for the Fairfax Country Club will try to demonstrate that the legislature had a narrow objective when it enacted § 33: to prevent neighborhood rowdyism at establishments that serve only liquor. The legislature, therefore, was not trying to regulate the more moderate kind of drinking that normally takes place at membership clubs where food and liquor are often served together. The opponent, on the other hand, will argue that the legislature had a broader purpose in enacting § 33: to decrease the consumption of liquor by all citizens on certain days. The legislature, therefore, did not intend to exclude drinking at a membership club.

2. FINDING LEGISLATIVE HISTORY

In tracing legislative history, you are looking for documents such as bills, hearing transcripts, proposed amendments, and committee reports. Unfortunately, it is often very difficult to trace the legislative history of *state* statutes. The documents are sometimes poorly preserved, if at all.

Techniques for Tracing the Legislative History of State Statutes

1. Examine the historical data beneath the statute in the statutory code (see Exhibit 11.24). Amendments are usually listed there.
2. For an overview of codification information about your state, check the introductory pages in the first volume of the statutory code, or the beginning of the volume where your statute is found, or the beginning of the Shepard's volume that will enable you to shepardize the statutes of that state.
3. Ask your librarian if there is a book (sometimes called a **legislative service**) that covers your state legislature. If one exists, it will give the bill numbers of statutes, proposed amendments, names of committees that considered the statute, etc. If such a text does not exist for your state, ask the librarian how someone finds the legislative history of a current state statute in your state.

continued

Techniques for Tracing the Legislative History of State Statutes—continued

4. Contact the committees of both houses of the state legislature that considered the bill. The office of your local state representative or state senator might be able to help you identify these committees. If your statute is not too old, staff members on these committees may be able to give you leads to the legislative history of the statute. Ask if any committee reports were written. Ask about amendments, etc.

5. Ask your librarian (or a local politician) if there is a law revision commission for your state. If so, contact it for leads.

6. Is there a state law library in your area? If so, contact it for leads.

7. Check the law library and drafting office of the state legislature for leads.

8. Cases interpreting the statute sometimes give the legislative history of the statute, or portions of it. To find cases interpreting a statute, check the Notes of Decisions after the statute in the statutory code (see Exhibit 11.24) and shepardize the statute (see Checklist #4b on shepardizing a statute, page 612).

9. You may also find leads to the legislative history of a statute in legal periodical literature on the statute (see Checklist #6, page 620), in annotations on the statute (see Checklist #3, page 601), in treatises on the statute (see Checklist #8, page 622), and in loose-leaf services on the statute (see Checklist #5, page 616). Phone and mail research might also provide some leads (see Checklist #9, page 623).

It is easier to trace the legislative history of a *federal* statute, since the documents are generally more available.

Techniques for Tracing the Legislative History of a Federal Statute

1. Examine the historical data at the end of the statute in the *United States Code* (U.S.C.), in the *United States Code Annotated* (U.S.C.A.), and in the *United States Code Service* (U.S.C.S.).

2. You will also find the **PL** (Public Law) **number** of the statute at the end of the statute printed in U.S.C./U.S.C.A./U.S.C.S. This PL number will be important for tracing legislative history. (Note that each amendment to a statute will have its own PL number.)

3. Step one in tracing the legislative history of a federal statute is to find out if the history has already been compiled by someone else. Ask your librarian. The Library of Congress compiles legislative histories. If the statute deals with a particular federal agency, check with the library or law department of that agency in Washington, D.C., or in the regional office nearest you to see if it has compiled the legislative history. Also check with special interest groups or associations that are directly affected by the statute. They may have compiled the legislative history, which might be available to you. (One question you can ask through phone and mail research is whether the expert knows if any-

one has compiled the legislative history of the statute. See Checklist #9 on doing phone and mail research, page 623.) Ask your librarian if there is a *Union List of Legislative Histories* for your area. This list tells you what area libraries have compiled legislative histories on federal statutes.

4. The following texts are useful in tracing the legislative history of federal statutes:
   - *U.S. Code Congressional and Administrative News* (see Table 4)
   - *CCH Congressional Index*
   - *Congressional Information Service (CIS) Annual*
   - *Digest of Public General Bills and Resolutions*
   - *House Journal and Senate Journal*
   - *Congressional Quarterly*
   - *Congressional Monitor*
   - *Monthly Catalog of U.S. Government Publications.*
   - *Information Handling Service (legislative histories on microfiche)*

5. Contact both committees of Congress that considered the legislation. Ask for leads to legislative history. (They may be able to send you committee reports, hearing

Techniques for Tracing the Legislative History of a Federal Statute—continued

transcripts, etc.) Ask staff people in the office of your U.S. Senator and Representative for help.

6. Cases interpreting the statute sometimes give the legislative history of the statute. To find cases interpreting the statute, check the Notes of Decisions after the statute in the U.S.C.A. and in the U.S.C.S. Also, shepardize the statute (see Checklist #4b on shepardizing a statute, page 612).

7. Find out if there is an annotation on the statute. See the "Table of Laws, Rules, and Regulations" in the last volume of *ALR Index.* (See Exhibit 11.18 and Checklist #3 on finding and updating annotations, page 601.)

8. You may also find leads to the legislative history of a statute in legal periodical literature (see Checklist #6, page 620), in legal treatises on the statute (see Checklist #8, page 622), in loose-leaf services on the statute (see Checklist #5, page 616), and through phone and mail research (see Checklist #9, page 623).

9. To try to find a discussion of your statute in Am. Jur. 2d, a legal encyclopedia, check a separate volume called *Table of Statutes, Rules, and Regulations Cited.*

10. Examine your statute in its session law form in *United States Statutes at Large* for possible leads (page 544).

11. Check legislative histories online through WESTLAW and LEXIS.

Section S
MONITORING PROPOSED LEGISLATION

Occasionally, you will be asked to **monitor a bill** currently before the legislature that has relevance to the caseload of the law office where you work. If you work for a corporation, you may be asked to monitor bills that affect the business of the company. Large corporations often hire *lobbyists* whose sole function is to monitor and try to influence the content of proposed legislation. To monitor a bill means to determine its current status in the legislature and to keep track of all the forces that are trying to enact, defeat, or modify the bill.

Techniques for Monitoring Proposed Legislation

1. Begin with the legislature. Find out what committee in each chamber of the legislature (often called the Senate and House) is considering the proposed legislation. Also determine whether more than two committees are considering the entire bill or portions of it.

2. Ask committee staff members to send you copies of the bill in its originally proposed form and in its amended forms.

3. Determine whether the committees considering the proposed legislation have written any reports on it and, if so, whether copies are available.

4. Determine whether any hearings have been scheduled by the committees on the bill. If so, try to attend. For hearings already conducted, see if they have been **transcribed** (a word-for-word recording).

5. Find out the names of people in the legislature who are working on the bill: legislators "pushing" the bill, legislators opposed to it, staff members of the individual legislators working on the bill, and staff members of the committees working on the bill. Ask for copies of any position papers or statements.

6. The local bar association may have taken a position on the bill. Call the association. Find out what committee of the bar is involved with the subject matter of the bill. This committee may have written a report on the bar's position on the bill. If so, try to obtain a copy.

7. Is an administrative agency of the government involved with the bill? Identify the agency with jurisdiction over the subject matter of the bill. Find out who in the

continued

Techniques for Monitoring Proposed Legislation—continued

agency is working on the bill and whether any written reports of the agency are available. Determine whether the agency has a Legislative Liaison Office.

8. Who else is lobbying for or against the bill? What organizations are interested in it? Find out if they have taken any written positions.

9. What precipitated consideration of the bill by the legislature? Was there a court opinion that prompted the legislative action? If so, you should know what the opinion said.

10. Are any other legislatures in the country contemplating similar legislation? Some of the ways of finding out include the following:

    (a) Look for legal periodical literature on the subject matter of the bill (see Checklist #6, page 620).

    (b) Check loose-leaf services, if any, covering the subject matter of the bill (see Checklist #5, page 616)—these services often cover proposed legislation in the various legislatures.

    (c) Check legal treatises on the subject matter of the bill (see Checklist #8, page 622).

    (d) Organizations such as bar associations, public interest groups, business associations, etc. often assign staff members to perform state-by-state research on what the legislatures are doing. Such organizations may be willing to share this research with you.

    (e) Find out if there is a Council of Governments in your area. It may have done the same research mentioned in (d) above.

    (f) Contact an expert for leads to what other legislatures are doing (see Checklist #9, page 623).

Section T
READING AND FINDING CONSTITUTIONAL LAW

READING CONSTITUTIONAL LAW

The **constitution** sets out the fundamental ground rules for the conduct of the government in the geographical area over which the government has authority or jurisdiction. The constitution defines the branches of the government, establishes basic rights of citizens, and covers matters that the framers considered important enough (such as limitations on the power to tax) to be included in the constitution. (See Exhibit 6.1 in chapter 6.) The United States Constitution does this for the federal government, and the state constitution does it for the state government. In reading *constitutional law,* a number of guidelines can be helpful:

1. *Thumb through the headings of all the sections or articles of the constitution or glance through the table of contents.* How is the document organized? What subjects did the framers want covered by the constitution? A quick scanning of the section headings or table of contents is a good way to obtain an overview of the structure of the text.

2. *The critical sections or articles are those that establish and define the powers of the legislative, judicial, and executive branches of government in the geographic area covered by the Constitution.* Who passes, interprets, and executes the law? For the United States Constitution, "all legislative Powers granted herein shall be vested in a Congress" (art. I, § 1); "the judicial Power of the United States, shall be vested in one supreme Court, and in such inferior Courts as the Congress may from time to time ordain and establish" (art. III, § 1); and "the executive Power shall be vested in a President of the United States of America" (art. II, § 1). The exact scope of these powers, as enunciated elsewhere in the Constitution, has been and continues to be an arena of constant controversy and litigation.

3. *The amendments to the Constitution change or add to the body of the text.* The main vehicle for changing the constitution is the amendment process, which itself is defined in the constitution. Some constitutions, for example, can be amended by a vote of the people in a general election. A condition for most amendments is that they must be approved by one or more sessions of the legislature. Constitutional amendments usually appear at the end of the document.

4. *Constitutions are written in very broad terms.* There are, of course, exceptions to this, particularly with respect to the constitutions of local governments. In the main, however, a common characteristic of constitutional provisions is their broad language. How would you interpret the following section?

> Congress shall make no laws respecting an establishment of religion, or prohibiting the free exercise thereof; or abridging the freedom of speech, or of the press; or of the right of the people to assemble, and to petition the Government for a redress of grievances.

How many words in this provision do you *not* understand? What is an "establishment"? If the school board requires a "moment of silence" at the beginning of each day, is the school board establishing a religion? What does "abridging" mean? If a government official leaks secret documents to the press, and the government tries to sue the press to prevent the publication of the documents, has the "freedom" of the press been abridged? If the people have a right to "assemble," could the government pass a law prohibiting all gatherings of three or more people at any place within one thousand yards of the White House gates? The questions arising from the interpretation of constitutional law are endless; tens of thousands of court opinions exist on questions such as these. The broader the language, the more ambiguous it is, and therefore the greater the need for interpretation.

5. *One of the central questions for the interpreter of constitutional law is, what meaning did the authors intend?* Common sense dictates that when language is ambiguous, the ambiguity may be resolved in part by attempting to determine what the author of the language intended by it. What was the author's meaning? In what context was the author writing? Does the context shed any light on what was meant? This kind of analysis is fundamental to legal reasoning whether the document is a constitution, a statute, a regulation, or a case. It is particularly difficult to do, however, for a constitution written over a hundred years ago.

Finding the *original intent* of the authors of the constitution, however, is not the only method used to interpret particular provisions of the constitution. Another approach is to view the constitution as a "living" document that must be interpreted in the light of the needs of modern society. The danger in this view is that too much can be read into the constitution based on the personal philosophies of individual judges. The charge is that these individuals rewrite the constitution under the guise of interpreting it to fit modern society. This debate, of course, adds to the controversy and the volume of constitutional law.

FINDING CONSTITUTIONAL LAW

Techniques for Finding Constitutional Law

1. Start with the text of the constitution itself. It is usually found at the beginning of the statutory code of the jurisdiction. (The federal Constitution is in U.S.C./ U.S.C.A./U.S.C.S.).

2. Use the CARTWHEEL to help you use the general index of the statutory code and the separate index for the

continued

Techniques for Finding Constitutional Law—continued

constitution itself. (See Exhibit 11.12.) Also check the table of contents material for the constitution in the statutory code.

3. Following the text of individual constitutional provisions there are often Notes of Decisions containing summaries of cases interpreting the constitution. Some of these notes can run hundreds of pages. Check any available index or table of contents covering these notes.

4. Sheppardize the constitutional provision. The set of Shepard's to use is the same set you use for sheppardizing a statute. (See Checklist #4b on sheppardizing a statute, page 612.)

5. Annotations. Find annotations in A.L.R., A.L.R.2d, etc. on the constitutional provisions in which you are interested. (See Exhibit 11.17 and Checklist #3 on finding and updating annotations, page 601.)

6. Digests. Go to the *United States Supreme Court Digest* (West) (page 525). Also use the various West digests that cover other jurisdictions. (The American Digest System, of course, covers all jurisdictions.) Use the Descriptive Word Index (DWI) of a digest to locate relevant key numbers. (See Checklist #2 on using West digests, page 595.) (For cases on the U.S. Constitution, you can also go to the non-West digest—the *United States Supreme Court Digest, Lawyers Ed.*, page 525.)

7. Legal treatises. Find legal treatises on the entire constitution or on the specific portions of the constitution in which you are interested. Numerous such treatises exist. (See Checklist #8 on finding legal treatises, page 622.)

8. Legal periodical literature. Go to the two indexes to legal periodical literature: ILP and CLI. Use them to help you locate what you need among the vast periodical literature on the constitution. (See Checklist #6 on finding legal periodical literature, page 620.)

9. Loose-leaf services. Find out if there are loose-leaf services on the area of the constitution in which you are interested. (See Checklist #5 on loose-leaf services, page 616.)

10. Phone and mail research. Contact an expert. (See Checklist #9 on phone and mail research, page 623.)

11. *Words and Phrases.* Identify specific words or phrases within the constitutional provision you are examining. Find court definitions of these words or phrases in the multivolume legal dictionary, *Words and Phrases.*

12. Legal encyclopedias. Find discussions of constitutional law in Am. Jur. 2d and in C.J.S. (See Checklist #7 on legal encyclopedias, page 621.)

13. Sheppardize every case you found that interprets the constitution. (See Checklist #4a on sheppardizing a case, page 609.)

Section U
FINDING ADMINISTRATIVE LAW

An **administrative regulation** is a rule or law of an administrative agency that explains or carries out the statutes and executive orders that govern the agency. (See Exhibit 6.1 in chapter 6.)

There are many agencies writing regulations, but few of them have coherent systems of organizing and distributing the regulations. A major exception is the federal agencies whose regulations are first published in the *Federal Register;* many are then codified in the *Code of Federal Regulations.*

Normally, an agency does not have the power to write regulations unless it has specific statutory authority to do so. An examination of the statute giving the agency this authority can be helpful in understanding the regulations themselves. In theory, the statutes of the legislature establish the purpose of the agency and define its overall policies, but leave to the agency (through its regulations) the task of filling in the specifics of administration. Regulations, therefore, tend to be very detailed.

The other major kind of administrative law is the **administrative decision.** This is a resolution of a controversy between a party and an administrative agency involving the application of the regulations, statutes, or executive orders that govern the agency. (It is also called an *administrative ruling.* See Exhibit 6.1 in chapter 6.) Not many agencies publish their decisions in any systematic order; some agencies do not publish them at all. Regulatory agencies, such as the Federal Communications Commission and state environmental agencies, often do a better job at publishing their decisions than other agencies.

The federal government and most states have an **Administrative Procedure Act.** This is a statute that governs the steps that an agency must take to write a regulation or issue an administrative decision. Examples of these steps include publishing a notice of a proposed regulation, allowing affected parties to participate in a hearing that leads to an administrative decision, etc. Part of legal research in administrative law should address the question of whether the agency properly complied with the Administrative Procedure Act on such steps.

Techniques for Finding Administrative Law

1. Start with the agency itself. Call or visit the agency. There may be a regional or district office near you. Contact the library, the law department, or the public information section in the agency. Ask for a list of the agency's publications, such as regulations, decisions, annual reports. Also ask where these materials are located. Find out if you can come to the agency and use the materials. Ask about brochures describing the agency's functions, which can be sent to you.

2. Whenever an agency official is reluctant to let you have access to any publications of the agency, you may have to do separate research to find out whether you are entitled to access—under the federal *Freedom of Information Act* and its state equivalent, for example.

3. Many federal administrative regulations are printed in the *Code of Federal Regulations* (C.F.R.), which are usually printed first in their proposed form in the *Federal Register* before they are enacted by the agency. The C.F.R. comes out in a new edition every year. There are four main ways to locate regulations in the C.F.R.:

   (a) *The C.F.R. Index and Finding Aids* volume. This is a single-volume pamphlet that is reissued every year.

   (b) *The Index to the Code of Federal Regulations* published by Congressional Information Service (CIS).

   (c) Loose-leaf services. As indicated earlier, there are numerous loose-leaf services covering many federal agencies and some state agencies. These services usually give extensive references to administrative regulations and decisions. (See Checklist #5, page 616.)

   (d) An online search through WESTLAW and LEXIS. Also check the monthly and annual indexes within the *Federal Register.*

   If you find no federal regulations on point in the C.F.R. or in the *Federal Register,* you should check whether the agency has regulations, rules, bulletins, etc., that are published elsewhere. (See technique 1.)

4. Once you have found a federal regulation on point in the C.F.R., do the following:

   (a) Shepardize the regulation. (See Checklist #4c on shepardizing a regulation, page 614.)

   (b) Find the statute that is the *authority* for that regulation. Read this statute in U.S.C./U.S.C.A./U.S.C.S. Make sure the regulation does not contradict, go beyond the scope of, or otherwise violate the statute that the regulation is supposed to implement:

   • If you have a regulation and want to find out what statute is the authority for that regulation, look for the *authority* reference beneath the regulation in the C.F.R. (or at the beginning of the cluster of regulations in C.F.R. of which your regulation is a part).

   • If you have a statute and want to find out if there are any regulations implementing that statute, check the Parallel Table of Authorities and Rules in a volume called *CFR Index and Finding Aids* that accompanies the C.F.R. (and is also published separately by Lawyers Co-op as part of U.S.C.S.).

   (c) Once you have found a regulation in the C.F.R., you must find out if the regulation has been *affected* in any way (changed, revoked, added to, renumbered) by subsequent material printed in the *Federal Register.* This is done by checking your C.F.R. cite in:

   • The monthly pamphlet called *LSA: List of Sections Affected.*

   • The "CFR Parts Affected" table in the daily *Federal Register* from the date of the latest *LSA* pamphlet to the current date. (The "Reader Aids" section of the *Federal Register* has this table in a cumulative list.)

   The *LSA* pamphlet and the "CFR Parts Affected" table will tell you what pages of the *Federal Register* contain material that affects your regulation in the C.F.R. (You need to do this only until the next annual edition of the C.F.R. comes out, since anything affecting the regulation during the preceding year will be incorporated in the next edition of C.F.R.)

continued

Techniques for Finding Administrative Law—continued

(d) Find out if there is an annotation on your regulation. Shepardize the regulation. Annotations in A.L.R., A.L.R.2d, etc. are among the "citing materials" of Shepard's. Also, check the "Table of Laws, Rules, and Regulations" in the last volume of the *ALR Index* (see Exhibit 11.18).

5. *State* administrative agency regulations are much more difficult to find and update. Few states have an administrative code as comprehensive as the C.F.R. For most state agencies, you must check with your law library and with the agency itself (see technique 1 above) on how the regulations are printed, found, and updated.

6. When federal or state administrative *decisions* are printed, they will often be found in separate volumes for each agency. Also check loose-leaf services that cover a particular agency. (See Checklist #5, page 616.)

7. The *Federal Register* and the C.F.R. can also be found on WESTLAW and LEXIS.

Section V
FINDING LOCAL LAW

Find out if your city or county has a *municipal code* containing local *charters, ordinances,* etc. (For definitions of these categories of law, see Exhibit 6.1 in chapter 6.) Many charters are also printed in the state's statutory code. Check with your law librarian. Also call city hall, the city council, or the county commissioner's office. Speak with the public information officer or the law department. Ask about the local publications of your city or county. What is printed? Where is it found? How often is it printed? How is it updated?

The following are other items to check:

- Legal periodical literature on local issues such as zoning, municipal bonds, etc. (see Checklist #6 on legal periodical literature, page 620).
- The Shepard's volumes for a particular state will enable you to shepardize local charters and ordinances.
- Digests can be used to find case law on charters and ordinances (see Checklist #2 on digests, page 595).
- Annotations on *local law* in A.L.R., A.L.R.2d, A.L.R.3d, A.L.R.4th, and A.L.R.5th (see Checklist #3 on annotations, page 601).
- Treatises on local law (see Checklist #8 on legal treatises, page 622).
- Am. Jur. 2d and C.J.S. have discussions on local law (see Checklist #7 on legal encyclopedias, page 621).
- Loose-leaf services cover aspects of local law (see Checklist #5 on loose-leaf services, page 616).
- Local legal newspapers often cover charter provisions, new ordinances, etc.
- Phone and mail research; contact an expert (see Checklist #9 on phone and mail research, page 623).
- *Ordinance Law Annotations* (published by Shepard's) summarizes court opinions that have interpreted ordinances.

Section W
FINDING RULES OF COURT

You must always check the *rules of court* governing practice and procedure before a *particular* court. These rules will tell you how to file a request for an extension of time, the number of days a defendant has to answer a complaint, the format of a complaint or appellate brief, etc.

Techniques for Finding Rules of Court

Rules of Court for State Courts:

- Check your state statutory code for the text of the rules.
- Ask your librarian if there is a rules service company that publishes an updated edition of state rules of court.
- Find out if the court itself publishes its own rules.
- Shepardize rules of court in the same set of Shepard's you use to shepardize a statute (see Checklist #4b, page 612).
- For case law on the rules of court, check the digests for your state (see Checklist #2 on digests, page 595).
- Check local practice books, formbooks, or other treatises (see Checklist #8 on legal treatises, page 622).
- Check with an expert (see Checklist #9 on phone and mail research, page 623).

Rules of Court for Federal Courts:

- Check the U.S.C./U.S.C.A./U.S.C.S., such as title 28, title 18 (Appendix).

- Shepardize federal rules of court in *United States Citations, Statute Edition* (page 540).
- For case law on rules of court, check the digests, such as *Federal Practice Digest* 4th (see Checklist #2 on digests, page 595).
- Check the Federal Rules Service.
- Check special treatises on the federal rules such as:
  Moore's *Federal Practice.*
  Wright and Miller, *Federal Practice and Procedure.*
- Find annotations on the federal rules of court. Check the "Table of Laws, Rules, and Regulations" in the last volume of the *CFR Index* (see Checklist #3, page 601).
- Check legal periodical literature on the federal rules of court (see Checklist #6 on legal periodical literature, page 620).
- Check Am. Jur. 2d and C.J.S. on the federal rules of court (see Checklist #7 on legal encyclopedias, page 621).
- Check with an expert (see Checklist #9 on phone and mail research, page 623).

Section X
FINDING INTERNATIONAL LAW

Techniques for Finding International Law

1. In general, check:

- The yearly U.S. Statutes at Large (page 544), which contain U.S. treaties
- *United States Treaties and Other International Acts*
- *Treaties and Other International Acts Series*
- *United States Treaties and Other International Agreements*
- WESTLAW's database, USTREATIES
- LEXIS's ITRADE, INLAW, etc., libraries
- Blaustein and Flanz, *Constitutions of the Countries of the World*
- *CCH Tax Treaties*

- *Treaties in Force*
- *Department of State Bulletin*
- *United Nations Treaty Series*
- Catalog of U.S. publications
- *International Legal Materials*
- Szladits, *Bibliography on Foreign and Comparative Law: Books and Articles in English*

For other texts summarizing and commenting on treaties and international law generally, see Checklist #8 on legal treatises, page 622.

continued

Techniques for Finding International Law—continued

2. Legal periodical literature. There is extensive periodical literature on international law, both in general legal periodicals and in specialty periodicals devoted to international law exclusively. (See Checklist #6, page 620.)

3. Loose-leaf services, such as *CCH Tax Treaties,* mentioned above. (See Checklist #5 on loose-leaf services, page 616.)

4. American case law on international law. Check the digests. (See Checklist #2 on digests, page 595.)

5. Case law of foreign countries. Statutory law of other countries. Go to the international law section of a large law library.

6. Annotations on international law. (See Checklist #3 on annotations, page 601.)

7. Legal encyclopedias. For material on international law in Am. Jur. 2d and in C.J.S., see Checklist #7, page 621.

8. Phone and mail research. (See Checklist #9 on contacting experts, page 623.)

9. See *Restatement (Second) of Foreign Relations Law of the United States.*

10. Shepardize all treaties. Go to *Shepard's United States Citations, Statute Edition* (page 540).

11. *Martindale-Hubbell Law Dictionary*—Digest volume. Contains brief summaries of the law of many countries (page 535).

Section Y
THE THIRD LEVEL OF RESEARCH: VALIDATION

Earlier (page 588) we mentioned the three levels of legal research:

- Background research
- Specific fact research
- Validation research

In Exhibit 11.14, we examined the steps for conducting *background research* on an area of law that is new to you. In Section O (page 590) of this chapter, we examined the techniques of *specific fact research* through a series of extensive checklists. If you have done a comprehensive job on the first two stages of research, you may also have completed most of the third stage—**validation research.**

PERSPECTIVE OF THE OTHER SIDE

At the validation stage, you insure that everything you want to use from your research is still good law. This means making sure that the law is current and has not been affected by any later laws that you have not yet found. A good way to approach validation research is to take the perspective of the other side. Suppose that you have helped do some of the research for an appellate brief. It has been filed in court and served on the attorney for the other side. Your brief is handed over to a researcher in the law office of your opponent. That person will do the following:

- Read the full text of all *primary authority* (see Exhibit 11.15) on which you rely to see if you have interpreted the statutes, cases, regulations, etc., properly; to see whether you have taken quotations out of the context, etc.
- *Shepardize* the statutes, cases, regulations, etc., that you cite to find out whether the law is still valid (page 602).

- Read the *secondary authority* (see Exhibit 11.7 and Exhibit 11.8) that you cite to see whether you have interpreted the legal treatise, legal periodical article, etc., properly; to see whether you have taken quotations out of context, etc.
- Look for *other* applicable primary authority that you failed to mention.
- Look for *other* applicable secondary authority that you failed to mention.

Proper validation research means that you will be able to predict what this imaginary researcher will find when he or she checks your research through these steps. In short, at the validation stage of your research you must ask yourself:

- Have I found everything I should have found?
- Is everything I found good law?
- Have I properly interpreted what I found?

The answer to the first two questions should be *no* if:

- You did an incomplete job of *CARTWHEELING* the indexes of all the sets of books mentioned in the checklists and techniques in this chapter (see Exhibit 11.12).
- You failed to shepardize cases, statutes, constitutional provisions, rules of court, ordinances, treaties, etc., as called for in these checklists and techniques (see Checklists #4a, 4b, and 4c).
- You failed to take other standard validation steps, such as updating regulations in C.F.R. through the *LSA* pamphlet and the proper tables in the *Federal Register* (page 641).

TIME TO STOP?

At the outset of your research, the difficulty you face is often phrased as: "Where do I begin?" As you resolve this difficulty, another one emerges: "When do I stop?" Once the research starts flowing, you are sometimes faced with a mountain of material, and yet you do not feel comfortable saying to yourself that you have found everything there is to be found. See Exhibit 11.26 for some guidelines on handling this concern. With experience, you will begin to acquire a clearer sense of when it is time to stop. But it is rare for you to know this with any certainty. You will always have the suspicion that if you pushed on just a little longer, you would find something new and more on point than what you have come up with to date. Also, there is no way around the reality that comprehensive research requires a substantial amount of time. It takes time to dig. It takes more time to dig comprehensively.

> Someone "who tries to respond to a motion or brief without conducting fresh research is courting sanctions or a malpractice suit."
>
> —United States Court of Appeals for the Seventh Circuit, *Continental Illinois Securities Litigation v. Continental Illinois Corp.*, 962 F.2d 566, 570 (7th Cir. 1995)

Exhibit 11.26   Guidelines to Determine When to End Your Legal Research

1. *Instructions from your supervisor.* You must, of course, live within time guidelines imposed by your supervisor. You cannot spend the rest of your career in the law library working on one problem! If your supervisor has not set specific time guidelines for the research project, ask him or her to do so as soon as you determine that the project is going to take a significant amount of time. This may be an opportunity for the supervisor to narrow the focus of the project or to redirect your energies entirely.

2. *Repetition.* If you find that all the different avenues you are taking in the law library appear to be leading to the same primary and secondary authority, it may be time to stop. This repetition may be a good indication that you have already found what there is to find.

continued

Exhibit 11.26	**Guidelines to Determine When to End Your Legal Research—continued**

3. *Comprehensive via checklists.* Work with checklists to be sure that you are covering all the bases in the law library. One indication of when it is time to stop is when you are able to check off everything on your checklists.

Section Z
ANNOTATED BIBLIOGRAPHY AND RESEARCH PROBLEMS

An **annotated bibliography** is a report giving a list of library material on a particular topic, with a brief description of how the material relates to the topic. An annotated bibliography on contributory negligence, for example, would list the major cases, statutes, periodical articles, etc. and would explain in a sentence or two what each says about contributory negligence. The same would be true of an annotated bibliography on a set of facts that you are researching. If the facts present more than one research issue, you would do an annotated bibliography for each issue, or you would subdivide a single annotated bibliography into sections so that it would be clear to the reader which issue you are covering at any given place in the bibliography. The annotated bibliography is, in effect, a progress report on your research. It will show your supervisor the status of your research. (The following instructions mainly cover the preparation of an annotated bibliography for a topic that requires the application of state and local law. The same instructions, however, would be used when doing the bibliography on a federal topic. The exception would be instruction #9, which calls for local ordinances. For all other instructions below, replace the word *state* with the word *federal* when researching a federal topic.)

Instructions for Preparing an Annotated Bibliography

1. CARTWHEEL the topic of your annotated bibliography.
2. *Annotated* here simply means that you provide some description of everything you list in the bibliography—not a long analysis, just a sentence or two explaining why you included it. If you find no relevant material in any of the following sets of books, specifically say so in your report.
3. Hand in a report that will cover what you find on the topic in the sets of books mentioned in the following instructions.
4. Statutes. Go to your state code. Make a list of the statutes on the topic. For each statute, give its citation and a brief quotation from it to show that it deals with the topic.
5. Constitutions. Go to your state constitution (usually found within your state code). Make a list of the con-

stitutional provisions on the topic. For each provision, give its citation and a brief quotation from it to show that it deals with the topic.
6. Cases. If you found statutes or constitutional provisions on the topic, check to see if there are any cases summarized in the Notes of Decisions (see Exhibit 11.24) *after* these statutes or provisions. Select several cases that deal with the topic. For each case you select, give its citation and a brief quote from the case summary in the Notes of Decisions to show that it deals with the topic.
7. Digests. Go to the Descriptive Word Index of digests (page 595). Make a list of key topics that deal with the topic. (See page 523.)
8. Rules of court. Go to the rules of court that cover courts in your state (page 643). Make a list of the rules,

Instructions for Preparing an Annotated Bibliography—continued

if any, that deal with the topic. For each rule, give its citation and a brief quotation from it to show that it deals with the topic.

9. Ordinances. Go to the ordinances that cover your city or county (page 642). Make a list of the ordinances, if any, that deal with the topic. For each ordinance, give its citation and a brief quotation from it to show that it deals with the topic.

10. Administrative regulations. Are there any state agencies that have jurisdiction over any aspect of the topic? If so, list the agencies. If your library has the regulations of the agencies, make a list of the regulations, if any, that deal with the topic. For each major regulation, give its citation and a brief quote from it to show that it deals with the topic (page 641).

11. A.L.R., A.L.R.2d, A.L.R.3d, A.L.R.4th, A.L.R.5th, A.L.R. Fed. Go to these six sets of books (see Exhibit 11.17). Try to find one annotation in *each* set that deals with your topic. Give the citation of the annotations in each set. Flip through the pages of each annotation and try to find the citation of one case from a state court of your state, or from a federal court with jurisdiction over your state. Give the citation of the case.

12. Legal periodical literature. Use the *Index to Legal Periodicals* and the *Current Legal Index* to locate four legal periodical articles that deal with the topic (page 617). Try to find at least two relevant articles in each index. Give the citation of the articles. Put a check mark next to the citation if your library has the legal periodical in which the article is located.

13. Legal treatises. Go to your card catalog or computer index (page 591). Find any two legal treatises (page 622) that cover your topic. Give the citation of the treatises. Sometimes you may not find entire books on the topic. The topic may be one of many subjects in a broader treatise.

14. Loose-leaf texts. Are there any loose-leaf services on this topic (page 616)? Check the card catalog or computer index and ask the librarian. For each loose-leaf, give its citation and explain how it covers the topic.

15. *Words and Phrases*. Go to this multivolume legal dictionary (page 545). In this dictionary, locate definitions, if any, of the major words and phrases involved in your topic. Limit yourself to definitions from court opinions of your state, if any.

16. Shepardize every case, statute, or constitutional provision you find to make sure it is still valid (page 602).

17. Other material. If you come across other relevant material not covered in the above instructions, include it in the bibliography as well.

18. When in doubt about whether to include something in the bibliography, include it.

19. There is no prescribed format for the bibliography. One possible outline format you can use is as follows:

Topic: _____

A. Statutes (Instructions 4 and 16)
B. Constitutions (Instructions 5 and 16)
C. Cases (Instructions 6, 7, and 16)
D. Digests (Instruction 7)
E. Rules of court (Instruction 8)
F. Ordinances (Instruction 9)
G. Administrative regulations (Instruction 10)
H. A.L.R., A.L.R.2d, A.L.R.3d, A.L.R.4th, A.L.R.5th, A.L.R. Fed. (Instruction 11)
I. Legal periodical literature (Instruction 12)
J. Legal treatises (Instruction 13)
K. Loose-leaf texts (Instruction 14)
L. *Words and Phrases* (Instruction 15)
M. Other material (Instruction 17)

RESEARCH PROBLEMS

🏛 *A s s i g n m e n t   1 1 . 1 3*

Prepare an annotated bibliography on the following topics:

(a) Common-law marriage
(b) Negligence liability of a driver of a car to his or her guest passenger
(c) Negligence liability of paralegals
(d) Overtime compensation for paralegals
(e) Sex discrimination
(f) The felony-murder rule

(g) Default judgment

(h) Worker's compensation for injury on the way to work

(i) Fact situation assigned by your instructor

🏛 *A s s i g n m e n t   1 1 . 1 4*

In the problems that follow, include citations that support every position you take in your responses. In analyzing and researching some of the problems below, you may find it difficult to proceed unless you know more facts about the problem. In such situations, clearly state the missing facts that you need to know. In order to proceed with the analysis and research, you can assume that certain facts exist as long as you state what your factual assumptions are, *and* your assumptions are reasonable given the facts that you have.

(a) In your state, what entity (e.g., legislature, committee, court, agency) has the authority to prescribe rules and regulations on who can and who cannot practice law?

(b) List the kinds (or levels) of courts (local, state, or federal) that sit in your state and identify the major powers of each court; i.e., indicate what kinds of cases each court can hear.

(c) In your state, find a statute or court opinion that defines the following words or phrases:

    (i) Summons

    (ii) In personam

    (iii) Mandamus

    (iv) Exhaustion of administrative remedies

    (v) Judgment

    (vi) Jurisdiction

    (vii) Warrant

(d) Mary Adams works for a National Welfare Rights Organization (N.W.R.O.) chapter in your state. She is a paralegal. An N.W.R.O. member, Mrs. Peterson, has a complaint against a local welfare department branch concerning her public assistance check. Mary Adams goes to a hearing with Mrs. Peterson to represent her. The hearing officer tells Mary that she cannot represent Mrs. Peterson since she (Mary) is not an attorney. Is the hearing officer correct?

(e) Using the statutory codes of five different states (one of which must be your own state), find out how old a male and female must be to marry without consent of parent or guardian in each of the states.

(f) Go to any statutory code that has a pocket part. Starting with the first few pages of the pocket part, identify any three statutes that have totally repealed *or* partially modified the corresponding three statutes in the body of the bound text. Describe what the repeal or modification was. (*Note:* You may have to compare the new section in the pocket part with the old section in the body of the text in order to describe the change.)

In the following problems, use the state law *of your state* whenever you determine from your research that state law governs the problem.

(g) John Jones was sent to a state mental hospital after being declared mentally ill. He has been institutionalized for the last five years. In his own view, he is not now mentally ill. The hospital disagrees. What can John do? What steps might he take to try to get out?

(h) Peter Thomas is convicted of petty larceny. At the time of sentencing, his attorney asks the court to grant probation in lieu of a prison term. The judge replies, "Since Mr. Thomas has had three prior felony convictions (and since one of them was for attempted rape), I could not grant him probation even if I wanted to. I sentence him to a year in prison." On appeal, the attorney argues that the judge was incorrect in ruling that she had no power to grant probation to Mr. Thomas. Is the attorney correct?

(i) Mrs. Peterson invites a neighbor to her house for dinner. Mrs. Peterson's dog bites the neighbor. Is Mrs. Peterson responsible for the injury?

(j) Sam, age fifteen, goes to a used car lot. He signs a purchase agreement on a used car: $500 down and $100 a month for the next ten months. One day after the purchase, Sam allows a friend to drive the car. The friend demolishes the car in an accident. When Sam tells the used car dealer about the accident, he is told that he must still make all payments until the purchase price has been paid. Is the dealer right?

(k) An elderly woman presented the following facts to you during a legal interview. She and her husband moved into their house in 1946. Next to the house is a vacant lot. She does not know who owns the lot. She planted a small vegetable and flower garden on this lot and built a small fence around the garden. She has continued to cultivate this garden for the past twenty-seven years. Neighbors regard this garden as hers. Since her husband's death last fall, men in the neighborhood have been trying to use the garden area as a place to store their old car parts. She is troubled by this. What are her rights?

(l) Dorothy Rhodes and John Samualson are the parents of Susan Samualson. (Dorothy married Robert Rhodes after divorcing John Samualson.) Dorothy died after separating from Robert Rhodes. Susan's father has disappeared.

   Mr. and Mrs. Ford were neighbors of the Rhodes. Susan lived with the Fords for a long period of time while her mother was having marital difficulties. A court granted the Fords custody and guardianship in 1988. The Social Security Administration sent Susan the Social Security benefits she was entitled to on the death of her mother. In 1990, the Fords formally adopted Susan, but did not inform the Social Security office of this; they did not know that they had to. When the Social Security office learned of the adoption, they terminated the payments for Susan and informed the Fords that the money she had received since the adoption would have to be returned.

   The Fords and Susan want to know what substantive and procedural rights they have.

(m) Jane Smith owns a small shoe repair shop. The city sanitation department determines that Jane is a carrier of a typhoid germ. She herself does not have typhoid fever, but others could become infected with the fever by coming in contact with her. The city orders Jane's shop to be closed. She and her husband are not allowed to leave the shop until arrangements can be made to transfer them to a hospital.

   (i) Can the city quarantine Jane and her husband?
   (ii) If they enter a hospital quarantine, can they be forced to pay the hospital bill?
   (iii) Can they recover loss of profits due to the closing of their business?

(n) The Henderson family owns a $140,000 home next door to a small grocery store. The store catches fire. The firefighters decide that to get at the fire from all angles, they must break through the Henderson home, which is not on fire. Damage to the Henderson home from the activity of the firefighters comes to $40,000. Who pays for this damage?

(o) Bill and Mary are married with two children. They are happily married except for one ongoing quarrel. Bill is upset with Mary because she goes bowling every Friday night. Mary is disturbed with Bill because he plays cards every Tuesday night. To resolve their difficulty, they reach the following agreement: Bill will give up his Tuesday night cards if Mary will give up her Friday bowling. On Friday, Mary stays home. On the following Tuesday, however, Bill plays cards. He declares that he wants to continue the card playing. Mary wants him to live up to his agreement and brings a suit in court against him, charging breach of contract. (Assume that neither wants a divorce.) What result?

(p) After a series of serious accidents in which numerous riders are hurt, a bill is placed before the city council that would require all motorcyclists to wear protective helmets whenever riding. Is the bill constitutional?

(q) As a measure to enforce a standard of dental care, a bill is proposed that all the drinking water in the state be fluoridated and every citizen be required to visit a dentist at least once a year. Is this bill constitutional?

(r) Tom Jones has terminal lung cancer. Modern technology, however, can keep him alive indefinitely. Tom requests that the hospital official no longer use the technology. He wants to die. What are his rights?

(s) Alice Brown is seventeen years old. She is a self-styled hippie, who refuses to work. Alice's parents tell her that they will fully finance a college education for her. She refuses. The parents go to court and ask that their daughter be forced to go to college and avoid ruining her life. What result?

(t) In 1942 James Fitzpatrick died, leaving an estate of $50,000. The executor tried to locate the heirs. In 1943 the probate court closed the estate and distributed the money to the heirs who were known at the time. In 1986, an individual who says he is an heir appears. He wants to go to court to reopen the estate and claim his share of the inheritance. What result?

(u) Mary is the sole beneficiary of her father's will. Another sister is intentionally left out of the will by her father. There are no other heirs. Mary murders her father. Who gets his estate?

(v) The board of education is alarmed over increasing disturbances in the public schools. The superintendent of schools proposes that the board adopt a regulation that would authorize the school nurse, under the direction of the principal, to administer an oral tranquilizer to disruptive pupils so that they could be rendered "relatively passive" and responsive to school guidance. Discuss the legality of the regulation.

(w) The state claims that public assistance costs are bringing the finances of the state to the brink of bankruptcy. It is proposed that all children of parents receiving public assistance be required to attend vocational classes as part of their regular school curriculum. Discuss the legality of the regulation.

(x) Most kosher meat stores accept the United Kosher Butchers Association (UKBA) as the authoritative certifier that "all the religious requirements have been thoroughly observed." Associated Synagogues (AS) certifies caterers as authentic carriers of kosher food. AS refuses to certify caterers who buy meat from stores certified by the UKBA because the latter refuses to submit to supervision by the rabbinical committee of AS. Many caterers then withdraw their patronage from stores supervised by UKBA. What legal action, if any, can the UKBA take?

(y) The town of Salem has a population of 2,000. A group of avowed homosexuals moves into the area. They begin to run for public offices, with some success. The old-time townspeople become very upset. A state law gives courts the power to hospitalize mentally ill individuals. The mayor of Salem files petitions in court to have the homosexuals declared mentally ill and institutionalized. Discuss any law that might apply to these facts.

(z) Mary Perry belongs to a religion that believes that medical problems can be resolved through spiritual meditation. Her son Paul is ten years old. One day at school, Paul is rushed to a hospital after collapsing. Mrs. Perry is called at home. When she arrives at the hospital, she is told that Paul will require emergency surgery. She refuses to give her consent. The doctor tells her that if the operation is not performed within the next twenty-four hours, Paul will die. Mrs. Perry responds by saying that "God will cure my son." What legal action, if any, can be taken to protect Paul's rights and to protect Mrs. Perry's rights?

Chapter Summary

The law is changing every day. The only dependable way to find out about all of these changes is through legal research. Research skills will take time and determination to master. A useful first step is to compile a list of definitions or functions of the major research terms (such as citation, citator, cumulative, and headnote), and the major sets of research materials (such as A.L.R., *Corpus Juris Secundum*, Federal Reporter 3d, U.S.C.A., and WESTLAW).

You need to know where to find law libraries in your community, particularly depository libraries. Within these libraries, you will find the following kinds of authority that courts consider in reaching a decision: primary authority, which consists of laws such as statutes and cases; secondary authority, which consists of nonlaws such as law review articles and legal encyclopedias; mandatory authority, which a court *must* rely on; and persuasive authority, which a court has discretion to accept or reject.

A citation is an "address" where authority can be found in a library. *The Bluebook: A Uniform System of Citation* tells you what to abbreviate in the citation, where spaces and commas must be inserted, in what order the information in the citation must be provided, when to include a parallel cite, etc. Most courts do not follow the Bluebook; a court may have its own rules of citation that it follows. Yet a very large number of supervising attorneys and teachers will ask you to follow the Bluebook. When cite checking, you identify inaccuracies in citation form, shepardize the authorities cited, check the accuracy of any quotations referred to in the citations, etc.

Many law books have standard features. Each time you come across a new law book or set of law books, you should check features such as the copyright page, which contains the latest copyright date; and the forward or preface, which may give a general description of how to use the book. The tables or lists at the beginning of the book will help you understand terms, symbols, or signals used in the book. Check also for updating features, (such as pocket parts), various tables of contents, and index features that may be available.

The CARTWHEEL is a technique that helps you use the often poorly organized indexes (and tables of contents) of law books. The technique assumes that the entry you first check in the index (or table) leads you nowhere, and that you must now think of some other entries to check that might be more productive. The CARTWHEEL is designed to help you identify these other entries.

There are three levels of legal research: background research, in which you start identifying the basic vocabulary and the major principles of an area of the law that is relatively new to you; specific fact research, in which you look for primary and secondary authority covering the facts of a client's case; and validation research, in which you check the current validity of whatever authority you initially believed was relevant to the problem you are researching. Occasionally, aspects of all three levels of research will be going on simultaneously.

A competent legal researcher knows how to use the major search tools or resources:

- Card catalog (or the computer catalog) to find what is available in the library you are using
- Digests to find case law
- Annotations to find case law
- Shepard's to shepardize cases, statutes, and regulations in order to validate cited material and to find citing material such as case law
- Loose-leaf services to give you leads to, and explanations of, primary authority
- Legal periodical literature to give you leads to, and explanations of, primary authority
- Legal encyclopedias to give you leads to, and explanations of, primary authority
- Legal treatises to give you leads to, and explanations of, primary authority
- Phone and mail research to give you leads to, and explanations of, primary authority

The major CALR (Computer Assisted Legal Research) tools are WESTLAW and LEXIS. (In chapter 13, we will cover them in greater detail.)

These major search tools or resources will often lead you to more than one kind of primary authority: opinions, statutes (plus legislative history), constitutions, administrative law, local law, rules of court, and international law.

KEY TERMS

depository library, 507
act, 512
administrative code, 512
advance sheet, 512
annotations, 513
annotated reporters, 513
online, 513
legal encyclopedia, 514
annotated, 514
annotated statutory code, 514
bill, 514
slip law, 514
blue book, 515
appellate briefs, 515
amicus curiae brief, 515
casebook, 516
case, 516
opinion, 516
reports, 516
reporter, 516
official reporter, 516
unofficial reporter, 516
star paging, 516
Internet, 517
CD-ROM, 517
regional reporters, 518
special edition state
   reporters, 518
headnotes, 520
ultrafiche, 520
citation, 521
parallel cite, 521
public domain citation, 521
citator, 521
code, 520
codify, 521
cumulative, 522
digest, 522

abstracts, 523
squibs, 523
key number system, 523
regional digest, 525
formbook, 529
legal treatise, 529
hornbook, 530
World Wide Web, 530
interstate compact, 532
legal dictionary, 532
legal newsletters, 532
legal newspapers, 533
legal periodicals, 533
law reviews, 533
law journals, 533
legal thesaurus, 534
legislation, 534
loose-leaf service, 534
law directory, 535
microforms, 535
nutshell, 536
pocket part, 536
record, 537
Restatements, 537
American Law Institute, 537
rules of court, 537
court rules, 537
edition, 537
series, 537
session laws, 537
shepardize, 538
slip law, 541
statutory code, 541
slip opinion, 541
authority, 547
primary authority, 547
secondary authority, 547
mandatory authority, 548
persuasive authority, 548

nonauthority, 548
enacted law, 548
legislative intent, 548
on point, 549
analogous, 549
overrule, 550
stare decisis, 550
conflicts of law, 550
subject-matter jurisdiction, 550
personal jurisdiction, 550
Full Faith and Credit, 551
dictum, 551
plagiarism, 554
first impression, 555
caption, 561
et al., 565
litigation status, 565
in re, 566
docket number, 566
writ of certiorari, 566
nominative reporter, 566
pinpoint cite, 567
popular name, 568
generic citation, 576
electronic citation, 576
public domain citation, 576
cite checking, 577
supra, 578
infra, 578
title page, 579
copyright page, 580
table of cases, 580
table of statutes, 580
statutory history table, 581
CARTWHEEL, 583
committee reports, 589
KF call number, 591
trace a key number, 595

DWI, 595
superseded annotation, 600
supplemented annotation, 600
cited material, 604
citing material, 604
syllabus (Shepard's), 606
session law cite, 611
codified cite, 611
et seq., 613
case notes, 617
black letter law, 620
CALR, 623
query, 625
common law, 626
on all fours, 625
Notes of Decisions, 627
Historical Note, 628
Id., 630
mandatory statute, 633
discretionary statute, 633
Popular Name Table, 633
legislative history, 634
legislative service, 635
PL number, 636
monitor a bill, 637
transcribed, 637
constitution, 638
administrative regulation, 640
administrative decision, 640
Administrative Procedure Act, 641
validation research, 644
annotated bibliography, 646

Appendix 11.A   Bibliography of Legal Research and Citation Guides on State Law

Alabama

H. Johnson & T. Coggins, *Guide to Alabama State Documents . . .* (American Ass'n of Law Libraries, 1993).

G. Schrader, *Alabama Law Bibliography* (Barrister Press, 1990).

L. Kitchens, *Alabama Practice Materials,* 82 Law Library Journal 703 (1990).

Alaska

A. Ruzicka, *Alaska Legal and Law Related Publications* (American Ass'n of Law Libraries, 1984).

Arizona

K. Shimpock-Vieweg & M. Alcorn, *Arizona Legal Research Guide* (Hein, 1992).

R. Teenstra et al., *Survey of Arizona Law-Related Documents* (American Ass'n of Law Libraries, 1984).

A. Torres, *Arizona Practice Materials,* 80 Law Library Journal 577 (1988).

K. Fitzhugh, *Arizona Practice Materials,* 81 Law Library Journal 277 (1989).

Arkansas

L. Foster, *Arkansas Legal Bibliography* (American Ass'n of Law Libraries, 1988).

California

D. Martin, *California Law Guide,* 3d (Butterworth, 1995).

D. Henke, *California Law Guide, 2d* (Parker, 1976, 1995 Supp.).

V. Mackay & L. Peritore, *California Government Publications and Legal Resources* (American Ass'n of Law Libraries, 1991).

K. Castetter, ed., *Locating the Law: A Handbook for Non-Librarians, 2d* (So. Calif. Ass'n of Law Libraries, 1989).

T. Dabagh, *Legal Research Guide for California Practice* (Hein 1985).

M. Fink, *Research in California Law, 2d* (Dennis, 1964).

R. Formichi, *California Style Manual, 3d* (1986).

J. Hanft, *Legal Research in California, 2d* (Bankcroft, 1996).

B. Ochal, *California Current State Practice Materials,* 74 Law Library Journal 281 (1981).

Colorado

G. Alexander et al. *Colorado Legal Resources* (American Ass'n of Law Libraries, 1987). *See also* 16 Colorado Lawyer 1795 (1987).

S. Weinstein, *Colorado Legal Source Materials—1981,* 10 Colorado Lawyer 1816 (August 1981).

Connecticut

L. Cheeseman & A. Bielefield, *Connecticut Legal Research Handbook* (Conn. Law Book Co., 1992).

S. Bysiewicz, *Sources of Connecticut Law* (Butterworth, 1987).

D. Voisinet et al., *Connecticut State Legal Documents* (American Ass'n of Law Libraries, 1985).

District of Columbia

L. Chanin et al., *Legal Research in the District of Columbia . . .* (Hein, 1995).

C. Ahearn, *Selected Information Sources for the District of Columbia, 2d* (American Ass'n of Law Libraries, 1985).

Florida

M. Kaplan et al., *Guide to Florida Legal Research, 4th* (Fla. Bar, Cont. Legal Education, 1994).

N. Martin, *Florida Legal Research and Source Book* (D&S Publishers, 1990).

E. Tribble & C. Beane, eds., *Guide to Florida Legislative Publications & Information Sources, 3d* (Capitol, 1990).

C. Roehrenbeck, *Florida Legislative Histories* (D&S Publishers, 1986).

Florida Style Manual (Fla. State Univ. Law Review, 1991).

Georgia

L. Chanin & S. Cassidy, *Guide to Georgia Legal Research and Legal History* (Harrison, 1990).

R. Stillwagon, *Georgia Legal Documents* (American Ass'n of Law Libraries, 1991).

Hawaii

R. Kahle, *How to Research Constitutional, Legislative and Statutory History in Hawaii* (Hawaii Legislative Reference Bureau, 1986).

J. Dupont & B. Keever, *The Citizens Guide: How to Use Legal Materials in Hawaii* (1983).

Idaho

P. Cervenka et al., *Idaho Law-Related State Documents* (American Ass'n of Law Libraries, 1989).

L. Seeger, *Idaho Practice Materials,* 87 Law Library Journal 534 (1995).

Illinois

L. Wendt, *Illinois Legal Research Manual* (Butterworth, 1989).

C. Nyberg et al., *Illinois State Documents* (American Ass'n of Law Libraries, 1986).

L. Wendt, *Researching Illinois Legislative Histories,* 1982 Southern Illinois University Law Journal 601.

Indiana

L. Fariss & K. Buckley, *An Introduction to Indiana State Publications for the Law Librarian* (American Ass'n of Law Libraries, 1982).

Iowa

A. Secrest, *Iowa Legal Documents Bibliography* (American Ass'n of Law Libraries, 1990).

Kansas

J. Custer, *Kansas Legal Research & Reference Guide, 2d* (Kansas Bar Ass'n, 1997).

M. Wisnecki, *Kansas State Documents for Law Libraries* (American Ass'n of Law Libraries, 1984).

Kentucky

A. Torres, *Kentucky Practice Materials,* 84 Law Library Journal 509 (1992).

W. Gilmer, *Guide to Kentucky Legal Research, 2d* (State Bar Library, 1985).

Louisiana

W. Chiang, *Louisiana Legal Research, 2d* (Butterworth, 1990).

M. Hebert, *Louisiana Legal Documents and Related Publications* (American Ass'n of Law Libraries, 1990).

M. Cunningham, *Guide to Louisiana and Selected French Materials and Citation,* 67 Tulane Law Review 1305 (1993).

—continued

Appendix 11.A Bibliography of Legal Research and Citation Guides on State Law—continued

Maine

W. Wells, *Maine Legal Research Guide* (Tower Publishing, 1989).

M. Seitzinger, *Uniform Maine Citations* (1983).

Maryland

M. Miller, *Ghost Hunting: Finding Legislative Intent in Maryland* (Md. State Law Library, 1984).

L. Davis, *An Introduction to Maryland State Publications* (American Ass'n of Law Libraries, 1981).

L. Chanin, *Legal Research in the District of Columbia, Maryland, and Virginia* (Hein, 1995).

Massachusetts

M. Botsford et al., *Handbook of Legal Research in Massachusetts* (Mass. Continuing Legal Education, 1988).

L. McAuliffe & S. Steinway, *Massachusetts State Documents Bibliography* (American Ass'n of Law Libraries, 1985).

Michigan

R. Beer & J. Field, *Michigan Legal Literature, 2d* (Hein, 1991).

N. Bosh, *Research Edge* (Institute of Continuing Legal Education, 1993).

J. Doyle, *Michigan Citation Manual* (Hein, 1986).

S. Yoak & M. Heinen, *Michigan Legal Documents* (American Ass'n of Law Libraries, 1982).

Legal Research Guide for Michigan Libraries (Mich. Ass'n of Law Libraries, 1982).

D. Johnson, *Michigan Practice Materials*, 73 Law Library Journal 672 (1980).

J. Doyle, *Michigan Citation Manual* (1986).

Minnesota

M. Baum & M. Nelson, *Guide to Minnesota State Documents . . .* (American Ass'n of Law Libraries, 1986).

A. Soderberg & B. Golden, *Minnesota Legal Research Guide* (Hein, 1985).

Mississippi

B. Cole, *Mississippi Legal Documents . . .* (American Ass'n of Law Libraries, 1987).

Missouri

M. Nelson, *Guide to Missouri State Documents . . .* (American Ass'n of Law Libraries, 1991).

Montana

S. Jordan, *Montana Practice Materials*, 84 Law Library Journal 299 (1992).

Nebraska

M. Fontenot et al., *Nebraska State Documents Bibliography* (American Ass'n of Law Libraries, 1988).

P. Hill, *Nebraska Legal Research and Reference Manual* (Butterworth, 1983).

Nevada

K. Henderson, *Nevada State Documents Bibliography . . .* (American Ass'n of Law Libraries, 1984).

New Jersey

C. Allen, *A Guide to New Jersey Legal Bibliography . . .* (Rothman, 1984).

P. Axel-Lute, *New Jersey Legal Research Handbook, 2d* (NJ Institute for Continuing Legal Education, 1985).

C. Senezak, *New Jersey State Publications* (American Ass'n of Law Libraries, 1984).

Manual on Style (NJ Administrative Office of the Courts, 1979).

New Mexico

P. Wagner & M. Woodward, *Guide to New Mexico State Publications, 2d* (American Ass'n of Law Libraries, 1991).

New York

R. Carter, *Legislative Intent in New York State* (NY State Library, 1981).

R. Carter, *New York State Constitution: Sources of Legislative Intent* (Rothman, 1988).

S. Dow & K. Spencer, *New York Legal Documents* (American Ass'n of Law Libraries, 1985).

E. Gibson, *New York Legal Research Guide* (Hein, 1988).

Brown, *An Annotated Bibliography of Current New York State Practice Materials*, 73 Law Library Journal 28 (1980).

New York Rules of Citation, 2d (St. John's Law Review, 1991).

North Carolina

J. McKnight, *North Carolina Legal Research Guide* (Rothman, 1994).

T. Steele & D. Diprisco, *Survey of North Carolina State Legal and Law-Related Documents* (American Ass'n of Law Libraries, 1987).

North Dakota

For All Intents and Purposes: Essentials in Researching Legislative Histories (ND Legislative Council, 1981).

Ohio

C. Corcas, *Ohio Legal and Law-Related Documents . . .* (American Ass'n of Law Libraries, 1986).

D. Gold, *A Guide to Legislative History in Ohio* (Ohio Legislative Service Comm'n, 1985).

Ohio Legal Resources . . . 4th (Ohio Library Council, 1996).

M. Putnam & S. Schaefgen, *Ohio Legal Research Guide* (Hein, 1996).

Manual of the Forms of Citation Used in the Ohio Official Reports (Ohio Supreme Court, 1992).

Style Manual (Ohio Northern Univ. Law Review, 1980).

Oklahoma

C. Corcas, *Oklahoma Legal and Law-Related Documents . . .* (American Ass'n of Law Libraries, 1983).

Oregon

L. Buhman et al., *Bibliography of Law-Related Oregon Documents* (American Ass'n of Law Libraries, 1986).

Pennsylvania

J. Fishman, *Bibliography of Pennsylvania Law: Secondary Sources* (Pa. Legal Resources Institute, 1992).

J. Fishman, *An Introduction to Pennsylvania Publications . . .* (American Ass'n of Law Libraries, 1986). *See also* 78 Law Library Journal 74 (1986).

C. Moreland & E. Surrency, *Research in Pennsylvania Law, 2d* (Oceana, 1965).

Guide to Citation (PA, Commonwealth Court, 1981).

Appendix 11.A Bibliography of Legal Research and Citation Guides on State Law—continued

Rhode Island

C. McConaghy, *Selective Bibliography for the State of Rhode Island* (American Ass'n of Law Libraries, 1993).

Legal Research in Rhode Island (RI Law Institute, 1989).

South Carolina

P. Benson, *A Guide to South Carolina Legal Research and Citation* (SC Bar Continuing Legal Education, 1991).

R. Mills & J. Schultz, *South Carolina Legal Research Handbook* (Hein, 1976).

South Dakota

D. Jorgensen, *South Dakota Legal Documents* (American Ass'n of Law Libraries, 1988).

D. Jorgensen, *South Dakota Legal Research Guide* (Hein, 1988).

Tennessee

L. Laska, *Tennessee Legal Research Handbook* (Hein, 1977).

D. Picquet & R. Best, *Law and Government Publications of the State of Tennessee* (American Ass'n of Law Libraries, 1988).

L. Laska, *Tennessee Rules of Citation* (1982).

Texas

M. Allison & K. Schleuter, *Texas State Documents for Law Libraries* (American Ass'n of Law Libraries, 1986).

K. Gruben & J. Hambleton, *A Reference Guide to Texas Law and Legal History, 2d* (Butterworth, 1987).

P. Permenter & S. Ratliff, *Guide to Texas Legislative History* (Legislative Reference Library, 1986).

K. Gruben, *An Annotated Bibliography of Texas Practice Materials*, 74 Law Library Journal 87 (1981).

Texas Law Review Manual on Style, 7th (1992).

Texas Rules of Form, 8th (1992).

Utah

K. Staheli, *Utah Practice Materials*, 87 Law Library Journal 50 (1995).

Vermont

V. Wise, *A Bibliographic Guide to the Vermont Legal System, 2d* (American Ass'n of Law Libraries, 1991).

Virginia

J. Eure, *A Guide to Legal Research in Virginia* (Va. Law Foundation, 1989).

J. Lichtman & J. Stinson, *A Law Librarian's Introduction to Virginia State Publica-tions* (American Ass'n of Law Libraries, 1988).

L. Chanin, *Legal Research in the District of Columbia, Maryland, and Virginia* (Hein, 1995).

Washington State

S. Burson, *Washington State Law-Related Publications* (American Ass'n of Law Libraries, 1984).

M. Cerjan, *Washington Legal Researchers Deskbook* (Wash. Law School Foundation, 1994).

West Virginia

S. Stemple et al., *West Virginia Legal Bibliography* (American Ass'n of Law Libraries, 1990).

Wisconsin

R. Danner, *Legal Research in Wisconsin* (Univ. of Wash, Extension Law Dept, 1980).

J. Oberla, *An Introduction to Wisconsin State Documents . . .* (American Ass'n of Law Libraries, 1987).

Wyoming

N. Greene, *Wyoming State Legal Documents* (American Ass'n of Law Libraries, 1985).

Chapter **12**

LEGAL WRITING

▶ *Chapter Outline*

Section A
KINDS OF LEGAL WRITING

A law office prepares a number of different kinds of writing:

- Letters
- Memoranda of law
- Appellate briefs
- Instruments
- Pleadings

The first three will be discussed later in the chapter. Here is an overview of the other two:

Instruments: An **instrument** is a formal document that gives expression to a legal act or agreement. Examples of instruments include contracts, deeds, wills, leases, bonds, notes, and mortgage agreements. Many formbooks and computer programs provide models for drafting such instruments. Except for simple contracts, an attorney will rarely write an instrument from scratch. The starting point is almost always a standard form or model, which is adapted to the particular facts of the client.

Pleadings: **Pleadings** are formal statements of claims and defenses that are exchanged between parties involved in litigation. The major pleadings are the complaint (see Exhibit 10.12 in chapter 10 for an example), answer, counterclaim, reply to counterclaim, cross-claim, and third-party complaint. Formbooks and computers are also heavily used in drafting pleadings. Companies sell software that contains sample pleadings ready to be filled in and adapted to the needs of particular clients. Or, the office may simply adapt old pleadings from its computer files. Practices such as family law and bankruptcy often use repetitive pleadings. Their files, if properly organized in the computer database, can quickly generate pleadings needed for new clients. Standard word processing can then be used to make needed adaptations with relative ease for most cases.

Section B
LETTER WRITING

A law office writes many garden variety letters every day, such as a letter requesting information (see Exhibit 12.1), a letter demanding payment, a letter notifying someone that the office represents a particular person or company, a cover letter that tells the recipient you are sending ("enclosing") a document or other physical object in the letter or package. For guidelines on letter writing in general, see Exhibit 12.2.

One of the major categories of letters a law office often writes is the **confirmatory letter** in which you confirm that something important has been done or said. For example:

"This is to confirm that you have agreed to accept $5,000 in full settlement of the contract dispute between . . . ."

"Thank you for coming in Tuesday to discuss the extension of insurance coverage for the employees in the Southeast region of your company's operations. I want to state my understanding of what took place at the meeting. Please let me know if this is consistent with your understanding. . . ."

Exhibit 12.1 **Sample Letter**

Gordon, Davis & Kildare
8268 Prestwick Drive
Boston, MA 02127
617-268-1899
617-268-9203 (fax)

Mary Gordon, Esq.
John Davis, Esq.
Lance Kildare, Esq.

March 13, 1997
RE: Massy Ford v. Cuttler
97-3456

Brenda A. Sarbanes
Vice President
Dennison Research Institute
74 Statler Road
Belmont, MA 02177

Dear Ms. Sarbanes:

Our office represents Charles Cuttler in a stock distribution suit against Massy Ford, Inc. I understand that your company provides marketing research used in litigation. I want to obtain some information about your services.

Do you have any literature you could send me on the kind of research you do? How are your fees determined? Finally, do you have any examples of reports you have prepared in the past that we could see?

To give you an idea of our practice, I am enclosing our firm brochure. Thank you for your consideration.

Sincerely,

Sean Williams
Paralegal

cc: Edith Jenkins

Encl.
SW:ebw

Exhibit 12.2 **Guidelines on Letter Writing**

1. Obtain clear instructions from your supervisor on (a) the purpose of the letter, (b) who will sign it, and (c) the date you should have a draft available for that person.

2. Determine if the office has any models for your letter. In the past, has the office ever sent out this kind of letter? If so, read them. Ask your supervisors if the letters are good examples, and if you should use them as a guide.

3. In form, your letter must be perfect. Here are the components to include:

   - **Heading** The heading is the letterhead, often preprinted. It contains the full name, address, and phone number of your law office. It is usually centered at the top of the page.
   - **Date** Give the full date (month, day, year) that the letter will be sent out. It is often placed at the right margin under the heading.
   - **Recipient** This is the full name, title, and address of the person who will be receiving the letter. It is often placed at the left margin.
   - **RE:** This is a brief statement that indicates the case to which the letter pertains, and occasionally the major theme of the letter (e.g., "RE: Henderson v. Jones, Civ. 92.179. Request for Extension of Time to File Responsive Declaration"). It is placed at either the right margin or the left margin.
   - **Salutation** Here you address the recipient "Dear . . ." A colon (:) follows the last name of this person. If he or she is a doctor, professor, or important public official, use his or her title. The salutation often starts at the left margin on the line under the address.
   - **Identification Line** In the first line of the letter, let the reader know who is sending the letter, unless this is already obvious to the recipient because of prior contact.
   - **Purpose Line** Shortly after the identification line, briefly tell the reader the main purpose of the letter.
   - **Body** In the main body of the letter, you explain the purpose of the letter in greater detail.
   - **Request Line** If you are asking the recipient to do something, be sure there is a specific request line in the letter that makes this clear.
   - **Closing** Here you conclude the letter. This should be a separate paragraph. Say something like, "If you have any questions about this matter, please do not hesitate to contact me." or "Thank you for your consideration in this matter." On the next line write, "Sincerely" or "Very truly yours." Place the name and title of the signer of the letter below the space for his or her signature.
   - **Copies Sent** If you are sending a copy of the letter to someone, indicate this by saying "cc:" followed by the name of the person(s) receiving the copy ("cc" stands for carbon copies; this abbreviation is still used even though carbon is seldom the method used today to make copies). Suppose you send out copies of the letter, but you do not want the recipient to know this. On the recipient's letter, you say nothing about copies. On the office copy of the letter, say "bcc:" (blind carbon copy) followed by the name of the people getting the copies. In this way, only your copy of the letter indicates who received copies. The main letter is silent ("blind") on this point.
   - **Enclosures** If you are enclosing anything with the letter, say, "Encl." If enclosing more than one item, say, "Encls."
   - **Initials** If someone else typed the letter for you, place your initials in capital letters, followed by a colon (:) and the initials (in lowercase) of the person who did the typing.

4. Grammatically, your letter must be perfect. There should be no spelling errors.

5. If the letter is to be sent to a client or another individual who is not an attorney, do not use technical words unless you define them in the letter. The only exception is when prior contact with the recipient leaves no doubt that he or she understands the words.

6. Avoid long sentences. There of course is no law specifying the number of words you should use in a sentence. Keep in mind, however, that shorter sentences are easier to understand, *particularly when dealing with technical subjects*. After you write a sentence, force yourself to decide whether the sentence would be clearer if you broke it into two or more shorter sentences (see Section E later in this chapter).

This kind of letter is important because it provides written confirmation of matters that might be subject to misunderstanding with the passage of time. It is also a good way to provide a record for the file. In this sense, a confirmatory letter is similar to a "memo to the file" in which you communicate something about the case that has taken place, e.g., the substance of a recent telephone conversation or the result of some research in the law library. A memo of this kind might not be important enough to send to a supervisor, but should be in the file where anyone working on the case will have access to it when using the file. The confirmatory letter is different, of course, since it goes to someone outside the office in an effort to prompt him or her to voice any disagreements with the contents of the letter.

In an **opinion letter,** the office writes to its client to explain the application of the law and advise the client what to do. Such letters try to clarify technical material. Unlike a brief or memorandum, the opinion letter does not make extensive reference to court opinions or statutes. The client's need is for clear, concise, practical advice.

🏛   *A s s i g n m e n t   1 2 . 1*

Prepare a letter for each of the following situations. You will need more facts to complete the letters (e.g., the address of the recipient, your address, and more details on the purpose of the letter). You can make up any of these facts as long as they are reasonably consistent with the facts provided. In each case, your supervisor is an attorney who wants you to draft the letter for his or her signature.

(a) The office represents Richard Clemens, who is a plaintiff in an automobile accident case against George Kiley. The latter's insurance company has offered to settle for $10,000. Draft a letter to Richard Clemens in which you tell him about the offer and ask him to call you so that you can schedule an appointment with your supervisor to discuss the offer. Point out that the supervisor is not pleased with the low amount of the offer, but that the decision on whether to accept it will be entirely up to the client.

(b) Draft a letter to a client who failed to appear at two meetings last month with her attorney (your supervisor) at the office to discuss her case. The client is Diane Rolark. She is very wealthy. The office hopes to keep her as a client in the future on other cases. Hence, the office does not want to antagonize her. The letter should remind her of the next appointment with her attorney (three weeks from today).

(c) Write an opinion letter to a client, James Duband, in which you explain any legal concept that you have learned in another course. Assume that this concept is relevant to the case of this client, and that the client has written the office asking your supervisor to explain the concept as it pertains to his case.

S e c t i o n   C
MEMORANDUM OF LAW

A **memorandum of law** is a written analysis of a legal problem. (The plural is memoranda; the shorthand is memo.) More specifically, it is a written explanation of how the law applies to a given set of facts. There are two main kinds of memoranda: (1) an internal or interoffice memorandum, and (2) an external or advocacy memorandum. The differences are outlined in Exhibit 12.3.

INTEROFFICE MEMORANDUM OF LAW	EXTERNAL MEMORANDUM OF LAW
Exhibit 12.3 **Characteristics of Interoffice and External Memoranda of Law**	
• Emphasizes both the strengths and the weaknesses of the client's position on each issue (objective)	• Emphasizes the strengths but minimizes or ignores the weaknesses of the client's position on each issue (adversary)
• Emphasizes both the weaknesses and the strengths of the opposing party's known or anticipated position on each issue (objective)	• Emphasizes the weaknesses but minimizes or ignores the strengths of the opposing party's position on each issue (adversary)
• Predicts the court's or the agency's probable decision on each issue	• Argues for a favorable decision on each issue
• Recommends the most favorable strategy for the client to follow	

1. *Interoffice Memorandum of Law:* The main audience of your **interoffice memorandum of law** is your supervisor; the memo is an internal document.[1] Your goal in the memo is to analyze the law in order to make a *prediction* of how a court or other tribunal will resolve the dispute in the client's case. It is extremely important that this memo present the strengths *and weaknesses* of the client's case. The supervisor must make strategy decisions based in part on what you say in the memo. Hence the supervisor must have a realistic picture of what the law is. Many students find it very difficult to present strengths and weaknesses in the same memo. They devote the vast majority of their memo to arguments that favor one side. This kind of writing is inappropriate in an interoffice memorandum of law. Force yourself to find arguments that support both sides—no matter which side is the client of your office and no matter which side you think should win. A hallmark of the professional is the ability to step back and assess a problem objectively. This means being able to analyze strengths and weaknesses of both sides.

2. *External or Advocacy Memorandum of Law:* The main audience of your **external memorandum of law** is someone outside the office, usually a judge or official in an administrative agency. Your goal in this memo is to try to convince the reader to take a certain action in the client's case. Hence, the memo is an *advocacy* document. In it, you are highlighting the strengths of the client's case and the weaknesses of the opponent's case.

   Different terminology is sometimes used for this kind of memo:

   • **Points and Authorities Memorandum:** An external memorandum submitted to a trial judge or hearing officer.
   • **Trial Memorandum:** An external memorandum submitted to a trial judge (also called a trial brief).
   • **Hearing Memorandum:** An external memorandum submitted to a hearing officer or administrative law judge within an administrative agency.

   When the document is submitted to an appellate court, it is called an appellate brief. The structure of the appellate brief is considered later in the chapter.

---

[1]Sometimes it is referred to as an **intraoffice memorandum of law** because it stays within the office.

Most of the discussion that follows is on the internal interoffice memo. The external advocacy memo is mentioned only when there are significant differences.

STRUCTURE OF AN INTEROFFICE MEMORANDUM OF LAW

What is the format or structure of an interoffice memorandum of law? The cardinal guideline is: Find out what format your supervisor prefers. There may be office memos in old files that you can use as models. If your supervisor does not express a preference, consider using the following format:

1. Heading
2. Statement of the assignment
3. Issues
4. Facts
5. Discussion or analysis
6. Conclusion
7. Recommendations
8. Appendix

1. Heading

The **heading** of the memo contains basic information about you and the nature of the memo:

a. A **caption** centered at the top of the page stating the kind of document it is (Interoffice Memorandum of Law)
b. The name of the person to whom the memo is addressed (usually your supervisor)
c. Your name (the author of the memo)
d. The date the memo was completed and submitted
e. The name of the case (client's name and opponent, if any)
f. The office file number
g. The court **docket number** (if the suit has already been filed and the clerk of the court has assigned a docket number)
h. The subject matter of the memo following the notation **RE:**, meaning "in the matter of" or "concerning"

The example in Exhibit 12.4 illustrates how this information might be set forth in a memo written on behalf of client Brown, who is suing Miller.

Note that the subject-matter description (RE) in this example briefly indicates the nature of the question you are treating in the memorandum. This information is needed for at least two reasons. First, the average law office case file contains a large number of documents, often including several legal memoranda. A heading that at least briefly indicates the nature of the subject of each memorandum makes it easier to locate the

---

Exhibit 12.4 **Heading of Interoffice Memorandum**

Interoffice Memorandum of Law

TO: Jane Patterson, Esq.
FROM: John Jackson, Paralegal
DATE: March 13, 1994   RE: Whether substituted service is
CASE: Brown v. Miller   allowed under Civil Code
OFFICE FILE NUMBER: 94-1168   § 34-403(g)
DOCKET NUMBER: C-34552-94

memorandum in the client's file. Second, your memo might be examined sometime in the future, long after the case is over. Many offices keep copies of old office memoranda in files or in computer databases. They are cataloged by subject matter for reference in future cases. The subject-matter heading on the memo facilitates the cataloging, filing, and retrieving of such memos.

Including the date on which the memorandum was completed and submitted is important for similar reasons. While your analysis and conclusions may have been accurate at the time the memorandum was written, the law may have changed by the time the memorandum is examined again. When the reader sees the date of the memorandum, he or she will know from what date subsequent legal research will be needed.

2. Statement of the Assignment

Soon after you are given an interoffice memorandum assignment, you should write out what you are asked to do. State the parameters of the assignment. If limitations or restrictions were imposed (e.g., not to cover a particular issue), include them in your written statement. If you have any difficulty writing the statement, consult with your supervisor immediately. The time to clarify what you are to do—and what you are not to do—is before you spend extensive amounts of time researching, analyzing, and writing. Here is an example:

> **Statement of Assignment**
> You have asked me to prepare a memorandum of law limited to the question of whether our client, Joan Davis, is required to return the overpayment she received from the Department of Revenue and Disbursements. You asked me to discuss Ohio law only.

Include this statement of the assignment after the heading. The value of clearly articulating the boundary lines of the memo cannot be overemphasized.

3. Issues

On phrasing issues, see page 349.

Often you must state and discuss certain issues *on the assumption* that the court or agency will decide against you on prior issues that you discuss early in the memorandum. Suppose that the client is a defendant in a negligence action. The first issue may concern the liability of the defendant: Was the defendant negligent or not? The memorandum will cover the liability question and will attempt to demonstrate in the discussion or analysis of this issue why the defendant is *not* liable. All the evidence and authority supporting nonliability will be examined under this issue. At the time the memorandum is written, of course, this issue will not have been resolved. Hence, you must proceed *on the assumption* that the client will lose the first issue and be prepared for other issues that will then arise. For example, all issues concerning damages (how much money must be paid to a plaintiff who has successfully established liability) need to be anticipated and analyzed in the event that the liability issue is lost. The statement of the damage issue in the memorandum should be prefaced by language such as:

> In the event that we lose the first issue, then we must discuss the issue of . . . .

or

> On the assumption that the court finds for [the other party] on the liability issue, the damages question then becomes whether . . . .

No matter how firmly you believe in your prediction of what a court or agency will do on an issue, be prepared for what will happen in the event that your prediction eventually proves to be erroneous. This must be done in an internal memorandum, in an external memorandum (hearing or trial), and in an appellate brief.

4. Facts

Your statement of the facts of the client's case is one of the most important components of the memorandum. You should take great pains to see that it is concise, highly accurate, and well organized.

a. *Conciseness:* An unduly long fact statement only frustrates the reader. Try to eliminate any unnecessary facts from the statement. One way of doing this is to carefully review your fact statement *after* you have completed your analysis of the issues. If your statement contains facts that are not subsequently referred to in your analysis, it may be that those facts are not particularly relevant to your memorandum and can be eliminated in your final draft. Otherwise, go back and discuss them in your analysis.

b. *Accuracy:* In many instances you will be drafting the memorandum for an attorney who is preparing to go before a court or agency for the first time; there may be no prior proceedings. Hence, there will be no record and no official findings of fact. The temptation will be to indulge in wishful thinking—to ignore adverse facts and to assume that disputed facts will be resolved in favor of the client. Do not give in to this temptation. You must assess the legal consequences of favorable *and* unfavorable facts. If a particular fact is presently unknown, put aside your writing, if possible, and investigate whatever evidence exists to prove the fact one way or the other. If it is not practical to conduct an investigation at the present time, then you should provide an analysis of what law will apply based on your most reasonable estimate of what an investigation may uncover. (When you get to the recommendations section of the memo, be sure to include investigation that the office should undertake later.) The need for accuracy does not mean that you should fail to state the facts in the light most favorable to the client. It simply means that you must be careful to avoid making false or misleading statements of fact.

c. *Organization:* A disorganized statement of facts not only prevents the reader from understanding the events in question but also interferes with an understanding of your subsequent analysis. In general, it is best to start with a short one- or two-sentence summary of the nature of the case. If the case has already been in court, include the prior proceedings to date in this summary. Then provide a *chronological* statement of the detailed facts. Occasional variations from strict chronological order can be justified as long as they do not interfere with the flow of the story.

5. Discussion or Analysis

Here you present the law and explain its applicability to the facts. In other words, you try to answer the issues. For memos that require interpretation of statutes, the following organizational structure is suggested:

- State the entire section or subsection of the statute that you are analyzing. Include only what must be discussed in the memo. If the section or subsection is long, you may want to place it in an appendix to the memo. If you are going to discuss more than one section or subsection, treat them separately in different parts of the memo unless they are so interrelated that they must be discussed together.
- Break the statute into its elements. (An element is a portion of a rule that is a precondition of the applicability of the entire rule.) List each element separately. (See "Organizing a Memorandum of Law" in Exhibit 7.1 in chapter 7.)

- Briefly tell the reader which elements will be in contention and why. In effect, you are telling him or her why you have phrased the issue(s) the way you did earlier in the memo.
- Go through each element you have identified, one at a time, spending most of your time on the elements that are most in contention.
- For the elements not in contention, simply tell the reader why you think there will not be any dispute about them. For example, you anticipate that both sides probably will agree that the facts clearly support the applicability or nonapplicability of the element.
- For the elements in contention, present your interpretation of each element; discuss court opinions that have interpreted the statute, if any; discuss regulations and administrative decisions that have interpreted the statute, if any; discuss the legislative history of the statute, if available (page 634); discuss scholarly interpretation of the statute, if any.
- Give opposing viewpoints for the elements in contention. Try to anticipate how the other side will interpret these elements. For example, what counterarguments will the other side probably make through court opinions or legislative history?

6. Conclusion

Give your personal opinion on which side has the better arguments. Do not state any new arguments in the conclusion. Simply state your own perspective on the strengths and weaknesses of your arguments.

7. Recommendations

State recommendations you feel are appropriate in view of the analysis and conclusion that you have provided. For example, further facts should be investigated, further research should be undertaken, a letter should be written to the agency involved, the case should be litigated or settled, etc.

8. Appendix

At the end of the memo, include special items, if any, that you referred to in the memo, such as photographs, statistical tables, or the full text of statutes.

What follows is an interoffice memorandum of law that conforms with this structure. Assume that the supervisor wants this memorandum within a few hours after it is given to you. You are asked to provide a preliminary analysis of a statute. Hence, at this point there has been no time to do any research on the statute, although the memo should indicate what research will be needed.

```
                      INTEROFFICE MEMORANDUM OF LAW

TO: Mary Jones, Esq.                  RE: Whether Donaldson has
FROM: Paul Vargas, Paralegal              violated § 17
DATE: March 23, 1990
CASE: Department of Sanitation v. Jim Donaldson
OFFICE FILE NUMBER: 90-114
DOCKET NUMBER: (none at this time; no action has been filed)
```

A. ASSIGNMENT

You have asked me to do a preliminary analysis of 23 State Code Ann. § 17 (1980) to assess whether our client, Jim Donaldson, has violated this statute. No research on the statute has been undertaken thus far, but I will indicate where such research might be helpful.

B. LEGAL ISSUE

When a government employee is asked to rent a car for his agency, but uses the car for personal business before he signs the lease, has this employee violated § 17, which prohibits the use of "property leased to the government" for nonofficial purposes?

C. FACTS

Jim Donaldson is a government employee who works for the State Department of Sanitation. On February 12, 1990, he is asked by his supervisor, Fred Jackson, to rent a car for the agency for a two-year period. At the ABC Car Rental Company, Donaldson is shown several cars available for rental. He asks the manager if he could test drive one of the cars for about 15 minutes before making a decision. The manager agrees. Donaldson then drives the car to his home in the area, picks up a TV, and takes it to his sister's home. When he returns, he tells the manager that he wants to rent the car for his agency. He signs the lease and takes the car to the agency. The supervisor, however, finds out about the trip that Donaldson made to his sister with the TV. He is charged with a violation of § 17. Since he is a new employee at the agency, he is fearful that he might lose his job.

D. ANALYSIS

Donaldson is charged with violating 23 State Code Ann. § 17 (1980), which provides as follows:

§17. Use of Government Property
An employee of any state agency shall not directly or indirectly use government property of any kind, including property leased to the government, for other than officially approved activities.

To establish a violation of this statute, the following elements must be proven:

(1) An employee of any state agency
(2) (a) shall not directly use government property of any kind including property leased to the government, or
    (b) shall not indirectly use government property of any kind including property leased to the government
(3) for other than officially approved activities

The main problem in this case will be the second element.

(1) Employee of a state agency
Donaldson works for the State Department of Sanitation, which is clearly a "state agency" under the statute.

(2) Use of property leased to the government

The central issue is whether Donaldson used property leased to the government. (The rented car was not owned by the government. Hence it was not "government property." And Donaldson acted "directly" rather than "indirectly," such as by causing someone else to drive the car.) There should be no dispute that when Donaldson drove the car to his sister's, he directly used property. But was it "property leased to the government"?

Donaldson's best argument is a fairly strong one. His position will be that when he made the trip to his sister, he had not yet signed the lease. He would argue that "leased" means contractually committed to rent. Under this definition, the car did not become property leased to the government until after he returned from his sister's house. No costs were incurred by the government because of the test drive. Rental payments would not begin until the car was rented through the signing of the lease.

The supervisor, on the other hand, will argue for a broader definition of "leased"— that it means the process of obtaining a contractual commitment to rent, including the necessary steps leading up to that commitment. Under this definition, the car was leased to Donaldson when he made the unauthorized trip. The test drive was arguably a necessary step in making the decision to sign a long-term leasing contract.

The goal of the legislature in enacting § 17 should be kept in mind when trying to determine the meaning of any of the language of § 17. The legislature was trying to avoid the misuse of government resources. Public employees should not take advantage of their position for private gain. To do so would be a violation of the public trust. Yet this is what Donaldson did. While on the government payroll, he obtained access to a car and used it for a private trip. Common sense would lead to the conclusion that leasing in § 17 is not limited to the formal signing of a leasing contract. Anything that is necessarily part of the process of signing that contract should be included. The legislature wanted to prevent the misuse of government resources in all necessary aspects of the leasing of property.

It is not clear from the facts whether the manager of the ABC Rental Company knew that Donaldson was considering the rental on behalf of a government agency when he received permission to take the test drive. The likelihood is that he did know it, although this should be checked. If the manager did know, then Donaldson probably used the fact that he was a government employee to obtain the permission. He held himself out as a reliable individual because of the nature of his employment. This reinforces the misuse argument under the broader definition of "leased" presented above.

I have not yet checked whether there are any court opinions or agency regulations interpreting § 17 on this point. Nor have I researched the legislative history of the statute. All this should be done soon.

```
(3) Officially Approved Activities
   Nothing in the facts indicates that Donaldson's supervisor,
Fred Jackson, gave him any authorization to make the TV trip.
Even if Jackson had authorized the trip, it would probably not
be "officially" approved, since the trip was not for official
(i.e., public) business.
```

```
E. CONCLUSION
   Donaldson has the stronger argument based on the language of the
statute. The property simply was not "leased" at the time he made
the TV trip. I must admit, however, that the agency has some very
good points in its favor. Unlike Donaldson's technical argument,
the agency's position is grounded in common sense. Yet on balance,
Donaldson's argument should prevail.
```

```
F. RECOMMENDATIONS
   Some further investigation is needed. We should find out whether
the ABC Rental Company manager knew that Donaldson was a
government employee at the time he asked for the test drive. In
addition, legal research should be undertaken to find out if any
court opinions and agency regulations exist on the statute. A
check into the legislative history of § 17 is also needed.
   Finally, I recommend that we send a letter to Donaldson's
supervisor, Fred Jackson, explaining our position. I have attached
a draft of such a letter for your signature in the event you deem
this action appropriate.
   There is one matter that I have not addressed in this memo.
Donaldson is concerned that he might lose his job over this
incident. Assuming for the moment that he did violate § 17, it is
not at all clear that termination would be an appropriate
sanction. The statute is silent on this point. Let me know if you
want me to research this issue.
```

🏛 *A s s i g n m e n t   1 2 . 2*

The Pepsi Cola Bottling Company is authorized to do business in Florida. It wishes to prevent another Florida company from calling itself the Pepsi Catsup Company because this name violates § 225.25. The Pepsi Catsup Company denies that its name is in violation of this statute. The Secretary of State has the responsibility of enforcing this statute.

48 State Code Ann. § 225.25 (1979). The name of a company or corporation shall be such as will distinguish it from any other company or corporation doing business in Florida.

Your supervisor asks you to prepare a preliminary memorandum of law on the applicability of this statute. The office represents the Pepsi Catsup Company. Do no legal research at this time, although you should point out what research might be helpful. After you complete the memo, draft a letter to the Secretary of State giving the position of your office on the applicability of the statute. (You can make up the names and addresses of the people involved as well as any dates that you need.)

Farrell, Grote, & Schweitzer
Attorneys at Law
724 Central Plaza Place
West Union, Ohio 45693
513-363-7159

Timothy Farrell, Esq.
Angela Grote, Esq.
Clara Schweitzer, Esq.

March 25, 1990
RE: James Donaldson
90-114

Frederick Jackson
Field Supervisor
Department of Sanitation
3416 34th St. NW
West Union, Ohio 45693

Dear Mr. Jackson:

Our firm represents Mr. James Donaldson. As you know, some question has arisen as to Mr. Donaldson's use of a car prior to the time he was asked to rent it for your agency on February 12, 1990. Our understanding is that he was asked to go to the ABC Car Rental Company in order to rent a car that was needed by your agency, and that he did so satisfactorily.

Your agency became responsible for the car at the moment Mr. Donaldson signed the lease for the car rental. What happened prior to the time the lease was signed is not relevant. The governing statute (§17) is quite explicit. It forbids nonofficial use of property "leased" to the government. Such use did not occur in this case. No one has questioned Mr. Donaldson's performance of his duty once he "leased" the car.

If additional clarification is needed, we would be happy to discuss the matter with you further.

Sincerely,

Timothy Farrell, Esq.

TF:ps

Section D
APPELLATE BRIEF

The word *brief* has several meanings.

First, to *brief* a case is to summarize its major components, such as key facts, issues, reasoning, disposition. (See Exhibit 7.1 in chapter 7.) Such a brief is your own summary of a court opinion for later use.

Second, a **trial brief** is an attorney's set of notes on how he or she will conduct the trial. The notes will be on the opening statement, witnesses, exhibits, direct and cross-examination, closing argument, etc. The trial brief is not submitted to the court nor to the other side. A *trial memorandum* on points of law might be submitted, but not the trial brief, which contains counsel's strategy. (This trial memorandum, however, is sometimes referred to as a trial brief. In such instances, the trial brief consists of arguments of law rather than the tactical blueprint for the conduct of the trial.)

Third, the **appellate brief** is the formal written argument to a court of appeals on why a lower court's decision should be affirmed, modified, or reversed. It is submitted to the appellate court and to the other side. The appellate brief is one of the most sophisticated kinds of legal writing in a law office.

The first appellate brief that is usually submitted is the *appellant's* brief. The **appellant** is the party initiating the appeal. Then the *appellee's* brief is filed in response. The appeal is taken against the **appellee** (sometimes called the **respondent**). Finally, the appellant is often allowed to submit a **reply brief** to counter the position taken in the appellee's brief.

Occasionally, a court will permit a nonparty to the litigation to submit an appellate brief. This is referred to as an ***amicus curiae*** (friend of the court) brief (page 515). The *amicus* brief advises the court on how to resolve the controversies before it.

Not all appellate briefs have the same structure. Rules of court often specify what structure or format the brief should take, the print size, number of the copies to be submitted, etc. The following are the major components of many appellate briefs:

(a) *Caption:* The caption states the names of the parties, the name of the court, the court file or docket number, and the kind of appellate brief it is. The caption goes on the front cover of the brief (page 515).

(b) *The Statement of Jurisdiction:* In this section of the brief, there is a short statement explaining the subject-matter jurisdiction of the appellate court. For example:

> This Court has jurisdiction under 28 U.S.C. § 1291 (1967).

The jurisdiction statement may point out some of the essential facts that relate to the jurisdiction of the appellate court, such as how the case came up on appeal. For example:

> On January 2, 1978, a judgment was entered by the U.S. Court of Appeals for the Second Circuit. The U.S. Supreme Court granted certiorari on February 6, 1978. 400 U.S. 302.

Later in the brief there is a Statement of the Case that often includes more detailed jurisdictional material.

(c) *Table of Contents:* The table of contents is an outline of the major components of the brief, including **point headings,** and the pages in the brief on which everything begins. A point heading is the party's conclusion it wants the court to adopt for a particular issue. The function of the table of contents is to provide the reader with quick and easy access to each portion of the brief. Because the page numbers will not be known until the brief is completed, the table of contents is the last section of the brief to be written. The following excerpt from the respondent's brief illustrates the structure of a table of contents that includes the point headings as part of the "argument."

TABLE OF CONTENTS

(d) *Table of Authorities:* The **table of authorities** lists all the cases, statutes, regulations, administrative decisions, constitutional provisions, charter provisions, ordinances, court rules, and secondary authority relied on in the brief. All the cases are listed in alphabetical order, all the statutes are listed in alphabetical and numerical order, etc. The page numbers on which each of these authorities is discussed in the brief are presented so that the table acts as an index to these authorities.

Example:

TABLE OF AUTHORITIES

	Page
CASES:	
Smith v. Jones, 24 F.2d 445 (5th Cir. 1974) 2, 4, 12	
Thompson v. Richardson, 34 Miss. 650, 65 So. 109 (1930) 3, 9	
Etc.	

TABLE OF AUTHORITIES

Page

CASES:

Smith v. Jones, 24 F.2d 445 (5th Cir. 1974)............ 2, 4, 12

Thompson v. Richardson, 34 Miss. 650, 65 So. 109
  (1930) 3, 9

Etc.

TABLE OF AUTHORITIES—continued

Page

CONSTITUTIONAL PROVISIONS

Art. 5, Miss. Constitution 12, 17

Art. 7, Miss. Constitution 20

Etc.

STATUTES

Miss. Code Ann. § 23(b) (1978) 2, 8, 23

(e) *Questions Presented:* The label used for the **questions presented** section of the brief
varies. Other names for it include "Points Relied on for Reversal," "Points in Error,"
"Assignments of Error," "Issues Presented," etc. Regardless of the label, its substance
is essentially the same: it is a statement of the legal issues that the party wishes the
appellate court to consider and decide.

(f) *Statement of the Case:* In the **statement of the case,** the dispute and lower court
proceedings to date are summarized, the essential facts of the case are presented,
and (often) the jurisdictional data are included.

Example:

These are actions based upon the Federal Tort Claims Act, 28
U.S.C. § 1346(b), initiated by the appellants, Garrett
Freightlines, Inc. and Charles R. Thomas in the United States
District Court for the District of Idaho. The appellant alleged
that appellee's employee, Randall W. Reynolds, while acting within
the scope of his employment, negligently caused injury to
appellants. The United States denied that the employee was acting
within the scope of his employment.

On March 27, 1973, appellant Garrett made a motion for limited
summary judgment as to whether Reynolds was acting within the
scope of his employment when the collision occurred. The actions
of Garrett and Thomas were consolidated by order of the court, and
appellee later moved for summary judgment (see trial transcript,
page 204).

The District Court held that under the authority of dicta in
Berrettoni v. United States, 436 F.2d 1372 (9th Cir. 1970),
Reynolds was not within the scope of his employment when the
accident occurred and granted appellee's motion for summary
judgment. It is from that order and judgment that the injured now
appeals.

> Staff Sergeant Reynolds was a career soldier in the United States Military and, until November 9, 1970, stationed at Fort Rucker, Alabama. On or about July 30, 1970, official orders directed that Reynolds be reassigned to the Republic of Vietnam. . . .

(g) *Summary of Argument:* The major points to be made in the brief are summarized in this section.

(h) *Argument:* Here the attorney explains the legal positions of the client presented in the order of the point headings listed in the table of contents. All the primary and secondary authority relied on is analyzed.

(i) *Conclusion:* The conclusion states what action the attorney is asking the appellate court to take.

(j) *Appendixes:* The appendixes contain excerpts from statutes, or other primary authority, excerpts from the trial, charts, descriptions of exhibits entered into evidence at the trial, etc.

Section E
SOME WRITING GUIDELINES

I believe that [the legal profession does] not use plain language for two reasons: time and fear. Time is the enemy of brevity as evidenced by a quotation I am certain many of us remember: "Please excuse the length of this letter; I did not have time to be brief." Fear, however, is an unavoidable concern to lawyers—we tremble at the thought of saying it differently than it has been said for years. Thus, "in the event that" still prevails [over] "if." William Nussbaum, *Afraid to Change?* 69 The Florida Bar Journal 6 (December 1995).

Lawyers like to throw around jargon and flowery language because it makes them feel self-important and prestigious. George Hathaway quoted by Debbie Laskey, *Legalese . . . Is It English?* 20 At Issue 14 (San Francisco Ass'n of Legal Assistants, May 1993).

1. *Do not use circumlocutions.*

A **circumlocution** is a pair of words that have the same effect. Here is a list of circumlocutions commonly found in the law. Avoid using them. Pick one of the words and discard the other.

Do not say:	*Say:*	*Or say:*
alter and change	alter	change
any and all	any	all
by and with	by	with
each and every	each	every
final and conclusive	final	conclusive
full and complete	full	complete
made and entered into	made	entered
null and void	null	void
order and direct	order	direct
over and above	over	above
sole and exclusive	sole	exclusive

type and kind	type	kind
unless and until	unless	until

2. *Omit excess language.*

If language adds nothing to the sentence, don't use it. There is an easy test to find out if your phrase, clause, or sentence is carrying excess baggage. Remove it and ask yourself whether you have altered the meaning or emphasis desired. If not, keep it out.

Compare the sentences in these two columns:

A	*B*
Your maximum recovery is $100 under the provisions of the Warsaw Convention.	Your maximum recovery is $100 under the Warsaw Convention.

When we remove "the provisions of" from the first sentence, we lose neither meaning nor emphasis. Hence, we don't need it.

Use the language in the second column unless you have a valid reason to use the language in the first column:

Do not say:	*Say:*
(1) all of the	(1) all the
(2) by means of	(2) by *or* with
(3) does not operate to	(3) does not
(4) during the course of	(4) during
(5) in the time of	(5) during
(6) in order to	(6) to
(7) or in the alternative	(7) or
(8) period of time	(8) period *or* time
(9) provision of law	(9) law
(10) State of New Jersey	(10) New Jersey
(11) until such time as	(11) until

3. *Use shorter words when longer ways of expressing the same idea add nothing.*

Use the language in the second column unless you have a valid reason to use the language in the first column:

Do not say:	*Say:*
(1) adequate number of	(1) enough
(2) prohibited from	(2) shall not
(3) at such time as	(3) when
(4) during such time as	(4) while
(5) enter into a contract	(5) contract (verb)
(6) for the duration of	(6) during
(7) for the purpose of	(7) for
(8) for the purpose of entering	(8) to enter
(9) for the reason that	(9) because
(10) give consideration to	(10) consider
(11) give recognition to	(11) recognize
(12) have need of	(12) need

(13) in case	(13) if
(14) in a number of	(14) in some
(15) in cases in which	(15) when
(16) in connection with	(16) in *or* on
(17) in regard to	(17) about
(18) in relation to	(18) about *or* toward
(19) in the case of	(19) if *or* in
(20) in the event of	(20) if
(21) in the matter of	(21) in *or* on
(22) in the majority of instances	(22) usually
(23) in view of	(23) because *or* since
(24) is able to	(24) can
(25) is applicable	(25) applies
(26) is binding on	(26) binds
(27) is dependent on	(27) depends on
(28) is entitled to	(28) may
(29) is in attendance at	(29) attends
(30) is permitted to	(30) may
(31) is required to	(31) shall
(32) is unable to	(32) cannot
(33) is directed to	(33) shall
(34) it is your duty to	(34) you shall
(35) make an appointment of	(35) appoint
(36) make a determination of	(36) determine
(37) make application	(37) apply
(38) make payment	(38) pay
(39) make provision for	(39) provide for
(40) on a few occasions	(40) occasionally
(41) on behalf of	(41) for
(42) on the part of	(42) by *or* among
(43) provided that	(43) if
(44) subsequent to	(44) after
(45) with reference to	(45) on

4. *Use a less complicated or less fancy way of expressing the same idea.*

   Use the language in the second column unless you have a valid reason to use the language in the first column:

Do not say:	*Say:*
(1) accorded	(1) given
(2) afforded	(2) given
(3) cause it to be done	(3) have it done *or* do it
(4) contiguous to	(4) touching
(5) deem	(5) consider
(6) endeavor (as a verb)	(6) try
(7) evince	(7) show
(8) expiration	(8) end
(9) expires	(9) ends
(10) have knowledge of	(10) know

(11) forthwith	(11) immediately
(12) in accordance with	(12) under
(13) in the event of	(13) if
(14) in the event that	(14) if
(15) in the interest of	(15) for
(16) is applicable	(16) applies
(17) is authorized to	(17) may
(18) is directed to	(18) shall
(19) is empowered to	(19) may
(20) is entitled (for a name)	(20) is called
(21) is hereby authorized	(21) may
(22) is not prohibited	(22) may
(23) per annum	(23) per year
(24) provided that	(24) if
(25) render service	(25) give service

🏛 *A s s i g n m e n t   1 2 . 3*

Rewrite any of the following sentences that contain language that can be simplified without interfering with the effectiveness of the sentence.

(a) You are required to pay the fine.

(b) The period of time you have to render assistance is three months.

(c) For the duration of construction, it shall be unlawful for a person to enter or to attempt entry.

(d) If you are unable to enter into a contract with him for the materials, the oral commitment is still binding on you.

(e) She consulted with a lawyer with respect to possible litigation.

(f) She accepted the appointment due to the fact that she was qualified.

(g) It is green in color.

(h) Ask the witness questions about the bills.

(i) Judge Jones is currently on the bench.

5. *Use action verbs.*

Wherever possible, draft your sentences to use action verbs instead of participles, gerunds, and other noun or adjective forms. Action verbs are shorter and more direct.

Do not say:	*Say:*
(1) give consideration to	(1) consider
(2) give recognition to	(2) recognize
(3) have knowledge of	(3) know
(4) have need of	(4) need
(5) in the determination of	(5) determine
(6) is applicable	(6) applies
(7) is dependent on	(7) depends on
(8) is in attendance at	(8) attends
(9) make an appointment of	(9) appoint

(10) make application	(10) apply
(11) make payment	(11) pay
(12) make provision for	(12) provide for

6. *Use active voice.*

Use **active voice** rather than **passive voice** by making the doer of the action the subject and main focus of the sentence. Compare the sentences in the following two columns:

A *(passive voice)*	B *(active voice)*
The decision was announced by the judge.	The judge announced the decision.
The report will be prepared.	I will prepare the report.
The court was cleared.	The clerk cleared the court.
By Friday the bridge will have been blown up by the workers.	By Friday, the workers will have blown up the bridge.
The strike was ended by the injunction.	The injunction ended the strike.

The verbs in the sentence in the "A" column are in the passive voice. The verbs in the sentence in the "B" column are in the active voice. What are the differences between these two kinds of sentences?

Sentences with verbs in the *passive voice* have the following characteristics:

- The doer of the action is either unknown or given less emphasis than what was done.
- The doer of the action, if referred to at all, is mentioned after the action itself.
- The subject of the sentence receives the action. The subject is acted upon.

If you do not mention the doer of the action in the sentence, the verb form is a **truncated passive.** In the following sentence, for example, you don't know who fired Jim:

Jim was fired at noon.

Sentences with verbs in the *active voice* have the following characteristics:

- The doer of the action is the important focus.
- The doer of the action is mentioned before the action itself.
- The subject of the sentence performs the action. The subject is the doer of the action.

The passive voice is often less effective because it is less direct and often less clear. It can dilute the forcefulness of a statement.

Weak: It is no longer allowed to take library books overnight.

Better: The law library no longer allows you to take books overnight.

Or: The law library no longer allows borrowers to take books overnight.

The action in these sentences is the prohibition on taking books overnight. In the rewrite, we know who has performed this action—the law library. In the first sentence, we are not sure. The subject (and center of attention) in the rewrite is the law library; the subject (and center of attention) in the first sentence is the prohibition—the action.

Assignment 12.4

Rewrite any of the following sentences that use the passive voice. If you need to add any facts to the sentences to identify the doer of the action, you may make them up.

(a) As the semester came to a close, the students prepared for their exams.
(b) Examinations are not enjoyed.
(c) No drugs were prescribed after the operation.
(d) It has been determined that your license should be revoked.
(e) Consideration is being given this matter by the attorney.
(f) It is believed by district officials that the expense is legal.
(g) The fracture was discovered by the plaintiffs in 1992.

7. *Use positive statements.*

Phrase something positively rather than negatively whenever possible.

Do not say:	*Say:*
It is not difficult to imagine.	It is easy to imagine.
The paper is not without flaws.	The paper has flaws.

8. *Avoid verbosity.*

Avoid unnecessary words.[2] Compare the following versions of the same sentence:

He consulted *with* a doctor *in regard to his injuries.*	He consulted a doctor *about* his injuries.
He drove to the left *due to the fact* that the lane was blocked.	He drove to the left *because* the lane was blocked.
This product is used for *hair-dyeing purposes.*	This product is used to *dye hair.*
The continuance was requested *in order to obtain the presence of a witness who was not then available.*	The continuance was requested *because a witness was unavailable.*

Read these sentences, with and without the italicized words.

The court directed a verdict in favor of the defendant *and against the plaintiff.* (Verdicts for defendants usually are against the plaintiff.)

The car was green *in color.* (This distinguishes it from the car that was green in size!)

A delivery was made every Tuesday *on a regular weekly basis.* (What does *every Tuesday* mean if not weekly and regularly?)

9. *Use shorter sentences.*

As indicated at the end of Exhibit 12.2, there is no rule on how long a sentence must be. Yet in general we can say that the longer a sentence is, the more

---

[2]Grey, *Writing a Good Appellate Brief*, 88 Case and Comment 44, 48–50 (No. 6, November/December 1983). Reprinted by special permission. Copyrighted © 1983 by the Lawyers Cooperative Publishing Co.

difficult it is to follow. Too many long sentences ask too much of the reader. This is not to say that a reader cannot understand such sentences. It simply means that you are taxing the patience of readers when you subject them to long, involved sentences.

Unfortunately, sentences are almost always too long in legal writing. Here is an example from a legal memorandum. In the rewrite, we have broken a fifty-four–word sentence into four smaller, more readable sentences:

Weak: Claims for child support were not fully and finally adjudicated pursuant to a North Carolina divorce judgment where the North Carolina court did not have personal jurisdiction over the husband and could not adjudicate any child support claims without jurisdiction and therefore Florida is not precluded from collecting monies from the husband toward arrearages.

Better: The North Carolina divorce judgment did not fully and finally adjudicate the claims for child support. The court in this state did not have personal jurisdiction over the husband. It could not adjudicate any child support claims without jurisdiction. Florida is therefore not precluded from collecting monies from the husband toward arrearages.

Other examples:

Weak: In May of 1995, a district personnel administrator informed Mary Miller that the district had decided to transfer her to a different school which was a decision that was based on information Miller provided, however the administrator had never talked to Miller in person prior to the decision.

Better: In May of 1995, a district personnel administrator informed Mary Miller that the district decided to transfer her to a different school. The district based its decision on information Miller provided. The administrator, however, never talked to Miller in person prior to the decision.

Weak: Her new job at the firm as the legal administrator in charge of personnel and finances was enjoyable, lucrative, educational, and challenging, but confusing and frightening at times.

Better: Her new job at the firm as legal administrator in charge of personnel and finances was enjoyable, lucrative, educational, and challenging. It was also confusing and frightening at times.

Weak: The final issue for discussion concerns the status of the national and international parties that has been the main stumbling block in the contract negotiations thus far.

Better: The final issue for discussion is the status of the national and international parties. This issue has been the main stumbling block in contract negotiations thus far.

Weak: There is no need for you to submit a revised report to the Board unless you wish to include new matter which should have been included in an earlier report provided that the new matter covers only procedural issues except for those procedural issues that have already been resolved by the commission.

Better: You do not have to submit a revised report to the Board. An exception is when you wish to include new matter on procedural issues that should have been included in an earlier report. These procedural issues must not be ones that the Commission has already resolved.

🏛 ## Assignment 12.5

Rewrite any of the following sentences that are too long.

(a) The board can, within sixty days of the receipt of a certification from the secretary, take action to return ownership to persons of corporations certified as owners from whom the property was acquired by expropriation or by purchase under threat of expropriation.

(b) A short time later, as George approached the intersection of Woodruff and Fuller, someone in the middle of the street started shooting, but George kept driving when he heard about fifteen shots that sounded like different guns firing, one of which hit his Pontiac, damaging the front windshield and dashboard.

(c) By way of illustration, presidential candidate Ross Perot and basketball player Michael Jordan arguably may have achieved such pervasive fame as to have become public figures for all purposes, while Dr. Jack Kevorkian may have voluntarily placed himself into the public controversy over euthanasia and physician-assisted suicide so as to have become a public figure for a limited range of issues.

10. *Be careful with pronoun references.*

Use pronouns only where the nouns to which the pronouns refer are unmistakably clear. Using pronouns with ambiguous referents can confuse the meaning of a sentence. If the pronoun could refer to more than one person or object in a sentence, repeat the name of the person or object to avoid ambiguity.

Do Not Say: After the administrator appoints a deputy assistant, he shall supervise the team. [Who does the supervising? The administrator or the deputy? If the latter is intended, then:]

Say: After the administrator appoints a deputy assistant, the deputy assistant shall supervise the team.

11. *Avoid sexism in language.*

Avoid gender-specific language when the intent is to refer to both sexes. If neutral language is not available, rewrite the sentence to avoid the problem.

Gender-Specific Language	*Gender-Neutral Alternatives*
(1) businessman	(1) executive, member of the business community
(2) chairman	(2) chairperson, chair
(3) draftsman	(3) drafter
(4) man	(4) person, human, humankind
(5) man-hours	(5) worker hours
(6) mankind	(6) humanity
(7) manpower	(7) work force, personnel
(8) workmen's compensation	(8) worker's compensation

Chapter Summary

A law office prepares many different kinds of writing. Instruments such as deeds, contracts, and other agreements are formal documents that accomplish specific legal results. Pleadings such as complaints, answers, and cross-claims state claims, defenses, and other positions of parties in litigation. Confirmatory letters seek verification that something important has been done or said. Opinion letters provide legal advice to a client. An interoffice memorandum of law analyzes the law for other members of the office. An external memorandum of law (for example, a "points and authorities" memorandum) analyzes the law for someone outside the office, such as a hearing officer. A case brief is a summary of the major parts of a court opinion. A trial brief is an attorney's set of notes on how he or she intends to conduct a trial. An appellate brief is an argument submitted to an appellate court on why the decision of a lower court should be affirmed, modified, or reversed.

The major components of an internal memorandum of law are the heading, the statement of the assignment, the issues, the facts, the discussion or analysis, the conclusion, and the recommendations.

The major components of an appellate brief are the caption, the statement of jurisdiction, the table of contents, the table of authorities, the questions presented, the statement of the case, the summary of the argument, the argument, the conclusion, and the appendixes.

Following a number of important guidelines will increase the clarity and effectiveness of any kind of writing. Avoid circumlocutions, omit excess language, use action verbs and active voice, express something positively whenever possible, use shorter sentences, make pronoun referents clear, and avoid sexist language.

KEY TERMS

instrument, 658
pleadings, 658
confirmatory letter, 658
opinion letter, 661
memorandum of law, 661
interoffice memorandum of law, 662
intraoffice memorandum of law, 662

external memorandum of law, 662
points and authorities memorandum, 662
trial memorandum, 662
hearing memorandum, 662
heading, 663
caption, 663
docket number, 663

RE, 663
trial brief, 671
appellate brief, 671
appellant, 671
appellee, 671
respondent, 671
reply brief, 671
amicus curiae, 671
point heading, 671

table of authorities, 672
questions presented, 672
statement of the case, 672
circumlocution, 672
active voice, 678
passive voice, 678
truncated passive, 678

AN INTRODUCTION TO THE USE OF COMPUTERS IN A LAW OFFICE*

► *Chapter Outline*

*Portions of an earlier edition of this chapter were written with Dale Hobart, Director of Legal Assistant Program and Assistant Director of Academic Computing, Ferris State College.

Section A
LAW OFFICES, COMPUTERS, AND PARALEGALS

"The practice of law has changed more in the last 20 years than in the last two centuries. Not only is most of that change attributable to advanced technology, but it does not appear to be anywhere near slowing down."
—Stacey Hunt, May 1995

It is very doubtful that you will work in an office without computers. In many medium and large law offices, computers dominate the practice of law and the management of the law office. If you flip through the pages of a bar association magazine or legal newspaper, you will probably find that two-thirds of the advertising is from computer manufacturers, vendors, and consultants. Paralegals are an integral part of this computer environment, as demonstrated by the survey presented in Exhibit 13.1 and by the following comments of paralegals on their experiences with computers.

Exhibit 13.1 **Survey on Computer Use**	
Percentage of paralegals with computers in their office	97.3%
Percentage of paralegals with computers at home that can be used for work	53.7%
Percentage of paralegals who use computers for word processing	96.0%
Percentage of paralegals who use computers for document control and data management	76.8%
Percentage of paralegals who use computers for research	71.9%

Source: 1995 Employment and Salary Survey, Los Angeles Paralegal Association.

PARALEGAL COMMENTS: GENERAL

"These amazing little machines are filled with micro-chips, circuit boards, disks, and many other magical parts about which I know nothing! What I do know is how much more efficient I am with my PC."[1]

"In the last few years, the computer has become a desirable, if not indispensable, tool of the legal profession, and, in fact, it is somewhat ironic that this new tool has caused typing skills to enjoy a comeback in popularity. Efficient use of the computer keyboard not only facilitates drafting of legal pleadings but also the use of a variety of software programs. While word processing programs are the programs most widely used by legal assistants, [other software used includes:] programs for file organization, document retrieval, calculation, spreadsheet formulation, and research. . . ."[2]

CORPORATE LAW

Some paralegals have become adept at tailoring general business programs, such as spreadsheet and database management programs, to different areas of legal practice.

---

[1]Eastwick, *JLA's Seminar/Workshop on Personal Computers in the Law Office,* JLA News 4, Issue 12 (Jacksonville Legal Assistants, January 1988).
[2]Schueneman, *Software Brings Typing Back to the Future,* 3 TALAFAX 3, No. 3 (Tucson Ass'n of Legal Assistants, 1991).

"When I worked . . . for a major corporation, I was responsible for the shareholder relations program. This required monthly analysis of the company's shareholder base. Rather than have a transfer agent compile the information for a handsome fee, I prepared the report on an IBM PC using Lotus 1-2-3."[3]

CRIMINAL LAW

"We were confronted with more than 300 boxes of documents stored in a depository in Houston" that contained evidence that had to be classified so that it would be available for the trial attorney. To do that, the attorney "started building a data base, using teams of paralegals to code and input the information." The judge allowed the attorney to connect his computer and fax machine in the courtroom with the computer and fax machine in the law office. In effect, the attorney was "wired into the network back at the office, which is staffed with paralegals who have access to all kinds of information which can be faxed or sent by computer back into the courtroom immediately."[4]

ESTATES AND TRUSTS

Ann Cook, legal assistant at Pepper, Hamilton & Scheetz of Philadelphia, saw a demonstration of a software package for fiduciary accounting and immediately began urging her firm to move in that direction. "After seeing it, I was no longer satisfied writing the same information several times for each different purpose when all I had to do was input it once and then push buttons. . . . We've now expanded our system to do estate planning calculations which manually were cumbersome and expensive to produce. Eventually, we would like to connect our system into a data bank like Standard & Poors, so that we can get instant evaluations of stock and bond values."[5]

INSURANCE

In the case management area, Norman Strizek works with insurance firms. He has "created databases so they can track separately every litigation case they're involved in, and [identify] which law firm is handling each part; what they're billed each quarter; the status of the litigation; responsible attorneys and paralegals, with phone numbers; due dates of different filings and who is handling each. It helps the insurer manage all their litigation."[6]

LITIGATION

"When the portable PC is not used for data retrieval, the legal assistant can use it to take notes." Julie Hoff, a litigation legal assistant for ten years, "cites an example of a legal assistant who put her portable to work in an efficient manner during a recent trial in Minneapolis. While the witness was testifying, the legal assistant summarized the proceedings on her portable computer. At the end of each day, she printed her notes and they were used in the preparation of [cross] examination for the next day and for future witnesses."[7]

"I never leave home without my laptop!" says Laurie Roselle, the Litigation Paralegal Manager at Rogers & Wells in New York. She "types in taxis, commutes with her desktop

> "Not so many years ago, computers were fancy tools only big firms could afford. Even firms with computers were inclined to keep them out of sight, off the polished oak desks of their lawyers, many of whom made it a point of pride not to be able to type. Those days are gone forever."
> —Paul Reidinger, American Bar Association Journal (1991)

---

[3]B. Bernardo, *Paralegal* (Peterson's Guides, 1990).
[4]Keeva, *Document Analysis in Criminal Litigation,* 76 American Bar Ass'n Journal 80 (May 1990).
[5]Troop, *Paralegals Are Taking the Lead Through Computers,* 2 Legal Assistant Today 21 (Winter 1985).
[6]Milano, *Novel Way Paralegals Are Using Computers,* 8 Legal Assistant Today 22, 110 (March/April 1991).
[7]*Law Office Trends: Portable PCs in the Courtroom,* Merrill Advantage 6 (Spring 1989).

portable, pulls cases and does actual memos." She says, "You have to use every minute—and you can bill the time."[8]

PROFESSIONAL RESPONSIBILITY

Jane Palmer is the conflict-of-interest specialist at Hogan and Hartson in Washington D.C. Working under the supervision of an attorney, Jane spends "more than half her time at the computer on requests for information." She "does all the research on every prospective client" for the firm's offices in Washington D.C., Maryland, Virginia, London, and Brussels "to find out who are the related parties in the matter they are bringing." She "uses her database to see if Hogan and Hartson has ever represented any party on any side of the matter, or been adverse to them. The databases are a client list, accounting and billing information, and addresses." "I draw on that for searches, and add to it every day, updating the information." Building on the accounting department's database, Palmer uses Informatics, software designed for conflicts, which connects to accounting and is used for both functions.[9]

TORTS

"Moving on to a tetracycline case involving five pharmaceutical firms, he computerized 40,000 documents. . . ." His "team did the coding."[10]

McCarthy, Palmer, Volkema & Becker is a plaintiff's tort litigation firm in Columbus Ohio. "Computers are an important part of the legal assistants' daily work environment. In place of the message slips and paper memos, the desks of the attorneys and paralegals are adorned with personal computers. Since the firm's beginning, all of the attorneys, legal assistants, secretaries and receptionists have been networked. All telephone messages are transferred from the receptionist via E-mail (Electronic Mail). The main function of the computer, however, is as a warehouse for client file information. The attorney and legal assistant can access the computer from the name and phone number of the judge, opposing counsel, adjuster, treating physician or expert, without pulling a large file from the filing cabinet. An electronic calendar is also available on the system. Firm members now have a means for scheduling meetings with more than one attorney and/or legal assistant without leaving their desks. The computer will notify the person . . . of any conflicts. No more telephone tag or running from one calendar to another."[11]

Section B
SURVIVAL STRATEGIES

When you walk into your first paralegal job, be prepared to encounter some sophisticated equipment. Our goal in this chapter is not to make you an expert in any particular product or system, but rather to provide you with some of the fundamentals so that you will be in a better position to benefit from the inevitable on-the-job training in the computer products and systems used by a particular law office. We will assume in this chapter that you are a beginner. Even if you are well-versed in computers generally, you'll

---

[8]Milano, see footnote 6 at p. 23.
[9]Milano, see footnote 6 at p. 24.
[10]Milano, see footnote 6 at p. 24.
[11]Overly, *Innovations in Law Office Automation,* 6 LACO Letter 12 (Legal Assistants of Central Ohio, December 1990).

be a beginner with respect to computer programs that have been (and will be) designed for law offices. Our starting point is a series of survival strategies presented in Exhibit 13.2. As we begin our exploration of computer use in the practice of law, keep these strategies in mind.

Exhibit 13.2   **Computer Survival Strategies: A Paralegal Tackles a New Program in the Law Office**

Stage I: Identify Your "Help" Resources

- Line up in-house support. Find out who in the office already knows how to use the program. Ask them if they would be willing to answer your questions about it. If possible, they should be people other than—or in addition to—your supervisor.
- Ask if the program you will be using has an 800 number that you can use for assistance. Free phone service may be available for a period of time after the office purchases the program or equipment. If not, find out if the office has purchased a service agreement that allows unlimited calls during the period of the agreement.
- Ask if the program has an **online tutorial** that explains the basics. If so, ask someone to start the tutorial for you.
- Ask if the program has a **HELP key** that can be used while you are running the program. If so, ask how to use it.
- Find the manual for the program (called the **documentation**). Turn to the index, if one exists. Select some familiar terms in the index, such as capitalization. Turn to the pages for such items and try to follow the instructions provided for them. In short, start with "easy" tasks.
- Find out if the supermarket-style bookstores in your area sell "how-to" books on the program you will be using in the office. Scores of such books exist for many of the most popular word processing, spreadsheet, and database programs. Buy one of these books and study it on your own.
- Start a computer notebook in which you write definitions of new terms, steps to follow for certain tasks, steps you took just before you seemed to make a mistake, questions that you want to ask someone later, etc.
- Expect to learn a new vocabulary. (*Boot,* for example, has nothing to do with what goes on your foot.)

Stage II: Learn the Big Seven Tasks

Learn the seven essential tasks that apply to most programs:

- How to turn on the computer, call up or **load** the program, and start using it

- How to create a new document or file with the program
- How to save a document or file
- How to retrieve a document or file that was created and saved earlier
- How to make a copy of the document or file
- How to turn on the printer and print a document or file
- How to exit from the program and turn the computer off

Stage III: Take the Initiative

- Find out if your local paralegal association is offering a seminar on computer use. Attend it. If none is planned, call the president of the association and suggest that one be offered.
- Read the local bar association journals to find out what computer seminars are offered by the bar or by **CLE** (Continuing Legal Education) groups. Attend some that are relevant to your job.
- Photocopy a chapter from the computer manual (documentation) at the office. Take the chapter home and read it over the weekend.
- Ask librarians in your area how you can find magazine reviews of the program that you use. Read these reviews.
- Find out if there is a **users group** in your area that meets every month to discuss the program, such as a WordPerfect Users Group. Attend the meetings of this group.
- Find out if there is a **listserv** on the Internet where you can read comments, questions, and answers (called postings) about the program from people who use it all over the world. Spend a few minutes each day at work or at home reading these postings. Once you are comfortable with the listserv, ask your own questions about the program and watch for answers from across town, another city, or another continent.
- Organize a "specialty section" of your paralegal association that consists of paralegals who use the program. Members of this section would meet periodically to learn from each other and to discuss common problems with the program.

Section C
TERMINOLOGY

The world of the computer, like the world of law, has its own language. Initially, this language can be very confusing. Persistence and time, however, will help rectify this problem. First we begin with some basic definitions:

Hardware: The computer and its physical parts. Hardware is what you take out of the box and plug together when you buy a computer system. It is any part of the system that can be physically touched other than the floppy disks or diskettes (see definitions below).

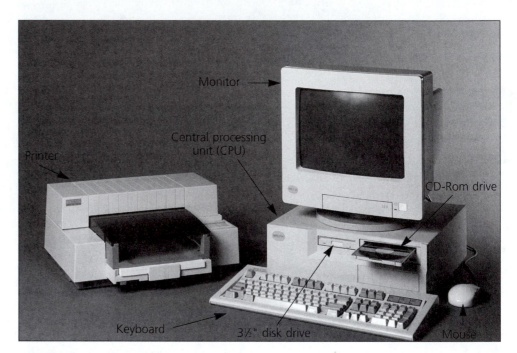

Typical desktop computer hardware

The heart of the computer is the **central processing unit (CPU).** It is the "brain" of a computer system. Its "chips" and other components coordinate all of the other parts of the system and perform the main functions of receiving and processing information or data.

IBM was the first manufacturer of the **personal computer,** which is simply a computer small enough to fit on a desk (see *microcomputer* below). IBM set the standard. A computer of another manufacturer is said to be **IBM-compatible** (also called a **clone**) if it can read data created by an IBM computer or use software created for an IBM computer. **Compatibility** simply means being able to work together. It refers to the extent to which computers of different manufacturers can read each other's data or use each other's software. Apple Computer's Macintosh, on the other hand, is not IBM-compatible. Special equipment and software are usually needed before these two types of computers can exchange data or use the same software. Most law offices use IBM or IBM-compatible computers.

Back Up: To copy information that a computer uses. (Copies should be made regularly in case the original is destroyed.)

CD-ROM: Compact Disk Read-Only Memory. An information storage system much like a compact disk or cassette sold in music stores. It uses optical technology or laser beams to store and allow you to read large quantities of information on a small disk. You cannot add any information to most CD-ROM disks; you can only read the information through your computer screen or monitor (hence the phrase *read only*). Advances in technology, however, now allow information to be added to some disks (i.e., you can *write to* the disk). CD-ROM disks are inserted in an internal or external CD-ROM drive, depending on whether the drive is within the main chassis of the computer (that houses the CPU) or sits outside as a stand-alone device.

CD-ROM disks

Command: A word or character typed into the computer to tell the computer what to do next.

Data: Information of any type that can be used by computers. The data may consist of numbers, words, or pictures.

Disk Drive (also called a disk): In this chapter, we will use the term *disk drive* (rather than disk) to describe the part of your hardware that is used to store and retrieve programs and information to and from diskettes (see definition below). The disk drive has the capability of placing program information on a diskette. This is often referred to as *writing information to the diskette.* The disk drive also has the capability of "reading" the information from the diskette into the computer. If the information is a *program,* the program can then be "run" (see definition below) by the computer. Disk drives can be hard or floppy. A **floppy disk** drive is one that can use diskettes. The diskettes can be easily inserted and removed from the disk drive. **Hard disks,** on the other hand, cannot be removed without taking the hardware apart. Furthermore, they have a much greater memory capacity than diskettes. A 400-megabyte hard disk, for example, will be able to hold approximately 400 million **bytes** of information—about 200,000 pages of text. (One byte is the storage equivalent of one letter of the alphabet, or one punctuation mark, or one blank space.) It could take hundreds of **diskettes** to store the same amount of data.

Sometimes diskettes are called disks, floppy disks, or just **floppies.** In this chapter, the term *diskette* will be used. A diskette is a flat 3½-inch or 5¼-inch piece of plastic that is covered with the same magnetic substance used on a magnetic tape. See Exhibit 13.3. Information is placed on the diskette in a manner similar to the way music is stored on a compact disk or cassette. The information can be a program or data to be used by a program. This information can then be read into the computer for the computer to use.

E x h i b i t 1 3 . 3   **Floppy Disks**

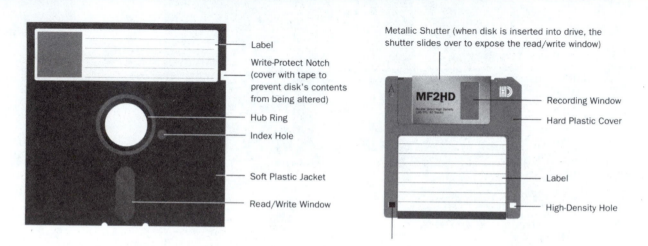

Source: Susan Baumann and Meredith Flynn, *Microcomputers and Information Technology* 93 (West Publishing Co., 1996).

File: A file refers to any information that a computer can use and that is stored or kept together as a group. A file can consist of data or a program. (For the meaning of file in a database program, see Exhibit 13.8.)

k: A measure of capacity. Each k equals one kilobyte, which is 1,024 bytes (see definition of *byte* above). The letter k often refers to the amount of information that can be kept on your diskette. It can also refer to the work area in the computer. The work area is the amount of space available to the computer for keeping programs and information that will be used:

- **Kilobyte** (k): one thousand bytes (approximately)
- **Megabyte** (Mb): one million bytes (approximately)
- **Gigabyte** (Gb): one billion bytes (approximately)

Not long ago, 64k was considered a great deal of memory (see definition below). Today, some popular programs require more than 4 megabytes (4Mb)!

Language: A program that allows a computer to understand commands and carry them out. Examples of languages include BASIC, COBOL, and Pascal. Most computer users do *not* need to be programmers to run the vast majority of computer programs used in a law office.

Laptop: A portable computer that can be powered by rechargeable batteries. The battery life is often two to four hours before recharging is needed. Smaller laptops are called *notebooks,* or *subnotebooks,* and *palmtops.* Battery-operated portable printers are also available.

Typical laptop computer

Load: To move or transfer a program or information from a disk drive into the computer.

Macro: A keyboard technique for performing something routine. Suppose, for example, that every time you write a letter, you start by typing your name, full address, and phone number. It takes about 100 keystrokes to do this (you have a long name). To cut down on this labor, you tell the computer that every time you type the letters HEADING, you want your full name, address, and phone number to appear on the screen. You have now replaced 100 keystrokes with 7 (HEADING) by creating a macro, which is simply any previously saved set of keystrokes that will accomplish what you have assigned to it. You have to type your name, address, and phone number only once when you create the macro called HEADING. Macros can be used to accomplish many of the routine tasks that you perform in creating documents, moving text, doing math calculations, etc. You decide what keystrokes will call up the macro (in our example, you could have saved even more labor by telling the computer that the single keystroke **H** will give you your full name, address, and phone number), and you decide what these keystrokes will do. Macros are a great time-saving aid.

Memory: The area inside a computer that temporarily holds programs and data, which are instantly erased when you shut off the computer—unless they have been properly saved.

Microcomputer: A computer (often called a personal computer) that is small enough to fit on a desk. The term is not clearly defined because the power of small computers has increased dramatically in the past few years.

Modem: A device that allows one computer to send and receive information using regular telephone lines. In most computer systems the modem is internal—within the main chassis.

Monitor: A TV-like device that is part of the hardware of the computer. On the screen the monitor displays whatever commands you type at the keyboard—and displays information in response to those commands.

Operating System: A program that is in charge of what is displayed on the screen, what is sent to the printer, and all other facets of the operation of a computer. In effect, the operating system serves the function of traffic cop or central manager. A variety of operating systems are available, such as DOS or MS-DOS, OS/2, UNIX, GEOS, HFS (Macintosh), and NextStep. In some of the systems, you type certain commands on the keyboard. In others, you use a small pointer device called a **mouse** to point to pictures (graphics or **icons**; see Exhibit 13.4) on the screen that stand for the same kind of commands that you

---

Exhibit 13.4   Icons in Windows 95 That Are "Clicked On" with a Mouse

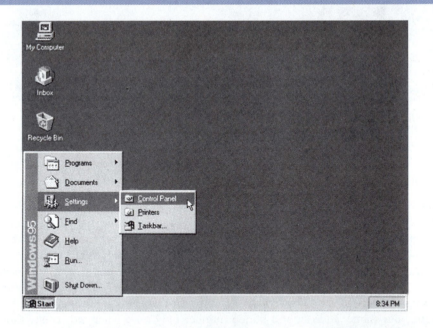

---

would otherwise "type in." To execute the command, you push (or *click*) a button on the mouse. An important development in this area is **Windows** from Microsoft. This is a *graphics-based* (as opposed to a mere text-based or character-based) program for IBM-compatible computers that works along with DOS. It is a mouse-pointer program that allows a user to run several large programs (such as word processing, database management, spreadsheet) simultaneously. To take advantage of this **multitasking** capacity, a number of the older operating systems are issuing what they call their *windows-based* operating system. Furthermore, many software manufacturers are rushing to release versions of their products for the *windows environment,* e.g., WordPerfect for Windows.

Printer: You use a printer to obtain a *hard copy* (on paper) of what you have generated on your computer. Many different kinds of printers are available:[12]

- **Dot Matrix Printer:** This printer uses tiny pins that press against or punch a ribbon to create a pattern of dots.
- **Daisy Wheel Printer:** This printer uses a "daisy wheel," a device (resembling a flower) that contains the alphabet and other characters on spokes. The printer spins the wheel to find the character, which then strikes the ribbon.

Daisy wheel

- **Ink Jet Printer:** This printer sprays a stream of ink on paper to produce the print. The ink comes from a cartridge rather than a ribbon.

Laser printer: HP LaserJet III Printer

- **Laser Printer:** This printer uses a laser beam of light to reproduce images. Special cartridges are needed to print text or graphics. It operates very much like a copy

---

[12]Electronic Industries Ass'n, *How to Buy a Personal Computer,* 14 (1990).

machine. Because of their versatility, speed, and high quality, laser printers have become standard in law offices.

One of the advantages of laser printers (and some ink jet printers) is the ability to choose different **fonts** (the design of the letters) and **points** (the size of the letters). There are often numerous font styles and point sizes to choose from. For example:

This is printed in a 10 point, Arial font (regular).

This is printed in a 13 point, Arial font (regular).

This is printed in an 8 point, Times New Roman font (italics).

This is printed in a 17 point, Times New Roman font (regular).

● Exhibit 13.5 shows the beginning of a motion that is being typed. Note that the title of the motion is in a different point size than the rest of the page. It is also in capital letters ("all caps") and in **bold,** which simply means darker print.

Run: To cause a program to be loaded into the computer from a disk drive and to begin performing its task.

Exhibit 13.5 **Computer Screen Showing Text with a Font in Different Point Sizes**

WordPerfect - [c:\...\m.wpd - unmodified]

File Edit View Insert Format Table Graphics Tools Window Help

Times New Roman ▾ 12 pt ▾ Styles ▾ Left ▾ 1.0 ▾ Tables ▾ Columns ▾ 100% ▾

In the United States District Court

Paul J. Vitolo,   )
                    Plaintiff,   )
)
)   Case Number 96-2345
       -vs-   )
)
Quaker West, Inc.,   )
                    Defendant.   )

MOTION FOR SUMMARY JUDGMENT

COMES NOW the defendant, Quaker West, Inc. and moves the Court for an Order to

grant summary judgment in the favor of defendant.

Insert   HP LaserJet IIP (Win)   Select May 9, 1995   8:48PM Pg 1 Ln 1.82" Pos 1"

Source: Brent Roper, *Using Computers in the Law, 2d,* 62 (West Publishing Co., 1996).

Save: To cause a program or data that are in the computer memory to be moved to or stored on a diskette or hard drive.

Scanner: A scanner is a machine that allows you to enter data into a computer directly from the printed page (called a **hard copy**) without typing the data. Most scanners look and operate like photocopy machines. You place a piece of paper (e.g., a page from a book) on the flat glass surface of the scanner. When you press the start button on the scanner, it scans the paper and enters the data on the paper into the computer. You can then use your word processing program to change the text that you have scanned and thereby incorporate it into the document you are preparing. In effect, the scanner allows you to enter text into the computer without typing it word by word. You can also scan images such as a company logo or a photograph of an accident scene.

Software: The word *software* means a program (also called an **application**) that allows you to perform tasks such as word processing, database management, and spreadsheet calculations. To use a program, you must get it into the computer. This is usually done by transferring the program into the computer from a diskette or, more commonly, from the hard drive on which the program has been permanently installed.

Scanner

Tape Backup System: A device that allows you to "back up" and store data on magnetic tape kept on tape cartridges.

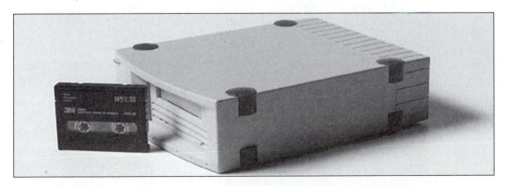

Tape backup system

Section D
SOFTWARE

Four basic types of software are available:

- Word processing
- Database management
- Spreadsheets
- Communications

A fifth and the latest kind of software consists of a combination of all four.

1. WORD PROCESSING

Word processing is a software program that allows you to enter, edit, store, and retrieve data. The software is referred to as a *word processor.* The most elemental difference between a word processor and a manual or electric typewriter becomes apparent when you prepare a document for the first time. For example, unlike a traditional typist, the computer user does not listen for a bell to know whether he or she is at the end of a line. The computer will automatically move a word down to the next line when the end of a line is reached. This feature is called **word wrap.** There is no need to pause or slow down. The only time you strike the "return" key is at the end of a paragraph. When a typing error is made at the computer keyboard, there is no need to reach for the bottle of "white out." Nor is there ever a need to worry about a messy final draft caused by insertions or corrections. With the computer you simply go back and correct the error(s). If you left out a letter or sentence, you can easily insert it. The line, in effect, opens up to allow this insertion. If you typed the wrong letter, you can quickly type the correct one directly over the wrong one. If there are too many letters, just press the delete key over the excess letters. Furthermore, there is no need to worry about what such changes will do to paragraph alignment. The computer will take care of it. The task of typing becomes infinitely easier. Someone with limited typing skills soon becomes a confident and competent typist. (See Exhibit 13.6 for a list of common word processing terms.)

Exhibit 13.6	**Frequently Used Word Processing Terms**
TERM	**DEFINITION**
Automatic pagination	A feature that enables a word processor to number the pages of the printed copy automatically.
Block	A group of characters, such as a sentence or paragraph.
Block movement	A feature that allows the user to define a block of text and then perform a specific operation on the entire block. Common block operations include block move, block copy, block save, and block delete.
Boldface	Heavy type; for example, **this is boldface.**
Character	A letter, number, or symbol.
Character enhancement	Underlining, boldfacing, subscripting, and superscripting.
Control character	A coded character that does not print but is part of the command sequence in a word processor.

Exhibit 13.6	Frequently Used Word Processing Terms—continued

TERM	DEFINITION
Cursor	The marker on the display screen indicating where the next character can be displayed when typed.
Default setting	A value used by the word processor when it is not instructed to use any other value.
Deletion	A feature by which a character, word, sentence, or larger block of text can be removed from the existing text.
Editing	The act of changing or amending text.
Footer	Text that is stored separately from the main text and printed at the bottom of each page.
Format	The layout of a page; for example, the number of lines and the margin settings.
Global	An instruction that will be carried out throughout an entire document. For example, change the word "avenue" to "street" everywhere in the document.
Header	Text that is stored separately from the main text and printed at the top of each page.
Incremental spacing	A method by which the printer inserts spaces between words and letters to produce justified margins; also called microspacing.
Insertion	A feature in which a character, word, sentence, or larger block of text is added to the existing text.
Justification	A feature that makes lines of text even at the margins.
Menu	A list of commands or prompts on the display screen.
Print formatting	The function of a word processor that communicates with the printer to tell it how to print the text on paper.
Print preview	A feature that enables the user to view on the screen a general representation of how the document will look when printed.
Screen formatting	A function of a word processor that controls how the text will appear on the screen.
Scrolling	Moving a line of text onto or off the screen.
Search and find	A routine that searches for, and places the cursor at, text you want to locate in the document.
Search and replace	A routine that searches for specified text and replaces it with other text.
Status line	A message line above or below the text area on a display screen that gives format and system information.
Subscript	A character that prints below the usual text baseline. For example, the number 7 in the following phrase is in subscript: Court$_7$.
Superscript	A character that prints above the usual text baseline. For example, the number 7 in the following phrase is in superscript: Court^7.
Text buffer	An area set aside in memory to hold text temporarily.
Text editing	The function of a word processor that enables the user to enter and edit text.
Text file	A file that contains text, as opposed to a program.

Exhibit 13.6	Frequently Used Word Processing Terms—continued
TERM	**DEFINITION**
Word wrap	The feature in which a word is moved automatically to the beginning of the next line if it goes past the right margin.
WYSIWYG	What You See (on the screen) Is What You Get (when the screen is printed).

Source: S. Mandell, *Introduction to Computers Using the IBM and MS-DOS PCs with Basic,* 3d 216 (West Publishing Co., 1991).

Easy text entry is just the beginning. Once a document has been put into the computer, it can be used over and over again. Standard paragraphs can be saved, modified, and inserted whenever needed. Documents can be designed so that names are entered once and then automatically included in the final output at fifty different locations. Standard documents can be rearranged by moving paragraphs and sentences within the document. Large or small parts of a document may be moved, deleted, or duplicated to create the final document.

A helpful feature on many word processors is the **spell checker.** After a document has been typed, you can activate a spelling program. Different types of spelling programs exist, all of which are based on a large number of words in the program's dictionary. The simpler programs place a mark on any word *not* contained in the program's dictionary. You have probably misspelled such words. You can then review and correct the marked words as needed. More sophisticated spelling programs not only mark a word that is not in the program's dictionary, but also present several possible correct spellings. Spell checkers are great for catching transposed letters, easily overlooked by a proofreader. (You will be told, for example, that you need to change the spelling of th*ie*r to th*ei*r.) Be aware that a spell checker will not tell you that you used "to" when you should have used "two" or "too." Since all these words are correctly spelled, they will not be marked by the program.

Word processors can print a document in many formats. The type can be **right justified** (meaning that the right-hand margin of the text is straight) or have a ragged right edge. Left margins can be set at many different places throughout the document. (See Exhibit 13.7 for other ways of arranging text.) Pages can be numbered or unnumbered, and the numbering can start with any digit you choose. Most word processors can include footnotes and keep the textual material that has been footnoted on the same page with the footnote even if you later insert a lot of material on this page. Word processors can place the same heading at the top of each page without your having to retype the heading for all the pages in the document.

Most word processors come with the capability of creating indexes for the document. You simply mark the word or phrase that is to be included in the index and run the index part of the program. An index is then created with all the page numbers for the location of the word or phrase.

One of the useful features of word processors is **merging.** This is "the process of combining a form with a list of variables to automatically produce a document. For instance, if you want to send the same letter to a large number of clients, but you want the letter to be personalized, you can use the merge feature found in most word processors to do

Exhibit 13.7 Arranging Text with a Word Processor

Here is an example of text created on a word processor that is *left justified* only. Note that the text is straight along the left margin, but ragged along the right margin.	Left justification
Here is an example of text created on a word processor that is *right justified* only. Note that the text is ragged along the left margin, but straight along the right margin.	Right justification
Here is an example of text created on a word processor that has *full justification.* Note that the text is straight along both the left margin and the right (except for the last line).	Full justification
Here is an example of text created on a word processor that uses the *left indent* feature. Note that the entire text is indented from the left margin. (The text is also left justified only.)	Left indent
Here is an example of text created on a word processor that uses the *double indent* feature. Note that the entire text is indented the same amount from both the left margin and the right margin. (The text is also left justified only.)	Double indent
Here is an example of text created on a word processor that uses the *hanging indent* feature. Note that the first line hangs or "sticks out" to the left. (The text is also left justified only.)	Hanging indent
Here is an example of text created on a word processor that uses *first line indent.* Note that only the first line is indented in traditional paragraph format. (The text is also left justified only.)	First line indent

this quickly."[13] You start with the body of the letter, which will be the same *(constant)* for each client. The differences *(variables)* will be the name and address of the client and the salutation line ("Dear . . ."). The merger involves two files: the *primary file* containing the constant information (the body of your form letter), and the *secondary file* containing the variable information, which you typed earlier. By inserting special codes (^F1, ^F2, ^E,

---

[13]Brent Roper, *Using Computers in the Law, 2d* 134 (West Publishing Co., 1996).

etc.) in the document in the primary file, you will be instructing the computer to go to the secondary file, find the variable data with the same special codes, and bring them over (merge them) into the form in the primary file. In a very short time, you have created and can now print a large number of personalized letters.

Many magazines review word processors and other software programs. Go to the library and find at least three reviews on a software program that you will be using. Read them carefully. Often, you will find a consensus among the reviews.

Examples of computer magazines that review software programs

2. DATABASES

Database software is used to store and organize information. The information is entered into the database in an organized manner so that the computer can extract it, reorganize it, consolidate it, summarize it, and create reports from it. As a business management tool in a law office, a database is used for timekeeping, calendars, ticklers, billing, and client records. (See Exhibit 13.8.) As a case management tool, it can be used for document control in cases that have a large number of documents that must be indexed and cross-referenced. Also, as we shall see, WESTLAW and LEXIS are services that consist of hundreds of databases used for legal research.

Entering information into the database usually requires someone to sit at a terminal and manually type in the information. (Alternatively, *scanners* may be available to enter text without typing.) If the database is to contain documents, each document entered will

| *Exhibit 13.8* | Frequently Used Database Management Terms |

TERM	DEFINITION
Database	A grouping of independent files into one integrated whole that can be accessed through one central point; a database is designed to meet the information needs of a wide variety of users within an organization.
Data manager	A data management software package that consolidates data files into an integrated whole, allowing access to more than one data file at a time.
Data redundancy	The repetition of the same data in several different files.
Field	A subdivision of a record that holds a meaningful item of data, such as an employee number.
Record	A collection of related data fields that constitute a single unit, such as an employee record.
File	A group of related data records, such as employee records.

Source: S. Mandell, *Introduction to Computers Using the IBM and MS-DOS PCs with Basic, 3d* 514–15 (West Publishing Co., 1991).

need an ID code, a brief description of the document, and index words for it. One of the major features of a database is that it can serve as a large index, thereby allowing rapid retrieval of information.

Once all the data have been entered, the database can be used to retrieve, compare, or compile information. To perform any of these functions, you need to search the database. There are two ways to search a database: *key word* searches and *full text* searches.

A **key word search** is like looking through the index of a book. The database program will build an index using information that it is told to use for the index. The computer searches through this index and displays all information associated with the key word. For example, assume that you create a database to keep the membership list for your national paralegal association, and you instruct the database program that you want an index created using the *state* in the address of members of the association. You could then ask the computer to list all members from Ohio or any other state. This type of search can be completed very quickly. The quality of the results of such a search depends on how well indexed the database is. If the person who made the list of index words for each document did not do a very good job, the search will not be very productive. Poor indexing causes either too little or too much information to be reported from a key word search.

The second way to search a database is called a **full text search.** With this type of search, the computer will examine *all* the information stored by the database program, not just the contents of an index. Suppose, for example, you are working on a complex bankruptcy case. Thousands of documents have been entered (typed or scanned) into the computer database, e.g., depositions, letters, company bills, and balance sheets. A full text search would examine every word in every one of these documents to locate specific information. For example, you could ask the computer to find documents:

- that contain the name "Ajax Company"
- that mention the "sale of stock"
- that mention the year "1990"

Once you "run" such searches, the computer will display a list of every document that contains your search terms anywhere in the document. Of course, for large and complex cases, it can be enormously expensive and time-consuming to enter every litigation document into a database, even if sophisticated scanners are used. An alternative is to create summaries of every document and place these summaries into a database rather than the complete documents. A full text search can then be made of the summaries.

Every search in a database must have **search criteria** that tell the computer what to search for and where to search for it. Many large databases allow search criteria that use the words AND, OR, and NOT. A search criteria using such words might be:

GUN AND ROBBERY AND NOT BANK

With these criteria, a search of the database would return a list of documents for which the summary had the words *gun* and *robbery* but would exclude any summary that also contained the word *bank*. The problem with this type of search is that if one document used the word *holdup* instead of *robbery*, that document would not be found by the search. To find that document, the following search criteria must be used

GUN AND (ROBBERY OR HOLDUP) AND NOT BANK

The parentheses show that the OR applies only to *robbery* and *holdup*. If you did not think of the word *holdup* at the time you phrased your search request, an important document would be missed because you did not use the same words as the person who wrote the summary for the database. In a moment, we will examine how search requests are made on the major legal research services, WESTLAW and LEXIS.

Most database programs can perform several simple tasks. Calendar control is one of them. A database is very efficient in keeping trial docket and appointment calendars for a law office. (See Exhibit 13.9.) Each attorney can receive a printed calendar of appointments for the day. All office calendars can be kept on one computer so that scheduling can be done without creating time conflicts among the attorneys.

A database could also be designed to print out a list of all the cases for the office where the statute of limitations is due to expire during the coming month.

Exhibit 13.9 Docket Control Database

DOCKET CONTROL DATABASE

DATE OF EVENT	EVENT	CASE NAME	PLACE OF EVENT	FIRST WARNING	SECOND WARNING
01/13/98	Trial	Black v. Neal	Court #3	12/13/97	01/02/98
01/24/98	Appt/Sanders	Smith v. Jones	Office	01/02/98	01/20/98
01/30/98	Depo/Defend.	King v. Hill	Def. Off.	01/15/98	01/25/98
02/01/98	Setlmnt. Mtg.	Berg v. Rob	J. Black's	01/20/98	01/28/98
02/03/98	Deadln-MSJ	Hope v. Hope	Office	01/23/98	01/30/98
03/01/98	Trial	Doe v. Doe	Court #12	01/02/98	02/01/98

Before the scheduled date of the event (first column), the responsible attorneys are given a number of warnings or alerts by this scheduling database program.

Source: Brent Roper, *Using Computers in the Law,* 2d 211 (West Publishing Co., 1996).

Name, address, family status, phone numbers, case type, and other pertinent information for all the clients of a law firm can be kept in a database. This information could be used for mass mailings of informational letters about certain types of cases to those clients. The database can also be used to identify the types of cases handled by different attorneys in the office and the completion time for each type. This information is very helpful in making management and marketing decisions for the law firm. (For examples of reports based on such databases, see Exhibits 14.11 and 14.12 in chapter 14.)

The computer is even more useful for more complex tasks. A good database program can make timekeeping and billing more efficient. Many database programs are designed specifically to perform timekeeping and billing tasks. For different clients, these programs can handle multiple rates for attorneys and paralegals. We will examine this in more detail in chapter 14 on law office administration.

The database also makes it possible to analyze which types of cases are more profitable to the law firm and which people are more productive in terms of billed hours. Of course, there are other factors that must still be evaluated subjectively. The attorney who brings in new clients for the law firm (often called a **rainmaker**) could very well show up poorly on a billable-hours evaluation if someone else in the office does the actual work on the clients this attorney brings in. Like all other tools, the numbers produced by a computer must be evaluated in perspective.

Databases can be very useful for document control. For example, they can keep track of the content and location of thousands of documents in an antitrust case. Document control programs were once available only for large computers and were very expensive. Consequently, document control with computers was used only in very large cases. Today, programs have been developed that enable small computers to perform many document control functions.

WESTLAW and LEXIS

(See also page 624 in chapter 11.) WESTLAW and LEXIS are commercial services that are available to anyone who wishes to perform (and pay for) **CALR**—Computer Assisted Legal Research. As we saw in chapter 11, these services can give you access to a vast amount of material, such as the full text of federal and state court opinions, federal and state statutes, federal and state administrative regulations, loose-leaf services, legal treatises, legal periodical articles, directories of attorneys, and financial data. West Publishing Company, which offers WESTLAW,[14] and Reed Elsevier, which offers LEXIS, have user agreements that must be signed before you will be allowed to use their services. The agreement establishes the fees to be paid for the different services available. You gain access to these services by using your regular computer (or a custom terminal), which is connected by telephone lines to computers with vast storage capabilities. Data are thereby searched **online,** which means being connected to a host computer system or information service—usually through normal telephone lines.

Assume that you are working on a case involving a client who developed cancer after smoking for many years. You want to know if the client can bring a product liability claim against the tobacco company. One of the first things you need to decide is whether you want to search for cases, statutes, regulations, secondary sources, etc. Assume that you want to find court cases written by any state court in your state. You then need to go to the database in WESTLAW or LEXIS that contains such cases. Once there, the next step is to formulate a question—called a **search query**—for the computer. The query would ask the computer to find cases involving product liability and cigarettes.

---

[14]The assistance of Laura C. Mickelson is gratefully acknowledged for the material on WESTLAW.

There are two ways to formulate queries in WESTLAW and LEXIS. You can use either **Boolean**[15] language or natural (associative) language. Boolean searches are more traditional and more commonly used. Hence we will examine them first.

Here is an example of a query that could be used in WESTLAW for our tobacco case:

```
cigar! tobacco smok! /p product strict! /5 liab!
```

Later, we will examine the meaning of such queries and how to write them. For now, we simply want to give you an overview of what is available.

The screen in Exhibit 13.10 shows a recent case *(Forster v. R. J. Reynolds Tobacco Co.)* that would be retrieved by WESTLAW, using the above query. It assumed that you asked

---

Exhibit 13.10

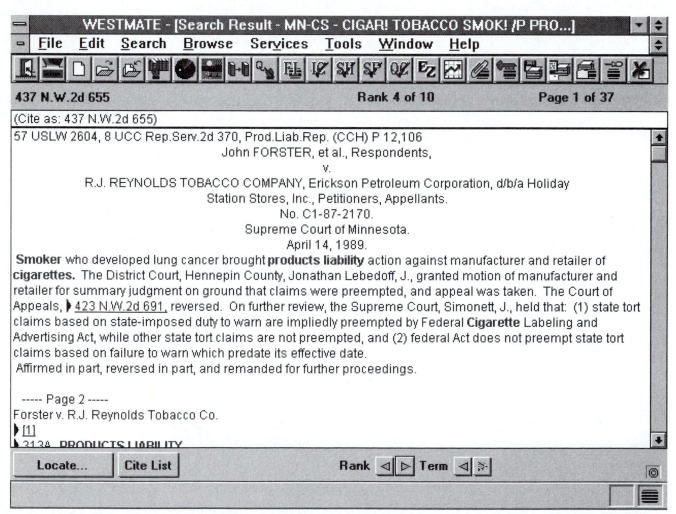

Case retrieved by WESTLAW, with search words in bold print. Note that at the top of the screen you find the database (MN-CS) and the query used.

---

[15]A Boolean search is one that allows words to be specifically included or excluded through operatives such as AND, OR, and NOT.

WESTLAW for Minnesota cases (found in its database, MN-CS). After looking at a large number of such cases, you might want to ask the computer to give you a list of citations of every case that fits your query. The screen in Exhibit 13.11 presents such a list. (It includes the *Forster* case as well as others that fit the query.) If you have a printer connected to your computer, you can ask for a printout of the data on any of these screens.

Exhibit 13.11

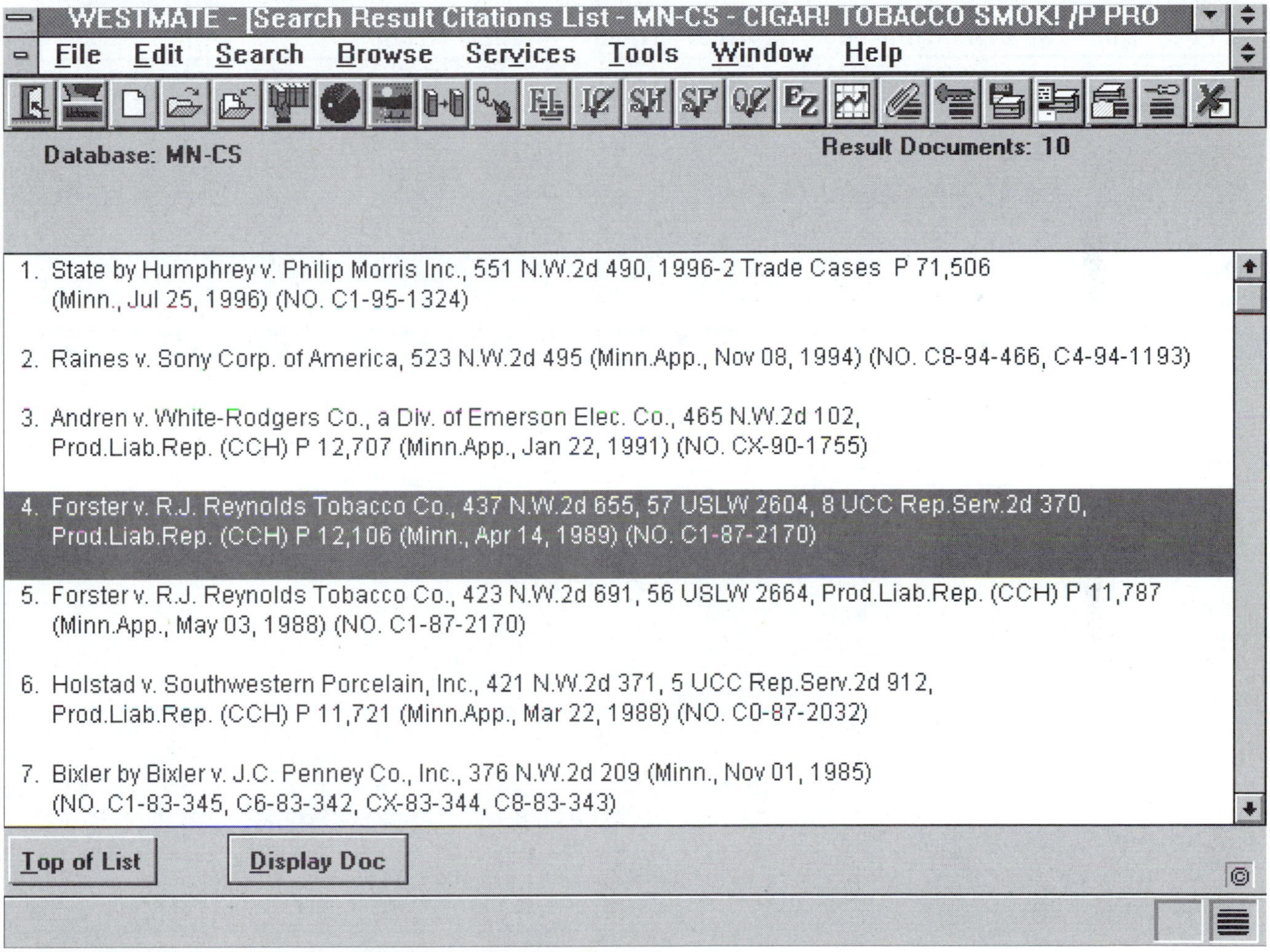

WESTMATE - [Search Result Citations List - MN-CS - CIGAR! TOBACCO SMOK! /P PRO

File   Edit   Search   Browse   Services   Tools   Window   Help

Database: **MN-CS**   Result Documents: **10**

1. State by Humphrey v. Philip Morris Inc., 551 N.W.2d 490, 1996-2 Trade Cases P 71,506 (Minn., Jul 25, 1996) (NO. C1-95-1324)

2. Raines v. Sony Corp. of America, 523 N.W.2d 495 (Minn.App., Nov 08, 1994) (NO. C8-94-466, C4-94-1193)

3. Andren v. White-Rodgers Co., a Div. of Emerson Elec. Co., 465 N.W.2d 102, Prod.Liab.Rep. (CCH) P 12,707 (Minn.App., Jan 22, 1991) (NO. CX-90-1755)

4. Forster v. R.J. Reynolds Tobacco Co., 437 N.W.2d 655, 57 USLW 2604, 8 UCC Rep.Serv.2d 370, Prod.Liab.Rep. (CCH) P 12,106 (Minn., Apr 14, 1989) (NO. C1-87-2170)

5. Forster v. R.J. Reynolds Tobacco Co., 423 N.W.2d 691, 56 USLW 2664, Prod.Liab.Rep. (CCH) P 11,787 (Minn.App., May 03, 1988) (NO. C1-87-2170)

6. Holstad v. Southwestern Porcelain, Inc., 421 N.W.2d 371, 5 UCC Rep.Serv.2d 912, Prod.Liab.Rep. (CCH) P 11,721 (Minn.App., Mar 22, 1988) (NO. C0-87-2032)

7. Bixler by Bixler v. J.C. Penney Co., Inc., 376 N.W.2d 209 (Minn., Nov 01, 1985) (NO. C1-83-345, C6-83-342, CX-83-344, C8-83-343)

Top of List   **Display Doc**

List of cases retrieved by WESTLAW. The case we have been examining is document no. 4 on this list.

Almost every citation to a case that you obtain through CALR can be taken to a traditional law library where you can read the case in a reporter volume. Of course, you can also read the case on the computer screen or you can read a printout of the case, but it is usually cheaper to read material in a library volume than to read it online. The computer is excellent for searching, but not necessarily for extensive reading.

The *Forster* case was decided in 1989. Suppose that you wanted to know what has happened to the case since 1989. Has it been overruled? Has it been cited by other courts? WESTLAW has four different updating or validation services that can give you further information about cases like *Forster*. They are Insta-Cite, Shepard's PreView, Shepard's Citations (see Exhibit 13.12), and QuickCite, which allows you to update Shepard's PreView and Shepard's Citations.

Exhibit 13.12

WESTMATE - [Shepard's - 437 N.W.2d 655]			▼ ▲
File Edit Search Browse Services Tools Window Help			▲ ▼

Total References: 38

Citations to: **437 N.W.2d 655**
Forster v R.J. Reynolds Tobacco Co. 1989
Coverage: To view coverage information, press Coverage button.

Ret. No.	Analysis	Citation	Headnote No.
1	▸ Shep Same Text	(8 UCC Rep.Serv.2d 370)	
2	SC Same Case	423 N.W.2d 691	
3		458 N.W.2d 417, 419	
4		467 N.W.2d 625, 630	
5		520 N.W.2d 388, 390	
6	D Distinguished	540 N.W.2d 870, 873	
7	F Followed	547 N.W.2d 105, 107	
.	D Distinguished	108:285 Finance and Commerce 30	
.	F Followed	109:107 Finance and Commerce 18	
10		505 U.S. 504, 509	3
11	J Dissenting Opin	505 U.S. 504, 542	
12		120 L.Ed.2d 407, 418	3
13	J Dissenting Opin	120 L.Ed.2d 407, 439	
14		112 S.Ct. 2608, 2613	3
15	J Dissenting Opin	112 S.Ct. 2608, 2631	
..		60 USLW at 4705	3

View Doc.   **Locate...**   **Coverage**   ©

Shepard's in WESTLAW

In litigation, there is often a need to find experts who may be able to provide consultation and, if needed, deposition or trial testimony.[16] One of the specialized searches that can be performed by computer is a search for such experts. Exhibit 13.13 presents an example of the results of this kind of search from the Forensic Services Directory (FSD) database in WESTLAW.

---

[16]See Runde, *Computer Assisted Legal Research,* 10 Facts and Findings 13 (NALA, July/August 1983).

Exhibit 13.13

```
WESTMATE v6.0 - [Search Result - FSD - CANCER! CARCINI & TRIAL]      _ □ ×
File  Edit  Search  Browse  Services  Tools  Window  Help          _ ₽ ×

Chapman, Judy-Anne W.          Rank 1 of 2          Page 1 of 1

                    GENERAL PROFESSIONAL DISCIPLINES
                         CONSULTING SCIENTISTS
                          MEDICINE & HEALTH
                           PHYSICAL HEALTH
              Medical Research, Clinical Trials & Biostatistics



Chapman, Judy-Anne W.
11 Dayman Court
Kitchener, Ontario
Canada N2M 3A1
(519) 579-2996

Specialties: Biometry; Cancer research; Mortality or incidence data; Clinical trials; Case-control studies.
Affiliation: Independent Consultant Degrees and Licenses: PhD.
END OF DOCUMENT





    Locate...    Cite List                  Rank  ◁ ▷  Term  ◁ ▷        ⊚
```

Search for expert witnesses in WESTLAW

LEXIS works in a similar way, with many of the same features. Suppose, for example, that you wanted cases in which a juror concealed his or her bias. You would instruct LEXIS to find cases in which the word *bias* appears in proximity to the words *juror* and *conceal* or *concealed*. See Exhibit 13.14.

Once you have examined a number of these cases, you can ask the service to display a list of citations of all the cases discovered when LEXIS fulfilled your search request. See Exhibit 13.15.

FORMULATING A QUERY

We turn now to one of the critical skills in using WESTLAW and LEXIS: formulating a research question or *query*. Our examination of this skill will explore the following topics:

(a) Universal character (*) and root expander (!) for WESTLAW and LEXIS

(b) WESTLAW queries:

Exhibit 13.14

```
LEXIS-NEXIS Research Software Version 4.1 - [Text]
 File  Edit  Search  View  Browse  Services  Image  Window  Help
```

467 U.S. 1025, *; 104 S. Ct. 2885, **;
1984 U.S. LEXIS 125, ***1; 81 L. Ed. 2d 847

resentenced to life imprisonment, and the trial court denied a motion for a new
trial, finding that practically no publicity had been given to the case between
the two trials, that little public interest was shown during the second trial,
and that the jury was without bias. The Pennsylvania [***2] Supreme Court
affirmed the conviction and the trial court's findings. Respondent then sought
habeas corpus relief in Federal District Court, claiming that his conviction had
been obtained in violation of his right under the Sixth and ...

OPINION:

    ... [*1030] [**2888] [***11]   a separate concurring opinion in which he
suggested that the "constitutional standard which for 175 years has guided the
lower courts" in this area be rejected.   <=16> 710 F.2d, at 972. Rather than
hinge disqualifications of a juror on whether he has a fixed opinion of guilt
that he cannot lay aside. Judge Stern would bar any juror who admitted any
opinion as to guilt. Moreover, no jury could be empaneled where more than 25%
of the veniremen state that they held an opinion concerning the defendant's
guilt. This would raise such doubts as to the sincerity of those who claimed no
opinion as to suggest concealed bias, Judge Stern wrote.

- - - - - - - - - - - - - - - - - -End Footnotes- - - - - - - - - - - - - - - - - -

```
Clien.. 19-64549                    Lit./File. GENFED;LS
Ready                                      NJM              CD Wednesday, December 18, 1996
```

Case retrieved in LEXIS, with search words highlighted

- The OR connector
- The AND connector (&)
- The sentence connector (/s)
- The paragraph connector (/p)
- The BUT NOT connector (%)
- The numerical connector (/n)
- Phrase searching (" ")

(c) LEXIS queries:

- The OR connector
- The AND connector
- The sentence connector (/s)
- The paragraph connector (/p)

E x h i b i t   1 3 . 1 5

LEXIS-NEXIS Research Software Version 4.1 - [Text]

File   Edit   Search   View   Browse   Services   Image   Window   Help

Level 1 - 19 CASES

5. PRESS-ENTERPRISE CO. v. SUPERIOR COURT OF CALIFORNIA FOR RIVERSIDE, No.
84-1560, SUPREME COURT OF THE UNITED STATES, 478 U.S. 1; 106 S. Ct. 2735; 1986
U.S. LEXIS 120; 92 L. Ed. 2d 1; 54 U.S.L.W. 4869; 13 Media L. Rep. 1001,
February 26, 1986, Argued,   June 30, 1986. Decided

6. PATTON v. YOUNT, No. 83-95, SUPREME COURT OF THE UNITED STATES, 467 U.S.
1025; 104 S. Ct. 2885; 1984 U.S. LEXIS 125; 81 L. Ed. 2d 847; 52 U.S.L.W. 4896,
  February 28, 1984, Argued,   June 26, 1984, Decided

7. McDONOUGH POWER EQUIP., INC. v. GREENWOOD, No. 82-958, SUPREME COURT OF THE
UNITED STATES, 464 U.S. 548; 104 S. Ct. 845; 1984 U.S. LEXIS 22; 78 L. Ed. 2d
663; 52 U.S.L.W. 4126,   November 28, 1983, Argued,   January 18, 1984. Decided

8. RUSHEN v. SPAIN, No. 82-2083, SUPREME COURT OF THE UNITED STATES, 464 U.S.
114; 104 S. Ct. 453; 1983 U.S. LEXIS 11; 78 L. Ed. 2d 267; 52 U.S.L.W. 3452,
December 12, 1983, Decided

9. SMITH v. PHILLIPS, No. 80-1082, SUPREME COURT OF THE UNITED STATES, 455 U.S.
209; 102 S. Ct. 940; 1982 U.S. LEXIS 69; 71 L. Ed. 2d 78; 50 U.S.L.W. 4169,
November 9, 1981, Argued,   January 25, 1982, Decided

Clien.. 19-64549   Lit./File. GENFED/LS

Ready   NJM   CD Wednesday, December 18, 1996

List of cases retrieved in LEXIS. The juror bias case is document no. 6 on the list.

- The numerical connector (w/n)
- The AND NOT connector
- Phrase searching

(d) Field searches:

- Title search
- Synopsis search
- Topic search
- Digest search
- Judge search

(e) WIN and Freestyle

(f) Find and read

(a) Universal Character (*) and Root Expander (!) for WESTLAW and LEXIS

An important technique in the formulation of queries in either WESTLAW or LEXIS is the proper use of the asterisk (*) as a **universal character,** and the exclamation mark (!) as a **root expander.** The discussion below of these and other query-formulation techniques will cover searches for cases, although the techniques are generally applicable when searching any kind of document available in the databases and files of WESTLAW and LEXIS.

The Universal Character (*)   Suppose that you asked the computer to find cases that contained the following word anywhere in the case:

```
marijuana
```

This search will not find a case that spelled the word *marihuana.* If, however, you changed your query to:

```
mari*uana
```

you would pick up cases under both spellings. The asterisk stands for any character or letter. Hence the above search would also pick up cases that contain the words *maribuana, marituana,* or *marizuana*—if such words exist in any of the cases in the database or file you are searching. Since the asterisk stands for any character, it is called the universal character. It is most commonly used when searching for cases that contain a proper name you are having trouble spelling. If, for example, you were looking for cases decided by a judge whose name is spelled *Falen* or *Falon,* you can enter the query as:

```
fal*n
```

You are not limited to one universal character per word. For example, the following search:

```
int**state
```

will give you cases containing the word *interstate* and cases containing the word *intrastate.* Similarly, the query:

```
s****holder
```

will give you cases containing the word *stockholder,* cases containing the word *stakeholder,* and cases containing the word *shareholder.*

Root Expander (!)   Next we consider the exclamation mark (!) as a root expander. When this mark is added to the root of a word, it acts as a substitute for one or more characters or letters. If your query is:

```
litig!
```

you will find cases containing one or more of the following words: litig, litigable, litigate, litigated, litigating, litigation, litigator, litigious, litigiousness. The root expander is quite powerful and can be overused. The query:

```
tax!
```

will lead you to cases containing any one or more of the following words: tax, taxability, taxable, taxation, taxational, taxes, taxi, tax-deductible, tax-exempt, tax-free, taxicab, taxidermy, taxidermist, taxied, taximeter, taximetrics, taxing, taxis, taxiway, taxol, taxon, taxonomist, taxonomy, taxpayer, taxy, taxying. This will undoubtedly lead to cases that are beyond the scope of your research problem.

Plurals   It is not necessary to use universal characters or the root expander to obtain the plural of a word. The query:

```
guest
```

will give you cases containing the word *guest* and cases containing the word *guests*. The query *memorandum* will give you cases containing the word *memoranda* and those containing the word *memorandums*. The same is true for other irregular plurals. The query *child* will give you cases containing the word *child* as well as those containing the word *children*. Entering the singular form of a word will automatically also search the plural form of that word.

Next we will focus on special guidelines for formulating WESTLAW queries and LEXIS queries.

(b) WESTLAW Queries

When formulating a query in WESTLAW (or in LEXIS), **connectors** can be used to show the relationship between the words in the query. Connectors link query words together to give the query more direction. Some of the main connectors in WESTLAW are:

- The OR connector
- The AND connector (&)
- The sentence connector (/s)
- The paragraph connector (/p)
- The BUT NOT connector (%)
- The numerical connector (/n)

After explaining how to use each of these connectors, we will examine how to search for phrases on WESTLAW through the use of quotation marks (" ") in queries.

The OR Connector   The simplest connector in WESTLAW is OR, which can be expressed by typing the word *or* between two words, or by leaving a blank space between the words. This connector instructs WESTLAW to treat the two words as alternatives and to find cases that contain either or both words. Hence, the query:

```
doctor or physician
```

or the query:

```
doctor physician
```

will find the following cases:

- A case that contains both the word *doctor* and the word *physician*[17]
- A case that contains the word *doctor*, but not the word *physician*
- A case that contains the word *physician*, but not the word *doctor*

Similarly, the query:

```
attorney or lawyer or counsel
```

or the query:

```
attorney lawyer counsel
```

---

[17]In all of these examples, remember that the service will retrieve cases containing these words and their plurals, such as physician, physicians; doctor, doctors.

will find the following cases:

- A case that contains all three words: *attorney* and *lawyer* and *counsel*
- A case that contains the word *attorney* but not the words *lawyer* or *counsel*
- A case that contains the words *attorney* and *lawyer* but not the word *counsel*
- A case that contains the words *attorney* and *counsel* but not the word *lawyer*
- A case that contains the word *lawyer* but not the words *attorney* or *counsel*
- A case that contains the words *lawyer* and *attorney* but not the word *counsel*
- A case that contains the words *lawyer* and *counsel* but not the word *attorney*
- A case that contains the word *counsel* but not the words *attorney* or *lawyer*
- A case that contains the words *counsel* and *lawyer* but not the word *attorney*
- A case that contains the words *counsel* and *attorney* but not the word *lawyer*

The AND Connector (&)   When you use the & connector in your WESTLAW query, you are asking WESTLAW to find cases that contain every word joined by &. The query:

`paralegal & fee`

will find cases in which the word *paralegal* and the word *fee* are found anywhere in the case, no matter how close or far apart they appear in the case. The query will not find cases containing only one of these words.[18]

The Sentence Connector (/s)   The sentence connector (/s) requires the search words to appear in the same sentence in the case.[19] The query:

`paralegal /s termin!`

will find cases in which the word *paralegal* is found in the same sentence as the word *terminable* or *terminal* or *terminate* or *terminating* or *termination* or *terminator* or *terminology* or *terminus*. Here are examples of two sentences from two different cases that this query would retrieve:

Case #1:

   "The **paralegal** did not receive notice of the allegation until the letter of **termination** arrived the next day."

Case #2:

   "The patient's **terminal** condition was negligently diagnosed in a report obtained by the **paralegal** of the opposing counsel."[20]

The Paragraph Connector (/p)   The paragraph connector (/p) requires the search words to appear in the same paragraph in the case. The query:

`paralegal /p certif!`

will find cases in which the word *paralegal* is found in the same paragraph as the word *certifiable* or *certificate* or *certified* or *certification* or *certifier* or *certify* or *certifying*.

---

[18]It is also possible to write this query as *paralegal and fee* (rather than use the ampersand—&), but this is not recommended.

[19]The sentence connector (/s) and the paragraph connector (/p) are referred to as the *grammatical connectors*.

[20]Note that in case #2, the order in which the search terms appear in the sentence is not the order of the words in the query itself. If you want to limit the search to cases that contain the search words in the sentence in the order presented in the query, you would phrase the query as follows: paralegal +s termin!

The BUT NOT Connector (%)   The BUT NOT connector (%) excludes everything that follows the percentage mark, %. The query:

```
paralegal % fee
```

or

```
paralegal but not fee
```

will find every case in which the word *paralegal* appears, except for those cases in which the word *fee* plus the word *paralegal* appear. Perhaps you are looking for every case that mentions the word *paralegal* other than those involving paralegal fees or attorney fees.

The Numerical Connector (/n)   The numerical connector (/n)[21] requires search words to appear within a specified number[22] of words of each other in the case. The query:

```
paralegal /5 license*
```

will retrieve any case in which the word *paralegal* appears within five words of the word *license,* or within five words of the word *licensed.* Here is an example of a line from a case that this query would retrieve:

```
". . . the paralegal had no license from the state."
```

A case with the following line, however, would *not* be retrieved by this query because there are more than five words between the search words of the query:

```
". . . paralegals as well as notaries and process servers are not
licensed."
```

Phrase Searching (" ")   Thus far, our examples of queries have involved searches for individual words in cases. Suppose, however, that you wanted to search for phrases such as drug addict, habeas corpus, or legal assistant. If your query was:

```
legal assistant
```

WESTLAW would interpret the space between these two words to mean OR. Hence, it will retrieve

- Any case in which the word *legal* appears but the word *assistant* does not appear
- Any case in which the word *assistant* appears but the word *legal* does not appear
- Any case in which both the word *legal* and the word *assistant* appear

This could lead to thousands of cases, the vast majority of which would have nothing to do with legal assistants.[23] To avoid this problem, we need a way to tell WESTLAW not to interpret the space between the search words to mean OR. This is done by placing quotation marks around any phrase (or group of words) that you want WESTLAW to search as a unit. Hence our query should read:

```
"legal assistant"
```

In a moment, we will see that LEXIS does *not* require quotation marks when conducting a phrase search since LEXIS does not interpret every space as an OR.

---

[21]The numerical connector can also be expressed as w/n. For example: paralegal w/5 fee.
[22]Up to 255.
[23]WESTLAW will probably flash a message on the screen warning you that your search query may retrieve a large number of cases and suggesting that you rephrase your query to make it narrower.

(c) LEXIS Queries

When using LEXIS, connectors are also used in formulating a query. While there are many similarities between the connectors in WESTLAW and in LEXIS, there are also differences. Some of the main connectors in LEXIS are:

- The OR connector
- The AND connector
- The sentence connector (/s)
- The paragraph connector (/p)
- The numerical connector (w/n)
- The AND NOT connector

After examining these connectors, we need to compare how to search for phrases in LEXIS and in WESTLAW.

The OR Connector   The OR connector tells LEXIS to treat the two words joined by OR as alternatives. The query:

```
merger or acquisition
```

will find the following cases:

- A case that contains both the word *merger* and the word *acquisition*
- A case that contains the word *merger* but not the word *acquisition*
- A case that contains the word *acquisition* but not the word *merger*

Hence the OR connector in LEXIS is similar to the OR connector in WESTLAW, except that LEXIS does *not* interpret a space between two words as an OR.

The AND Connector   When you use the AND connector in your LEXIS query, you are asking LEXIS to find cases that contain every word joined by AND, no matter how close or far apart they appear in the case. The query:

```
paralegal and fee
```

will find cases in which the word *paralegal* and the word *fee* appear. The query will not find cases containing only one of these words. (In WESTLAW, the preferred way to achieve this result is by using the & connector.)

The Sentence Connector (/s)   The sentence connector (/s) requires the search words to appear in the same sentence in the case. The query:

```
boston /s strangler
```

will find cases in which the word *boston* is found in the same sentence as the word *strangler*.

The Paragraph Connector (/p)   The paragraph connector (/p) requires the search words to appear in the same paragraph in the case. The query:

```
murder /p drug
```

will find cases in which the word *murder* is found in the same paragraph as the word *drug*.

The Numerical Connector (w/n)   The numerical connector (w/n) or (/n) of LEXIS requires search words to appear within a designated number of words of each other in the case. The query:

> paralegal w/5 license

will retrieve any case in which the word *paralegal* appears within five words of the word *license.*[24]

The AND NOT Connector   The AND NOT connector in a LEXIS query excludes everything that follows *and not.* The query:

> paralegal and not fee

will find every case in which the word *paralegal* appears, except for those cases in which the word *fee* plus the word *paralegal* appear.[25]

Phrase Searching   Recall that phrase searching in WESTLAW required the use of quotation marks around any phrase, since WESTLAW interprets spaces between words to mean OR. This is *not* so in LEXIS, since LEXIS does not equate spaces with ORs. Hence to search for a phrase in LEXIS, you do not have to use quotation marks around the phrase. Simply state the phrase. The query:

> legal assistant

will not lead you to any cases in which the word *legal* appeared but not the word *assistant,* and vice versa.

𐄏 *A s s i g n m e n t   1 3 . 1*

Below you will find five separate queries. If they were used in either WESTLAW or LEXIS, what words in the documents would they find?

(a) para!

(b) assign!

(c) crim!

(d) legis!

(e) e****e

---

[24]The number (n) of words that can be used as the numerical connector in LEXIS is any number up to 255. But LEXIS does not count words such as *the, be,* and *to.* LEXIS considers them "noise words." The numerical connector in WESTLAW also goes up to 255. See footnote 22. But WESTLAW counts every word. In the LEXIS numerical query, if you want the words in the case to appear in the order in which the words are listed in the query, use the pre/n connector. For example: paralegal pre/5 license. See also footnote 20.

[25]Another way to phrase this query is: paralegal but not fee. The latter phrasing would make this LEXIS connector the same as the connector in WESTLAW that serves this function.

Assignment 13.2

On page 704, the following query was given as an example of a WESTLAW query:

```
cigar! tobacco smok! /p product strict! /5 liab!
```

Explain this query. State what the symbols mean. What is the query designed to find? Assume that you are using the query to find cases in one of the databases of WESTLAW.

Assignment 13.3

You are looking for cases in which a paralegal is charged with the unauthorized practice of law.
(a) Write the query for WESTLAW.
(b) Write the query for LEXIS.

Assignment 13.4

You are looking for cases in which a law firm illegally failed to pay overtime compensation to its paralegals.
(a) Write the query for WESTLAW.
(b) Write the query for LEXIS.

Assignment 13.5

You would like to know what the courts in your state have said about paralegals.
(a) Write several queries for WESTLAW.
(b) Write several queries for LEXIS.

(d) Field Searches

In addition to full text searches, both WESTLAW and LEXIS allow you to conduct searches that are limited to information found in certain parts of cases or other documents. On LEXIS, these parts are called **segments.** The segments of cases are: name, court, writtenby, dissentby, counsel, number, etc. On WESTLAW, these parts are called **fields.** The fields of cases are: title, synopsis, topic, digest, judge, etc. Here is a fuller explanation and some examples of field searches on WESTLAW:

Field Searches on WESTLAW

Title (abbreviated *ti*). The title field contains only the names of the parties to a case. Use this field to retrieve a case if you know the case name. The computer will quickly retrieve your case and display it so you can either read it online or print it to read at a later time. Suppose, for example, that the title of the case you wanted to read was

Pennzoil v. Texaco. Once you select the database you want, a title field search for this case would be as follows:

```
ti(pennzoil & texaco)
```

Synopsis (abbreviated *sy*).   The synopsis field contains a summary of the case prepared by the editorial staff of WESTLAW. This summary includes the facts presented by the case, the holding of the lower court, the issues on appeal, and the resolution of those issues. The names of majority, concurring, and dissenting judges are also included in the synopsis field. Since general legal concepts are used to describe the issues before the court, this is a good field in which to run a conceptual search. A conceptual search is helpful for finding cases that fall into a legal category or classification, such as domicile, adverse possession, or product liability. The digest field (to be considered below) also allows you to conduct a search via concepts. Hence it is often worthwhile to combine the synopsis and digest fields in a single search. For example:

```
sy,di("product liability")
```

Topic (abbreviated *to*).   Each small-paragraph summary in the West digests (page 552) is assigned a topic classification, such as criminal law, bankruptcy, and divorce. West has tens of thousands of cases summarized under these topics. If you already know a topic classification, you can conduct a WESTLAW search that is limited to this topic field. For example:

```
to(criminal)
to(bankruptcy)
```

```
to(divorce)
to("product liability")
```

Digest (abbreviated *di*).   In addition to a topic classification, every small-paragraph case summary in a West digest contains the name or title of the case, the name of the court that decided it, the citation of the case, and the rest of the summary itself, known as a headnote (page 529). All of this information (topic, title, court, citation, headnote) is contained within what is called the digest field of WEST-LAW. Here is an example of a search in this field:

```
di(paralegal)
```

This search will find every case that has the word paralegal anywhere in a small-paragraph case summary of a West digest. To make sure that your search finds cases mentioning legal assistants as well as those mentioning paralegals, the search would be:

```
di(paralegal "legal assistant")
```

As indicated above, it is often wise to combine searches in the digest and synopsis fields.

Judge (abbreviated *ju*).   If you wanted to find cases written by a particular judge, e.g., Justice William Brennan, you could conduct a search in the judge field:

```
ju(brennan)
```

When run in the database containing opinions of the United States Supreme Court (sct), this search will give you every majority opinion written by Justice Brennan.

(e) WIN and Freestyle

Thus far we have been covering *Boolean* searches in which you broaden or narrow your search query by using connectors such as AND, OR, and NOT. There is now a simpler method. WESTLAW and LEXIS use different terms to describe this alternative:

WESTLAW: **WIN** (WESTLAW Is Natural), a "natural language" method of writing a search query.

LEXIS: **Freestyle,** a "plain English" method of writing a search query.

Under both methods, you simply write out a question using everyday language. For example, instead of writing:

```
cigar! tobacco smok! /p product strict! /5 liab!
```

you would write:

```
Can strict product liability be imposed for harm caused by smok-
ing cigarettes?
```

Both WESTLAW and LEXIS have a built-in thesaurus that will allow you to select synonyms and closely related words if the ones you used are not productive.

This kind of search is not a substitute for a Boolean search. Natural or plain English searches work best when you are searching general issues at the beginning of your research. Eventually, you may need to refine your search by switching to a search that uses Boolean language.[26]

(f) Find and Read

Suppose that you already have the citation of a case or other document, and you simply want to read it. But you are not in a traditional law library that has the bound volumes you need. If you have access to WESTLAW or LEXIS, there is a relatively easy way to retrieve what you want. On WESTLAW, use the *find* command (abbreviated *fi*). On LEXIS, use the *lexstat* command (abbreviated *lxt*) when you are looking for a statute and the *lexsee* command (abbreviated *lxe*) when you are looking for cases or any other documents available through this route.

Here are four examples that use the *find* command of WESTLAW to retrieve documents in the Supreme Court Reporter (sct), the United States Code Annotated (usca), the Code of Federal Regulations (cfr), and the Federal Register (fr). All of these examples assume that you already know the volume, page, and section numbers indicated. You simply want to find these documents and read them on your computer screen.

```
fi 97 sct 451
fi 18 usca 1968
fi 9 cfr 11.24
fi 52 fr 22391
```

The first example below uses the *lexstat* command of LEXIS to locate a statute in United States Code Service (uscs), and the next three examples use the *lexsee* command to locate material in Columbia Law Review (colum l rev), American Law Reports, Federal (alrfed), and an IRS Revenue Ruling (rev rul). Again, all of these examples assume that you already know the volume, page, and section numbers indicated.

```
lxt 11 uscs 101
lxe 87 colum l rev 1137
lxe 44 alrfed 148
lxe rev rul 88-2
```

3. SPREADSHEET PROGRAMS

Most law offices can easily see the usefulness of word processing and database programs. The usefulness of a **spreadsheet,** however, is a little more difficult to appreciate. A spreadsheet is a computerized accounting ledger or table used for financial calculations and for recording transactions. Spreadsheets can be helpful for almost any project that requires the use or manipulation of numbers. They are good management tools for creating budgets and tracking expenses of a law firm. Most spreadsheet programs have built-in functions that will make intricate calculations, such as determining present net value, loan repayment schedules, averages, and many other statistical functions.

A spreadsheet allows you to create large groups of interrelated numbers. Once this is done, changing one of the numbers allows you to see what happens to all the others. A spreadsheet can quickly recalculate the values of all the numbers that are dependent on

---

[26]Roper, *Using Computers in the Law, 2d* 302 (see note 13).

the one that was changed. (See Exhibit 13.16.) For example, with a spreadsheet you can create a program that will calculate the size of payments on a loan based on the amount, length, and interest rate that apply to the loan. If you change the numbers displayed on the screen for the amount, for the length, or for the interest rate of the loan, the spreadsheet will recalculate the payment size.

Exhibit 13.16   Frequently Used Spreadsheet Terms

TERM	DEFINITION
Cell	A storage location within a spreadsheet that is used to store a single piece of information relevant to the spreadsheet.
Coordinates	The column letter and row number that define the location of a specific cell.
Formula	A mathematical expression used in a spreadsheet.
Label	Information used for describing some aspect of a spreadsheet. A label can be made up of alphabetic or numeric information, but no arithmetic can be performed on a label.
Value	A single piece of numeric information used in the calculations of a spreadsheet.
Window	The portion of a worksheet that can be seen on the computer display screen.

Source: S. Mandell, *Introduction to Computers Using the IBM and MS-DOS PCs with Basic, 3d* 409 (West Publishing Co., 1991).

A spreadsheet consists of a series of boxes called *cells.* Numbers and other information can be placed directly into the boxes from the keyboard. Once the information is stored in a box, it can be a source for formulas in other boxes. When a box containing a formula is displayed on the screen, the result of the formula is seen, not the formula itself. If any of the numbers in the boxes used by a formula are changed, the display for the box with the formula will reflect this change. For example, let us assume that we have a small spreadsheet program with three boxes. (Large, sophisticated spreadsheets can have thousands of boxes.) Each of our three boxes has a name that refers to the information in the box. We will name our boxes A, B, and C.

If we place the number 5 in box A and the number 2 in box B, we can then combine this information in box C by entering the formula A + B into box C.

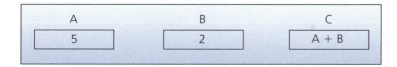

Box C will then display the number 7.

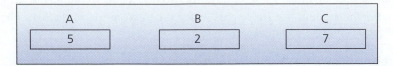

We can change the formula in box C to read (A + B) * 2 (here, the * means *times* on most computers).

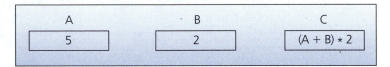

C will now read 14.

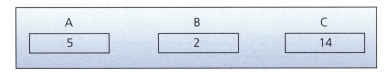

Now if we change the number in box A from 5 to 4, box C will read 12. [(4 + 2) * 2 = 12.]

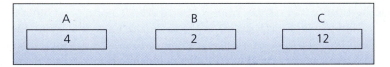

Let's make our small spreadsheet example slightly more complicated. Place the number 2 in box A. Then place the formula A + 2 in box B. Box B will now contain the number 4 [2 + 2 = 4]. We could now place the formula A * B in box C. Box C would now display the number 8 [2 * 4 = 8].

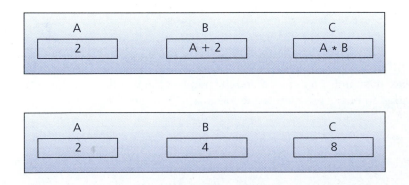

Any time we change the number in box A, the numbers displayed in both box B and box C will change. If the number 4 is placed in box A, box B will show the number 6 [4 + 2 = 6], and box C will display the number 24 [6 * 4 = 24].

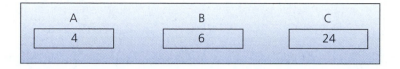

On a large spreadsheet, many cells (boxes) can depend on information from formulas in other cells. Therefore, a spreadsheet program can be used to create sophisticated models and project formulas.

When creating large models, you must guard against making circular references. For example, place the formula (A * C) in box B and the formula (A * B) in box C.

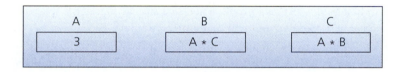

No matter what number is entered in box A, box B looks to box C for information and box C looks to box B for information. Some spreadsheet programs will get stuck on these two formulas and stop dead. Other spreadsheets will run through the calculations for the two boxes ten or twenty times and then stop.

The capability of a spreadsheet to perform a whole series of calculations based on formulas and numbers makes it possible for you to do in minutes or seconds what once took accountants hours or days. The spreadsheet is perfect for doing what users call "what ifs." Suppose you were considering the purchase of a small garage and wanted to figure out what the monthly payments would be. Three factors determine the size of the payments: the interest rate, the length of the mortgage, and the amount of the loan. Using the proper financial formulas, you could create a spreadsheet that would let you enter an interest rate, the number of years, and the amount that you wished to borrow. In seconds the spreadsheet would display the monthly mortgage payment based on those numbers. You can then play "what if" and change one or more of the numbers to see what happens to the payment level when the interest rate goes down, the length of the mortgage increases, the amount of the loan is greater, etc. (See Exhibit 13.17.)

A spreadsheet used as a "what if" device can be very helpful in a law office for working out damage projections and settlement offers, particularly structured settlements where the payments are spread over a period of time and take account of the value of money in the future according to an agreed-on formula. Once the relationship of the various elements of damages is determined, different interest and inflation assumptions can be tested. You can determine how these assumptions will influence the amount of damages that would be necessary in a particular case. For example, assume you are trying to project lost wages of an injured plaintiff. Interrelated formulas can be created to determine this damage calculation. One of the formulas would project potential salary over the working life of the person, starting with the current salary and adding increases over time. Each increase would be a percentage of the salary. The formula can allow for changing

> *Exhibit 13.17*   **Spreadsheet Mortgage Cost Display**
>
> Real Estate Financial Analysis
>
> | | |
> |---|---|
> | Garage Price: | $35,900.00 |
> | Downpayment: | 1,795.00 |
> | Amount Financed: | $34,105.00 |
> | Interest Rate %: | 9.75 |
> | Number of Yrs Financed: | 20.00 |
> | Monthly Payment: | $323.49 |

the percent increase so that different increase assumptions may be tested quickly. Another formula can take the results from the salary calculations and determine how many dollars would be needed today to create an amount equal to the future income. Various rates of return can be tested with this formula. Used in a similar manner, a spreadsheet can be productive for estate planning and real estate projections.

Most of the current spreadsheet programs have the capability of creating graphs from the numbers they produce. They can create line, bar, and pie charts in many different formats. Bar charts can be made to appear three dimensional or can be stacked one above the other. If the computer has a color monitor, the bars representing different items can be displayed in various colors.

Many applications for spreadsheets can be obtained by purchasing a **template** to perform the needed task. A template is a predefined formula or format. A federal income tax template, for example, contains all the lines and forms of a tax return. The template covers each part of the tax form on which information must be entered, and calculates the taxes based on the information entered. The template then prints the form as a completed tax return. Templates are available for almost any type of business calculation. There are small bookkeeping programs, purchase-lease comparison programs, linear regression programs, and many others.

⚜ *Assignment 13.6*

Barklay is a freelance paralegal. He shares an office with three others: Adams, Cordier, and Davis. The office expenses are rent, phone, electricity, gas, postage meter, and secretarial service. They agree to the following allocation of expenses: rent will be $185 per person; the cost of electricity and gas will be split evenly among the four of them; everything else will be apportioned according to actual use and cost.

Different people will have the job of making the actual payments: Barklay will pay the phone and secretarial bills; Adams will pay the rent; Cordier will pay the electricity and gas bills; and Davis will pay the postage bill. At the end of every month, each will make an accounting of what was paid. They will then calculate who owes what to whom based on their agreement of how expenses are to be allocated.

Here are the figures for last month. Adams ran up $122 in phone calls, Barklay $85, Cordier $77, and Davis $19. Postage use was $22.50 for Adams, $14.20 for Barklay, $66.85 for Cordier, and $10.31 for Davis. The bill for secretarial services showed that Adams owes $118.00, Barklay $100.33, Cordier $84, and Davis $44. The electric bill was $29.03. The gas bill was $11.16.

The bills were paid on time. In Parts I and II of this assignment, you will be setting up a spreadsheet to calculate each person's share of the expenses, using the following basic structure as a guide:

	A	B	C	D
	Adams	**Barklay**	**Cordier**	**Davis**

Row

1	Rent				
2	Amt. Paid				
3	Bal. Due				
4	Phone				
5	Amt. Paid				
6	Bal. Due				
7	Electricity				
8	Amt. Paid				
9	Bal. Due				
10	Gas				
11	Amt. Paid				
12	Bal. Due				
13	Postage				
14	Amt. Paid				
15	Bal. Due				
16	Secretarial				
17	Amt. Paid				
18	Bal. Due				
19	Grand Totals Due from Each				

Part I

For each category of expense, fill in the figures you were given for last month. Do not do any math at this time, but state the formulas that you would use to arrive at all of the mathematical calculations. For example, if you must divide $11.16 by 4, phrase the formula as follows: (11.16/4). Or, if you must add Row 13 for all four individuals, phrase the formula as follows: (A13+B13+C13+D13). Next, do all the calculations based on your formulas.

Part II

Assume that there is a 3 percent tax on the phone calls over and above the amounts stated. Change your spreadsheet setup accordingly.

4. COMMUNICATIONS

Communications software makes it possible to call up WESTLAW or LEXIS to do legal research over telephone lines. Such programs also make it possible to contact people or businesses and communicate with their computers. You can send or receive letters, statistical information, programs, or insults! Anything that can be put on paper or into a computer can be sent from one computer to another over telephone lines.

For successful computer communications, two components are necessary: a modem and communications software. A *modem* is a piece of hardware that is plugged into your computer on one end and into your telephone line on the other. The modem controls the transmission of information over telephone lines. The communications software controls the information sent to the modem that is to be transmitted over telephone lines. When two computers are transmitting information to one another over telephone lines, each one must have a modem and a communications program. The two modems transmit the information that they are told to send by the communications software.

For the modems to be able to do this, they must be "speaking" with the same code and "talking" at the same speed. Most modems sold today use the same code, but they do not all communicate at the same speed. Some can communicate at more than one speed. The speed of transmission is stated in terms of **baud** or the **baud rate.** Twelve hundred baud is the minimum used today; most modems can transmit and receive information at this speed. If large amounts of information are being sent, however, 1,200 baud is very slow. The higher the baud rate, the less time it takes to send the same information. Today's high-speed standard is 36,600 baud. As modem technology improves, higher baud modems will become available. The only drawback to higher (faster) baud rates is that the error rate may go up with the speed. When more information is squeezed into the same space, the equipment used must be more sensitive. Unfortunately, sensitive equipment may be less able to distinguish static from the information being sent on the telephone line. Therefore, at higher transmission rates, the information is more likely to become garbled. This problem must be controlled by the communications software.

5. COMBINATIONS

We have examined four types of programs: word processing, database management, spreadsheets, and communications. You can now obtain software packages that contain all four types in one program. These are often called **integrated packages.** Such programs require computers with large amounts of memory. The reason for creating an integrated package is to simplify the process of moving information from one application to another. If, for example, you have information in your database that you wish to manipulate with a spreadsheet program, an integrated package will help you achieve this goal by moving the information from a format that a database understands to one that a spreadsheet understands.

📖 *A s s i g n m e n t   1 3 . 7*

Each student will make a presentation in front of the class on a computer product—a hardware or software product. You can select your own product, but it must be approved in advance by your teacher.

The setting will be a mock meeting of members of a law firm (attorney, paralegals, and secretaries) who have assembled to listen to you. You have come to the meeting to make a sales presentation on the product.

You have several objectives:

(a) *To introduce yourself.* You are the representative of the company that makes the product. Use your own name. Make up some brief facts about yourself as representative, such as how long you have been with the company.

(b) *To provide something visual about the product.* You do not have to bring the product with you. Try to obtain a brochure on it. If one is not available, try to obtain a photo of the product. For example, you might be able to photocopy an ad that has a picture of the product. At the very least, you should prepare a diagram or drawing of the product or of some important aspect of it. Circulate the brochure, photo, ad, diagram, or drawing to the group while you are talking.

(c) *To describe the product.* State what the product does. What is its purpose? How is it used in a law office? What are its benefits? Who is supposed to use it in the office? How will the product improve efficiency or increase profit? How does the product compare with competing products on the market? How much does it cost? Try to cover as many of these areas as possible.

The product you select must meet the following characteristics:

- It is a brand product that is currently on the market.
- It is a product that is either designed exclusively for law offices or is widely used in law offices.
- It is not a product that you work with every day (if you already work in a law office). The goal of this assignment is to force yourself to learn about a *new* product and to communicate what you have learned to others.
- It is a product that no one else in the class has covered in a presentation. (The teacher will enforce this guideline by approving the products in advance.)

The best starting point in locating a product is to go to any law library and look through ads in bar association journals (state or national) and ads in legal newspapers (state or national). Many of these ads have 800 numbers you can call for more information. Once you have identified a product, ask a librarian how you can find out if any reviews of that product have been published. (Manufacturers of the product are often very willing to send you copies of favorable reviews.) You might also obtain a lead to products by talking to someone who works in a law office.

No one is expected to have intimate familiarity with the product (although you may want to give a contrary impression as part of your sales presentation).

Your goal is to provide information about the product that you learn by:

- Reading ads
- Reading brochures
- Talking with company representatives (locally, if available, or via an 800 number)
- Reading reviews
- Talking with someone in a law office in your area that already uses the product

---

🏛 *Assignment 1 3 . 8*

Smith, Smith & Smith is a twenty-attorney law firm that was established thirty years ago. It employs eight paralegals, ten secretaries, a librarian, a receptionist, a file clerk, and a part-time maintenance worker. The firm handles a great variety of cases: personal injury litigation, worker's compensation, government contracts, antitrust, domestic relations, estates and trusts, taxation, bankruptcy, commercial law, etc.

The founder and leader of the firm is John Smith, who practiced law with his father in the 1920s before he set up the present firm with his two children, Mary and David Smith. They are full partners in the firm.

For years, John Smith practiced law "the old-fashioned way." "If it was good enough for my father," he is fond of saying, "it's good enough for me." The consequence of this attitude is that Smith, Smith & Smith is managed today in almost the same manner that it was run thirty years ago. Almost everything is done by hand. All the secretaries have typewriters. John agreed to purchase electric typewriters only five years ago. These machines do nothing but type. There are a few dictaphones, but they are seldom used.

Payroll, billing, document control, etc. are all done by hand. The law firm consists of a suite of fifty rooms, almost half of which contain nothing but records and files.

Six months ago John Smith died. Mary and David are now in full control of the firm. At a recent bar association meeting, Mary and David listened to a presentation on the use of computers in the practice of law. Mary was fascinated by the presentation and is ready to restructure the law firm by introducing computers throughout the office. David (who believed that his father and grandfather were incapable of making a mistake) is skeptical. David does not see any reason to change the way the firm practices law. Yet he agrees that the idea of computer use is worth exploring.

Mary and David agree to hire you as a computer consultant. You specialize in giving advice to attorneys in the use of computers in the management of a law firm and in the practice of law.

(a) Name some areas where you think Smith, Smith & Smith might be able to use computers in the office. Explain why.

(b) What do you think some of David's objections might be to the introduction of computers in these areas? How would you respond to these objections?

Section E
THE INTERNET

"Every paralegal will eventually use the Internet. It is only a question of time."
—James Powers, May 1996

The **Internet** is one of the most exciting developments in the history of computers. Approximately 40 million people around the world can and do access the enormously flexible communication Internet medium. That figure is expected to grow to 200 million Internet users by the year 1999.[27] The Internet is a massive collection of networks—a network of networks. A **network** is two or more computers (and other devices) that are connected by telephone lines, fiber optic cables, satellites, or other systems in order to share messages, other data, software, and hardware. It isn't difficult to envision how the Internet works "since it parallels, to some extent, how our worldwide, and even national telephone system works. When you place a call to someone in the United States outside your local phone company's service area, you dial a single number (with an area code), and the phone rings at the other end. You do not need to know that you're really using the systems of several phone companies, all of whom have agreed with one another how they're going to bill for connections so that they can all go through unimpeded by differences in each system. The Internet works in much the same way. All of the individuals running the various networks that are connected to it have agreed with one another on a common set of specifications, or **protocols,** in order for information to flow from one network to another."[28] A protocol is a set of standards that allows computers to communicate with each other.

The Internet was developed in the 1960s by the U.S. Department of Defense to link a handful of computers in the event of a nuclear attack. The idea was to design a system that would allow communication over a number of different routes between linked computers. Thus, a message sent from a computer in Washington, D.C. to a computer in Palo Alto, California, might first be sent to a computer in Philadelphia, and then be forwarded

---

[27] *American Civil Liberties Union v. Reno,* 929 F. Supp. 824 (E.D. Pa. 1996).

[28] Will Sadler, *Introduction to the Internet,* 65 The Bar Examiner 45, 46 (May 1995).

to a computer in Pittsburgh, and then to Chicago, Denver, and Salt Lake City, before finally reaching Palo Alto. If the message could not travel along that path (because of military attack, simple technical malfunction, or other reason), the message would automatically (without human intervention or even knowledge) be rerouted, perhaps, from Washington, D.C. to Richmond, and then to Atlanta, New Orleans, Dallas, Albuquerque, Los Angeles, and finally to Palo Alto. This type of transmission and rerouting would likely occur in a matter of seconds.[29]

When the government no longer needed this link, it, in effect, turned the system over to the public. Hence no single entity—academic, corporate, governmental, or nonprofit—administers the Internet. It exists and functions because hundreds of thousands of separate operators of computers and computer networks independently decided to use common data transfer protocols to exchange communications and information with other computers (which in turn exchange communications and information with still other computers). There is no centralized storage location, control point, or communications channel for the Internet, and it would not be technically feasible for a single entity to control all of the information conveyed on the Internet.[30]

Some have called the Internet the most important new communication medium in decades. "The Internet attracts educational institutions doing research, commercial organizations advertising their products electronically, sports networks, artists, musicians, financial analysts, television networks, lawyers, and . . . governments." Small wonder that many use the metaphor "information superhighway" to describe the Internet.[31]

Why are attorneys interested in the Internet? First of all, many of their clients are on the Internet. Very few large businesses today do not have an Internet address where consumers can find out about their products and organizational structure. Second, the Internet is an additional way for attorneys to communicate with each other. And finally, while the Internet is not ready to replace giants such as WESTLAW and LEXIS, it provides a great deal of legal, financial, and other information on a cost-efficient basis.

To use the Internet, you need a computer, a modem, a regular telephone line, and an Internet account through an access or service provider.[32] Examples of commercial or fee-based providers are America Online, CompuServe, Microsoft Network, and Prodigy. If you are part of a university, you may be able to gain access to the Internet through the university's direct connection.

In addition to using the national commercial online services, individuals can also access the Internet using some (but not all) of the thousands of local dial-in computer services, often called **bulletin board systems** or "BBSs." Individuals, nonprofit organizations, advocacy groups, and businesses can offer their own dial-in computer "bulletin board" service where friends, members, subscribers, or customers can exchange ideas and information. BBSs range from single computers with only one telephone line into the computer (allowing only one user at a time), to single computers with many telephone lines into the computer (allowing multiple simultaneous users), to multiple linked computers each servicing multiple dial-in telephone lines (allowing multiple simultaneous users). Some (but not all) of these BBSs offer direct or indirect links to the Internet. Some BBSs charge users a nominal fee for access, while many others are free to individual users.[33]

---

[29] *American Civil Liberties Union v. Reno,* 929 F. Supp. at 832.
[30] Id. at 832.
[31] Sadler, *Introduction to the Internet,* 65 The Bar Examiner at 45.
[32] Roper, *Using Computers in the Law, 2d,* 313.
[33] *American Civil Liberties Union v. Reno,* 929 F. Supp. at 833–34.

Here is an overview of some of the main components and services available on the Internet.

1. E-MAIL (ONE-TO-ONE MESSAGING)

Electronic mail (**e-mail**) is a message sent by one computer to another. Many individuals send e-mail over the Internet, making it one of the system's most popular features.[34] In seconds, you can send private messages to another computer user in the next room or around the world. (By comparison, the traditional "paper mail" delivery services such as the U.S. Post Office and overnight delivery services are condescendingly referred to as "snail mail.") To send e-mail, you and your recipient need an address. E-mail addresses have two parts: a **user name** and a location or **domain name.** The two names are separated by an @ sign (pronounced "at"). For example:

```
wptech@corel.com
smith@research.westlaw.com
```

The user name (to the left of the @) is the account name of the user. The domain name (to the right of the @) is the name of a system or location. The period (pronounced "dot") at the end of the address gives you the **domain identifier,** which tells you the type of organization it is. Here are the major domain identifiers:

```
.com  (commercial organization)
.edu  (educational institution)
.gov  (government office or entity)
.mil  (military office or entity)
.org  (almost everything else)
```

The typical components of an e-mail message are the sender's address (FROM), the recipient's address (TO), the date of the message, a one-line summary of the message or its topic (SUBJECT), and the message itself. Most e-mail programs allow you to save or store messages (called **archiving**), print them, forward them to multiple recipients, etc.

2. LISTSERV (ONE-TO-MANY MESSAGING)

One of the fascinating benefits of the Internet is becoming a member of a **listserv.** This is an automatic mailing list service consisting of a list of individuals interested in receiving and sending e-mail to each other on a particular topic of mutual interest. Once you subscribe to the list, you can receive messages relevant to the topic. You can then reply to the message and have the reply distributed to everyone on the mailing list. By allowing the list members to read everyone else's e-mail in this way, the service enables them to keep abreast of developments or events in a particular subject area. Most listserv-type mailing lists automatically forward all incoming messages to all mailing list subscribers.[35]

The Internet has thousands of such mailing list services, collectively with hundreds of thousands of subscribers. Pick the ones you want to join. For example, you could join one that consists of paralegals who work in corporate law. They might talk about paralegal salary and overtime issues peculiar to corporate employers, as well as issues of substantive corporate law.

---

[34]You don't need the Internet to send e-mail. Companies such as America Online and CompuServe allow users to send each other e-mail independent of as well as through the Internet.
[35]*American Civil Liberties Union v. Reno,* 929 F. Supp. at 834.

Here are some examples of questions that might be posed on different listservs. On a paralegal listserv, a paralegal asks:

> "I'm thinking about taking either NALA's CLA exam or the NFPA's PACE exam. Have any of you taken both exams? Is there benefit in taking both? Neither?"

A California paralegal who is a member of a real estate listserv, asks:

> "We have a client who bought and sold land in Georgia in 1979. I'm trying to find a copy of the standard purchase agreement used by the Georgia Association of Real Estate Agents in the 1970s before they radically changed the format of the contract. Anyone in Georgia who can help me? If you can fax me a copy (619-456-9103), you would save my life. Help!"

At the beginning of the week, a New York attorney in immediate need of Mississippi regulations sends out the following urgent e-mail plea to the members of his listserve:

> "I am looking for Mississippi Department of Health regulations pertaining to abortion, nursing, birthing, and home healthcare facilities. I didn't find them on the Mississippi State home page, LEXIS, or WESTLAW. The Mississippi Department of Health can't supply them until Friday. Anyone willing to FedEx the relevant regulations using our firm's account number?"

Someone who uses the WordPerfect word processor sends this e-mail to the members of a WordPerfect listserv:

> "I just purchased the 7.0 upgrade. Twice while using spell check, the system locked up on me. Has this happened to anyone else? Any suggestions on avoiding this?"

Depending on the number of members in the listserv, you could receive scores of replies. It is not uncommon for people who have been helped to send "thanks-for-saving-my-life" messages to the group. Even if you don't ask any questions yourself, you will probably find it instructive—and fun—to read the questions and answers others are sending each other.

Listservs (and other communication forums) often use shorthand communication. Here are some of the commonly used acronyms and their meanings:

BFN: Bye For Now

FAQ: Frequently Asked Questions

FWIW: For What It's Worth

IMHO: In My Humble Opinion

IMNHO: In My Not-so-Humble Opinion

IMO: In My Opinion

NOYB: None Of Your Business

PITA: Pain in The . . . Derrière

PMJI: Pardon My Jumping In

ROTFL: Rolling On The Floor Laughing

TIA: Thanks In Advance

TPTB: The Powers That Be

TTFN: Ta-Ta For Now

TTYL: Talk To You Later

3. DISTRIBUTED MESSAGE DATABASES (NEWSGROUPS)

Similar in function to listservs—but quite different in how communications are transmitted—are **distributed message databases** such as "USENET newsgroups." User-sponsored newsgroups are among the most popular and widespread applications of Internet services and cover all imaginable topics of interest to users. Like listservs, newsgroups are open discussions and exchanges on particular topics. Users, however, can access the database at any time and need not subscribe to the discussion mailing list in advance, as they do with listservs. Some USENET newsgroups are "moderated" (i.e., one person screens messages for relevance to the topics under discussion), but most newsgroups are open access—unmoderated. Responses to messages, like the original messages, are automatically distributed to all other computers receiving the newsgroup or forwarded to a moderator in the case of a moderated newsgroup. The dissemination of messages to USENET servers around the world is an automated process that does not require direct human intervention or review. There are newsgroups on more than 15,000 different subjects. Collectively, almost 100,000 new messages (or "articles") are posted to newsgroups each day.[36] See Exhibit 13.18 for a list of some of the law-related newsgroups.

Exhibit 13.18	**Law-Related Internet Newsgroups**
INTERNET ADDRESS	**DESCRIPTION**
clari.news.gov.taxes	Tax laws, trials, etc.
clari.news.law	General group for law-related issues
clari.news.law.civil	Civil trials and litigation
clari.news.law.profession	Lawyers, judges, etc.
clari.news.law.supreme	U.S. Supreme Court rulings and news
misc.legal	Legalities and the ethics of law
misc.taxes	Tax laws and advice

Source: Brent Roper, *Using Computers in the Law, 2d* 315 (West Publishing Co., 1996).

4. REAL-TIME COMMUNICATION

In addition to transmitting messages that can be read or accessed later, individuals on the Internet can engage in an immediate dialog, in "real time," with other people on the Internet. In its simplest form, "talk" allows one-to-one communications, and **Internet Relay Chat** (or IRC) allows two or more individuals to type messages to each other that appear almost immediately on the others' computer screens. IRC is analogous to a telephone party line, but uses a computer and keyboard rather than a telephone. With IRC, however, at any one time thousands of different party lines are available, with collectively tens of thousands of users engaging in conversations on a huge range of subjects. More-

[36]Id. at 835.

over, one can create a new party line to discuss a different topic at any time. Some IRC conversations are "moderated" or include "channel operators." In addition, commercial online services such as America Online, CompuServe, Microsoft Network, and Prodigy have their own "chat" systems allowing their members to converse.[37]

5. WORLD WIDE WEB

The **World Wide Web** is a tool that allows you to navigate locations on the Internet that are often linked by **hypertext.** Hypertext is a method of displaying and linking information located in different places in the same document or in different documents. On a page on the World Wide Web, you will see words or pictures that are highlighted, perhaps by being in a different color. When you click on the words or picture, you are sent to another location on the Internet. Suppose, for example, you are on the World Wide Web site of the NFPA (the National Federation of Paralegal Associations). One of the pages on this site is the "Legal Resources" page. See Exhibit 13.19. Note the fifteen resources

Exhibit 13.19   **Information Options on the World Wide Web Site of the National Federation of Paralegal Associations (NFPA)**

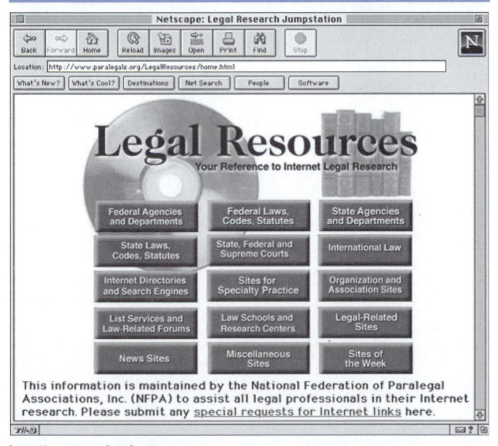

http://www.paralegals.org
Web Site of the National Federation of Paralegal Associations

---

[37]Id. at 835.

available on this page. By clicking any of these fifteen options, you will be sent to over 1,000 other Web sites on the Internet that will help you do factual and legal research. Do you want information on federal statutes? Click the option called "Federal Laws, Codes, Statutes" at the top of the second column. Do you want information about the Federal Trade Commission? Click the option called "Federal Agencies and Departments" at the top of the first column. For another example, see Exhibit 13.20, the **home page** Web site

Exhibit 13.20   **Information Options on the World Wide Web Site of the American Bar Association**

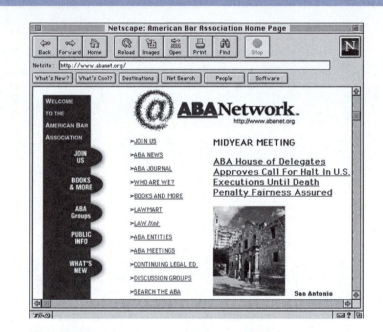

http://www.abanet.org
Web Site of the American Bar Association

of the American Bar Association. (A home page is the page on the Internet, usually the opening page, that introduces a computer user to the site of an organization or individual.) Do you want to know if the ABA is conducting any CLE (Continuing Legal Education) seminars on law firm billing practices? Click the "CONTINUING LEGAL ED" option on the screen. Do you want information about the work of the Legal Assistant Committee of the ABA? Try clicking "ABA ENTITIES," which will lead you to a large list of the various sections, divisions, and committees of the ABA. As you can see, hypertext gives you quick and easy access to a great many resources.

Addresses on the World Wide Web are identified by their **URL,** or Uniform Resource Locator. For examples of Web addresses, see Exhibit 13.21.

One final word before leaving our discussion of the Internet. More and more attorneys are establishing a presence on the Internet. See Exhibit 13.22. This is one way for attorneys to let the world (literally) know who they are, what services they provide, and how

Exhibit 13.21   Relevant Web Sites

LEGAL SITES	ADDRESS
Attorney Yellow Pages	www.newquest.com/attorney/altindex.htm
Chicago-Kent College of Law	www.kentlaw.edu
Cornell Legal Information Institute	www.law.cornell.edu
Federal Judicial Center	earth.fjc.gov
Hieros Gamos (Lex Mundi)	www.hg.org
Indiana School of Law at Bloomington	www.law.indiana.edu
Int'l Ass'n of Constitutional Law	www.eur.nl/iacl
Law Journal Extra!	www.ljx.com
Legal List (Lawyers Co-op)	www.lcp/The-Legal-List/TLL-home.html
Lexis Counsel Connect	www.counsel.com
More Law	http://www.morelaw.com
National Center for State Courts	oyez.ncsc.dni.us
Seamless Web	seamless.com
Shepard's Citations	http://www.shepards.com
Thomas (Congress)	http://thomas.gov
United States Federal Judiciary	www.uscourts.gov
West Publishing Company	www.westpub.com

SEARCH ENGINES (FOR GENERAL SEARCHES)	ADDRESS
Alta Vista	http://www.altavista.com
Excite	http://www.excite.com
Infoseek	http://www.infoseek.com
Lycos	http://www.lycos.com
Magellan	http://www.mckinley.com
OpenText	http://www.opentext.com
WebCrawler	http://www.webcrawler.com
Yahoo	http://www.yahoo.com

ASSOCIATIONS	ADDRESS
American Association of Law Libraries	http://www.lawlib.wuacc.edu
American Bar Association	www.abanet.org
Canadian Bar Association	cba.org/abc
National Association of Legal Assistants	http://www.nala.org
National Association of Legal Secretaries	http://www.nals.org
National Association of Paralegal Associations	http://www.paralegals.org

they can be reached. This is an added bonus for paralegals seeking employment. In addition to checking traditional law directories such as *Martindale-Hubbell,* paralegals can learn a great deal about law firms where they are applying for work by reading whatever information is available about a law firm on its Web site.

Exhibit 13.22   Finding Law Firms and Attorney Profiles on the Internet

Examples of attorney home pages on the World Wide Web. Such pages can include color graphics, video, sound clips, and hypertext links to other relevant sites on the Internet.

Chapter Summary

Like almost every other aspect of our society, the law office has been substantially altered by the computer. Since there is a tremendous diversity in computer products available, it is unlikely that any paralegal will walk into a new office, particularly a large one, and be totally familiar with all of the hardware and software programs in use. Hence, you must expect to go through a large and ongoing dose of on-the-job computer training. Standard survival techniques can help, such as finding out if any of the products have an 800-number helpline that you can call, taking advantage of online tutorials, and using HELP keys.

Fairly soon you should learn a relatively small list of computer terms. The list includes hardware, software, back-up, data, hard disk drive, operating system, modem, laser printer, etc. The four major kinds of software programs are word processing, database management, spreadsheets, and communications. A fifth kind combines the other four.

Word processing software is a substitute for the traditional typewriter, bottle of "white-out," and scissors that were once used to cut-and-paste a report together. Now you can use the word processor to type the text of a report, to insert additional text, to move text around, and to make other corrections on a computer screen (monitor) so that you can see the finished product before the report is printed. This feature, plus many others, makes word processing the most widely used software in offices and homes throughout the country.

Database software allows you to store, organize, and retrieve a large body of information. The office can design its own database, and it can purchase access to commercial databases such as WESTLAW and LEXIS. One of the critical skills in this area is the ability to formulate a question, or query, for the computer to answer. Most queries ask the computer to find data within a designated database. In formulating a query using Boolean language, you need to know how to use the universal character (*) and the root expander (!). You also need to know when to use connectors (such as the OR connector, the AND connector, and the numerical connector) to specify the relationship among the search words in the query in order to give the search more direction. You also need to know how to search for phrases, how to conduct field and segment searches, and how to perform simple "find" searches when you already have the citation to something you want to read.

Recently, a more natural way to phrase queries by using plain English has been developed. WESTLAW calls its method WIN (WESTLAW Is Natural); LEXIS calls its method Freestyle.

Spreadsheet software allows you to make financial calculations and solve mathematically oriented problems with much greater ease than with traditional calculators. Endless "what if" questions can be answered based on variables entered into the program.

Communications software makes it possible for computers to "talk" with each other, through a modem over telephone lines. Finally, software exists that allows the user to combine or integrate word processing, database management, spreadsheets, and communications capabilities.

The Internet has been a major development in the computer revolution. Internet users have access to a vast network of resources at a reasonable cost. They can also communicate with each other by e-mail, listservs, newsgroups, and real-time communication. The power of hypertext has made the World Wide Web the dominant vehicle for navigating the resources of the Internet.

KEY TERMS

online tutorial, 687
HELP key, 687
documentation, 687
load, 687
CLE, 687
users group, 687
listserv, 687
hardware, 688
central processing unit (CPU), 688
personal computer, 688
IBM-compatible, 688
clone, 688
compatibility, 688
back up, 688
CD-ROM, 689
command, 689
data, 689
disk drive, 689
floppy disk, 689
hard disks, 689
bytes, 689
diskettes, 690
floppies, 690
file, 690
k, 690

kilobyte, 690
megabyte, 690
gigabyte, 690
language, 690
laptop, 691
load, 691
macro, 691
memory, 691
microcomputer, 692
modem, 692
monitor, 692
operating system, 692
mouse, 692
icons, 692
Windows, 692
multitasking, 692
printer, 693
dot matrix printer, 693
daisy wheel printer, 693
ink jet printer, 693
laser printer, 693
fonts, 694
points, 694
bold, 694
run, 694
save, 695

scanner, 695
hard copy, 695
software, 695
application, 695
tape backup system, 695
word processing, 696
word wrap, 696
spell checker, 698
right justified, 698
merging, 698
database, 700
key word search, 701
full text search, 701
search criteria, 702
rainmaker, 703
CALR, 703
online, 703
search query, 703
Boolean, 704
universal character (*), 710
root expander (!), 710
connectors, 711
segments, 716
fields, 716
WIN, 717
Freestyle, 717

spreadsheet, 718
template, 722
baud, 724
baud rate, 724
integrated packages, 724
Internet, 726
network, 726
protocol, 726
bulletin board systems (BBSs), 727
e-mail, 728
user name, 728
domain name, 728
domain identifier, 728
archiving, 728
listserv, 728
distributed message databases, 730
Internet Relay Chat (IRC), 730
World Wide Web, 731
hypertext, 731
home page, 732
URL, 732

Chapter 4

INTRODUCTION TO LAW OFFICE ADMINISTRATION*

*Portions of this chapter were originally written with Robert G. Baylor, Business Manager at Manatt, Phelps, Rothenberg, and Tunney, Los Angeles. Others who have reviewed this chapter and provided valuable commentary include Dorothy B. Moore, Kathleen M. Reed, Michele A. Coyne, Patsy R. Pressley, Deborah L. Thompson, and Shawn A. Jones.

Section A
The Practice of Law in the Private Sector

There are over 700,000 attorneys in the United States—one for every 360 citizens. This is double the number in 1970. By the year 2000 the number is expected to grow to 1,000,000.[1]

About 70 percent of attorneys practice in private law offices. Another 10 percent work for corporations in corporate practice. The remainder practice in the public sector for government, for legal aid and legal service offices, or for organizations such as unions, trade associations, and public interest groups, or they do not practice law at all. In this chapter, our primary focus will be on attorneys who practice law in relatively large private offices, although we will also look at other practice settings as well.

In the private sector, law is practiced in a variety of settings:

- Sole practice
- Office-sharing arrangement
- Partnership
- Professional corporation
- Limited liability entity
- Corporate law department

SOLE PRACTICE

A **sole practice** (also called a solo practice) often refers to an attorney who practices alone. More accurately, it means a *sole proprietorship* in which one attorney owns and manages the firm. Anyone who works for this attorney, including another attorney, is an employee who receives a salary. They are not entitled to a share of the profits of the office in addition to a salary.

Sole practitioners can be generalists or specialists. A generalist is the equivalent of a doctor in general practice. An attorney who is a **general practitioner** often tries to handle all kinds of cases. If, however, the case is unusually complex or if the attorney is very busy with other cases, he or she might consult with an attorney in another office or refer the case to another attorney. Other sole practitioners specialize. Their practice might be limited, for example, to tax, criminal, or patent and trademark cases, or—more commonly—to personal injury cases.

Most sole practitioners have very few employees. There is a secretary, who often performs many paralegal functions along with the traditional clerical responsibilities of typing, filing, and reception work. He or she may also perform bookkeeping chores. The most common job title of this individual is "legal secretary," although occasionally he or she will be known as a "paralegal/secretary." You will sometimes find job ads for small offices seeking paralegals with clerical skills. These skills are often phrased more positively as administrative or word processing skills, but they are, in essence, clerical. In recent years, however, many sole practitioners have begun to hire one or more paralegals who have minimal or no clerical duties.

The office may also have a **law clerk.** This is a full- or part-time law office employee who is studying to be an attorney or who has graduated from law school and is waiting to pass the bar examination. (If this person is not paid, he or she is usually called a **legal intern.**) In addition, the office may employ one or more other attorneys. Again, in a sole practice, these attorneys do not share in the profits of the office.

---

[1]Stanton, *Stepping Up to the Bar,* 35 Occupational Outlook Quarterly 3 (Spring 1991).

OFFICE-SHARING ARRANGEMENT

It can be very expensive to start a practice, particularly in high-rent areas of the country. Often a sole practitioner will allow other attorneys (e.g., those newly admitted to the bar) to use the facilities of the office in exchange for some nonpaid help on the practitioner's cases. In more formal **office sharing,** two or more attorneys with independent practices share the use and cost of administration such as rent, copy machine, other equipment, library, secretarial help, etc. They do not practice law together as a partnership or corporation, although they may assist each other during periods of vacation, illness, or other emergencies. To avoid the conflict-of-interest and confidentiality problems discussed in chapter 5, the attorneys (and any of their employees) must be careful in selecting clients and discussing their cases with each other.

PARTNERSHIP

A **law partnership** is a group of individuals who practice law jointly and share in the profits and losses of the venture. If the partnership is relatively large, it will probably be organized into a series of departments based on client needs (such as an antitrust department, a litigation department, etc.) and will be managed through a series of committees (such as a recruitment committee, a library committee, a records committee) based on the variety of support services available to the attorneys. See Exhibit 14.1 for an example of the organization structure of a large law firm.

A large partnership can include a number of different categories of attorneys, the most common of which are:

- Partners
- Associates
- Staff attorneys
- Of counsel
- Contract attorneys

1. Partners

Partners contribute the capital that is needed to create the firm and to expand it as needed. They decide whether to merge with other firms and, indeed, whether to go out of business altogether. Partners share the profits and losses of the firm pursuant to an elaborate partnership agreement. They decide how the firm should be managed, when to take on new partners, what attorneys, paralegals, and other employees to hire, etc. Most of this is done through a variety of administrative staff. In short, the partners own the firm. A firm may have different categories of partners (for example, senior partner and junior partner) depending on such factors as the amount of capital the attorney contributed to the firm and how involved he or she is in the firm's management. As we will see, a distinction is also sometimes made between equity and nonequity partners.

Generally, partners are not on salary in the traditional sense, although they do receive a periodic **draw,** which is an advance against profits in some firms and an overhead expense in others.

2. Associates

Associates are attorney employees of the firm who are hoping to become partners. Often, they are hired right out of law school while studying for the bar examination. As students, they may have worked for the firm as a *law clerk.* Other associates, however, are hired from other law firms. They are known as **lateral hires.** (When partners and paralegals switch law firms, they also are referred to as lateral hires.) After a certain number of years at the firm, e.g. seven, associates are usually considered for partnership. If they are

Exhibit 14.1 Large Law Firm Organization Chart: An Example

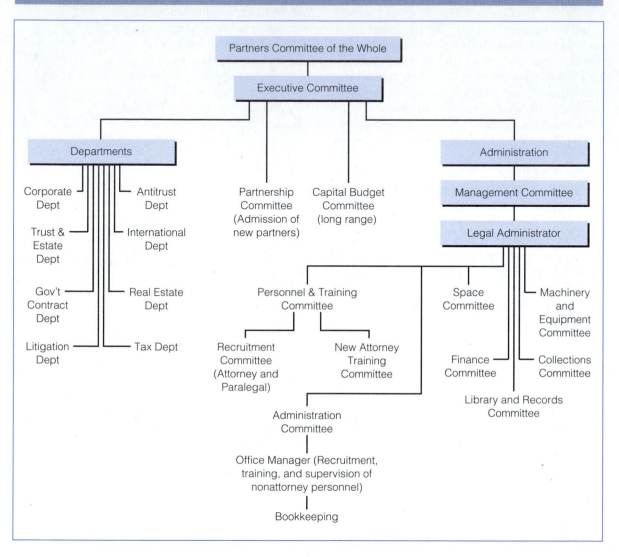

Partners Committee of the Whole

Executive Committee

Departments

- Corporate Dept
- Antitrust Dept
- Trust & Estate Dept
- International Dept
- Gov't Contract Dept
- Real Estate Dept
- Litigation Dept
- Tax Dept

Partnership Committee (Admission of new partners)

Capital Budget Committee (long range)

Personnel & Training Committee

- Recruitment Committee (Attorney and Paralegal)
- New Attorney Training Committee

Administration Committee

Office Manager (Recruitment, training, and supervision of nonattorney personnel)

Bookkeeping

Administration

Management Committee

Legal Administrator

- Space Committee
- Machinery and Equipment Committee
- Finance Committee
- Collections Committee

Library and Records Committee

---

passed over for partner, they often leave the firm to practice elsewhere, although a few may be invited to stay as a **permanent associate** or a **senior associate.**

Some firms are moving away from the "up-or-out" system that adds great tension to the ranks of associates. To encourage good people to stay, the firms have created different tiers of partners. For example, a firm might create the category of **nonequity partner** or **income partner,** to be distinguished from the **equity partner** or **capital partner.** The latter is a full partner in the sense of owning the firm and sharing in its profits and losses. A nonequity or income partner, on the other hand, is an individual who has not made, or who does not aspire to become, a full partner. In effect, he or she is often little more than a permanent associate with a more inviting title.

Hence paralegals are not the only workers who are concerned by a lack of career ladders in the legal profession. As we saw in chapters 1 and 3, the paralegal field has been slowly developing career ladders, e.g., from case clerk to paralegal to senior paralegal and paralegal supervisor. Attorneys also want career ladders beyond the traditional associate-partner regime. Equally slowly, the profession has been responding to this need.

3. Staff Attorneys

Staff attorneys (sometimes called **second-tier attorneys**) are hired with the understanding that they will never be considered for partnership. This is what distinguishes them from associates.

4. Of Counsel

There is no fixed definition of an attorney who is **of counsel** to a firm. He or she may be a semiretired partner, a part-time attorney, or a full-time attorney who is considering a long-term relationship with the firm. Not all firms use the title "of counsel." Some prefer "special counsel" or simply "counsel."

5. Contract Attorneys

Contract attorneys (sometimes called **project attorneys**) are hired when the firm has a temporary shortage of attorneys or needs expertise in a certain area for a limited period. Often paid on an hourly basis, the contract attorney is not a full-time employee.

PROFESSIONAL CORPORATIONS

In most states, it is possible for attorneys to incorporate their practice of law as a **professional corporation** (P.C.), e.g., "Jamison & Jamison, P.C." This is done primarily for tax purposes. From a tax and estate-planning perspective, it is often more advantageous to organize as a corporation than as a partnership. Another important feature of a corporation is **limited liability.** This simply means that if you lose a lawsuit that arises out of your business activities, the winner of the lawsuit can collect only out of the assets of the business; he or she cannot reach your personal assets such as your home. If your personal assets are reachable, then you have full **personal liability.** Like any corporation, a professional corporation has stockholders (the owners), directors, and officers—all of whom are attorneys. The operation of a professional corporation is practically identical to the operation of a traditional partnership. A client would hardly notice the difference.

LIMITED LIABILITY ENTITY

Recently, a new form of organization has been developed—the **limited liability entity.** It can be a limited liability company (LLC) or a limited liability partnership (LLP). These entities are hybrid structures in that they combine features of a corporation and a partnership. In most, but not all, states, a law firm can be organized as an LLC or an LLP. Like a corporation, a limited liability entity allows limited liability for its owners, but the entity is treated like a partnership for income tax purposes.[2]

CORPORATE LEGAL DEPARTMENTS

Many large corporations have a **corporate legal department** (sometimes called the *law department*) headed by a **general counsel** who may also be a vice-president of the company. Other attorneys in this office can include deputy or associate general counsel, senior

---

[2]Brent Roper, *Practical Law Office Management* 27 (West Publishing Co., 1995).

attorneys, staff attorneys, etc. They are the **in-house attorneys** who handle the day-to-day tasks of advising the company on legal matters. They have one client—the corporation that hires them and that pays them a salary. Frequently, paralegals work with these attorneys. In 1983, the ratio of paralegals to attorneys was 0.15-to-1. In 1994 the ratio had doubled to 0.3-to-1. The average number of paralegals per department was 5.1.[3] Other support personnel may include legal administrators, legal secretaries, word processing and data processing operators, clerks, librarians, and record managers. There are, of course, no client fees. Funds to operate the department come directly from the corporate treasury. When expertise is needed, such as trial experience in a certain specialty, the general counsel will hire "outside" attorneys from law firms if the expertise is not available "in-house."

Section B
THE LEGAL ADMINISTRATOR AND THE LEGAL ASSISTANT MANAGER: OVERVIEW OF ADMINISTRATION IN A LARGE LAW FIRM

The practice of law is a profession, but it is also a business. The larger the practice, the more likely its business component will be managed by individuals whose main or sole responsibility is administration. While the owners of a law firm have ultimate responsibility for administration, they often delegate this responsibility to others. For example, there may be a **managing partner,** often an attorney with a small case load or none at all. More and more firms are hiring new categories of management personnel who are not attorneys. We will focus on two such individuals: the **legal administrator** and the **legal assistant manager.** One way to obtain an overview of management is to examine the job descriptions of such individuals.

The legal administrator works under the supervision of the managing partner or of a management committee of the firm. The range of this person's responsibility, and of the business component of the practice of law, can be seen in the job description in Exhibit 14.2.

Exhibit 14.2 **Legal Administrator: Job Description (Association of Legal Administrators)**

Summary of Responsibilities

The legal administrator manages the planning, marketing, and business functions, as well as the overall operations, of a law office. He or she reports to the managing partner or the executive committee and participates in management meetings. In addition to having general responsibility for financial planning and controls, personnel administration (including compensation), systems, and physical facilities, the legal administrator also identifies and plans for the changing needs of the organization, shares responsibility with the appropriate partners for strategic planning, practice management, and marketing, and contributes to cost-effective management throughout the organization.

continued

---

[3]Wilber, *Support Staffing Ratios,* National Law Journal S6 (May 20, 1991); *Staffing Additions and Reductions,* Illinois Legal Times 24 (August 1995).

E x h i b i t   1 4 . 2   **Legal Administrator: Job Description (Association of Legal Administrators) —continued**

WHETHER DIRECTLY OR THROUGH A MANAGEMENT TEAM, THE LEGAL ADMINISTRATOR IS RESPONSIBLE FOR MOST OR ALL OF THE FOLLOWING:

Financial Management:

- ☐ Planning
- ☐ Forecasting
- ☐ Budgeting
- ☐ Variance analysis
- ☐ Profitability analysis
- ☐ Financial reporting
- ☐ Operations analysis
- ☐ General ledger accounting
- ☐ Rate analysis
- ☐ Billing and collections
- ☐ Cash flow control
- ☐ Banking relationships
- ☐ Investment
- ☐ Tax planning and reporting
- ☐ Trust accounting
- ☐ Payroll and pension plans
- ☐ Other related functions

Systems Management:

- ☐ Systems analysis
- ☐ Operational audits
- ☐ Procedures manual
- ☐ Cost-benefit analysis
- ☐ Computer systems design
- ☐ Programming and systems development
- ☐ Information services
- ☐ Records and library management
- ☐ Office automation
- ☐ Document construction systems
- ☐ Information storage and retrieval
- ☐ Telecommunications
- ☐ Litigation support
- ☐ Conflict-of-interest docket systems
- ☐ Legal practice systems
- ☐ Other related services

Facilities Management:

- ☐ Lease negotiations
- ☐ Space planning and design
- ☐ Office renovation

- ☐ Purchasing and inventory control
- ☐ Reprographics
- ☐ Reception/switchboard services
- ☐ Telecommunications
- ☐ Mail messenger services
- ☐ Other related functions

Human Resource Management:

- ☐ Recruitment, selection, and placement
- ☐ Orientation, training, and development
- ☐ Performance evaluation
- ☐ Salary and benefits administration
- ☐ Employee relations
- ☐ Motivation and counseling
- ☐ Discipline
- ☐ Termination
- ☐ Worker's compensation
- ☐ Personnel data systems
- ☐ Organization analysis
- ☐ Job design, development of job descriptions
- ☐ Resource allocation
- ☐ Other human resource management functions for the legal and support staff

AS A MEMBER OF THE LEGAL ORGANIZATION'S MANAGEMENT TEAM, THE LEGAL ADMINISTRATOR MANAGES AND/OR CONTRIBUTES SIGNIFICANTLY TO THE FOLLOWING:

General Management:

- ☐ Policymaking
- ☐ Strategic and tactical planning
- ☐ Business development
- ☐ Risk management
- ☐ Quality control
- ☐ Organizational development
- ☐ Other general management functions

Practice Management:

- ☐ Attorney recruiting
- ☐ Attorney training and development
- ☐ Legal assistant supervision
- ☐ Work-product quality control

continued

Exhibit 14.2	**Legal Administrator: Job Description (Association of Legal Administrators) —continued**

☐ Professional standards
☐ Substantive practice systems
☐ Other related functions

Marketing:
☐ Management of client-profitability analysis

☐ Forecasting of business opportunities
☐ Planning client development
☐ Marketing legal services: enhancement of the firm's visibility and image in the desired markets

Job Requirements

Knowledge: Has familiarity with legal or other professional service organizations, and experience in managing business operations, including planning, marketing, financial and personnel administration, and management of professionals.

Skills and Abilities: Able to identify and analyze complex issues and problems in management, finance, and human relations, and to recommend and implement solutions. Able to manage office functions economically and efficiently, and to organize work, establish priorities, and maintain good interpersonal relations and communications with attorneys and support staff. Excellent supervisory and leadership skills, as well as skills in written and oral communication. Demonstrated willingness and ability to delegate.

Education: Graduation from a recognized college or university with major coursework in business administration, finance, data processing, or personnel management, or comparable work experience.

Again, this job description fits an individual who works for a law office that is fairly large. The support staff for such an office can also be quite extensive. Here are some examples:[4]

Administrative Support Staff in a Large Law Office

Legal Administrator	Secretaries
Legal Assistant Manager	Data Processing Operators
Personnel Manager	Word Processing Supervisor
Records Information Manager	Word Processors
Employee Benefits Manager	Proofreaders
Recruiter	Docket Clerks
Director of Marketing	Computer Specialists
Facilities Manager	Equipment Managers
Risk Manager	File Room Clerks
Office Manager	Librarian
Financial Manager	Library Aides
Credit/Collections Manager	Messengers/Pages
Chief Financial Officer/Comptroller	Copy Room Clerks
Bookkeepers	Mail Clerks
Analysts	Purchasing Clerks

---

[4]R. Green, ed., *The Quality Pursuit* 69 (American Bar Association, 1989).

Payroll Specialists
Accounts Payable Clerk
Accounts Receivable Clerk
Time and Billing Assistants

Receptionists
Telephone Operators
Reservation Clerks

Prominent on this list is the legal assistant manager, whose job description is presented in Exhibit 14.3.

Exhibit 14.3   **Legal Assistant Manager**

Legal Assistant Manager: Job Description Attorneys' Guide to Practicing with Legal Assistants
(State Bar of Texas, 1986)*

General Responsibilities:

The legal assistant manager has overall responsibility for administration of the program. Formal training programs responsive to the needs of the various sections and to the professional development of legal assistants are identified and established by this individual. He or she works with the supervising attorneys, providing assistance in staffing and in resolving legal assistant–related conflicts between sections and between individuals.

Specific Duties:

A. Development and utilization of legal assistant skills

  1. Work with the supervising attorneys. Become and remain familiar with the nature and amount of work done by each lawyer in the firm.

  2. Work with the supervising attorney. Develop and submit to the Practice Management Committee a written analysis of each lawyer's work, identify the portions that should be performed by a legal assistant, and update this information on an annual basis.

  3. Develop a training program for the supervising attorneys.

4. Develop a short introductory presentation for lawyers in each section to demonstrate the types of tasks for which legal assistants should be used.

5. Meet with each new attorney in the firm to explain the legal assistant program, thus insuring the utilization of legal assistants by new attorneys.

6. Develop an orientation program for new legal assistants and conduct orientation sessions with each new legal assistant.

7. Develop an in-house training program for all new legal assistants and conduct or supervise the training provided by others.

8. Receive notice of each lawsuit docketed in the Litigation Section and assign a legal assistant to each lawsuit.

9. Assign legal assistants to all files that require the assistance of a legal assistant.

10. Receive notice of the assignment of all or major parts of "Special Projects" to attorneys, and assign a legal assistant to each "Special Project."

11. Monitor the progress of legal assistant use in each section and develop changes in the legal assistant support program as needed.

12. Consult with each legal assistant and each supervising attorney

---

*The job title used in the Guide is Legal Assistant Coordinator. Legal Assisntant Manager or Paralegal Manager is more common, however.

continued

Exhibit 14.3   Legal Assistant Manager—continued

individually at appropriate intervals to identify problems and possible solutions.

13. Conduct monthly meetings of the legal assistants to keep them informed.

14. Work with the supervising attorney in the development of written procedures for inclusion in the firm's manual concerning the use of legal assistants.

15. Evaluate the need for support staff for legal assistants and work with firm administrator to insure that legal assistants have adequate support.

B. Legal assistant supervision

1. Supervise the development of procedure manuals for legal assistants in each section for review by the supervising attorneys.

2. Review legal assistant time records to insure proper preparation and to monitor workloads.

3. Coordinate the evaluations of legal assistants.

4. With the respective supervising attorneys, conduct a performance interview with each legal assistant.

5. Insure that all section staff meetings and similar meetings are open to legal assistants.

6. Monitor both the quality and the quantity of work assignments to legal assistants.

C. Reporting

Prepare and submit to the Practice Management Committee a quarterly report showing:

1. Approximate hours spent by each legal assistant on work from each lawyer.

2. The number of assignments carried out by each assigned legal assistant for each lawyer.

3. The same information for backup work done by the legal assistants in each section.

D. Professional development for legal assistants

1. Set objectives for and help plan in-house professional instruction for legal assistants.

2. Review all notices received in the firm regarding seminars.

3. Develop and implement schedules of continuing in-house and outside training for each legal assistant to insure timely completion of required formal and enhancement instruction.

E. Personnel

1. Recruit, interview, and hire legal assistants.

2. Maintain a personnel file for each legal assistant.

3. Anticipate and help correct unsatisfactory assignments and inadequate or inappropriate staffing.

4. Assign backup responsibility after consultation with legal assistants and supervising attorneys.

5. Provide assistance in resolving legal assistant conflicts between individuals.

6. Evaluate office space requirements for legal assistants and work with firm administration in providing office space for legal assistants.

Section C
EXPENSES

How does a large law firm spend the fee income that it receives? A number of organizations conduct surveys to answer this question. One of the largest is the Altman Weil Pensa

Survey of Law Firm Management. Some of the highlights of one of its recent surveys are presented in Exhibit 14.4. The data were collected from 647 law firms with more than 16,000 attorneys.

Exhibit 14.4   Survey of Law Firm Economics

Between 1985 and 1990, the average overhead cost per attorney rose to $93,648, an increase of 51%. The average law firm spent:

- $34,121 per attorney for support staff (excluding paralegals). This constituted 16.5% of the gross revenue of the firm. This is the same percentage as in 1984. (Apparently, the large investment in law office automation between 1984 and 1990 did *not* result in significant net staff cost savings.)
- $28,718 per attorney for general expenses, such as insurance of all kinds, printing, meetings, postage, and office supplies not charged to clients. This constituted 13.9% of the gross revenue of the firm, an increase of 69% between 1985 and 1990.
- $8,323 per attorney for paralegals. This constituted 4.0% of gross revenue, an increase of 67% between 1984 and 1990.
- $15,462 per attorney for occupancy expenses. This constituted 7.5% of gross revenue, an increase of 49% between 1985 and 1990.
- $4,672 per attorney for equipment. This constituted 2.3% of gross revenue, an increase of 10% between 1985 and 1990.
- $2,352 per attorney for library and reference expenses. This constituted 1.1% of gross revenue, an increase of 33% between 1984 and 1990.

The median number of billable hours were:

- 1,706 for partners/shareholders in 1990; 1,722 in 1995
- 1,820 for associates in 1990; 1,813 in 1995
- 1,400 for paralegals in 1989; 1,412 in 1995

The billing rates were:

- $102 per hour for attorneys with less than two years of experience (1995)
- $198 per hour for attorneys with over twenty years of experience (1995)
- $55 per hour for paralegals in 1990; $66 per hour in 1995

Section D
TIMEKEEPING

Abraham Lincoln's famous statement that a "lawyer's time is his stock in trade" is still true today. Effective **timekeeping** is critical to the success of a law firm. In some firms, it is an obsession, as typified by the following story. A senior partner in a very prestigious Wall Street law firm walked down the corridor to visit the office of another senior partner. Upon entering the room, he was startled to find his colleague on the floor writhing in pain, apparently due to a heart attack. Standing there, he could think of only one thing to say to him: "Howard, are your time sheets in?" [5]

---

[5]Margolis, *At the Bar*, New York Times B13 (September 7, 1990).

In some firms, the pressures of the clock on attorneys and paralegals can be enormous:

> [Y]oung lawyers often are shocked to discover their new employer's time expectations. Many firms in major cities require as many as 2,400 billable hours per year. When one considers that many full-time employees outside of the law only *work* 2,000 hours per year, the time commitment required by these firms is staggering.[6]
>
> The cry for billable hours is thought by many to be at the heart of much of the problem. Many legal assistants as well as attorneys have quotas of billable hours. Zlaket [the President of the State Bar of Arizona] stated that some firms require 2,200 hours a year and he deems this to be outrageous. He suggested that this only leads to padding of bills and time sheets, and it leads to unnecessary work that will be paid by somebody.[7]

The ethical dimensions of this problem are considered in chapter 5. Here our concern is the administration of the timekeeping and billing system.

To gain an understanding of how a timekeeping and billing system might work in many large law firms, we will now trace the accounting route taken by a client's *case* (sometimes called a *matter*) within a law firm. After the initial client interview, the accounting starting point can be a **New File Worksheet** (see Exhibit 14.5). It is also sometimes referred to as a

---

[6]Walljasper, *I Quit!* Wisconsin Lawyer 16 (March 1990).
[7]Morris, *Join the Effort to Restore Respect to the Legal Profession,* The Digest 3 (Arizona Paralegal Ass'n, April 1989).

Exhibit 14.5 **New File Worksheet**	Billing No. _____
	Date _____ Opened _____ Closed

New File

Client (Check one)
____ INDIVIDUAL

_____
Last   First   Middle Initial

____ ENTITY
_____
(Use complete name & common abbreviations; place articles [e.g., The] at end.)

____ CLASS ACTION
_____
(File Name, ex.: Popcorn Antitrust Litigation)

Matter (Check One)
____ NON-LITIGATION _____

____ LITIGATION _____

_____ Approved for litigation by—MUST BE INITIALED by submitting attorney!!

Nature of the Case
Area of law code ____   Summary of work or dispute: _____
_____

Client Contact (N/A for Class Actions)
Name: _____
Company: _____
Street: _____
City, State, Zip: _____
Telephone: _____

Exhibit 14.5 **New File Worksheet—continued**	Billing No. _____
	Date _____ Opened _____ Closed

Billing Address (N/A for Class Actions)

Name: _____

Company: _____

Street: _____

City, State, Zip: _____

Telephone: _____

Team Information (Use initials)

_____ _____ _____   Managing Attorney(s) (for non-litigation cases only)

_____ _____ _____   Bill Review Attorney(s)

_____ _____ _____   Originating Attorney(s)

_____   Calendar Attorney (for litigation cases only)

_____   Legal Assistant (for litigation cases only)

_____   Secretary to Calendar Attorney (for litigation cases only)

Referral Source (Check one)

____ Existing Client   _____

(Name)

____ Non-Firm Attorney   _____

(Name)

____ Firm Attorney or Employee   _____

____ Martindale-Hubbell

____ Other   _____

Fee Agreement (Check those that apply)

___ Hourly

___ Contingent _____%

___ Fee Petition

___ Fixed Fee $_____ or Fixed Range from $_____ to $_____

___ Retainer $_____

___ Letter of Retainer sent by _____ on _____

___ ___   (Initials)   (Date)

Statement Format (Check those that apply)

Do you want identical disbursements grouped?   _____ Yes _____ No

Do you want attorney hours reflected on *each* time entry?   _____ Yes _____ No

Do you want fees extended on *each* time entry?   _____ Yes _____ No

---

Conflict Check

Conflict Check Completed By: _____   Date: _____

(Initials)

Conflict Check Not Needed: _____

(Initials of Submitting Person)

Check One:

_____ No conflicts

_____ Potential conflict with the following existing parties (from computer system):

_____

_____

(Or attach computer printout from Conflict Check System.)   *continued*

Exhibit 14.5 New File Worksheet—continued	Billing No. _____
	Date _____ Opened _____ Closed

*New Adverse Parties:

_____
_____
_____

*New Related Parties (for Class Actions, Named Plaintiffs Only):

_____
_____
_____

*Will be entered into computer system by Bus. Dept. *AFTER* approval by Managing Partner.

Closed File

Date Closed: _____   **Atty. or Sec. Initials:** _____

_____ Attach Pleadings and/or File Indexes. If indexes are not available, attach brief description of what is contained in the file(s). SEND FILES, THIS FORM, AND INDEX TO FILE ROOM.

Routing Lists

(Initial)

	New File:	Date:	Closed File:	Date:
Submitted by	_____	_____	_____	_____
Sec. of Submitting Person	_____	_____	_____	_____
Managing Partner	_____	_____	_____	_____
Business Department	_____	_____	_____	_____
File Department	_____	_____	_____	_____
Firm Newsletter	_____	_____	_____	_____
Docket for Litigation	_____	_____	_____	_____
EnviroLaw (Computer Center) Add?	_____			
IdeaLaw (Computer Center) Add?	_____			
JobLaw (Computer Center) Add?	_____			
Pulse—See Fred Farrell				

New Matter Sheet or a *New Business Sheet.* The New File Worksheet becomes the source document for the creation of all the necessary accounting records involved in working on a client's case or matter.

Attorneys and paralegals must keep an accurate account of the time they spend on behalf of a client. An example of a form they can use is the **Daily Time Sheet** (see Exhibit 14.6). This sheet becomes the journal from which all time entries are posted to individual client ledger pages.

Law firms normally use tenths of an hour (in increments of six minutes) as the base unit for the measurement of time, although a few firms still use one-fourth of an hour as their base for recording time. **Hourly Time and Rate Charts** (see Exhibit 14.7) can later be used to translate these time fractions into dollars and cents for billing purposes; or this can be quickly accomplished by computer. Attorneys and paralegals note their activities on the Daily Time Sheet each time during the day that they work on a particular matter. The information from these Daily Time Sheets can then be typed on **time tickets** (see Exhibit 14.8) or into a computer database.

These time tickets are usually perforated or shingled. For offices still using a manual system, this facilitates easy separation so that they can be subsequently sorted into alphabeti-

Exhibit 14.6 Daily Time Sheet

DAILY SERVICE REPORT OF: DATE:

ANS –Answer	DEPO –Deposition	K –Contract	O –Order	RES –Research
APP –Appearance or Attending	DIC –Dictation	L –Legal	OP –Opinion	REV –Revision
ARG –Argue or Argument	DOC –Document	LT –Letter to	P –Preparation	S –Settlement
BR –Brief	DR –Drafting	LF –Letter from	PL –Plaintiff	TF –Telephone from
COMP –Complaint	F –Facts	MT –Memorandum to	PR –Praecipe	TT –Telephone to
CW –Conference–Office	FL –File	MF –Memorandum from	PRT –Pretrial	TR –Trial
CWO –Conference–Outside Office	H –Hearing	MOT –Motion	R –Reading and Review	TRV –Travel
DEF –Defendant	INV –Investigation	NEG –Negotiation	REL –Release	W –Witness
DEM –Demurrer	INT –Interview			

CLIENT (State billing division or department)	MATTER	DESCRIPTION OF WORK (Use abbreviations above)	TIME Hours	10ths

Exhibit 14.7 Hourly Time × $ Hourly Rate

TIME / RATE:	$20	$25	$30	$35	$40	$45	$50	$55	$60	$65	$70	$75
0.10 hour	2 00	2 50	3 00	3 50	4 00	4 50	5 00	5 50	6 00	6 50	7 00	7 50
0.20	4 00	5 00	6 00	7 00	8 00	9 00	10 00	11 00	12 00	13 00	14 00	15 00
0.30	6 00	7 50	9 00	10 50	12 00	13 50	15 00	16 50	18 00	19 50	21 00	22 50
0.40	8 00	10 00	12 00	14 00	16 00	18 00	20 00	22 00	24 00	26 00	28 00	30 00
0.50	10 00	12 50	15 00	17 50	20 00	22 50	25 00	27 50	30 00	32 50	35 00	37 50
0.60	12 00	15 00	18 00	21 00	24 00	27 00	30 00	33 00	36 00	39 00	42 00	45 00
0.70	14 00	17 50	21 00	24 50	28 00	31 50	35 00	38 50	42 00	45 50	49 00	52 50
0.80	16 00	20 00	24 00	28 00	32 00	36 00	40 00	44 00	48 00	52 00	56 00	60 00
0.90	18 00	22 50	27 00	31 50	36 00	40 50	45 00	49 50	54 00	58 50	63 00	67 50
1.00 hour	20 00	25 00	30 00	35 00	40 00	45 00	50 00	55 00	60 00	65 00	70 00	75 00
2.00	40 00	50 00	60 00	70 00	80 00	90 00	100 00	110 00	120 00	130 00	140 00	150 00
3.00	60 00	75 00	90 00	105 00	120 00	135 00	150 00	165 00	180 00	195 00	210 00	225 00
4.00	80 00	100 00	120 00	140 00	160 00	180 00	200 00	220 00	240 00	260 00	280 00	300 00
5.00	100 00	125 00	150 00	175 00	200 00	225 00	250 00	275 00	300 00	325 00	350 00	375 00
6.00	120 00	150 00	180 00	210 00	240 00	270 00	300 00	330 00	360 00	390 00	420 00	450 00
7.00	140 00	175 00	210 00	245 00	280 00	315 00	350 00	385 00	420 00	455 00	490 00	525 00
8.00	160 00	200 00	240 00	280 00	320 00	360 00	400 00	440 00	480 00	520 00	560 00	600 00
9.00	180 00	225 00	270 00	315 00	360 00	405 00	450 00	495 00	540 00	585 00	630 00	675 00
10.00 hours	200 00	250 00	300 00	350 00	400 00	450 00	500 00	550 00	600 00	650 00	700 00	750 00

Exhibit 14.8 Time Ticket

DATE	NAME	CLIENT	MATTER	CLIENT REFERENCE NUMBER	TIME

DESCRIPTION:

Posted:

Exhibit 14.9 Master Ledger Card

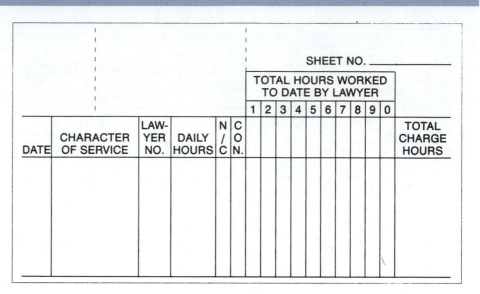

DATE	CHARACTER OF SERVICE	LAW-YER NO.	DAILY HOURS	N / C	C O N.	TOTAL HOURS WORKED TO DATE BY LAWYER										TOTAL CHARGE HOURS
						1	2	3	4	5	6	7	8	9	0	

SHEET NO. _____

cal order for quick posting to client ledger cards. The tickets can be processed in several different ways. One is to retain the individual tickets in an open tray in alphabetical order for eventual retrieval and tabulation for billing; another would be to use gummed backs for pasting directly onto a client ledger card; or the ticket may be used as a source document for transcribing onto a **Master Ledger Card** (see Exhibit 14.9); or the ticket could be keyed directly from the Daily Time Sheet of the attorney or paralegal and used as an input document for the firm's computerized system.

If you have never kept close track of your time, you will find that the task requires a great deal of effort and discipline; it does not come naturally to most of us. The key to performing the task effectively is to do it consistently and comprehensively until it becomes second nature.

Tory Barcott, a Certified Legal Assistant in Anchorage, makes a number of important points about timekeeping:

> It "sometimes scares me a little to contemplate clients paying" $10.00 or more "for every six minutes of our time." To survive in this world, the legal assistant must possess the accuracy and efficiency of a Swiss watch. "I keep one of those small, cheap, adhesive digital clocks where it can't be missed or covered with paperwork. Sticking it to my phone, in the middle of my desk, works best for me. The first step in performing any task is to record the time on my time sheet. I do this before retrieving the file, making a phone call," or going to meet a supervising attorney. The clock is also helpful in recording the time when a task is interrupted by anything unrelated to the current client matter. "I take notes on the start and stop times exactly as displayed on my digital clock." Some Saturdays, while absently attending to household chores, I'll glance at the clock and catch myself thinking, "that floor took only 0.4 to clean." This is a sure sign that the discipline of timekeeping has been internalized![8]

For other recommendations on effective timekeeping, see Exhibit 14.10.

Computer programs have been developed to provide assistance in keeping track of time. In one program, for example, you use a menu on the screen to tell the computer the fol-

---

[8]Barcott, *Time Is Money*, AALA News (Alaska Ass'n of Legal Assistants, April 1990).

Exhibit 14.10   Effective Timekeeping Techniques

- Always have your time sheet and pen at your side, ready for entries.
- If available, use a dictating machine for time only. Regularly tell the machine what you are doing—for example, as soon as you hang up the phone.
- When you begin a project, make a list of each task involved. Note the time you begin each task. Note the time of interruptions and the completion time. If additional tasks are needed for the project, add them to the list.
- In addition to a project list of tasks to be completed over a period of days, weeks, or longer, compile a *daily to-do list*. This will help you organize your day and focus on the time dimensions of what you do.
- Whenever possible, complete a project before moving on to another one. This facilitates timekeeping.
- Conduct your own study of your nonbillable hours, such as interruptions, pro bono work, interoffice conferences on administrative matters, breaks, clerical work, lunch. At the end of a pre-determined period, e.g., two weeks, identify the largest categories of your nonbillable time. Determine whether you can do anything to cut this time down. You may want to show your study to a supervisor to encourage him or her to delegate some of your nonbillable tasks to others who do not bill by the hour, or who bill at a lower rate than you do.

Sources: Rucker, *Effective Timekeeping: A Legal Assistant's Point of View,* Newsletter (Houston Legal Assistants Ass'n, August 1987); Serrano, *The Member Connection,* Facts & Findings 7 (NALA, December 1986).

lowing information (with relatively few keystrokes): what project you are working on, whether the time is billable, what client the project is for, the nature of the work you are doing, the time you begin the project, the times you are interrupted, and the completion time. An internal computer clock keeps track of the time until you tell it to stop and resume. You can also "input" costs connected with the case, such as postage and photocopying charges. The data you enter into the computer can be sent to the accounting department and to the supervising attorney for eventual billing. The computer can use the data in other ways as well, as the following discussion demonstrates.

Computers can take an initial item of data such as the following transaction:

Attorney Smith met with client ACME to discuss research needs, 2 hours, July 2

and use the data over and over again in various ways. For example, the data may be sorted by attorney to give a listing of all the hours worked by the attorney on that day, or in that month for all clients. It may be sorted by client to give a listing of all the hours worked for a particular client. It may be used to produce a preliminary or final bill. The data may be merged with other data to price the hours spent and to provide additional billing information. The same data may be matched with other data to list the total hours billed for the client that year or even total hours still unbilled. The *Meeting With Client* might be encoded as MWC and the firm, for whatever reason, might build statistics on how much meeting with clients occurred for all clients. . . .

Computerization not only allows one entry to provide a great deal of output but it speeds the entry. Special codes can be used for such items as the name of the lawyer (Smith), the name of the client (ACME) and the type of work done (e.g., MWC). The user may not even need to enter a billing rate ($150 per hour) since some systems can automatically search the lawyer or client information to find a rate. Or, the system may look at the transaction code (Processed *Application for State Trademark* abbreviated as AST) and disregard all hourly rates, using the $1,500 fixed fee automatically associated with that type of work. Some computer systems can keep track of the hours spent on all trademark cases, multiply by the lawyer's basic rate and determine at the end of the year if the $1,500 fee is profitable for this type of work.

Entry by computer is also faster and easier. Computers prompt the operator for information and require it before allowing the operator to move on. The details are often immediately verified to see if they are consistent with other data in the computer. Correction speed is also improved. If a lawyer sees a printout of the work done for a client and realizes that there was an error, it can be easily corrected without much retyping. For example if an entry were made for a meeting with a client, when the meeting was actually with the client's witness, the error can usually be changed with a single entry. And all other places where the data are used are automatically changed as well.[9]

Time spent by paralegals and attorneys on tasks for which clients cannot be asked to pay is called **nonbillable time.** Examples of such tasks include general file maintenance or learning to operate a new data processing program that the firm is implementing throughout the office, helping to develop standard forms, and taking lunch breaks. **Pro bono work** is also nonbillable. This consists of legal services provided without cost, usually for an **indigent** (i.e., poor) individual or organization. A firm's regular clients cannot be asked to pay for pro bono work the office does for others. The firm needs to know how many billable and nonbillable hours paralegals and attorneys have accumulated over a particular period of time. Computer programs are very helpful in allowing timekeepers such as paralegals and attorneys to indicate which tasks fall into which category. They can also produce clear graphs that present this information in summary form. An example is the chart in Exhibit 14.11, which was generated by a popular computer timekeeping program from Timeslips, Inc.

Exhibit 14.11	**Bar Chart Showing Billable versus Unbillable Hours for Each Timekeeper**

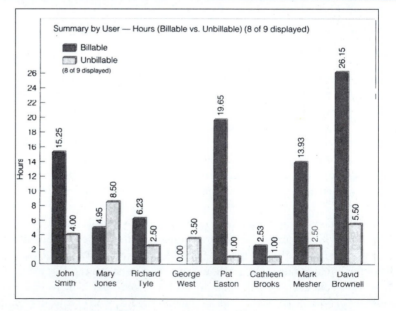

Source: Courtesy Timeslips Corporation.

---

[9]Adapted from P. Maggs & J. Sprowl, *Computer Applications in the Law* 172–74 (1987).

Law firms also set *targets* on how many billable hours they hope to obtain from partners, associates, and paralegals. Exhibit 14.12 shows different formats that computers can help generate to provide a graphic presentation of these expectations.

Exhibit 14.12	**Billable Hour Expectations: Timekeeper Productivity Report**

AVERAGE BILLABLE HOURS BY TIMEKEEPER

	Jan	Feb	Mar	Apr	May	Jun
Partners	128	132	127	134	144	141
Associates	170	163	175	170	159	179
Paralegals	118	111	120	119	121	108

YEAR-TO-DATE SUMMARY

	Target	Average Year-to-Date	Variance
Partners	140	134	−4%
Associates	165	169	+2%
Paralegals	125	116	−7%

Source: Jeff Coburn, *Creating Financial Reports That Partners Will Read.* Reprinted with permission from *Legal Management,* November/December, 1995, vol. 14, page 40, published by the Association of Legal Administrators, Vernon Hills, Illinois.

Section E
KINDS OF FEES

Most fees are based on the amount of time spent in providing legal services. Yet there are alternatives. Here is an overview of fee arrangements.

CLOCK-BASED FEES

1. Hourly Rate

An **hourly rate fee** is based on the number of attorney hours worked. Paralegals usually have a separate hourly rate covering their time.

2. Blended Hourly Rate

In many instances a partner and an associate, who have different hourly rates, may work on the same case. The bill to the client could break the fee down by rates. For example: $600 for two hours spent by Smith (a partner who bills at $300 an hour), and $450 for three hours spent by Jacob (an associate who bills at $150 an hour). An alternative is to charge a **blended hourly rate.** This is a single hourly rate that is based on a blend or mix of partner and associate rates. For example, to calculate the blended hourly rate, the firm might take the average of the normal rate charged by the partner and associate working on the case. In some states the firm is allowed to add a paralegal's time into this blended hourly rate.

3. Bundled/Unbundled Hourly Rate

The most common hourly rate is a **bundled rate,** which means that the rate covers the attorney's time plus the cost of his or her **overhead.** The latter consists of the operating expenses of a business such as the cost of office space, furniture, equipment, insurance, and clerical staff. An **unbundled rate** would break out the attorney's time. A client who wants unbundled services may be handling part of the case himself or herself, and may simply want an attorney to look over some documents or to provide legal advice. The client may not want full-service (i.e., bundled) legal representation and hence pays an unbundled rate.

ALTERNATIVES

Many individuals are not happy with billing that is controlled by the clock, as reflected in the following comments made by a business client who often hires attorneys:

> [We] have to look not only at the service and quality of law firms with which we do business but also at the linkage between price and performance. Hourly billing provides no such linkage. It is an accounting device. There is no credible economic theory underlying the hourly billing method, and for that reason, we no longer accept it as the sole, or even predominant, method of pricing legal services.
>
> In fact, hourly billing pushes the economic incentives in the wrong direction—weakening rather than strengthening the bonds between performance and pay. It also pushes law firms to near-obsession with billable hours. And this in turn supports the great unwritten rule of all law practices: those who want to get ahead must tally up the hours. This is first and foremost dubious economics. The number of hours spent on a matter is no measure of productivity. Productivity is better measured by results, including both outcome and time-frame. Linking the economic structure . . . to true measures of productivity—or value—will benefit both the firms and the client.[10]

---

[10]Matteucci, *What the Heck Is "Value Billing" Anyway?* 18 The Montana Lawyer 2 (November 1992). See also Ricker, *The Vanishing Hourly Fee,* 80 American Bar Ass'n Journal 66 (March 1994); Marcotte, *Billing Choices,* 75 American Bar Ass'n Journal 38 (November 1989): *Value Billing Popularity,* Tennessee Bar Journal 9 (January/February 1990).

While billing by the hour is likely to remain an important method of financing legal services in most kinds of cases, there are alternatives, as suggested by this client. These alternatives are either to abandon the clock or to use it as only one factor in determining the fee.

A great deal of discussion centers on what is called **value billing.** This means that the fee is not based solely on the time required to perform the work but also takes into account factors such as the following:[11]

- The nature of the services provided.
- The complexity, novelty, and difficulty of the question.
- The time pressure under which the services were provided.
- The time limitations imposed by the client.
- The amount of responsibility assumed by the firm.
- The extent to which the services provided precluded the firm from taking other clients.
- The amount of money involved in the matter.
- The nature and length of the firm's relationship with the client.
- The efficiency with which the services were performed.
- The results achieved.

Using factors such as these, a number of different fee arrangements have been devised. Here is an overview of these arrangements, some of which overlap:

1. Fixed Fee

A **fixed fee** is a flat fee for the service—a set figure regardless of the amount of time needed to complete the service. The fixed fee can be a specific sum or a percentage of the recovery.

2. Capped Fee

Under a **capped fee,** the firm bills an hourly rate, but the total bill will not exceed a predetermined budgeted amount.

3. Task-Based Billing

Under **task-based billing** (also called *unit billing* or *project billing*), the law firm charges a specific sum for each legal task it performs (e.g., drafting a complaint, conducting a deposition), often without regard to how long it takes to perform that task.

4. Hourly Plus Fixed Fee

With an **hourly plus fixed fee,** the firm charges an hourly rate until the nature and scope of the legal problem are identified; thereafter a fixed fee is charged for services provided.

5. Volume Discounts

The hourly or fixed fee might be reduced if the client gives the office a large amount of business, particularly when the office is able to reduce its own costs by standardization of work. A bill reduced for such reasons is called a **discounted hourly fee** or a volume discount.

6. Contingency Billing

The traditional **contingent fee** is a fee that is dependent—contingent—on the outcome of the case. The fee could be a fixed amount or a percentage of the amount the plaintiff wins in the litigation. This kind of fee is most often used in personal injury litigation. Contingency billing, however, is now being used in many other kinds of cases. Suppose, for

---

[11]G. Emmett Raitt, *What if Your Client Used Value Billing?* Orange County Lawyer 37 (April 1992).

example, an attorney is hired to handle a contract dispute the client is having with one of its suppliers. Under a contingent billing arrangement with the attorney, "the law firm takes on part of the risk of the transaction. If the transaction fails to go through, the law firm bills the client either a pre-negotiated sum or a small portion of the actual billable hours. Conversely, if the deal is successful, the firm bills the client either a higher pre-negotiated sum or a premium."[12]

A premium is sometimes referred to as **incentive billing** (or a *performance bonus*). The attorney receives an increased fee for achieving an exceptional result such as settling a case for an amount that exceeds a target set by the plaintiff-client and attorney.

Most contingent fees are earned by the plaintiff's attorney. A **defense contingent fee** (also called a *negative contingency*) is a fee for the defendant's attorney that is dependent on the outcome of the case. Most often the fee is a fixed amount.

7. Retroactive Negotiated Fee

Occasionally, a client and attorney might agree to finalize the fee *after* the services are provided. This is called a **retroactive negotiated fee.** When the case is over, the attorney and client agree on the value of the services provided and set the fee accordingly.

Section F
BILLING

In addition to fees for services, a law firm usually recovers out-of-pocket expenses (called **disbursements** or costs) that the firm incurs while working on the case, e.g., court filing costs, witness fees, copying charges, long-distance phone calls, out-of-town transportation, and lodging for attorneys and paralegals.

The fees and costs to be paid by the client should be spelled out in the **retainer.** Unfortunately, not everyone uses this word in the same way. Its meaning should be made clear in the agreement between attorney and client. In a general sense, a retainer is the contract of employment that establishes the attorney-client relationship. (For a sample retainer, see Exhibit 8.1 in chapter 8.) More specifically, it sometimes refers to an amount of money (or other property) paid by the client as a form of deposit or advance payment against future fees and costs. Additional money is paid only when the deposit or advance runs out. The agreement should specify whether such money or other assets from the client are refundable if the client terminates the relationship because he or she decides not to pursue the matter.

The actual billing process differs from firm to firm, and occasionally differs from case to case within the same firm. Client billing sometimes occurs only after the matter is completed. More commonly, a client is billed monthly, quarterly, or semiannually. An administrator in the firm usually works with the billing attorney to prepare the bill. When a matter is called for billing, the administrator may prepare a billing memorandum (the **draft bill**), which specifies the disbursements of the firm in connection with the matter, plus the amount of time each attorney and paralegal has spent on the matter (along with the billing rate of each). For example:[13]

- *Attorney Jones: $1,000.* This attorney, who has a billing rate of $200 an hour, spent five hours on the matter ($5 \times \$200 = \$1,000$).
- *Attorney Sampson: $1,200.* This attorney, who has a billing rate of $150 an hour, spent eight hours on the matter ($8 \times \$150 = \$1,200$).

---

[12]Michele Coyne, *Alternatives to Customary Billing Practices,* The LAMA Manager 19 (Legal Assistant Management Ass'n, Summer 1991).

[13]Darby, *Of Firms and Fees: The Administrator's Role,* 8 Legal Management 34, 39 (March/April 1989).

- *Paralegal Kelly: $600.* This paralegal, who has a billing rate of $60 an hour, spent ten hours on the matter (10 × $60 = $600).

The billing attorney has three choices: (1) Bill the total of the actual amounts. In our example, this would produce a bill of $2,800 ($1,000 + $1,200 + $600). (2) **Write down** the matter by subtracting a certain amount, e.g., $300. This would produce a bill of $2,500. (3) **Write up** the matter by adding an amount, e.g., $600. This would produce a bill of $3,400. This adjustment downward or upward is known as **valuing the bill.** An increase is sometimes called a *premium adjustment;* a decrease, a *discount adjustment.* The decision to adjust is based on factors such as the potential liability exposure of the firm (leading to a write-up) and the relative inexperience of an attorney or paralegal working on the matter (leading to a write-down). If, for example, recently hired attorneys or paralegals take an unusually long time to complete a task they have not performed before, a write-down may be appropriate so that the client does not have to bear the full cost of their on-the-job training.

See Exhibit 14.13 for an example of a bill sent to a client covering work of attorneys and paralegals on a matter.

E x h i b i t   1 4 . 1 3   **Bill Sent to Client Involving Attorney and Paralegal Services**

Rubin, Rinke, Pyeumac & Craigmoyle
1615 Broadway, Suite 1400
Oakland, California 94612-2115
(415) 444-5316
Tax ID 94-2169491

April 10, 1996

IBM Corporation
Norm Savage
3133 Northside Parkway
Atlanta GA   33033

Statement for Professional Services Rendered

Re: Chapter 11   (IBM-1)
　　Reorganization

Description of services

04/17/96   Receipt and review of contracts regarding Armonk home
　　　　　 office liquidation.

04/18/96   Meeting with opposing attorney regarding court appearance
　　　　　 in Atlanta in late October of 1996.

04/21/96   Receipt and review of depositions from seven
　　　　　 hundred forty three (743) claimants to Austin plant
　　　　　 parking facilities.

04/22/96   Meeting with officers of the corporation to discuss
　　　　　 liquidation of office furniture in all branch offices. Scheduling
　　　　　 of 2,000 simultaneous garage sales in marketing managers'
　　　　　 driveways to be advertised during next year's Super Bowl.

Total for legal services rendered $1,797.50

continued

Exhibit 14.13 Bill Sent to Client Involving Attorney and Paralegal Services—continued

	Hours	Rate	
Partners	6.00	250	1,500.00
Paralegals	3.50	85	297.50

Reimbursable expenses

04/17/96	Lunch meeting with three opposing attorneys.	185.17
04/27/96	Atlanta Bankruptcy Court filing fee due September 1, 1996.	55.00
04/29/96	Photocopies.	5.69
04/29/96	Long distance telephone charges.	36.90
	Total expenses	$282.76
	Total current charges	$2,080.26

Source: Computer Software for Professionals, Inc., LEGALMASTER

Section G
ADMINISTRATIVE REPORTS

The managers of a law firm need to know what everyone in the firm is doing. Many attorneys routinely complete a form similar to that illustrated in Exhibit 14.14, the Work

Exhibit 14.14 Work Summary

[ ] Can Handle More Work
[ ] Have All the Work
     I Can Handle
[ ] Need Help
Report of:

* C (Work Completed Since Last Report)
WP (Work in Progress)
IA (Matter Is Inactive)
Date:

Client	Matter	Description of Work [Designate Specialty Work by Symbol (S)]	Date Assgnd	Partner	Status*

Summary. Paralegals also fill out Work Summary sheets, depending on the nature of the work they're doing. If they are working for many attorneys in one department, the department head and the paralegal supervisor, if any, often require copies of the Work Summary report in order to keep track of the work being done.

There are different types of administrative reports based on timekeeping, billing, and work summary data. Some of the more common reports used by law firms are outlined in Exhibit 14.15.

Exhibit 14.15   Administrative Reports

- *Aged Accounts Receivable Report.* A report showing all cases that have outstanding balances due and how long these balances are past due. For example, the report may state how many of the total receivables (i.e., accounts due and payable) are less than 30 days old, how many are 30–59 days old, how many are 60–90 days old, and how many are more than 90 days old. (Also called a firm utilization report.) (See Exhibit 14.16.)
- *Timekeeper Productivity Report.* A report showing how much billable and nonbillable time is being spent by each timekeeper. (See Exhibit 14.12.)
- *Case-Type Productivity Report.* A report showing which types of cases in the firm (e.g., bankruptcy, personal injury, criminal) are most profitable. (Also called a practice analysis report.)
- *Fee Analysis Report.* A report on the fees generated by client, by area of law, by law firm branch office, and by individual attorney. The report helps the firm identify which cases, offices, and attorneys are profitable and which are not.
- *Work-in-Progress Report.* A report that provides the details of unbilled hours and costs per timekeeper, including client totals.
- *Cash Receipts Report.* A report that describes the income received in a day, week, month, quarter, or year. The cash receipts can be compared with the amount of projected income for a specific time period.
- *Client Investment Summary Report.* A report of the total amount billed and unbilled, with a calculation of the actual costs of providing legal services for a particular client.
- *Budget Performance Report.* A report that compares a firm's actual income and expenditures with budgeted or projected income and expenditures. (See Exhibit 14.17 for an example of a budget statement keyed to the budget allocations for the year to date.)

Sources: Brent Roper, *Practical Law Office Management* 183ff. (West Publishing Company, 1995); Pamela Everett, *Fundamentals of Law Office Management* 284ff (West Publishing Company, 1994).

Of particular interest to paralegals are reports generated from timekeeping records that analyze how much time paralegals are investing in client matters. This analysis is similar to the analysis the firm performs on the time invested by attorneys. Management uses these data to evaluate where the profit centers are, whether costs need to be contained, whether work is properly allocated among attorneys and among paralegals, which attorneys and paralegals are in line for salary increases and bonuses, etc.

Exhibit 14.16	Aged Accounts Receivable Billed— Not Yet Collected

Billing Attorney	Client Name	Legal Services	Disburse-ments	Total Due		Current To 30 Days	31–60 Days	61–90 Days	91–180 Days	More Than 6 Mos. Old
	(Alphabetic listing by client)	$	$	$		$	$	$	$	$
	.									
	.									
	.									
	.									
	TOTAL, ALL CLIENTS	$	$	$		$	$	$	$	$
	% Distribution	%	%	100%		%	%	%	%	%
	TOTAL RECAP BY BILLING ATTORNEY				% to total					
	(Total by billing lawyer)	$	$	$	%	$	$	$	$	
	.				%					
	.				%					
	.				%					
	TOTAL ALL LAWYERS				100%					

Section H
The Procedures Manual in a Small Office: Mail, Copying, and Filing

Law offices often have a procedures manual to cover different aspects of law office administration. The following excerpts are from a manual in a relatively small firm.[14]

INCOMING MAIL

Mail procedures must provide some fairly straightforward routines for handling incoming mail. In addition to sorting mail by addressee, the individual responsible for the morning mail (usually a secretary) should:

1. Date-stamp *everything* with the "Received" stamp. Exceptions are books received on approval or original documents such as deeds that have been mailed to the office for recording or filing elsewhere. Whenever possible, stamp the date in the same location on every document. This will make it easier for someone to read the dates when perusing a large file.

2. When an incoming document requires reference to previous papers, place the appropriate file with it.

3. If you can draft a response to the incoming document, place it with the document.

4. Return receipts for certified mail should be stapled to the copies of the documents to which they correspond.

5. File the following documents immediately without circulation:

   - Pocket parts to books in the library.
   - All loose-leaf page supplements.
   - The paperback supplements to the state statutes and the United States Code Annotated or United States Code Service.

---

[14]Adapted from Light, *The Procedure Manual: Mail, Copying and Filing Rules,* 26 The Practical Lawyer 71 (January 1980). Copyright 1980 by the American Law Institute. Reprinted with permission of The Practical Lawyer.

Exhibit 14.17   Income Statement with Budget

11/16/86   CLARK, LOWREY & SMITH
PERIOD 9   ATTORNEYS AT LAW   PAGE 1

INCOME STATEMENT WITH BUDGET

ACCT NO	DESCRIPTION	CURRENT PERIOD				YEAR TO DATE			
		THIS YEAR	%	BUDGET	%	THIS YEAR	%	BUDGET	%
	INCOME								
	INCOME ACCRUAL								
400	FEES: INCOME FROM CLIENTS	42356.00		19000.00		229247.57		228000.00	
460	OTHER INCOME/RECEIPTS	1836.23		700.00		9232.88		8400.00	
480	INCOME PRODUCING PROPERTY	.00		350.00		3790.00		4200.00	
	TOTAL INCOME ACCRUAL	44192.23		20050.00		242270.37		240600.00	
	EXPENSES								
	PAYROLL								
500	SALARY: SECRETARIAL	2975.30	6.7	1500.00	7.5	17851.00	7.4	18000.00	7.5
501	SALARY: WORD/DATA PROC.	1100.00	2.5	650.00	3.2	7556.45	3.1	7800.00	3.2
502	SALARY: PARALG & CLERKS	1875.18	4.2	2000.00	10.0	20632.15	8.5	24000.00	10.0
503	SALARY: ATTORNEYS	11400.00	25.8	6000.00	29.9	68400.00	28.2	72000.00	29.9
504	SALARY: OTH NON-OWN EMPL	1050.00	2.4	700.00	3.5	7804.00	3.2	8400.00	3.5
	TOTAL PAYROLL	18400.48	41.6	10850.00	54.1	122244.40	50.5	130200.00	54.1
	NON-PAYROLL EMPLOYEE COSTS								
510	FICA & UNEMPLOY TAXES	838.77	1.9	420.00	2.1	5038.77	2.1	5020.00	2.1
514	RETIREMENT BENEFITS	746.00	1.7	370.00	1.8	4446.00	1.8	4440.00	1.8
518	TRAINING & EDUCATION	250.00	.6	300.00	1.5	3660.00	1.5	3600.00	1.5
519	OTHER EMPLOYEE COSTS	.00	.0	150.00	.7	1674.00	.7	1800.00	.7
	TOTAL NON-PAYROLL EMPL COST	1834.77	4.2	1240.00	6.2	14818.77	6.1	14860.00	6.2
	OCCUPANCY EXPENSES								
520	OFFICE RENT	2940.00	6.7	750.00	3.7	10290.00	4.2	9000.00	3.7
521	PARKING	240.00	.5	80.00	.4	1003.85	.4	960.00	.4
523	REAL EST TAXES & INS	382.00	.9	185.00	.9	2245.78	.9	2200.00	.9

Source: Computer Legal Systems, Inc.

6. For informational purposes, prepare a "Daily Checks and Bills Received" sheet using the format in Exhibit 14.18.

Incoming mail may have to be photocopied and distributed to others—for example, to paralegals for specific assignments or to clients for their information. In some firms, special stamps are used such as the following:

FOR INFORMATION ONLY—NO ACTION REQUIRED

COPYING CHARGES

Failure to record legitimate copying charges for later billing to the client constitutes a drain on the firm's financial resources.

1. Register on the alphabetical list that is kept on or near the copying machine the client's name, if not already there, and the number of copies.

Exhibit 14.18   Daily Checks and Bills Received

Received on January 6, 1998

CHECKS

Hammerlee	(title search)	$1,380.00
Mid-Penn	136.55 C.A.	3,961.43
PNB	164.80 C.A.	724.80
Kalp, Arn	2.25 C.A.	62.25

BILLS

Wagners	(clips and rubber stamps)	12.72

Rec'd vol. 97 of *Supreme Court Reporter*   N/C

2. Copies that are not to be charged to any client should be noted as "office" copies or "N/C" copies.
3. On at least a monthly basis, the member of the staff who is responsible for copy charges should post them to the respective client accounts.

FILING SYSTEM

Rules and Comments

The importance of a good filing system cannot be overestimated. Lost and misplaced papers are the obvious result of a poor system. But the damage can run even deeper. Deadlines can be missed, leading to one of the most common causes of malpractice claims against attorneys. Hours may be lost in ferreting through files for crucial documents that cannot be found. Appellate briefs might be poorly prepared because files are not in a readily usable form that would allow drafters to gather information and prepare the briefs in an orderly fashion. Particular tasks might be overlooked because attorneys, often subconsciously, dread having to search for needed information or simply do not know how to tell a member of the staff to compile what is needed.

Some firms use an exclusively **alphabetical filing system.** For example, all the documents for the Allan Construction Corporation case would be filed just before all the documents for the Allenson estate case. Such a system is not as effective as a **numerical filing system** accompanied by an *alphabetical card index.* Here is an example of the categories of cases (or client matters) that could be used in a numerical filing system:

001–099	Large clients
100–199	Wills and estate planning
200–349	Real estate: purchase and sale
350–399	Estate administration and trusts
400–499	Domestic relations, excluding divorce and custody masterships
500–549	Personal injury, including worker's compensation
600–649	Litigation, excluding personal injury
700–749	Corporations and partnerships
750–799	Financing, bonds, industrial developments, and similar matters
800–849	Tax, excluding estate planning
900–999	Miscellaneous files not appropriate for any other category
1000–1499	Printed forms, applications, and other miscellaneous documents
1500–1999	Bar association and non-client-related matters
2000–2049	Bankruptcy

2100–2149   Divorce and custody masterships and arbitration panels
2200–2299   Criminal matters

The missing numbers (e.g., 550–599) are not needed for the categories of client matters currently in the office. As new categories emerge, they can be assigned the unused numbers.

These numerical categories vary widely from office to office according to size and type of practice. Large firms spread the brackets and use higher numbers. A two-digit number representing the year would precede each of the number categories. Hence, 96.287 would be a real estate matter opened in 1996. Anytime a significant block of cases does not fit within a particular category, it is relatively easy to create a new category.

A numerical filing system with an alphabetical card index is preferable since it:

- Reduces the misplacement of files. For some reason, individuals are more likely to place files in correct numerical order than in correct alphabetical order. For example, a purely alphabetical system would have difficulty handling the industrial development project for a client named Jones who owns North Marine Industries involving a local development agency bearing the acronym SIFT. While someone looking for this file may think of the project as "Jones: SIFT-North Marine Industries," others may look for the file under "North Marine Industries: SIFT." Cross-referencing within a card index (see below) almost eliminates this problem when a numerical filing system is used.
- Permits the grouping of files by subject matter, such as litigation or real estate. Such a system can be useful if, for example, the firm wants to contact all clients for whom wills were prepared within the past five years.
- Allows easier reference on memoranda, correspondence, and client lists. It is certainly simpler to jot "86.267" on a title abstract sheet than "Stankiewicz: Purchase of Real Estate (1986).
- Allows cross-referencing within the card index. The index cards *can* be alphabetical. You can create cards under any variety of headings that you think a user might try to use. Each card would refer to the files under their numerical entry.
- Automatically brings old files to the front of the filing system, acting almost as a tickler system.
- Allows the immediate identification of the year of a particular file by the first two digits of the file index, such as "86.589" for a 1986 file.
- Facilitates the differentiation of files that may have confusingly similar designations. "Kelly: Personal Injury (1981)" and "Kelly: Property Settlement Agreement (1983)" would probably be stored next to one another in an *alphabetical* system and would have the tendency not only to be filed in the wrong alphabetical order but to attract each other's papers. But in a *numerical* system, although the index cards would probably be neighbors, the folders would be physically separated in the file cabinet, making the misplacing of documents among the files less likely.[15]
- Adapts to computerization, when that time comes (see next section).
- Eases the handling of closed files. Under an alphabetical system, when the firm is ready to "retire" a particular file, two choices are available—continue to file alphabetically or switch to a sequential numbering system for closed files, with files placed one after the other as they are closed, regardless of their alphabetical designations. The first choice leads to the situation in which all the files from I through Z have to be

---

[15]One possible difficulty with a numerical filing system is the confusion of file 91.325 with file 92.325. The multicolored file folders that are available from stationery suppliers offer a ready solution to this potential problem. If blue folders were used for 1991, red for 1992, and green for 1993, a file is not likely to be misplaced, and if it is in the wrong spot, it will stand out. In order to have the benefit of a fully integrated system, color-matching index cards should be used for the alphabetical index.

moved if H grows rapidly (for example, nobody anticipated that the Half-Penny National Bank would become the firm's most active client). The second alternative requires an alphabetical card index to allow for the retrieval of particular closed files. The index would already exist under the numerical system.

Depending on the size of the office, a library-like system may be needed in which files are checked out of the file room in much the same manner that books are checked out of a library. While administratively burdensome, this system at least insures an ability to trace missing files. Overly strict measures, however, might backfire. For example, an attempt to prevent attorneys from ever holding files in their office might discourage them from initially storing any of their files in the filing room.

Closed Files

The filing cabinets in the main office contain only files on which work is being done, on which work is likely to be done in the near future, or that are likely to be used for reference in a current matter. Closed file procedures are designed to save active file space as well as allow for easy retrieval of retired information. Theoretically, if the firm's practice is stable, its main filing cabinets should maintain a constant size, while the real accumulation of paper occurs in the closed file storage area.

Generally, only the billing attorney may declare a file closed. Such a decision is not crucial or irreversible because the file can be retrieved easily. It is better to close a file than to keep it around. The fewer the active files, the more manageable the filing system.

When a file is to be closed, one way to do it is to:

1. Assign a CF (closed file) number to the file. This will be the next number for the year, with the first file closed during the calendar year 1996 receiving the number CF 96.001.
2. Place the CF number on the file's alphabetical index cards.
3. Write the CF number on the file label.
4. Place the file in the "upstairs" CF filing drawer. The upstairs CF filing drawer contains recently closed files that might still be needed. These files are sent upstairs for a time, before being relegated to the basement or other permanent storage area.

The closed files are permanently stored in boxes clearly labeled with the first and last CF file number. To retrieve a closed file, simply check the alphabetical index card, obtain the CF number, and find the file in storage. In some firms, closed files are placed on microfilm after a designated time. Most of the original file is then destroyed. Future access and copying of such files are achieved through microfilm readers and printers.

You might wonder why law firms go through the expense of keeping old files. First of all, the files might be useful in future cases. Rather than reinvent the wheel, a firm can "dig out" some of its old discovery documents (e.g., interrogatories), pleadings (e.g., complaint), and instruments (e.g., mortgage, separation agreement) and adapt them for use in current client cases. More importantly, there is a need to avoid legal liability. Some states impose an ethical obligation on a law firm to preserve records of account funds and other property for a specific period of time, e.g., six years, after termination of the representation. Clients have been known to sue attorneys for carelessly failing to safeguard the documents in their files. It is not always clear who owns which documents—the client, the attorney, or both. But a careful attorney would rather have the file ready to turn over than litigate who was entitled to what documents. A Florida ethics opinion offers the following advice:

> With regard to the disposal of files, we believe that the length of time a file should be maintained depends largely on the contents of the file itself. However, if [an attorney desires] to dispose of a file, we believe the client should be notified and asked to pick up the material or give authority to dispose of it in case there is any question. Opinion 63-3.

Section I
COMPUTER-BASED RECORDS MANAGEMENT SYSTEM IN A LARGE OFFICE

Some large law firms have hundreds of thousands of documents in their active files and many more in their closed files. A card index system would not be the most efficient way to manage this quantity of material. For those in charge of files (sometimes called **records information managers**), new technology is now available, as illustrated in the following description of how one office made the transition to computers.

How One Law Firm Automated Its Records Management

Patricia Patterson, Director of Legal Information Services, Schiff Hardin & Waite, Chicago, Illinois
21 American Association of Law Libraries Newsletter 291 (April 1991)

By the end of the next decade, it is likely that all records managers will have considered, tested, or installed some sort of computer-based records management system. From the smallest to the most complex central file system, computer automation offers the possibility of a cost-effective method for increasing management efficiency. . . .

When I assumed the responsibilities of the Schiff Hardin and Waite Records Department, I inherited a large problem. Data entry operators had been employed three years prior to my arrival to capture our 350,000 3 × 5 card file information onto magnetic tape. The Records Department was behind in its duties of opening new files, tracking file locations, and checking for conflicts of interest. In addition, the Records Department still had two people keying all of the file card and cross reference card information into batches of data onto magnetic type. Management directed me to guide the department into the twenty-first century by installing a computer system capable of using the data that the firm had spent significant time and money on over the previous four years. My background was in library management, and I was responsible for the Schiff library, so I was accustomed to working with large volumes of information.

My first task was to select a computer company to convert the data stored on nine reels of magnetic tape. We needed this data reformatted into a structure that could be loaded to an online database. Over 350,000 records of data had been keyed with very little control over checking the validity of client numbers, dates, attorney numbers, etc. Previous computer consultants employed by Schiff had not

thoroughly planned for the next step. That being the case and with the keying of data nearly complete, an implementation decision was needed.

At that time, we contacted the firm of Micom Systems, Inc., of North Muskegon, Michigan. Micom had been doing custom programming and computer services work for law firms since 1969. Their proposal to convert our data to a database format and clean up the duplicate entries and as much of the erroneous editing as possible was accepted by the firm in the fall of 1987. Micom, using its IBM 4341 computer and IBM assembler language, converted the data by January 1988.

My next task was to select an online database on which to use our newly converted data. After researching all of the records management software packages on the market, we concluded that they were inappropriate for our application. Because of Micom's knowledge of our data and experience with online law firm systems, we selected them to develop our records management system. With our data now ready for use, and after years of keying in the data, we were naturally anxious for the system to be operational. However, Schiff's two IBM System 36s were filled to capacity with litigation support and accounting functions. There was no room for a 250 million-character records management system on either of our two computer systems. Therefore, we chose to install communications equipment and a dedicated baud line to Micom's IBM mainframe 200 miles from our Chicago office.

Micom personnel studied our information storage and reporting needs. They then designed our system to meet current, as well as future, needs. Operational requirements and key functions of the system included:

1. All data from the conversion loaded and accessible.
2. User-friendly system with a short learning curve.
3. An adaptable system that could be changed quickly and easily.

4. Online interactive with additions, changes, and deletions immediately available.
5. Online conflict of interest searching with results printed on demand.
6. File cards and labels printed online using local printers.
7. Accommodation of the complex structured file identification system Schiff already had in place.

As I will list later on, the records management system has many features that address our information needs. The key ones, previously stated, were the driving force behind Micom selecting IBM CSP (Cross System Product) as its development language. Because of CSP's ability to run across IBM platforms, Micom could develop and initially run the system on their IBM mainframe. Then when Schiff installs an IBM AS/400 or networked IBM PS/2s, Micom can port the system to run on either of these computer systems. This software portability across platforms was a positive factor in our decision to use Micom to develop our system.

The Schiff requirements for an automated records management system originated from attorney needs and expectations. Accurate and thorough conflict checking is a necessity and rates the highest priority. Our system provides timely and complete new client screening based on all of the data stored in the records management system. Our attorneys need rapid opening of new files and swift retrieval of stored files. We have the ability to track folders and identify files easily and quickly with very few keystrokes or screen changes. Quick locating of a client's file folders is important whether the file is located in someone's office or in a box at an off-site storage facility. Attorney and secretary requests for file locations and identifications are handled by our staff of 11 using this system. Most requests of this type are handled by phone. New, revised, or additional file labels are printed on demand by the Records Center staff.

Our system has performed as we had hoped it would, allowing us to proceed with add-on enhancements. For example, we are now in the installation phase of a **bar coding** subsystem. This will enable us to print a bar code label with a unique client/matter number for each file created in the Records Center. Using a fixed scanner in our Records Department, we will scan the bar codes of all folders that leave the Records Center. Both the location and file folder identification will be scanned online directly into the computer system. All file folders leaving the Records Center at night will be batch-scanned into an IBM PS/2 and transferred to the IBM mainframe the next morning. Periodically we will scan all folders in attorneys' offices using portable, hand-held scanners. This procedure will give us the ability to track folder movements between attorney offices.

One feature of our system which saves additional time is the box storage system. This system tracks all box storage; both on, and off-site. Folder movement into and out of boxes is monitored, as are all pick-ups and deliveries. This system provides us with reports of all pick-ups and deliver-

Scanning coded files in records department

ies by date to enable us to verify our warehouse service bill more easily.

The Conflict of Interest System deserves more comment. This system is fully integrated into our Records Management System. Our personnel can hot key to the full text search process at any time. Then, using . . . commands, they can completely search our file records data. The data is displayed in our record structure format with the "hits" highlighted. We also have the ability to print any or all of the occurrences immediately. This efficient system has saved us countless hours of work.

While you may not be ready to adopt the automated records system that I have described, I hope the process we went through at Schiff Hardin and Waite will alert you to the advantages offered by computerized records management systems. Just be certain that the system you select addresses your specific information needs. The future is upon us, and we must knowledgeably embrace the technology on which it is based.

🏛 *A s s i g n m e n t   1 4 . 1*

In the practice of law, time is money. Hence you must develop the discipline of recording your time. Supervisors will later decide what portions of your time are billable—and to what clients. Step one is to compile a record of your time.

To practice this discipline, fill out a Daily Time Sheet for a day that you select. On *one* sheet of paper, record (in a chart form that you design) everything (approximately) that you do *in six-minute* intervals over a continuous eight-hour period. Once you design your chart, *it should take you no more than about fifteen minutes to fill it out* during the eight-hour period. You do not, however, fill it out at one time; you fill it out contemporaneously as you go through the tasks you are keeping track of throughout the eight hours.

Select an eight-hour period in which you are engaged in a fairly wide variety of activities. If possible, avoid an eight-hour period that contains any single activity lasting over two hours. Draw a chart covering the eight-hour period. At the top of the chart, place your name, the date of the eight-hour period that you used, and the starting/ending times of the eight-hour period. The period can be within a school day, a workday, a day of leisure, etc.

Using abbreviations, make specific entries on your activities within the eight hours—in six-minute intervals. For example, "Reading a chapter in a real estate school text" might be abbreviated as RE-R. "Driving to school" might be abbreviated as D-Sch. "Purely personal matters" (such as taking a shower) might be abbreviated as PPM. You decide what the abbreviations are. On the back of the sheet of paper containing the chart, explain what the abbreviations mean. When an activity is repeated in more than one six-minute interval, simply repeat the abbreviation.

One format for the chart might be a series of vertical and horizontal lines on the sheet of paper. This will give you a small amount of space on which to insert your abbreviations for each six-minute interval. Design the chart any way that you want, keeping in mind the goal of the exercise: to enable someone else to know what you did within the eight-hour period.

In Exhibit 14.6, there is an example of a Daily Time Sheet used in a law office. Note that the last column says "hours" and "10ths." A 10th of an hour is six minutes. Do *not* follow the format in Exhibit 14.6. Use the guidelines listed above, e.g., place your abbreviations on the other side of the sheet of paper that you submit.

Assignment 14.2

Mary Davis is a paralegal who has been working at the law firm of Smith & Smith for five years. The firm consists of two attorneys, Sam and Karen Smith, a husband and wife attorney team. There is one other employee, Jane Jones, who has just been hired as a paralegal trainee. This person, a high school graduate, was a homemaker for fifteen years. She has had no outside employment or training. The firm has one secretary who spends most of his time typing bills to be sent to clients and acting as the receptionist.

Smith & Smith has a family-law practice, handling mostly divorces. It takes two main kinds of cases: (1) contested divorces, where the husband and wife cannot agree on one or more critical issues (such as custody, property division, or amount of alimony); and (2) uncontested divorces, where everything is agreed on. While most of the firm's clients are plaintiffs who have filed for divorce, the firm also represents defendants on occasion.

Uncontested cases involve a fair amount of paperwork plus at least one court appearance, where the attorney obtains the approval of the court for what the parties have agreed to do. Contested cases involve extensive paperwork and many court appearances in which the disputed issues are resolved by the court—unless a settlement is eventually reached by the parties.

Almost every case requires the preparation of the following documents:

- Retainer (in which the client hires the firm)
- Intake Memorandum (reporting on a long interview with the client, during which extensive information is obtained about spouses, children, addresses, employment, facts of marriage, length of time in the county, bank accounts, residences, cars, other property owned, family health conditions, kinds of insurance, stocks, bonds, pension plans, debts already incurred, budget data, etc.)
- Complaint (stating the grounds for divorce)
- Answer (responding to the complaint)
- Letters to opposing counsel requesting information
- Motions to the court requesting temporary alimony or maintenance, child custody and support, and attorney fees
- Motion for a Restraining Order (to prevent either side from transferring assets and to prevent harassment)
- Motion to Produce (a formal request that the other side turn over designated items, such as pay stubs, copies of tax returns, bank statements, and insurance policies)
- Agreement on Property Division, Custody, and Support (uncontested cases only, unless a settlement is eventually reached in contested cases)
- Interrogatories (in which one party sends written questions to the other)
- A Notice of Deposition (informing the other to appear at a designated place, such as at the office of one of the attorneys, to answer questions)
- Proposed Final Decree of Dissolution of the Marriage

In the office, Mary prepares the Intake Memorandum based on an interview that she conducts with the client. This occurs after the retainer is signed and one of the attorneys goes over the case with the client. Mary prepares the first draft of all the other documents listed above.

Mary conducts the intake interview with the client alone. Since she has done so many of these interviews, she knows from memory what questions to ask. When she was first hired, she watched the attorneys interview and thereby learned what to ask and how to conduct an interview on her own. Whenever anything unusual came up during the interview, she left the room to find one of the attorneys for guidance. She took extensive notes on what the client said and later typed her notes for the Intake Memorandum.

Whenever Mary needed to draft one of the documents, she went to the firm's closed-case files to try to find a model that she could adapt. Since she had legal research skills, she also sought help from practice texts (such as formbooks) found in the law library. The more experienced Mary became, however, the less she had to resort to the old files and the law library. The attorneys were amazed at her ability to find and retain whatever she needed to prepare so many different kinds of documents. They developed tremendous trust in Mary. For many cases, the documents never seemed to vary except for the names of the parties and particular financial figures. A fair number of times, however, different situations arose—for example, the parties had prior marriages or a child was retarded and therefore required special care following the divorce. Starting from scratch, Mary used her experience and skills to draft the proper documents to accommodate these situations.

Mary was also responsible for opening case files for all new clients. Each time the firm accepted a client, she took an accordion folder and typed the name of the client on it. Scattered throughout the folder were handwritten notes (from Mary or the attorney in charge of the case) describing some event that was relevant to the case. The documents were not placed in the folder in any particular order. This, however, did not create much difficulty since Mary was so familiar with all of the files. Only occasionally were things lost or misfiled.

The reason that the firm has decided to hire another paralegal is that Mary has announced that in six months she is going to leave the firm for another position. The receptionist also gave notice that he is leaving. Neither is dissatisfied with the firm; it is simply time to move on. The firm tried to find an experienced paralegal to replace Mary, but could not. Hence it just hired Jane Jones who, as indicated, has had no experience or training. The firm will replace the receptionist with a full-time typist and a full-time receptionist who will also be available for messenger assignments.

The firm is in a panic. The caseload is increasing at a rapid pace. There is some talk of hiring an additional attorney who has just graduated from law school and passed the bar, but no definite decision has yet been made. The big worry is the effect of Mary's departure in six months.

Sam Smith's solution is to have Jane Jones, the paralegal trainee, follow Mary around, observing everything Mary does during her last six months in the hope of absorbing as much as possible.

Karen Smith has a different approach. "Why don't we create some management systems and then train everyone on them?" Sam is very skeptical, but willing to listen.

Assume that you work for a law office management consulting firm. Karen and Sam Smith have asked you to prepare a report on how the office can systematize and manage its divorce practice so that Jane Jones—and *anyone* else—can come in, learn the system on their own (or almost on their own), and become functioning members of the team.

State how you would go about handling this task. If you think more than one system is needed, describe what they are. What facts do you want to obtain on how the firm now operates? How would you go about getting these facts? State any problems that you anticipate in obtaining these facts and how these problems might be resolved. Then describe what you would do with what you learn. State how the system or systems would operate. Give examples. Detail any problems you anticipate in implementing the system or systems and how these problems might be handled. If you feel that the firm needs different kinds of equipment, describe what is needed and how it would be used within the system or systems that you propose. State the benefits that the system(s) might provide. Also describe any difficulties that might exist in the system(s). In short, provide a comprehensive but realistic report. Don't try to oversell what you propose. Assume that the main audience of your report will be attorneys who are uninformed about the management dimensions of a law office.

Chapter Summary

Our examination of law office administration began with an overview of the different settings in which attorneys practice law in the private sector in the United States and of the different kinds of attorneys found in each setting.

A sole practice consists of one attorney who owns the practice even if he or she employs other attorneys. The others do not share in the profits of the firm. To save on expenses, several sole practitioners may enter into an office-sharing arrangement under which the attorneys share expenses for office space, secretarial help, library materials, etc.

In a partnership, the equity or capital partners share in the profits and losses of the firm and control its management, often through a committee or department structure. Associates are attorneys in the firm who hope one day to be invited to become partners. There are, however, special categories of associates created for those who do not become partners, such as senior associate and permanent associate.

Other categories of attorneys who might be hired by a law firm include staff attorneys, of-counsel attorneys, and contract attorneys. For tax and estate-planning purposes, many states allow attorneys to practice law as a professional corporation. There is little practical difference, however, between the administration of a partnership and a professional corporation. The newest format for law firms is the limited liability company (LLC) and the limited liability partnership (LLP). They help avoid personal liability for law firm debts and provide tax-filing advantages.

Finally, some attorneys practice law in the legal departments of corporations. They are employees of the corporation, which is their sole client.

Large law offices may have many nonattorney employees to help manage the office. Among the most prominent is the legal administrator. Also, if there are more than a few paralegals in the office, a legal assistant manager is often hired to help administer the office's system for recruiting, hiring, training, and monitoring the progress of paralegals.

There is considerable pressure on attorneys and paralegals to keep precise track of their time. The accounting records and financial health of the law firm depend on it. A number of different fee arrangements exist: clock-based (e.g., hourly rate, blended hourly rate, bundled rate, unbundled rate); and alternatives that stress value billing (e.g., fixed fee, capped fee, task-based billing, hourly plus fixed fee, discounted hourly fee, contingent fee, and retroactive negotiated fee.) The method of paying the bill (including disbursements) should be spelled out in the retainer. The amount actually paid by a client is not determined until there has been a valuing of the bill, which might result in a write-up, a write-down, or no change.

An efficient law firm uses administrative reports to help it keep track of and manage the practice. Among the most important are the aged accounts receivable report, timekeeper productivity report, case-type productivity report, fee analysis report, work-in-progress report, cash receipts report, client investment summary report, and the budget performance report.

A busy law firm receives a great deal of mail, does a great amount of copying, and files a great many documents. It is important for the paralegal to learn what method the firm uses for these tasks. While some offices file alphabetically, many firms have found that numerical filing is more effective. Offices with large caseloads, and hence many documents to file and store, often use a computerized system of record management.

KEY TERMS

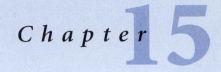

Chapter 15

INFORMAL AND FORMAL ADMINISTRATIVE ADVOCACY

► *Chapter Outline*

Section A
THE NATURE OF ADVOCACY

Advocacy is the process by which an individual attempts to influence the behavior of others according to predetermined goals. Advocacy is a basic component of everyday life; we are frequently advocates for ourselves and for others. Note, for example, the advocacy involved, or potentially involved, in the following circumstances:

1. At a supermarket checkout counter, a clerk tells a customer that the price of tomatoes is 49¢ a pound. The customer replies, "But the sign back there said 39¢ a pound." The clerk says, "I'm sorry, but the price is 49¢."
2. A student goes to the teacher to say that a term paper should have been graded "A" rather than "B."
3. A tenant tells the landlord that a $500 a month rent increase is ridiculous because the building has been steadily deteriorating.
4. An individual applying for a driver's license is told that he filled out his application incorrectly and that he must wait a week before he will be allowed to fill out another one. The individual feels that his application is not incorrect and that, even if it is, he should not have to wait a week to do it over.
5. An employee has been laid off from her job. She calls the unemployment insurance bureau and asks to be sent forms so that she can fill out a claim. The clerk tells her that no forms can be sent through the mail. She asks the clerk if an exception can be made in her case because she has not been feeling very well and her doctor has told her to stay in bed. The clerk says there are no exceptions.
6. A homeowner has been away on a vacation. Upon his return, he finds that his house has been burglarized. When he goes to the police station to report the crime, he asks the desk sergeant why his neighborhood has not been receiving better protection in view of all the burglaries that have been occurring in the area lately. The sergeant replies that there are not enough police available to patrol the neighborhood adequately. The homeowner is not satisfied with this response and asks to see the precinct captain.

The customer, student, tenant, applicant, employee, and homeowner all have complaints. They are complainants. They are not satisfied with something. Their natural response is to make an *argument* for better service. In so doing, they become advocates for the goals or objectives that they are seeking. Advocacy does not always require courtrooms, judges, and attorneys; all that is needed is a complaint, a complainant, and someone who should be able to act on the complaint.

The distinction between *formal* and *informal advocacy* is primarily one of degree. Generally, the more the setting looks like a court procedure (for example, with a hearing officer present, evidence or testimony taken, or written decisions issued), the more formal it is. As we saw in chapter 6, an administrative agency's quasi-judicial powers are often exercised through hearings that have many similarities to courtroom proceedings. A **quasi-judicial proceeding** is one in which the agency acts similar to a court when resolving a dispute between a citizen and the agency (such as between a welfare recipient and welfare department) or between two or more citizens under the control of the agency (e.g., two students in the same school or two inmates in the same prison who are having a dispute). If you are representing yourself or someone else at such a hearing, you are engaged in formal advocacy.

Our first concern in this chapter is *in*formal advocacy that occurs (a) in connection with administrative agencies not involving formal hearings or (b) outside the realm of administrative agencies altogether, as in the supermarket example at the beginning of this chapter. Our primary focus will be the informal advocacy techniques that can be used when confronting employees of *any* organization—for example, a public agency such as a social security office or a private business such as an insurance company.

Paralegals often have contact with organizations that require the application of informal advocacy techniques. The following are several examples:

- Determining the names and addresses of the principal shareholders of a corporation
- Gaining access to the records of an agency or of a company
- Obtaining copies of forms from the Securities and Exchange Commission on the disclosure and reporting requirements of a corporation
- Writing to or visiting an agency or company to obtain its position on a matter involving a client
- Trying to convince a caseworker or a social worker that the action the agency has taken (or that it proposes to take) is illegal or ill-advised

A paralegal can meet resistance in any and all of these situations. The basic techniques of informal advocacy should help in handling this resistance.

Section B
THE TECHNIQUES OF INFORMAL ADVOCACY

Exhibit 15.1 presents a summary of nineteen techniques of informal advocacy that are sometimes useful when trying to obtain action from an administrative agency or from any large organization. The techniques are listed in the approximate order of effectiveness. Of course, whether a particular technique will be effective depends on what you are trying to accomplish, whom the technique is directed against, and how well you execute the technique. In general, though, the techniques at the beginning of Exhibit 15.1 are more likely to be effective than those at the end. Do you agree?

Exhibit 15.1   Techniques of Informal Advocacy

1. *Put your cards on the table.* Be direct and completely aboveboard in telling the agency official what your position is and what you want.
2. *Insist on adequate service.* Point out to the agency official that the purpose of the agency is service and that this principle should guide the official's actions.
3. *Ask for authorization.* Insist that the agency official show you the regulation, law, or other authority that supports the action taken or proposed by the agency.
4. *Climb the chain of command.* Normally, everyone has a boss who can overrule decisions made by those beneath him or her. When you are dissatisfied with the decision or action of an employee, "appeal," or com-plain "up the chain of command," to the employee's supervisor and to the supervisor's supervisor, if needed.
5. *Insist on common sense.* Convey to the agency official the impression that common sense dictates your position—in addition to or despite regulations or technicalities that might be cited against you.
6. *Take the role of the tired, battered, helpless citizen.* Do not insist on anything. Play dumb; act exhausted; act in such a way that the agency official will think, "This person needs help;" act as if everyone else has given you the runaround and that you are praying that this offi-

continued

Exhibit 15.1 Techniques of Informal Advocacy—continued

cial (whom you have not dealt with before) will finally give you a sympathetic ear—and some help.

7. *Cite a precedent.* Point out to the agency official (if it is true) that your case is not unusual because the agency has granted what you want to others under the same or similar circumstances in the past.

8. *Find the points of compromise.* Ferret out the negotiable points in the dispute and determine whether you can bargain your way to a favorable result.

9. *Uncover the realm of discretion.* Take the position that rules do not exist until they are applied, and that agency officials often have wide discretion in applying rules despite claims that their hands are tied by the rules.

10. *Demonstrate the exception.* Insist on the uniqueness of your client's situation. Show agency officials that the general rule they are using to deny your client a benefit is inapplicable.

11. *Cite the law.* Show the agency official that you know what administrative regulations apply to the case. Also cite statutes and other laws to demonstrate your point.

12. *Be a buddy.* Show agency officials that you are not an enemy, that you respect and like them, and that you are aware how difficult their job is.

13. *Make clear that you and your office are going to fight this case all the way up.* Make the agency official aware

of how important the case is. Point out that you are thinking about taking the case to a formal agency hearing and that your office may go to court, if necessary.

14. *Redefine the problem.* If you can't solve a problem, redefine it—as long as you can still achieve what the client seeks. For example, stop trying to qualify the client for program "Z" if program "Y" will serve the client equally well (or almost so) and the problems of qualifying the client for "Y" are not as great as you'll face by continuing to insist on "Z."

15. *Do a favor to get a favor.* Be willing to do something (within reason) for the person from whom you are seeking something.

16. *Seek the support of third parties.* Before you make your position known, gather the support of individuals or groups within and outside the agency so you can demonstrate that you are not alone.

17. *Preach.* Lecture the civil servant. Tell the agency what it should or should not be doing.

18. *Embarrass the official.* Show the agency official that you do not respect him or her. Do it in such a way that the official is made to look silly.

19. *Demonstrate anger and hostility.* Be completely open about the bad feelings you have concerning what is being done or proposed.

Effective advocacy involves other concerns as well:

Advocacy

I. *Threshold Concerns*

    1. Define your goals in order of priority.
    2. Decide when to intervene.

II. *Self-Evaluation of Techniques Used*

    1. Are you making yourself clear?
    2. Are you creating more problems than you are solving?
    3. Are you accomplishing your goal?

III. *Adaptation.* Are you flexible enough to shift your technique?

IV. *Recording*

    1. Describe what you saw.
    2. Describe what you did.

The focus of the first threshold concern is the priority of goals. This concern, of course, would not be applicable if the assignment you are given contains only one goal, such as obtaining a copy of a record at the agency or organization. Sometimes, however, an assignment contains a variety of objectives at the outset, or a single-objective assignment subsequently blossoms into tasks involving more than one goal. In that case, priorities must be set. If you try to do everything, you may end up accomplishing nothing. Every technique of informal advocacy will probably fail if you have unrealistic expectations of what can be accomplished.

The second threshold issue is to decide when to intervene with the advocacy techniques. The decision to intervene involves a strategic judgment about when it would be most appropriate to seek what you are after at the agency or organization. In most situations, a sense of timing is very important. For example, suppose that you must contact the complaint bureau of an agency that is relatively new to you. One approach would be simply to walk up to the complaint bureau and delve right into the matter that brought you there. Another approach would be to try to find out something about the bureau *before* going to it. There may be some literature available on the structure of the agency that will provide you with at least a general idea of what to expect. You may be able to talk to attorneys or other paralegals who have had prior contact with the bureau. Suppose you learn that two agency employees rotate their work at the bureau and that one employee has a reputation of being more cooperative than the other. You may decide not to go to the bureau until this employee is on duty. In short, you decide to postpone your contact with the bureau until circumstances are most favorable to the objective you are seeking.

As you use any of the techniques in Exhibit 15.1, you must simultaneously judge the *effectiveness* of the technique in light of what you are trying to accomplish. Are you making yourself clear? Are you complicating rather than resolving things? Are you getting through? Are you comfortable with the technique you are using? Does it clash with your personality? Are you pacing yourself properly? Is your insistence on immediate success interfering with proceeding step-by-step along the road toward progress?

One of the major signs of ineffective advocacy is becoming so involved in the case that you begin to take roadblocks and defeat *personally.* Everyone agrees that objectivity is a good quality—and most of us claim to possess this quality in abundance. The unfortunate fact, however, is that *we tend to lose objectivity as friction increases.* We allow our careers and our lifestyles to be threatened when someone says to us, "You can't do that." We rarely admit that we can be so threatened. We justify our response by blaming someone else for insensitivity, stupidity, or unfairness.

Once you have disciplined yourself to identify the techniques you are using and evaluate their effectiveness, you must be flexible enough to *adapt* your techniques and shift to more effective techniques, when needed.

Finally, the paralegal usually will have a recording responsibility. Almost every case you work on must be heavily documented in the office files. Your efforts at informal advocacy should be included in those files.

🏛 Class Exercise 15.A

In each role-playing exercise, there are two characters: C (the complainant) and E (the agency employee). Students from the class will be assigned one or the other role. In each setting, C is seeking something from E. E is uncooperative. The objective of E is to antagonize C (within reason) to the point where C loses objectivity. The objective of C is to refrain from losing his or her objectivity.

(a) At 4:30 P.M., C goes to the Department of Motor Vehicles to apply for a license. E tells C that the office closes at 5:00 P.M. and the application procedure takes forty-five minutes. E refuses to let C apply.

(b) At the post office, C tries to buy $400 worth of first-class stamps. E tells C that no individual customer can buy over $100 worth of stamps per day.

(c) C goes to the Bureau of Vital Statistics and requests a copy of his mother's birth certificate. E tells C that no citizen can obtain the birth certificate of another person without the written permission of the person. C's mother is ill in a hospital a thousand miles away. C wants the record without going through the bother of obtaining this permission.

Those members of the class who are not participating in the role-playing exercises should identify and evaluate the techniques of informal advocacy that C uses.

We now examine informal advocacy techniques in the context of the following fact situation:

> You are in your own home or apartment. You receive a letter from the gas company stating that your gas will be shut off in ten days if you do not pay your bill. Your spouse tells you that all the bills have already been paid. You call the gas company, and when you question the clerk, she says to you, "I'm sorry sir, our records reflect an unpaid bill. You must pay the bill immediately." To try to straighten matters out, you take a trip to the utilities office.

In the dialogue that follows, the complainant is his own advocate. "C" will stand for complainant and "E" will stand for the various company employees. As you read the dialog, ask yourself how effective is C's advocacy.

E: Can I help you?

C: Yes, I want to see someone about a problem with my bill.

E: I'm sorry, sir, but the customer complaint division closed at 2 P.M. You'll have to come back or call tomorrow.

C: Closed! Well, let me see someone about terminating the gas service altogether.

E: All right, would you step right over to the desk?

TECHNIQUE: *If you can't solve a problem, redefine the problem* to manageable proportions if, on balance, it is consistent with your objectives. (See Exhibit 15.1.)

The client is taking a risk. He cannot get to the complaint division so he is going to try to achieve his objective through the termination division. He has substituted one problem (getting to the complaint division) for another problem (getting to the termination division) in the hope of expressing his grievances.

E: Can I help you?

C: Yes, I want to terminate my gas if I can't get this problem straightened out.

E: You'll have to go over to the bill complaint division, sir.

C: Look, stop sending me somewhere else! Either I get this straightened out or else!

TECHNIQUE: *Demonstrate anger and hostility.* This is a dangerous tactic to employ. It is a fact of life, however, that some people respond to this kind of pressure. (See Exhibit 15.1.)

C: Aren't you here to serve the public?

TECHNIQUE: *Insist on adequate service.* Point out that the organization exists to serve and that you need better service. (See Exhibit 15.1.)

E: There are rules and procedures that we all must abide by and. . . .

C: Your responsibility is to take care of the public!

TECHNIQUE: *Preach.* Perhaps the most common way people try to change other people is to lecture them, to tell them what they should or should not be doing.

TECHNIQUE: *Embarrass the official.* Make the agency official look silly and unworthy of respect.

At this point, has the complainant lost all objectivity? What risks are being taken? Do you think the complainant is aware of what he is doing? If you asked him whether he's being effective, what do you think his response would be? Is he more involved with the "justice" of his case than with the effectiveness of his approach?

C: I'd like to speak to your supervisor. Who is in charge of this office?
E: Well, Mr. Adams is the unit director. His office is right over there.
C: Fine.

TECHNIQUE: *Climb the chain of command.* Everyone has a boss who can overrule his or her subordinate's decisions. If you're unhappy about a decision, complain "up the chain of command," to the top if necessary.

E: Can I help you?
C: I want to speak to Mr. Adams about a complaint. Tell him that it is very important.
E: Just a moment. *[She goes into Mr. Adams' office for a few moments and then returns.]* You can go in, sir.
C: Mr. Adams?
E: Yes, what can I do for you? I understand you are having a little problem.
C: It's about this bill. I have been talking to person after person in this office without getting any response. I'm going in circles. I need to talk to someone who is not going to send me to someone else!

TECHNIQUE: *Take the role of the tired, battered, helpless citizen.*

E: Well, let me see what I can do. I've asked the secretary to get your file. . . . Here it is. The records say that you haven't paid several months' bills. Our policy here is to terminate utility service if payment is delinquent sixty days or more.
C: What policy is that? Could I see a copy of this policy and what law it is based on?

TECHNIQUE: *Ask for authorization.* Make the agency show you the regulation, law, or authority that allegedly backs up the action it has taken or says it will take.

What risk is the complainant taking by resorting to this technique? Is the complainant suggesting to Mr. Adams that he does not trust him? How would you have asked for authorization in this situation? Does the request for authorization always have to be made in a hostile manner?

E: Well, I'll be glad to show you the brochure.
C: I would like to see it and also the law it is based on. My position, Mr. Adams, is that my wife has paid the bills.
E: Well our records don't reflect it.
C: The canceled checks have not all come back from the bank yet. I would like a photocopy of your file on me. Under the law, I am entitled to it.

TECHNIQUE: *Cite the law.* Demonstrate that you know what regulations and other laws apply to the case.

E: You do have this right, but only if you make the request in writing.
C: Let's be reasonable. I'm making the request in person. That should be sufficient.

TECHNIQUE: *Insist on common sense.* You need to show the agency official that your position makes good common sense, even if regulations or technicalities go against you.

C: Surely, your rule calling for a written request can't apply when the person making the request is right in front of you.

TECHNIQUE: *Interpret the law.* Regulations, statutes, and cases often are susceptible to more than one meaning; identify and argue for the meaning most favorable to your cause.
TECHNIQUE: *Demonstrate the exception.* Insist that your situation is unique, not governed by the general rule.

C: Don't you have the power to waive this rule in such a case?

TECHNIQUE: *Uncover the realm of discretion.* Argue that rules do not exist until they are applied and that in the application of rules, agency officials often have a lot of latitude as to how they interpret them in spite of their claim that their hands are tied by the rules.

E: Well, all right, I'll see if I can't get a copy run off for you while you are here, but it will take a little time and I must point out that it's highly irregular.
C: Now, Mr. Adams, I understand that you are a very busy man and that you have responsibilities more demanding than listening to people like me all day.

TECHNIQUE: *Be a buddy.* Show the agency official that you are not his enemy and that you respect and like him and that you are aware of how difficult his job is.

Here the complainant has obviously shifted his tactic; he is no longer antagonistic. Consciously or unconsciously, he has made an evaluation of how successful his techniques have been thus far and has decided on a different course of action. What risk is he running in making this shift?

C: All I want is a two-week extension of time so that I can collect the proof needed to show you that the bill has been paid.

TECHNIQUE: *Put your cards on the table.* Tell the agency official, directly and openly, what your position is and what you want.

E: Well, we seldom give extensions. The situation must be extreme. I don't know. . . .
C: Mr. Adams, suppose we forget my request for a copy of the records for the time being. All I want is two weeks.

TECHNIQUE: *Find the points of compromise.* Look for the negotiable points and figure out whether you can bargain your way to a good result.

E: I don't think so.
C: Well, Mr. Adams, it's either that or I'm going to go to court. All I'm asking for is some fair treatment. There's a principle involved and I intend to fight for it.

TECHNIQUE: *Make clear that you are going to fight this case all the way up.* Make the agency official aware of how important this case is. When you have grounds to back you, point out that you are thinking about taking the case to a formal hearing and, if necessary, to court.

E: I'm sorry you feel that way, but we have our rules here. It would be chaos if we broke them every time someone asked for it.
C: Good day, Mr. Adams. *[You leave the office, resolved never to come back alone.]*

TECHNIQUE: *Seek the support of third parties.* Gather the support of individuals or groups within and outside the agency so that you can demonstrate that you are not alone.

Has the complainant failed? Was he a "bad" advocate? Has he accomplished anything? Should he give up? Do you think he will? If he does not, do you think he has learned (or that he should have learned) enough about the utility company to come back next time better equipped to handle his problem? If he comes back, what approach should he take and whom should he see? Should he see the supervisor of Mr. Adams, for example?

🏛 *C l a s s   E x e r c i s e   1 5 . B*

Following are two exercises for role-playing. The instructor will select students to play the roles indicated. The rest of the class will evaluate the role-playing through questions that follow the statement of the exercises.

(a) A paralegal is asked by his supervisor to file some papers in court. They must be filed by 5:00 P.M. that day. At 4:15 P.M. the paralegal takes the papers to the office of the court clerk. The clerk determines that the papers are in order except that the attorney forgot to sign one of them. It would take the paralegal more than an hour to go back to obtain the signature and return to court. The paralegal asks the clerk to accept the *other* papers. The clerk refuses since all the papers are closely interrelated. The paralegal tells the clerk that this happened once before and the clerk (another one) accepted the papers that were properly executed. The clerk refuses.

(b) A parent (acting as her own advocate) asks the principal for a meeting on her child. The child has been selected to be sent to another school nearby. The parent is opposed to this transfer. The principal tells her that she will have to go talk to an official at the City Board of Education about the matter. The parent persists in demanding a meeting with the principal. She wants to know, for example, the position of the principal on the transfer, but the principal wants to avoid controversy and therefore refers her to the City Board.

Evaluation

1. What advocacy technique did the paralegal start out using?
2. On a scale of 1 to 10, how effective was this technique? ("10" is very effective; "1" is very ineffective.) Give reasons for your score.
3. When the sequence ended, what advocacy technique was the paralegal using? How would you score this technique?
4. What shifts in technique, if any, did the paralegal make? Score each technique.
5. On a scale of 1 to 10, how effective was the paralegal's overall performance?
6. According to the agency official, what was the problem?
7. According to the paralegal, what was the problem?
8. What, if anything, was standing in the way of communication between them?
9. How could this communication problem have been overcome?
10. Was the paralegal objective, or did the paralegal take anything personally? Explain.
11. Was the agency official taking anything personally? Explain.
12. If the agency official took anything personally, how did the paralegal deal with this?
13. What do you think the paralegal *should* have done about this?
14. Describe the most positive aspects of what you saw the paralegal do.
15. Describe the least effective aspects of what you saw the paralegal do.
16. As specifically as possible, list all the advocacy techniques that you observed the paralegal use that you haven't already mentioned.

17. Reexamine the list of nineteen informal advocacy techniques in Exhibit 15.1. Do you think that any techniques should be added to the list? If so, how would you rate the general effectiveness of the techniques that you would add?

Section C
PROCEDURAL DUE PROCESS

Where paralegals are authorized by law to engage in *formal advocacy* by representing clients at administrative hearings (see chapter 4 and appendix E), it is one of the great challenges that they enjoy. In this chapter, we will explore some of the skills required to perform this task effectively.

The subject matter of a hearing, as well as its procedure, can range from the very simple to the very complex. Our approach will be to examine a relatively simple hearing, after identifying the components of procedural due process when a government agency and a citizen have a dispute.

When a government agency and a citizen have a serious dispute, basic fairness may require a number of procedural safeguards for the citizen. These safeguards are known as **procedural due process.**

> Tom is a civilian employee of the army. One day he receives a call from the manager of the division who says, "I have just finished reading the report of the assistant manager. Based on my own observations and on this report, it is clear to me that you have been using the agency car for your own personal use. I have decided to fire you."

As a matter of fairness and common sense, what is wrong with the manager's approach? Assume that Tom denies the charge and that this is the first time he has heard anything about an alleged improper use of an agency car. The *substantive* question is whether Tom used the car improperly. The *procedural* question is whether the agency's method of resolving this problem is fair. The latter is a question of procedural due process.

In Exhibit 15.2 you will find some of the visceral responses that Tom or any citizen might make, plus their legal translation in terms of procedural safeguards.

As a matter of constitutional law, a citizen is not entitled to all ten components of procedural due process outlined in Exhibit 15.2 in every dispute he or she has with a government agency. What procedural safeguards are required? The answer differs from agency to agency depending on the seriousness of the dispute. In a welfare hearing, for example, all ten safeguards *are* required whenever a welfare recipient wishes to challenge a decision of

Exhibit 15.2	**Procedural Due Process: Procedural Safeguards**
VISCERAL RESPONSE	**LEGAL TRANSLATION**
"Before I was fired, I should have been told the agency thinks I used the car illegally."	1. *Notice.* To enable you to prepare a response, you should be given adequate advance **notice** of the charge against you.

continued

Exhibit 15.2	Procedural Due Process: Procedural Safeguards—continued

VISCERAL RESPONSE	LEGAL TRANSLATION
"Show me the report the assistant manager wrote on me so that I can see what he's talking about. And tell me what observations you [the manager] made to arrive at this conclusion."	2. *Examination of evidence.* In order to respond to the evidence against you, you should be able to see what that evidence is.
"Before you fire me, give me a chance to explain myself."	3. *Hearing.* You should be given a formal meeting or **hearing,** where you can present your case.
"I want to present my case before someone other than the assistant manager or the manager."	4. *Hearing officer free of legal bias.* The hearing officer should be uninvolved—free of **legal bias.** The person making the charge against you, or giving any evidence against you, should not be making the final decision as to whether the charge is true. (The accuser should not be the executioner.)
"If someone has something to say against me, I want to hear it from this person's own mouth, and I want to be able to ask him questions myself."	5. *Confrontation and cross-examination.* Whoever is accusing you or giving any evidence against you should be required to do so in your presence **(confrontation).** You should be able to ask this person questions about his or her allegations **(cross-examination).**
"I want to be able to bring my own counsel to help me."	6. *Legal representation.* You should have the right to representation by an attorney or an attorney-substitute of your own choosing.
"I've had some unrelated troubles on the job in the past, plus some personal problems at home, but that has nothing to do with my use of the car."	7. *Relevancy of evidence.* The hearing officer should consider only relevant evidence. **Relevancy** refers to anything reasonably related to establishing the truth or falsity of the charge.
"My co-worker knows everything do with agency cars. I want to bring him to the hearing."	8. *Presentation of own witnesses.* You should be given the opportunity to present your own witnesses and any other evidence that supports your position.
"I want to see the decision in writing."	9. *Written decision with reasons.* To enable you to prepare an appeal, you should be given the decision in writing as well as the reasons for the decision.
"I want to be able to appeal."	10. *Appeal.* You should be given the right to **appeal** the decision to another individual or body.

the welfare department to terminate public assistance. This is so because of the extreme consequences that could result from this termination. The more extreme the possible consequences, the more procedural safeguards the law imposes on the conduct of hearings to determine whether those consequences should be imposed.

Section D
AN AGENCY PROBLEM

Fact Situation

George Temple was born on January 1, 1955. His parents, Mr. and Mrs. Sam Temple, live at 435 West 100th Street, New York, New York. He was graduated from high school in 1977 and spent six months at Wentworth Technical Institute in Boston before dropping out. He came back to live with his parents in February of 1978. But while in Boston, he began using drugs. He smoked pot regularly and experimented with LSD and heroin. After returning to New York on April 15, 1988, he got a job with the Thomas TV Repair Shop at 90 South Side Avenue, Queens. The boss, John Adams, fired George on June 1, 1988, because he suspected George of being an addict and of stealing.

On June 30, 1988, George married Ann Fuller. George began using drugs more often. Ann realized that he was not going to be able to support her and their expected child. When the child was born on January 2, 1989, she decided to go to the Amsterdam Welfare Center to apply for public assistance. She did so on January 10, 1989. The caseworker, Brenda Marshall, asked Ann what her husband did for a living. Ann answered that he took odd jobs "off and on," since he was sick. The caseworker asked if he was an addict. Ann was scared and answered *no.* The caseworker said that she would need more information about Ann's husband's employment history and condition before her application could be processed and approved. Ann left the center confused and frustrated. She never returned.

In the meantime, George was arrested on March 13, 1989, for possession of a dangerous drug in the third degree. He "took a plea" for attempted petty larceny and spent four months at Green Haven Prison. When he got out on July 13, 1989, he went to live with his wife at 758 West 85th Street. While George was in prison, Ann worked as a waitress. During this time, her mother-in-law cared for the child. Ann was laid off from work on August 1, 1989.

George did not want to settle down with a job. He began using drugs again. He wanted to stop but couldn't.

On September 1, 1989, George went to Exodus House, a voluntary drug rehabilitation center in New York City. He left after only two days, claiming that the program demanded too much from him. For example, he would have had to live at Exodus House, which he refused to do. On September 25, 1989, he went to Reality House, another voluntary rehabilitation center at 2065 Amsterdam Avenue. This was not a live-in program; members stayed there from 9 to 5. On October 1, 1989, he left this program because his urine test came back positive, meaning that he was still using drugs. He left rather than be confronted with the results of this urine test.

On October 2, 1989, he obtained a job with the ABC Truck Company and worked there part-time until February 15, 1990, when he was fired for being late.

On February 16, 1990, he went back to Reality House, but failed to attend every day. On March 1, 1990, he went to the Amsterdam Welfare Center to apply for welfare for himself and his family. The caseworker, Linda Stout, asked him why he could not get a job. He said he was an addict attending Reality House. Linda Stout was skeptical. She demanded verification that he was regularly attending Reality House. George went back to Reality House to speak to his therapist, John Hughey. Mr. Hughey told him that he could not give him a letter stating that he was a member of the program until he began to attend more often.

On March 15, 1990 Linda Stout contacted Brenda Marshall, the caseworker who had previously interviewed George's wife on January 10, 1989. Brenda told Linda that Mrs. Temple told her that her husband was *not* an addict.

In the meantime, George still had trouble getting a letter from Reality House stating that he was a "member" of the program. On March 17, 1990, Linda Stout called John Hughey at Reality House, who told her that George was not coming in every day. On March 18, 1990, she closed George's case, declaring him ineligible for welfare for failure to demonstrate need. She concluded that the welfare regulation authorizing public assistance to addicts attending rehabilitation programs did not apply to George.

Section E
PRELIMINARY CONSIDERATIONS

Your first responsibility as the paralegal assigned to this case is to help the office decide when and how to intervene. George comes in and tells you that he wants to fight the decision of the caseworker, Linda Stout. He wants a hearing. Is this an appropriate strategy? What alternatives exist? What about informal advocacy? Would you first want to call or visit Linda Stout? Brenda Marshall? John Hughey? Linda Stout's boss? Brenda Marshall's boss? John Hughey's boss? If so why? Is the time ripe to intervene by asking for a formal hearing?

Suppose that you decide to give informal advocacy a try, but it does not work. The welfare department still refuses to declare George eligible. Therefore, in consultation with your supervisor, you decide to ask for a hearing.

In preparing for a hearing, there are a number of preliminary considerations:

1. *Define your issues.* What are the issues in George's case? What would you have to show in order to qualify him for welfare? What are the points in doubt? Two questions come to mind: (1) Is George an addict? And (2) is he a member of a drug rehabilitation center? If you showed that George was an addict, would he be sent to jail or to a hospital? Is this a real danger? How would you find out? Linda Stout demanded verification from George that he was a member of Reality House. Can you identify two reasons she would ask for this? Is she saying that if George is not a member of a drug rehabilitation program, he probably is not an addict? Or is she saying that he cannot obtain welfare unless he is a member of such a program even if he is an addict? Which is the case? How would you find out? What other issues exist? What legal research should be done?

2. *Draft the request for the hearing.* In welfare cases, paralegals often draft the letter to the agency requesting the *hearing.* The client signs this letter. The request is extremely important since it can be a major determinant of what the issues at the hearing will be. How broadly or narrowly should an issue be stated? How many issues should be presented? These are questions of strategy that are answered largely in the light of what you think you might be able to prove at the hearing.

   When a response to the letter of request is received, you will know whether a hearing has been granted on the issues requested. If not satisfied with this response, you should consult with your supervisor on ways to challenge the response before the hearing is held. If satisfied, preparation should be geared accordingly.

   A careful definition and a thorough understanding of what the issues are can be critical for the following reasons:

    a. At the hearing, the other side or the hearing officer may raise matters outside the scope of the issues of the hearing. You can object, based on the wording of the request for the hearing and the response received to the request.

    b. If an office attorney is going to appeal the final decision of the hearing in court, the starting point in preparing for the appeal is often an analysis of what the issues of the hearing were supposed to be.

3. *Engage in continuing efforts to resolve the case through informal advocacy.* It is almost always preferable to try to solve a problem informally so that the time and expense of formal hearings and court proceedings can be avoided. At the time of the request for a formal hearing in this case, you determined that informal advocacy would not be effective. The agency, however, can always change its mind, particularly when it realizes that the client is serious about fighting the case. Throughout the preparations for the hearing, you should try to be in continued contact with employees of the agency involved in the case. In these contacts, you may be able to bring to the agency's attention new factors that may cause it to reevaluate its position. The result may be a reversal of the agency's decision or the negotiation of a settlement between agency and client, eliminating the need for a hearing altogether. You must be constantly aware of this option.

4. *Familiarize yourself with agency procedures in advance.* There is no better way to prepare for a hearing than to see one in operation before you conduct your own. You might "tag along" as the assistant of another advocate conducting a hearing. Take extensive notes on procedure and strategy. Later on, organize your notes into an outline covering the procedures that governed the hearing as well as the strategy that both sides used.

    Some agencies have prehearing conferences, during which the advocates for both sides sit down (in advance of the hearing) to narrow the issues and determine whether a solution can be reached without a formal hearing. When available, this can be a valuable meeting. If the agency does not have prehearing conferences as a matter of course, why not ask for one anyway? Besides being a vehicle to attempt a solution, the conference is an excellent way to learn more about the agency's case and hence be better prepared for the hearing, if it is held.

5. *Try to respond to the client's emergency needs, if any, while waiting for a hearing decision.* In a welfare case, the recipient should not be left destitute while the agency makes a decision following a hearing. Emergency assistance of a temporary nature may be available in the interim. Suppose that you are representing a client in a worker's compensation case. While the hearing is going on, you may be able to help this individual obtain public assistance or, possibly, union benefits. To the extent feasible, be alert to a client's total needs and do not simply zero in on narrow legal questions. Of course, you have limited time available and must set priorities on what you can do. Very often you can be of help simply by referring the client to other resources in the community.

6. *Make sure that the client has given you proper authorization to act on his or her behalf.* The law office may have a standard form for the client to sign authorizing you to represent the client at the agency proceeding. In addition, you should have the client sign a waiver-of-confidentiality statement authorizing you to examine all documents the agency possesses that pertain to the case. A similar statement may permit you to gain access to needed doctor or hospital records.

7. *Make a request in writing that the agency send you, in advance, copies of all documents that it intends to rely on at the hearing.* Are you curious about what documents the welfare department will be using at the hearing to prove its case against George? Ask the

department to send you copies of these documents in advance of the hearing. Would this be a fair request? In many situations, the law will back up such a request. What documents would you be interested in seeing? Their entire file on George? Their most recent policy statement on addicts? What else? (Suppose the agency wanted *you* to send them copies of the documents you will be using? What would you do?)

8. *Find out as much as you can about the witnesses the agency intends to call at the hearing.* Usually, the agency will tell you in advance what witnesses it will call to support its position. Often these witnesses are willing to talk to you before the hearing, particularly if they are agency employees. This is frequently an excellent way to discover more details about the agency's case and how the agency intends to establish that case at the hearing. Your approach should be casual. Do not say to these witnesses, "What testimony are you going to give at the hearing next week?" Rather, deal with points of information: "I understand that you know George Temple. Could I ask when you last spoke to him?" Etc.

9. *Make sure that you have completed all necessary field investigation before the hearing.* What facts do you think need to be checked? What are you unsure of? Are you convinced that George is an addict? What *is* an addict? Someone currently using drugs? What kinds of drugs? How would you find out? Are you also unsure about George's relationship with Reality House? What is a "member"? How many definitions of "member" might exist? Do George, Linda Stout, and John Hughey each define it differently? Would you want to check this out? How often does George go to Reality House? What other items should you investigate? Before the hearing, would you want to make a request to the agency that it state its position on George's case in writing? What would you do with such a document? Use *fact particularization* to help identify factual questions that you need to pursue through investigation and subsequent client interviews (see Exhibits 8.4 and 8.5 in chapter 8).

10. *Study the law governing your case.* It goes without saying that you must be thoroughly familiar with the law, particularly the agency regulations that may be applicable to the case. A good deal of legal research may be necessary before you even request a hearing. Some aspects of the law governing the case may be unclear due to ambiguities in regulations, statutes, or cases. Part of the task of preparation is to identify these ambiguities and to map out a strategy on how to deal with them if they arise at the hearing.

   Bring photocopies of relevant regulations, statutes, or cases with you to the hearing. In addition, summarize, in your own words, the sections of these documents that you believe will be most pertinent.

11. *Determine what witnesses you want to call and prepare them.* Who should be present at the hearing to help George make his case? Should George be present? Why? Should John Hughey be present? Why? How about the boss of John Hughey? Do you want George's wife to be present? The tests that you should use in deciding whether to ask a witness to be present are: Does the witness have something to say that would help George make his case, and would the witness be able to say it? Someone may have important points to make but be so frightened at the thought of going to a hearing that he or she is, in effect, unavailable. Suppose you have a witness whom you want to call, but the person has an acute stuttering problem. How would you handle this?

   Tell your witnesses what the hearing is all about to set their mind at ease. To be willing and valuable participants, they must trust you. Tell them why you want them to come. (You do not have to use words such as "witness" and "testimony" if these would frighten them.) Get them to role-play part of the proceeding with you. A brief role-playing experience can be very helpful. Explain that the other side may want to ask some questions after you introduce them and ask your own questions. Be sure that your witnesses understand what the issues are. They may try to use the occasion to begin a tirade about everything under the sun. This could be damaging, though you may determine as a matter of strategy to let the witnesses "unload" to some extent.

You must be careful not to place your witnesses in embarrassing situations. Whenever you think that a question you want to ask might be embarrassing or damaging to your witnesses, check it out with your supervisor before the hearing. What about George's addiction? Can you think of any questions you might ask that could create difficulties for him?

12. *Assemble all the documentary evidence that you want to introduce at the hearing. Determine how you will lay the foundation for each item of evidence—that is, how you will show that it is relevant to the issues of the hearing.* What documents do you want to present at the hearing on behalf of George? Do you want a letter from Exodus House stating that he once attended the program? If so, why? What would it prove? Do you want a letter from Reality House? Saying what? Would you ask them to write down all of the dates that George did attend that program? Would it help or hurt to obtain a letter from ABC Truck Company stating that George once worked there? Is it relevant? Suppose that you could arrange a doctor's examination of George. Would you want to use the results of this examination at the hearing? What would it depend on?

13. *Draft an outline of how you intend to present your case at the hearing.* The great danger of preplanning, of course, is that the unexpected almost always "fouls up" your preliminary plan. It nevertheless is helpful to have a tentative plan in mind, *as long as you do not slavishly try to follow it.* Flexibility is always key.

A useful approach is to arrange all the facts according to a chronological history. Every client's story has a beginning, middle, and end. Your outline should attempt to tell George's story in this way. Simple as this may seem, it is not easy to do. At the hearing, people will raise points out of sequence. These points often have to be dealt with, but if you have prepared your chronology carefully, you at least have something to come back to after treating this other point.

Draft a preliminary outline of your strategy in conducting George's hearing. What points do you want to make? What documents or witnesses will you use to help you make these points? Arrange the entire sequence chronologically.

Confusion over the precise issue or issues of the hearing is one of the major frustrations you might experience in conducting formal hearings. This can arise in a number of ways: (a) the original request for a hearing or the agency's response to it was not precise enough; (b) the hearing officer refuses to hear testimony on an issue that you were prepared to argue; (c) your own witness raises an issue that you are not prepared to argue; (d) subissues are raised by either side, the relevance of which are dependent on the establishment of other major issues or subissues that have not yet been established; or (e) you make the dangerous assumption that everyone is focused on the same issue.

Issue control, therefore, is critical. How do you identify the issue in the most favorable light for your client? How do you make sure everyone is on the same wavelength with respect to the issues of the hearing? What do you do when new issues are raised? How do you keep from becoming paralyzed when the issue on which you have based your entire case is taken away from you, not by a failure to prove the issue but by a decision of the hearing officer about what's relevant to the hearing?

Again, the answer to these questions is "preplanned flexibility." As you prepare for the hearing, you must do such a thorough job of anticipating the unexpected that you are ready to meet *any* new challenge, even if it is your own witness who poses the challenge.

Suppose that at George's hearing, the welfare department begins by making a major issue of George's poor employment record. They want to prove that he should enter a state vocational training program. What do you do? You should have anticipated this during your preparation, particularly due to the informal contacts that you had with the agency before the hearing. If for some reason this new position takes you by surprise, or if any other issue comes up that you feel is irrelevant, you have a number of options:

(a) Argue that the other side is being unfair; the agency should have let you know about its new position in advance.

(b) Argue that the issues at the hearing should conform to the issues defined in the letter granting the hearing.

(c) Ask for a postponement.

(d) After you have made your protest and lost, do the best you can with the issues that the hearing officer decides will be discussed.

14. *Make sure that the hearing officer does not have a legal bias.* The hearing officer should not have been involved in the agency's initial decision against the client, the decision that led to the necessity of asking for a hearing. Normally, this will not be a problem, since the hearing officer will usually be employed within a separate unit of the agency.

15. *If, after you request the hearing, it becomes clear that you need more time to prepare, ask for a postponement of the hearing.* Do not be rushed into a hearing unless it is absolutely necessary. Ask for a postponement and be prepared to back up your request with reasons (e.g., you are waiting for a letter to arrive that you want to produce at the hearing).

16. *Make sure that the client and the witnesses know when and where the hearing is to be held.*

Section F
HEARSAY, OPINIONS, AND RELEVANCE

Generally, the technical rules of evidence that are scrupulously followed in court proceedings (see chapter 10) do not apply to administrative hearings. The standard rule is that hearings are conducted "informally." Nevertheless, you should have an understanding of some concepts of evidence, because they do come up in hearings despite the general rule of informality.

As we shall see when we cover direct and cross-examination, you should (1) know when your witness or a witness for the other side is speaking from firsthand or personal knowledge as opposed to second- or thirdhand knowledge (**hearsay**), and (2) know when the witness is stating a fact as opposed to an opinion. It is important to know these distinctions not because a hearing officer will exclude hearsay evidence or opinion evidence, but because your case is always strengthened when your own witness speaks from personal knowledge of the facts. You tend to weaken the case of the other side when you can point out (through cross-examination) that a witness for the opposition is speaking from hearsay or is relating opinions as opposed to facts. If you ask your witness to state an opinion or conclusion, be sure your witness has already stated the underlying facts that support the opinion. (For an overview of principles of evidence, see section I in chapter 9.)

ꙮ **A s s i g n m e n t   1 5 . 1**

For each statement made by the witness below, answer the following questions:

(a) Is the witness talking from firsthand (personal) knowledge? Secondhand? Thirdhand?

(b) Is the witness stating a fact or an opinion?

(c) What questions would you ask the witness so that the same information would come out in a different way?

    (1) "My caseworker is rude."

    (2) "My caseworker called me a liar."

    (3) "I am eligible for public assistance."

    (4) "My son told me that the caseworker reported me to the supervisor."

    (5) "I need welfare."

    (6) "My mother can't pay my rent."

    (7) "I'm too sick to join the job training program."

    (8) "That job does not suit me."

    (9) "My husband does not contribute to the support of my family."

   (10) "I did report to the job employment agency."

   (11) "I was told that no jobs were available."

   (12) "You must give me seven days' notice before you terminate me."

Another critical concern of evidence is relevance: only evidence that is relevant to the issues at the hearing should be considered by the hearing officer. Something is relevant if it (reasonably) tends to prove or disprove a matter in dispute. Very often common sense is a clear guide on whether something is relevant. The fact that I am in Chicago is not at all relevant to whether or not it is raining in New York; but the fact that I am in Chicago is relevant to whether or not I *know* if it is raining in New York. In a large number of situations, however, the borderline between relevance and irrelevance is thin. On the question of whether or not George Temple "regularly attends" a drug rehabilitation center, is it relevant that he often plays in baseball games? Is it relevant he has an ulcer? Is his age relevant? Hearing officers will generally lean in the direction of admitting something into evidence if its relevance is at least probable; they are more inclined to let evidence in than to exclude it.

Whenever the hearing officer or the representative of the other side objects to an item of evidence that you plan to introduce, you must be prepared to argue its relevance by explaining how it will contribute to reaching a resolution of the issues. If this approach does not seem to be successful, make a basic "fairness pitch" by asking that you be allowed to present your client's case in the best manner that you can. In effect you are saying, "Don't push me on technicalities; give me some time to show you why this is important. It may not be clear to you now why it is important, but I'll make it clear to you shortly."

Another consideration is the extent to which the evidence you want to produce would be burdensome on the proceeding. You must be reasonable. You cannot try to introduce one thousand pages of canceled receipts and bills, for example, if it is not quite clear that every item is needed to make your case.

Section G
INTRODUCTION TO THE EXAMINATION OF WITNESSES

Before the examination of witnesses begins, be sure that you know who everyone in the hearing room is. The hearing officer may ask everyone to state his or her name and connection with the case. If the hearing officer does not, you should ask that this be done.

Another preliminary is the opening statement made by each side. When it is your turn to begin, your opening statement should briefly cover the following:

1. Your understanding of what the issues at the hearing are
2. A summary of what you are going to establish at the hearing through your witnesses and other evidence
3. The result the client is seeking from the hearing

After the opening statements, the next step is the examination of witnesses.

You conduct the **direct examination** of your own witnesses (George, for example) and the **cross-examination** of the witnesses presented by the other side (the agency employee, Linda Stout, for example). After you have directly examined your own witnesses, the other side can cross-examine them. After the other side has directly examined their own witnesses, you can cross-examine them. Each side directly examines its own witnesses and cross-examines the witnesses of the other side. When you directly examine a witness, it simply means that you are the first person to ask questions of that witness.

Normally, one side presents its entire case and then the other side presents its case. The main time you talk when the other side is presenting its case is when you are cross-examining its witnesses, and vice versa.

After a side has cross-examined a witness, the other side (the one that originally examined the witness directly) is sometimes allowed to conduct a **redirect examination** to cover points raised in the cross-examination.

Sequence:

I. *You Present Your Side*

- You direct-examine your own witnesses.
- They cross-examine your witnesses.
- You conduct a redirect examination of your own witnesses to cover points they raised in their cross-examination.

II. *They Present Their Side*

- They direct-examine their own witnesses.
- You cross-examine their witnesses.
- They conduct a redirect examination of their own witnesses to cover points you raised in your cross-examination.

This may all sound highly technical. Some hearings are, in fact, conducted this formally. Others are not. You must be prepared to deal with both settings.

To call a witness does not necessarily mean that the person stands in a witness box or is "sworn in." In all probability, everyone will remain in his or her own seat and will not be asked to take an oath. Furthermore, the technical words "direct," "cross," and "redirect" examination may not and need not be used. Simpler language can be used:

Direct Examination
"Sir (addressed to the hearing officer) I would like to ask (name of witness) a few questions."

Cross-Examination
"I would like the opportunity to ask (name of witness) some questions if (name of advocate on the other side) is finished with her own questions."

Redirect Examination
"After I asked (name of witness) some questions, Ms. (name of advocate representing the other side) asked some questions of her own, and while I was listening, a few other impor-

tant and pertinent points occurred to me. I would like to ask a few final questions of (name of witness), if I could."

It does not make any difference what labels are used, as long as you take every allowable opportunity to make your points.

S e c t i o n H
DIRECT EXAMINATION

Reduced to its simplest level, direct examination means nothing more than being first to interview or talk to someone concerning what he or she knows about an event. A direct examination has three components:

1. *Introduction:* Who is the witness, where does he or she live, where does he or she go to school or work?
2. *Connection to event:* What relationship does the witness have to the events at issue in the hearing?
3. *Testimony on event:* What does this witness have to say about the events at issue in the hearing?

GUIDELINES ON CONDUCTING DIRECT EXAMINATION

1. The witness on direct examination is *your* witness. You call this witness to give testimony. You are always very cordial to the witness. You never ask anything that might embarrass him or her.
2. Let the witness tell his or her own story in his or her own words. The story should flow naturally.
3. Ask the witness to speak loudly and clearly. If the witness says something that may not be clear to others, ask him or her to state it again, even though it may have been perfectly clear to *you* what was said.
4. Encourage the witness to let you know if he or she does not understand a question.
5. In the introduction of the witness, let the witness give the basic facts about himself or herself. Instead of saying, "This is John Smith of . . .," you should ask the witness to state his name, address, occupation, etc.
6. Before you ask the witness to state what he or she knows about an event, ask questions to establish his or her relationship or connection to the event. If the witness is a doctor, for example, before you ask his or her opinion of the client's medical condition, you should ask if the doctor has treated the patient. Before you ask a neighbor whether or not the client earns money as a private babysitter at home, you should ask the witness questions to establish that he or she is a close neighbor of the client and often visits the client during the day. By so doing, you will be *laying the foundation for the relevance of the witness's testimony.*
7. It is often helpful to structure your questions to the witness so that he or she tells the story chronologically from beginning to end. Discourage jumping from topic to topic if the narrative is becoming confusing.
8. When the witness is stating things from firsthand knowledge, emphasize the fact that it is firsthand, personal knowledge.
9. When the witness is stating things from secondhand (or hearsay) knowledge, de-emphasize the fact that it is not firsthand knowledge. When you prepare a witness to testify, encourage him or her to preface his or her statements by saying "to the best of my knowledge."

10. When your witness must state conclusions or opinions, you should structure your questions so that you first bring out all the supporting facts on which the witness has relied in forming the opinions or conclusions.

11. Be aware of the danger of open-ended questions such as, "Tell us what happened." Very often such questions are invitations to ramble. Confusion can result. The more effective kind of questions are structured to require a brief and concise answer. Use an open-ended question only when you are sure that the witness is able to handle it. (On the different kinds of questions, see Exhibit 8.8 in chapter 8.)

12. Very often a witness, particularly the client, has a need to vent his or her feelings. When this happens, the witness often becomes emotional and raises issues that may not be relevant. You must make a decision when this happens. On the one hand, it is the client's hearing and—as a matter of fairness—he or she should have the opportunity to speak his or her mind. It can be very frustrating if questioners keep steering the client away from what he or she has been waiting a long time to say. On the other hand, you do not want the client to say anything that may be damaging to the case. You must understand the client psychologically. The best strategy is to determine in advance whether the client is inclined to become emotional. If so, then your responsibility is to make the client aware of the consequences of this occurring at the hearing. In the final analysis, the client must decide; it is his or her case that's on the line, not yours.

13. You may want to introduce certain documents into evidence after you have asked the witness questions that will reveal facts demonstrating the documents' relevance. That is, you establish a foundation for the documents through your questioning. Once the foundation has been laid, you *introduce* the documents by asking the hearing officer to make them part of the record and by giving copies to the agency's representative. Then you resume your direct examination of the witness.

14. The hearing officer may interrupt you with questions of his or her own for the witness. The officer, of course, has the right to do this. You may, however, want to tell the hearing officer politely that you will treat the subject matter of his or her question in "just a few moments."

15. The advocate for the other side may try to interrupt you with questions. Normally, he or she does *not* have this right. Politely ask the hearing officer if you can finish your own questions before the other side asks any questions on cross-examination.

16. Try to anticipate what the other side will want to question your witness about on cross-examination, and try to cover these points in your own direct examination.

17. Expect the unexpected. Your witness may say things that you never anticipated. You have to be flexible enough to deal with whatever comes your way.

Class Exercise 15.C

Role-play the following situations in class. The instructor will select one student to take the part of the person conducting the direct examination and someone else to role-play the person being questioned. The latter should make up answers that are generally consistent with the situation stated. (Review the material in chapter 8 on fact particularization as a guide to formulating questions. See Exhibit 8.5.) Conduct a:

(a) Direct examination (DE) of another student concerning the most frustrating aspect of his or her last job

(b) DE of a teenager who just drove home the family car with a big dent on the side

(c) DE of a pupil who has been charged with fighting

(d) DE of a welfare recipient on his claim that he has tried to find suitable work but has been unable to do so

(e) DE of George Temple

Section I
CROSS-EXAMINATION

Before covering guidelines on cross-examination, you should review chapter 9 on investigation. Restudy the evaluation of testimonial and physical evidence and the checklist on the validity of physical (tangible) evidence. (See Exhibits 9.6 and 9.7.) Many of the considerations discussed in the investigation chapter apply to cross-examination at hearings.

GUIDELINES ON CONDUCTING CROSS-EXAMINATION

1. Be courteous to the witness even though you may be tempted, indeed baited, into attacking him or her personally. On cross-examination during a court trial, an attorney is allowed to ask **leading questions,** in which an answer is suggested in the questions themselves. On direct examination, the attorney is generally not allowed to ask leading questions of his or her own witnesses. Compare the following questions:

   - "Did you speak to your doctor?"
   - "Did your doctor tell you that you needed medication?"

   The second question is leading because it suggests an answer—the need for medication. Since the rules of evidence and procedure are not as strict in administrative hearings as they are in trials, you will probably not have to worry about when leading questions can be used. Nevertheless you should be aware of when you or your opponent is using this kind of question. The natural tendency of advocates is to try to ask such questions of adverse witnesses during cross-examination. Overuse, however, can be unnecessarily antagonistic.

2. Be sure that it is clear to you who the witness is and what relationship he or she has to the events at issue in the hearing. This may not have been brought out clearly enough while this witness was being direct-examined by the agency representative.

3. If during the direct examination, this witness said something based on secondhand knowledge (or if it was not clear to you whether it was said from personal or secondhand knowledge), ask about it on cross-examination. Be sure that your questions force the witness to admit that no firsthand knowledge exists when this is so.

4. If, during the direct examination, this witness stated conclusions without providing any facts to support them, ask this witness on cross-examination about these conclusions. Probe the underlying facts that support them—according to the witness. Do *not* use this tactic, however (nor the one mentioned in guideline 3 above), if you are absolutely certain that the witness has valid facts to support the conclusions or opinions even though they were not brought out on direct examination. You do *not* want to give an opposing witness the opportunity to *reinforce* damaging evidence.

5. If it is a fact (or if you are reasonable in suspecting it is a fact) that the witness has a bias (something personal) against the client, you should try to bring this out on cross-examination. This, of course, will be very difficult and somewhat dangerous to do. No one wants to admit that he or she is not being objective. Probably the best that you can do on cross-examination is to raise some doubts about the objectivity

of the witness's testimony (by asking questions about any prior hostility that may have existed between the client and the witness, for example) even though you may not be able to establish bias conclusively.

6. The point made about bias *against* someone applies to bias *in favor of* a person. A witness can lose objectivity because of partisanship and friendship as well as because of hostility.

7. If the witness is reading from any papers during cross-examination, politely ask the witness what he or she is reading from and request that you be shown a copy. If needed, ask for a few moments to read it before you continue your cross-examination. If the witness is reading from a document that was not sent to you before the hearing (and you requested that the agency send you *all* records that it was going to rely on at the hearing), you should object.

8. Sometimes the witness will read from official agency records. These records often refer to statements made by individuals who work for the agency but who are not present at the hearing. The agency representative will try to introduce these records into evidence. Again, you should bring out, through your questioning, the fact that the witness is not speaking from firsthand knowledge when referring to records of which he or she is not the author. In addition, you should complain that, as a matter of fairness, authors of critically important statements in the records should be present at the hearing so that you can confront and cross-examine them. If you are not allowed to cross-examine them, you should request that their statements not become part of the hearing proceedings.

9. If, during cross-examination, the witness raises points that surprise you (for a reason other than your own sloppy preparation), you should ask the hearing officer to exclude the matter because of unfair surprise or to postpone the hearing to give you more time to prepare the client's response to the new point.

10. In courtroom proceedings, it is often the rule that you cannot raise new matters on cross-examination; you can cross-examine a witness only within the scope of the testimony this witness gave on direct examination. If, for example, the witness testifies only about food stamp eligibility on direct examination, the attorney conducting the cross-examination cannot ask questions about an invasion of privacy claim. This technical rule, however, almost *never* applies to administrative hearings. You should nonetheless be aware of it, since the advocate for the agency may improperly try to apply the technical rule against you while you are cross-examining a witness. You usually do *not* have to limit your questioning on cross-examination to the scope of what was brought out by the other side on direct examination. Normally, however, it is a good practice not to raise new matters on cross-examination unless you have no alternative. Use direct examination to make all your major points. Use cross-examination as a vehicle to challenge positions of the other side and to buttress the points you have made on direct examination.

11. On cross-examination you are questioning witnesses who are normally hostile to your client, although this is not always so. Do not antagonize them unnecessarily. You may find that on cross-examination the witness is willing, either consciously or not, to make statements that are very favorable to your client.

12. As a corollary to point 11, do not be unduly aggressive or defensive. Make your case positively by direct examination. Do not rely exclusively on establishing your case negatively by trying to show on cross-examination that the witnesses for the other side are foolish.

13. Do not help the other side by asking questions on cross-examination that you know (or reasonably anticipate) will produce damaging statements. (See also guideline 4 above.)

14. You do not have to conduct a cross-examination of a witness (a) if nothing he or she said on direct examination is unclear to you or to the hearing officer or (b) if you do not think you can prompt the witness to contradict or discredit his or her position. In such a case, it would be better to rely solely on what you were able to establish on direct examination.

15. Remain loose and flexible; anticipate the unexpected.

⚖ Class Exercise 15.D

Role-play the following situations in class. The instructor will select students to play the roles involved. The witness should make up answers that are generally consistent with the situation stated. (Review the material in chapter 8 on fact particularization as a guide to formulating questions. See Exhibit 8.5.)

(a) On direct examination, the witness testified that Mr. Smith was drunk. Conduct a cross-examination of this witness.

(b) On direct examination, the witness (a social worker) testified that she feels the client is an unfit mother. When she visited the client, the house was dirty, the children were sick, and there was no food in the refrigerator. Conduct a cross-examination of this witness.

(c) On direct examination, the witness (a social worker) testified that an unemployed client should be able to obtain employment for the following reasons: the children are old enough for day care services, the client is basically healthy in spite of occasional headaches, and jobs are available (or at least job-training programs are available). Conduct a cross-examination of this witness.

Section J
CLOSING THE HEARING AND PREPARING FOR AN APPEAL

At the end of all the questioning and presentation of evidence, ask the hearing officer to let you sum up with your version of what happened. State what you think you proved, state what you think the other side failed to prove. Specifically, state again what result you seek for the client. If you think that the hearing was inconclusive because you were unfairly surprised by what the other side did or because the other side failed to bring individuals to the hearing who were sufficiently acquainted with the case, then:

- Ask for a decision for the client because of these factors; or
- At the very least, ask for an adjournment. The hearing can resume after you have had a chance to study the matter that the other side unfairly surprised you with, or after the other side brings individuals to the hearing who should have been there.

Many hearings are either transcribed or tape-recorded by the agency. Every word of the hearing, therefore, is preserved. Normally, the law office for which you work will be able to purchase a typed copy of the transcript or a copy of the tape. This record made of the hearing becomes the basis of a court appeal if the client is dissatisfied with the decision. You must understand the relationship between what happens at the hearing and a possible subsequent court appeal. To a very large extent, you are responsible for **making a record** for the attorney to use on appeal.

Attorneys who have litigated cases following administrative hearings should acquaint you with the mechanics of the court appeal process. If possible, you should try to read a copy of an old appellate brief that cites testimony taken at an administrative hearing so that you can see the connection between the hearing and the court action.

In some administrative hearings, an advocate waives any objection that he or she has to what takes place at the hearing *unless he or she specifically objects on the record at the agency hearing.* A **waiver** can mean that the attorney cannot later raise the point on appeal in court.

To avoid such waivers, then you must be familiar with the technique of objecting for the record. When you have an objection to make during the hearing, you should do so simply by saying to the hearing officer, "Sir, I would like to object" and briefly state what you are objecting to and the reasons. It is not necessary to object constantly to the same point. If the hearing officer decides against you and you object once, it is usually unnecessary to object again every time the agency representative brings up what you objected to.

With few exceptions, courts do not allow clients to appeal an issue in court unless the agency involved has been given the opportunity to resolve the issue within the agency's own hearing structure. This is the doctrine of **exhausting administrative remedies.** For example, at a welfare hearing, a client might claim that he or she failed to receive a check that was due *and* that the caseworker is harassing him or her with unauthorized home visits. At the hearing, if the only issue discussed concerned the check, then the visitation issue cannot be appealed in court since the client has not exhausted administrative remedies as to this issue. Another hearing may have to be brought on the visitation issue before it can be raised in court. You must be aware of this problem as a matter of issue control.

🏛 *Assignment 15.2*

Read each situation. State whether you would raise any objection. If so, state the reasons for your objection. Also, answer any other questions asked in the problem situation.

(a) On direct examination, a witness of the agency representative says that your client "is a liar."

(b) On direct examination, a witness of the agency representative reads from a piece of paper. You are not sure what the paper is.

(c) On direct examination, a witness of the agency representative says that he or she was told by another caseworker that the client had a secret bank account. On cross-examination of this same witness, what line of questions should you pursue?

(d) Before the hearing began, you requested that the agency send you all the documents that the agency intended to rely on at the hearing. The agency never did. Should you refer to this fact at the beginning of the hearing? If so, how?

(e) Same as (d) above, except that when you mention at the beginning of the hearing that the records were never sent, the agency representative hands you forty pages of records.

(f) Same as (d) above except that when you mention at the beginning of the hearing that the records were never sent, the agency representative responds by saying that the records are confidential.

(g) On direct examination of your witness, the agency representative keeps interrupting with questions of his or her own.

(h) While the agency representative is talking to the hearing officer, he or she uses some legal language that you do not understand.

(i) While talking to the hearing officer, the agency representative hands him or her a document that announces a new agency regulation.

🏛 *C l a s s   E x e r c i s e   1 5 . E*

Role-play the George Temple hearing in class. As a starting point, use the facts presented on page 786. Participants can make up other facts as they go along, as long as they are generally consistent with the facts given. The instructor will select students to play the parts of the various roles, such as hearing officer, paralegal for George, paralegal for the agency, and witnesses. The paralegals should review the material on fact particularization as a guide in formulating questions (see chapter 8). The rest of the class should observe and take notes on how the paralegals conduct themselves. What did they do well? What went wrong? How should it have been handled?

C h a p t e r   S u m m a r y

Advocacy takes place all the time. It is an everyday process by which all citizens—not just attorneys—attempt to influence or change the actions of others at one time or another. Informal advocacy occurs outside of courts or other tribunals where hearings are held to resolve controversies that the participants have not been able to resolve informally.

Advocates try many techniques of informal advocacy, with varying degrees of success. Among the most common are the following: placing your cards on the table; insisting on adequate service; seeking the support of third parties; being a buddy; finding the points of compromise; insisting on common sense; demonstrating the exception; uncovering the realm of discretion; asking for authorization; citing the law; redefining the problem; showing anger and hostility; preaching; climbing the chain of command; embarrassing the official; making clear that you will fight the case; taking the role of the tired, battered, helpless citizen; doing a favor to get a favor; and citing a precedent. While using any of these techniques, you need to evaluate your effectiveness and modify the techniques based on this evaluation.

Whenever the government takes an action that seriously affects a citizen, such as denying or removing a benefit, basic fairness may require a number of procedural safeguards. These requirements are referred to as *procedural due process*. While not applicable to every situation, the safeguards include notice, hearing, personal appearance at the hearing, the absence of legal bias, representation, relevance of the evidence, opportunity to examine the evidence, opportunity to present your own witnesses, a decision in writing, and an opportunity to appeal.

When paralegals are allowed to represent clients at administrative hearings, preparation requires careful defining of the issues, drafting the requests or demand for the hearing, continuation of informal advocacy, familiarity with the procedures to be used at the hearing and with the substantive law that will govern the client's case, attention to a client's emergency needs, proper authorization from the client, efforts to obtain access to agency documents and witnesses before the hearing, finalizing field investigation, preparation of your own witnesses, organization of documentary evidence, and the design of a flexible outline of your presentation. While most hearings are conducted less formally than a court proceeding, the paralegal should be familiar with the evidentiary difficulties involving hearsay, opinion testimony, and relevance. (These areas are discussed more fully in chapter 9.)

The standard format of an administrative hearing is as follows: direct examination of a witness by the side that calls the witness; cross-examination of that witness by the other side; and redirect examination of the witness by the side that called the witness. Normally, any objections that are not made during the hearing are waived and hence cannot be the basis of a court appeal after administrative remedies have been exhausted.

KEY TERMS

advocacy, 776
quasi-judicial proceeding, 776
procedural due process, 784
notice, 784

hearing, 785
legal bias, 785
confrontation, 785
relevancy, 785
appeal, 785

hearsay, 791
direct examination, 793
cross-examination, 793
redirect examination, 793
leading questions, 796

making a record, 798
waiver, 799
exhausting administrative remedies, 799

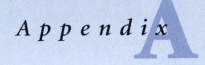

BIBLIOGRAPHY

ARTICLES, BOOKS, REPORTS, ETC. ON PARALEGALS

ABBREVIATIONS:

AAfPE = American Association for Paralegal Education
ABA = American Bar Association
ABAJ = American Bar Association Journal
ALA = Association of Legal Administrators
ALR = American Law Reports
F&F = Facts and Findings (a journal of NALA)
JPE&P = Journal of Paralegal Education and Practice
    (a journal of AAfPE)
LADJ = Los Angeles Daily Journal (legal newspaper)
LAMA = Legal Assistants Management Association
LAT = Legal Assistant Today (a magazine on paralegal
    issues)

LM = Legal Management (magazine of ALA)
LOEM = Law Office Economics and Management (a legal
    journal)
LOMAR = Law Office Management & Administrative Report
NALA = National Association of Legal Assistants
NALS = National Association of Legal Secretaries
NFPA = National Federal of Paralegal Associations
NLJ = National Law Journal (a legal newspaper)
NPR = National Paralegal Reporter (a journal of NFPA)
PLI = Practicing Law Institute

INDEX TO BIBLIOGRAPHY

(The numbers below refer to specific entries in the
bibliography.)

(The numbers below refer to specific entries in the bibliography.)—cont.

(The numbers below refer to specific entries in the bibliography.)—cont.

BIBLIOGRAPHY

A

1. *AAfPE Addresses PACE Exam at NFPA Conference* by A. McCoin, 9 The Paralegal Educator 5 (AAfPE, June 1995).

2. *ABA Commission Finds Widespread Nonlawyer Usage* by S. Cohn, 11 LAT 22 (July/Aug. 1994).

3. *The ABA Has Spoken: Will the Nonlawyer Practice Report Make a Difference?* by M. Curriden, 13 LAT 62 (Jan./Feb. 1996).

4. *ABA May Target Paralegals for Membership* by M. Curriden, 11 LAT 23 (Jan./Feb. 1994).

5. *The ABA Nonlawyer Practice Report* by M. Curriden, 13 LAT 89 (Nov./Dec. 1995).

6. *ABA Report* by P. Bailey, 22 F&F 33 (NALA, Issue 4, 1995) (ABA Commission on Non-Lawyer Practice).

7. *ABA Says Paralegal Costs Should Be Counted in Fee Awards* by S. Cohn, 11 LAT 22 (Jan./Feb. 1994).

8. *ABA Struggles with Right Role for Nonlawyers* by T. Carter, LADJ, 1 (May 2, 1994). (limited licensing, regulation)

9. *The ABC's of Databases* by P. Eyres, 14 LAT 38 (Sept./Oct. 1996).

10. *The ABC's of Overtime Pay* by D. Orlik, 4 LAT 37 (July/Aug. 1987).

11. *Activities of Insurance Adjusters as Unauthorized Practice of Law,* 29 ALR 4th 1156 (1967).

12. *Activities of Law Clerks Illegal Practice of Law,* 13 ALR 3rd 1137 (1967).

13. *Administrative Law Guide for Paralegals* by W. Van Duyne (Wiley, 1994).

14. *The Administrative Legal Assistant: A Nuts and Bolts View of Complex Toxic Tort Litigation Management* by B. Gagnon, 16 F&F 24 (NALA, Mar. 1990).

15. *After Slump, Paralegal Work on Rebound: They Faced Less Dire Layoffs than Associates . . . ; Surviving the Downturn* by T. Weidlich, 16 NLJ 1 (Apr. 25, 1994).

16. *Alleviate the Full-Time Press* by M. Messmer, 15 LM 29 (ALA, Sept./Oct. 1996). (hiring temporary paralegals)

17. *Alliances: What Are They? How Do They Work?*, 20 F&F 23 (NALA, Issue 4, 1993). (California, Missouri, Virginia)

18. *All of These People are Paralegals: If They Say They Are* by M. Curriden, 13 LAT 24 (Sept./Oct. 1995). (disbarred attorney, prisoners, credentials)

19. *All That She Can Be: Army Paralegal* by C. Estrin, 12 LAT 34 (Nov./Dec. 1994).

20. *Alternate Dispute Resolution Provides Challenging Role for Legal Assistants* by F. Whiteside, 9 LAT 28 (May/June 1992).

21. *Alternate Sentencing: A Case Study: What a Paralegal Can Do to Improve the Criminal Justice Process* by M. Courlander, 3 LAT 16 (Winter 1986).

22. *Analyzing Medical Records* by L. Clark, 11 LAT 84 (May/June 1994).

23. *The Annual LAMA (Legal Assistant Management Association) Conference* by P. Perry, 10 LAT 76 (Mar./Apr. 1993).

24. *Another First for the State Bar of Texas: Specialty Certification of Legal Assistants* by L. Thomas, 57 Texas Bar Journal 58 (Jan. 1994).

25. *Answers to Eight Stupid Interviewing Questions* by A. Dewitt, 12 LAT 76 (Sept./Oct. 1994).

26. *Appearance by Paralegal on Behalf of Debtor at Creditors' Meeting Constitutes the Unauthorized Practice of Law,* 9 Inside Litigation 21 (Feb. 1995).

27. *Approaches for Continuing Legal Education of Paralegals* by T. Calvocoressi & R. Villanova, 7 JPE&P 43 (1990).

28. *Arbitration in a Union Setting* by M. Simmons, 18 F&F 28 (Nov. 1991).

29. *Are Computers Replacing Lawyers? No, but a Growing Volume of Good Lay-Level Software Is Creating "Instant Paralegals" and Cutting into Billable Hours,* 11 Lawyer's PC 1 (Jan. 1994).

30. *Are Firms Losing Paralegals as a Last Source of Leverage?* 94 LOMAR 3 (Dec. 1994).

31. *Are Legal Administrators Professionals?* by R. Yegge, LM 20 (ALA, Nov./Dec. 1992).

32. *Are Legal Assistants a Profession? Yes: Judge Us by What We Do; No: Wishing Doesn't Make it So* by M. Boerder & P. O'Brien, 11 LAT 31 (Mar./Apr. 1994).

33. *Are Paralegals Content to Be a Sub-Profession?* by M. Thomas, 20 NPR 7 (NFPA, Fall 1995).

34. *Are You a Team Player?* by S. Hunt, 13 LAT 76 (Mar./Apr. 1996). (litigation)

35. *Are You Ready for Cyberspace?* by A. Yelin, 12 LAT 32 (May/June 1995). (Internet)

36. *Arizona State Bar OK's Non-Lawyer Practitioners,* Bar Leader 4 (Mar./Arp. 1994).

37. *The Art of Audit Letters* by D. Bogen, 13 LAT 80 (Mar./Apr. 1996). (legal writing)

38. *The Art of Managing Your Support Staff* by the Section of Economics of Law Practice (ABA, 1986).

39. *The Art of On-Line Factual Discovery* by R. Leiter, 13 LAT 80 (Sept./Oct. 1995).

40. *The Art of Summarizing Depositions* by L. Clark, 11 LAT 144 (Sept./Oct. 1993).

41. *Assisting with the Representation of the Buyer in a Residential Purchase* by K. Dunn, 19 F&F 30 (NALA, Nov. 1992).

42. *The A to Z of CLE (Continuing Legal Education)* by K. Perry, 11 LAT 96 (Jan./Feb. 1994).

43. *Attorneys' Fees: Cost of Services Provided by Paralegals or the Like as Compensable Element of Award in State Court* 73 ALR 4th 938 (1987).

44. *Attorneys' Guide to Practicing with Legal Assistants,* 2d ed. (State Bar of Texas, 1992).

45. *Attorney's Splitting Fees with Other Attorneys or Laymen as Grounds for Disciplinary Proceeding,* 6 ALR 3rd 1446 (1966).

46. *The Authorized Practice of Legal Reference Service* by M. Mosley, 87 Law Library Journal 203 (1995).

47. *Automated Deposition Summaries with Summation II* by L. Moore, 21 F&F 40 (NALA, Aug. 1994).

48. *Automated Litigation Support Databases* by B. McNamara, 20 F&F 6 (NALA, Feb. 1994).

B

49. *Balancing Parenthood and a Paralegal Career* by C. Steinberg, 10 LAT 94 (July/Aug. 1993).

50. *Bankruptcy Clients and the Role of the Legal Assistant,* 20 F&F 14 (NALA, Nov. 1993).

51. *Bankruptcy Court Denies Reimbursement For Chapter 7 Trustee's Paraprofessional,* 9 Inside Litigation 30 (Aug. 1995).

52. *Bankruptcy Law and Practice: A Guide for Paralegals,* 3d ed. by S. Berger (Wiley, 1994).

53. *Bankruptcy Paralegal Regulation . . . Legitimate Legal Assistance Options for the Pro Se Bankruptcy Debtor* by M. Testerman, 23 California Bankruptcy Journal 37 (1996).

54. *Bankruptcy Petition Preparation Services: The Nonlawyer Provider of Bankruptcy Legal Services. Angel or Vulture?* by J. Cristol, 2 American Bankruptcy Institute Law Review 353 (Winter 1994).

55. *Bar Chiefs Protect the Guild* by M. France, the NLJ, A1 (August 7, 1995). (reaction to ABA Commission)

56. *Bar Membership and Guidelines Update* by C. Pederson, 22 F&F 8 (NALA, Issue 4, 1995).

57. *Bar Seeks to Protect Public with Non-Lawyer Practice Rules* by J. Calle, 30 Arizona Attorney 10 (Mar. 1994).

58. *A Battle for a Better Life* by B. Baker, 11 LAT 122 (Sept./Oct. 1993). (AIDS, Atlanta, Georgia, pro bono)

59. *Behind Door Number Three* by D. Kartson, 12 LAT 66 (Mar./Apr. 1995). (legal vendors)

60. *Be Steps Ahead of Other [Job] Candidates: Understand the Interview Game* by C. Reitz, 5 LAT 24 (Mar./Apr. 1988).

61. *The Best Firms to Work For* by W. Webb, 13 LAT 52 (Mar./Apr. 1996). (benefits, work environment, salary, assignments, Ohio, New York, Michigan, Arkansas, New Hampshire, Colorado, California, Texas)

62. *The Best Legal Software for Paralegals,* 13 LAT 32 (May/June 1996).

63. *Better Resumes for Attorneys & Paralegals* by A. Lewis & D. Saltman (Barron's, 1986).

64. *Beyond the Chinese Wall* by S. Cohn, 13 LAT 46 (Nov./Dec. 1995). (ethics, conflict of interest)

65. *The Big Question in 1993 Seems to Be Where Are the Jobs for Paralegals, Particularly Entry-Level Candidates Entering a Tight Job Market* by S. Widoff, 10 LAT 144 (Mar./Apr. 1993).

66. *Bill Seeks Registration of Legal Techs: Three-year Study Would Identify Services and Number of Paralegals* by T. Dresslar, LADJ 3 (Mar. 4, 1993).

67. *Billing for Paraprofessional Services* by T. McCormick, New Jersey Lawyer 20 (No. 136, Sept./Oct. 1990).

68. *A Bit About UPL* by S. Kaiser, 20 NPR 26 (NFPA, Fall 1995). (unauthorized practice of law, ethics)

69. *The Boom in Going Bust: Opportunities for Paralegals in Bankruptcy Law* by V. Safran, 9 LAT 98 (May/June 1992).

70. *Broadening the Paralegal Horizons* by L. Gray, 20 NPR 9 (NFPA, Spring 1996). (alternative careers, service providers, mediation)

71. *Brownstein's Legal-Assistant Blues: D. C. Firm Must Pay Staff for Back Hours* by R. Schmidt, Legal Times, S35 (Apr. 11, 1994).

72. *The Buddy System* by H. Samborn, 12 LAT 78 (Sept./Oct. 1994). (mentors, senior paralegals)

73. *Building a Strong Attorney-Paralegal Team* by N. Cattie & T. Vesper, 27 Trial 24 (Jan. 1991).

74. *Building a Strong Working Relationship with New Associates* by C. Tokumitsu, 10 LAT 38 (May/June 1993).

75. *Building Self-Management Skills* by D. Petropulos, 11 LAT 151 (Sept./Oct. 1993).

76. *Build Respect: Be an Assertive Professional* by L. Bourget, 4 LAT 40 (Jan./Feb. 1987).

77. *The Business of Confidentiality: What Everyone Doesn't Need to Know* by J. Levin (Estrin Pub. 1992).

78. *The Business Side of Freelance Paralegals* by S. Kligerman, 18 NPR 8 (NFPA, Summer 1994).

C

79. *Calculating Profit from Associates and Paralegals,* 58 The Journal of the Kansas Bar Ass'n 5 (Apr. 1989).

80. *California Attorney Held Responsible for Paralegal's Conflict of Interest* by V. Cope, 25 Trial 21 (Dec. 1989).

81. *The California Certification Program for Legal Assistants* by T. Brewster, 21 F&F 24 (NALA, Issue 4, 1994).

82. *California Narrows the Ethical Wall; Pennsylvania Expands It* by D. Orlik, 10 LAT 144 (May/June 1993).

83. *California Paralegal's Checklist Guide* by J. Wilson (Parker, 1994).

84. *California Paralegal's Guide,* 4th ed. by Z. Mack (Parker, 1993).

85. *Calling All Volunteers* by S. Cauldron, 12 LAT 44 (Mar./Apr. 1995). (pro bono)

86. *Call the ~~Doctor!~~ Nurse!: The Role of the Legal Nurse Consultant in the Litigation Process* by M. Atkins, 19 San Francisco Attorney Magazine 20 (Dec. 1993/ Jan. 1994).

87. *Canadian Legal Assistants Enjoy Growth & Recognition* by P. Hicks, 15 NPR 4 (NFPA, Spring 1991).

88. *Can You Bill Two Clients for the Same Hour's Work?* 11 LAT 26 (May/June 1994).

89. *Capitalizing on Legal Assistants in Columbia, South Carolina* by T. Howard, 5 LAT 40 (Nov./Dec. 1987).

90. *Career Alternatives for Paralegals* by F. Whiteside, 10 LAT 38 (Jan./Feb. 1993).

91. *Career Guide* (Legal Assistants of Central Ohio, 1993).

92. *A Career of One's Own* by P. Eyres, 12 LAT 44 (Jan./Feb. 1995). (freelance paralegal, computers)

93. *A Career of Service: Pro Bono Opportunities* by F. Whiteside, 10 LAT 106 (Sept./Oct. 1992).

94. *Career Opportunities for Legal Assistants in Corporations* by J. McIntyre, 10 LAT 64 (Nov./Dec. 1992).

95. *Career Paths for Paralegal Assistants in Corporate Legal Departments* by R. Homes & T. Caples, 14 Legal Economics 59 (ABA, July/Aug. 1988).

96. *The Case for Legal Technicians: They Provide an Affordable Option for Those Who Can't Afford Lawyers* by J. Berger, LADJ 6 (Dec. 22, 1992).

97. *CBA (Colorado Bar Association) Legal Assistants Committee Proposed Guidelines for the Utilization of Legal Assistants* (Feb. 1986).

98. *CBA (Colorado Bar Association) Legal Assistants Committee Survey Report,* 9 Colorado Lawyer 482 (1980).

99. *Certification Exams in Your Future?* by D. Petropulos, 13 LAT 80 (Jan./Feb. 1996).

100. *Certification Proposed In South Dakota* by J. Polsinelli, 7

NPR 12 (NFPA, Spring 1983).

101. *Certification v. Certificate* by L. Klessig, 17 F&F 32 (NALA, Fall 1990).

102. *Challenges of Government Jobs: Opportunities for Paralegals* by T. Howard, 8 LAT 84 (May/June 1991).

103. *Changing Economy Shaping New Trends for Paralegals* by M. Isgett, 16 NPR 2 (NFPA, Spring, 1992).

104. *Changing Jobs: Ethical Considerations* by V. Voisin, 15 F&F 12 (NALA, Mar. 1989).

105. *Charting a Path through the Tax Research Maze?* by A. Yelin, 12 LAT 48 (Mar./Apr. 1995).

106. *Chinese Walls: A Means of Avoiding Law Firm Disqualification When a Personally Disqualified Lawyer Joins the Firm* by M. Moser, 3 Georgetown Journal of Legal Ethics 399 (1990).

107. *Choice for Legal Services: Consumer Need for Legal Technicians Is Increasing* by R. Smith, 52 Oregon State Bar Bulletin 26 (June 1992).

108. *Chronology of Non-Lawyer Practice Rules* by L. Shely, 30 Arizona Attorney 15 (Mar. 1994).

109. *Cigarette Papers. (Merrell Williams, Former Paralegal at Louisville, Kentucky's Wyatt, Tarrant and Combs Sued for Allegedly Taking Tobacco Industry Documents with Him When He Left Firm* by A. Blum, NLJ 2 (Dec. 20, 1993).

110. *Cite Checking Made Painless* by C. Griffith, 11 LAT 52 (May/June 1994).

111. *CLA (Certified Legal Assistant) Study Guide* by Florida Legal Assistants, Inc. (Butterworths, 1986).

112. *The Clerical Trap* by B. Kumpe, 14 LAT 56 (Sept./Oct. 1996). (finding employment, secretarial jobs, typing)

113. *Client? Client? Who is the Client?* by D. Orlik, 12 LAT 78 (Nov./Dec. 1994). (ethics)

114. *The Client's Viewpoint on Paralegals* by W. Redd, 8 West Virginia Lawyer 19 (Apr. 1995).

115. *The Client Wants to Know* by D. Orlik, 14 LAT 90 (Sept./Oct. 1996). (ethics, malpractice)

116. *A Closer Look* by S. Johnston, Bar Leader 21 (Oct. 1993). (legal technicians)

117. *Code Crackdown: Bankruptcy Trustees Use Law to Police (Nonlawyer) Petition Preparers* by H. Samborn, 82 ABAJ 18 (May 1996).

118. *Code of Ethics* by P. Stout, 21 F&F 31 (NALA, Issue 4, 1994).

119. *Colloquium on Nonlawyer Practice before Federal Administrative Agencies,* 37 Administrative Law Review 359 (1985).

120. *Columbus Bar Association Associate Membership for Paralegals,* 9 NPR 11 (NFPA, Feb. 1985).

121. *Comments Invited on Proposed Paralegal Rules,* 20 Montana Lawyer 13 (Jan. 1995).

122. *Commercial Real Estate: The Team Approach* by C. Holler, 19 F&F 46 (NALA, Nov. 1992).

123. *Committee Report* by New York County Lawyers' Ass'n, Committee on Legal Assistants (Oct. 14, 1993).

124. *Community Courts* by W. Statsky, 3 Capital University Law Review 2 (1974).

125. *Companies Can Handle IP [Intellectual Property] Matters Themselves; Much [IP] Work Can Be Delegated to a Paralegal* by L. Whitney, NLJ, C13 (Oct. 17, 1994).

126. *Company Finds a Lifeboat in a Flood of Asbestos Litigation; Paralegals Play Key Role* by B. Feder, Chicago Daily Law Bulletin 1 (July 6, 1993).

127. *Compensation and Benefits Survey* (ALA, 1995).

128. *Competition from Outside the Profession* by D. Trigoboff, 81 ABAJ 18 (Apr. 1995). (accountants, bankers)

129. *Complex Litigation and Paralegals: An Effective Combination* by D. Johnson, 16 NPR 20 (NFPA, Spring, 1992).

130. *Components of Ethics for Legal Support Staff* by J. Anderson, The Docket 14 (NALS, Fall 1995).

131. *Computerized Digesting: A Time-Saver . . .* by L. Hill, 16 NPR 28 (NFPA, Spring, 1992).

132. *Computerized Litigation Support for Paralegals* by D. Kartson (Wiley, 1993).

133. *Computer Programs and Systems Optimize Legal Assistant Productivity* by M. Bjorkman & T. Torgerson, 70 Michigan Bar Journal 1154 (Nov. 1991).

134. *Computers and Charting to Conquer Complex Cases* by D. Kelley, 20 F&F 18 (NALA, Nov. 1993).

135. *Conducting a CLA (Certified Legal Assistant) Litigation Specialty Study Group* by S. McInnis, 16 F&F 18 (NALA, Jan. 1990).

136. *Conducting an Effective Interview: How to Hire the Right Person for the Job* by J. Bassett, 7 LAT 56 (May/June 1990).

137. *Conducting Effective Client Conferences* by K. Reade, 11 LAT 58 (May/June 1994). (interviewing of clients)

138. *Confessions of a Male Paralegal* by M. Russell, 13 NPR 15 (NFPA, Summer 1988).

139. *Conflicts and Confidences: Codes Address Ethics for Paralegals and Impact on Lawyers* by H. Samborn, 82 ABAJ 24 (June 1996).

140. *Conflicts of Interest Rules: What Guidance for Paralegals* by T. Hull, 11 JPE&P 1 (Spring 1995).

141. *Confidentiality and the Corporate Paralegal* by A. Schneeman, 11 LAT 113 (Mar./Apr. 1994).

142. *Congratulations: You've Been Laid Off* by C. Estrin, 10 LAT 128 (July/Aug. 1993).

143. *Conn. Paralegal Wages Near U.S. Average,* 16 The

Connecticut Law Tribune 13 (Feb. 26, 1990).

144. *Constitutional Law in the Paralegal Curriculum* by D. Jarratt, 9 JPE&P 125 (1993).

145. *Constructing a Contract* by S. Morrell, 22 F&F 24 (NALA, Aug. 1995).

146. *Construction Litigation for Paralegals* by D. Zalewski (Wiley, 1993).

147. *Contract Paralegals Saved Boston Edison $1 Million* by D. Horan, Corporate Legal Times 32 (June 1993).

148. *Coping with the World Trade Center Bombing Disaster* by S. Conn, 10 LAT 86 (July/Aug. 1993). (danger to paralegals at work)

149. *Corporate Formation for Legal Assistants* by P. Dris (Wiley, 1995).

150. *The Corporate Paralegal* by J. Bassett, 8 LAT 21 (Nov./Dec. 1990).

151. *The Corporate Paralegal and Litigation* by A. Schneeman, 10 LAT 118 (Mar./Apr. 1993).

152. *Corporate Paralegal's Role in Commercial Financial Transactions* by J. Rebuck, 16 NPR 8 (NFPA, Spring, 1992).

153. *Counsel Behind Bars: Jailhouse Lawyers . . .* by Kroll, 7 Calif. Lawyer 34 (June 1987).

154. *Court-Awarded Paralegal Fees: An Update* by M. Lee, 5 JPE&P 11 (Oct. 1988).

155. *Court Orders Legal Technicians to Stop Practicing Law* by G. Blankenship, The Florida Bar News 9 (May 1, 1993).

156. *Create Your Own Career Path* by G. Malone, 4 LAT 33 (July/Aug. 1987).

157. *Creative Computer Careers* by C. Estrin, 12 LAT 26 (May/June 1995).

158. *Criminal Defendant's Representation by Person Not Licensed to Practice Law as Violation of Right to Counsel* by J. Zitter, 19 ALR 5th 351 (1994).

159. *Crisis of Conscience* by S. Caudron, 12 LAT 73 (Sept./Oct. 1994). (personal conflicts with clients, ethics)

160. *Crossing State Lines with Your Certificate,* by S. Widoff, 11 LAT 38 (Mar./Apr. 1994).

161. *Crumbling Fortress* by J. Podgers, 79 ABAJ 50 (Dec. 1993). (independent paralegals, unauthorized practice of law)

162. *Custody Cases from A to Z* by T. Bullard & B. Walker, 13 LAT 38 (July/Aug. 1996). (family law, paralegal/attorney team)

D

163. *DA-Elect Praises Paralegals: [Los Angeles District Attorney Garcetti] Promises Opportunities and More Work for Them* by M. Stevenson, LADJ, 11 (Nov. 23, 1992).

164. *Dallas Paralegal Pro Bono Legal Clinics* by F. Whiteside, 15 NPR 6 (NFPA, Fall 1990).

165. *Dangerous Office; Liaisons* by L. Lowndes, 11 LAT 64 (Sept./Oct. 1993). (office dating, sexual harassment)

166. *DAs [District Attorneys] Consider Legal Assistants,* 9 NDAA Bulletin 4 (National District Attorneys Ass'n, Mar./Apr. 1990).

167. *Data on Paralegals Reveal Errors in Conventional Wisdom* by G. Crouse, 12 Of Counsel 31 (May 3–17, 1993).

168. *A Day in the Life* by G. Stern, 13 LAT 44 (May/June 1996). (New York)

169. *Dealing Effectively with Divorce Clients* by M. McAuliffe, 3 LAT 39 (Summer 1986).

170. *Dealing with Corporate Service Companies* by C. McKown, 12 LAT 62 (Nov./Dec. 1994).

171. *Dealing with Difficult Clients* by G. Stern, 13 LAT 58 (Mar./Apr. 1996).

172. *Dealing with the Personal Injury Client* by S. Danelson, 10 LAT 148 (Jan./Feb. 1993).

173. *Dealing with Troubled Employees* by P. Perry, 9 LAT 78 (May/June 1992).

174. *Death Row Paralegals* by M. Curriden, 11 LAT 34 (July/Aug. 1994). (criminal Law)

175. *Defining Law Practice (Whether Paralegals Engage in Unauthorized Practice of Law)* by G. Hazard, NLJ, A23 (Apr. 22, 1996).

176. *Defining Mediation and Its Use for Paralegals* by A. Chasen, 9 JPE&P 61 (1993).

177. *Defining the Unauthorized Practice of Law* by A. Morrison, 4 Nova Law Journal 363 (1980).

178. *Defining Paralegal Ethics* by H. Samborn, 12 LAT 64 (Jan./Feb. 1995).

179. *Delaware Corporate Practice for the Paralegal* by C. Nemeth (G. Bisel Co.).

180. *Delegate to Your Legal Assistant* by M. Gaige, 5 Maine Bar Journal 98 (Mar. 1990).

181. *The Delivery of Legal Services by Non-Lawyers* by D. Rhode, 4 Georgetown Journal of Legal Ethics 209 (1990).

182. *Demand for Paralegals Mushrooms* by R. Lee, Texas Lawyer 6 (Jan. 8, 1990).

183. *Deposition Manual for Paralegals,* 2d ed. by C. Greene (Wiley, 1993).

184. *Deposition Summarizing: Pain or Pleasure?* by S. Dickson, 16 NPR 28 (NFPA, Summer, 1992).

185. *Deregulation of the Practice of Law: Panacea or Placebo?* by M. Munro, 42 Hastings Law Journal 203 (1990).

186. *Developing a Paralegal Training Program for Legal Aid*

Western Australia: Conception to Inception by
P. Hosie, 13 Journal of Professional Legal Education
111 (June 1995).

187. *Developing a Strategy for Witness Interviews* by
L. Clark, 10 LAT 65 (Jan./Feb. 1993).

188. *A Dialogue on the Unauthorized Practice of Law* by
Hunter & Klonoff, 25 Villanova Law Review 6
(1979–1980). (licensing)

189. *Did You Say Expansion of Duties?* by S. Cohron, 21
F&F 34 (NALA, Issue 4, 1994).

190. *A Different Road to Success* by K. Beer, 20 NPR 28
(NFPA, Summer 1996). (corporate law)

191. *Directions in Legal Assistant Training and Education* by
L. Jevahirian & K. Kustron, 75 Michigan Bar Journal 38
(Jan. 1996).

192. *Disciplinary Action against Attorney for Aiding or
Assisting Another Person in Unauthorized Practice of
Law,* 41 ALR 4th 361 (1985).

193. *Discover Four "Hot" Buttons That Increase Job Satisfaction* by S. Ruble, 16 NPR 32 (NFPA, Summer, 1992).

194. *Discovery: Interviewing and Investigation* by
Michael A. Pener (Pearson, 1992).

195. *Disqualified: Switching Sides by Legal Assistants in
Litigation* by S. Goldberg, 77 ABAJ 88 (Oct. 1991).
(California, conflict of interest, ethics)

196. *DOJ (Dept. of Justice) Probes Law Firms: Paralegal
Who Copied Tobacco Company Documents Subpoenaed*
by M. Curriden 80 ABAJ 14 (June 1994).

197. *Don't Get Burnt: When the Attorney You Work For Burns
Out* by S. Caudron, 13 LAT 54 (July/Aug. 1996).

198. *Don't Let Your Staff Do Wrong* by D. Walther,
13 Family Advocate 40 (ABA, Spring 1991).

199. *Do Paralegals and Attorneys Really Follow the Same Ethical Code?* by D. Orlik, 10 LAT 138 (Nov./Dec. 1992).

200. *Do We Want Paralegal Judges?* by A. Smith, New York
Law Journal 2 (Apr. 21, 1987).

201. *Do You Need Professional Liability Insurance?* by
P. Perry, 10 LAT 58 (July/Aug. 1993).

202. *Do Your Confidences Go Out the Window When Your
Employees Go Out the Door?* by K. Randall,
42 Hastings Law Journal 1667 (1991).

203. *Drafting of Will or Other Estate Planning Activities as
Illegal Practice of Law,* 22 ALR 3rd 1112 (1968).

204. *A Dream Job* by N. Kording, 14 LAT 48 (Nov./Dec.
1996). (corporate legal departments, employment
benefits)

205. *DUI Handbook for Paralegals* by S. Ruble (Legal Publications). (criminal law)

206. *Duties of the Litigation Paralegal* by S. Bettis,

23 F&F 6 (NALA, Aug. 1996).

207. *Duties and Opportunities as a Corporate Legal Assistant*
by P. Harris, 18 F&F 22 (NALA, Jan. 1992).

E

208. *Earning a Living Independently* by H. Samborn,
12 LAT 42 (Mar./Apr. 1995). (freelance paralegals)

209. *Educating Students about the Transition from School to
Work* by J. Kaiser, 3 Journal of Paralegal Education 13
(Oct. 1986).

210. *The Education and Utilization of Paralegals in the
Practice of Immigration Law* by A. Wernick,
7 JPE&P 23 (1990).

211. *The Education of Legal Paraprofessionals: Myths, Realities and Opportunities* by W. Statsky, 24 Vanderbilt
Law Review 1083 (1971).

212. *Effective and Ethical Use of Legal Assistants* by
T. Fagan, 15 The Colorado Lawyer 659 (1986).

213. *The Effective Use of Legal Assistants* by Bennett,
35 The Practical Lawyer 25 (June 1989).

214. *The Effective Utilization of Legal Assistants* by V. Kunz
(Western Dakota Ass'n of Legal Assistants, 1990).
(North Dakota)

215. *8 Good Reasons to Become a CLA,* 22 F&F 25 (NALA,
Issue 4, 1995).

216. *11 Ways Computers Can Make You More Efficient* by
B. Roper, 9 LAT 38 (May/June 1992).

217. *Embezzler's Paralegal Job Riles N.C. Bar* by C. Frank,
11 Bar Leader 25 (Sept./Oct. 1985).

218. *Emotional Abuse in the Workplace* by C. Estrin,
13 LAT 78 (Mar./Apr. 1996). (career advice)

219. *An Employer's Assessment of Legal Assistant Candidates*
by L. Wertheim & S. Sommers, 6 JPE&P 49 (1989).

220. *The End of the Lawyer Monopoly: What Will It Look
Like?* by S. Elias & R. Warner, 12 NPR 20 (NFPA,
Spring 1988).

221. *Enhancing Computer Proficiency at Your Firm* by
B. Baber, 13 LAT 68 (May/June 1996).

222. *Ensuring Attorney/Paralegal Team Excellence* by
G. Green, 38 The North Carolina State Bar Quarterly
33 (Winter 1991).

223. *Establishing Yourself as a Professional* by J. Bassett,
8 LAT 41 (May/June 1991).

224. *Estate Planning and Administration for Paralegals* by
C. Nemeth (Wiley, 1993).

225. *Ethical Checklist for the Freelance Paralegal* by D. Orlik,
18 NPR 17 (NFPA, Summer 1994).

226. *Ethical Concerns in Hiring Temporary Legal Service
Providers* by D. Templeton, 16 NPR 4 (NFPA,
Summer, 1992).

227. *Ethical Considerations in the Use of Paralegals in Your Office* by C. Gilsinan, 30 The St. Louis Bar Journal 14 (Summer, 1983).

228. *Ethical Considerations of Employing Paralegals in Florida* by J. Lehan, 52 The Florida Bar Journal 14 (Jan. 1979).

229. *Ethical Guidelines for Legal Assistants in Iowa* (Iowa State Bar Ass'n, Mar. 1988).

230. *Ethical Responsibility of Lawyers for Deception by Undercover Investigators . . .* by D. Isbell & L. Salvi, 8 Georgetown Journal of Legal Ethics 791 (1995).

231. *Ethical Standards for Legal Assistants* by V. Voisin, 70 Michigan Bar Journal 1178 (Nov. 1991).

232. *The Ethical Wall: Its Application to Paralegals* by the National Federation of Paralegal Associations (PLI Litigation Course Handbook Series No. H4-5192, 1993).

233. *Ethics and Professional Responsibility for Legal Assistants,* 2d ed. by T. Cannon (Little Brown, 1996).

234. *Ethics and the Contract Paralegal* by D. Orlik, 13 LAT 90 (July/Aug. 1996).

235. *Ethics for the Legal Assistant,* 3d ed. by D. Orlik (Marlin Hill, 1994).

236. *Ethics: Practical Applications for a Law Firm's Support Staff—Part II* by J. Friedlund-Lovely, The Colorado Lawyer 707 (Apr. 1992).

237. *Evidence Handbook for Paralegals* by C. Nemeth (Wiley, 1993).

238. *The Evolving Role of the Paralegal* (New Jersey State Bar Ass'n, 1991).

239. *Examining the Issue of Paralegal Regulation* by R. Sova, 75 Michigan Bar Journal 34 (Jan. 1996).

240. *The Expanding Role of the Legal Assistant in New York State,* New York State Bar Association, Law Office Economics Committee (1982).

241. *Expanding Paralegal Roles* by T. Brewster, 22 F&F 8 (NALA, Issue 4, 1995).

242. *Expanding the Role Your Paralegals Play* by C. Tokumitsu, 8 LAT 33 (Mar./Apr. 1991).

243. *Expectations for Women on the Job Are Different* by C. Estrin, 10 LAT 148 (May/June 1993).

244. *Exempt from Overtime Pay . . . Page & Addison* by D. Ridgway, 8 The West Virginia Lawyer 16 (Feb. 1995). See also 19 NPR 31 (NFPA, Spring 1995).

245. *Expanding Your Role in a Corporate Securities Setting* by S. Koonz, 10 LAT 46 (Nov./Dec. 1992).

F

246. *Face to Face: Client Interviewing Techniques for the Legal Assistant* by R. Bilz, 5 LAT 55 (Jan./Feb. 1988).

247. *Fee-Shifting Statutes and Paralegal Services* by

A. Piazza, 2 Journal of Legal Education 141 (Apr. 1985).

248. *Fee Splitting with Nonlawyers,* 12 Journal of the Legal Profession 139 (1987).

249. *Finally! A Comprehensive Legal Assistant Utilization Survey* by S. Adams, 10 The LAMA Manager 10 (Sept. 1994).

250. *Final Report* by N.Y. State Bar Ass'n, Ad Hoc Committee on Nonlawyer Practice (May 1995).

251. *Final Report,* Task Force on Nonlawyer Practice of Law, Washington State Bar Ass'n (Oct. 29, 1995).

252. *Final Report: Unauthorized Practice of Law Committee,* Nebraska State Bar Ass'n (Apr. 4, 1994).

253. *Finding a Future in Paralegal Management* by L. Roselle, 9 LAT 78 (Jan./Feb. 1992).

254. *Finding a Job in 1995: What's Hot, What's Not* by B. Rosen, 12 LAT 34 (Jan./Feb. 1995).

255. *Finding Her Way through a Cloud of Smoke* by M. Curriden, 12 LAT 60 (Jan./Feb. 1995). (document control, tobacco case)

256. *Finding the Needle in the Medical Records Haystack* by M. Mason, 11 LAT 82 (Sept./Oct. 1993).

257. *Five Tips for a Successful Move to the Bankruptcy Field* by S. Walsh, 10 LAT 118 (Jan./Feb. 1993).

258. *Five Ways to Commit Malpractice with Your Computer* by D. Vangariff, 19 NPR 27 (NFPA, Fall 1994).

259. *Five Ways to Digest a Deposition* by C. Tokumitsu, 9 LAT 84 (Mar./Apr. 1992).

260. *Fixed Salary for Paralegal Indicated Employee Status,* 80 Journal of Taxation 183 (Mar. 1994).

261. *The Florida Certification Program for Legal Assistants* by K. Foos, 21 F&F 19 (NALA, Issue 4, 1994).

262. *Florida Ethics Guide for Legal Assistants* by R. Troutman (Florida Bar, Continuing Legal Education, 1986).

263. *Florida Ethics Guide for Legal Assistants and Attorneys Who Utilize Legal Assistants* by C. Adorno (Florida Bar, Continuing Legal Education, 1992).

264. *Florida's Program: State Certification* by K. Foos, 21 F&F 19 (NALA, Issue 4, 1994).

265. *Florida Report of Legal Technician Committee: Summary* by K. Maxwell, 19 F&F 6 (NALA, Issue 4, 1992).

266. *FLSA (Fair Labor Standards Act): Exempting Paralegals from Overtime Pay* by A. Engel, 74 Washington University Law Quarterly 253 (1996).

267. *Focus on Corporate Practice: Legal Assistants and Legal Opinion Due Diligence* by C. Drozd, 7 JPE&P 63 (1990).

268. *Forms of Operating A Paralegal Business* by D. Baldwin & F. Whiteside, 17 NPR 42 (NFPA, Winter 1992).

269. *For The People: Paralegals in the Criminal Justice System* by S. Ruble, 18 NPR 14 (NFPA, Spring 1992).

270. *Fourteen Ways to Manage Conflict in Your Office* by G. Tolchinsky, 10 LAT 110 (July/Aug. 1993).

271. *The Freelance Legal Assistant* by P. Davidson, 70 Michigan Bar Journal 1184 (Nov. 1991).

272. *The Freelance Legal Assistant* by G. Lucas, 21 F&F 33 (NALA, Aug. 1994).

273. *The Free-Lance Legal Assistant and Ethics* by K. Hill, 2 LAT 15 (Winter 1985).

274. *The Freelance Legal Secretary* by P. Garcia, 38 The Docket 13 (NALS, Sept./Oct. 1989).

275. *The Freelancer's Marketing Plan* by P. Everett, 13 LAT 65 (Mar./Apr. 1996).

276. *From Computer Reluctance to Expertise: a Paralegal's Experience* by J. Frazier, 10 Lawyer's PC 1 (July 1993).

277. *From the Reference Desk to the Jailhouse: Unauthorized Practice of Law and Librarians* by Y. Brown, 13 Legal Reference Services Quarterly 31 (1994).

278. *Functional Division of the American Legal Profession: The Legal Paraprofessional* by C. Selinger, 22 Journal of Legal Education 22 (1969).

279. *Fundamentals of Effective Legal Writing* by M. Faulk, 9 LAT 59 (Nov./Dec. 1991).

280. *Fundamentals of Law Office Management* by P. Everett (West, 1994).

281. *Fundamentals of Paralegalism*, 3d ed. by T. Eimerman (Little Brown, 1992).

282. *The Future of Paralegal Education* by Q. Johnstone, 6 JPE&P 27 (1989).

G

283. *General Guidelines for the Utilization of the Services of Legal Assistants by Attorneys* (State Bar of Texas, 1981, 1993).

284. *Georgia Paralegals Make Move Toward "Inevitable" Regulation* by J. Okrasinski, Fulton County Daily Report 6 (Aug. 30, 1991).

285. *Get Ready for Future Shock* by L. Martin-Bowen, 18 NPR 28 (NFPA, Spring 1994). (computers, law office management)

286. *Get the Recognition You Deserve* by P. Pressley, 13 LAT 62 (Nov./Dec. 1995).

287. *Getting a Handle on Legislative Research* by S. Caudron, 12 LAT 55 (Nov./Dec. 1994).

288. *Getting over the Entry Level Hump: Finding That First Legal Assistant Job with Sole Practitioners* by C. French, 22 F&F 19 (NALA, Aug. 1995).

289. *Getting Primed for the Internet* by G. Miller, 19 NPR 21 (NFPA, Summer 1995).

290. *Getting Started as an Independent Paralegal*, 2d ed. by R. Warner (Nolo Press, 1993), (audio tape).

291. *Going After the Deadbeats: Paralegals in Child Support Enforcement* by M. Scott, 19 NPR 16 (NFPA, Summer 1995).

292. *Going for Paralegal Gold* by J. Murry, 3 LAT 18 (Fall 1985). (Wash. D.C. paralegals)

293. *Going from Good to Great* by D. Bogen, 14 LAT 48 (Sept./Oct. 1996). (performance, career development, assertiveness)

294. *The Golden Age of Paralegals and Risk Managers: Acceptance, Appreciation and Shared Goals* by R. Martin, 9 West Virginia Lawyer 18 (Nov. 1995).

295. *Grass Roots Structure Is Basis for NFPA Power* by C. Aglialoro, 16 NPR 12 (NFPA, Summer, 1992).

296. *Griping vs. Negotiating: Techniques and Tactics for Achieving Your Goals* by S. Wendel, 4 LAT 51 (May/June 1987).

297. *A Guide for Legal Assistants: Roles, Responsibilities, Specializations*, 2d ed. by M. Gowen (PLI, 1991).

298. *Guidelines and Procedures for Obtaining ABA Approval of Legal Assistant Education Programs* by the ABA Standing Committee on Legal Assistants (1992).

299. *Guidelines for Allowing Paralegal Costs*, 16 Fair$hare 9 (June 1996).

300. *Guidelines for Practicing with Paralegals*, Missouri Rules of Professional Conduct (1987, 1992).

301. *Guidelines for the Use of Legal Assistants* (part of Rules of Professional Conduct, 1993). (Indiana)

302. *Guidelines for the Use of Legal Assistant Services* by the State Bar of New Mexico (1980). See also New Mexico Supreme Court, *Rules Governing Legal Assistant Services*, Rules 20-101 to 20-114 (1986); Judicial Pamphlet 16.

303. *Guidelines for the Utilization by Lawyers of the Services of Legal Assistants*, South Carolina Bar, Committee on Economics and Law Office Management (1980).

304. *Guidelines for the Utilization by Lawyers of the Service of Legal Assistants*, New York State Bar Ass'n (1976).

305. *Guidelines for the Utilization of Legal Assistants*, Colorado Bar Ass'n Legal Assistant Committee. See also 18 The Colorado Lawyer 2097 (Nov. 1989).

306. *Guidelines for the Utilization of Legal Assistants*, Supreme Court of the State of South Dakota, Rule 92-5 (1992).

307. *Guidelines for the Utilization of Legal Assistants in Kansas*, Kansas Bar Ass'n Committee on Legal Assistants (1988).

308. *Guidelines for the Utilization of Non-Lawyers in Rendering Legal Services*, North Carolina State Bar (1986, revised 1992); see also 39 North Carolina State Bar Quarterly 3 (Summer, 1992).

309. *Guidelines for Use of Attorney Assistants As Approved By ISBA Assembly* (1977). (Illinois State Bar Ass'n)

310. *Guidelines for Use of Legal Assistants,* Rhode Island Supreme Court, Provisional Order No. 18 (1993, revised 1990); 31 Rhode Island Bar Journal 19 (Apr. 1983).

311. *Guidelines for Use of Legal Assistant Services* (State Bar of New Mexico, 1980).

312. *Guidelines for Utilization of Legal Assistants Services,* 57 Michigan Bar Journal 334 (1978).

H

313. *Handbook for Utilization of Legal Assistants* (Nebraska Ass'n of Legal Assistants, 1992).

314. *Handbook on Paralegal Utilization* (California Alliance of Paralegal Assn's, 1992).

315. *Handling the Auto Accident Case: The Paralegal in Action* by J. Mulvin, 9 LAT 93 (Jan./Feb. 1992).

316. *Hard Choices: Dealing with Ethical Dilemmas on the Job* by C. Milano, 9 LAT 72 (Mar./Apr. 1992).

317. *Healthcare Law as a Legal Specialty,* 22 F&F 19 (NALA, May 1995).

318. *Helping Legal Assistants to Help Themselves* by P. Saucier, 9 LM 28 (ALA, Sept./Oct. 1990). (billable hours)

319. *Help! . . . Can My Office Use a Legal Assistant?* by J. Work, 57 Texas Bar Journal 42 (Jan. 1994).

320. *Help! Service Companies Come to the Rescue of Drowning Legal Assistants* by C. McKown, 4 LAT 24 (Mar./Apr. 1987).

321. *Hereinafter Go Hence . . . And Write More Clearly* by B. Rosen, 13 LAT 34 (Jan./Feb. 1996).

322. *Hide & Seek for Assets: The Life of a Probate Paralegal* by H. Walker, 5 LAT 38 (Mar./Apr. 1988).

323. *Hiring Legal Staff: Determining Cost and Value* by T. Brooks & W. Hackett (ABA, 1990).

324. *A History of the American Bar* by C. Warren (Little Brown, 1966).

325. *Hot Job of the 90s? 1995 Salary Survey Results* by J. Barge & G. Gladwell, 13 LAT 24 (Jan./Feb. 1996).

326. *Hot Tips for Interviewing Witnesses* by J. Bassett, 9 LAT 23 (Sept./Oct. 1991).

327. *Hours on the Rise* by R. Morrow, 12 LAT 44 (Nov./Dec. 1994). (billable hours, salaries)

328. *How Attorneys Can Utilize Legal Assistants at Trial* by L. Clark, 11 LAT 53 (Jan./Feb. 1994).

329. *How Firms Successfully Hire Staffers: . . . Junior Associate, Paralegal and Secretary* by K. Yusko, NLJ B11 (May 1, 1995).

330. *How Legal Assistants Can Aid You with Real Estate Foreclosures* by C. Burns, 63 Journal of the Kansas Bar Ass'n 18 (May 1994).

331. *How to Assign a Task Clearly* by R. Feferman, 13 Legal Economics 62 (ABA, Apr. 1987).

332. *How to Avoid the Top 10 Mistakes Paralegals Make on the Job* by C. Tokumitsu, 9 LAT 26 (Nov./Dec. 1991).

333. *How to Communicate Effectively with Attorneys* by L. Badertscher, 9 LAT 134 (Mar./Apr. 1992).

334. *How to Evaluate the Qualifications of Legal Assistants: What's Wrong with This Ad?* by T. Clarke, 30 Arizona Attorney 28 (May 1994).

335. *How to Find a Few Good Expert Witnesses* by K. Shimpock-Vieweg, 10 LAT 80 (May/June 1993).

336. *How to Get Out of the Typing* by M. Policzer, 11 LAT 70 (Jan./Feb. 1994).

337. *How to Handle Hostile Work Environment Cases* by A. Dewitt, 11 LAT 46 (July/Aug. 1994). (sexual harassment)

338. *How to Keep the Client Informed* by N. Nelson, 14 LM 14 (no. 2) (ALA, Mar./Apr. 1995).

339. *How to Land Your First Paralegal Job* by A. Wagner (Estrin 1992).

340. *How to Maximize Profits, Lower Your Stress Level,* 20 F&F 16 (NALA, Feb. 1994). (Santa Clara, California)

341. *How to Negotiate a Good Raise* by I. Hill, 8 LAT 53 (May/June 1991).

342. *How to Open a Solo Practitioner's Law Office* by J. Watkins, 10 LAT 102 (July/Aug. 1993).

343. *How to Serve a Civil Summons* by L. Clark, 12 LAT 48 (Sept./Oct. 1994).

344. *How to Set Up a Mock Trial* by R. Bergman, 10 LAT 102 (Sept./Oct. 1992).

345. *How to Survive in a Law Firm* by D. Graves, J. Levin, & N. Pulsifer (Wiley, 1993).

346. *How to Use Legal Assistants to Enforce Commercial Secured Claims* by J. Verellen, 33 Practical Lawyer 9 (Dec. 1987).

347. *How to Wage Peace* by T. McGowan, 2 LAT 22 (Winter 1985). (friction with secretaries)

348. *How to Write an Interoffice Legal Memorandum* by W. Putman, LAT 120 (Nov./Dec. 1993).

I

349. *The Ideal Freelance Paralegal Service* by P. Everett & A. Penny, 12 LAT 76 (Mar./Apr. 1995).

350. *If You're Smart, Why Aren't You in Law School?* by L. Hardwick, 4 LAT 27 (May/June 1987).

351. *Illinois State Bar Association Position Paper on Use of Attorney Assistants in Real Estate Transactions* (May 16, 1984).

352. *The Immigration Paralegal* by J. Mason, 8 LAT 76 (Nov./Dec. 1990).

353. *Improving Access to Justice: The Future of Paralegal Professionals* (Australia Institute of Criminology, 1991).

354. *In California, It's Better to Stay Put Than to Switch: A Paralegal's Past Forces New Boss to Drop Cases* by B. Motamedi, 7 LAT 37 (May/June 1990).

355. *"Independent Contractors" May Really be "Employees"* by M. Bryant & P. Vaccaro, 14 LM 14 (no. 1) (ALA, Jan./Feb. 1995). (freelance paralegals)

356. *Independent Paralegal Career Tracks* by C. Estrin, 12 LAT 28 (Jan./Feb. 1995).

357. *Independent Paralegals* by G. Gladwell, 15 LAT 62 (May/June 1995).

358. *Independent Paralegals: Friends in Need or Foes at the Gate?* by J. Middlemiss, 17 Canadian Lawyer 26 (Feb. 1993).

359. *The Independent Paralegal's Handbook: How to Provide Legal Services without Going to Jail,* 3d ed. by R. Warner (Nolo Press, 1994).

360. *Independent Paralegals: Working for the Public* by C. Elias-Jermany, 9 LAT 102 (Mar./Apr. 1992).

361. *The Independents Movement* by K. Withem, 11 LAT 40 (Nov./Dec. 1993).

362. *The Inherent Power of the Courts to Regulate the Practice of Law* by T. Albert, 32 Buffalo Law Review 525 (1983).

363. *Inmate Involvement in Prison Legal Services* by W. Statsky (ABA Resource Center on Correctional Law and Legal Services, 1974).

364. *In re Petition to Amend Code of Professional Responsibility,* 327 So. 2d 15 (Florida 1975).

365. *In re Unauthorized Practice of Law Rules Proposed by the South Carolina Bar,* 422 So. 2d 123 (1992).

366. *INS Concludes "Visa Consultants" May Not Represent Persons in Immigration Hearings* by S. Cohn, 10 LAT 18 (Jan./Feb. 1993).

367. *In Search of the True Freelance Paralegal* by P. Everett, 12 LAT 22 (Nov./Dec. 1994).

368. *The Inside Story: Working with Prominent Attorneys* by P. Helou, 10 LAT 36 (Mar./Apr. 1993). (litigation, client contact)

369. *Is Law School Worth It?* by C. Milano, 10 LAT 68 (Jan./Feb. 1993).

370. *The Institute of Legal Executives* by G. Schrader, 4 JPE&P 19 (Oct. 1987). (England)

371. *Intellectual Property Guide for Paralegals* by V. Atkinson (Wiley, 1994).

372. *Interviewing: The Employer Perspective* by C. Kauffman, 7 The LAMA Manager 11 (LAMA, Winter 1991).

373. *Interviewing to Rave Reviews in the '90s* by C. Estrin, 11 LAT 80 (Mar./Apr. 1994). (job interviews, employment)

374. *In the Matter of the Adoption of a New Rule Relating to the Utilization of Legal Assistants,* South Dakota Supreme Court Rule 92-5 (1992).

375. *In the Spirit of Public Spirit: A Blueprint for the Rekindling of Lawyer Professionalism,* American Bar Association (1986); 112 Federal Rules Decisions 243 (1986).

376. *ISBA (Illinois State Bar Association Assembly) Approves Rules Governing Use of Legal Assistants* by D. Gill, Chicago Daily Law Bulletin 1 (June 27, 1988).

377. *Issues in Paralegalism: Education, Certification, Licensing, Unauthorized Practice* by P. Haskell, 15 Georgia Law Review 631 (1981).

378. *Is Technology Taking Away Paralegal Jobs?* by J. Barge, 13 LAT 40 (May/June 1996).

379. *Is There Life after the Law Firm?* by C. Estrin, 8 LAT 65 (May/June 1991).

380. *Is There True Diversity in the Workplace?* by L. Gray, 19 NPR 10 (NFPA, Spring 1995). (Asian, black, male paralegals, minorities)

381. *It's a Keeper: Recruiting, Motivating and Keeping Effective Support Staff* by S. O'Brien, 15 LM 37 (ALA, Sept./Oct. 1996).

382. *It's 10 P.M.: Do You Know Where Your Life Went?* by B. Rosen, 13 LAT 40 (Nov./Dec. 1995). (overtime)

383. *It's Time to Open the Legal Profession* by J. Scalone, 49 Washington State Bar News 41 (Mar. 1995).

J

384. *Jailhouse Lawyers: Nuisance or Necessity?* by A. Love, The Philadelphia Lawyer, 31 (Sept. 1993).

385. *J. D.s Accepted, Paralegals Preferred* by C. Rogovin, 13 LAT 26 (July/Aug. 1996). (attorney/paralegal competition for jobs)

386. *Job Growth for Paralegals Seen Better Than for Lawyers* by E. Adams, New York Law Journal 1 (July 22, 1994).

387. *Job Hoppers: There's Hope* by M. Harmon, 13 LAT 46 (Jan./Feb. 1996). (résumé, switching jobs, job hunt)

388. *The Job Search: Strategies for Marketing Your Skills* by D. Mortensen, 9 LAT 128 (May/June 1992).

389. *Judging Credentials: Nonlawyer Judges and the Politics of Professionalism* by D. Provine (Univ. of Chicago Press, 1986).

390. *The Juggling Act* by S. Gladwell, 14 LAT 24 (Sept./Oct. 1996). (workload, working for more than one attorney)

K

391. *Keeping Focused: Total Time Management* by J. Moore, 12 LAT 56 (July/Aug. 1995). (paralegal effectiveness)

392. *Kentucky Supreme Court Rule 3.700* (1979). (proper utilization of legal assistants)

L

393. *LAFLA (Legal Aid Foundation of Los Angeles) Paralegal Arrested While Giving Out Fliers* by S. Parker, LADJ 1 (Feb. 25, 1991).

394. *LAMA [Legal Assistant Management Association] Conference Highlights: Wave of the Future* by P. Kerley, 9 LAT 117 (Mar./Apr. 1992).

395. *LAMA [Legal Assistant Management Association] Study Offers Insight into Maximizing The Use of Legal Assistants,* 96 LOMAR 1 (Feb. 1996).

396. *Law Clerks and the Unauthorized Practice of Law,* 46 Chicago-Kent Law Review 214 (1969).

397. *Law Firm Diversification and Affiliation Between Lawyers and Nonlawyer Professionals* by D. Pitofsky, 3 Georgetown Journal of Legal Ethics 885 (1990).

398. *Law Firms in the 21st Century* by M. Curriden, 13 LAT 38 (Sept./Oct. 1995). (computers)

399. *Law Office Management: Leveraging with Legal Assistants* by E. Clark, 25 Arizona Attorney 36 (Oct. 1989).

400. *The Law of the Jungle* by C. Estrin, 14 LAT 68 (Sept./Oct. 1996). (office politics, career development).

401. *Law School: Legal Education in America from the 1850s to the 1980s* by R. Stevens (Univ. of North Carolina Press, 1983)

402. *The Lawyer and the Legal Assistant,* The Legal Assistants (Joint) Committee of the Oregon State Bar (1988).

403. *The Lawyer and the Legal Assistant* by Oregon State Bar (1988).

404. *The Lawyer from Antiquity to Modern Times* by R. Pound (West, 1953).

405. *Lawyers Aiding Nonlawyers in the Unlawful Practice of Law,* Oregon State Bar Bulletin, 37 (Feb./Mar. 1990).

406. *Lawyer's Professional Responsibility Obligations Concerning Paralegals* by Connecticut Bar Ass'n Inter-Committee Group to Study the Role of Paralegals, 59 Connecticut Bar Journal 425 (Dec. 1985).

407. *Lawyers to Prosecute Paralegals* by K. Makin, 13 LAT 22 (May/June 1996). (Ontario, Canada)

408. *Lawyer vs. Paralegal: Who Does What?,* 140 New Jersey Law Journal 998 (June 12, 1995).

409. *Lawyers Who Skip Law School* by M. Curriden, 81 ABAJ 28 (Feb. 1995).

410. *The Lay Advocate* by Sparer, 43 University of Detroit Law Journal 493 (1966).

411. *Layman's Assistance to Party in Divorce Proceeding as Unauthorized Practice of Law,* 12 ALR 4th 656 (1982).

412. *Lay Practice before Administrative Tribunals: Clarification Needed* by Pollack, 66 Michigan Bar Journal 675 (1987).

413. *Learning about Learning: 20 Years of Paralegal Education* by H. Samborn, 11 LAT 88 (Jan./Feb. 1994).

414. *Learning Styles and Paralegal Studies* by B. Nagle & P. Lechman-Woznick, 11 JPE&P 67 (Spring 1995).

415. *Leaving the Typewriter Behind* by D. Bebb, 12 LAT 56 (Sept./Oct. 1994). (legal secretary)

416. *Legal Advice Revisited* by D. Orlik, 13 LAT 82 (Nov./Dec. 1995).

417. *Legal & Paralegal Services on Your Home-Based PC* by K. Hussey (Windcrest-McGraw-Hill, 1994).

418. *Legal Assistant as Law Librarian* by J. Lewek, 17 F&F 28 (NALA, Mar. 1991).

419. *The Legal Assistant as Librarian* by N. Wendt, 6 LAT 19 (Sept./Oct. 1988).

420. *Legal Assistant Community Awaits Results of ABA Nonlawyer Hearings* by S. Cohn, 11 LAT 19 (Sept./Oct. 1993).

421. *The Legal Assistant Division* by A. Dunkin, 57 Texas Bar Journal 39 (Jan. 1994).

422. *Legal Assistant Division Created,* 22 F&F 10 (NALA, Issue 4, 1995). (New Mexico)

423. *Legal Assistant Education* by D. Dye, 38 Journal of the Missouri Bar 111 (Mar. 1982).

424. *The Legal Assistant: Guidelines for the Future* by George Shoemaker, 45 Texas Bar Journal 326 (1982).

425. *The Legal Assistant in a Small Law Firm* by D. Holliday, 63 Journal of the Kansas Bar Ass'n 7 (June/July 1994).

426. *A Legal Assistant Is Elected Probate Judge* by T. Howard, 5 LAT 32, (Mar./Apr. 1988).

427. *The Legal Assistant Letter Book* by S. von Matt Stoddard (Estrin, Prentice-Hall, 1994).

428. *"Legal Assistant" Losing Clout? Increasing Trend to Become "Paralegal"* by S. Cohn, 13 LAT 14 (Sept./Oct. 1995). (job titles)

429. *The Legal Assistant Manager as Mentor* by D. Thompson, 12 LAT 68 (July/Aug. 1995).

430. *Legal Assistant Pleads Guilty in Client Thefts* by J. Pittman, LADJ 3 (Apr. 15, 1992).

431. *Legal Assistant Professional, Educational and Career-Related Organizations* by G. Schrader, 8 JPE&P 63 (1991).

432. *Legal Assistant Professionalism in the Decade of Confusion* by C. Embry, 20 F&F 30 (NALA, Nov. 1993).

433. *A Legal Assistant Program Evaluation Design* by J. Snell & D. Green, 4 JPE&P 53 (Oct. 1987).

434. *Legal Assistant Programs: A Guide to Effective Program Implementation and Maintenance* (ABA, 1978).

435. *The Legal Assistant Role at the High-Tech, Multi-Media Trial* by D. Jarchow, 19 NPR 8 (NFPA, Fall 1994).

436. *Legal Assistants: A Growing Role in the Practice of Law*

in Alabama by K. Rasmussen, 52 The Alabama Lawyer 214 (July 1991).

437. *Legal Assistants: Answers to Common Questions* by S. Keaton-Hardin, 57 Texas Bar Journal 35 (Jan. 1994).

438. *Legal Assistants as Law Office Managers* by Kreipe, 59 The Journal of the Kansas Bar Ass'n 19 (July 1990).

439. *Legal Assistants at 21: Self Assured and Professional* by R. Martin, 22 F&F 26 (NALA, Issue 4, 1995).

440. *Legal Assistants Can Increase Your Profits* by P. Ulrich, 69 ABAJ 1634 (Nov. 1983).

441. *Legal Assistants Can Join St. Louis Bar* by F. Silas, 10 Bar Leader 26 (Jan./Feb. 1985).

442. *Legal Assistants Division Proposes Voluntary Certification Program,* 49 Texas Bar Journal 886 (1986).

443. *Legal Assistant's Guide to Alternative Dispute Resolution* by J. Quan (Clark Boardman/Callaghan, 1994).

444. *The Legal Assistant's Handbook,* 2d ed. by T. Brunner et al. (Bureau of National Affairs, 1988). See also 19 California Western Law Review 226 (Fall 1982).

445. *Legal Assistants: Has The Time Arrived for State-by-State Licensing? Yes: Enhance Professionalism* by H. Samborn; *No: Another Roadblock* by T. Rudy, 78 ABAJ 42 (Dec. 1992).

446. *Legal Assistants Increase Productivity* by M. Douglass, 45 The Alabama Lawyer 334 (Nov. 1984).

447. *Legal Assistants in Northern Michigan* by C. Andary, 68 Michigan Bar Journal 398 (May 1989).

448. *Legal Assistants in Probate Administration* by M. Mulligan & S. Grabert, 30 The St. Louis Bar Journal 28 (Summer, 1983).

449. *Legal Assistants Listed on Letterheads?* by B. Kent, 60 Journal of the Kansas Bar Association 15 (Feb./Mar. 1991).

450. *Legal Assistants—Look at What They Can Do for You!* by C. Given, 9 West Virginia Lawyer 22 (Mar. 1996).

451. *Legal Assistants: Measuring Profitability* by Green, 14 Legal Economics 26 (ABA, Mar. 1988).

452. *Legal Assistants Report Salary Increases Despite Sluggish Economy,* Wisconsin Lawyer, 9 (July 1993).

453. *Legal Assistants: Saving Time and Resources for Lawyers and Clients,* 57 Texas Bar Journal 28 (Jan. 1994).

454. *Legal Assistants Share the Spotlight at Historic Minneapolis Firm* by T. Howard, 4 LAT 16 (Mar./Apr. 1987).

455. *Legal Assistants Supervising Lawyers* by T. Howard, 4 LAT 28 (July/Aug. 1987).

456. *Legal Assistants: Their Place in Your Law Practice* by C. Johnson, 51 Oklahoma Bar Journal 2827 (Nov. 29, 1980).

457. *Legal Assistant's Time to Be Included in Award of Rea-sonable Attorney Fees in Florida,* 13 F&F 24 (NALA, Aug. 1986).

458. *Legal Assistants Will Increase Your Income* by H. Draper, 62 Michigan Bar Journal 1083 (Dec. 1983).

459. *Legal Assistants Will Increase Your Income* by P. Ulrich, 69 ABAJ 1634 (Nov. 1983).

460. *Legal Assistant Utilization in Connecticut Law Firms* by S. Endleman, 55 Connecticut Bar Journal 324 (Aug. 1981).

461. *The Legal Assistant: Your Profit Center* by A. Callum, 69 Michigan Bar Journal 558 (1990).

462. *Legal Ethics for Paralegals and the Law Office* by L. Morrison & G. DeCiani (West, 1995).

463. *Legal Investigation & Informal Discovery* by K. Andrews, 7 LAT 36 (July/Aug. 1990).

464. *The Legal Nurse Consultant: The Newest Member of the Litigation Team* by J. McHugh, 18 NPR 18 (NFPA, Summer 1994).

465. *Legal Nurse Consultants* by B. Faherty, 41 Medical Trial Technique Quarterly 228 (1994).

466. *Legal Paraprofessionals and Unauthorized Practice,* 8 Harvard Civil Rights–Civil Liberties Law Review 104 (1973).

467. *Legal Profession Faces Rising Tide of Nonlawyer Practice,* by J. Podgers, 79 ABAJ 51 (Dec. 1993); also in 30 Arizona Attorney 24 (Mar. 1994).

468. *Legal Secretaries and the Conflict of Interest Rule* by I. Schein, 14 Advocates' Quarterly 81 (July 1992). (Canada)

469. *The Legal Secretary: an Anachronism of the 21st Century?* by L. Iannelli, 61 Florida Bar Journal 23 (Mar. 1987).

470. *Legal Services by Non-Lawyers,* 20 F&F 11 (NALA, Issue 4, 1993).

471. *Legal Technicians* by S. Johnston, Bar Leader 19 (Sept./Oct. 1993).

472. *Legal Technicians Are Not the Answer: More Lawyers Is* by P. O'Brien, LADJ 6 (Dec. 22, 1992).

473. *Legal Techs Face Regulation* by R. Resnick, NLJ 3 (June 22, 1992).

474. *Let the Consumer Choose: Does Government Protect or Harm the Consumers by Allowing Them to Choose a Non-Lawyer?* by J. Stubenvoll, 52 Oregon State Bar Bulletin 21 (June 1992).

475. *Letterhead Communication of Paralegal Position,* 36 LOEM 407 (Fall 1995).

476. *The Leveraged Legal Assistant* by L. Werthheim, 5 LAT 22 (Nov./Dec. 1987). (profitability)

477. *Leveraging for the 1990s* by C. Kretchmer, 21 F&F 28 (NALA, Aug. 1994).

478. *Leveraging Paralegals,* 96 Partner's Report 13 (Jan. 1996). See also 95 Partner's Report 13 (July 1995).

479. *Leveraging with Legal Assistants,* A. Greene, editor (ABA, 1993); see also 39 Mississippi Lawyer 23 (Apr./May 1993) and 35 LOEM 105 (Spring 1994).

480. *Life after Layoff* by J. Bassett, 10 LAT 45 (Nov./Dec. 1992).

481. *Life as an Inmate Legal Assistant,* 13 LAT 86 (Jan./Feb. 1996); and 13 LAT 86 (Mar./Apr. 1996).

482. *Life in a Small Firm* by C. Estrin, 13 LAT 70 (Sept./Oct. 1995).

483. *Life Outside the Law Firm: Non-Traditional Careers for Paralegals* by K. Treffinger (Delmar, 1995).

484. *Limited Licensing: Historical Perspectives* (NFPA, 1989).

485. *Limited Practice Officer* by J. Johnson & D. Ridgway, NPR 18 (NFPA, Winter 1991). (Washington State)

486. *The Limited Practice Rule: Its Track Record after Four Years* by Fuller, 40 Washington State Bar News 15 (Oct. 1986).

487. *Litigation Case Management for Legal Assistants* (PLI, 1993).

488. *Litigation Guide for Paralegals: Research and Drafting,* 2d ed. by C. Osborne (Wiley, 1994).

489. *The Litigation Legal Assistant—from Case Inception to Pretrial* by K. Gooze, 75 Michigan Bar Journal 50 (Jan. 1996).

490. *Litigation Legal Assistants—Saving Time and Money for the Litigator!* by L. Sifuentes, 4 Nevada Lawyer 24 (June 1996).

491. *Litigation Nightmares* by C. Steinberg, 11 LAT 74 (Sept./Oct. 1993).

492. *Litigation Organization and Management for Paralegals* by L. Randall (Wiley, 1993).

493. *Litigation Paralegal* by P. Signey (Wiley, 1989, 1993).

494. *The Litigation Paralegal,* 2d ed. by J. McCord (West, 1992).

495. *Litigation Support Imperatives for the '90s* by J. Brazier, 3 Practical Litigator 11 (Nov. 1992).

496. *Long-Overlooked Paralegals Need a Sexier Self-Image* by C. Estrin, LADJ 7 (Sept. 12, 1991).

497. *Looking at Alternative Services: The Lawyer/Non-Lawyer Wall Continues to Erode* by R. Resnick, NLJ, 1 (June 10, 1991).

498. *Looking for a Job Is a Job* by K. Allen, 15 NPR 22 (NFPA, Spring 1991).

499. *Looking Forward: A More Professional Future* by A. Bailus, 10 LAT 86 (Nov./Dec. 1992).

500. *Los Angeles Pro Bono Paralegals Expand Community Crisis Services* by D. Childs, 16 NPR 26 (NFPA, Spring, 1992).

501. *The Louisiana Certification Program for Legal Assistants* by S. Smith, 21 F&F 21 (NALA, Issue 4, 1994).

502. *Lower Paralegal Rates, Real Profits Fuel Law Firm Leverage in the 1990s* by C. Collins, 14 Of Counsel 1 (Aug. 7, 1995).

M

503. *Make the Most of Legal Assistants in Tax Practice* by F. Berall, 2 Practical Tax Lawyer 59 (Winter 1988).

504. *Making a Paralegal a Starting Player on a Litigation Trial Team* by B. Swearingen, 19 F&F 32 (NALA, Feb. 1993).

505. *Making a Placement Agency Work for You* by D. Rothfield, LAT 88 (Sept./Oct. 1992).

506. *Making Sure Paralegals Meet Their Billable Goals,* 95 LOMAR 1 (June 1995).

507. *Making the Jump to Attorney at Law* by S. Caudron, 12 LAT 69 (Jan./Feb. 1995).

508. *Management of Legal Assistants: The Ethical Obligations of the Attorney,* 26 Arizona Attorney 27 (Jan. 1989).

509. *The Manager's Manual* (LAMA, 1991).

510. *The Manager's Perspective* by C. Estrin, 13 LAT 42 (July/Aug. 1996).

511. *Managing Associates and Legal Assistants* by M. Magness, 40 Practical Lawyer 25 (June 1994).

512. *Managing Paralegals as a Human Resource* by M. George, 4 LAT 26 (Jan./Feb. 1987).

513. *Managing the Difficult Client* by N. Nelson, 20 F&F 20 (NALA, Feb. 1994).

514. *Manual for Legal Assistants,* 2d ed. by NALA (West, 1992).

515. *Manual for the Lawyer's Assistant,* 2d ed. by NALS (West, 1988).

516. *Measuring Progress: How Far Have We Come?* by C. Bruno, 10 LAT 38 (Nov./Dec. 1992). (paralegal history)

517. *Mediation: An Effective Tool in Law Firm Management* by T. Burnett, 14 LM 51 (ALA, Mar./Apr. 1995).

518. *Medical Malpractice Guide for Paralegals* by S. Danelson (Wiley, 1993).

519. *Meet Needs with Nonlawyers: It Is Time to Accept Lay Practitioners—and Regulate Them* by D. Rhode, 82 ABAJ 104 (Jan. 1996).

520. *Michigan Firm Views Its Paralegals as "Full Members" of the Team* by T. Sarb, 2 Law Firm Partnership & Benefits Report 5 (Aug. 1996).

521. *Michigan Guidelines for the Utilization of Legal Assistant Services,* State Bar Board of Commissioners (1993); 72 Michigan Bar Journal 563 (June, 1993).

522. *Missouri Guidelines for Practicing with Paralegals* (Missouri Bar Ass'n, 1987).

523. *Model Guidelines for the Utilization of Legal Assistant Services* (ABA, Standing Committee on Legal Assistants, Mar. 1, 1991). Reprinted in 8 JPE&P 1 (1991).

524. *Model Standards and Guidelines for Utilization of Legal Assistants Annotated,* 17 F&F 48 (NALA, Fall 1990).

525. *Modern Investigation for the Paralegal* by T. Rimer (Westpointe Publishing Co.).

526. *Modern Legal Ethics* by C. Wolfram (West, 1986).

527. *More Firms Use Paralegal Managers* by L. Jevahirian, 13 NLJ 23 (Feb. 25, 1991).

528. *Motivating Paralegals* by P. Pressley, 11 LAT 42 (Jan./Feb. 1994).

529. *The Myths and Realities of Freelancing* by P. Everett & A. Penny, 11 LAT 26 (July/Aug. 1994).

N

530. *NALA and Arizona Affiliates File Brief on Work Product,* 17 F&F 18 (NALA, Jan. 1991). (attorney-client privilege, paralegal work product)

531. *NALA Model Standards and Guidelines* by K. Sanders-West, 2 LAT 9 (Summer 1985); see also 20 F&F 35 (NALA, Issue 4, 1993).

532. *NALA's Statement to ABA Commission on Non-Lawyers,* 22 F&F 4 (NALA, Career Chronicle 1994).

533. *NALS Probate Handbook for the Lawyer's Assistant* (West, 1993).

534. *The National Federation of Paralegal Associations [NFPA] Is Currently Considering the Endorsement of Model Legislation That Would Permit Legal Assistants to Be Licensed in Certain Practice Areas and to Perform Duties Usually Reserved for Attorneys,* 9 Of Counsel 15 (Oct. 1990).

535. *National Groups: What Do They Do? Paralegals Often Ambivalent about Two Different Organizations. [National Association of Legal Assistants, National Federation of Paralegal Associations]* by M. Stevens, LADJ 13 (Sept. 28, 1992).

536. *National Groups Worth the Cost?: Whether Local Paralegal Groups Need Affiliation with National Organizations* by M. Stevenson, LADJ 12 (Aug. 24, 1992).

537. *National Reporter on Legal Ethics and Professional Responsibility* (1982–   ).

538. *National Survey of Compensation for Legal Assistant Managers & Legal Assistants,* 6th ed. (LAMA, 1994).

539. *National Survey Provides Insight into Specialty Areas* by L. Hangley, 16 NPR 16 (NFPA, Summer 1992).

540. *National Regulation of Nonlawyer Practice* by P. Young, 57 Texas Bar Journal 28 (Jan. 1994).

541. *National Salary Survey and Overview* by G. Gladwell, 13 LAT 48 (Sept./Oct. 1995).

542. *Nature of Legal Services or Law-Related Services Which May Be Performed for Others by Disbarred or Suspended Attorney,* 87 ALR 3rd 279 (1978).

543. *Nebraska State Bar Fights "Bright Line Rule"* by L. Mares, 13 LAT 14 (May/June 1996).

544. *Negotiated Salaries: The Undeclared War?* by C. Estrin, 9 LAT 136 (May/June 1992).

545. *The Nevada Legal Needs Study* by Downey Research Associates, State Bar of Nevada Study Committee (May 1994).

546. *New Career Opportunities in the Paralegal Profession* by R. Berkey (Arco, 1983).

547. *New Health Professionals: The Physician Assistant and Advanced Nurse Practitioner in Texas,* 22 South Texas Law Journal 132 (1982).

548. *New Mexico Rules Governing the Practice of Law, Rule 20-102(A)* (1989). (defining legal assistant)

549. *New Surveys Look at Paralegal Pay in Light of DOL [Department of Labor] Exemption Ruling,* 94 LOMAR 1 (July 1994).

550. *New York Negligence: A Practical Guide for Paralegals* (Moran Publishing Co., 19_).

551. *NFPA Report Reveals More African-Americans Entering Paralegal Profession* by M. Dowdy, 9 LAT 25 (May/June 1992).

552. *1992 Legal Assistant Today Salary Survey Results?* by C. Milano, 9 LAT 60 (May/June 1992).

553. *1993 Legal Assistant Today Salary Survey Results* by C. Milano, 10 LAT 48 (May/June 1993).

554. *1994 Survey and Related Materials on the Unauthorized Practice of Law/Nonlawyer Practice* (ABA, Aug. 1996).

555. *1995 National Utilization and Compensation Survey Report,* 22 F&F 18 (NALA, Issue 4, 1995).

556. *No, I'm Not Your Attorney* by P. Sevin, 13 LAT 50 (July/Aug. 1996). (male paralegals)

557. *Nonlawyer Activities in Law-Related Situations* (ABA Commission on Nonlawyer Practice, 1995).

558. *Nonlawyer Activity in Law-Related Situations,* 2 Texas Paralegal Journal 25 (Nov 1995). (ABA commission)

559. *Non-Lawyer Debate Escalating in Light of Unmet Legal Needs* by B. Kueuk, 211 The Daily Record (Maryland Lawyer) 269 (Nov. 18, 1995).

560. *Non-Lawyer Legal Technicians* by D. Nuffer, 7 Utah Bar Journal 6 (Oct. 1994).

561. *The Nonlawyer Partner: Moderate Proposals Deserve a Chance* by S. Gilbert & L. Lempert, 2 Georgetown Journal of Legal Ethics 383 (1988).

562. *Nonlawyer Practice: An Expanding Role* by D. Tenenbaum, 67 Wisconsin Lawyer 12 (Nov. 1994).

563. *Nonlawyer Practice before Federal Administrative Agencies Should Be Discouraged* by Heiserman, 37 Administrative Law Review 375 (1985).

564. *Nonlawyer Practice before Federal Administrative Agencies Should be Encouraged* by Rose, 37 Administrative Law Review 363 (1985).

565. *Nonlawyer Practice before the Immigration Agencies* by Holmes, 37 Administrative Law Review 417 (1985).

566. *Non-Lawyer Practice Rules: No Turning Back* by J. Simmons, 30 Arizona Attorney, 19 (Mar. 1994).

567. *Nonlawyer Practice: Will GP's [General Practitioner's] Survive the Onslaught?* by A. Garwin, 10 The Compleat Lawyer 31 (Fall 1993).

568. *The Nonlawyer Provider of Bankruptcy Legal Services: Angel or Vulture?* by A. Cristol, 2 ABI Law Review 353 (1993).

569. *Nonlawyers Are Not the Answer* by T. Curtin, 80 ABAJ 128 (Apr. 1994).

570. *Nonlawyers as Legal Practitioners* by C. Jones, 17 Journal of the Legal Profession 287 (1992). (ethics, nonattorney partners, unauthorized practice of law)

571. *Nonlawyers in the Business of Law* by T. Andrews, 40 Hastings Law Journal 577 (1989).

572. *Nonlawyers Should Not Practice Law* by R. Ostertag, 82 ABAJ 116 (May 1996).

573. *Notice of Public Hearings: Texas Voluntary Certification of Legal Assistants*, 48 Texas Bar Journal 1358 (1985).

574. *Novel Ways Paralegals Are Using Computers* by C. Milano, 8 LAT 22 (Mar./Apr. 1991).

O

575. *Odd Man Out* by S. Goldberg, 11 LAT 58 (Jan./Feb. 1994). (male paralegals)

576. *Offering Low-Cost Services, Paralegal Firms Gain Foothold Despite Opposition from Lawyers* by G. Kang, Chicago Daily Law Bulletin 1 (July 15, 1992).

577. *Office Politics* by A. Stern, 7 LAT 61 (May/June 1990).

578. *Office Politics: In-House "Kissing"* by C. Estrin, 9 LAT 106 (Nov./Dec. 1991).

579. *Older Paralegals Entering Work Force at Rapid Pace* by S. Cohn, 9 LAT 26 (May/June 1992).

580. *$100,000 a Year for Paralegals?* by P. Marcotte, 73 ABAJ 19 (Oct. 1987).

581. *Onward and Upward for Legal Assistants; Trends in Legal Employment: A View of the Region's Legal Job Market)* by S. Danelson, New Jersey Law Journal S6 (Sept. 12, 1994).

582. *On Your Own: . . . Freelance Paralegal* by R. Cook, 18 NPR 31 (NFPA, Summer 1994).

583. *Opportunities in Paralegal Careers* by A. Fins (National Textbook Co., 1979).

584. *Oregon State Bar Certifies Legal Assistants*, 17 LOEM 118 (Sept. 1976).

585. *The Organization and Management of a Study Group for the CLA Certifying Examination* by E. Stanton, 18 F&F 6 (NALA, Jan. 1992).

586. *The Other Side of the Mountain* by B. Baber, 14 LAT 32 (Nov./Dec. 1996). (debtors, creditors, bankruptcy paralegals)

587. *Out of the Closet, into the Firm* by S. Caudron, 12 LAT 64 (Sept./Oct. 1994). (homosexual paralegals)

588. *Outsourcing and Other Trends in Law Firm Libraries* by K. Shimpock-Vieweg, 13 LAT 64 (Sept./Oct. 1995).

589. *Outsourcing Deposition Summaries . . .* by H. Kaskel, LM 78 (ALA, Mar./Apr. 1994).

590. *Overcoming the Fear of Legal Writing* by S. McInnis, 17 F&F 38 (NALA, Jan. 1991).

591. *Overcrowding Plagues Field* by G. Sea, Houston Chronicle, 1L (Oct. 2, 1988).

592. *Overtime Pay* by S. Caudron, 13 LAT 50 (Jan./Feb. 1996).

P

593. *Parajudges and the Administration of Justice* by Clark, 24 Vanderbilt Law Review 1167 (1971).

594. *Paralegal Abuse: Is Your Boss Asking Too Much?* 12 LAT 59 (Sept./Oct. 1994). (ethics)

595. *Paralegal Advocacy before Administrative Agencies* by W. Statsky, 4 University of Toledo Law University Review 439 (1973).

596. *Paralegal Advocates for Low Income Elderly*, 20 NPR 26 (NFPA, Winter 1995). (pro bono)

597. *(Para) Legal Aid: What Sort of Assignments Can You Delegate to Nonlawyer Assistants?* by A. Garwin, 79 ABAJ 101 (July 1993).

598. *Paralegal Alleges Attorney Failed to Protect Interests* by L. Blau, LADJ, 2 (Apr. 4, 1995). (California)

599. *The Paralegal: An Effective Part of the Legal Service Team* by J. Harwell, 23 Tennessee Bar Journal 37 (July/Aug. 1987).

600. *The Paralegal: A New Career* by R. Deming (Elsevier/Nelson Books, 1980).

601. *Paralegal: An Insider's Guide to the Fastest-Growing Occupation in the 1990s* by B. Bernardo (Peterson's Guides, 1993).

602. *The Paralegal as Patron* by K. Carlson, 84 Law Library Journal 567 (1992).

603. *Paralegal Billing*, 95 Partner's Report 8 (Nov. 1995).

604. *Paralegal Billing Trends* by J. Mello, 11 LAT 126 (Sept./Oct. 1993).

605. *The Paralegal Book of Letters* (Wiley, 1994).

606. *The Paralegal Boom,* by K. Liebler, 12 Pennsylvania Lawyer 12 (Apr. 1990).

607. *Paralegal Burnout: Challenging Work Wanted* by Frank, 70 ABAJ 30 (Dec. 1984).

608. *Paralegal Career Advancement* by J. Reinard, 6 JPE&P 1 (1989).

609. *The Paralegal Career Guide,* 2d ed. by C. Estrin (Wiley, 1996).

610. *Paralegal Careers* by W. Fry (Enslow Publishers, 1986).

611. *Paralegal Certification: State Bar to Petition Supreme Court for Adoption of Rules,* 20 Montana Lawyer 7 (Oct. 1994).

612. *Paralegal Compensation and Benefits Survey,* 20 NPR 30 (NFPA, Fall 1995).

613. *Paralegal Degree Program Offers Prisoners Hope,* New York Times 40 (Dec. 1, 1985).

614. *Paralegal Discovery: Procedures and Forms,* 2d ed. by Pat Medina (Wiley, 1994).

615. *Paralegal Drafting Guide* by D. McClellan (Wiley, 1993).

616. *Paralegal Education Programs* by D. Petropulos, 11 LAT 47 (Jan./Feb. 1994).

617. *Paralegal Education: Standards or Standardization?* by D. Petropulos, 12 LAT 24 (Jan./Feb. 1995).

618. *Paralegal Education: The Educator's Perspective* by R. Marquardt, 40 The Mississippi Lawyer 13 (Nov./Dec. 1993).

619. *Paralegal Employment Opportunities in State Government* by M. Baker & T. Eimermann, 6 JPE&P 9 (1989).

620. *Paralegal Entrepreneurs* by C. Estrin, 12 LAT 34 (July/Aug. 1995). (legal vendors, service companies, freelance paralegal)

621. *The Paralegal Factor* by B. Palermo, 9 California Lawyer 47 (June 1989). (paralegal billing)

622. *Paralegal Fights to Use Secret Tobacco Papers, (Merrell Williams Sues Tobacco Industry for Fraud* by A. Jewell, Chicago Daily Law Bulletin 1 (Jan. 3, 1994).

623. *Paralegal Forms Disk Library* (Wiley, 1994).

624. *Paralegal Growth Paralleled 1980s Law-Firm Expansion* by M. Goldberg, 26 Trial 97 (May 1990).

625. *Paralegal Guide to Automobile Accident Cases* by J. Murvin (Wiley, 1995).

626. *Paralegal Guide to Intellectual Property* by V. Atkinson (Wiley, 1994).

627. *The Paralegal in Army Legal Practice* by R. Black, Army Lawyer, 70 (Nov. 1990).

628. *The Paralegal in Practice* by A. Clinton, 23 The Arkansas Lawyer 22 (Jan. 1989).

629. *Paralegalism: A Still Evolving Profession* by W. Peters, 40 Mississippi Lawyer 18 (Nov./Dec. 1993).

630. *Paralegalism: The United Profession,* by J. Farinacci, 8 JPE&P 148 (1991).

631. *The Paralegal Job-Hunting Handbook* (National Capital Area Paralegal Ass'n, 1982, 1985).

632. *The Paralegal Job Market: Going Strong!* by W. Webb, 13 LAT 58 (July/Aug. 1996).

633. *Paralegal Job Search Guides* by T. Coyle, 9 LAT 106 (May/June 1992). (book reviews)

634. *Paralegal/Librarian Needed* by A. Yelin, 13 LAT 62 (Sept./Oct. 1995).

635. *Paralegal Litigation Forms and Procedures,* 2d ed. by M. Fawcett (Wiley, 1995).

636. *Paralegal Malpractice: New Profession, New Responsibility* by M. Moon, 18 Trial 40 (Jan. 1982); *see also* 6 NPR 1.

637. *Paralegal Management Handbook* by M. Brophy (Wiley, 1993).

638. *Paralegal Managers: Surviving the '90s* by P. Pressley, 10 LAT 34 (May/June 1993).

639. *Paralegal Opportunities in Environmental Law* by A. Parisi, 8 LAT 83 (Jan./Feb. 1991).

640. *Paralegal Overtime* by R. Cassidy, 57 Texas Bar Journal 32 (Jan. 1994). Reprinted in 20 F&F 46 (NALA, Feb. 1994).

641. *Paralegal Overtime?* by J. Browning, 21 F&F 26 (NALA, Issue 4, 1994).

642. *Paralegal Parallax: Are Legal Technicians Parasites? Or Are Lawyers Just Paranoid?* by D. Olin, 10 California Lawyer 20 (Nov. 1990).

643. *Paralegal Personnel for Attorneys General's Offices* (National Ass'n of Attorneys General, May 1976).

644. *Paralegal Placement Executive Speaks Out* by J. Hosea, 14 NPR 14 (NFPA, Spring 1990).

645. *Paralegal Power* by K. Dunn, 11 Compleat Lawyer 24 (ABA, Winter 1994). (delegation, divorce, family law)

646. *Paralegal Practice and Procedure,* 3d ed. by D. Larbalestrier (Prentice-Hall, 1994).

647. *The Paralegal Profession* by N. Shayne (Oceana, 1977).

648. *The Paralegal Profession* by Brown, 19 Howard Law Journal 117 (1976).

649. *Paralegal Profitability Enhancement* by L. Leraul, 27 LOEM 448 (1987).

650. *Paralegal Programs: An Educational Alternative for Law Librarians* by C. Harris, 77 Law Library Journal 171 (1984–85).

651. *Paralegal Prowess: What Is It? Who Has It?* by L. Martin-Bowen, 19 NPR 8 (NFPA, Summer 1995).

652. *Paralegal Public Interest Law Clinic* by M. Taylor & T. Farrell, 11 JPE&P 29 (Spring 1995).

653. *Paralegal Representation before the Social Security*

Administration by S. Humphreys, 9 JPE&P 24 (1993).

654. *Paralegal Representation of Persons before State Administrative Agencies* by T. Aaron, 10 NPR 4 (NFPA, Oct. 1985).

655. *Paralegal's Acceptance and Utilization Increasing in Indy's Legal Community* by D. Brandt, The Indiana Lawyer 1 (No. 5, June 20–July 3, 1990).

656. *Paralegals and Administrative Assistants for Prosecutors* by J. Stein & B. Hoff (National District Attorneys Ass'n, 1974).

657. *Paralegals and Lawyers—A Team Approach* by K. Dulin, 32 Trial 62 (Jan. 1996).

658. *Paralegals and Sublegals: Aids to the Legal Profession* by Holme, 46 Denver Law Journal 392 (1969).

659. *Paralegals and the Imputed Disqualification Rule* by M. Schairer, 7 JPE&P 1 (1990).

660. *Paralegals Are an Integral Part of the Team* by S. Kligerman, New Jersey Lawyer, 1651 (Oct. 15, 1993).

661. *Paralegals: A Resource for Defenders and Correctional Services* by J. Stein (U.S. Gov't Printing Office, No. 027-000-00399-1) (Dec. 1976).

662. *Paralegals Average $14,000 to Start, Bring Profits to Firm* by Reskin, 70 ABAJ 52 (Dec. 1984).

663. *Paralegals Can Be More Profitable Than Associates* by A. Jones, 16 The Montana Lawyer 7 (Dec. 1990).

664. *Paralegals, Clients, Fees: Informing the Client and Billing the Client for Paralegal Work* by J. Honohan, 51 The Iowa Lawyer 23 (Aug. 1991).

665. *The Paralegal's Desk Reference* by S. Albrecht (Arco 1993).

666. *Paralegal Seen Taking Jobs from Associates* by B. Winter, 68 ABAJ 527 (May 1982).

667. *Paralegal Sentenced for Theft* by M. Harris, LADJ 4 (May 18, 1994).

668. *Paralegals: Entitled to Overtime Rates* by C. Quasebarth, 5 West Virginia Lawyer 21 (Feb. 1992).

669. *Paralegal Services and Awards of Attorneys' Fees* by Stahl & Smith, Arizona Bar Journal 21 (Oct./Nov. 1984).

670. *Paralegal's-Eye View of Law Firm Follies,* LADJ 6 (Oct. 21, 1994).

671. *Paralegals: Getting Everything in Order* by E. Coari, 39 Louisiana Bar Journal 265 (Nov. 1991).

672. *Paralegal's Guide to Dallas/Fort Worth Law-Related Careers* (Scrivener Publications, 1989).

673. *Paralegal's Guide to Manhattan Law Firms* by G. Pirozzi (West Heath Press, 1988).

674. *The Paralegal's Guide to U.S. Government Jobs: How to Land a Job in 70 Law-Related Careers,* 7th ed. (Federal Reports, 1996).

675. *Paralegal's Guide to Veterans' Administration Advocacy* by K. Snyder, 23 Clearinghouse Review 236 (July 1989).

676. *Paralegals: Has Pandora's Box Been Opened?: Survey of Trends in Law Office Management* by L. Thompson, 46 Washington State Bar News 27 (Sept. 1992).

677. *Paralegals Have a Definition Problem; They Worry That Public Confuses Them with Legal Technicians* by M. Stevenson, LADJ 13 (Sept. 21, 1992).

678. *Paralegals' Hidden Assets: Recovery of Paralegal Fees* by B. Lilly, 22 The Colorado Lawyer 715 (Apr. 1993).

679. *Paralegals in Australia* by J. Johnson, 15 NPR 8 (NFPA, Spring 1991).

680. *Paralegals in Law School . . .* by R. Margolis, 22 Student Lawyer 14 (Oct. 1993).

681. *Paralegals in Northern Michigan—Should Their Future Be Part of Yours?* by D. McDonald, 74 Michigan Bar Journal 416 (May 1995).

682. *Paralegals in Rural Africa,* A. Dieng, ed. (International Commission of Jurists, Switzerland, Feb. 1990).

683. *Paralegals in Texas Get Certified by the Bar* by S. Johnston, 19 Bar Leader 7 (Nov./Dec. 1994).

684. *Paralegals in the Bush* by Conn & Hippler, 3 UCLA-Alaska Law Review 85 (1973).

685. *Paralegals in the Corporate Setting* by J. Campbell, 30 The St. Louis Bar Journal 22 (Summer 1983).

686. *Paralegals in The 1990s: Fewer Jobs, More Specialists, Innovative Training* by L. Smith, 11 Of Counsel 9 (Apr. 1992).

687. *Paralegals: Invaluable Lawyer Support* by K. Berning, 1 Nevada Lawyer 20 (Mar. 1993).

688. *Paralegals Make "Partner"* by D. Bogen, 13 LAT 50 (May/June 1996). (career ladders, perks, salary)

689. *Paralegals—Nine; Attorneys—One* by R. Morrow, 13 LAT 34 (Mar./Apr. 1996). (small law firms)

690. *Paralegals Online,* 13 LAT 84 (Mar./Apr. 1996).

691. *Paralegals: Out of the Shadows and Into the Light* by D. Vitucci, Report 22 (Cincinnati Bar Ass'n, Feb. 1991).

692. *Paralegals, Out-of-Work Lawyers, and High-Rolling Consultants* by L. Smith, 14 Of Counsel 2 (Oct. 16, 1995).

693. *Paralegals: Powerful Performers in a Changing Legal World* by J. Bourgoin, 24 Colorado Lawyer 1193 (Sept. 1995).

694. *Paralegals Serve as Hollywood's Police* by D. Ricker, LADJ, S13 (May 30, 1995).

695. *A Paralegal Speaks on Professional Issues* by J. Hughbanks, 2 Probate and Property 33 (May/June 1988).

696. *Paralegals: Powerful Performers in a Changing Legal World* by L. Bourgoin & S. Davis, 24 Colorado Lawyer 2193 (Sept. 1995).

697. *Paralegals: Progress and Prospects of a Satellite Occupation* by Q. Johnstone (Greenwood Press, 1985).

698. *A Paralegal's Role in Insurance Defense Litigation* by S. Bullock, 17 F&F 60 (NALA, May 1990).

699. *The Paralegal's Role in Mergers and Acquisitions* by A. Schneerman, 12 LAT 65 (Nov./Dec. 1994).

700. *Paralegals: Should Legal Technicians Be Allowed to Practice Independently?* by D. Chalfie, 77 ABAJ 40 (Mar. 1991).

701. *Paralegals Struggle for Right to Practice* by M. Hall, LADJ 1 (July 31, 1992). (Nevada)

702. *Paralegal Survey Reveals Rising Salaries,* 27 Arizona Attorney 9 (Nov. 1990).

703. *Paralegals Taking a Bite Out of Associates' Work* by H. Rosen, 134 New Jersey Law Journal 195 (May 17, 1993).

704. *Paralegals: The Good, the Bad and the Ugly* by G. Mund, 2 American Bankruptcy Institute Law Review 337 (1994).

705. *Paralegals: The Making of a Profession* by C. Gilsinan & S. Pope, 30 The St. Louis Bar Journal 6 (Summer 1983).

706. *Paralegals: The National and State Outlook* by R. Beard, 18 Arkansas Lawyer 189 (Oct. 1984).

707. *Paralegal Trial Handbook,* 2d ed. by B. Hudson (Wiley, 1995).

708. *Paralegals: Untapped Potential for Performance and Profit* by P. Potter, 40 North Carolina State Bar Quarterly 16 (Summer 1993).

709. *Paralegals: Valuable Members of the Legal Team* by J. Baker, 23 The Colorado Lawyer 2295 (Oct. 1994).

710. *Paralegal Value May Decline as Associates Get More Profitable,* 95 Compensation & Benefits for Law Offices 6 (Apr. 1995).

711. *Paralegals vs. Attorneys: The Competition Escalates* by H. Samborn, 12 LAT 36, 39 (Sept./Oct. 1994). (associates)

712. *Paralegal Who Copied Tobacco Company Documents Subpoenaed* by M. Curriden, 80 ABAJ 14 (June 1994).

713. *Paralegal: Wills, Trusts and Estates* by P. Carter (D&E Publishers, 1982). (Florida)

714. *Paralegals Win Greater Latitude in Switching Firms; Ethics Panel Approves Use of "Wall" to Protect Client Confidences* by S. Riss, New Jersey Law Journal 5 (Aug. 10, 1992).

715. *Paralegal Wins Appeal in Suit against Judge* by M. Stapleton, Chicago Daily Law Bulletin 3 (June 2, 1995).

716. *Professional Responsibility for Nonlawyers,* Professional Responsibility Committee of the Philadelphia Bar Association (1989).

717. *Paraprofessionals' Compensation must Be Based on Prevailing Local Market Rates,* 7 Inside Litigation 23 (Sept. 1993).

718. *Paraprofessionals: Expanding the Legal Service Delivery Team* by W. Statsky, 24 Journal of Legal Education 397 (1972).

719. *Pay Parity for Paralegals of Both Sexes, Study Finds* by A. Grene, Chicago Daily Law Bulletin 3 (Feb. 24, 1994). (salary survey)

720. *The Performance Review* by S. Caudron, 11 LAT 50 (Nov./Dec. 1993). (evaluation)

721. *The Permanent Temporary* by S. Tetrault, 11 LAT 56 (July/Aug. 1994).

722. *Perry Mason They're Not: But "Legal Technicians" Are Cutting into the Establishment's Market* by M. Shao, Business Week, 83 (Nov. 20, 1989). (independent paralegals)

723. *Personal-Bankruptcy Bar Attacks Low-Cost Services by Paralegals* by J. Woo, Wall Street Journal 36 (Jan. 12, 1994).

724. *Personal Injury Paralegal,* 2d ed. by S. Atwood (Wiley, 1994).

725. *Personal Problems on the Job: The Ultimate Conflict of Interest* by C. Estrin, 10 LAT 83 (Mar./Apr. 1993).

726. *A Piece of Your Business: Competition from Nonlawyer "Technicians"—Cause for Alarm?* by G. Yuda, 15 The Pennsylvania Lawyer 6 (May 1993).

727. *Plain Language for the Legal Assistant: Preparing Enclosure Letters* by S. McIntyre, 75 Michigan Bar Journal 73 (Jan. 1996).

728. *Policing the Profession* by D. Orlik, 13 LAT 90 (Mar./Apr. 1996). (ethics)

729. *Policing the Professional Monopoly: A Constitutional and Empirical Analysis of Unauthorized Practice Prohibitions* by D. Rhode, 34 Stanford Law Review 1 (1981).

730. *Position Paper on Use of Attorney Assistants in Real Estate Transactions* (Illinois State Bar Ass'n, May 1984).

731. *Post-Law School Job (of Attorney) May Be as Paralegal . . . Where Work Tough to Find* by H. Samborn, 81 ABAJ 14 (Mar. 1995).

732. *Poverty Law for the '90s: Business Is Booming for Storefront Paralegals on the Poor Side of Town* by T. Sisco, 15 California Lawyer 31 (June 1995).

733. *The Power of the Influential Paralegal* by M. Haines, New Jersey Law Journal 19 (June 29, 1994).

734. *Power to the Paralegal* by R. Morrow, 11 LAT 56 (Mar./Apr. 1994). (associates, leveraging)

735. *Practical Ethics for Paralegals and the Law Office* by

L. Morrison (West, 1995).

736. *Practical Law Office Management* by B. Roper (West, 1995).

737. *Practice before Administrative Agencies and the Unauthorized Practice of Law* by V. Baur, 15 Federal Bar Journal 103 (1955).

738. *Practice by Non-Lawyers before the National Labor Relations Board* by Gall, 15 Federal Bar Journal 222 (1955).

739. *Practice by Non-Lawyers before the United States Patent Office* by Bailey, 15 Federal Bar Journal 211 (1955).

740. *Practicing Law in Germany* by R. Loomis, 11 WSPA Findings and Conclusions 6 (Washington State Paralegal Ass'n, Jan. 1995). (paralegals in Germany)

741. *Practicing Law without a License* by R. Bilz, 20 F&F 34 (NALA, Nov. 1993).

742. *Practicing Law without a License: Is It Time for the Bar to Drop Its Opposition to Independent Paralegals? No: Keeping Standards High Protects the Public* by F. Apicella; *Yes: Monopolizing the Market Serves No One* by W. Fry; 81 ABAJ 36 (Jan. 1995).

743. *Practicing with Paralegals* (Missouri Bar Legal Assistants Committee, 1989, 1992).

744. *Practicing with Paralegals: Answers to Frequently Asked Questions and the Missouri Bar Guidelines,* Missouri Bar Committee on Legal Assistants (1989).

745. *Preparing Your Client for Mediation* by L. Massey, 10 LAT 115 (Mar./Apr. 1993).

746. *Preserving a Client's Confidences* by L. Emert, 19 F&F 38 (NALA, Feb. 1993).

747. *Preventive Law and the Paralegal* by L. Brown, 24 Vanderbilt Law Review 1181 (1971).

748. *Prisoner Access to Justice and Paralegals* by B. Kempinen, 14 New England Journal on Criminology & Civil Confinement 67 (Winter 1988).

749. *Pro Bono Is for Legal Assistants, Too* by R. Yegge & W. Moore, 15 NPR 8 (NFPA, Fall 1990). Reprinted in 17 F&F 12 (NALA, July 1990).

750. *Pro Bono Update: Legal Assistants Making Great Strides* by J. Holmgren, 21 F&F 44 (NALA, Issue 4, 1994).

751. *Professional Ethics in Texas* by P. Powell-Lane, 16 NPR 18 (NFPA, Summer 1992).

752. *Professionalism in Perspective: Alternative Approaches to Nonlawyer Practice* by D. Rhode, 22 New York University Review of Law and Social Change 701 (1996).

753. *The Professionalization of the Legal Assistant* by D. Green, 7 JPE&P 35 (1990).

754. *Professional Negligence, Paralegals and Modern Legal Ethics between the Bookends* by H. Cohen, 11 The Journal of the Legal Profession 143 (1986).

755. *The Professional Paralegal Job Search* by C. French (Little Brown, 1995).

756. *Professional Responsibility and the Family Law Legal Assistant* by S. Andress, 12 LAT 30 (Nov./Dec. 1994). (ethics)

757. *Professional Responsibility for Nonlawyers,* Philadelphia Bar Ass'n, Professional Responsibility Committee (1989).

758. *Professional Teamwork between Attorney and Secretary* by Ralston, 14 Legal Economics 25 (ABA, Sept. 1988).

759. *Profitability Formulas and Paralegal/Associate Comparisons* by J. Tate, 31 LOEM 462 (Winter 1991). See also 15 NPR 18 (NFPA, Spring 1991).

760. *Programming for the Classroom* by J. Johnson, 11 JPE&P 79 (Spring 1995).

761. *Progressive Paralegal Planning* by C. Acree, 29 The Colorado Lawyer 725 (1991).

762. *Prohibition on NonLawyer Practice* by the Ass'n of the Bar of the City of New York, Committee on Professional Responsibility (Mar. 1995).

763. *Proper Hiring & Use of a Paralegal Professional: An Attorney's Perspective* by H. Davidson, 40 Mississippi Lawyer 9 (Nov./Dec. 1993).

764. *The Proper Scope of Nonlawyer Representation in State Administrative Proceedings* by G. Stevens, 43 Vanderbilt Law Review 245 (1990).

765. *Proposal to Regulate Montana's Paralegals Needs More Discussion,* by J. Balyeat, 20 Montana Lawyer 3 (Nov. 1994).

766. *Proposed Guidelines for the Utilization of Legal Assistants,* 15 The Colorado Lawyer 183 (1986).

767. *Proposed Rules Would Govern State's Paralegal Profession* by C. Bronson, 19 Montana Lawyer 7 (June 1994).

768. *Propriety and Effect of Corporation's Appearance Pro Se through Agent Who Is Not Attorney* by J. Zitter, 8 ALR 5th 653 (1992).

769. *Prostitution v. Bates-Stamping: Law Firms Fail to Make Use of Paralegals* by K. Spring, 20 Law Practice Management 58 (ABA, Sept. 1994).

770. *Providing Inmate Advocacy on a Shoestring: Former Prison Paralegals to Dispense Advice to Current Prisoners* by J. Kanige, New Jersey Law Journal 5 (Oct. 12, 1992).

771. *Proving Up Legal Assistant Time as Part of Attorneys' Fees* by L. Thomas, 57 Texas Bar Journal 38 (Jan. 1994).

Q

772. *Qualities of an Effective Litigation Paralegal* by L. Clark, 10 LAT 123 (Mar./Apr. 1993).

773. *A Quick Look at Paralegal Master's Programs* by S. Widoff, 13 LAT 89 (Jan./Feb. 1996).

774. *A Quick Look at . . . the CLA Exam* by R. Thompson, 12 LAT 32 (Jan./Feb. 1995). (Certified Legal Assistant)

R

775. *Reaching for New Heights in Excellence: NFPA's 20th Anniversary Celebration* by D. Healy, 19 NPR 12 (NFPA, Fall 1994).

776. *Real Estate Foreclosure: Paralegal Practice and Procedure* by C. Nemeth (Wiley, 1994).

777. *The Real Estate Paralegal* by D. Johnson, 8 LAT 73 (Mar./Apr. 1991).

778. *Recommendations to Attorneys for the Use of Legal Assistants* (Illinois State Bar Ass'n, 1988).

779. *Recoverability of Legal Assistant Time in Attorney Fee Applications* by S. Koran, 9 JPE&P 1 (1993).

780. *Recovery of Legal Assistant Fees in Litigation* by C. Smith, 30 Trial 59 (Sept. 1994).

781. *Recruiting, Interviewing, and Hiring Legal Assistants* by A. Dodds, 57 Texas Bar Journal 40 (Jan. 1994).

782. *Re-Engineering Your Career* by C. Estrin, 13 LAT 76 (Jan./Feb. 1996).

783. *Refighting the First Amendment* by M. Curriden, 12 LAT 46 (July/Aug. 1995). (civil rights, constitutional law, paralegal functions)

784. *Registering Legal Assistants* by J. Noll & K. Buss, 5 Bar Bulletin, Issue 7 (Seattle–King County Bar Ass'n, Mar. 1987).

785. *Regulation of Paralegals: An Upcoming Issue* by D. Latorraca, 22 Colorado Lawyer 493 (Mar. 1993).

786. *Removing the Veil of Mystery from the CLA Exam* (Certified Legal Assistant) by Dunn, 18 F&F 38 (NALA, July 1991).

787. *Reporting Ethical Violations* by D. Orlik, LAT 39 (July/Aug. 1992).

788. *Report of Legal Assistants Section Survey Results* by K. Neher et al., 75 Michigan Bar Journal 30 (Jan. 1996).

789. *Report of the Connecticut Bar Association Special Inter-Committee Group to Study the Role of Paralegals* (Dec. 11, 1985).

790. *Report of the Legal Technician Study Committee,* The Florida Bar (1992).

791. *Report of the Special Committee on Non-Lawyer Practice,* The Florida Bar (1994).

792. *Report of the Specialized Legal Assistants Study Committee,* Minnesota Supreme Court (Feb. 18, 1994).

793. *Report of the State Bar of California Commission on Legal Technicians* (State Bar of California, July 1990).

794. *Report of the Task Force on Paralegals* (Ontario Ministry of the Attorney General, 1990). (Canada)

795. *Representing the Injured Worker* by S. Danelson, 9 LAT 103 (Jan./Feb. 1992).

796. *Representation of Clients before Administrative Agencies: Authorized or Unauthorized Practice of Law?* 15 Valparaiso University Law Review 567 (1981).

797. *Requirements for Paralegals? No: Experience Is What Counts* by M. Provost, 11 LAT 25 (May/June 1995).

798. *Researching Professional Ethics for Lawyers* by R. Leiter, 10 LAT 127 (Mar./Apr. 1993).

799. *Responsibilities of Bankruptcy Legal Assistants,* 20 F&F 10 (NALA, Nov. 1993).

800. *Résumés for Paralegals and Other People with Legal Training* by R. Berkey (Arco, 1984).

801. *Retaining a Paralegal,* 80 ABAJ 70 (Jan. 1994). (Alaska, computers)

802. *The Retention of Limitations on the Out-of-Court Practice of Law by Independent Paralegals* by C. Selinger, 9 Georgetown Journal of Legal Ethics 879 (1996).

803. *Revitalization of the Legal Profession through Paralegalism,* 30 Baylor Law Review 841 (1978).

804. *The Rhode Island Paralegal Association Hosts Conference,* 33 Island Bar Journal 43 (June/July 1985).

805. *Rhode Island Supreme Court Provisional Order No. 18* (1983). (covering legal assistants)

806. *Right of Juvenile Court Defendant to Be Represented during Court Proceedings by Parent,* 11 ALR 4th 719 (1982).

807. *A Risky Stand-in? Paralegals at Realty Closings* by F. Silas, 69 ABAJ 1812 (Dec. 1983).

808. *The RMLAA (Rocky Mountain Legal Assistants Association) Employment and Salary Survey: A 1990 Paralegal Profile* by B. Lilly, 19 The Colorado Lawyer 2213 (Nov. 1990).

809. *The Role of a Government Legal Assistant in Eminent Domain* by E. Cousineau, 21 F&F 8 (NALA, Aug. 1994).

810. *The Role of a Legal Assistant in Real Estate Practice* by E. Mahoney, 70 Michigan Bar Journal 1160 (Nov. 1991).

811. *The Role of a Paralegal in Estate Administration* by M. Levine, The Compleat Lawyer 27 (ABA, Winter 1994). (delegation, divorce, family law)

812. *The Role of Paralegals in Inmate Litigation* by F. Devine, 5 JPE&P 1 (Oct. 1988).

813. *The Role of Paralegals in Real Estate Transactions,* 68 Illinois Bar Journal 391 (Feb. 1980).

814. *The Role of the Legal Assistant in Family Law Matters* by B. Miller & S. Babboni-Stripp, 75 Michigan Bar Journal 54 (Jan. 1996).

815. *The Role of the Legal Assistant (Paralegal) in Iowa* by the Iowa State Bar Ass'n (1979).

816. *The Role of the Paralegal in the Civil Commitment Process* by R. Lockwood, 10 Capital University Law Review 721 (Summer 1981).

817. *A Roundtable Discussion with Legal Assistant Managers* by M. Curriden, 11 LAT 61 (Mar./Apr. 1994).

818. *Rules of Professional Conduct, Use of Legal Assistants* (Indiana Bar Ass'n, 1993).

819. *Running with Hares and Chasing with the Hounds: The Emerging Dilemma of Paralegal Mobility* by R. Marquardt, 2 Journal of Legal Education 57 (Oct. 1984).

S

820. *Salaried Personnel: Are They Really Exempt from Minimum Wage and Overtime Requirements?* by P. Stewart, 9 LM 11 (ALA, Jan./Feb. 1990).

821. *The Salary Wars: Paralegals Could Come Out the Winners* by R. McCroskey, 4 LAT 37 (May/June 1987).

822. *Sale of Books or Forms . . . as Unauthorized Practice of Law,* 71 ALR 3rd 1000 (1976).

823. *School Trains Jail-House Lawyers* by D. Horine, The LADJ (Mar. 26, 1991).

824. *Searching for a Job? Here Are Some Helpful Hints* by M. Vaneecke, 13 F&F 20 (NALA, Apr. 1987).

825. *Seating a Jury: The Role of the Legal Assistant* by P. Robtoy, 23 F&F 10 (NALA, Aug. 1996).

826. *The Secretarial Advantage, Law Students, Paralegal Tasks, Flexible Hours Are Part of New Approach* by B. Morgenstern, 81 ABAJ 75 (Jan. 1995).

827. *Secretaries, Legal Assistants Assume New Roles as Automation Forces Changes* by A. Rossheim, 10 Of Counsel 4 (July 1991).

828. *"Senior Paralegal" Is More Than Just a Title* by B. Grajski, 125 New Jersey Law Journal 14 (Apr. 19, 1990).

829. *Senior Paralegals Counsel Newcomers: Computer Litigation Support Can Help* by D. Bernhard, 9 LM 48 (ALA, Mar./Apr. 1990).

830. *Separate Fee Awards for Paralegals: Jenkins v. Missouri, Revisited* by T. Wright, 44 Rhode Island Bar Journal 23 (May 1996).

831. *Settle or Take It to Court: The Paralegal's Role in Preparing a Case for Settlement* by S. Danelson, 11 LAT 90 (May/June 1994).

832. *Sex and the Legal Assistant* by D. Orlik, 12 LAT 30 (Mar./Apr. 1995). (ethics)

833. *Sexual Harassment* by D. Orlik, 9 LAT 126 (Jan./Feb. 1992). (ethics)

834. *Sexual Harassment: Curbing the Law Profession's Dirty Secret* by P. Perry, LAT 60 (Sept./Oct. 1992).

835. *Shooting Ourselves in the Foot* by W. Weston, 10 The Compleat Lawyer 38 (Fall 1993). (legal technicians)

836. *Should Law Societies "Prosecute the Hell" out of Independent Paralegal Firms?* by P. Pevato, 7 Journal of Law & Social Policy 215 (Fall 1991).

837. *Should Nonlawyers Provide Legal Services* by M. Brockmeyer, 27 Maryland Bar Journal 12 (July/Aug. 1994).

838. *Should Paralegals Have More Responsibility?* by D. Austern, 23 Trial 19 (May 1987).

839. *Should Paralegals Prepare Wills?* 24 Maryland Bar Journal 38 (Jan./Feb. 1991).

840. *Should the ABA or Anyone Else Be Involved in Approving or Accrediting Paralegal Training Programs?,* 1 LAT 14 (Spring 1984).

841. *Should You Rat on Your Boss?* by P. Perry, 10 LAT 62 (Mar./Apr. 1993).

842. *The Side-Switching Staff Person in a Law Firm* by S. Kalish, 15 Hamline Law Review 35 (1991). (ethics, conflict of interest)

843. *Skadden Paralegal Named in Fraud Case; Trio Alleged to Have Used Firm's Information* by D. Pines, New York Law Journal 1 (Oct. 16, 1992).

844. *Slugging It Out for Justice* by J. Murry, 1 LAT 20 (Summer 1984). (Rosemary Furman and the Florida Bar)

845. *The Smoking Gun* by J. Dwight, 12 LAT 87 (Jan./Feb. 1995). (paralegal in fiction)

846. *Software and Hard Choices: Interactive Legal Software Should Be Considered before Independent Paralegals Are Licensed* by C. James, 52 Oregon State Bar Bulletin 15 (July 1992).

847. *Software Helps Replace Lawyer Hours with Paralegal Hours* by D. Black, 12 Lawyer's PC 5 (July 1995).

848. *Solo Practitioner Does Away with Secretary* by D. Elmes, Lawyers Weekly USA, 6 (Jan. 16, 1994).

849. *A Solution to the Evaluation Dilemma* by C. Bast, 11 JPE&P 41 (Spring 1995). (paralegal education, legal writing)

850. *Solving the Most Common Personnel Problems* by J. Bassett, 10 LAT 78 (July/Aug. 1993).

851. *Some Paralegals Earn $55,000: Survey,* Chicago Daily Law Bulletin 1 (Feb. 23, 1988).

852. *So What Is a Lawyer Anyway?: The Fight Over Non-Lawyers . . .* by R. Samborn, 15 NLJ 1 (June 21, 1993).

853. *So, You Want to Become a Litigation Support Manager?* by D. Kartson, 13 LAT 34 (Sept./Oct. 1995).

854. *Standard Industrial Classification Manual* by Executive Office of the President, Office of Management and Budget, 369 (1987). (listing paralegals as providing "miscellaneous business services")

855. *Standards and Guidelines for the Utilization of Legal*

Assistants in Kansas (Kansas Bar Ass'n Committee on Legal Assistants, Dec. 2, 1988).

856. *Standing Out from the Competition* by C. Estrin, 10 LAT 138 (Jan./Feb. 1993). (employment search)

857. *Starting a Law Firm: The Paralegal's Role* by D. Miranda, 19 NPR 39 (NFPA, Summer 1995).

858. *Starting and Managing Your Own Business: A Freelancing Guide for Paralegals* by D. Socol (Wiley, 1994).

859. *State Bar Bans Practice by Nonlawyer Legal Technicians* by M. Hall, LADJ 10 (June 15, 1993).

860. *State Bar Membership and Guidelines* by C. Pederson, 21 F&F 9 (NALA, Issue 4, 1994).

861. *State Certification Programs* by J. Cormier, 20 F&F 28 (NALA, Issue 4, 1993). (Louisiana, Florida)

862. *State Liable for Guard's Harassment of Paralegal* by G. Spencer, New York Law Journal 1 (July 14, 1995).

863. *Status of Mid-South Paralegals and Their Utilization of Office Technology* by S. McKee, 33 LOEM 76 (Spring 1992). (Memphis Tennessee survey)

864. *Staying Out of the Briar Patch: Ethical Considerations and the Legal Assistant* by M. Wise, 57 Texas Bar Journal 30 (Jan. 1994).

865. *Storefront Paralegals and UPL* by S. Caudron, 12 LAT 48 (Nov./Dec. 1994). (unauthorized practice of law, ethics, freelance paralegals)

866. *Strategies for Training Legal Assistants in the Law Firm* by R. Bike, 10 LAT 58 (Jan./Feb. 1993).

867. *Studying for the Certified Legal Assistant Exam* by C. Udell, 21 F&F 30 (NALA, Aug. 1994).

868. *Successful Law Practice with Paralegals* by the New Hampshire Bar Association (1992). See also *Guidelines for the Utilization of the Services of Legal Assistants* (1977) and Rule 35 of the *New Hampshire Supreme Court Administrative Rule.*

869. *Successful Paralegal Utilization* by R. Simkins, 21 Massachusetts Lawyers Weekly 2409 (Apr. 26, 1993).

870. *Suit Settles over Arrest of Paralegals* by S. Parker, LADJ 1 (Sept. 9, 1993).

871. *Summary of the Arizona Dawson Case and How It Affects Legal Assistants* by T. Hyland, 19 F&F 16 (NALA, Issue 4, 1992).

872. *Superfund and the Legal Assistant* by K. Crank, 70 Michigan Bar Journal 1162 (Nov. 1991). (environmental law)

873. *Supervision of Non-Lawyer Employees: The Hidden Ethical Obligation* by W. Steele, 58 Texas Bar Journal 798 (Sept. 1995).

874. *The Support Staff Role in Marketing* by S. Yost, 9 The Compleat Lawyer 3 (ABA, Spring 1992).

875. *Survey of Legal Assistants Shows Field Increasing in Numbers,* 31 LOEM 94 (1990).

876. *Survey Results of Paralegal Instructors* by J. Hosea, 15 NPR 8 (NFPA, Summer 1990). (paralegals as teachers)

877. *Survey Says Role of Paralegals Is Growing as Law Firms Watch Costs,* 36 LOEM (Summer 1995).

878. *Surviving the Downturn: After Slump, Paralegal Work on Rebound; They Faced Less Dire Layoffs Than Associates and Billable Hours Are Up* by T. Weidlich, NLJ, 1 (Apr. 25, 1994).

879. *Surviving the Split* by G. Gladwell, 14 LAT 20 (Nov./Dec. 1996). (law firm dissolves/splits into other firms)

880. *Systemization and the Legal Assistant in the Law Office* by Endacott, 54 Nebraska Law Review 46 (1975).

T

881. *Take Charge of Your Career* by C. Estrin, 11 LAT 40 (July/Aug. 1994).

882. *Take the Bar and Beat Me: An Irreverent Look at Law School and Career Choices for Pre-laws, Paralegals, Law Students and the People Who Once Loved Them* by R. Woodcock (Career Press, 1991). *See also* 20 Student Lawyer 13 (May 1992) and 33 LOEM 100 (Spring 1992).

883. *A Tale of Two Legal Assistants,* 22 F&F 21 (NALA, Issue 4, 1995). (survival tips)

884. *Task-Based Billing: The Wave of the Future* by J. Neath, 14 LM 20 (ALA, Mar./Apr. 1995).

885. *Task Force Report: A Plan to License Limited Law Advisors . . .* by K. Tichnor, 52 Oregon State Bar Bulletin 10 (June 1992).

886. *Taxation without Representation* by D. Healy, 19 NPR 8 (NFPA, Winter 1994). (paralegal membership in bar associations)

887. *Taylor v. Chubb: The Decision That Almost Wasn't* by B. Wilkinson, 22 F&F 15 (NALA, Issue 4, 1995). (Oklahoma, paralegal fees)

888. *Teaching Corrections Law to Corrections Personnel* by W. Statsky, 37 Federal Probation 42 (June 1973).

889. *Techniques for Supervising Paralegals* by W. Statsky, 22 The Practical Lawyer 81 (Nov. 4, 1976). Reprinted in Law Office Management Manual No. 5, p. 27 (ABA-ALI, 1984).

890. *Television Commercial Portrays Paralegal in a Negative Light* by B. Schultz, 13 NPR 7 (NFPA, Winter 1989).

891. *Temporary Employment* by C. Toncray, 15 NPR 9 (NFPA, Winter 1991).

892. *Ten Secrets of Efficient Litigation Paralegals* by C. Tokumitsu, 10 LAT 46 (Sept./Oct. 1992).

893. *Ten Thousand Documents and Counting* by A. Miro, 13 LAT 40 (Mar./Apr. 1996). (litigation, computers, discovery)

894. *Ten Tips for Effectively Assisting at Trial* by D. Patrick, 8 LAT 22 (Sept./Oct. 1990).

895. *Ten Tips for Working with Clients* by L. Massey, 11 LAT 92 (July/Aug. 1994). (family law)

896. *Ten Ways to Find the Law in 50 States* by M. Talley, 9 LAT 118 (Jan./Feb. 1992).

897. *Ten Ways to Make Paralegals More Profitable* by E. Wesemann, 134 Pittsburgh Legal Journal 20 (Apr. 1986).

898. *Test Your Knowledge of Ethics* by S. Tolle, 21 F&F 38 (NALA, Aug. 1994).

899. *Texas Makes Solicitation a Felony,* 79 ABAJ 32 (Sept. 1993).

900. *Texas Opts for NALA CLA by Default* by J. Browning, 15 F&F 27 (NALA, Fall 1988).

901. *There Goes the Monopoly: The California Proposal to Allow Nonlawyers to Practice Law,* 44 Vanderbilt Law Review 179 (1991).

902. *There's Trouble Right Here in Florida, But There Is No Easy Answer: Nonlawyer "Legal Technicians" Providing Legal Services* . . . by A. Dimond, 66 Florida Bar Journal 7 (Sept. 1992).

903. *Things Your Ex-Secretaries Didn't Tell You* by B. Rosen, 17 Law Practice Management 50 (ABA, July/Aug. 1991).

904. *Three Who Dare* . . . *to Defend Those Who Can't Defend Themselves* by L. Martin-Bowen, 18 NPR 12 (NFPA, Fall 1993). (disability law, social security, public benefits law)

905. *Time for Firms to Take Another Look at Legal Assistant Mgrs.?* 94 Compensation & Benefits for Law Offices 5 (Oct. 1994).

906. *A Time to Work, a Time to Play* by K. Withem, 11 LAT 76 (Jan./Feb. 1994). (burnout, recreation, stress, Seattle, Washington State)

907. *Tips and Traps for the New Paralegal* by A. Wagner, 8 LAT 78 (Mar./Apr. 1991).

908. *Tips for Interviewing Witnesses on a Custody Case* by L. Massey, 9 LAT 54 (Mar./Apr. 1992).

909. *Tips for Investigating Automobile Accidents* by J. Lehe, 11 LAT 100 (Sept./Oct. 1993).

910. *Tips for Managing Your Unbillable Time* by S. Reilly, 18 NPR 18 (NFPA, Fall 1993).

911. *Tips on Hiring and Training Paralegals* by C. Tupis, 7 LAT 53 (July/Aug. 1990).

912. *To Be or Not to Be (Exempt)* by D. Patrick, 10 LAT 36 (Sept./Oct. 1992).

913. *Today's Paralegal* by Maryland State Bar Ass'n Special Comm. on Paralegals, 27 Maryland Bar Journal 20 (July/Aug. 1994).

914. *To Hire or Not to Hire* by B. Gagnon, 13 LAT 66 (Jan./Feb. 1996).

915. *Tools for the Freelance Paralegal* by J. McIntyre, 10 LAT 112 (May/June 1993).

916. *Tort Liability of Legal Paraprofessionals and Lawyers Who Utilize Their Services* by Wade, 24 Vanderbilt Law Review 1133 (1971).

917. *Total Quality Management Programs* by H. Samborn, 12 LAT 40 (Nov./Dec. 1994). (client service, law office management)

918. *To the Rescue: Paralegals/Legal Assistants* by R. Kerl, 35 Advocate 7 (Idaho Bar Ass'n, Mar. 1992).

919. *Trading Places* by S. Hunt, 13 LAT 46 (Mar./Apr. 1996). (small law firm, large law firm)

920. *Training Attorneys to Utilize Legal Assistants* by M. Gaige, 19 F&F 10 (NALA, Nov. 1992).

921. *The Training of Community Judges* by W. Statsky, 4 Columbia Human Rights Law Review 401 (1972).

922. *Trials of the Decade* by S. Caudron, 13 LAT 26 (Mar./Apr. 1996). (litigation)

923. *Twelve Prominent Paralegals* by C. Bruno, 10 LAT 74 (Nov./Dec. 1992).

924. *Twelve Techniques for Selling Yourself at a Job Interview* by J. Bassett, 9 LAT 40 (Jan./Feb. 1992).

925. *Two Appeals Courts Rule Paralegal Fees Recoverable at Market Rate* by S. Cohn, 11 LAT 24 (July/Aug. 1994). (California, Pennsylvania)

926. *Two Looks at Pay Strategies for Legal Assistants,* 94 Compensation & Benefits for Law Offices 1 (June 1994).

U

927. *The Ultimate Evaluation* by S. Vonn Matt Stoddard, 14 LAT 78 (Sept./Oct. 1996). (employment evaluations, job performance)

928. *Unauthorized Practice and Legal Assistants* by Whidden, 13 The Journal of the Legal Profession 327 (1988).

929. *Unauthorized Practice and Pro Se Divorce: An Empirical Analysis,* 86 Yale Law Journal 104 (1976).

930. *Unauthorized Practice of Administrative Proceedings* by D. Jordan, Journal of the Missouri Bar 539 (Oct./Nov. 1992).

931. *The Unauthorized Practice of Law and the Legal Assistant* by D. Orlik, 2 Journal of Legal Education 120 (Apr. 1985).

932. *Unauthorized Practice of Law by Insurance Claims Adjusters* by Jordan, 10 The Journal of the Legal Profession 171 (1985).

933. *Unauthorized Practice of Law: Does Anyone Know What It Is?* by K. Currier, 8 JPE&P 21 (1991).

934. *The Unauthorized Practice of Law: Do Good Fences Really Make Good Neighbors?* by Christensen, 1980 American Bar Foundation Research Journal 159.

935. *Unauthorized Practice of Law in Immigration,* University of Alabama Law School Journal of Legal Profession 151 (1987).

936. *The Unauthorized Practice of Law in Immigration* by A. Ashbrook, 5 Georgetown Journal of Legal Ethics 237 (1991).

937. *Unauthorized Practice of Law: Protection or Protectionism?* by D. Tenenbaum, 67 Wisconsin Lawyer 14 (Sept. 1994).

938. *Under New Mismanagement: The Problem of Non-Lawyer Equity Partnership in Law Firms* by C. Carson, 7 Georgetown Journal of Legal Ethics 593 (1994).

939. *Understanding Law Firm Culture* by S. Caudron, 12 LAT 50 (July/Aug. 1995). (management)

940. *The Undiscovered Field: Being an Employee Benefits Paralegal* by E. Spielman, 11 LAT 112 (Nov./Dec. 1993).

941. *The Un-Specialist* by D. Bogen, 14 LAT 26 (Nov./Dec. 1996). (generalist paralegal)

942. *Unsupervised Probate: Ultimate Legal Assistant Utilization* by M. Burgner, 21 F&F 12 (NALA, Aug. 1994).

943. *Unwanted Arrival* by S. McArthur, 52 Oregon State Bar Bulletin 19 (June 1992). (proposal to license legal technicians)

944. *Unwritten Rules: A Guide to Successfully Working with Attorneys* by N. Pulsifer (Estrin, 1992).

945. *USA On the Road Again: The Logistics of Working on an Out-of-Town Trial* by J. Dwight, 12 LAT 54 (May/June 1995).

946. *Use of Lay Representatives,* 58 Michigan Law Review 456 (1960).

947. *The Use of Legal and Technical Assistants by Administrative Law Judges in Administrative Proceedings* by Mathias, 1 The Administrative Law Journal 107 (1987).

948. *The Use of Legal Assistants in a Small Office* by V. Nicholas, Arizona Bar Journal 36 (Oct. 1978).

949. *Use of Mock Trials in Paralegal Education* by K. Houser, 9 JPE&P 107 (Apr. 1993).

950. *The Use of Paralegal Assistants in Divorce Practice* by P. Grove, 4 American Journal of Family Law 41 (Spring 1990).

951. *Use of Paralegals Makes Good Economic Sense,* 69 ABAJ 1626 (1983).

952. *Using Legal Assistants in Estate Planning* by G. Cohen, 30 The Practical Lawyer 73 (Oct. 1984).

953. *Using Paralegals in Pre-Trial Litigation* by L. Zimet, 14

954. *Using Paralegals in Small and Mid-Sized Law Firms* by D. Howard, 5 JPE&P 67 (Oct. 1988).

955. *U.S. Paralegal Shot Twice in Moscow Violence, Baker and McKenzie Reports* by L. Duncan, Chicago Daily Law Bulletin 1 (Oct. 5, 1993).

956. *Utilization of Legal Assistants in the Private Law Firm* by Klessing, 58 Wisconsin Bar Bulletin 33 (1985).

957. *Utilization: The Legal Assistant's Perspective* by D. Hammack, 40 Mississippi Lawyer 11 (Nov./Dec. 1993).

Legal Economics 63 (ABA, Mar. 1988).

V

958. *Validity of Will Drawn by Layman Who, in So Doing, Violated Criminal Statute Forbidding Such Activities by One Other Than Licensed Attorneys,* 18 ALR 2d 918 (1951).

959. *Vertical Expansion of the Legal Service Team* by Smith, 56 ABAJ 664 (July 1970).

960. *Volunteering Your Paralegal Services* by F. Whiteside, 10 LAT 70 (Mar./Apr. 1993). (pro bono)

W

961. *Walt Disney World Company's Legal Assistants: Their Role in the Show* by Miquel, 16 F&F 29 (NALA, Jan. 1990).

962. *War Stories from the Job-Hunt Front* by C. McGraw 11 LAT 64 (Jan./Feb. 1994).

963. *Washington State Bar Defines Paralegals* by H. Samborn, 12 LAT 16 (Mar./Apr. 1995).

964. *Welcome to the Club* by S. Cohn, 13 LAT 54 (Sept./Oct. 1995). (bar membership)

965. *What Activities of Stock or Securities Broker Constitute Unauthorized Practice of Law,* 34 ALR 3d 1305 (1970).

966. *What a Legal Secretarial Coordinator Can Do for Your Practice* by E. Dietel, 38 Practical Lawyer 15 (Oct. 1992).

967. *What Ever Happened in Minnesota?,* 21 F&F 50 (NALA, Issue 4, 1994). (regulation)

968. *What Exactly Is Confidentiality?* by D. Orlik, 9 LAT 174 (May/June 1992).

969. *What Is a Legal Assistant Manager and Why Do You Need One?* by E. Feldman, 34 LOEM 277 (Fall 1993).

970. *"What Is a Paralegal, Anyway?"* by D. L. Taylor, 37 Advocate 22 (Idaho Bar Ass'n, July 1994).

971. *What Is a Technician?* by D. Braddock, 39 Occupational Outlook Quarterly 38 (Spring 1995).

972. *What Is the Profit from Associates and Paralegals?* 62 Wisconsin Lawyer 6 (Apr. 1989).

973. *What's Hot, What's Not: Legal Assistant Hiring Trends* by D. Patrick, 9 LAT 44 (Mar./Apr. 1992).

974. *What's Hot, What's Not: Recruiters Report on Hiring*

Trends by D. Patrick, 10 LAT 48 (Mar./Apr. 1993).

975. *What's Hot, What's Not: The Latest Hiring Trends* by D. Patrick, 11 LAT 74 (Mar./Apr. 1994).

976. *What to Do about Paralegals* by S. Thom, 27 Law Society Gazette 34 (Mar. 1993). (Canada)

977. *What to Expect in Your First Ten Years as a Legal Assistant* by C. Estrin, 10 LAT 126 (Nov./Dec. 1992).

978. *What You Don't Know CAN Hurt You* by B. Rosen, 12 LAT 24 (July/Aug. 1995). (ethics) (legal advice)

979. *What You Had to Say: Independent Paralegal Services* by G. Gladwell, 12 LAT 62 (May/June 1995).

980. *What Your Law Office Management Professor Never Told You* by C. Elwell, 5 LAT 66 (Nov./Dec. 1987).

981. *What Your Office Support Staff and You Need to Know about Professional Responsibility for Nonlawyer Assistants* by D. O'Roark, 54 Kentucky Bench & Bar 40 (Fall 1993).

982. *What Your Paralegals Always Wanted to Tell You but Didn't Dare Because They Needed the Job: A Paralegal Gets a Chance to Talk Back* by F. Dowell, 60 Kentucky Bench & Bar 23 (Spring 1996).

983. *When Is a Paralegal Really a Paralegal?* by R. Lais, 32 Orange County Lawyer 6 (May 1990).

984. *When Legal Assistants Change Jobs: Ethical Issues and Solutions* by D. Kowalski, 75 Michigan Bar Journal 42 (Jan. 1996).

985. *When Paralegals = Profit$* by L. Martin-Bowen, 18 NPR 14 (NFPA, Summer 1994).

986. *When the Want Ad Won't Do: How to Find a Job without Using the Classifieds* by C. Milano, 11 LAT 98 (Nov./Dec. 1993).

987. *When Time Ran Out for the California Alliance* by W. Vogeler, 12 LAT 36 (Nov./Dec. 1994). (San Francisco)

988. *When You're Asked to Lie,* by D. Orlik, 11 LAT 84 (July/Aug. 1994).

989. *Where Are the Jobs for Entry-Level Paralegals?* by S. Widoff, 10 LAT 144 (Mar./Apr. 1993).

990. *Where Do I Go from Here?* by C. Estrin & D. Wagner (Estrin Publishing, 1992).

991. *Where Do Legal Assistants Fit In?* by C. Trethewy, 52 Oregon State Bar Bulletin 24 (June 1992).

992. *Where We are Today: Non-Lawyer Legal Practice in Arizona* by L. Shely, 30 Arizona Attorney, 11 (Feb. 1994).

993. *Who Can Practice Law?* by J. Podgers, 79 ABAJ 113 (Apr. 1993).

994. *Who Gets the Best Jobs?* by C. Milano, 8 LAT 39 (Sept./Oct. 1990).

995. *The Whole Truth: Witness Preparation Instructions for Paralegals* by M. Gaige, 23 F&F 18 (NALA, Aug. 1996).

996. *Who Should Practice Law?* by P. Hickell, 52 Oregon State Bar Bulletin 9 (June 1992).

997. *Who Should Regulate Lawyers?* by D. Wilkins, 105 Harvard Law Review 799 (1992).

998. *Why Aren't More Attorneys Using Paralegals?* by K. Neher, 13 LAT 58 (Jan./Feb. 1996). (Michigan)

999. *Why Do the Courts Often Deny Paralegal Fees in Attorney Applications for Fees?* by S. Kligerman, 20 NPR 29 (NFPA, Winter 1995).

1000. *Working for the Prosecution* by D. Orlik, 13 LAT 90 (Jan./Feb. 1996). (ethics)

1001. *Working Scared* by S. Caudron, 13 LAT 24 (Nov./Dec. 1995). (violence on job)

1002. *Working Together to Make Things Better?* by L. Martin-Bowen, 19 NPR 12 (NFPA, Winter 1994). (bar ass'n membership)

1003. *Working with Bar Committees* by G. Davis, 20 F&F 40 (NALA, Issue 4, 1993). (Mississippi, Virginia, Arizona, unauthorized practice of law, ethics)

1004. *Working with Legal Assistants,* P. Ulrich & R. Mucklestone, eds. (ABA, 1980, 1981).

1005. *Working with Legal Assistants: Professional Responsibility* by Ulrich & Clarke, 67 ABAJ 992 (1981).

1006. *Writing the Perfect Résumé* by A. Dewitt, 11 LAT 62 (July/Aug. 1994).

1007. *Writing Tips: Memo or Brief* by K. Miller, 13 LAT 76 (Nov./Dec. 1995).

1008. *Writing Witness Statements that Win Cases* by K. Wilkoff, 12 LAT 51 (Sept./Oct. 1994).

Y

1009. *Your First 100 Days on the Job* by F. Kanofsky, 12 LAT 60 (July/Aug. 1995). (office politics, survival skills)

1010. *Your Secretary: Paralegal in Disguise* by Sternin, 88 Case & Comment 12 (July/Aug. 1983).

1011. *You Want It When?* by C. Estrin, 14 LAT 62 (Nov./Dec. 1996). (client service)

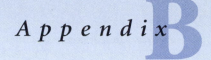

PARALEGAL ASSOCIATIONS AND RELATED ORGANIZATIONS

PARALEGAL ASSOCIATIONS (NATIONAL)

(Membership statistics, where known, are presented in brackets.)

National Association of Legal Assistants
   [17,000]
1516 South Boston, Suite 200
Tulsa, OK 74119-4013
918-587-6828
918-582-6772 (fax)
e-mail: nala@mail.webtek.com
Internet: http://www.nala.org

Federation of Paralegal Associations
   [17,500]
32 West Bridlespur Terrace
P.O. Box 33108
Kansas City, MO 64114-0108
816-941-4000
800-989-NFPA (info. on buying liability
   insurance)
816-941-2725 (fax)
e-mail: info@paralegals.org
Internet: http://www.paralegals.org

The National Association of Legal Assistants (NALA) and the National Federation of Paralegal Associations (NFPA) have numerous affiliated local paralegal associations. NALA affiliates are indicated by one asterisk (*) below; NFPA affiliates are indicated by two asterisks (**). Associations without an asterisk are unaffiliated at the present time.

PARALEGAL ASSOCIATIONS (STATE)

CAUTION: The addresses of many local paralegal associations change often. Very few of the associations have business offices. Most rent a P.O. box number and keep all association files in the home of an active paralegal member or in an available file cabinet of the law office where he or she works. If one of the addresses below turns out to be unproductive, (1) try the alternative address provided, if any; (2) check with your program director; (3) ask your classmates if they have a different address; (4) ask a working paralegal in your area; (5) contact the national office of NALA or NFPA if the association is affiliated with either; and (6) contact the association that is geographically closest to the one you are trying to contact and ask if it knows the current address. Also follow these steps if an association is listed below with no address.

ALABAMA

Alabama Association of Legal Assistants
(*) [215]
P.O. Box 55921
Birmingham, AL 35255

Alabama Association of Legal Assistants
(*) [215]
% Linda Reid, CLA
Sirote & Permutt
P.O. Box 55727
Birmingham, AL 35255

Mobile Association of Legal Assistants [50]
P.O. Box 1988
Mobile, AL 36633

ALASKA

Alaska Association of Legal Assistants (**)
[150]
P.O. Box 101956
Anchorage, AK 99510-1956
e-mail: Alaska@paralegals.org

Fairbanks Association of Legal Assistants (*)
P.O. Box 73503
Fairbanks, AK 99707

Fairbanks Association of Legal Assistants (*)

ARIZONA

Arizona Association of Professional
Paralegals (**) [56]
P.O. Box 430
Phoenix, AZ 85001
e-mail: Arizona@paralegals.org

Arizona Paralegal Association (*)
P.O. Box 392
Phoenix, AZ 85001
602-258-0121

Arizona Paralegal Association (*)
Debra Frazee, CLAS
Baird, Williams, Davis & Smith
340 E. Palm Lane, Suite 275
Phoenix, AZ 85004

Legal Assistants of Metropolitan Phoenix (*)
P.O. Box 13005
Phoenix, AZ 85002

Legal Assistants of Metropolitan Phoenix (*)
% Fawn Barnes, CLA
Maricopa County Attorney's Office
301-W. Jefferson, 9th Floor
Phoenix, AZ 85003

Tucson Association of Legal Assistants (*)
P.O. Box 257
Tucson, AZ 85702

Tucson Association of Legal Assistants (*)
% Shirley Welch, CLA
W.J. Harrison & Associates
3561 E. Sunrise, Suite 201
Tucson, AZ 85718

ARKANSAS

Arkansas Association of Legal
Assistants (*)
P.O. Box 2162
Little Rock, AR 72203

Arkansas Association of Legal
Assistants (*)
% Cynthia Schroeder
Wright, Lindsay & Jennings
200 W. Capitol Ave., Suite 2200
Little Rock, AR 72201-3699

CALIFORNIA

California Alliance of Paralegal
Associations [4,000]
P.O. Box 2234
San Francisco, CA 94126
415-576-3000

Commission for Advanced California
Paralegal Specialization
(specialty testing)
P.O. Box 22433
Santa Barbara, CA 93121

California Association of Independent
Paralegals (**) [230]
39120 Argonaut Way, Suite 114
Fremont, CA 94538
e-mail: CAIndependent@paralegals.org
http://www.caip.org

Central Coast Legal Assistant
Association [70]
P.O. Box 93
San Luis Obispo, CA 93406

Central Valley Paralegal Association
P.O. Box 4086
Modesto, CA 95352

Channel Cities Legal Assistants Association
P.O. Box 1260
Santa Barbara, CA 93120

Inland Counties Paralegal Association
P.O. Box 143
Riverside, CA 92502

Kern County Paralegal Association [63]
P.O. Box 2673
Santa Barbara, CA 93120

Legal Assistants Association of Santa
Barbara (*)

P.O. Box 2695
Santa Barbara, CA 93120
805-965-7319

Legal Assistants Association of Santa
Barbara (*)
% Tracy Anderson
City Attorney's Office
De La Guerra Plaza
Santa Barbara, CA 93101

Long Beach Paralegal Association
P.O. Box 32242
Long Beach, CA 90832

Los Angeles Paralegal Association [1000]
P.O. Box 8788
Calabasas, CA 91372
818-347-1001

Marin Association of Legal Assistants
P.O. Box 4165
San Rafari, CA 94913

National Association for Independent
Paralegals
635 5th St., West
Sonoma, CA 95476

Orange County Paralegal Association (*)
[480]
P.O. Box 8512
Newport Beach, CA 92658
714-744-7747
e-mail: Misty1@ix.netcom.com

Paralegal Association of San Mateo County
250 Wheeler Ave.
Redwood City, CA 94061

Paralegal Association of Santa Clara
County (*)
P.O. Box 26736
San Jose, CA 95159

Paralegal Association of Santa Clara
County (*)
San Jose, CA

Redwood Empire Legal Assistants
P.O. Box 143
Santa Rosa, CA 95402

Sacramento Association of Legal Assistants
(**) [182]
P.O. Box 453
Sacramento, CA 95812-0453
916-763-7851
e-mail: Sacramento@paralegals.org

San Diego Association of Legal Assistants
(**) [254]

P.O. Box 87449
San Diego, CA 92138-7449
619-491-1994

San Francisco Association of Legal
    Assistants (**) [756]
P.O. Box 2110
San Francisco, CA 94126-2110
415-777-2390
415-333-9045 (fax)
e-mail: SanFrancisco@paralegals.org

San Joaquin Association of Legal
    Assistants (*)
P.O. Box 1306
Fresno, CA 93715

San Joaquin Association of Legal
    Assistants (*)
% Melinda McConnell
Sierra Paralegal Services
3729 N. Claremont
Fresno, CA 93727

Sequoia Paralegal Association
P.O. Box 3884
Visalia, CA 93278

Ventura County Association of Legal
    Assistants (*)
P.O. Box 24229
Ventura, CA 93002

Ventura County Association of Legal
    Assistants (*)
% Joyce Muller
Law Office of Tom Buford
56 E. Main St., Suite 200
Ventura, CA 93001

West Coast Association of Paralegals (**)
One World Trade Center, #32242
Long Beach, CA 90832-2242
310-460-2939

CANADA

Alberta Association of Legal Assistants
700, 401 9th Ave. SW
P.O. Box 2010
Calgary, AB T2P 2M2

Canadian Association of Legal Assistants
P.O. Box 967
Station "B"
Montreal, Quebec H3B 3K5

Institute of Law Clerks of Ontario
97 Front St., NW, Suite 160
Toronto, Ontario M5J 1E6
416-366-2731

Manitoba Association of Legal
    Assistants
1L-300 Roslyn Road
Winnipeg, Manitoba R3L 0H4

COLORADO

Association of Legal Assistants of
    Colorado (*) [106]
% Brenda Mientka, CLAS
105 East Vermijo Ave., Suite 415
Colorado Springs, CO 80903

Legal Assistants of Western Slope (*)
% Jennifer LeBlanc
Mathis & Masters
P.O. Box 1487
Montrose, CO 81402

Rocky Mountain Paralegal
    Association (**) [346]
P.O. Box 1835
Arvada, CO 80001-1835
303-369-1606
e-mail: RMLAA@paralegals.org

CONNECTICUT

Central Connecticut Paralegal
    Association (**) [331]
P.O. Box 230594
Hartford, CT 06123-0594

Connecticut Association of Paralegals (**)
    [124]
P.O. Box 134
Bridgeport, CT 06601-0134

Legal Assistants of Southeastern
    Connecticut [55]
P.O. Box 409
New London, CT 06320

New Haven County Association of
    Paralegals (**) [133]
P.O. Box 862
New Haven, CT 06504-0862

DELAWARE

Delaware Paralegal Association (**) [251]
P.O. Box 1362
Wilmington, DE 19899
e-mail: Delaware@paralegals.org

DISTRICT OF COLUMBIA

National Capital Area Paralegal
    Association (**) [755]
P.O. Box 86171
Gaithersburg, MD 20886-6171

202-659-0243
e-mail: ncapa2nkj@aol.com
e-mail: NationalCapital@paralegals.org

FLORIDA

Broward County Paralegal Association
% Leigh M. Williams
Ruden, Barnett, McClosky
P.O. Box 1900
Ft. Lauderdale, FL 33302

Central Florida Paralegal Association (*)
P.O. Box 1107
Orlando, FL 32802
407-672-6372

Dade Association of Legal Assistants (*)
14027 S.W. 84th St.
Miami, FL 33183

Florida Legal Assistants, Inc. (*) [800]
11812A North 56th St.
Tampa, FL 33617
800-433-4352
813-985-2044

Gainesville Association of Legal
    Assistants (*)
Gainesville, FL

Jacksonville Legal Assistants (*)
P.O. Box 52264
Jacksonville, FL 32201

Paralegal Association of Florida (**)
6265 West Sample Rd., #297
Fort Lauderdale, FL 33067
e-mail: Florida@paralegals.org

Pensacola Legal Assistants (*)
% Deborah Johnson
Levin, Middlebrooks & Mabie
226 S. Palafox St.
Pensacola, FL 32581

Volusia Association of Legal Assistants (*)
P.O. Box 15075
Daytona Beach, FL 32115-5075

GEORGIA

Georgia Paralegal Association (**) [556]
P.O. Box 1802
Atlanta, GA 30301
770-433-5252
e-mail: Georgia@paralegals.org

Georgia Legal Assistants (*)
% Elaine Streat, CLA

Law Offices of Jimmy Boatright
P.O. Box 580
Alma, GA 31510-0580

Southeastern Association of Legal
  Assistants of Georgia (*)
Pooler, GA

South Georgia Association of Legal
  Assistants (*)
P.O. Box 181
Nashville, GA 31639

HAWAII

Hawaii Association of Legal Assistants (**)
  [150]
P.O. Box 674
Honolulu, HI 96809
e-mail: Hawaii@paralegals.org

IDAHO

Gem State Association of Legal
  Assistants (*)
Filer, ID

Idaho Association of Legal Assistants [54]
P.O. Box 1254
Boise, ID 83701

Intermountain Paralegal Association
P.O. Box 6009
Pocatello, ID 83205-6009

ILLINOIS

Central Illinois Paralegal Association (*)
P.O. Box 1948
Bloomington, IL 61702-1948

Central Illinois Paralegal Association (*)
Tuscola, IL

Heart of Illinois Paralegal Association (*)
Peoria, IL

Illinois Paralegal Association (**) [1385]
P.O. Box 8089
Bartlett, IL 60103
630-837-8088
630-837-8096 (fax)

INDIANA

Indiana Legal Assistants (*)
℅ Stephenie Veach
Gerling Law Office
519 Main St. Walkway
Evansville, IN 47730

Indiana Paralegal Association (**) [300]
P.O. Box 44518
Federal Station
Indianapolis, IN 46204
317-767-7798
e-mail: Indiana@paralegals.org

Michiana Paralegal Association (**) [38]
P.O. Box 11458
South Bend, IN 46634
e-mail: Michiana@paralegals.org

Northeast Indiana Paralegal
  Association (**) [92]
P.O. Box 13646
Ft. Wayne, IN 46865

IOWA

Iowa Association of Legal Assistants [400]
P.O. Box 335
Des Moines, IA 50302-0335

KANSAS

Kansas Association of Legal Assistants (*)
  [138]
P.O. Box 47031
Wichita, KS 67201

Kansas Association of Legal Assistants (*)
  [138]
℅ Connie Kennedy
Coleman Company
3600 North Hydraulic
Wichita, KS 67219

Kansas Paralegal Association (**) [202]
P.O. Box 1675
Topeka, KS 66601
e-mail: ksparalegals@ink.org
e-mail: Kansas@paralegals.org
Internet: http://www.ink.org/public/klas

KENTUCKY

Greater Lexington Paralegal Association
  (**) [71]
P.O. Box 574
Lexington, KY 40586
e-mail: Lexington@paralegals.org

Kentucky Paralegal Association
P.O. Box 2675
Louisville, KY 40201

Kentucky Paralegal Association
P.O. Box 760
Salyersville, KY 41465

Louisville Association of Paralegals (**)
  [201]

P.O. Box 962
Louisville, KY 40201
e-mail: Louisville@paralegals.org

Western Kentucky Paralegals (*)
P.O. Box 1737
Paducah, KY 42002-1737

LOUISIANA

Baton Rouge Paralegal Association
P.O. Box 306
Baton Rouge, LA 70821

Lafayette Paralegal Association
P.O. Box 2775
Lafayette, LA 70502

Louisiana State Paralegal Association (*)
P.O. Box 249
Lecompte, LA 71346

Louisiana State Paralegal Association (*)
℅ Karen Greer, CLAS
Cook, Yancey, King & Galloway
P.O. Box 22260
Shreveport, LA 71120-2260

New Orleans Paralegal Association (**)
  [190]
P.O. Box 30604
New Orleans, LA 70190
504-467-3136
e-mail: NewOrleans@paralegals.org

Northwest Louisiana Paralegal
  Association (*)
Shreveport, LA

Southwest Louisiana Paralegal Association
P.O. Box 1143
Lake Charles, LA 70602

MAINE

Maine State Association of Legal
  Assistants (*)
P.O. Box 7554
Portland, ME 04112

Maine State Association of Legal
  Assistants (*)
℅ Lawrence Yerxa
McEachern & Thornhill
10 Walker St.
Kittery, ME 03904

MARYLAND

Maryland Association of Paralegals
  (**) [170]

P.O. Box 13244
Baltimore, MD 21203
410-576-2252
e-mail: Maryland@paralegals.org

MASSACHUSETTS

Berkshire Association for Paralegals and
Legal Secretaries
℅ Nancy Schaffer
Stein, Donahue & Zuckerman
54 Wendell Ave.
Pittsfield, MA 01201

Central Massachusetts Paralegal
Association (**) [91]
P.O. Box 444
Worcester, MA 01614

Massachusetts Paralegal Association (**)
[800]
5 Grant St.
Framingham, MA 01701-6708
508-879-4001
e-mail: Massachusetts@paralegals.org

Western Massachusetts Paralegal
Association (**) [65]
P.O. Box 30005
Springfield, MA 01103

MICHIGAN

Legal Assistants Association of Michigan (*)
5785 S. Aylesbury
Waterford, MI 48327
e-mail: golaam@aol.com

Michigan Bar Association
Legal Assistant Section [400]
306 Townsend St.
Lancing, MI 48933
517-372-9030

MINNESOTA

Arrowhead Association of Legal Assistants
P.O. Box 221
Duluth, MN 55801

Minnesota Paralegal Association (**) [698]
8030 Old Cedar Ave. S., Suite 225
Bloomington, MN 55425
612-853-0272
612-854-1402 (fax)
e-mail: Minnesota@paralegals.org
Internet: http://www.winternet.com/
~rgaddes/mpaHome.htm

St. Cloud Area Legal Services
P.O. Box 896
St. Cloud, MN 56302

MISSISSIPPI

Gulf Coast Paralegal Association
942 Beach Dr.
Gulfport, MS 39507

Mississippi Association of Legal
Assistants (*)
P.O. Box 966
600 Heritage Bldg.
Jackson, MS 39205

Mississippi Association of Legal
Assistants (*)
℅ Elizabeth Woods
Lake, Tindall & Thackston
P.O. Box 1789
Jackson, MS 39215-1789

Paralegal Association of Mississippi
P.O. Box 22887
Jackson, MS 39205

MISSOURI

Gateway Paralegal Association
P.O. Box 50233
St. Louis, MO 63105

Joplin Metropolitan Paralegal Association
Joplin, MO

Kansas City Paralegal Association (**)
[389]
P.O. Box 13223
Kansas City, MO 64199
913-381-4458
913-381-9308 (fax)
e-mail: KansasCity@paralegals.org

Mid-Missouri Paralegal Association
Jefferson City, MO

Northwest Missouri Paralegal Association
(*) [30]
P.O. Box 6002
St. Joseph, MO 64506

Southwest Missouri Paralegal Association
[80]
Springfield, MO

St. Louis Association of Legal Assistants (*)
P.O. Box 69218
St. Louis, MO 63169-0218

MONTANA

Montana Association of Legal
Assistants (*)
P.O. Box 9016
Missoula, MT 59807-9016

Montana Paralegal Association
P.O. Box 601
Billings, MT 59103

NEBRASKA

Nebraska Association of Legal
Assistants (*)
P.O. Box 24943
Omaha, NE 68124

Nebraska Association of Legal
Assistants (*)
℅ Mary Bronson
Kutak Rock
1650 Farnam
Omaha, NE 68102-6000

NEVADA

Clark County Organization of Legal
Assistants (*)
P.O. Box 1103
Las Vegas, NV 89125

Clark County Organization of Legal
Assistants (*)
℅ Harry Heck, CLA
Kummer, Kaempker, Bonner & Renshaw
3800 Howard Hughes Pkwy, 7th Floor
Las Vegas, NV 89101

Sierra Nevada Association of Paralegals (*)
P.O. Box 40638
Reno, NV 89504

Sierra Nevada Association of Paralegals (*)
℅ Tawney Waldo, CLA
Jones, Jones, Close & Brown, Ltd.
290 S. Arlington Ave., Suite 200
Reno, NV 89501

NEW HAMPSHIRE

Paralegal Association
of New Hampshire (*)
P.O. Box 728
Manchester, NH 03105-0725

Paralegal Association
of New Hampshire (*)
℅ Marla Snow
Devine, Millimet & Branch, P.A.
P.O. Box 719
Manchester, NH 03105-0719

NEW JERSEY

Central Jersey Paralegal Association
Manalapan, NJ

Legal Assistants Association of New Jersey
(*) [260]
P.O. Box 142
Caldwell, NJ 07006

Legal Assistants Association of New Jersey
(*) [260]
% Kandi Moncelsi, CLA
Law Office of Steven Greenberg
West Orange, NJ 07052

New Jersey Paralegal Association
232 Inza Street
Highland PK, NJ 08904

Paralegal Council (**) [120]
Prudential Insurance Company Of America
751 Broad St.
Newark, NJ 07102

South Jersey Paralegal Association (**)
[170]
P.O. Box 355
Haddonfield, NJ 08033
e-mail: SouthJersey@paralegals.org

NEW MEXICO

Legal Assistants of New Mexico (**) [71]
P.O. Box 1113
Albuquerque, NM 87103-1113

Southwestern Association of Legal
Assistants (*)
% Karen Pilgreen
The Title Company
P.O. Box 2949
Ruidoso, NM 88345

NEW YORK

Adirondack Paralegal Association [46]
% Bartlett, Pontiff, Stewart
One Washington St.
P.O. Box 2168
Glen Falls, NY 12801-0012

Albany Legal Assistants Association [100]
P.O. Box 244
Albany, NY 12201-0244

Albany Legal Assistants Association [100]
% Carol Hotchkiss
Ruberti, Girvin & Ferlazzo, P.C.
100 State St.
Albany, NY 12207-2829

Central New York Paralegal Association
% Bond, Shoeneck, and Kink
One Lincoln Center
Syracuse, NY 13204

Legal Professionals of Dutchess County
51 Maloney Rd.
Wappingers Falls, NY 12590

Long Island Paralegal Association (**)
[113]
1877 Bly Road
East Meadow, NY 11554-1158
e-mail: lipa@inteltec.com

Manhattan Paralegal Association (**)
[250]
521 Fifth Ave., 17th Fl.
New York, NY 10175
212-330-8213
e-mail: Manhattan@paralegals.org

Onondaga County Legal Assistants
East Syracuse, NY

Paralegal Association of Rochester (**)
[198]
P.O. Box 40567
Rochester, NY 14604
716-234-5923
e-mail: Rochester@paralegals.org

Southern Tier Association of Paralegals
(**) [45]
P.O. Box 2555
Binghamton, NY 13902
607-772-9262

Westchester County Paralegal Association
White Plains, NY

Western New York Paralegal Association
(**) [252]
P.O. Box 207
Niagara Square Station
Buffalo, NY 14202
716-635-8250
e-mail: WesternNewYork@paralegals.org
e-mail: western@moran.com

West/Rock Paralegal Association (**) [60]
P.O. Box 668
New City, NY 10956
e-mail: WestRock@paralegals.org

NORTH CAROLINA

Cumberland County Paralegal Association
P.O. Box 1358
Fayetteville, NC 28302

Metrolina Paralegal Association (*)
P.O. Box 36260
Charlotte, NC 28236

Metrolina Paralegal Association (*)
% Marcia Siuda, CLA

Bell, Seltzer, Park & Gibson
P.O. Drawer 34009
Charlotte, NC 28234

North Carolina Paralegal Association (*)
P.O. Box 28554
Raleigh, NC 27611

North Carolina Paralegal Association (*)
% Sharon Wall
Lawyers Title Company of North Carolina
P.O. Box 309
Raleigh, NC 27602

Professional Legal Assistants [1000]
120 Penmarc Dr., #118
P.O. Box 31951
Raleigh, NC 27603
919-821-7762

Raleigh Wake Paralegal Association
P.O. Box 1427
Raleigh, NC 27602

Triad Paralegal Association
Drawer U
Greensboro, NC 27402

NORTH DAKOTA

Red River Valley Legal Assistants (*)
P.O. Box 1954
Fargo, ND 58107

Red River Valley Legal Assistants (*)
% Linda Johnson, CLA
Fjevre Law Firm
P.O. Box 8
Morehead, ND 58560

Western Dakota Association of Legal
Assistants (*)
P.O. Box K
Dickinson, ND 58602-8305

Western Dakota Association of Legal
Assistants (*)
P.O. Box 484
Minot, ND 58702-0484

OHIO

Cincinnati Paralegal Association (**) [280]
P.O. Box 1515
Cincinnati, OH 45201
513-244-1266
e-mail: Cincinnati@paralegals.org

Cleveland Paralegal Association (**) [226]
P.O. Box 5496
Cleveland, OH 44101
216-575-6090

Greater Dayton Paralegal Association (**)
[115]
P.O. Box 515
Mid-City Station
Dayton, OH 45402
e-mail: Dayton@paralegals.org

Northern Ohio Paralegal Association (**)
[93]
P.O. Box 80068
Akron, OH 44308-0068
e-mail: NEOhio@paralegals.org

Paralegal Association of Central Ohio (**)
[268]
P.O. Box 15182
Columbus, OH 43215-0182
614-224-9700
e-mail: CentralOhio@paralegals.org

Toledo Association of Legal Assistants (*)
[176]
P.O. Box 1322
Toledo, OH 43603-1322

Toledo Association of Legal Assistants (*)
[176]
% Gidget DiRienz
Owens-Corning
Fiberglass Tower, T-26
Toledo, OH 43659

OKLAHOMA

Central Oklahoma Association of Legal
Assistants
P.O. Box 2146
Oklahoma City, OK 73101-2146

Oklahoma Paralegal Association (*)
P.O. Box 96002
Oklahoma City, OK 73096

Tulsa Association of Legal Assistants (*)
[340]
P.O. Box 1484
Tulsa, OK 74101-1484

Tulsa Association of Legal Assistants (*)
[340]
% Gayla LeBow, CLA
The Williams Companies
Legal Department
P.O. Box 1400
Tulsa, OK 74102

OREGON

Oregon Paralegal Association (**)
P.O. Box 8523
Portland, OR 97207

503-796-1671
e-mail: Oregon@paralegals.org

Pacific Northwest Legal Assistants (*)
P.O. Box 1835
Eugene, OR 97440

PENNSYLVANIA

Berks County Paralegal Association
% Berks County Bar Association
544 Court St.
Reading, PA 19601
215-375-4591

Central Pennsylvania Paralegal Association
(**) [97]
P.O. Box 11814
Harrisburg, PA 17108

Chester County Paralegal Association (**)
P.O. Box 295
West Chester, PA 19381-0295

Keystone Alliance of Paralegal Associations
(1400)
P.O. Box 344
Pittsburgh, PA 15230

Keystone Legal Assistant Association (*)
RR 1, Box 873
Landisburg, PA 17030-9747

Lancaster Area Paralegal Association
% Rosemary Merwin
Gibble, Kraybill & Hess
41 East Orange St.
Lancaster, PA 17602

Lycoming County Paralegal Association
(**)
P.O. Box 991
Williamsport, PA 17701

Philadelphia Association of Paralegals (**)
2 Penn Center Plaza, Suite 200
Philadelphia, PA 19102
215-854-6352
e-mail: Philadelphia@paralegals.org

Pittsburgh Paralegal Association (**) [436]
P.O. Box 2845
Pittsburgh, PA 15230
412-255-1070

Wilkes-Barre Area Group
West Hazelton, PA

York County Paralegal Association (**)
[54]
P.O. Box 2584
York, PA 17405-2584

PUERTO RICO

Puerto Rico Association of Legal Assistants
P.O. Box 4225
San Juan, PR 00936

RHODE ISLAND

Rhode Island Paralegal Association (**)
[208]
P.O. Box 1003
Providence, RI 02901

SOUTH CAROLINA

Charleston Association of Legal
Assistants (*)
P.O. Box 1511
Charleston, SC 29402

Charleston Association of Legal
Assistants (*)
% Tanya Greene
Sinkler & Boyd
160 East Bay St.
Charleston, SC 29401

Columbia Legal Assistant Association (**)
[157]
P.O. Box 11634
Columbia, SC 29211-1634

Greenville Association of Legal
Assistants (*)
P.O. Box 10491 F.S.
Greenville, SC 29603

Paralegal Association of Beaufort
County (*)
P.O. Box 5668
Hilton Head Island, SC 29938

Paralegal Association of the Pee Dee (**)
P.O. Box 5592
Florence, SC 29502

Tri-County Paralegal Association (*)
P.O. Box 62691
Charleston, SC 29419-2691
e-mail: vst@wiselaw.com
Internet: http://www.concentric.net/~tcpa

Tri-County Paralegal Association (*)
% Rhonda McCraw, CLA
Law Office of Leonel Lofton
174 East Bay St., Suite 302
P.O. Box 62691
Charleston, SC 29402

SOUTH DAKOTA

South Dakota Legal Assistants Association
(*) [100]

% Dennyce Korb, CLA
Quinn, Eiesland, Day & Barker
P.O. Box 9335
Rapid City, SD 57709-9335
605-343-6400

TENNESSEE

East Tennessee Association of Legal
  Assistants
3370 Jackson Circle, S.E.
Cleveland, TN 37311

Greater Memphis Legal Assistants (*)
% Olivia Roleson
Evans & Petree
81 Monroe Ave., Suite 600
Memphis, TN 38103

Memphis Paralegal Association (**) [71]
P.O. Box 3646
Memphis, TN 38173-0646

Middle Tennessee Paralegal Association
  [145]
P.O. Box 198006
Nashville, TN 37219

Tennessee Paralegal Association (*)
P.O. Box 11172
Chattanooga, TN 37401

Tennessee Paralegal Association (*)
% Glenda DeLozier, CLA
Butler, Vines & Babb
P.O. Box 2649
Knoxville, TN 37901

Tennessee Valley Legal Assistants
  Association
507 Gay Street, S.W.
Knoxville, TN 37902

TEXAS

Legal Assistants Division [2300]
State Bar of Texas
P.O. Box 12487
Austin, TX 78711
512-463-1437

Legal Assistants Division [2300]
State Bar of Texas
P.O. Box 1375
Manchaca, TX 78652
512-280-1776 (Texas Paralegal Journal)
e-mail: slinky@io.com (Texas Paralegal
  Journal)
e-mail: laddir@flash.net

Alamo Area Professional Legal Assistants
  [155]
P.O. Box 524
San Antonio, TX 78292
210-231-5791

Capital Area Paralegal Association (*)
  [295]
P.O. Box 773
Austin, TX 78767-0773
512-505-6822

Capital Area Paralegal Association (*)
  [295]
% Nancy McLaughlin, CLAS
Law Office of William Schmidt
707 West 18th St.
Austin, TX 78701-1113

Dallas Area Paralegal Association (**)
  [750]
P.O. Box 12533
Dallas, TX 75225-0533
972-991-0853
e-mail: Dallas@paralegals.org

El Paso Association of Legal Assistants (*)
  [87]
P.O. Box 121
El Paso, TX 79941

El Paso Association of Legal Assistants (*)
  [87]
% Julie Suarez
Rio Grande Council of Governments
1100 North Stanton
El Paso, TX 79902

Fort Worth Paralegal Association (*) [339]
P.O. Box 17021
Fort Worth, TX 76102
817-336-FWPA

Galveston Area Legal Assistants
  Association [23]
P.O. Box 1319
Galveston, TX 77553

Greater Denton Legal Assistants
  Association [30]
% Mandy Smithers
Counsel to the Sheriff
127 N. Woodrow Land
Denton, TX 76205

Houston Association of Legal Assistants
  [1335]
P.O. Box 90398
Houston, TX 77290-0398
713-580-7722

713-580-1451 (fax)

Legal Assistants Association/Permian Basin
  (*) [60]
P.O. Box 10683
Midland, TX 79702

Legal Assistants Association/Permian Basin
  (*) [60]
% Robyn Glass-Miller, CLA
Woerndle, Patterson, Strain & Miller
1004 Big Spring
Midland, TX 79701

Legal Assistants Professional Association
  (Brazos Valley)
P.O. Box 925
Madisonville, TX 79702

Northeast Texas Association of Legal
  Assistants (*) [67]
P.O. Box 2284
Longview, TX 75606

Northeast Texas Association of Legal
  Assistants (*) [67]
% Pamela Luker, CLAS
Roberts Hill & Calk, P.C.
2020 Bill Owens Pkwy, Suite 200
Longview, TX 75604

Nueces County Association of Legal
  Assistants (*) [70]
P.O. Box 208
Corpus Christi, TX 78403

Southeast Texas Association of Legal
  Assistants (*) [125]
P.O. Box 813
Beaumont, TX 77704

Southeast Texas Association of Legal
  Assistants (*) [125]
% Shannon Hyde, CLA
Benchenstein & Oxford
P.O. Drawer 150
Beaumont, TX 77704

Texarkana Association of Legal Assistants
  (*) [40]
P.O. Box 6671
Texarkana, TX 75505

Texas Panhandle Association (*) [56]
P.O. Box 1127
Amarillo, TX 79105

Texas Panhandle Association (*) [56]
% Laina Bartlow, CLA
Hinkle, Cox, Eaton
P.O. Box 9238
Amarillo, TX 79105

Tyler Area Association of Legal Assistants
(*) [94]
P.O. Box 1178
Tyler, TX 75710

Tyler Area Association of Legal Assistants
(*) [94]
℅ Alice Rogers, PLS, CLA
Bain, Files, Allen
P.O. Box 2013
Tyler, TX 75710

West Texas Association of Legal Assistants
(*) [44]
P.O. Box 93103
Lubbock, TX 79493

West Texas Association of Legal Assistants
(*) [44]
℅ Teresa McGaa, CLA
Lamb County District Clerk
P.O. Box 689
Littlefield, TX 79339

UTAH

Legal Assistants Association of Utah (*)
P.O. Box 112001
Salt Lake City, UT 84147
801-531-0331

Legal Assistants Association of Utah (*)
℅ Kathy Scott-Thalmann, CLAS
Strong & Hanni
9 Exchange Pl., Suite 800
Salt Lake City, UT 84111

VERMONT

Vermont Paralegal Association (**)
P.O. Box 6238
Rutland, VT 05702

VIRGINIA

American Academy of Legal Assistants
1022 Park Ave. N.E.
Norton, VA 24273

Central Virginia Legal Assistant
Association
P.O. Box 4461
Lynchburg, VA 24502

Fredericksburg Association of Legal
Assistants
P.O. Box 7818
Fredericksburg, VA 22404-7818

Peninsula Legal Assistants (*)
P.O. Box 12888

Newport News, VA 23612-2888

Richmond Association of Legal Assistants
(*) [186]
P.O. Box 384
Richmond, VA 23218

Richmond Association of Legal Assistants
(*) [186]
℅ Jane Nuttall
Hon. Douglas Tice
P.O. Box 676
Richmond, VA 23206

Roanoke Valley Paralegal Association [70]
P.O. Box 1505
Roanoke, VA 24005
703-224-8000

Shenandoah Valley Paralegal Association
P.O. Box 88
Harrisonburg, VA 22801

Southside Virginia Paralegal Association
P.O. Box 2751
Danville, VA 24541

Tidewater Association of Legal
Assistants (*)
P.O. Box 3566
Norfolk, VA 23514-3566

Tidewater Association of Legal
Assistants (*)
℅ Colleen Hagy, CLA
U.S. Attorney's Office
101 W. Main St., Suite 8000
Norfolk, VA 23510

Virginia Alliance of Legal Assistant
Associations
P.O. Box 2125
Richmond, VA 23218-2125

VIRGIN ISLANDS

Virgin Islands Paralegal Association (*)
P.O. Box 6276
St. Thomas, VI 00804

Virgin Islands Paralegal Association (*)
P.O. Box 6376, EGS
Charlotte, Amali, VI 00804

WASHINGTON

Association of Paralegals and Legal
Assistants of Washington State (*)
℅ Sheila White, CLAS
Metropolitan Mortgage & Securities
929 Sprague Avenue West

Spokane, WA 92204

Columbia Basin Paralegal Association (*)
Kennewick, WA

Washington State Paralegal Association
(**) [450]
5500 Olympic Dr., Suite 105, Box 269
Gig Harbor, WA 98335
800-288-WSPA (9772)
206-851-2557
206-265-2983 (fax)
e-mail: Washington@paralegals.org

WEST VIRGINIA

Legal Assistants of West Virginia (*) [270]
P.O. Box 3422
Charleston, WV 25334

Legal Assistants of West Virginia (*) [270]
℅ Mary Hamilton
Hunt & Wilson
P.O. Box 2506
Charleston, WV 25329

West Virginia Association of Legal
Assistants
℅ Paula Houston
Volk, Frankovitch, Anetakis
3000 Boury Center
Wheeling, WV 26003

WISCONSIN

Madison Area Legal Assistants
Association (*)
℅ Christine Durow
Boardman, Suhr, Curry & Field
P.O. Box 927
Madison, WI 53701-0927

Paralegal Association of Wisconsin (**)
[372]
P.O. Box 92882
Milwaukee, WI 53202
414-272-7168
e-mail: Wisconsin@paralegals.org

WYOMING

Legal Assistants of Wyoming (*)
℅ Nancy Hole
Brown & Drew
123 West First St.
Casper, WY 82601

Legal Assistants of Wyoming (*)
℅ Wendy Soto-Martin, CLA
Patrick Hacker & Associates

2515 Pioneer Ave.
Cheyenne, WY 82001-3022

OTHER ORGANIZATIONS

(For addresses of state and local bar associations, see Appendix C.)

American Association for Paralegal
Education
P.O. Box 40244
Overland Park, KS 66204
913-381-4458
e-mail: sabanskes@aol.com
Internet: http://www.aafpe.org/

American Association of Law Libraries
53 W. Jackson Blvd., Suite 940
Chicago, IL 60604
312-939-4764
e-mail: aallhq@aol.com

American Association of Legal Nurse
Consultants [1,400]
500 North Michigan Ave., Suite 1400
Chicago, IL 60611
312-670-0550

American Association of Petroleum
Landsmen
4100 Fossil Creek Blvd.
Fort Worth, TX 76137
817-847-7700

American Bar Association
750 N. Lake Shore Dr.
Chicago, IL 60611
312-988-5000
312-988-5618 (Legal Assistants)
e-mail: legalassts@attmail.com
312-988-5619 (Law Practice Management)
800-285-2221 (book orders)
800-322-INET (ABA/NET/INET)
800-621-6159 (AMBAR)
312-988-5822 (Legal Technology Advisory
Council)

American Corporate Legal Assistants
Association
5003 Willowbend
Houston, TX 77035

American Paralegal Association
P.O. Box 35233
Los Angeles, CA 90035

Americans for Enforcement of Attorney
Ethics

P.O. Box 417-120
Chicago, IL 60641-7120
708-453-0080

American Society for Information Science
8720 Georgia Ave., Suite 501
Silver Spring, MD 20910
301-495-0900

American Society of Notaries
918 16th St., NW
Washington, D.C. 20006
202-955-6162

American Society of Questioned
Document Examiners
11420 SW 88th St. #206
Miami, FL 33176
703-285-2482

Association for Information and Image
Management
1100 Wayne Ave., Suite 1100
Silver Spring, MD 20910

Association of American Law Schools
1201 Connecticut Ave., NW
Washington, D.C. 20036
202-296-8851

Association of Commercial Records Centers [540]
P.O. Box 20518
Raleigh, NC 27619
800-336-9793

Association of Computer Support
Specialists
218 Huntington Rd.
Bridgeport, CT 06608
203-332-1524

Association of Continuing Legal Education
Administrators
2001 6th Ave., Suite 500
Seattle, WA 98121
206-448-0433

Association of Federal Investigators
1612 K. St., NW, Suite 506
Washington, D.C. 20006
202-466-7288

Association of Legal Administrators
175 E. Hawthorn Parkway, Suite 325
Vernon Hills, IL 60061-1428
847-816-1212
847-816-1213 (fax)

Association of Records Managers and
Administrators [11,000]

4200 Somerset Dr., Suite 215
Prairie Village, KS 66208
913-341-3808
800-913-3808 (U.S.)
800-422-2762 (Canada)

Association of Transportation
Practitioners [1600]
(New name: Association for Transportation Law)
19564 Club House Road
Gaithersburg, MD 20879
301-670-6733

Center for Computer-Assisted Legal
Instruction
University of Minnesota School of Law
229 19th Ave., S
Minneapolis, MN 55455
612-373-5352

Coalition for Consumer and Paralegal
Rights
1714 Stockton St., Suite 400
San Francisco, CA 94133

Council of Better Business Bureaus
4200 Wilson Blvd., Suite 800
Arlington, VA 22203
703-276-0100

Council of International Investigators
P.O. Box 266
Palmer, MA 01069-0266
413-283-7003
800-852-5073

Federal Administrative Law Judges
Conference
2020 Penn. Ave. NW, Suite 717
Washington, D.C. 20006-8002
202-633-0042

Federal Criminal Investigators Association
P.O. Box 1256
Detroit, MI 48231
512-229-5610

HALT (Help Abolish Legal Tyranny)—
An Organization of Americans
for Legal Reform
1319 F. St. NW, Suite 300
Washington, D.C. 20004
202-347-9600
http://www.halt.org

Independent Association of Questioned
Document Examiners
403 W. Washington
Red Oak, IA 51566
712-623-9130

Institute for Court Management
1331 17th St., Suite 402
Denver, CO 80202
303-293-3063

Institute of Judicial Administration
1 Washington Square S
New York, NY 10012
212-998-6196

Institute of Legal Executives
Kempson Manor
Kempson, Bedford, England

International Association of Arson
    Investigators
5428 Del Maria Way
Louisville, KY 40291
502-491-7482

International Association of Auto Theft
    Investigators
255 S. Vernon
Dearborn, MI 48124
313-561-8583

International Association of Credit Card
    Investigators
1620 Grant Ave.
Novato, CA 94945
415-897-8800

Investigators Open Network [400]
2111 E. Baseline, Suite F7
Tempe, AZ 85283
800-338-3463

Law Technology Product News
345 Park Ave.
New York, NY 10010
800-888-8300

Legal Assistant Management Association
638 Prospect Ave.
Hartford, CT 06105-4298
860-586-7507
860-586-7550 (fax)
e-mail: lamaoffice@aol.com
Internet: http://www.lamanet.org

Legal Assistant Today
3520 Cadallac Ave., Suite E
Costa Mesa, CA 92626
714-755-5450
800-394-2626

Legal Services Corporation
750 First St., NE
Washington, D.C. 20004
202-336-8810

Medical Library Association
6 N. Michigan Ave., Suite 300
Chicago, IL 60602-4895
312-419-9094

National American Indian Court Judges
    Association
1000 Connecticut Ave., Suite 1206
Washington, D.C. 20036
202-296-0685

National Association for Law Placement
1666 Connecticut Ave., NW, Suite 325
Washington, D.C. 20009
202-667-1666
800-324-NALS

National Association of Certified Fraud
    Examiners
716 West Ave.
Austin, TX 78701
512-478-9070
800-245-3321

National Association of Document
    Examiners
20 Nassau St.
Princeton, NJ 08542
609-924-8193

National Association of Enrolled Agents
6000 Executive Blvd., Suite 205
Rockville, MD 20852
800-424-4339

National Association of Law Firm
    Marketing Administrators
60 Revere Dr., Suite 500
Northbrook, IL 60062
708-480-9641

National Association of Legal Investigators
    [700]
P.O. Box 3254
Alton, IL 62002
618-465-4400
800-266-6254

National Association of Legal Investigators
    [700]
P.O. Box 516
Newport, OR 97365
503-265-6966

National Association of Legal Secretaries
2250 East 73rd St., Suite 550
Tulsa, OK 74136
918-493-3540
800-756-NALS
Internet: http://www.nals.org

National Association of Legal Vendors
    [214]
8080 N. Central Expressway, Suite 400
Dallas, TX 75206
214-891-8559

National Association of Paralegal
    Personnel
℅ Ross Multi Management
P.O. Box 8202
Northfield, IL 60093
312-973-7712

National Association of Professional
    Process Servers [850]
P.O. Box 4547
Portland, OR 97208
503-222-4180
800-477-8211

National Association of Professional
    Process Servers
306 H. St., NE
Washington, D.C. 20002
202-547-5710

National Association of Traffic Accident
    Reconstructionists and Investigators
P.O. Box 61208
King of Prussia, PA 19406
610-992-9817

National Black American Paralegal
    Association
P.O. Box 28024
Washington, DC 20038-8024
202-452-7485

National Center for Automated
    Information Retrieval
165 E. 72nd St., Suite B
New York, NY 10021
212-249-0760

National Court Reporters Association
    [18,000]
822 Old Courthouse Rd.
Vienna, VA 22182-3808
703-556-6272
800-272-6272

National Indian Paralegal Association
7524 Major Ave. N.
Brooklyn Park, MN 55443

National Law Firm Marketing
    Administrators
60 Revere Dr., Suite 500
Northbrook, IL 60062
708-480-9641

National Legal Assistant Conference
  Center
2444 Wilshire Blvd., Suite 301
Santa Monica, CA 90403

National Notary Association
8236 Emmet Ave.
P.O. Box 7184
Canoga Park, CA 91309
818-713-4000
800-876-6827
e-mail: Natlnotary@aol.com

National Organization of Social Security
  Claimants Representatives
19 E. Central Ave., 2nd Floor
Pearl River, NY 10965
800-431-2804

National Paralegal Association
P.O. Box 406
Solebury, PA 18963
215-297-8333

National Resource Center for Consumers
  of Legal Services
1444 Eye St. NW
Washington, D.C. 20005
202-842-3503

National Shorthand Reporters Association
118 Park St. SE
Vienna, VA 22180
703-281-4677

NOLO Press
950 Parker St.

Berkeley, CA 94710
510-549-4648
800-992-6656
http://www.nolo.com

Professional Legal Assistants [1000]
120 Penmarc Dr., #118
P.O. Box 31951
Raleigh, NC 27603
919-821-7762

Society of Professional Investigators
80 8th Ave., Suite 303
New York, NY 10011
212-807-5658

World Council of Defense Investigators
512-320-8818

ASSOCIATIONS OF ATTORNEYS

STATE AND LOCAL BAR ASSOCIATIONS

ALABAMA

Alabama State Bar
415 Dexter St.
P.O. Box 671
Montgomery, AL 36101
205-269-1515

Birmingham Bar Association
2021 2d Ave. N.
Birmingham, AL 35203
205-251-8006

ALASKA

Alaska Bar Association
510 L. St., No. 602
P.O. Box 100279
Anchorage, AK 99510
907-272-7469

ARIZONA

State Bar of Arizona
111 W. Monroe St.
Phoenix, AZ 85003-1742
602-252-4804

Maricopa County Bar Association
303 E. Palm Lane
Phoenix, AZ 85004
602-257-0522

ARKANSAS

Arkansas Bar Association
400 W. Markham
Little Rock, AR 72201
501-375-4605
http://www.arkbar.com/

CALIFORNIA

State Bar of California
555 Franklin St.
San Francisco, CA 94102
415-561-8200
http://www.calbar.org/

Bar Association of San Francisco
685 Market St., #700
San Francisco, CA 94105
415-267-0709

Beverly Hills Bar Association
300 S. Beverly Dr., Suite 201
Beverly Hills, CA 90212
310-553-6644

Eastern Alameda County Bar Association
360 22nd St., Suite 800
Oakland, CA 94612
510-893-7160

Lawyers' Club of Los Angeles
601 W. 5th St., Suite 203
Los Angeles, CA 90017-2000
213-624-4223

Lawyers' Club of San Francisco
685 Market St., Suite 750
San Francisco, CA 94105
415-882-9150

Los Angeles County Bar Association
617 S. Olive St., 2nd Floor
P.O. Box 55020
Los Angeles, CA 90055
213-896-6424
http://www.lacba.org

Orange County Bar Association
601 Civic Center Dr. West
Santa Ana, CA 92701-4002
714-541-6222

Sacramento County Bar Association
901 H. St., Suite 101
Sacramento, CA 95814
916-448-1087

San Diego County Bar Association
1333 Seventh Ave.
San Diego, CA 92101
619-231-0781
http://www.sddt.com/files/law/bar/bar.html

Santa Clara County Bar Association
4 N. Second St., Suite 400
San Jose, CA 95113
408-287-2557

COLORADO

Colorado Bar Association
1900 Grant St., Suite 950
Denver, CO 80203
303-860-1115
http://www.usa.net/cobar/index.html

Denver Bar Association
1900 Grant St., Suite 950
Denver, CO 80203-4309
303-860-1115

San Luis Valley Bar Association
http://www.rmii.com/slv/courts/bar.htm

CONNECTICUT

Connecticut Bar Association
101 Corporate Pl.
Rocky Hill, CT 06067
203-721-0025
http://www.ctbar.org

Hartford County Bar Association
61 Hungerford St.
Hartford, CT 06106
203-525-8106

DELAWARE

Delaware Bar Association
1225 King St.
Wilmington, DE 19801
302-658-5279

DISTRICT OF COLUMBIA

District of Columbia Bar
1250 H St. NW, 6th Floor
Washington, D.C. 20005-3908
202-737-4700

Bar Association of the District of
    Columbia
1819 H. St. NW, 12th Floor
Washington D.C. 20006-3690
202-223-6600

FLORIDA

The Florida Bar
650 Apalachee Parkway
Tallahassee, FL 32399-2300
904-561-5600
http://www.FLABAR.org

Dade County Bar Association
123 N.W. First Ave., Suite 214
Miami, FL 33128
305-371-2220

Hillsborough County Bar Association
315 E. Madison, Suite 1010
Tampa, FL 33602
813-226-6431

Orange County Bar Association
880 N. Orange Ave., Suite 100
Orlando, FL 32801
407-422-4551

GEORGIA

State Bar of Georgia
800 The Hurt Bldg.
50 Hunt Plaza
Atlanta, GA 30303
404-527-8755

Atlanta Bar Association
100 Peachtree St. NW, Suite 2500
Atlanta, GA 30303
404-521-0781

Cobb County Bar Association
http://www.kuesterlaw.com/cobb

GUAM

Guam Bar Association
259 Martyr St.

Agana, GU 96910
011-671-472-6848

HAWAII

Hawaii State Bar Association
1136 Union Mall
Penthouse 1, 9th Floor
Honolulu, HI 96813
808-537-1868

IDAHO

Idaho State Bar
P.O. Box 895
525 W. Jefferson St.
Boise, ID 83701
208-334-4500

ILLINOIS

Illinois State Bar Association
424 S. Second St.
Springfield, IL 62701
217-525-1760
800-252-8908
312-726-8775 (Chicago)
800-442-ISBA
http://www.illinoisbar.org

The Chicago Bar Association
321 S. Plymouth Ct.
Chicago, IL 60604
312-554-2000

The Chicago Council of Lawyers
220 S. State St., Suite 800
Chicago, IL 60604
312-427-0710

Illinois Trial Lawyers Association
110 W. Edwards St.
P.O. Box 5000
Springfield, IL 62705
217-789-0755
800-252-8501

INDIANA

Indiana State Bar Association
230 E. Ohio St., 4th Floor
Indianapolis, IN 46204
317-639-5465
http://www.iquest.net/isba/

Indianapolis Bar Association
10 West Market St., Suite 440
Indianapolis, IN 46204
317-269-2000

IOWA

Iowa State Bar Association
521 E. Locust
Des Moines, IA 50309
515-243-3179

KANSAS

Kansas Bar Association
1200 Harrison St.
P.O. Box 1037
Topeka, KS 66612
913-234-5696
http://www.ink.org/public/cybar/

KENTUCKY

Kentucky Bar Association
514 West Main St.
Frankfort, KY 40601-1883
502-564-3795
http://www.kybar.org/

Louisville Bar Association
717 W. Main St.
Louisville, KY 40202
502-583-5314

LOUISIANA

Louisiana State Bar Association
601 St. Charles Ave.
New Orleans, LA 70130
504-566-1600

Louisiana Trial Lawyers Association
442 Europe St.
P.O. Drawer 4289
Baton Rouge, LA 70821
504-383-5554

New Orleans Bar Association
228 St. Charles Ave., Suite 1223
New Orleans, LA 70130-2612
504-525-7432

MAINE

Maine State Bar Association
124 State St.
P.O. Box 788
Augusta, ME 04332-0788
207-622-7523

MARYLAND

Maryland State Bar Association
520 W. Fayette St.
Baltimore, MD 21201
410-685-7878
http://www.charm.net/msba/

Bar Association of Baltimore City
111 N. Calvert St., Suite 627
Baltimore, MD 21202
410-539-5936

Bar Association of Montgomery County
27 W. Jefferson St.
Rockville, MD 20850
301-424-3454

MASSACHUSETTS

Massachusetts Bar Association
20 West St.
Boston, MA 02111-1218
617-542-3602

Boston Bar Association
16 Beacon St.
Boston, MA 02108
617-742-0615

MICHIGAN

State Bar of Michigan
306 Townsend St.
Lansing, MI 48933-2083
517-372-9030
http://www.michbar.org

Detroit Bar Association
2380 Penobscot Bldg.
Detroit, MI 48226
313-961-6120

Michigan Trial Lawyers Association
501 S. Capitol Ave., Suite 405
Lansing, MI 48933-2327
517-482-7740

Oakland County Bar Association
760 S. Telegraph, Suite 100
Bloomfield, MI 48302-0181
810-334-3400

MINNESOTA

Minnesota State Bar Association
514 Nicollet Mall, Suite 300
Minneapolis, MN 55402
612-333-1183
800-292-4152

Hennepin County Bar Association
514 Nicollet Mall, Suite 350
Minneapolis, MN 55402
612-340-0022

Ramsey County Bar Association
322 Minnesota St., E-1312
St. Paul, MN 55101
612-222-0846

MISSISSIPPI

Mississippi State Bar
643 N. State St.
P.O. Box 2168
Jackson, MS 39225-2168
601-948-4471

MISSOURI

The Missouri Bar
326 Monroe
P.O. Box 119
Jefferson City, MO 65102
314-635-4128
http://www.gopher.connect.more.net/

Bar Association of Metropolitan
    Saint Louis
One Metropolitan Sq., Suite 1400
St. Louis, MO 63102
314-421-4134

Kansas City Metropolitan Bar Association
1125 Grand Ave., Suite 400
Kansas City, MO 64106
816-474-4322

MONTANA

State Bar of Montana,
46 N. Last Chance Gulch
P.O. Box 577
Helena, MT 59624
406-442-7660

NEBRASKA

Nebraska State Bar Association
635 S. 14th St., 2nd Floor
P.O. Box 81809
Lincoln, NE 68501
402-475-7091

NEVADA

State Bar of Nevada
201 Las Vegas Blvd., Suite 200
Las Vegas, NV 89101
702-382-2200

NEW HAMPSHIRE

New Hampshire Bar Association
112 Pleasant St.
Concord, NH 03301
603-224-6942
http://www.nh.com/legal/nhbar/

NEW JERSEY

New Jersey State Bar Association
New Jersey Law Center

One Constitution Sq.
New Brunswick, NJ 08901-1500
908-249-5000
http://www.njsba.com

Bergen County Bar
61 Hudson St.
Hackensack, NJ 07601
201-488-0044

Camden County Bar Association
P.O. Box 1027
Mid-Atlantic Building
Broadway & Cooper Streets
Camden, NJ 08101
609-964-3420

Essex County Bar Association
One Newark Center, 16th Floor
Newark, NJ 07102
201-622-6207

NEW MEXICO

State Bar of New Mexico
P.O. Box 25883
Albuquerque, NM 87125
505-842-6132
800-876-6227

New Mexico Trial Lawyers' Association
    Foundation
P.O. Box 301
Albuquerque, NM 87103
505-243-6003

NEW YORK

New York State Bar Association
One Elk St.
Albany, NY 12207
518-463-3200
http://www.nysba.org

Association of the Bar of the City of
    New York
42 W. 44th St.
New York, NY 10036
212-382-6620
http://www.abcny.org/

Bar Association of Erie County
1450 Statler Towers
Buffalo, NY 14202
716-852-8687

Bar Association of Nassau County
15th and West Streets
Mineola, NY 11501
516-747-4070
http://infoshop.com/ncba/

Brooklyn Bar Association
23 Remsen St.
Brooklyn, NY 11201-4212
718-624-0675

Monroe County Bar Association
One Exchange St., 5th Floor
Rochester, NY 14614
716-546-1817

New York County Lawyers Association
14 Vesey St.
New York, NY 10007
212-267-6646

New York State Defenders Association
518-465-3524
http://www.nysda.org/

New York State Trial Lawyers Association
132 Nassau St.
New York, NY 10038
212-349-5890
http://www.nystla.org/

Queens County Bar Association
90-35 148th St.
Jamaica, NY 11435
718-291-4500

Suffolk County Bar Association
560 Wheeler Rd.
Hauppauge, NY 11788-4357
516-234-5511

Westchester County Bar Association
300 Hamilton Ave., Suite 400
White Plains, NY 10601
914-761-3707

NORTH CAROLINA

North Carolina State Bar
208 Fayetteville Street Mall
Raleigh, NC 27605
919-828-4260

North Carolina Bar Association
P.O. Box 12806
Raleigh, NC 27608
919-677-0561
http://www.barlinc.org/

Mecklenburg County Bar
438 Queens Road
Charlotte, NC 28207
704-375-8624

10th Judicial District Bar Association
P.O. Box 10625
Raleigh, NC 27605
919-677-9903

NORTH DAKOTA

State Bar Association of North Dakota
P.O. Box 2136
Bismarck, ND 58502
701-255-1404
800-472-2685

OHIO

Ohio State Bar Association
1700 Lake Shore Drive
Columbus, OH 43216-6562
614-487-2050

Cincinnati Bar Association
35 E. 7th St., 8th Floor
Cincinnati, OH 45202-2492
513-381-8213

Cleveland Bar Association
113 St. Clair Ave. NE
Cleveland, OH 44114-1253
216-696-3525

Columbus Bar Association
175 South 3rd St.
Columbus, OH 43215-5134
614-221-4112
http://www.smartpages.com/cba/

Cuyahoga County Bar Association
500 The Terminal Tower
50 Public Square
Cleveland, OH 44113-2303
216-621-5112

OKLAHOMA

Oklahoma Bar Association
1901 N. Lincoln
Oklahoma City, OK 73105
405-524-2365
800-522-8065

Oklahoma County Bar Association
119 W. Robinson, Suite 240
Oklahoma City, OK 73102
405-236-8421

Oklahoma Trial Lawyers Association
http://pwr.com/otla/otlal.html

Tulsa County Bar Association
1446 South Boston
Tulsa, OK 74119
918-584-5243

OREGON

Oregon State Bar
P.O. Box 1689

Lake Oswego, OR 97035
503-620-0222

Multnomah Bar Association
630 SW Fifth Ave., Suite 200
Portland, OR 97204
503-222-3275

PENNSYLVANIA

Pennsylvania Bar Association
100 South St.
P.O. Box 186
Harrisburg, PA 17108
717-238-6715

Allegheny County Bar Association
Kopper's Building, 4th Floor
426 7th Ave.
Pittsburgh, PA 15219
412-261-6161
http://www.acba.lm.com

Lancaster Bar Association
http://www.law.vill.edu/bar/lanbar/

Philadelphia Bar Association
1101 Market St., 11th Floor
Philadelphia, PA 19107-2911
215-238-6338
http://www.philabar.org

PUERTO RICO

Puerto Rico Bar Association
P.O. Box 1900
San Juan, PR 00902
809-721-3358

RHODE ISLAND

Rhode Island Bar Association
115 Cedar St.
Providence, RI 02903
401-421-5740

SOUTH CAROLINA

South Carolina Bar
950 Taylor St.
P.O. Box 698
Columbia, SC 29202
803-799-6653

SOUTH DAKOTA

State Bar of South Dakota
222 E. Capitol
Pierre, SD 57501
605-224-7554
http://www.sdbar.org

TENNESSEE

Tennessee Bar Association
3622 W. End Ave.
Nashville, TN 37205-2403
615-383-7421
http://www.tba.org

Nashville Bar Association
221 Fourth Ave. N., Suite 400
Nashville, TN 37219-2100
615-242-9272

TEXAS

State Bar of Texas
1414 Colorado
P.O. Box 12487
Austin, TX 78711
512-463-1400
800-204-2222
800-532-3947 (ethics hotline)

Dallas Bar Association
2101 Ross Ave.
Dallas, TX 75201
214-969-7066

Houston Bar Association
1001 Fannin, Suite 1300
Houston, TX 77002-6708
713-759-1133

San Antonio Bar Association
Bexar County Courthouse, 5th Floor
San Antonio, TX 78205
512-227-8822

Travis County Bar Association
700 Lavaca, Suite 602
Austin, TX 78701
512-472-0279

UTAH

Utah State Bar
645 S. 200 East, Suite 310
Salt Lake City, UT 84111
801-531-9077
http://www.utahbar.org

VERMONT

Vermont Bar Association
35-37 Court St.
P.O. Box 100
Montpelier, VT 05601
802-223-2020
800-642-3153

VIRGINIA

Virginia State Bar
707 E. Main St., Suite 1120
Richmond, VA 23219-2803
804-775-0500

Virginia Bar Association
701 E. Franklin St., Suite 1515
Richmond, VA 23219
804-644-0041

Fairfax Bar Association
4110 Chain Bridge Rd., Suite 303
Fairfax, VA 22030
703-246-2740

VIRGIN ISLANDS

Virgin Islands Bar Association
P.O. Box 4108
Christiansted, VI 00822
809-778-7497

WASHINGTON

Washington State Bar Association
2001 6th Ave.
500 Westin Bldg.
Seattle, WA 98121-2599
206-727-8200
http://www.wsba.org

King County Bar Association
900 4th Ave., Suite 600
The Bank of California Bldg.
Seattle, WA 98164
206-624-9365
http://www.owt.com/kcba/

WEST VIRGINIA

West Virginia State Bar
2006 Kanawha Blvd. E
Charleston, WV 25311
304-558-2456
http://www.wvbar.org

West Virginia Bar Association
904 Security Bldg., 101 Capitol St.
Charleston, WV 25307
304-342-1474

West Virginia Trial Lawyers Association
P.O. Box 3968
Charleston, WV 25339
304-344-0692

WISCONSIN

State Bar of Wisconsin
402 W. Wilson

Madison, WI 53703
608-257-3838
800-362-8096
800-728-7788
http://www.wisbar.org/home.htm

Milwaukee Bar Association
533 E. Wells St.
Milwaukee, WI 53202
414-274-6760

WYOMING

Wyoming State Bar
500 Randall Ave.
P.O. Box 109
Cheyenne, WY 82003
307-632-9061

OTHER ATTORNEY ASSOCIATIONS

American Academy of Appellate Lawyers
15245 Shady Grove Rd., Suite 130
Rockville, MD 20850
301-258-9210

American Academy of Adoption Attorneys
P.O. Box 33053
Washington, D.C. 20033
202-331-1955

American Academy of Healthcare
   Attorneys
American Hospital Association
1 N. Franklin
Chicago, IL 60606
312-422-3700

American Academy of Matrimonial
   Lawyers
20 N. Michigan Ave., Suite 540
Chicago, IL 60602
312-263-6477

American Association of Public Welfare
   Attorneys
810 1st St. NE, Suite 500
Washington, D.C. 20002
202-682-0100

American Bar Association
750 N. Lake Shore Dr.
Chicago, IL 60611
312-988-5000
800-285-2221
202-331-2200 (Washington, D.C. office)
317-264-8340 (Indianapolis office)
http://www.abanet.org

American Blind Lawyers Association
1010 Vermont Ave. NW
Washington, D.C. 20005
202-393-3666
800-424-8666

American Board of Professional Liability
  Attorneys
175 E. Shore Rd.
Great Neck, NY 11023
516-487-1990

American Board of Trial Advocates
16633 Ventura Blvd., Suite 1015
Encino, CA 91436
318-501-3250

American Civil Liberties Union
122 Maryland Ave., NE
Washington, DC 20002
202-544-1681

American College of Probate Counsel
2716 Ocean Park Blvd., Suite 1080
Santa Monica, CA 90405
213-450-2033

American College of Real Estate Lawyers
733 15th St. NW, Suite 700
Washington, D.C. 20005
202-393-1344

American College of Trial Lawyers
10886 Wilshire Blvd.
Los Angeles, CA 90024
213-879-0143

American Corporate Counsel Association
1225 Connecticut Ave., Suite 202
Washington, D.C. 20036
202-296-4523

American Immigration Lawyers
  Association
1400 I St. NW, Suite 1200
Washington, D.C. 20005
202-371-9377
http://aila.org

American Intellectual Property Law
  Association
2001 Jefferson Davis Hwy., Suite 203
Arlington, VA 22202
703-415-0780
http://www.aipla.org/

Asian American Legal Defense and
  Education Fund
99 Hudson St.
New York, NY 10013
212-966-5932

Association of Defense Trial Attorneys
600 Jefferson Bank Bldg.
Peoria, IL 61602
309-676-0400

Association of Federal Defense Attorneys
http://www.afda.org/

Association of Immigration Attorneys
291 Broadway, Suite 1000
New York, NY 10007
212-227-2522

Association of Life Insurance Counsel
200 East Berry St.
Fort Wayne, IN 46801
219-455-2000

Association of Transportation Practitioners
(new name: Association for Transportation
  Law)
19564 Club House Road
Gaithersburg, MD 20879
301-670-6733

Association of Trial Lawyers of America
1050 31st St. NW
Washington, D.C. 20007
202-965-3500
800-424-2727
http://www.atlanet.org/

Black Entertainment & Sports Lawyers
  Association
111 Broadway
New York, NY 10006
212-587-0300

Childrens Defense Fund
25 E. St., NW
Washington, DC 20001
202-628-8787
800-CDF-1200

Commercial Law League of America
150 N. Michigan Ave., Suite 600
Chicago, IL 60601
312-781-2000

Cuban American Legal Defense and
  Education Fund
2119 Webster St.
Fort Wayne, IN 46802
219-745-5421

Decalogue Society of Lawyers
179 W. Washington St., Suite 350
Chicago, IL 60602
312-263-6493

Defense Research & Trial Lawyers
  Association

750 N. Lake Shore Dr., Suite 500
Chicago, IL 60611
312-944-0575

Disability Rights Education and Defense
  Fund
2212 6th St.
Berkeley, CA 94710
510-644-2555

Federal Bar Association
1815 H. St. NW, Suite 408
Washington, D.C. 20006-3697
202-638-0252
http://www.access.digex.net/`fedbar/index.
  html

Federal Circuit Bar Association
1300 I St. NW, Suite 700
Washington, D.C. 20005
202-408-4002

Federal Communications Bar Association
1722 Eye St. NW, Suite 300
Washington, D.C. 20006
202-833-2684
http://www.fcba.org/

Federal Energy Bar Association
1350 Connecticut St. NW, Suite 300
Washington, D.C. 20036
202-223-5625

Federation of Insurance & Corporate
  Counsel
15 Ridge Rd.
Marblehead, MA 01945
617-639-0698

Gay and Lesbian Advocates and
  Defenders
P.O. Box 218
Boston, MA 02112
617-426-1350

Hispanic National Bar Association
1634 Eye St. NW, Suite 901
Washington, DC 20006
202-628-7147
202-887-3560

Incorporated Society of Irish/American
  Lawyers
15140 Farmington Rd.
Livonia, MI 48154
810-766-5454

Inter-American Bar Association
1889 F. St. NW, Suite 450
Washington D.C. 20006-4499
202-789-2747

International Academy of Trial Lawyers
210 S. 1st St., Suite 206
San Jose, CA 95113
408-275-6767

International Association of Defense
Counsel
20 N. Wacker Dr., Suite 3100
Chicago, IL 60606
312-368-1494

International Federation of Women
Lawyers
186 5th Ave.
New York, NY 10010
212-206-1666

International Legal Defense Counsel
111 S. 15th St., 24th Floor
Philadelphia, PA 19102
215-977-9982

International Society of Barristers
3586 E. Huron Dr.
Ann Arbor, MI 48104
313-763-0165

International Trade Commission Trial
Lawyers Association
815 Connecticut Ave. NW, Suite 601
Washington, D.C. 20006
202-659-5070

Judge Advocates Association
1815 H. St. NW
Washington, D.C. 20006-3604
202-628-0979

La Raza Lawyers Association of
San Francisco
2601 Mission St., Suite 2601
San Francisco, CA 94110
415-285-7426

Lawyer-Pilots Bar Association
P.O. Box 685
Poolesville, MD 20837
301-972-7700

Lawyers Committee for Civil Rights Under
Law
1450 G. St., Suite 400
Washington, DC 20005
202-662-8600

Maritime Law Association of the United
States
195 Broadway
New York, NY 10007
212-341-7244
504-561-1311

Mexican-American Legal Defense and
Education Fund
634 S. Spring St., 11th Floor
Los Angeles, CA 90014
213-629-2512

NAACP Legal Defense and Education Fund
1275 K. St. NW, Suite 301
Washington, D.C. 20005
202-682-1300

National Academy of Elder Law Attorneys
1730 E. River Rd., Suite 107
Tucson, AZ 85718
http://www.naela.com/elderlaw/

National Asian Pacific American Bar
Association
1215 4th Ave. S
Seattle, WA 98134
206-292-9988
http://www.napaba.org/

National American Indian Court Judges
Association
1000 Connecticut Ave. NW
Washington D.C. 20036
202-296-0685

National Association of Attorneys General
444 N. Capitol St. NW, Suite 339
Washington, D.C. 20001
202-434-8054

National Association of Black Women
Attorneys
506 5th St. NW
Washington, D.C. 20001
202-966-9693

National Association of Bond Attorneys
911 N. Elm St., Suite 129
Hinsdale, IL 60521
708-920-0160
http://www.qadas.com/nabl/

National Association of College &
University Attorneys
One Dupont Circle, Suite 620
Washington, D.C. 20036
202-833-8390

National Association of Counsel for
Children
1205 Oneida St.
Denver, CO 80220
303-321-3963

National Association of County Civil
Attorneys
440 1st St. NW

Washington, D.C. 20001
202-393-6226

National Association of Criminal Defense
Lawyers
1627 K. St. N.W.
Washington, D.C. 20006
202-872-8688

National Association of Railroad Trial
Counsel
88 Alma Real Dr., Suite 103A
Pacific Palisades, CA 90272
213-459-7659

National Association of Retail Collection
Attorneys
1515 N. Warson, Suite 109
St. Louis, MO 63132
800-633-6069

National Association of Securities and
Commercial Law Attorneys
1301 K. St., NW, Suite 650
Washington, DC 20005
202-789-3963

National Association of Women Judges
300 Newport Ave.
Williamsburg, VA 23187-8798
804-253-2000

National Association of Women Lawyers
750 N. Lake Shore Dr.
Chicago, IL 60611
312-988-6186

National Bar Association
1225 11th St. NW
Washington, D.C. 20001
202-842-3900

National Conference of Black Lawyers
2 W. 125th St.
New York, NY 10027
212-864-4000

National District Attorneys Association
99 Canal Center Plaza, Suite 510
Alexandria, VA 22314
703-549-9222

National Employment Lawyers Association
600 Harrison St., Suite 535
San Francisco, CA 94107
415-227-4655

National Gay Rights Advocates
540 Castro St.
San Francisco, CA 94114
415-863-3624

National Health Lawyers Association
1120 Connecticut Ave. NW, Suite 950
Washington, D.C. 20036
202-833-1100

National Lawyers Club
1815 H. St. NW
Washington, D.C. 20006
202-638-3200

National Legal Aid & Defender Association
1625 K. St. NW, Suite 800
Washington, D.C. 20006
202-452-0620

National Organization of Bar Counsel
541 N. Fairbanks Court
Chicago, IL 60611
312-988-5000
http://ourworld.compuserve.com/home-
   pages/nobc/

National Women's Law Center
1616 P. St. NW
Washington, D.C. 20036
202-328-5160

Native American Rights Fund
1712 N. St. NW
Washington, D. C. 20036
202-785-4166

National Lesbian and Gay Law
   Association
P.O. Box 77130
National Capital Station
Washington, D.C. 20013-7130
202-389-0161

NOW Legal Defense and Education Fund
99 Hudson St., 12th Fl.
New York, NY 10013
212-925-6635

Puerto Rican Bar Association
888 Grand Concourse, Suite 1-0
Bronx, NY 10451
212-292-8201

Puerto Rican Legal Defense & Education
   Fund
99 Hudson St., 24th Floor
New York, NY 10013
212-219-3360

Scandinavian American Lawyers
   Association
4177 Garrick
Warren, MI 48071
810-757-4177

Serbian-American Bar Association
20 N. Nacher Dr., Suite 2520
Chicago, IL 60626

Sports Lawyers Association
11250-8 Roger Bacon Dr.
Reston, VA 22090
703-437-4377

Transportation Lawyers Association
3310 Harrison
Topeka, KS 66611
913-266-7014

Volunteer Lawyers for the Arts
1 E. 53d St., 6th Fl.
New York, NY 10022
212-319-2787
212-977-9270

Women's Legal Defense Fund
218 W. 40th St., Room 203
New York, NY 10018
212-730-7412

MISCELLANEOUS

American Arbitration Association
140 W. 51st St.
New York, NY 10020
212-484-4100

American Judicature Society
25 East Washington St.
Chicago, IL 60602
312-558-6900

American Law Institute
4025 Chestnut St.
Philadelphia, PA 19104-3099
215-243-1600

American Prepaid Legal Services Institute
750 N. Lake Shore Dr.
Chicago, IL 60611
312-988-5751

Association of American Law Schools
1201 Connecticut St. NW, Suite 800
Washington, D.C. 20036-2065
202-296-8851

Computer Law Association
3028 Javier Rd., Suite 500E
Fairfax, VA 22031
703-560-7747

Environmental Law Institute
1616 P St. NW, Suite 200
Washington, D.C. 20036

Institute for Mediation and Conflict
   Resolution
425 W. 144th St., 4th Fl.
New York, NY 10031
212-690-5700

Lawyers' Committee for Civil Rights
   Under Law
1450 G St. NW, Suite 400
Washington, D.C. 20005
202-783-0857

Legal Services Corporation
750 First St. NE
Washington, D.C. 20002
202-336-8800

National Association for Law Placement
1666 Connecticut Ave. NW, Suite 325
Washington, D.C. 20009
202-667-1666

National Association for Public
   Interest Law
1118 22nd St. NW, 3rd Floor
Washington, D.C. 20036
202-466-3686

National Association of Bar Executives
c/o ABA Division for Bar Services
541 North Fairbanks Court
Chicago, IL 60611
312-988-5361

National Association of Legal Search
   Consultants
1200 G St. NW, Suite 760
Washington, D.C. 20005
202-347-1917

National Center for Law and Deafness
Gallaudet University
800 Florida Ave. NE
Washington, D.C. 20002
202-651-5373

National Center for Law and Learning
   Disabilities
P.O. Box 368
Cabin John, MD 20818
301-469-8308

National Center for State Courts
300 Newport Ave.
Williamsburg, VA 23185
804-253-2000

National Clearinghouse for Legal Services
205 W. Monroe
Chicago, IL 60606

312-263-3830
800-621-3256

National Clients Council
2617 Martha St.
Philadelphia, PA 19125
215-686-2913

National Conference of Bar Examiners
333 N. Michigan, Suite 1025
Chicago, IL 60601
312-641-0963

National Conference of Commissioners on
Uniform State Laws
676 North St. Clair St., Suite 1700
Chicago, IL 60611
312-915-0195

National Conference of Women's Bar
Associations
P.O. Box 77

Edenton, NC 27932-0077
919-482-8202

National Institute for Citizen Education in
the Law
711 G St. SE
Washington, D.C. 20003
202-546-6644

National Institute for Trial Advocacy
Notre Dame Law School
Notre Dame, IN 46556
219-239-6322

National Legal Center for the Medically
Dependent and Disabled
50 S. Meridian St., Suite 605
Indianapolis, IN 46204
317-632-6245

National Resource Center for Consumers
of Legal Services
1444 Eye St. NW
Washington, D.C. 20005
202-842-3503

Office of Personnel Management
1900 E St. NW
Washington, D.C. 20415
202-606-1800

Western Center for Law and Poverty
3701 Wilshire Blvd.
Los Angeles, CA 90010
213-487-7211

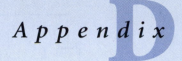

FEDERAL GOVERNMENT ORGANIZATION CHART

THE GOVERNMENT OF THE UNITED STATES

THE CONSTITUTION

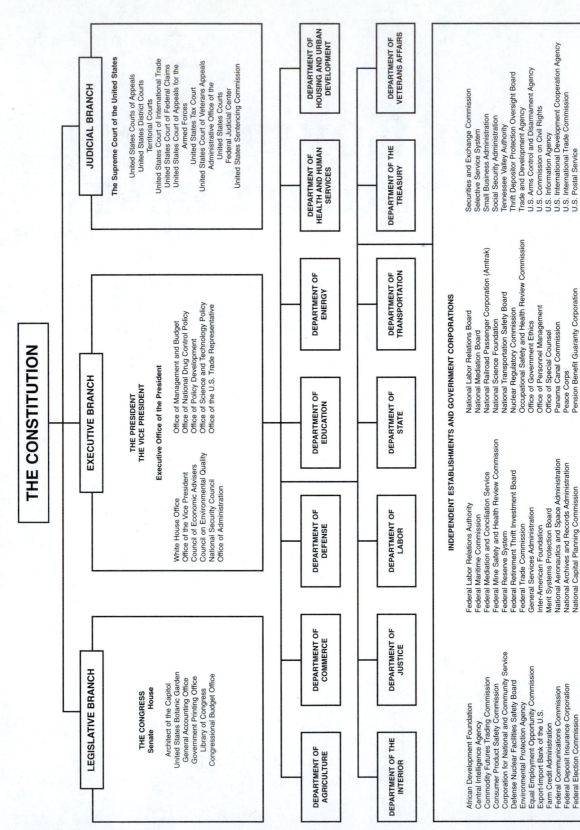

LEGISLATIVE BRANCH

THE CONGRESS
Senate   House

Architect of the Capitol
United States Botanic Garden
General Accounting Office
Government Printing Office
Library of Congress
Congressional Budget Office

EXECUTIVE BRANCH

THE PRESIDENT
THE VICE PRESIDENT

Executive Office of the President

White House Office
Office of the Vice President
Council of Economic Advisers
Council on Environmental Quality
National Security Council
Office of Administration

Office of Management and Budget
Office of National Drug Control Policy
Office of Policy Development
Office of Science and Technology Policy
Office of the U.S. Trade Representative

JUDICIAL BRANCH

The Supreme Court of the United States

United States Courts of Appeals
United States District Courts
Territorial Courts
United States Court of International Trade
United States Court of Federal Claims
United States Court of Appeals for the
Armed Forces
United States Tax Court
United States Court of Veterans Appeals
Administrative Office of the
United States Courts
Federal Judicial Center
United States Sentencing Commission

DEPARTMENT OF AGRICULTURE

DEPARTMENT OF COMMERCE

DEPARTMENT OF DEFENSE

DEPARTMENT OF EDUCATION

DEPARTMENT OF ENERGY

DEPARTMENT OF HEALTH AND HUMAN SERVICES

DEPARTMENT OF HOUSING AND URBAN DEVELOPMENT

DEPARTMENT OF THE INTERIOR

DEPARTMENT OF JUSTICE

DEPARTMENT OF LABOR

DEPARTMENT OF STATE

DEPARTMENT OF TRANSPORTATION

DEPARTMENT OF THE TREASURY

DEPARTMENT OF VETERANS AFFAIRS

INDEPENDENT ESTABLISHMENTS AND GOVERNMENT CORPORATIONS

African Development Foundation
Central Intelligence Agency
Commodity Futures Trading Commission
Consumer Product Safety Commission
Corporation for National and Community Service
Defense Nuclear Facilities Safety Board
Environmental Protection Agency
Equal Employment Opportunity Commission
Export-Import Bank of the U.S.
Farm Credit Administration
Federal Communications Commission
Federal Deposit Insurance Corporation
Federal Election Commission
Federal Emergency Management Agency
Federal Housing Finance Board

Federal Labor Relations Authority
Federal Maritime Commission
Federal Mediation and Conciliation Service
Federal Mine Safety and Health Review Commission
Federal Reserve System
Federal Retirement Thrift Investment Board
Federal Trade Commission
General Services Administration
Inter-American Foundation
Merit Systems Protection Board
National Aeronautics and Space Administration
National Archives and Records Administration
National Capital Planning Commission
National Credit Union Administration
National Foundation on the Arts and the Humanities

National Labor Relations Board
National Mediation Board
National Railroad Passenger Corporation (Amtrak)
National Science Foundation
National Transportation Safety Board
Nuclear Regulatory Commission
Occupational Safety and Health Review Commission
Office of Government Ethics
Office of Personnel Management
Office of Special Counsel
Panama Canal Commission
Peace Corps
Pension Benefit Guaranty Corporation
Postal Rate Commission
Railroad Retirement Board

Securities and Exchange Commission
Selective Service System
Small Business Administration
Social Security Administration
Tennessee Valley Authority
Thrift Depositor Protection Oversight Board
Trade and Development Agency
U.S. Arms Control and Disarmament Agency
U.S. Commission on Civil Rights
U.S. Information Agency
U.S. International Development Cooperation Agency
U.S. International Trade Commission
U.S. Postal Service

Source: United States Government Manual 1996/1997.

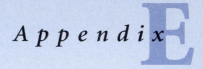

SURVEY OF NON-LAWYER PRACTICE BEFORE FEDERAL ADMINISTRATIVE AGENCIES

STANDING COMMITTEE ON LAWYERS' RESPONSIBILITY FOR CLIENT PROTECTION AND THE AMERICAN BAR ASSOCIATION CENTER FOR PROFESSIONAL RESPONSIBILITY (FEBRUARY 1985)

I. BACKGROUND

The American Bar Association Standing Committee on Lawyers' Responsibility for Client Protection disseminated this survey to thirty-three (33) federal administrative agencies in late August 1984. The survey was intended to provide background information on the experiences of agencies permitting nonlawyer practice (other than for purposes of self-representation). During September and October ninety-seven percent (97%) of the agencies responded either over the phone or by mail following initial contact with their Offices of General Counsel. The ABA Center for Professional Responsibility tabulated the results in October 1984.

II. BRIEF ANALYSIS AND CONCLUSIONS

We found that the overwhelming majority of agencies studied permit nonlawyer representation in both adversarial and nonadversarial proceedings.* However, most of them seem to encounter lay practice very infrequently (in less than 5 percent of adjudications), while only a few encounter lay practice as often as lawyer practice. Thus, although universally permitted, lay practice before federal agencies rarely occurs.

---

*A proceeding is adversarial if there is an opposing side in the controversy, whether or not the other side is represented. A proceeding is nonadversarial if only one side is appearing before the agency official.

Few of the responding agencies comprehensively monitor or control the lay practice that does occur. Only about twenty percent (20%) require nonlawyers to register with the agency before permitting them to practice. Registration procedures may range from simply listing nonlawyers' names to more formalized certifying or licensing procedures, which may include testing and character reviews. Proceedings in most of these agencies tend to require highly technical or specialized knowledge. Registration insures that lay representation meets an appropriate level of quality and competence. In at least one agency, registration insures that nonlawyer representatives will charge only nominal fees or no fees at all.

No agencies indicated that they would discipline nonlawyers differently from lawyers, although they clearly have an additional ability to pursue sanctions against lawyers through external disciplinary mechanisms. Only a few agencies indicated any special need for nonlawyer discipline. Most reported they had not encountered any problems with misconduct by nonlawyers or any inability of nonlawyers to meet appropriate ethical standards (though fewer than a third of the agencies studied have actually defined any specific ethical standards). Of those that voiced complaints about nonlawyers' skills in representation, most indicated that the problem they encounter most frequently is nonlawyers' lack of familiarity with procedural rules and tactics. The majority of responses suggest that nonlawyers do not pose any special practice problems, nor do they receive any special disciplinary consideration. Overall, the concern for nonlawyers' competence and ethical conduct seems limited, perhaps because nonlawyer practice is not widespread.

III. METHODOLOGY

Throughout the survey our questions focused on lay representation (other than self-representation) occurring in adjudicatory proceedings. In question 1, in which we asked whether agencies permitted nonlawyer representation, we attempted to distinguish between adversarial and nonadversarial proceedings. Our distinction did not prove particularly informative because all agencies permitting nonlawyer practice (97 percent) allow such practice in both arenas.

Question 2 sought the methods by which agencies control or limit those practicing before them. The responses vary considerably from agency to agency. Questions 3 and 4 requested statistics concerning the frequency of nonlawyer practice. Many of the agencies indicated that statistics were unavailable. These responses also vary considerably. The results of questions 1 through 4 are tabulated in Chart 1.

Chart 1   Regulations Governing Nonlawyer Representation, Frequency, and Type of Practice

Agency	Statute/ Regulation Permitting Appearance	Permits Nonlawyer Adversarial Representation?	Permits Nonlawyer Nonadversarial Representation?	Provisions Limiting or Governing Practice	Frequency of Nonlawyer Representation	Change in Frequency of Nonlawyer Rep. w/in Past 6 Years	Most Common Type(s) of Nonlawyer Representation
Board of Immigration Appeals: Immigration and Naturalization Serv.	8 CFR § 292.1–3	Yes	Yes	"Accredited representative"[1] working for "recognized organization"[2] may charge only nominal fees. "Reputable individual"[3] may not charge fees	No statistics available	No statistics available	One time only by family member/ friend; charitable, religious, or social service organization
Civil Aeronautics Board	14 CFR § 300.1–6 14 CFR § 302.11	Yes	Yes	None	Fewer than 6 appearances per yr., less than 1% of appearances[4]	None	Economic consultants for corporations
Comptroller of the Currency	12 CFR § 19.3	Yes[5]	Yes	Nonlawyer may be required to file a power of attorney or show to the satisfaction of the Comptroller the possession of requisite qualifications	None	None	None
Consumer Product Safety Comm'n	16 CFR § 1025.61 et seq.	Yes	Yes	Filing and approval of proof of qualifications See 16 CFR § 1025.65	Very infrequent, 2–5% of appearances	None	Nonfee by industry rep., consultant, or private service agency

Chart 1 Regulations Governing Nonlawyer Representation, Frequency, and Type of Practice—Continued

Agency	Statute/Regulation Permitting Appearance	Permits Nonlawyer Adversarial Representation?	Permits Nonlawyer Nonadversarial Representation?	Provisions Limiting or Governing Practice	Frequency of Nonlawyer Representation	Change in Frequency of Nonlawyer Rep. W/in Past 6 Years	Most Common Type(s) of Nonlawyer Representation
Dep't of Agric., Agricultural Marketing Serv.	7 CFR § 50.27	Yes	Yes	None	Fewer than 3 appearances per yr., less than 1% of appearances	Decreased,[6] no statistics available	Economist/accountant providing assistance prior to appearance
Dep't of Commerce, Office of Secretary	Those of other agencies governing appearances before administrative bodies, e.g., MSPB, 5 CFR Part 1201	Yes	Yes	Reasonable atty fees for litigated matters set by agency; maximum atty fees for settlement set at $75/hr.; government pays fees to winning atty	No statistics available	No statistics available	Nonfee by union reps.
Dep't of Commerce, Patent and Trademark Office	35 U.S.C. §§ 31–33	Yes	Yes	Only registered[7] practitioners permitted to practice	Less than 16% of appearances[8]	None	Repeated practice for a fee by registered agents

[1] May become accredited by the Department of Immigration Appeals (D.I.A.) by submitting an application through a recognized organization for review of character and fitness and experience with and knowledge of immigration law. No formal testing requirement or licensing fee.

[2] Typically, a religious, charitable, or social service organization becomes recognized by submitting an application for approval to the D.I.A. assuring that it will charge only nominal fees and assess no representation charges.

[3] Typically, a family member or friend submits declaration that he or she charges no fee, has a preexisting relationship with immigrant-applicant, and appears only on individual basis at request of immigrant-applicant.

[4] Although nonlawyer practice [is] not discouraged, complexity of agency proceedings tends to require specialized legal practice. Typical parties, large corporations or businesses, tend to hire lawyers.

[5] Permitted but lay representation rare because of complex proceedings and substantial rights or amounts of money involved.

[6] In agency's early history, economists provided a substantial amount of representation because of the economic nature of agency proceedings. As proceedings become more sophisticated, economists began aiding lawyers rather than assuming primary responsibility for legal representation. Representation by economists is now rare, and lawyers handle the bulk of representation.

[7] Nonlawyers become registered by passing a character and fitness review and an examination. Nonlawyers having served four years in the examining corps of the Patent and Trademark Office (P.T.O.) may waive the exam. See 57 CFR § 1.341.

[8] Nonlawyers comprise about 16% of registered practitioners, but not all registered practitioners appear before P.T.O., so that nonlawyers probably appear in less than 16% of patent applications filed with P.T.O.

Agency	Regulation			Fees	Appearances		Examples
Dep't of Health and Human Services, Food and Drug Admin.	32 CFR §§ 12.40, 12.45	Yes	Yes	None	No appearances in recent years	None	None
Dep't of Justice, Drug Enforcement Admin.	21 CFR § 1316.50	Yes	N/A, all proceedings adversarial	None	2 to 3 appearances per yr., 5% of appearances[9]	None	One time only by officer/employee of small family-owned business
Dep't of Justice Foreign Claims Settlement Comm'n	45 CFR § 500.1-6	No	No[10]	Lawyer's fees set by statute at 10% of claim award and deducted from award	N/A[11]	N/A[11]	Family member providing assistance prior to appearance
Dep't of Labor, Benefits Review Board	20 CFR § 802.201(b) 20 CFR §802.202	Yes	N/A, all proceedings adversarial	Employer pays fee for successful claimant represented by lawyer; claimant pays fee when represented by nonlawyer; lawyer may acquire lien against award; nonlawyers may not.[12] Professional status is criterion for determining fees.[13]	2–4% of appearances	None	Repeated practice for fee
Dep't of Labor, Employees Compensation Appeals Board	20 CFR § 501.11	Yes	N/A, all proceedings adversarial	All fees approved by board	Appear as frequently as lawyers	None	One time only by family member/friend; repeated practice for a fee

Chart 1 Regulations Governing Nonlawyer Representation, Frequency, and Type of Practice—Continued

Agency	Statute/ Regulation Permitting Appearance	Permits Nonlawyer Adversarial Representation?	Permits Nonlawyer Nonadversarial Representation?	Provisions Limiting or Governing Practice	Frequency of Nonlawyer Representation	Change in Frequency of Nonlawyer Rep. w/in Past 6 Years	Most Common Type(s) of Nonlawyer Representation
Dep't of Labor, National Railroad Adjustment Board	45 U.S.C. § 3153	Yes	N/A	Only entities identified in 45 U.S.C. § 151 allowed to practice	Almost 100% of appearances	None	Industry employees
Dep't of Labor, Wage and Appeals Board	20 CFR § 725.362(a) 20 CFR § 725.365 20 CFR § 725.366(b)	Yes	N/A	Fees must be reasonably commensurate with services performed;[14] attorney's fee deducted from award; employer pays fee for successful claimant represented by lawyer; claimant prep fee when represented by nonlawyer; lawyer may require lien against award, nonlawyers may not.[15]	3% of appearances; as in 180 cases/yr.	Decrease due to investigations by Office of Inspector General into unauthorized receipt of fees	One time only by family member or friend; repeated practice for fee; assistance prior to appearance

[9]Appearances are by the employees or officers of small family-owned businesses, analogous to pro se appearances.
[10]The agency only allows "representation" by bar members. Family members may sometimes assist in preparation of claims or at oral hearings, typically where elderly parent has language barrier problems.
[11]No nonlawyer representation allowed.
[12]These policies may tend to discourage lay representation.
[13]Typically approved rates for nonlawyers are less than half of those attorneys receive.
[14]See 20 CFR § 725.366(b) (black lung) and 20 CFR § 702.132 (longshore).
[15]These policies may tend to discourage lay representation.

Dep't of Transportation, Maritime Admin.	46 CFR § 201.21	Yes	Yes	Only registered nonlawyers permitted to practice	Very infrequent	None	One time only by family member/ friend; nonlawyer assistance prior to appearance
Federal Deposit Ins. Corp.	12 CFR § 308.04	Yes	Yes	Only qualified nonlawyers permitted to represent	10 to 20 appearances per yr., 5% of appearances	50% decrease	Engineering firm assisting in technical nonadversarial proceeding
Federal Energy Regulatory Comm'n	18 CFR § 385.2101	Yes	Yes	None	1 or 2 per yr.	None	
Federal Maritime Comm'n	46 CFR § 502.30	Yes	Yes	Only registered nonlawyers permitted to appear[16]	.5 to 1% of appearances	None	One time only by family member/ friend; nonfee by industry rep., consultant or private service agency
Federal Mine Safety & Health Review Comm'n	29 CFR § 2700.3(b)	Yes, at trial hearings before Administrative Law Judges (ALJ); at appellate reviews before commissioners	N/A	Nonlawyer may practice only if party, "representative of miners,"[17] or owner, partner, full time officer or employee of party–business entity; otherwise permitted to appear for limited purpose in special proceedings	5–10% of appearances	None	Nonfee by industry rep., consultant or private service agency

Chart 1   Regulations Governing Nonlawyer Representation, Frequency, and Type of Practice—Continued

Agency	Statute/Regulation Permitting Appearance	Permits Nonlawyer Adversarial Representation?	Permits Nonlawyer Nonadversarial Representation?	Provisions Limiting or Governing Practice	Frequency of Nonlawyer Representation	Change in Frequency of Nonlawyer Rep. w/in Past 6 Years	Most Common Type(s) of Nonlawyer Representation
General Accounting Office	31 U.S.C. § 731–732; 4 CFR §§ 11 and 28; GAO Orders 2713.2, 2752.1, and 2777.1	Yes, in adverse actions, grievance proceedings, and discrimination complaints	Yes	Nonlawyers not permitted fees; government pays fees to winning representatives[18]	Very infrequent	Not aware of any	
Internal Revenue Serv. fied	13 CFR Part 10; 31 U.S.C. § 330; Treasury Dept. Circular 230	Yes	Yes	Noncertified public accountant and nonlawyer must become enrolled agent[19] to practice	As frequent as lawyer representation[20]	Increased, no statistics available	Repeated practice for fee by certified public accountant or enrolled agent
Interstate Commerce Comm'n	49 CFR § 1103	Yes	Yes	Fee limitations,[21] only registered nonlawyer permitted to practice,[22] however, self-representation is allowed without registration	1,600 nonlawyers now registered and account for 5% of appearances.[23]	Decreased,[24] no statistics available	Repeated practice for a fee
National Credit Union Admin.	12 CFR § 747	Yes	Yes	None	No statistics available	Decreased, no statistics available	Credit union representatives

[16]Certificates of registration are issued on payment of $13.00 processing fee and completion of application form indicating sufficient educational qualifications and recommendations. There is no testing or formal licensing.

[17]See generally 30 CFR § 40.1(b).

[18]As provided in discrimination statutes, backpay act, and appeals authorized by law.

[19]Nonlawyers and noncertified public accountants become enrolled agents by (1) passing a character and fitness review, and (2) successful completion of special enrollment examination testing on federal taxation and related matters, or (3) former employment with the IRS, provided duties qualify the individual. Lawyers and certified public accountants may practice without enrollment.

[20]Includes representation by certified public accountants as well as enrolled agents.

[21]Practitioners may not overestimate the value of services, accept compensation from party other than client, make contingent fee arrangements, or divide fees with laypersons. See 49 CFR § 1103.70.

[22]To become registered applicant must (1) meet educational and experience requirements, (2) undergo character and fitness review, (3) pass exam administered by the agency testing knowledge in the field of transportation, and (4) take an oath. See 49 CFR § 1103.3.

[23]Figure includes appearances in rulemaking as well as adjudicatory proceedings.

[24]Deregulation has reduced the caseload while proceedings have become more complex, creating a greater need for legal expertise.

National Labor Relations Board		Yes	Yes	None	Infrequent	None	
National Mediation Board	None, agency governed by 29 CFR § 1200 et seq.	N/A, all proceedings adversarial	Yes	None	200 appearances per yr., appear twice as frequently as lawyers	Decreased, no statistics available	Union representative
National Transportation Safety Board	49 CFR § 821 49 CFR § 831 49 CFR § 845	Yes	Yes	In adjudication, lawyer representation is encouraged; in investigation, lawyer participation is discouraged because technical expertise required; parties[25] participate in investigations	Very infrequent except at investigatory levels	None	Manufacturers at investigatory levels
Occupational Safety and Health Comm'n	29 CFR § 2200.22	Yes	N/A, all proceedings adversarial	Optional simplified procedures to encourage self-representation by small businesses	20% of appearances[26]	20% decrease[27]	Nonlegal employee representing employer; union representative
Small Business Admin.	13 CFR § 121.11 13 CFR § 134.16	Yes	N/A, all proceedings adversarial	None	Less than 1% of appearances[28]	None	

Chart 1 Regulations Governing Nonlawyer Representation, Frequency, and Type of Practice—Continued

Agency	Statute/Regulation Permitting Appearance	Permits Nonlawyer Adversarial Representation?	Permits Nonlawyer Nonadversarial Representation?	Provisions Limiting or Governing Practice	Frequency of Nonlawyer Representation	Change in Frequency of Nonlawyer Rep. w/in Past 6 Years	Most Common Type(s) of Nonlawyer Representation
Social Security Admin.	42 USC § 406(a) 29 CFR	Yes, tentatively as part of experiment; generally agency has no adversarial proceedings	Yes	Claimants advised of advantages of representation at hearing level;[29] fees set by agency;[30] attorney fees are withheld from awards[31]	Appear in 13% of total hearings or in 25–30% of hearings with representation	None, although lawyer representation increased by 56% since 1978[32]	One time only by family member/friend; repeated practice for fee; nonfee rep. by legal services paralegal
U.S. Customs Serv.	None	Yes	Yes	None	5 to 15% of caseload volume	None	Repeated practice for fee by licensed customs brokers and former customs officials
U.S. Environmental Protection Agency	40 CFR § 124 40 CFR § 164.30 40 CFR § 22.10	Yes	N/A	None	No appearances	None	None

25 "Parties" includes manufacturers, unions, operators and other regulatory agencies.

26 Statistic includes pro se representation.

27 Nonlawyer practice accounted in 1980 for 40% of the agency's caseload but decreased in 1982–83 to 20%. Decrease may result from increasing complexity in cases causing claimants to seek legal representation.

28 Figure excludes pro se appearances in size and Standard Industrial Classification (SIC) Appeals. Approximately 50% of size and SIC appeals are conducted pro se by nonlawyers.

29 When hearing request [is] filed, agency sends a letter to unrepresented claimant describing advantages of representation. Attached to letter is a list of organizations which may provide representation. The list includes lawyer referral services, legal aid groups, law schools, etc.

30 The agency sets all fees based on criteria listed in 20 CFR § 404.1725(b), including extent and type of services, complexity of case, level of skill and competence required in performing services, time spent, results achieved, level at which representative became involved, and amount requested.

31 When decision is entered in favor of a claimant represented by a lawyer in a Title II or Black Lung case, normally 25% of the benefits awarded are withheld. After agency has set the fee, it forwards fee directly to the lawyer from the amount withheld. If attorney's fees exceed the amount withheld, the lawyer must seek the remainder from the claimant. If the attorney's fees are less than the amount withheld, the claimant receives the remainder. Nonlawyer representatives do not have this withholding benefit.

32 In fiscal year 1978 lawyers appeared in 32% of hearings; nonlawyers in 12%. In fiscal year 1983 lawyers appeared in 50% of hearings; nonlawyers in 13%. Though the letter discussed in footnote 29 does not exclusively reference lawyers' services, this list may attribute to the increase in lawyer representation. Lawyers also have a high success rate before the agency as well as the advantage of award withholdings to secure fees in Title II and Black Lung cases (see footnote 31).

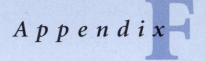
STATE SURVEY: OPINIONS, RULES, STATUTES, AND REPORTS ON PARALEGAL ETHICS AND RELATED TOPICS

The following fifty-state summary covers paralegals and other nonattorneys. The purpose of the summary is to give an overview of the kinds of issues that have arisen. It is *not* meant to describe the current state of the law or provide the current ethics regulations of any particular state. Keep in mind that the rules governing paralegals are undergoing considerable change. See Section F of chapter 5 on how to do legal research to determine the current ethics rules that apply to your state.[1]

ALABAMA

ETHICAL RULES AND GUIDELINES IN ALABAMA

Under Rule 7.6 of the Rules of Professional Conduct, the title "Legal Assistant" is acceptable on a business card that also contains an attorney's or a law firm's name. The title of the nonattorney employee should be legibly and prominently displayed in close proximity to the employee's name. Cards that visually present an attorney's or law firm's name so prominently that they obscure the employee's nonattorney status are prohibited. An earlier ethics opinion preferred the title, *non-lawyer assistant,* since *paralegal* could be a misleading title. Alabama State Bar, *Opinion 86-04* (3/17/86). See also *Opinion 86-120* (12/2/86).

When a paralegal signs a letter to a nonattorney, the paralegal's name should be followed by one of these titles: *nonlawyer assistant, nonlawyer paralegal,* or *nonlawyer investigator.* Alabama State Bar, *Opinion 87-77* (6/16/87).

---

[1]Some of the citations in this survey are to WESTLAW documents (designated WL), which are provided when a more traditional citation is unavailable. In some instances, however, the WL citation is simply an additional reference provided for convenience.

It is improper to include the name of a nonattorney assistant on the letterhead of law firm stationery. Alabama State Bar, *Opinion 83-87* (5/23/83).

The business card of a legal secretary can list the fact that she has been certified by passing an examination of the National Association of Legal Secretaries. Alabama State Bar, *Opinion 90-01* (1/17/90).

When a plaintiff's law firm hires an investigator who worked for a defense law firm, the plaintiff's law firm must withdraw from all cases in which the investigator previously worked, unless the defense law firm consents and its clients consent. Screening the investigator from such cases is not enough. Alabama State Bar, *Opinion 89-41* (4/5/89). See also *Opinion 89-91* (8/7/89) on job switching by a secretary and the effectiveness of a Chinese Wall (screening) around her, and Alabama State Bar, *Opinion 91-01* (5/7/91) (reasonable measures to prevent the disclosure of confidential information *will* allow a law firm to continue to employ a part-time secretary/bookkeeper who is also employed by another firm).

An attorney cannot allow his paralegal to ask questions of debtors at meetings of creditors in bankruptcy cases. Alabama State Bar, *Opinion 89-76* (9/20/90).

Paralegals may draft documents if supervised by an attorney, but they cannot make court appearances or give legal advice. Alabama State Bar, *Opinion 86-120* (12/2/86).

An attorney engaged in collection work may not pay his lay employees on a commission basis. *Opinion of the General Counsel* (2/3/88, revised 2/14/90).

Nonattorney independent contractors who sell legal research services to attorneys are not engaged in the unauthorized practice of law. Alabama State Bar, *Opinion 90-04* (1/18/90).

Other Alabama State Bar Opinions involving nonattorneys: *86-101* (10/30/86); *86-124* (12/15/86); *87-31* (5/20/87); *87-38* (3/6/87); *87-129* (12/31/87); *87-135* (10/30/87); *75-151* (2/4/88); *88-03* (2/4/88); *89-92* (9/25/89); *98-18* (2/21/90). See also Birmingham Bar Ass'n, *Opinion 88-4* (7/8/88).

DEFINING THE PRACTICE OF LAW IN ALABAMA

§ 34-3-6 *(Michie's Alabama Code)* . . . (b) For the purposes of this chapter, the practice of law is defined as follows: Whoever, (1) In a representative capacity appears as an advocate or draws papers, pleadings or documents, or performs any act in connection with proceedings pending or prospective before a court or a body, board, committee, commission or officer constituted by law or having authority to take evidence in or settle or determine controversies in the exercise of the judicial power of the state or any subdivision thereof; or (2) For a consideration, reward or pecuniary benefit, present or anticipated, direct or indirect, advises or counsels another as to secular law, or draws or procures or assists in the drawing of a paper, document or instrument affecting or relating to secular rights; or (3) For a consideration, reward or pecuniary benefit, present or anticipated, direct or indirect, does any act in a representative capacity in behalf of another tending to obtain or secure for such other the prevention or the redress of a wrong or the enforcement or establishment of a right; or (4) As a vocation, enforces, secures, settles, adjusts or compromises defaulted, controverted or disputed accounts, claims or demands between persons with neither of whom he is in privity or in the relation of employer and employee in the ordinary sense; is practicing law.

PARALEGALS (AND OTHER NONATTORNEYS) IN COURT

- *Ex Parte Moody,* 1996 WL 342284 (Court of Criminal Appeals of Alabama, 1996) (an indigent defendant representing himself in a criminal case does not have a constitutional right to the services of a paralegal).

- *Grimsley v. State,* 632 So. 2d 547 (Court of Criminal Appeals of Alabama, 1993) (the attorney-client privilege did not apply to statements made by the defendant to an investigator hired by a paralegal).
- *Blankenship v. City of Hoover,* 590 So. 2d 245 (Supreme Court of Alabama, 1991) (the propriety of a conversation between a paralegal and the secretary of the trial judge).

ALASKA

ETHICAL RULES AND GUIDELINES IN ALASKA

A suspended attorney may work as a paralegal, but only under the supervision of an attorney in good standing. He or she may not have a direct relationship with a client. Alaska Bar Ass'n, *Ethics Opinion 84-6* (8/25/84).

Under the supervision or review of an attorney, a legal assistant can investigate claims and have contact with insurance agents regarding the settlement of claims in worker's compensation cases under the supervision or review of an attorney. Alaska Bar Ass'n, *Ethics Opinion 73-1* (10/6/73).

Paralegal employees of attorneys may not conduct worker's compensation hearings. Alaska Bar Ass'n, *Ethics Opinion 84-7* (8/25/84). Note: this Opinion was *reversed* on 11/9/84.

DEFINING THE PRACTICE OF LAW IN ALASKA

Rule 63. *Rules of the Alaska Bar Association.* For purposes of Alaska Statutes § 08.08.230 [making unauthorized practice of law a misdemeanor], "practice of law" is defined as: (a) representing oneself by words or conduct to be an attorney, and, if the person is authorized to practice law in another jurisdiction but is not a member of the Alaska Bar Association, representing oneself to be a member of the Alaska Bar Association; and (b) either (i) representing another before a court or governmental body which is operating in its adjudicative capacity, including the submission of pleadings, or (ii), for compensation, providing advice or preparing documents for another which effect legal rights or duties.

PARALEGALS (AND OTHER NONATTORNEYS) IN COURT

- *Nielson v. Benton,* 903 P.2d 1049 (Supreme Court of Alaska, 1995) (paralegal fees and Alaska Rule of Civil Procedure 82(b) (2)).
- *Frontier Companies of Alaska v. Jack White Co.,* 818 P.2d 645 (Alaska Supreme Court, 1991) (paralegal fees).
- *Pederson-Szafran v. Baily,* 837 P.2d 124 (Alaska Supreme Court, 1992) (paralegal in state government claims she was blacklisted).
- *State v. M.,* 3AN-S93-1602 (an Anchorage paralegal is charged with forging a client's signature on four court documents in a criminal matter; she pleads guilty to a charge of hindering a prosecution).

ARIZONA

ETHICAL RULES AND GUIDELINES IN ARIZONA

The letterhead of an attorney or law firm can list nonattorney support personnel if their nonattorney status is made clear. State Bar of Arizona, *Ethics Opinion 90-03* (3/16/90). This overrules *Opinion 84-14* (10/5/84), which held to the contrary. The latter opinion also said that a separate letterhead for paralegals is not allowed).

A corporation consisting of independent contractor paralegals and a salaried attorney employee is impermissible. State Bar of Arizona, *Opinion 82-18* (12/1/82). It is unethical for an attorney to associate with a nonattorney-operated eviction service; there would be inadequate attorney supervision of the nonattorneys and improper sharing of fees with nonattorneys. State Bar of Arizona, *Ethics Opinion 93-01* (2/18/93).

A law firm can ethically compensate one of its nonattorney employees by a base monthly fee plus quarterly bonuses measured by a percentage of the firm's increased revenues derived from areas the nonattorney employee was hired to develop. State Bar of Arizona, *Ethics Opinion 90-14* (10/17/90).

Other State Bar of Arizona Opinions involving nonattorneys: *Ethics Opinion 86-7* (2/26/86) (it is ethically improper for an attorney to cooperate with a nonattorney "consulting service" that provided expert testimony to its customers for a contingent fee); *Ethics Opinion 82-18* (12/1/82) (it is ethically improper for an attorney to be a salaried employee—not an owner—of a paralegal-run corporation that contracted with attorneys to provide legal services on an as-needed basis); *Opinion 84-4* (3/28/84); *Opinion 87-13* (6/17/87).

DEFINING THE PRACTICE OF LAW IN ARIZONA

State Bar of Arizona v. Arizona Land Title and Trust Co., 366 P.2d 1, 8–9 (Supreme Court of Arizona, 1961): In the light of the historical development of the lawyer's functions, it is impossible to lay down an exhaustive definition of "the practice of law" by attempting to enumerate every conceivable act performed by lawyers in the normal course of their work. We believe it sufficient to state that those acts, whether performed in court or in the law office, which lawyers customarily have carried on from day to day through the centuries must constitute "the practice of law."

PARALEGALS (AND OTHER NONATTORNEYS) IN COURT

- *Styles v. Ceranski*, 916 P.2d 1164 (Court of Appeals of Arizona, 1996) (propriety of communication by a defense paralegal with an employee of the plaintiff without consent of the plaintiff's attorney).
- *In the Matter of Miller*, 872 P.2d 661 (Supreme Court of Arizona, 1994) (discipline of attorney for failure to supervise paralegals).
- *In Re Galbasini*, 789 P.2d 971 (Supreme Court of Arizona, 1990) (discipline of attorney for failure to supervise nonattorney employees.)
- *Smart Industries Corp. v. Superior Court*, 876 P.2d 1176 (Court of Appeals of Arizona, 1994) (disqualification of a plaintiff's attorney when he hired a legal assistant who once worked for the defendant's attorney).
- *Samaritan Foundation v. Goodfarb*, 862 P.2d 870 (Supreme Court of Arizona, 1993) (defendant's attorney hires a nurse paralegal who interviews hospital employees in a medical malpractice case; the statements of the employees are not within the hospital's attorney-client privilege).
- *Bustamonte v. Ryan*, 856 P.2d 1205 (Court of Appeals of Arizona, 1993) (paralegal assistance to prison inmates).
- *Lewis v. Casey*, 116 S. Ct. 2174 (U.S. Supreme Court, 1996) (paralegal assistance to prison inmates).
- *Aries v. Palmer Johnson, Inc.*, 735 P.2d 1373 (Court of Appeals of Arizona, 1987) (recoverability of paralegal fees).
- *State v. Murray*, 906 P.2d 542 (Supreme Court of Arizona, 1995) (becoming a paralegal is not a mitigating factor in a charge of murder!).

ARKANSAS

ETHICAL RULES AND GUIDELINES IN ARKANSAS

"The paralegal should never be placed in a position to decide what information takes priority over other information or to make decisions which affect the client." This function should never be delegated to a paralegal, even though "sometimes a fine line exists in the area of professional judgment." Paralegals need "specific guidelines," preferably in writing, in carrying out responsibilities. *The Paralegal in Practice* by A. Clinton, chairperson of the Paralegal Committee of the Arkansas Bar Ass'n, 23 Arkansas Lawyer 22 (January 1989).

DEFINING THE PRACTICE OF LAW IN ARKANSAS

Arkansas Bar Association v. Block, 323 S.W.2d 912, 914, 915 (Supreme Court of Arkansas, 1959): Research of authorities by able counsel and by this court has failed to turn up any clear, comprehensible definition of what really constitutes the practice of law. Courts are not in agreement. We believe it is impossible to frame any comprehensive definition of what constitutes the practice of law. Each case must be decided upon its own particular facts. . . . "The practice of law consists in no small part of work performed outside of any court and having no immediate relation to proceedings in court. It embraces the giving of legal advice on a large variety of subjects and the preparation of legal instruments covering an extensive field.

In re Arkansas Bar Association Rules and Regulations for Mandatory Continuing Legal Education, 792 S.W.2d 874, 882 (Supreme Court of Arkansas, 1990): The practice of law shall be defined as any service rendered, regardless of whether compensation is received therefor, involving legal knowledge or legal advice. It shall include representation, provision of counsel, advocacy, whether in or out of court, rendered with respect to the rights, duties, regulations, liabilities, or business relations of one requiring the legal services.

PARALEGALS (AND OTHER NONATTORNEYS) IN COURT

- *Herron v. Jones*, 637 S.W.2d 569 (Supreme Court of Arkansas, 1982) (conflict of interest allegation; an employee—a legal secretary—switches law firms in the same case; court refuses to disqualify current employer because confidentiality was not breached).
- *Simmons v. Lockhart*, 931 F.2d 1226 (U.S. Court of Appeals, 8th Circuit, 1991) (recoverability of paralegal fees).
- *In re Anderson*, 851 S.W.2d 408 (Supreme Court of Arkansas, 1993) (attorney surrenders his license to practice law after a drug conviction and then goes to work as a paralegal in his father's law firm; readmission denied).
- *In re Lee*, 806 S.W.2d 382 (Supreme Court of Arkansas, 1991) (disbarred attorney as paralegal and investigator).
- *Andrews v. Carol Turnage Personnel Agency*, 1988 WL 24750 (Court of Appeals of Arkansas, 1988) (contract dispute over payment of placement fee to a paralegal employment agency).
- *Carton v. Missouri Pacific Railroad Co.*, 865 S.W.2d 635 (Supreme Court of Arkansas, 1993) (juror did not have to be removed from a jury because she was a cousin of the paralegal for one of the attorneys).
- *Walters Law Firm v. Director*, 1993 WL 375361 (Court of Appeals of Arkansas, 1993) (paralegal who left law firm was entitled to unemployment compensation since she did not leave voluntarily or without good cause).

● *Beech Abstract Guaranty Co. v. Bar Association of Arkansas,* 624 S.W.2d 900 (Supreme Court of Arkansas, 1959) (nonattorneys drafting real estate documents as the unauthorized practice of law).

CALIFORNIA

ETHICAL RULES AND GUIDELINES IN CALIFORNIA

When a paralegal is authorized to represent a client before the Workers' Compensation Appeals Board, a law firm can use its paralegal to represent a client of the firm before this Board if the client consents and the firm supervises the paralegal. State Bar of California, *Opinion 1988-103.*

Attorneys must take steps to insure that nonattorney employees understand their obligation not to disclose client confidences and secrets. State Bar of California, *Opinion 1979-50* (1979).

A nonattorney can use a business card if it is used for identification rather than for solicitation of business. Los Angeles County Bar Ass'n, *Opinion 381.*

A law firm can pay a bonus to its paralegal as long as the bonus does not involve a sharing of legal fees. Los Angeles County Bar Ass'n, *Opinion 457* (11/20/89).

A nonprofit legal services center for the elderly cannot advertise in a local newspaper the availability of "legal help" from "para-legal aides" trained by a local attorney. Legal help implies legal services. San Diego Bar Ass'n, *Opinion 1976-9* (7/1/76).

A business that provides paralegal services to the public should have attorney supervision except for some purely ministerial tasks. San Diego Bar Ass'n, *Opinion 1983-7.*

Other State Bar of California opinion involving nonattorneys: *Opinion 1988-97* (lay signatory on client trust account). Other Los Angeles County Bar Ass'n opinions involving nonattorneys: *Opinion 457* (payment of bonus to a paralegal); *Opinion 391; Opinion 444.*

DEFINING THE PRACTICE OF LAW IN CALIFORNIA

California v. Landlords Professional Services, 264 Cal. Rptr. 548, 550 (Court of Appeals, 4th District, 1990): Business and Professions Code section 6125 states: "No person shall practice law in this State unless he is an active member of the State Bar." Business and Professions Code section 6126, subdivision (a), provides: "Any person advertising or holding himself or herself out as practicing or entitled to practice law or otherwise practicing law who is not an active member of the State Bar, is guilty of a misdemeanor." The code provides no definition for the term "practicing law." . . . "[A]s the term is generally understood, the practice of law is the doing and performing services in a court of justice in any manner depending therein throughout its various stages and in conformity with the adopted rules of procedure. But in a larger sense it includes legal advice and counsel and the preparation of legal instruments and contracts by which legal rights are secured although such matter may or may not be depending in court." . . . [N]onetheless . . . "ascertaining whether a particular activity falls within this general definition may be a formidable endeavor." . . . In close cases, the courts have determined that the resolution of legal questions for another by advice and action is practicing law "if difficult or doubtful legal questions are involved which, to safeguard the public, reasonably demand the application of a trained legal mind."

PARALEGALS (AND OTHER NONATTORNEYS) IN COURT

● *In re Complex Asbestos Litigation,* 283 Cal. Rptr. 732 (California Court of Appeals, 1st District, 1991) (a paralegal who switches jobs might cause the disqualification of his or her new employer to represent clients about whom the paralegal obtained confidential information while working at a prior (opposing) law firm; a rebuttable presumption exists that the paralegal shared this information with the new employer; the most likely way for the new employer to rebut this presumption, and hence to avoid disqualification, is to show that when the paralegal was hired, a Chinese Wall was built around the paralegal with respect to any cases the paralegal worked on while at the prior employment). (See page 282 in chapter 5.)

- *Devereux v. Latham & Watkins,* 38 Cal. Rptr. 2d 849 (California Court of Appeals, 2nd District, 1995) (litigation paralegal sues her former law firm employer after the paralegal testified against the law firm in an overbilling case).
- *Oakland v. McCullough,* 53 Cal. Rptr. 2d 531 (California Court of Appeals, 1st District, 1996 (a claim for paralegal fees is rejected because of a failure to provide documentation in support of the claim).
- *Guinn v. Dotson,* 28 Cal. Rptr. 2d 409 (California Court of Appeals, 4th District, 1994 (award of paralegal fees).

COLORADO

ETHICAL RULES AND GUIDELINES IN COLORADO

The names of support personnel can be printed on law firm letterhead, and they can be given their own business card as long as they reveal clearly that they are not attorneys. Colorado Bar Ass'n, *Formal Ethics Opinion 84* (4/90).

Paralegals must disclose their nonattorney status to everyone at the outset of any professional relationship. They should be given no task that requires the exercise of unsupervised legal judgment. They can write letters and sign correspondence on attorney letterhead as long as their nonattorney status is clear and the correspondence does not contain legal opinions or give legal advice. They can have their own business cards with the name of the law firm on them if their nonattorney status is made clear. The services performed by the paralegal must supplement, merge with, and become part of the attorney's work product. Colorado Bar Ass'n, *Guidelines for the Utilization of Legal Assistants* (1986).

A law firm can use a paralegal to represent clients at administrative proceedings when authorized by statute and when the practice of law is not involved. To ensure competent representation, the attorney must train and supervise the paralegal. Colorado Bar Ass'n, *Opinion 79* (2/18/89).

An attorney shall continually monitor and supervise the work of assistants to assure that the services they render are performed competently and efficiently. Colorado Bar Ass'n, *Ethics Opinion 61* (10/23/82).

An attorney may not participate with nonattorneys in preparing and marketing estate planning documents when the venture consists of the unauthorized practice of law. Colorado Bar Ass'n, *Opinion 87* (7/14/90).

DEFINING THE PRACTICE OF LAW IN COLORADO

Unauthorized Practice of Law Committee of the Supreme Court of Colorado v. Prog, 761 P.2d 1111, 1115 (Supreme Court of Colorado, 1988): The determination of what acts do or do not constitute the practice of law is a judicial function. . . . While recognizing the difficulty of formulating and applying an all-inclusive definition of the practice of law, we have stated that "generally one who acts in a representative capacity in protecting, enforcing, or defending the legal rights and duties of another and in counseling, advising and assisting him in connection with these rights and duties is engaged in the practice of law."

PARALEGALS (AND OTHER NONATTORNEYS) IN COURT

- *B. B. v. Colorado*, 785 P.2d 132, 139 (Supreme Court of Colorado, 1990) (paralegals and the attorney-client privilege).
- *People v. Lowery*, 894 P.2d 758, 759 (Supreme Court of Colorado, 1995) (paralegal subjected to sexual harassment on the job).
- *People v. Fry*, 875 P.2d 222 (Supreme Court of Colorado, 1994) (failure of an attorney to supervise his paralegal as the unauthorized practice of law).
- *People v. Felker*, 770 P.2d 402 (Supreme Court of Colorado, 1989) (attorney disciplined for allowing nonattorney employee to give a client legal advice).
- *American Water Development v. City of Alamosa*, 874 P.2d 352 (Supreme Court of Colorado, 1994) (award of paralegal fees).
- *In Re Stromberg*, 161 Bankruptcy Reports 510 (U.S. Bankruptcy Court, Colorado District, 1993) (paralegal fees not allowed for babysitting services performed by paralegal).

CONNECTICUT

ETHICAL RULES AND GUIDELINES IN CONNECTICUT

The names of paralegals can be printed on law firm letterhead, and they may have their own business card if their nonattorney status is made clear. Connecticut Bar Ass'n, *Opinion 85-17* (11/20/85).

It is proper for a law firm to use paralegals as messengers to transfer documents and funds to and from real estate closings. The paralegals can also communicate information or questions between the attorneys involved. The paralegals must not comment on the legal implications of the documents, negotiate, or supervise the closing. Connecticut Bar Ass'n, *Informal Opinion 96-16* (7/3/96) (1996 WL 405034).

It is unethical for an attorney to instruct his nonattorney employee to make misrepresentations to the public. Connecticut Bar Ass'n, *Informal Opinion 95-4* (1/6/95) (1995 WL 170147).

Attorneys are responsible for the mistakes of their paralegals and must make sure they have the education, knowledge, and ability to perform delegated tasks competently. Paralegals cannot conduct real estate closings nor supervise the execution of wills. [See, however, *Informal Opinion 96-16* above.] They should not accept or reject cases or set fees "if these tasks entail any discretion on the part of the paralegal." Attorneys can list paralegals on attorney letterhead if the listing is not deceptive and the paralegal's status is clearly identified. Paralegals must not divulge information concerning a client. Even if the client consents to divulging the information, the information must not be used to the disadvantage of the client. Attorneys must not split fees with paralegals nor enter partnerships with them. Connecticut Bar Ass'n, Special Inter-Committee Group, *Lawyers' Professional Responsibility Obligations Concerning Paralegals*, 59 Connecticut Bar Journal 425 (1985).

DEFINING THE PRACTICE OF LAW IN CONNECTICUT

Grievance Committee of the Bar of Fairfield County v. Dacey, 222 A.2d 339, 347, 348, 22 A.L.R.3d 1092 (Supreme Court of Connecticut, 1966): Attempts to define the practice of law have not been particularly successful. The reason for this is the broad field covered. The more practical approach is to consider each state of facts and determine whether it falls within the fair intendment of the term. . . .

State Bar Ass'n of Connecticut v. the Connecticut Bank and Trust Co., 140 A.2d 863, 870, 69 A.L.R.2d 394 (Supreme Court of Errors of Connecticut, 1958): The practice of law consists in no small part of work performed outside of any court and having no immediate relation to proceedings in court. It embraces the giving of legal advice on a large variety of subjects and the preparation of legal instruments covering an extensive field. Although such transactions may have no direct connection with court proceedings, they are always subject to subsequent involvement in litigation. They require in many aspects a high degree of legal skill and great capacity for adaptation to difficult and complex situations. No valid distinction can be drawn between the part of the work of the lawyer which involves appearance in court and the part which involves advice and the drafting of instruments.

PARALEGALS (AND OTHER NONATTORNEYS) IN COURT

- *Rivera v. Chicago Pneumatic Tool Co.,* 1991 WL 151892 (Connecticut Superior Court, 8/5/91) (trial court denies a motion to disqualify the plaintiff's attorney who hired a paralegal formerly employed by defendant's attorney even though the paralegal had been extensively involved in litigation concerning the defendant; there must be a sufficient Chinese Wall built around such a paralegal to insure that confidences are not divulged).
- *Gazda v. Olin Corp.,* 5 CSCR 227 (1/18/90) (legal secretary switches firms; disqualification denied where reasonable efforts were taken to insure that the nonattorney employee would not divulge any confidences she might have acquired).
- *Puglio v. Puglio,* 559 A.2d 1159 (Appellate Court of Connecticut, 1989) (a paralegal can testify in a foreclosure case on behalf of a mortgagee even though the paralegal had been involved in the preparation of the mortgagee's case).
- *Monroe v. Horwitch,* 820 F. Supp. 682 (U.S. District Court for Connecticut, 1993) (paralegal advertises for legal services in uncontested divorce cases and is charged with the unauthorized practice of law).
- *Gibbs v. Southwestern Investment Corp.,* 705 F. Supp. 738 (U.S. District Court for Connecticut, 1989) (award of paralegal fees).

DELAWARE

ETHICAL RULES AND GUIDELINES IN DELAWARE

A law firm cannot allow its paralegal to represent a client before the Industrial Accident Board on a worker's compensation case. Delaware State Bar Ass'n, *Opinion 1985-3.*

A nonattorney law clerk cannot work on a case where the other side is represented by the clerk's former employer. The clerk must be screened from involvement in the case. Delaware State Bar Ass'n, *Opinion 1986-1.*

It is not the unauthorized practice of law for a paralegal to forward documents to a court and to write a letter requesting a hearing as long as the paralegal's status is clear. The paralegal can also gather factual information and draft documents under the supervision of an attorney. Finally, the paralegal can attend a mediation session of the Family Court without an attorney present as long as no legal advice is given. Board on the Unauthorized Practice of Law of the Supreme Court of Delaware, *In re Nancy Stone,* UPL-91-22 (12/20/91) (Order signed by R. Balotti, Chairman).

DEFINING THE PRACTICE OF LAW IN DELAWARE

Delaware State Bar Ass'n v. Alexander, 386 A.2d 652, 661, 12 A.L.R.4th 637 (Supreme Court of Delaware, 1978): In general, one is deemed to be practicing law whenever he furnishes to another advice or service under circumstances which imply the possession and use of legal knowledge and skill. The practice of law includes "all advice to clients, and all actions taken for them in matters connected with the law. . . . Practice of law includes the giving of legal advice and counsel, and the preparation of legal instruments and contracts of which legal rights are secured. . . . Where the rendering of services for another involves the use of legal knowledge or skill on his behalf where legal advice is required and is availed of or rendered in connection with such services these services necessarily constitute or include the practice of law." . . . "In determining what is the practice of law, it is well settled that it is the character of the acts performed and not the place where they are done that is decisive. The practice of law is not, therefore, necessarily limited to the conduct of cases in court but is engaged in whenever and wherever legal knowledge, training, skill and ability are required."

PARALEGALS (AND OTHER NONATTORNEYS) IN COURT

- *In the Matter of the Estate of Ross,* 1996 WL 74731 (Court of Chancery of Delaware, 1996) ("In an age in which attorney fees are high, it is always welcome to see that good use is made of paralegals, with a resulting benefit to the client.").
- *Welsh & Katz, Ltd. v. Imaging Management Associates,* 1996 WL 280888 (Superior Court of Delaware, 1996) (award of paralegal fees).
- *McMackin v. McMackin,* 651 A.2d 778 (Family Court of Delaware, 1993) (award of paralegal fees).
- *In the Matter of Mekler,* 672 A.2d 23 (Supreme Court of Delaware, 1995) (suspended attorney can act as a paralegal but cannot have any contact with clients or prospective clients).

DISTRICT OF COLUMBIA

ETHICAL RULES AND GUIDELINES IN THE DISTRICT OF COLUMBIA

A paralegal who switches firms must be screened from any cases involving clients represented by both firms. This will protect confidences and avoid imputed disqualification. D.C. Bar, *Opinion 227* (21 Bar Report 2, August/September 1992).

Nonattorneys can have a business card that prints the name of the law firm where they work as long as their nonattorney status is clear. D.C. Bar, *Opinion 19.* See also *Speaking of Ethics,* Bar Report, 2 (February/March 1988).

A law firm can share a "success fee" with nonattorney experts on a case. *Opinion 233* (Bar Report, 2, June/July 1993).

A nonattorney *can* be a partner in a law firm. Hence a District of Columbia law firm *can* share fees with nonattorneys under the guidelines of Rule 5.4. For example, a lobbyist or an economist could form a partnership with an attorney. The nonattorney must agree to abide by the Rules of Professional Conduct. Rule 5.4, *Model Rules of Professional Conduct.*

A nonattorney who is an officer, director, or employee of a corporation can appear for that corporation in the settlement of any landlord-and-tenant case. If, however, the corporation files an answer, cross-claim, or counterclaim, the corporation must be represented by an attorney. D.C. Court of Appeals, Rule 49(c) (8), *Rules of the District of Columbia Court of Appeals.*

Other ethical opinions of the D.C. Bar involving nonattorneys: *172* (4/15/86); *176* (10/21/86); *182* (5/19/87); *201* (4/18/89); *203* (6/20/89).

PARALEGALS (AND OTHER NONATTORNEYS) IN COURT

- *In Re Ryan,* 670 A.2d 375 (District of Columbia Court of Appeals, 1996) (attorney disciplined in part because of her overreliance on paralegals who had no paralegal training).

- *In Re Davis*, 650 A.2d 1319 (District of Columbia Court of Appeals, 1994) (disbarred attorney ordered to perform 250 hours of community service as a paralegal).
- *Hampton Courts Tenants Ass'n v. DC Rental Housing Commission*, 599 A.2d 1113, 1118 (District of Columbia Court of Appeals, 1991) ("Hours are not reasonably expended . . . if an attorney . . . performs tasks normally performed by paralegals. . . ." citing *Action on Smoking v. CAB*, 724 F.2d 211, 220-21 (D.C. Cir. 1984)).

FLORIDA

ETHICAL RULES AND GUIDELINES IN FLORIDA

Paralegals can have their own business cards. They may also be listed on a law firm's letterhead, but a title indicating their nonattorney status should appear beneath their name. Attorneys should not hold their paralegals out as "certified" if they are not. Florida Bar, *Opinion 86-4* (8/1/86). See also Florida Bar, *Opinion 71-39* (10/20/71) (nonattorney employee can use the law firm's name on his business card).

When a nonattorney changes jobs to an opposing law firm, the old and new employer must admonish him or her not to reveal any confidences or secrets obtained during prior employment, and the new employer must take steps to insure there is no breach of confidentiality by this employee. Florida Bar, *Opinion 86-5* (8/1/86).

A law firm can allow a nonattorney to conduct a real estate closing if certain conditions are met, e.g., an attorney is available (in person or by telephone) to answer legal questions, the nonattorney performs only ministerial acts (he or she must not give legal advice or make any legal decisions), and the client consents to having the closing handled by a nonattorney. Florida Bar, *Opinion 89-5* (11/89) (overruling *Opinion 73-43*).

Preparing living trust documents constitutes the practice of law. It is the unauthorized practice of law for a nonattorney to decide whether a living trust is appropriate, and to prepare and execute the documents involved. *Florida Bar Re: Advisory Opinion on Non-lawyer Preparation of Living Trusts*, 613 So. 2d 426 (Supreme Court of Florida, 1992). See also *Florida Bar Re: Advisory Opinion on Nonlawyer Preparation of Residential Leases Up to One Year in Duration*, 602 So. 2d 914 (Supreme Court of Florida 1992) and *Florida Bar Re: Nonlawyer Preparation of and Representation of Landlord in Uncontested Residential Evictions*, 605 So. 2d 868 (Supreme Court of Florida 1992).

It is ethically improper for a law firm to delegate to nonattorneys the handling of negotiations with adjusters on claims of the firm's clients. Florida Bar, *Ethics Opinion 74-35* (9/23/74). But the nonlawyer employee can transmit information from the attorney. "For example, the nonlawyer employee may call the adjuster and inform the adjuster that the attorney will settle the matter for X. If the adjuster comes back with a counteroffer, the nonlawyer employee must inform the attorney. The employee cannot be given a range in which to settle." *Ethically Speaking* 15, The Florida Bar News (9/15/91).

An attorney can allow a supervised nonattorney to conduct an initial interview of a prospective client if his or her nonattorney status is disclosed to the client and only factual information is obtained. Florida Bar, *Opinion 88-6* (4/15/88).

Other Florida Bar Opinions involving nonattorneys: *Opinion 88-15* (sharing office space with nonattorneys); *Opinion 87-11* (4/15/88) (nonattorney signing pleadings); *Opinion 70-62* (2/12/71) (a law firm cannot delegate anything that requires personal judgment to a nonattorney employee); *Opinion 68-58* (1/17/69) (nonattorney employees of a law firm can be part of a retirement plan funded from firm profits); *Opinion 73-41* (3/11/74) (nonattorneys cannot take depositions); *Opinion 76-33* (3/15/77) (an attorney must not overbill for paralegal time).

DEFINING THE PRACTICE OF LAW IN FLORIDA

The Florida Bar v. Brumbaugh, 355 So. 2d 1186, 1191-92 (Supreme Court of Florida, 1978): Although persons not licensed as attorney are prohibited from practicing law within this state, it is somewhat difficult to define exactly what constitutes the practice of law in all instances. This Court has previously stated that: ". . . if the giving of such advice and performance of such services affect important rights of a person under the law, and if the reasonable protection of the rights and property of those advised and served requires that the persons giving such advice possess legal skill and a knowledge of the law greater than that possessed by the average citizen, then the giving of such advice and the performance of such services by one for another as a course of conduct constitute the practice of law." This definition is broad and is given content by this Court only as it applies to specific circumstances of each case. We agree that "any attempt to formulate a lasting, all encompassing definition of 'practice of law' is doomed to failure for the reason that under our system of jurisprudence such practice must necessarily change with the ever changing business and social order."

PARALEGALS (AND OTHER NONATTORNEYS) IN COURT

- *The Florida Bar v. Florida Service Bureau*, 581 So. 2d 900 (Supreme Court of Florida, 1991) (it is not the unauthorized practice of law for nonattorneys to give assistance to landlords by explaining what the eviction procedure entails as long a they don't give legal advice; the "information given was no greater than that which anyone could glean from reading the eviction statute").
- *Florida Bar v. Carter*, 502 So. 2d 904 (Florida Supreme Court, 1987) (attorney suspended for failing to supervise his nonattorney personnel).
- *Florida Bar v. Lawless*, 640 So. 2d 1098 (Supreme Court of Florida, 1994) (attorney fails to supervise paralegal properly).
- *United States v. Pepper's Steel*, 742 F. Supp. 641 (U.S. District Court, Southern District of Florida, 1990) (although a paralegal accidentally delivered documents to the opposing party [!], the documents are still protected by the attorney-client privilege).
- *Whitlow v. South Georgia Natural Gas Co.*, 650 So. 2d 637 (District Court of Florida, 1995) (award of paralegal fees).
- *Florida Bar v. Furman*, 376 So. 2d 378 (Florida Supreme Court, 1979) (see discussion of the *Furman* case on page 188 of chapter 4).
- *Esquire Care, Inc. v. Maguire*, 532 So. 2d 740 (Florida District Court, 1988) (nonattorney switches jobs; disqualification not required).
- *Lackow v. Walter E. Heller & Company Southeast, Inc.*, 466 So. 2d 1120 (Florida District Court, 1985) (nonattorney switches jobs; disqualification required).

GEORGIA

ETHICAL RULES AND GUIDELINES IN GEORGIA

It is the unauthorized practice of law for a law firm to allow a nonattorney to conduct a real estate closing. State Bar of Georgia, *Opinion 86-5* (5/12/89).

An attorney should not allow a paralegal to correspond with an adverse party (or the latter's agents) on the attorney's letterhead if the letter discusses legal matters that suggest or assert claims. (Routine contacts with opposing counsel not involving the merits of the case are, however, permitted.) *Advisory Opinion 19* (7/18/75).

An attorney may delegate tasks to a paralegal that ordinarily comprise the practice of law, but only if the attorney has direct contact with the client and maintains "constant supervision" of the paralegal. The paralegal can render specialized advice on scientific or technical topics. The paralegal cannot negotiate with parties or opposing counsel on substantive issues. The paralegal's name may not appear on the letterhead or office door. The paralegal must not sign any pleadings, briefs, or other legal documents to be presented to a court. The paralegal can have a business card with the name of the firm on it if the word *paralegal* is clearly used to indicate nonattorney status. Unless previous contacts would justify the paralegal in believing that his or her nonattorney status is already known, the paralegal should begin oral communications, either face-to-face or on the telephone, with a clear statement that he or she is a paralegal employee of the law firm. Georgia, *Advisory Opinion 21* (9/16/77, revised 1983).

Another State Bar of Georgia opinion involving nonattorneys: *82-2* (11/10/88).

DEFINING THE PRACTICE OF LAW IN GEORGIA

§ 15-19-50 *(Code of Georgia)*: The practice of law in this state is defined as: (1) Representing litigants in court and preparing pleadings and other papers incident to any action or special proceedings in any court or other judicial body; (2) Conveyancing; (3) The preparation of legal instruments of all kinds whereby a legal right is secured; (4) The rendering of opinions as to the validity or invalidity of titles to real or personal property; (5) The giving of any legal advice; and (6) Any action taken for others in any matter connected with the law.

PARALEGALS (AND OTHER NONATTORNEYS) IN COURT

- *Peters v. Hyatt Legal Services,* 469 S.E.2d 481 (Court of Appeals of Georgia, 1996) (a paralegal is sued for legal malpractice along with the law firm).
- *Jones v. Armstrong Cork Co.,* 630 F.2d 324 (U.S. Court of Appeals, 5th Circuit, 1980) (calling someone a "paralegal" does not necessarily mean he or she is a paralegal for purposes of awarding paralegal fees).
- *Cullins v. Georgia Dept. of Transportation,* 827 F. Supp. 756, 762 (M.D. Georgia, 1993) ("paralegal costs are recoverable as a part of . . . attorney's fees and expenses but only to the extent such work is the type traditionally performed by an attorney. Otherwise, paralegal expenses are separately unrecoverable overhead expenses").
- *Mitcham v. Blalock,* 447 S.E.2d 83 (Court of Appeals of Georgia, 1994) (award of paralegal fees).
- *Grinsted v. Houston County School District,* 826 F. Supp. 482 (M.D. Georgia, 1993) (award of paralegal fees).

HAWAII

ETHICAL RULES AND GUIDELINES IN HAWAII

An attorney may list a paralegal on professional cards, letterhead, and professional notices or announcement cards as long as the employee is identified as a paralegal or legal assistant. A paralegal can use a business card identifying him or her as an employee of the law firm. A paralegal can sign correspondence as a paralegal. Hawaii Supreme Court Disciplinary Board, *Formal Opinion 78-8-19* (6/28/84). See also *Opinion 78-8-19-Supp.*

DEFINING THE PRACTICE OF LAW IN HAWAII

Oahu Plumbing and Sheet Metal, Ltd. v. Kona Construction, Inc., 590 P.2d 570, 574 (Supreme Court of Hawaii, 1979): While no statute defines "practice of law", it has been stated that the "practice of law" "consists, among other things, of . . . the rendition of any service to a third party, affecting the legal rights (whether concerning persons or property) of such party, where such . . . rendition of service requires the use of any degree of legal knowledge, skill or advocacy." *Hawaii House Journal 1955,* 28th Terr. Leg. Reg. Sess., S.C. Rep. 612 at 783.

PARALEGALS (AND OTHER NONATTORNEYS) IN COURT

- *Feher v. Dep't of Labor and Industrial Relations,* 561 F. Supp. 757, 766 (U.S. District Court for Hawaii, 1983) ("using paralegals . . . is cost-efficient and should be encouraged").
- *Tirona v. State Farm Mutual Insurance Co.,* 821 F. Supp. 632 (U.S. District Court for Hawaii, 1993) (paralegal fees denied when most of the services performed by paralegals were clerical in nature).
- *Stewart v. Sullivan,* 810 F. Supp. 1102 (U.S. District Court for Hawaii, 1993) (award of paralegal fees).
- *Hawaii v. Liuafi,* 623 P.2d 1271 (Intermediate Court of Appeals of Hawaii, 1981) (paralegal assistance to prisoners).
- *Oahu Plumbing and Sheet Metal, Ltd. v. Kona Construction, Inc.,* 590 P.2d 570 (Supreme Court of Hawaii, 1979) (it is the unauthorized practice of law for a nonattorney officer of a corporation to represent the corporation in litigation).

IDAHO

ETHICAL RULES AND GUIDELINES IN IDAHO

An attorney must not share fees with nonattorneys. The attorney can request compensation for the work of a paralegal or other laypersons acting under his or her supervision as long as the request specifies that laypersons performed the work. Idaho State Bar, *Formal Ethics Opinion 125.*

A law firm cannot list legal assistants on its letterhead. Idaho State Bar, *Formal Opinion 109* (11/30/81).

Attorneys must not split fees with nonattorneys. Idaho State Bar Committee on Ethics, *Opinion 117* (3/14/86).

DEFINING THE PRACTICE OF LAW IN IDAHO

Idaho State Bar v. Meservy, 335 P.2d 62, 64 (Supreme Court of Idaho, 1959): The practice of law as generally understood, is the doing or performing services in a court of justice, in any matter depending [sic] therein, throughout its various stages, and in conformity with the adopted rules of procedure. But in a larger sense, it includes legal advice and counsel, and the preparation of instruments and contracts by which legal rights are secured, although such matter may or may not be depending [sic] in a court. . . . The drafting of . . . documents . . . or the giving of advice and counsel with respect thereto, by one not a licensed attorney at law, would constitute an unlawful practice of law, whether or not a charge was made therefor, and even though the documents or advice are not actually employed in an action or proceeding pending in a court. I.C. § 3-104.

PARALEGALS (AND OTHER NONATTORNEYS) IN COURT

- *Idaho State Bar v. Jenkins,* 816 P.2d 335 (Supreme Court of Idaho, 1991) (an attorney was not sanctioned when his paralegal unethically solicited clients for the law firm, but without the knowledge or ratification of her attorney employer; hence there was no violation of Rule 5.3 of the code of ethics).
- *Kyle v. Beco Corp.,* 707 P.2d 378 (Supreme Court of Idaho, 1985) (a party before the Industrial Commission must be represented by an attorney, if represented at all; the

Idaho Supreme Court is the final arbiter on who can practice law in this state; the legislature cannot allow nonattorneys to practice law before an administrative agency).

- *Coleman v. Idaho,* 762 P.2d 814, 817 (Supreme Court of Idaho, 1988) (prison officials may not constitutionally prevent inmate paralegals from assisting illiterate inmates).
- *Chapman v. Idaho,* 918 P.2d 602 (Court of Appeals of Idaho, 1996) (paralegal assistance to prisoners).
- *Cornett v. Donovan,* 51 F.3d 894 (U.S. Court of Appeals, 9th Cir. 1995) (paralegal assistance to involuntarily committed patients).
- *Idaho State Bar v. Williams,* 893 P.2d 202 (Supreme Court of Idaho, 1995) (disbarred attorney as paralegal).

ILLINOIS

ETHICAL RULES AND GUIDELINES IN ILLINOIS

Paralegal names can be printed on a firm's letterhead. The nonattorney status of the employee must be indicated. Illinois State Bar Ass'n, *Opinion 87-1* (9/8/87). This apparently overrules an earlier opinion that prohibited placing a nonattorney name on letterhead. *Opinion 350.*

Supervising attorneys must be sure their paralegals understand the rules of ethics governing attorneys. Paralegals can have contact with clients but a direct attorney/client relationship remains primary. Paralegals must preserve confidentiality and make sure the paralegal's work does not benefit the client's adversaries. Attorneys may charge clients for paralegal services, but they may not form partnerships with paralegals. Illinois State Bar Ass'n, *Recommendations to Lawyers for the Use of Legal Assistants* (1988).

An attorney can charge an hourly rate for paralegal work, but not for "expenses" that include an hourly rate for a salaried paralegal. Illinois State Bar Ass'n, *Opinion 86-1* (7/7/86).

A paralegal cannot handle phone calls involving legal matters of her law firm while at a collection agency that is one of the clients of the law firm. The law firm would not be able to supervise the paralegal. Illinois State Bar Ass'n, *Opinion 88-8* (3/15/89).

Attorney assistants can prepare standardized deeds and other real estate documents; correspond with any party, but only to obtain factual information; and assist at real estate closings, but only in the company of a supervising attorney. Illinois State Bar Ass'n, *Position Paper on Use of Attorney Assistants in Real Estate Transactions* (approved by Board of Governors, 5/16/84).

It is the unauthorized practice of law for a nonattorney to represent an employer before the Illinois Department of Employment Security in an unemployment compensation case in which the nonattorney prepares and presents evidence. The employer must be represented by an attorney. An attorney does not aid in the unauthorized practice of law by continuing to represent his client when the other side is represented by a nonattorney. Illinois State Bar Ass'n, *Advisory Opinion 93-15* (3/94).

Sharing fees with a nonattorney via profit-sharing is proper provided the sharing is based on a percentage of overall firm profit and is not tied to fees in a particular case. Illinois State Bar Ass'n, *Opinion 89-5* (7/17/89).

A paralegal can conduct a real estate closing without his or her attorney-supervisor present if no legal advice is given, if all the documents have been prepared in advance, if the attorney-supervisor is available by telephone to provide help, and if the other attorney consents. Chicago Bar Ass'n (1983).

Legal assistants can be listed on law firm letterhead or on the door as long as their nonattorney status is clear. Chicago Bar Ass'n, *Opinion 81-4.*

DEFINING THE PRACTICE OF LAW IN ILLINOIS

Indiana-Michigan Corp. v. Estate of Piper, 375 N.E.2d 477, 478 (Appellate Court of Illinois, First District, Fifth Division, 1978): Although the Illinois Supreme Court has not expressly defined "the practice of law," it has indicated that the following definition is substantially correct: "Practicing as an attorney or counselor at law, according to the laws and customs of our courts, is the giving of advice or rendition of any sort of service by any person, firm or corporation when the giving of such advice or rendition of such service requires the use of any degree of legal knowledge or skill."

In re Herrera, 194 Bankruptcy Reporter 178, 191 (U.S. Bankruptcy Court, Northern District of Illinois, 1996): The Illinois Supreme Court has defined the practice of law as constituting "the preparation of pleadings, and other papers incident to actions and special proceedings, and the management of such actions and proceedings on behalf of clients before judges and courts, and, in addition, conveyancing, the preparation of legal instruments of all kinds, and, in general, all advice to clients, and all action taken for them in matters connected with the law."

§ 205/1. (705 *Illinois Compiled Statutes Annotated*): 1. No person shall be permitted to practice as an attorney or counselor at law within this State without having previously obtained a license for that purpose from the Supreme Court of this State. No person shall receive any compensation directly or indirectly for any legal services other than a regularly licensed attorney. . . . Any person practicing, charging or receiving fees for legal services within this State, either directly or indirectly, without being licensed to practice as herein required, is guilty of contempt of court and shall be punished accordingly, upon complaint being filed in any Circuit Court of this State. . . . Nothing in this Act shall be construed to prohibit representation of a party by a person who is not an attorney in a proceeding before the Illinois State Labor Relations Board or the Illinois Local Labor Relations Board under the Illinois Public Labor Relations Act, as now or hereafter amended, the Illinois Educational Labor Relations Board under the Illinois Educational Labor Relations Act, as now or hereafter amended, the State Civil Service Commission, the local Civil Service Commissions, or the University Civil Service Merit Board, to the extent allowed pursuant to rules and regulations promulgated by those Boards and Commissions.

PARALEGALS (AND OTHER NONATTORNEYS) IN COURT

- *In re Estate of Divine,* 635 N.E.2d 581 (Appellate Court of Illinois, 1994) (attorney supervisors are liable for the actions of their paralegals, but the latter should not be liable for the actions of their supervisors; a paralegal does not have an independent fiduciary duty to a law firm client).
- *Kapco Mfg. Co., Inc. v. C&O Enterprises, Inc.,* 637 F. Supp. 1231 (U.S. District Court, Northern District for Illinois, 1985) (disqualification of a law firm is not required simply because it hired a law office manager-secretary who had worked for opposing party at another law firm).
- *Shortino v. Illinois Telephone Co.,* 665 N.E.2d 414, 419 (Appellate Court of Illinois, 1996) (just because an experienced attorney is paid $350 an hour while appearing in court, he or she should not also be paid $350 per hour for tasks that could easily be done by . . . paralegals . . . at a lower hourly rate).
- *In re Marriage of Ahmad,* 555 N.E.2d 439 (Appellate Court of Illinois, 1990) (award of paralegal fees).
- *In the Matter of Continental Illinois Securities Litigation,* 962 F.2d 566 (U.S. Court of Appeals, 7th Circuit, 1992) (paralegal services can be compensated at market rates).

- *Boettcher v. Fournie Farms, Inc.,* 612 N.E.2d 969 (Appellate Court of Illinois, 1993) (confidential communications made by a client to the paralegal of the client's attorney are protected by the attorney-client privilege).
- *In re Discipio,* 645 N.E.2d 906 (Supreme Court of Illinois, 1994) (a suspended or disbarred attorney should not act as a paralegal).
- *Lawline v. American Bar Ass'n,* 956 F.2d 1378 (U.S. Court of Appeals, Seventh Circuit, 1992) (Illinois paralegals and others try to sue the ABA and the Illinois Supreme Court for antitrust violations in their rules on the unauthorized practice of law).
- *People v. Alexander,* 202 N.E.2d 841 (Appellate Court of Illinois, 1964) (a nonattorney can appear in court for purposes of handling ministerial acts such as submitting agreed or stipulated matters) (see discussion of this case on page 193 in chapter 4).

INDIANA

ETHICAL RULES AND GUIDELINES IN INDIANA

Rules of Professional Conduct, Use of Legal Assistants (1993). *Guideline 9.1*: An attorney must supervise the work of the legal assistant. Independent legal assistants, to wit, those not employed by a specific firm or by specific attorney are prohibited. *Guideline 9.2*: An attorney may delegate any task to a legal assistant so long as that task is not prohibited by law. The attorney must be responsible for the work product of the legal assistant. *Guideline 9.3*: An attorney cannot delegate to a legal assistant the tasks of establishing the attorney-client relationship, setting fees, or giving legal opinions to a client. *Guideline 9.4*: The attorney has the duty to make sure the client, the courts, and other attorneys know the legal assistant is not an attorney. *Guideline 9.5*: The legal assistant's name and title can appear on the attorney's letterhead and business card that also identifies the attorney's firm. *Guideline 9.6*: The attorney must take reasonable measures to ensure the legal assistant preserves client confidences. *Guideline 9.7*: The attorney can charge for the work performed by the legal assistant. *Guideline 9.8*: An attorney may not split fees with a legal assistant nor pay legal assistants for referring legal business. An attorney may compensate a legal assistant based on the quantity and quality of the legal assistant's work and the value of that work to a law practice, but the legal assistant's compensation may not be contingent, by advance agreement, upon the profitability of the attorney's practice. *Guideline 9.9*: An attorney who employs a legal assistant should facilitate the legal assistant's participation in appropriate continuing legal education and pro bono publico activities. *Guideline 9.10*: All attorneys who employ legal assistants in the State of Indiana shall assure that such legal assistants conform their conduct to be consistent with the following ethical standards: (a) A legal assistant may perform any task delegated and supervised by an attorney so long as the attorney is responsible to the client, maintains a direct relationship with the client, and assumes full professional responsibility for the work product. (b) A legal assistant shall not engage in the unauthorized practice of law. (c) A legal assistant shall serve the public interest by the improvement of the legal system. (d) A legal assistant shall achieve and maintain a high level of competence, as well as a high level of personal and professional integrity and conduct. (e) A legal assistant's title shall be fully disclosed in all business and professional communications. (f) A legal assistant shall preserve all confidential information provided by the client or acquired from other sources before, during, and after the course of the professional relationship. (g) A legal assistant shall avoid conflicts of interest and shall disclose any possible conflict to the employer or client, as well as to the prospective employers or clients. (h) A legal assistant shall act within the bounds of the law, uncompromisingly for the benefit of the client. (i) A legal assistant shall do all things incidental, necessary, or expedient for the attainment of the ethics and responsibilities imposed by statute or rule of court. (j) A legal assistant shall be governed by the American Bar Association *Model Code of Professional Responsibility* and the American Bar Association *Model Rules of Professional Conduct.*

Paralegal names can be printed on a firm's letterhead if their nonattorney status is clear. The attorneys and nonattorneys must be distinguished clearly. Indiana Bar Ass'n, *Opinion 9* (1985) (overruling *Opinion 5*).

Paralegals may have a business card as long as their capacity is stated and the identity of their employing attorney is disclosed. Indiana Bar Ass'n, *Opinion 8* (1984).

An attorney aids an accountant in the unauthorized practice of law if the attorney prepares blank legal forms for the accountant who will help his clients fill them out without any attorney supervision. Indiana Bar Ass'n, *Opinion 2* (1995). See also *Opinion 4* (1992).

DEFINING THE PRACTICE OF LAW IN INDIANA

In the Matter of Fletcher, 655 N.E.2d 58, 60 (Supreme Court of Indiana, 1995): It is the province of this Court to determine what acts constitute the practice of law. . . . The practice of law includes "the doing or performing services in a court of justice, in any matter depending therein, throughout its various stages . . . [b]ut in a larger sense it includes legal advice and counsel. . . ." The core element of practicing law is the giving of legal advice to a client and placing oneself in the very sensitive relationship wherein the confidence of the client, and the management of his affairs, is left totally in the hands of the attorney. . . . The practice of law includes the appearance in court representing another.

PARALEGALS (AND OTHER NONATTORNEYS) IN COURT

- *Whitehead v. Indiana,* 511 N.E.2d 284 (Supreme Court of Indiana, 1987) (paralegal allowed to sit at counsel's table during trial).
- *Johnson v. Naugle,* 557 N.E.2d 1339 (Court of Appeals of Indiana, 1990) (paralegal costs not recoverable as part of attorney fees) (but see § 1-1-4-6 (a) *West's Annotated Indiana Code,* allowing recovery of paralegal fees (1996)].
- *Alston v. DeBruyn,* 13 F.3d 1036 (U.S. Court of Appeals, Seventh Circuit, 1994) (paralegal assistance in prison).
- *Miller v. Duffib,* 637 F. Supp. 496 (U.S. District Court, Northern District for Indiana, 1986) (court refuses to appoint lay advocate for inmate for court contacts).

IOWA

ETHICAL RULES AND GUIDELINES IN IOWA

A legal assistant who has passed the CLA exam (Certified Legal Assistant) of the Nat'l Ass'n of Legal Assistants may *not* sign law firm correspondence with the designation "CLA, Legal Assistant" or "Certified Legal Assistant," since the public might be misled about his or her nonattorney status. A reader might think that *CLA* was a legal degree. Iowa State Bar Ass'n, *Opinion 88-5* (9/9/88) and *Opinion 88-19* (6/8/89). It is proper, however, to sign the letter with the titles "Legal Assistant" or "Paralegal." *Opinion 89-22* (12/8/89).

Paralegals and other nonattorney employees may not be listed on the law firm letterhead. Iowa State Bar Ass'n, *Opinion 87-18* (2/2/88). The office of the county public defender may not list the names of nonattorney personnel on its letterhead. *Opinion 89-35* (12/14/89).

A paralegal can have his or her own business card. An attorney must take steps to insure his or her paralegal preserves client confidentiality; there must be no intentional or casual breaches. Iowa State Bar Ass'n, Legal Assistant Committee, *Ethical Guidelines for Legal Assistants in Iowa* (1988).

A sign outside the door of a law firm may not list the name of nonattorney employees even though they are called *legal assistants*. Iowa State Bar Ass'n, *Opinion 89-23* (12/26/88). A law firm may not list its paralegals or other nonattorney employees in law directories such as Martindale-Hubbell. Iowa State Bar Ass'n, *Opinion 92-33* (5/27/93).

In oral communications, a paralegal should disclose his or her nonattorney status at the outset of the conversation. *Iowa Code of Professional Responsibility,* EC 3-6, subparagraph 5.

As an incentive, a law firm can pay a paralegal a percentage of the total income it earns as long as the compensation relates to the firm's profits and not the receipt of specific legal fees. Iowa State Bar Ass'n, *Opinion 90-9* (8/23/90).

It would be the unauthorized practice of law for a paralegal to represent a client in Small Claims Court. Iowa State Bar Ass'n, *Opinion 89-30* (12/8/89) and *Opinion 88-18* (2/20/89). Nor can a nonattorney represent someone before the city Civil Service Commission. *Opinion 92-18* (12/3/92).

In a Section 341 bankruptcy proceeding, a paralegal cannot sit with a debtor at the counsel table in the absence of the paralegal's supervising attorney. The paralegal can help the debtor find things in the schedule, but cannot counsel the debtor. Iowa State Bar Ass'n, *Opinion 92-24* (2/28/93).

A retired attorney who is still licensed cannot function as a paralegal in a law office. Iowa State Bar Ass'n, *Opinion 94-1* (9/13/94).

Other Iowa State Bar Ass'n Opinions involving nonattorneys: *87-28* (5/16/88); *88-25* (6/8/89); *89-3* (9/6/89); *90-20* (8/23/90).

DEFINING THE PRACTICE OF LAW IN IOWA

The Committee on Professional Ethics and Conduct of the Iowa State Bar v. Baker, 492 N.W.2d 695, 700, 701 (Supreme Court of Iowa, 1992): This court has refrained from attempting an all-inclusive definition of the practice of law. Rather it decides each case in this area largely on its own particular facts. . . . "It is neither necessary nor desirable to attempt the formulation of a single, specific definition of what constitutes the practice of law." However, the practice of law includes, but it is not limited to, representing another before the courts; giving of legal advice and counsel to others relating to their rights and obligations under the law; and preparation or approval of the use of legal instruments by which legal rights of others are either obtained, secured or transferred even if such matters never become the subject of a court proceeding. Functionally, the practice of law relates to the rendition of services for others that call for the professional judgment of a lawyer. The essence of the professional judgment of the lawyer is his educated ability to relate the general body and philosophy of law to a specific legal problem of a client; and thus, the public interest will be better served if only lawyers are permitted to act in matters involving professional judgment. Where this professional judgment is not involved, nonlawyers, such as court clerks, police officers, abstracters, and many governmental employees, may engage in occupations that require a special knowledge of law in certain areas. But the services of a lawyer are essential in the public interest whenever the exercise of professional legal judgment is required. In short, the practice of law includes the obvious: representing another before the court. But the practice of law includes out-of-court services as well. For example, one who gives legal advice about a person's rights and obligations under the law is practicing law. Or one who prepares legal instruments affecting the rights of others is practicing law. Or one who approves the use of legal instruments affecting the rights of others is practicing law. Practically speaking, professional judgment lies at the core of the practice of law. When lawyers use their educated ability to apply an area of the law to solve a specific problem of a client, they are exercising professional judgment. The phrase "educated ability" . . . refers to the system of analysis lawyers learn in law school. They learn to recognize issues first and then how to solve those issues in an ethical manner, using their knowledge of the law. . . . [L]awyers determine what the issues are and use their knowledge of the law to solve them in an ethical way. This is the art of exercising professional judgment.

PARALEGALS (AND OTHER NONATTORNEYS) IN COURT

- *Committee on Professional Ethics . . . v. Lawler,* 342 N.W.2d 486 (Supreme Court of Iowa, 1984) (attorney disciplined for fee splitting with a nonattorney and failing to supervise his paralegal).
- *Collins v. Hoke,* 705 F.2d 959 (U.S. Court of Appeals, 8th Circuit, 1983) (disabled widower has a right to be represented by a nonattorney at administrative hearing).
- *Committee on Professional Ethics . . . v. Zimmerman,* 465 N.W.2d 288 (Supreme Court of Iowa, 1991) (attorney confused on how to bill for paralegal time; attorney disciplined for charging excessive and duplicative fees).
- *Foxley Cattle Co. v. Grain Dealers . . . ,* 142 Federal Rules Decisions 677, 681 (U.S. District Court, Southern District for Iowa, 1992) (attorney's claim for 8.8 hours to prepare a motion is excessive; "[t]his document easily could have been prepared by a legal assistant in two to three hours.").
- *Houghton v. Sipco, Inc.,* 828 F. Supp. 631 (U.S. District Court, Southern District for Iowa, 1993) (the award of paralegal fees is not designed to be a full employment program for paralegals; there was inadequate documentation for the requested award of paralegal fees).
- *In re Marriage of Grauer,* 478 N.W.2d 83, 85 (Court of Appeals of Iowa, 1991) ("We do not believe that it takes six to twelve months of paralegal training to learn to use a fax machine. . . .").
- *Landals v. George A. Rolfes Co.,* 454 N.W.2d 891, 898 (Supreme Court of Iowa, 1990) (award of paralegal fees).
- *Teleconnect v. Ensrud,* 55 F.3d 357 (U.S. Court of Appeals, 8th Circuit, 1995) (paralegal charged with breaching confidential communications).

KANSAS

ETHICAL RULES AND GUIDELINES IN KANSAS

Legal assistants may be listed on law firm letterhead if their nonattorney status is clear and they have achieved some minimal training as a legal assistant over and above that customarily given legal secretaries. Supervised nonattorney employees may also have their own business cards. Kansas Bar Ass'n, *Opinion 92-15* (12/2/92). This overrules *Opinion 88-02)* (7/15/88), which did *not* allow legal assistant names on attorney letterhead. See also *Opinion 82-38* (11/4/82).

A legal assistant can use a business card that prints the name of his or her law firm if the legal assistant is identified as such. Kansas Bar Ass'n, *Opinion 85-4.* Overrules *Opinion 84-18.*

Clients must be fully informed that the legal assistant is not an attorney. An attorney shall not share legal fees with a legal assistant, meaning that no form of compensation must be tied to a particular fee. A legal assistant shall not be compensated for recommending an attorney. At the beginning of a professional contact, the legal assistant should disclose that he or she is not an attorney. A legal assistant can sign correspondence on law firm letterhead if the signature is followed by a designation that makes clear he or she is not an attorney. If an attorney accepts a case in which the legal assistant has a conflict of interest, the attorney should exclude the legal assistant from participating in that case. The client must be told of this conflict. Kansas Bar Ass'n Committee on Legal Assistants, *Standards and Guidelines for the Utilization of Legal Assistants in Kansas* (12/2/88).

DEFINING THE PRACTICE OF LAW IN KANSAS

Kansas v. Williams, 793 P.2d 234, 240 (Supreme Court of Kansas, 1990): In determining what constitutes the "practice of law" no precise, all-encompassing definition is advisable, even if it were possible. Every matter asserting the unauthorized practice of law must be considered on its own facts on a case-by-case basis. . . . "As the term is generally understood, the practice of law is the doing or performing of services in a court of justice, in any matter depending therein, throughout its various stages, and in conformity to the adopted rules of procedure. But in a larger sense it includes legal advice and counsel, and the preparation of legal instruments and contracts by which legal rights are secured, although such matters may or may not be depending in a court." . . . . [T]he practice of law [is] "the rendition of services requiring the knowledge and application of legal principles and technique to serve the interests of another with his consent." . . . "It is clearly the prerogative of the Supreme Court to define the practices of law: It is unnecessary here to explore the limits of judicial power conferred by [Article 3, Sec. 1, of the Kansas Constitution], but suffice it to say that the practice of law is so intimately connected and bound up with the exercise of judicial power in the administration of justice that the right to regulate the practice naturally and logically belongs to the judicial department of the government. . . . Included in that power is the supreme court's inherent right to prescribe conditions for admission to the Bar, to define, supervise, regulate and control the practice of law, whether in or out of court, and this is so notwithstanding acts of the legislature in the exercise of its police power to protect the public interest and welfare.

PARALEGALS (AND OTHER NONATTORNEYS IN COURT)

- *Dorner v. Polsinelli, White, Vardeman & Shalton, P.C.,* 856 F. Supp. 1483 (U.S. District Court for Kansas, 1994) (paralegal/office coordinator sues her former law firm for failure to pay overtime compensation).
- *Hawkins v. Dennis,* 905 P.2d 678 (Supreme Court of Kansas, 1995) (attorney blames paralegal for errors).
- *In the Matter of Wilkinson,* 834 P.2d 1356 (Supreme Court of Kansas, 1992) (disbarred attorney can work as a paralegal or law clerk; the work must be exclusively of a preparatory nature).
- *Aig Life Insurance Co. v. Johnson,* 1996 WL 422297 (U.S. District Court for Kansas, 1996) (a party may take the deposition of the paralegal employed by opposing counsel).
- *Brown v. Unified School District No. 501,* 878 F. Supp. 1430 (U.S. District Court for Kansas, 1995) (time spent by volunteer paralegals would not be included in award of attorney's fees).
- *Ortega v. City of Kansas City,* 659 F. Supp. 1201 (U.S. District Court for Kansas, 1987) (paralegal's presence at trial was not necessary; therefore, paralegal fees for time spent at trial are denied).

KENTUCKY

ETHICAL RULES AND GUIDELINES IN KENTUCKY

The letterhead of an attorney can include the name of a paralegal. An attorney's name can appear on the business card of a paralegal if the latter's nonattorney status is clear. An attorney shall not share, on a proportionate basis, legal fees with a paralegal. When dealing with a client, a paralegal must disclose at the outset that he or she is not an attorney. This disclosure must be made to anyone who may have reason to believe that the paralegal is an attorney or is associated with an attorney. Kentucky Paralegal Code, *Supreme Court Rule 3.700.*

Without client consent, it is unethical for an attorney to charge a client for paralegal services when the attorney's contract with the client calls for a statutory-set fee, a lump-sum fee, or a contingent fee. The attorney who charges an hourly rate *can* charge for paralegal services, which may be separately stated. Kentucky Bar Ass'n, *Opinion E-303* (5/85).

To avoid disqualification, a law firm that hires a paralegal who brings a conflict of interest because of prior employment must screen the paralegal from the case in which the conflict arises, and take other steps to avoid a breach of confidentiality. Kentucky Bar Ass'n, *Opinion E-308* (1985).

A suspended attorney may work in a law firm as a paralegal after the period of his suspension has expired, even if he has not been reinstated. Kentucky Bar Ass'n, *Opinion E-336* (9/89).

A paralegal cannot appear in court on motion day or for the motion docket. Kentucky Bar Ass'n, *Opinion E-266* (11/82).

A lay assistant cannot take (i.e., conduct) a deposition. Kentucky Bar Ass'n, *Opinion E-341.*

Independent paralegals cannot provide legal services to the public without attorney supervision. Kentucky Bar Ass'n, *Opinion U-45* (1992).

A nonattorney cannot represent a corporation except in small claims court. Kentucky Bar Ass'n, *Opinion E-344* (1991).

A nonattorney nurse ombudsman cannot represent a nursing home patient before an administrative agency unless federal law allows it. Kentucky Bar Ass'n, *Opinion U-46* (1994).

DEFINING THE PRACTICE OF LAW IN KENTUCKY

§ 3.020 *(Rules of the Kentucky Supreme Court)*: The practice of law is any service rendered involving legal knowledge or legal advice, whether of representation, counsel or advocacy in or out of court, rendered in respect to the rights, duties, obligations, liabilities, or business relations of one requiring the services. But nothing herein shall prevent any natural person not holding himself out as a practicing attorney from drawing any instrument to which he is a party without consideration unto himself therefor. An appearance in the small claims division of the district court by a person who is an officer of or who is regularly employed in a managerial capacity by a corporation or partnership which is a party to the litigation in which the appearance is made shall not be considered an unauthorized practice of law.

PARALEGALS (AND OTHER NONATTORNEYS) IN COURT

- *Wyatt, Tarrant & Combs v. Williams,* 892 S.W.2d 584 (Supreme Court of Kentucky, 1995) (paralegal works on tobacco litigation at law firm; when the paralegal stopped working at the firm, he took copies of some of the tobacco litigation documents with him; law firm seeks injunction against the paralegal to prevent disclosure of the contents of these "stolen" documents).
- *Kentucky Bar Ass'n v. Legal Alternatives, Inc.,* 792 S.W.2d 368 (Supreme Court of Kentucky, 1990) (independent paralegals sued for unauthorized practice of law).
- *In re Belknap, Inc.,* 103 Bankruptcy Reporter 842, 844 (U.S. Bankruptcy Court, W.D. Kentucky, 1989) (in the award of fees: "Senior partners should not perform services which could be as competently performed by associates or paralegals; paralegals should not be used to perform tasks which are clerical in nature.").

- *Jackson v. The Law Firm of O'Hara, Ruberg . . .* , 875 F.2d 1224 (U.S. Court of Appeals for the 6th Circuit, 1989) (paralegal fees plus 20 percent).
- *Kendrick v. Bland,* 586 F. Supp. 1536 (U.S. District Court, Western District for Kentucky, 1984) (inmate paralegals).

LOUISIANA

DEFINING THE PRACTICE OF LAW IN LOUISIANA

§ 37:212 *(West's Louisiana Statutes Annotated):* A. The practice of law means and includes: (1) In a representative capacity, the appearance as an advocate, or the drawing of papers, pleadings or documents, or the performance of any act in connection with pending or prospective proceedings before any court of record in this state; or (2) For a consideration, reward, or pecuniary benefit, present or anticipated, direct or indirect; (a) The advising or counseling of another as to secular law; (b) In behalf of another, the drawing or procuring, or the assisting in the drawing or procuring of a paper, document, or instrument affecting or relating to secular rights; (c) The doing of any act, in behalf of another, tending to obtain or secure for the other the prevention or the redress of a wrong or the enforcement or establishment of a right; or (d) Certifying or giving opinions as to title to immovable property or any interest therein or as to the rank or priority or validity of a lien, privilege or mortgage as well as the preparation of acts of sale, mortgages, credit sales or any acts or other documents passing titles to or encumbering immovable property.

B. Nothing in this Section prohibits any person from attending to and caring for his own business, claims, or demands; or from preparing abstracts of title; or from insuring titles to property, movable or immovable, or an interest therein, or a privilege and encumbrance thereon, but every title insurance contract relating to immovable property must be based upon the certification or opinion of a licensed Louisiana attorney authorized to engage in the practice of law. Nothing in this Section prohibits any person from performing, as a notary public, any act necessary or incidental to the exercise of the powers and functions of the office of notary public, as those powers are delineated in Louisiana Revised Statutes of 1950, Title 35, Section 1, et seq.

C. Nothing in this Section shall prohibit any partnership, corporation, or other legal entity from asserting any claim, not exceeding five thousand dollars, or defense pertaining to an open account or promissory note, or suit for eviction of tenants on its own behalf in the courts of limited jurisdiction on its own behalf through a duly authorized partner, shareholder, officer, employee, or duly authorized agent or representative. No partnership, corporation, or other entity may assert any claim on behalf of another entity or any claim assigned to it.

PARALEGALS (AND OTHER NONATTORNEYS) IN COURT

- *Louisiana State Bar v. Edwins,* 540 So. 2d 294 (Supreme Court of Louisiana, 1989) (an attorney can be disbarred for delegating too much to a paralegal and for failing to supervise the paralegal).
- *Louisiana State Bar v. Lindsay,* 553 So. 2d 807 (Supreme Court of Louisiana, 1989) (an attorney charged with professional misconduct tries to shift the blame to his paralegal).
- *In re Harrington,* 608 So. 2d 631 (Supreme Court of Louisiana, 1992) (attorney fails to supervise paralegal who improperly prepares a letter on a case; the attorney fails to insure that the paralegal's conduct was compatible with the professional obligations of a lawyer).

- *Hertz Corp. v. Caulfield,* 796 F. Supp. 225 (U.S. District Court, Eastern District for Louisiana, 1992) (award of $50 per hour for paralegal time is excessive).
- *Salsbury v. Salsbury,* 658 So. 2d 734 (Court of Appeals of Louisiana, 1995) (award of paralegal fees).
- *Louisiana v. Kaltenbach,* 587 So. 2d 779 (Court of Appeals of Louisiana, 1991) (anti-lawyer group that taught the law to others was not engaged in the unauthorized practice of law).
- *United States v. Cabra,* 622 F.2d 182 (5th Cir. 1980) (it is improper to impound a paralegal's trial notes taken during a federal trial).

MAINE

ETHICAL RULES AND GUIDELINES IN MAINE

The names of paralegals can be printed on a firm's letterhead as long as it is not misleading. Maine Board of Overseers of the Bar, *Opinion 34* (1/17/83).

An attorney cannot form a partnership or professional corporation with a nonattorney to provide legal and nonlegal services to clients. Maine Board of Overseers of the Bar, *Opinion 79* (5/6/87).

Other Opinions of the Maine Board of Overseers of the Bar involving nonattorneys: *69* (3/17/86); *99* (9/6/89); *102* (2/2/90).

DEFINING THE PRACTICE OF LAW IN MAINE

§ 807. *(Maine Revised Statutes Annotated):* 1. Prohibition. No person may practice law or profess to practice law within the State or before its courts, or demand or receive any remuneration for those services rendered in this State, unless that person has been admitted to the bar of this State and has complied with section 806-A, or unless that person has been admitted to try cases in the courts of this State under Section 802. . . . 3. Application. This section shall not be construed to apply to: . . . B. A person pleading or managing that person's own cause in court; C. An officer or authorized employee of a corporation, partnership, sole proprietorship or governmental entity, who is not an attorney, but is appearing for that organization: (1) In an action cognizable as a small claim under Title 14, chapter 738. . . . G. A person who is not an attorney, but is representing a party in any hearing, action or proceeding before the Workers' Compensation Board as provided in Title 39-A, section 317; . . . .

PARALEGALS (AND OTHER NONATTORNEYS) IN COURT

- *Maine v. DeMotte,* 669 A.2d 1331 (Supreme Judicial Court of Maine, 1996) (Chinese Wall built around paralegal to prevent disclosure of privileged communications and a conflict of interest).
- *Rich v. Zitnay,* 644 F.2d 41 (U.S. Court of Appeals for the 1st Circuit, 1981) (paralegal assistance to inmates).
- *Federal Deposit Insurance Corp. v. Singh,* 148 Federal Rules Decisions 6, 9 (U.S. District Court for Maine, 1993) (the "[r]eimbursement for any paralegal services which constitute "the practice of law" under Maine law is prohibited"). See also *Weinberger v. Great Northern Nekoosa Corp.,* 801 F. Supp. 804, 823 (U.S. District Court for Maine, 1992).
- *First NH Banks Granite State v. Scarborough,* 615 A.2d 248, 251 (Supreme Judicial Court of Maine, 1992) (allows paralegal fees; we "adopt no talismanic formula with regard to the inclusion of paralegal fees").
- *Wilcox v. Stratton Lumber, Inc.,* 921 F. Supp. 837, 847 (U.S. District Court for Maine, 1996) (parties "seek to bill an excessive amount of paralegal time for unnecessary effort").

Maryland

ETHICAL RULES AND GUIDELINES IN MARYLAND

Legal assistants can have business cards as long as their legal assistant status is designated. Maryland Bar Ass'n, *Ethics Opinion 77-28* (10/18/76).

An attorney can list the names of paralegals on office letterhead or on the office door as long as their nonattorney status is designated. Maryland Bar Ass'n, *Ethics Opinion 81-69* (5/29/81).

A nonattorney once worked for attorney #A. She now works for attorney #B. These attorneys are opponents on a case in litigation. This case was underway when the nonattorney worked for attorney #A. If effective screening (i.e., a "Chinese Wall") is used to insulate the nonattorney from the case, attorney #B does not have to withdraw from the litigation. Maryland Bar Ass'n, *Ethics Docket 90-17* (1990).

An attorney can hire a freelance paralegal as long as the latter is supervised at all times by the attorney who takes steps to insure there is no disclosure of client confidences. Maryland Bar Ass'n, *Opinion 86-83* (7/23/86).

It is unethical to pay a bonus to a paralegal for bringing business to the office. Maryland State Bar Ass'n, *Ethics Docket 86-57* (2/12/86).

An attorney cannot divide a fee with a nonattorney. Maryland Bar Ass'n, *Opinion 86-59* (2/12/86).

A legal assistant cannot be paid a percentage of the recovery in a case on which the assistant works. Maryland Bar Ass'n, *Ethics Opinion 84-103* (1984).

An attorney can rent office space to a nonattorney as long as confidentiality of the attorney's clients is not compromised. Maryland Bar Ass'n, *Ethics Opinion 89-45* (6/12/89).

It is unethical for a sole practitioner to hire as a paralegal his disbarred former associate. The public would think the paralegal is an attorney. Maryland State Bar Ass'n, *Ethics 79-41*. On the same issue, see *Attorney Grievance Commission of Maryland v. James,* 666 A.2d 1246 (Court of Appeals of Maryland, 1995).

Other Maryland Bar Ass'n Opinions involving nonattorneys: *84-6* (7/20/76); *86-45* (9/11/86); *86-69* (7/15/86); *88-56* (3/13/88); *89-18* (3/23/89); *89-64* (8/11/89); *90-26* (2/21/90).

DEFINING THE PRACTICE OF LAW IN MARYLAND

In the Matter of Mark W., 491 A.2d 576, 579 (Court of Appeals of Maryland, 1985): Numerous definitions of what constitutes practice of law are to be found. . . . [The definitions] have not been particularly successful. . . . The more practical approach is to consider each state of facts and determine whether it falls within the fair intendment of the term.

Attorney Grievance Commission of Maryland v. Hallmon, 681 A.2d 510, 514 (1996 WL 492984) (Court of Appeals of Maryland, 1996): This Court has always found it difficult to craft an all encompassing definition of the "practice of law." To determine what is the practice of law we must look at the facts of each case and determine whether they "fall [ ] within the fair intendment of the term." . . . The purpose of Rule 5.5 [prohibiting the unauthorized practice of law] "is to protect the public from being preyed upon by those not competent to practice law— from incompetent, unethical, or irresponsible representation." . . . That "goal . . . is achieved, in general, by emphasizing the insulation of the unlicensed person from the public and from tribunals such as courts and certain administrative agencies." To determine whether an individual has engaged in the practice of law, the focus of the inquiry should "be on whether the activity in question required legal knowledge and skill in order to apply legal principles and precedent." . . . "Functionally, the practice of law relates to the rendition of services for others that call for the professional judgment of a lawyer." . . . "Where trial work is not involved but the preparation of legal documents, their interpretation, the giving of legal advice, or the application of legal principles to problems of any complexity, is involved, these activities are still the practice of law."

PARALEGALS (AND OTHER NONATTORNEYS) IN COURT

- *Attorney Grievance Commission of Maryland v. Wright,* 507 A.2d 618, 622, 623 (Court of Appeals of Maryland, 1986) (tasks were performed by paralegals "without detailed direction and under minimal supervision by way of review of the final product"; the dollar value of non-legal work "is not enhanced just because a lawyer does it").
- *Sheppard v. Riverview Nursing Centre, Inc.,* 870 F. Supp. 1369, 1380 (U.S. District Court for Maryland, 1994) (paralegal fees reduced; "The Court regards the 33.7 hours [the paralegal] spent outlining and summarizing various depositions to be excessive and unnecessary in this straightforward case").
- *In re Ward,* 190 Bankruptcy Reporter 242, 248 (U.S. Bankruptcy Court for Maryland, 1995) ("[w]hen seeking compensation for clerical services performed by an attorney or a paralegal, an applicant must provide sufficient information enabling the court to make a determination as to why such services were performed by an attorney or paralegal as opposed to a paralegal or secretary, respectively").
- *Buffington v. Baltimore County,* 913 F.2d 113 (U.S. Court of Appeals for the 4th Circuit, 1990) (award of paralegal fees).
- *Microsoft Corp. v. Gray Computer,* 910 F. Supp. 1077, 1084 (U.S. District Court for Maryland, 1995) (role of paralegal working for Microsoft in trademark infringement case).
- *ACLU of Maryland v. Wicomico County,* 999 F.2d 780, 787 (U.S. Court of Appeals for the 4th Circuit, 1993) (a paralegal's "contact visits" with inmates are withdrawn; "the right to ply the paralegal's trade does not per se entail a concomitant right to freely enter federal prisons to do so").
- *Carlson v. NCOP Academy for Paralegals,* 1995 WL 819050 (U.S. District Court for Maryland, 1995) (suit involving the National Academy for Paralegals—an inmate organization, which has categories of membership based on passing a criminal law examination).
- *Attorney Grievance Commission of Maryland v. Hallmon,* 1996 WL 492984 (Court of Appeals of Maryland, 1996) (attorney charged with aiding the unauthorized practice of law by one of his nonattorney employees).

MASSACHUSETTS

ETHICAL RULES AND GUIDELINES IN MASSACHUSETTS

Paralegal names can be printed on a firm's letterhead if their nonattorney status is clear. Massachusetts Bar Ass'n, *Ethics Opinion 83-10* (11/29/83).

A paralegal can sign his or her name on law firm letterhead. Massachusetts Bar Ass'n, *Ethics Opinion 73-2.*

A law firm cannot pay its office administrator (a nonattorney) a percentage of the firm's profits in addition to his fixed salary. Massachusetts Bar Ass'n, *Opinion 84-2* (1984).

DEFINING THE PRACTICE OF LAW IN MASSACHUSETTS

In re Opinion of the Justices, 194 N.E. 313, 317, 318 (Supreme Judicial Court of Massachusetts, 1935): Practice of law under modern conditions consists in no small part of work performed outside of any court and having no immediate relation to proceedings in court. It embraces conveyancing, the giving of legal advice on a large variety of subjects, and the preparation and execution of legal instruments covering an extensive field of business and trust relations and other affairs. Although these transactions may have no direct connection with court proceedings, they are always subject to become involved in litigation. They require in many aspects a high degree of legal skill, a wide experience with men and affairs, and great capacity for adaptation to difficult and complex situations. These "customary functions of an attorney or counsellor at law . . . bear an intimate relation to the administration of justice by the courts. No valid distinction, so far as concerns the questions set forth in the order, can be drawn between that part of the work of the lawyer which involves appearance in court and that part which involves advice and drafting of instruments in his office. The work of the office lawyer is the groundwork for future possible contests in courts. It has profound effect on the whole scheme of the administration of justice. It is performed with that possibility in mind, and otherwise would hardly be needed. In this country the practice of law includes both forms of legal service; there is no separation, as in England, into barristers and solicitors. It is of importance to the welfare of the public that these manifold customary functions be performed by persons possessed of adequate learning and skill, of sound moral character, and acting at all times under the heavy trust obligation to clients which rests upon all attorneys. . . .

Individuals have been permitted to manage, prosecute or defend their own actions, suits, and proceedings, and to defend prosecutions against themselves except when the public welfare demanded otherwise, and this does not constitute the practice of law. . . . The occasional drafting of simple deeds, and other legal instruments when not conducted as an occupation or yielding substantial income may fall outside the practice of the law. The gratuitous furnishing of legal aid to the poor and unfortunate without means in the pursuit of any civil remedy, as matter of charity, the search of records of real estate to ascertain what may there be disclosed without giving opinion or advice as to the legal effect of what is found, the work of an accountant dissociated from legal advice, do not constitute the practice of law. There may be other kindred pursuits of the same character. All these activities, however, lie close to the border line and may easily become or be accompanied by practice of the law. The giving of advice as to investments in stocks, bonds and other securities, in real or personal property, and in making tax returns falls within the same category.

PARALEGALS (AND OTHER NONATTORNEYS) IN COURT

- *Britt v. Rosenberg*, 665 N.E.2d 1022, 1023 (Appeals Court of Massachusetts, 1996) (paralegal lies to court and opposing counsel about why the plaintiff failed to appear).
- *DeVaux v. American Home Assurance Co.*, 444 N.E.2d 355 (Massachusetts Supreme Judicial Court, 1983) (nonattorney employee negligently misfiles a letter seeking legal assistance; client sues attorney for legal malpractice after the statute of limitations runs out on her claim).
- *Williams v. Resolution GGF OY*, 630 N.E.2d 581, 583 (Supreme Judicial Court of Massachusetts, 1994) (paralegal encourages others to believe he is an attorney).
- *Crance v. Commissioner of Public Welfare*, 507 N.E.2d 751, 753 (Supreme Judicial Court of Massachusetts, 1987) (award of paralegal fees where the paralegal's work was not merely ministerial but required the exercise of judgment).
- *EEOC v. Green*, 76 F.3d 19 (U.S. Court of Appeals for the 1st Circuit, 1996) (paralegal sues her law firm for sexual harassment).
- *In re Grand Jury Proceedings*, 786 F.2d 3 (U.S. Court of Appeals for the 1st Circuit, 1986) (grand jury subpoena against paralegal; court orders incarceration).

- *In re Smuggler's Beach Properties,* 149 Bankruptcy Reporter 740, 743 (U.S. Bankruptcy Court, Eastern District for Massachusetts, 1993) (failure to delegate appropriate tasks to paralegals may warrant reduction in attorney fees).
- *In re Cumberland Farms, Inc.,* 154 Bankruptcy Reporter 9, 11 (U.S. Bankruptcy Court, District for Massachusetts, 1993) (attorney rewarded for its efficiency in using paralegals).

MICHIGAN

ETHICAL RULES AND GUIDELINES IN MICHIGAN

State Bar Board of Commissioners, *Michigan Guidelines for the Utilization of Legal Assistant Services* (1993) (72 Michigan Bar Journal 563 (June, 1993)). *Guideline 1:* An attorney must take reasonable steps to ensure that his or her legal assistant complies with the ethical rules governing Michigan attorneys. *Guideline 2:* The attorney must directly supervise and evaluate assigned tasks. A legal assistant may not convey to persons outside the law firm the legal assistant's opinion on the applicability of laws to particular cases. Legal documents on which a legal assistant works must be signed by an attorney. *Guideline 3:* An attorney cannot delegate to legal assistants the task of establishing an attorney-client relationship or the fee to be paid. *Guideline 4:* A legal assistant may be identified on attorney letterhead and on business cards that mention the law firm's name. *Guideline 5:* The attorney should take reasonable measures to ensure that no conflict of interest is presented arising out of the legal assistant's current or prior employment, or from the legal assistant's other business or personal interests. *Guideline 6:* An attorney can charge a client for legal assistant time if the client consents. *Guideline 7:* An attorney must not split fees with a legal assistant nor pay a legal assistant for referring legal business. A legal assistant can be included in a firm's retirement plan even if based on a profit-sharing arrangement. *Guideline 8:* The attorney should facilitate the legal assistant's participation in continuing legal education and public service activities.

Business cards and law firm letterhead can list the name of nonattorney employees with titles such as *legal assistant* or *paralegal.* The public must not be confused as to their nonattorney status. State Bar of Michigan, *Opinion RI-34* (10/25/89).

A law firm may pay a legal assistant compensation based on a set salary and a percentage of the net profits of the practice area in which the legal assistant is involved as long as no payments are made based on fees generated from particular clients. State Bar of Michigan, *Opinion RI-143* (8/25/92).

It is not possible for an attorney to give quality supervision to twenty-four paralegals located at six separate sites in the state. State Bar of Michigan, *Opinion R-1* (12/16/88).

An attorney's paralegal can represent clients in administrative hearings where authorized by law. The attorney must make sure that this paralegal acts ethically in providing this representation. State Bar of Michigan, *Opinion RI-125* (4/17/92). See also *Opinion RI-103* (10/9/91).

An attorney may not establish a business employing a paralegal who will sell will and trust forms where the paralegal will probably provide consultation and advice to clients. State Bar of Michigan, *Opinion RI-191* (2/14/94).

An attorney cannot avoid all direct client contact by obtaining all information about and from the client through the attorney's paralegal. State Bar of Michigan, *Opinion RI-128* (4/21/92).

When nonattorney employees with access to the files move to another law firm, a Chinese Wall may have to be built around them to prevent the imputed disqualification of the new firm. State Bar of Michigan, *Opinion R-4* (9/22/89).

A paralegal works for a legal service organization that represents a plaintiff in a case against a potential defendant who is the paralegal's fiancé. The organization is not disqualified if the paralegal is screened from the case and the client (the plaintiff) is made aware of this relationship and consents. State Bar of Michigan, *Opinion CI-1168* (12/10/86). See also *Opinion R-115* (1/31/92) (Chinese Wall built around secretary who switches firms).

An attorney is prohibited from representing a client if one of his nonattorney employees will become a witness who will give testimony that is not consistent with the interests of the attorney's client. State Bar of Michigan, *Opinion RI-26* (7/19/89).

Information collected by a legal assistant during an interview is protected against disclosure by the attorney-client privilege. State Bar of Michigan, *Opinion RI-123* (3/13/92).

Other State Bar of Michigan opinions involving nonattorneys: *CI-1155* (7/25/86); *CI-1203* (8/5/88); *R-6* (12/15/89); *RI-36* (11/20/89); *RI-55* (8/1/90).

DEFINING THE PRACTICE OF LAW IN MICHIGAN

State Bar of Michigan v. Cramer, 249 N.W.2d 1, 6-7 (Supreme Court of Michigan, 1976): [T]he Legislature has not seen fit to define what constitutes the "practice of law", and, accordingly, "[t]he formidable task of constructing a definition of the practice of law has largely been left to the judiciary. . . ." We are still of the mind that any attempt to formulate a lasting, all encompassing definition of "practice of law" is doomed to failure "for the reason that under our system of jurisprudence such practice must necessarily change with the ever changing business and social order . . . ." No essential definition of the practice of law has been articulated and the descriptive definitions which have been agreed upon from time to time have only permitted disposition of specific questions. These definitions have been relatively helpful in counseling conduct but have provided no sure guide for the public's protection. A broad definition of the "practice of law" embraces virtually all commercial areas of human endeavor. This, of course, will not do. "It cannot be urged, with reason, that a lawyer must preside over every transaction where written legal forms must be selected and used by an agent for one of the parties. Such a restriction would so paralyze business activities that very few transactions could be expeditiously consummated. . . ." The result of this inability to fashion a definition of "practice of law" to fit every situation "has been a line of decisions consistent only in their inconsistency as the courts have sought to accommodate the need for public protection through restricting the practice of law to members of the bar with the economic and practical realities of modern society."

PARALEGALS (AND OTHER NONATTORNEYS) IN COURT

- *Michigan v. Hurst*, 517 N.W.2d 858, 862-3 (Court of Appeals of Michigan, 1994) (the "defendant's supplemental appellate brief . . . prepared by an apparently competent legal assistant, sufficiently apprised this court of the finer points of defendant's arguments").
- *In the Matter of Bright*, 171 Bankruptcy Reporter 799, 802 (U.S. Bankruptcy Court, Eastern District for Michigan, 1994) (bankruptcy trustee charges paralegal with the unauthorized practice of law in helping the debtor; a disclaimer that one is "only providing 'scrivener' or 'paralegal' services is irrelevant if the nonlawyer in fact engages in the unauthorized practice of law).

- *State Bar of Michigan v. Cramer,* 249 N.W.2d 1 (Supreme Court of Michigan, 1976) (the unauthorized practice of law and the sale of do-it-yourself divorce kits).
- *Knop v. Johnson,* 977 F.2d 996 (U.S. Court of Appeals for the 6th Circuit, 1992) (paralegal assistance for inmates).
- *Glover v. Johnson,* 75 F.3d 264 (U.S. Court of Appeals for the 6th Circuit, 1996) (paralegal assistance for inmates).
- *Gibbs v. Hopkins,* 10 F.3d 373 (U.S. Court of Appeals for the 6th Circuit, 1993) (the nonattorney "jailhouse lawyer").
- *Bodenhamer Building Corp. v. Architectural Research Corp.,* 989 F.2d 213 (U.S. Court of Appeals for the 6th Circuit, 1993) (award of paralegal fees).
- *Cobb Publishing Co. v. Hearst Corp.,* 907 F. Supp. 1038 (U.S. District Court, Eastern District for Michigan, 1995) (Chinese Wall to prevent disqualification of law firm due to conflict of interest; memo sent to all attorneys, paralegals, and other staff to stay away from the contaminated employee).
- *Kearns v. Ford Motor Co.,* 114 Federal Rules Decisions 57 (U.S. District Court, Eastern District for Michigan, 1987) (paralegal gives copy of privileged litigation documents to someone with whom she was having a romantic relationship).

MINNESOTA

ETHICAL RULES AND GUIDELINES IN MINNESOTA

Paralegal names can be printed on a firm's letterhead, on business cards, on professional announcement cards, office signs, telephone directory listings, law lists, and legal directory listings, if their nonattorney status is clear. Paralegals, so identified, may sign correspondence on behalf of the law firm if acting under an attorney's direction. But they cannot be named on pleadings under any identification. Minnesota Bar Ass'n, *Ethics Opinion 8* (6/26/74; amended 6/18/80 and 12/4/87). On letterheads, see also *Opinion 93* (6/7/84).

It is improper for a lawyer to permit any nonattorney employee to accept a gratuity offered by a court reporting service or other service for which the client is expected to pay unless the client consents. Minnesota Lawyers Professional Responsibility Board, *Opinion Number 17* (6/18/93).

DEFINING THE PRACTICE OF LAW IN MINNESOTA

§ 481.02 *(Minnesota Statutes Annotated):* Subdivision 1. Prohibitions. It shall be unlawful for any person or association of persons, except members of the bar of Minnesota admitted and licensed to practice as attorneys at law, to appear as attorney or counselor at law in any action or proceeding in any court in this state to maintain, conduct, or defend the same, except personally as a party thereto in other than a representative capacity, or, by word, sign, letter, or advertisement, to hold out as competent or qualified to give legal advice or counsel, or to prepare legal documents, or as being engaged in advising or counseling in law or acting as attorney or counselor at law, or in furnishing to others the services of a lawyer or lawyers, or, for a fee or any consideration, to give legal advice or counsel, perform for or furnish to another legal services, or, for or without a fee or any consideration, to prepare, directly or through another, for another person, firm, or corporation, any will or testamentary disposition or instrument of trust serving purposes similar to those of a will, or, for a fee or any consideration, to prepare for another person, firm, or corporation, any other legal document, except as provided in subdivision 3. . . .

Subdivision 3. Permitted actions. The provisions of this section shall not prohibit: . . . (2) a person from drawing a will for another in an emergency if the imminence of death leaves insufficient time to have it drawn and its execution supervised by a licensed attorney-at-law. . . . (5) any bona fide labor organization from giving legal advice to its members in matters arising out of their employment. . . . (14) the delivery of legal services by a specialized legal assistant in accordance with a specialty license issued by the supreme court before July 1, 1995. . . .

Subdivision 3a. Real estate closing services. Nothing in this section shall be construed to prevent a real estate broker, a real estate salesperson, or a real estate closing agent, as defined in section 82.17, from drawing or assisting in drawing papers incident to the sale, trade, lease, or loan of property, or from charging for drawing or assisting in drawing them, except as hereafter provided by the supreme court. . . .

Subdivision 7. Lay assistance to attorneys. Nothing herein contained shall be construed to prevent a corporation from furnishing to any person lawfully engaged in the practice of law, such information or such clerical service in and about the attorney's professional work as, except for the provisions of this section, may be lawful, provided, that at all times the lawyer receiving such information or such services shall maintain full, professional and direct responsibility to the attorney's clients for the information and services so received. . . .

PARALEGALS (AND OTHER NONATTORNEYS) IN COURT

- *Vinje v. Brink* . . . , 1992 WL 358685 (Court of Appeals of Minnesota, 1992) (full-time paralegal at law firm is fired after the paralegal tried to sell his services to other law firms as a contract paralegal).
- *In Re Rubin,* 484 N.W.2d 786 (Supreme Court of Minnesota, 1992) (attorney disciplined for permitting a legal assistant to back-date a signature on a deed).
- *Minnesota v. Richards,* 456 N.W.2d 260 (Supreme Court of Minnesota, 1990) (a county attorney's office is not disqualified from prosecuting the defendant merely because the office hired a paralegal who had previously interviewed for a job with defense counsel).
- *In re Mille Lacs County Attorney Salary and Budget v. County Board of Commissioners,* 422 N.W. 2d 291 (Court of Appeals of Minnesota, 1988) (comparison of the role of a legal secretary and a paralegal).
- *Rose v. Neubauer,* 407 N.W.2d 727 (Court of Appeals of Minnesota, 1987) (paralegal files complaint and interrogatories without knowledge of attorney).
- *Narum v. Eli Lilly,* 914 F. Supp. 317 (U.S. District Court for Minnesota, 1996) (affidavit of paralegal, who was also a nurse, is inadmissible because of its unsupported conclusions).
- *Diocese of Winona v. Interstate Fire and Casualty Company,* 916 F. Supp. 923 (U.S. District Court for Minnesota, 1995) (award of paralegal fees).

Mississippi

ETHICAL RULES AND GUIDELINES IN MISSISSIPPI

Paralegal names can be printed on a firm's letterhead if their nonattorney status is clear. The paralegal should not be called a *paralegal associate* since in common usage the term *associate* carries a connotation of being an attorney in a law firm. Mississippi Bar Ass'n, Opinion 93 (6/7/84).

An attorney can pay a paralegal a bonus based on the number of her hours billed and collected in excess of a designated minimum. A nonattorney compensation or retirement plan can be based in whole or in part on a profit-sharing arrangement. Mississippi State Bar, *Opinion 154* (9/12/89).

A legal assistant can use the initials *CLA* (Certified Legal Assistant) or *CLAS* (Certified Legal Assistant Specialist) after their names on law firm letterhead as long as the designation is accompanied by language indicating that the legal assistant is not an attorney. These initials indicate the legal assistant has passed the test and met the other requirements of the National Association of Legal Assistants. Mississippi State Bar, *Opinion 223* (1/19/95).

A disbarred or suspended attorney cannot work as an attorney or paralegal. Mississippi State Bar, *Opinion 96* (6/7/84). See also *Opinion 171.*

DEFINING THE PRACTICE OF LAW IN MISSISSIPPI

Darby v. Mississippi State Board of Bar Admissions, 185 So.2d 684, 687 (Supreme Court of Mississippi, 1966): The practice of law includes the drafting or selection of documents, the giving of advice in regard to them, and the using of an informed or trained discretion in the drafting of documents to meet the needs of the person being served. So any exercise of intelligent choice in advising another of his legal rights and duties brings the activity within the practice of the legal profession. . . . The element of compensation for such services may be a factor in determining whether specified conduct constitutes the practice of law, but it is not controlling. The character of the service and its relation to the public interest determines its classification, not whether compensation is charged for it. . . . The objective of both the legislature and the courts in supervising admissions to the bar is the protection of the public against injuries from acts or services, professional in nature, constituting the practice of law, and done or performed by those not deemed to be qualified to perform them. A gratuitous service by a licensed doctor or lawyer is none the less professional. The welfare of the public is the principal consideration. . . . A statute makes it . . . unlawful for any person to engage in the practice of law without a license, stating that any person "who shall for a fee or reward or promise, directly or indirectly," write any paper to be filed in a proceeding or dictate a bill of sale, deed, deed of trust, mortgage, contract, or will, or make or certify to any abstract of title, "shall be held to be engaged in the practice of law." *Miss. Code Ann.* § 8682 (1956).

PARALEGALS (AND OTHER NONATTORNEYS) IN COURT

- *Ivy v. K.D. Merchant,* 666 So. 2d 445 (Supreme Court of Mississippi, 1995) (inmate paralegal assistance; paralegal fined $25 for assisting an inmate who filed a frivolous lawsuit).
- *Williams v. Mississippi State Bar Ass'n,* 492 So. 2d 578 (Supreme Court of Mississippi, 1986) (a disbarred attorney should not act as a paralegal).
- *Minnick v. Mississippi,* 551 So. 2d 77, 101 (Supreme Court of Mississippi, 1988) (lawyer should not use a paralegal "to do his dirty work" in communicating with the other side).
- *Mississippi State Chapter Operation Push v. Mabus,* 788 F. Supp. 1406, 1421 (U.S. District Court, Northern District for Mississippi, 1992) (award of paralegal fees criticized: it "is unnecessary to have three paralegals assisting at trial"; "using three paralegals when one would be sufficient").
- *In re White,* 171 Bankruptcy Reporter 554 (U.S. Bankruptcy Court, Southern District for Mississippi, 1994) (attorney fees reduced; "too many lawyers are spending too much time on this case"; they "used paralegals to perform secretarial tasks").
- *Martin v. Mabus,* 734 F. Supp. 1216 (U.S. District Court, Southern District for Mississippi, 1990) (award of paralegal fees).

- *Sykes v. Grantham*, 567 So. 2d 200 (Supreme Court of Mississippi, 1990) (paralegal member of the Mississippi State Parole Board).

MISSOURI

ETHICAL RULES AND GUIDELINES IN MISSOURI

Missouri Bar Ass'n, *Guidelines for Practicing with Paralegals* (1987) (1992). Scope and Purposes of Guidelines: The recognition of a paralegal as a professional member of the legal community is one of the purposes of these Guidelines. *Guideline I:* An attorney shall not assist a paralegal in the performance of an activity that constitutes the unauthorized practice of law. There are regulations that permit lay persons to represent clients at certain administrative agencies. *Guideline II:* An attorney shall not share fees with a paralegal except that the paralegal may be included in a compensation or retirement plan based in whole or part on a profit-sharing arrangement. Paralegal compensation cannot be tied to the existence or amount of a particular fee. A paralegal cannot be paid for recommending or referring business to an attorney. An attorney shall not form a partnership with a paralegal if any of the activities of the partnership consist of the practice of law. An attorney shall not practice law in the form of a business in which a paralegal owns an interest, or in which a paralegal is a corporate director or officer, or if the paralegal has the right to direct or control the professional judgment of the attorney. *Guideline III:* (a) Law firm partners must make reasonable efforts to ensure that the law firm has in effect measures giving reasonable assurance that the paralegal's conduct is compatible with the professional obligations of an attorney. (b) An attorney with direct supervisory authority over a paralegal shall make reasonable efforts to ensure that the paralegal's conduct is compatible with the professional obligations of an attorney. (c) An attorney is responsible for conduct of a paralegal that would be unethical if engaged in by an attorney (1) if the attorney orders, or with the knowledge of the specific conduct, ratifies the paralegal's conduct; or (2) if the attorney (whether a partner or an attorney who directly supervises the paralegal) knows of the conduct of the paralegal at a time when its consequences can be avoided or mitigated but fails to take reasonable remedial action. (d) An attorney shall give the paralegal appropriate instruction and supervision concerning the ethical aspects of the paralegal's employment, particularly regarding the obligation not to disclose information (confidential or otherwise) relating to representation of a client. A copy of these Guidelines and the Missouri Rules of Professional Conduct shall be delivered to or discussed with the paralegal immediately upon employment of the paralegal. *Guideline IV:* (a) An attorney shall instruct the paralegal to disclose at the outset of any professional dealings for the attorney with clients, the public, or other attorneys that he or she is a paralegal. (b) The name of a paralegal may appear on the letterhead of a law firm, on business cards, or any other method of communicating the identity of personnel as long as the name is clearly delineated as a paralegal. If the client indicates confusion as to the role of the paralegal, the attorney must describe the functions of the paralegal. A paralegal may sign correspondence on attorney letterhead as long as the signature is followed by an appropriate identifying designation as a paralegal. No communication shall contain claims concerning the paralegal's status or authority in relationship to the attorney employing the paralegal.

An attorney cannot allow a paralegal to accompany a client to a deposition. Missouri Bar Ass'n, *Informal Opinion* (8/15/75). C. Gilsinan, *Ethical Considerations . . .* , 30 St. Louis Bar Journal 15 (Summer 1983). (Note, however, that Judge Dolan of the Scott County

33rd Judicial Circuit recently ruled that a paralegal *could* attend a deposition conducted by her supervising attorney.)

A paralegal cannot answer a docket call of an attorney. Missouri Bar Ass'n, *Informal Opinion 1* (7/9/82)

Paralegal names cannot appear on attorney letterhead. Missouri Bar Ass'n, *Informal Opinion 13* (8/22/77) and *Opinion 14* (5/23/80). (The Guidelines above, however, now allow this.)

It would be an improper splitting of a fee with a paralegal if an attorney agrees not to pay a paralegal unless an entire particular fee is collected. Missouri Bar Ass'n, *Informal Opinion 20* (6/16/78).

DEFINING THE PRACTICE OF LAW IN MISSOURI

§ 484.010. *(Vernon's Annotated Statutes):* 1. The "practice of the law" is hereby defined to be and is the appearance as an advocate in a representative capacity or the drawing of papers, pleadings or documents or the performance of any act in such capacity in connection with proceedings pending or prospective before any court of record, commissioner, referee or any body, board, committee or commission constituted by law or having authority to settle controversies.

2. The "law business" is hereby defined to be and is the advising or counseling for a valuable consideration of any person, firm, association, or corporation as to any secular law or the drawing or the procuring of or assisting in the drawing for a valuable consideration of any paper, document or instrument affecting or relating to secular rights or the doing of any act for a valuable consideration in a representative capacity, obtaining or tending to obtain or securing or tending to secure for any person, firm, association or corporation any property or property rights whatsoever.

PARALEGALS (AND OTHER NONATTORNEYS) IN COURT

- *Logan v. Hyatt Legal Plans, Inc,* 874 S.W.2d 548 (Missouri Court of Appeals, 1994) (paralegal works for a law firm that represents the wife in a divorce action; paralegal has an affair with the husband of this client (!); paralegal is charged with disclosing confidential strategy information to her lover).
- *Missouri v. Jenkins,* 109 S. Ct. 2463 (U.S. Supreme Court, 1989) (award of paralegal fees; see discussion on page 25 in chapter 1).
- *In re Kroh Brothers . . . ,* 105 Bankruptcy Reporter 515, 529 (U.S. Bankruptcy Court, Western District for Missouri, 1989) (in a request for attorney fees, the attorney fails to explain why some of the tasks performed by attorneys "were not performed by a paralegal").
- *Newport v. Newport,* 759 S.W.2d 630, 637 (Missouri Court of Appeals, 1988) (award of paralegal fees).
- *Buckman v. Buckman,* 857 S.W. 2d 313 (Missouri Court of Appeals, 1993) (award of paralegal fees).
- *In the Matter of Kinghorn,* 764 S.W.2d 939 (Supreme Court of Missouri, 1989) (an attorney charged with ethical violations cannot assert in mitigation his reliance on a paralegal).
- *Dudley v. Shaver,* 770 S.W.2d 712 (Missouri Court of Appeals, 1989) (inmate paralegals).
- *American Inmate Paralegal Ass'n v. Cline,* U.S. Court of Appeals for the 8th Circuit, 1988) (inmate paralegal association brings civil rights action against prison).

MONTANA

ETHICAL RULES AND GUIDELINES IN MONTANA

An attorney must not split a fee with a nonattorney. State Bar of Montana *Opinion (1)* (9/13/85).

It is unethical for a law firm to pay "runners" to recommend the law firm to injured railroad workers. State Bar of Montana, *Opinion No. 930927* (1994), 19 Montana Lawyer 15 (1/94).

Attorneys are responsible for the work product of their paralegal employees. There is no need to establish a bureaucracy to provide additional regulation on who can be a paralegal and how they can be used. *In the Matter of the Proposed Adoption of Rules Relating to Paralegals and Legal Assistants,* No. 94-577 (Supreme Court of Montana, (7/17/95).

PARALEGALS (AND OTHER NONATTORNEYS) IN COURT

- *Sparks v. Johnson,* 826 P.2d 928 (Supreme Court of Montana, 1992) (nonattorneys cannot practice in the lower Montana courts).
- *Head v. Central Reserve Life . . . ,* 845 P.2d 735 (Supreme Court of Montana, 1993) (award of paralegal fees).
- *In re Sirefco, Inc.,* 144 Bankruptcy Reporter 495, 497 (U.S. Bankruptcy Court for the District of Montana, 1992) (paralegal fees disallowed; the paralegal's work in this case was duplicative and not beneficial; the attorney failed to establish that the paralegal's work "was not merely secretarial in nature.")
- *Harris v. Maloughney,* 827 F. Supp. 1488 (U.S. District Court for Montana, 1993) (nonattorney legal assistance to inmates).
- *In re Semenza,* 121 Bankruptcy Reporter 56 (U.S. Bankruptcy Court for the District of Montana, 1990) (paralegals are not "professional persons" within the meaning of the Bankruptcy Code; paralegals do not have to be licensed in Montana).

NEBRASKA

ETHICAL RULES AND GUIDELINES IN NEBRASKA

Paralegals can be listed on law firm letterhead if their nonattorney status is clear. Nebraska State Bar Ass'n, *Opinion 88-2.*

Several attorneys who are not partners, associates, or otherwise affiliated with each other, share office space and share nonattorney personnel. They represent clients who are opposite each other in cases. This is not improper if the clients are aware of and consent to the arrangement, and if steps are taken to ensure confidentiality—such as preventing common access to case files and preventing the nonattorneys from working both sides on a case. Nebraska State Bar Ass'n, *Opinion 89-2.*

Hiring someone who has worked for an opposing law firm in matters related to a particular case automatically disqualifies the hiring firm from the case. A Chinese Wall or cone of silence erected around an attorney, law clerk, paralegal, secretary or other ancillary staff member is insufficient to prevent disqualification due to a conflict of interest and appearance of impropriety. Nebraska State Bar Ass'n, *Opinion 94-4.*

DEFINING THE PRACTICE OF LAW IN NEBRASKA

Nebraska . . . v. Butterfield 111 N.W.2d 543, 545 (Supreme Court of Nebraska, 1961): The Supreme Court of this state has the inherent power to define and regulate the practice of law in this state. . . . While an all-embracing definition of the term "practicing law" would involve great difficulty, it is generally defined as the giving of advice or rendition of any sort of service by a person, firm, or corporation when the giving of such advice or rendition of such service requires the use of any degree of legal knowledge or skill. . . . In an ever-changing economic and social order, the "practice of law" must necessarily change, making it practically impossible to formulate an enduring definition. . . . In determining what constitutes the practice of law it is the character of the act and not the place where the act is performed that is the controlling factor. . . . Whether or not a fee is charged is not a decisive factor in determining if one has engaged in the practice of law.

PARALEGALS (AND OTHER NONATTORNEYS) IN COURT

- *State ex rel. Creighton University v. Hickman,* 512 N.W.2d 374 (Nebraska Supreme Court, 1994) (attorney works on a case and is disbarred; he then goes to work as a legal assistant to do discovery work for the opposing attorney on the same case; the new employer is disqualified from continuing on the case).
- *Nebraska v. Thierstein,* 371 N.W.2d 746 (Nebraska Supreme Court, 1985) (a legal assistant must be supervised by an attorney).
- *Nebraska v. Garvey,* 457 N.W.2d 297 (Supreme Court of Nebraska, 1990) (suspended attorney ordered to perform fifty hours of pro bono paralegal work).
- *El Tabech v. Gunther,* 869 F. Supp. 1146 (U.S. District Court for Nebraska, 1994) (award of paralegal fees).
- *Weaver v. Clarke,* 933 F. Supp. 831 (1996 WL 388547) (U.S. District Court for Nebraska, 1996) (award of paralegal fees).
- *Klinger v. Nebraska Dept. of Correctional Services,* 909 F. Supp. 1329 (U.S. District Court for Nebraska, 1995) (award of paralegal fees).
- *Reutcke v. Dahm,* 707 F. Supp. 1121 (U.S. District Court for Nebraska, 1988) (legal training for inmate paralegals).
- *Davis v. Parratt,* 608 F. 2d 717 (U.S. Court of Appeals for the 8th Circuit, 1979) (inmate paralegal is not entitled to attorney fees).

NEVADA

PARALEGALS (AND OTHER NONATTORNEYS) IN COURT

- *Greenwell v. Paralegal Center,* 836 P.2d 70 (Supreme Court of Nevada, 1992) (injunction granted against a typing service for the unauthorized practice of law, but the court orders the state bar to investigate the alleged unavailability of legal services for low- and middle-income Nevadans).
- *Pioneer Title v. State Bar,* 326 P.2d 408 (Supreme Court of Nevada, 1958) (some simple legal services may be so necessary that they could properly be provided by nonattorneys if they would otherwise be unavailable).
- *Hunter v. Moran,* 128 Federal Rules Decisions 115, 116 (U.S. District Court for Nevada, 1989) (an attorney should not delegate to a paralegal the task of attempting to resolve a discovery dispute).
- *Snell v. Reno Hilton Resort,* 930 F. Supp. 1428 (U.S. District Court for Nevada, 1996) (award of paralegal fees).
- *Herbst v. Humana Health Insurance of Nevada,* 781 P.2d 762 (Supreme Court of Nevada, 1989) (award of paralegal fees; 359 hours of work performed by paralegals on the case).

- *In re Ginji*, 117 Bankruptcy Reporter 983, 993 (U.S. Bankruptcy Court for Nevada, 1990) (award of paralegal fees; work that "was done by an attorney which should have been done by a paralegal . . . shall be billed at a lower rate").
- *Housewright v. Simmons*, 729 P.2d 499 (Supreme Court of Nevada, 1986) (inmate paralegals).

NEW HAMPSHIRE

ETHICAL RULES AND GUIDELINES IN NEW HAMPSHIRE

Rule 35 of the *New Hampshire Supreme Court Administrative Rule. Rule 1:* Paralegals must not give legal advice, but they can, with adequate attorney supervision, provide information concerning legal matters. *Rule 2:* An attorney may not permit a legal assistant to represent a client in judicial or administrative proceedings unless authorized by statute, court rule or decision, administrative rule or regulation, or customary practice. *Rule 3:* A paralegal shall not be delegated any task that requires the exercise of professional legal judgment. The attorney must supervise the paralegal. *Rule 4:* An attorney must take care that the legal assistant does not reveal information relating to representation of a client or use such information to the disadvantage of the client. *Rule 5:* An attorney shall not form a partnership with a paralegal if any part of the partnership consists of the practice of law. *Rule 6:* An attorney shall not share fees with a paralegal but can include the paralegal in a retirement plan based on a profit-sharing arrangement. *Rule 7:* A paralegal's name may not be included on the letterhead of an attorney. A paralegal can have a business card that prints the name of the law firm where he or she works, if the card indicates the paralegal's nonattorney capacity and the firm does not use the paralegal to solicit business for the firm improperly. *Rule 8:* When dealing with clients, attorneys, or the public, the paralegal must disclose at the outset that he or she is not an attorney. *Rule 9:* An attorney must exercise care to prevent a legal assistant from engaging in conduct that would involve the attorney unethical conduct.

A law firm cannot list legal assistants on its letterhead. New Hampshire Bar Ass'n, *Ethics Opinion 1982-3/20* (3/17/83).

Paralegals must avoid communications that involve the offering of legal advice, which is the exclusive function of the attorney. New Hampshire Bar Ass'n, *Successful Law Practice with Paralegals* (1992). See also *Guidelines for the Utilization of the Services of Legal Assistants* (1977).

DEFINING THE PRACTICE OF LAW IN NEW HAMPSHIRE

New Hampshire v. Settle, 480 A.2d 6, 8 (Supreme Court of New Hampshire, 1984): The only statutory definition of the unauthorized practice of law is provided in RSA 311:7 which states: "No person shall be permitted commonly to practice as an attorney in court unless he has been admitted by the court. . . ." The defendant argues that unless an individual is actually practicing in court, his conduct is not proscribed by the statute. We cannot read RSA 311:7 to limit the unauthorized practice of law to those instances in which an individual has physically appeared in the courtroom to represent a litigant. At the very least, this provision also encompasses the filing of documents in the court system. . . . There is no "single factor to determine whether someone is engaged in the unauthorized practice of law . . . [Rather, such a] determination must be made on a case-by-case basis."

PARALEGALS (AND OTHER NONATTORNEYS) IN COURT

- *Kalled's Case,* 607 A.2d 613 (Supreme Court of New Hampshire, 1992) (excessive billing by an attorney such as charging the client for 1,489 hours of paralegal time at $60 per hour).
- *Van Dorn Retail Management, Inc. v. Jim's Oxford Shop, Inc.,* 874 F. Supp. 476, 490 (U.S. District Court for New Hampshire, 1994) (paralegal fees reduced; "attorneys and paralegals duplicated their efforts"; paralegals "performed clerical functions").
- *New Hampshire v. Gordon,* ___ A.2d ___ (Supreme Court of New Hampshire, 1996) (1996 WL 425508) (paralegal student claims attorney-client privilege covers incriminating statements he made to his paralegal instructor).

New Jersey

ETHICAL RULES AND GUIDELINES IN NEW JERSEY

New Jersey has added an additional subsection to Rule 5.3 of the *Model Rules of Professional Conduct* that is not in the ABA *Model Rules.* The N.J. addition is (c)(3): Attorneys must make a "reasonable investigation of circumstances that would disclose past instances of conduct by the nonlawyer" that are "incompatible with the professional obligations of an attorney, which evidence a propensity for such conduct."

It is not the unauthorized practice of law for a nonattorney broker to conduct residential real estate closings and settlements without attorneys as long as the broker notifies the buyer and seller of the risk of not having attorney representation and of the conflicting interest that brokers and title companies have. *In re Opinion No. 26 of Committee on Unauthorized Practice of Law,* 1995 WL 121535.

It is unethical for attorneys to hire a paralegal to screen calls of prospective clients to determine whether the case involves "good liability and damages." The paralegal would discuss the claims of the callers and make a determination of whether to refer the case to an attorney. This is the unauthorized practice of law. New Jersey Supreme Court Advisory Committee on Professional Ethics, *Opinion 645* (10/4/90) (126 New Jersey Law Journal 894) (1990 WL 441602). In agreement: *Opinion 6* (10/4/90) of the New Jersey Supreme Court Advisory Committee on Attorney Advertising.

A paralegal can have a business card as long as the name of the employing law firm is also printed on it. New Jersey Supreme Court Advisory Committee on Professional Ethics, *Opinion 647* (1990) (126 New Jersey Law Journal 1525) (1990 WL 441612).

The names of paralegals may be printed on attorney letterhead and in advertisements. "[T]he respect accorded paralegals and the work they perform has increased immeasurably over the last 10 to 15 years." New Jersey Supreme Court Committee on Attorney Advertising, *Opinion 16* (1/24/94) (136 New Jersey Law Journal 375) (1994 WL 45949). This opinion superseded *Opinion 296* (1975).

Nonattorney employees of the county welfare agency may represent litigants before the Office of Administrative Law. New Jersey Supreme Court Advisory Committee on Professional Ethics, *Opinion 580* (2/27/86).

Paralegals can sign law firm correspondence concerning routine tasks such as gathering factual information and documents. They should not sign correspondence to clients, adverse attorneys, or tribunals. Minor exceptions are allowed such as "a purely routine request to a court clerk for a docket sheet." New Jersey Supreme Court Advisory Committee on Professional Ethics *Opinion 611* (2/23/88) (121 New Jersey Law Journal 301) (1988 WL 356368).

A paralegal switches jobs between law firms that opposed each other in litigation. The paralegal worked on the litigation while at the former firm. The new employer is not disqualified if a Chinese Wall is built around the paralegal and she would work for an attorney who has no involvement in the litigation. Also, her office would be located in another end of the building. New Jersey Supreme Court Advisory Committee on Professional Ethics, *Opinion 665* (8/3/92) (131 New Jersey Law Journal 1074) (1992 WL 465626) modifying the per se prohibition announced in *Opinion 546* (11/8/84) (114 New Jersey Law Journal 496) (1984 WL 140946). See also *Opinion 633* (11/2/89) (a law firm litigating tobacco cases can hire a nonattorney who had been involved in tobacco litigation at another firm if the nonattorney had no substantial responsibility in the tobacco litigation at the other firm, obtained no confidential information concerning the litigation, and is screened from such litigation at the present firm).

Other New Jersey Advisory Committee on Professional Ethics opinions involving nonattorneys: *296* (2/6/75) (has been superseded): *296 Supplement* (2/12/76): *461* (2/12/81): *553* (1/24/85); *598* (3/26/87); *631* (10/12/89).

DEFINING THE PRACTICE OF LAW IN NEW JERSEY

In re Opinion No. 24 of the Committee on the Unauthorized Practice of Law, 607 A.2d 962, 966 (Supreme Court of New Jersey, 1992): No satisfactory, all-inclusive definition of what constitutes the practice of law has ever been devised. None will be attempted here. That has been left, and wisely so, to the courts when parties present them with concrete factual situations. . . . "What is now considered the practice of law is something which may be described more readily than defined." . . . Essentially, the Court decides what constitutes the practice of law on a case-by-case basis. . . . The practice of law is not subject to precise definition. It is not confined to litigation but often encompasses "legal activities in many non-litigious fields which entail specialized knowledge and ability." Therefore, the line between permissible business and professional activities and the unauthorized practice of law is often blurred. . . . There is no question that paralegals' work constitutes the practice of law. N.J.S.A. 2A:170-78 and 79 deem unauthorized the practice of law by a nonlawyer and make such practice a disorderly-persons offense. However, N.J.S.A. 2A:170-81(f) excepts paralegals from being penalized for engaging in tasks that constitute legal practice if their supervising attorney assumes direct responsibility for the work that the paralegals perform. N.J.S.A. 2A:170-81(f) states: Any person or corporation furnishing to any person lawfully engaged in the practice of law such information or such clerical assistance in and about his professional work as, except for the provisions of this article, may be lawful, but the lawyer receiving such information or service shall at all times maintain full professional and direct responsibility to his client for the information and service so rendered. Consequently, paralegals who are supervised by attorneys do not engage in the unauthorized practice of law.

PARALEGALS (AND OTHER NONATTORNEYS) IN COURT

- *In re Opinion No. 24*, 607 A.2d 962 (Supreme Court of New Jersey, 1992) (see page 283 in chapter 5) (attorneys may delegate tasks to paralegals whether the paralegal is employed by the attorney or is an independent paralegal who is retained by the attorney as long as the attorney maintains a direct relationship with his or her clients, supervises the paralegal's work, and is responsible for the paralegal's work product). This opinion overruled *Opinion 24* (1990) of the New Jersey Unauthorized Practice of Law Committee, which said that attorneys cannot hire paralegals as independent contractors because of the difficulty of providing them with needed day-to-day supervision and the danger of conflict-of-interest because the paralegals work for different attorneys.
- *Infante v. Gottesman*, 558 A.2d 1338 (Superior Court of New Jersey, 1989) (it is unethical for an attorney to form a partnership and split fees with a paralegal/investigation service).

- *Argila v. Argila,* 607 A.2d 675, 679 (Superior Court of New Jersey, 1992) (the application for paralegal fees failed to provide the qualifications of the paralegals and data on the prevailing market rate for paralegals).
- *Hawkins v. Harris,* 661 A.2d 284 (Supreme Court of New Jersey, 1995) (statements made by investigators can be privileged).
- *Buccilli v. Timby, Brown, Timby,* 660 A.2d 1261 (Superior Court of New Jersey, 1995) (New Jersey paralegal who worked for a Pennsylvania law firm claims she was fired because she told the firm she was subjected to sexual harassment, she intended to file a workers' compensation claim, and she objected to the lack of attorney supervision of her work and being asked to forge her attorney's name to court documents).
- *Prisoners' Legal Association v. Roberson,* 822 F. Supp. 185 (U.S. District Court for New Jersey, 1993) (inmate paralegals). *Jones v. Lilly,* 37 F.3d 964 (U.S. Court of Appeals for the 3rd Circuit, 1994) (inmate paralegal).
- *Valentine v. Beyer,* 850 F.2d 951 (U.S. Court of Appeals for the 3rd Circuit, 1988) (inmates challenge adequacy of paralegal program).
- *United States v. Barber,* 808 F. Supp. 361 (U.S. District Court for New Jersey, 1992) (disbarred attorney acts as paralegal).

NEW MEXICO

ETHICAL RULES AND GUIDELINES IN NEW MEXICO

A paralegal shall disclose to all persons with whom he or she communicates—at the beginning of any dealings with them—that the paralegal is not an attorney. The word *associate* should not be used when referring to a paralegal since it might be interpreted as an attorney-associate. A lawyer must ensure that the paralegal preserves the confidences and secrets of a client and that no personal, social, or business interest of the paralegal creates a conflict of interest with a client. Paralegals should not recommend that their law firm be retained. An attorney shall not share fees nor form a partnership with a paralegal. The compensation of a paralegal shall not include a percentage of profits or fees received from clients referred to the attorney by the paralegal. A paralegal's name cannot be printed on the letterhead of an attorney. A paralegal can have a business card that prints the name of the law firm as long as his or her nonattorney status is clear. A paralegal can sign correspondence on attorney letterhead as long as his or her nonattorney status is disclosed by a title such as *legal assistant* or *paralegal.* An attorney should not assign tasks beyond the competence of a paralegal. "In addition, a lawyer should explain to the legal assistant that the legal assistant has a duty to inform the lawyer of any assignment which the assistant regards as beyond his capability." New Mexico Supreme Court, *Rules Governing Legal Assistant Services,* Rules 20-101 to 20-114 (1986); Judicial Pamphlet 16; State Bar of New Mexico, *Guidelines for the Use of Legal Assistant Services* (1980).

Attorneys must tell clients how much services to be rendered by office nonattorneys will cost. Advisory Opinions Committee of the State Bar of New Mexico, *Opinion 1990-4* (6/9/90).

Other opinion of the Advisory Opinions Committee of the State Bar of New Mexico involving nonattorneys: *Opinion 1983-3.*

DEFINING THE PRACTICE OF LAW IN NEW MEXICO

State Bar of New Mexico v. Guardian Abstract and Title Company, Inc., 575 P.2d 943, 948 (Supreme Court of New Mexico, 1978):The authority of the Supreme Court to define and regulate the practice of law is inherently contained in the grant of judicial power to the courts by the Constitution. . . . There is no comprehensive definition of what constitutes the practice of law in our basic law or the cases. This Court has specifically declined to take on the onerous task. . . . We have declined to define what constitutes the practice of law because of the infinite number of fact situations which may be presented, each of which must be judged according to its own circumstances. . . . "[R]endering a service that requires the use of legal knowledge" or "preparing instruments and contracts by which legal rights are secured" would be indicia of the practice of law. . . . Defining the practice of law is an extremely difficult task, which we find unnecessary to undertake at this time. The line between what constitutes practicing law and what is permissible business and professional activity by non-lawyers is indistinct. . . . The answer may be determined only from a consideration of the acts or service performed in each case. Generally, . . . courts hold that whenever, as incidental to another transaction or calling, a layman, as part of his regular course of conduct resolves legal questions for another at his request and for a consideration by giving him advice or by taking action for and in his behalf, the layman is "practicing law," but only if difficult or doubtful legal questions are involved, which, to safeguard the public, reasonably demand the application of a trained legal mind. . . . What is a difficult or doubtful question of law demanding the application of a trained legal mind is not to be measured by the comprehension of a trained legal mind but by the understanding thereof which is possessed by a reasonably intelligent layman who is reasonably familiar with similar transactions. The test must be applied in a common-sense way which will protect primarily the interest of the public and not hamper or burden such interest with impractical and technical restrictions which have no reasonable justification.

Rule 20-102 *(New Mexico Rules of Court)*. DEFINITIONS
As used in these guidelines:

A. A "legal assistant" is a person, qualified through education, training or work experience, who is employed or retained by a lawyer, law office, governmental agency or other entity in a capacity or function which involves the performance, under the ultimate direction and supervision of an attorney, of a specifically-delegated substantive legal work, which work, for the most part, requires a sufficient knowledge of legal concepts that, absent such assistant, the attorney would perform the task; and

B. practice of law, insofar as court proceedings are concerned, includes:
(1) representation of parties before judicial or administrative bodies; (2) preparation of pleadings and other papers, incident to actions and special proceedings; (3) management of such actions and proceedings; and (4) noncourt-related activities, such as: (a) giving legal advice and counsel; (b) rendering a service which requires use of legal knowledge or skill; and (c) preparing instruments and contracts by which legal rights are secured.

PARALEGALS (AND OTHER NONATTORNEYS) IN COURT

- *In the Matter of Martinez,* 754 P.2d 842 (New Mexico Supreme Court, 1988) (attorney suspended for failing to supervise a paralegal to insure that the conduct of the paralegal comported with the ethical obligations of the attorney).
- *In the Matter of Rawson,* 833 P.2d 235 (New Mexico Supreme Court, 1992) (disbarred attorney can act as paralegal).
- *Aragon v. Westside Jeep/Eagle,* 876 P.2d 235 (Supreme Court of New Mexico, 1994) (law firm fails to file a notice of appeal and the appeal was dismissed; the firm alleges that the failure to file was caused by a "clerical difficulty" of its paralegal who had a heavy workload and was busy training a new employee when the notice of appeal should have been filed).

- *Robbins v. Budke,* 739 F. Supp. 1479 (D. New Mexico, 1990) (role of paralegal at psychiatric hospital).
- *Bustamonte v. Albuquerque Police Dept,* 1991 WL 125307 (award of paralegal fees).

NEW YORK

ETHICAL RULES AND GUIDELINES IN NEW YORK

New York State Bar Ass'n, *Guidelines for Utilization of Legal Assistants by Attorneys* (1976). *Guideline I:* An attorney cannot permit his or her legal assistant to engage in the unauthorized practice of law. *Guideline II:* An attorney may permit his or her legal assistant to perform certain functions otherwise prohibited when and only to the extent authorized by statute, court rule, court decision, administrative rule or regulation. *Guideline III:* The attorney must retain a direct relationship with the client, supervise the legal assistant's performance, and remain fully responsible for all actions taken and not taken by his or her legal assistant. *Guideline IV:* The attorney should exercise care that his or her legal assistant preserves and refrains from using any confidences or secrets of a client, and should instruct the legal assistant not to disclose or use any such confidences or secrets. *Guideline V:* An attorney shall not form a partnership with a legal assistant if any part of the firm's activities consists of the practice of law, nor shall an attorney share legal fees with a legal assistant. The legal assistant can, however, be included in a retirement plan even though based in whole or part on a profit-sharing arrangement. *Guideline VI:* The letterhead of an attorney shall not include the name of his or her legal assistant. [Note: This prohibition has been changed by *Opinion 500* referred to below.] The attorney's name can be printed on the business card of a legal assistant as long as his or her legal assistant status is clearly indicated. *Guideline VII:* When dealing with a client, the legal assistant must disclose at the outset that he or she is not an attorney. The same is true when dealing with a court, an agency, an attorney, or the public if there is any reason for believing he or she is an attorney or associated with an attorney. *Guideline VIII:* Unless otherwise provided by law, the propriety of the utilization of legal assistants by attorneys shall be governed by opinions of the Committees on Professional Ethics and Unlawful Practice of Law that have jurisdiction.

Paralegal names *can* be printed on a firm's letterhead if their nonattorney status is clear. New York State Bar Ass'n, *Ethics Opinion 500* (12/6/78) (1978 WL 14163).

The titles *paralegal* and *senior paralegal* are acceptable, but the following titles are unacceptable because they are ambiguous: *paralegal coordinator, legal associate, public benefits advocate, legal advocate, family law advocate, housing law advocate, disability benefits advocate,* and *public benefits specialist.* The public might be misled about the nonattorney status of the people with these titles. New York State Bar Ass'n, *Ethics Opinion 640* (1992) (1992 WL 450730).

There are circumstances in which an attorney can send his or her paralegal to attend a real estate closing alone. The attorney must determine that the closing calls for "merely ministerial" as opposed to discretionary duties, must be sure the background of the paralegal makes him or her suitable to attend, and must have a plan to cope for the unforeseen such as being available by telephone to the paralegal. "[F]rom an ethical standpoint, the lawyer who assigns a non-lawyer to work on a client's matter had better be right about the suitability of that task for delegation, and the suitability of that employee for the task at hand." New York State Bar Ass'n, *Opinion 677* (12/12/95) (1995 WL 870964).

A paralegal cannot conduct a deposition or supervise the execution of a will. New York State Bar Ass'n, *Ethics Opinion 304* (1973) and *Ethics Opinion 343.*

An attorney can give credit or recognition to a nonattorney for work performed in the preparation of a brief, as long as his or her nonattorney status is clear. New York State Bar Ass'n, *Ethics Opinion 299.*

An attorney cannot allow a nonattorney to engage in settlement negotiations or to appear at a pretrial conference. Bar Ass'n of Nassau County, *Opinion 86-40* (9/12/89).

A nonattorney can attend a real estate closing to perform ministerial functions involving only formalities. His or her nonattorney status must be disclosed at the closing. Bar Ass'n of Nassau County, *Opinion 86-43* (10/21/86); reaffirmed in *Opinion 90-13* (3/18/90).

An attorney cannot divide a fee with a paralegal who brings clients to the attorney. Bar Ass'n of Nassau County, Opinion 87-37 (10/1/87).

Nonattorneys cannot be referred to as *associates* of an attorney. Bar Ass'n of Nassau County, Opinion 88-34 (9/29/88).

Nonattorneys can be printed on attorney letterhead if such employees are clearly described and identified as nonattorneys. Bar Ass'n of Nassau County, *Opinion 91-32* (1991) (accountants); *Opinion 87-14* (1987) (paralegals).

An attorney may not represent a defendant in a criminal case when the complainant in the case is an investigator whom the attorney used in an unrelated case. There would be an appearance of impropriety in such a representation. Bar Ass'n of Nassau County, *Opinion 89-1* (1/18/89).

An attorney cannot form a partnership with a nonattorney to practice law. An attorney who shares an office with a nonattorney must avoid misleading the public into believing the nonattorney is an attorney. Ass'n of the Bar of the City of New York, *Opinion 1987-1* (2/23/87).

A law firm may issue an announcement that it has hired a law student or other nonattorney. Ass'n of the Bar of the City of New York, *Opinion 1996-2* (2/26/96) (1996 WL 93063).

Attorneys must effectively supervise their nonattorney employees, refrain from aiding or encouraging them to engage in the unauthorized practice of law, be sure that they maintain client confidences, and that the public is not misled by their nonattorney status. Ass'n of the Bar of the City of New York, *Opinion 1995-1* (7/6/95) (1995 WL 607778).

Paralegals can be listed on the letterhead of a law firm and on a business card that prints the name of the law firm (without printing the name of the supervising attorney) as long as their nonattorney status is indicated. New York County Lawyers' Ass'n, *Opinion 673* (12/23/89).

DEFINING THE PRACTICE OF LAW IN NEW YORK

New York State Bar Association, *Opinion 633* (5/3/92) (1992 WL 348745): The Code does not specifically define what constitutes the practice of law, but EC 3-5 states that "[f]unctionally, the practice of law relates to the rendition of services for others that calls for the professional judgment of a lawyer."

Gemayel v. Seaman, 533 N.E.2d 245, 248, 536 N.Y.S.2d 406, 409 (Court of Appeals of New York, 1988): The "practice" of law reserved to duly licensed New York attorneys includes the rendering of legal advice as well as appearing in court and holding oneself out to be a lawyer. . . . Additionally, such advice or services must be rendered to particular clients. . . . *State v. Winder,* 348 N.Y.S.2d 270, 272 (1973): This is the essential of legal practice—the representation and the advising of a particular person in a particular situation.

PARALEGALS (AND OTHER NONATTORNEYS) IN COURT

- *People v. Mitchell*, 461 N.Y.S.2d 267 (Supreme Court, Appellate Division, 4th Dept., 1982) (statements made in a law office waiting room to a paralegal in the attorney's absence are not privileged).
- *Fine v. Facet Aerospace Products Co.*, 133 Federal Rules Decisions 439 (U.S. District Court, Southern District for New York, 1990) (handwritten notes made by a paralegal on a document in the course of discovery in another case are protected from disclosure under the work product doctrine).
- *Glover Bottled Gas Corp. v. Circle M. Beverage Barn*, 514 N.Y.S.2d 440 (Supreme Court, Appellate Division, 2d Dept., 1987) (attorney is disqualified after hiring a paralegal who worked on specific litigation while previously employed by the opposing counsel in the litigation).
- *First Deposit Nat'l Bank v. Moreno*, 606 N.Y.S.2d 938 (City Court of the City of New York, New York County, 1993) (a claim for paralegal fees must itemize what was done and how much time was spent by attorneys and by others; "paralegals often competently perform certain services equivalent to those done by attorneys, while generally charging their time at a lesser rate than attorneys, thus benefitting those who pay the fees").
- *United States Football League v. National Football League*, 887 F.2d 408 (U.S. Court of Appeals for the 2d Circuit, 1989) (award of paralegal fees; $1,042,888 sought).
- *In the Matter of Law Offices of Schlesinger*, 509 N.Y.S.2d 983 (Surrogate Court, Queens County, 1986) (paralegal fees in decedent's estate case).
- *Hicks v. Russi*, 632 N.Y.S.2d 341 (Supreme Court, Appellate Division, 4th Dept., 1995) (the state cannot prevent an ex-offender from working as a paralegal on criminal cases).
- *In the Matter of Yankopoulos*, 478 N.Y.S.2d 633 (Supreme Court, Appellate Division, 1st Dept., 1984) (the state cannot revoke a paralegal's commission as a notary public based on his alleged unauthorized practice of law).
- *Day v. Morgenthau*, 909 F.2d 75 (U.S. Court of Appeals for the 2d Circuit, 1990) (paralegal arrested and incarcerated for being in the wrong area of the criminal court; paralegal sues for false arrest and malicious prosecution).
- *Abbasi v. Herzfeld & Rubin*, 863 F. Supp. 144 (U.S. District Court, Southern District for New York, 1994) (terminated paralegal alleges age and disability discrimination).
- *Reid v. New York*, 570 F. Supp. 1003 (U.S. District Court, Southern District for New York, 1983) (allegation of discrimination in the state civil service examination for the positions of Legal Assistant I and Legal Assistant II).
- *Arvelo v. Multi Trucking, Inc.*, 599 N.Y.S.2d 301 (Supreme Court, Appellate Division, 2d Dept., 1993) (client seeks to set aside negotiated settlement on the ground that the attorney's paralegal made a mistake in believing further approval of the settlement was needed).
- *United States v. Hooper*, 43 F.3d 26 (U.S. Court of Appeals for the 2d Circuit, 1994) (a paralegal's mistake on the deadline for filing a criminal appeal is not "excusable neglect" justifying permission to file the appeal late; the paralegal thought she had thirty days to file rather than ten).
- *Bank Brussels Lambert v. Credit Lyonnais*, 160 Federal Rules Decisions 437 (U.S. District Court, Southern District for New York, 1995) (paralegal mistake in turning over privileged documents to opponent).
- *In the Matter of Rosales*, 598 N.Y.S.2d 302 (Supreme Court, Appellate Division, 2d Dept., 1993) (attorney disciplined for allowing his paralegal to accept $30,000 in cash at a closing in order to avoid paying taxes on the amount).

- *In the Matter of Saltz,* 536 N.Y.S.2d 126 (Supreme Court, Appellate Division, 2d Dept, 1988) (attorney disciplined for lying when he claimed that his paralegal "doctored" divorce papers).
- *Paralegal Institute, Inc. v. American Bar Ass'n,* 475 F. Supp. 1123 (U.S. District Court, Southern District for New York, 1979) (paralegal school charges ABA with antitrust violations).
- *Perez v. Chater,* 77 F.3d 41 (U.S. Court of Appeals for the 2d Circuit, 1996) (paralegal represents client at social security disability hearing).

North Carolina

ETHICAL RULES AND GUIDELINES IN NORTH CAROLINA

Guidelines for the Utilization of Non-Lawyers in Rendering Legal Services, North Carolina State Bar (1986, revised 1992) 39 North Carolina State Bar Quarterly 3 (Summer 1992). Opening Statement: Paralegals "are now routinely engaged in activities which until recently were felt to be the exclusive province of lawyers." *Guideline 1:* An attorney must not permit an assistant to engage in the practice of law. *Guideline 2:* An attorney may not permit an assistant to appear on behalf of a client in court or before an agency or board, in person or on record, except to the extent permitted by the North Carolina General Statutes and a rule of a particular court, agency, or board. *Guideline 3:* An attorney must require that an assistant, when dealing on behalf of the attorney with a client, court, attorney, or the public disclose at the outset that he or she is not an attorney. An attorney must insure that his or her assistant does not communicate directly with a party known to be represented by an attorney, without that attorney's consent. *Guideline 4:* A partner in a law firm shall make reasonable efforts to insure that the firm has in effect measures giving reasonable assurance that the assistant's conduct is compatible with the professional obligations of the attorney. Attorneys with responsibility for the management of the firm must familiarize legal assistants with all provisions of the North Carolina ethics code that relate to the work they will be doing, particularly the duty to preserve the confidentiality of information received incident to the representation of clients. *Guideline 5:* An attorney having direct supervisory authority over an assistant shall make reasonable efforts to insure that the assistant's conduct is compatible with the professional obligations of the attorney. *Guideline 6:* An attorney must maintain an active and direct relationship with the client, supervise the assistant's performance of duties, and remain fully responsible for the work performed. A paralegal should inform the responsible attorney of all significant actions and services performed by the paralegal. Thorough supervision by an attorney is necessary to insure the assistant is not engaging in the unauthorized practice of law or other unethical conduct. *Guideline 7:* An attorney must insure that no interest or relationship of the assistant impinges upon the services rendered to the client. In the event that the interest of a legal assistant might materially limit or adversely affect the attorney's representation of a prospective or current client, the attorney must decline or discontinue the representation. Attorneys should make sure their assistants clearly understand their professional and ethical responsibilities with respect to conflict of interest. If an attorney accepts a matter in which the assistant may have a conflict of interest, the attorney should exclude the assistant from participation in any services performed in connection with that matter. The client should be told of this conflict. When using independent paralegals, the attorney must use special care to insure that they are performing competently and ethically. *Guideline 8:* An attorney shall not form a partnership or other business entity with an assistant for the practice of law. Attorneys must not share fees with a nonattorney. The compensation of a paralegal shall not include a percentage of the fees received by the attorney, but assistants can be included in a retirement plan based in whole or part on a profit-sharing arrangement. A paralegal shall receive no compensation for referring matters to the attorney. *Guideline 9:* The letterhead or business card of an attorney may include the names of a nonattorney if the assistant's capacity is clearly indicated. An assistant may sign correspondence on an attorney's letterhead as long as his or her title clearly indicates his or her nonattorney status, e.g., "paralegal" or "legal assistant."

A legal assistant can be listed on the letterhead of an attorney's stationery. "To ensure that the public is not led to believe that a nonlawyer is eligible to practice law, the nonlawyer's limited capacity should be clearly set forth on the letterhead." The paralegal can be a disbarred attorney. North Carolina State Bar, *RPC 126* (4/17/92) (1992 WL 754062).

A paralegal switches jobs. She now works for an attorney whose client opposes a party represented by the paralegal's former employer who says the paralegal worked on the case while there. The former employer seeks the disqualification of the current employer on the case. The request is denied. The imputed disqualification rules in Rule 5.11 do not apply to nonlawyers. But the current employer "must take extreme care" to ensure the paralegal is "totally screened" from the case even if her involvement in the case at the prior employment was negligible. North Carolina State Bar, *RPC 176* (7/21/94) (1994 WL 899356). In agreement: *RPC 74* (10/20/89) (1989 WL 550603).

An attorney may not pay a paralegal a percentage of fees as a bonus. A bonus for productivity can be given, but not as a percentage of fees. North Carolina State Bar, *RPC 147* (1/15/93) (1992 WL 753129).

A legal assistant can communicate and negotiate with a claims adjuster if directly supervised by an attorney. However, "[u]nder no circumstances should the legal assistant be permitted to exercise independent legal judgment regarding the value of the case, the advisability of making or accepting any offer of settlement or any other related matter." North Carolina State Bar, *RPC 70* (10/20/89).

An attorney may use the services of an independent paralegal title searcher as long as this paralegal is properly supervised. North Carolina State Bar, *RPC 216* (1995). (Note: a proposal to require extensive supervision was not adopted.)

An attorney can represent a client in an action to abate a nuisance even though his paralegal may be called as a witness against the opponent. North Carolina State Bar, *Revised RPC 213* (10/20/95) (1995 WL 853891).

An attorney may not permit his paralegal to examine or represent a witness at a deposition. North Carolina State Bar, *RPC 183* (10/21/94) (1994 WL 901318).

DEFINING THE PRACTICE OF LAW IN NORTH CAROLINA

§ 84-2.1 *(General Statutes of North Carolina):* The phrase "practice law" as used in this Chapter is defined to be performing any legal service for any other person, firm or corporation, with or without compensation, specifically including the preparation or aiding in the preparation of deeds, mortgages, wills, trust instruments, inventories, accounts or reports of guardians, trustees, administrators or executors, or preparing or aiding in the preparation of any petitions or orders in any probate or court proceeding; abstracting or passing upon titles, the preparation and filing of petitions for use in any court, including administrative tribunals and other judicial or quasi-judicial bodies, or assisting by advice, counsel, or otherwise in any legal work; and to advise or give opinion upon the legal rights of any person, firm or corporation: Provided, that the above reference to particular acts which are specifically included within the definition of the phrase "practice law" shall not be construed to limit the foregoing general definition of the term, but shall be construed to include the foregoing particular acts, as well as all other acts within the general definition.

PARALEGALS (AND OTHER NONATTORNEYS) IN COURT

- *North Carolina v. Cummings,* 389 S.E.2d 66, 74 (Supreme Court of North Carolina, 1990) (paralegal allowed to testify about hearsay statement of victim made during intake interview).
- *Lea Co. v. North Carolina Board of Transportation,* 374 S.E.2d 868 (Supreme Court of North Carolina, 1989) (paralegal fees denied; the paralegal work in this case was largely clerical in nature and therefore part of ordinary office overhead to be subsumed in the hourly attorney rate).
- *Spell v. McDaniel,* 852 F.2d 762 (U.S. Court of Appeals for the 4th Circuit, 1988) (award of paralegal fees challenged).
- *Bounds v. Smith,* 97 S. Ct. 1491 (U.S. Supreme Court, 1977) (inmate paralegals).
- *In re Grand Jury Investigation,* 142 Federal Rules Decisions 276 (U.S. District Court, Middle District for North Carolina, 1992) (paralegal part of team that allegedly turns over documents protected by attorney-client privilege).

NORTH DAKOTA

DEFINING THE PRACTICE OF LAW IN NORTH DAKOTA

Ranta v. McCarney, 391 N.W.2d 161, 162, 163 (Supreme Court of North Dakota, 1986): Practice of law under modern conditions consists in no small part of work performed outside of any court and having no immediate relation to proceedings in court. It embraces conveyancing, the giving of legal advice on a large variety of subjects, and the preparation and execution of legal instruments covering an extensive field of business and trust relations and other affairs. Although these transactions may have no direct connection with court proceedings, they are always subject to become involved in litigation. They require in many aspects a high degree of legal skill, a wide experience with men and affairs, and great capacity for adaptation to difficult and complex situations. These "customary functions of an attorney or counsellor at law" . . . bear an intimate relation to the administration of justice by the courts. No valid distinction . . . can be drawn between that part which involves appearance in court and that part which involves advice and drafting of instruments in his office. The work of the office lawyer is the ground work for future possible contests in courts. It has profound effect on the whole scheme of the administration of justice. It is performed with that possibility in mind, and otherwise would hardly be needed. . . . It is of importance to the welfare of the public that these manifold customary functions be performed by persons possessed of adequate learning and skill, of sound moral character, and acting at all times under the heavy trust obligation to clients which rests upon all attorneys. The underlying reasons which prevent corporations, associations and individuals other than members of the bar from appearing before the courts apply with equal force to the performance of these customary functions of attorneys and counsellors at law outside of courts. . . . If compensation is exacted either directly or indirectly, "all advice to clients, and all action taken for them in matters connected with the law," constitute practicing law.

PARALEGALS (AND OTHER NONATTORNEYS) IN COURT

- *In the Matter of Nassif,* 547 N.W.2d 541 (Supreme Court of North Dakota, 1996) (attorney disciplined for allowing untrained "paralegals" to recruit and advise clients, negotiate fees, and perform unsupervised legal work for clients).

- *In the Matter of Johnson,* 481 N.W.2d 225 (Supreme Court of North Dakota, 1992) (disbarred attorney is not allowed to practice as a paralegal).
- *Nat'l Farmers Union . . . v. Souris River Telephone . . . ,* 75 F.3d 1268 (U.S. Court of Appeals for the 8th Circuit, 1996) (award of paralegal fees).
- *Gassler v. Rayl,* 862 F.2d 706 (U.S. Court of Appeals for the 8th Circuit, 1988) (inmate paralegal assistance).

OHIO

ETHICAL RULES AND GUIDELINES IN OHIO

A legal assistant can sign law firm correspondence on law firm stationery as long as his or her nonattorney status is clearly indicated. Board of Commissioners on Grievances and Discipline *Opinion 89-11* (4/14/89) (1989 WL 535016).

Nonattorneys *cannot* be listed on law firm letterhead. They can, however, have business cards as long as their nonattorney status is clear. Board of Commissioners on Grievances and Discipline, *Opinion 89-16* (6/16/89) (1989 WL 535021).

A retired or inactive attorney may not perform the duties of a paralegal since such attorneys "may not render any legal service for an attorney" in active status. Board of Commissioners on Grievances and Discipline, *Opinion 92-4* (2/14/92) (1992 WL 739414). But a suspended or disbarred attorney can act as a paralegal. *Opinion 90-06.* (4/20/90) (1990 WL 640501).

Law firm letterhead *can* print the names and titles of nonattorney employees as long as their nonattorney status is clear, and they are listed separately from the attorneys. Columbus Bar Ass'n, *Opinion (6)* (11/17/88).

Law firm letterhead *can* print the names and titles of nonattorney employees, and the latter can also have their own business card as long as their nonattorney status is made clear. Cleveland Bar Ass'n, *Opinion 89-1* (2/25/89).

DEFINING THE PRACTICE OF LAW IN OHIO

Cincinnati Bar Ass'n v. Estep, 657 N.E.2d 499, 500 (Supreme Court of Ohio, 1995): The practice of law is not limited to the conduct of cases in court. It embraces the preparation of pleadings and other papers incident to actions and special proceedings and the management of such actions and proceedings on behalf of clients . . . and in general all advice to clients and all action taken for them in matters connected with the law. . . . One who gives legal advice to others with the expectation of being compensated therefor engages in the practice of law.

PARALEGALS (AND OTHER NONATTORNEYS) IN COURT

- *Cincinnati Bar v. Estep,* 657 N.E.2d 499 (Supreme Court of Ohio, 1995) (it is the unauthorized practice of law for a nonattorney to represent a client before the Ohio Bureau of Workers' Compensation).
- *Office of Disciplinary Counsel v. Ball,* 618 N.E.2d 159 (Supreme Court of Ohio, 1993) (attorney disciplined for failing to supervise secretary/paralegal).
- *In re Oakes,* 135 Bankruptcy Reporter 511 (U.S. Bankruptcy Court, Northern District for Ohio, 1991) (paralegal fees reduced to the extent that fees were sought for doing work of a clerical nature).
- *Bowling v. Pfizer,* 922 F. Supp. 1261 (U.S. District Court, Southern District for Ohio, 1996) (award of paralegal fees).

- *Ron Scheiderer & Associates v. City of London*, ___ N.E.2d ___ (Court of Appeals of Ohio, 1996) (1996 WL 435312) (award of paralegal fees; when "properly supervised, legal assistants may decrease litigation expenses, and their use should not be discouraged").
- *Crawford v. Sylvania Marketplace Co.*, 655 N.E.2d 284 (Court of Common Pleas of Ohio, 1995) (alleged misconduct by paralegal who was a member of the jury).
- *Malone v. Academy of Court Reporting*, 582 N.E.2d 54 (Court of Appeals of Ohio, 1990) (suit by paralegal students).
- *Palmer v. Westmeyer*, 549 N.E.2d 1202 (Court of Appeals of Ohio, 1988) (a paralegal cannot be charged with legal malpractice since she is not an attorney).
- *Knecht v. Collins*, 903 F. Supp. 1193 (U.S. District Court, Southern District for Ohio, 1995) (inmate paralegals).
- *Riley v. Heckler*, 585 F. Supp. 278 (U.S. District Court, Southern District for Ohio, 1984) (paralegal represents claimant at social security disability hearing).

OKLAHOMA

DEFINING THE PRACTICE OF LAW IN OKLAHOMA

Edwards v. Hert, 504 P.2d 407, 416, 417 (Supreme Court of Oklahoma, 1972): [P]ractice of law: the rendition of services requiring the knowledge and the application of legal principles and technique to serve the interests of another with his consent. . . . [It is] unnecessary that we should . . . have defined 'practice of law' to include specific acts as a prerequisite to the exercise of the proper jurisdiction of the judicial department. . . . This is not to say that there may not be problems in respect to particular facts, or to the sound discretion which is ours in policing the practice of law. . . . But certainly it is unnecessary that we should attempt to anticipate every such problem and to write a detailed code describing every possible situation before the courts may exercise their unquestionable authority. . . . [A] service which otherwise would be a form of the practice of law does not lose that character merely because it is rendered gratuitously. . . . "[I]t is not a prerequisite that a fee should be paid before the relation of attorney and client may exist" . . . . [A]n unlicensed practitioner's performance of legal service is not sanctified by his failure to require pay. . . . It has been urged upon us that acts which properly are part of the lawyer's work also may form an integral part of the legitimate activity of another calling, and that, for performance of these acts by an unlicensed person, incidental to such an independent vocation, penalties should not be inflicted upon the theory that thereby he practices law. To a certain extent, this contention is sound. "There is authority for the proposition that the drafting of documents, when merely incidental to the work of a distinct occupation, is not the practice of law, although the documents have legal consequences." . . . The "distinction between law practice and that which is not may be determined only from a consideration of the acts of service performed in each case." . . . If the practitioner of the "distinct occupation" goes beyond the determination of legal questions for the purpose of performing his special service, and, instead, advises his patron as to the course to be taken to secure a desired legal status, he is engaged in the practice of law. The title searcher is exempt if he performs his task "without giving opinion or advice as to the legal effect of what is found." . . . The work of the accountant is exempt only if it is "dissociated from legal advice." One who, in the exercise of a commission to draw a conveyance, selects language designed to create a certain effect is practicing law. . . . So is one who draws estate plans, involving legal analysis. . . A layman who draws a will for another necessarily is practicing law. . . . So is one who draws legal instruments or contracts. . . . A layman who evaluates a claim, and undertakes to settle it, based upon applicable legal principles, is practicing law. . . . A bank which furnishes "legal information or legal advice with respect to investments, taxation, stocks, bonds, notes or other securities or property" is involved in "a considerable practice of law," despite the argument that this is an incident to the investment trade.

PARALEGALS (AND OTHER NONATTORNEYS) IN COURT

- *Taylor v. Chubb Group of Insurance Companies,* 874 P.2d 806, 809 (Supreme Court of Oklahoma, 1994) (award of paralegal fees is for substantive legal work, not for copying documents or for performing other secretarial tasks; a party must "prove that the charges made for nonattorney's time covered work that a lawyer would have had to perform but for the performance of such services by a legal assistant" at a lower total charge than a lawyer would have charged; a legal assistant may interview clients; draft pleadings and other documents; carry out conventional and computer legal research; research public documents; prepare discovery requests and responses; schedule depositions and prepare notices and subpoenas; summarize depositions and other discovery responses; coordinate and manage document production; locate and interview witnesses; organize pleadings, trial exhibits and other documents; prepare witness and exhibit lists; prepare trial notebooks; prepare for attendance of witnesses at trial; and assist lawyers at trials).
- *Brown v. Ford,* 905 P.2d 223 (Supreme Court of Oklahoma, 1995) (paralegal alleges sexual harassment by attorney at work).
- *Fitter v. Shalala,* 1993 WL 332306 (U.S. Court of Appeals for the 10th Circuit, 1993) (duties of administrative law judge when claimant for supplemental security income is represented at the hearing by a paralegal).
- *Battle v. Anderson,* 457 F. Supp. 719 (U.S. District Court for Oklahoma, 1978) (inmate paralegals).

OREGON

ETHICAL RULES AND GUIDELINES IN OREGON

An attorney can list nonattorneys (e.g., a legal assistant, an office manager) on the law firm's letterhead. Oregon State Bar Ass'n, *Formal Opinion 1991-65* (7/91) (1991 WL 279132).

Two law firms who oppose each other on cases can employ the same nonattorney part time if he or she has no access to the confidences or secrets of either firm. An example would be the mutual employment of a messenger. If they both hired the same legal assistant, however, this access would probably exist. Oregon State Bar Ass'n, *Formal Opinion 1991-44* (7/91) (1991 WL 279229).

An attorney can hire a suspended or disbarred attorney as a paralegal as long as the person does not practice law and there is no sharing of fees with him or her. Oregon State Bar Ass'n, *Formal Ethics Opinion 1991-24* (1991 WL 279165).

It is unethical for an attorney to let his legal assistant draft pleadings that the attorney would sign but not review prior to filing. Oregon State Bar Ass'n, *Formal Opinion 1991-20* (7/91) (1991 WL 279161).

Nonattorneys in an estate-planning service are engaged in the unauthorized practice of law when they give legal advice to clients in connection with the service, even if an attorney reviews and executes the documents involved. Oregon State Bar, *Opinion 523* (3/89).

Nonattorney employees can have their own business cards that contain the name of their attorney-employer. Oregon State Bar, *Opinion 295* (7/75).

A paralegal can write and sign letters on attorney letterhead. Oregon State Bar, *Opinion 349* (6/77) and *Opinion 295* (7/75).

A paralegal cannot take depositions. Oregon State Bar, *Opinion 449* (7/80).

Other relevant opinions of the Oregon State Bar: *Opinion 208* (6/6/72); *Opinion 435*.

A well-trained legal assistant can do almost anything an attorney can do. However, a legal assistant cannot accept a case, set a fee, give legal advice, or represent a client in judicial proceedings. The Legal Assistants (Joint) Committee of the Oregon State Bar, *The Lawyer and the Legal Assistant* (1988).

DEFINING THE PRACTICE OF LAW IN OREGON

Oregon State Bar v. Security Escrows, Inc., 377 P.2d 334, 337 (Supreme Court of Oregon, 1962): We must hold that the legislature has not attempted to define the practice of law, and, accordingly, there is no need to inquire whether it has the power to do so. Before we may proceed with the case at bar, however, it is necessary to have before us enough of a definition so that we can decide whether the court below should have issued the injunction. We must mark out at least enough of the boundaries of the practice of law so that we can decide whether or not the activities complained of fall within them, leaving to future cases such other definitional problems as may remain unresolved. There have been numerous attempts elsewhere to define the practice of law. None has been universally accepted. The Arizona Supreme Court has said that an exhaustive definition is impossible. Perhaps it is. . . . Documents creating legal rights abound in the business community. The preparation of some of these documents is the principal occupation of some lawyers. The preparation of business documents also occupies part of the time of accountants, automobile salesmen, insurance agents, and many others. The practice of law manifestly includes the drafting of many documents which create legal rights. It does not follow, however, that the drafting of all such documents is always the practice of law. The problem, as is frequently the case, is largely one of drawing a recognizable line. Here the line must be drawn between those services which laymen ought not to undertake and those services which laymen can perform without harm to the public. . . . [A footnote of the court quotes from] Black's Law Dictionary (1957): "Practice of law. Not limited to appearing in court, or advising and assisting in the conduct of litigation, but embracing the preparation of pleadings, and other papers incident to actions and special proceedings, conveyancing, the preparation of legal instruments of all kinds, and the giving of all legal advice to clients. . . . It embraces all advice to clients and all actions taken for them in matters connected with the law."

PARALEGALS (AND OTHER NONATTORNEYS) IN COURT

- *Mendoza v. SAIF,* 859 P.2d 582 (Court of Appeals of Oregon, 1993) (an attorney does not establish "good cause" for failure to file a request for a hearing by arguing that he told his legal assistant twice to file it but she failed to do so).
- *Richmark Corp. v. Timber Falling Consultants,* 126 Federal Rules Decisions 58 (U.S. District Court for Oregon, 1989) (paralegal mistakenly sends privileged documents to opposing counsel; attorney failed to supervise paralegal properly).
- *In the Matter of Griffith,* 913 P.2d 695 (Supreme Court of Oregon, 1995) (disbarred attorney acts as paralegal at his old law firm).
- *Bartsch v. Kulongoski,* 906 P.2d 815 (Supreme Court of Oregon, 1995) (the phrases "independent legal technicians" and "independent paralegals" on a ballot initiative conveyed a sense of weighty legal significance that was false and misleading because these phrases had no established meaning in the law).
- *In re Conduct of Morin,* 878 P.2d 393 (Supreme Court of Oregon, 1994) (it is not the unauthorized practice of law for paralegals to give seminars on living trusts and answer general questions about living trust packages; it is the unauthorized practice of law for the paralegal to advise clients or potential clients on legal matters specific to them or to help them select among the legal forms available).

- *Robins v. Scholastic Book Fairs*, 928 F. Supp. 1027 (U.S. District Court for Oregon, 1996) (paralegal fees reduced; 210 hours spent by paralegals were excessive in a straightforward case).

PENNSYLVANIA

ETHICAL RULES AND GUIDELINES IN PENNSYLVANIA

Paralegals can sign letters on attorney letterhead if their nonattorney status is indicated. A supervised paralegal can correspond with the attorney for the opponent. Pennsylvania Bar Ass'n, *Opinion 80-46.*

A document is protected by the attorney-client privilege even if a paralegal mistakenly sends the document to the opposing attorney. Pennsylvania Bar Ass'n, *Opinion 94-11B.*

An attorney's letterhead can print the name of paralegals or other nonattorneys if their nonattorney status is indicated. Pennsylvania Bar Ass'n, *Opinion 85-145* (11/14/85).

A paralegal can have a business card with the title of *legal assistant.* The card can list the name of the law firm. Pennsylvania Bar Ass'n, *Opinion 80-15.*

A law student who has not taken and passed the bar examination is a paralegal and cannot practice law. Pennsylvania Bar Ass'n, *Opinion 86-97* (5/27/87).

An attorney cannot hire an independent paralegal to do accident investigations if the paralegal is not a licensed private detective. Pennsylvania Bar Ass'n, *Opinion 87-31* (6/87).

An attorney cannot allow a paralegal to conduct a deposition even if the attorney prepares the questions to be asked. Pennsylvania Bar Ass'n, *Opinion 87-127* (12/87).

Other opinions of the Pennsylvania Bar Ass'n involving nonattorneys: *87-102; 89-145; 90-65; 91-88; 92-115; 93-100; 93-132.*

Philadelphia Bar Ass'n, Professional Responsibility Committee, *Professional Responsibility for Nonlawyers* (1989). *Guideline 1:* Consider all work of the office confidential, even public knowledge about a client. Do not discuss the business of your office or your firm's clients with any outsider unless you have specific authorization from an attorney. It is illegal and unethical to disclose or to use any information about a company that might be of significance to the securities market in financial transactions such as the purchase or sale of stocks, bonds or other security. *Guideline 2:* A paralegal may not sign papers to be filed in court, ask questions at a deposition, or handle court appearances. A client with whom the paralegal has developed rapport will often ask the paralegal questions such as, "What do you think my chances of recovery are?" Such questions seek advice and the paralegal should refer them to an attorney. *Guideline 3:* If an attorney allows a nonattorney to sign letters on law firm stationery, a descriptive title such as *legal assistant* should be used to clearly indicate the nonattorney's position. *Guideline 4:* If you interview a witness who does not have his or her own attorney, explain who you are and who your office represents. You cannot give the witness any advice except to secure his or her own attorney. If the opposing party has an attorney, you cannot talk with that party without his or her attorney's permission. You might also need this permission to talk to any employees of the opposing party. *Guideline 5:* A paralegal must be truthful when dealing with others on behalf of a client. *Guideline 6:* If the law firm has possession of a client's money or other property, it must be kept completely separate from the attorney's or law firm's money or property, and a proper accounting must be maintained.

An attorney should explain to his paralegal the ethical importance of not breaching client confidentiality and seek to preclude any deliberate or inadvertent disclosures by the paralegal. Philadelphia Bar Ass'n, *Opinion 94-7* (5/94) (1994 WL 187066).

A paralegal can use a business card bearing the name of the law firm provided his or her nonattorney status is clearly designated. Philadelphia Bar Ass'n, *Opinion 74-1* (1974).

Law firm letterhead can include the names of paralegals as long as their nonattorney status is clear. "Terms such as *legal assistant* and *paralegal* suggest specialized training at a recognized school or resulting from some years of experience, and should be used only by persons possessing the requisite training or experience." Committee of the Philadelphia Bar Ass'n, *Opinion 87-18* (6/25/87) (1987 WL 109743).

A paralegal can draft a demand letter as long as an attorney supervises the work product to check its accuracy and the paralegal identifies him/herself as a paralegal. Philadelphia Bar Ass'n, *Ethical Opinion 90-5* (4/90) (1990 WL 303921).

A professional corporation that practices law cannot have a nonattorney as a corporate officer. Philadelphia Bar Ass'n, *Opinion 86-76* (6/19/86).

An attorney can accept referrals from a bilingual paralegal even though the paralegal charges the client for translation and investigation services. Philadelphia Bar Ass'n, *Opinion 88-15* (6/27/88) (1988 WL 236395).

Disqualification of a law firm can be avoided if the firm has in place adequate screening devices to require a nonattorney employee to maintain the confidences gained in a prior job. Philadelphia Bar Ass'n, *Opinion 80-77* (1980); *80-119.*

Other opinions of the Professional Guidance Committee of the Philadelphia Bar Ass'n involving nonattorneys: *80-14* (1980); *81-44; 86-162* (12/18/86); *87-3* (5/8/87); *87-6* (5/5/87); *87-21* (9/8/87); *89-1* (3/89): *89-5* (3/89); *90-5* (6/90); *92-22* (1992); *93-7* (7/93).

Attorney letterhead cannot list paralegals or legal assistants as these titles do not necessarily identify graduates of properly accredited courses of study. Allegheny County Bar Ass'n, *Ethical Opinion 1* (10/81).

DEFINING THE PRACTICE OF LAW IN PENNSYLVANIA

Vohlman v. Western Pennsylvania Hospital, 652 A.2d 849, 851, 852 (Superior Court of Pennsylvania, 1994): While the rules and laws proscribing the unauthorized practice of law are clear, defining the abstract boundaries of the "practice of law" would be an elusive, complex task, "more likely to invite criticism than to achieve clarity." . . . This is so because the practice of law may well be used in a different sense for various purposes. "Where . . . a judgment requires the abstract understanding of legal principles and a refined skill for their concrete application, the exercise of legal judgment is called for. While at times the line between lay and legal judgments may be a fine one, it is nevertheless discernible. Each given case must turn on a careful analysis of the particular judgment involved and the expertise that must be brought to bear on its exercise. . . . See 7 *American Jurisprudence 2d,* Attorneys at Law § 1 (1980) ("practice of law . . . embraces the preparation of pleadings and other papers incident to actions and special proceedings, the management of such actions and proceedings on behalf of clients before judges and courts").

§ 2524 *(Pennsylvania Consolidated Statutes Annotated):* (a) General rule. Except as provided in subsection (b), any person, including, but not limited to, a paralegal or legal assistant, who within this Commonwealth shall practice law, or who shall hold himself out to the public as being entitled to practice law, or use or advertise the title of lawyer, attorney at law, attorney and counselor at law, counselor, or the equivalent in any language, in such a manner as to convey the impression that he is a practitioner of the law of any jurisdiction, without being an attorney at law or a corporation complying with 15 Pa.C.S. Ch. 29 (relating to professional corporations), commits a misdemeanor of the third degree upon a first violation. A second or subsequent violation of this subsection constitutes a misdemeanor of the first degree. . . .

(b)(2) This subsection shall not be interpreted to preclude the use of clerks, secretaries, administrators, bookkeepers, technicians and other assistants who are not usually and ordinarily considered by law, custom and practice to be rendering legal services nor to preclude the use of any other person who performs all his employment under the direct supervision and control of a person duly admitted to practice law. A person shall not, under the guise of employment, render legal services unless duly admitted to practice law. . . .

PARALEGALS (AND OTHER NONATTORNEYS) IN COURT

- *Brown v. Hammond,* 810 F. Supp. 644 (U.S. District Court, Eastern District for Pennsylvania, 1993) (paralegal dismissed for disclosing illegal billing practices) (see text of case on page 260 in chapter 5).
- *Paralegal v. Lawyer,* 783 F. Supp. 230 (U.S. District Court, Eastern District for Pennsylvania, 1992) (paralegal claims wrongful discharge for disclosing a backdated letter).
- *In re Busy Beaver Building Centers,* 19 F.3d 833 (U.S. Court of Appeals for the 3rd Circuit, 1994) (award of paralegal fees in bankruptcy case; extensive discussion of the role of the litigation paralegal as opposed to a legal secretary; amicus brief filed by the National Federation of Paralegal Associations; trial court disallowed compensation for those services performed by paralegals that it considered "purely clerical functions" and therefore part of an attorney's overhead for which there can be no separate payment; on appeal this decision was reversed; page 838: "if the court were to disallow paralegal assistance on such matters, the paralegal profession would suffer a major setback, and attorneys would instead perform those services but at greater expense" to the client; the standard on what paralegal services are compensable will be whether such services are compensable in nonbankruptcy cases: whether nonbankruptcy attorneys typically charge and collect from their clients fees for the kind of services in question, and the rates charged and collected therefor; the case was sent back to the lower court to apply this standard).
- *Schofield v. Trustees of the University of Pennsylvania,* 919 F. Supp. 821, 829 (U.S. District Court, Eastern District for Pennsylvania, 1996) (paralegal fees reduced for time paralegal spent at trial; "It is . . . difficult to justify the need for a paralegal to sit in on the trial").
- *Turiano v. Schnarrs,* 904 F. Supp. 400 (U.S. District Court, Middle District for Pennsylvania, 1995) (inmates as paralegals).
- *Randt v. Rynkiewicz,* 671 A.2d 228, 235 (Superior Court of Pennsylvania, 1996) (judge not required to excuse—"recuse"—himself from the case even though his son worked for defense counsel in the case as a paralegal).
- *Cruz v. Pennsylvania Board of Probation and Parole,* 623 A.2d 381 (Commonwealth Court of Pennsylvania, 1993) (paralegal seeks to represent a parolee before the Board of Probation and Parole).
- *In re Stone,* 166 Bankruptcy Reporter 269 (U.S. Bankruptcy Court, Western District for Pennsylvania, 1994) (paralegal charged with unlicensed practice of law in helping bankruptcy clients).
- *In re Gunn,* 171 Bankruptcy Reporter 517 (U.S. Bankruptcy Court, Eastern District for Pennsylvania, 1994) (paralegal formerly charged with unlicensed practice of law allowed to work for bankruptcy attorney on condition that he repay his former clients and inform all future clients of his prior misconduct).
- *Falcon Oil Co. v. Dept of Environmental Services,* 609 A.2d 876 (Commonwealth Court of Pennsylvania, 1992) (attorney tries to blame his secretary for failing to file a timely appeal).

- *Ezold v. Wolf, Block Schoor . . .* , 983 F.2d 509, 543 (U.S. Court of Appeals for the 3rd Circuit, 1992) (working conditions of paralegals challenged).
- *Buccilli v. Timby, Brown, Timby,* 660 A.2d 1261 (Superior Court of New Jersey, 1995) (New Jersey paralegal who worked for Pennsylvania law firm claims she was fired because she told the firm she was subjected to sexual harassment, she intended to file a workers' compensation claim, and she objected to the lack of attorney supervision of her work and being asked to forge her attorney's name to court documents).
- *In re Mitchell,* 901 F.2d 1179 (U.S. Court of Appeals for the 3rd Circuit, 1990) (a suspended attorney can act as a paralegal but cannot have any contact with clients).
- *In re Anonymous,* 27 D.B. 89, 5 D. & C. 4th 77 (Disciplinary Board of the Supreme Court of Pennsylvania, January 16, 1990) (it is not unethical for an attorney to employ as a paralegal an attorney who is not permitted to practice law in Pennsylvania—because of suspension and later disbarment—and to permit the paralegal to have client contact).

RHODE ISLAND

ETHICAL RULES AND GUIDELINES IN RHODE ISLAND

In contacts with clients, courts, agencies, attorneys, or the public, paralegals must disclose at the outset that they are not attorneys. They can assist at a real estate closing. They can sign correspondence as long as their nonattorney status is clear and the letter does not give legal advice or substantive instructions to a client. They can use a business card with the name of the law firm on it if their nonattorney status is disclosed. An attorney shall not form a partnership with a paralegal if any part of the partnership involves the practice of law. A paralegal cannot share legal fees or be compensated for referring matters to an attorney. An attorney cannot hire a suspended or disbarred attorney as a paralegal (or an attorney who has resigned because of a breach of ethics). Rhode Island Supreme Court, *Provisional Order No. 18* (2/1/83), Revised 10/31/90.

A law firm's letterhead must place the title *legal assistant* after the name of an attorney who is licensed in another state but who is ineligible to sit for the Rhode Island bar examination because he was graduated from an unaccredited law school. Ethics Advisory Panel of the Rhode Island Supreme Court, *Opinion 93-28* (5/12/93). See also *Opinion 92-6* (1992) where the term *legal assistant* is preferred over *paralegal* for nonattorney employees.

An attorney may not hire a suspended or disbarred attorney as a paralegal. Ethics Advisory Panel of the Rhode Island Supreme Court, *Opinion 90-12* (2/27/90): *Opinion 91-64* (9/19/91).

Other opinions of the Ethics Advisory Panel of the Rhode Island Supreme Court involving nonattorneys: *88-4* (4/15/88); *87-3* (1/8/88); *88-7* (5/13/88); *91-42* (7/18/91).

DEFINING THE PRACTICE OF LAW IN RHODE ISLAND

§ 11-27-2 *(Rhode Island Statutes):* The term "practice law" as used in this chapter shall be deemed to mean the doing of any act for another person usually done by attorneys at law in the course of their profession, and, without limiting the generality of the foregoing, shall be deemed to include the following: (1) The appearance or acting as the attorney, solicitor, or representative of another person before any court, referee, master, auditor, division, department, commission, board, judicial person, or body authorized or constituted by law to determine any question of law or fact or to exercise any judicial power, or the preparation of pleadings or other legal papers incident to any action or other proceeding of any kind before or to be brought before the court or other body; (2) The giving or tendering to another person for a consideration, direct or indirect, of any advice or counsel pertaining to a law question or a court action or judicial proceeding brought or to be brought; (3) The undertaking or acting as a representative or on behalf of another person to commence, settle, compromise, adjust, or dispose of any civil or criminal case or cause of action; (4) The preparation or drafting for another person of a will, codicil, corporation organization, amendment, or qualification papers, or any instrument which requires legal knowledge and capacity and is usually prepared by attorneys at law.

PARALEGALS (AND OTHER NONATTORNEYS) IN COURT

- *United States v. Brandon,* 17 F.3d 409 (U.S. Court of Appeals for the 1st Circuit, 1994) (court refuses to appoint a paralegal for the defendant in a criminal case).
- *Lamphere v. Brown University,* 610 F.2d 46 (U.S. Court of Appeals for the 1st Circuit, 1979) (law firm uses voluntary paralegals; lower court improperly grants paralegal fees at approximately three times the amount the law firm paid them).
- *Mokover v. Neco Enterprises,* 785 F. Supp. 1083 (U.S. District Court for Rhode Island, 1992) (award of paralegal fees; duplication of services).
- *In re Almacs,* 178 Bankruptcy Reporter 598 (U.S. Bankruptcy Court for Rhode Island, 1995) (some of the paralegal charges are for tasks that are clerical in nature and should be treated as overhead rather than as separate paralegal fees).
- *In re Swansea,* 155 Bankruptcy Reporter 28 (U.S. Bankruptcy Court for Rhode Island, 1993) (in determining paralegal compensation, a distinction must be made between legitimate paralegal tasks as opposed to clerical ministerial tasks performed by paralegals).
- *Jacobs v. Mancuso,* 825 F.2d 559 (U.S. Court of Appeals for the 1st Circuit, 1987) (award of paralegal fees).

South Carolina

ETHICAL RULES AND GUIDELINES IN SOUTH CAROLINA

South Carolina Bar, *Guidelines for the Utilization by Lawyers of the Services of Legal Assistants* (12/11/81). *Guideline I:* An attorney shall not permit his or her legal assistant to engage in the unauthorized practice of law. *Guideline II:* A legal assistant may perform certain functions otherwise prohibited when and to the extent permitted by court or administrative agency. *Guideline III:* A legal assistant can perform services for the lawyer if (a) the client understands that the legal assistant is not an attorney, (b) the attorney supervises the legal assistant, and (c) the attorney is fully responsible for what the legal assistant does or fails to do. *Guideline IV:* The attorney must instruct the legal assistant to preserve the confidences and secrets of a client and shall exercise care that the legal assistant does so. *Guideline V:* An attorney shall not form a partnership with a legal assistant if any part of the partnership consists of the practice of law. Nor shall an attorney share, on a proportionate basis, legal fees with a legal assistant. The legal assistant, however, can be included in a retirement plan even though based in whole or in part on a profit-sharing arrangement. A legal assistant shall not be paid, directly or indirectly for referring legal matters to an attorney. *Guideline VI:* The letterhead of an attorney may not include the name of a legal assistant, but a legal assistant can have a business card that prints the name of his or her attorney as long as the legal assistant's capacity or status is clearly indicated. A legal assistant can sign letters on an attorney's letterhead as long as the legal assistant's signature is followed by an appropriate designation (e.g., "legal assistant") so that it is clear the signer is not an attorney. *Guideline VII:* An attorney shall require a legal assistant, when dealing with a client, to disclose at the outset that he or she is not an attorney. This disclosure is also required when the paralegal is dealing with a court, administrative agency, attorney, or the public if there is any reason for their believing the legal assistant is an attorney or is associated with an attorney. This guideline applies even in administrative agencies where the legal assistant is allowed to represent clients. *Guideline VIII:* Except as otherwise provided by law, any grievances or complaints of the use of legal assistants by attorneys shall be referred for action to the Board of Commissioners on Grievances and Discipline.

Nonattorney employees can have their own business cards as long as the title *legal assistant* is used on the card. The name of the law firm can also be printed on the card but only if the legal assistant performs significant duties outside the law office. South Carolina Bar, *Opinion 88-6.*

An attorney can hire a legal assistant with a criminal record for vehicular manslaughter but cannot hire a legal assistant who is a lawyer who has been disciplined. South Carolina Bar, *Opinion 87-6.*

An attorney can hire nonattorneys to fill in preprinted real estate forms and do title searches as long as they are supervised by the attorney and the attorney maintains direct contact with clients. South Carolina Bar, *Opinion 88-2* (6/88). On title searches, see also *Opinion 78-26* (10/78).

It is the unauthorized practice of law for a nonattorney to have an ownership interest, along with an attorney, in a corporation that drafts and provides real estate documents if the nonattorney controls any of the legal services provided. South Carolina Bar, *Opinion 84-3* (9/85).

Other opinions of the Ethics Advisory Committee of the South Carolina Bar involving nonattorneys: *86-5; 88-14; 88-18.*

DEFINING THE PRACTICE OF LAW IN SOUTH CAROLINA

The South Carolina Medical Malpractice Joint Underwriting Association v. Froelich, 377 S.E.2d 306, 307 (Supreme Court of South Carolina, 1989): Conduct constituting the practice of law includes a wide range of activities. It is too obvious for discussion that the practice of law is not limited to the conduct of cases in courts. According to the generally understood definition of the practice of law in this country, it embraces the preparation of pleadings and other papers incident to actions and special proceedings and the management of such actions and proceedings on behalf of clients before judges and courts, and in addition conveyancing, the preparation of legal instruments of all kinds, and in general all advice to clients and all action taken for them in matters connected with the law.

PARALEGALS (AND OTHER NONATTORNEYS) IN COURT

- *Lucas v. Guyton,* 901 F. Supp. 1047, 1059 (U.S. District Court for South Carolina, 1995) (the "court observed Ms. Pope to be a diligent and very able paralegal who assisted in many respects during the trial including reading the depositions of Plaintiff's death row witnesses, taking notes throughout the proceeding and, on numerous occasions, conferring with counsel during his presentation of the case").
- *Andersdon v. Tolbert,* 473 S.E.2d 456 (Court of Appeals of South Carolina, 1996) (award of paralegal fees).
- *Alexander S. v. Boyd,* 929 F. Supp. 925 (U.S. District Court for South Carolina, 1995) (paralegal fees).

- *In re Unauthorized Practice of Law Rules Proposed by the South Carolina Bar*, 422 S.E.2d 123 (Supreme Court of South Carolina, 1992) (a business can be represented by a nonattorney employee in civil magistrate's court proceedings; a South Carolina state agency may authorize nonattorneys to appear and represent clients before the agency; an arresting police officer—a nonattorney—may prosecute traffic offenses in magistrate's court and in municipal court).
- *In re Easler*, 272 S.E.2d 32, 32-3 (Supreme Court of South Carolina, 1980) (the activities of a paralegal do not constitute the practice of law as long as they are limited to work of a preparatory nature).
- *South Carolina v. Robinson*, 468 S.E.2d 290 (Supreme Court of South Carolina, 1996) (injunction against paralegal who advertises in yellow pages—"If your civil rights have been violated, call me"—as a paralegal and represents clients in court; § 40-5-80 of the *South Carolina Code Annotated* allows a nonattorney to represent another in court if the permission of the court is first obtained—"with leave of the court"—but the paralegal in this case did not always obtain this permission).
- *In the Matter of Jenkins*, 468 S.E.2d 869 (Supreme Court of South Carolina, 1996) (attorney disciplined for asking her paralegal to notarize a forged signature).
- *Robinson v. Tyson*, 461 S.E.2d 397, 399 (Court of Appeals of South Carolina, 1995) (data on starting salaries for paralegals in 1980s).
- *Williams v. Leeke*, 584 F.2d 1336 (U.S. Court of Appeals for the 4th Circuit, 1978) (inmate paralegals).

South Dakota

ETHICAL RULES AND GUIDELINES IN SOUTH DAKOTA

South Dakota Supreme Court Rule 92-5, *In the Matter of the Adoption of a New Rule Relating to the Utilization of Legal Assistants* (1992); *South Dakota Statutes* § 16-18-34. An attorney must assure that a legal assistant is trained and competent to perform assigned tasks. The status of a legal assistant must be disclosed. The tasks assigned a legal assistant must not require the exercise of unsupervised legal judgment. An attorney must instruct the legal assistant about the standards of confidentiality and the other ethical standards governing attorneys. A legal assistant can write and sign correspondence on attorney letterhead as long as no legal opinion or advice is given. Legal assistants may be mentioned by name and title on attorney letterhead and on business cards that identify the attorney's firm. An attorney must take reasonable measures to prevent conflicts of interest created by the legal assistant's personal interests and other employment. There must be no splitting of fees with legal assistants nor paying them for a referral of legal business. A legal assistant's pay cannot, by advance agreement, be contingent on the profitability of the attorney's practice. To be a legal assistant in South Dakota, a person must meet minimum educational qualifications or a designated number of years of experience and in-house training.

It is unethical for an attorney to give 5% of the fees collected from clients referred by a nonattorney. State Bar of South Dakota, *Opinion 94-12.*

A law firm can list paralegals on their letterhead (referring to graduates of law school who have not yet passed the bar exam). State Bar of South Dakota, *Opinion 90-10* (9/22/90).

DEFINING THE PRACTICE OF LAW IN SOUTH DAKOTA

Persche v. Jones, 387 N.W.2d 32, 36 (Supreme Court of South Dakota, 1986): Practicing law "is not limited to conducting litigation, but includes giving legal advice and counsel, and rendering services that require the use of legal knowledge or skill and the preparing of instruments and contracts by which legal rights are secured, whether or not the matter is pending in a court."

PARALEGALS (AND OTHER NONATTORNEYS) IN COURT

- *In re French,* 162 Bankruptcy Reporter 541 (U.S. Bankruptcy Court for South Dakota, 1994) (disclosures by a debtor to a paralegal of the debtor's attorney are not protected by the attorney-client privilege).
- *In re Grenoble Apartments,* 152 Bankruptcy Reporter 608, 610 (U.S. Bankruptcy Court for South Dakota, 1993) (the rate a court will award for paralegal fees is not higher if the case the paralegal is working on is complex).
- *In re Yankton College,* 101 Bankruptcy Reporter 151, 159 (U.S. Bankruptcy Court for South Dakota, 1989) ("Paraprofessional Billing": if paralegal work is to be compensated, the qualifications of the paralegal should be established to justify the charge; "[s]imply classifying a secretary as a paralegal for billing purposes does not justify compensating secretary time" which should be part of overhead).
- *Cody v. Hillard,* 599 F. Supp. 1025 (U.S. District Court for South Dakota, 1984) (inmates as paralegals).

TENNESSEE

ETHICAL RULES AND GUIDELINES IN TENNESSEE

If appropriate screening devices are in place, and Client "A" consents, an entire law firm need not be disqualified from representing that Client simply because a "tainted" attorney in the firm once worked at another firm that represented client "B" in a case adverse to Client "A." Furthermore, "the disqualification rules and screening procedures are applicable to lawyer, law clerk, paralegal, and legal secretary." Board of Professional Responsibility of the Supreme Court of Tennessee, *Formal Ethics Opinion 89-F-118* (3/10/89). Note: this Opinion may overrule *Formal Ethics Opinion 87-F-110* (6/10/87), which disqualified a law firm because of a "tainted" paralegal who switched jobs even though screening mechanisms were in place. The validity of *Opinion 89-F-110* is also in doubt because of *King v. King* (see discussion below).

It is the unauthorized practice of law for an attorney to allow his or her paralegal to appear at a Section 341 meeting of creditors in bankruptcy cases to ask questions of debtors, unless a court expressly authorizes it. Board of Professional Responsibility of the Supreme Court of Tennessee, *Advisory Ethics Opinion 92-A-473 (a)* (5/12/92) confirming *Opinion 92-A-475* (1/91). See *In re Kincaid* below, which *does* authorize it.

It is the unauthorized practice of law for an attorney to allow his or her paralegal to appear in court at docket calls on behalf of the attorney to schedule cases. Board of Professional Responsibility of the Supreme Court of Tennessee, *Formal Ethics Opinion 85-F-94* (5/6/85).

A suspended attorney should not act as a paralegal. Board of Professional Responsibility of the Supreme Court of Tennessee, *Ethics Opinion 83-F-50* (8/12/83).

It is the unauthorized practice of law for an unsupervised independent paralegal to provide the public with the service of filling out legal documents such as bankruptcy petitions, uncontested divorce petitions, wills, and premarital agreements for a fee. Attorney General of Tennessee, *Opinion 92-01* (1/9/92).

DEFINING THE PRACTICE OF LAW IN TENNESSEE

§ 23-3-101 *(Tennessee Code Annotated):* (1) "Law business" means the advising or counseling for a valuable consideration of any person, firm, association, or corporation, as to any secular law, or the drawing or the procuring of or assisting in the drawing for a valuable consideration of any paper, document or instrument affecting or relating to secular rights, or the doing of any act for a valuable consideration in a representative capacity, obtaining or tending to secure for any person, firm, association or corporation any property or property rights whatsoever, or the soliciting of clients directly or indirectly to provide such services; and (2) "Practice of law" means the appearance as an advocate in a representative capacity or the drawing of papers, pleadings or documents or the performance of any act in such capacity in connection with proceedings pending or prospective before any court, commissioner, referee or any body, board, committee or commission constituted by law or having authority to settle controversies, or the soliciting of clients directly or indirectly to provide such services.

PARALEGALS (AND OTHER NONATTORNEYS) IN COURT

- *King v. King,* 1989 WL 122981 (Court of Appeals of Tennessee, 1989) (motion to disqualify the defendant's law firm is denied; the defendant hired a person who was once a secretary for the plaintiff's attorney, but there were no breaches of confidentiality by the secretary at the new firm: the court relied on *Ethics Opinion 87-F-110,* but pointed out differences in the positions of legal secretaries and paralegals).
- *In re Kincaid,* 146 Bankruptcy Reporter 387 (U.S. Bankruptcy Court, Western District for Tennessee, 1992) (a nonattorney regularly employed by a corporate-creditor could appear on behalf of the employer at a creditors' meeting in a bankruptcy case and question debtors without engaging in unauthorized practice of law).
- *Davis v. Brady,* 1993 WL 430137 (9 F.3d 107) (U.S. Court of Appeals for the 6th Circuit, 1993) (attorney hires freelance paralegal; if the paralegal "dropped the ball," it would be treated as the attorney's responsibility).
- *Budoff v. Holiday Inns, Inc.,* 732 F.2d 1523 (U.S. Circuit Court for the 6th Circuit, 1984) (new trial ordered after paralegal of attorney has a conversation with a relative of a juror during the trial).
- *Alexander v. Inman,* 903 S.W.2d 686, 704 (Court of Appeals of Tennessee, 1995) (the request to the court for an award of fees for paralegal services explained the services they provided in such general terms "that no finder of fact would be able to determine whether they were required or reasonable").
- *Chandler v. Secretary . . . ,* 792 F.2d 70, 73 (U.S. Court of Appeals for the 6th Circuit, 1986) (it is not true that an attorney will be compensated at paralegal rates if the attorney is asking for compensation for a task he could have delegated to an experienced paralegal).
- *Overton v. Wimberly,* 1996 WL 138231 (Court of Appeals of Tennessee, 1996) (client sues attorney and his legal assistant for fraud).
- *Austin Power Co. v. Thompson,* 1996 WL 73815 (Court of Appeals of Tennessee, 1996) (litigation paralegal called as witness).
- *Tuggle v. Barksdale,* 641 F. Supp. 34 (U.S. District Court, Western District for Tennessee, 1985) (use of inmate paralegals—jailhouse lawyers).

TEXAS

ETHICAL RULES AND GUIDELINES IN TEXAS

State Bar of Texas, *General Guidelines for the Utilization of the Services of Legal Assistants by Attorneys* (January 22, 1993). *Guideline I:* An attorney should ensure that a legal assistant does not give legal advice or otherwise engage in the unauthorized practice of law. *Guideline II:* The attorney must take reasonable measures to ensure that the legal assistant's conduct is consistent with the Texas rules of ethics. *Guideline III:* An attorney may, with the client's consent, perform supervised functions authorized by law and ethics. *Guideline IV:* When dealing with others, the status of the legal assistant must be disclosed at the outset. *Guideline V:* The attorney must not assign functions to a legal assistant that require the exercise of independent professional legal judgment. The attorney must maintain a direct relationship with the client. The attorney is responsible for the actions taken and not taken by a legal assistant. *Guideline VI:* An attorney may not delegate to a legal assistant responsibility for establishing the attorney-client relationship, setting fees, or giving legal advice to a client. *Guideline VII:* An attorney must instruct the legal assistant to preserve the sanctity of all confidences and secrets and take reasonable measures to ensure that this is done. *Guideline VIII:* The attorney should take reasonable measures to prevent conflicts of interest resulting from a legal assistant's other employment or interests. *Guideline IX:* An attorney can charge and bill for a legal assistant's time but may not share legal fees with a legal assistant. *Guideline X:* An attorney may not split legal fees with a legal assistant nor pay a legal assistant for the referral of legal business. A legal assistant's compensation cannot be contingent, by advance agreement, upon the profitability of the attorney's practice. *Guideline XI:* The legal assistant can have a business card that names the firm as long as the status of the legal assistant is included on the card. The attorney must take reasonable measures to ensure that the card is not used in a deceptive way for unethical solicitation.

———————

Law firm letterhead can print the name of legal assistants and can indicate that they have been certified (with a notation that they are legal assistants and are not licensed to practice law). State Bar of Texas, *Opinion 436* (6/20/86), which overrules *Opinion 390.*

A legal assistant can write a letter on the law firm's letterhead as long as he or she signs as a legal assistant. The letter should not contain legal advice, judgment, strategy, or settlement negotiations. Such letters should be signed by an attorney. State Bar of Texas, *Opinion 381* (3/75).

A legal assistant may have a business card with the law firm's name appearing on it provided the status of the legal assistant is clearly disclosed. State Bar of Texas, *Opinion 403* (1982).

The name of an employee can be printed on an outdoor sign of a law firm as long as the nonattorney status of the employee is clear on the sign. Professional Ethics Committee of the State Bar of Texas, *Opinion 437* (6/20/86).

It is unethical for attorneys to take a case in which they know or believe that they may have to call their nonattorney employee as an expert witness. State Bar of Texas, *Opinion 516* (6/2/95).

A legal assistant switches sides between law firms who are opposing each other on a case. The new employer is not disqualified if he takes steps to ensure there will be no breach of confidentiality by the legal assistant. State Bar of Texas, *Opinion 472* (6/20/91).

Other opinions of the Professional Ethics Committee of the State Bar of Texas involving nonattorneys: *438* (3/16/87); *458* (3/11/88).

When an attorney fails to supervise his paralegal, the attorney is responsible for the malpractice of the paralegal, such as the theft of client funds by the paralegal. "In the future, you should establish greater controls over your paralegals. " Dallas Bar Ass'n, *Opinion 1989-5.*

DEFINING THE PRACTICE OF LAW IN TEXAS

§ 81.101 *Vernon's Texas Statutes and Codes Annotated:* (a) In this chapter the "practice of law" means the preparation of a pleading or other document incident to an action or special proceeding or the management of the action or proceeding on behalf of a client before a judge in court as well as a service rendered out of court, including the giving of advice or the rendering of any service requiring the use of legal skill or knowledge, such as preparing a will, contract, or other instrument, the legal effect of which under the facts and conclusions involved must be carefully determined.

(b) The definition in this section is not exclusive and does not deprive the judicial branch of the power and authority under both this chapter and the adjudicated cases to determine whether other services and acts not enumerated may constitute the practice of law.

PARALEGALS (AND OTHER NONATTORNEYS) IN COURT

- *Phoenix Founders, Inc. v. Marshall,* 887 S.W.2d 831, 834 (Supreme Court of Texas, 1994) (see page 281 in chapter 5) (there is a rebuttable presumption that a nonattorney who switches sides in ongoing litigation, after having gained confidential information at the first firm, will share the information with members of the new firm; but the presumption may be rebutted to avoid disqualification upon a showing that sufficient precautions, e.g., building a Chinese Wall, to guard against any disclosure of confidences).
- *Arzate v. Hayes,* 915 S.W.2d 616, 619 (Court of Appeals of Texas, 1996) (when a paralegal switches law firms, the presumption that confidential information has been disclosed is rebutted upon a showing that sufficient precautions have been taken by the new firm to guard against disclosure of confidential matters; the precautions were taken in this case).
- *State Bar of Texas v. Faubion,* 821 S.W.2d 203 (Court of Appeals of Texas, 1991) (it was unethical for an attorney to pay a paralegal/investigator up to one-third of the fees generated from particular cases on which the paralegal worked; a bonus is proper if it is not based on a percentage of the law firm's profits or on a percentage of particular legal fees).
- *Reich v. Page & Addison,* 1994 WL 143208 (U.S. District Court, Northern District for Texas, 1994) (overtime pay). See discussion of this case on page 233 in chapter 4.
- *Stewart Title Guaranty Co. v. Aiello,* 911 S.W.2d 463 (Court of Appeals of Texas, 1995) (award of paralegal fees).
- *In re Witts,* 180 Bankruptcy Reporter 171, 173 (U.S. Bankruptcy Court, Eastern District for Texas, 1995) (attorney cannot recover paralegal rates for such clerical tasks as organizing files, proofreading and revising documents, faxing and copying).
- *Toyota Motor Sales v. Heard,* 774 S.W.2d 316, 318 (Court of Appeals of Texas, 1989) (the attorney work product privilege extends to materials prepared in anticipation of litigation by the attorney's paralegal).
- *Sims v. Texas,* 735 S.W.2d 913 (Court of Appeals of Texas, 1987) (paralegal not allowed to sit at counsel's table during trial).
- *Gill v. Gill,* 657 F. Supp. 1394 (U.S. District Court, Western District for Texas, 1987) (there is a need for Hispanic paralegals who can assist Hispanic prisoners).

- *Petroleos Mexicanos v. Crawford Enterprises, Inc.,* 826 F.2d 392 (U.S. Court of Appeals for the 5th Circuit, 1987) (court appoints paralegal as a special master to monitor a company's discovery compliance).
- *Vargas v. Texas,* 859 S.W.2d 534 (Court of Appeals of Texas, 1993) (paralegal as juror).
- *Kendall v. Whataburger, Inc.,* 759 S.W.2d 751 (Court of Appeals of Texas, 1988) (paralegal as presiding juror who gave legal opinions during jury deliberations).
- *Rea v. Cofer,* 879 S.W.2d 224 (Court of Appeals of Texas, 1994) (former client sues attorney and paralegal for legal malpractice).
- *Bair v. Hagans,* 838 S.W.2d 677 (Court of Appeals of Texas, 1992) (attorney blames paralegal's illness for neglect in handling a case).
- *Masterson v. Cox,* 886 S.W.2d 436 (Court of Appeals of Texas, 1994) (paralegal sues attorney for slander for calling the paralegal a homosexual).

Utah

ETHICAL RULES AND GUIDELINES IN UTAH

A lawyer may not use the word "associate" in its name if there are no associated attorneys in the firm even if it "employs one or more associated nonattorneys such as paralegals or investigators." Utah State Bar, *Opinion Number 138* (1/27/94).

A law firm may not split fees with nonattorneys, but may include nonattorney employees in a compensation or retirement plan as long as compensation is not tied to particular fees and the nonattorney has no controlling interest in the firm. Utah State Bar, *Opinion Number 139* (1/27/94).

A nonattorney may be listed on the letterhead of an attorney as long as the nonattorney's status is clear. Utah State Bar, *Opinion Number 131* (5/20/93).

DEFINING THE PRACTICE OF LAW IN UTAH

Utah State Bar v. Summerhayes & Hayden, 905 P.2d 867, 869, 870 (Supreme Court of Utah, 1995): The practice of law, although difficult to define precisely, is generally acknowledged to involve the rendering of services that require the knowledge and application of legal principles to serve the interests of another with his consent. . . . It not only consists of performing services in the courts of justice throughout the various stages of a matter, but in a larger sense involves counseling, advising, and assisting others in connection with their legal rights, duties, and liabilities. . . . It also includes the preparation of contracts and other legal instruments by which legal rights and duties are fixed. . . . This Court has the exclusive authority to regulate the practice of law in Utah. . . . This authority includes the power to determine what constitutes the practice of law and to promulgate rules to control and regulate that practice. There is little in Utah case law that assists the determination of which specific acts, beyond the representation of another's legal interests in a court of law, constitute the practice of law. What constitutes the practice of law in any given situation requires a case-by-case decision, and therefore, each case must be evaluated to determine whether the particular acts involved constitute the practice of law.

PARALEGALS (AND OTHER NONATTORNEYS) IN COURT

- *Barnard v. Utah State Bar,* 857 P.2d 917 (Supreme Court of Utah, 1993) (attorney charged with unauthorized practice of law for using paralegals to help clients file their own divorces).
- *Utah v. Long,* 844 P.2d 381 (Court of Appeals of Utah, 1992) (attorney disciplined for failing to supervise his legal assistant who gave a client incorrect legal advice).

- *Anderson v. Secretary of Health and Human Services,* 80 F.3d 1500 (U.S. Court of Appeals for the 10th Circuit, 1996) (paralegal costs denied where no documentation—other than the statement of the lead attorney—was submitted on what the paralegal did).
- *Baldwin v. Burton,* 850 P.2d 1188, 1200 (Supreme Court of Utah, 1993) ("allowing recovery for legal assistant fees promotes lawyer efficiency and decreases client litigation costs").
- *Law Offices of David Paul White v. Industrial Commission of Utah,* 778 P.2d 21 (Court of Appeals of Utah, 1989) (nonattorney employee denied unemployment because she was fired for "just cause" due to her conduct on the job).
- *Gold Standard, Inc. v. American Barrick Resources Corp.,* 805 P.2d 164, 169 (Supreme Court of Utah, 1990) (a nonattorney's work in preparation for litigation is protected by the attorney work-product rule).

VERMONT

ETHICAL RULES AND GUIDELINES IN VERMONT

A law firm cannot continue to represent a defendant in a civil case after hiring a nonattorney employee who had previously performed extensive work on the same case while employed by the law firm representing the plaintiff. Vermont Bar Ass'n, *Opinion 85-8* (1985).

In a conversation with a nonattorney employee, if a prospective client threatens to kill someone, the employee who believes the threat can warn the potential victim. Vermont Bar Ass'n, *Opinion 86-3.*

An attorney represents a client in a real estate transaction where the opposing party is the spouse of a paralegal who works for that attorney. The attorney is not disqualified from the case if the client is told about the paralegal's relationship to the spouse, and if the paralegal does not work on the case. Vermont Bar Ass'n, *Opinion 87-15* (1987).

A paralegal works for an attorney who represents the plaintiff in a case. The paralegal also works in a court diversion program that processed the brother of the defendant in this case. What this brother did or didn't do is relevant to the case between the plaintiff and defendant. The attorney can still represent this plaintiff, but the paralegal should be screened from the case and must not tell the attorney any secrets he learned in the diversion program. Vermont Bar Ass'n, *Opinion 89-4.*

A firm is not disqualified from handling a case because a paralegal employed in the firm formerly was employed in a paralegal training clinic that provided representation to an opposing party in litigation handled by the firm even though the paralegal had some involvement in the representation as long as the paralegal has no present involvement in the case and conveys no confidential information to firm attorneys. Vermont Bar Ass'n, *Opinion 78-2* (1978).

Other Vermont Bar Ass'n opinions involving nonattorneys: *Opinion 87-8* (nonattorney employee poses as a disinterested third party in a letter to the plaintiff to gain information about the suit); *Opinion 85-9.*

DEFINING THE PRACTICE OF LAW IN VERMONT

In re Welch, 185 A.2d 458, 459 (Supreme Court of Vermont, 1962): In general, one is deemed to be practicing law whenever he furnishes to another advice or service under circumstances which imply the possession and use of legal knowledge and skill. The practice of law includes "all advice to clients, and all actions taken for them in matters connected with the law." . . . Practice of law includes the giving of legal advice and counsel, and the preparation of legal instruments and contracts of which legal rights are secured. . . . Where the rendering of services for another involves the use of legal knowledge or skill on his behalf—where legal advice is required and is availed of or rendered in connection with such services—these services necessarily constitute or include the practice of law. . . . We cannot over-emphasize the necessity of legal training in the proper drafting of legal documents and advice relating thereto. The absence of such training may result in legal instruments faulty in form and contents, and also lead to a failure of purpose, litigation, and expense.

PARALEGALS (AND OTHER NONATTORNEYS) IN COURT

- *In re S.T.N. Enterprises, Inc.,* 70 Bankruptcy Reporter 823 (U.S. Bankruptcy Court for Vermont, 1987) (court will reduce an attorney's rate of compensation for performing tasks that could have been performed by a paralegal at a lower rate).
- *McSweeney v. McSweeney,* 618 A.2d 1332 (Supreme Court of Vermont, 1992) (it is not the unauthorized practice of law for nonattorney employees of the Office of Child Support to prepare and file complaints and motions in child support cases before a magistrate [4 V.S.A. § 464,] but they cannot handle URESA cases involving interstate support issues before a magistrate).
- *Nash v. Coxon,* 583 A.2d 96 (Supreme Court of Vermont, 1990) (court refuses to order payment of inmate's paralegal correspondence course).
- *Hohman v. Hogan,* 458 F. Supp. 669 (U.S. District Court for Vermont, 1978) (paralegal assistance to inmates).
- *Berry v. Schweiker,* 675 F.2d 464 (U.S. Court of Appeals for the 2d Circuit, 1982) (paralegal represents client at disability benefits hearing).

VIRGINIA

ETHICAL RULES AND GUIDELINES IN VIRGINIA

A paralegal shall not communicate with clients, outside attorneys, or the public without disclosing his or her nonattorney status. *Code of Professional Responsibility, DR 3-104(E).*

An attorney is not required to withdraw from a case as long as a nonattorney employee does not disclose confidential information learned while she worked for an opposing attorney. Standing Committee on Legal Ethics of the Virginia State Bar, *Opinion 745* (1985).

An attorney represents a client in a case in which the attorney's former nonattorney employee will testify against this client. The attorney is not disqualified from representing this client as long as the client is informed of this situation and still wants the attorney to represent him. Standing Committee on Legal Ethics of the Virginia State Bar, *Opinion 891* (4/1/87).

A law firm can print the names of nonattorney employees on its letterhead as long as their nonattorney status is clear. These employees can participate in a profit sharing plan of the firm as part of a compensation or retirement program. Standing Committee on Legal Ethics of the Virginia State Bar, *Opinion 762* (1/29/86). See also *Opinion 970* (9/30/87) (attorney may list name and title of firm's chief investigator as long as listing includes affirmative statement that investigator is not licensed to practice law).

An attorney must not split fees with nonattorneys, but they can be paid a bonus that is based on profit-sharing. Standing Committee on Legal Ethics of the Virginia State Bar, *Opinion 806* (6/25/86).

A law firm engaged in collection work can pay its nonattorney employee a percentage of profits from the collections received plus a salary. Standing Committee on Legal Ethics of the Virginia State Bar, *Opinion 885* (3/11/87).

It is unethical for a nonattorney employee of a law firm to contact prospective collections clients in order to suggest that they hire the law firm for their collections work. Standing Committee on Legal Ethics of the Virginia State Bar, *Opinion 1290* (10/25/89).

A "real estate paralegal company" can provide assistance to an attorney in closing real estate loans that have been referred to this company by the closing attorney. This is not the unauthorized practice of law as long as designated procedures are followed. Unauthorized Practice of Law Committee, *Opinion 147* (4/19/91).

It is not the unauthorized practice of law for a nonattorney to give a judicial officer information (present facts) that concerns the weight of the evidence in bail cases. Unauthorized Practice of Law Committee, *Opinion 186* (9/7/95).

It is not the unauthorized practice of law for a paralegal to appear in court to collect monies resulting from a garnishment as long as this appearance only involves a ministerial or clerical act. Unauthorized Practice of Law Committee, *Opinion 72* (12/12/84).

A suspended attorney who was a sole practitioner may not continue to employ a paralegal in his office since this paralegal would not have attorney supervision in what he does. Unauthorized Practice of Law Committee, *Opinion 137* (1/8/90). See also DR 3-101(C) and *Opinion 934* (6/16/87) (a disbarred attorney cannot be employed as a paralegal by an attorney with whom the disbarred was previously associated).

A paralegal's name can be printed on the door of the paralegal's private office as long as it does not create the impression that the paralegal is an attorney. Unauthorized Practice of Law Committee, *Opinion 225* (5/21/73) and *Opinion 326* (6/19/79).

A private law firm employs a paralegal whose husband is an attorney who represents the government in cases against clients of the law firm. The law firm can continue to employ this paralegal, but it must tell its clients and the court of the relationship between the paralegal and the government attorney. Unauthorized Practice of Law Committee, *Opinion 358* (3/10/80).

An attorney can instruct his paralegal to call a prospective defendant to ask if it manufactures a particular product. This does not violate the rule against contacting the other side since there is no litigation underway. The call is part of proper investigation. Unauthorized Practice of Law Committee, *Opinion 1190* (1/4/89). See also *Opinion 1504* (12/14/92) (paralegal can contact opponent to obtain information under Virginia Freedom of Information Act) and *Opinion 1639* (4/24/95) (OK for paralegal to contact the other side to provide information as a courtesy).

Other opinions of the Standing Committee on Legal Ethics of the Virginia State Bar involving nonattorneys: *806* (1986); *823* (9/19/86); *875* (1/30/87); *909* (4/1/87); *946* (6/25/87); *1003* (11/24/87); *1054* (3/29/88); *1077* (5/23/88); *1258* (7/25/89); *1276* (10/3/89); *1288* (10/19/89).

DEFINING THE PRACTICE OF LAW IN VIRGINIA

Part Six: Section I: (B) *(Rules of the Supreme Court of Virginia):* (a) preamble to Part Six: Section I: (B) . . . defines the practice of law as: (1) advising another, not his regular employer, for direct or indirect compensation, in any matter involving the application of legal principles to factors or purposes, or desires; (2) preparation for another, not his regular employer, with or without compensation, legal instruments of any character; or (3) representing the interest of another, with or without compensation, before any tribunal judicial, administrative, or executive.

PARALEGALS (AND OTHER NONATTORNEYS) IN COURT

- *Musselman v. Willoughby Corp.*, 337 S.E.2d 724 (Supreme Court of Virginia, 1985) (paralegal negligence asserted in legal malpractice case brought by client against attorney).

- *EEOC v. American Nat'l Bank,* 625 F.2d 1176 (U.S. Court of Appeals for the 4th Circuit, 1981) (role of paralegal in racial discrimination case).
- *Kaufhold v. Bright,* 835 F. Supp. 294 (U.S. District Court, Western District for Virginia, 1993) (inmate who attended paralegal correspondence school sues the parole board for impeding his potential employment as a paralegal).
- *Tanksley v. Garrett,* 175 Bankruptcy Reporter 434 (U.S. Bankruptcy Court, Western District for Virginia, 1994) (United States Trustee seeks to enjoin a law firm from allowing a paralegal to represent clients at Section 341 bankruptcy hearing).
- *Trimper v. City of Norfolk,* 58 F.3d 68 (U.S. Court of Appeals for the 4th Circuit, 1995) (award of paralegal fees).
- *Martin v. Cavalier Hotel Corp.,* 48 F.3d 1343, 1360 (U.S. Court of Appeals for the 4th Circuit, 1995) (paying for thirty hours of paralegal time for "jury observation" is excessive; there was no reasonable necessity for other paralegals to attend forty-seven hours of trial proceedings).

VIRGIN ISLANDS

Virgin Islands Court Case Involving Paralegals:

An attorney who has been suspended from practice before a federal court of appeals can work on a federal case as a paralegal if supervised by an attorney in good standing and there is no contact with clients. *In re Mitchell,* 901 F.2d 1179, 1190 (U.S. Court of Appeals for the 3rd Circuit, 1990).

WASHINGTON STATE

ETHICAL RULES AND GUIDELINES IN WASHINGTON STATE

A disbarred attorney cannot be employed as a paralegal. Washington State Bar Ass'n, *Opinion 184* (1990).

An attorney cannot let a collection agency use his name on court documents unless the attorney provides legal assistance on each particular case. Rubber-stamping legal papers of nonattorneys is unethical. Washington State Bar Ass'n, *Opinion 18* (1952) and *Opinion 76* (1960).

DEFINING THE PRACTICE OF LAW IN WASHINGTON STATE

Washington v. Hunt, 880 P.2d 96, 99, 100 (Court of Appeals of Washington, 1994): [T]he term "practice of law" includes not only the doing or performing of services in a court of justice, in any matter depending therein, throughout its various stages, and in conformity with the adopted rules of procedure, but in a larger sense includes legal advice and counsel, and the preparation of legal instruments and contracts by which legal rights are secured. . . . [T]he selection and completion of form legal documents, or the drafting of such documents, including deeds, mortgages, deeds of trust, promissory notes and agreements modifying these documents constitutes the practice of law. . . . Also, when "one determines for the parties the kinds of legal documents they should execute to effect their purpose, such is the practice of law." . . . Services which are ordinarily performed by licensed lawyers and that involve legal rights and obligations were held to be the practice of law. . . . "It is the nature and character of the service performed which governs whether given activities constitute the practice of law", not the nature or status of the person performing the services. . . . If the activities in question are the practice of law, then the question is whether the person practicing law is authorized to do so. . . . As the Washington Supreme Court has stated, "there is no such thing as a simple legal instrument in the hands of a layman."

PARALEGALS (AND OTHER NONATTORNEYS) IN COURT

● *Washington v. Hunt*, 880 P.2d 96 (Court of Appeals of Washington, 1994) (independent paralegal charged with the unauthorized practice of law).

● *In the Matter of Gillingham*, 896 P.2d 656 (Supreme Court of Washington, 1995) (discipline of attorney for failure to supervise paralegal).

● *Storseth v. Spellman*, 654 F.2d 1349 (U.S. Court of Appeals for the 9th Circuit, 1981) (paralegal assistance to inmates; jailhouse lawyers).

● *Absher Construction Co. v. Kent School District*, 917 P.2d 1086 (Court of Appeals of Washington, 1995) (award of paralegal fees at $67 per hour; no recovery for duplicating and delivering documents).

● *In re Berglund Construction Co.*, 142 Bankruptcy Reporter 947 (U.S. Bankruptcy Court, Eastern District for Washington, 1992) (compensation of paralegal in bankruptcy case).

WEST VIRGINIA

ETHICAL RULES AND GUIDELINES IN WEST VIRGINIA

Anything delegated to a nonattorney must lose its separate identity and be merged in the service of the attorney. When communicating with persons outside the office, a paralegal "must disclose his status as such." Nonattorneys can sign letters on law firm stationery as long as their nonattorney status is clearly indicated. *Legal Ethics Inquiry No. 76-7* (3 W.Va. State Bar Journal, Spring 1977).

A corporation can be represented by a nonattorney in Magistrates Court. "Any party to a civil action in a magistrate court may appear and conduct such action in person, by agent or by attorney. . . . [T]he appearance by an agent shall not constitute the unauthorized practice of law. . . ." (W. Va. Code § 50-4-4a). West Virginia State Bar Committee on Unlawful Practice, *Advisory Opinion 93-001*.

DEFINING THE PRACTICE OF LAW IN WEST VIRGINIA

West Virginia State Bar v. Early, 109 S.E.2d 420, 431 (Supreme Court of West Virginia, 1959): The courts in numerous decisions in different jurisdictions have undertaken to define and designate what constitutes the practice of law; but it is generally recognized that it is extremely difficult, perhaps impossible, to formulate a precise and completely comprehensive definition of the practice of law or to prescribe limits to the scope of that activity. It is clear, however, that a licensed attorney at law in the practice of his profession generally engages in three principal types of professional activity. These types are legal advice and instructions to clients to inform them of their rights and obligations; preparation for clients of documents requiring knowledge of legal principles which is not possessed by an ordinary layman; and appearance for clients before public tribunals, which possess the power and authority to determine rights of life, liberty and property according to law, in order to assist in the proper interpretation and enforcement of law. . . . "The practice of law is not limited to the conduct of cases in courts. It embraces the preparation of pleadings and other papers incident to actions and special proceedings and the management of such actions and proceedings on behalf of clients before judges and courts, and in addition conveyancing, the preparation of legal instruments of all kinds, and in general all advice to clients and all action taken for them in matters connected with the law."

West Virginia Code Rules, "Practice of Law Definition": In general, one is deemed to be practicing law whenever he or it furnishes another advice or service under circumstances which imply the possession or use of legal knowledge and skill. More specifically but without purporting to formulate a precise and completely comprehensive definition of the practice of law or to prescribe limits to the scope of that activity, one is deemed to be practicing law whenever (1) one undertakes, with or without compensation and whether or not in connection with another activity, to advise another in any matter involving the application of legal principles to facts, purposes or desires; (2) one undertakes, with or without compensation and whether or not in connection with another activity, to prepare for another legal instruments of any character; or (3) one undertakes, with or without compensation and whether or not in connection with another activity, to represent the interest of another before any judicial tribunal or officer, or to represent the interest of another before any executive or administrative tribunal, agency or officer otherwise than in the presentation of facts, figures or factual conclusions as distinguished from legal conclusions in respect to such facts and figures. Nothing in this paragraph shall be deemed to prohibit a lay person from appearing as agent before a justice of the peace or to prohibit a bona fide full-time lay employee from performing legal services for his regular employer (other than in connection with representation of his employer before any judicial, executive or administrative tribunal, agency or officer) in matters relating solely to the internal affairs of such employer, as distinguished from such services rendered to or for others. (Amended by order adopted June 27, 1961.)

PARALEGALS (AND OTHER NONATTORNEYS) IN COURT

- *Office of Disciplinary Counsel v. Battistelli,* 465 S.E.2d 644 (Supreme Court of Appeals of West Virginia, 1995) (suspended attorney can work as a paralegal, but must have no contact with clients).
- *Stacy v. B. O. Stroud,* 845 F. Supp. 1135, 1145 (U.S. District Court, Southern District for West Virginia, 1993) (award of attorney fees; "Delegating appropriate tasks to paralegals reduces the overall costs of . . . litigation.").
- *In re Heck's, Inc.,* 112 Bankruptcy Reporter 775 (U.S. Bankruptcy Court, Southern District for West Virginia, 1990) (objections filed to claims for paralegal fees).
- *Roush v. Roush,* 767 F. Supp. 1344 (U.S. District Court, Southern District for West Virginia) (civil rights complaint filed against paralegal is dismissed).

WISCONSIN

ETHICAL RULES AND GUIDELINES IN WISCONSIN

Law firm letterhead can include the names of paralegals as long as their nonattorney status is made clear. State Bar of Wisconsin, *Opinion E-85-6* (10/85).

The office of the district attorney and the office of a circuit judge can share the services of a paralegal as long as the paralegal is supervised so as to maintain the confidentiality of each office. State Bar of Wisconsin, *Opinion E-86-13* (9/24/86).

A paralegal can have a business card containing the law firm's name, but cannot be listed on the law firm's letterhead. State Bar of Wisconsin, *Opinion E-75-22.* (Note: *Opinion E-85-6* changes the letterhead portion of *E-75-22.*)

A paralegal can be listed on law firm letterhead. State Bar of Wisconsin, *Opinion E-85-6.*

A paralegal who is a licensed real estate broker cannot appear at a real estate closing. "If a paralegal from the attorney's office appears at the closing, it will *seem* that he is there in a legal capacity." State Bar of Wisconsin, *Opinion E-80-2.*

A law firm can hire a litigation paralegal who will also provide court reporting services to other attorneys. State Bar of Wisconsin, *Opinion E-86-19* (12/12/86).

DEFINING THE PRACTICE OF LAW IN WISCONSIN

§ 757.30 *(Wisconsin Statutes Annotated):* (1) Every person, who without having first obtained a license to practice law as an attorney of a court of record in this state, as provided by law, practices law within the meaning of sub. (2), or purports to be licensed to practice law as an attorney within the meaning of sub. (3), shall be fined not less than $50 nor more than $500 or imprisoned not more than one year in the county jail or both, and in addition may be punished as for a contempt.

(2) Every person who appears as agent, representative or attorney, for or on behalf of any other person, or any firm, partnership, association or corporation in any action or proceeding in or before any court of record, court commissioner, or judicial tribunal of the United States, or of any state , or who otherwise, in or out of court, for compensation or pecuniary reward gives professional legal advice not incidental to his or her usual or ordinary business, or renders any legal service for any other person, or any firm, partnership, association or corporation, shall be deemed to be practicing law within the meaning of this section.

(3) Every person who uses the words attorney at law, lawyer, solicitor, counselor, attorney and counselor, proctor, law, law office, or any equivalent words in connection with his or her name or any sign, advertisement, business card, letterhead, circular, notice, or other writing, document or design, the evident purpose of which is to induce others to believe or understand the person to be authorized to practice law or who in any other manner represents himself or herself either verbally or in writing, directly or indirectly, as authorized to practice law in this state, shall be deemed to be purporting to be licensed to practice law as an attorney within the meaning of his section. . . .

PARALEGALS (AND OTHER NONATTORNEYS) IN COURT

- *In the Matter of Hinnawi,* 549 N.W.2d 245 (Supreme Court of Wisconsin, 1996) (a suspended or disbarred attorney may not work as a paralegal, SCR 22.26).
- *In re Webster,* 120 Bankruptcy Reporter 111 (U.S. Bankruptcy Court, Eastern District for Wisconsin, 1990) (injunction against nonattorney for engaging in unauthorized practice of law in providing bankruptcy services).
- *In the Matter of Leaf,* 476 N.W.2d 13 (Supreme Court of Wisconsin, 1991) (attorney assists a nonattorney associate in the unauthorized practice of law).
- *Nowicki v. Ullsvik,* 69 F.3d 1320 (U.S. Court of Appeals for the 7th Circuit, 1995) (paralegal challenges Wisconsin's law on unauthorized practice as unconstitutional) (See also 56 F.3d 782).
- *Wisconsin v. Town of Turtle Lake,* 526 N.W.2d 784 (Court of Appeals of Wisconsin, 1994) (award of paralegal fees).
- *Hutchison v. Amateur Electronic Supply,* 42 F.3d 1037, 1048 (U.S. Court of Appeals for the 7th Circuit, 1994) (fee award reduced for "failure to utilize paralegals").
- *EEOC v. Accurate Mechanical Contractors, Inc.,* 863 F. Supp. 828 (U.S. District Court, Eastern District for Wisconsin, 1994) (paralegal fees are limited to work performed by paralegals that would otherwise be performed by an attorney).
- *Purdy v. Security Savings . . . ,* 727 F. Supp. 1266, 1270 (U.S. District Court, Eastern District for Wisconsin, 1989) (it is "clearly excessive" to claim six and a half hours of paralegal time to cite check a document with only 40 citations in it).
- *United States v. Windfelder,* 790 F.2d 576 (U.S. Court of Appeals for the 7th Circuit, 1986) (government subpoenas paralegal in tax case).
- *Piper v. Popp,* 482 N.W.2d 353 (Supreme Court of Wisconsin, 1992) (inmate paralegal assistance).

WYOMING

DEFINING THE PRACTICE OF LAW IN WYOMING

Rule 12 *(Wyoming Rules of Court)*
(4) "Practice of law" means advising others and taking action for them in matters connected with law. It includes preparation of legal instruments and acting or proceeding for another before judges, courts, tribunals, commissioners, boards or other governmental agencies. (Student Practice Rule)

PARALEGALS (AND OTHER NONATTORNEYS) IN COURT

- *Brooks v. Zebre,* 792 P.2d 196, 220 (Supreme Court of Wyoming, 1990) (a "lawyer who approaches a represented third party without going through counsel should be severely punished. And this is so though the lawyer uses a law representative or paralegal to do his dirty work").
- *Mendicino v. Whitchurch,* 565 P.2d 460, 478 (Supreme Court of Wyoming, 1977) (a suspended attorney shall not participate in the practice of law as an attorney or paralegal).
- *Van Riper v. Wyoming,* 882 P.2d 230 (Supreme Court of Wyoming, 1994) (felony defendant with paralegal training defends himself).
- *Wyoming v. Brown,* 805 P.2d 830 (Supreme Court of Wyoming, 1991) (award of paralegal fees).
- *Baker v. Bowen,* 707 F. Supp. 481 (U.S. District Court for Wyoming, 1989) (award of paralegal fees).

Paralegal Business Cards

Most paralegals have their own business card. As indicated in Chapter 5 and in Appendix F, it is ethical for an attorney to allow a paralegal employee to have a business card that also prints the name of the employer. Here are several examples of such cards in use today:

Connie Butler
LEGAL ASSISTANT

LAW OFFICES
SHOOK, HARDY & BACON LLP
ONE KANSAS CITY PLACE
1200 MAIN STREET
KANSAS CITY, MISSOURI 64105-2118

TELEPHONE (816) 474-6550
FAX (816) 421-5547

N.J. (201) 622-6200
N.Y. (212) 964-7979

VALERIE A. BURKE
LEGAL ASSISTANT · ESTATE ADMINISTRATION

ORLOFF, LOWENBACH, STIFELMAN & SIEGEL
A PROFESSIONAL CORPORATION
COUNSELLORS AT LAW
101 EISENHOWER PARKWAY
ROSELAND, NEW JERSEY 07068

JOYCE M. CHARLES
LEGAL ASSISTANT
SCHATZ PAQUIN
LOCKRIDGE GRINDAL & HOLSTEIN

100 WASHINGTON AVENUE S.
MINNEAPOLIS, MINNESOTA 55401
612-339-6900
FAX 612-339-0981

1301 K STREET, N.W.
EAST TOWER, SUITE 650
WASHINGTON, D.C. 20005
202-789-3970
FAX 202-789-2961

SAMUEL H. BAYLESS
ATTORNEY AT LAW

CHARLENE B. CARROLL
LEGAL ASSISTANT

DIRECT DIAL
(210) 270-8627
FAX (210) 226-5154

112 EAST PECAN STREET, SUITE 900
SAN ANTONIO, TEXAS 78205-1542

OWENS CORNING WORLD HEADQUARTERS
ONE OWENS CORNING PARKWAY
TOLEDO, OHIO 43659
419.248.6926 FAX 419.325.1926 OR 419.248.7044
INTERNET: gidget.dirienz@owenscorning.com

GIDGET DIRIENZ
SENIOR LEGAL ASSISTANT

OWENS CORNING

CELIA C. ELWELL
Legal Assistant

The City of
OKLAHOMA CITY

OFFICE OF THE MUNICIPAL COUNSELOR
200 NORTH WALKER, 309 MUNICIPAL BLDG.
OKLAHOMA CITY, OK 73102

405/297-2695
FAX 405/297-2118

SAN DIEGO VOLUNTEER LAWYER PROGRAM, INC.
AIDS Legal Services Project

Debra D. Roback
Paralegal II

1305 Seventh Avenue, Suite #100
San Diego, CA 92101
Business: (619) 238-8100 · FAX: (619) 238-8145

SCHUREMAN, FRAKES, GLASS & WULFMEIER
ATTORNEYS AND COUNSELORS

440 E. CONGRESS, FOURTH FLOOR
DETROIT, MICHIGAN 48226

CHRISTINE C. SCHULTZ
LEGAL ASSISTANT

(313) 961-1500

---

the**Principal**
Financial Group

Cynthia M. Switzer
Legal Assistant

Des Moines, Iowa 50392-0300
(515) 248-4360
FAX (515) 248-3011

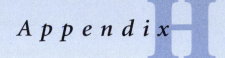

FEDERAL DEPOSITORY LIBRARIES

Paralegals often have a need to find a law library. (See section G in chapter 11.) One option, although only a partial one, is to try to find and use a *federal depository library*. The federal government has an agreement with hundreds of public and private libraries throughout the country. It provides these libraries with free copies of *federal* laws such as the statutes of Congress, the administrative regulations of federal agencies, and the opinions of federal courts. In exchange, these libraries (with certain exceptions such as court libraries) agree to give the general public free access to these materials. This does *not* mean that the library must give you access to its entire collection; the access must be to all the federal publications it receives free from the federal government. Here is a list of these libraries for your state.[1] Call the number listed to find out the exact location of the library and whether there are any access restrictions.

---

[1]See Superintendent of Documents, U.S. Government Printing Office, *Federal Depository Library Directory* (December 1996).

ABBREVIATIONS

(states are abbreviated by their postal abbreviation, e.g., AL is Alabama)

C = College	Hq = Headquarters	Ref = Reference
Cntr = Center	Info = Information	S = State
Comm = Community	Inst = Institute	Sc = School
Comm'n = Commission	Intl = International	Sec = Section
Ct = Court	Jr = Junior	So = Southern
Cy = County	L = Library	St = Saint
Dept = Department	Mt = Mountain	Sys = System
Div = Division	Mun = Municipal	Tech = Technical or Technology
Doc = Documents	No = Northern	U = University
Exec = Executive	Off = Office	U/ = University of; at
Gov = Government	P = Public	We = Western
Fed = Federal	Pub = Publications	X = Extension

ALABAMA

Auburn	Birmingham	Birmingham So CL	205-856-8524
Auburn U Draughon L	Birmingham PL	205-226-4750	Samford U Davis L
334-844-1702	205-226-3620	Jefferson S Comm C	205-870-2847

Enterprise
  Enterprise S Jr C
  334-347-2623 x271
Fayette
  Bevill S Comm C
  205-932-3221 x514
Florence
  U/North AL Collier L
  205-760-4469
Gadsden
  Gadsden PL
  205-549-4699
Huntsville
  U/AL/Huntsville L
  205-895-6526
Jacksonville
  Jacksonville SU Cole
  205-782-5238
Maxwell Air Base
  Air UL/LSAS
  334-953-5042
Mobile
  Mobile PL
  334-434-7078
  Spring Hill C
  334-380-3880
  U/South AL
  334-460-7024
Montgomery
  AL PL Service
  334-213-3900
  AL Supreme Ct Law L
  334-242-4347
  Auburn U/Montgomery
  334-244-3650
Normal
  AL A&M U Drake L
  205-851-5760
Troy
  Troy SUL Wallace
  334-670-3869
Tuscaloosa
  U/AL Gorgas L
  205-348-6047
  U/AL Sc of Law L
  205-348-1107
Tuskegee
  Tuskegee U Frissell
  334-727-8891

ALASKA

Anchorage
  Anchorage Law L
  907-264-0585

Anchorage Loussac L
  907-562-7323
  Dept of Interior
  907-271-5025
  U/AK/Anchorage
  907-786-1874
Fairbanks
  U/AK/Fairbanks
  907-474-7624
Juneau
  AK SL
  907-465-2920
  U/AK Southeast Eagan
  907-465-6585
Ketchikan
  U/AK Ketchikan CL
  907-225-4722

ARIZONA

Apache Junction
  Apache Junction PL
  602-983-0204
Coolidge
  Central AZ C
  520-426-4280
Flagstaff
  No AZ U Cline L
  520-523-6805
Glendale
  Glendale PL
  602-930-3531
Mesa
  Mesa PL
  602-644-2207
Phoenix
  AZ Dept L Archives
  602-542-3701
  Grand Canyon U
  602-589-2494
  Maricopa Cy L
  602-506-2957
  Phoenix PL
  602-261-4636
Prescott
  Yavapai CL
  520-776-2274
Tempe
  AZ SU Hayden L
  602-965-3390
  AZ SU Law L
  602-965-4860
Tucson
  Tuscon-Pima PL
  520-791-4393

U/AZ C of Law L
  520-621-1413
  U/AZ Main L
  520-621-6441
Winslow
  Northland Pioneer C
  520-289-4633 x228
Yuma
  Yuma Cy L District
  520-782-1871 x2

ARKANSAS

Arkadelphia
  Ouachita Baptist U
  501-245-5122
Batesville
  Lyons C Mabee L
  501-698-4205
Clarksville
  U/Ozarks Dobson L
  501-979-1382
Conway
  U of Central AR
  501-450-3129
Fayetteville
  U/AR U L
  501-575-5516
  U/AR Sc of Law L
  501-575-5604
Little Rock
  AR SL Govt Pub
  501-682-2869
  AR Supreme Ct L
  501-682-2147
  Central AR L Sys
  501-370-5952
  U/AR/Ottenheimer L
  501-569-8444
  U/AR/Pulaski Cy Law L
  501-324-9970
Magnolia
  So AR U Magale L
  501-235-5066
Monticello
  U/AR/Monticello L
  501-460-1080
Pine Bluff
  U/AR/Pine Bluff L
  501-543-8415
Russelville
  AR Tech U Tomlinson L
  501-968-0289
Searcy
  Harding U Brackett L

501-279-4354
State University
  AR SU/Jonesboro Ellis
  501-972-5706
Walnut Ridge
  Williams Baptist C
  501-886-6741 x130

CALIFORNIA

Anaheim
  Anaheim PL
  714-254-1880
Arcadia
  Arcadia PL
  818-821-5569
Arcata
  Humboldt SUL
  707-826-3419
Bakersfield
  CA SU Stiern L
  805-664-3231
  Kern Cy L Sys
  805-861-2136
Berkeley
  U/CA/Berkeley Main L
  510-642-2569
  U/CA/Berkeley Law L
  510-642-0900
Carson
  CA SU/Dominguez UL
  310-516-3758
  Carson Regional L
  310-830-0901
Chico
  CA SU/Chico Miriam L
  916-898-5710
Claremont
  Claremont C Mouth L
  909-621-8800
Culver City
  Culver City L
  310-559-2994
Davis
  U/CA/Davis Shields L
  916-752-1624
  U/CA/Davis Law L
  916-752-3340
Downey
  Downey City L
  310-904-7364
Fresno
  CA SU/Fresno
  209-278-2335
  Fresno Cy Free L
  209-488-2976

Fullerton
  CA SU/Fullerton UL
  714-773-3449
Garden Grove
  Orange Cy PL
  714-530-0711
Hayward
  CA SU/Haywood L
  510-885-3765
Ingelwood
  Inglewood PL Serials
  310-412-5380
Irvine
  U/CA/Irvine Main L
  714-824-7234
La Jolla
  UC/San Diego Geisel
  619-534-3336
La Verne
  U/La Verne C Law L
  909-392-2717
Lakewood
  Angelo Iacoboni PL
  310-866-1777
Lancaster
  Lancaster PL
  805-948-5029
Long Beach
  CA SU/Long Beach L
  310-985-4027
  Long Beach PL
  310-570-6944
Los Angeles
  CA SU/Los Angeles
  213-343-3960
  Los Angeles Cy Law L
  213-629-3531
  Los Angeles PL
  213-228-7000
  Loyola Law Sc L
  213-736-1177
  Occicdental C Clapp
  213-259-2810
  Southwestern U Law L
  213-738-6725
  US Ct of Appeals L
  213-894-3636
  UC/LA U Research L
  310-825-3135
  UC/LA Law L
  310-825-6414
  U/So CA Doheny L
  213-740-2339
  U/So CA Law L
  213-740-6482

Whittier C Law L
  213-938-3621
Malibu
  Pepperdine U Payson
  310-456-4238
Menlo Park
  Dept of Interior L
  415-329-5027
Montebello
  Montebello Regional
  213-722-6551
Monterey
  US Naval Knox L
  408-656-2485
Monterey Park
  Bruggemeyer L
  818-307-1379
Northridge
  CA S/Northridge
  818-677-2285
Norwalk
  Norwalk Regional L
  310-868-0775
Oakland
  Oakland PL Doc Dept
  510-238-3138
Ontario
  Ontario City L
  909-988-8481 x221
Palm Springs
  Palm Springs PL
  619-323-8294
Pasadena
  CA Inst Tech
  818-395-6419
  Pasadena PL
  818-405-4052
Pleasant Hill
  Contra Costa Cy L
  510-646-6434
Redding
  Shasta Cy L
  916-225-5769
Redlands
  U/Redlands Armacost
  909-335-4021
Redwood City
  Redwood City PL
  415-780-7061
Reseda
  West Valley Regional
  818-345-4394
Richmond
  Richmond PL
  510-620-6561

Riverside
  Riverside City & Cy L
  909-782-5202
  U/CA/Riverside
  909-787-3226
Sacramento
  CA SL Govt Pub
  916-654-0069
  CA SU/Sacramento L
  916-278-5673
  Sacramento Cy Law L
  916-440-6012
  Sacramento PL Central
  916-264-2972
  U/Pacific Law L
  916-739-7131
San Bernadino
  San Bernadino Law L
  909-885-3020
  San Bernadino Cy L
  909-387-5718
San Diego
  San Diego Cy Law L
  619-531-3906
  San Diego Cy L Hq
  619-945-5116
  San Diego PL Central
  619-236-5813
  San Diego SU Love L
  619-594-5832
  UC/San Diego Geisel
  619-534-3336
  U of San Diego Law L
  619-260-6813
San Francisco
  CA Supreme Ct L
  415-396-9439
  Golden Gate U Law L
  415-442-6683
  San Francisco PL
  415-557-4488
  San Francisco SUL
  415-338-7324 x273
  US Ct of Appeals L
  415-744-9590
  U/CA Hastings Law L
  415-565-4751
  U/San Francisco L
  415-666-2040
San Jose
  San Jose SU Clark L
  408-924-2770
San Leandro
  San Leandro PL
  510-577-3491

San Luis Obispo
  CA Polytechnic SUL
  805-756-1364
San Marcos
  CA SU/San Marcos
  619-750-3287
San Mateo
  C of San Mateo L
  415-574-6100
San Rafael
  Marin Cy Free L
  415-499-6058
Santa Ana
  Orange Cy Law L
  714-834-3004
  Santa Ana PL
  714-647-5264
Santa Barbara
  U/CA/Santa Barbara
  805-893-3133
Santa Clara
  Santa Clara UL
  408-554-5385
Santa Cruz
  U/CA/Santa Cruz L
  408-459-2347
Santa Rosa
  Sonoma Cy PL
  707-545-0831
Stanford
  Stanford U Jonsson L
  415-723-2727
  Stanford U Law L
  415-725-0800
Stockton
  PL of Stockton
  209-937-8221
Thousand Oaks
  CA Luthern UL
  805-493-3250
Torrance
  Torrence PL
  310-618-5959
Turlock
  CA CU Stanislaus L
  209-667-3233
Valencia
  Valencia L
  805-259-8332
Vallejo
  Solano Cy L Sys
  707-553-5568
Ventura
  Ventura Cy L
  805-652-7525

Visalia
  Tulare Cy Free L
  209-733-6952
Walnut
  Mount San Antonio CL
  909-594-5611 x428
West Covina
  West Covina Regional
  818-962-1507
Whittier
  Whittier C Wardman L
  310-907-4297

COLORADO

Alamosa
  Adams SCL
  719-589-7781
Aurora
  Aurora PL
  303-739-6630
Boulder
  U/CO/Boulder Govt L
  303-492-8834
  U/CO/Boulder Law L
  303-492-3522
Broomfield
  Eisenhower PL
  303-438-6208
Colorado Springs
  CO C Tutt L
  719-389-6660
  U/CO L
  719-593-3295
Denver
  Auraria L
  303-556-8372
  CO Supreme Ct L
  303-837-3720
  Denver PL
  303-640-6249
  Regis U Dayton L
  303-458-4031
  US Courts L
  303-844-3951
  U/Denver Penrose L
  303-871-2905
  U/Denver Law L
  303-871-6206
Fort Collins
  CO SUL Doc Dept
  970-491-1881
Golden
  CO Sc of Mines L
  303-273-3695
Grand Junction

Grand Junction PL
  970-241-5251
  Mesa SC Tomlinson L
  970-248-1860
Greeley
  U/No CO Michener L
  970-351-2987
Gunnison
  Western SC Savage L
  970-943-7012
La Junta
  Otero Jr C Wheeler L
  719-384-6882
Lakewood
  Jefferson Cy PL
  303-232-9507
Pueblo
  Pueblo L District L
  719-543-9601
  U/So CO L
  719-549-2333
USAF Academy
  USAF Academy L
  719-472-4774

CONNECTICUT

Bridgeport
  Bridgeport PL
  203-576-7403
Danbury
  Western CT SU Haas L
  203-837-9112
Hamden
  Quinnipiac C Law L
  203-287-3314
Hartford
  CT SL
  860-566-2507
  Hartford PL
  860-293-6000
  Trinity CL
  860-297-2270
  U/CT Sc of Law L
  860-241-4637
Middletown
  Weseyan U Olin L
  860-685-3882
New Britain
  Central CT SU L
  860-832-2066
New Haven
  So CT SU Buley L
  203-392-5745
  Yale U Goldman Law L
  203-432-1606

Yale U Mudd L
  203-432-3209
New London
  CT C Shain L
  860-439-2655
  US Coast Guard L
  860-444-8515
Stamford
  Ferguson L
  203-964-1000 x221
Storrs
  U/CT Babbidge L
  860-486-2513
Waterbury
  Silas Bronson PL
  203-574-8225
  Teikyo Post UL
  203-596-4560
West Haven
  U/West Haven L
  203-932-7178
Willimantic
  Eastern CT SUL
  860-465-4470

DELAWARE

Dover
  DE Div of L Govt Doc
  302-739-4748
  DE SU Jason L
  302-739-3571
Georgetown
  DE Tech & Comm Betez
  302-856-9033
Newark
  U/DE L
  302-831-2965
Wilmington
  Widener U Law L
  302-477-2114

DISTRICT OF COLUMBIA

American U Law L
  202-274-4352
Catholic U Law L
  202-319-5136
Comtroller L
  202-874-4720
DC Ct of Appeals L
  202-879-2767
DC PL Doc Dept
  202-727-1117
Dept/Commerce L
  202-482-5511

Dept/Education L
  202-219-2322
Dept/Housing L
  202-708-2370
Dept/Justice Main L
  202-514-3775
Dept/Labor L
  202-219-6992
Dept/State Law L
  202-647-4130
Dept/State L IS/OIS
  202-647-3002
Dept/Army Pentagon L
  703-697-4301
Dept/Interior L
  202-208-5815
Dept/Navy L
  202-433-4132
Dept/Treasury L
  202-622-0990
Dept/Transportation
  202-366-0746
Dept/Veterans L
  202-273-8523
EEOC L
  202-663-4630
Fed Election Comm'n L
  202-219-3312 x381
Fed Energy . . . Comm'n L
  202-208-2179
Fed Mine Safety L
  202-653-5459
Fed Reserve L
  202-452-3283
GAO Info Cntr
  202-512-5180
Georgetown UL
  202-687-7467
Georgetown U Law Cntr
  202-662-9140
George Washington UL
  202-994-6304
George Washington UL
  202-994-7338 (Law)
GSA L
  202-501-0001
Library of Congress
  202-707-5690 (Govt)
  202-707-7456 (CRS)
National Defense UL
  202-287-9111
Pension Benefit . . .
  202-326-4004
President, Exec Off
  202-395-3654

US Coast Guard Law L
202-267-2536
US Ct of Appeals L
202-633-8603
202-273-0400
USIA Info Cntr
202-619-4888
US Postal Service L
202-268-2900
US Senate L
202-224-7106
US Supreme Ct L
202-479-3170

FLORIDA

Boca Raton
  FL Atlantic UL
  561-367-3785
Bradenton
  Manatee Cy PL
  941-748-5555
Clearwater
  Clearwater PL Sys
  813-462-6800 x257
Cocoa
  Brevard Cy L Sys
  407-633-1915
Coral Gables
  U/Miami Richter L
  305-284-3155
Daytona Beach
  Volusia Cy PL Cntr
  904-257-6036
De Land
  Stetson U duPont L
  904-822-7185
Fort Lauderdale
  Broward Cy Main L
  954-357-7438
  Nova Southeastern U
  954-452-6202 (Law)
Fort Pierce
  Indian River Comm C
  407-462-4757
Gainesville
  U/FL C of Law L
  904-392-0417
  U/FL Libraries
  352-392-0367
Jacksonville
  Jacksonville PL
  904-630-2424
  Jacksonville UL
  904-745-7267 x726
  U/No FL Carpenter L

904-646-2617
Key West
  FL Keys Comm C Cntr
  305-296-9081 x210
Lakeland
  Lakeland PL
  941-284-4280
Leesburg
  Lake-Sumter Comm CL
  352-365-3563
Melbourne
  FL Inst of Tech L
  407-768-8000 x753
Miami
  FL Intl U Park L
  305-348-2481
  Miami-Dade PL Doc Div
  305-375-5575
  St Thomas UL Doc Dept
  305-628-6667
North Miami
  FL Intl UL
  305-940-5726
Orlando
  U/Central FL L-Doc
  407-823-2593
Palatka
  St Johns River Comm C
  904-325-6627
Panama City
  Bay Cy PL
  904-872-7507
Pensacola
  U/West FL Pace L
  904-474-2410
Saint Petersburg
  St Petersburg PL
  813-893-7928
  Stetson UC Law L
  813-345-1121 x227
Sarasota
  Selby PL
  941-316-1183
  U/So FL/Sarasota L
  941-359-4300
Tallahassee
  FL A&M U Coleman L
  904-599-3714
  FL SU Stozier L
  904-644-6061
  FL SUC of Law L
  904-644-4095
  FL Supreme Ct L
  904-488-8919
  SL of FL

904-487-2651
Tampa
  Tampa-Hillsborough PL
  813-273-3628
  U/So FL L
  813-974-9875
  U/Tampa Kelce L
  813-253-6231
Winter Park
  Rollins C Olin L
  407-646-2507

GEORGIA

Albany
  Dougherty Cy PL
  912-431-2910
Americus
  Georgia Southwestern
  912-931-2259
Athens
  U/GA Sc of Law L
  706-542-3825
  U/GA Libraries
  706-542-8949
Atlanta
  Atlanta U Woodruff L
  404-522-8980 x110
  Atlanta-Fulton PL
  404-730-4636
  Emory U Woodruff L
  404-727-6880
  Emery U Law L
  404-727-6797
  GA Inst of Tech
  404-894-4519
  GA S Law L
  404-656-3468
  GA SU Pullen L
  404-651-2185
  GA SUC of Law L
  404-651-2478
  US Ct of Appeals L
  404-331-2510
Augusta
  Augusta C Reese L
  706-737-1748
  Medical C of GA L
  706-721-3441
Brunswick
  Brunswick-Glynn L
  912-267-1213
Corrollton
  SU of West GA L
  770-836-6495
Columbus

Columbus SU Schwob L
  706-568-2042
Dahlonega
  North GA C Stewart L
  706-864-1516
Dalton
  Dalton C L Cntr
  706-272-2474
Kennesaw
  Kennesaw SUL
  770-423-6213
Macon
  Mercer U Main L
  912-752-2960
  Mercer U Sc of Law L
  912-752-2334
Milledgeville
  GA C Russell L
  912-453-5573
Mount Berry
  Berry C Memorial L
  706-236-2221 x243
Savannah
  Chatham . . . Regional L
  912-652-3615
Smyrna
  Smyrna PL
  404-431-2860
Statesboro
  GA So U Henderson L
  912-681-5117
Valdosta
  Valdosta SC Odum L
  912-333-7149

GUAM

Agana
  Flores . . . Guam PL
  671-477-9777
Mangilao
  U/Guam Kennedy L
  671-734-6882

HAWAII

Hilo
  U/HI/Hilo Mookini L
  808-933-3525
Honolulu
  HI Medical L
  808-536-9302
  HI SL Fed Doc
  808-586-3477
  Municipal Ref . . . Cntr
  808-523-4577
  Supreme Ct Law L

808-539-4964
U/HI Hamilton L
808-956-8230
U/HI Sc of Law L
808-956-7583
Laie
  Brigham Young U/HI
  808-293-3877
Lihue
  Lihue PL
  808-241-3222
Pearl City
  Leeward Comm CL
  808-455-0379
Wailuku
  Wailuku PL
  808-243-5566

IDAHO

Boise
  Boise PL
  208-345-4023
  Boise SUL
  208-385-3559
  ID SL
  208-334-2150
  ID Supreme Ct S Law L
  208-334-3316
Caldwell
  Albertson C of ID L
  208-459-5524
Lewiston
  Lewis-Clark SCL
  208-799-2236
Moscow
  U/ID L Govt Doc Div
  208-885-6344
  U/ID C of Law L
  208-885-6521
Nampa
  Northwest Nazarene C
  208-467-8607
Pocatello
  ID SU Oboler L
  208-236-2907
Rexburg
  Ricks C McKay
  208-356-2367
Twin Falls
  C of So ID L
  208-733-9554 x250

ILLINOIS

Bloomington
  IL Wesleyan UL

309-556-3010
Bourbonnais
  Olivet Nazarene U
  815-939-5354
Carbondale
  So IL U/Carbondale
  618-453-8708 (Lesar)
  So IL U/Carbondale
  618-453-2708 (Morris)
Carlinville
  Blackburn CL
  217-854-3231 x431
Carterville
  Logan C Resources
  618-985-3741
Champaign
  U/IL Law L
  217-244-3041
Charleston
  Eastern IL U Booth L
  217-581-6092
Chicago
  Campbell L/US Courts
  312-435-5660
  Chicago-Kent C of Law
  312-906-5600
  Chicago PL Govt Pub
  312-747-4500
  Chicago SU Douglas L
  312-995-2284
  DePaul U Law L
  312-362-6894
  Field Museum L
  312-922-9410 x282
  IL Inst of Tech L
  312-567-3616
  312-906-5600 (Law)
  John Marshall Law L
  312-427-2737
  Loyola/Chicago Cudahy
  312-508-2654
  Loyola/Chicago Law L
  312-915-7205
  Northeastern IL U
  312-794-2613
  Northwestern U Law L
  312-503-7344
  U/Chicago Regenstein
  312-702-8767
  U/Chicago Law L
  312-702-0211
  U/IL/Chicago L Doc
  312-996-2738
De Kalb
  No IL U Founders L

815-753-9841
  No IL UC of Law L
  815-753-0505
Decatur
  Decatur PL Govt Doc
  217-424-2900
Des Plaines
  Oakton Comm CL
  708-635-1644
Edwardsville
  So ILL U Lovejoy L
  618-692-2615
Elsah
  Principia C Brooks L
  618-374-5074
Evanston
  Northwestern UL
  847-491-3130
Freeport
  Freeport PL
  815-233-3000
Galesburg
  Galesburg PL
  309-343-6118
Jacksonville
  MacMurray CL
  217-479-7011
Lake Forest
  Lake Forest CL
  847-735-5074
Lebanon
  McKendree CL
  618-537-6950
Lisle
  IL Benedictine C
  708-829-6050
Macomb
  Western IL U
  309-298-2722
Moline
  Black Hawk CL
  309-796-1311 x128
Monmouth
  Monmouth C Hewes L
  309-457-2190
Mount Carmel
  Wabash Valley C
  618-262-8641 x324
Mount Prospect
  Mount Prospect PL
  847-253-5675
Normal
  IL SU Milner L
  309-438-3451
Oak Park

Oak Park PL
708-383-8200
Oglesby
  IL Valley Comm CL
  815-224-2720 x396
Palos Hills
  Moraine Valley C
  708-974-5234
Peoria
  Bradley UL
  309-677-2840
  Peoria PL
  309-672-8844
River Forest
  Rosary C Crown L
  708-524-6875
Rockford
  Rockford PL
  815-965-6731
Romeoville
  Lewis UL
  815-838-0500 x530
South Holland
  So Suburban CL
  708-210-5751
Springfield
  IL SL Fed Doc Dept
  217-782-7596
Streamwood
  Poplar Creek PL
  708-837-6800
University Park
  Governors SUL
  708-534-4113
Urbana
  U/IL Doc L
  217-333-1056
Wheaton
  Wheaton C Buswell L
  708-752-5169
Woodstock
  Woodstock PL
  815-338-0542

INDIANA

Anderson
  Anderson PL Govt Pub
  317-641-2456
  Anderson UL
  317-641-4280
Bloomington
  IN UL
  812-855-6924
  IN U Sc of Law L
  812-855-9666

Crawfordsville
 Wabash C Lilly L
 317-361-6361
Evansville
 Evansville . . . Cy PL
 812-428-8218
 U/So IN Rice L
 812-464-1907
Fort Wayne
 Allen Cy PL
 219-424-7241 x331
 IN U/Purdue U
 219-481-6506
Franklin
 Franklin CL
 317-738-8160
Gary
 Gary PL Main L
 219-886-2484
 IN U/Northwest Campus
 219-980-6608
Greencastle
 DePauw U West L
 317-658-4444
Hammond
 Hammond PL
 219-852-2241
Hanover
 Hanover C Duggan L
 812-866-7164
Huntington
 Huntington CL
 219-356-6000 x106
Indianapolis
 Butler U Irwin L
 317-940-9235
 IN SL Doc Sec
 317-232-3679
 IN Supreme Ct Law L
 317-232-2557
 IN U/Indianapolis
 317-274-1932 (Law)
 IN U/Purdue UL
 317-274-0469
 Indianapolis . . . Cy L
 317-269-1733
Kokomo
 IN U Kokomo Cntr
 317-455-9521
Muncie
 Muncie SU Bracken L
 317-285-1110
 Muncie PL
 317-747-8204
New Albany

IN U/Southeast L
 812-941-2489
Notre Dame
 U/Notre Dame Law L
 219-631-5664
 U/Notre Dame L
 219-631-6043
Rensselaer
 St Joseph CL
 219-866-6210
Richmond
 Earlham C Lilly L
 317-983-1404
 Morrisson-Reeves L
 317-966-8291
South Bend
 IN U/South Bend L
 219-237-4442
Terre Haute
 IN SU L
 812-237-2629
Valparaiso
 Valparaiso U Law L
 219-465-7866
 Valparaiso U
 219-464-5366
West Lafayette
 Perdue U HSSE L
 317-494-2837

IOWA

Ames
 IA SU Parks L
 515-294-3642
Cedar Falls
 U/Northern IA L
 319-273-6327
Cedar Rapids
 Cedar Rapids PL
 319-398-5123
Council Bluffs
 Council Bluffs PL
 712-323-7553
Davenport
 Davenport PL
 319-326-7902
Des Moines
 Drake U Law L
 515-271-3883
 Drake U Cowles L
 515-271-2113
 PL of Des Moines
 515-283-4152 x323
 SL of IA Doc Sec
 515-281-4102

Dubuque
 Carnegie-Stout PL
 319-589-4225
 Loras C Wahlert L
 319-588-7042
Fayette
 Upper IA UL
 319-425-5217
Grinnell
 Grinnell CL
 515-269-3350
Iowa City
 U/IA C of Law L
 319-335-9040
 U/IA L Govt Pub
 319-335-5926
Lemoni
 Graceland C Smith L
 515-784-5361
Mason City
 North IA Comm CL
 515-421-4327
Mount Vernon
 Cornell C Cole L
 319-895-4265
Orange City
 Northwestern CL
 712-737-7238
Sioux City
 Sioux City PL
 712-252-5669 x221

KANSAS

Atchison
 Benedictine CL
 913-367-5340 x251
Baldwin City
 Baker U Collins L
 913-594-8389
Colby
 Colby Comm CL
 913-462-3984
Dodge City
 Dodge City Comm C
 316-227-9287
Emporia
 Emporia SU White L
 316-341-5049
Hays
 Ft. Hays SUL
 913-628-4340
Hutchinson
 Hutchinson PL
 316-663-5441 x122
Kansas City

Kansas City Comm CL
 913-596-9650
Lawrence
 U/KS Govt Doc
 913-864-4660
 U/KS Law Sc L
 913-864-3025
Manhattan
 KS SU Farrell L
 913-532-7449
Overland Park
 Johnson Cy L
 913-495-2400
Pittsburg
 Pittsburg SU Axe L
 316-235-4889
Salina
 KS Wesleyan UL
 913-827-5541 x412
Topeka
 KS S Historical L
 913-272-8681
 KS SL Statehouse
 913-296-3296
 Washburn U/Topeka Law
 913-231-1010 x178
Wichita
 Witchita SU Ablah L
 316-689-3155

KENTUCKY

Ashland
 Ashland Comm CL
 606-329-2999 x572
Barbourville
 Union C Weeks . . . L
 606-546-4151 x224
Bowling Green
 Western KY U Helm L
 502-745-6175 x612
Columbia
 Lindsey Wilson CL
 502-384-8102
Crestview Hills
 Thomas More CL
 606-344-3615
Danville
 Centre C Doherty L
 606-238-5278
Frankfort
 KY SL Service Div
 502-564-8300 x334
 KY S Law L
 502-564-4848

KY SU Blazer L
502-227-6857
Hazard
Hazard Comm CL
606-436-5721
Highland Heights
No KY U Steely L
606-572-5456
Lexington
U/KY King L
606-257-8397
U/KY Law L
606-323-4906
Louisville
Louisville Free PL
502-574-1611
U/Louisville L
502-852-6760
U/Louisville Law L
502-852-0729
Morehead
Morehead SUL
606-783-2160
Murray
Murray SUL
502-762-4799
Owensboro
KY-Wesleyan CL
502-926-3111 x135
Richmond
Eastern KY UL
606-622-1791
Williamsburg
Cumberland CL
606-539-4329

LOUISIANA

Baton Rouge
LA SU Middleton L
504-388-4019
LA SU Law Cntr
504-388-4957
So U Law Cntr L
504-771-2194
So U A&M C Cade L
504-771-2853
SL of LA
504-342-4913
Eunice
LA SU/Eunice L
318-457-7311 x387
Hammond
Southeastern LA UL
504-549-3966
Lafayette

U/Southwestern LA L
318-482-6030
Lake Charles
McNeese SU Frazar L
318-475-5736
Leesville
Vernon Parish L
800-737-2231
Monroe
Northeast LA UL
318-342-1065
Natchitoches
Northwestern SUL
318-357-4574
New Orleans
Law L of LA
504-568-5705
Loyola U Law L
504-861-5548
Loyola UL
504-865-2158
New Orleans PL
504-596-2583
Our Lady Holy Cross C
504-394-7744
So U/New Orleans L
504-286-5224
Tulane UL
504-865-5683
Tulane U Sc of Law L
504-865-5994
U/New Orleans Long L
504-286-7277
US Ct of Appeals L
504-589-6510
Xavier UL
504-483-7309
Pineville
Pineville C Norton L
318-487-7201
Ruston
LA Tech U Prescott L
318-257-4962
Shreveport
LA SU/Shreveport L
318-797-5069
Shreve Memorial L
318-226-5888
Thibaux
Nicholls SUL
504-448-4670

MAINE

Augusta
ME Law & Ref L

207-287-1600
ME SL Doc
207-287-5600
Bangor
Bangor PL
207-947-8336
Brunswick
Bowdoin CL
207-725-3298
Castine
ME Maritime Academy
207-326-2263
Lewiston
Bates C Ladd L
207-786-6271
Orono
U/ME Fogler L
207-581-1673
Portland
Portland PL
207-871-1736
U/ME Sc of Law L
207-780-4351
Presque Isle
U/ME/Presque Isle L
207-768-9594
Sanford
Louis Goodall L
207-324-5982
Waterville
Colby C Miller L
207-872-3463 x330

MARYLAND

Annapolis
MD S Law L
410-974-3395
US Naval Academy L
410-293-2420
Baltimore
Enoch Pratt Free L
410-396-5426
Goucher C Rogers L
410-337-6212
Johns Hopkins U
410-516-8360
Morgan SU Soper L
410-319-3642
US Ct of Appeals L
410-962-0997
U/Baltimore L
410-837-4274
U/Baltimore Law L
410-837-4559

U/MD Sc of Law L
410-706-6502
Bel Air
Harford Comm CL
410-836-4131
Beltsville
Dept/Agriculture L
301-504-5479
Bethesda
National L Medicine
301-496-6075 x609
Uniformed Services
301-295-3350
Catonsville
U/MD/Baltimore L
410-455-2358
Chestertown
Washington CL
410-778-7288
College Park
U/MD McKeldin L
301-405-9165
Cumberland
Allegany C of MD L
301-724-7700 x276
Frostburg
Frostburg SU Ort L
301-687-4426
Patuxent River
Naval Air Warfare L
301-342-1931
Rockville
Montgomery Cy L
301-217-3863
Salisbury
Salisbury SUL
410-543-6520
Silver Spring
Dept/Commerce NOAA L
301-713-2607 x124
Towson
Towson SU Cook L
410-830-2462
Westminster
Western MD CL
410-857-2287

MASSACHUSETTS

Amherst
Amherst C Frost L
413-542-2676
U/MA/Amherst UL
413-545-2765

Boston
  Boston Athenaeum L
  617-227-0270
  Boston PL Govt Doc
  617-536-5400 x226
  Boston U Sc of Law L
  617-353-3151
  Northeastern UL
  617-373-2354
  SL of MA Doc Dept
  617-727-6279
  Social Law L
  617-523-0018 x520
  Suffolk U Law L
  617-573-8609
  US Ct of Appeals L
  617-223-9044
Brookline
  PL of Brookline
  617-730-2369
Cambridge
  Harvard C Lamont L
  617-495-2479
  Harvard C Law Sc L
  617-495-3170
  MIT L
  617-253-5677
Chestnut Hill
  Boston C O'Neill L
  617-552-3221
Chicopee
  C of Our Lady of Elms
  413-594-2761 x297
Lowell
  U/MA/Lowell
  508-934-4589
Medford
  Tuffs U Tisch L
  617-627-3460
Milton
  Curry C Levin L
  617-333-2177
New Bedford
  New Bedford Free PL
  508-991-6280
Newton Center
  Boston C Law Sc L
  617-552-4406
North Dartmouth
  U/MA/Dartmouth L
  508-999-8678
North Easton
  Stonehill CL
  508-230-1238
Springfield

MA Trial Ct Law L
  413-748-7923
  Springfield City L
  413-263-6800 x213
  Western New England
  413-782-1309 (Law)
Waltham
  Brandeis UL
  617-736-4670
Wellesley
  Wellesley CL
  617-283-2100
Wenham
  Gordon C
  508-927-2300 x433
Williamstown
  Williams C Sawyer L
  413-597-2514
Worcester
  American Antiquarian
  508-753-3311
  U/MA Medical L
  508-856-6857
  Worcester PL
  508-799-1663

MICHIGAN

Albion
  Albion CL
  517-629-0384
Allendale
  Grand Valley SUL
  616-895-3500
Alma
  Alma C Monteith L
  517-463-7227
Ann Arbor
  U/MI Law L
  313-764-9324 x932
  U/MI Hatcher L
  313-764-0410
Benton Harbor
  Benton Harbor PL
  616-926-6139 x12
Clinton Township
  Macomb Cy L
  810-286-6660
Dearborn
  Henry Ford Comm CL
  313-845-6377
Detroit
  Detroit C of Law L
  313-226-0159
  Detroit PL
  313-833-1025

Marygrove CL
  313-862-8000 x212
  U/Detroit Law L
  313-596-0241
  U/Detroit McNichols L
  313-993-1071
  Wayne SUL
  313-577-1603
  Wayne SU Law L
  313-577-6166
Dowagiac
  Southwestern MI CL
  616-782-1205
East Lansing
  MI SU Main L
  517-353-8707
Farmington Hills
  Oakland Comm C
  810-471-7580
Flint
  Flint PL
  810-767-6740
Grand Rapids
  Calvin C Hekman L
  616-957-6307
  Grand Rapids PL
  616-456-3600
Houghton
  MI Tech UL
  906-487-2506
Jackson
  Jackson District L
  517-788-4316
Kalamazoo
  Kalamazoo PL
  616-342-9837 x240
  Western MI UL
  616-387-5208
Lansing
  L of MI Govt Doc
  517-373-1300
  Thomas Cooley Law L
  517-371-5140 x618
Livonia
  Livonia PL
  313-421-7338
  Schoolcraft CL
  313-462-4440
Madison Heights
  Madison Heights PL
  810-588-7763
Marquette
  No MI U Olson L
  906-227-2112
Monroe

Monroe Cy L Sys
  313-241-5277 x17
Mount Pleasant
  Central MI U Park L
  517-774-3414
Muskegon
  Hackley PL
  616-722-7276
Petoskey
  North Central MI CL
  616-348-6615
Pontiac
  Oakland Cy L
  810-858-0738
Port Huron
  St Clair Cy L
  810-987-7327
Rochester
  Oakland U Kresge L
  810-370-4426
Royal Oak
  Royal Oak PL
  810-541-1470
Saginaw
  Hoyt PL
  517-755-0904
Sault Ste. Marie
  Lake Superior SU
  906-635-2167
Traverse City
  Northwestern MI CL
  616-922-1065
University Center
  Delta CL
  517-686-9560
Warren
  Warren PL
  810-751-5377
Ypsilanti
  Eastern MI UL
  313-487-2280

MINNESOTA

Bemidji
  Bemidji SU Clark L
  218-755-3342
Blaine
  Anoka Cy L
  612-784-1100
Collegeville
  St John's UL
  320-363-2125
Duluth
  Duluth PL Doc Sec

218-723-3802
U/MN/Duluth L
218-726-7881
Eagan
　Dakota Cy L
　612-688-1500
Edina
　Hennepin Cy L
　612-830-4933
Mankato
　Mankato SUL
　507-389-5154
Marshall
　Southwest SUL
　507-537-6176
Minneapolis
　Minneapolis PL
　612-372-6534
　U/MN Law Sc L
　612-625-4309
　U/MN Wilson L
　612-624-5073
Moorhead
　Moorhead SUL
　218-236-2349
Morris
　U/MN/Morris
　612-589-6171
Northfield
　Carleton CL
　507-663-4266
　St Olaf CL
　507-646-3795
Roseville
　Ramsey Cy PL
　612-631-0494
Saint Cloud
　St Cloud SU
　612-255-2086
Saint Paul
　Hamline U Sc of Law L
　612-641-2397
　MN S Law L
　612-296-2775
　St Paul PL Govt Pub
　612-292-6178
　U/MN/St Paul L
　612-624-1212
　Wm Mitchell Law L
　612-290-6424
Saint Peter
　Gustavus Adolphus CL
　507-933-7556
Winona

Winona SUL
507-457-5146

MISSISSIPPI

Cleveland
　Delta SUL
　601-846-4431
Columbus
　MS U for Women L
　601-329-7695
Hattiesburg
　U/So MS Cook L
　601-266-4249
Jackson
　Jackson SUL
　601-968-2123
　Millsaps CL
　601-974-1072
　MS C Sc of Law L
　601-949-5674
　MS L Comm'n Doc Sec
　601-359-1036
　Supreme Ct of MS L
　601-359-3672
Lorman
　Alcorn SU Boyd L
　601-877-6350
Mississippi State
　MS SU Mitchell L
　601-325-7660
University
　U/MS Law L
　601-232-7361 x306
　U/MS Williams L
　601-232-7465

MISSOURI

Cape Girardeau
　Southeast MO SUL
　573-651-2756
Columbia
　U/MO/Columbia L
　314-882-6733
　U/MO/Columbia Law L
　314-884-6362
Fulton
　Westminster CL
　314-592-1378
Hillsboro
　Jefferson CL
　314-789-3951 x163
Jefferson City
　Lincoln U Page L
　314-681-5503

MO SL
573-751-3615
MO Supreme Ct L
314-751-2636
Joplin
　Joplin So SCL
　417-625-9335
Kansas City
　Kansas City MO PL
　816-221-9650 x83
　Rockhurst CL
　816-501-4131
　U/MO/Kansas City L
　816-235-2630 (Law)
　U/MO/Kansas City L
　816-235-1534
Kirksville
　Truman SUL
　816-785-4051
Liberty
　Wm Jewell CL
　816-781-7700 x546
Maryville
　Northwest MO SUL
　816-562-1591
O'Fallon
　St Charles City-Cy L
　314-978-7926
Rolla
　U/MO/Rolla L
　314-341-4007
Saint Charles
　Lindenwood CL
　314-949-4820
Saint Joseph
　River Bluffs L
　816-232-8151
Saint Louis
　Maryville UL
　314-529-9595
　St Louis Cy L
　314-997-7602
　St Louis PL Govt Info
　314-539-0375
　St Louis UL
　413-977-3105
　St Louis U Law L
　314-977-2756
　US Ct of Appeals L
　314-539-2930
　U/MO/St Louis L
　314-516-5061
　Washington U Law L
　314-935-6484

Washington U Olin L
314-935-4021
Springfield
　Drury C Olin L
　417-873-7337
　Southwest MO SUL
　417-836-4532
Warrensburg
　Central MO SUL
　816-543-4149

MONTANA

Billings
　MT SU/Billings L
　406-657-1662
Bozeman
　MT SU/Bozeman L
　406-994-3171
Butte
　MT Tech of U/MT L
　406-496-4281
Havre
　Mt SU/No Vande L
　406-265-3706 x303
Helena
　Carroll C Corette L
　406-447-4344
　MT SL
　406-444-3004
　S Law L of MT
　406-444-3636
Missoula
　U/MT Mansfield L
　406-243-6700

NEBRASKA

Blair
　Dana CL
　402-426-7332
Crete
　Doane C Perkins L
　402-826-8287
Fremont
　Midland Luthern CL
　402-721-5480 x625
Kearney
　U/NE/Kearney L
　308-865-8542
Lincoln
　NE L Comm'n Fed Doc
　402-471-4016
　NE SL
　402-471-3189

U/NE/Lincoln Law L
402-472-3547
U/NE/Lincoln Love L
402-472-4473
Omaha
Creigton U Law L
402-280-5541
Creigton U Reinert
402-280-2978
Omaha PL
402-444-4817
U/NE/Omaha UL
402-554-3202
Scottsbluff
Scottsbluff PL
308-630-6250
Wayne
Wayne SC Conn L
402-375-7263

NEVADA

Carson City
NV SL & Archives
702-687-8330
NV Supreme Ct L
702-687-5140
Elko
Elko Cy L
702-738-3077
Great Basin C
702-753-2222
Las Vegas
Clark Cy Law L
702-455-4696
Las Vegas-Clark Cy
702-382-3493
U/NV/Las Vegas
702-895-3904
Reno
NV Historical L
702-688-1191
U/NV Judicial C Law L
702-784-6039
U/NV/Reno L
702-784-6500 x257
Washoe Cy L Govt Doc
702-785-4507

NEW HAMPSHIRE

Concord
F. Pierce Law Cntr L
603-228-1541 x176
NH Law L
603-271-3777

NH SL Ref & Info
603-271-2144
Durham
U/NH Diamond L
603-862-1777
Hanover
Dartmouth C Baker L
603-646-2546
Henniker
New England CL
603-428-2344
Manchester
Manchester City L
603-624-6550
NH C Shapiro L
603-668-2211
St Anselm CL
603-641-7306
Nashua
Nashua PL
603-594-3412

NEW JERSEY

Bayonne
Bayonne Free PL
201-858-6980
Brighton
Cumberland Cy L
609-453-2210
Camden
Rutgers U Robeson L
609-225-6034
Rutgers U Law Sc L
609-225-6173
East Brunswick
East Brunswick PL
908-390-6767
East Orange
East Orange PL
201-266-5612
Elizabeth
Free PL/Elizabeth
908-354-6060 x203
Glassboro
Rowan C of NJ
609-256-4965 x49
Hackensack
Johnson Free PL
201-343-4169 x18
Irvington
Irvington PL
201-372-6400
Jersey City

Jersey City PL
201-547-4517
Jersey City SCL
201-200-3137
Lawrenceville
Rider U Moore L
609-896-5115
Madison
Drew UL
201-408-3588
Mahwah
Rampo C Potter L
201-529-7500 x790
Morristown
C of St Elizabeth L
201-605-7037
Mount Holly
Burlington Cy L
609-267-9660
New Brunswick
Rutgers UL
908-932-7526
Newark
Newark PL
201-733-7815
Rutgers U Dana L
201-648-5910
Rutgers U Law L
201-648-5849
Saton Hall U Law L
201-642-8589
Newton
Susses Cy L
201-948-3660
Phillipsburg
Phillipsburg Free L
908-454-3712
Plainfield
Plainfield PL
908-757-1111
Pomona
Stockton SC of NJ
609-652-4532
Princeton
Princeton UL
609-258-3701
Randolph
Cy C of Morris
201-328-5296
Shrewsbury
Monmouth Cy L
908-842-5995
South Orange
Seton Hall UL

201-761-9438
Teaneck
Fairleigh Dickinson
201-692-2290
Toms River
Ocean Cy CL
908-255-0392 x228
Trenton
NJ SL US Doc
609-292-6259
Trenton Free PL
609-392-7188
Upper Montclair
Montclair SCL
201-655-7145
West Long Branch
Monmouth UL
908-571-3450
Woodbridge
Free PL/Woodbridge
908-634-4450

NEW MEXICO

Albuquerque
U/NM Health L
505-277-2311
U/NM General L
505-277-5441
U/NM Sc of Law L
505-277-5135
Hobbs
NM Jr C Pannell L
505-392-5473
Las Cruces
NM SU Branson L
505-646-3737
Las Vegas
NM Highlands UL
505-454-3404
Portales
Eastern NM UL
505-562-2650
Santa Fe
NM SL
505-827-3824
NM Supreme Ct Law L
505-827-4850
Silver City
Western NM UL
505-538-6485
Socorro
NM Inst of Mining L
505-835-5740

NEW YORK

Albany
Albany Law Sc L
518-445-2390
NY SL
518-474-5355
SU/NY/Albany UL
518-442-3558

Binghamton
Binghamton UL
607-777-4907 x461

Brockport
SU/NY/Brockport L
716-395-2197

Bronx
Fordham UL Pub Doc
718-817-3586
Lehman CL
718-960-8580
SU/NY Maritime L
718-409-7231

Bronxville
Sarah Lawrence CL
914-395-2474

Brooklyn
Brooklyn CL Govt Doc
718-951-5332
Brooklyn Law Sc L
718-780-7973
Brooklyn PL Central
718-780-7747
Brooklyn PL Business
718-722-3333
Pratt Inst L
718-636-3686

Brookville
Long Island UL
516-299-2142 x284

Buffalo
Buffalo & Erie PL
716-858-8900
SU/NY/Buffalo Law L
716-645-2047
SU/NY/Buffalo L
716-645-2821

Canton
St Lawrence UL
315-379-5451

Corning
Corning Comm CL
607-962-9251

Cortland
SUC/Cortland L

607-753-2590

Delhi
SUC of Tech L
607-746-4635

East Islip
East Islip PL
516-286-1600 x325

Elmira
Elmira CL
607-735-1862

Farmingdale
SU/NY/Farmingdale L
516-420-2420

Flushing
Queens C/CUNY Law L
718-575-4240
Queens CL
718-997-3700

Garden City
Adelphi UL
516-877-3587

Geneseo
SU/NY/Geneseo L
716-245-5595

Hamilton
Colgate U Case L
315-824-7194

Hempstead
Hofstra U Law Sc L
516-463-5905
Hofstra U Axinn L
516-463-5972

Huntington
Touro C Law Sc L
516-421-2244 x325

Ithaca
Cornell U Olin L
607-255-4144
Cornell U Mann L
607-255-5406
Cornell U Law Sc L
607-255-9577

Jamaica
Queens Borough PL
718-990-0769
St John's U Law L
718-990-1896
St John's UL
718-990-6161 x545

Kings Point
US Merchant Marine L
516-773-5503

Long Island City
LaGuardia Comm CL

718-482-5425

Middletown
Middletown Thrall L
914-341-5454

Mount Vernon
Mount Vernon PL
914-668-1840

New Paltz
SUC/New Paltz L
914-257-3709

New York City
City C/CUNY L
212-650-5073
C of Insurance L
212-962-4111 x312
Columbia U Law Sc L
212-854-3743
Columbia U Lehman L
212-854-5002
Cooper Union L
212-353-4186
Fordham U Kissam L
212-636-6906
Medical L Cntr/NY
212-427-1630
NY Law Inst L
212-732-8720
NY Law Sc L
212-431-2150
NY PL Astor
212-930-0724
NY PL Hunt's Point
212-340-0888
NY U Law L
212-998-6326
NY U Bobst L
212-998-2600
US Ct of Appeals L
212-791-1052
Yeshiva U Pollack L
212-960-5378
Yeshiva U Law L
212-790-0220

Newburgh
Newburgh Free L
914-561-1985

Niagara Falls
Niagara Falls PL
716-286-4882

Oakdale
Dowling CL Govt Doc
516-244-3282

Oneonta
SUC/Oneonta L

607-436-2465

Oswego
SU/NY/Oswego L
315-341-4267

Plattsburgh
SUC/Plattsburgh L
518-564-5190

Potsdam
Clarkson U Burnap L
315-268-2297
SUC/Potsdam L
315-267-3328

Poughkeepsie
Vassar C Thompson L
914-437-5766

Purchase
SU/NY Purchase L
914-251-6405

Rochester
Rochester-Monroe PL
716-428-7300
U/Rochester Rhees L
716-275-4468

Saint Bonaventure
St Bonaventure UL
716-375-2164

Saratoga Springs
Skidmore CL
518-584-5000 x272

Schenectady
Union C Schaffer L
518-388-6635

Southampton
Long Island UL
516-287-8379

Sparkill
St Thomas Acquinas
914-398-4216

Staten Island
Wagner CL
718-390-3401

Stony Brook
SU/NY Stony Brook L
516-632-7161

Syracuse
Onondaga Cy PL
315-435-1900
Syracuse U Byrd L
315-443-4176
Syracuse U Law L
315-443-9560

Troy
Troy PL
518-274-7071 x9

Uniondale
  Nassau L Sys
  516-292-8920
Utica
  SU/NY Inst of Tech
  315-792-7245
  Union PL
  315-735-2279
West Point
  US Military Academy
  914-938-2230
White Plains
  Pace U Sc of Law L
  914-422-4273
Yonkers
  Yonkers PL
  914-476-1255
Yorktown Heights
  Mercy CL
  914-962-6100 x222

NORTH CAROLINA

Asheville
  U/NC/Asheville L
  704-251-6111
Boiling Springs
  Gardner-Webb UL
  704-434-4290
Boone
  Appalachian SUL
  704-262-2820
Buies Creek
  Campbell UL
  910-893-1465
Chapel Hill
  U/NC Everel Law L
  919-962-1194
  U/NC Davis L
  919-962-1151
Charlotte
  PL of Charlotte
  704-336-2725
  Queens C Everett L
  704-337-2401
  U/NC/Charlette L
  704-547-2243
Cullowhee
  Western Carolina UL
  704-227-7380
Davidson
  Davidson CL
  704-892-2154
Durham

Duke U Perkins L
  919-660-5851
  Duke U Law L
  919-613-7121
  NC Central U Law L
  919-560-3320
  NC Central UL
  919-560-6097
Elon College
  Elon C McEwen L
  910-584-2159
Fayetteville
  Fayetteville SUL
  910-486-1752
Greensboro
  NC A&T SUL
  910-334-7753
  U/NC Jackson L
  910-334-5251
Greenville
  East Carolina UL
  919-328-6533
Laurinburg
  St Andrews CL
  910-277-5047 x289
Lexington
  Davidson Cy PL
  704-242-2040
Mount Olive
  Mount Olive CL
  919-658-7168
Pembroke
  Pembroke SUL
  910-521-6655
Raleigh
  NC SU Hill L
  919-515-3280
  NC Supreme Ct L
  919-733-3425
  SL/NC
  919-733-3270
Rocky Mount
  NC Wesleyan CL
  919-985-5233 x283
Salisbury
  Catawba CL
  704-637-4448
Wilmington
  U/NC Randall L
  910-395-3277
Wilson
  Barton C Hackney L
  919-399-6502
Winston-Salem

Forsyth Cy PL
  910-727-2220
  Wake Forest UL
  910-759-4520
  910-759-5478

NORTH DAKOTA

Bismarck
  Bismarck Veteran PL
  701-222-6410
  ND SL
  701-328-4622
  ND Supreme Ct Law L
  701-328-2227
  S Historical Soc
  701-328-2668
Dickinson
  Dickinson SUL
  701-227-2135
Fargo
  ND SUL
  701-231-8886
Grand Forks
  U/ND Fritz L
  701-777-3316
Minot
  Minot SU Olson L
  701-858-3296
Valley City
  Valley City SUL
  701-845-7277

OHIO

Ada
  Ohio Northern Law L
  419-772-2254
Akron
  Akron-Summit Cy PL
  216-643-9000
  U/Akron Sc of Law L
  216-972-7330
  U/Akron Bierce L
  216-972-7494
Alliance
  Mount Union CL
  800-992-6682 x384
Ashland
  Ashland UL
  419-289-5410
Athens
  Ohio U Alden L
  614-593-2718
Bluffton
  Bluffton CL

419-358-3275
Bowling Green
  Bowling Green SUL
  419-372-2142
Canton
  Malone C Cattell L
  216-471-8324
Chardon
  Chardon PL
  216-285-7601
Cincinnati
  PL of Cincinnati
  513-369-6932
  U/Cincinnati L
  513-556-1874
  U/Cincinnati Law L
  513-556-8078
  US Ct of Appeals L
  513-684-2678
Cleveland
  Case Western Law L
  216-368-5206
  Case Western Smith L
  216-368-6512
  Cleveland PL
  216-623-2870
  Cleveland SUL
  216-687-2487
  Cleveland SU Law L
  216-287-6877
  Municipal Ref L
  216-664-2656
Columbus
  Capital UL
  614-236-6436
  Capital U Law Sc L
  614-445-8836 x160
  Columbus Metro L
  614-645-2710
  OH SU C of Law L
  614-292-9463
  OH SU Main L
  614-292-6175
  OH Supreme Ct L
  614-466-1520
  SL/OH Doc Dept
  614-644-7051
Dayton
  Dayton ... PL
  513-227-9500 x311
  U/Dayton Roesch L
  513-229-4263
  Wright SUL
  513-873-2533

Delaware
 OH Wesleyan UL
 614-368-3242
Elyria
 Elyria PL
 216-323-5747
Findlay
 U/Findlay Shafer L
 419-424-4762
Gambier
 Kenyon CL
 614-427-5658
Granville
 Denison UL
 614-587-6682
Hiram
 Hiram CL
 216-569-5358
Kent
 Kent SUL
 330-672-2159
Marietta
 Marietta CL
 614-376-4543
Marion
 Marion PL Fed Doc
 614-382-3951
Middletown
 Middletown UL
 513-727-3293
New Concord
 Muskingum CL Doc
 614-826-8152
Oberlin
 Oberlin CL Doc Dept
 216-775-8285 x238
Oxford
 Miami U King L
 513-529-3340
Portsmouth
 Shawnee SUL
 614-355-2321
Rio Grande
 U/Rio Grande L
 614-245-7344
Springfield
 Clark Cy PL
 513-328-6903
Steubenville
 Franciscan UL
 614-283-6366
 PL/Steubenville
 614-282-9782
Tiffin
 Heidelberg CL

419-448-2104
Toledo
 Toledo-Lucas Cy PL
 419-259-5245
 U/Toledo Carlson L
 419-530-2171
 U/Toledo C of Law L
 419-530-2733
University Heights
 John Carroll UL
 216-397-1635
Westerville
 Otterbein CL
 614-823-1115
Westlake
 Westlake Porter PL
 216-871-2600
Wilmington
 Wilmington CL
 513-382-6661 x297
Wooster
 C of Wooster L
 216-263-2279
Worthington
 Worthington PL
 614-645-2626
Youngstown
 PL of Youngstown
 216-744-8636 x45
 Youngstown SUL
 216-742-3126

OKLAHOMA
Ada
 East Central UL
 405-332-8000 x368
Alva
 Northwestern OK SL
 405-327-8572
Bethany
 So Nazarene U
 405-491-6350
Durant
 Southeastern OK SUL
 405-924-0121 x256
Edmond
 U/Central OK L
 405-341-2980 x290
Enid
 PL of Enid Cy
 405-234-6313
Langston
 Langston UL
 405-466-3292

Lawton
 Lawton PL
 405-581-3450
Norman
 U/OK Bizzell L
 405-325-1832
 U/OK Law L
 405-325-4673
Oklahoma City
 Metro L Sys
 405-236-0571
 OK City UL
 405-521-5073
 OK Dept L US Govt
 405-521-2502 x253
Shawnee
 OK Baptist U
 405-878-2262
Stillwater
 OK SU Low L
 405-744-6546
Tahlequah
 Northeastern SUL
 918-456-5511 x324
Tulsa
 Tulsa City-Cy L
 918-596-7946
 U/Tulsa Law L
 918-631-2461
 U/Tulsa McFarlin L
 918-631-2874

Weatherford
 Southwestern OK SL
 405-774-3031

OREGON
Ashland
 So OR SCL
 541-552-6851
Bend
 Central OR Comm CL
 503-383-7560
Corvallis
 OR SU Kerr L
 503-737-2761
Eugene
 U/OR L
 541-346-3070
 U/OR Law L
 541-346-3097
Forest Grove
 Pacific UL
 503-359-2835
Klamath Falls

OR Inst of Tech L
 541-885-1772
La Grande
 Eastern OR SCL
 503-962-3540
McMinnville
 Linfield CL
 503-434-2518
Monmouth
 Western OR SCL
 503-838-8899
Pendleton
 Blue Mt Comm CL
 503-276-1260 x213
Portland
 Dept/Energy BPA L
 503-230-4171
 Lewis & Clark CL
 503-768-7285
 Multnomah Cy L
 503-248-5234
 Northwestern Law L
 503-768-6776
 Portland SUL
 503-725-4123
 Reed C Houser L
 503-777-7554
Salem
 OR SL
 503-378-4277 x7119
 OR Supreme Ct Law L
 503-986-5640
 Willamette UL
 503-370-6312
 Willamette U Law L
 503-370-6386 x400

PENNSYLVANIA
Allentown
 Muhlenberg CL
 610-821-3600
Altoona
 Altoona Area PL
 814-946-0417
Bethel Park
 Bethel Park PL
 412-835-2207
Bethlehem
 Lehigh UL
 610-758-3053
Bloomsburg
 Bloomsburg U/PA L
 717-389-4224
Blue Bell
 Montgomery Cy Comm

215-641-6594
Bradford
  U/Pittsburgh/Bradford
  814-362-7617
Broomall
  Marple PL
  610-356-1510
California
  Calif/U/PA L
  412-938-4049
Carlisle
  Dickinson CL
  717-245-1747
  Dickinson Law L
  717-240-5226
Cheyney
  Cheyney UL
  610-399-2060
Collegeville
  Ursinus CL
  610-409-3607
Coraopolis
  Robert Morris CL
  412-262-8272
Doylestown
  Bucks Cy Free L
  215-348-9082
East Stroudsburg
  East Stroudsburg UL
  717-422-3150
Erie
  Erie Cy L Sys
  814-451-6927
Greenville
  Theil CL
  412-589-2127
Harrisburg
  SL of PA Law Pub
  717-787-2327
  Widener U Law L
  717-541-3933
Haverford
  Haverford CL
  610-896-1169
Indiana
  Indiana U/PA L
  412-357-4892
Johnstown
  Cambria Cy L Sys
  814-536-5131
Lancaster
  Franklin & Marshall
  717-291-4217
Lewisburg
  Bucknell UL

717-524-1462
Mansfield
  Mansfield UL
  717-662-4673
Meadville
  Allegheny CL
  814-332-3769
Millersville
  Millersville UL
  717-872-3617
Monessen
  Monessen PL
  412-684-4750
New Castle
  New Castle PL
  412-658-6659
Newtown
  Bucks Cy Comm CL
  215-968-8013
Norristown
  Montgomery Cy PL
  610-278-5110
Philadelphia
  Free L of Phil.
  215-686-5330
  St Joseph UL
  610-660-1904
  Temple U Law L
  215-204-1195
  Temple U Paley L
  215-204-8231
  U/PA L
  215-898-7555
  U/PA Law L
  215-898-7853
  US Ct of Appeals L
  215-597-2009
Pittsburgh
  Allegheny Cy Law L
  412-350-5353
  Carnegie L
  412-237-1893
  Carnegie L Govt Doc
  412-622-3175
  Dept/Energy Mines L
  412-892-4431
  Duquesne U Law L
  412-396-5016
  LaRoche CL
  412-367-9300 x170
  U/Pittsburgh L
  412-648-3300
  U/Pittsburgh Law L
  412-648-1324
Pottsville

Pottsville Free PL
  717-622-8880 x17
Reading
  Reading PL
  610-655-6355
Scranton
  Scranton PL
  717-348-3009
Shippensburg
  Shippensburg UL
  717-532-1634
Slippery Rock
  Slippery Rock UL
  412-738-2638
Swarthmore
  Swarthmore CL
  610-328-8477
University Park
  PA SU Pattee L
  814-865-4861
Villanova
  Villanova Law L
  610-519-7020
Warren
  Warren PL
  814-723-4650
West Chester
  West Chester UL
  610-436-2869
Williamsport
  Lycoming CL
  717-321-4053
Youngwood
  Westmoreland Comm C
  412-925-4100

RHODE ISLAND

Barrington
  Barrington PL
  401-247-1920
Kingston
  U/RI L
  401-792-2606
Newport
  US Naval War CL
  401-841-4551
Providence
  Brown UL
  401-863-2522
  Providence CL
  401-865-2581
  Providence PL
  401-455-8005
  RI CL
  401-456-9604

RI SL
  401-277-2473
RI S Law L
  401-277-3275
Warwick
  Warwick PL
  401-739-5440
Westerly
  Westerly PL
  401-596-2877
Woonsocket
  Woonsocket PL
  401-769-9044 x123

SOUTH CAROLINA

Aiken
  U/SC/Aiken L
  803-641-3320
Charleston
  Charleston So UL
  803-863-7946
  C of Charleston L
  803-953-8009
  Citadel Military CL
  803-953-5128
Clemson
  Clemson UL
  864-656-5174
Columbia
  Benedict C
  803-253-5180
  SC SL Doc Dept
  803-734-8666
  U/SC L
  803-777-4841
  U/SC Law L
  803-777-5942
Conway
  Coastal Carolina UL
  803-349-2400
Due West
  Erskine CL
  864-379-8898
Florence
  Florence Cy L
  803-662-8424 x11
  Francis Marion UL
  803-661-1310
Greenville
  Furman UL
  864-294-3203
  Greenville Cy L
  864-242-5000 x241
Greenwood

Lander UL
864-229-8365
Lancaster
U/SC/Lancaster L
803-285-7471
Orangeburg
SC SUL
803-536-7045
Rock Hill
Winthrop UL
803-323-4501
Spartanburg
Spartanburg Cy PL
864-596-3505

SOUTH DAKOTA

Aberdeen
No SU William L
605-626-2645
Brookings
SD SU Briggs L
605-688-5576
Pierre
SD SL Fed Doc Dept
605-773-3131
SD Supreme Ct L
605-773-4898
Rapid City
Rapid City PL
605-394-4171
SD Sc of Mines L
605-394-2418
Sioux Falls
Augustana CL
605-336-4921
Sioux Falls PL
605-367-7082
Spearfish
Black Hills SUL
605-642-6358
Vermillion
U/SD Weeks L
605-677-6085

TENNESSEE

Bristol
King CL
423-652-4795
Chattanooga
Chattanooga Cy L
423-757-5351
US TVA Corporate L
423-751-7439
Clarksville
Austin Peay SUL

615-648-7346
Cleveland
Cleveland S Comm CL
423-478-6209
Columbia
Columbia S Comm CL
615-540-2552
Cookeville
TN Tech UL
615-372-3841
Jackson
Lambuth UL
901-425-3290
Jefferson City
Carson-Newman CL
423-471-3337
Johnson City
East TN SUL
423-929-5334
Knoxville
Knox Cy PL Sys
423-544-5723
U/TN/Knoxville L
423-974-6870
U/TN/Knoxville Law L
423-974-4381
Martin
U/TN/Martin L
901-587-7073 x706
Memphis
Memphis-Shelby PL
901-725-8893
U/Memphis Law L
901-678-2426
U/Memphis UL
901-678-2206
Murfreesboro
Middle TN SUL
615-898-2817
Nashville
Fisk UL
615-319-8640
PL of Nashville
615-862-5842
TN SL & Archives
615-741-2561
TN SUL
615-963-5201
Vanderbily UL
615-322-2838
Vanderbilt U Law L
615-322-2568
Sewanee
U/South duPont L
615-598-1702

TEXAS

Abilene
Abilene Christian UL
915-674-2477
Hardin-Simmons UL
915-670-1512
Arlington
Arlington PL
817-459-6905
U/TX/Arlington L
817-273-3000 x496
Austin
TX S Law L
512-463-1722
TX S L US Doc
512-463-5455
U/TX/Austin Law L
512-471-7250
U/TX/Austin Perry
512-495-4250
U/TX/Austin Wasserman
512-495-4400
Baytown
Lee C Resource Cntr
713-425-6276
Beaumont
Lamar U Gray L
409-880-8261
Brownwood
Howard Payne UL
915-649-8602 x560
Canyon
West TX A&M UL
806-656-2204
College Station
TX A&M UL
409-845-3826
Commerce
East TX SUL
903-886-5726
Corpus Christi
TX A&M U L
512-994-2609
Corsicana
Navarro C
903-874-6501
Dallas
Dallas Baptist UL
214-333-5320
Dallas PL Govt Pub
214-670-1468
So Methodist UL
214-768-2331
Denton
U/North TX L

817-565-2870
Edinburg
U/TX Pan American L
210-381-3304
El Paso
El Paso PL Govt Doc
915-543-5433
U/TX/El Paso L
915-747-5685
Fort Worth
Fort Worth PL
817-871-7724
Tx Christian UL
817-921-7669
Galveston
Rosenberg L
409-763-8854 x130
Garland
Nicholson L Sys
214-205-2503
Houston
Houston PL Govt Doc
713-236-1313
North Harris C
713-443-5707
Rice U Fondren L
713-527-8101 x258
South TX C of Law L
713-646-1720
TX So U Law L
713-313-7125
U/Houston/Clear Lake
713-283-3910
U/Houston L
713-743-9781
U/Houston Law L
713-743-2335
Huntsville
Sam Houston SUL
409-294-1629
Irving
Irving PL Sys
214-721-2608
Kingsville
TX A&M UL
512-595-3319
Laredo
Laredo Comm CL
210-721-5270
Longview
Longview PL
903-237-1356
Lubbock
TX Tech UL
806-742-2268

TX Tech U Law L
806-742-3883
Nacogdoces
Stephen Austin SUL
409-468-4217
Richardson
U/TX/Dallas L
214-883-2918
San Angelo
Angelo SUL
915-942-2141
San Antonio
Palo Alto C
210-921-5087
San Antonio CL
210-733-2477
San Antonio PL
210-207-2500
St Mary's UL
210-436-3441
St Mary's U Law L
210-436-3435
Trinity UL
210-736-7430
U/TX/San Antonio L
210-691-4573
San Marcos
Southwest TX SUL
512-245-3686
Seguin
TX Luthern CL
210-372-8100
Sherman
Austin CL Cntr
903-813-2556
Texarkana
Texarkana CL
903-838-6514 x414
Victoria
U/Houston L
512-788-6283
Waco
Baylor UL
817-755-2157
Baylor U Law L
817-755-2168
Wichita Falls
Midwestern SUL
817-689-4177

UTAH

Cedar City
So UT UL
801-865-5156

Ephraim
Snow CL
801-283-4021 x363
Logan
UT SUL
801-797-2684
Ogden
Weber SUL
801-626-6766
Provo
Brigham Young Law L
801-378-6658
Brigham Young Lee L
801-378-5838
Salt Lake City
U/UT Law L
801-581-6438
U/UT Marriott L
801-581-8394
U/UT . . . Science L
801-581-5534
UT SL
801-466-5888
UT Supreme Ct Law L
801-538-1045

VERMONT

Burlington
U/VT Bailey-Howe L
802-656-2542
Castleton
Castleton SCL
802-468-5611 x257
Johnson
Johnson SC Dewey L
802-635-2356 x274
Lydonville
Lyndon SCL
802-626-6450
Middlebury
Middlebury CL
802-388-3711 x549
Montpelier
VT Dept/Libraries
802-828-3268
Northfield
Norwich UL
802-485-2168
South Royalton
VT Law Sc Cornell L
802-763-8303 x244

VIRGIN ISLANDS

Saint Croix
Florence Williams PL

809-773-5715
Saint Thomas
U/VI L
809-693-1367

VIRGINIA

Alexandria
Dept/Navy
703-325-9565
Arlington
George Mason U Law L
703-993-8062
US Patent . . . Office
703-308-0810
Blacksburg
VA Polytechnic L
540-231-9232
Bridgewater
Bridgewater CL
540-828-5415
Charlottesville
U/VA Alderman L
804-924-3133
U/VA Morris Law L
804-924-3504
Chesapeake
Chesapeake PL Sys
804-547-6591
Danville
Danville Comm C
804-797-8555
Emory
Emory & Hency CL
540-944-6209
Fairfax
George Mason UL
703-993-2210
Fredericksburg
Mary Washington CL
540-654-1148
Hampden-Sydney
Hampden-Sydney CL
804-223-6193
Hampton
Hampton UL
804-727-5371
Harrisonburg
James Madison UL
540-568-6929
Lexington
VA Military Inst L
540-464-7296
Washington & Lee UL
540-463-8644
Washington & Lee UL

540-463-8544 (Law)
Martinsville
Patrick Henry Comm C
540-638-8777 x228
Norfolk
Norfolk PL Sys
804-664-7337
Old Dominion UL
757-683-4178
US Armed Forces CL
804-444-5155 x532
Petersburg
VA SUL
804-524-5582
Quantico
FBI Academy L
703-640-1135
Marine Corps UL
703-784-4409
Reston
Dept/Interior L
703-648-4302
Richmond
L of VA
804-786-2175
US Ct of Appeals L
804-771-2219 x223
U/Richmond
804-289-8668
U/Richmond Law Sc L
804-289-8225
VA Commonwealth UL
804-828-1104
VA S Law L
804-786-2075
Roanoke
Hollins C Fishburn
540-362-6091
Salem
Roanoke C Fintel L
540-375-2295
Williamsburg
C of Wm & Mary L
804-221-3064
C of Wm & Mary Law L
804-221-3244
Wise
Clinch Valley CL
540-328-0150

WASHINGTON

Bellevue
King Cy Bellevue L
206-684-6600
Bellingham

West WA U Wilson L
360-650-3075

Cheney
East WA U Kennedy L
509-359-2263

Des Moines
Highline Comm CL
206-878-3710 x232

Ellensburg
Central WA U
509-963-1541

Everett
Everett PL Doc Sec
206-259-8000

Olympia
Evergreen SC Evans L
360-866-6000 x625
WA State Law L
360-357-2135
WA State L Govt Pub
360-753-4027

Port Angeles
North Olympic L Sys
360-452-9259

Pullman
WA SU Holland L
509-335-8516

Seattle
Seattle PL Govt Pub
206-386-4139
US Ct of Appeals L
206-553-4475
U/WA Suzzallo L
206-543-1937
U/WA Gallagher Law L
206-543-6794

Spokane
Gonzaga U Law L
509-328-4220 x375
Spokane PL Doc Dept
509-626-5336

Tacoma
Seattle U Law L
206-591-2975
Tacoma PL Doc Div
206-591-5666
U/Puget Sound
206-756-3216

Vancouver
Fort Vancouver Reg L
360-695-1566

Walla Walla
Whitman C Penrose L

509-527-5918

WEST VIRGINIA

Athens
Concord C Marsh L
304-384-5371

Bluefield
Bluefield SCL
304-327-4055

Charleston
Kanawha Cy PL
304-343-4646 x231
WV L Comm'n Ref L
304-558-2045
WV Supreme Ct Law L
304-558-2607

Elkins
Davis & Elkins CL
304-637-1359

Fairmont
Fairmont SCL
304-367-4121

Huntington
Marshall U Morrow L
304-696-2342

Institute
WV SC Jordan L
304-766-3116

Montgomery
WV Inst/Technology
304-442-3241

Morgantown
WV UL Govt Doc
304-293-3051

Salem
Salem-Teikyo UL
304-782-5232

Shepherdstown
Shepherd CL
304-876-2511 x420

Weirton
Mary H Weir PL
304-797-8510

Wheeling
Wheeling Jesuit CL
304-243-4341

WISCONSIN

Appleton
Lawrence U Mudd L
414-832-6752

Beloit
Beloit C Morse L

608-363-2544

Eau Claire
U/WI/Eau Claire L
715-836-3859

Fond du Lac
Fond du Lac PL
414-929-7080

Green Bay
U/WI/Green Bay L
414-465-2388

La Crosse
La Crosse PL
608-789-7122
U/WI/La Crosse L
608-785-8313

Madison
Madison PL
608-266-6350
S Hist Society L
608-264-6525
U/WI/Madison L
608-262-9852
U/WI/Madison Law L
608-262-3394
WI S Law L
608-266-1600

Milwaukee
Alverno CL Center
414-382-6062
Marquette U Law L
414-288-7092
Medical C/WI Wehr L
414-456-8302
Milwaukee PL
414-286-3073
Mount Mary CL
414-258-4810 x341
U/WI/Milwaukee L
414-229-4659

Oshkosh
U/WI/Oshkosh Polk L
414-424-3347

Platteville
U/WI/Platteville L
608-342-1758

Racine
Racine PL Doc
414-636-9217

Ripon
Ripon C Lane L
414-748-8752

River Falls
U/WI/River Falls L

715-425-3874

Sheboygan
Mead PL
414-459-3435

Stevens Point
U/WI/Stevens Point
715-346-3726

Superior
Superior PL
715-394-8860
U/WI/Superior
715-394-8512

Waukesha
Waukesha PL
414-524-3682

Wausau
Marathon Cy PL
715-847-5530

Whitewater
U/WI/Whitewater L
414-472-1032

WYOMING

Casper
Natrona Cy PL
307-237-4935

Cheyenne
WY SL
307-777-6333
WY S Law L
307-777-7509

Gillette
Campbell Cy PL
307-682-0115

Laramie
U/WY Coe L
307-766-2070
U/WY Law L
307-766-5730

Powell
Northwest CL
307-754-6207

Riverton
Central WY CL
307-856-9291 x116

Rock Springs
Western WY Comm CL
307-382-1700

Sheridan
Sheridan CL
307-674-6446 x213

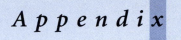

COURTS

This appendix lists the telephone numbers of the highest state court and the major state appellate courts in every state. Also included are the numbers of every major federal trial court (e.g., the United States District Court, the United States Bankruptcy Court) and every major federal appellate court (e.g., the United States Court of Appeals) that sit within the state.

ABBREVIATIONS

/: of
Appl: Appellate
Apps: Appeals
Civ: Civil
Cir: Circuit
Crim: Criminal
Ct: Court

Dept: Department
Dist: District
Div: Division
Inter: Intermediate
Intl: International
Jud: Judicial
Super: Superior

US: United States
USBC: United States Bankruptcy Court
USCA: United States Court of Appeals
USDC: United States District Court
USSC: United States Supreme Court

ALABAMA

AL Supreme Ct
205-242-4609
AL Ct/Civ Apps
205-242-4093
AL Ct/Crim Apps
205-242-4590
USDC Northern AL
205-731-1701
USDC Middle AL
205-223-7308
USDC Southern AL
205-690-2371
USBC Northern AL
205-731-1614
USBC Middle AL
205-223-7250
USBC Southern AL
205-441-5391

ALASKA

AK Supreme Ct
907-264-0607

AK Ct/Apps
907-264-0607
USDC
907-271-5568
USBC
907-271-2655

ARIZONA

AZ Supreme Ct
602-542-9300
AZ Ct/Apps Div I
602-542-4821
AZ Ct/Apps Div II
602-628-6954
USDC
602-514-7101
USBC
602-640-5800

ARKANSAS

AR Supreme Ct
501-682-6849
AR Ct/Apps

501-682-6849
USDC Eastern AR
501-324-5351
USDC Western AR
501-783-6833
USBC
501-324-6357

CALIFORNIA

CA Supreme Ct
415-396-9400
CA Ct/Apps 1st Dist
415-396-9600
CA Ct/Apps 2d Dist
213-897-2307
CA Ct/Apps 3d Dist
916-654-0209
CA Ct/Apps 4th Dist
619-645-2842
CA Ct/Apps 5th Dist
209-445-5491
CA Ct/Apps 6th Dist
408-277-1004

USCA (9th Cir)
415-744-9800
USDC Northern CA
415-556-3031
USDC Eastern CA
916-498-5415
USDC Central CA
213-894-3535
USDC Southern CA
619-557-6348
USBC Northern CA
415-705-3200
USBC Eastern CA
916-498-5525
USBC Central CA
213-894-6046
USBC Southern CA
619-557-5620

COLORADO

CO Supreme Ct
303-861-1111
CO Ct/Apps

303-861-1111
USCA (10th Cir)
303-844-3157
USDC
303-844-3433
USBC
303-844-0236

CONNECTICUT

CT Supreme Court
203-566-6234
CT Ct/Apps
203-566-6234
USDC
203-773-2140
USBC
203-240-3675

DELAWARE

DE Supreme Ct
302-739-4155
USDC
302-573-6170
USBC
302-573-6174

DISTRICT OF COLUMBIA

DC Ct/Apps
202-879-2725
US Supreme Court
202-479-3000
USCA (DC Cir)
202-273-0300
USCA (Federal Cir)
202-633-6550
US Ct/Federal Claims
202-219-9657
US Ct/Intl Trade
212-264-2814
US Ct/Military Apps
202-761-1448
US Ct/Veterans Apps
202-501-5970
Multi-District Panel
202-273-2800
US Tax Ct
202-606-8754
USDC
202-273-0594
USBC
202-273-0046

FLORIDA

FL Supreme Ct
904-488-0125
FL Ct/Apps 1st Dist

904-488-6152
FL Ct/Apps 2d Dist
813-499-2290
FL Ct/Apps 3d Dist
305-229-3200
FL Ct/Apps 4th Dist
407-647-7200
FL Ct/Apps 5th Dist
904-255-8600
USDC Northern FL
904-942-8826
USDC Middle FL
904-232-2854
USDC Southern FL
305-536-4131
USBC Northern FL
904-942-8933
USBC Middle FL
813-243-5134
USBC Southern FL
305-536-4320

GEORGIA

GA Supreme Ct
404-656-3470
GA Ct/Apps
404-656-3450
USCA (11th Cir)
404-331-6187
USDC Northern GA
404-331-6496
USDC Middle GA
912-752-3497
USDC Southern GA
912-662-4281
USBC Northern GA
404-331-6886
USBC Middle GA
912-752-3506
USBC Southern GA
912-662-4100

HAWAII

HI Supreme Ct
308-539-4919
HI Inter Ct/Apps
808-539-4919
USDC
808-541-1300
USBC
808-522-8100

IDAHO

ID Supreme Ct
208-334-2210

ID Ct/Apps
208-334-2210 USDC
208-334-1361
USBC
208-334-1361

ILLINOIS

IL Supreme Ct
217-782-2035
IL Appl Ct 1st Dist
312-793-5510
IL Appl Ct 2d Dist
708-695-3750
IL Appl Ct 3d Dist
815-434-5050
IL Appl Ct 4th Dist
217-782-2586
IL Appl Ct 5th Dist
618-242-3120
USCA (7th Cir)
312-435-5850
USDC Northern IL
312-435-5670
USDC Central IL
217-492-4020
USDC Southern IL
618-482-9371
USBC Northern IL
312-435-5587
USBC Central IL
217-492-4551
USBC Southern IL
618-482-9365

INDIANA

IN Supreme Ct
317-232-1930
IN Ct/Apps
317-232-1930
USDC Northern IN
219-236-8260
USDC Southern IN
317-226-6670
USBC Northern IN
219-236-8247
USBC Southern IN
317-226-6710

IOWA

IA Supreme Ct
515-281-5911
IA Ct/Apps
515-281-5911
USDC Northern IA
319-364-2447

USDC Southern IA
515-284-6248
USBC Northern IA
319-362-9696
USBC Southern IA
515-284-6230

KANSAS

KS Supreme Ct
913-296-3229
KS Ct/Apps
913-296-3229
USDC
316-269-6491
USBC
316-269-6486

KENTUCKY

KY Supreme Ct
502-564-4720
KY Ct/Apps
502-573-7920
USDC Eastern KY
606-233-2503
USDC Western KY
502-582-5156
USBC Eastern KY
606-233-2608
USBC Western KY
502-582-5145

LOUISIANA

LA Supreme Ct
504-568-5707
LA Ct/Apps 1st Cir
504-342-1500
LA Ct/Apps 2d Cir
318-227-3701
LA Ct/Apps 3d Cir
318-433-9403
LA Ct/Apps 4th Cir
504-568-4700
LA Ct/Apps 5th Cir
504-361-6399
USCA (5th Cir)
504-589-6514
USDC Eastern LA
504-589-4471
USDC Middle LA
504-389-0321
USDC Western LA
318-676-4273
USBC Eastern LA
504-589-6506
USBC Middle LA

504-389-0211
USBC Western LA
318-676-4267

MAINE

ME Supreme Ct
207-822-4146
USDC
207-780-3356
USBC
207-780-3482

MARYLAND

MD Ct/Apps
410-974-3341
MD Ct/Special Apps
410-974-3646
USDC
410-962-2600
USBC
410-962-2688

MASSACHUSETTS

MA Supreme Jud Ct
617-557-1020
MA Apps Ct
617-725-8106
USCA (1st Cir)
617-223-9057
USDC
617-223-9152
USBC
617-565-6050

MICHIGAN

MI Supreme Ct
517-373-0120
MI Ct/Apps
517-373-0786
USDC Eastern MI
313-226-7200
USDC Western MI
616-456-2381
USBC Eastern MI
313-226-3622
USBC Western MI
616-456-2693

MINNESOTA

MN Supreme Ct
612-296-2581
MN Ct/Apps
612-296-2581
USDC
612-290-3212

USBC
612-348-1855

MISSISSIPPI

MS Supreme Ct
601-359-3694
USDC Northern MS
601-234-1971
USDC Southern MS
601-965-4439
USBC Northern MS
601-369-2596
USBC Southern MS
601-965-5301

MISSOURI

MO Supreme Ct
314-751-4144
MO Ct/Apps Southern
417-895-6811
MO Ct/Apps Western
816-889-3600
MO Ct/Apps Eastern
314-340-6967
USCA (8th Cir)
314-359-3609
USDC Eastern MO
314-539-2315
USDC Western MO
816-426-2811
USBC Eastern MO
314-425-4222
USBC Western MO
816-426-2811

MONTANA

MT Supreme Ct
406-444-3858
USDC
406-247-7000
USBC
406-782-3354

NEBRASKA

NE Supreme Ct
402-471-3731
NE Ct/Apps
402-471-3731
USDC
402-221-4761
USBC
402-221-4687

NEVADA

NV Supreme Ct
702-687-5180

USDC
702-388-6351
USBC
702-388-6257

NEW HAMPSHIRE

NH Supreme Ct
603-271-2646
USDC
603-225-1423
USBC
603-666-7626

NEW JERSEY

NJ Supreme Ct
609-984-7791
NJ Super Ct Appl Div
609-292-4693
USDC
201-645-3730
USBC
201-645-3930

NEW MEXICO

NM Supreme Ct
505-827-4860
NM Ct/Apps
505-827-4925
USDC
505-766-2851
USBC
505-766-2051

NEW YORK

NY Ct/Apps
518-455-7700
NY Appl Div 1st Dept
212-340-0400
NY Appl Div 2d Dept
718-875-1300
NY Appl Div 3d Dept
518-474-3609
NY Appl Div 4th Dept
716-428-1000
USCA (2d Cir)
212-791-0103
USDC Northern NY
315-448-0501
USDC Southern NY
212-637-0136
USDC Eastern NY
718-330-2105
USDC Western NY
716-846-4211
USBC Northern NY

518-431-0188
USBC Southern NY
212-668-2867
USBC Eastern NY
718-330-2188
USBC Western NY
716-846-4130

NORTH CAROLINA

NC Supreme Ct
919-733-3723
NC Ct/Apps
919-733-3561
USDC Eastern NC
919-856-4370
USDC Middle NC
910-333-5347
USDC Western NC
704-344-6200
USBC Eastern NC
919-237-0248
USBC Middle NC
910-333-5647
USBC Western NC
704-344-6103

NORTH DAKOTA

ND Supreme Ct
701-328-2221
ND Ct/Apps
701-328-2221
USDC
701-250-4295
USBC
701-239-5120

OHIO

OH Supreme Ct
614-466-5201
OH Ct/Apps 1st Dist
513-632-8811
OH Ct/Apps 2d Dist
513-225-4464
OH Ct/Apps 3d Dist
419-223-1861
OH Ct/Apps 4th Dist
614-355-8258
OH Ct/Apps 5th Dist
216-438-0765
OH Ct/Apps 6th Dist
419-245-4755
OH Ct/Apps 7th Dist
216-740-2180
OH Ct/Apps 8th Dist
216-443-6350

OH Ct/Apps 9th Dist
216-643-2250
OH Ct/Apps 10th Dist
614-462-3624
OH Ct/Apps 11th Dist
216-675-2650
OH Ct/Apps 12th Dist
513-425-6609
USCA (6th Cir)
513-684-2953
USDC Northern OH
216-522-4359
USDC Southern OH
614-469-5835
USBC Northern OH
216-522-7555
USBC Southern OH
513-225-7274

OKLAHOMA

OK Supreme Ct
405-521-2163
OK Ct/Crim Apps
405-521-2163
OK Ct/Civ Apps
405-521-2163
USDC Northern OK
918-581-7796
USDC Eastern OK
918-687-2471
USDC Western OK
405-231-4792
USBC Northern OK
918-581-7183
USBC Eastern OK
918-758-0126
USBC Western OK
405-231-5542

OREGON

OR Supreme Ct
503-278-6005
OR Ct/Apps
503-278-6005
USDC
503-326-2202
USBC
503-326-2231

PENNSYLVANIA

PA Supreme Ct
412-565-2816
PA Super Ct
215-560-5801
PA Commonwealth Ct

717-783-1743
USCA (3d Cir)
215-597-2995
USDC Eastern PA
215-597-7704
USDC Middle PA
717-347-1795
USDC Western PA
412-644-3528
USBC Eastern PA
215-597-7704
USBC Middle PA
717-826-6450
USBC Western PA
412-644-2700

PUERTO RICO

USDC
809-766-6477
USBC
809-766-5123

RHODE ISLAND

RI Supreme Ct
401-277-3263
USDC
401-528-5100
USBC
401-528-4487

SOUTH CAROLINA

SC Supreme Ct
803-734-1080
SC Ct/Apps
803-734-1890
USDC
803-765-5816
USBC
803-765-5436

SOUTH DAKOTA

SD Supreme Ct
605-773-3511
USDC
605-338-5566
USBC
605-330-4541

TENNESSEE

TN Supreme Ct
615-594-6700
TN Ct/Crim Apps
615-741-2681
TN Ct/Apps Eastern
615-594-6700

TN Ct/Apps Middle
615-741-2681
TN Ct/Apps Western
901-423-5840
USDC Eastern TN
615-545-4228
USDC Middle TN
615-736-5498
USDC Western TN
901-544-3317
USBC Eastern TN
615-752-5163
USBC Middle TN
615-736-5590
USBC Western TN
901-544-3202

TEXAS

TX Supreme Ct
512-463-1312
TX Ct/Crim Apps
512-463-1551
TX Ct/Civ Apps 1st
713-655-2700
TX Ct/Civ Apps 2d
817-884-1900
TX Ct/Civ Apps 3d
512-463-1733
TX Ct/Civ Apps 4th
210-220-2635
TX Ct/Civ Apps 5th
214-653-7382
TX Ct/Civ Apps 6th
903-798-3046
TX Ct/Civ Apps 7th
806-342-2650
TX Ct/Civ Apps 8th
915-546-2240
TX Ct/Civ Apps 9th
409-835-8402
TX Ct/Civ Apps 10th
817-757-5200
TX Ct/Civ Apps 11th
817-629-2638
TX Ct/Civ Apps 12th
903-593-8471
TX Ct/Civ Apps 13th
512-888-0416
TX Ct/Civ Apps 14th
713-655-2800
USDC Northern TX
214-767-0787
USDC Southern TX
713-250-5500
USDC Eastern TX

903-592-8195
USDC Western TX
210-229-6550
USBC Northern TX
214-767-9180
USBC Southern TX
713-250-5500
USBC Eastern TX
903-592-1212
USBC Western TX
210-229-5187

UTAH

UT Supreme Ct
801-538-1044
UT Ct/Apps
801-578-3950
USDC
801-524-5160
USBC
801-524-5157

VERMONT

VT Supreme Ct
802-828-3276
USDC
802-951-6301
USBC
802-747-7625

VIRGINIA

VA Supreme Ct
804-786-2251
VA Ct/Apps
804-371-8428
USCA (4th Cir)
804-771-2213
USDC Eastern VA
703-557-5127
USDC Western VA
703-857-2224
USBC Eastern VA
908-771-2878
USBC Western VA
703-857-2391

VIRGIN ISLANDS

USDC
809-774-0640

WASHINGTON STATE

WA Supreme Ct
206-357-2077
WA Ct/Apps Div 1
206-464-7750

WA Ct/Apps Div 2
206-593-2970
WA Ct/Apps Div 3
509-456-3082
USDC Eastern WA
509-353-2150
USDC Western WA
206-553-5598
USBC Eastern WA
509-353-2404
USBC Western WA
206-553-2751

WEST VIRGINIA

WVA Ct/Apps
304-558-2601
USDC Northern WVA
304-636-1445
USDC Southern WVA
304-342-5154
USBC Northern WVA
304-233-1655
USBC Southern WVA
304-342-5154

WISCONSIN

WI Supreme Ct
608-266-1880
WI Ct/Apps
698-266-1880
USDC Eastern WI
414-297-3372
USDC Western WI
608-264-5156
USBC Eastern WI
414-297-3293

USBC Western WI
608-264-5158

WYOMING

WY Supreme Ct
307-777-7316
USDC
307-772-2145
USBC
307-772-2191

STATE RESOURCES

ABBREVIATIONS

ADA: Attorney Disciplinary Agency, e.g., Board of Professional Responsibility, State Bar Counsel

BBB: Better Business Bureau in capital or major city in state (900 calls cost 95¢ per minute)

BRA: Bank Regulatory Agency

BSA: To check the Bill Status in Legislature (Assembly)

BSH: To check the Bill Status in Legislature (House)

BSL: To check the Bill Status in Legislature (both houses)

BSS: To check the Bill Status in Legislature (Senate)

CLE: Continuing Legal Education of state bar association

CLU: Civil Liberties Union Office (ACLU state chapter)

CPA: Consumer Protection Agency

CSE: Child Support Enforcement Agency

CVC: Crime Victims Compensation Resources

EEO: Equal Employment Opportunity Office, State

GPO: Government Printing Office (federal) in the State

IRA: Insurance Regulatory Agency

ISG: Information on State Government (phone directory)

LAR: Locating Accident Reports (involving motor vehicles)

LCR: Locating Criminal Records

LSO: Legal Service Office (state coordinating office for legal aid and legal service offices serving the poor; if none, the phone number is for one of the largest offices in state serving the poor)

OCR: Office of Civil Rights

OSO: Office of State Ombudsman (investigates citizen complaints against state agencies)

OWI: Office of Women's Issues in State (civil rights, employment, etc.)

POL: Professional and Occupational Licensing Agency in State

SAG: State Attorney General

SBA: State Bar Association (for phone numbers and addresses of state and local bar associations, see also Appendix C)

SCA: State Court Administration, Office of

SCR: State Corporate Records (mandatory filings of corporations)

SCS: State Civil Service (see also Appendix 2.B at the end of chapter 2)

SLE: State Law Enforcement (state criminal investigations)

SLL: State Law Library or government publications division of large general public library or one of large public law libraries in the state (see also Appendix H, Federal Depository Libraries)

SOS: Secretary of State

SPD: State Public Defender (statewide office or office in one of the state's largest cities)

SRA: Securities Regulatory Agency

STI: State Tourism Information
SUI: State Unemployment Insurance
SVS: State Vital Statistics (information on obtaining birth, death, marriage, and divorce records)
URA: Utilities Regulatory Agency
WCA: Workers Compensation Administration

ALABAMA

ADA:	205-269-1515
BBB:	334-262-5606
BBB:	800-544-4714
BRA:	334-242-3452
BSH:	205-242-7627
BSS:	205-242-7826
CLE:	205-348-6230
CLU:	205-262-0304
CPA:	334-242-7334
CPA:	800-392-5658
CSE:	334-242-9300
CVC:	334-242-4007
GPO:	295-731-1056
IRA:	334-269-3550
ISG:	334-242-8000
LAR:	205-242-4241
LCR:	205-242-4244
LSO:	205-264-1471
OSO:	334-242-7994
SAG:	334-242-7300
SBA:	205-269-1515
SCA:	334-242-0300
SCR:	334-242-5324
SCS:	334-242-3389
SPD:	205-262-4421
SLE:	334-242-4394
SLL:	334-242-4347
SOS:	205-242-7205
SRA:	800-222-1253
STI:	800-ALABAMA
SUI:	334-242-8025
SVS:	334-613-5300
URA:	334-242-5207
URA:	800-392-8050
WCA:	334-242-2868

ALASKA

ADA:	907-272-7469
BBB:	907-562-0704
BRA:	907-465-2521
BRA:	800-770-4833
BSL:	907-465-3867
CLE:	907-272-7469
CLU:	907-276-7133
CPA:	907-276-3550
CVC:	907-465-3040
CSE:	907-269-6800
EEO:	907-269-7495
IRA:	907-465-2515
ISG:	907-269-7460
LAR:	907-465-4335
LCR:	907-269-5765
LSO:	907-276-8282
OCR:	907-276-7474
OSO:	907-465-4970
POL:	907-465-2538
SAG:	907-465-3600
SBA:	907-272-7469
SCA:	907-264-0547
SCR:	907-465-2521
SCS:	907-465-4430
SLE:	907-465-4322
SLL:	907-465-2920
SOS:	907-465-3520
SPD:	907-264-4400
SRA:	907-465-2521
STI:	907-465-2010
SUI:	907-465-2711
SVS:	907-465-3393
URA:	907-276-6222
WCA:	907-465-2790

ARIZONA

ADA:	602-252-4804
BBB:	602-622-7651
BBB:	800-696-2827
BRA:	602-255-4421
BRA:	800-544-0708
BSH:	602-542-4221
BSS:	602-542-3559
CLE:	602-252-4804
CLU:	602-254-3339
CPA:	602-542-3702
CPA:	800-352-8431
CSE:	602-274-7646
CVC:	602-542-4911
EEO:	602-542-3711
IRA:	602-912-8444
ISG:	602-542-4900
LAR:	602-223-2000
LCR:	602-223-2233
LSO:	602-252-3432
OCR:	602-542-5263
OWI:	602-542-1755
SAG:	602-542-4266
SBA:	602-252-4804
SCA:	602-542-9301
SCR:	602-542-3931
SCS:	602-542-5482
SLE:	602-223-2359
SLL:	602-542-3701
SOS:	602-542-0681
SPD:	602-740-5300
SRA:	602-542-4242
STI:	800-842-8257
SUI:	602-542-6578
SVS:	602-255-2501
URA:	602-542-3935
URA:	800-222-7000
WCA:	602-631-2000

ARKANSAS

ADA:	501-664-8658
BBB:	501-664-7274
BBB:	800-482-8448
BRA:	501-324-9019
BSH:	501-375-7771
BSS:	501-682-6107
CLE:	501-375-3957
CLU:	501-374-2660
CPA:	501-682-2341
CPA:	800-482-8982
CSE:	501-682-6169
CVC:	501-682-1323
EEO:	501-682-2242
IRA:	501-686-2945
IRA:	800-852-5494
ISG:	501-682-3000
LAR:	501-221-8236
LCR:	501-221-8233
LSO:	501-376-8015
SAG:	501-682-2007
SBA:	501-375-4605
SCA:	501-376-6655
SCR:	501-682-1010
SCS:	501-682-1823
SLE:	501-221-8200
SLL:	501-682-2869
SOS:	501-682-1010
SPD:	501-340-6120
SRA:	501-324-9260
STI:	800-NATURAL
SUI:	501-682-2121
SVS:	501-661-2371
URA:	501-682-1453
URA:	800-482-1164
WCA:	501-682-3930

CALIFORNIA

ADA:	213-580-5000
ADA:	800-843-9053
BBB:	415-243-9999
BRA:	415-263-8506
BRA:	800-622-0620
BSA:	916-445-3614
BSS:	916-445-4251
CLE:	510-642-3973
CLU:	213-487-1720
CLU:	415-621-2493
CPA:	916-445-1254
CPA:	800-344-9940
CSE:	916-654-1556
CVC:	916-323-3432
EEO:	916-227-2873
GPO:	213-239-9844
GPO:	415-512-2770
IRA:	916-445-5544
IRA:	800-927-4357
ISG:	916-657-9900
LCR:	916-227-3460
LSO:	213-252-3922
LSO:	415-627-0200
OCR:	916-227-2873
OSO:	916-445-0255
OWI:	916-445-3175
POL:	916-445-4465
SAG:	916-324-5437
SBA:	415-561-8200
SCA:	415-396-9100

SCR: 916-657-5448
SCS: 916-322-5193
SLE: 916-324-5437
SLL: 916-654-0069
SOS: 916-653-7244
SPD: 916-322-2676
SRA: 213-736-2741
STI: 800-TO-CALIF
SUI: 916-654-8210
SVS: 916-445-1719
URA: 415-703-3703
URA: 800-649-7570
WCA: 415-975-0700

COLORADO

ADA: 303-893-8121
BBB: 303-758-2212
BRA: 303-894-7575
BSL: 303-866-3055
CLE: 303-860-0608
CLU: 303-861-2258
CPA: 303-866-5189
CSE: 303-866-5994
CVC: 303-239-4402
EEO: 303-894-2997
GPO: 303-844-3964
GPO: 719-544-3142
IRA: 303-894-7499
ISG: 303-866-5000
LAR: 303-623-9463
LCR: 303-239-4208
LSO: 303-837-1321
OCR: 303-894-7830
OSO: 303-866-2885
POL: 303-894-7855
SAG: 303-866-3052
SBA: 303-860-1115
SCA: 303-837-3668
SCR: 303-894-2251
SCS: 303-866-3221
SLE: 303-239-4300
SLL: 303-640-6249
SOS: 303-894-2200
SPD: 303-620-4888
SRA: 303-894-2320
STI: 800-433-2656
SUI: 303-620-4718
SVS: 303-692-2248
URA: 303-894-2000
WCA: 303-620-4700

CONNECTICUT

ADA: 203-566-4163
BBB: 203-374-6161

BRA: 203-240-8299
BRA: 800-831-7225
BSL: 203-240-8888
CLE: 203-721-0025
CLU: 203-247-9823
CPA: 203-566-2534
CPA: 800-842-2649
CSE: 203-424-5251
CVC: 203-529-3089
EEO: 203-566-4895
IRA: 203-297-3998
ISG: 203-566-2211
LAR: 203-238-6637
LCR: 202-238-6151
LSO: 203-297-0760
OCR: 203-566-4895
OWI: 203-566-5702
POL: 203-566-4999
SAG: 203-566-2026
SBA: 203-721-0025
SCA: 203-566-4461
SCR: 203-566-2448
SCS: 203-566-3081
SLE: 203-265-2373
SLL: 860-566-2507
SOS: 203-566-2739
SPD: 203-566-5328
SRA: 203-240-8299
STI: 800-CT-BOUND
SUI: 203-566-4288
SVS: 203-509-7895
URA: 203-827-1553
URA: 800-382-4586
WCA: 203-334-6000

DELAWARE

ADA: 302-571-8703
BBB: 302-996-9200
BRA: 302-739-4235
BRA: 800-638-3376
BSL: 302-739-4471
CLE: 302-658-5278
CLU: 302-654-3966
CPA: 302-727-7120
CSE: 202-577-4800
CVC: 302-995-8383
EEO: 302-577-3950
IRA: 302-739-4251
IRA: 800-282-8611
ISG: 302-251-5030
LAR: 302-739-5931
LCR: 302-739-5880
LSO: 302-575-0660
OCR: 302-577-3485
OSO: 302-577-3210

OWI: 302-761-8005
POL: 302-739-4522
SAG: 302-577-3838
SBA: 302-658-5279
SCA: 302-577-2480
SCR: 302-739-3077
SCS: 302-739-4195
SLE: 302-739-5911
SLL: 302-739-4748
SOS: 302-739-4111
SPD: 302-577-3230
SRA: 302-577-2515
STI: 800-441-8846
SUI: 302-761-8350
SVS: 302-739-4721
URA: 302-739-4247
URA: 800-282-8574
WCA: 302-761-8176

DISTRICT OF COLUMBIA

ADA: 202-638-1501
BBB: 202-393-8000
BRA: 202-727-1563
BSL: 202-724-8050
CLE: 202-223-6600
CLU: 202-457-0800
CPA: 202-727-7120
CSE: 202-724-5610
EEO: 202-939-8780
GPO: 202-512-0132
GPO: 202-653-5075
IRA: 202-727-8000
ISG: 202-727-1000
LAR: 202-727-1159
LCR: 202-879-1372
LSO: 202-682-2700
LSO: 202-628-1161
OCR: 202-939-8780
OWI: 202-939-8083
POL: 202-727-7480
SAG: 202-727-6248
SBA: 202-737-4700
SCA: 202-879-1700
SCS: 202-727-6406
SLE: 202-727-4218
SLL: 202-707-5690
SOS: 202-727-6306
SPD: 202-628-1200
SRA: 202-626-5105
STI: 800-422-8644
SUI: 202-639-1163
SVS: 202-727-0682
URA: 202-626-5125
WCA: 202-576-6265

FLORIDA

ADA: 904-561-5600
ADA: 800-342-8060
ADA: 800-874-0005
BBB: 813-957-0093
BBB: 800-957-0093
BRA: 904-488-0286
BRA: 800-848-3792
BSL: 904-488-4371
CLE: 904-222-5286
CLU: 305-576-2336
CPA: 904-488-2221
CPA: 800-435-7352
CSE: 904-922-9590
CVC: 904-488-0848
EEO: 904-488-7082
GPO: 904-353-0569
IRA: 904-922-3100
IRA: 800-342-2762
ISG: 904-488-1234
LAR: 904-488-5017
LCR: 904-488-6236
LSO: 904-385-7900
OCR: 904-488-5905
OSO: 904-488-8253
OWI: 904-922-0252
POL: 904-488-6982
SAG: 904-487-1963
SBA: 904-561-5600
SCA: 904-922-5081
SCR: 904-487-6000
SCS: 904-922-5449
SLE: 904-488-8771
SLL: 904-487-2651
SOS: 904-922-0234
SPD: 904-488-2458
SRA: 904-488-9805
SRA: 800-372-8792
STI: 904-487-1462
SUI: 904-921-3889
SVS: 904-359-6970
URA: 904-423-6040
URA: 800-342-3552
WCA: 904-488-2514

GEORGIA

ADA: 404-527-8720
BBB: 404-688-4910
BRA: 404-986-1633
BSH: 404-656-5015
BSS: 404-656-5040
CLE: 404-521-0781
CLU: 404-523-5399
CPA: 404-651-8600

CPA: 800-869-1123
CSE: 404-657-3856
CVC: 404-321-4060
EEO: 404-656-1736
GPO: 404-347-1900
IRA: 404-656-2070
ISG: 404-656-2000
LAR: 404-624-7660
LCR: 404-244-2601
LSO: 404-656-6021
OCR: 404-651-9115
POL: 404-656-3900
SAG: 404-656-4585
SBA: 404-527-8755
SCA: 404-656-5171
SCS: 404-656-2705
SLE: 404-244-2501
SLL: 404-656-3468
SOS: 404-656-2881
SPD: 404-656-4585
SRA: 404-656-2894
STI: 800-VISIT-GA
SUI: 404-656-3050
SVS: 404-656-4750
URA: 404-656-4512
URA: 800-282-5813
WCA: 404-656-2034

HAWAII

ADA: 808-521-4591
BBB: 808-942-2355
BRA: 808-586-2820
BSH: 808-586-6400
BSS: 808-586-6720
CLE: 808-956-6551
CLU: 808-545-1722
CPA: 808-586-2636
CSE: 808-587-3698
CVC: 808-587-1143
EEO: 808-586-8636
IRA: 808-586-2790
IRA: 800-586-2790
ISG: 808-586-2211
LCR: 808-587-3106
LSO: 808-536-4302
OCR: 808-586-8636
OSO: 808-587-0770
OWI: 808-586-5758
POL: 808-586-2850
SAG: 808-586-1500
SBA: 808-537-1868
SCA: 808-539-4910
SCR: 808-586-2850
SCS: 808-587-1100

SLE: 808-586-1500
SLL: 808-586-3477
SOS: 808-586-0255
SPD: 808-586-2200
SRA: 808-586-2744
SRA: 800-468-4644
STI: 800-464-2924
SUI: 808-586-9069
SVS: 808-586-4600
URA: 808-586-2020
WCA: 808-586-9151

IDAHO

ADA: 208-342-8958
BBB: 208-342-4649
BRA: 208-334-3313
BSL: 208-334-2475
CLE: 208-342-8958
CLU: 208-344-5243
CPA: 208-334-2424
CPA: 800-432-3545
CSE: 208-334-6515
CVC: 208-334-2400
EEO: 208-334-2873
IRA: 208-334-4320
IRA: 800-721-3272
ISG: 208-334-2411
LAR: 208-334-8101
LCR: 208-327-7130
LSO: 208-336-8980
OCR: 208-334-2873
OWI: 208-334-4673
POL: 208-334-3233
SAG: 208-334-2400
SBA: 208-334-4500
SCA: 208-334-2246
SCR: 208-334-2301
SCS: 208-334-2263
SLE: 208-884-7003
SLL: 208-334-2150
SLL: 208-334-3316
SOS: 208-334-2300
SPD: 208-364-2180
SRA: 208-334-3684
STI: 800-635-7820
SUI: 208-334-6466
SVS: 208-334-5976
URA: 208-334-3912
WCA: 208-334-6000

ILLINOIS

ADA: 312-346-0690
BBB: 900-225-5222

BRA: 217-785-2837
BSL: 217-782-3944
CLE: 217-787-2080
CLU: 312-427-7330
CPA: 217-782-0244
CPA: 800-642-3112
CSE: 219-524-4602
CVC: 217-782-7101
EEO: 312-814-6284
GPO: 312-353-5133
IRA: 217-785-5049
ISG: 217-782-2000
LAR: 217-525-5994
LCR: 217-740-2655
LSO: 312-341-1071
OCR: 312-814-6245
OSO: 217-782-0244
OWI: 217-785-8652
POL: 217-785-0822
SAG: 312-814-2503
SBA: 217-525-1760
SCA: 217-785-2125
SCR: 217-782-4909
SCS: 217-782-3379
SLE: 217-782-4593
SLL: 217-782-7596
SOS: 217-782-2201
SPD: 217-782-7203
SRA: 217-782-2256
SRA: 800-628-7937
STI: 800-223-0121
SUI: 312-793-5700
SVS: 217-782-6554
URA: 217-782-7907
WCA: 312-814-6556

INDIANA

ADA: 317-232-1807
BBB: 800-637-2188
BBB: 800-552-4631
BRA: 317-232-3955
BRA: 800-382-4880
BSL: 317-232-9856
CLE: 317-637-9102
CLU: 317-635-4059
CPA: 317-232-6330
CPA: 800-382-5516
CSE: 317-232-4894
CVC: 317-232-7103
EEO: 317-232-8029
IRA: 317-232-2395
IRA: 800-622-4461
ISG: 317-232-1000
LAR: 317-232-8286

LCR: 317-232-8262
LSO: 317-631-9410
OCR: 317-232-2600
OWI: 317-276-0313
POL: 317-232-3997
SAG: 317-233-4386
SBA: 317-639-5465
SCA: 317-232-2542
SCR: 317-232-6587
SCS: 317-232-3059
SLE: 317-232-8241
SLL: 317-232-3679
SLL: 317-232-2557
SOS: 317-232-6536
SPD: 317-232-2475
SRA: 317-232-6681
SRA: 800-223-8791
STI: 800-289-6646
SUI: 317-233-5661
SVS: 317-383-6701
URA: 317-232-2701
URA: 800-851-4268
WCA: 317-232-3808

IOWA

ADA: 515-243-3179
BBB: 515-243-8137
BRA: 515-285-4014
BSH: 515-281-5381
BSL: 515-281-4961
BSS: 515-281-5308
CLE: 515-243-3179
CPA: 515-281-5926
CSE: 515-281-5767
CVC: 515-281-5044
EEO: 515-281-4121
IRA: 515-281-4025
ISG: 515-281-5011
LAR: 515-237-3070
LCR: 515-281-5138
LSO: 515-243-2151
OCR: 515-281-4121
OSO: 515-281-3592
OWI: 515-281-4467
POL: 515-281-5602
SAG: 515-281-3053
SBA: 515-243-3179
SCA: 515-281-5241
SCR: 515-281-5204
SCS: 515-281-3351
SLE: 515-281-6203
SLL: 515-281-4102
SOS: 515-281-5204
SPD: 515-281-8841

SRA: 515-281-4441
STI: 800-345-IOWA
SUI: 515-281-4986
SVS: 515-281-6762
URA: 515-281-5979
WCA: 515-281-5934

KANSAS

ADA: 913-296-2486
BBB: 913-232-0454
BRA: 913-296-2266
BSL: 913-296-5292
CLE: 913-234-5696
CPA: 913-296-3751
CPA: 800-432-2310
CSE: 913-296-3237
CVC: 913-296-2359
EEO: 913-296-5000
IRA: 913-296-7829
IRA: 800-432-2484
ISG: 913-296-0111
LAR: 913-296-3671
LCR: 913-232-6000
LSO: 913-233-2068
OCR: 913-296-3206
OSO: 913-296-3232
POL: 913-296-3053
SAG: 913-296-2215
SBA: 913-234-5696
SCA: 913-296-4873
SCR: 913-296-4564
SCS: 913-296-4278
SLE: 913-296-8200
SLL: 913-296-3296
SLL: 913-296-3257
SOS: 913-296-4575
SPD: 913-296-1833
SRA: 913-296-3307
STI: 800-2-KANSAS
SUI: 913-296-2118
SVS: 913-296-1414
URA: 913-271-3166
URA: 800-662-0027
WCA: 913-296-3441

KENTUCKY

ADA: 502-564-3795
BBB: 502-583-6546
BBB: 800-388-2222
BRA: 502-564-3390
BSL: 502-564-8100
CLE: 502-583-5314
CLU: 502-581-1181

CPA: 502-564-2200
CPA: 800-432-9257
CSE: 502-564-2285
CVC: 502-564-2290
EEO: 502-595-4024
IRA: 502-564-6088
ISG: 502-564-3130
LAR: 502-227-8700
LCR: 502-227-8717
LSO: 606-233-3057
OCR: 502-595-4024
OSO: 502-564-5497
OWI: 502-564-6643
POL: 502-564-3296
SAG: 502-564-7600
SBA: 502-564-3795
SCA: 502-573-2350
SCR: 502-564-3490
SCS: 502-564-4460
SLE: 502-695-6300
SLL: 502-564-4848
SOS: 502-564-3490
SPD: 502-564-5213
SRA: 502-573-3390
STI: 800-225-TRIP
SUI: 502-564-2900
SVS: 502-564-4212
URA: 502-564-3940
URA: 800-772-4636
WCA: 502-564-5500

LOUISIANA

ADA: 504-523-1414
BBB: 504-528-9277
BRA: 504-925-4660
BSH: 504-342-2395
BSS: 504-342-6245
CLE: 504-566-1600
CLE: 800-421-5722
CLU: 504-522-0617
CPA: 504-342-9638
CSE: 504-342-0286
CVC: 504-342-7013
IRA: 504-342-1259
ISG: 504-342-6600
LAR: 504-925-6156
LCR: 504-925-6095
LSO: 504-525-2996
OCR: 504-342-1532
OSO: 504-925-7956
OWI: 504-922-0960
POL: 504-342-0138
SAG: 504-342-7013
SBA: 504-566-1600

SCA: 504-568-5747
SCR: 504-342-4479
SCS: 504-342-8272
SLE: 504-342-6744
SLL: 504-342-4912
SOS: 504-342-4479
SPD: 504-342-7013
SRA: 504-568-5515
STI: 800-33-GUMBO
SUI: 504-342-3013
SVS: 504-586-8353
URA: 504-342-6687
URA: 800-256-2413
WCA: 504-342-7558

MAINE

ADA: 207-622-1121
BBB: 207-878-2715
BRA: 207-624-8570
BSL: 207-289-1692
CLE: 207-622-7523
CLU: 207-774-5444
CPA: 207-624-8527
CPA: 800-332-8529
CSE: 207-287-2886
EEO: 207-624-6050
IRA: 207-582-8707
IRA: 800-300-5000
ISG: 207-582-9500
LAR: 207-287-3397
LCR: 207-624-7009
LSO: 207-774-4753
OCR: 207-624-6050
POL: 207-624-8603
SAG: 207-626-8800
SBA: 207-622-7523
SCA: 207-822-0793
SCS: 207-287-3761
SLE: 207-626-8800
SOS: 207-626-8400
SLL: 207-287-1600
SLL: 207-287-5600
SRA: 207-582-8760
STI: 800-533-9595
SUI: 207-287-3377
SVS: 207-624-5445
URA: 207-287-3831
URA: 800-452-4699
WCA: 207-287-3751

MARYLAND

ADA: 410-474-7841
ADA: 800-492-1660
BBB: 900-225-5222

BRA: 410-333-6812
BSL: 410-841-3787
BSL: 800-492-7122
CLE: 410-328-6730
CLU: 410-889-8555
CPA: 410-528-8662
CSE: 410-767-7606
EEO: 410-767-8561
GPO: 301-953-7974
IRA: 410-333-1782
IRA: 800-492-6116
ISG: 410-841-3886
LAR: 410-298-3390
LCR: 410-764-4501
LSO: 410-539-5340
OCR: 410-767-8561
OWI: 410-767-7137
POL: 410-333-6200
SAG: 301-576-6300
SBA: 410-685-7878
SCA: 410-974-2141
SCR: 410-225-1184
SCS: 410-225-4715
SLE: 410-653-4219
SLL: 410-974-3395
SOS: 410-974-2229
SPD: 410-767-8479
SRA: 410-576-6360
STI: 800-543-1036
SUI: 410-767-2000
SVS: 410-767-0158
URA: 410-767-8000
URA: 800-492-0474
WCA: 410-767-0829

MASSACHUSETTS

ADA: 617-357-1860
BBB: 617-426-9000
BBB: 800-4BBB-811
BRA: 617-727-2102
BRA: 800-495-BANK
BSH: 617-722-2356
BSS: 617-722-1276
CLE: 617-482-2205
CLU: 617-482-3170
CPA: 617-727-2200
CSE: 617-577-7200
CVC: 617-727-5200
EEO: 617-727-7441
GPO: 617-720-4180
IRA: 617-521-7777
ISG: 617-727-2121
LAR: 617-351-9000
LCR: 617-727-0090

LSO: 617-357-5757
OCR: 617-727-3990
OSO: 617-727-6250
OWI: 617-727-3040
POL: 617-727-3074
SAG: 617-727-2200
SBA: 617-542-3602
SCA: 617-727-8383
SCR: 617-727-2800
SCS: 617-727-1556
SLE: 508-820-2350
SLL: 617-727-6279
SOS: 617-727-9180
SPD: 617-482-6212
SRA: 617-269-5428
SRA: 800-269-5428
STI: 800-447-MASS
SUI: 617-626-6600
SVS: 617-753-8600
URA: 617-727-3500
WCA: 617-727-4900

MICHIGAN

ADA: 313-961-6585
BBB: 810-644-9100
BBB: 800-684-3222
BRA: 517-373-3460
BSH: 517-373-0135
BSL: 517-373-0170
BSS: 517-373-2400
CLE: 313-764-0533
CLE: 800-922-6516
CLU: 313-961-4462
CPA: 517-373-1140
CSE: 517-373-0130
CVC: 517-373-7373
EEO: 517-373-3020
GPO: 313-226-7816
IRA: 517-373-0240
ISG: 517-373-1837
LAR: 517-322-6092
LCR: 517-322-1955
LSO: 313-964-4130
OCR: 517-335-3164
OWI: 517-373-2884
POL: 517-373-1253
SAG: 517-373-1110
SBA: 517-372-9030
SCA: 517-373-0130
SCR: 517-334-6212
SCS: 517-373-3020
SLE: 517-336-6157
SLL: 517-373-1300
SOS: 517-373-2510

SPD: 313-256-9833
SRA: 517-334-6212
STI: 800-543-2YES
SUI: 313-876-5000
SVS: 517-335-8676
URA: 517-334-6445
URA: 800-292-9555
WCA: 517-373-3480

MINNESOTA

ADA: 612-296-3952
ADA: 800-657-3601
BBB: 612-699-1111
BRA: 612-296-2135
BSH: 612-296-6646
BSS: 612-296-0504
CLE: 612-339-6453
CLU: 612-522-2824
CPA: 612-296-3353
CSE: 612-297-9232
CVC: 612-266-6642
EEO: 612-296-5665
IRA: 612-296-2488
ISG: 612-296-6013
LAR: 612-296-2045
LCR: 612-642-0673
LSO: 612-332-1441
OCR: 612-296-5665
OSO: 612-296-6196
OWI: 612-296-8590
POL: 612-296-3528
SAG: 612-296-6196
SBA: 612-333-1183
SCA: 612-296-2474
SCR: 612-296-2097
SCS: 612-296-8366
SLE: 612-642-0600
SLL: 612-296-2775
SOS: 612-296-2079
SPD: 612-627-6980
SRA: 612-296-4026
STI: 800-657-3700
SUI: 612-296-1692
SVS: 612-623-5121
URA: 612-296-7124
URA: 800-657-3782
WCA: 612-296-6490

MISSISSIPPI

ADA: 601-946-4471
BBB: 601-987-8282
BRA: 601-359-1031
BRA: 800-844-2499

BSH: 601-359-3358
BSL: 601-359-3719
BSS: 601-359-3229
CLE: 601-948-4471
CLU: 601-355-6465
CPA: 601-359-4230
CPA: 800-281-4418
CSE: 601-359-4861
CVC: 601-359-6766
IRA: 601-359-3569
IRA: 800-562-2957
ISG: 601-359-1000
LAR: 601-987-1260
LSO: 601-944-0765
POL: 601-359-1350
SAG: 601-359-3692
SBA: 601-948-4471
SCA: 601-359-3697
SCR: 601-359-1350
SCS: 601-359-2704
SLE: 601-987-1490
SLL: 601-359-1036
SLL: 601-359-3672
SOS: 601-359-1350
SPD: 601-969-7156
SRA: 601-359-6371
STI: 800-927-6378
SUI: 602-354-8711
SVS: 601-960-7982
URA: 601-961-5400
URA: 800-356-6428
URA: 800-356-6429
URA: 800-356-6430
WCA: 601-987-4200

MISSOURI

ADA: 314-635-7400
BBB: 314-531-3300
BBB: 800-497-4222
BRA: 314-751-3242
BRA: 800-722-3321
BSH: 314-751-2979
BSL: 314-751-4633
BSS: 314-751-4666
CLE: 314-635-4128
CLU: 314-361-2111
CPA: 314-751-3321
CPA: 800-392-8222
CSE: 573-751-4301
CVC: 573-526-6006
EEO: 573-751-3325
GPO: 816-765-2256
IRA: 314-751-2640
IRA: 800-726-7390

ISG: 573-889-2011
LAR: 314-751-3313
LCR: 314-751-3313
LSO: 314-367-1700
OCR: 573-751-3325
OSO: 573-751-3222
OWI: 573-751-0810
POL: 573-751-1081
SAG: 573-751-3321
SBA: 314-635-4128
SCA: 573-751-3585
SCR: 573-751-3200
SCS: 573-751-3053
SLE: 573-751-4905
SLL: 573-751-3615
SOS: 573-751-4936
SPD: 573-526-5210
SRA: 314-751-4136
SRA: 800-751-4136
STI: 800-877-1234
SUI: 573-751-3643
SVS: 573-751-6383
URA: 314-751-3243
URA: 800-392-4211
WCA: 573-751-4231

MONTANA

ADA: 406-444-2608
BRA: 406-444-2091
BSL: 406-444-3064
CLE: 406-442-7660
CLU: 406-248-1086
CPA: 406-444-4312
CSE: 406-444-6856
CVC: 406-444-3653
EEO: 406-444-2284
IRA: 406-444-2040
IRA: 800-332-6148
ISG: 406-444-2511
LAR: 406-444-3278
LCR: 406-444-3625
LSO: 406-442-9830
OCR: 406-444-2884
OSO: 406-444-3468
OWI: 406-444-3111
POL: 406-444-3737
SAG: 406-444-2026
SBA: 406-442-7660
SCA: 406-444-2621
SCR: 406-444-3665
SCS: 496-444-3871
SLE: 406-444-2026
SLL: 406-444-3636
SOS: 406-444-2034

SPD: 406-444-4122
SRA: 406-444-2040
SRA: 800-332-6148
STI: 800-228-4307
SUI: 406-444-3555
SVS: 406-444-2614
URA: 406-444-6199
WCA: 406-444-6518

NEBRASKA

ADA: 402-475-7091
ADA: 800-927-0117
BBB: 402-476-8855
BRA: 402-471-2171
BSL: 402-471-2271
CLE: 402-475-7091
CLU: 402-476-8091
CPA: 402-471-2682
CSE: 402-471-9626
CVC: 402-471-2194
EEO: 402-471-2024
IRA: 402-471-4642
ISG: 402-471-2311
LAR: 402-479-4645
LCR: 402-471-4545
LSO: 402-435-2161
OCR: 402-471-2024
OSO: 402-471-2035
OWI: 402-471-2039
POL: 402-471-2115
SAG: 402-471-2682
SBA: 402-475-7091
SCA: 402-471-3730
SCR: 402-471-4079
SCS: 402-471-2075
SLE: 402-471-4545
SLL: 402-471-3189
SOS: 402-471-2554
SPD: 402-441-7631
SRA: 402-471-3445
STI: 800-228-4307
SUI: 402-475-8451
SVS: 402-471-2873
URA: 402-471-3101
URA: 800-526-0017
WCA: 402-471-2568

NEVADA

ADA: 702-322-8999
BBB: 702-735-6900
BRA: 702-687-4260
BSA: 702-687-5742
CLE: 702-329-4100
CLU: 702-366-1226

CPA: 702-486-7355
CPA: 800-992-0900
CSE: 702-687-4128
CVC: 702-486-6492
EEO: 702-486-7161
IRA: 702-687-4270
IRA: 800-992-0900
ISG: 702-687-5000
LAR: 702-687-5300
LCR: 702-687-5203
LSO: 702-386-1070
OCR: 702-486-7161
OSO: 702-687-6300
SAG: 702-687-4170
SBA: 702-382-2200
SCA: 702-687-5076
SCR: 702-687-5203
SCS: 702-687-4050
SLE: 702-687-4412
SLL: 702-687-5160
SOS: 702-687-5203
GPD: 702-687-4880
SRA: 702-486-2440
STI: 800-NEVADA-8
SUI: 702-687-4635
SVS: 702-687-4740
URA: 702-486-2600
WCA: 702-687-5284

NEW HAMPSHIRE

ADA: 603-224-5828
BBB: 603-224-1991
BRA: 603-271-3561
BSH: 603-271-2548
BSL: 603-271-2239
BSS: 603-271-3420
CLE: 603-224-6942
CLU: 603-225-3080
CPA: 603-271-3641
CSE: 603-271-4427
CVC: 603-271-3671
EEO: 603-271-2767
IRA: 603-271-2261
ISG: 603-271-1110
LAR: 603-271-2128
LCR: 603-271-2535
LSO: 603-225-4700
OCR: 603-271-2767
OWI: 603-271-2660
POL: 603-271-3242
SAG: 603-271-3655
SBA: 603-224-6942
SCA: 603-271-2521
SCR: 603-271-3242

SCS: 603-271-3261
SLE: 603-271-2575
SLL: 603-271-3777
SOS: 603-271-3242
SPD: 603-224-1236
SRA: 603-271-1463
STI: 800-258-3608
SUI: 603-224-3311
SVS: 603-271-4651
URA: 603-271-2431
URA: 800-855-1155
WCA: 603-271-3174

NEW JERSEY

ADA: 609-292-8750
BBB: 609-588-0808
BRA: 609-292-3420
BSL: 609-292-4840
CLE: 908-249-5100
CLU: 201-642-2086
CPA: 201-504-6534
CSE: 609-588-2401
CVC: 201-648-2107
EEO: 609-777-0919
IRA: 609-984-2444
ISG: 609-292-2121
LAR: 609-882-2000
LCR: 609-882-2000
LSO: 609-292-6262
OCR: 609-984-3100
OSO: 609-292-7087
OWI: 609-292-8840
POL: 201-504-6200
SAG: 609-292-4925
SBA: 908-249-5000
SCA: 609-984-0275
SCR: 609-530-6400
SCS: 609-292-4144
SLE: 609-292-8740
SLL: 609-292-6259
SOS: 609-777-2535
SPD: 609-292-8827
SRA: 201-504-3600
STI: 800-JERSEY-7
SUI: 609-292-2460
SVS: 609-292-8085
URA: 201-648-2027
URA: 800-621-0241
WCA: 609-292-2414

NEW MEXICO

ADA: 505-842-5781
BBB: 505-844-0500
BBB: 800-873-2224

BRA: 505-827-7100
BSL: 505-986-4600
CLE: 505-842-6132
CLE: 800-432-6976
CLU: 505-266-5915
CPA: 505-827-6060
CPA: 800-678-1508
CSE: 505-827-7200
CVC: 505-841-9437
EEO: 505-827-6838
IRA: 505-827-4648
IRA: 800-947-4722
ISG: 800-825-6639
LAR: 505-827-9300
LCR: 505-827-9181
LSO: 505-243-6282
OCR: 505-827-6838
OSO: 505-827-3050
OWI: 505-841-8921
POL: 505-827-7199
SAG: 505-827-6000
SBA: 505-842-6132
SCA: 505-827-4800
SCR: 505-827-4202
SCS: 505-827-8120
SLE: 505-827-9003
SLL: 505-827-3824
SOS: 505-827-3600
SPD: 505-827-3900
SRA: 505-827-7140
STI: 800-545-2040
SUI: 505-841-8657
SVS: 505-827-0121
URA: 505-827-6940
WCA: 505-841-6000

NEW YORK

ADA: 518-474-8816
BBB: 900-225-5222
BRA: 212-618-6642
BRA: 800-522-3330
BSL: 518-455-7506
CLE: 518-463-3200
CLE: 800-582-2452
CLU: 212-944-9800
CLU: 212-382-0557
CPA: 518-474-5481
CPA: 800-788-9898
CSE: 518-474-9081
CVC: 518-457-8658
EEO: 518-457-3701
GPO: 212-264-3825
IRA: 212-602-2488
IRA: 800-342-3736

ISG: 518-474-2121
LAR: 518-474-2381
LCR: 518-457-6043
LSO: 212-431-7200
OCR: 212-961-8400
OSO: 518-474-0050
OWI: 212-417-5842
POL: 518-473-4909
SAG: 518-474-7330
SBA: 518-463-3200
SCA: 518-474-7469
SCR: 518-474-0050
SCS: 518-457-3701
SLE: 518-457-6721
SLL: 518-474-5355
SOS: 518-474-0050
SPD: 518-474-7330
SRA: 212-416-8200
STI: 800-CALL-NYS
SUI: 518-457-2741
SVS: 518-474-3077
URA: 518-474-2530
URA: 800-342-3377
WCA: 718-802-6666

NORTH CAROLINA

ADA: 919-828-4620
BBB: 704-527-0012
BBB: 800-222-0950
BRA: 919-733-3016
BSL: 919-733-7779
CLE: 919-828-0561
CLU: 919-273-1641
CPA: 919-733-7741
CSE: 919-571-4120
CVC: 919-733-7974
EEO: 919-733-0205
IRA: 919-733-2004
IRA: 800-662-7777
ISG: 919-733-1110
LAR: 919-733-7250
LCR: 919-662-4500
LSO: 919-856-2121
OCR: 919-733-7996
OSO: 919-733-5017
OWI: 919-733-2455
SAG: 919-733-3377
SBA: 919-828-4620
SCA: 919-733-7107
SCR: 919-733-4201
SCS: 919-733-7108
SLE: 919-662-4500
SLL: 919-733-3270
SOS: 919-733-5140

SPD: 919-560-3282
SRA: 919-733-3924
SRA: 800-688-4507
STI: 800-VISIT-NC
SUI: 919-733-7546
SVS: 919-733-3000
URA: 919-733-4249
WCA: 919-733-4820

NORTH DAKOTA

ADA: 701-224-3348
BRA: 701-328-9933
BSL: 701-224-2916
CLE: 701-255-1404
CLU: 701-280-2349
CPA: 701-224-2210
CPA: 800-472-2600
CSE: 701-328-5493
CVC: 701-328-6390
EEO: 701-328-2660
IRA: 701-328-3548
IRA: 800-247-0560
ISG: 701-328-2000
LAR: 701-224-2603
LCR: 701-221-5500
LSO: 701-222-2110
OCR: 701-328-2660
OWI: 701-258-2251
POL: 701-328-2905
SAG: 701-328-2210
SBA: 701-255-1404
SCA: 701-328-2221
SCR: 701-328-4284
SCS: 701-328-3290
SLE: 701-328-6180
SLL: 701-328-4622
SOS: 701-328-2900
SRA: 701-224-2910
SRA: 800-297-5124
STI: 800-435-5663
SUI: 701-328-2833
SVS: 701-328-2360
URA: 701-328-2400
WCA: 701-328-3800

OHIO

ADA: 614-461-0256
ADA: 800-589-5256
BBB: 614-486-6336
BBB: 800-362-0494
BRA: 614-466-2932
BSL: 614-466-8842
CLE: 614-487-2050
CLE: 614-487-8585

CLU: 614-228-8951
CPA: 614-466-4986
CPA: 800-282-0515
CSE: 614-752-6561
CVC: 614-466-5610
EEO: 614-752-9271
GPO: 216-522-4922
GPO: 614-469-6956
IRA: 614-644-2473
IRA: 800-522-0071
ISG: 614-466-2000
LAR: 614-752-1575
LCR: 614-466-8204
LSO: 614-299-6364
OCR: 614-466-2785
OWI: 614-466-4496
POL: 614-644-7053
SAG: 614-466-3376
SBA: 614-487-2050
SCA: 614-466-2653
SCR: 614-466-3084
SCS: 614-466-3455
SLE: 614-466-3375
SLL: 614-644-7051
SOS: 614-466-2655
SPD: 614-466-5394
SRA: 614-644-7381
STI: 800-BUCKEYE
SUI: 614-466-8032
SVS: 614-466-2533
URA: 614-466-3292
URA: 800-686-7826
WCA: 614-466-8751

OKLAHOMA

ADA: 405-524-2365
BBB: 405-239-6081
BRA: 405-521-2783
BSH: 405-524-2711
BSS: 405-524-5668
CLE: 405-524-2365
CLE: 800-522-8065
CLU: 405-524-8511
CPA: 405-521-4274
CSE: 405-521-3646
CVC: 405-521-5811
EEO: 405-521-2177
IRA: 405-521-2991
IRA: 800-522-0071
ISG: 405-521-2011
LAR: 405-425-2193
LCR: 405-848-6724
LSO: 405-557-0020
OCR: 405-521-3441

OWI: 918-581-2801
SAG: 405-521-3921
SBA: 405-524-2365
SCA: 405-521-2318
SCR: 405-521-3911
SCS: 405-521-2177
SLE: 405-425-2424
SLL: 405-521-2502
SOS: 405-521-3911
SPD: 405-329-4222
SRA: 405-235-0230
STI: 800-652-OKLA
SUI: 405-557-7200
SVS: 405-271-8056
URA: 405-521-2267
URA: 800-522-8154
WCA: 405-557-7600

OREGON

ADA: 503-620-0222
ADA: 800-452-8260
BBB: 800-488-4166
BRA: 503-378-4140
BSL: 503-378-1233
CLE: 503-620-0222
CLE: 800-452-8260
CLU: 503-227-3186
CPA: 503-378-4732
CSE: 503-986-6083
CVC: 503-378-5348
EEO: 503-731-4873
GPO: 503-221-6217
IRA: 503-378-4636
ISG: 503-378-3131
LAR: 503-945-5000
LCR: 503-378-3070
LSO: 503-234-1534
OCR: 503-731-4873
OSO: 503-378-5116
OWI: 503-725-5889
POL: 503-378-4100
SAG: 503-378-6002
SBA: 503-620-0222
SCA: 503-986-5900
SCR: 503-986-2205
SCS: 503-378-3020
SLE: 503-378-3720
SLL: 503-378-4277
SOS: 503-378-4139
SPD: 503-378-3349
SRA: 503-378-4387
STI: 800-547-7842
SUI: 503-378-3208
SVS: 503-731-4109

URA: 503-378-6611
URA: 800-522-2404
WCA: 503-945-7500

PENNSYLVANIA

ADA: 717-731-7038
BBB: 412-456-2700
BBB: 800-225-5222
BRA: 717-787-6991
BRA: 800-PA-BANKS
BSL: 717-787-3392
CLE: 717-238-6715
CLE: 800-932-4637
CLU: 215-592-1513
CPA: 717-787-9707
CPA: 800-441-2555
CSE: 717-783-8729
CVC: 717-783-5153
EEO: 717-783-1130
GPO: 215-636-1900
GPO: 412-644-2721
IRA: 717-787-2317
ISG: 717-787-2121
LAR: 717-783-5516
LCR: 717-783-5592
LSO: 717-236-9486
OCR: 717-787-4410
OWI: 717-787-8128
POL: 717-783-7194
SAG: 717-787-3391
SBA: 717-238-6715
SCA: 215-560-6337
SCR: 717-783-9210
SCS: 717-787-5545
SLE: 717-783-5558
SLL: 717-787-2327
SOS: 717-787-7630
SPD: 717-255-2746
SRA: 717-787-8061
SRA: 800-600-0007
STI: 800-VISIT-PA
SUI: 717-787-1745
SVS: 412-656-3100
URA: 717-783-7349
URA: 800-782-1110
WCA: 717-783-5421

PUERTO RICO

ADA: 809-721-3358
BBB: 809-756-5400
BRA: 809-723-3131
CLE: 809-727-1930
CPA: 809-721-0940
CPA: 809-721-2900

CSE: 787-767-1500
EEO: 787-754-2105
IRA: 809-722-8686
LSO: 809-728-8686
OCR: 787-764-8779
OSO: 787-724-7373
OWI: 787-722-2907
POL: 787-722-2122
SAG: 809-721-7700
SBA: 809-721-3358
SCA: 787-763-3358
SCS: 787-721-4300
SLE: 787-724-7000
SOS: 787-723-4344
SRA: 809-723-3131
SUI: 787-754-5375
SVS: 787-726-1027
URA: 809-758-6264

RHODE ISLAND

ADA: 401-277-3270
BBB: 401-785-1213
BRA: 401-277-2405
BSL: 401-277-3580
CLU: 401-831-7171
CPA: 401-274-4400
CPA: 800-852-7776
CSE: 401-464-2421
CVC: 401-274-4400
EEO: 401-227-3090
IRA: 401-277-2233
ISG: 401-277-2000
LAR: 401-444-1143
LCR: 401-274-2238
LSO: 401-331-4665
OCR: 401-277-2080
OSO: 401-277-2080
OWI: 401-277-6105
POL: 401-277-2827
SAG: 401-274-4400
SBA: 401-421-5740
SCA: 401-277-2251
SCR: 401-277-3040
SCS: 401-277-2160
SLE: 401-444-1111
SLL: 401-277-3275
SOS: 401-277-2357
SPD: 401-274-4400
SRA: 401-277-3048
STI: 800-556-2484
SUI: 401-277-3649
SVS: 401-277-2812
URA: 800-341-1000
WCA: 401-277-3097

SOUTH CAROLINA

ADA: 803-734-2038
BBB: 803-254-2525
BRA: 803-734-2001
BSL: 803-737-2923
CLE: 803-799-6653
CLU: 803-799-5151
CPA: 803-734-3970
CSE: 803-734-5760
CVC: 803-737-8125
EEO: 803-737-4812
IRA: 803-737-6150
IRA: 800-768-3467
ISG: 803-734-1000
LAR: 803-251-2969
LCR: 807-337-9000
LSO: 802-352-0034
OCR: 802-353-6336
OSO: 803-734-0457
OWI: 803-734-9144
POL: 803-734-9600
SAG: 803-734-3970
SBA: 803-799-6653
SCA: 803-734-1800
SCR: 803-734-2170
SCS: 803-737-0900
SLE: 803-896-7136
SLL: 803-734-8666
SOS: 803-734-2170
SPD: 803-734-1330
SRA: 803-734-1087
STI: 800-868-2492
SUI: 803-737-2617
SVS: 803-734-4810
URA: 803-737-5110
URA: 800-922-1531
WCA: 803-737-5744

SOUTH DAKOTA

ADA: 605-224-0282
BRA: 605-773-3421
BSL: 605-773-4498
CLE: 605-224-7554
CPA: 605-773-4400
CPA: 800-300-1986
CSE: 605-773-3641
CVC: 605-773-3478
EEO: 605-773-3148
IRA: 605-773-3563
ISG: 605-773-3011
LAR: 605-773-3868
LCR: 605-773-3331
LSO: 605-342-7171

LSO: 605-224-6274
OCR: 605-773-4493
OSO: 605-773-3661
POL: 605-773-3178
SAG: 605-773-3215
SBA: 605-224-7554
SCA: 604-733-3474
SCS: 605-773-3148
SLE: 605-773-3332
SLL: 605-773-3131
SOS: 605-773-3537
SPD: 605-394-2181
SRA: 605-773-4823
STI: 800-732-5682
SUI: 605-622-2340
SVS: 605-773-3361
URA: 605-773-3201
URA: 800-332-1782
WCA: 605-773-3101

TENNESSEE

ADA: 615-361-7500
BBB: 615-242-4222
BBB: 901-795-1300
BRA: 615-741-2236
BSH: 615-361-7500
BSL: 615-741-3511
CLE: 615-383-7421
CLU: 615-320-7142
BSS: 615-741-2730
CPA: 615-741-3491
CPA: 800-342-8385
CSE: 615-741-3241
CVC: 615-741-7328
EEO: 615-741-2649
IRA: 615-741-2218
IRA: 800-342-4029
ISG: 615-741-3011
LAR: 615-741-3954
LCR: 615-741-0430
LSO: 615-244-6610
OCR: 615-741-5825
POL: 615-741-3449
SAG: 615-741-3492
SBA: 615-383-7421
SCA: 615-741-2687
SCR: 615-741-0584
SCS: 615-741-2958
SLE: 615-741-0430
SLL: 615-741-2561
SOS: 615-741-2819
SPD: 615-741-5562
SRA: 800-863-9177
STI: 800-636-7600

SUI: 615-741-2131
SVS: 615-532-2600
URA: 615-741-3668
URA: 800-342-8359
WCA: 615-741-2395

TEXAS

ADA: 512-463-1400
BBB: 512-445-2911
BBB: 800-592-4433
BRA: 512-475-1300
BSL: 512-463-1252
CLE: 512-463-1437
CLU: 512-477-5849
CPA: 512-463-2070
CSE: 512-463-2181
CVC: 512-463-1929
EEO: 512-837-8534
GPO: 214-767-0076
GPO: 713-228-1187
IRA: 512-463-6464
IRA: 800-252-3439
ISG: 512-463-4630
LAR: 512-465-2296
LCR: 512-465-2079
LSO: 512-476-7244
OCR: 512-837-8534
OSO: 512-463-1782
OWI: 512-475-2615
POL: 512-463-3173
SAG: 512-463-2100
SBA: 512-463-1400
SBA: 800-204-2222
SCA: 512-463-1625
SCR: 512-466-3570
SCS: 512-479-4700
SLE: 512-465-2000
SLL: 512-463-1722
SOS: 512-463-5701
SPD: 915-546-8185
SRA: 512-305-8300
STI: 800-8888-TEX
SUI: 512-463-2652
SVS: 512-458-7111
URA: 512-458-0100
WCA: 512-448-7962

UTAH

ADA: 801-531-9077
BBB: 801-487-4656
BBB: 800-456-3907
BRA: 801-538-8830
BSL: 801-538-1032
CLE: 801-531-9077

CLU: 801-521-9289
CPA: 801-530-6001
CPA: 800-721-7233
CSE: 801-536-8901
CVC: 801-533-4000
EEO: 801-530-6921
IRA: 801-538-3874
IRA: 800-439-3805
ISG: 801-538-3000
LAR: 801-965-4428
LCR: 801-965-4561
LSO: 801-328-8891
OCR: 801-530-6921
OSO: 801-538-1000
OWI: 801-538-3027
POL: 801-530-6039
SAG: 801-538-1149
SBA: 801-531-9077
SCA: 801-538-3806
SCR: 801-530-6027
SCS: 801-538-3080
SLE: 801-965-4463
SLL: 801-466-5888
SOS: 801-538-1520
SPD: 801-532-5444
SRA: 800-721-SAFE
STI: 800-200-1160
SUI: 801-536-7423
SVS: 801-538-6360
URA: 801-530-6716
WCA: 801-538-6800

VERMONT

ADA: 802-828-3368
BBB: 617-426-9000
BBB: 800-4BBB-811
BRA: 802-828-3301
BSL: 802-828-2231
CLE: 802-223-2020
CLU: 802-223-6304
CPA: 802-828-3171
CSE: 802-241-2319
CVC: 802-828-3374
EEO: 802-241-2450
IRA: 802-828-4884
ISG: 802-828-1110
LAR: 802-828-2050
LCR: 802-244-8727
LSO: 802-863-5620
OCR: 802-828-3171
OSO: 802-828-3333
OWI: 802-828-2851
POL: 802-828-2363
SAG: 802-828-3171
SBA: 802-223-2020

SCA: 802-828-3278
SCR: 802-828-2386
SCS: 802-828-3491
SLE: 802-244-8781
SLL: 802-828-3268
SOS: 802-828-2148
SPD: 802-828-3168
SRA: 802-828-3420
STI: 800-837-6668
SUI: 802-828-4100
SVS: 802-863-7275
URA: 802-828-2358
WCA: 802-828-2286

VIRGINIA

ADA: 804-775-0500
BBB: 804-648-0016
BRA: 804-371-9657
BRA: 800-552-7945
BSH: 804-786-8826
BSL: 804-786-0553
BSS: 804-786-2366
CLE: 804-979-5644
CLU: 804-644-8022
CPA: 804-786-2116
CPA: 800-451-1525
CSE: 804-692-1900
CVC: 804-786-8718
EEO: 804-225-2237
IRA: 804-371-9694
IRA: 800-552-7945
ISG: 804-786-0000
LAR: 804-367-6600
LCR: 804-674-2084
LSO: 804-782-9438
OCR: 804-225-2292
OWI: 804-786-7765
POL: 804-367-8519
SAG: 804-786-2071
SBA: 804-775-0500
SCA: 804-786-6455
SCR: 804-371-9608
SCS: 804-225-2237
SLE: 804-674-2087
SLL: 804-786-2075
SOS: 804-786-2441
SPD: 804-225-3297
SRA: 804-371-9051
SRA: 800-552-7945
STI: 800-VISIT-VA
SUI: 804-786-3001
SVS: 804-786-6202
URA: 804-371-9608
URA: 800-552-7945
WCA: 804-367-8666

VIRGIN ISLANDS

ADA: 809-778-7497
BRA: 809-774-2991
CSE: 809-774-5666
CPA: 809-774-3130
EEO: 809-773-1994
IRA: 809-774-2991
OCR: 809-776-2485
URA: 809-776-1291

WASHINGTON

ADA: 206-448-0307
BBB: 509-328-2100
BRA: 360-753-6520
BRA: 800-372-8303
BSL: 206-753-6804
CLE: 206-448-0433
CLU: 206-624-2184
CPA: 360-753-6210
CPA: 800-551-4636
CSE: 360-586-3162
CVC: 360-902-5310
EEO: 360-753-5368
GPO: 206-553-4270
IRA: 360-753-3616
ISG: 360-753-5000
LAR: 206-586-2638
LCR: 206-705-5100
LSO: 509-838-6773
OCR: 360-753-6770
OSO: 360-753-6200
OWI: 360-753-5540
POL: 360-902-3600
SAG: 360-753-6200
SBA: 206-727-8200
SCA: 360-753-3365
SCR: 360-753-7121
SCS: 360-753-5368
SLE: 360-753-6540
SLL: 360-357-2135
SOS: 360-753-7121
SPD: 206-296-7583
SRA: 360-902-8760
SRA: 800-372-8303
STI: 800-544-1800
SUI: 360-902-9500
SVS: 360-753-5936
URA: 360-753-6423
URA: 800-586-8208
WCA: 360-902-4200

WEST VIRGINIA

ADA: 304-348-2456
BRA: 304-558-2294

BRA: 800-642-9056	SRA: 304-558-2257	OCR: 608-266-6860	CSE: 307-777-6948
BSH: 304-357-3200	STI: 800-CALL-WVA	OSO: 608-266-1212	CVC: 307-635-4050
BSL: 304-558-8905	SUI: 304-558-2630	OWI: 608-266-2219	EEO: 307-777-6730
BSS: 304-357-7800	SVS: 304-558-2931	POL: 304-266-8609	IRA: 307-777-7402
CLE: 304-293-2470	URA: 304-340-0300	SAG: 608-266-1221	IRA: 800-438-5768
CLU: 304-755-5978	URA: 800-344-5113	SBA: 608-257-3838	ISG: 307-777-7011
CPA: 304-558-8986	WCA: 304-558-2630	SCA: 608-266-6828	LAR: 307-777-4450
CPA: 800-558-0184		SCR: 608-266-3590	LCR: 307-777-7523
CSE: 304-558-3780	**WISCONSIN**	SCS: 608-266-9820	LSO: 307-634-1566
CVC: 304-558-2021		SLE: 608-266-1671	OCR: 307-777-6730
EEO: 304-558-0400	ADA: 608-267-7274	SLL: 608-266-1600	POL: 307-777-6300
IRA: 304-348-3386	BBB: 414-273-0123	SOS: 608-266-8888	SAG: 307-777-7841
IRA: 800-642-9004	BRA: 608-266-1621	SPD: 608-266-0087	SBA: 307-632-9061
ISG: 304-558-3456	BRA: 800-452-3328	SRA: 608-266-3431	SCA: 307-777-7581
LAR: 304-746-2128	BSL: 608-266-9960	SRA: 800-47-CHECK	SCR: 307-777-5334
LCR: 304-746-2277	CLE: 608-257-3838	STI: 800-432-TRIP	SCS: 307-777-6713
LSO: 304-342-6814	CLU: 414-272-4032	SUI: 608-266-7074	SLE: 307-777-7181
OCR: 304-558-2616	CPA: 608-224-4939	SVS: 608-266-1939	SLL: 307-777-7509
OWI: 304-348-0070	CPA: 800-422-7128	URA: 800-225-7729	SOS: 307-777-5333
SAG: 304-558-2021	CSE: 608-266-3035	WCA: 608-266-1340	SPD: 307-777-6498
SBA: 304-558-2456	CVC: 608-266-6470		SRA: 307-777-7370
SCA: 304-558-0145	EEO: 608-266-6860	**WYOMING**	STI: 800-CALL-WYO
SCR: 304-558-6000	GPO: 414-297-1304		SUI: 307-235-3200
SCS: 304-558-3950	IRA: 608-266-0103	ADA: 307-632-9061	SVS: 307-777-7591
SLE: 304-746-2111	IRA: 800-236-8517	CPA: 307-777-7874	URA: 307-777-7427
SLL: 304-558-2607	ISG: 608-266-2211	BRA: 307-777-7797	WCA: 307-777-6750
SOS: 304-558-6000	LAR: 608-266-8753	BSL: 307-777-7881	
SPD: 304-348-3905	LCR: 608-266-7314	CLE: 307-632-9061	
	LSO: 414-291-5480	CLU: 307-745-3729	

LEGAL MATERIALS ON THE INTERNET

For a list of other Internet addresses that provide access to law and law-related material, see Exhibit 13.21 in chapter 13. Here's a brief sampling of what's available:

- ABANet:

  http://www.abanet.org

  This is the site of the American Bar Association that contains information on its sections and divisions (including the Legal Assistant Division), news releases, and a calendar of events. Some of the publications of the ABA and a list of Internet discussion groups hosted by the ABA are also included.

- Arent, Fox, Kintner, Plotkin & Kahn, Washington D.C.:

  http://www.arentfox.com

  This site was voted one of the "Best of the Web" sites in the category of large law firms by the legal newsletter *legal.online*. Approximately 3,000 people visit the site every day. Law firm sites often contain profiles of personnel in the firm, areas of practice, special accomplishments, and other information found in a firm's brochure. The Arent Fox site also has a "Feature of the Month" that examines a particular legal subject in depth.

- Chicago-Kent Guide to Legal Resources:

  http://Kentlaw.edu/lawnet/lawlinks.html

  This site provides instructions on finding legal materials on the Internet. In addition, you are given lists covering computer law, family law, environmental law, human rights, health law, federal government, state government, etc.

- Counsel Connect Web:

  http://www.counsel.com

  This online service has links to other legal resources on the Internet. There are also online seminars on legal topics conducted for subscribers.

- Federal Court Locator:

  http://www.law.vill.edu/Fed-Ct/fedcourt.html

This site provides information on the U.S. Supreme Court, the U.S. Courts of Appeals, and the federal agencies that work with these courts, e.g., the U.S. Department of Justice and the U.S. Sentencing Commission.

- Federal Web Locator:

  http://www.law.vill.edu/Fed.Agency/fedwebloc.html

  This is an index of all the Internet sites covering the federal government.

- FindLaw:

  http://www.findlaw.com

  This site is a comprehensive legal research site called a "one-stop shopping center." It was voted one of the "Best of the Web" sites in the category of overall research by the legal newsletter *legal.online*. The index of FindLaw contains numerous links to legal resources on the Internet. Its LawCrawler feature allows you to search for key terms in the contents of other Internet sites as well as within FindLaw itself.

- GPO Access:

  http://www.acess.gpo.gov/su_docs

  This site provides comprehensive coverage of information on the executive branch of the federal government including the full text of the *Federal Register,* GAO reports, and Comptroller General Decisions. Data on Congress are also included.

- LawCrawler:

  http://www.lawcrawler.com

  A search tool ("engine") devoted to legal topics. See also FindLaw above.

- Law Group Network, Lawyers Legal Research:

  http://www.llr.com

  This site has an extensive database of court opinions, including all opinions of the U.S. Supreme Court since 1900, all opinions of the U.S. Courts of Appeals since 1992, and all recent opinions of the highest appellate court in every state. It also has numerous links to other kinds of laws, law firms, financial services, e-mail addresses, etc.

- Law Journal Extra, U.S. Courts of Appeals:

  http://www.ljextra.com/public/daily/coaall.html

  This site contains current opinions of the U.S. Courts of Appeals, including the U.S. Court of Appeals for the Federal Circuit.

- Law Journal Extra, Practice Areas:

  http://www.ljextra.com/Practice.pointer.html

  This site provides links to statutes, opinions, and related materials for specific areas in which attorneys practice.

- Law Journal Extra, State Courts:

  http://www.ljextra.com/courthouse/states.html

This site contains state law resources including the state court rules of selected states and materials from the National Conference of Commissioners on Uniform State Laws.

- Law Journal Extra, U.S. Supreme Court:

  http://www.ljextra.com/courthouse/supindex.html

  This site provides links to federal laws including opinions of the U.S. Supreme Court, federal statutes governing federal procedure, and news involving the U.S. Supreme Court.

- Legal Information Institute of Cornell Law School:

  http://www.law.cornell.edu

  Here you obtain access to recent opinions of the U.S. Supreme Court, an index of opinions of the U.S. Courts of Appeal, the current U.S. Code, e-mail addresses, etc.

- LEXIS Counsel Connect's LAWlinks:

  http://www.counsel.com

  This site provides links to federal and state laws, classified ads from legal newspapers, stock quotations, law library materials (including the Library of Congress), etc.

- Moye, Giles, O'Keefe, Vermeire & Gorrell, Denver:

  http://www.mgovg.com

  This site was voted one of the "Best of the Web" sites in the category of medium-sized law firms by the legal newsletter *legal.online*. It contains the full text of a number of legal treatises on banking and commercial law. The site also has a "Funny Stuff" feature covering humorous transcripts and "war stories."

- P-LAW Legal Resource Locator:

  http://www.dorsai.org/p-law

  This locator provides links to federal and state research sites, statistical data, and specialized research on a variety of topics.

- Tax Prophet:

  http://www.taxprophet.com

  This site contains links to numerous other tax resources on the Internet as well as columns, newsletters, and articles on tax planning and law. The site is arranged to be a useful teaching tool for attorneys and the general public. It includes a forms-based questionnaire you can use to help distinguish between an employee and an independent contractor for tax purposes. A law firm that uses independent paralegals might find this feature helpful.

- U.S. House of Representatives, Internet Law Library:

  http://www.law.house.gov

  This site contains the full text of the USC (United States Code) and the CFR (Code of Federal Regulations). Historical documents are included such as the Constitution, Declaration of Independence, *Federalist Papers,* etc. You can also gain access to the federal budget, *Congressional Record,* hearings of congressional committees, House and Senate committee reports, presidential documents, etc. In addition, there are links to state laws, treaties, and the catalogs of law school libraries.

- Villanova Center for Information Law and Policy:

  http://www.law.vill.edu

  This site has links to the Federal Web Locator on the federal government, Federal Court Locator on the federal courts, and State Court Locator on state courts.

- WWW Virtual Law Library:

  http://law.indiana. edu/law//lawindex.html

  This site provides a connection to a great deal of legal material on various sites. You are led to law firms, law schools, federal government information, state government information, international law, etc.

OTHER USEFUL SITES

- Alta Vista (general search engine):

  http://www.altavista.digital.com

- Internal Revenue Service:

  http://www.irs.ustreas.gov/prod

- Internet Sleuth (Law):

  http://www.isleuth.com/lega.html

- Lawyers Weekly:

  http://www.lweekly.com

- Legal List:

  http://www.lcp.com/The-Legal-List/TLL-home.html

- Martindale-Hubbell:

  http://www.martindale.com

- Securities & Exchange Commission:

  http://www.sec.gov/index.html

- Thomas (federal legislative information):

  http://thomas.loc.gov

- U.S. Federal Courts Finder:

  http://www.law.emory.edu/FEDCTS

- WashLaw Web (an indexer of legal sites):

  http://www.lawlib.wuacc.edu

- West's Legal News:

  http://www.westlaw.com/wlntop/front.htm

- West Publishing Company:

  http://www.westpub.com

- Yahoo (general search engine):

  http://www.yahoo.com

FEDERAL JOB INFORMATION

There are a number of ways to obtain information about paralegal and other employment opportunities in the federal government. (See chapter 2.) The methods listed here are sponsored by the United States Office of Personnel Management.

TOUCH-SCREEN COMPUTERS

Touch-screen computers that provide on-line information about federal jobs worldwide are available at the following locations. At these kiosks you can also request application packages.

ALABAMA: Huntsville
520 Wynn Dr., NW.

ALASKA: Anchorage
Federal Bldg., 222 W. 7th Ave.,
Rm. 156

ARIZONA: Phoenix
VA Medical Center, 650 E. Indian
School Rd., Bldg. 21, Rm. 141

ARKANSAS: Little Rock
Federal Bldg., 700 W. Capitol, 1st
Floor Lobby

CALIFORNIA: Sacramento
1029 J St., Rm. 202

COLORADO: Denver
12345 W. Alameda Pkwy., Room 101,
Lakewood

CONNECTICUT: Hartford
Federal Bldg., 450 Main St., Rm. 133

DISTRICT OF COLUMBIA: Washington, D.C., Theodore Roosevelt Federal Bldg., 1900 E St., NW, Rm. 1416

FLORIDA: Miami
Downtown Jobs and Benefits Center,
Florida Job Service Center, 401 NW.
2nd Ave., Suite N-214

Orlando
Florida Job Service Center, 1001
Executive Center Dr., First Floor

GEORGIA: Atlanta
Richard B. Russell Federal Bldg., Main
Lobby, Plaza Level, 75 Spring St., SW.

HAWAII: Honolulu
Federal Bldg., 300 Ala Moana Blvd.,
Rm. 5316

Fort Shafter
Department of Army, Army Civilian
Personnel Office, Army Garrison,
Bldg. T-1500

ILLINOIS: Chicago
77 West Jackson Blvd., 1st Floor Lobby

INDIANA: Indianapolis
Minton-Capehart Federal Bldg., 575
N. Pennsylvania St., Rm. 339

LOUISIANA: New Orleans
Federal Bldg., 423 Canal St., 1st Floor
Lobby

MAINE: Augusta
Federal Office Bldg., 40 Western Ave.

MARYLAND: Baltimore
George H. Fallon Bldg., Lombard St. &
Hopkins Plaza, Lobby

MASSACHUSETTS: Boston
Thomas P. O'Neill, Jr., Federal Bldg.,
10 Causeway St., 2nd Floor

MICHIGAN: Detroit
477 Michigan Ave., Rm. 565

MINNESOTA: Twin Cities
Bishop Henry Whipple Federal Bldg.,
1 Federal Dr., Rm. 501, Ft. Snelling

MISSOURI: Kansas City
Federal Bldg., 601 E. 12th St., Rm. 134

NEW HAMPSHIRE: Portsmouth
Thomas McIntyre Federal Bldg., 80
Daniel St., 1st Floor Lobby

NEW JERSEY: Newark
Peter J. Rodino Federal Bldg., 970 Broad St., 2nd Floor near cafeteria

NEW MEXICO: Albuquerque
New Mexico State Job Service, 501 Mountain Rd., Lobby

NEW YORK: Albany
Leo W. O'Brian Federal Bldg., Clinton Ave. & North Pearl, Basement Level

Buffalo
Thaddeus T. Dulski Federal Bldg., 111 West Huron St., 9th Floor

New York City
Jacob K. Javits Federal Bldg., 26 Federal Plaza, Lobby

New York City
290 Broadway, Lobby

Syracuse
James M. Hanley Federal Bldg., 100 S. Clinton St.

OHIO: Dayton
Federal Bldg., 200 W. 2nd St., Rm. 509

OKLAHOMA: Oklahoma City
Career Connection Center, 7401 NE. 23rd St., (Effective NLT 02/01/96)

OREGON: Portland
Federal Bldg., Rm. 376, 1220 SW. Third Ave.

PENNSYLVANIA: Harrisburg
Federal Bldg., 228 Walnut St., Rm. 168

Philadelphia
William J. Green, Jr., Federal Bldg., 600 Arch St.

Pittsburgh
Federal Bldg., 1000 Liberty Ave., 1st Floor Lobby

Reading
Reading Postal Service, 2100 N. 13th St.

PUERTO RICO: San Juan
U.S. Federal Bldg., 150 Carlos Chardon Ave., Rm. 328

RHODE ISLAND: Providence
380 Westminster, Mall Lobby

TENNESSEE: Memphis
Naval Air Station Memphis, Transition Assistance Center, 7800 3rd Ave., Bldg. South 239, Millington

TEXAS: Dallas
Federal Bldg., 1st Floor Lobby, 1100 Commerce St.

El Paso
Federal Bldg., 700 East San Antonio St., Lobby

Houston
Mickey Leland Federal Bldg., 1919 Smith St., 1st Floor Lobby

San Antonio
Federal Bldg., 1st Floor Lobby, 727 East Durango, (Effective NLT 01/19/96)

Texas Employment Commission Office, 1248 Austin Highway

UTAH: Salt Lake City
Utah State Job Service, 720 South 2nd East

VERMONT: Burlington
Federal Bldg., 11 Elmwood Ave., 1st Floor Lobby

VIRGINIA: Norfolk
Federal Bldg., 200 Granby St.

WASHINGTON: Seattle
Federal Bldg., 915 Second Ave., Rm. 110

Also visit your local *state* employment service office. There you might find information on current federal job listings. Depending on the state, the list may be on a printed report, on microfiche, or on computer.

PHONE INFORMATION

An automated phone system provides 24-hour, seven-day-a-week information about current employment opportunities in the federal government (Career America Connection). There are two ways to obtain this phone information. From anywhere in the country you can call the following number:

912-757-3000

Alternatively, you can call the number at whichever of the following centers is closest to you:

Alabama, Huntsville: 205-837-0894
California, San Francisco: 415-744-5627
Colorado, Denver: 303-969-7050
District of Columbia:
 202-606-2700

Georgia, Atlanta: 404-331-4315
Hawaii, Honolulu: 808-541-2791
Illinois, Chicago: 312-353-6192
Michigan, Detroit: 313-226-6950
Minnesota, Twin Cities: 612-725-3430

Missouri, Kansas City: 816-426-5702
North Carolina, Raleigh: 919-790-2822
Ohio, Dayton: 513-225-2720
Pennsylvania, Philadelphia: 215-597-7440

Texas, San Antonio: 210-805-2402
Virginia, Norfolk: 804-441-3355
Washington, Seattle: 206-553-0888

COMPUTER BULLETIN BOARD

To use the computer bulletin board to obtain information about federal job opportunities, call the following number:

912-757-3100

To use this system, you need a personal computer equipped with a modem and communications software, along with a telephone line.

INTERNET

Here are some of the ways to obtain information about federal job opportunities through the Internet:

Telnet:

FJOB.MAIL.OPM.GOV

File Transfer Protocol:

FTP.FJOB.MAIL.OPM.GOV

Internet Mail:

INFO@FJOB.MAIL.OPM.GOV

USA JOBS Web Site:

HTTP:WWW.USAJOBS.OPM.GOV

The USA Jobs web site, like all of the employment information delivery systems, will provide: access to the Federal Jobs Database of worldwide opportunities, full-text job announcements for positions in the database, answers to frequently asked federal employment questions via delivery of Employment Info Line fact sheets, and access to electronic and hard copy application forms.

HOW TO START A FREELANCE PARALEGAL BUSINESS

by Linda Harrington

The best way to get into business is to do it, not talk forever about it. In fact, you may be doing it before you know that you are actually running a business.

The conservative approach to getting into freelance business is to take work on the side while you maintain a salaried position. When your side business interferes with your job, then you must decide whether the business is enticing enough to promote. If it is not, give up the business, keep the salaried job, and be thankful to have learned a lesson—in an undramatic way—about running a business.

If the business is satisfying and if you enjoy it, the time has come to devote more time and energy to it. Therefore, you will be resigning your salaried job to tackle a business.

Perhaps you have impressed your current employer enough so that he, she, or it will be one of your clients after you resign.

PRELIMINARY CONSIDERATIONS IN GETTING STARTED

Don't begin a freelance business unless and until you have acquired enough experience to be an expert in something. So the first question is: What is your area of expertise? The second question is: Will this area generate some cash for you if you go freelance? One of the areas to avoid is claimants' personal injury work where it's contingent, that is, where the attorney will get a fee contingent upon success in court. It has been my experience that attorneys will pay you when they get paid on a case. So, if you're working for an attorney who will pay you when that attorney gets paid and that attorney loses the case, it's likely you won't get paid.

I work in probate. Everyone knows that death and taxes are inevitable. That being the case, I find it a very lucrative and interesting area.

An extremely important aspect of being a freelance paralegal is having a network. A network can be one of two kinds: first, a network of prior employers who respect your skills a lot and will use you when you go freelance; second, the network of your peers that's developed through paralegal associations and contacts. Both are equally important; one does not substitute for the other. I found that my activities in the local association have been extremely rewarding. They have given me leadership opportunities, the ability to learn current law from the people who work in large law firms, and a chance to meet friends who have the same kind of responsibilities I do. For the most part, my job leads have come from people I worked for before I became a freelancer.

The other part of the network to explore is the school system. The local paralegal programs can assist you a great deal in establishing a freelance business. For one thing you can offer to teach a course in your area of expertise. Second, if you're teaching, you're meeting people who will one day be your peers—and that's expanding your professional network. Third, many paralegal programs have work-study experiences available for the students. The students are placed in offices where they get on-the-job training. I have lots of them come to my office. That keeps my overhead down. I give the students on-the-job training in all aspects of probate and death taxes, and in return, I have people to staff my office. It benefits the school, my office, and the students as well. So there are resources, lots of resources, available from the local schools.

I want to stress again the importance of having a high level of expertise before venturing into your own business. I have seen a lot of people come out of paralegal training programs and not get their dream job. They then decide that they're going to open freelance business operations without knowing very much about the practical reality of dealing with attorneys, not to mention the practical reality of working as a paralegal. *I did not realize that you need about four or five years' experience in your field before attempting to go freelance.* The first reason, of course, is that you want to have strength in your practice area and be able to handle some of the problems that you will later encounter as a freelance paralegal.

The second reason is that you have to learn what working with attorneys is like. You have to know about their personalities, and have to be able to manage the problems that they often present. I tell all my students that attorneys now have to pass "arrogance" before they are allowed to take the bar exam, and you have to learn how to deal with this attitude in as cheerful a manner as you possibly can. Dealing with attorneys is just as important an area of expertise to develop as any other aspect of expertise in a practice field. If you're going to go freelance, you will have to be able to handle hundreds of attorneys calling you up, each one considering himself or herself the most important person in the world. You have to deal with that reality.

The most important things I had to learn were to keep a sense of humor and to remember to be compulsive. Some people say that I'm a workaholic; I prefer to state that I work hard. I work very, very hard. The things that most people think are available in freelance work are independence and free time. The reality is that they don't always exist. If your office does not get the work done, the buck stops with you. You can't blame your staff. The final responsibility rests on your shoulders. If everybody else leaves and the computer breaks down, you still must perform. If you don't get the work done, you face the possibility of jeopardizing your entire business operation.

OTHER PRACTICAL SUGGESTIONS

Step 1. Have business cards printed. The cards should state your name, specialty area, and telephone number.

Have a business answering service that provides a real, live voice to a caller, not a recording. It is reassuring to a potential customer to hear "a live one" on the line. Limit the service to the hours 9–5 to keep the cost of the service down.

Have "call waiting" installed by the phone company so that one phone line can handle several calls at once by a mere flick of a button. Also, have "call forward" installed. This feature enables you to have incoming calls automatically forwarded to the telephone number of your choice. If you are waiting for an important call but have a visit to make, you can have your call forwarded to your destination automatically.

Step 2.   Systematize your operation immediately. The systems you will need include:

1. Calendar system
2. Timekeeping system
3. Billing system
4. Filing system for both open and closed matters
5. Procedural manual for your specialty area

A *calendar system* should include a master calendar that is easily spotted among clutter; a pocket calendar, which you must carry at all times; and some sort of statute-of-limitations reminder system. Many companies offer calendar systems at relatively low cost. Two are Safeguard Business Systems and Lawfax System.

A *timekeeping system* should include a master time record repository (separate from the case file) and time slips, and should allow you to make decisions on the standard charges for services and costs. It is easiest to assign a set charge for a particular service, subject to increases for complications or quirks. For example, typical time charges will be incurred for telephone calls. Assign a minimum charge for each call. Each duty should have a minimum charge assigned to it. In this way, your billing will reflect all applicable charges for the particular service involved in the transaction as well as your research, investigation, and other "write up" expenses. Costs such as photocopies should also reflect the time involved to perform the service. Therefore, standard mark-up for costs is advisable. Naturally, these are matters that are internal to the business. Therefore, establish your standards and then keep your mouth shut.

A *billing system* should include a retainer, which is received when the case work comes in, and a statement for services submitted at an advantageous time and in a personal manner, which makes it clear that the bill is an important document to the sender. Set up a system for billing that is realistic. If your clients are most likely to pay on the 30th of the month, send your bills on the 25th. If your clients will not pay the bill until the receipts from the case are received, bill at the end of the work. Billing is as much psychology as anything else. Figure out when the client will want to pay and bill at that time.

A *filing system* for open cases will include a repository for current case documents, an identification system for file labels, and a place for the files to be stored. Each case needs a case matter sheet that generally describes the client, the case, and the work to be done, as well as the billing arrangements between you and the client. Casework can be stored in file folders, in binders, in boxes, and a number of other places. Make sure that all cases are stored in the same fashion and that the case files are easily located.

Closed cases should be stored and retained. A closed file system should be a numerical system. For this type of system, you need file folders, a rolodex to store the case name and closed file number (retained in alphabetical order by case), and a central register to show the numbers used for previously closed files, so that the number chosen for a closed file will not have been used previously.

A *procedural manual* will contain standard correspondence sent for the particular areas of law you specialize in, standard (completed) court forms used in your field, and instructions to others about processing the documents. A procedural manual can also contain information concerning special and standard requirements of area courts, if your work involves preparing and filing court papers. The latter will help you avoid procedural errors and will save time, if you update regularly.

Step 3.   Fix your goals and prepare to stick to them.

Fixing a goal involves knowing why you want to run a business. There are many reasons to want to be in business for yourself. Some are ego gratification—now you are going to get recognition for how great you've always known you are; free time—now you can set your own hours and go to the beach whenever you want; money—now you are going to get a piece of the action and get rich.

Caution: *be prepared for reality.* All of your original goals will change if you are still in business one year later. Most of the people you work for will never be impressed by your brilliance—you said you could do the work, you did do the work, so what's the big deal? If you are successful, the last thing you will have is free time. Even in the beginning, your clients will want to see you or talk to you when *they* want to do so, not when you want them to. Most attorneys feel that if you only knew that they wanted to talk to you, you would jump to attention at four in the morning and be grateful for the phone call. All the money you earn will be hard earned. When you finally do earn money, some of it will go to your staff, some to your landlord, some to the IRS, and some to you.

To keep your wits about you, you must budget and you must set limits. How much of what you want do you have to receive in order to stick with it? If you want ego gratification, how many clients have to tell you you are great to make the business worthwhile? If you want free time, how much free time do you have to have to make the business worthwhile? If you want money, how much profit must you make for the business to be worthwhile? The "how much" is your minimum. Obviously, the sky is the limit.

If you do not get your minimum, are you willing to quit? If not, do not go into business.

Do not count on new business to get you by. Count on the status quo as far as income is concerned to figure out how much money you will make by December 31 and budget accordingly. If you need income from the business to pay your personal bills, how much do you need monthly? Does this leave any money to run the business? Of the money that is left, how much will be required for telephone, answering service, supplies, and other fixed expenses? Now how much is left? Use the rest for expansion of your business (equipment purchases, personnel, etc.).

Step 4.   Develop realistic employee relationships.

If you have done everything you can do to avoid hiring your first employee, but you are having difficulty keeping pace with your work or finding the time off you desire, then it is time to hire help.

Accept what you are. You are the owner of a very small business and cannot offer big-firm benefits, bonuses, or vacations to your prospective employee. Also, you are a person who wishes to protect your business position; you do not want to hand your business over to a potential competitor. Last, you are a person who has certain expectations concerning job performance, productivity, and attendance. You have developed your own ideas about what constitutes a good job in your field.

Do not hire a friend. Being someone's boss does not improve a friendship when you also own the business.

Hire someone trainable. A trainable person is likely to be a recent graduate from a paralegal school. The fact that an applicant has sought education in the field and completed some or all of it is a strong indication that the person has an interest in the field and a desire for practical experience.

Do not hire someone just like you. You are the person who decided to start up the business, who worked (slaved?) to get it going, who knows everything, and who does not want to work so hard now. If you hire someone just like you, you will have two people not wanting to work so hard (you and your employee) *or* one who wants to start a business and has access to all your clients.

Establish a trial employment first. Whether you're hiring a work-study student at minimum wage from a local paralegal program or hiring an experienced person from some other source, set a review period or termination period for the relationship. Tell your employee what that period is and stick to it.

Be realistic about your employee. Because you are a small business, you cannot compete with larger firms that will offer your employee a better deal after the employee has experience and training. Therefore, accept the fact that the employee will probably move on. Tell the employee that you accept this fact and will help the person find a better position after the training has been completed (one to two years, usually). This will motivate the employee to learn as much as possible and to do a good job. This will also help you avoid taking the job move personally.

Be sure you understand the tax and insurance requirements for your employee. You must have an employer I.D. number; you must withhold taxes and social security and state disability insurance; you must file quarterly reports with the taxing authorities and provide your employee with a W-2 at year end; you must have Worker's Compensation Insurance; and you must make employer contributions to the unemployment fund and to social security. Each employee's salary is hardly your total cost in keeping that employee.

Have your employee work on your premises. This is essential at least during the training period, so that you can become familiar with the employee's work habits and control work production.

Review the employee's time slips. The time slip review will tell you how long a particular job takes the employee to perform, how many hours during the day the employee devotes to office matters, and how the cases are progressing.

Fire the hopeless. When you know that an employee is not going to work out, do not wait for the realization to come to the employee. It never will. Call the person in to your office, look the person in the eyes, and tell the person how wonderful he or she is and how many fantastic qualities he or she has and how unfortunate it is that the job is so miserable for such a terrific individual and that the job just isn't good enough for such a talented person. *Or* call the person in and tell him or her that the employment is not working out and that you wish to ask for his or her resignation to avoid the stigma to the employee of being fired. *Or* call the person in and tell him or her that you can no longer tolerate his or her presence and that he or she is fired. However you do it, be sure that it gets done as soon as you have given up hope for improvement. That's your money that your employee is taking home every two weeks. Nothing rankles so much as feeling that you are paying for a mistake again and again.

Reward the hearty. Go out to lunch for a chat and pay the bill. Send the employee home early or give him or her a surprise day off after a hard week. Leave town yourself and let him or her have the office to himself or herself. Give bonuses when a difficult case is completed. Give a raise of a day off. Compliment the employee for work well done.

Accept criticism. Your employee will probably be compelled to express criticism of the systems in your office or, perhaps, your own style. So what? This is how good ideas get born. Think about the recommendations and, if they are good ones, change your office systems.

CONCLUSION

The worst way to get into business is to assume that there is no way you can fail (90 percent of all new businesses do fail, the Small Business Administration says), buy the most expensive equipment, rent the most costly office space, get the most sophisticated telephone system, and generally count on the birds in the bushes before they land in your hand. Hope that you are able to start building your business slowly so that you will have time to learn about building and problem solving. Give it a good try. If it works out and you like it, keep going. If it works out and you do not like it, or if it does not work out, then give it up and congratulate yourself on having given it a good try.

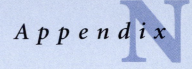

"LEGAL ASSISTANT DAY"

In many states, governors and mayors have issued proclamations that set aside a particular day or week to honor paralegals. Here are two examples:

The State of Maryland

Proclamation

From the Governor of the State of Maryland

PARALEGAL WEEK
OCTOBER 6 - 12, 1996

WHEREAS, A paralegal is a trained professional who is dedicated to providing proficient and substantive legal assistance to attorneys, the court system, the business community and to the public; and

WHEREAS, The paralegal profession is a rapidly growing professional both in the number of veteran specialists and entry level graduates; and

WHEREAS, Paralegals constitute an increasingly significant component of the State's legal system; and

WHEREAS, The National Capital Area Paralegal Association is a Charter Member of the National Federation of Paralegal Associations and has been serving the legal needs of the people of our state for twenty-two years... and, Maryland is proud to salute the outstanding work these dedicated professionals are doing on behalf of our citizens.

NOW, THEREFORE, I, PARRIS N. GLENDENING, GOVERNOR OF THE STATE OF MARYLAND, do hereby proclaim October 6 - 12, 1996 as PARALEGAL WEEK in Maryland, and do commend this observance to all of our citizens.

Given Under My Hand and the Great Seal of the State of Maryland, this 6th day of October One Thousand Nine Hundred and Ninety-six

Parris N. Glendening
Governor

John T. Willis
Secretary of State

OFFICIAL MEMORANDUM
STATE OF TEXAS
OFFICE OF THE GOVERNOR

The legal assistant is a vital part of the operations of any office or organization. He or she must perform a variety of duties in an efficient, professional manner and have a broad knowledge of many subjects.

The legal assistant strives to maintain a high standard of professionalism with continued educational growth and development. These individuals understand the importance of their position and take great pride in their performance.

The State Bar of Texas also realizes the invaluable contributions of these assistants to the legal system in our state. The Legal Assistants Division of the State Bar was created to better facilitate and coordinate the services these individuals provide; October 23, 1990 marks the ninth anniversary of the establishment of that division.

Therefore, I, William P. Clements, Jr., Governor of Texas, do hereby find it fitting and proper to designate October 23rd, 1990 as:

LEGAL ASSISTANTS DAY

in Texas and urge the appropriate recognition thereof.

In official recognition whereof, I hereby affix my signature this

___10th___ day of ___October___, 19 _90_ .

Governor of Texas

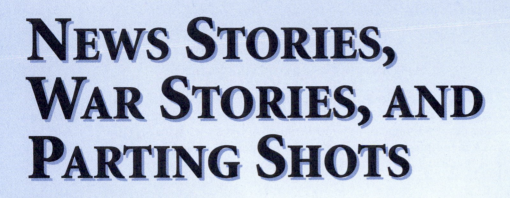

NEWS STORIES, WAR STORIES, AND PARTING SHOTS

LEGAL ASSISTANT ELECTED PROBATE JUDGE

In November 1987, Arlene G. Keegan, a legal assistant, was elected Probate Judge in the town of Litchfield, Connecticut. A law degree is not required to be a Probate Judge in Connecticut. Judge Keegan handles a wide variety of cases. In one case, for example, family members argued that their mother was incompetent when she prepared her will. "It was a tough decision, because I had to get in the middle of a situation with family members pulling against a close friend of the decedent." "I get to deal with a lot of people, and I find people totally intriguing." Howard, *A Legal Assistant Is Elected Probate Judge*, 5 Legal Assistant Today 32 (March/April 1988).

Former Legal Assistant, now Probate Judge Arlene Keegan, at the courthouse in Litchfield, Connecticut.

PARALEGAL APPOINTED CHAIRMAN OF BAR ASSOCIATION COMMITTEE

In 1989, the Colorado Bar Association appointed Joanna Hughbanks "to serve as chairman of the Legal Assistants Committee of the Colorado Bar Association." Ms. Hughbanks is an independent paralegal in Denver. She is believed to be the first nonattorney to chair a standing committee of a bar association. Letter from Christopher R. Brauchi, President of the Colorado Bar Association, to Joanna Hughbanks, 6/27/89.

PARALEGAL APPOINTED BANKRUPTCY TRUSTEE

A Fort Worth paralegal, Twalla Dupriest, was appointed by the Bankruptcy Court as trustee for the estate of T. Cullen Davis, who was one of the wealthiest men in the United States. Twalla was responsible for gathering all of Davis's assets for the purpose of repaying creditors and presided at the meetings of creditors. *Paralegal Appointed Trustee to Cullen Davis Estate,* Newsletter, Dallas Ass'n of Legal Assistants, (Sept. 1987).

FREELANCE PARALEGAL NAMED PRO BONO PARALEGAL OF THE YEAR

A freelance paralegal, Jim Carrao of Dallas, was named Pro Bono Paralegal of the Year by the Dallas Bar Association and Legal Services of North Texas, Inc. for donating 176 hours of his time to help provide legal services to the poor. Parchman, *Communiqué,* AAPLA Advocate 17 (Alamo Area Professional Legal Assistants, Inc., July/August 1991).

PARALEGAL RUNS FOR THE LEGISLATURE

Rosemary Mulligan, an Illinois paralegal, ran for a seat in the Illinois House of Representatives in 1990 against an incumbent. The election was held in a district in a suburb of Chicago. The vote was so close that it was declared a tie. By law, such elections are decided by lottery—a toss of the coin. Although the paralegal won the toss, a court later declared her opponent the victor after reviewing some disputed ballots. *Toss of Coin to Decide Race in Illinois,* A12 (New York Times, 7/18/90).

PARALEGAL SUED FOR CIVIL RIGHTS VIOLATIONS

A Kentucky paralegal was sued, along with a prosecutor, for civil rights violations. In the complaint, an automobile dealership alleged that the prosecutor and paralegal fraudulently conspired to obtain the business records of the plaintiff. The paralegal allegedly caused an invalid and unenforceable subpoena duces tecum to be issued in order to illegally obtain the records of the dealership. Hectus, *Paralegal Sued for Civil Rights Violations,* One Voice (Kentucky Paralegal Ass'n, March/April 1991).

PARALEGAL CHARGED WITH INSIDER TRADING

A twenty-four-year-old paralegal was charged with insider trading by the Securities and Exchange Commission. The complaint against the paralegal alleged that she had access to confidential information pertaining to the proposed merger of a client of the firm where she worked. She "tipped" her friends by giving them confidential information. The friends then used this information to earn $823,471 through the purchase of 65,020 shares. A civil complaint sought damages of $3.29 million. The paralegal was fired by the law firm. *SEC v. Hurton,* Civ. #89–1070, DC Mass. (5/16/89); *Federal Securities and Corporate Developments,* 21 Securities & Law Report (5/21/89).

A $90,000,000 Mistake!

Several years ago, a paralegal for Prudential inadvertently left off the last three zeros on a mortgage used to secure a $92,885,000 loan made by Prudential to a company that is now bankrupt. As a result of the mistake, Prudential was left with only a $92,885 lien. Prudential's attorneys have asked the U.S. Bankruptcy Court in New York City to ignore the mistake—and restore the zeros. 17 *At Issue* (San Francisco Legal Assistants Ass'n, Dec. 1990).

Paralegal Convicted

Mershan Shaddy was an independent paralegal in San Diego. He charged clients $180 to handle uncontested divorces, plus $50 if property had to be divided, and $30 for each child. He was arrested after an undercover investigator posed as a divorce client and secretly recorded him giving legal advice in violation of the California law against the unauthorized practice of law. He was convicted and sentenced to forty-five days in jail. *Paralegal's Role in Legal System Stirs a Debate,* San Diego Union B-1 (March 29, 1990).

Billionaire Paralegal Prefers Prison to Filling Out Time Sheets

Michael Milken, the billionaire "junk bond king," went to prison for illegal activities stemming from his Wall Street career. While still under the jurisdiction of federal prison and parole authorities, Milken worked for three weeks as a paralegal in a law firm. He did not enjoy the experience. Comparing prison to the law firm, he told reporters that he would rather have other people keep track of his time than to have to "fill out those . . . time sheets every day." *News Across the Country,* KLAS Action (Kansas Legal Assistants Society, December/January 1994).

Did the Paralegal Work 43 Hours on January 10?

Hotel magnate Leona Helmsley (infamous for her wealth and her comment, "only little people pay taxes") sued a New York law firm for $35 million because she claimed they submitted fraudulent bills for fees and expenses. Among the allegedly fraudulent items cited in the suit was a bill for 43 hours of work charged by a paralegal for one day—January 10. Andrew Blum, *The Empress Strikes Back,* p. A6, The National Law Journal (July 11, 1994).

Don't Be Photographed in That T-Shirt

An insurance company challenged a bill for attorney and paralegal time submitted by the Los Angeles law firm of Latham & Watkins. During a court proceeding on the dispute, the company embarrassed the firm by introducing into evidence a photograph of the paralegal working on the case while wearing a T-Shirt that read "Born to Bill." *Take Note of This*, p. 9, California Paralegal (January/March 1992)

LAW FIRM SUES ITS FORMER PARALEGAL

Richard Trotter once worked as a paralegal for a Denver law firm. He wrote a book called *A Toothless Paper Tiger* about his experiences at the law firm. The book alleged that the firm improperly authorized him and other paralegals at the firm to perform the work of attorneys. The law firm sought an injunction to prevent the release of the book. Hicks, *Law Firm Fights Book by Former Employee,* National Law Journal 39 (August 6, 1990).

PARALEGAL ALLEGED TO HAVE STOLEN THE SMOKING GUN IN TOBACCO LITIGATION

Suits against tobacco companies by smokers have become one of the major litigation battles of the decade. In the middle of the storm is a paralegal, Merrell Williams, who once worked for the Louisville law firm of Wyatt, Tarrant & Combs, the largest law firm in Kentucky. The firm represents Brown & Williamson Tobacco Corporation, maker of Kool and Viceroy. While Williams worked at the firm, he secretly photocopied and distributed confidential internal memos, letters, and other documents between the law firm and its client. They allegedly demonstrate that the company knew about the danger of smoking, but tried to cover it up. The news media made extensive use of this material, which was made available to them. Wyatt, Tarrant & Combs has obtained an injunction against Williams to prevent him from revealing anything more about what he learned while he was a paralegal at the firm—even to the attorney Williams hired to represent him. "The evidence that this paralegal could provide could be most damaging to the tobacco companies," said J. Lee, former president of the Association of Trial Lawyers of America. In 1996, a smoker won a $750,000 judgment against Brown & Williamson. If this judgment is upheld on appeal, it will be the first time the cigarette industry has paid damages. According to the *New York Times,* this was "the first case to successfully introduce the so-called Brown & Williamson documents—papers spirited away from the company that indicate it knew for decades that cigarettes were harmful." The *New York Times Magazine,* 31 (October 20, 1996). In the meantime the tobacco company has sued Williams. "They say Williams broke his employment contract, which requires confidentiality, and stole photocopies of documents from the law office." An ex-smoker himself, Williams has undergone quadruple bypass surgery and has sued Brown & Williamson for his health problems. Mark Curriden, *DOJ (Department of Justice) Probes Law Firms: Paralegal Who Copied Tobacco Company Documents Subpoenaed,* 80 American Bar Association Journal 14 (June 1994); Mark Curriden, *It Started with a Paralegal,* 13 Legal Assistant Today 18 (May/June 1996).

PARALEGAL ORDERED TO PAY $925,000 IN ATTORNEY FEES

Los Angeles Superior Court Judge Arnold Gold dismissed the sexual harassment lawsuit brought by a paralegal, Elizabeth Saret-Cook, against her former law firm employer, Gilbert, Kelly, Crowley & Jannett. *Saret-Cook v. Gilbert, Kelly,* BC116590. She alleged that she had been harassed after getting pregnant with the child of an attorney at the firm, Clifford Woosley. Calling her suit "frivolous" and "completely without merit," the judge ordered the paralegal to pay $925,000 in attorney fees to the law firm and to Woosley. According to court documents, the law firm had earlier offered to settle the suit for

$400,000, but Saret-Cook refused the offer. Rebecca Liss, *Paralegal Ordered to Pay Fees in Harassment Case*, 2 Los Angeles Daily Journal (September 27, 1996).

Law Firm Settles Suit Brought by Paralegals

A class action was brought by paralegals and clerical workers who claimed that the Oakland firm where they worked failed to pay them overtime compensation. The case was eventually settled for $170,000, which was distributed among the paralegals and clerical workers. Ziegler, *Firm Settles Suit on Overtime for Paralegals*, San Francisco Banner Daily Journal (1/25/89).

"Will the Legal Assistant Please Tell the Court the Facts of the Case?"

At a paralegal association meeting in Houston, Judge Lynn Hughes, a federal District Court judge, recently drew a "big laugh" concerning an incident in her courtroom. During a hearing, she watched a "Big Gun" senior partner constantly turn to his associate for information on the facts of the case. This associate, in turn, would ask his legal assistant for this information. Finally, Judge Hughes asked the legal assistant to stand up and tell the court the facts of the case! *National News . . . Houston Legal Assistants Association*, 21 Outlook 5 (Illinois Paralegal Ass'n, Spring 1991).

"Then You Should Have Used a Paralegal!"

At oral argument before the United States Supreme Court in a case on paralegal fees, an attorney was interrupted by Justice Thurgood Marshall during the attorney's description of the custom of billing in New Orleans. In the following fascinating excerpt from the transcript of the oral argument, a clearly irritated Justice Marshall suggested that the attorney was unprepared because he did not have a paralegal working with him on the case:

JUSTICE MARSHALL: Is all that in the record?
ATTORNEY: I'm sorry. . . .
JUSTICE MARSHALL: Is that in the record?
ATTORNEY: I'm not. . . .
JUSTICE MARSHALL: What you've just said, that the custom of billing and all in New Orleans, is that in the record?
ATTORNEY: I think it is Justice Marshall.
JUSTICE MARSHALL: You think? Didn't you try the case?
ATTORNEY: I tried the case, but whether or not that particular item is in the record, it is certainly in the briefs, but. . . .
JUSTICE MARSHALL: Then you should have used a paralegal!

Official Transcript Proceedings Before The Supreme Court of the United States, Arthur J. Blanchard, petitioner V. James Bergerson, et al., Case 87–1485, page 25 (11/28/88).

The Perfect Recipe

"To one paralegal, add a pound of variety, eight ounces of flexibility, four ounces of creativity, and a healthy sense of humor. The result? One cost-effective, efficient litigation paralegal." Vore, *A Litigation Recipe*, On Point (Nat'l Capital Area Paralegal Ass'n, Nov. 1990).

PARALEGAL TRAPPED

A paralegal, on his way to an assignment on another floor, became trapped in an elevator just after getting on. Fellow employees gathered around the elevator door. The time-conscious paralegal called out from inside the elevator, "Is this billable or nonbillable time?" *A Lighter Note,* MALA Advance 15 (Summer 1989).

SUSPENSE NOVEL ABOUT A PARALEGAL BY A PARALEGAL

E. P. Dalton has published *Housebreaker,* a novel by David Linzee, who has worked as a litigation paralegal. It is about Megan Lofting. "Megan used to be a probate paralegal at a Connecticut law firm. She used to try hard never to do something wrong. But then she was unjustly fired. Now a big-time criminal is offering her a chance to make a fortune, and to strike back at the client who got her fired, and the lawyer—once her lover—who let it happen." *The First Suspense Novel Ever About a Paralegal . . . by a Former Paralegal,* 4 Viewpoint 10 (Massachusetts Paralegal Ass'n, July/August 1987).

THE COST OF WHAT?

Recently, a paralegal was given an unusual assignment by her supervising attorney. She was asked to determine how much it would cost to purchase a penguin! *How Much Does a Penguin Cost?* SJPA Reporter, p. 3 (South Jersey Paralegal Ass'n, Sept. 1990).

PARALEGAL WATCHES EXORCISM

Kevin McKinley is a paralegal at a West Palm Beach law firm that represented a defendant in a murder case. While working on the case, Kevin found an urn in the room of the defendant where the latter allegedly practiced voodoo and black magic. The family of the defendant was concerned that if the urn was opened in the courtroom, the spirit within it would harm those attending the trial. Hence an exorcism was performed to remove the defendant's control over this spirit. Kevin's assignment was to be a witness at this exorcism. *Columbus Dispatch* (January 6, 1991).

THE PARALEGAL FLORAL STRATEGY

A litigation legal assistant was given the task of serving a subpoena on a defendant who was unlikely to open the door. She came up with a creative approach. On her way to the defendant's house, she stopped at a flower shop and picked up a plant. Upon her arrival, she rang the doorbell. The defendant looked out, saw a person with flowers, opened the door, and was presented with a plant . . . and a subpoena! Anderson, *In the Line of Duty,* MALA Advance 17 (Minnesota Ass'n of Legal Assistants, Spring 1991).

WANTED: ADVENTUROUS PARALEGAL UNDER 107 POUNDS

The following want ad appeared in the classified section of a San Francisco legal newspaper. "ADVENTUROUS PARALEGAL. Travel in pvt. aircraft around the country up to 3 wks/mo. investigating franchise cases. Duties incl: client interviews, lgl research & witness invest. Your weight max: 107 lbs. (flight requirement)." *Daily Journal Classifieds,* 18, The Daily Journal (May 17, 1993).

WANTED: PARALEGAL WITH MINIMUM OF 203 YEARS OF EXPERIENCE

A paralegal placement agency is seeking a person "w/at least 203 yrs exp in paralegal field." The ad was either a typo or the first step in getting recognition in the next edition of the Guinness record book. *Employment Registry,* Reporter, p. 11 (Los Angeles Paralegal Ass'n, June 1993).

I DON'T BELIEVE HE SAID THAT

- "I told him that I'm a paralegal. He thinks I am a lawyer who jumps out of planes"— in parachutes. *Compendium* (Orange County Paralegal Ass'n, Oct. 1990).
- When asked what to do for your secretary when she needs recognition but doesn't deserve a raise, the attorney answered, "Make her a paralegal!" *The Question of Paralegals,* 20 The Legal Investigator 35 (2/91).
- At a cocktail party, Therese Carey was introduced to a middle-aged businessman. He asked her what she did for a living. Answering that she was a legal assistant, Therese enthusiastically explained her duties. After her response, the man turned to her and earnestly said, "Say, you know, with your background, have you ever considered becoming a paralegal?" Burdett, *Rodney Dangerfield: You're Not Alone,* Newsletter 2, Rhode Island Paralegal Ass'n (Jan. 1987).

BUMPER STICKER AWARD

The Alaska Association of Legal Assistants had a bumper sticker contest. The top three winners were as follows:

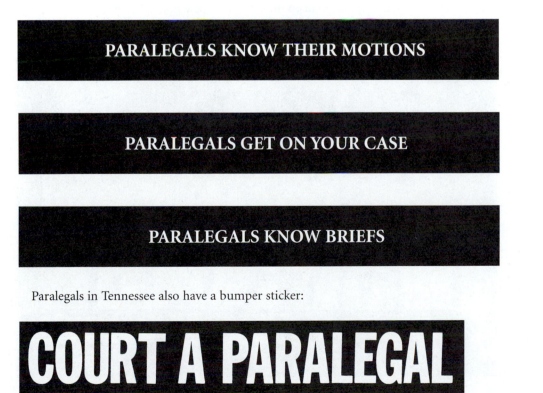

PARALEGALS KNOW THEIR MOTIONS

PARALEGALS GET ON YOUR CASE

PARALEGALS KNOW BRIEFS

Paralegals in Tennessee also have a bumper sticker:

COURT A PARALEGAL

THE ULTIMATE STATUS SYMBOL

A California paralegal has found a unique way to assert her presence. She ordered a vanity plate that will force everyone on the freeway to take notice:

"What It Is That I Do"

A. Pergola, Newsletter, Rocky Mountain Legal Assistants Association (June 1980)

The World of Attorneys

- "I served with General Washington in the legislature of Virginia before the revolution, and during it, with Dr. Franklin in Congress. . . . If the present Congress errs in too much talking, how could it do otherwise in a body to which the people send 150 lawyers, whose trade it is to question everything, yield nothing & talk by the hour?" *Autobiography 1743–1790*, Thomas Jefferson.
- If a man were to give another man an orange, he would say, simply, "Have an orange." But if the transaction were entrusted to an attorney, he would say: "I hereby give, grant, bargain and sell to you, all my right, title and interest in, of, and to said orange, together with all its rind, skin, juice, pulp, and pips, and all rights and advantages therein, with full power to bite, cut, and otherwise eat of the same, or give the same away, with or without the rind, skin, juice, pulp, and pips, anything hereinbefore or hereinafter, or in any other deed or deeds, instrument or instruments, of whatever kind or nature whatsoever to the contrary in any wise notwithstanding." Hirsch, *Pittsburgh Legal Journal.*

- A document recently filed in the United States Bankruptcy Court in Tennessee contained the following language: "Debtors hereby amend the Amendment to Second Amended and Restated Disclosure Statement, Third Amended and Restated Plan of Reorganization, and Amendment to Third Amended and Restated Plan of Organization as follows. Wherever the name 'Mortgage Company' appears in the Amendment to Second Amended and Restated Disclosure Statement, Third Amended and Restated Plan of Reorganization and Amendment to Third Amended and Restated Plan of Organization, the name 'Bank' shall be inserted in lieu thereof." *The Reporter,* 15 (Delaware Paralegal Ass'n, May/June 1991).

- Question: How many lawyers does it take to change a light bulb? Answer: Three senior partners to contemplate the history of light; two junior partners to check for conflicts of interest; ten associates to do the research on the anti-trust implications of using a particular brand, on the cost-benefits of electric lighting versus candle light, on the health aspects of incandescent versus fluorescent bulb lighting, on the electric components that make light bulbs work, etc. And, of course, a paralegal to screw the bulb into the socket! *On the Lighter Side,* Par·Spectives 5, Paralegal Ass'n of Rochester (May 1990).

MURPHY'S LAW FOR PARALEGALS

1. The day you wear comfortable, ugly old shoes is the day you are called into the managing partner's office or have to meet with an important client.
2. The day you wear attractive, stylish pumps that pinch your toes, bite your instep, and chafe your heels is the day that you have to serve papers at Nick Tahou's in an unpaved part of the county.
3. The night when you have a date, theater tickets, or fifteen dinner guests due at 7:30 is the night you are asked to stay late.
4. The day your car is in the garage and you carpooled is the day that you receive a 15-hour project that has to be done before you go home.
5. Your mother, your spouse, your significant other, or your bookie always calls when the boss is standing in your office.
6. Clients that work near you never have to sign anything. The number of documents that need to be signed by a client increases in proportion to the number of miles between their home or office and your office.
7. Whatever you lost is what everyone must have immediately.
8. Whatever can't be found was last in the possession of a paralegal.
9. Whatever needs to be hand delivered or picked up is always beyond the messenger's responsibility.
10. The day you have liverwurst and onion for lunch is the day that you have to attend an unscheduled meeting with an important client or another attorney.
11. The volume of Carmody-Wait 2nd that you require to prepare a motion is always missing from the library.
12. Nobody ever asks you about subjects with which you are familiar. If you are an expert on the mating habits of mosquitoes, you will be asked to digest a deposition or prepare research about the malfunction of the farabus and ullie pin connection in Yugoslavian lawnmowers.

Ciaccia, *Murphy's Laws for Paralegals,* 9 Newsletter 12 (Dallas Ass'n of Legal Assistants, Sept. 1985).

GLOSSARY

AAfPE American Association for Paralegal Education.

ABA American Bar Association.

Abstract A summary of something; an overview. *See also* Digests.

Accounts Receivable A list of who owes money to the office, how much, how long the debt has been due, etc.

Accreditation The process by which an organization evaluates and recognizes a program of study (or an institution) as meeting specified qualifications or standards.

Acquit To find not guilty.

Act *See* Statute.

Ad Damnum The amount of damages claimed in the complaint.

Ad Hoc For the specific or special purpose at hand.

Adjudication The process by which a court resolves a legal dispute through litigation. The verb is *adjudicate*.

Ad Litem For the purposes of this litigation.

Administrative Agency A unit of government whose primary mission is to carry out or administer the statutes of the legislature and the executive orders of the chief of the executive branch.

Administrative Code A collection of administrative regulations organized by subject matter rather than by date.

Administrative Decision A resolution of a controversy between a party and an administrative agency involving the application of the regulations, statutes, or executive orders that govern the agency. Sometimes called a *ruling*.

Administrative Hearing A proceeding at an administrative agency presided over by a hearing officer (e.g., an Administrative Law Judge) to resolve a controversy.

Administrative Law Judge (ALJ) A hearing officer who presides over a hearing at an administrative agency.

Administrative Procedure Act (APA) The statute that governs procedures before federal administrative agencies. Many states have their own APA for state agencies.

Administrative Regulation A law of an administrative agency designed to explain or carry out the statutes and executive orders that govern the agency. Also called a *rule*.

Admiralty Law An area of the law that covers accidents and injuries on navigable waters. Also called *maritime law*.

Admissible Evidence Evidence that a judge will allow a jury to consider.

Admission by a Party-Opponent An earlier statement by a party that is now offered in court by an opponent. (An exception to the hearsay rule.)

Admonition A nonpublic declaration that the attorney's conduct was improper. This does not affect his or her right to practice. Also called a *private reprimand*.

ADR Alternative dispute resolution.

Ad Valorem According to value; for example, a tax based on the value of the property being taxed.

Advance Sheet A pamphlet that comes out before (in advance of) a later volume.

Adversarial Involving the presence of an opponent or adversary.

Adversarial Hearing A proceeding in which both parties to a controversy appear before a judge.

Adversarial Memorandum *See* External Memorandum, Memorandum of Law.

Adversarial System Justice and truth have a greater chance of being achieved when the parties to a controversy appear before a neutral judge (on their own or through a representative or advocate) to present their conflicting positions.

Adverse Interests Opposing purposes or claims.

Adverse Judgment A judgment or decision against you.

Advice *See* Professional Judgment.

Advocacy An attempt to influence actions of others.

Affiant *See* Affidavit.

Affidavit   A written statement of fact in which a person (called the *affiant*) swears that the facts in the statement are true.

Affiliate Member   *See* Associate Member.

Affirmation of Professional Responsibility   A statement of the ethical guidelines of the National Federation of Paralegal Associations.

Affirmative Defense   A defense that is based on new factual allegations by the defendant not contained in the plaintiff's allegations.

Aged Accounts Receivable Report   A report showing all cases that have outstanding balances due and how long these balances are past due. (Also called *firm utilization report.*)

Agency Practitioner   An individual authorized to practice before an administrative agency. This individual often does not have to be an attorney.

ALA   Association of Legal Administrators.

Allegation   A claimed fact.

ALS   Automated (computerized) litigated support.

Alternate   An extra juror who will take the place of a regular juror if one becomes incapacitated during the trial.

Ambulance Chasing   Aggressively going to individuals with potentially good claims as plaintiffs (e.g., personal injury victims) to encourage them to hire a particular attorney. If the attorney uses someone else to do the soliciting, the latter is called a *runner*. If this other person uses deception or fraud in the solicitation, he or she is sometimes called a *capper* or a *steerer*. *See also* Court Runner.

Amicus Curiae Brief   A friend-of-the-court brief. An appellate brief submitted by someone who is not a party to the litigation.

Analogous   Similar or alike, although there are differences. Also referred to as *on point*.

Analogy   Similar in some respects but different in others. A comparison of similarities and differences.

Annotate   To provide notes or commentary. A text is annotated if such notes and commentary are provided along with the text.

Annotated Bibliography   A bibliography that briefly states why you included each entry in the bibliography.

Annotated Code/Annotated Statutes   A collection of statutes organized by subject matter rather than by date, along with notes and commentary.

Annotated Reporter   A set of books that contains the full text of court opinions plus commentary (annotations) on them.

Annotation   A set of notes or commentaries on something; for example, the research notes found within the annotated reporter, *American Law Reports*.

Answer   The pleading that responds to or answers the allegations of the complaint.

Antitrust Law   The law governing unlawful restraints of trade, price fixing, and monopolies.

APA   *See* Administrative Procedure Act.

Appeal as a Matter of Right   The appeal of a case that an appellate court must hear; it has no discretion on whether to take the appeal.

Appearance   Going to court to act on behalf of a party to the litigation. The first time this is done, the attorney files a *notice of appearance.*

Appellant   The party bringing an appeal because of dissatisfaction with something the lower tribunal did.

Appellate Brief   A party's written argument to a court of appeals covering the issues that relate to claimed errors that occurred during the trial or other lower court proceeding. A document submitted to an appellate court in which a party seeks to approve, modify, or reverse what a lower court has done. The brief is filed in an appeals court and served on opposing parties.

Appellate Jurisdiction   The power of a court to hear an appeal of a case from a lower tribunal to determine whether it made any errors of law.

Appellee   The party against whom an appeal is brought. Also called the *respondent.*

Appendixes   Additions to a volume or document printed after the body of the text.

Apprentice   A person in training for an occupation under the supervision of a full member of that occupation.

Approval   The recognition that comes from accreditation, certification, licensure, or registration. The ABA uses *approval* as a substitute for the word *accreditation.*

Approval Commission   A group of individuals who investigate whether a paralegal school meets the criteria for approval established by the ABA.

Arbitration   In lieu of litigation, both sides agree to allow a neutral third party to resolve their dispute.

Arraignment   A court proceeding in which the defendant is formally charged with a crime and enters a plea.

Arrest   To take someone into custody in order to bring him or her before the proper authorities.

Assertive   Confident, prepared, and tactfully demonstrative about one's accomplishments and needs.

Assigned Counsel   A private attorney appointed by the court to represent an individual who cannot afford to hire an attorney. If the attorney is a government employee handling criminal cases, he or she is often called a *public defender.*

Associate   An attorney employee of a law firm who hopes eventually to become a partner.

GLOSSARY 1005

Associated Pertaining to an attorney who is an associate in a law firm.

Associate Member A nonattorney who is allowed to become part of—but not a full member of—a bar association. Sometimes called *affiliate member*.

At Common Law (1) All the case law and statutory law in England and in the American colonies before the American Revolution. (2) Judge-made law that exists until changed by statute. *See also* Common Law.

Attestation Clause A clause stating that a person saw a witness sign a document.

Attorney Attestation A signed statement by an attorney that a paralegal applying for membership in a paralegal association meets designated criteria of the association, e.g., is employed as a paralegal.

Attorney-Client Privilege A client and an attorney can refuse to disclose communications between them whose purpose was to facilitate the provision of legal services for the client.

Attorney General The chief attorney for the government. *See also* Opinion of the Attorney General.

Attorney of Record The attorney who has filed a notice of appearance. *See also* Appearance.

Attorney Work Product *See* Work-Product Rule.

At Will *See* Employment at Will.

Authentication Evidence that a writing or other physical item is genuine and is what it purports to be.

Authority Anything that a court could rely on in reaching its decision.

Authorized Practice of Law Services constituting the practice of law that a nonattorney has authorization to provide. *See also* Practice of Law, Professional Judgment.

Automatic Pagination A feature that enables a word processor to number printed pages automatically.

AV Rated The highest rating given to a law firm by the *Martindale-Hubbell Law Directory*.

Baby Attorney A condescending term for an attorney with little or no experience, usually a first-year associate.

Background Research Checking secondary sources to give you a general understanding of an area of law that is new to you.

Backup To copy information.

Bail A sum of money or other property deposited with the court to insure that the defendant will reappear in court at designated times.

Bailiff A court employee who keeps order in the courtroom and renders general administrative assistance to the judge.

Bankruptcy Petition Preparer A person, other than an attorney or an employee of an attorney, who prepares for compensation a bankruptcy petition or other document for filing by a debtor in a United States Bankruptcy Court or a United States District Court.

Bar Prevent or stop.

Bar Coding A series of lines of different widths that can be read by a scanner.

Barratry Stirring up quarrels or litigation; persistently instigating lawsuits, often groundless ones. The illegal solicitation of clients.

Barrister A lawyer in England who represents clients in the higher courts.

Bar Treaties Agreements between attorneys and other occupations that identify the law-related activities of these other occupations that will not be considered the unauthorized practice of law.

Bates Stamping Using a stamp that places a sequential number on documents. The stamp is manufactured by the Bates Company.

Baud Rate A unit of measurement used to indicate the speed of transmission over a modem.

Below (1) The lower tribunal that heard the case before it was appealed. (2) Later in the document.

Bene In proper legal form; legally sufficient.

Best Evidence Rule To prove the contents of a private writing, the original writing should be produced unless it is unavailable.

Beyond a Reasonable Doubt There is no reasonable doubt that every element of the crime has been established. Reasonable doubt is such doubt as would cause prudent persons to hesitate before acting in matters of importance to themselves.

Bias An inclination or tendency to think and perhaps to act in a certain way; a prejudice. A person *without* bias is objective.

Bicameral Having two houses in the legislature. If there is only one house, it is *unicameral*.

Bill A proposed statute.

Billable Tasks Those tasks requiring time that can be charged to a client. A *billable hour* is time spent on a client's case for which the client can be charged.

Billing Memorandum A draft of a client bill that states disbursements, time expended, and billing rates of those working on the matter. *See also* Portable Billings.

Black Letter Law A statement of a fundamental or basic principle of law.

Blended Hourly Rate A rate is set depending on the mix of partners and associates (and sometimes the paralegals) working on the case. *See also* Fee.

Blind Ad A want ad that does not print the name and address of the prospective employer. The contact is made through a third party, e.g., the newspaper.

Block A group of characters, e.g., a word, a sentence, a paragraph. Block movement is a feature of a word processor that allows the user to define a block of text and then do something with that block, e.g., move it, delete it.

Bluebook (1) The *Uniform System of Citation,* the bible of citation form. (2) The *National Reporter Blue Book,* a source for parallel cites. (3) The *A.L.R. Bluebook of Supplemental Decisions,* a set of books that allows you to update the annotations in *A.L.R. First.*

Board of Appeals The unit within an administrative agency to which a party can appeal a decision of the agency.

Boilerplate Standard language that is commonly used in a certain kind of document. Standard verbiage.

Boldface Heavier or darker than normal type.

Bona fide Good faith.

Bond A sum of money deposited in court to insure compliance with a requirement.

Bonus A payment beyond one's regular salary, usually as a reward or recognition. *See also* Incentive Billing.

Boolean Search A search that allows words to be specifically included or excluded through operatives such as AND, OR, and NOT.

Brief (1) Shorthand for appellate brief. A document submitted to an appellate court in which a party seeks to approve, modify, or reverse what a lower court has done. A party's written argument to a court of appeals covering the issues that relate to claimed errors that occurred during the trial or other lower court proceeding. (2) A document submitted to any court in support of a particular position. (3) A summary of the main or essential parts of a court opinion. (4) Shorthand for a trial brief, which is an attorney's personal notes on how to conduct a trial.

Brief of a Case A set of notes on the essential parts of a court opinion, e.g., facts, issues, holding, reasoning.

Budget Performance Report A report that compares a firm's actual income and expenditures with budgeted or projected income and expenditures.

"Bugs" Manufacturing or design errors that exist in products such as computer hardware or software.

Bulletin Board An inexpensive, relatively small, user-run version of a commercial information service.

Bundled/Unbundled An hourly rate is *bundled* if overhead is included in this rate. It is *unbundled* if the various charges are broken out separately. *See also* Fee.

Burden of Proof The responsibility of proving a fact at trial.

Business Entry An out-of-court statement found in business records made in the regular course of business by someone whose duty is to make such entries. (An exception to the hearsay rule.)

Byte The storage equivalent of one letter, one punctuation mark, or one blank space typed into the computer.

CALR Computer-Assisted Legal Research.

Capital Partner *See* Income Partner.

Capped Fee *See* Fee.

Capper *See* Ambulance Chasing.

Caption of Appellate Brief The front of an appellate brief that prints the name of the parties, the name of the court, the docket number, and the kind of appellate brief it is.

Caption of Complaint The top of a complaint that identifies the names of the parties, the court in which the action is brought, the number assigned by the court, etc.

Caption of Opinion The title of an opinion (usually consisting of the names of the parties), the name of the court that wrote it, the docket number, the date of decision—all printed just before the opinion begins.

Career Ladder A formal promotion structure within a company or office.

CARTWHEEL A technique designed to help you think of a large variety of words and phrases to check in the index and table of contents of a law book.

CAS California Advanced Specialist, a person who has passed the California Advanced Specialty Exam.

Case (1) A legal matter in dispute or potential dispute. (2) The written decision of a court. *See also* Opinion.

Casebook A law-school textbook containing numerous edited court opinions.

Case Clerk An assistant to a paralegal; an entry-level paralegal.

Case Manager An experienced legal assistant who can coordinate or direct legal assistant activities on a major case or transaction.

Case Note A summary of and commentary on a court opinion in a law review.

Case-Type Productivity Report A report showing which types of cases in the firm (e.g., bankruptcy, personal injury, criminal) are most profitable. (Also called a practice analysis report.)

Cash Receipts Report A report that describes the income received in a day, week, month, quarter, or year. The cash receipts can be compared with the amount of projected income for a specific time period.

Cause of Action Facts that give a party the right to judicial relief. A legally acceptable reason for suing.

CD-ROM Compact Disk Read-Only Memory. An information

storage system that uses optical technology or laser beams to store and allow you to read large quantities of information.

CEB Continuing education of the bar.

Cell A storage location within a spreadsheet, used to store a single piece of information that is relevant to the spreadsheet.

Censure A formal disapproval or declaration of blame. *See also* Reprimand.

Central Processing Unit (CPU) The "brain" of the computer that coordinates all of the other parts of the computer system and performs the main functions of receiving and processing information or data.

Certificated Having met the qualifications for certification from a school or training program.

Certification The process by which a nongovernmental organization grants recognition to a person who has met the qualifications set by that organization. *See also* Specialty Certification.

Certified Having complied with or met the qualifications for certification.

Certified Legal Assistant (CLA) The title bestowed by the National Association of Legal Assistants on a paralegal who has passed the CLA exam and has met other criteria of NALA. *See also* Specialty Certification.

Certified PLS A Certified Professional Legal Secretary. This status is achieved after passing an examination and meeting other requirements of NALS, the National Association of Legal Secretaries.

Certiorari *See* Writ of Certiorari.

CFLA Certified Florida Legal Assistant. To earn this title, a paralegal must first pass the CLA (Certified Legal Assistant) exam of NALA and then pass a special exam on Florida law.

Challenge for Cause A request to exclude someone from a jury for a specified reason. *See also* Peremptory Challenge.

Champerty Promoting someone else's litigation, often by helping to finance the litigation in exchange for a share in the recovery.

Character A letter, number, or symbol. Character enhancement includes underlining, boldfacing, subscripting, and superscripting.

Chargeable Hour Schedule A report that summarizes hours invested by attorneys and paralegals, usually on a monthly basis.

Charge to Jury Instructions to the jury on how to go about determining the facts and reaching its verdict.

Charter The fundamental law of a municipality or other local unit of government authorizing it to perform designated governmental functions.

Checks and Balances An allocation of governmental powers whereby one branch of government can block or check what another branch wants to do and thereby maintain a balance of powers among the branches.

Chinese Wall Steps taken to prevent a tainted employee (attorney, paralegal, or secretary) from having any contact with the case of a particular client in the office. The employee is tainted because he or she has a conflict of interest with that client. A Chinese wall is also called an *ethical wall*. A tainted employee is also called a *contaminated employee*. Once the Chinese wall is set up around the tainted employee, the latter is referred to as a *quarantined employee*.

Churning Providing services beyond what the circumstances warrant for the primary purpose of generating fees and commissions.

Circumstantial Evidence Evidence of one fact from which another fact can be inferred.

Citation A reference to any material printed on paper or stored in a computer database. It is the "address" where you can locate and read the material. *See also* Parallel Cite, Pinpoint Cite, Public Domain Citation.

Citator A book containing lists of citations that can help you assess the current validity of an item and can give you leads to additional laws.

Cite (1) A citation. (2) To give the volume number, page number, or other information that will enable you to locate written material in a library.

Cite Checking Reading every cite in a document to determine whether the format of the cite conforms to the citation rules being used (e.g., the Bluebook rules), whether the quotations in the cite are accurate, etc.

Cited Material The case, statute, regulation, or other document that you are shepardizing.

Citing Material The case, article, or annotation that mentions whatever you are shepardizing, i.e., that mentions the cited material.

Civil Dispute One private party suing another, or a private party suing the government, or the government suing a private party for a matter other than the commission of a crime.

Civil Law Any law other than criminal law. The law governing the resolution of disputes (a) between persons or (b) between persons and the government other than for the prosecution of a crime.

Civil Law System The legal system of many Western European countries other than England. (England and America have a common law system.) A civil law system places a greater emphasis on statutory or code law than the common law system.

CLA *See* Certified Legal Assistant.

Claims-Made Policy Insurance that covers only claims actually filed (i.e., made) during the period in which the policy is in effect.

CLAS Certified Legal Assistant Specialist (an advanced certification status of NALA).

CLE Continuing Legal Education. Undertaken after an individual has received his or her primary education or training in a law-related occupation.

Clergy-Penitent Privilege A member of the clergy and a penitent can refuse to disclose communications between them that relate to spiritual counseling or consultation.

Clerk The court employee who assists judges with record keeping and other administrative duties. *See also* Law Clerk.

Client Investment Summary Report A report of the total amount billed and unbilled, with a calculation of the actual costs of providing legal services for a particular client.

Clinical Education Training programs in which students work on real cases under supervision.

Clone See IBM-compatible.

Closed-Ended Question A narrowly structured question that often can be answered in one or two words. Also called a *directed question*.

Closing The event during which steps are taken to finalize the transfer of an interest in property.

Code A set of rules, organized by subject matter.

Codefendants More than one defendant sued in the same civil case. More than one defendant prosecuted in the same criminal case.

Code of Ethics and Professional Responsibility A statement of the ethical guidelines of the National Association of Legal Assistants.

Codified To arrange laws by subject matter regardless of when they were enacted.

Coding Taking specified information from documents that will be used as part of a computer index to those documents.

Command An instruction typed into a computer.

Commingling Mixing general law firm funds with client funds in a single account.

Common Law (1) Judge-made law in the absence of controlling statutory or other higher law. (2) Case law; all court opinions. (3) The legal system we inherited from England. (4) All the case law and statutory law in England and in the American colonies before the American Revolution. *See also* At Common Law; Enacted Law.

Common Representation *See* Multiple Representation.

Communications A program that allows computers to communicate with each other, usually through telephone lines. *See also* Modem.

Compatibility Being able to work together. Computers of different manufacturers are compatible if they can read each other's data or use each other's software.

Competence, Attorney Having the knowledge and skill that is reasonably necessary to represent a particular client.

Competent (evidence) Capable of giving testimony because the person understands the obligation to tell the truth, has the ability to communicate, and has knowledge of the topic of his or her testimony.

Complaint The pleading filed by the plaintiff that tries to state a claim or cause of action against the defendant.

Concurrent Jurisdiction The power of a court to hear a particular kind of case, along with other courts that could also hear it.

Concurring Opinion An opinion written by less than a majority of the judges on the court that agrees with the *result* reached by the majority but not with all of its reasoning.

Conference Committee A committee made up of members of both houses of the legislature that meets to try to resolve differences in the versions of a bill that each house passed.

Confidential That which should not be revealed; pertaining to information that others do not have a right to receive.

Conflict of Interest The presence of divided loyalty that actually or potentially places a person at a disadvantage even though this person is owed undivided loyalty. Also called *divided loyalty*.

Conflicts Check A determination of whether a conflict of interest exists that might disqualify a law office from representing a client or from continuing the representation. The person performing this check full-time is often called a *conflicts specialist*.

Conflicts of Law An area of the law that determines what law applies when a choice must be made between the laws of different, coequal legal systems, e.g., two states.

Confrontation The right to face your accuser.

Connectors Characters, words, or symbols used to show the relationship between the words and phrases in a query.

Constitution The fundamental law that creates the branches of government and that identifies basic rights and obligations.

Contaminated Having an employee who brings a conflict of interest to the office. *See also* Chinese Wall.

Contest To challenge.

Contingent Fee A plaintiff's fee that is dependent on the outcome of the case. A *defense contingent fee* (also called a *negative contingency*) is a fee for the defendant's attorney that is dependent on the outcome of the case.

Continuing Legal Education (CLE) Legal training a person receives after completing his or her primary or formal education.

Contract Attorney *See* Project Attorney.

Contract Paralegal A self-employed paralegal who often works for several different attorneys on a freelance basis. *See also* Freelance Paralegal.

Control Character A coded character that does not print but is part of the command sequence in a word processor.

Coordinates   In a spreadsheet program, the column letter and row number that define the location of a specific cell.

Corporate Counsel   The chief attorney of a corporation. Also called the *general counsel*.

Corporate Legal Department   The law office within a corporation containing salaried attorneys (in-house attorneys) who advise and represent the corporation.

Counterclaim   A claim or cause of action against the plaintiff stated in the defendant's answer.

Court of First Instance   A trial court; a court with original jurisdiction.

Court Runner   A messenger used primarily to deliver and pick up documents and files from the courts. *See also* Ambulance Chasing.

Credentialization   A form of official recognition based on one's training or employment status.

Credible   Believable.

Criminal Dispute   A suit brought by the government for the alleged commission of a crime.

Cross-claim   Usually, a claim by one codefendant against another.

Cross-examination   Questioning the witness called by the other side after direct examination.

Cumulative   That which repeats earlier material and consolidates it with new material. A cumulative supplement contains new supplemental material and repeats earlier supplemental material.

Cured   Corrected.

Curriculum Vitae   A résumé.

Cursor   The marker on the display screen indicating where the next character can be displayed when typing resumes.

Daisy Wheel Printer   A printer that uses a device resembling a flower that contains the alphabet and other characters on spokes.

Damages   An award of money paid by the wrongdoer to compensate the person who has been harmed.

Data   Information that can be used by a computer.

Database   A program used to store and organize information; a grouping of independent files into one integrated whole that can be accessed through one central point.

Data Manager   A data management software package that consolidates data files into an integrated whole, allowing access to more than one data file at a time.

Data Redundancy   The repetition of the same data in several different files.

Decision   *See* Administrative Decision, Opinion.

Declaration against Interest   An out-of-court statement made by a nonparty to the litigation that is against the interest of that nonparty. (An exception to the hearsay rule.)

Declaration of Bodily Feelings   An out-of-court statement or utterance made spontaneously about the person's present bodily condition. (An exception to the hearsay rule.)

Declaration of Present Sense Impression   An out-of-court statement that describes an event while it is being observed by the person making the statement. (An exception to the hearsay rule.)

Declaration of State of Mind   An out-of-court statement made about the person's present state of mind. (An exception to the hearsay rule.)

Declaratory Judgment   A court decision establishing the rights and obligations of the parties but not ordering them to do or to refrain from doing anything.

Declination Letter   *See* Letter of Disengagement.

Dedicated Word Processor   A system that can perform only word processing tasks.

Deep Pocket   Slang for the person or organization with enough money or other assets to be able to pay a judgment.

De Facto   In fact; actually. Exercising power even though not by law or proper authority.

Default Judgment   A judgment for the plaintiff because the defendant failed to appear or to file an answer before the deadline.

Default Setting   A value used by the word processor when it is not instructed to use any other value.

Defense   A response to a claim of the other party, setting forth reason(s) the claim should be denied. The response may be an allegation of facts and/or a presentation of a legal theory.

Defense Contingent Fee   *See* Contingent Fee.

De Jure   Lawful; in compliance with the requirements of the law.

"Delegatitis"   An inordinate fear of delegating tasks to others.

Deletion   A feature of a word processor that allows you to remove a character, word, sentence, or larger block of text from the existing text.

Demurrer   Even if the plaintiff proved all the facts stated in the complaint, a cause of action would not be established.

De Novo   Anew; starting over.

Denturist   A nondentist who produces and dispenses removable dentures directly to the public.

Deponent   *See* Deposition.

Deposition   A pretrial discovery device consisting of a question-and-answer session involving a party or witness designed to assist the other party prepare for trial. The person who is questioned is called the *deponent*.

Depository Library   A private or public library that receives free federal government publications to which it must allow the general public access.

Depo Summarizer   An employee whose main job is digesting discovery documents, particularly depositions.

Dictum   A statement made by a court that was not necessary to resolve the specific legal issues before the court. The plural of dictum is dicta.

Digest by Person   A summary of the information in a document pertaining to a certain individual.

Digest by Subject   A summary of the information in a document pertaining to a certain topic or subject.

Digesting   Summarizing discovery documents. *See also* Depo Summarizer.

Digests   (1) Volumes that contain summaries of court opinions. These summaries are sometimes called *abstracts* or *squibs*. (2) Volumes that contain summaries of annotations in A.L.R., A.L.R.2d, A.L.R.3d, etc.

Directed Question   *See* Closed-Ended Question.

Directed Verdict   An order by the court that the jury reach a verdict for the party making the motion on the ground that the other side, which has just rested its case, has failed to produce enough convincing evidence to establish a cause of action.

Direct Evidence   Evidence that tends to establish a fact (or to disprove a fact) without the need for an inference.

Direct Examination   The first questioning of a witness you have called.

Disbarment   The temporary or permanent termination of the right to practice law.

Disbursements   Out-of-pocket expenses.

Disciplinary Rule (DR)   *See* Model Code of Professional Responsibility.

Discount Adjustment   A write-down (decrease) in the bill.

Discoverable   Obtainable through one of the devices of pretrial discovery, e.g., interrogatories.

Discovery   Pretrial devices designed to assist a party prepare for trial. *See* Deposition, Interrogatories.

Disengagement   *See* Letter of Disengagement.

Disinterested   Not working for one side or the other in a controversy or other legal matter; not deriving benefit if one of the sides prevails.

Disk Drive   Hardware used to store and retrieve programs and information to and from diskettes.

Diskette   A flat piece of plastic on which information can be placed or removed by the computer.

Dismissal without Prejudice   A dismissal based on procedural, not substantive, grounds. The party can try to bring the case again.

Disqualification   *See* Vicarious Disqualification.

Dissenting Opinion   An opinion that disagrees with the result and the reasoning used by the majority.

District Court   *See* United States District Court.

Diversity of Citizenship   The parties to the litigation are citizens of different states, and the amount in controversy exceeds the amount specified by federal statute. This diversity gives jurisdiction to a United States District Court.

Divided Loyalty   *See* Conflict of Interest.

Docket Number   The number assigned to a case by the court.

Doctor-Patient Privilege   A doctor and a patient can refuse to disclose any confidential (private) communications between them that relate to medical care.

Documentation   The manual on operating a computer; the accompanying documents.

Document Clerk   An individual whose main responsibility is to organize, file, code, or digest litigation or other client documents.

Dot Matrix Printer   A printer that uses tiny pins that press against or punch a ribbon to create a pattern of dots.

Double Density   The disk drive can store information on the diskette in condensed mode.

Downtime   The period during which the computer is unavailable because of technical difficulties.

DR   Disciplinary Rule. *See* Model Code of Professional Responsibility.

Draft   (1) To write. (She *drafted* a memorandum.) (2) A document in one of its preliminary stages. (I was asked to proofread a *draft* of a contract before it was printed.)

Draft Bill   *See* Billing Memorandum.

Draw   A partner's advance against profits.

Dual Sided   The disk drive is capable of writing on both sides of the diskette.

DWI   Descriptive Word Index, an index to the digests of West.

Dying Declaration   An out-of-court statement concerning the causes or circumstances of death made by a person whose death is imminent. (An exception to the hearsay rule.)

EC   Ethical Consideration. *See* Model Code of Professional Responsibility.

Editing   In word processing, the function of changing or amending text.

Edition   A version of a text that is usually a revision of an earlier version.

EEOC Equal Employment Opportunity Commission, a federal agency that investigates job discrimination.

Electronic Citation *See* Public Domain Citation.

Element A portion of a rule that is a precondition of the applicability of the entire rule. The *element in contention* is an element of the rule about which the parties cannot agree. The disagreement may be over the meaning of the element or how it applies to the facts.

Employment at Will An employment that can be terminated by the employer or employee at any time for any reason.

Enacted Law Law written by the legislature (statutes), by the people (constitutions), and by an administrative agency (regulations). Law that is not the product of litigation or adjudication. *See also* Adjudication.

En Banc The entire membership of the court; by the entire court.

Encyclopedia *See* Legal Encyclopedia.

Enrolled Agent An individual authorized to represent taxpayers at all administrative proceedings within the Internal Revenue Service—this person does not have to be an attorney.

Enrollment *See* Registration.

Entry-Level Certification Certification of individuals who have just begun their careers.

Equity Partner A full owner of a law firm. *See also* Income Partner.

Estate All the property left by a decedent from which his or her debts can be paid.

Et al. And others.

Ethical Consideration (EC) *See* Model Code of Professional Responsibility.

Ethical Wall *See* Chinese Wall.

Ethics Rules that embody standards of behavior to which members of an organization are expected to conform.

Et Seq. And following.

Evidence Anything that is offered to help establish or disprove a factual position. A separate determination must be made on whether a particular item of evidence is relevant or irrelevant, admissible or inadmissible, etc.

Excited Utterance An out-of-court statement relating to a startling event or condition made while the declarant was under the stress of excitement caused by the event or condition. (An exception to the hearsay rule.)

Exclusive Jurisdiction The power of a court to hear a particular kind of case, to the exclusion of other courts.

Execution Carrying out or enforcing a judgment.

Executive Branch The branch of government that carries out, executes, or administers the law.

Executive Department Agency An administrative agency that exists within the executive branch of government, often at the cabinet level.

Executive Order A law issued by the chief executive pursuant to specific statutory authority or to the executive's inherent authority to direct the operation of governmental agencies.

Executor The person named in a will who has the responsibility of carrying out the terms of the will. (Called the *executrix,* if a woman.)

Exempt Employee An employee who is not entitled to overtime compensation under the Fair Labor Standards Act because the employee is a professional, administrative, or executive employee. The U.S. Department of Labor asserts that paralegals are nonexempt, except for paralegal managers.

Exhausting Administrative Remedies Going through all methods available in an administrative agency to resolve a dispute before asking a court to review what the agency did.

Exhibit An item of physical or tangible evidence offered to the court for inspection.

Existing Physical or Mental Condition, Statement of An out-of-court statement of a then-existing physical or mental condition.

Ex Parte Involving one party only.

Ex Parte Hearing A hearing at which only one party is present. A court order issued at such a hearing is an *ex parte order.*

Ex Post Facto After the fact.

External/Adversary Memorandum of Law A memorandum written primarily for individuals outside the office to convince them to take a certain course of action. *See also* Memorandum of Law.

Fact Particularization A technique designed to help you list numerous factual questions in order to obtain a comprehensive picture of all the facts that are relevant to a legal matter.

Fact Pleading A statement of every ultimate (i.e., essential) fact in the complaint.

Facts & Findings A periodical of the National Association of Legal Assistants.

Fair Labor Standards Act The federal statute that regulates conditions of employment such as when overtime compensation must be paid. *See also* Exempt Employee.

Federalism The division of powers between the federal government and the state governments.

Federal Question A legal question that arises from the application of the United States Constitution, a statute of Congress, or a federal administrative regulation.

Fee The amount charged for services rendered. An *hourly rate fee* is based on the number of hours worked. A *blended hourly rate* is a single hourly rate that is based on a blend or mix of partner, associate, and sometimes paralegal rates. A *bundled rate* covers the attorney's time plus the cost of his or her overhead. An *unbundled rate* consists of the cost of the attorney's time without considering overhead costs. A *fixed fee* is a flat fee for the service regardless of the amount of time needed to complete it. A *capped fee* is an hourly rate leading to a total bill that will not exceed a predetermined amount. An *hourly plus fixed fee* is an hourly rate charged until the nature and scope of the legal problem are identified, at which time a fixed fee is charged for services provided thereafter. *See also* Contingent Fee, Fee-Generating Case, Fee Splitting, Incentive Billing, Task-Based Billing, Value Billing.

Fee Analysis Report A report on the fees generated by client, by area of law, by law firm branch office, and by individual attorney.

Fee-Generating Case The case of a client who can pay a fee out of the damages awarded or from his or her independent resources.

Fee Splitting A single client bill covering the fee of two or more attorneys who are not in the same firm.

Felony A crime punishable by a sentence of one year or more.

Field A subdivision of a record that holds a meaningful item of data, e.g., an employee number.

Field Search In WESTLAW, a search that is limited to a certain part of cases in its databases.

File A group of related data records, e.g., employee records.

Filed To deposit a pleading, motion, or other formal document with an official, often a court clerk. What is filed, frequently becomes a public record.

Firm Utilization Report See Aged Accounts Receivable Report.

First Impression New; that which has come before the court for the first time.

First Instance, Court of A trial court; a court with original jurisdiction.

Fixed Fee A flat fee for services. A set amount paid regardless of the amount of time needed to complete it. *See also* Fee.

Floppy Disk A disk drive that can use diskettes.

Fonts The design of letters.

Format In word processing, the layout of the page, e.g., the number of lines and margin settings.

Formbook A manual that contains forms, checklists, practice techniques, etc. Sometimes called a *practice manual* or *handbook*.

Formula A mathematical expression that is used in a spreadsheet.

Forum The court where the case is to be tried.

Forwarding Fee *See* Referral Fee.

FRCP Federal Rules of Civil Procedure.

Freedom of Information Act A statute that gives citizens access to certain information in the possession of the government.

Freelance Paralegal A self-employed paralegal who works for several different attorneys, or a self-employed paralegal who works directly for the public. Also referred to as an *independent paralegal*.

Friendly Divorce A divorce proceeding in which the parties have no significant disputes between them.

Full-Text Search A search through all of the information (usually every word) in a database.

Functional Résumé A résumé that clusters skills and talents together regardless of when they were developed.

General Counsel The chief attorney in a corporate law department.

General Jurisdiction The power of the court (within its geographic boundaries) to hear any kind of case, with certain exceptions.

General Practitioner An attorney who handles any kind of case.

General Schedule (GS) The pay-scale system used in the federal government.

Generic Citation A citation to material based on a system that is not dependent on traditional volume and page numbers. Also called a *public domain citation*. It is medium neutral. If the references are to documents online, it is called an *electronic citation*.

Geographic Jurisdiction The area of the state or country over which a court has power to render decisions.

Gigabyte One billion bytes (approximate).

Global In word processing, an instruction that will be carried out throughout the document.

Go Bare To engage in an occupation or profession without malpractice insurance.

GOD The Great Overtime Debate. *See* Exempt Employee.

Grand Jury A special jury whose duty is to hear evidence of felonies presented by the prosecutor to determine whether there is sufficient evidence to return an indictment against the defendant and cause him or her to stand trial on the charges.

Grounds Reasons.

Group Legal Services A form of legal insurance in which members of a group pay a set amount on a regular basis, for which they receive designated legal services. Also called *prepaid legal services*.

GS *See* General Schedule.

Guideline Suggested conduct that will help an applicant obtain accreditation, certification, licensure, registration, or approval.

HALT Help Abolish Legal Tyranny, an organization that seeks to reform the legal profession, primarily by eliminating the monopoly of attorneys over the practice of law.

Handbook   *See* Formbook.

Harassment   *See* Hostile Environment, Harassment, Quid Pro Quo Harassment.

Hard Copy   A printed page on which text and/or graphics appear.

Hard Disk   A disk drive that cannot be removed without taking the hardware apart.

Hardware   The computer and its physical parts.

Header   In word processing, a piece of text that is stored separately from the text and printed at the top of each page.

Headhunter   Someone who tries to locate people to work in a particular office.

Heading   The beginning of a memorandum that lists who the memo is for, who wrote it, what it is about, etc.

Headnote   A small-paragraph summary of a portion of a court opinion, written by a private publisher.

Hearing Examiner   One who presides over an administrative hearing.

Hearing Memorandum   A memorandum of law submitted to a hearing officer.

Hearsay   Testimony in court, or written evidence, of a statement made out of court when the statement is offered to show the truth of matters asserted therein, and thus relying for its value on the credibility of the out-of-court asserter.

Historical Note   Information on the legislative history of a statute printed after the text of the statute.

Holding   A court's answer to one of the legal issues in the case. Also called a *ruling*.

Hornbook   A treatise that summarizes an area of the law.

Hostile Environment Harassment   Pervasive unwelcome sexual conduct or sex-based ridicule that unreasonably interferes with an individual's job performance or creates an intimidating, hostile, or offensive working environment.

Hourly Plus Fixed Fee   *See* Fee.

Hourly Rate Fee   *See* Fee.

Hypertext   A method of displaying and linking information located in different places in the same document or in different documents.

Hypothetical   Not actual or real, but presented for purposes of discussion or analysis; based on an assumed set of facts; based on a hypothesis.

Hypothetical Question   A question in which the interviewee is asked to respond to a set of assumed facts provided by the interviewer.

IBM-compatible Computer   A computer—called a clone—that is not manufactured by IBM but can read data created by an IBM computer or use software an IBM computer can use.

Icon   A picture or graphic that is "clicked" on with a mouse in order to execute it.

Id.   The same citation as immediately above.

Imaging   Creating images of an original document through scanning or other techniques.

Impaired Attorney   An attorney with a drug or alcohol problem.

Impaneled   Selected, sworn in, and seated.

Impeach   To challenge; to attack the credibility of.

Imputed Disqualification   *See* Vicarious Disqualification.

Incentive Billing   The attorney receives an increased fee for achieving an exceptional result such as settling a case for an amount that exceeds a target set by the client and attorney. Also called a *performance bonus.*

Income Partner   A special category of partner who does not own the firm in the sense of a full equity or capital partner. Also called a *permanent associate* and a *nonequity partner.*

Incremental Spacing   In word processing, a method by which the printer inserts spaces between words and letters to produce margins that are justified. Also called *microspacing.*

Independent Contractor   One who operates his or her own business and contracts to do work for others who do not control the details of how that work is performed.

Independent Paralegal   *See* Freelance Paralegal.

Independent Regulatory Agency   An administrative agency (often existing outside the executive department) created to regulate an aspect of society.

Indexing   Identifying the page numbers on which certain topics appear in a document.

Indictment   A formal document issued by a grand jury accusing the defendant of a crime. *See also* Grand Jury.

Indigent   Without funds to hire legal counsel. Impoverished.

Inferior Court   A lower court.

Information   A document accusing the defendant of a crime (used in states without a grand jury).

Informational Interview   An interview in which you find out about a particular kind of employment. It is *not* a job interview.

Information and Belief   To the best of my knowledge; good faith understanding.

Infra   Below, mentioned or referred to later in the document.

In-house Attorney   An attorney who is an employee of a business corporation. *See* Corporate Legal Department.

In Issue   In dispute or question.

Initial Appearance   The first criminal court appearance by the accused during which the court (a) informs him or her of the charges, (b) makes a decision on bail, and (c) determines the date of the next court proceeding.

Ink Jet Printer   A printer that uses a stream of ink sprayed on paper to produce the print.

In Personam Jurisdiction   *See* Personal Jurisdiction.

In Propria Persona   (In Pro Per) In one's own proper person. *See also* Pro Se.

In Re   In the matter of.

Insertion   In word processing, a feature by which a character, word, sentence, or larger block of text is added to the existing text.

Insider Trading   Transacting in shares of a publicly held corporation by persons with inside or advance information on which the trading is based.

Instrument   A formal document that gives expression to a legal act or agreement, e.g., a mortgage.

Intake Memo   A memorandum that summarizes the facts given by a client upon becoming a client of the office.

Integrated Bar Association   A state bar association to which an attorney must belong in order to practice law in the state. Also called a *mandatory* or *unified bar association.*

Integrated Package   A software program that enables the user to use more than one kind of program simultaneously, e.g., word processing, database management, spreadsheet.

Intellectual Property Law   The law governing patents, copyrights, trademarks, and trade names.

Interim Suspension   A temporary suspension, pending the imposition of final discipline.

Interlocutory Appeal   An appeal of a trial court ruling before the trial court reaches its final judgment.

Intermediate Appellate Court   A court with appellate jurisdiction to which parties can appeal before they appeal to the highest court in the judicial system.

Intern   *See* Legal Intern.

Internal/Interoffice Memorandum of Law   A memorandum written for members of one's own office. *See also* Memorandum of Law.

Internet   A special network of networks to which millions of individual computer users have access.

Interrogatories   A pretrial discovery device consisting of written questions sent by one party to another to assist the sender of the questions in preparing for trial.

Interstate Compact   An agreement between two or more states governing a problem of mutual concern.

Intra-agency Appeal   An appeal within an administrative agency, before the case is appealed to a court.

Investigation, Legal   The process of gathering additional facts and verifying presently known facts in order to advise a client about solving or avoiding a legal problem.

Jailhouse Lawyer   A paralegal in prison, usually self-taught, who has a limited right to practice law by giving legal advice to fellow inmates if the prison does not provide adequate alternatives for legal services. Also known as a *writ writer.*

Jargon   Technical language; language that does not have an everyday meaning.

Job Bank   A service that lists available jobs, usually available only to members of an organization.

Joint and Several Liability   Legally responsible together and individually.

Judgment   The final conclusion of a court. The judgment will resolve the legal dispute before the court or will decide what further proceedings are needed to resolve the dispute.

Judgment Creditor   The party to whom damages must be paid.

Judgment Debtor   The party who must pay damages.

Judgment NOV (Notwithstanding the Verdict)   A judgment by the trial judge that is contrary to the verdict reached by the jury.

Judgment on the Merits   A decision on the substance of the claims raised.

Judicial Branch   The branch of government with primary responsibility for interpreting laws and resolving disputes that arise under them.

Judicial Review   The power of a court to refuse to enforce a law because it is in conflict with the constitution.

Jump Cite   *See* Pinpoint Cite.

Jurisdiction   The power of a court. *See also* Geographic Jurisdiction, Subject-Matter Jurisdiction.

Jury Panel   *See* Panel.

Justification   In word processing, a feature for making lines of text even at the margins.

K   A measure of capacity in a computer system.

Kardex   A file in which the library records the volume numbers and dates of incoming publications that are part of subscriptions.

Key Fact   A critical fact; a fact that was essential to the holding of the court.

Key Number   A general topic and a number of a subtopic. It is the heart of the system used by West to organize the millions of small-paragraph summaries of court opinions in its digests.

Key-Word Search   A search through a list of specified words that function like an index to a database.

Kilobyte   One thousand bytes (approximately).

Label   Information used for describing some aspect of a spreadsheet.

LAMA   Legal Assistant Management Association.

Landmen   Paralegals who work in the area of oil and gas law. Also called *land technicians.*

Language   A program that allows a computer to understand commands and to carry them out.

Laptop   A portable computer that can be powered by rechargeable batteries. Smaller laptops are called notebooks, subnotebooks, and palmtops.

Laser Printer   A printer that uses a laser beam of light to reproduce images.

Lateral Hire   An attorney, paralegal, or secretary who has been hired from another law office.

Law Clerk   An attorney's employee who is in law school studying to become an attorney or who has graduated from law school and is waiting to pass the bar examination. In Ontario, Canada, a law clerk is a trained professional doing independent legal work, which may include managerial duties, under the direction and guidance of a lawyer, and whose function is to relieve a lawyer of routine and administrative matters and to assist a lawyer in the more complex ones.

Law Directory   A list of attorneys.

Law Review   A legal periodical published by a law school. Sometimes called a *law journal.*

Lay Opinion Evidence   The opinion of someone who is not an expert.

LCP   Louisiana Certified Paralegal, a person who has passed the Louisiana Certified Paralegal Exam.

Leading Question   A question that suggests an answer within the question.

Legal Administrator   An individual, usually a nonattorney, with broad management responsibility for a law office.

Legal Advice   The application of laws or legal principles to the facts of a particular client's case. *See also* Professional Judgment.

Legal Analysis   The application of rules of law to facts in order to answer a legal question or issue. The goal is to solve a legal dispute, to prevent such a dispute from arising, or to prevent the dispute from getting worse.

Legal Assistant   *See* Paralegal.

Legal Assistant Clerk   A person who assists a legal assistant in clerical tasks such as document numbering, alphabetizing, filing, and any other project that does not require substantive knowledge of litigation or of a particular transaction. *See also* Document Clerk.

Legal Assistant Division   A few state bar associations, e.g., Texas, have established special divisions that paralegals can join as associate members.

Legal Assistant Manager   A person who is responsible for recruiting, interviewing, and hiring legal assistants and spends little or no time working on client cases as a legal assistant. He or she may also be substantially involved in other matters pertaining to legal assistants, e.g., training, monitoring work assignments, designing budgets, and overseeing the billing of paralegal time. Also known as a *paralegal manager.*

Legal Bias   *See* Bias.

Legal Encyclopedia   A multivolume set of books that alphabetically summarizes almost every major legal topic.

Legal Executive   A trained and certified employee of a solicitor in England; the equivalent of an American paralegal but with more training and credentials.

Legal Insurance   *See* Group Legal Services.

Legal Intern   A person who works (usually unpaid) in a law office while still a student.

Legal Investigation   *See* Investigation.

Legal Issue   A question of law; a question of what the law is, or what the law means, or how the law applies to a set of facts. If the dispute is over the truth or falsity of the facts, it is referred to as a *question of fact* or a *factual dispute.*

Legalman   A nonattorney in the Navy who assists attorneys in the practice of law.

Legal Technician   A self-employed paralegal who works for several different attorneys, or a self-employed paralegal who works directly for the public. Sometimes called an *independent paralegal* or a *freelance paralegal.*

Legal Treatise   A book written by a private individual (or by a public individual writing as a private citizen) that provides an overview, summary, or commentary on a legal topic.

Legislation   (1) The process of making statutory law. (2) A statute.

Legislative Branch   The branch of government with primary responsibility for making or enacting the law.

Legislative History   All of the events that occur in the legislature before a bill is enacted into a statute.

Letterhead   The top part of stationery, which identifies the name and address of the office (often with the names of selected employees).

Letter of Disengagement   A letter sent to a client formally notifying him or her that the attorney will no longer be representing the client. The letter severs the attorney-client relationship. Also called a *declination letter*.

Letter of Nonengagement   A letter sent to a prospective client that explicitly states that the attorney will not be representing him or her.

Leverage   The ability to make a profit from the income-generating work of others.

LEXIS   The legal research computer service of Reed Elsevier Co.

Liable   Legally responsible.

Licensed Independent Paralegal   A paralegal who holds a limited license. *See* Limited Licensure.

Licensure   The process by which an agency of government grants permission to persons meeting specified qualifications to engage in an occupation and often to use a particular title.

Limited Jurisdiction   The power of a court to hear only certain kinds of cases. Also called *special jurisdiction*.

Limited Liability   If you have limited liability and lose a lawsuit that arises out of your business activities, the winner of the lawsuit can collect only out of the assets of the business; he or she cannot reach your personal assets such as your home. If your personal assets are reachable, then you have full *personal liability*.

Limited Liability Entity   A limited liability company (LLC) or a limited liability partnership (LLP) that allows limited liability for its owners, but is treated like a partnership for income tax purposes.

Limited Licensure   The process by which an agency of government grants permission to persons meeting specified qualifications to engage in designated activities that are now customarily (although not always exclusively) performed by another license holder, i.e., that are part of someone else's monopoly.

Limited Practice Officer   A nonattorney in Washington State who has the authority to select and prepare designated legal documents pertaining to real estate closings.

Lis Pendens   A pending suit.

Listserv   A program that manages computer mailing lists automatically. This includes receiving and distributing messages from and to the members of the list.

Litigation   The formal process of resolving legal controversies through special tribunals established for this purpose. The major tribunal is a court.

Load   To move a program or information from a disk drive into the computer.

Lodestar   A method of calculating an award of attorney fees authorized by statute. The number of reasonable hours spent on the case is multiplied by a reasonable hourly rate. Other factors might also be considered above the lodestar in setting the fee, e.g., the quality of representation, any delay in receiving payment, and the risk at the outset of the litigation that the prevailing attorney will receive no fee.

Loose-leaf Service   A three-ring (or post) binder containing pages that can be easily inserted or taken out. The service covers current information on a broad or narrow topic.

Macro   Prerecorded keystrokes that print text and/or execute commands.

Magistrate   A judicial officer having some but not all the powers of a judge.

Majority Opinion   The opinion whose result and reasoning are supported by at least half plus one of the judges on the court.

Malpractice   Serious wrongful conduct committed by an individual, usually a member of a profession.

Managing Partner   The partner of a firm who has day-to-day responsibility for running the administrative aspects of the firm.

Mandate   The order of the court.

Mandatory Authority   Whatever a court must rely on in reaching its decision.

Mandatory Bar Association   *See* Integrated Bar Association.

Marital Communications   A husband and a wife can refuse to disclose communications between them during the marriage.

Maritime Law   *See* Admiralty Law.

Market Rate   The prevailing rate in the area.

Martindale-Hubbell   A national directory of attorneys.

Med-arb   In lieu of litigation, the parties to a dispute try arbitration after mediation is unsuccessful.

Mediation   In lieu of litigation, a neutral third party (the mediator) tries to encourage the parties to a dispute to reach a compromise.

Megabyte   One million bytes (approximately).

Memorandum of Law   A memorandum is simply a note, a comment, or a report. A legal memorandum is a written explanation of what the law is and how it might apply to a fact situation.

Memorandum Opinion   A court opinion, usually a short one, that does not name the judge who wrote the opinion. Also called a *per curiam* opinion.

Memory   The area inside the computer that contains programs and data that the programs help generate.

Mental Condition   *See* Declaration of State of Mind; Existing Physical or Mental Condition.

Menu   In word processing and other programs, a list of commands or prompts on the display screen.

Merge Printing In word processing and other programs, a feature that allows a user to combine whole files and to place data from one file into specified locations in another.

Merging The process of combining a form with a list of variables to automatically produce a document.

Microcomputer A computer small enough to fit on a desk. Also called a *personal computer.*

Microfiche *See* Microform.

Microform Images or photographs that have been reduced in size. Microforms can be *microfilms,* which store material on reels or cassettes, or *microfiche* and *ultrafiche,* which store material that has been reduced by a factor of 100 or more on a single sheet of film.

Minimum-Fee Schedule A published list of fees recommended by a bar association.

Misdemeanor A crime punishable by a sentence of less than a year.

Model Code of Ethics and Professional Responsibility A statement of ethical guidelines of the National Federation of Paralegal Associations.

Model Code of Professional Responsibility An earlier edition of the ethical rules governing attorneys recommended by the American Bar Association. The Model Code consisted of Ethical Considerations (ECs), which represented the objectives toward which each attorney should strive, and Disciplinary Rules (DRs), which were mandatory statements of the minimum conduct below which no attorney could fall without being subject to discipline.

Model Guidelines for the Utilization of Legal Assistant Services Ethical guidelines recommended by the American Bar Association for the ethical use of paralegals by attorneys.

Model Rules of Professional Conduct The current set of ethical rules governing attorneys recommended by the American Bar Association. These rules revised the ABA's earlier rules found in the *Model Code of Professional Responsibility.*

Model Standards and Guidelines for Utilization of Legal Assistants A statement of ethical and related guidelines of the National Association of Legal Assistants.

Modem A device that allows a computer to send and receive information using regular telephone lines.

Monitor A display screen; a TV-like device used to display what is typed at the keyboard and the response of the computer.

Monitoring Legislation Finding current information on the status of a proposed statute in the legislature.

Mouse A clicking device used as a partial substitute for typing commands into a computer.

Movant The party who formally requests a court to do something.

Multiple Representation Representing more than one side in a legal matter or controversy. Also called *common representation.*

Multitasking Having the capacity to run several large programs simultaneously.

NALA National Association of Legal Assistants.

NALS National Association of Legal Secretaries. *See also* Certified PLS.

National Paralegal Reporter A periodical of the National Federation of Paralegal Associations.

Negative Contingency *See* Contingent Fee.

Neighborhood Legal Service Office A law office that serves the legal needs of the poor, often publicly funded.

Network Several computers connected together to share printers or hard disk drives.

Networking Establishing contacts with a relatively large number of people who might be helpful to you now or in the future. Similarly, you become such a contact for others.

NFPA National Federation of Paralegal Associations.

NJC Neighborhood Justice Center.

Nolle Prosequi A statement by the prosecutor that he or she is unwilling to prosecute the case.

Nominative Reporter A reporter volume that is identified by the name of the person responsible for compiling and printing the opinions in the volume.

Nonadversarial Proceeding Only one party appears in the proceeding, or both parties appear but they have no real controversy between them.

Nonbillable Time Time spent by paralegals and attorneys on tasks for which clients cannot be asked to pay.

Nonengagement *See* Letter of Nonengagement.

Nonequity Partner *See* Income Partner.

Nonexempt Employee An employee who must be paid overtime compensation.

Nonrebuttable Presumption *See* Presumption.

Notary Public A person who witnesses (i.e., attests to the authenticity of) signatures, administers oaths, and performs related tasks. In Europe, a notary often has more extensive authority.

Notebook *See* Laptop.

Notes of Decisions Summaries of court opinions that have interpreted a statute. The notes are printed after the statute in annotated codes.

Notice of Appearance *See* Appearance.

Notice Pleading A short and plain statement of the claim showing that the pleader is entitled to relief.

NOV *See* Judgment NOV.

Nutshell A legal treatise (written in pamphlet form) that summarizes a topic that is covered in a law school course.

Oath A sworn statement that what you say is true.

Objectivity *See* Bias.

Occurrence Policy Malpractice insurance that covers all occurrences (e.g., a negligent error or omission) during the period the policy is in effect, even if the claim is not actually filed until after the policy expires.

Of Counsel An attorney with a special status in the firm, e.g., a semiretired partner.

Office Sharing Attorneys with their own independent practices who share the use and cost of administration such as rent, copy machine, etc.

Official Reporter A reporter that is published under the authority of the government, often printed by the government itself. An unofficial reporter is printed by a private or commercial publisher without specific authority from the government.

OJT On-the-job training.

On All Fours The facts are exactly the same, or almost the same.

Online Being connected to a host computer system or information service—usually through the telephone lines.

On Point Relevant; covering the facts of your case or research problem. *See also* Analogous.

Open-Ended Question A broad, unstructured question that cannot be answered by one or two words.

Operating System A program that controls the overall operation of the computer, allowing it to do anything.

Opinion A court's written explanation of how it applied the law to the facts before it to resolve a legal dispute. Also called a *case*. Opinions are printed in volumes called *reporters*.

Opinion Letter A letter to a client explaining the application of the law and advising the client what to do.

Opinion of the Attorney General Formal legal advice given by the chief law officer of the government to another government official or agency.

Ordinance A law passed by the local legislative branch of government (e.g., city council).

Original Jurisdiction The power of a court to hear a particular kind of case initially. A trial court has original jurisdiction.

Outside Counsel An attorney used by a company who is not an employee of the company.

Outstanding Still unresolved; still unpaid.

Overhead The operating expenses of a business, e.g., cost of office space, furniture, equipment, insurance, clerical staff.

PACE Paralegal Advanced Certification Exam, a voluntary certification exam of the National Federation of Paralegal Associations that tests advanced proficiency.

Padding Adding something without justification.

Palmbook *See* Laptop.

Panel (1) A group of judges, usually three, who decide a case. The group is often part of a court that consists of a larger number of judges. (2) A list of individuals summoned for jury duty; from this list, juries for particular trials are selected. (3) A group of attorneys available in a group legal services plan. (4) Members of a commission.

Paralegal A person with legal skills who works under the supervision of an attorney or who is otherwise authorized to use those skills; this person performs tasks that do not require all the skills of an attorney and that most secretaries are not trained to perform. Synonymous with *legal assistant*.

Paralegal Manager *See* Legal Assistant Manager.

Paralegal Specialist A job classification in the federal government.

Parallel Cite An additional citation where you can find the same written material in the library.

Parallelism Using a consistent (i.e., parallel) grammatical structure when phrasing logically related ideas in a list.

Paraphrase To phrase something partly or entirely in your own words.

Parol Evidence Rule Oral evidence cannot be introduced to alter or contradict the contents of a written document if the parties initially intended the written document to be a complete statement of the agreement.

Partner, Full An attorney who contributes the capital to create the firm and to expand it, who shares the profits and losses of the firm, who controls the management of the firm, and who decides whether the firm will go out of existence.

Partnership A group of individuals who practice law jointly and who share in the profits and losses of the venture.

People The state or government.

Percentage Fee The fee is a percentage of the amount involved in the transaction or award.

Per Curiam By the court. A per curiam opinion is a court opinion, usually a short one, that does not name the judge who wrote the opinion. Also called a *memorandum opinion*.

Peremptory Challenge A request to exclude someone from a jury without stating a reason for the request. *See also* Challenge for Cause.

Performance Bonus   *See* Incentive Billing.

Personal Computer   *See* Microcomputer.

Personal Jurisdiction   The court's power over a particular person. Also called *in personam jurisdiction*.

Personal Liability   *See* Limited Liability, Vicarious Liability.

Personal Recognizance   The release of a defendant charged with a crime after a personal promise to return to court at a designated time. No bail is deposited.

Persuasive Authority   Whatever a court relies on in reaching its decision that it is not required to rely on.

Petition   (1) A formal request or motion. (2) A complaint.

Physical Condition   *See* Existing Physical or Mental Condition.

Physical Evidence   That which can be seen or touched. Also called *tangible evidence*.

Physician Assistant   An individual who is qualified by academic and clinical training to provide patient care services under the supervision and responsibility of a doctor of medicine or osteopathy.

PI Cases   Personal injury (tort) cases.

Pinpoint Cite   A reference to a specific page number in a document, e.g., a case, in addition to the page number where the document begins. In some documents, the pinpoint reference is to a specific paragraph number in the document. Also called a *jump cite*.

Plaintiff   The party initiating the lawsuit.

Plea Bargaining   An attempt to avoid a criminal trial by negotiating a plea, e.g., the defendant agrees to plead guilty to a lesser charge than initially brought.

Plead   To deliver a formal statement or response.

Pleading   A formal document that contains allegations and/or responses of the parties in a trial. The major pleadings are the complaint and answer.

PL Number   Public Law number.

Plotter   A device that will hold a pen to a piece of paper and draw lines as instructed by commands you enter into the computer.

PLS   Professional Legal Secretary. *See also* Certified PLS.

Pocket Part   An insert that fits into a small pocket built into the inside back (and occasionally front) cover of a bound volume.

Pocket Veto   A rejection of a bill passed by the legislature without an explicit veto from the chief executive. He or she does nothing with the bill, and the legislature adjourns within ten weekdays after he or she receives it.

Point Heading   A party's conclusion to one of its major arguments it is making in an appellate brief.

Points   The size of letters.

Points and Authorities Memorandum   A memorandum of law submitted to a judge or hearing officer. Sometimes called a *trial memorandum*.

Poll   To question jurors individually in open court as to whether each agrees with the verdict announced by the foreman.

Popular Name   A statute that is identified by the name of a person, place, or topic rather than simply by a title and section number.

Portable Billings   Fees that an attorney brings with him or her when he or she changes law firms.

Practical Manual   *See* Formbook.

Practice Analysis Report   *See* Case-Type Productivity Report.

Practice of Law   Performing services that require the professional judgment of an attorney on a person's specific legal problem. Representing someone, drafting legal documents for someone, or giving someone legal advice.

Praecipe   A formal request to the court (usually made through the clerk) that something be done.

Prayer for Relief   The request for damages or other form of relief.

Present Sense Impression, Statement of   An out-of-court statement describing or explaining an event or condition made while the declarant was perceiving the event or condition or immediately thereafter. (An exception to the hearsay rule.)

Pre-evaluation Memo   A memorandum sent to a supervisor before a formal evaluation in which the employee lists the following information (since the last formal evaluation): major projects, functions on those projects, names of co-workers on the projects, evidence of initiative, quotations on the quality of work, etc.

Preliminary Hearing   A hearing during which the state is required to produce sufficient evidence to establish that there is probable cause to believe the defendant committed the crimes charged.

Premium Adjustment   A write-up (increase) of a bill.

Prepaid Legal Services   *See* Group Legal Services.

Preponderance of the Evidence   It is more likely than not that the fact is as alleged.

Presumption   An assumption that a certain fact is true. It is rebuttable if the court will consider evidence that it is false, and nonrebuttable if no such contrary evidence will be considered.

Pretrial Conference   A meeting between the judge (or magistrate) and the attorneys to prepare the case for trial and perhaps to make one last effort to settle the case.

Prima Facie   On the face of it; that which would be legally sufficient, if believed, to support a verdict.

Primary Authority   Any *law* that a court could rely on in reaching its decision.

Print Formatting   The function of a word processor that communicates with the printer to tell it how to print the text on paper.

Print Review   In word processing, a feature that enables you to view a general representation on the screen of how the document will look when printed.

Private Law   *See* Statute.

Private Law Firm   A law firm that generates its income from the fees of individual clients.

Private Reprimand   *See* Admonition.

Private Sector   An office where the funds come from client fees or the corporate treasury.

Private Statute   *See* Statute.

Privilege   A special benefit, right, or protection. In the law of evidence, a privilege is the right to refuse to testify or to prevent someone else from testifying.

Privilege against Self-Incrimination   Persons cannot be compelled to testify in a criminal proceeding or to answer incriminating questions that directly or indirectly connect themselves to the commission of a crime.

Probable Cause   A reasonable basis to believe that the defendant is guilty of the crime(s) charged.

Probate   (1) To bring a will before the proper court to prove it is genuine. (2) The act of proving that a will is genuine.

Probation   Supervised punishment in the community in lieu of incarceration. In the field of ethics, probation means: to allow an attorney to continue to practice, but under specified conditions, e.g., submit to periodic audits, make restitution to a client.

Pro Bono Publico   For the public good. *Pro bono* work refers to work performed free.

Procedural Due Process   Procedural protections that are required before the government can take away or refuse to grant liberty or a public benefit.

Procedural Law   The rules that govern the mechanics of resolving a dispute in court or in an administrative agency, e.g., a rule on the time a party has to respond to a complaint.

Process   *See* Service of Process.

Professional Corporation   The organization of a law practice as a corporation.

Professional Judgment   Relating or applying the general body and philosophy of law to a specific legal problem. When communicated to a client, the result is known as *legal advice*.

Project Attorney   An attorney who works either part-time or full-time over a relatively short period. Also referred to as a *contract attorney*.

Project Billing   *See* Task-Based Billing.

Pro Per   *See* Pro Se.

Pro Se   Appearing or representing oneself; acting without representation. This person is said to be proceeding *in properia persona*—in one's own proper person. The abbreviation is *pro per*.

Prosecution   (1) Bringing and processing criminal proceedings against someone. (2) The attorney representing the government in a criminal case, also called the *prosecutor*. (3) Bringing and processing of civil proceedings against someone.

Prosecutor   The attorney representing the government in a criminal case.

Public Benefits   Government benefits.

Public Censure   *See* Reprimand.

Public Defender   A government attorney who represents indigent (i.e., low-income) people charged with crimes. *See also* Assigned Counsel.

Public Domain   Free; accessible to anyone at no cost.

Public Domain Citation   A citation that is medium neutral. To find the material in the citation, you do not have to use the traditional volume and page numbers of a commercial publisher such as West. Also called a generic citation. If the reference is to documents online, the public domain citation is called an *electronic citation*.

Public Law   *See* Statute.

Public Sector   An office where the funds come from charity or the government.

Public Statute   *See* Statute.

Quarantined Paralegal   *See* Chinese Wall.

Quasi-adjudication   An administrative decision of an administrative agency that has characteristics of a court opinion.

Quasi-independent Agency   An administrative agency that has characteristics of an executive department agency and of an independent regulatory agency.

Quasi-judicial   Like or similar to a court.

Quasi-legislation   A regulation of an administrative agency that has characteristics of the legislation (statutes) of a legislature.

Query   A question that asks a computer to find something in its database.

Question of Law/Question of Fact   *See* Legal Issue.

Quid Pro Quo Harassment   Using submission to or rejection of unwelcome sexual conduct as the basis for making employment decisions affecting an individual.

Rainmaker   A person who brings fee-generating cases into the office.

RE   Concerning

Reasonable Doubt   Such doubt as would cause prudent persons to hesitate before acting in matters of importance to themselves.

Reasonable Fee   A fee that is not excessive in light of the amount of time and labor involved, the complexity of the case, the experience and reputation of the attorney, the customary fee charged in the locality for the same kind of case, etc.

Rebuttable Presumption   *See* Presumption.

Receivables   Accounts due and payable.

Record   (1) The official collection of all the trial pleadings, exhibits, orders, and word-for-word testimony given during the trial. (2) A collection of data fields that constitute a single unit, e.g., employee record.

Redirect Examination   Questioning your own witness (i.e., one you called) after cross-examination by the other side of that witness.

Referendum   A vote by the electorate on a proposed constitutional provision or statute. A direct vote by voters in the general public on proposed laws.

Referral Fee   A fee received by an attorney from another attorney to whom the first attorney referred a client. Also called a *forwarding fee.*

Regional Digest   A digest that summarizes court opinions that are printed in full in its corresponding regional reporter.

Regional Reporter   A reporter that contains state court opinions of states within a region of the country.

Registered Agent   An individual authorized to practice before the United States Patent Office. He or she does not have to be an attorney.

Registration   The process by which individuals or institutions list their names on a roster kept by an agency of government or by a nongovernmental organization. The agency or organization will often establish qualifications for the right to register and determine whether applicants meet these qualifications. Also called *enrollment.*

Regulation   Any governmental or nongovernmental method of controlling conduct. *See also* Administrative Regulation.

Relevance   That which reasonably has a bearing on something; that which tends to help establish a fact as true or as false, as present or as missing. Evidence is relevant when it reasonably tends to make the existence of a fact more probable or less probable than it would be without that evidence.

Remand   Send the case back to a lower tribunal with instructions from the appellate court.

Reply Brief   An appellate brief of the appellant that responds to the appellate brief of the appellee.

Reporter   A set of law books that contains the full text of court opinions. *See also* Annotated Reporter, Official Reporter.

Reprimand   A public declaration that an attorney's conduct was improper. This does not affect his or her right to practice. Also called a *censure* and a *public censure.*

Request for Admissions   A pretrial discovery device consisting of a series of written factual statements that a party is asked to affirm or deny.

Res Gestae Exceptions   Exceptions to the hearsay rule that consist of statements or utterances closely connected to or concurrent with an occurrence.

Res Judicata   A judgment on the merits will prevent the same parties from relitigating the same cause of action on the same facts.

Respondeat Superior   Let the superior answer. An employer is responsible for the wrongs committed by an employee within the scope of employment.

Respondent   *See* Appellee.

Restatements   A series of volumes that attempt to formulate existing law in a given area.

Retainer   (1) The contract that formally establishes the attorney-client relationship. It states the nature and cost of the services to be rendered. (2) An amount of money (or other property) paid by the client as a deposit or advance against future fees, expenses, and costs of representation.

Review   To examine in order to determine whether any errors of law were made. *See also* Appellate Jurisdiction.

Right Justified   In word processing, an even right side margin.

Root Expander (!)   The exclamation mark stands for one or more characters or letters added to the root of a word.

Rule   *See* Administrative Regulation, Rules of Court.

Rule-Making Function   Writing administrative regulations.

Rule of Three   Gross revenue generated through paralegal billing should equal three times a paralegal's salary.

Rules of Court   The procedural laws that govern the mechanics of litigation before a particular court. Also called *court rules.*

Ruling   *See* Administrative Decision, Holding.

Run   To cause a program to (1) be loaded into the computer from a disk drive and (2) begin to perform its task.

Runner   *See* Ambulance Chasing, Court Runner.

Sanction   (1) A penalty or punishment imposed for unacceptable conduct. (2) To authorize or give approval.

Satisfy   To comply with a legal obligation.

Save   To cause a program or data in the computer memory to be moved or stored on a diskette or hard drive.

Scanner   A machine that allows you to enter data and graphics into a computer directly from a printed page without typing the data.

Scienter   Knowingly.

Scope Note   The summary of coverage of a topic within a West digest.

Screen Formatting   In word processing and other programs, a feature that controls how the text will appear on the screen.

Scrivener   Professional copyist; a typist.

Scrolling   In word processing and other programs, moving a line of text onto or off the screen.

Search and Find   In word processing and other programs, a routine that searches for and places the cursor at a specified string of characters.

Search and Replace   In word processing and other programs, a routine that searches for a specified string of characters and replaces it with another string.

Search Criteria/Query   A computer research question; what you ask the computer in order to find something in a database.

Secondary Authority   Any *nonlaw* that a court could rely on in reaching its decision.

Second Chair   A seat at the counsel's table in the courtroom used by an assistant to the trial attorney during the trial.

Second-Tier Attorney   *See* Staff Attorney.

Section (§)   A portion of a statute, regulation, or book.

Segment Search   In LEXIS, a search that is limited to a certain part of cases in its databases.

Self-Interest   *See* Statement Against Self-Interest.

Self-Regulation   A process by which members of an occupation or profession establish and administer the rules on who can become a member and when members should be disciplined.

Senior Legal Assistant   An experienced legal assistant with the ability to supervise or train other legal assistants. He or she may have developed a specialty in a practice area.

Series   A set of books with its own internal volume-numbering system. When a new series in the set begins, the volume number starts again with 1.

Service Company   A business that sells particular services, usually to other businesses.

Service of Process   *Process* is the means used by the court to acquire or exercise its power or jurisdiction over a person. *Service of process* is the formal notification given to a defendant that a suit has been initiated against him or her and that he or she must respond to it.

Session Law Cite   The citation to a statute that has not yet been printed in a code and therefore is organized chronologically. *See also* Codified.

Settlement Work-up   A summary of the major facts in the case presented in a manner designed to encourage the other side (or its liability insurance company) to settle the case. Also called a *Settlement Brochure.*

Sexual Harassment   *See* Hostile Environment, Harassment, Quid Pro Quo Harassment.

Shepardizing   Using the volumes (or online resources) of *Shepard's Citations* to obtain the data available in these volumes (or online resources), e.g., whether a case has been appealed, whether a statute has been repealed.

Situs   Location.

Slip Law   A single act passed by the legislature and printed separately, often in a small pamphlet. It is the first official publication of the act.

Slip Opinion   A single court opinion, which for many courts is the first printing of the case.

Software   Computer programs for performing tasks such as word processing and database management.

Sole Practice   A single attorney owns and manages the law firm.

Solicitor   (1) A lawyer in England who handles day-to-day legal problems of clients with only limited rights to represent clients in certain lower courts. *See also* Barrister. (2) In the United States, some high government attorneys are called solicitors, e.g., the Solicitor-General of the United States who argues cases before the United States Supreme Court for the federal government.

Special Edition State Reporter   A reporter that prints the court opinions of one state, which are also printed within the regional reporter that covers that state.

Special Interest Group   An organization that serves a particular group of people, e.g., a union.

Special Jurisdiction   *See* Limited Jurisdiction.

Specialty Certification   Official recognition of competency in a particular area of law. The National Association of Legal Assistants, for example, has a specialty certification program to recognize a person as a Certified Legal Assistant Specialist (CLAS). A paralegal must first become a Certified Legal Assistant (CLA), and then pass one of NALA's specialty exams. *See also* Certified Legal Assistant.

Spell Checker   A computer software program that checks the spelling of words entered through a word processing program.

Spontaneous Declaration   An out-of-court statement or utterance made spontaneously during or immediately after an exciting event by an observer. (An exception to the hearsay rule.)

Spreadsheet   A ledger or table used for financial calculations and for the recording of transactions.

Squibs   *See* Digests.

Staff Attorney   A full-time attorney who has no expectation of becoming a full partner. Sometimes called a *second-tier* attorney.

Staffing Agency   An employment agency providing part-time employees for businesses. Often the business pays the agency, which in turn pays the employee.

Standard Form   A preprinted form used frequently for various kinds of transactions or proceedings.

Standard of Proof   A statement of how convincing a version of a fact must be before the trier of facts can accept it as true.

Stare Decisis   Courts should decide similar cases in the same way unless there is good reason for the court to do otherwise. A reluctance to reject precedent—prior opinions.

Star-Paging   A notation (e.g., an asterisk or star) next to text within a page of an unofficial reporter that indicates where the same text is found in an official reporter. *See also* Official Reporter.

Statement Against Self-Interest   An out-of-court statement made by a nonparty (who is now unavailable as a witness) if the statement was against the financial interest of the declarant at the time it was made. (An exception to the hearsay rule.)

State Question   A legal question that arises from the application of the state constitution, a state statute, or a state administrative regulation.

Stating a Cause of Action   Including in a pleading those facts which, if proved at trial, would entitle the party to win (assuming the other party does not plead and prove any defenses that would defeat the effort).

Status Line   In word processing and other programs, a message line above or below the text area on a display screen that gives format and system information.

Statute   A law passed by the legislature declaring, commanding, or prohibiting something. The statute is contained in a document called an *act*. If the statute applies to the general public or to a segment of the public, it is called a *public law* or *public statute*. If the statute applies to specifically named individuals or to groups—and has little or no permanence or general interest—it is called a *private law* or *private statute*.

Statute in Derogation of the Common Law   A statute that changes the common law. *See* Common Law.

Statute of Limitations   The period within which the lawsuit must be commenced or it can never be brought.

Statutory Code   A collection of statutes organized by subject matter rather than by date.

Stay   To delay enforcement or execution of a judgment.

Steerer   *See* Ambulance Chasing.

Stipulated   Agreed to.

Sua Sponte   Voluntarily; of its own will.

Subject-Matter Jurisdiction   The power of the court to resolve a particular category of dispute.

Subnotebook   *See* Laptop.

Subpoena   A command to appear at a certain time and place to give testimony.

Subpoena Duces Tecum   A command that specific documents or other items be produced.

Subscript   In word processing and other programs, a character that prints below the usual text baseline.

Subscription   The signature of the attorney who prepared the complaint.

Substantive Law   The nonprocedural rules that define or govern rights and duties.

Summary   Quick, expedited, without going through a full adversarial hearing.

Summary Judgment, Motion for   A request by a party that a decision be reached on the basis of the pleadings alone, without going through an entire trial, because there is no dispute on any material facts.

Summons   A formal notice from the court ordering the defendant to appear and answer the plaintiff's complaint. *See also* Service of Process.

Superior Court   Usually a trial court.

Superscript   In word processing and other programs, a character that prints above the usual text baseline.

Superseded   Outdated and replaced.

Supervising Legal Assistant   Someone who spends about 50 percent of his or her time supervising other legal assistants and about 50 percent on client cases as a legal assistant.

Supplemented   Added to.

Supra   Above, mentioned or referred to earlier in the document.

Supremacy Clause   The clause in the United States Constitution that gives the federal government supremacy over state and local governments in regulating designated areas.

Supreme Court   The highest court in a judicial system. (In New York, however, the supreme court is a trial court.)

Surrogate Courts   A special court with subject-matter jurisdiction over wills, probate, guardianships, etc.

Suspension   The removal of an attorney from the practice of law for a specified minimum period, after which the attorney can apply for reinstatement.

Sustain   To affirm the validity of.

"Swoose" Syndrome   Being recognized as part of the clerical staff in some respects and as part of the professional staff in others.

Syllabus   (1) A one-paragraph summary of an entire court opinion, usually written by a private publisher rather than by the court. (2) In *Shepard's Citations,* the syllabus refers to the headnotes of an opinion that summarize a portion of the opinion.

System   An organized method of performing a recurring task.

Table of Authorities   A list of the authorities a party is citing in a document, e.g., cases, statutes, law review articles.

Table of Cases   A list of all the cases printed or referred to in the volume, and where they are found in the volume.

Table of Statutes   A list of all the statutes printed or referred to in the volume, and where they are found in the volume.

Tainted   Having a conflict of interest; contaminated. *See also* Chinese Wall.

Tangible Evidence   *See* Physical Evidence.

Tape Backup System   A device that allows you to "back up" and store data on magnetic tape kept on tape cartridges.

Task-Based Billing   The law firm charges a specific sum for each legal task it performs (e.g., draft a complaint, conduct a deposition), often without regard to how long it takes to perform that task. Also called *unit billing* or *project billing.*

Template   A set of formulas created to perform a designated task.

Testimonial Evidence   That which someone says.

Text Buffer   In word processing and other programs, an area set aside in memory to hold text temporarily.

Text Editing   In word processing and other programs, the function that enables the user to enter and edit text.

Text File   In word processing and other programs, a file that contains text, as opposed to a program.

Third-Party Complaint   A complaint filed by the defendant against a third party.

Tickler   A reminder system that helps office staff remember important deadlines.

Timekeeper Productivity Report   A report showing how much able and nonbillable time is being spent by each timekeeper.

Page   A page at the beginning of a book that lists the name book, the author(s), publisher, etc. On this page, or on the e, the latest copyright date of the book is printed.

Key Number   *See* Key Number.

ate wrong or injury other than a breach of contract sion of a crime, although some breaches of contract also constitute torts.

Traditional Paralegal   A paralegal who works under the supervision of an attorney.

Transcribed   Copied or written out, word for word.

Transcript   A word-for-word account.

Treatise   *See* Legal Treatise.

Treaty   An international agreement between two or more foreign governments.

Trial Book   *See* Trial Brief.

Trial Brief   An attorney's set of notes on how to conduct a trial, often placed in a *trial notebook.* Sometimes called a *trial manual* or *trial book.*

Trial de Novo   A totally new fact-finding hearing.

Trial Manual   *See* Trial Brief.

Trial Memorandum   *See* Points and Authorities Memorandum.

Trial Notebook   A collection of documents, arguments, and strategies that an attorney plans to use during a trial. Sometimes referred to as the *trial brief.* (It can mean the notebook in which the trial brief is placed.)

Ultrafiche   *See* Microform.

Unauthorized Practice of Law   Performing acts that constitute the practice of law by someone not authorized to perform such acts. *See also* Practice of Law, Professional Judgment.

Unbundled Rate   *See* Fee.

Uncodified   Organized chronologically rather than by subject matter.

Unicameral   *See* Bicameral.

Unified Bar Association   *See* Integrated Bar Association.

Uniform State Law   A proposed statute presented to all the state legislatures by the National Conference of Commissioners on Uniform State Laws.

Unit Billing   *See* Task-Based Billing.

United States Court of Appeals   The main federal appellate court just below the United States Supreme Court.

United States District Court   The main federal trial court.

United States Supreme Court   The highest court in the federal judicial system.

Universal Character (*)   The asterisk stands for any character or letter in a query.

Unofficial Reporter   *See* Official Reporter.

User Group   Individuals using the same computer product who meet to discuss their experiences with it.

Utterance   *See* Excited Utterance.

Vacate   (1) To annul or put an end to. (2) To move out.

Validation Research   Using citators and other sources to check the current validity of every authority you intend to rely on in your document.

Value   A single piece of numeric information used in the calculations of a spreadsheet.

Value Billing   A method of charging a client for legal services that is not totally dependent on the number of hours spent. The amount of the bill may also depend on such factors as the complexity of the case and the results achieved.

Valuing the Bill   Determining whether there should be a write-up or a write-down of the bill.

Venue   The place of the trial.

Verdict   The final conclusion of the jury.

Verification   An affidavit stating that a party has read the complaint and swears that it is true to the best of his or her knowledge.

Veto   A rejection by the chief executive of a bill passed by the legislature. See also Pocket Veto.

Vicarious Disqualification   A law firm cannot continue to represent a client or cannot accept a new client because it has hired someone (attorney, paralegal, or secretary) who has a conflict of interest with that client.

Vicarious Liability   Being responsible because of what someone else has wrongfully done or wrongfully failed to do. See also Limited Liability.

Virtual Representation   In word processing and other programs, screen formatting that enables the user to see on the screen exactly how the printed output will look.

Voir Dire   The oral examination of prospective jurors for purposes of selecting a jury.

Wage and Hour Division   The unit within the U.S. Department of Labor that administers the Fair Labor Standards Act, which governs overtime compensation and related matters. See also Exempt Employee, Fair Labor Standards Act.

Waiver   The loss of a right or privilege because of an explicit rejection of it or because of a failure to claim it at the appropriate time.

Warrant   An order from a judicial officer authorizing an act, e.g., the arrest of an individual, the search of property.

WESTLAW   The legal research computer service of West Publishing Co.

Window   In a spreadsheet program, the portion of a worksheet that can be seen on the computer display screen.

Word Processor   A computerized system of entering, editing, storing, retrieving, etc. data.

Word Wrap   A word is automatically moved to the next line if it goes past the right margin.

Work-in-Progress Report   A report that provides the details of unbilled hours and costs per timekeeper, including client totals.

Work-Product Rule   Notes, working papers, memoranda, or similar documents and tangible things prepared by the attorney in anticipation of litigation are not discoverable. See also Discoverable.

World Wide Web (www)   Multimedia documents on the Internet where you can access other documents through hypertext.

Write Down   Deduct an amount from the bill.

Write Up   Add an amount to the bill.

Writ of Certiorari   An order by an appellate court requiring a lower court to certify the record of a lower court proceeding and to send it up to the appellate court, which has decided to accept an appeal of the proceeding. The writ is used in a case in which the appellate court has discretion to accept or reject the appeal.

Writ Writer   See Jailhouse Lawyer.

WYSIWYG   What You See (on the screen) Is What You Get (when the screen is printed).

INDEX

PARALEGAL ASSOCIATIONS: LOCAL

1. Determine how many paralegal associations exist in your state (or in any state where you hope to work). See Appendix B.

2. Photocopy the following form, fill out one form for each association you identify in step one, and mail the form to each association.

Date: _____

Dear Paralegal Association:

    I am a student at the following paralegal school:

_____

Would you be kind enough to answer the following questions:

    1. Can paralegal students be members of your association? If so, what are the dues for students?

    2. Does your association have a mentor program where an experienced paralegal member provides guidance or advice to new members?

    3. Do you have a student rate for subscriptions to your newsletter?

    4. Does your association have a job bank service? If so, can student members take advantage of this service?

    5. Would your association consider conducting a "Career Day" in which experienced paralegal members of your association describe work in different employment settings in the state?

Any other information you can send me about the association would be greatly appreciated.

    I hope to hear from you.

Sincerely,

_____

My Address: _____

_____

_____

Source: Statsky, *Introduction to Paralegalism* (West)

PARALEGAL ASSOCIATIONS: NATIONAL

Please send me information about the Federation.

My Name and Address:

_____

_____

_____

Clip this form and mail to:

Nat'l Federation of Paralegal
   Associations
32 West Bridlespur Terrace
P.O. Box 33108
Kansas City, MO 64114-0108

Statsky, *Introduction to Paralegalism* (West)

Please send me information about NALA.

My Name and Address:

_____

_____

_____

Clip this form and mail to:

Nat'l Association of
   Legal Assistants
1516 South Boston, Suite 200
Tulsa, OK 74119-4013

Statsky, *Introduction to Paralegalism* (West)